ACCOUNTING TRENDS & TECHNIQUES

U.S. GAAP Financial Statements

Best Practices in Presentation and Disclosure

SIXTY-SIXTH EDITION

Copyright © 2012 by
American Institute of Certified Public Accountants, Inc.
New York, NY 10036-8775

1 2 3 4 5 6 7 8 9 0 AAP 1 9 8 7 6 5 4 3 2

ISSN 1531-4340   01-04-13

ISBN 978-1-93735-141-0

Notice to readers: This book does not represent an official position of the American Institute of Certified Public
Accountants, and it is distributed with the understanding that the authors and publisher are not rendering legal,
accounting, or other professional services via this publication.

Director, Accounting & Auditing Publications: Amy Eubanks
Senior Technical Manager: Doug Bowman
Technical Manager: Anjali Patel
Developmental Editor: David Cohen
Project Manager: Charlotte Ingles

Recognition

The 2012 edition of *U.S. GAAP Financial Statements—Best Practices in Presentation and Disclosure* was developed by

Raymond J. Petrino, CPA
Content Matter Expert

David J. Cohen
Developmental Editor
AICPA Publications Product Development

Anjali V. Patel, CPA
Technical Manager
AICPA Accounting and Auditing Publications

Keira A. Kraft, CPA
Technical Manager
AICPA Accounting and Auditing Publications

Special acknowledgment and sincere thanks are due to the following individuals for their efforts, without whom this book would not be possible:

Mark Bond
Sandy Carlin
Caroline Carr
Lisa Hopson

Stephanie Jordan
Kathy Keough
Gene P. Leporiere
Karen Venturini

About This Edition of *U.S. GAAP Financial Statements—Best Practices in Presentation and Disclosure*

AICPA's flagship product has a new name: *U.S. GAAP Financial Statements—Best Practices in Presentation and Disclosure (Best Practices in Presentation and Disclosure)*. Formerly *Accounting Trends & Techniques, Best Practices in Presentation and Disclosure* continues to provide the same outstanding, essential content that users have depended on for over 60 years. The name has changed simply to provide users with a clearer sense of what this product delivers: presentation and disclosure examples carefully selected by AICPA experts accompanied by just the right amount of reporting guidance and relevant financial statement trends. This book remains the best source for reporting and disclosure examples from real world financial statements, providing accounting professionals with an invaluable resource for incorporating new and existing accounting and reporting guidance into financial statements using presentation techniques adopted by companies across numerous industries, all of which are headquartered in the United States.

Organization and Content

This 2012 edition surveyed annual reports of 500 entities of various sizes representing over 100 industries with fiscal periods ending between January and December 2011. The industry classifications of survey entities (as shown in Table 1-1 in section 1) were obtained from Morningstar, Inc.

To provide you with the most useful and comprehensive look at current financial reporting presentation and disclosure, this book is topically organized and offers the following:

- Examples taken from the surveyed annual reports illustrating financial statement presentation and virtually every required U.S. GAAP disclosure.
- Descriptive guidance that includes current reporting requirements under U.S. generally accepted accounting principles (GAAP). U.S. GAAP is generally considered to be the requirements of the Financial Accounting Standards Board (FASB) *Accounting Standards Codification*™ (ASC). Select Securities and Exchange Commission (SEC) guidance is also included.
- Statistical tables that track reporting trends.
- Detailed indexes.

Illustrative Reporting Examples

AICPA leverages its decades of experience as the CPA national membership organization to select the most useful, comprehensive presentation and disclosure examples, which comprise the majority of this book. Every edition of *Best Practices in Presentation and Disclosure* includes all new annual report excerpts that were chosen to be particularly relevant and useful to financial statement preparers in illustrating current reporting practices.

Because survey entities may present disclosures on specific topics within different footnotes in their annual filings, including those ostensibly about a separate accounting topic, the excerpts presented herein to illustrate a given topic may have been taken from footnotes about other topics.

Guidance

Discerning, plain English guidance covers the significant U.S. GAAP accounting and financial statement reporting requirements in narrative form. These narratives use common headings (recognition and measurement, presentation, and disclosure) to achieve a consistent presentation throughout all the sections. Although not a substitute for the authoritative accounting and reporting standards, the reporting guidance herein encapsulates the complex requirements to facilitate your understanding of the content. The related authoritative sources for each requirement are cited within the narratives (for example, FASB ASC 310, *Receivables*, or Regulation S-K).

SEC rules and interpretative releases may expand, modify, or decrease accounting and disclosure requirements for foreign private issuers, regardless of whether they file their annual financial statements with the SEC in Forms 10-K, 20-F, or 40-F (Canadian issuers). Therefore, it is critical to consider SEC requirements, as well as those of FASB ASC, when reviewing the financial statements of SEC registrants. A general reference to FASB ASC in this publication does not include the SEC materials. When requirements are taken from an SEC rule or regulation, that rule or regulation will be cited directly.

Reporting Trends

Statistical tables present reporting trends across the available choices in recognition, measurement, presentation, and disclosure in such diverse reporting matters as financial statement format and terminology and the treatment of transactions and events reflected in the financial statements. To distinguish them from content excerpted from a survey entity's financial statements, these tables are presented with a shaded background.

Indexes

Indexes in this edition include the "Appendix of 500 Entities," which alphabetically lists each of the 500 survey entities included in the current edition and notes where in the text excerpts from their annual reports can be found; the "Index of Authoritative Accounting & Auditing Guidance," which provides for easy cross-referencing of pronouncements to the applicable descriptive narratives; and a detailed "Subject Index," which is fully cross-referenced to all significant topics included throughout the narratives.

FASB ASC

Because FASB ASC is the source of authoritative U.S. GAAP for nongovernmental entities, in addition to guidance issued by the SEC, the guidance herein refers only to the appropriate FASB ASC reference for all standards.

Note that the effective dates of recently released guidance affect the timing of its inclusion in the financial statements of the survey entities, thereby affecting the availability of illustrative excerpts for potential inclusion in each edition of *Best Practices in Presentation and Disclosure*. This 2012 edition includes survey entities having fiscal years ending within calendar year 2011. Technical guidance for which this edition supplies illustrative annual report excerpts includes the following, among other recently issued guidance:

- Accounting Standards Update (ASU) No. 2011-09, *Compensation—Retirement Benefits—Multiemployer Plans (Subtopic 715-80): Disclosures about an Employer's Participation in a Multiemployer Plan*
- ASU No. 2011-08, *Intangibles—Goodwill and Other (Topic 350): Testing Goodwill for Impairment*
- ASU No. 2010-29, *Business Combinations (Topic 805): Disclosure of Supplementary Pro Forma Information for Business Combinations (a consensus of the FASB Emerging Issues Task Force)*
- ASU No. 2010-28, *Intangibles-Goodwill and Other (Topic 350): When to Perform Step 2 of the Goodwill Impairment Test for Reporting Units with Zero or Negative Carrying Amounts (a consensus of the FASB Emerging Issues Task Force)*

Convergence of U.S. GAAP and IFRSs

Converging the standards of FASB and the International Accounting Standards Board (IASB) continues to be a primary focus of both organizations' boards throughout 2012. The commitment for global convergence gained momentum in 2002, when FASB and the IASB signed what is known as the Norwalk Agreement. At that meeting, FASB and IASB pledged to use their best efforts to (a) make their existing financial reporting standards fully compatible as soon as is practicable, and (*b*) coordinate their future work programs to ensure that, once achieved, compatibility is maintained. That agreement was reaffirmed in a February 2006 Memorandum of Understanding (MoU), which was based on the following three principles:

- Convergence of accounting standards can best be achieved through the development of high quality, common standards over time.
- Trying to eliminate differences between two standards that are in need of significant improvement is not the best use of FASB's and IASB's resources—instead, a new common standard should be developed that improves the financial information reported to investors.
- Serving the needs of investors means that FASB and IASB should seek convergence by replacing standards in need of improvement with jointly developed new standards.

At a joint meeting in April 2008, FASB and the IASB again affirmed their commitment to developing common, high quality standards, and agreed on a path to completing the MoU projects, including projected completion dates. In September 2008, and again in April 2011, the two boards jointly published an update of their 2006 MoU to report the progress they had made since. During 2011, the boards regularly updated project completion dates as difficulties in completing projects arose. Some projects (for example, Income Taxes) were removed from the convergence schedules when the boards agreed that convergence was unlikely to be achieved in the short time available, whereas other projects have reached the exposure draft milestone. FASB and the IASB expect to issue final joint standards in their major convergence projects by mid-2013. Each board believes that these standards, when completed, would improve the quality, consistency, and comparability of financial information for investors and capital markets around the world.

Lastly, in May 2011, the SEC produced a work plan to outline how convergence efforts may be carried out. Many of the panelists from a roundtable discussion held in July 2011 favored the "condorsement" approach, whereby FASB would endorse new IFRSs one at a time, instead of following a "Big Bang" approach of converging several IFRSs at one time. In November 2011, the SEC released a staff paper that summarizes the current status of convergence projects and groups them by both short term and long term, as well as level of priority. Currently, the three projects that are of greater priority are financial instruments, revenue recognition, and leases. Refer to www.sec.gov for the full version of the staff paper.

In July 2012, the SEC published its final staff report on the Work Plan, which focuses on the arguments for and against various forms of adoption of global accounting standards. When assessing the implications of incorporating IFRSs in the U.S. financial reporting system, the SEC concluded that while international standards have improved in comprehensiveness, there are still some gaps, especially in the areas of insurance, extractive industries, and rate-regulated industries. The report also states that the costs of full IFRS adoption remain to be among the most significant costs required from an accounting perspective, and that companies questioned whether the benefits would justify such a full-scale transition. While the report does not contain information leading to any decision the SEC has made regarding incorporation of IFRSs, the staff expects that the SEC and others in the United States will remain involved with the development and application of IFRS.

Related Products

U.S. GAAP Financial Statements—Best Practices in Presentation and Disclosure is the flagship product in the AICPA's *Accounting Trends & Techniques* series; it is also available in an interactive, online format. Other titles in the *Accounting Trends & Techniques* series include

- *IFRS Financial Statement—Best Practices in Presentation and Disclosure*
- *Employee Benefit Plans Financial Statement—Best Practices in Presentation and Disclosure*
- *Not-for-Profit Entities Financial Statement—Best Practices in Presentation and Disclosure*

Notice

This book is a nonauthoritative practice aid and is not designed to provide a comprehensive understanding of all the requirements contained in U.S. GAAP. The guidance provided herein may not discuss all relevant accounting guidance on a given topic and should not be relied upon for its completeness. Users are encouraged to consult FASB ASC for complete, authoritative discussion of U.S. GAAP. Users are also encouraged to consult the complete body of SEC rules and regulations for regulatory requirements. In addition, this book does not include reporting requirements relating to other matters such as internal control or agreed-upon procedures.

Authoritative guidance on accounting treatments in accordance with U.S. GAAP can be made only by reference to the FASB ASC, which is copyright of the FAF and can be acquired directly from FASB.

This book has not been reviewed, approved, disapproved, or otherwise acted on by any senior technical committee of the AICPA and does not represent official positions or pronouncements of the AICPA.

The use of this publication requires the exercise of individual professional judgment. It is not a substitute for the original authoritative accounting and auditing guidance. Users are urged to refer directly to applicable authoritative pronouncements, when appropriate. As an additional resource, users may call the AICPA Technical Hotline at 1.877.242.7212.

Feedback

We hope that you find this edition to be informative and useful. Please let us know! What features do you like? What do you think can be improved or added? We encourage you to submit your comments and questions to Anjali Patel, using the following contact information. All feedback is greatly appreciated and kept strictly confidential.

Anjali Patel—Professional Publications
AMERICAN INSTITUTE OF CERTIFIED PUBLIC ACCOUNTANTS
220 Leigh Farm Road
Durham, NC 27707-8110
Telephone: 919.402.4580
E-mail: apatel@aicpa.org

You can also contact the Accounting and Auditing Publications team of the AICPA directly via e-mail at

A&Apublications@aicpa.org

TABLE OF CONTENTS

Section		Paragraph
1	General Topics	.01-.161
	Survey Entities	.01-.06
	General Financial Statement Considerations	.07-.42
	Recognition and Measurement	.07-.13
	Presentation	.14-.17
	Disclosure	.18-.22
	Presentation and Disclosure Excerpts	.23-.42
	Plain English References	.23-.24
	Specific FASB ASC References	.25
	Quarterly Financial Data	.26
	Selected Information for Five Years	.27
	Forward-Looking Information	.28
	Liquidity and Capital Resources	.29
	New Accounting Standards	.30
	Market Risk Information	.31
	Critical Accounting Policies	.32
	Disclosure of Accounting Policies	.33
	Nature of Operations	.34-.35
	Description of Business	.36
	Use of Estimates	.37-.38
	Significant Accounting Policies and Estimates	.39
	Vulnerability Due to Certain Concentrations	.40-.42
	Segment Reporting	.43-.49
	Presentation	.43-.46
	Presentation and Disclosure Excerpts	.47-.49
	Segment Information	.47-.49
	Accounting Changes and Error Corrections	.50-.76
	Presentation	.50-.56
	Disclosure	.57-.58
	Presentation and Disclosure Excerpts	.59-.76
	Change in Accounting Principle: Pension and Other Postretirement Benefits	.59
	Change in Accounting Principle: Business Combinations	.60
	Change in Accounting Principle: Interest and Penalties for Uncertain Tax Positions	.61
	Change in Accounting Principle: Inventory	.62
	Change in Accounting Principle: Revenue Recognition	.63
	Change in Accounting Principle: Transfers of Financial Assets and Variable Interest Entities	.64-.65
	Change in Accounting Principle: Multiemployer Pension Plans	.66-.67
	Change in Accounting Principle: Comprehensive Income	.68
	Change in Accounting Principle: Goodwill	.69
	Change in Accounting Principle: Troubled Debt Restructuring	.70

Section   **Paragraph**

1   General Topics—continued

Change in Accounting Principle: Consolidation .... .71
Change in Accounting Estimates .... .72-.73
Correction of Errors .... .74-.76
Consolidation .... .77-.85
Recognition and Measurement .... .77-.79
Presentation .... .80-.81
Disclosure .... .82-.83
Presentation and Disclosure Excerpts .... .84-.85
Consolidation .... .84-.85
Business Combinations .... .86-.92
Recognition and Measurement .... .86
Disclosure .... .87-.88
Presentation and Disclosure Excerpts .... .89-.92
Business Combinations .... .89-.92
Commitments .... .93-.102
Disclosure .... .93
Presentation and Disclosure Excerpts .... .94-.102
Restrictive Covenants .... .94-.98
Leasing Commitments .... .99
Sales/Marketing Agreements .... .100
Royalty, Licensing, and Marketing Obligations .... .101
Purchase Agreements .... .102
Contingencies .... .103-.116
Recognition and Measurement .... .103-.105
Presentation and Disclosure Excerpts .... .106-.116
Legal Matters .... .106
Tax Contingencies .... .107-.108
Environmental Matters .... .109-.110
Self-Insurance .... .111
Investigations and Regulatory Action .... .112
Warranties .... .113
Tax Credits and Other Tax Carryforwards .... .114
Net Operating Loss and Tax Credit Carryforwards .... .115
Value-Added Tax Credits .... .116
Financial Instruments .... .117-.135
Recognition and Measurement .... .117-.118
Disclosure .... .119-.130
Presentation and Disclosure Excerpts .... .131-.135
Financial Guarantees and Indemnifications—Line of Credit .... .131-.132
Derivative Financial Instruments—Interest Rate Hedging Instruments .... .133
Derivative Financial Instruments—Forward Contracts .... .134
Standby Letters of Credit .... .135
Fair Value .... .136-.140
Recognition and Measurement .... .136-.138

Section   **Paragraph**

1   General Topics—continued

                           Disclosure .... .139

                    Presentation and Disclosure Excerpts .... .140

                           Fair Value Measurements .... .140

             Subsequent Events .... .141-.151

                    Recognition and Measurement .... .141

                    Disclosure .... .142-.143

                    Presentation and Disclosure Excerpts .... .144-.151

                           Notes .... .144

                           Term Loan & Credit Facilities .... .145

                           Litigation .... .146

                           Discontinued Operations .... .147-.148

                           Restructuring .... .149

                           Acquisitions .... .150

                           Restricted Stock and Performance Share Grants .... .151

             Related Party Transactions .... .152-.158

                    Disclosure .... .152

                    Presentation and Disclosure Excerpts .... .153-.158

                           Transaction Between Reporting Entity & Investee .... .153

                           Major Stockholder Transactions .... .154

                           Transaction Between Reporting Entity and Officer/Director ... .155

                           Transaction Between Reporting Entity and Variable Interest Entity ..... .156

                           Transactions With Related Parties .... .157

                           Merger Agreement and Exchange Agreement .... .158

             Inflationary Accounting .... .159-.161

                    Disclosure .... .159-.160

                    Presentation and Disclosure Excerpts .... .161

                           Inflationary Accounting .... .161

2   Balance Sheet and Related Disclosures   .01-.189

             General Balance Sheet Considerations .... .01-.07

                    Presentation .... .01-.03

                    Disclosure .... .04-.06

                    Presentation and Disclosure Excerpts .... .07

                           Reclassifications .... .07

             Cash and Cash Equivalents .... .08-.10

                    Presentation .... .08

                    Disclosure .... .09

                    Presentation and Disclosure Excerpts .... .10

                           Reclassifications .... .10

             Marketable Securities .... .11-.24

                    Recognition and Measurement .... .11-.13

                    Presentation .... .14

                    Disclosure .... .15-.21

                    Presentation and Disclosure Excerpts .... .22-.24

Section   **Paragraph**

2   Balance Sheet and Related Disclosures—continued

      Marketable Securities—Available-for-Sale Securities .... .22

      Marketable Securities—Held-to-Maturity Securities .... .23

      Marketable Securities—Trading Securities .... .24

    Current Receivables .... .25-.30

     Presentation .... .25

     Disclosure .... .26

     Presentation and Disclosure Excerpts .... .27-.30

      Receivables from Related Parties .... .27

      Finance Receivables .... .28

      Insurance Claims .... .29

      Sale of Assets—Escrow Receivable .... .30

    Receivables Sold or Collateralized .... .31-.37

     Recognition and Measurement .... .31-.33

     Disclosure .... .34

     Presentation and Disclosure Excerpts .... .35-.37

      Receivables Sold or Collateralized .... .35-.37

    Inventory .... .38-.47

     Recognition and Measurement .... .38-.39

     Presentation .... .40

     Disclosure .... .41-.44

     Presentation and Disclosure Excerpts .... .45-.47

      First-In First-Out .... .45

      Last-In First-Out .... .46

      Average Cost .... .47

    Other Current Assets .... .48-.57

     Presentation .... .48-.49

     Presentation and Disclosure Excerpts .... .50-.57

      Deferred Taxes .... .50

      Advances .... .51

      Assets Held for Sale .... .52

      Current Assets of Discontinued Operations .... .53

      Costs and Estimated Earnings in Excess of Billings .... .54

      Derivatives .... .55

      Content Rights .... .56

      Prepaid Expenses .... .57

    Property, Plant, and Equipment .... .58-.64

     Recognition and Measurement .... .58-.59

     Presentation .... .60-.61

     Disclosure .... .62

     Presentation and Disclosure Excerpts .... .63-.64

      Property, Plant, and Equipment .... .63-.64

    Equity Method and Joint Ventures .... .65-.72

     Recognition and Measurement .... .65

     Presentation .... .66

Section   **Paragraph**

2   Balance Sheet and Related Disclosures—continued

                    Disclosure .... .67-.68

                        Presentation and Disclosure Excerpts .... .69-.72

                            Equity Method .... .69-.70

                            Cost Method .... .71

                            Fair Value .... .72

                    Noncurrent Receivables .... .73-.76

                        Presentation .... .73-.74

                        Presentation and Disclosure Excerpts .... .75-.76

                            Long-Term Receivables .... .75

                            Notes Receivable .... .76

                    Intangible Assets .... .77-.92

                        Recognition and Measurement .... .77-.79

                        Presentation .... .80

                        Disclosure .... .81-.83

                        Presentation and Disclosure Excerpts .... .84-.92

                            Goodwill .... .84-.85

                            Trademarks and Other Intangibles .... .86

                            Merchandising Rights and Other Intangibles .... .87

                            Customer Contracts and Related Customer Relationships .... .88

                            Technology .... .89

                            Software .... .90

                            Licenses .... .91

                            In-Process Research and Development (IPR&D) .... .92

                    Other Noncurrent Assets .... .93-.106

                        Recognition and Measurement .... .93

                        Disclosure .... .94-.95

                        Presentation and Disclosure Excerpts .... .96-.106

                            Assets of Discontinued Operations .... .96

                            Pension Asset .... .97

                            Deferred Compensation Arrangements .... .98

                            Deposits .... .99

                            Long-Term Deferred Income Tax Asset .... .100

                            Cash Surrender Value of Life Insurance .... .101

                            Derivatives .... .102

                            Retail Real Estate .... .103

                            Software .... .104

                            Debt Issuance Costs .... .105

                            Contracts .... .106

                    Short-Term Debt 107.111

                        Presentation .... .107

                        Disclosure .... .108-.109

                        Presentation and Disclosure Excerpts .... .110-.111

                            Short-Term Debt .... .110-.111

Section   **Paragraph**

2   Balance Sheet and Related Disclosures—continued
              Trade Accounts Payable .... .112-.114
                 Recognition and Measurement .... .112
                 Presentation .... .113
                 Disclosure .... .114
              Employee-Related Liabilities .... .115.-120
                 Presentation .... .115
                 Disclosure .... .116-.117
                 Presentation and Disclosure Excerpts .... .118-.120
                    Employee-Related Liabilities .... .118-.120
              Income Tax Liability .... .121-.124
                 Presentation .... .121
                 Disclosure .... .122
                 Presentation and Disclosure Excerpts .... .123.-124
                    Income Taxes Payable .... .123-.124
              Current Amount of Long-Term Debt .... .125-.128
                 Presentation .... .125
                 Disclosure .... .126
                 Presentation and Disclosure Excerpts .... .127-.128
                    Current Amount of Long-Term Debt .... .127-.128
              Other Current Liabilities .... .129-.144
                 Presentation .... .129-.130
                 Presentation and Disclosure Excerpts .... .131-.144
                    Dividends .... .131
                    Advance Payments from Customers .... .132
                    Deferred Income Taxes .... .133
                    Warranties .... .134
                    Billings in Excess of Costs and Estimated Earnings .... .135
                    Restructuring .... .136
                    Self-Insurance Reserves .... .137
                    Deferred Net Revenue .... .138
                    Environment .... .139
                    Acquisition-Related Items .... .140
                    Litigation .... .141
                    Derivatives .... .142
                    Returns, Rebates and Incentives .... .143
                    Asset Retirement Obligation .... .144
              Long-Term Debt .... .145-.152
                 Presentation .... .145
                 Disclosure .... .146-.148
                 Presentation and Disclosure Excerpts .... .149-.152
                    Unsecured .... .149
                    Collateralized .... .150
                    Convertible .... .151
                    Covenants .... .152

Section   **Paragraph**

2   Balance Sheet and Related Disclosures—continued

           Credit Agreements .... .153-.155

               Disclosure .... .153

               Presentation and Disclosure Excerpts .... .154-.155

                   Credit Agreements .... .154-.155

           Long-Term Leases .... .156-.163

               Recognition and Measurement .... .156

               Presentation .... .157-.158

               Disclosure .... .159

               Presentation and Disclosure Excerpts .... .160-.163

                   Lessee Leases .... .160-.162

                   Lessor Leases .... .163

           Other Noncurrent Liabilities .... .164-.181

               Presentation .... .164-.170

               Presentation and Disclosure Excerpts .... .171-.181

                   Deferred Income Taxes .... .171

                   Taxes Payable .... .172

                   Tax Uncertainties .... .173

                   Insurance .... .174

                   Discontinued Operations .... .175

                   Warranty .... .176

                   Environmental .... .177

                   Asset Retirement Obligations .... .178

                   Litigation .... .179

                   Derivatives .... .180

                   Deferred Credits .... .181

           Accumulated Other Comprehensive Income .... .182-.189

               Presentation .... .182-.183

               Presentation and Disclosure Excerpts .... .184-.189

                   Accumulated Other Comprehensive Income—Equity Section of Balance Sheet .... .184-.185

                   Accumulated Other Comprehensive Income—Statement of Changes in Equity .... .186-.187

                   Accumulated Other Comprehensive Income—Notes to Consolidated Financial

                       Statements .... .188-.189

3   Income Statement   .01-.100

           Income Statement Format .... .01-.03

               Presentation .... .01-.02

               Presentation and Disclosure Excerpts .... .03

                   Reclassifications .... .03

           Revenues and Gains .... .04-.18

               Recognition and Measurement .... .04-.06

               Presentation and Disclosure Excerpts .... .07-.18

                   Revenues .... .07

                   Interest .... .08

                   Dividends .... .09

Section		Paragraph
3	Income Statement—continued	
	Royalty Revenue	.10
	Equity in Earnings of Affiliates	.11
	Gain on Asset Disposals	.12
	Bargain Purchase Gain	.13
	Litigation	.14
	Derivatives	.15
	Investment Gains	.16
	Insurance Recoveries	.17
	Gains on Extinguishment of Debt	.18
	Expenses and Losses	.19-.44
	Presentation	.19-.20
	Presentation and Disclosure Excerpts	.21-.44
	Selling, General, and Administrative	.21
	Research, Development, and Engineering	.22
	Exploration	.23
	Advertising	.24
	Taxes Other Than Income Taxes	.25
	Provision for Losses	.26
	Warranty	.27
	Interest	.28
	Interest and Penalties Related to Unrecognized Tax Benefits	.29
	Accretion on Asset Retirement Obligation	.30
	Write-down of Assets	.31
	Restructuring	.32
	Intangible Asset Amortization	.33
	Foreign Currency	.34
	Software Amortization	.35
	Litigation	.36
	Equity in Losses of Investees	.37
	Environmental	.38
	Sale of Receivables	.39
	Mergers and Acquisitions	.40
	Change in Fair Value of Derivatives	.41
	Change in Fair Value	.42
	Impairment of Intangibles	.43
	Loss on Extinguishment of Debt	.44
	Pensions and Other Postretirement Benefits	.45-.53
	Recognition and Measurement	.45
	Disclosure	.46-.48
	Presentation and Disclosure Excerpts	.49-.53
	Defined Benefit Plans	.49
	Defined Contribution Plans	.50
	Supplemental Retirement Plans (SERP)	.51
	Multi-Employer Plans	.52

Section   **Paragraph**

3   Income Statement—continued

Plan Amendment .... .53

Postemployment Benefits .... .54-.55

  Recognition and Measurement .... .54

  Presentation and Disclosure Excerpts .... .55

    Postemployment Benefits .... .55

Employee Compensatory Plans .... .56-.64

  Recognition and Measurement .... .56

  Presentation and Disclosure Excerpts .... .57-.64

    Stock Option Plans .... .57

    Stock Award Plans .... .58

    Savings and Investment Plans .... .59

    Employee Stock Purchase Plans (ESPP) .... .60

    Deferred Compensation Plans .... .61

    Incentive Compensation Plans .... .62

    Employee Stock Ownership Plans (ESOP) .... .63

    Profit Sharing Plans .... .64

Depreciation Expense .... .65-.71

  Recognition and Measurement .... .65-.66

  Disclosure .... .67-.68

  Presentation and Disclosure Excerpts .... .69-.71

    Straight-Line and Accelerated Method .... .69-.70

    Units-of-Production Method .... .71

Income Taxes .... .72-.78

  Recognition and Measurement .... .72

  Disclosure .... .73

  Presentation and Disclosure Excerpts .... .74-.78

    Expense Provision .... .74

    Credit Provision .... .75

    Operating Loss and Tax Credit Carryforwards .... .76-.77

    Taxes on Undistributed Earnings .... .78

Construction-Type and Production-Type Contracts .... .79-.83

  Recognition and Measurement .... .79-.80

  Presentation and Disclosure Excerpts .... .81-.83

    Construction and Production Type Contracts .... .81-.83

Discontinued Operations .... .84-.91

  Recognition and Measurement .... .84-.85

  Presentation .... .86-.88

  Presentation and Disclosure Excerpts .... .89-.91

    Business Component Disposals .... .89-.90

    Adjustment of Gain or Loss .... .91

Extraordinary Items .... .92-.98

  Recognition and Measurement .... .92

  Presentation .... .93-.95

  Presentation and Disclosure Excerpts .... .96-.98

Section   **Paragraph**

3   Income Statement—continued
                         Extraordinary Items .... .96
                         Unusual Items .... .97-.98
              Earnings Per Share .... .99-.100
                  Presentation .... .99
                  Presentation and Disclosure Excerpts .... .100
                      Earnings per Share .... .100

4   Comprehensive Income   .01-.20
              Comprehensive Income in Annual Filings .... .01-.20
                  Recognition and Measurement .... .01
                  Presentation .... .02-.07
                  Presentation and Disclosure Excerpts .... .08-.20
                      Combined Statement of Income and Comprehensive Income .... .08
                      Separate Statement of Comprehensive Income .... .09
                      Statement of Comprehensive Income Included With Statement of Changes
                          in Stockholders' Equity .... .10
                      Tax Effect Disclosure in the Notes .... .11
                      Tax Effect Disclosure on the Face of the Financial Statements .... .12
                      Foreign Currency Translation .... .13
                      Pension and Postretirement Adjustments .... .14-.15
                      Net Change in Unrealized Gains and Losses on Available-for-Sale Securities .... .16
                      Gains and Losses on Derivatives Held as Cash Flow Hedges .... .17-.18
                      Reclassification Adjustments .... .19-.20

5   Stockholders' Equity   .01-.63
              Format of Stockholders' Equity in Annual Filings .... .01-.19
                  Presentation .... .01-.03
                  Disclosure .... .04-.07
                  Presentation and Disclosure Excerpts .... .08-.19
                      Stock Option Awards and Employee Stock Purchase Plan (ESPP) ..... .08
                      Common Stock Issued to Employees .... .09
                      Common Stock Issued in a Public Offering .... .10
                      Common Stock Issued for an Acquisition .... .11
                      Common Stock Issued Upon Conversion of Convertible Debt .... .12
                      Warrants .... .13
                      Tax Benefits of Stock-Based Compensation .... .14
                      Equity-Based Compensation Expenses .... .15
                      Share Repurchase Program .... .16
                      Dividends .... .17
                      Conversion of Common Shares .... .18
                      Redemption of Convertible Preferred Stock .... .19
                  Common Stock .... .20-.21
                      Disclosure .... .20-.21

Section			**Paragraph**

5   Stockholders' Equity—continued

Preferred Stock .... .22-.26
- Presentation .... .22-.23
- Disclosure .... .24-.25
- Presentation and Disclosure Excerpts .... .26
  - Preferred Stock .... .26

Dividends .... .27-.31
- Presentation .... .27-.29
- Presentation and Disclosure Excerpts .... .30-.31
  - Cash Dividends .... .30
  - Non-Cash Dividends .... .31

Stock Splits .... .32-.35
- Recognition and Measurement .... .32-.33
- Presentation and Disclosure Excerpts .... .34-.35
  - Stock Split .... .34
  - Reverse Stock Split .... .35

Changes to Retained Earnings .... .36-.46
- Recognition and Measurement .... .36
- Presentation .... .37-.41
- Presentation and Disclosure Excerpts .... .42-.46
  - Change in Accounting Principle .... .42
  - Correction of an Error or Misstatement .... .43-.44
  - Other Changes in Retained Earnings: Share Repurchase Programs .... .45
  - Other Changes in Retained Earnings: Stock Split .... .46

Spinoffs .... .47-.49
- Recognition and Measurement .... .47-.48
- Presentation and Disclosure Excerpts .... .49
  - Spinoffs .... .49

Treasury Stock .... .50-.53
- Presentation .... .50-.52
- Presentation and Disclosure Excerpts .... .53
  - Treasury Stock .... .53

Other Components of Stockholders' Equity .... .54-.63
- Presentation .... .54-.55
- Disclosure .... .56-.58
- Presentation and Disclosure Excerpts .... .59-.63
  - Unearned Compensation .... .59
  - Deferred Compensation .... .60
  - Stock Compensation .... .61
  - Warrants .... .62
  - Noncontrolling Interest .... .63

6   Statement of Cash Flows .01-.44
- General .... .01-.12
  - Presentation .... .01-.05

Section   **Paragraph**

6   Statement of Cash Flows—continued

                     Disclosure .... .06-.08
                     Presentation and Disclosure Excerpts .... .09-.12
                         Cash and Cash Equivalents .... .09
                         Foreign Currency Cash Flows .... .10
                         Interest and Income Tax Payments .... .11
                         Noncash Activities .... .12
                     Cash Flows From Operating Activities .... .13-.27
                         Presentation .... .13-.18
                         Presentation and Disclosure Excerpts .... .19-.27
                             Direct Method .... .19
                             Indirect/Reconciliation Method .... .20
                             Adjustments to Reconcile Net Income: Depreciation and Amortization .... .21
                             Adjustments to Reconcile Net Income: Gain/Loss on Discontinued Operations/
                                 Sale of Business .... .22
                             Adjustments to Reconcile Net Income: Restructuring Expense .... .23
                             Adjustments to Reconcile Net Income: Cash Surrender Value .... .24
                             Adjustments to Reconcile Net Income: Deferred Taxes .... .25
                             Adjustments to Reconcile Net Income: Settlement of Receivables and Related
                                 Charges .... .26
                             Adjustments to Reconcile Net Income: Impairment/Write-Down of Assets .... .27
                     Cash Flows From Operating Activities .... .28-.36
                         Presentation .... .28
                         Presentation and Disclosure Excerpts .... .29-.36
                             Acquisitions .... .29
                             Investments .... .30
                             Business Combinations .... .31
                             Sale of Discontinued Operations .... .32
                             Capitalized Software .... .33
                             Restricted Cash .... .34
                             Insurance Proceeds .... .35
                             In-Process Research & Development (IPRD) .... .36
                     Cash Flows From Financing Activities .... .37-.44
                         Presentation .... .37
                         Presentation and Disclosure Excerpts .... .38-.44
                             Debt Proceeds/Repayments .... .38
                             Capital Stock Proceeds/Payments .... .39
                             Stock-Based Compensation .... .40
                             Dividends .... .41
                             Debt Issuance Costs .... .42
                             Financial Instrument Settlements—Credit Facility .... .43
                             Issuance of Noncontrolling Interest .... .44

7   Independent Auditors' Report .... .01-.60
                     Presentation in Annual Report .... .01-.02

Section **Paragraph**

7 Independent Auditors' Report—continued

Presentation .... .01-.02

Title and Addressee .... .03-.04

Presentation .... .03-.04

Auditors' Reports .... .05-.15

Presentation .... .05-.12

Nonissuers .... .05-.08

Issuers .... .09-.12

Presentation and Disclosure Excerpts .... .13-.15

PricewaterhouseCoopers LLP Auditors' Report .... .13

Statement of Operations and Comprehensive Income .... .14

Statement of Changes in Shareholders' Equity .... .15

Reference to the Report of Other Auditors .... .16-.23

Presentation .... .16-.22

Nonissuers .... .16-.19

Issuers .... .20-.22

Presentation and Disclosure Excerpts .... .23

Reference to Other Auditors .... .23

Uncertainties .... .24-.27

Presentation .... .24-.25

Presentation and Disclosure Excerpts .... .26-.27

Going Concern .... .26

Fresh-Start Accounting .... .27

Lack of Consistency .... .28-.41

Presentation .... .28-.35

Nonissuers .... .28-.29

Issuers .... .30-.35

Presentation and Disclosure Excerpts .... .36-.41

Correction of Errors and Restatement .... .36

Pension and Other Postretirement Benefit Obligations .... .37

Variable Interest Entities .... .38

Trade Receivables Securitization .... .39

Comprehensive Income .... .40

Multiple Deliverable Revenue Arrangements .... .41

Emphasis of a Matter .... .42-.43

Presentation .... .42

Presentation and Disclosure Excerpts .... .43

Emphasis of a Matter .... .43

Departures From Unqualified Opinions .... .44

Presentation .... .44

Reports on Comparative Financial Statements .... .45

Presentation .... .45

Opinion Expressed on Supplementary Financial Information .... .46-.47

Presentation .... .46

Presentation and Disclosure Excerpts .... .47

Section   **Paragraph**

7   Independent Auditors' Report—continued
                          Supplementary Financial Information .... .47
                 Dating of Report .... .48-.50
                      Presentation .... .48-.49
                          Nonissuers .... .48
                          Issuers .... .49
                      Presentation and Disclosure Excerpts .... .50
                          Dating of Report .... .50
                 Auditors' Reports on Internal Control Over Financial Reporting .... .51-.57
                      Presentation .... .51-.53
                      Presentation and Disclosure Excerpts .... .54-.57
                          Separate Report on Internal Control .... .54
                          Combined Report on Financial Statements and Internal Control .... .55
                          Audit Report with Specific Items Excluded .... .56
                          Ineffective Internal Controls .... .57
                 General Management And Special-Purpose Committee Reports .... .58-.60
                      Presentation .... .58
                      Presentation and Disclosure Excerpts .... .59-.60
                          Report of Management on Financial Statements .... .59
                          Report of the Audit Committee .... .60

LIST OF TABLES

Table   **Paragraph**

Table 1-1: Industry Classifications of Survey Entities 1.04
Table 1-2: Filing Classification of Survey Entities 1.05
Table 1-3: Size of Survey Entities by Amount of Revenue 1.06
Table 1-4: FASB ASC Referencing 1.13
Table 1-5: Disclosure of Accounting Policies 1.22
Table 1-6: Segment Information 1.46
Table 1-7: Accounting Changes and Error Corrections 1.58
Table 1-8: Business Combination Disclosures 1.88
Table 1-9: Contingencies 1.105
Table 1-10: Financial Instruments—Financial Guarantees/Indemnifications 1.126
Table 1-11: Financial Instruments—Interest Rate Contracts 1.127
Table 1-12: Financial Instruments—Foreign Currency Contracts 1.128
Table 1-13: Financial Instruments—Commodity Contracts 1.129
Table 1-14: Financial Instruments—Other Financial Instruments 1.130
Table 1-15: Subsequent Events 1.143
Table 2-1: Balance Sheet Classification 2.06
Table 2-2: Fair Value Inputs for Debt and Equity Securities 2.21
Table 2-3: Inventory Cost Determination 2.43
Table 2-4: Inventory Cost Determination—Use of LIFO 2.44
Table 2-5: Other Current Assets 2.49

Table   **Paragraph**

Table 2-6: Noncurrent Investments—Carrying Bases 2.68

Table 2-7: Intangible Assets 2.82

Table 2-8: Intangible Assets Amortization Period 2.83

Table 2-9: Other Noncurrent Assets 2.95

Table 2-10: Other Current Liabilities 2.130

Table 2-11: Long-Term Debt 2.148

Table 2-12: Other Noncurrent Liabilities—Related to Employees 2.168

Table 2-13: Other Noncurrent Liabilities—Deferred Credits 2.169

Table 2-14: Other Noncurrent Liabilities—Other Than Employee Related and Deferred Credits 2.170

Table 2-15: Accumulated Other Comprehensive Income—Presentation of Component Balances 2.183

Table 3-1: Frequently Disclosed Gains and Other Income 3.06

Table 3-2: Expenses and Losses—Other Than Cost of Goods Sold 3.20

Table 3-3: Depreciation Methods 3.68

Table 3-4: Method of Accounting for Construction-Type and Production-Type Contracts 3.80

Table 3-5: Unusual Items 3.94

Table 3-6: Extraordinary Items 3.95

Table 4-1: Comprehensive Income—Reporting Statement 4.05

Table 4-2: Other Comprehensive Income—Components 4.06

Table 4-3: Comprehensive Income—Tax Effect Disclosure 4.07

Table 5-1: Format of Changes in Stockholders' Equity 5.06

Table 5-2: Presentation of Changes in Additional Paid-In Capital 5.07

Table 5-3: Common Stock 5.21

Table 5-4: Preferred Stock 5.25

Table 5-5: Dividends 5.29

Table 5-6: Credits and Charges to Additional Paid-In Capital 5.41

Table 5-7: Treasury Stock—Balance Sheet Presentation 5.52

Table 5-8: Other Stockholders' Equity Accounts 5.58

Table 6-1: Presentation of Interest and Income Tax Payments 6.08

Table 6-2: Method of Reporting Cash Flows From Operating Activities 6.16

Table 6-3: Cash Flows From Operating Activities—Income Statement Reconciling Items 6.17

Table 6-4: Cash Flows From Operating Activities—Balance Sheet Reconciling Items 6.18

Table 7-1: Information Related to Auditor's and Management's Reports 7.11

Table 7-2: Internal Control Framework 7.12

Table 7-3: References to Uncertainties in Auditors' Reports 7.25

Table 7-4: References to Lack of Consistency in Auditors' Reports 7.35

Section 1: General Topics

SURVEY ENTITIES

1.01 In years prior to fiscal year 2008, 600 entities were used in the survey. All tables of significant accounting trends will be based on a survey of 500 entities for the 2008–11 fiscal years and 600 entities for the years prior to fiscal year 2008.

1.02 All 500 entities included in the survey are registered with the Securities and Exchange Commission (SEC). Many of the survey entities have securities traded on one of the major stock exchanges: 80 percent on the New York Stock Exchange and 19 percent on NASDAQ. The remaining entities were traded on the American Stock Exchange or "over-the-counter" exchanges.

1.03 Each year, entities are selected from the latest Fortune 1000 listing to replace those entities that were deleted from the survey (see the "Appendix of 500 Entities" for a comprehensive listing of the 500 entities). Generally, entities are deleted from the survey when they are acquired; become privately held and, therefore, are no longer registered with the SEC; fail to timely issue a report; or cease operations.

1.04

TABLE 1-1: INDUSTRY CLASSIFICATIONS OF SURVEY ENTITIES

	2011	2010
Basic Materials/Agricultural Inputs	3	3
Basic Materials/Aluminum	1	1
Basic Materials/Building Materials	9	10
Basic Materials/Chemicals	9	9
Basic Materials/Coal	2	2
Basic Materials/Copper	1	1
Basic Materials/Gold	1	1
Basic Materials/Industrial Metals & Minerals	2	2
Basic Materials/Lumber & Wood Production	2	2
Basic Materials/Paper & Paper Products	6	7
Basic Materials/Specialty Chemicals	6	7
Basic Materials/Steel	8	8
Communication Services/Pay TV	3	3
Communication Services/Telecom Services	6	7
Consumer Cyclical/Advertising Agencies	2	2
Consumer Cyclical/Apparel Manufacturing	9	9
Consumer Cyclical/Apparel Stores	4	4
Consumer Cyclical/Auto & Truck Dealerships	2	2
Consumer Cyclical/Auto Manufacturers	1	1
Consumer Cyclical/Auto Parts	8	8
Consumer Cyclical/Broadcasting—TV	1	1
Consumer Cyclical/Department Stores	6	6
Consumer Cyclical/Footwear & Accessories	5	7
Consumer Cyclical/Home Furnishings & Fixtures	9	10
Consumer Cyclical/Home Improvement Stores	2	2
Consumer Cyclical/Leisure	6	7
Consumer Cyclical/Lodging	3	3

1.04

TABLE 1-1: INDUSTRY CLASSIFICATIONS OF SURVEY ENTITIES—*(continued)*

	2011	2010
Consumer Cyclical/Luxury Goods	2	2
Consumer Cyclical/Marketing Services	1	1
Consumer Cyclical/Media—Diversified	6	6
Consumer Cyclical/Packaging & Containers	8	9
Consumer Cyclical/Personal Services	3	3
Consumer Cyclical/Publishing	8	8
Consumer Cyclical/Recreational Vehicles	4	4
Consumer Cyclical/Residential Construction	10	10
Consumer Cyclical/Resorts & Casinos	3	3
Consumer Cyclical/Restaurants	9	10
Consumer Cyclical/Rubber & Plastics	4	4
Consumer Cyclical/Specialty Retail	11	12
Consumer Cyclical/Textile Manufacturing	1	1
Consumer Defensive/Beverages—Brewers	1	1
Consumer Defensive/Beverages—Soft Drinks	3	3
Consumer Defensive/Beverages—Wineries & Distilleries	3	2
Consumer Defensive/Confectioners	1	1
Consumer Defensive/Department Stores	1	1
Consumer Defensive/Discount Stores	5	5
Consumer Defensive/Education & Training Services	2	2
Consumer Defensive/Farm Products	6	6
Consumer Defensive/Food Distribution	2	2
Consumer Defensive/Grocery Stores	9	9
Consumer Defensive/Household & Personal Products	10	11
Consumer Defensive/Packaged Foods	14	14
Consumer Defensive/Pharmaceutical Retailers	3	3
Consumer Defensive/Tobacco	4	4
Energy/Oil & Gas Drilling	0	1
Energy/Oil & Gas E&P	5	5
Energy/Oil & Gas Equipment & Services	4	4
Energy/Oil & Gas Integrated	6	6
Energy/Oil & Gas Refining & Marketing	4	4
Financial Services/Banks—Global	2	0
Financial Services/Banks—Regional—US	1	0
Financial Services/Capital Markets	2	0
Financial Services/Credit Services	2	0
Financial Services/Insurance—Diversified	2	0
Financial Services/Insurance—Life	2	0
Healthcare/Biotechnology	1	1
Healthcare/Diagnostics & Research	1	1
Healthcare/Drug Manufacturers—Major	7	7
Healthcare/Health Care Plans	4	3
Healthcare/Medical Care	2	2
Healthcare/Medical Devices	5	5
Healthcare/Medical Distribution	2	2
Healthcare/Medical Instruments & Supplies	9	10
Industrials/Aerospace & Defense	12	12

(continued)

1.04

TABLE 1-1: INDUSTRY CLASSIFICATIONS OF SURVEY ENTITIES—(continued)

	2011	2010
Industrials/Airlines	3	0
Industrials/Business Equipment	7	7
Industrials/Business Services	14	13
Industrials/Conglomerates	4	4
Industrials/Diversified Industrials	33	33
Industrials/Engineering & Construction	6	6
Industrials/Farm & Construction Equipment	7	7
Industrials/Industrial Distribution	3	3
Industrials/Integrated Shipping & Logistics	2	2
Industrials/Metal Fabrication	4	4
Industrials/Railroads	2	1
Industrials/Rental & Leasing Services	2	2
Industrials/Security & Protection Services	1	1
Industrials/Staffing & Outsourcing Services	5	6
Industrials/Tools & Accessories	5	5
Industrials/Truck Manufacturing	2	2
Industrials/Trucking	3	3
Industrials/Waste Management	2	2
Real Estate/REIT—Industrial	3	3
Technology/Communications Equipment	7	7
Technology/Computer Distribution	2	2
Technology/Computer Systems	5	5
Technology/Consumer Electronics	2	2
Technology/Contract Manufacturers	2	2
Technology/Data Storage	4	4
Technology/Electronic Components	6	8
Technology/Electronic Gaming & Multimedia	1	1
Technology/Electronics Distribution	2	2
Technology/Information Technology Services	4	4
Technology/Internet Content & Information	3	3
Technology/Scientific & Technical Instruments	3	3
Technology/Semiconductor Equipment & Materials	3	3
Technology/Semiconductor Memory	2	2
Technology/Semiconductors	10	10
Technology/Software—Application	8	8
Technology/Software—Infrastructure	3	4
Technology/Solar	1	1
Total Entities	**500**	**500**

1.05

TABLE 1-2: FILING CLASSIFICATION OF SURVEY ENTITIES*

Table 1-2 shows the filing classifications of the survey entities.

	2011
Smaller reporting company	4
Non-accelerated filer	5
Accelerated filer	55
Large accelerated filer	436
Total	**500**

* Note: 2011 was the first year these data were tracked in Accounting Trends & Techniques, so no prior year data are available.

1.06

TABLE 1-3: SIZE OF SURVEY ENTITIES BY AMOUNT OF REVENUE*

Table 1-3 indicates the relative size of the survey entities as measured by dollar amount of revenue.

	2011
Less than $500,000,000	13
Between $500,000,001 and $1,000,000,000	18
Between $1,000,000,001 and $2,000,000,000	53
Between $2,000,000,001 and $3,000,000,000	64
Between $3,000,000,001 and $4,000,000,000	48
Between $4,000,000,001 and $5,000,000,000	33
Between $5,000,000,001 and $10,000,000,000	100
Between $10,000,000,001 and $50,000,000,000	130
More than $50,000,000,000	41
Total Entities	**500**

* Note: Due to a shift in the categories of entity size in this edition, no prior year data are available.

GENERAL FINANCIAL STATEMENT CONSIDERATIONS

RECOGNITION AND MEASUREMENT

1.07 Financial Accounting Standards Board (FASB) *Accounting Standards Codification* (ASC) 105-10-05-2 explains that if the necessary guidance for a transaction or event is not specified within a source of authoritative generally accepted accounting principles (GAAP), an entity should first consider accounting principles for similar transactions or events within a source of authoritative GAAP for that entity and then consider nonauthoritative guidance from other sources. When those accounting principles either prohibit the application of the accounting treatment to the particular transaction or event or indicate that the accounting treatment should not be applied by analogy, an entity should not follow those accounting principles.

1.08 FASB ASC 105-10-05-3 explains that accounting and financial reporting practices not included in FASB ASC are nonauthoritative. FASB Concept Statements are not considered authoritative sources of GAAP, and no preference is given to the FASB Concept Statements over other nonauthoritative sources. FASB ASC does not state that consistency with the FASB Concept Statements in connection with an entity's application of an accounting treatment is necessary. Sources of nonauthoritative accounting guidance include the following:

- Practices that are widely recognized and prevalent, either generally or in the industry
- FASB Concept Statements
- AICPA Issues Papers
- International Financial Reporting Standards (IFRSs) of the International Accounting Standards Board
- Pronouncements of professional associations or regulatory agencies
- Technical Questions and Answers included in AICPA *Technical Practice Aids*
- Accounting textbooks, handbooks, and articles

The appropriateness of other sources of accounting guidance depends on its relevance to particular circumstances, the specificity of the guidance, the general recognition of the issuer or author as an authority, and the extent of its use in practice.

1.09 As discussed in FASB ASC 105-10-05-1, GAAP, as codified in FASB ASC, includes the rules and interpretive releases of the SEC as sources of authoritative GAAP as a convenience to SEC registrants. In addition to SEC rules and interpretive releases, the SEC staff issues Staff Accounting Bulletins that represent practices that the staff follows when administering SEC disclosure requirements. SEC staff announcements and observer comments made at meetings of the Emerging Issues Task Force publicly announce the staff's views on certain accounting issues for SEC registrants.

1.10 In June 2009, FASB issued the last FASB statement referenced in that form: FASB Statement No. 168, *The FASB Accounting Standards Codification™ and the Hierarchy of Generally Accepted Accounting Principles—a replacement of FASB Statement No. 162*. This standard established FASB ASC as the source of authoritative U.S. accounting and reporting standards for nongovernmental companies, in addition to guidance issued by the SEC, and was effective for financial statements issued for interim and annual periods ending after September 15, 2009.

1.11 In FASB ASC's Notice to Constituents (NTC), FASB suggests the use of plain English references to describe broad FASB ASC topics going forward in financial statements and related footnote disclosures. FASB provides the following example of plain English references in the NTC when referring to the requirements of FASB ASC 815, *Derivatives and Hedging*: "as required by the Derivatives and Hedging Topic of the FASB Accounting Standards Codification."

1.12 A natural business year is the period of 12 consecutive months that end when the business activities of an entity have reached the lowest point in their annual cycle. In many instances, the natural business year of an entity ends December 31.

1.13

TABLE 1-4: FASB ASC REFERENCING

Table 1-4 indicates the method in which the survey entities referenced FASB ASC.

	Number of Entities		
	2011	2010	2009
Plain English references throughout....................	334	350	236
Specific FASB ASC references throughout..........	84	78	98
Dual referencing (use of both plain English and specific references is the same paragraph, typically by using a parenthetical).....................	21	34	35
Mix of both plain English and FASB ASC references..........	61	38	—
Legacy referencing to old standard names only (for example, SFAS No. 157).............................	—	—	2
Pre-codification financial statements....................	—	—	129
Total Entities.............................	**500**	**500**	**500**

PRESENTATION

1.14 Rule 14a-3 of the Securities Exchange Act of 1934 states that annual reports furnished to stockholders in connection with the annual meetings of stockholders should include audited financial statements: balance sheets as of the end of the two most recent fiscal years and statements of income and cash flows for each of the three most recent fiscal years. Rule 14a-3 also states that the following information, as specified in SEC Regulation S-K should be included in the annual report to stockholders:

- Selected quarterly financial data
- Changes in, and disagreements with, accountants on accounting and financial disclosure
- Summary of selected financial data for the last five years
- Description of business activities
- Segment information
- Listing of company directors and executive officers
- Market price of, and dividends on, the company's common stock for each quarterly period within the two most recent fiscal years
- Management's discussion and analysis (MD&A) of financial condition and results of operations
- Quantitative and qualitative disclosures about market risk

1.15 FASB ASC 205-10-45-2 states only that it is ordinarily desirable for an entity to present the statement of financial position; the income statement; and the statement of changes in equity for one or more preceding years, in addition to those of the current year.

1.16 Paragraphs 3–4 of FASB ASC 205-10-45 require these statements to be comparable, and any exceptions to comparability should be described as required by FASB ASC 250, *Accounting Changes and Error Corrections*. An entity is required to repeat, or at least refer to, any notes to financial statements, other explanations, or accountants' reports that contain qualifications for prior years that appeared in the comparative statements when originally issued, to the extent this information remains significant. Multiple rules set forth in SEC Regulation S-X provide guidance to SEC registrants on the form and ordering of financial statements, the presentation of amounts, the omission of certain items, and requirements for supplemental schedules. Rule 14a-3 requires that annual reports to stockholders should include comparative balance sheets and statements of income and cash flows for each of the three most recent fiscal years. All the survey entities are SEC registrants and conformed to the aforementioned requirements of Rule 14a-3.

1.17 FASB ASC permits an entity to offset a liability with an asset only when the following certain conditions discussed in FASB ASC 210-20-45-1 are met:
- Each of two parties owes the other determinable amounts.
- The reporting party has the right to set off the amount owed with the amount owed by the other party.
- The reporting party intends to set off.
- The right of setoff is enforceable by law.

Author's Note

In December 2011, FASB issued Accounting Standards Update (ASU) No. 2011-11, *Balance Sheet (Topic 210): Disclosures about Offsetting Assets and Liabilities*, to enhance comparability of financial statements prepared in accordance with GAAP and IFRS. The amendments in this update will enhance disclosures by requiring improved information about financial instruments and derivative instruments that are either (*a*) offset in accordance with either FASB ASC 210-20-45 or 815-10-45 or (*b*) subject to an enforceable master netting arrangement or similar agreement, irrespective of whether they are offset in accordance with either of the aforementioned FASB ASC sections. The additional disclosures will enable financial statement users to better understand the effect of such arrangements on their financial position. Entities are required to apply the amendments in this ASU for annual reporting periods beginning on or after January 1, 2013, and interim periods within those annual periods. As a result of the effective date of this ASU, the excerpts appearing later in this section may not reflect all or some of these revisions.

DISCLOSURE

1.18 SEC Regulations S-X and S-K and AU section 431, *Adequacy of Disclosure in Financial Statements* (AICPA, *Professional Standards*), state the need for adequate disclosure in financial statements. Normally, the financial statements alone cannot present all information necessary for adequate disclosure without considering appended notes that disclose information. All surveyed entities provided footnote disclosures to their financial statements.

1.19 FASB ASC 235, *Notes to Financial Statements*, sets forth guidelines about the content and format of disclosures of ac-

counting policies. FASB ASC 235-10-50-1 requires that the significant accounting policies of an entity be presented as an integral part of the financial statements of the entity. FASB ASC 235-10-50-6 states that the preferable format is to present a summary of significant accounting policies preceding notes to financial statements or as the initial note under the same or a similar title.

1.20 FASB ASC 205-10-50-1 requires an entity to provide information explaining changes due to reclassifications or other reasons that affect the manner of, or basis for, presenting corresponding items for two or more periods. FASB ASC 250-10 does not require an entity to present an opening balance sheet of the earliest period presented when an entity retrospectively applies a change in accounting policy or restates to correct an error.

1.21 FASB ASC 275, *Risks and Uncertainties*, requires reporting entities to disclose information about the risks and uncertainties resulting from the nature of their operations, the use of estimates in preparing financial statements, and significant concentrations in certain aspects of the entity's operations.

1.22

TABLE 1-5: DISCLOSURE OF ACCOUNTING POLICIES

Table 1-5 shows the nature of information frequently disclosed in summaries of accounting policies and the number of survey entities disclosing such information.

	Number of Entities		
	2011	2010	2009
Revenue recognition	491	491	485
Consolidation policy	459	473	477
Use of estimates	461	476	476
Property	481	484	475
Cash equivalents	477	485	474
Depreciation methods	480	488	456
Amortization of intangibles	389	395	456
Interperiod tax allocation	206	314	449
Impairment	451	457	436
Financial instruments	387	433	435
Inventory pricing	412	430	429
Stock-based compensation	402	425	414
Translation of foreign currency	383	389	383
Nature of operations	387	403	365
Earnings per share calculation	278	327	297
Accounts receivable	326	351	349
Advertising costs	241	258	244
Employee benefits	212	263	229
Research and development costs	166	202	185
Credit risk concentrations	153	220	181
Fiscal years	151	171	150
Environmental costs	127	150	129
Capitalization of interest	87	114	98
Market risk concentrations	73	N/C*	N/C*
Income taxes	447	N/C*	N/C*

* N/C = Not compiled. Line item was not included in the table for the year shown.

PRESENTATION AND DISCLOSURE EXCERPTS

Plain English References

1.23

INTEL CORPORATION (DEC)

NOTES TO CONSOLIDATED FINANCIAL STATEMENTS

Note 3—Accounting Changes (in part)

2011

In the first quarter of 2011, we adopted new standards for revenue recognition with multiple deliverables. These new standards change the determination of whether the individual deliverables included in a multiple-element arrangement may be treated as separate units for accounting purposes. Additionally, these new standards modify the method by which revenue is allocated to the separately identified deliverables. The adoption of these new standards did not have a significant impact on our consolidated financial statements.

In the first quarter of 2011, we adopted new standards that remove certain tangible products and associated software from the scope of the software revenue recognition guidance. The adoption of these new standards did not have a significant impact on our consolidated financial statements.

In the fourth quarter of 2011, we adopted amended standards that simplify how entities test goodwill for impairment. These amended standards permit an assessment of qualitative factors to determine whether it is more likely than not that the fair value of a reporting unit in which goodwill resides is less than its carrying value. For reporting units in which this assessment concludes that it is more likely than not that the fair value is more than its carrying value, these amended standards eliminate the requirement to perform goodwill impairment testing. The adoption of these amended standards did not have an impact on our consolidated financial statements.

Note 4—Recent Accounting Standards

In May 2011, the Financial Accounting Standards Board (FASB) issued amended standards to achieve a consistent definition of fair value and common requirements for measurement of and disclosure about fair value between U.S. generally accepted accounting principles and International Financial Reporting Standards. For assets and liabilities categorized as Level 3 and recognized at fair value, these amended standards require disclosure of quantitative information about unobservable inputs, a description of the valuation processes used by the entity, and a qualitative discussion about the sensitivity of the measurements. In addition, these amended standards require that we disclose the level in the fair value hierarchy for financial instruments disclosed at fair value but not recorded at fair value. These new standards are effective for us beginning in the first quarter of 2012; early adoption of these standards is prohibited. We do not expect these new standards to significantly impact our consolidated financial statements.

In 2011, the FASB issued amended standards to increase the prominence of items reported in other comprehensive income. These amendments eliminate the option to present components of other comprehensive income as part of the statement of changes in stockholders' equity and require that all changes in stockholders' equity—except investments by, and distributions to, owners—be presented either in a single continuous statement of comprehensive income or in two separate but consecutive statements. These new standards are effective for us beginning in the first quarter of 2012 and are to be applied retrospectively. These amended standards will impact the presentation of other comprehensive income but will not impact our financial position or results of operations.

1.24

UNISYS CORPORATION (DEC)

NOTES TO CONSOLIDATED FINANCIAL STATEMENTS

Note 5—Recent Accounting Pronouncements and Accounting Changes

Effective January 1, 2011, the company adopted two accounting standards issued by the Financial Accounting Standards Board (FASB) that amend revenue recognition guidance. The first standard supersedes certain prior accounting guidance and requires an entity to allocate arrangement consideration at the inception of an arrangement to all of its deliverables based on their relative standalone selling prices (i.e., the relative-selling-price method). The standard eliminates the use of the residual method of allocation and requires the relative-selling-price method in all circumstances in which an entity recognizes revenue for an arrangement with multiple deliverables subject to this standard. The second standard amends prior software revenue recognition accounting guidance by excluding from the scope of such prior guidance tangible products that contain both software elements and non-software elements that function together to deliver the tangible product's essential functionality. The company has adopted the new standards prospectively for revenue arrangements entered into or materially modified on or after January 1, 2011. In certain of the company's arrangements, revenue was previously deferred for certain deliverables included in multiple element arrangements where the arrangements also included undelivered services for which the company was unable to demonstrate fair value pursuant to previous standards. The new standards require deliverables for which revenue was previously deferred to be separated and recognized as delivered, rather than combined with undelivered items and recognized over the longest service delivery period.

If the new standards were applied to transactions entered into or materially modified in the year ended December 31, 2010, it would not have resulted in a material change to the company's reported revenue for 2010. The company is not able to reasonably estimate the effect of adopting these standards on future periods as the impact will vary based on the nature and volume of new or materially modified deals in any given period.

On October 1, 2011, the company adopted FASB amendments issued in September 2011 to authoritative accounting guidance to simplify how companies test for goodwill impairment. The amendments permit a company to continue to perform quantitative analyses or to first assess qualitative factors to determine whether it is more likely than not (defined as having a likelihood of more than 50 percent) that the fair value of a reporting unit is less than its carrying amount as a basis for determining whether it is necessary to perform the two-step goodwill impairment test described by current accounting rules. Previous accounting guidance required an entity to test goodwill for impairment, on at least an annual basis, by comparing the fair value of a reporting unit with its carrying amount. If the fair value of a reporting unit is less than its carrying amount, then a second step of the test must be performed to measure the amount of impairment loss, if any. Under the amendments, a company is not required to calculate the fair value of a reporting unit unless the company determines that it is more likely than not that its fair value is less than its carrying amount. Adoption of the amendments did not have a material impact to the company's consolidated financial statements.

In June 2011, the FASB issued authoritative guidance that amends previous guidance for the presentation of comprehensive income. It eliminates the current option to present other comprehensive income in the statement of changes in equity. Under this revised guidance, an entity will have the option to present the components of net income and other comprehensive income in either a single continuous statement of comprehensive income or in two separate but consecutive financial statements. The new standard is to be applied retrospectively and is effective for the company beginning in the first quarter of 2012. The company is currently evaluating the alternatives for adopting the guidance. Other than the change in presentation, the company has determined that these changes will not have an impact on its consolidated financial statements.

In May 2011, the FASB issued authoritative guidance that amends previous guidance for fair value measurement and disclosure requirements. The revised guidance changes certain fair value measurement principles, clarifies the application of existing fair value measurements and expands the disclosure requirements, particularly for Level 3 fair value measurements. This standard is effective for the company beginning in the first quarter of 2012. The company is currently evaluating the impact of this guidance, but does not anticipate a material impact to its consolidated financial statements upon adoption.

Specific FASB ASC References

1.25

THE BON-TON STORES, INC. (JAN)

NOTES TO CONSOLIDATED FINANCIAL STATEMENTS

(In thousands except share and per share data)

Note 1—Summary of Significant Accounting Policies (in part)

Property, Fixtures and Equipment: Depreciation and Amortization (in part)

Costs of major remodeling and improvements on leased stores are capitalized as leasehold improvements. Leasehold improvements are amortized over the shorter of the accounting lease term or the useful life of the asset. Capital leases are recorded at the lower of fair market value or the present value of future minimum lease payments. Capital leases are amortized in accordance with the provisions codified within Accounting Standards Codification ("ASC") Subtopic 840-30, *Leases—Capital Leases*.

ASC Section 360-10-35, *Property, Plant and Equipment—Overall—Subsequent Measurement* ("ASC 360-10-35"), requires the Company to test a long-lived asset for recoverability whenever events or changes in circumstances indicate that its carrying value may not be recoverable. If the undiscounted cash flows associated with the asset are insufficient to support the recorded asset, an impairment loss is recognized for the amount (if any) by which the carrying amount of the asset exceeds the fair value of the asset. Cash flow estimates are based on historical results, adjusted to reflect the Company's best estimate of future market and operating conditions. Estimates of fair value are determined through various techniques, including discounted cash flow models and market approaches, as considered necessary. As a result of this evaluation, asset impairment charges, which resulted in a reduction in the carrying amount of certain store and distribution center properties of $1,738, $5,717 and $17,853, were recorded in 2010, 2009 and 2008, respectively (see Note 2).

Goodwill and Intangible Assets (in part)

In accordance with the provisions codified within ASC Section 350-20-35, *Intangibles—Goodwill and Other—Goodwill—Subsequent Measurement* ("ASC 350-20-35"), and ASC Section 350-30-35, *Intangibles—Goodwill and Other—General Intangibles Other than Goodwill—Subsequent Measurement* ("ASC 350-30-35"), goodwill and other intangible assets that have indefinite lives, respectively, are reviewed for impairment at the reporting unit level at least annually or when events or changes in circumstances indicate it is more likely than not that the carrying value of these assets exceeds their implied fair values. Intangible assets subject to amortization are reviewed for impairment in accordance with ASC 360-10-35. Based on its reporting structure, management has determined the Company has one reporting unit for purposes of applying ASC 350-20-35 and ASC 350-30-35. Fair value is determined using a discounted cash flow analysis, which requires certain assumptions and estimates regarding industry economic factors and future profitability of acquired businesses. The Company's policy is to conduct impairment testing based on its most current business plans, which reflect anticipated changes in the economy and the industry.

Income Taxes (in part)

Income taxes are accounted for under the asset and liability method, pursuant to ASC Topic 740, *Income Taxes* ("ASC 740"). Deferred tax assets and liabilities are recognized for the future tax consequences attributable to differences between the financial statement carrying amounts of existing assets and liabilities and their respective tax bases and operating loss and tax credit carryforwards. Deferred tax assets and liabilities are measured using enacted tax rates expected to apply to taxable income in the years in which those temporary differences are expected to be recovered or settled. The effect on deferred tax assets and liabilities of a change in tax rates is recognized in income in the period that includes the enactment date. ASC 740 requires an assessment of whether valuation allowances are needed against deferred tax assets based upon consideration of all available evidence using a "more likely than not" standard. The Company reported valuation allowances of $126,333 and $140,452 at January 29, 2011 and January 30, 2010, respectively (see Note 16).

Share-Based Compensation

The Company recognizes share-based compensation pursuant to ASC Topic 718, *Compensation—Stock Compensation* ("ASC 718"). The Company measures the cost of grantee services received in exchange for an award of equity instruments based on the grant date fair value of the award, and recognizes that cost over the period that the grantee is required to provide service in exchange for the award. For stock option awards, the Company estimates grant date fair value using the Black-Scholes option valuation model.

Earnings Per Share (in part)

Effective February 1, 2009, the Company adopted certain new provisions now codified within ASC Topic 260, *Earnings Per Share* ("ASC 260"), pursuant to which unvested share-based payment awards that contain nonforfeitable rights to dividends or dividend equivalents, whether paid or unpaid, are considered participating securities and are included in the computation of earnings per share ("EPS") according to the two-class method if the impact is dilutive. The Company's unvested restricted shares and restricted stock units are considered participating securities. However, in the event of a net loss, participating securities are excluded from the calculation of both basic and diluted EPS. All prior-period EPS data presented was adjusted retrospectively to conform to these provisions of ASC 260, which, for 2008, had no effect on the previously reported basic and diluted earnings per share.

Recently Issued Accounting Standards

In January 2010, the Financial Accounting Standards Board ("FASB") issued Accounting Standards Update ("ASU") No. 2010-06, *Fair Value Measurements and Disclosures (Topic 820): Improving Disclosures about Fair Value Measurements* ("ASU 2010-06"), which requires new disclosures regarding recurring or nonrecurring fair value measurements. Entities are required to separately disclose significant transfers into and out of Level 1 and Level 2 measurements in the fair value hierarchy and the reasons for the transfers, and to provide information on purchases, sales, issuances and settlements on a gross basis in the reconciliation of Level 3 fair value measurements. In addition, entities must provide fair value measurement disclosures for each class of assets and liabilities and, for Level 2 or Level 3 measurements, disclose the valuation technique and inputs used in determining fair value for each class. ASU 2010-06 impacts disclosure requirements only. The Company adopted ASU 2010-06 in the first quarter of 2010, with the exception of the additional information in the reconciliation of Level 3 assets and liabilities, which will be effective in 2011. There were no transfers into or out of Level 1 or 2 of the fair value hierarchy in 2010.

In December 2009, the FASB issued ASU No. 2009-17, *Consolidation (Topic 810): Improvements to Financial Reporting by Enterprises Involved with Variable Interest Entities* ("ASU 2009-17"), which changed the accounting for variable interest entities ("VIEs"). These changes require an entity to (1) perform an analysis to determine if the entity has a variable interest in a VIE; (2) initially determine and reassess, on an ongoing basis, whether an entity is the primary beneficiary of a VIE; (3) eliminate the solely quantitative approach previously required in determining the primary beneficiary of a VIE in favor of a qualitatively focused analysis; and (4) provide enhanced disclosures regarding an entity's involvement in a VIE. The Company adopted the provisions of this update in 2010. The adoption of ASU 2009-17 did not have a material impact on the Company's consolidated financial statements.

Quarterly Financial Data

1.26

UNIVERSAL CORPORATION (MAR)

NOTES TO CONSOLIDATED FINANCIAL STATEMENTS

(All dollar amounts are in thousands, except per share amounts or as otherwise noted)

Note 16—Unaudited Quarterly Financial Data

Unaudited quarterly financial data for the fiscal years ended March 31, 2011 and 2010, is provided in the table below. Due to the seasonal nature of the Company's business, management believes it is generally more meaningful to focus on cumulative rather than quarterly results.

	First Quarter	Second Quarter	Third Quarter	Fourth Quarter
Fiscal Year Ended March 31, 2011				
Sales and other operating revenues	$538,916	$664,188	$688,208	$680,215
Gross profit	102,237	133,274	154,044	118,778
Net income	24,418	53,783	57,585	28,764
Net income attributable to Universal Corporation	25,320	51,831	52,298	27,116
Earnings available to Universal Corporation common shareholders after dividends on convertible perpetual preferred stock	21,608	48,118	48,586	23,403
Earnings per share attributable to Universal Corporation common shareholders:				
Basic	0.89	2.00	2.05	1.00
Diluted	0.87	1.78	1.82	0.95
Cash dividends declared per share of convertible perpetual preferred stock	16.88	16.87	16.88	16.87
Cash dividends declared per share of common stock	0.47	0.47	0.48	0.48
Market price range of common stock:				
High	55.92	44.82	43.34	43.72
Low	38.38	35.44	37.05	37.74
Fiscal Year Ended March 31, 2010				
Sales and other operating revenues	$616,112	$647,918	$661,205	$566,503
Gross profit	139,364	147,343	144,664	110,894
Net income	43,804	54,672	48,474	23,395
Net income attributable to Universal Corporation	43,745	52,515	45,696	26,441
Earnings available to Universal Corporation common shareholders after dividends on convertible perpetual preferred stock	40,033	48,802	41,984	22,728
Earnings per share attributable to Universal Corporation common shareholders:				
Basic	1.60	1.97	1.70	0.93
Diluted	1.47	1.77	1.54	0.90
Cash dividends declared per share of convertible perpetual preferred stock	16.88	16.87	16.88	16.87
Cash dividends declared per share of common stock	0.46	0.46	0.47	0.47
Market price range of common stock:				
High	38.29	44.02	49.48	55.19
Low	29.27	33.46	41.27	45.36

Note: Earnings per share amounts for each fiscal year may not equal the total of the four quarterly amounts due to differences in weighted-average outstanding shares for the respective periods and to the fact that the Company's convertible perpetual preferred stock may be antidilutive for some periods.

Significant items included in the quarterly results were as follows:

- First Quarter 2011—restructuring costs of $0.9 million associated with voluntary early retirement offers aimed at reducing costs in the Company's U.S. operations. The restructuring costs reduced net income attributable to Universal Corporation by approximately $0.6 million and diluted earnings per share by $0.02.
- Second Quarter 2011—a $7.4 million reversal of a portion of a charge recorded in fiscal year 2005 to accrue a fine imposed by the European Commission on Deltafina, S.p.A., the Company's subsidiary in Italy, related to tobacco buying practices in Spain. The reversal reflected a favorable court decision in Deltafina's appeal of the fine and increased net income attributable to Universal Corporation by $4.8 million and diluted earnings per share by $0.17. The Company also recorded restructuring costs of approximately $2.0 million primarily related to voluntary early retirement offers in the Company's U.S. operations and voluntary and involuntary separations in various other locations. The restructuring costs reduced net income attributable to Universal

Corporation by $1.3 million and diluted earnings per share by $0.05.

- Third Quarter 2011—a $19.4 million gain on the assignment of farmer contracts and sale of related assets in Brazil to an operating subsidiary of one of the Company's major customers. The gain increased net income attributable to Universal Corporation by $12.6 million and diluted earnings per share by $0.44. The Company also recorded restructuring and impairment costs totaling $11.0 million during the quarter. Those costs primarily related to a decision to close the Company's leaf tobacco processing operations in Canada and sell the assets of the operations, but they also included costs associated with initiatives to restructure and downsize activities at various other locations. The restructuring and impairment costs reduced net income attributable to Universal Corporation by $7.5 million and diluted earnings per share by $0.26.
- Fourth Quarter 2011—restructuring and impairment costs totaling $7.5 million. The restructuring costs included pension curtailment and settlement charges related to the termination of a defined benefit pension plan with the closing of the operations in Canada, as well as costs associated with voluntary early retirement

offers in the Company's U.S. operations and voluntary and involuntary separations in various other locations. The restructuring and impairment costs reduced net income attributable to Universal Corporation by $4.8 million and diluted earnings per share by $0.17.

Selected Information for Five Years

1.27

THE MOSAIC COMPANY (MAY)

NOTES TO CONSOLIDATED FINANCIAL STATEMENTS

(In millions, except per share amounts)

Five Year Comparison

	\multicolumn{5}{c}{Years Ended May 31}
	2011	**2010**	**2009**	**2008**	**2007**
Statements of Operations Data:					
Net sales	$ 9,937.8	$ 6,759.1	$10,298.0	$ 9,812.6	$5,773.7
Cost of goods sold	6,816.0	5,065.8	7,148.1	6,652.1	4,847.6
Lower of cost or market write-down	—	—	383.2	—	—
Gross margin	3,121.8	1,693.3	2,766.7	3,160.5	926.1
Selling, general and administrative expenses	372.5	360.3	321.4	323.8	309.8
Restructuring loss (gain)	—	—	0.6	18.3	(2.1)
Other operating expenses	85.1	62.2	43.8	11.7	2.1
Operating earnings	2,664.2	1,270.8	2,400.9	2,806.7	616.3
Interest expense, net	5.1	49.6	43.3	90.5	149.6
Foreign currency transaction (loss)	(56.3)	(32.4)	(131.8)	(57.5)	(8.6)
Gain on sale of equity investment[a]	685.6	—	673.4	—	—
Other income (expense)	(17.1)	0.9	6.5	23.7	47.6
Earnings from consolidated companies before income taxes	3,271.3	1,189.7	2,905.7	2,682.4	505.7
Provision for income taxes	752.8	347.3	649.3	714.9	123.4
Earnings from consolidated companies	2,518.5	842.4	2,256.4	1,967.5	382.3
Equity in net earnings (loss) of nonconsolidated companies	(5.0)	(10.9)	100.1	124.0	41.3
Net earnings including non-controlling interests	2,513.5	831.5	2,356.5	2,091.5	423.6
Less: Net earnings (loss) attributable to non-controlling interests	(1.1)	4.4	6.3	8.7	3.9
Net earnings attributable to Mosaic	$ 2,514.6	$ 827.1	$ 2,350.2	$ 2,082.8	$ 419.7
Earnings per Common Share Attributable to Mosaic:					
Basic net earnings per share	$ 5.64	$ 1.86	$ 5.29	$ 4.70	$ 0.97
Diluted net earnings per share	$ 5.62	$ 1.85	$ 5.27	$ 4.67	$ 0.95
Average Shares Outstanding:					
Basic weighted average number of shares outstanding	$ 446.0	$ 445.1	$ 444.3	$ 442.7	$ 434.3
Diluted weighted average number of shares outstanding	447.5	446.6	446.2	445.7	440.3
Balance Sheet Data (At Period End):					
Cash and cash equivalents	$ 3,906.4	$ 2,523.0	$ 2,703.2	$ 1,960.7	$ 420.6
Total assets	15,786.9	12,707.7	12,676.2	11,819.8	9,163.6
Total long-term debt (including current maturities)	809.3	1,260.8	1,299.8	1,418.3	2,221.9
Total liabilities	4,125.0	3,959.3	4,161.0	5,065.2	4,957.4
Total equity	11,661.9	8,748.4	8,515.2	6,754.6	4,206.2
Other Financial Data:					
Depreciation, depletion and amortization	$ 447.4	$ 445.0	$ 360.5	$ 358.1	$ 329.4
Capital expenditures	1,263.2	910.6	781.1	372.1	292.1
Dividends per share[b]	0.20	1.50	0.20	—	—

[a] In fiscal 2011 we recorded a $685.6 million pre-tax gain on the sale of our equity method investment in Fosfertil. We recorded a $673.4 million pre-tax gain on the sale of our equity method investment in Saskferco in fiscal 2009. See further discussion in Note 10 to the Consolidated Financial Statements.

[b] In fiscal 2010 we paid a special dividend of $1.30 per share in addition to quarterly dividends of $0.05 per share.

Forward-Looking Information

1.28

BROWN-FORMAN CORPORATION (APR)

IMPORTANT INFORMATION ON FORWARD-LOOKING STATEMENTS

This report contains statements, estimates, and projections that are "forward-looking statements" as defined under U.S. federal securities laws. Words such as "aim," "anticipate," "aspire," "believe," "envision," "estimate," "expect," "expectation," "intend," "may," "potential," "project," "pursue," "see," "will," "will continue," and similar words identify forward-looking statements, which speak only as of the date we make them. Except as required by law, we do not intend to update or revise any forward-looking statements, whether as a result of new information, future events, or otherwise. By their nature, forward-looking statements involve risks, uncertainties and other factors (many beyond our control) that could cause our actual results to differ materially from our historical experience or from our current expectations or projections. These risks and other factors include, but are not limited to:

- declining or depressed economic conditions in our markets; political, financial, or credit or capital market instability; supplier, customer or consumer credit or other financial problems; bank failures or governmental debt defaults or nationalizations
- failure to develop or implement effective business and brand strategies and innovations, including route-to-consumer, and marketing and promotional activity
- unfavorable trade or consumer reaction to our new products, product line extensions, or changes in formulation, packaging or pricing
- inventory fluctuations in our products by distributors, wholesalers, or retailers
- competitors' pricing actions (including price reductions, promotions, discounting, couponing or free goods), marketing, category expansion, product introductions, entry or expansion in our markets, or other competitive activities
- declines in consumer confidence or spending, whether related to the economy (such as austerity measures, tax increases, high fuel costs, or higher unemployment), wars, natural or other disasters, weather, pandemics, security concerns, terrorist attacks or other factors
- changes in tax rates (including excise, sales, VAT, tariffs, duties, corporate, individual income, dividends, capital gains) or in related reserves, changes in tax rules (e.g., LIFO, foreign income deferral, U.S. manufacturing and other deductions) or accounting standards, or other restrictions affecting beverage alcohol, and the unpredictability and suddenness with which they can occur
- governmental or other restrictions on our ability to produce, import, sell, price, or market our products, including advertising and promotion in either traditional or new media; regulatory compliance costs
- business disruption, decline or costs related to reductions in workforce or other cost-cutting measures
- lower returns or discount rates related to pension assets, interest rate fluctuations, inflation or deflation
- fluctuations in the U.S. dollar against foreign currencies, especially the euro, British pound, Australian dollar, or Polish zloty
- changes in consumer behavior or preferences and our ability to anticipate and respond to them, including societal attitudes or cultural trends that result in reduced consumption of our products; reduction of bar, restaurant, hotel or other on-premise business or travel
- consumer shifts away from spirits or premium-priced spirits products; shifts to discount store purchases or other price-sensitive consumer behavior
- distribution and other route-to-consumer decisions or changes that affect the timing of our sales, temporarily disrupt the marketing or sale of our products, or result in implementation-related costs
- effects of acquisitions, dispositions, joint ventures, business partnerships or investments, or portfolio strategies, including integration costs, disruption or other difficulties, or impairment in the recorded value of assets (e.g. receivables, inventory, fixed assets, goodwill, trademarks and other intangibles)
- lower profits, due to factors such as fewer or less profitable used barrel sales, lower production volumes, decreased demand for products we sell, sales mix shift toward lower priced or lower margin SKUs, or cost increases in energy or raw materials, such as grain, agave, wood, glass, plastic, or closures
- natural disasters, climate change, agricultural uncertainties, environmental or other catastrophes, our suppliers' financial hardships or other factors that affect the availability, price, or quality of agave, grain, glass, energy, closures, plastic, water, wood, or finished goods
- negative publicity related to our company, brands, marketing, personnel, operations, business performance or prospects
- product counterfeiting, tampering, contamination, or recalls and resulting negative effects on our sales, brand equity, or corporate reputation
- significant costs or other adverse developments stemming from class action, intellectual property, governmental, or other major litigation; or governmental investigations of beverage alcohol industry business, trade, or marketing practices by us, our importers, distributors, or retailers

Liquidity and Capital Resources

1.29

AIRGAS, INC. (MAR)

MANAGEMENT'S DISCUSSION AND ANALYSIS OF FINANCIAL CONDITION AND RESULTS OF OPERATIONS

Liquidity and Capital Resources

Cash Flows

Net cash provided by operating activities was $275 million in fiscal 2011 compared to $600 million in fiscal 2010 and $583 million in fiscal 2009. The reduction in net cash provided by operating activities during fiscal 2011 was principally driven by the new accounting treatment for the Company's Securitization Agreement, which resulted in a $295 million use of cash in operating activities and a corresponding source of cash in financing activities in the current year. On April 1, 2010, the Company adopted new accounting guidance which affected the presentation of its trade receivables securitization program. Under the new guidance, proceeds received under the securitization are treated as secured borrowings, which are classified as a financing activity on the Consolidated Statement of Cash Flows, whereas previously they were treated as proceeds from the sale of trade receivables, which were classified as an operating activity on the Consolidated Statement of Cash Flows. Furthermore, the new accounting treatment resulted in the recognition of both the trade receivables securitized under the program and the borrowings they collateralize on the Company's Consolidated Balance Sheet, which led to a $295 million increase in trade receivables and long-term debt as of April 1, 2010. Accordingly, $295 million in new borrowings under the Securitization Agreement were classified as sources of cash under financing activities on the Company's Consolidated Statement of Cash Flows. Prior to April 1, 2010, these borrowings were treated as proceeds from the sale of trade receivables and reflected net of collections on the Consolidated Statement of Cash Flows as operating activities. Additionally, the $295 million increase in trade receivables was classified as a use of cash from operating activities.

The Company's underlying business activities generated strong operating cash flows during fiscal 2011. Net earnings adjusted for non-cash and non-operating items provided cash of $598 million in fiscal 2011 versus $541 million in fiscal 2010 and $605 million in fiscal 2009. Adjusted cash from operations, which essentially removes the impact of the fiscal 2011 change in accounting principle noted above and cash expenditures related to the Air Products unsolicited takeover attempt in fiscal 2011 and fiscal 2010 from the Company's net cash provided by operating activities, was $617 million in the current year as compared to $648 million in the prior year. The fiscal 2011 decline in the adjusted cash from operations reflected higher working capital requirements as a result of improving sales. Improving sales drove higher trade receivable and inventory levels as trade receivable collection rates and Days Sales Outstanding metrics improved slightly year over year, while inventory turns remained relatively consistent for both the current and prior year. Likewise, free cash flow of $387 million in the current year decreased from $412 million in the prior year for principally the same reasons.

Net cash used in investing activities during fiscal 2011 totaled $262 million and primarily consisted of cash used for capital expenditures. Capital expenditures were 6.0% of sales in fiscal 2011 as compared to 6.5% of sales in fiscal 2010 and 8.1% in fiscal 2009. Capital expenditures in all three fiscal years reflected investments in revenue generating equipment, such as cylinders and bulk tanks, as well as the development of the Company's highly customized SAP system. Capital expenditures in fiscal 2009 also reflected the completion of major capital projects, such as the New Carlisle, Indiana air separation unit and the carbon dioxide plant in Deer Park, Texas. Capital spending in fiscal 2010 reflected the completion of the Carrollton, Kentucky air separation unit. Capital expenditures in fiscal 2012 are expected to remain at approximately 6.0% of sales. Cash used in investing activities decreased $61 million from fiscal 2010 and $348 million from fiscal 2009 as a result of lower capital expenditures and fewer acquisition-related activities. During fiscal 2011, the Company paid $21 million to acquire eight businesses and settle holdback liabilities. The largest of the businesses acquired was Conley Gas, Ltd., a supplier of pure gases to the specialty gas industry, with historical annual sales of approximately $9 million. In fiscal 2010, the Company made acquisition-related cash payments of $81 million primarily associated with the purchase of six businesses, the largest of which was Tri-Tech, a Florida-based industrial gas and welding supply distributor with approximately $31 million in historical annual sales. During fiscal 2009, the Company paid $274 million to acquire 14 businesses, the largest of which was Refron, Inc., a distributor of refrigerant gases with historical annual sales of $93 million, and to settle acquisition holdback liabilities.

Financing activities used cash of $3 million in fiscal 2011 and $278 million in fiscal 2010. Financing activities provided cash of $31 million in fiscal 2009. As noted in the Financial Instruments section below, during fiscal 2011, the Company engaged in refinancing activities, which extended its average debt maturity to 3.6 years at March 31, 2011. In addition to refinancing its Prior Credit Facility, the Company also issued $250 million of 3.25% senior notes during fiscal 2011. The Company also authorized and completed a share repurchase plan in its fiscal fourth quarter, purchasing 4.8 million shares of treasury stock for $300 million. The treasury stock purchases were financed under the Credit Facility. The change in accounting principle for the Securitization Agreement noted above was reflected in proceeds from borrowings, but had no impact on the Company's net cash position. Absent the change in accounting principle, the Company borrowed a net $36 million during fiscal 2011. During fiscal 2010, the Company redeemed in full its $150 million 6.25% senior notes and purchased a significant portion of its 7.125% senior subordinated notes. Also in fiscal 2010, the Company issued $400 million of 4.5% senior notes and $300 million of 2.85% senior notes, using the net proceeds from both offerings to pay down its Prior Credit Facility. The Company repaid a net $254 million of debt during fiscal 2010. During fiscal 2009, the Company issued $400 million of 7.125% senior subordinated notes using the proceeds to pay down its Prior Credit Facility. The Company also purchased 2.4 million treasury shares for $120 million and completed a share repurchase plan in fiscal 2009. The Company also increased its per share dividend payouts to stockholders by 33% in fiscal 2011 and by 36% in fiscal 2010.

Dividends

The Company paid its stockholders quarterly cash dividends of $0.22 per share at the end of the first quarter and $0.25 per share at end of the second and third quarters of fiscal 2011. In the fourth quarter of fiscal 2011, the Company paid dividends of $0.29 per share. On May 17, 2011, the Company's Board of Directors declared a cash dividend of $0.29 per share, which is payable on June 30, 2011 to the stockholders of record as of June 15, 2011. During fiscal 2010, the Company paid regular quarterly cash dividends of $0.18 per share at the end of each of the first three quarters and $0.22 in the fourth quarter. During fiscal 2009, the Company paid regular quarterly cash dividends of $0.12 per share at the end of each of the first two quarters and $0.16 per share in the third and fourth quarters. Future dividend declarations and associated amounts paid will depend upon the Company's earnings, financial condition, loan covenants, capital requirements and other factors deemed relevant by management and the Company's Board of Directors.

Financial Instruments

Senior Subordinated Note Redemption

During fiscal 2011, the Company repurchased $30 million of its 2018 Notes at an average price of 110.6%. Losses on the early extinguishment of the 2018 Notes were $3.6 million for the year ended March 31, 2011 and related to the redemption premiums and write-off of unamortized debt issuance costs. During fiscal 2010, the Company repurchased $155 million of its 2018 Notes and redeemed in full the $150 million of 2004 Notes. The Company recognized losses on the early extinguishment of debt of $17.9 million in fiscal 2010. The losses related to the redemption premiums and the write-off of unamortized debt issuance costs.

Senior Credit Facility

On September 13, 2010, the Company entered into its new four-year $750 million Credit Facility. The Credit Facility consists of a $650 million U.S. dollar revolving credit line and a $100 million (U.S. dollar equivalent) multi-currency revolving credit line. The maturity date of the revolving credit lines is September 13, 2014. Under circumstances described in the Credit Facility, the revolving credit line may be increased by an additional $325 million, provided that the multi-currency revolving credit line may not be increased by more than an additional $50 million.

In connection with the entry by the Company into the Credit Facility, on September 13, 2010, the Company terminated its Prior Credit Facility, a senior credit facility with an aggregate commitment of $1.7 billion. All obligations under the Prior Credit Facility (including the term loans) were repaid in full using proceeds of the Credit Facility and other funds. As a result of the termination of the Prior Credit Facility, the Company recorded a loss on the early extinguishment of debt of $0.6 million for the year ended March 31, 2011 related to the write-off of unamortized debt issuance costs.

As of March 31, 2011, the Company had $374 million of borrowings under the Credit Facility, including $331 million under the U.S. dollar revolver and $43 million under the multi-currency revolver. The Company also had outstanding letters of credit of $41 million issued under the Credit Facility. The U.S. dollar revolver borrowings bear interest at the London Interbank Offered Rate ("LIBOR") plus 212.5 basis points.

The multi-currency revolver bears interest based on a spread of 212.5 basis points over the Euro currency rate applicable to each foreign currency borrowing. As of March 31, 2011, the average effective interest rates on the U.S. dollar revolver and the multi-currency revolver were 2.31% and 2.87%, respectively.

The Company also maintains a committed revolving line of credit of up to €5.0 million (U.S. $7.1 million) to fund its expansion into France. These revolving credit borrowings are outside of the Company's Credit Facility. At March 31, 2011, French revolving credit borrowings were €2.9 million (U.S. $4.1 million). The variable interest rates on the French revolving credit borrowings are based on the Euro currency rate plus 212.5 basis points. As of March 31, 2011, the effective interest rate on the French revolving credit borrowings was 2.98%. The French revolving line of credit was amended in February 2011 to extend the maturity date to December 31, 2011 and increase the borrowing capacity.

At March 31, 2011, the Credit Facility's financial covenant did not restrict the Company's ability to borrow on the unused portion of the Credit Facility. The Credit Facility contains customary events of default, including nonpayment and breach of covenants. In the event of default, repayment of borrowings under the Credit Facility may be accelerated. The Company's Credit Facility also contains cross-default provisions whereby a default under the Credit Facility could result in defaults under the senior and senior subordinated notes discussed below.

Total Borrowing Capacity

As of March 31, 2011, $335 million remained unused under the Company's Credit Facility. The Company believes that it has sufficient liquidity from cash from operations and under its revolving credit facilities to meet its working capital, capital expenditure and other financial commitments. The financial covenant under the Company's Credit Facility requires the Company to maintain a leverage ratio not higher than 3.5. The leverage ratio is a contractually defined amount principally reflecting debt and, historically, the amounts outstanding under the Securitization Agreement divided by a contractually defined Earnings Before Interest, Taxes, Depreciation and Amortization ("EBITDA") for the trailing twelve-month period with pro forma adjustments for acquisitions. The financial covenant calculations of the Credit Facility include the pro forma results of acquired businesses. Therefore, total borrowing capacity is not reduced dollar-for-dollar with acquisition financing. The leverage ratio measures the Company's ability to meet current and future obligations. At March 31, 2011, the Company's leverage ratio was 2.4.

The Company continually evaluates alternative financing and believes that it can obtain financing on reasonable terms. The terms of any future financing arrangements depend on market conditions and the Company's financial position at that time.

Money Market Loans

The Company has an agreement with a financial institution that provides access to short-term advances not to exceed $35 million. The agreement expires on December 1, 2011, but may be extended subject to renewal provisions contained in the agreement. The advances are generally overnight or for up to seven days. The amount, term and interest rate of an advance are established through mutual agreement with the financial institution when the Company requests such

SEC 1.29

an advance. At March 31, 2011, there were no advances outstanding under the agreement.

The Company also has an agreement with another financial institution that provides access to additional short-term advances not to exceed $35 million. The advances may be for one to six months with rates at a fixed spread over the corresponding LIBOR. At March 31, 2011, there were no advances outstanding under the agreement.

Senior Notes

On September 30, 2010, the Company issued $250 million of 3.25% senior notes due October 1, 2015 (the "2015 Notes"). The 2015 Notes were issued at a discount and yield 3.283%. The net proceeds from the sale of the 2015 Notes were used to reduce borrowings under the Company's revolving credit line under the Credit Facility. Interest on the 2015 Notes is payable semi-annually on April 1 and October 1 of each year. Additionally, the Company has the option to redeem the 2015 Notes prior to their maturity, in whole or in part, at 100% of the principal plus any accrued but unpaid interest and applicable make-whole payments.

At March 31, 2011, the Company had $400 million outstanding of the 2014 Notes. The 2014 Notes were issued at a discount and yield 4.527%. Interest on the 2014 Notes is payable semi-annually on March 15 and September 15 of each year. Additionally, the Company has the option to redeem the 2014 Notes prior to their maturity, in whole or in part, at 100% of the principal plus any accrued but unpaid interest and applicable make-whole payments.

At March 31, 2011, the Company had $300 million outstanding of the 2013 Notes. The 2013 Notes were issued at a discount and yield 2.871%. Interest on the 2013 Notes is payable semi-annually on April 1 and October 1 of each year. Additionally, the Company has the option to redeem the 2013 Notes prior to their maturity, in whole or in part, at 100% of the principal plus any accrued but unpaid interest and applicable make-whole payments.

The 2013, 2014 and 2015 Notes contain covenants that could restrict the incurrence of liens and limit sale and lease-back transactions.

Senior Subordinated Notes

At March 31, 2011, the Company had $215 million of its 2018 Notes outstanding. The 2018 Notes bear interest at a fixed annual rate of 7.125%, payable semi-annually on October 1 and April 1 of each year. The 2018 Notes have a redemption provision, which permits the Company, at its option, to call the 2018 Notes at scheduled dates and prices. The first scheduled optional redemption date is October 1, 2013 at a price of 103.563% of the principal amount.

During the year ended March 31, 2011, the Company incurred a one-time interest penalty payable to holders of the 2018 Notes in the amount of $2.6 million related to the late removal of the restrictive legend on these notes. The Company has classified these charges as interest expense.

The 2018 Notes contain covenants that could restrict the payment of dividends, the repurchase of common stock, the issuance of preferred stock, and the incurrence of additional indebtedness and liens.

Acquisition and Other Notes

The Company's long-term debt also includes acquisition and other notes, principally consisting of notes issued to sellers of businesses acquired, which are repayable in periodic installments. At March 31, 2011, acquisition and other notes totaled $9.9 million with an average interest rate of approximately 6% and an average maturity of approximately one year.

Trade Receivables Securitization

The Company participates in the Securitization Agreement with three commercial banks to which it sells qualifying trade receivables on a revolving basis. Effective April 1, 2010 under new accounting guidance, the Company's sale of qualified trade receivable is now accounted for as a secured borrowing under which qualified trade receivables collateralize amounts borrowed from the commercial banks. Trade receivables that collateralize the Securitization Agreement are held in a bankruptcy-remote special purpose entity, which is consolidated for financial reporting purposes. Qualified trade receivables in the amount of the outstanding borrowing under the Securitization Agreement are not available to the general creditors of the Company. The maximum amount of the Securitization Agreement is $295 million and it bears interest at approximately LIBOR plus 80 basis points. At March 31, 2011, the amount of outstanding borrowing under the Securitization Agreement has been classified as long-term debt on the Consolidated Balance Sheet. Amounts borrowed under the Securitization Agreement could fluctuate monthly based on the Company's funding requirements and the level of qualified trade receivables available to collateralize the Securitization Agreement. The Securitization Agreement expires in March 2013 and contains customary events of termination, including standard cross default provisions with respect to outstanding debt. The amount of outstanding borrowing under the Securitization Agreement at March 31, 2011 was $295 million.

Interest Rate Derivatives

The Company manages its exposure to changes in market interest rates. The Company's involvement with derivative instruments is limited to a) highly effective interest rate swap agreements used to manage well-defined interest rate risk exposures and b) treasury rate lock agreements used to fix the interest rate related to forecasted debt issuances. The Company monitors its positions and credit ratings of its counterparties and does not anticipate non-performance by the counterparties. Interest rate swap and treasury rate lock agreements are not entered into for trading purposes. The Company recognizes derivative instruments as either assets or liabilities at fair value on the Consolidated Balance Sheet. At March 31, 2011, the Company was party to a total of five interest rate swap agreements with an aggregate notional amount of $300 million.

The Company designates fixed interest rate swap agreements as cash flow hedges of interest payments on variable-rate debt associated with the Company's Securitization Agreement. For derivative instruments designated as cash flow hedges, the effective portion of the gain or loss on the derivative is reported as a component of accumulated other comprehensive income ("AOCI") and is reclassified into earnings in the same period or periods during which the hedged transaction affects earnings. Gains and losses on the derivative instruments representing hedge ineffectiveness are recognized in current earnings.

During fiscal 2011, fixed interest rate swaps with an aggregate notional amount of $250 million matured and at

March 31, 2011, the Company was not party to any fixed interest rate swap agreements.

For the year ended March 31, 2011, the fair value of the liability for the fixed interest rate swap agreements decreased and the Company recorded a corresponding adjustment to AOCI of $4.0 million, or $2.7 million after tax. For the year ended March 31, 2010, the fair value of the liability for the fixed interest rate swap agreements decreased and the Company recorded a corresponding adjustment to AOCI of $8.6 million, or $5.6 million after tax. The amount of gain or loss recorded in earnings as a result of hedge ineffectiveness related to the designated cash flow hedges was immaterial for the years ended March 31, 2011, 2010 and 2009.

In anticipation of the issuance of the 2015 Notes, the Company entered into a treasury rate lock agreement in July 2010, with a notional amount of $100 million, maturing on September 8, 2010. The treasury rate lock agreement was designated as a cash flow hedge of the semi-annual interest payments associated with the forecasted issuance of the 2015 Notes. When the treasury rate lock agreement matured, the Company incurred a loss of $2.6 million ($1.6 million after tax) which is reported as a component of AOCI and will be reclassified into earnings over the term of the 2015 Notes. For the year ended March 31, 2011, $258 thousand of the loss on the treasury rate lock was reclassified to interest expense. At March 31, 2011, the estimated loss recorded in AOCI on the treasury rate lock agreement that is expected to be reclassified into earnings within the next twelve months is $326 thousand, net of tax.

The Company also has variable interest rate swap agreements, which are designated as fair value hedges. For derivative instruments designated as fair value hedges, the gain or loss on the derivative as well as the offsetting gain or loss on the hedged item attributable to the hedged risk are recognized in current earnings.

At March 31, 2011, the Company had five variable interest rate swaps outstanding with a notional amount of $300 million. These variable interest rate swaps effectively convert the Company's $300 million of fixed rate 2013 Notes to variable rate debt. At March 31, 2011, these swap agreements required the Company to make variable interest payments based on a weighted average forward rate of 2.17% and receive fixed interest payments from the counterparties based on a fixed rate of 2.85%. The maturity of these fair value swaps coincides with the maturity date of the Company's 2013 Notes in October 2013. During the year ended March 31, 2011, the fair value of the variable interest rate swaps increased by $5.7 million to an asset of $5.1 million and was recorded in other non-current assets. The corresponding increase in the carrying value of the 2013 Notes caused by the hedged risk was $5.6 million and was recorded in long-term debt. The Company records the gain or loss on the hedged item (i.e., the 2013 Notes) and the gain or loss on the variable interest rate swaps in interest expense. The net gain or loss recorded in earnings as a result of hedge ineffectiveness related to the designated fair value hedges was immaterial for the years ended March 31, 2011 and 2010.

The Company measures the fair value of its interest rate swaps using observable market rates to calculate the forward yield curves used to determine expected cash flows for each interest rate swap agreement. The discounted present values of the expected cash flows are calculated using the same forward yield curve. The discount rate assumed in the fair value calculations is adjusted for non-performance risk, dependent on the classification of the interest rate swap as an asset or liability. If an interest rate swap is a liability, the Company assesses the credit and non-performance risk of Airgas by determining an appropriate credit spread for entities with similar credit characteristics as the Company. If, however, an interest rate swap is in an asset position, a credit analysis of counterparties is performed assessing the credit and non-performance risk based upon the pricing history of counterparty specific credit default swaps or credit spreads for entities with similar credit ratings to the counterparties. The Company does not believe it is at risk for non-performance by its counterparties. However, if an interest rate swap is in an asset position, the failure of one or more of its counterparties would result in an increase in interest expense and a reduction of earnings. The Company compares its fair value calculations to the fair values calculated by the counterparties for each swap agreement for reasonableness.

New Accounting Standards

1.30

MONSANTO COMPANY (AUG)

NOTES TO THE CONSOLIDATED FINANCIAL STATEMENTS

Note 3—New Accounting Standards

In September 2011, the FASB issued an amendment to the Intangibles-Goodwill and Other topic of the ASC. Prior to this amendment the company performs a two-step test as outlined by the ASC. Step one of the two-step impairment test is performed by calculating the fair value of the reporting unit and comparing the fair value with the carrying amount of the reporting unit. If the carrying amount of a reporting unit exceeds its fair value, then the company is required to perform the second step of the goodwill impairment test to measure the amount of the impairment loss, if any. Under this amendment, an entity has the option to first assess qualitative factors to determine whether it is necessary to perform the current two-step test. If an entity believes, as a result of its qualitative assessment, that it is more-likely-than-not that the fair value of a reporting unit is less than its carrying amount, the quantitative impairment test is required. Otherwise, no further testing is required. An entity can choose to perform the qualitative assessment on none, some or all of its reporting units. Moreover, an entity can bypass the qualitative assessment for any reporting unit in any period and proceed directly to step one of the impairment test, and then resume performing the qualitative assessment in any subsequent period. The amendment is effective for annual and interim goodwill impairment tests performed for fiscal years beginning after Dec. 15, 2011. Accordingly, Monsanto will adopt this amendment in fiscal year 2013. The company is currently evaluating the impact of adoption on the consolidated financial statements.

In June 2011, the FASB issued an amendment to the Comprehensive Income topic of the ASC. This amendment eliminates the option to present the components of other comprehensive income as part of the statement of changes in shareowners' equity. In addition, items of other comprehensive income that may be reclassified to profit or loss in the future are required to be presented separately from those that would never be reclassified. The amendment is effective for fiscal years beginning after Dec. 15, 2011, and interim periods within that year. Accordingly, Monsanto will adopt this amendment in first quarter fiscal year 2013. The company is currently evaluating the impact of adoption on the consolidated financial statements.

In May 2011, the FASB issued a new accounting standard update, which amends the fair value measurement guidance and includes some enhanced disclosure requirements. The most significant change in disclosures is an expansion of the information required for Level 3 measurements based on unobservable inputs. The amendment is effective for interim and annual periods beginning after Dec. 15, 2011. Accordingly, Monsanto will adopt this amendment in third quarter of fiscal year 2012. The company is currently evaluating the impact of adoption on the consolidated financial statements.

In June 2009, the FASB issued a standard that requires an analysis to determine whether a variable interest gives the entity a controlling financial interest in a variable interest entity. This statement requires an ongoing reassessment and eliminates the quantitative approach previously required for determining whether an entity is the primary beneficiary. This standard is effective for fiscal years beginning after Nov. 15, 2009. Accordingly, Monsanto adopted this standard on a prospective basis in fiscal year 2011.

In June 2009, the FASB issued a standard that removes the concept of a qualifying special-purpose entity (QSPE) from GAAP and removes the exception from applying consolidation principles to a QSPE. This standard also clarifies the requirements for isolation and limitations on portions of financial assets that are eligible for sale accounting. This standard is effective for fiscal years beginning after Nov. 15, 2009. Accordingly, Monsanto adopted this standard in fiscal year 2011.

In December 2007, the FASB issued a standard that requires an entity to clearly identify and present its ownership interests in subsidiaries held by parties other than the entity in the consolidated financial statements within the equity section but separate from the entity's equity. It also requires the amount of consolidated net income attributable to the parent and to the noncontrolling interest be clearly identified and presented on the face of the Statements of Consolidated Operations; changes in ownership interest be accounted for similarly, as equity transactions; and when a subsidiary is deconsolidated, any retained noncontrolling equity investment in the former subsidiary and the gain or loss on the deconsolidation of the subsidiary be measured at fair value. This statement is effective for financial statements issued for fiscal years beginning after Dec. 15, 2008. The provisions of the standard related to accounting for changes in ownership are to be applied prospectively, except for the presentation and disclosure requirements, which are to be applied retrospectively. Monsanto adopted this standard on Sept. 1, 2009, and the presentation and disclosure requirements of this standard were applied retrospectively to all periods presented. The adoption of this standard did not have a material impact on the consolidated financial statements, other than the following changes in presentation of noncontrolling interests:

- Consolidated net income was recast to include net income attributable to both the company and noncontrolling interests in the Statements of Consolidated Operations.
- Noncontrolling interests were reclassified from other liabilities to equity, separate from the parent's shareown-

ers' equity, in the Statements of Consolidated Financial Position.
- The Statements of Consolidated Cash Flows now begin with net income (including noncontrolling interests) instead of net income attributable to Monsanto Company, with net income from noncontrolling interests (previously, minority interests) no longer a reconciling item in arriving at net cash provided by operating activities, and the Statements of Consolidated Cash Flows were recast to include dividend payments to noncontrolling interests.
- Statements of Consolidated Shareowners' Equity and Comprehensive Income have been combined and were recast to include noncontrolling interests.

Market Risk Information

1.31

CABOT CORPORATION (SEP)

QUANTITATIVE AND QUALITATIVE DISCLOSURES ABOUT MARKET RISK

We are exposed to changes in interest rates and foreign currency exchange rates because we finance certain operations through long- and short-term borrowings and denominate our transactions in a variety of foreign currencies. Changes in these rates may have an impact on future cash flows and earnings. We manage these risks through normal operating and financing activities and, when deemed appropriate, through the use of derivative financial instruments.

We have policies governing our use of derivative instruments, and we do not enter into financial instruments for trading or speculative purposes.

By using derivative instruments, we are subject to credit and market risk. The derivative instruments are booked to our balance sheet at fair market value and reflect the asset or (liability) position as of September 30, 2011. If a counterparty fails to fulfill its performance obligations under a derivative contract, our exposure will equal the fair value of the derivative. Generally, when the fair value of a derivative contract is positive, the counterparty owes Cabot, thus creating a payment risk for Cabot. We minimize counterparty credit (or repayment) risk by entering into these transactions with major financial institutions of investment grade credit rating. As of September 30, 2011, the counterparties that we have executed derivatives with were rated between A- and AA-, inclusive, by Standard and Poor's. Our exposure to market risk is not hedged in a manner that completely eliminates the effects of changing market conditions on earnings or cash flow.

Interest Rate Risk

As of September 30, 2011, we had long-term debt, including the current portion, totaling $613 million, which has both variable and fixed interest rate components. We have entered into interest rate swaps as a hedge to a portion of our underlying debt instruments to effectively change the characteristics of the interest rate without changing the debt instrument. For fixed rate debt, interest rate changes affect the fair value, but do not impact earnings or cash flows. Conversely, for floating rate debt, interest rate changes generally do not affect the fair value, but do impact future earnings and cash flows, assuming other factors are held constant. As most of our long-term debt was issued at fixed rates, we use interest rate swaps as a means to achieve a different fixed-to-floating interest rate mix.

The table below summarizes the principal terms of our interest rate swap transactions, including the notional amount of the swap, the interest rate payment we receive from and pay to our swap counterparty, the term of the transaction, and its fair value at September 30, 2011.

Description	Notional Amount	Receive	Pay	Fiscal Year Entered Into	Maturity (Fiscal Year)	Fair Market Value at September 30, 2011 Asset/ (Liability)
						(USD)
Interest Rate Swaps— Fixed to Variable	USD 35 million	5.25% Fixed	U.S.-6 month LIBOR + 0.62%	2003	2013	3 million
	USD 8 million	8.28% Fixed	U.S.-6 month LIBOR + 3.14%	2007	2012	—
	USD 5 million	8.27% Fixed	U.S.-3 month LIBOR + 6.38%	2010	2012	—
	USD 5 million	8.27% Fixed	U.S.-3 month LIBOR + 6.38%	2010	2012	—
	USD 5 million	8.18% Fixed	U.S.-3 month LIBOR + 6.35%	2010	2012	—

Foreign Currency Risk

Our international operations are subject to certain risks, including currency exchange rate fluctuations and government actions. Currently, we have issued debt denominated in U.S. dollars and then entered into cross currency swaps that exchange our dollar principal and interest payments into a currency where we expect long-term, stable cash receipts. The following table summarizes the principal terms of our long-term foreign currency swap transactions, including the notional amount of the swap, the interest rate payment we receive from and pay to our swap counterparty, the term of the transaction and its fair market value at September 30, 2011.

Description	Net Notional Amount	Receive	Pay	Fiscal Year Entered Into	Maturity Year	Fair Market Value at September 30, 2011
						(USD)
Cross Currency Swaps	USD 140 million swapped to EUR 124 million	5.25% Fixed	5.43% Fixed	2003	2013	(32 million)
	USD 35 million swapped to EUR 31 million	US-6 month LIBOR	EUR-6 month LIBOR	2003	2013	(8 million)

Foreign currency exposures also relate to assets and liabilities denominated in foreign currencies other than the functional currency of a given subsidiary as well as the risk that currency fluctuations could affect the dollar value of future cash flows generated in foreign currencies. Accordingly, we use short-term forward contracts to minimize the exposure to foreign currency risk. These forward contracts typically have a duration of 30 days. At September 30, 2011, we had $65 million in net notional foreign currency contracts, which were denominated in the Australian dollar, British pound sterling, Canadian dollar, Euro, and Japanese yen. These forwards had a fair value of ($2 million) as of September 30, 2011. Of the $65 million in net notional foreign currency contracts, $12 million related to contracts denominated in Japanese yen which were designated as a fair value hedge. These hedge contracts had a fair value of ($1 million) at September 30, 2011.

In certain situations where we have a long-term commitment denominated in a foreign currency we may enter into appropriate financial instruments in accordance with our risk management policy to hedge future cash flow exposures.

Commodity Risk

Certain of our carbon black plants in Europe are subject to mandatory greenhouse gas emission trading schemes. Our objective is to ensure compliance with the European Union Emission Trading Scheme, which is based upon a Cap-and-Trade system that establishes a maximum allowable emission credit for each ton of CO_2 emitted. European Union Allowances ("EUA") originate from the individual EU member state's country allocation process and are issued by that country's government. A company that has an excess of EUAs based on the CO_2 emissions limits may sell EUAs in the Emission Trading Scheme and if they have a shortfall, a company can buy EUAs or Certified Emission Reduction ("CER") units to comply.

In order to limit the variability in cost to our European operations, we purchased CERs and sold EUAs which settle each December until 2012. The following table provides details of the derivatives held as of September 30, 2011 used to manage commodity risk.

Description	Net Notional Amount	Net Buyer/ Net Seller	Fiscal Year Entered into	Maturity (Fiscal Year)	Fair Market Value at September 30, 2011 Asset/(Liability)
					(USD)
EUAs	EUR 1 million	Net Seller	2008 & 2009	2012	1 million
CERs	EUR 1 million	Net Buyer	2008 & 2009	2012	(1) million

Critical Accounting Policies

1.32

SMITHFIELD FOODS, INC. (APR)

CRITICAL ACCOUNTING POLICIES AND ESTIMATES

The preparation of consolidated financial statements requires us to make estimates and assumptions. These estimates and assumptions affect the reported amounts of assets and liabilities and disclosure of contingent assets and liabilities at the date of the consolidated financial statements and the reported amounts of revenues and expenses during the reporting period. These estimates and assumptions are based on our experience and our understanding of the current facts and circumstances. Actual results could differ from those estimates. The following is a summary of certain accounting policies and estimates we consider critical. Our accounting policies are more fully discussed in Note 1 in "Item 8. Financial Statements and Supplementary Data."

Description	Judgments and Uncertainties	Effect if Actual Results Differ From Assumptions
Contingent Liabilities		
We are subject to lawsuits, investigations and other claims related to the operation of our farms, labor, livestock procurement, securities, environmental, product, taxing authorities and other matters, and are required to assess the likelihood of any adverse judgments or outcomes to these matters, as well as potential ranges of probable losses and fees. A determination of the amount of reserves and disclosures required, if any, for these contingencies are made after considerable analysis of each individual issue. We accrue for contingent liabilities when an assessment of the risk of loss is probable and can be reasonably estimated. We disclose contingent liabilities when the risk of loss is reasonably possible or probable.	Our contingent liabilities contain uncertainties because the eventual outcome will result from future events, and determination of current reserves requires estimates and judgments related to future changes in facts and circumstances, differing interpretations of the law and assessments of the amount of damages or fees, and the effectiveness of strategies or other factors beyond our control.	We have not made any material changes in the accounting methodology used to establish our contingent liabilities during the past three fiscal years. We do not believe there is a reasonable likelihood there will be a material change in the estimates or assumptions used to calculate our contingent liabilities. However, if actual results are not consistent with our estimates or assumptions, we may be exposed to gains or losses that could be material.
Marketing and Advertising Costs		
We incur advertising, retailer incentive and consumer incentive costs to promote products through marketing programs. These programs include cooperative advertising, volume discounts, in-store display incentives, coupons and other programs. Marketing and advertising costs are charged in the period incurred. We accrue costs based on the estimated performance, historical utilization and redemption of each program. Cash consideration given to customers is considered a reduction in the price of our products, thus recorded as a reduction to sales. The remainder of marketing and advertising costs is recorded as a selling, general and administrative expense.	Recognition of the costs related to these programs contains uncertainties due to judgment required in estimating the potential performance and redemption of each program. These estimates are based on many factors, including experience of similar promotional programs.	We have not made any material changes in the accounting methodology used to establish our marketing accruals during the past three fiscal years. We do not believe there is a reasonable likelihood there will be a material change in the estimates or assumptions used to calculate our marketing accruals. However, if actual results are not consistent with our estimates or assumptions, we may be exposed to gains or losses that could be material.

(continued)

Description	Judgments and Uncertainties	Effect if Actual Results Differ From Assumptions
Accrued Self Insurance We are self insured for certain losses related to health and welfare, workers' compensation, auto liability and general liability claims. We use an independent third-party actuary to assist in the determination of certain of our self-insurance liabilities. We and the actuary consider a number of factors when estimating our self-insurance liability, including claims experience, demographic factors, severity factors and other actuarial assumptions. We periodically review our estimates and assumptions with our third-party actuary to assist us in determining the adequacy of our self-insurance liability.	Our self-insurance liabilities contain uncertainties due to assumptions required and judgment used. Costs to settle our obligations, including legal and healthcare costs, could increase or decrease causing estimates of our self-insurance liabilities to change. Incident rates, including frequency and severity, could increase or decrease causing estimates in our self-insurance liabilities to change.	We have not made any material changes in the accounting methodology used to establish our self-insurance liabilities during the past three fiscal years. We do not believe there is a reasonable likelihood there will be a material change in the estimates or assumptions used to calculate our self-insurance liabilities. However, if actual results are not consistent with our estimates or assumptions, we may be exposed to gains or losses that could be material. A 10% increase in the estimates as of May 1, 2011, would result in an increase in the amount we recorded for our self-insurance liabilities of approximately $7.5 million.
Impairment of Long-Lived Assets Long-lived assets are evaluated for impairment whenever events or changes in circumstances indicate the carrying value may not be recoverable. Examples include a current expectation that a long-lived asset will be disposed of significantly before the end of its previously estimated useful life, a significant adverse change in the extent or manner in which we use a long-lived asset or a change in its physical condition. When evaluating long-lived assets for impairment, we compare the carrying value of the asset to the asset's estimated undiscounted future cash flows. Impairment is recorded if the estimated future cash flows are less than the carrying value of the asset. The impairment is the excess of the carrying value over the fair value of the long-lived asset. We recorded impairment charges related to long-lived assets of $9.2 million, $48.1 million (including $6.5 million of goodwill) and $70.9 million in fiscal 2011, 2010 and 2009, respectively.	Our impairment analysis contains uncertainties due to judgment in assumptions and estimates surrounding undiscounted future cash flows of the long-lived asset, including forecasting useful lives of assets and selecting the discount rate that reflects the risk inherent in future cash flows.	We have not made any material changes in the accounting methodology used to evaluate the impairment of long-lived assets during the last three years. We do not believe there is a reasonable likelihood there will be a material change in the estimates or assumptions used to calculate impairments of long-lived assets. However, if actual results are not consistent with our estimates and assumptions used to calculate estimated future cash flows, we may be exposed to future impairment losses that could be material.
Impairment of Goodwill and Other Non-Amortized Intangible Assets Goodwill impairment is determined using a two-step process. The first step is to identify if a potential impairment exists by comparing the fair value of a reporting unit with its carrying amount, including goodwill. If the fair value of a reporting unit exceeds its carrying amount, goodwill of the reporting unit is not considered to have a potential impairment and the second step of the impairment test is not necessary. However, if the carrying amount of a reporting unit exceeds its fair value, the second step is performed to determine if goodwill is impaired and to measure the amount of impairment loss to recognize, if any.	We estimate the fair value of our reporting units by applying valuation multiples and/or estimating future discounted cash flows. The selection of multiples and cash flows is dependent upon assumptions regarding future levels of operating performance as well as business trends and prospects, and industry, market and economic conditions.	We have not made any material changes in the accounting methodology used to evaluate impairment of goodwill and other intangible assets during the last three years. As of May 1, 2011, we had $793.3 million of goodwill and $348.0 million of other non-amortized intangible assets. Our goodwill is included in the following segments: • $216.1 million—Pork • $157.2 million—International • $420.0 million—Hog Production

(continued)

SEC 1.32

Description	Judgments and Uncertainties	Effect if Actual Results Differ From Assumptions

Impairment of Goodwill and Other Non-Amortized Intangible Assets—*(continued)*

The second step compares the implied fair value of goodwill with the carrying amount of goodwill. If the implied fair value of goodwill exceeds the carrying amount, goodwill is not considered impaired. However, if the carrying amount of goodwill exceeds the implied fair value, an impairment loss is recognized in an amount equal to that excess.

The implied fair value of goodwill is determined in the same manner as the amount of goodwill recognized in a business combination (i.e., the fair value of the reporting unit is allocated to all the assets and liabilities, including any unrecognized intangible assets, as if the reporting unit had been acquired in a business combination and the fair value of the reporting unit was the purchase price paid to acquire the reporting unit).

For our other non-amortized intangible assets, if the carrying value of the intangible asset exceeds its fair value, an impairment loss is recognized in an amount equal to that excess.

We have elected to make the first day of the fourth quarter the annual impairment assessment date for goodwill and other intangible assets. However, we could be required to evaluate the recoverability of goodwill and other intangible assets prior to the required annual assessment if we experience disruptions to the business, unexpected significant declines in operating results, divestiture of a significant component of the business or a decline in market capitalization. For example, in fiscal 2009, we performed an interim test of the carrying amount of goodwill related to our U.S. hog production operations due to significant losses incurred in our hog production operations, the deteriorating macro-economic environment, the continued market volatility and the decrease in our market capitalization.

A discounted cash flow analysis requires us to make various judgmental assumptions about sales, operating margins, growth rates and discount rates. When estimating future discounted cash flows, we consider the assumptions that hypothetical marketplace participants would use in estimating future cash flows. In addition, where applicable, an appropriate discount rate is used, based on our cost of capital or location-specific economic factors.

We experienced significant losses in our domestic hog production operations in fiscal 2009 and fiscal 2010 resulting primarily from record high grain prices. Our Hog Production segment returned to profitability in fiscal 2011. The fair value estimates of our Hog Production reporting units assume normalized operating margin assumptions based on long-term expectations and margins historically realized in the hog production industry.

The fair values of trademarks have been calculated using a royalty rate method. Assumptions about royalty rates are based on the rates at which similar brands and trademarks are licensed in the marketplace.

Our impairment analysis contains uncertainties due to uncontrollable events that could positively or negatively impact the anticipated future economic and operating conditions.

As a result of the first step of the 2011 goodwill impairment analysis, the fair value of each reporting unit exceeded its carrying value. Therefore, the second step was not necessary. A hypothetical 10% decrease in the estimated fair value of our reporting units would not result in a material impairment.

Our fiscal 2011 other non-amortized intangible asset impairment analysis did not result in an impairment charge. A hypothetical 10% decrease in the estimated fair value of our intangible assets would not result in a material impairment.

Income Taxes

We estimate total income tax expense based on statutory tax rates and tax planning opportunities available to us in various jurisdictions in which we earn income.

Federal income taxes include an estimate for taxes on earnings of foreign subsidiaries expected to be remitted to the United States and be taxable, but not for earnings considered indefinitely invested in the foreign subsidiary.

Deferred income taxes are recognized for the future tax effects of temporary differences between financial and income tax reporting using tax rates in effect for the years in which the differences are expected to reverse.

Valuation allowances are recorded when it is likely a tax benefit will not be realized for a deferred tax asset.

We record unrecognized tax benefit liabilities for known or anticipated tax issues based on our analysis of whether, and the extent to which, additional taxes will be due. This analysis is performed in accordance with the applicable accounting guidance.

Changes in tax laws and rates could affect recorded deferred tax assets and liabilities in the future.

Changes in projected future earnings could affect the recorded valuation allowances in the future.

Our calculations related to income taxes contain uncertainties due to judgment used to calculate tax liabilities in the application of complex tax regulations across the tax jurisdictions where we operate.

Our analysis of unrecognized tax benefits contain uncertainties based on judgment used to apply the more likely than not recognition and measurement thresholds.

We do not believe there is a reasonable likelihood there will be a material change in the tax related balances or valuation allowances. However, due to the complexity of some of these uncertainties, the ultimate resolution may result in a payment that is materially different from the current estimate of the tax liabilities.

To the extent we prevail in matters for which liabilities have been established, or are required to pay amounts in excess of our recorded liabilities, our effective tax rate in a given financial statement period could be materially affected. An unfavorable tax settlement may require use of our cash and result in an increase in our effective tax rate in the period of resolution. A favorable tax settlement could be recognized as a reduction in our effective tax rate in the period of resolution.

(continued)

Description	Judgments and Uncertainties	Effect if Actual Results Differ From Assumptions
Pension Accounting		

Pension Accounting

We provide the majority of our U.S. employees with pension benefits. We account for our pension plans in accordance with the applicable accounting guidance, which requires us to recognize the funded status of our pension plans in our consolidated balance sheets and to recognize, as a component of other comprehensive income (loss), the gains or losses and prior service costs or credits that arise during the period, but are not recognized in net periodic benefit cost.

We use an independent third-party actuary to assist in the determination of our pension obligation and related costs.

We generally contribute the minimum amount required under government regulations to our qualified pension plans. We funded $95.1 million, $62.6 million and $43.1 million to our qualified pension plans during fiscal 2011, 2010 and 2009, respectively. We expect to fund at least $61.8 million in fiscal 2012.

The measurement of our pension obligation and costs is dependent on a variety of assumptions regarding future events. The key assumptions we use include discount rates, salary growth, retirement ages/mortality rates and the expected return on plan assets.

These assumptions may have an effect on the amount and timing of future contributions. The discount rate assumption is based on investment yields available at year-end on corporate bonds rated AA and above with a maturity to match our expected benefit payment stream. The salary growth assumption reflects our long-term actual experience, the near-term outlook and assumed inflation. Retirement rates are based primarily on actual plan experience. Mortality rates are based on mandated mortality tables, which have flexibility to consider industry specific groups, such as blue collar or white collar. The expected return on plan assets reflects asset allocations, investment strategy and historical returns of the asset categories. The effects of actual results differing from these assumptions are accumulated and amortized over future periods and, therefore, generally affect our recognized expense in such future periods.

The following weighted average assumptions were used to determine our benefit obligation and net benefit cost for fiscal 2011:
- 6.00%—Discount rate to determine net benefit cost
- 5.85%—Discount rate to determine pension benefit obligation
- 8.00%—Expected return on plan assets
- 4.00%—Salary growth

If actual results are not consistent with our estimates or assumptions, we may be exposed to gains or losses that could be material. For example, the discount rate used to measure our projected benefit obligation decreased from 8.25% as of May 3, 2009 to 6.00% as of May 2, 2010, which was the primary cause for an increased net pension cost of $82.0 million in fiscal 2011.

An additional 0.50% decrease in the discount rate used to measure our projected benefit obligation would have caused a decrease in funded status of $82.8 million as of May 1, 2011, and would result in additional net pension cost of $9.2 million in fiscal 2012.

A 0.50% decrease in expected return on plan assets would result in a $4.8 million increase in net pension cost in fiscal 2012.

In addition to higher net pension cost, a significant decrease in the funded status of our pension plans caused by either a devaluation of plan assets or a decline in the discount rate would result in higher pension funding requirements.

Derivatives Accounting

See "Derivative Financial Instruments" above for a discussion of our derivative accounting policy.

Disclosure of Accounting Policies

1.33

AMERICAN INTERNATIONAL GROUP, INC. (DEC)

NOTES TO CONSOLIDATED FINANCIAL STATEMENTS

Note 2—Summary of Significant Accounting Policies

(a) Revenue Recognition and Expenses:

Premiums: Premiums for short duration contracts are recorded as written on the inception date of the policy. Premiums are earned primarily on a pro rata basis over the term of the related coverage. The reserve for unearned premiums includes the portion of premiums written relating to the unexpired terms of coverage. Reinsurance premiums under a reinsurance contract are typically earned over the same period as the underlying policies, or risks, covered by the contracts. As a result, the earning pattern of a reinsurance contract may extend up to 24 months, reflecting the inception dates of the underlying policies.

Reinsurance premiums ceded are expensed over the period the reinsurance coverage is provided in proportion to the risks to which they relate.

Premiums for long duration insurance products and life contingent annuities are recognized as revenues when due. Estimates for premiums due but not yet collected are accrued.

Policy fees: Policy fees represent fees recognized from universal life and investment-type products consisting of policy charges for the cost of insurance, policy administration charges, amortization of unearned revenue reserves and surrender charges.

Net investment income: Net investment income represents income primarily from the following sources in AIG's insurance operations and AIG Parent:

- Interest income and related expenses, including amortization of premiums and accretion of discounts on bonds with changes in the timing and the amount of expected principal and interest cash flows reflected in the yield, as applicable.
- Dividend income from common and preferred stock and distributions from other investments.
- Realized and unrealized gains and losses from investments in trading securities accounted for at fair value.
- Earnings from private equity funds and hedge fund investments accounted for under the equity method.
- The difference between the carrying amount of a life settlement contract and the life insurance proceeds of the underlying life insurance policy recorded in income upon the death of the insured.
- Changes in the fair values of AIG's interests in ML II, ML III, AIA and MetLife securities prior to sale.

Net realized capital gains (losses): Net realized capital gains and losses are determined by specific identification. The net realized capital gains and losses are generated primarily from the following sources:

- Sales of fixed maturity securities and equity securities (except trading securities accounted for at fair value), real estate, investments in private equity funds and hedge funds and other types of investments.

- Reductions to the cost basis of fixed maturity securities and equity securities (except trading securities accounted for at fair value) and other invested assets for other-than-temporary impairments.
- Changes in fair value of derivatives except for (1) those instruments at AIG Financial Products Corp. and AIG Trading Group Inc. and their respective subsidiaries (collectively, AIGFP), (2) those instruments that qualify for hedge accounting treatment when the change in the fair value of the hedged item is not reported in Net realized capital gains (losses), and (3) those instruments that are designated as economic hedges of financial instruments for which the fair value option has been elected.
- Exchange gains and losses resulting from foreign currency transactions.

Aircraft leasing revenue: Income from flight equipment under operating leases is recognized over the life of the lease as rentals become receivable under the provisions of the lease or, in the case of leases with varying payments, under the straight-line method over the noncancelable term of the lease. In certain cases, leases provide for additional payments contingent on usage. In those cases, rental income is recognized at the time such usage occurs, net of estimated future contractual aircraft maintenance reimbursements. Gains on sales of flight equipment are recognized in Other income when flight equipment is sold and the risk of ownership of the equipment is passed to the new owner.

Other income: Other income includes unrealized gains and losses on derivatives, including unrealized market valuation gains and losses associated with AIGFP's super senior credit default swap (CDS) portfolio, as well as income from the Direct Investment book.

Other income from the operations of the Direct Investment book and AIG's Other Operations category consists of the following:

- Change in fair value relating to financial assets and liabilities for which the fair value option has been elected.
- Interest income and related expenses, including amortization of premiums and accretion of discounts on bonds with changes in the timing and the amount of expected principal and interest cash flows reflected in the yield, as applicable.
- Dividend income from common and preferred stock and distributions from other investments.
- Changes in the fair value of trading securities and spot commodities sold but not yet purchased, futures, hybrid financial instruments, securities purchased under agreements to resell, and securities sold under agreements to repurchase for which the fair value option was elected.
- Realized capital gains and losses from the sales of available for sale securities and investments in private equity funds and hedge funds and other investments.
- Income earned on real estate based investments and related losses from property level impairments and financing costs.
- Exchange gains and losses resulting from foreign currency transactions.
- Reductions to the cost basis of securities available for sale for other-than-temporary impairments.
- Earnings from private equity funds and hedge fund investments accounted for under the equity method.
- Gains and losses recognized in earnings on derivatives for the effective portion and their related hedged items.

Policyholder benefits and claims incurred: Incurred claims and claims adjustment expenses for short duration insurance contracts consist of the estimated ultimate cost of settling claims incurred within the reporting period, including incurred but not reported claims, plus the changes in estimates of current and prior period losses resulting from the continuous review process, which are charged to income as incurred. Benefits for long duration insurance contracts consist of benefits paid and changes in future policy benefits liabilities. Benefits for universal life and investment-type products primarily consist of interest credited to policy account balances and benefit payments made in excess of policy account balances except for certain contracts for which the fair value option was elected, for which benefits represent the entire change in fair value (including derivative gains and losses on related economic hedges).

Interest credited to policyholder account balances: Represents interest on account-value-based policyholder deposits consisting of amounts credited on non-equity-indexed account values, accretion to the host contract for equity indexed products, and net amortization of sales inducements.

Amortization of deferred policy acquisition costs: Amortization of deferred policy acquisition costs represents amortization of short-duration and long-duration deferred policy acquisition costs:

- Short-duration policies: Policy acquisition costs are deferred and amortized over the period in which the related premiums written are earned, generally 12 months.
- Long-duration policies: Policy acquisition costs for participating life, traditional life and accident and health insurance products are generally deferred and amortized, with interest, over the premium paying period. Policy acquisition costs and policy issuance costs related to universal life, and investment-type products (investment-oriented products) are deferred and amortized, with interest, in relation to the incidence of estimated gross profits to be realized over the estimated lives of the contracts.

Aircraft leasing expenses: Aircraft leasing expenses consist of depreciation expense, impairment charges, fair value adjustments and lease-related charges on aircraft as well as selling, general and administrative expenses and other expenses incurred by ILFC.

Net (gain) loss on sale of properties and divested businesses: Includes gains or losses from the sales of businesses that do not qualify as discontinued operations and sales of previously occupied properties.

(b) Held-for-sale and discontinued operations: AIG reports a business as held for sale when management has approved or received approval to sell the business and is committed to a formal plan, the business is available for immediate sale, the business is being actively marketed, the sale is anticipated to occur during the ensuing year and certain other specified criteria are met. A business classified as held for sale is recorded at the lower of its carrying amount or estimated fair value less cost to sell. If the carrying amount of the business exceeds its estimated fair value, a loss is recognized. Depreciation is not recorded on assets of a business classified as held for sale. Assets and liabilities related to a business classified as held for sale are segregated in the Consolidated Balance Sheet and major classes are separately disclosed in the notes to the Consolidated Financial Statements commencing in the period in which the business is classified as held for sale.

AIG reports the results of operations of a business as discontinued operations if the business is classified as held for sale, the operations and cash flows of the business have been or will be eliminated from the ongoing operations of AIG as a result of a disposal transaction and AIG will not have any significant continuing involvement in the operations of the business after the disposal transaction. The results of discontinued operations are reported in Discontinued Operations in the Consolidated Statement of Operations for current and prior periods commencing in the period in which the business meets the criteria of a discontinued operation, and include any gain or loss recognized on closing or adjustment of the carrying amount to fair value less cost to sell.

(c) Investments:

Fixed maturity and equity securities: Bonds held to maturity are carried at amortized cost when AIG has the ability and positive intent to hold these securities until maturity. When AIG does not have the positive intent to hold bonds until maturity, these securities are classified as available for sale or as trading and are carried at fair value. None of AIG's fixed maturity securities met the criteria for held to maturity classification at December 31, 2011 or 2010.

Fixed maturity and equity securities classified as available for sale or as trading are carried at fair value. Unrealized gains and losses from available for sale investments in fixed maturity and equity securities are reported as a separate component of Accumulated other comprehensive income (loss), net of deferred acquisition costs and deferred income taxes, in Total AIG shareholders' equity. Realized and unrealized gains and losses from fixed maturity and equity securities classified as trading are reflected in Net investment income (for insurance subsidiaries) or Other income (for Direct Investment book). Investments in fixed maturities and equity securities are recorded on a trade-date basis.

Premiums and discounts arising from the purchase of bonds classified as available for sale are treated as yield adjustments over their estimated holding periods, until maturity, or call date, if applicable. For investments in certain residential mortgage-backed securities (RMBS), certain commercial mortgage-backed securities (CMBS) and certain collateralized debt obligations/asset backed securities (CDO/ABS), (collectively, structured securities), recognized yields are updated based on current information regarding the timing and amount of expected undiscounted future cash flows. For high credit-quality structured securities, effective yields are recalculated based on actual payments received and updated prepayment expectations, and the amortized cost is adjusted to the amount that would have existed had the new effective yield been applied since acquisition with a corresponding charge or credit to net investment income. For structured securities that are not high credit-quality, effective yields are recalculated and adjusted prospectively based on changes in expected undiscounted future cash flows. For purchased credit impaired (PCI) securities, at acquisition, the difference between the undiscounted expected future cash flows and the recorded investment in the securities represents the initial accretable yield, which is to be accreted into net investment income over the securities' remaining lives on a level-yield basis. Subsequently, effective yields recognized on PCI securities are recalculated and adjusted prospectively to reflect changes in the contractual benchmark interest rates on variable rate securities and any significant increases in undiscounted expected future cash flows arising due to reasons other than interest rate changes.

SEC 1.33

Trading securities include the investment portfolio of the Direct Investment book and the Maiden Lane Interests. Trading securities for the Direct Investment book are held to meet short-term investment objectives and to economically hedge other securities.

For discussion of AIG's other-than-temporary impairment policy, see Note 7 herein.

Mortgage and other loans receivable—net: Mortgage and other loans receivable include commercial mortgages, life insurance policy loans, commercial loans, other loans and notes receivable. Commercial mortgages, commercial loans, and other loans and notes receivable are carried at unpaid principal balances less credit allowances and plus or minus adjustments for the accretion or amortization of discount or premium. Interest income on such loans is accrued as earned.

Direct costs of originating commercial mortgages, commercial loans, and other loans and notes receivable, net of nonrefundable points and fees, are deferred and included in the carrying amount of the related receivables. The amount deferred is amortized to income as an adjustment to earnings using the interest method.

Mortgage and other loans receivable are considered impaired when collection of all amounts due under contractual terms is not probable. Interest income on such impaired loans is recognized as cash is received. For a discussion of the allowance for credit losses on mortgages and other loans receivable, see Note 8 herein.

Mortgage and other loans receivable also include life insurance policy loans, which are carried at unpaid principal amount. There is no allowance for policy loans because these loans serve to reduce the death benefit paid when the death claim is made and the balances are effectively collateralized by the cash surrender value of the policy.

Flight equipment primarily under operating leases—net: Flight equipment is stated at cost (adjusted for any impairment charges), net of accumulated depreciation. Major additions, modifications and interest on deposits during the construction phase are capitalized. Normal maintenance and repairs, airframe and engine overhauls and compliance with return conditions of flight equipment on lease are generally provided by and paid for by the lessee. Under the provisions of most leases for certain airframe and engine overhauls, the lessee is reimbursed for certain costs incurred up to but not exceeding contingent rentals paid to ILFC by the lessee. ILFC recognizes overhaul rentals received as revenue, net of estimated overhaul reimbursements. Any lessor maintenance contribution made by ILFC in conjunction with a lease of a used aircraft and in excess of overhaul rentals received from the lessee, is capitalized as lease incentives and amortized into lease revenue over the life of the lease. Maintenance performed by ILFC in the event of a repossession of an aircraft is capitalized to the extent the costs meet the recognition criteria for an asset. Depreciation of aircraft is generally computed on a straight-line basis over a useful life of 25 years to a residual value of approximately 15 percent of the cost of the asset.

Aircraft in the fleet are evaluated for impairment annually during the third quarter and whenever events or changes in circumstances indicate the carrying amount of an asset may not be recoverable. Recoverability of assets is measured by comparing the carrying amount of an asset to future undiscounted net cash flows expected to be generated by the asset. These evaluations for impairment are significantly affected by estimates of future net cash flows and other factors that involve uncertainty. There are a number of factors and circumstances that can influence (and increase) the potential for recognizing an impairment loss. A firm commitment to sell aircraft may result in aircraft being reclassified from held for use to held for sale for financial reporting purposes and would require an impairment assessment based on the aircraft's fair value. An increase in the likelihood of a sale transaction being completed could result in a similar impairment assessment if the probability of an aircraft sale becomes high enough to reduce the probability weighted expected undiscounted future cash flows to be realized from the aircraft to an amount that is less than its carrying value. In addition, changes in portfolio strategies, changes in demand for a particular aircraft type and changes in economic and market circumstances, including risk factors affecting the airline industry, can affect the impairment assessment.

When assets are retired or disposed of, the cost and associated accumulated depreciation are removed from the related accounts and the difference, net of proceeds, is recorded as a gain in Other income.

Other invested assets: Other invested assets consist primarily of investments by AIG's insurance operations in hedge funds, private equity funds, other investment partnerships and direct private equity investments. AIG's investments in life settlement contracts and its 33 percent interest in AIA are also included in Other invested assets.

Hedge funds, private equity funds and other investment partnerships in which AIG's insurance operations hold in the aggregate less than a five percent interest are reported at fair value. The change in fair value is recognized as a component of Accumulated other comprehensive income (loss). With respect to hedge funds, private equity funds and other investment partnerships in which AIG holds in the aggregate a five percent or greater interest or less than a five percent interest but in which AIG has more than a minor influence over the operations of the investee, AIG's carrying value is its share of the net asset value of the funds or the partnerships. The changes in such net asset values, accounted for under the equity method, are recorded in Net investment income. Direct private equity investments entered into for strategic purposes and not solely for capital appreciation or for income generation are also accounted for under the equity method.

In applying the equity method of accounting, AIG consistently uses the most recently available financial information provided by the general partner or manager of each of these investments, which is one to three months prior to the end of AIG's reporting period. The financial statements of these investees are generally audited annually.

Life settlement contracts are accounted for under the investment method. Under the investment method, AIG recognizes its initial investment in life settlement contracts at the transaction price plus all initial direct external costs. Continuing costs to keep the policy in force, primarily life insurance premiums, increase the carrying value of the investment. AIG recognizes income on individual life settlement contracts when the insured dies, at an amount equal to the excess of the contract proceeds over the carrying amount of the contract at that time. Contracts are reviewed for indications that the expected future proceeds from the contract would not be sufficient to recover AIG's estimated future carrying amount of the contract, which is the current carrying amount for the contract plus anticipated undiscounted future premiums and other capitalizable future costs. Any such contracts identified are written down to their estimated fair value.

AIG accounts for its investment in AIA under the fair value option with gains and losses recorded in Net investment income. See Note 7 herein for further information.

Also included in Other invested assets are real estate held for investment and aircraft asset investments held by non-Aircraft Leasing subsidiaries. See Note 7 herein for further information.

Short-term investments: Short-term investments consist of interest-bearing cash equivalents, time deposits, securities purchased under agreements to resell, and investments, such as commercial paper, with original maturities within one year from the date of purchase.

Securities purchased under agreements to resell (reverse repurchase agreements) generally are accounted for as collateralized lending transactions. These agreements are recorded at their contracted resale amounts plus accrued interest, other than those that are accounted for at fair value. Such agreements entered into by AIGFP are carried at fair value based on market observable interest rates. AIG's policy is to take possession of or obtain a security interest in securities purchased under agreements to resell. The value of reverse repurchase agreements that were accounted for as collateralized lending transactions was $7.0 billion at December 31, 2011. The fair value of securities collateral received by AIG was $6.8 billion at December 31, 2011, of which $122 million was repledged by AIG.

AIG minimizes the risk that counterparties to transactions might be unable to fulfill their contractual obligations by monitoring customer credit exposure and collateral value and generally requiring additional collateral to be deposited with AIG when necessary.

(d) Cash: Cash represents cash on hand and non-interest bearing demand deposits.

(e) Premiums and other receivables—net: Premiums and other receivables includes premium balances receivable, amounts due from agents and brokers and insureds, trade receivables for Direct Investment book and Global Capital Markets and other receivables. Trade receivables for Global Capital Markets include cash collateral posted to derivative counterparties that are not eligible to be netted against derivative liabilities. The allowance for doubtful accounts on premiums and other receivables was $484 million and $515 million at December 31, 2011 and 2010, respectively.

(f) Reinsurance assets—net: In the ordinary course of business, AIG uses both treaty and facultative reinsurance to minimize its net loss exposure to any single catastrophic loss event or to an accumulation of losses from a number of smaller events. AIG determines the portion of the incurred but not reported (IBNR) loss that will be recoverable under its reinsurance contracts by reference to the terms of the reinsurance protection purchased. This determination is necessarily based on the estimate of IBNR and accordingly, is subject to the same uncertainties as the estimate of IBNR. Reinsurance assets include the balances due from reinsurance and insurance companies under the terms of AIG's reinsurance agreements for paid and unpaid losses and loss expenses, ceded unearned premiums and ceded future policy benefits for life and accident and health insurance contracts and benefits paid and unpaid. Amounts related to paid and unpaid losses and benefits and loss expenses with respect to these reinsurance agreements are substantially collateralized. AIG remains liable to the extent that its reinsurers do not meet their obligation under the reinsurance contracts,

and as such, AIG regularly evaluates the financial condition of its reinsurers and monitors concentration of credit risk. The allowance for doubtful accounts on reinsurance assets was $365 million and $492 million at December 31, 2011 and 2010, respectively.

(g) Deferred policy acquisition costs: Policy acquisition costs represent those costs, including commissions, premium taxes and other underwriting expenses that vary with and are primarily related to the acquisition of new business.

Short-duration insurance contracts: Policy acquisition costs are deferred and amortized over the period in which the related premiums written are earned. DAC is grouped consistent with the manner in which the insurance contracts are acquired, serviced and measured for profitability and is reviewed for recoverability based on the profitability of the underlying insurance contracts. Investment income is not anticipated in assessing the recoverability of DAC. AIG assesses the recoverability of its DAC on an annual basis or more frequently if circumstances indicate an impairment may have occurred. This assessment is performed by comparing recorded unearned premiums to the sum of expected claims, claims adjustment expenses, unamortized DAC and maintenance costs. If the sum of these costs exceeds the amount of recorded unearned premiums, the excess is recognized as an offset against the asset established for DAC. This offset is referred to as a premium deficiency charge. Increases in expected claims and claims adjustment expenses can have a significant impact on the likelihood and amount of a premium deficiency charge.

Long-duration insurance contracts: Policy acquisition costs for participating life, traditional life and accident and health insurance products are generally deferred and amortized, with interest, over the premium paying period. Policy acquisition costs and policy issuance costs related to universal life, and investment-type products (investment-oriented products) are deferred and amortized, with interest, in relation to the incidence of estimated gross profits to be realized over the estimated lives of the contracts. Estimated gross profits are composed of net interest income, net realized investment gains and losses, fees, surrender charges, expenses, and mortality and morbidity gains and losses.

AIG uses a "reversion to the mean" methodology, which allows AIG to maintain its long-term assumptions, while also giving consideration to the effect of deviations from these assumptions occurring in the current period. A DAC unlocking is performed when management determines that key assumptions (e.g. market return, surrender rates, etc.) should be modified. The DAC asset is recalculated using the new assumptions. The use of a reversion to the mean assumption is common within the industry; however, the parameters used in the methodology are subject to judgment and vary within the industry. If estimated gross profits change significantly, DAC is recalculated using the new assumptions. Any resulting adjustment is included in income as an adjustment to DAC. DAC is grouped consistent with the manner in which the insurance contracts are acquired, serviced and measured for profitability and is reviewed for recoverability based on the current and projected future profitability of the underlying insurance contracts.

The DAC for investment-oriented products is also adjusted for changes in estimated gross profits that result from changes in the net unrealized gains or losses on fixed maturity and equity securities available for sale. Because fixed maturity and equity securities available for sale are carried at aggregate fair value, an adjustment is made to DAC equal

SEC 1.33

to the change in DAC amortization that would have been recorded if such securities had been sold at their stated aggregate fair value and the proceeds reinvested at current yields. For long-duration traditional business, if such reinvestment would not be sufficient to recover DAC and meet policyholder obligations an adjustment to DAC and additional future policy benefits for those products is recorded using current best estimates that incorporate a review of assumptions regarding mortality, morbidity, persistency, maintenance expenses and investment returns. The change in these adjustments, net of tax, is included with the change in net unrealized appreciation (depreciation) of investments that is credited or charged directly to Accumulated other comprehensive income (loss).

Value of Business Acquired (VOBA) is determined at the time of acquisition and is reported in the Consolidated Balance Sheet with DAC. This value is based on the present value of future pre-tax profits discounted at yields applicable at the time of purchase. For participating life, traditional life and accident and health insurance products, VOBA is amortized over the life of the business similar to that for DAC based on the assumptions at purchase. For universal life, and investment-oriented products, VOBA is amortized in relation to the estimated gross profits to date for each period.

For contracts accounted for at fair value, policy acquisition costs are expensed as incurred and not deferred or amortized.

See (v) Recent Accounting Standards—Future Application of Accounting Standards herein for changes related to deferred acquisition costs in 2012 due to the adoption of a new accounting standard that addresses the accounting for costs associated with acquiring or renewing insurance contracts.

(h) Derivative assets and derivative liabilities, at fair value: Interest rate, currency, equity and commodity swaps, credit contracts (including AIGFP's super senior credit default swap portfolio), swaptions, options and forward transactions are accounted for as derivatives recorded on a trade-date basis, and carried at fair value. Unrealized gains and losses are reflected in income, when appropriate. In certain instances, a contract's transaction price is the best indication of initial fair value. Aggregate asset or liability positions are netted on the Consolidated Balance Sheet only to the extent permitted by qualifying master netting arrangements in place with each respective counterparty. Cash collateral posted by AIG with counterparties in conjunction with transactions supported by qualifying master netting arrangements is reported as a reduction of the corresponding net derivative liability, while cash collateral received by AIG in conjunction with transactions supported by qualifying master netting arrangements is reported as a reduction of the corresponding net derivative asset.

(i) Other assets: Other assets consists of, prepaid expenses, including deferred advertising costs, sales inducement assets, deposits, other deferred charges, real estate, other fixed assets, capitalized software costs, goodwill, intangible assets other than goodwill, restricted cash, including net cash proceeds from the AIA initial public offering in 2010 and, at December 31, 2010, net cash proceeds from the ALICO sale held in escrow pending the Closing and a prepaid commitment fee asset related to the FRBNY Credit Agreement. The prepaid commitment fee asset related to the FRBNY Credit Agreement was amortized as interest expense ratably over the five-year term of the agreement, accelerated for actual pay-downs that reduce the total credit available. The remaining unamortized prepaid commitment fee asset of

$3.6 billion at December 31, 2010 was derecognized by AIG through earnings upon the closing of the Recapitalization on January 14, 2011.

Certain direct response advertising costs are deferred and amortized over the expected future benefit period. When AIG can demonstrate that its customers have responded specifically to direct-response advertising, the primary purpose of which is to elicit sales to customers, and when it can be shown such advertising results in probable future economic benefits, the advertising costs are capitalized. Deferred advertising costs are amortized on a cost-pool-by-cost-pool basis over the expected future economic benefit period and are reviewed regularly for recoverability. Deferred advertising costs totaled $78 million and $200 million at December 31, 2011 and 2010, respectively. The amount of expense amortized into income was $34 million, $40 million and $173 million, for the years ended 2011, 2010 and 2009, respectively.

AIG offers sales inducements, which include enhanced crediting rates or bonus payments to contract holders (bonus interest) on certain annuity and investment contract products. Sales inducements provided to the contractholder are recognized as part of the liability for policyholders' contract deposits in the Consolidated Balance Sheet. Such amounts are deferred and amortized over the life of the contract using the same methodology and assumptions used to amortize DAC. To qualify for such accounting treatment, the bonus interest must be explicitly identified in the contract at inception, and AIG must demonstrate that such amounts are incremental to amounts AIG credits on similar contracts without bonus interest, and are higher than the contract's expected ongoing crediting rates for periods after the bonus period. The deferred bonus interest and other deferred sales inducement assets totaled $766 million and $856 million at December 31, 2011 and 2010, respectively. The amortization expense associated with these assets is reported within Policyholder benefits and claims incurred in the Consolidated Statement of Operations. Such amortization expense totaled $201 million, $194 million and $215 million for the years ended December 31, 2011, 2010 and 2009, respectively.

All commodities are recorded at the lower of cost or fair value. The exposure to market risk may be reduced through the use of forwards, futures and option contracts. Lower of cost or fair value reductions in commodity positions and unrealized gains and losses in related derivatives are reflected in Other income.

See Note 12 herein for a discussion of derivatives.

The cost of buildings and furniture and equipment is depreciated principally on a straight-line basis over their estimated useful lives (maximum of 40 years for buildings and 10 years for furniture and equipment). Expenditures for maintenance and repairs are charged to income as incurred; expenditures for improvements are capitalized and depreciated. AIG periodically assesses the carrying value of its real estate for purposes of determining any asset impairment. Capitalized software costs, which represent costs directly related to obtaining, developing or upgrading internal use software, are capitalized and amortized using the straight-line method over a period generally not exceeding five years. Real estate, fixed assets and other long-lived assets are assessed for impairment when impairment indicators exist. Accumulated depreciation on real estate and other fixed assets was $3.8 billion and $3.6 billion at December 31, 2011 and 2010, respectively.

(j) Goodwill: Goodwill is the excess of the cost of an acquired business over the fair value of the identifiable net assets of the acquired business. Goodwill is tested for impairment annually, or more frequently if circumstances indicate an impairment may have occurred. Substantially all of AIG's goodwill is associated with and allocated to its Chartis segment at December 31, 2011.

The impairment assessment involves a two-step process in which an initial assessment for potential impairment is performed and, if potential impairment is present, the amount of impairment is measured (if any) and recorded. Impairment is tested at the reporting unit level.

Management initially assesses the potential for impairment by estimating the fair value of each of AIG's reporting units and comparing the estimated fair values with the carrying amounts of those reporting units, including allocated goodwill. The estimate of a reporting unit's fair value may be based on one or a combination of approaches including market-based earnings multiples of the unit's peer companies, discounted expected future cash flows, external appraisals or, in the case of reporting units being considered for sale, third-party indications of fair value, if available. Management considers one or more of these estimates when determining the fair value of a reporting unit to be used in the impairment test.

If the estimated fair value of a reporting unit exceeds its carrying value, goodwill is not impaired. If the carrying value of a reporting unit exceeds its estimated fair value, goodwill associated with that reporting unit potentially is impaired. The amount of impairment, if any, is measured as the excess of the carrying value of the goodwill over the implied fair value of the goodwill. The implied fair value of the goodwill is measured as the excess of the fair value of the reporting unit over the amounts that would be assigned to the reporting unit's assets and liabilities in a hypothetical business combination. An impairment charge is recognized in earnings to the extent of the excess. Chartis manages its assets on an aggregate basis and does not allocate its assets, other than goodwill, between its operating segments. Therefore, the carrying value of the reporting units was determined by

allocating the carrying value of Chartis to those units based upon an internal model.

During the third quarter of 2011, Chartis finalized its reorganization, operating design and related segment reporting changes. In connection with this reorganization, total goodwill of $1.4 billion was allocated between Commercial Insurance and Consumer Insurance based on their relative fair values as of September 30, 2011. Management tested the allocated goodwill for impairment and determined that the fair values of the Commercial Insurance and Consumer Insurance reporting units exceeded their carrying values at both September 30, 2011 and December 31, 2011 and therefore the goodwill of these reporting units was considered not impaired.

During 2010, AIG had performed goodwill impairment tests at March 31, June 30 and September 30, in connection with the announced sales of ALICO, AIG Star and AIG Edison and again at December 31, 2010.

During 2010, AIG determined that the fair value of ALICO was less than its carrying value. Based on the results of the goodwill impairment test, AIG determined that all of the goodwill allocated to ALICO should be impaired and, accordingly, recognized a goodwill impairment charge of $3.3 billion.

In connection with the announced sale of AIG Star and AIG Edison (the Reporting Unit) in 2010 and management's determination that the Reporting Unit met the held-for-sale criteria, management tested the $1.3 billion of goodwill of the Reporting Unit for impairment. AIG estimated the fair value of the Reporting Unit based on the consideration to be received pursuant to the agreement with Prudential Financial Inc. and determined the fair value to be less than its carrying value. Based on the results of the goodwill impairment test, AIG determined that all of the goodwill allocated to the Reporting Unit should be impaired and, accordingly, recognized a goodwill impairment charge of $1.3 billion in the third quarter of 2010.

At December 31, 2010, AIG performed its annual goodwill impairment test. Based on the results of the goodwill impairment test, AIG concluded that the remaining goodwill was not impaired.

The following table presents the changes in goodwill by reportable segment:

(In millions)	Chartis	Aircraft Leasing	Other	Total
Balance at December 31, 2009:				
Goodwill—gross	$ 2,480	$—	$ 7,192	$ 9,672
Accumulated impairments	(1,196)	—	(2,281)	(3,477)
Net goodwill	1,284	—	4,911	6,195
Increase (decrease) due to:				
Acquisition	33	—	—	33
Sales of business units	—	—	(69)	(69)
Other(a)	16	—	(86)	(70)
Goodwill impairment included in discontinued operations	—	—	(4,625)	(4,625)
Dispositions(b)	—	—	(131)	(131)

(continued)

(In millions)	Chartis	Aircraft Leasing	Other	Total
Balance at December 31, 2010:				
Goodwill—gross	$ 2,529	$—	$ 2,281	$ 4,810
Accumulated impairments	(1,196)	—	(2,281)	(3,477)
Net goodwill	$ 1,333	$—	$ —	$ 1,333
Increase (decrease) due to:				
Acquisition	3	15	8	26
Other[a]	14	—	—	14
Balance at December 31, 2011:				
Goodwill—gross	$ 2,546	$15	2,289	$ 4,850
Accumulated impairments	(1,196)	—	(2,281)	(3,477)
Net goodwill	$ 1,350	$15	$ 8	$ 1,373

[a] Includes foreign exchange translation and purchase price adjustments (PPA).
[b] Reflects the deconsolidation of AIA.

(k) Separate accounts: Separate accounts represent funds for which investment income and investment gains and losses accrue directly to the policyholders who bear the investment risk. Each account has specific investment objectives, and the assets are carried at fair value. The assets of each account are legally segregated and are not subject to claims that arise out of any other business of AIG. The liabilities for these accounts are equal to the account assets.

(l) Liability for unpaid claims and claims adjustment expense: The liability for unpaid claims and claims adjustment expense represents the accumulation of estimates for unpaid reported losses and includes provisions for IBNR losses. Because the reserves are based on estimates, the ultimate liability may be more or less than such reserves. The methods of determining such estimates and establishing resulting reserves are reviewed and updated periodically. If the estimate of reserves is determined to be inadequate or redundant, the increase or decrease is reflected in income. AIG discounts its loss reserves relating to workers' compensation business written by its U.S. domiciled subsidiaries as permitted by the domiciliary statutory regulatory authorities.

(m) Future policy benefits for life and accident and health insurance contracts and policyholder contract deposits: The liabilities for future policy benefits and policyholder contract deposits are established using assumptions described in Note 13 herein. Future policy benefits for life and accident and health insurance contracts include provisions for future dividends to participating policyholders, accrued in accordance with all applicable regulatory or contractual provisions. Also included in Future policy benefits are liabilities for annuities issued in structured settlement arrangements whereby a claimant has agreed to settle a general insurance claim in exchange for fixed payments over a fixed determinable period of time with a life contingency feature. Structured settlement liabilities are presented on a discounted basis because the settled claims are fixed and determinable. Policyholder contract deposits also include AIG's liability for (a) certain guarantee benefits accounted for as embedded derivatives at fair value, (b) annuities issued in a structured settlement arrangement with no life contingency and (c) certain contracts AIG elected to account for at fair value.

See Note 6 herein for additional fair value information.

(n) Other policyholder funds: Other policyholder funds are reported at cost and include any policyholder funds on deposit that encompass premium deposits and similar items.

(o) Income taxes: Deferred tax assets and liabilities are recorded for the effects of temporary differences between the tax basis of an asset or liability and its reported amount in the consolidated financial statements. AIG assesses its ability to realize deferred tax assets considering all available evidence, including the earnings history, the timing, character and amount of future earnings potential, the reversal of taxable temporary differences and prudent and feasible tax planning strategies available to the legal entities when recognizing deferred tax assets. See Note 22 herein for a further discussion of income taxes.

(p) Other liabilities: Other liabilities consist of other funds on deposit, other payables, securities sold under agreements to repurchase and securities and spot commodities sold but not yet purchased. AIG has entered into certain insurance and reinsurance contracts, primarily in its Chartis segment, that do not contain sufficient insurance risk to be accounted for as insurance or reinsurance. Accordingly, the premiums received on such contracts, after deduction for certain related expenses, are recorded as deposits within Other liabilities in the Consolidated Balance Sheet. Net proceeds of these deposits are invested and generate Net investment income. As amounts are paid, consistent with the underlying contracts, the deposit liability is reduced. Also included in Other liabilities are trade payables for the Direct Investment book and AIGFP, which include option premiums received and payables to counterparties that relate to unrealized gains and losses on futures, forwards, and options and balances due to clearing brokers and exchanges. Trade payables for Global Capital Markets include cash collateral received from derivative counterparties that is not contractually nettable against derivative assets.

Securities and spot commodities sold but not yet purchased represent sales of securities and spot commodities not owned at the time of sale. The obligations arising from such transactions are recorded on a trade-date basis and carried at fair value. Fair values of securities sold but not yet purchased are based on current market prices. Fair values of spot commodities sold but not yet purchased are based on current market prices of reference spot futures contracts traded on exchanges.

Liabilities arising from securities sold under agreements to repurchase securities (repurchase agreements) (other than those entered into by AIGFP) are generally treated as collateralized borrowing transactions and are recorded at their contracted repurchase amounts plus accrued interest.

Agreements to repurchase securities entered into by AIGFP are carried at fair value based on market-observable interest rates. As of December 31, 2011, the fair value of repurchase agreements accounted for as collateralized borrowing transactions was $563 million.

When AIG does not obtain cash proceeds sufficient to fund substantially all of the cost of purchasing identical replacement securities during the term of the contract (generally less than 90 percent of the security value), AIG accounts for the transaction as a sale of the security and reports the obligation to repurchase the security as a derivative contract that is recognized at fair value through earnings. When securities carried in the available for sale category are sold, AIG records a gain or loss in income. When securities accounted for at fair value are considered sold, no additional gain or loss is recognized.

The fair value of securities transferred under repurchase agreements accounted for as sales was $2.1 billion and $2.7 billion at December 31, 2011 and December 31, 2010, respectively.

As of December 31, 2011, the fair value of collateral posted by AIG for repurchase agreements totaled $2.8 billion, of which $2.7 billion could be repledged or resold by the counterparties. The market value of securities to be repurchased is monitored, and additional collateral is posted where appropriate.

Also included in Other liabilities are obligations under gold leases, which are accounted for as a debt host with an embedded gold derivative which are accounted for under the fair value option.

(q) Other long-term debt: AIG's funding consists, in part, of medium and long-term debt. Long-term debt is carried at the principal amount borrowed, net of unamortized discounts or premiums. See Note 15 herein for additional information. Long-term debt also includes liabilities connected to trust preferred stock principally related to outstanding securities issued by SunAmerica Financial Group, Inc. (SAFG, Inc.), a wholly owned subsidiary of AIG (formerly AIG Life Holdings, Inc.). Cash distributions on such preferred stock are accounted for as interest expense.

(r) Contingent liabilities: Amounts are accrued for the resolution of claims that have either been asserted or are deemed probable of assertion if, in the opinion of management, it is both probable that a liability has been incurred and the amount of the liability can be reasonably estimated. In many cases, it is not possible to determine whether a liability has been incurred or to estimate the ultimate or minimum amount of that liability until years after the contingency arises, in which case, no accrual is made until that time. See Note 16 herein for additional information.

(s) Foreign currency: Financial statement accounts expressed in foreign currencies are translated into U.S. dollars. Functional currency assets and liabilities are translated into U.S. dollars generally using rates of exchange prevailing at the balance sheet date of each respective subsidiary and the related translation adjustments are recorded as a separate component of Accumulated other comprehensive income (loss), net of any related taxes, in Total AIG shareholders' equity. Functional currencies are generally the currencies of the local operating environment. Financial statement accounts expressed in currencies other than the functional currency of a consolidated entity are translated into that entity's functional currency. Income statement accounts expressed in functional currencies are translated using average exchange rates during the period. The adjust-

ments resulting from translation of financial statements of foreign entities operating in highly inflationary economies are recorded in income. Exchange gains and losses resulting from foreign currency transactions are recorded in income.

(t) Noncontrolling Interests:

Nonvoting, callable, junior preferred interests held by Department of the Treasury and Nonvoting, callable, junior and senior preferred interests held by the FRBNY: Represent preferred interests in (i) at December 31, 2011, a wholly-owned SPV initially formed to hold the common stock of AIA and (ii) at December 31, 2010, two wholly-owned SPVs initially formed to hold common stock of AIA and ALICO at December 31, 2010. The preferred interests were measured at fair value on their issuance date. AIG transferred the preferred interests in the SPVs to the FRBNY in consideration for a $25 billion reduction of the FRBNY Credit Facility. The preferred interests initially had a liquidation preference of $25 billion and had a preferred return of five percent per year compounded quarterly through September 22, 2013 and nine percent thereafter. The preferred return is reflected in Income (loss) from continuing operations attributable to noncontrolling interests—Nonvoting, callable, junior and senior preferred interests in the Consolidated Statement of Operations. The difference between the preferred interests' fair value and the initial liquidation preference is being amortized and included in Net income (loss) from continuing operations attributable to noncontrolling interests—Nonvoting, callable, junior and senior preferred interests. These noncontrolling interests, other than the senior preferred interests in the ALICO SPV, which were redeemed in full, were transferred to the Department of the Treasury as part of the January 14, 2011 Recapitalization transactions.

Other noncontrolling interests: Includes the equity interests of third-party shareholders in AIG's consolidated subsidiaries and includes the preferred shareholders' equity in outstanding preferred stock of ILFC, a wholly owned subsidiary of AIG. Cash distributions on such preferred stock or equity interests are accounted for as interest expense. This preferred stock consists of 1,000 shares of market auction preferred stock (MAPS) in two series (Series A and B) of 500 shares each. Each of the MAPS shares has a liquidation value of $100,000 per share and is not convertible. The dividend rate, other than the initial rate, for each dividend period for each series is reset approximately every seven weeks (49 days) on the basis of orders placed in an auction, provided such auctions are able to occur. At December 31, 2011, there is no ability to conduct such auctions; therefore, the MAPS certificate of determination dictates that a maximum applicable rate, as defined in the certificate of determination, be paid on the MAPS. At December 31, 2011, the dividend rate for each of the Series A and Series B MAPS was 0.25 percent and 0.88 percent respectively.

(u) Earnings (loss) per share: Basic earnings or loss per share and diluted loss per share are based on the weighted average number of common shares outstanding, adjusted to reflect all stock dividends and stock splits. Diluted earnings per share is based on those shares used in basic earnings per share plus shares that would have been outstanding assuming issuance of common shares for all dilutive potential common shares outstanding, adjusted to reflect all stock dividends and stock splits.

See Note 17 herein for additional earnings (loss) per share disclosures.

(v) Recent Accounting Standards:

Future Application of Accounting Standards

Accounting for Costs Associated with Acquiring or Renewing Insurance Contracts

In October 2010, the Financial Accounting Standards Board (FASB) issued an accounting standard that amends the accounting for costs incurred by insurance companies that can be capitalized in connection with acquiring or renewing insurance contracts. The standard amends how to determine whether the costs incurred in connection with the acquisition of new or renewal insurance contracts qualify as deferred acquisition costs. The standard is effective for interim and annual periods beginning on January 1, 2012 with early adoption permitted. Prospective or retrospective application is also permitted.

AIG will adopt the standard retrospectively on January 1, 2012. Upon adoption, retrospective application will result in a reduction to opening retained earnings for the earliest period presented and a decrease in the amount of capitalized costs in connection with the acquisition or renewal of insurance contracts because AIG will only defer costs that are incremental and directly related to the successful acquisition of new or renewal business.

As a result of adopting this standard at January 1, 2012, AIG expects a pre-tax reduction of Deferred policy acquisition costs of approximately $4.9 billion and an after-tax decrease in AIG shareholders' equity of approximately $3.3 billion, which consists of a decrease in Retained earnings of approximately $3.7 billion partially offset by an increase in Accumulated other comprehensive income of $0.4 billion at January 1, 2012. The retrospective adoption will favorably affect Income (loss) from continuing operations before income taxes (benefit) by approximately $149 million, $90 million and $40 million for the years ended December 31, 2011, 2010, and 2009, respectively. The reduction in Deferred policy acquisition costs is primarily due to lower deferrals associated with unsuccessful efforts as well as advertising costs included in Deferred policy acquisition costs that no longer meet the criteria for deferral under the accounting standard.

Reconsideration of Effective Control for Repurchase Agreements

In April 2011, the FASB issued an accounting standard that amends the criteria used to determine effective control for repurchase agreements and other similar arrangements such as securities lending transactions. The standard modifies the criteria for determining when these transactions would be accounted for as secured borrowings (i.e., financings) instead of sales of the securities.

The standard removes from the assessment of effective control the requirement that the transferor have the ability to repurchase or redeem the financial assets on substantially the agreed terms, even in the event of default by the transferee. The removal of this requirement makes the level of collateral received by the transferor in a repurchase agreement or similar arrangement irrelevant in determining whether the transaction should be accounted for as a sale. Consequently, more repurchase agreements, securities lending transactions and similar arrangements will be accounted for as secured borrowings.

The guidance in the standard must be applied prospectively to transactions or modifications of existing transactions that occur on or after January 1, 2012. Early adoption is prohibited. Under this standard, which AIG adopted on January 1, 2012, $2.1 billion in repurchase agreements will continue to be accounted for as sales unless modifications of these transactions occur subsequent to adoption, which would result in an assessment of whether they should be accounted for as secured borrowings under the standard.

Common Fair Value Measurements and Disclosure Requirements in GAAP and IFRS

In May 2011, the FASB issued an accounting standard that amends certain aspects of the fair value measurement guidance in GAAP, primarily to achieve the FASB's objective of a converged definition of fair value and substantially converged measurement and disclosure guidance with International Financial Reporting Standards (IFRS). Consequently, when the standard becomes effective on January 1, 2012, fair value measurement and disclosure requirements under GAAP and IFRS will be consistent, with certain exceptions including the accounting for day one gains and losses, measuring the fair value of alternative investments using net asset value and certain disclosure requirements.

The standard's fair value guidance applies to all companies that measure assets, liabilities, or instruments classified in shareholders' equity at fair value or provide fair value disclosures for items not recorded at fair value. While many of the amendments are not expected to significantly affect current practice, the guidance clarifies how a principal market is determined, addresses the fair value measurement of financial instruments with offsetting market or counterparty credit risks and the concept of valuation premise (i.e., in-use or in exchange) and highest and best use, extends the prohibition on blockage factors to all three levels of the fair value hierarchy, and requires additional disclosures.

The standard is effective for AIG for interim and annual periods beginning on January 1, 2012. The new disclosure requirements must be applied prospectively. The standard will not have a material effect on AIG's consolidated financial condition, results of operations or cash flows.

Presentation of Comprehensive Income

In June 2011, the FASB issued an accounting standard that requires the presentation of comprehensive income either in a single continuous statement of comprehensive income or in two separate but consecutive statements. In the two-statement approach, the first statement should present total net income and its components, followed consecutively by a second statement that presents total other comprehensive income and its components. This presentation is effective January 1, 2012 and is required to be applied retrospectively.

Accounting Standards Adopted During 2011

Fair Value Measurements and Disclosures

In January 2010, the FASB issued an accounting standard that requires fair value disclosures about significant transfers between Level 1 and 2 measurement categories and separate presentation of purchases, sales, issuances, and settlements within the rollforward of Level 3 activity. Also, this fair value guidance clarifies the disclosure requirements about the level of disaggregation and valuation techniques and inputs. This guidance became effective for AIG beginning on January 1, 2010, except for the disclosures about purchases, sales, issuances, and settlements within the roll-forward of Level 3 activity, which became effective for AIG beginning on January 1, 2011. See Note 6 herein.

Consolidation of Investments in Separate Accounts

In April 2010, the FASB issued an accounting standard that clarifies that an insurance company should not combine any investments held in separate account interests with its interest in the same investment held in its general account when assessing the investment for consolidation. Separate accounts represent funds for which investment income and investment gains and losses accrue directly to the policyholders who bear the investment risk. The standard also provides guidance on how an insurer should consolidate an investment fund when the insurer concludes that consolidation of an investment is required and the insurer's interest is through its general account in addition to any separate accounts. The standard became effective for AIG on January 1, 2011. The adoption of this standard did not have a material effect on AIG's consolidated financial condition, results of operations or cash flows.

A Creditor's Determination of Whether a Restructuring is a Troubled Debt Restructuring

In April 2011, the FASB issued an accounting standard that amends the guidance for a creditor's evaluation of whether a restructuring is a troubled debt restructuring and requires additional disclosures about a creditor's troubled debt restructuring activities. The standard clarifies the existing guidance on the two criteria used by creditors to determine whether a modification or restructuring is a troubled debt restructuring: (i) whether the creditor has granted a concession and (ii) whether the debtor is experiencing financial difficulties. The standard became effective for AIG for interim and annual periods beginning on July 1, 2011. AIG applied the guidance in the accounting standard retrospectively for all modifications and restructuring activities that had occurred since January 1, 2011. For receivables that were considered impaired under the guidance, AIG was required to measure the impairment of those receivables prospectively in the first period of adoption. In addition, AIG must provide the disclosures about troubled debt restructuring activities in the period of adoption. The adoption of this standard did not have a material effect on AIG's consolidated financial condition, results of operations or cash flows. See Note 8 herein.

Testing Goodwill for Impairment

In September 2011, the FASB issued an accounting standard that amends the approach to testing goodwill for impairment. The standard simplifies how entities test goodwill for impairment by permitting an entity to first assess qualitative factors to determine whether it is more likely than not that the fair value of a reporting unit is less than its carrying amount as a basis for determining whether it is necessary to perform the quantitative, two-step goodwill impairment test. The standard is effective for annual and interim goodwill impairment tests performed for fiscal years beginning after December 15, 2011. Early adoption is permitted. AIG plans to adopt the standard in conjunction with its goodwill impairment testing performed in 2012. The adoption of the standard is not expected to affect AIG's consolidated financial condition, results of operations or cash flows.

Accounting Standards Adopted During 2010

Accounting for Transfers of Financial Assets

In June 2009, the FASB issued an accounting standard addressing transfers of financial assets that removes the concept of a qualifying special-purpose entity (QSPE) from the FASB Accounting Standards Codification and removes the exception that exempted transferors from applying the consolidation rules to QSPEs.

The standard was effective for interim and annual periods beginning on January 1, 2010 for AIG. Earlier application was prohibited. The adoption of this standard increased both assets and liabilities by approximately $1.3 billion as a result of consolidating two previously unconsolidated QSPEs. The adoption of this standard did not have a material effect on AIG's consolidated financial condition, results of operations or cash flows.

Consolidation of Variable Interest Entities

In June 2009, the FASB issued an accounting standard that amends the guidance addressing consolidation of certain variable interest entities with an approach focused on identifying which enterprise has the power to direct the activities of a variable interest entity that most significantly affect the entity's economic performance and has (1) the obligation to absorb losses of the entity or (2) the right to receive benefits from the entity. The standard also requires enhanced financial reporting by enterprises involved with variable interest entities.

The following table summarizes the two methods applied by AIG and the amount and classification in the Consolidated Balance Sheet of the assets and liabilities consolidated as a result of the adoption of the standard on January 1, 2010:

| | Transition Methods | | |
(In millions)	Fair Value Option	Carrying Value	Total
Assets:			
Bond trading securities, at fair value	$1,239	$1,262	$2,501
Mortgage and other loans receivable	—	1,980	1,980
Other invested assets	—	480	480
Other asset accounts	194	150	344
Assets held for sale	4,630	—	4,630
Total assets	$6,063	$3,872	$9,935

(continued)

SEC 1.33

(In millions)	Transition Methods		
	Fair Value Option	Carrying Value	Total
Liabilities:			
FRBNY commercial paper funding facility	$1,088	$ —	$1,088
Other long-term debt	—	1,533	1,533
Other liability accounts	1	31	32
Liabilities held for sale	4,525	—	4,525
Total liabilities	$5,614	$1,564	$7,178

The cumulative effect adjustment of electing the fair value option was not material to AIG's accumulated deficit.

The following table summarizes the excess of amounts previously recorded upon the consolidation of previously unconsolidated VIEs, as a result of the adoption of the standard on January 1, 2010:

(In billions)	
Assets	$8.2
Liabilities	7.1
Redeemable noncontrolling interest	1.1
Equity:	
Accumulated deficit	0.2
Accumulated other comprehensive income	(0.3)
Other noncontrolling interests	0.1
Total liabilities and equity	$8.2

In February 2010, the FASB also issued an update to the aforementioned accounting standard that defers the revised consolidation rules for variable interest entities with attributes of, or similar to, an investment company or money market fund. The primary effect of this deferral for AIG is that AIG will continue to apply the consolidation rules in effect before the amended guidance discussed above for its interests in eligible entities, such as certain mutual funds.

Accounting for Embedded Credit Derivatives

In March 2010, the FASB issued an accounting standard that amends the accounting for embedded credit derivative features in structured securities that redistribute credit risk in the form of subordination of one financial instrument to another. The standard clarifies how to determine whether embedded credit derivative features, including those in collateralized debt obligations (CDOs), credit-linked notes (CLNs), synthetic CDOs and CLNs and other synthetic securities (e.g., commercial and residential mortgage-backed securities issued by securitization entities that wrote credit derivatives), are considered to be embedded derivatives that should be analyzed for potential bifurcation and separate accounting or, alternatively, for fair value accounting in connection with the application of the fair value option to the entire hybrid instrument. AIG adopted the standard on July 1, 2010 and recorded a reclassification of $256 million of synthetic securities from Bonds available for sale to Bond trading securities and also reclassified a gain of $68 million from Accumulated other comprehensive income to Accumulated deficit as of July 1, 2010. Upon adoption, AIG accounts for its investments in synthetic securities otherwise requiring bifurcation at fair value, with changes in fair value recognized in earnings. The adoption of this standard did not have a material effect on AIG's consolidated financial condition, results of operations or cash flows.

Disclosure about the Credit Quality of Financing Receivables

In July 2010, the FASB issued an accounting standard that requires enhanced disclosures about the credit quality of financing receivables that are not measured at fair value. This guidance requires a greater level of disaggregated information about the credit quality of financing receivables and the related allowance for credit losses. In addition, this guidance requires disclosure of credit quality indicators, past due information, and modifications of financing receivables. The disclosures as of the end of a reporting period became effective for interim and annual reporting periods ended on or after December 15, 2010. The disclosures about activity that occurs during a reporting period became effective for interim and annual reporting periods beginning on or after December 15, 2010. In January 2011, the FASB issued an accounting standard that temporarily deferred the effective date for disclosures on modifications of financing receivables by creditors. In April 2011, the FASB issued an accounting standard that amended the guidance for a creditor's evaluation of whether a restructuring is a troubled debt restructuring. In addition, this guidance requires additional disclosures about a creditor's troubled debt restructuring activities in interim and annual periods beginning on July 1, 2011. See Accounting Standards Adopted During 2011 herein for further discussion.

Accounting Standards Adopted During 2009

Determining Whether an Instrument (or Embedded Feature) is Indexed to an Entity's Own Stock

In June 2008, the FASB issued an accounting standard that addresses how to determine whether a financial instrument (or embedded feature) is indexed to an entity's own stock and therefore may not be accounted for as a derivative instrument. AIG adopted the standard on January 1, 2009, which resulted in a $15 million cumulative effect adjustment to opening Accumulated deficit and a $91 million reduction in Additional paid-in capital.

Recognition and Presentation of Other-Than-Temporary Impairments

In April 2009, the FASB issued an accounting standard that requires a company to recognize the credit component of an other-than-temporary impairment of a fixed maturity security in earnings and the non-credit component in accumulated other comprehensive income when the company does not intend to sell the security or it is more likely than not that the company will not be required to sell the security prior to recovery. The standard also changed the threshold for determining when an other-than-temporary impairment has occurred on a fixed maturity security with respect to intent and ability to hold until recovery. The standard does not change the recognition of other-than-temporary impairment for equity securities. The standard requires additional disclosures in interim and annual reporting periods for fixed maturity and equity securities. See Note 7 herein for the expanded disclosures.

AIG adopted the standard on April 1, 2009 and recorded an after-tax cumulative effect adjustment to increase AIG shareholders' equity by $2.5 billion as of April 1, 2009, consisting of a decrease in Accumulated deficit of $11.8 billion and an increase to Accumulated other comprehensive loss of $9.3 billion, net of tax. The net increase in AIG's shareholders' equity was due to a reversal of a portion of the deferred tax asset valuation allowance for certain previous non-credit impairment charges directly attributable to the change in accounting principle (see Note 22 herein). The cumulative effect adjustment resulted in an increase of approximately $16 billion in the amortized cost of fixed maturity securities, which has the effect of significantly reducing the accretion of investment income over the remaining life of the underlying securities, beginning in the second quarter of 2009. The ef-

fect of the reduced investment income will be offset, in part, by a decrease in the amortization of deferred policy acquisition costs (DAC) and sales inducements assets (SIA).

The standard reduced the level of other-than-temporary impairment charges recorded in earnings for fixed maturity securities due to the following required changes in AIG's accounting policy for other-than-temporary impairments (see Note 7 herein for a more detailed discussion of the changes in policy):

- Impairment charges for non-credit (e.g., severity) losses are no longer recognized;
- The amortized cost basis of credit impaired securities will be written down through a charge to earnings to the present value of expected cash flows, rather than to fair value; and
- For fixed maturity securities that are not deemed to be credit-impaired, AIG is no longer required to assert that it has the intent and ability to hold such securities to recovery to avoid an other-than-temporary impairment charge. Instead, an impairment charge through earnings is required only when AIG has the intent to sell the fixed maturity security or it is more likely than not that AIG will be required to sell the security prior to recovery.

The following table presents the components of the change in AIG shareholders' equity at April 1, 2009 due to the adoption of the accounting standard for other-than-temporary impairments:

(In billions)	Accumulated Deficit	Accumulated Other Comprehensive Loss	AIG Shareholders' Equity
Increase (decrease) to:			
Net effect of the increase in amortized cost of available for sale fixed maturity securities	$16.1	$(16.1)	$ —
Net effect of related DAC, SIA and other insurance balances	(1.8)	1.8	—
Net effect on deferred income tax assets	(2.5)	5.0	2.5
Net increase in AIG shareholders' equity	$11.8	$ (9.3)	$2.5

Determining Fair Value When the Volume and Level of Activity for the Asset or Liability Have Significantly Decreased and Identifying Transactions That Are Not Orderly

In April 2009 the FASB issued an accounting standard that provides guidance for estimating the fair value of assets and liabilities when the volume and level of activity for an asset or liability have significantly decreased and for identifying circumstances that indicate a transaction is not orderly. The adoption of the standard on April 1, 2009, did not have a material effect on AIG's consolidated financial condition, results of operations or cash flows.

Measuring Liabilities at Fair Value

In August 2009, the FASB issued an accounting standard to clarify how the fair value measurement principles should be applied to measuring liabilities carried at fair value. The standard explains how to prioritize market inputs in measuring liabilities at fair value and what adjustments to market inputs are appropriate for debt obligations that are restricted from being transferred to another obligor. The standard was

effective beginning October 1, 2009 for AIG. The adoption of the standard did not have a material effect on AIG's consolidated financial condition, results of operations or cash flows.

Investments in Certain Entities that Calculate Net Asset Value per Share (or Its Equivalent)

In September 2009, the FASB issued an accounting standard that permits, as a practical expedient, a company to measure the fair value of an investment that is within the scope of the standard on the basis of the net asset value per share of the investment (or its equivalent) if that value is calculated in accordance with fair value as defined by the FASB. The standard also requires enhanced disclosures. The standard applies to investment companies that do not have readily determinable fair values such as certain hedge funds and private equity funds. The standard was effective for interim and annual periods ended after December 15, 2009. The adoption of the standard did not have a material effect on AIG's consolidated financial condition, results of operations or cash flows. See Note 6 herein for disclosure.

Nature of Operations

1.34

ARMSTRONG WORLD INDUSTRIES, INC. (DEC)

NOTES TO CONSOLIDATED FINANCIAL STATEMENTS

(Dollar amounts in millions)

Note 3—Nature of Operations

Building Products—produces suspended mineral fiber, soft fiber and metal ceiling systems for use in commercial, institutional and residential settings. In addition, our Building Products segment sources complementary ceiling products. Our products, which are sold worldwide, are available in numerous colors, performance characteristics and designs, and offer attributes such as acoustical control, rated fire protection and aesthetic appeal. Commercial ceiling materials and accessories are sold to ceiling systems contractors and to resale distributors. Residential ceiling products are sold in North America primarily to wholesalers and retailers (including large home centers). Suspension system (grid) products manufactured by Worthington Armstrong Venture ("WAVE") are sold by both us and WAVE.

Resilient Flooring—produces and sources a broad range of floor coverings primarily for homes and commercial and institutional buildings. Manufactured products in this segment include vinyl sheet, vinyl tile and linoleum flooring. In addition, our Resilient Flooring segment sources and sells laminate flooring products, vinyl tile products, vinyl sheet products, adhesives, and installation and maintenance materials and accessories. Resilient Flooring products are offered in a wide variety of types, designs, and colors. We sell these products worldwide to wholesalers, large home centers, retailers, contractors and to the manufactured homes industry.

Wood Flooring—produces and sources wood flooring products for use in new residential construction and renovation, with some commercial applications in stores, restaurants and high-end offices. The product offering includes pre-finished solid and engineered wood floors in various wood species, and related accessories. Virtually all of our Wood Flooring sales are in North America. Our Wood Flooring products are generally sold to independent wholesale flooring distributors and large home centers.

Cabinets—produces kitchen and bathroom cabinetry and related products, which are used primarily in the U.S. residential new construction and renovation markets. Through our system of Company-owned and independent distribution centers and through direct sales to builders, our Cabinets segment provides design, fabrication and installation services to single and multi-family homebuilders, remodelers and consumers. All of Cabinets' sales are in the U.S.

Unallocated Corporate—includes assets, liabilities, income and expenses that have not been allocated to the business units. Balance sheet items classified as Unallocated Corporate are primarily income tax related accounts, cash and cash equivalents, the Armstrong brand name, the U.S. prepaid pension cost and long-term debt. Expenses for our corporate departments and certain benefit plans are allocated to the reportable segments based on known metrics, such as specific activity, headcount, or net sales. The remaining items, which cannot be attributed to the reportable segments without a high degree of generalization, are reported in Unallocated Corporate.

For the Year Ended 2011	Building Products	Resilient Flooring	Wood Flooring	Cabinets	Unallocated Corporate	Total
Net sales to external customers	$1,237.5	$1,002.3	$483.3	$136.4	—	$2,859.5
Equity (earnings) from joint venture	(54.9)	—	—	—	—	(54.9)
Segment operating income (loss)[1]	226.1	15.8	43.4	(0.7)	(45.4)	239.2
Restructuring charges	1.5	6.8	(0.2)	—	0.9	9.0
Segment assets	935.6	575.9	329.5	46.3	1,107.4	2,994.7
Depreciation and amortization	57.8	32.3	10.5	2.2	11.0	113.8
Asset impairments	—	2.2	0.7	0.4	—	3.3
Investment in joint venture	141.0	—	—	—	—	141.0
Capital additions	101.5	43.1	9.8	0.5	6.7	161.6

For the Year Ended 2010	Building Products	Resilient Flooring	Wood Flooring	Cabinets	Unallocated Corporate	Total
Net sales to external customers	$1,135.5	$1,013.2	$479.1	$138.6	—	$2,766.4
Equity (earnings) from joint venture	(45.0)	—	—	—	—	(45.0)
Segment operating income (loss)[1]	171.0	13.1	(45.8)	(6.4)	(50.8)	81.1
Restructuring charges	3.2	13.9	0.9	—	4.0	22.0
Segment assets	931.4	582.6	340.7	47.9	1,019.8	2,922.4
Depreciation and amortization	62.5	38.6	26.4	2.0	13.8	143.3
Asset impairments	—	2.1	22.4	—	6.1	30.6
Investment in joint venture	188.6	—	—	—	—	188.6
Capital additions	47.7	24.0	12.2	3.0	5.8	92.7

(continued)

For the Year Ended 2009	Building Products	Resilient Flooring	Wood Flooring	Cabinets	Unallocated Corporate	Total
Net sales to external customers	$1,087.7	$1,031.7	$510.4	$150.2	—	$2,780.0
Equity (earnings) from joint venture	(40.0)	—	—	—	—	(40.0)
Segment operating income (loss)[1]	155.9	0.1	(5.9)	(18.3)	(41.2)	90.6
Segment assets	966.0	645.2	410.3	53.2	1,227.9	3,302.6
Depreciation and amortization	61.5	45.2	14.9	7.2	18.0	146.8
Asset impairments	—	3.0	18.0	—	—	21.0
Investment in joint venture	194.5	0.1	—	—	—	194.6
Capital additions	31.8	50.5	10.3	2.5	10.0	105.1

[1] Segment operating income (loss) is the measure of segment profit or loss reviewed by the chief operating decision maker. The sum of the segments' operating income (loss) equals the total consolidated operating income as reported on our income statement. The following reconciles our total consolidated operating income to earnings before income taxes. These items are only measured and managed on a consolidated basis:

	2011	2010	2009
Segment operating income	$239.2	$81.1	$90.6
Interest expense	48.5	21.2	17.7
Other non-operating expense	1.4	1.2	0.9
Other non-operating (income)	(3.8)	(8.0)	(3.2)
Earnings before income taxes	$193.1	$66.7	$75.2

Accounting policies of the segments are the same as those described in the summary of significant accounting policies.

The sales in the table below are allocated to geographic areas based upon the location of the customer.

Geographic Areas Net Trade Sales	2011	2010	2009
Americas:			
United States	$1,798.1	$1,742.4	$1,810.5
Canada	179.6	179.4	152.0
Other Americas	42.9	39.5	30.1
Total Americas	$2,020.6	$1,961.3	$1,992.6
Europe:			
Germany	$ 147.8	$ 146.3	$ 154.7
United Kingdom	85.6	79.9	94.1
Other Europe	317.0	334.0	347.3
Total Europe	$ 550.4	$ 560.2	$ 596.1
Pacific Rim:			
Australia	$ 86.1	$ 85.3	$ 63.4
China	73.6	57.1	47.2
Other Pacific Rim	128.8	102.5	80.7
Total Pacific Rim	$ 288.5	$ 244.9	$ 191.3
Total net trade sales	$2,859.5	$2,766.4	$2,780.0

Property, Plant and Equipment, Net

at December 31	2011	2010
Americas:		
United States	$656.3	$635.7
Other Americas	1.9	6.0
Total Americas	$658.2	$641.7
Europe:		
Germany	$113.7	$115.2
Other Europe	43.1	44.3
Total Europe	$156.8	$159.5
Pacific Rim:		
China	$ 58.3	$ 28.4
Other Pacific Rim	29.6	25.3
Total Pacific Rim	$ 87.9	$ 53.7
Total property, plant and equipment, net	$902.9	$854.9

Impairment testing of our tangible assets occurs whenever events or changes in circumstances indicate that the carrying amount of the assets may not be recoverable.

During the third quarter of 2011, we recorded an asset impairment charge of $2.2 million in selling, general and administrative ("SG&A") expense for a European Resilient Flooring office building. The fair value was determined by management estimates of market prices based upon information available, including offers received from potential buyers of the property (considered Level 3 inputs in the fair value hierarchy as described in Note 18 to the Consolidated Financial Statements).

During the fourth quarter of 2011, we recorded asset impairment charges of $1.1 million in SG&A expense for two previously occupied manufacturing facilities. We have been actively pursuing a sale of both facilities. The fair values were determined by management estimates and independent market valuations based on information available at that time. The valuation information included sales of similar facilities and estimates of market prices (considered Level 2 inputs in the fair value hierarchy) for these assets.

The Wood Flooring business recorded operating losses in 2010 and 2009 primarily due to non-cash impairment charges of $22.4 million and $18.0 million, respectively. The 2010 operating loss also included restructuring charges. See Note 15 to the Consolidated Financial Statements for further information on our restructuring charges. The Wood Flooring business had positive cash flows for both 2011 and 2010. There were no indicators of impairment for the tangible assets of the Wood Flooring business in 2011 and 2010.

During 2010, management decided to exit our corporate flight operations. As a result, we recorded a $6.1 million impairment charge in SG&A expense. The fair value was determined by management estimates and an independent valuation based on information available at that time. The valuation information included sales of similar equipment and estimates of market prices (considered Level 2 inputs in the fair value hierarchy) for these assets. We sold the corporate aircraft in the fourth quarter of 2010.

During the first quarter of 2010, we announced that one of our European metal ceilings manufacturing facilities would be shut down, which prompted us to perform an impairment test for this asset group. The carrying amount of the tangible assets was determined to be recoverable as the projected undiscounted cash flows exceeded the carrying value. We sold the facility in the third quarter of 2010.

During the second quarter of 2010, we recorded an asset impairment charge of $2.1 million in SG&A expense for a European Resilient Flooring warehouse facility due to the decline in the commercial property sector. The fair value was determined by management estimates of market prices available at that time. This data included sales and leases of comparable properties within similar real estate markets (considered Level 3 inputs in the fair value hierarchy). We sold the warehouse in the first quarter of 2011.

During the third quarter of 2010, we decided to close a ceilings plant, one of our previously idled Wood Flooring plants, portions of another previously idled Wood Flooring plant, and a Resilient Flooring facility. These facilities were shut down in 2010 or 2011. We concluded that an indicator of impairment existed for these asset groups, which prompted us to perform impairment analyses for these asset groups. In each case the carrying amount of the tangible assets was determined to be recoverable as the projected undiscounted cash flows, or estimated fair value of the assets, exceeded the carrying value.

In the third quarter of 2010, we announced our intention to exit the residential flooring business in Europe. We concluded that an indicator of impairment existed which prompted us to perform an impairment analysis. The carrying amount of the tangible assets was determined to be recoverable as the estimated fair value of the assets exceeded the carrying value. We sold the assets related to this business during the fourth quarter of 2010.

The Cabinets business incurred operating losses beginning in 2008 and continuing through 2011. In 2009, 2010 and 2011 the carrying amount of the tangible assets was determined to be recoverable as the projected undiscounted cash flows exceeded the carrying value.

1.35

TIFFANY & CO. (JAN)

NOTES TO CONSOLIDATED FINANCIAL STATEMENTS

A. Nature of Business

Tiffany & Co. (the "Company") is a holding company that operates through its subsidiary companies. The Company's principal subsidiary, Tiffany and Company ("Tiffany"), is a jeweler and specialty retailer whose principal merchandise offering is fine jewelry. The Company also sells timepieces, sterling silverware, china, crystal, stationery, fragrances and accessories. Through Tiffany and Company and other subsidiaries, the Company is engaged in product design, manufacturing and retailing activities.

Effective with the first quarter of 2010, management has changed the Company's segment reporting in order to align with a change in its organizational and management reporting structure. Specifically, the Company is now reporting results in Japan separately from the rest of the Asia-Pacific region, and results for certain "emerging market" countries that were previously included in the Europe and Asia-Pacific segments are now included in the "Other" non-reportable segment. Prior year results have been revised to reflect this change. The Company's reportable segments are as follows:

- Americas includes sales in TIFFANY & CO. stores in the United States, Canada and Latin/South America, as well as sales of TIFFANY & CO. products in certain markets through business-to-business, Internet, catalog and wholesale operations;
- Asia-Pacific includes sales in TIFFANY & CO. stores in Asia-Pacific markets (excluding Japan), as well as sales of TIFFANY & CO. products in certain markets through Internet and wholesale operations;
- Japan includes sales in TIFFANY & CO. stores, as well as sales of TIFFANY & CO. products through business-to-business, Internet and wholesale operations;
- Europe includes sales in TIFFANY & CO. stores, as well as sales of TIFFANY & CO. products in certain markets through Internet and wholesale operations; and
- Other consists of all non-reportable segments. Other consists primarily of wholesale sales of TIFFANY & CO. merchandise to independent distributors for resale in certain emerging markets (such as the Middle East and Russia) and wholesale sales of diamonds obtained through bulk purchases that were subsequently deemed not suitable for the Company's needs. In addition, Other includes earnings received from third-party licensing agreements.

Description of Business

1.36

AUTOMATIC DATA PROCESSING, INC. (JUN)

MANAGEMENT'S DISCUSSION AND ANALYSIS OF FINANCIAL CONDITION AND RESULTS OF OPERATIONS

Description of the Company and Business Segments

ADP is one of the world's largest providers of business outsourcing solutions. Leveraging over 60 years of experience, ADP offers a wide range of human resource ("HR"), payroll, tax and benefits administration solutions from a single source. ADP is also a leading provider of integrated computing solutions to auto, truck, motorcycle, marine, recreational vehicle ("RV") and heavy equipment dealers. The Company's reportable segments are: Employer Services, PEO Services and Dealer Services. A brief description of each segment's operations is provided below.

Employer Services

Employer Services offers a comprehensive range of HR information, payroll processing, time and labor management, and tax and benefits administration solutions and services, including traditional and Web-based outsourcing solutions, that assist employers in the United States, Canada, Europe, South America (primarily Brazil), Australia and Asia to staff, manage, pay and retain their employees. As of June 30, 2011, Employer Services assisted approximately 537,000 employers with approximately 628,000 payrolls. As of June 30, 2010, Employer Services assisted approximately 520,000 employers with approximately 614,000 payrolls. Employer Services categorizes its services as "payroll and payroll tax" and "beyond payroll." The payroll and payroll tax business represents the Company's core payroll processing and payroll tax filing business. The "beyond payroll" business represents services such as time and labor management, benefits administration, retirement recordkeeping and administration, and HR administration services. Within Employer Services, the Company collects client funds and remits such funds to tax authorities for payroll tax filing and payment services and to employees of payroll services clients.

PEO Services

PEO Services provides approximately 6,100 small and medium sized businesses with comprehensive employment administration outsourcing solutions through a co-employment relationship, including payroll, payroll tax filing, HR guidance, 401(k) plan administration, benefits administration, compliance services, health and workers' compensation coverage and other supplemental benefits for employees. Workers' compensation and employer's liability deductible reimbursement protection is provided to PEO Services by ADP Indemnity, Inc. ("ADP Indemnity"), a wholly-owned captive insurance company of Automatic Data Processing, Inc. whose results of operations are recorded in the "Other" segment. Premiums are charged to PEO Services by ADP Indemnity in exchange for which ADP Indemnity provides a policy to PEO Services that reimburses all workers' compensation and employer's liability claim expense resulting from worksite employee claims up to a $1 million per occurrence retention. At the beginning of each policy period, ADP Indemnity establishes the premium to be paid by PEO Services required to satisfy the expected ultimate workers' compensation claims within the $1 million per occurrence retention based upon historical loss experience and the expected workers' compensation loss estimate as determined by an independent actuary. PEO Services has secured specific per occurrence and aggregate stop loss reinsurance from a wholly-owned and regulated insurance carrier of American International Group, Inc. ("AIG") that covers all losses in excess of the $1 million per occurrence retention and also any aggregate losses within the $1 million retention that collectively exceed a certain level in each policy year. The cost of the per occurrence and aggregate stop loss insurance is paid by PEO Services directly to AIG's wholly-owned subsidiary and is incremental to the premium paid to ADP Indemnity. ADP's PEO Services business, TotalSource SM, is the largest PEO in the United States based on the number of worksite employees. TotalSource SM has 54 offices located in 23 states and serves approximately 241,000 worksite employees in all 50 states.

Dealer Services

Dealer Services provides integrated dealer management systems (such a system is also known in the industry as a "DMS"), digital marketing solutions, including website, sales leads, email, search, display and social media marketing services and other business management solutions to auto, truck, motorcycle, marine, RV and heavy equipment retailers in North America, Europe, South Africa, the Middle East, and the Asia Pacific region. Approximately 25,000 auto, truck, motorcycle, marine, RV and heavy equipment retailers in nearly 100 countries use our DMS products, other software applications, networking solutions, data integration, consulting and/or digital marketing services. As of June 30, 2010, Dealer Services provided DMS products to approximately 25,000 retailers in over 90 countries.

Use of Estimates

1.37

AMERICAN INTERNATIONAL GROUP, INC. (DEC)

NOTES TO CONSOLIDATED FINANCIAL STATEMENTS

1. Basis of Presentation and Significant Events (in part)

Use of Estimates

The preparation of financial statements requires the application of accounting policies that often involve a significant degree of judgment. AIG considers the accounting policies that are most dependent on the application of estimates and assumptions to be those relating to items considered by management in the determination of:

- estimates with respect to income taxes, including the recoverability of the deferred tax assets and the predictability of future tax planning strategies and operating profitability of the character necessary for their realization;
- recoverability of assets, including deferred policy acquisition costs (DAC), flight equipment, and reinsurance;
- insurance liabilities, including general insurance unpaid claims and claims adjustment expenses and future policy benefits for life and accident and health contracts;
- estimated gross profits for investment-oriented products;
- impairment charges, including other-than-temporary impairments on financial instruments and goodwill impairments;
- liabilities for legal contingencies; and
- fair value measurements of certain financial assets and liabilities, including credit default swaps (CDS) and AIG's economic interest in Maiden Lane II LLC (ML II) and equity interest in Maiden Lane III LLC (ML III) (together, the Maiden Lane Interests).

These accounting estimates require the use of assumptions about matters, some of which are highly uncertain at the time of estimation. To the extent actual experience differs from the assumptions used, AIG's consolidated financial condition, results of operations and cash flows could be materially affected.

1.38

BRUNSWICK CORPORATION (DEC)

NOTES TO CONSOLIDATED FINANCIAL STATEMENTS

Note 1—Significant Accounting Policies (in part)

Use of Estimates. The preparation of the consolidated financial statements in accordance with accounting principles generally accepted in the United States (GAAP) requires management to make certain estimates. Actual results could differ materially from those estimates. These estimates affect:

- The reported amounts of assets and liabilities at the date of the financial statements;
- The disclosure of contingent assets and liabilities at the date of the financial statements; and
- The reported amounts of revenues and expenses during the reporting periods.

Estimates in these consolidated financial statements include, but are not limited to:

- Allowances for doubtful accounts;
- Inventory valuation reserves;
- Reserves for dealer allowances;
- Warranty related reserves;
- Losses on litigation and other contingencies;
- Environmental reserves;
- Insurance reserves;
- Income tax reserves;
- Valuation of goodwill and other intangible assets;
- Valuation allowances on deferred tax assets;
- Reserves related to repurchase and recourse obligations;
- Impairments of long-lived assets;
- Reserves related to restructuring activities; and
- Postretirement benefit liabilities.

The Company records a reserve when it is probable that a loss has been incurred and the loss can be reasonably estimated. The Company establishes its reserve based on its best estimate within a range of losses. If the Company is unable to identify the best estimate, the Company records the minimum amount in the range.

Significant Accounting Policies and Estimates

1.39

APPLE INC. (SEP)

NOTES TO CONSOLIDATED FINANCIAL STATEMENTS

Note 1—Summary of Significant Accounting Policies

Apple Inc. and its wholly-owned subsidiaries (collectively "Apple" or the "Company") designs, manufactures, and markets mobile communication and media devices, personal computers, and portable digital music players, and sells a variety of related software, services, peripherals, networking solutions, and third-party digital content and applications. The Company sells its products worldwide through its retail stores, online stores, and direct sales force, as well as through third-party cellular network carriers, wholesalers, retailers and value-added resellers. In addition, the Company sells a variety of third-party iPhone, iPad, Mac, and iPod compatible products including application software, printers, storage devices, speakers, headphones, and various other accessories and supplies through its online and retail stores. The Company sells to consumers, small and mid-sized businesses, education, enterprise and government customers.

Basis of Presentation and Preparation

The accompanying consolidated financial statements include the accounts of the Company. Intercompany accounts and transactions have been eliminated. The preparation of these consolidated financial statements in conformity with U.S. generally accepted accounting principles ("GAAP") requires management to make estimates and assumptions that affect the amounts reported in these consolidated financial statements and accompanying notes. Actual results could differ materially from those estimates. Certain prior year amounts in the consolidated financial statements and notes thereto have been reclassified to conform to the current year's presentation.

The Company's fiscal year is the 52 or 53-week period that ends on the last Saturday of September. The Company's fiscal years 2011, 2010 and 2009 ended on September 24, 2011, September 25, 2010 and September 26, 2009, respectively, and included 52 weeks each. An additional week is included in the first fiscal quarter approximately every six years to realign fiscal quarters with calendar quarters. Fiscal year 2012 will end on September 29, 2012, and will span 53 weeks, with a 14th week added to the first quarter of 2012. Unless otherwise stated, references to particular years or quarters refer to the Company's fiscal years ended in September and the associated quarters of those fiscal years.

During the first quarter of 2011, the Company adopted the Financial Accounting Standard Board's ("FASB") new accounting standard on consolidation of variable interest entities. This new accounting standard eliminates the mandatory quantitative approach in determining control for evaluating whether variable interest entities need to be consolidated in favor of a qualitative analysis, and requires an ongoing reassessment of control over such entities. The adoption of this new accounting standard did not impact the Company's consolidated financial statements.

Revenue Recognition

Net sales consist primarily of revenue from the sale of hardware, software, digital content and applications, peripherals, and service and support contracts. The Company recognizes revenue when persuasive evidence of an arrangement exists, delivery has occurred, the sales price is fixed or determinable, and collection is probable. Product is considered delivered to the customer once it has been shipped and title and risk of loss have been transferred. For most of the Company's product sales, these criteria are met at the time the product is shipped. For online sales to individuals, for some sales to education customers in the U.S., and for certain other sales, the Company defers revenue until the customer

receives the product because the Company legally retains a portion of the risk of loss on these sales during transit. The Company recognizes revenue from the sale of hardware products, software bundled with hardware that is essential to the functionality of the hardware, and third-party digital content sold on the iTunes Store in accordance with general revenue recognition accounting guidance. The Company recognizes revenue in accordance with industry specific software accounting guidance for the following types of sales transactions: (i) standalone sales of software products, (ii) sales of software upgrades and (iii) sales of software bundled with hardware not essential to the functionality of the hardware.

The Company sells software and peripheral products obtained from other companies. The Company generally establishes its own pricing and retains related inventory risk, is the primary obligor in sales transactions with its customers, and assumes the credit risk for amounts billed to its customers. Accordingly, the Company generally recognizes revenue for the sale of products obtained from other companies based on the gross amount billed. For sales of third-party software applications for iPhone, iPad and iPod touch ("iOS devices") and Macs made through the App Store and the Mac App Store, the Company is not the primary obligor to users of the software, and third-party developers determine the selling price of their software. Therefore, the Company accounts for such sales on a net basis by recognizing only the commission it retains from each sale and including that commission in net sales in the Consolidated Statements of Operations. The portion of the sales price paid by users that is remitted by the Company to third-party developers is not reflected in the Company's Consolidated Statements of Operations.

The Company records deferred revenue when it receives payments in advance of the delivery of products or the performance of services. This includes amounts that have been deferred for unspecified and specified software upgrade rights and non-software services that are attached to hardware and software products. The Company sells gift cards redeemable at its retail and online stores, and also sells gift cards redeemable on the iTunes Store for the purchase of content and software. The Company records deferred revenue upon the sale of the card, which is relieved upon redemption of the card by the customer. Revenue from AppleCare service and support contracts is deferred and recognized over the service coverage periods. AppleCare service and support contracts typically include extended phone support, repair services, web-based support resources and diagnostic tools offered under the Company's standard limited warranty.

The Company records reductions to revenue for estimated commitments related to price protection and for customer incentive programs, including reseller and end-user rebates, and other sales programs and volume-based incentives. The estimated cost of these programs is recognized in the period the Company has sold the product and committed to a plan. The Company also records reductions to revenue for expected future product returns based on the Company's historical experience. Revenue is recorded net of taxes collected from customers that are remitted to governmental authorities, with the collected taxes recorded as current liabilities until remitted to the relevant government authority.

Revenue Recognition for Arrangements with Multiple Deliverables

For multi-element arrangements that include hardware products containing software essential to the hardware product's functionality, undelivered software elements that relate to the hardware product's essential software, and undelivered non-software services, the Company allocates revenue to all deliverables based on their relative selling prices. In such circumstances, the Company uses a hierarchy to determine the selling price to be used for allocating revenue to deliverables: (i) vendor-specific objective evidence of fair value ("VSOE"), (ii) third-party evidence of selling price ("TPE"), and (iii) best estimate of the selling price ("ESP"). VSOE generally exists only when the Company sells the deliverable separately and is the price actually charged by the Company for that deliverable. ESPs reflect the Company's best estimates of what the selling prices of elements would be if they were sold regularly on a stand-alone basis.

For sales of iPhone, iPad, Apple TV, for sales of iPod touch beginning in June 2010, and for sales of Mac beginning in June 2011, the Company has indicated it may from time-to-time provide future unspecified software upgrades and features to the essential software bundled with each of these hardware products free of charge to customers. Essential software for iOS devices includes iOS and related applications and for Mac includes Mac OS X and iLife. In June 2011, the Company announced it would provide various non-software services to owners of qualifying versions of iOS devices and Mac. The Company has identified up to three deliverables in arrangements involving the sale of these devices. The first deliverable is the hardware and software essential to the functionality of the hardware device delivered at the time of sale. The second deliverable is the embedded right included with the purchase of iOS devices, Mac and Apple TV to receive on a when-and-if-available basis, future unspecified software upgrades and features relating to the product's essential software. The third deliverable is the non-software services to be provided to qualifying versions of iOS devices and Mac. The Company allocates revenue between these deliverables using the relative selling price method. Because the Company has neither VSOE nor TPE for these deliverables, the allocation of revenue has been based on the Company's ESPs. Amounts allocated to the delivered hardware and the related essential software are recognized at the time of sale provided the other conditions for revenue recognition have been met. Amounts allocated to the embedded unspecified software upgrade rights and the non-software services are deferred and recognized on a straight-line basis over the estimated lives of each of these devices, which range from 24 to 48 months. Cost of sales related to delivered hardware and related essential software, including estimated warranty costs, are recognized at the time of sale. Costs incurred to provide non-software services are recognized as cost of sales as incurred, and engineering and sales and marketing costs are recognized as operating expenses as incurred.

The Company's process for determining its ESP for deliverables without VSOE or TPE considers multiple factors that may vary depending upon the unique facts and circumstances related to each deliverable. The Company believes its customers, particularly consumers, would be reluctant to buy unspecified software upgrade rights related to iOS devices, Mac and Apple TV. This view is primarily based on the fact that unspecified upgrade rights do not obligate the Company to provide upgrades at a particular time or at all, and do not specify to customers which upgrades or features will be delivered. The Company also believes its customers would be unwilling to pay a significant amount for access to the non-software services because other companies of-fer similar services at little or no cost to users. Therefore, the Company has concluded that if it were to sell upgrade rights or access to the non-software services on a standalone basis, including those rights and services attached to iOS devices, Mac and Apple TV, the selling prices would be relatively low. Key factors considered by the Company in developing the ESPs for software upgrade rights include prices charged by the Company for similar offerings, market trends for pricing of Mac and iOS compatible software, the Company's historical pricing practices, the nature of the upgrade rights (e.g., unspecified and when-and-if-available), and the relative ESP of the upgrade rights as compared to the total selling price of the product. The Company may also consider, when appropriate, the impact of other products and services, including advertising services, on selling price assumptions when developing and reviewing its ESPs for software upgrade rights and related deliverables. The Company may also consider additional factors as appropriate, including the pricing of competitive alternatives if they exist and product-specific business objectives. When relevant, the same factors are considered by the Company in developing ESPs for offerings such as the non-software services; however, the primary consideration in developing ESPs for the non-software services is the estimated cost to provide such services over the estimated life of the related devices, including consideration for a reasonable profit margin.

Beginning with the Company's June 2011 announcement of the upcoming release of the non-software services and Mac OS X Lion, the Company's combined ESP for the unspecified software upgrade rights and the right to receive the non-software services are as follows: $16 for iPhone and iPad, $11 for iPod touch, and $22 for Mac. The Company's ESP for the embedded unspecified software upgrade right included with each Apple TV is $5 for 2011 and $10 for fiscal years prior to 2011. Amounts allocated to the embedded unspecified software upgrade rights and the non-software services associated with iOS devices and Apple TV are recognized on a straight-line basis over 24 months, and amounts allocated to the embedded unspecified software upgrade rights and the non-software services associated with Macs are recognized on a straight-line basis over 48 months.

The Company's ESP for the software upgrade right included with each iPhone sold beginning with the introduction of iPhone in June 2007 through the Company's second quarter of 2010 was $25. Beginning in April 2010 in conjunction with the Company's announcement of iOS 4 for iPhone, the Company lowered its ESP for the software upgrade right included with each iPhone to $10. Beginning with initial sales of iPad in April 2010, the Company's ESP for the embedded software upgrade right included with the sale of each iPad is $10, and the Company's ESP for the embedded software upgrade right included with each iPod touch sold beginning in June 2010 is $5.

The Company accounts for multiple element arrangements that consist only of software or software-related products, including the sale of upgrades to previously sold software, in accordance with industry specific software accounting guidance. For such transactions, revenue on arrangements that include multiple elements is allocated to each element based on the relative fair value of each element, and fair value is determined by VSOE. If the Company cannot objectively determine the fair value of any undelivered element included in such multiple-element arrangements, the Company defers revenue until all elements are delivered and services have been performed, or until fair value can objectively be determined for any remaining undelivered elements. Beginning in July 2011, the sale of certain upgrades to Mac OS X and Mac versions of iLife include when-and-if-available upgrade rights for which the Company does not have VSOE. Therefore, beginning in July 2011 the Company defers all revenue from the sale of upgrades to the Mac OS and Mac versions of iLife and recognizes it ratably over 36 months.

Shipping Costs

For all periods presented, amounts billed to customers related to shipping and handling are classified as revenue, and the Company's shipping and handling costs are included in cost of sales.

Warranty Expense

The Company generally provides for the estimated cost of hardware and software warranties at the time the related revenue is recognized. The Company assesses the adequacy of its pre-existing warranty liabilities and adjusts the amounts as necessary based on actual experience and changes in future estimates.

Software Development Costs

Research and development costs are expensed as incurred. Development costs of computer software to be sold, leased, or otherwise marketed are subject to capitalization beginning when a product's technological feasibility has been established and ending when a product is available for general release to customers. In most instances, the Company's products are released soon after technological feasibility has been established. Therefore, costs incurred subsequent to achievement of technological feasibility are usually not significant, and generally most software development costs have been expensed as incurred.

The Company did not capitalize any software development costs during 2011 and 2010. In 2009, the Company capitalized $71 million of costs associated with the development of Mac OS X Version 10.6 Snow Leopard ("Mac OS X Snow Leopard"), which was released during the fourth quarter of 2009. The capitalized costs are being amortized to cost of sales on a straight-line basis over a three year estimated useful life of the underlying technology.

Total amortization related to capitalized software development costs was $30 million, $48 million and $25 million in 2011, 2010 and 2009, respectively.

Advertising Costs

Advertising costs are expensed as incurred. Advertising expense was $933 million, $691 million and $501 million for 2011, 2010 and 2009, respectively.

Share-Based Compensation

The Company recognizes expense related to share-based payment transactions in which it receives employee services in exchange for (a) equity instruments of the Company or (b) liabilities that are based on the fair value of the enterprise's equity instruments or that may be settled by the issuance of such equity instruments. Share-based compensation cost for restricted stock units ("RSUs") is measured based on the closing fair market value of the Company's common stock on the date of grant. Share-based compensation cost for stock options is estimated at the grant date based on each option's fair-value as calculated by the Black-Scholes-Merton ("BSM") option-pricing model. The Company recognizes share-based compensation cost as expense ratably on a straight-line basis over the requisite service period. The Company recognizes a benefit from share-based compensation in the Consolidated Statements of Shareholders' Equity if an incremental tax benefit is realized. In addition, the Company recognizes the indirect effects of share-based compensation on research and development tax credits, foreign tax credits and domestic manufacturing deductions in the Consolidated Statements of Operations. Further information regarding share-based compensation can be found in Note 6, "Shareholders' Equity and Share-based Compensation" of this Form 10-K.

Income Taxes

The provision for income taxes is computed using the asset and liability method, under which deferred tax assets and liabilities are recognized for the expected future tax consequences of temporary differences between the financial reporting and tax bases of assets and liabilities, and for operating losses and tax credit carryforwards. Deferred tax assets and liabilities are measured using the currently enacted tax rates that apply to taxable income in effect for the years in which those tax assets are expected to be realized or settled. The Company records a valuation allowance to reduce deferred tax assets to the amount that is believed more likely than not to be realized.

The Company recognizes the tax benefit from an uncertain tax position only if it is more likely than not the tax position will be sustained on examination by the taxing authorities, based on the technical merits of the position. The tax benefits recognized in the financial statements from such positions are then measured based on the largest benefit that has a greater than 50% likelihood of being realized upon settlement. See Note 5, "Income Taxes" of this Form 10-K for additional information.

Earnings Per Common Share

Basic earnings per common share is computed by dividing income available to common shareholders by the weighted-average number of shares of common stock outstanding during the period. Diluted earnings per common share is computed by dividing income available to common shareholders by the weighted-average number of shares of common stock outstanding during the period increased to include the number of additional shares of common stock that would have been outstanding if the potentially dilutive securities had been issued. Potentially dilutive securities include outstanding stock options, shares to be purchased under the employee stock purchase plan and unvested RSUs. The dilutive effect of potentially dilutive securities is reflected in diluted earnings per common share by application of the treasury stock method. Under the treasury stock method, an increase in the fair market value of the Company's common stock can result in a greater dilutive effect from potentially dilutive securities.

SEC 1.39

The following table sets forth the computation of basic and diluted earnings per common share for the three years ended September 24, 2011 (in thousands, except net income in millions and per share amounts):

	2011	2010	2009
Numerator:			
Net income	$ 25,922	$ 14,013	$ 8,235
Denominator:			
Weighted-average shares outstanding	924,258	909,461	893,016
Effect of dilutive securities	12,387	15,251	13,989
Weighted-average diluted shares	936,645	924,712	907,005
Basic earnings per common share	$ 28.05	$ 15.41	$ 9.22
Diluted earnings per common share	$ 27.68	$ 15.15	$ 9.08

Potentially dilutive securities representing 1.7 million, 1.6 million and 12.6 million shares of common stock for 2011, 2010 and 2009, respectively, were excluded from the computation of diluted earnings per common share for these periods because their effect would have been antidilutive.

Financial Instruments

Cash Equivalents and Marketable Securities

All highly liquid investments with maturities of three months or less at the date of purchase are classified as cash equivalents. The Company's marketable debt and equity securities have been classified and accounted for as available-for-sale. Management determines the appropriate classification of its investments at the time of purchase and reevaluates the designations at each balance sheet date. The Company classifies its marketable debt securities as either short-term or long-term based on each instrument's underlying contractual maturity date. Marketable debt securities with maturities of 12 months or less are classified as short-term and marketable debt securities with maturities greater than 12 months are classified as long-term. The Company classifies its marketable equity securities, including mutual funds, as either short-term or long-term based on the nature of each security and its availability for use in current operations. The Company's marketable debt and equity securities are carried at fair value, with the unrealized gains and losses, net of taxes, reported as a component of shareholders' equity. The cost of securities sold is based upon the specific identification method.

Derivative Financial Instruments

The Company accounts for its derivative instruments as either assets or liabilities and carries them at fair value.

For derivative instruments that hedge the exposure to variability in expected future cash flows that are designated as cash flow hedges, the effective portion of the gain or loss on the derivative instrument is reported as a component of accumulated other comprehensive income ("AOCI") in shareholders' equity and reclassified into income in the same period or periods during which the hedged transaction affects earnings. The ineffective portion of the gain or loss on the derivative instrument, if any, is recognized in current income. To receive hedge accounting treatment, cash flow hedges must be highly effective in offsetting changes to expected future cash flows on hedged transactions. For options designated as cash flow hedges, changes in the time value are excluded from the assessment of hedge effectiveness and are recognized in income. For derivative instruments that hedge the exposure to changes in the fair value of an asset or a liability and that are designated as fair value hedges, both the net gain or loss on the derivative instrument as well as the offsetting gain or loss on the hedged item attributable to the hedged risk are recognized in earnings in the current period. The Company had no fair value hedges in 2011, 2010 and 2009. The net gain or loss on the effective portion of a derivative instrument that is designated as an economic hedge of the net investment in a foreign operation is reported in the same manner as a foreign currency translation adjustment. For forward exchange contracts designated as net investment hedges, the Company excludes changes in fair value relating to changes in the forward carry component from its definition of effectiveness. Accordingly, any gains or losses related to this component are recognized in current income. Derivatives that do not qualify as hedges must be adjusted to fair value through current income.

Allowance for Doubtful Accounts

The Company records its allowance for doubtful accounts based upon its assessment of various factors. The Company considers historical experience, the age of the accounts receivable balances, credit quality of the Company's customers, current economic conditions, and other factors that may affect customers' ability to pay.

Inventories

Inventories are stated at the lower of cost, computed using the first-in, first-out method, or market. If the cost of the inventories exceeds their market value, provisions are made currently for the difference between the cost and the market value. The Company's inventories consist primarily of components and finished goods for all periods presented.

Property, Plant and Equipment

Property, plant and equipment are stated at cost. Depreciation is computed by use of the straight-line method over the estimated useful lives of the assets, which for buildings is the lesser of 30 years or the remaining life of the underlying building, up to five years for equipment, and the shorter of lease terms or ten years for leasehold improvements. The Company capitalizes eligible costs to acquire or develop internal-use software that are incurred subsequent to the preliminary project stage. Capitalized costs related to internal-use software are amortized using the straight-line method over the estimated useful lives of the assets, which range from three to five years. Depreciation and amortization expense on property and equipment was $1.6 billion, $815 million and $606 million during 2011, 2010 and 2009, respectively.

Long-Lived Assets Including Goodwill and Other Acquired Intangible Assets

The Company reviews property, plant and equipment and certain identifiable intangibles, excluding goodwill, for impairment. Long-lived assets are reviewed for impairment whenever events or changes in circumstances indicate the carrying amount of an asset may not be recoverable. Recoverability of these assets is measured by comparison of their carrying amounts to future undiscounted cash flows the assets are expected to generate. If property, plant and equipment and certain identifiable intangibles are considered to be impaired, the impairment to be recognized equals the amount by which the carrying value of the assets exceeds its fair market value. The Company did not record any significant impairments during 2011, 2010 and 2009.

The Company does not amortize goodwill and intangible assets with indefinite useful lives, rather such assets are required to be tested for impairment at least annually or sooner whenever events or changes in circumstances indicate that the assets may be impaired. The Company performs its goodwill and intangible asset impairment tests in the fourth quarter of each fiscal year. The Company did not recognize any goodwill or intangible asset impairment charges in 2011, 2010 and 2009. The Company established reporting units based on its current reporting structure. For purposes of testing goodwill for impairment, goodwill has been allocated to these reporting units to the extent it relates to each reporting unit.

The Company amortizes its intangible assets with definite lives over their estimated useful lives and reviews these assets for impairment. The Company is currently amortizing its acquired intangible assets with definite lives over periods generally ranging between three to seven years.

Fair Value Measurements

The Company applies fair value accounting for all financial assets and liabilities and non-financial assets and liabilities that are recognized or disclosed at fair value in the financial statements on a recurring basis. The Company defines fair value as the price that would be received from selling an asset or paid to transfer a liability in an orderly transaction between market participants at the measurement date. When determining the fair value measurements for assets and liabilities, which are required to be recorded at fair value, the Company considers the principal or most advantageous market in which the Company would transact and the market-based risk measurements or assumptions that market participants would use in pricing the asset or liability, such as risks inherent in valuation techniques, transfer restrictions and credit risk. Fair value is estimated by applying the following hierarchy, which prioritizes the inputs used to measure fair value into three levels and bases the categorization within the hierarchy upon the lowest level of input that is available and significant to the fair value measurement:

Level 1—Quoted prices in active markets for identical assets or liabilities.

Level 2—Observable inputs other than quoted prices in active markets for identical assets and liabilities, quoted prices for identical or similar assets or liabilities in inactive markets, or other inputs that are observable or can be corroborated by observable market data for substantially the full term of the assets or liabilities.

Level 3—Inputs that are generally unobservable and typically reflect management's estimate of assumptions that market participants would use in pricing the asset or liability.

The Company's valuation techniques used to measure the fair value of money market funds and certain marketable equity securities were derived from quoted prices in active markets for identical assets or liabilities. The valuation techniques used to measure the fair value of all other financial instruments, all of which have counterparties with high credit ratings, were valued based on quoted market prices or model driven valuations using significant inputs derived from or corroborated by observable market data.

In accordance with the fair value accounting requirements, companies may choose to measure eligible financial instruments and certain other items at fair value. The Company has not elected the fair value option for any eligible financial instruments.

Foreign Currency Translation and Remeasurement

The Company translates the assets and liabilities of its non-U.S. dollar functional currency subsidiaries into U.S. dollars using exchange rates in effect at the end of each period. Revenue and expenses for these subsidiaries are translated using rates that approximate those in effect during the period. Gains and losses from these translations are recognized in foreign currency translation included in accumulated other comprehensive income in shareholders' equity. The Company's subsidiaries that use the U.S. dollar as their functional currency remeasure monetary assets and liabilities at exchange rates in effect at the end of each period, and inventories, property, and nonmonetary assets and liabilities at historical rates. Gains and losses from these remeasurements were insignificant and have been included in the Company's results of operations.

Segment Information

The Company reports segment information based on the "management" approach. The management approach designates the internal reporting used by management for making decisions and assessing performance as the source of the Company's reportable segments. Information about the Company's products, major customers and geographic areas on a company-wide basis is also disclosed.

Vulnerability Due to Certain Concentrations

1.40

CARDINAL HEALTH, INC. (JUN)

NOTES TO CONSOLIDATED FINANCIAL STATEMENTS

1. Basis of Presentation and Summary of Significant Accounting Policies (in part)

Concentrations of Credit Risk and Major Customers. We maintain cash depository accounts with major banks throughout the world and invest in high quality short-term liquid instruments. Such investments are made only in instruments issued or enhanced by high quality institutions. These investments mature within three months and we have not incurred any related losses.

Our trade receivables, lease receivables, finance notes, and accrued interest receivables are exposed to a concentration of credit risk with customers in the retail and healthcare sectors. Credit risk can be affected by changes in reimbursement and other economic pressures impacting the hospital and acute care sectors of the healthcare industry.

Such credit risk is limited due to supporting collateral and the diversity of the customer base, including its wide geographic dispersion. We perform ongoing credit evaluations of our customers' financial conditions and maintain reserves for credit losses. Such losses historically have been within our expectations.

The following table summarizes all of our customers that individually account for at least 10 percent of revenue and their corresponding percent of gross trade receivables. The customers in the table below are serviced through our Pharmaceutical segment.

	Percent of Revenue			Percent of Gross Trade Receivables at June 30	
	2011	2010	2009	2011	2010
Walgreen Co.	23%	24%	24%	31%	32%
CVS Caremark Corporation	22%	22%	21%	20%	21%

We have entered into agreements with group purchasing organizations ("GPOs") which act as purchasing agents that negotiate vendor contracts on behalf of their members.

The following table summarizes the revenue that was derived from GPO members through the contractual arrangements established with Novation, LLC and Premier Purchasing Partners, L.P., our two largest GPO relationships in terms of revenue:

	Percent of Revenue		
	2011	2010	2009
GPO members	14%	15%	15%

Our trade receivable balances are with individual members of the GPO, and therefore no significant concentration of credit risk exists with these types of arrangements.

1.41

IDT CORPORATION (JUL)

NOTES TO CONSOLIDATED FINANCIAL STATEMENTS

Note 1—Description of Business and Summary of Significant Accounting Policies (in part)

Vulnerability Due to Certain Concentrations and International Operations

Financial instruments that potentially subject the Company to concentration of credit risk consist principally of cash, cash equivalents, certificates of deposit, investments in hedge funds and trade accounts receivable. The Company holds cash, cash equivalents and certificates of deposit at several major financial institutions, which often exceed FDIC insurance limits. Historically, the Company has not experienced any losses due to such concentration of credit risk. The Company's temporary cash investments policy is to limit the dollar amount of investments with any one financial institution and monitor the credit ratings of those institutions. While the Company may be exposed to credit losses due to the nonperformance of the holders of its deposits, the Company does not expect the settlement of these transactions to have a material effect on its results of operations, cash flows or financial condition.

Concentration of credit risk with respect to trade accounts receivable is limited due to the large number of customers in various geographic regions and industry segments comprising the Company's customer base. No single customer accounted for more than 10% of consolidated revenues in fiscal 2011 or fiscal 2010. However, the Company's five largest customers collectively accounted for 11.7% and 15.4% of its consolidated revenues from continuing operations in fiscal 2011 and fiscal 2010, respectively. The Company's customers with the five largest receivables balances collectively accounted for 27.3% and 31.7% of the consolidated gross trade accounts receivable at July 31, 2011 and 2010, respectively. This concentration of customers increases the Company's risk associated with nonpayment by those customers. In an effort to reduce such risk, the Company performs ongoing credit evaluations of its significant retail telecom, wholesale carrier and cable telephony customers. In addition, the Company attempts to mitigate the credit risk related to specific wholesale carrier customers by also buying services from the customer, in order to create an opportunity to offset its payables and receivables and reduce its net trade receivable exposure risk. When it is practical to do so, the Company will increase its purchases from wholesale customers with receivable balances that exceed the Company's payable in order to maximize the offset and reduce its credit risk.

IDT Energy reduces its credit risk by its participation in purchase of receivable programs for a significant portion of its receivables. Under purchase of receivable programs, utility companies provide billing and collection services, purchase IDT Energy's receivables and assume all credit risk without recourse to IDT Energy. IDT Energy's primary credit risk is therefore nonpayment by the utility companies. Certain of the utility companies represent significant portions of the Company's consolidated revenues and consolidated gross trade accounts receivable balance and such concentrations increase the Company's risk associated with nonpayment by those utility companies.

The Company is also subject to risks associated with its international operations, including fluctuations in exchange rates and trade accounts receivable collections. The Company regularly monitors the creditworthiness of its international customers and believes that it has adequately provided for any exposure to potential credit losses.

1.42

XILINX, INC. (MAR)

NOTES TO CONSOLIDATED FINANCIAL STATEMENTS

Note 2. Summary of Significant Accounting Policies and Concentrations of Risk (in part)

Concentrations of Credit Risk

Avnet, one of the Company's distributors, distributes the substantial majority of the Company's products worldwide. As of April 2, 2011 and April 3, 2010, Avnet accounted for 79% and 83% of the Company's total accounts receivable, respectively. Resale of product through Avnet accounted for 51%, 49% and 55% of the Company's worldwide net revenues in fiscal 2011, 2010 and 2009, respectively. The percentage of accounts receivable due from Avnet and the percentage of worldwide net revenues from Avnet are consistent with historical patterns.

Xilinx is subject to concentrations of credit risk primarily in its trade accounts receivable and investments in debt securities to the extent of the amounts recorded on the consolidated balance sheet. The Company attempts to mitigate the concentration of credit risk in its trade receivables through its credit evaluation process, collection terms, distributor sales to diverse end customers and through geographical dispersion of sales. Xilinx generally does not require collateral for receivables from its end customers or from distributors.

No end customer accounted for more than 10% of net revenues for any of the periods presented.

The Company mitigates concentrations of credit risk in its investments in debt securities by currently investing more than 94% of its portfolio in AA or higher grade securities as rated by Standard & Poor's or Moody's Investors Service. The Company's methods to arrive at investment decisions are not solely based on the rating agencies' credit ratings. Xilinx also performs additional credit due diligence and conducts regular portfolio credit reviews, including a review of counterparty credit risk related to the Company's forward currency exchange and interest rate swap contracts. Additionally, Xilinx limits its investments in the debt securities of a single issuer based upon the issuer's credit rating and attempts to further mitigate credit risk by diversifying risk across geographies and type of issuer. As of April 2, 2011, 52% and 48% of its investments in debt securities were domestic and foreign issuers, respectively. See "Note 4. Financial Instruments" for detailed information about the Company's investment portfolio.

As of April 2, 2011, less than 2% of the Company's $2.60 billion investment portfolio consisted of student loan auction rate securities and all of these securities are rated AAA with the exception of $3.8 million that were downgraded to an A rating during fiscal 2009. Nearly all of the underlying assets that secure these securities are pools of student loans originated under the FFELP, which are substantially guaranteed by the U.S. Department of Education. These securities experienced failed auctions in the fourth quarter of fiscal 2008 due to liquidity issues in the global credit markets. In a failed auction, the interest rates are reset to a maximum rate defined by the contractual terms for each security. The Company has collected and expects to collect all interest payable on these securities when due. During fiscal 2011 and 2010,

$20.2 million and $1.3 million, respectively, of these student loan auction rate securities were redeemed for cash by the issuers at par value. In addition, during fiscal 2011 the Company sold $10.8 million notional value of student loan auction rate securities and realized a $580 thousand loss. Because there can be no assurance of a successful auction in the future, the student loan auction rate securities are reclassified as long-term investments on the consolidated balance sheets. The maturity dates range from December 2027 to May 2046.

As of April 2, 2011, approximately 23% of the portfolio consisted of mortgage-backed securities. All of the mortgage-backed securities in the investment portfolio are AAA rated and were issued by U.S. government-sponsored enterprises and agencies.

The global credit and capital markets have continued to experience adverse conditions that have negatively impacted the values of various types of investment and non-investment grade securities, and have experienced volatility and disruption due to instability in the global financial system, uncertainty related to global economic conditions and concerns regarding sovereign financial stability. While general conditions in the global credit markets have improved, there is a risk that the Company may incur other-than-temporary impairment charges for certain types of investments should credit market conditions deteriorate or the underlying assets fail to perform as anticipated. See "Note 4. Financial Instruments" for a table of the Company's available-for-sale securities.

SEGMENT REPORTING

PRESENTATION

1.43   FASB ASC 280, *Segment Reporting*, requires that a public business enterprise report a measure of segment profit or loss, certain specific revenue and expense items, and segment assets. FASB ASC 280-10-05-1 requires that all public business enterprises report information about the revenues derived from the enterprise's products or services or groups of similar products and services; about the countries in which the enterprise earns revenues and holds assets; and about major customers, regardless of whether that information is used in making operating decisions. Even if a public company has only one operating segment, FASB ASC 280 requires that it report information about geographic areas and major customers. However, FASB ASC does not require an enterprise to report information that is impracticable to present because the necessary information is not available, and the cost to develop it would be excessive.

1.44   According to FASB ASC 280-10-50-1, an operating segment of a public entity has all of the following characteristics:
- It engages in business activities from which it may earn revenues and incur expenses, including revenues and expenses relating to transactions with other components of the same public entity.
- Its operating results are regularly reviewed by the public entity's chief operating decision maker to make decisions about resources to be allocated to the segment and assess its performance.
- Its discrete financial information is available.

1.45 FASB ASC 280-10-50-30 requires reconciliations of total segment revenues, total segment profit or loss, total segment assets, and other amounts disclosed for segments to corresponding amounts in the enterprise's general-purpose financial statements. FASB ASC 350-20-50-1 states that entities that report segment information should provide information about the changes in the carrying amount of goodwill during the period for each reportable segment.

1.46

TABLE 1-6: SEGMENT INFORMATION

Table 1-6 shows the type of segment information most frequently presented as an integral part of the financial statements of the survey entities.

	Number of Entities		
	2011	2010	2009
Industry Segments			
Revenue	420	408	386
Operating income or loss	381	362	291
Identifiable assets	341	306	312
Depreciation expense	346	331	339
Capital expenditures	308	305	311
Goodwill	273	230	235
Other, described	152	135	N/C*
Geographic Area			
Revenue	336	346	256
Operating income or loss	45	61	35
Identifiable assets	282	282	52
Depreciation expense	24	45	24
Capital expenditures	28	45	24
Goodwill	22	20	9
Other, described	41	47	N/C*
Entity Reports Segment Cash Flow	5	N/C*	N/C*
Entity Does Not Report by Segment	47	35	N/C*

* N/C = Not compiled. Line item was not included in the table for the year shown.

PRESENTATION AND DISCLOSURE EXCERPTS

Segment Information

1.47

HEWLETT-PACKARD COMPANY (OCT)

NOTES TO CONSOLIDATED FINANCIAL STATEMENTS

Note 19: Segment Information

Description of Segments

HP is a leading global provider of products, technologies, software, solutions and services to individual consumers, small- and medium-sized businesses ("SMB"), and large enterprises, including customers in the government, health and education sectors. Our offerings span personal computing and other access devices; multi-vendor customer services, including infrastructure technology and business process outsourcing, technology support and maintenance, application development and support services and consulting and integration services; imaging and printing-related products and services; and enterprise information technology infrastructure, including enterprise storage and server technology, networking products and solutions, IT management software, information management solutions and security intelligence/risk management solutions.

HP and its operations are organized into seven business segments for financial reporting purposes: the Personal Systems Group ("PSG"), Services, the Imaging and Printing Group ("IPG"), Enterprise Servers, Storage and Networking ("ESSN"), HP Software, HP Financial Services ("HPFS") and Corporate Investments. HP's organizational structure is based on a number of factors that management uses to evaluate, view and run its business operations, which include, but are not limited to, customer base, homogeneity of products and technology. The business segments are based on this organizational structure and information reviewed by HP's management to evaluate the business segment results.

HP has reclassified segment operating results for fiscal 2010 and fiscal 2009 to conform to certain fiscal 2011 organizational realignments. None of the changes impacts HP's previously reported consolidated net revenue, earnings from operations, net earnings or net earnings per share. Future changes to this organizational structure may result in changes to the business segments disclosed.

A description of the types of products and services provided by each business segment follows.

*   *Personal Systems Group* provides commercial PCs, consumer PCs, workstations, calculators and other related accessories, software and services for the commercial and consumer markets. Commercial PCs are optimized for commercial uses, including enterprise and SMB customers, and for connectivity and manageability in networked environments. Commercial PCs include the HP ProBook and HP EliteBook lines of notebooks and the Compaq Pro, Compaq Elite, HP Pro and HP Elite lines of business desktops, as well as the All-in-One Touchsmart and Omni PCs, HP Mini-Note PCs, retail POS systems, HP Thin Clients, and HP Slate Tablet PCs. Consumer PCs include the HP and Compaq series of multi-media consumer notebooks, desktops and mini notebooks, including the Touch-Smart line of touch-enabled all-in-one notebooks and desktops. HP's workstations are designed for users demanding enhanced performance, such as computer animation, engineering design and other programs requiring high-resolution graphics, and run on both Windows and Linux-based operating systems.

*   *Services* provides consulting, outsourcing and technology services across infrastructure, applications and business process domains. Services is divided into four main business units: Infrastructure Technology Outsourcing, Technology Services, Applications Services and Business Process Outsourcing. Infrastructure Technology Outsourcing delivers comprehensive services that encompass the data center and the workplace (desktop); network and communications; security, compliance and business continuity; and enterprise managed services. Technology Services provides consulting and support services, including mission

critical services, converged infrastructure services, networking services, data center transformation services and infrastructure services for storage, server and unified communication environments, as well as warranty support across HP's product lines. Applications Services helps clients revitalize and manage their applications assets through flexible, project-based consulting services and longer-term outsourcing contracts. These full life cycle services encompass application development, testing, modernization, system integration, maintenance and management. Business Process Outsourcing provides a broad array of enterprise shared services, customer relationship management services, financial process management services and administrative services.

- *Imaging and Printing Group* provides consumer and commercial printer hardware, supplies, media and scanning devices. IPG is also focused on imaging solutions in the commercial markets. These solutions range from managed print services and capturing high-value pages in areas such as industrial applications, outdoor signage, and the graphic arts business. Inkjet and Web Solutions delivers HP's consumer and SMB inkjet solutions (hardware, supplies, media, web-connected hardware and services) and develops HP's retail publishing and web businesses. It includes single function and all-in-one inkjet printers targeted toward consumers and SMBs, as well as retail publishing solutions, Snapfish and ePrintCenter. LaserJet and Enterprise Solutions delivers products, services and solutions to the medium-sized business and enterprise segments, including LaserJet printers and supplies, multi-function devices, scanners, web-connected hardware and services and enterprise software solutions, such as Exstream Software and Web Jetadmin. Managed Enterprise Solutions include managed print service products and solutions delivered to enterprise customers partnering with third-party software providers to offer workflow solutions in the enterprise environment. Graphics solutions include large format printing (Designjet and Scitex), large format supplies, WebPress supplies, Indigo printing, specialty printing systems and inkjet high-speed production solutions. HP's printer supplies offerings include LaserJet toner and inkjet printer cartridges, graphic solutions ink products and other printing-related media.

- *Enterprise Servers, Storage and Networking* provides server, storage, networking and, when combined with HP Software's Cloud Service Automation software suite, HP's CloudSystem. The CloudSystem enables infrastructure, platform and software-as-a-service in private, public or hybrid environments. Industry Standard Servers offers primarily entry-level and mid-range ProLiant servers, which run primarily Windows, Linux and Novell operating systems and leverage Intel and AMD processors. The business spans a range of product lines, including pedestal-tower servers, density-optimized rack servers and HP's BladeSystem family of server blades. Business Critical Systems offers HP Integrity servers based on the Intel Itanium-based processor as well as HP Integrity NonStop solutions. Business Critical Systems also offers scale-up x86 ProLiant Servers for scalability of systems with more than four industry standard processors. HP's Storage business offers a broad range of products including storage area networks, network attached storage, storage management software and virtualization technologies, StoreOnce data deduplication solutions, tape drives and tape libraries. HP's networking offerings include switch, router, wireless LAN and TippingPoint network security products.

- *HP Software* provides enterprise IT management software, information management solutions, and security intelligence/risk management solutions. Solutions are delivered in the form of traditional software licenses or as software-as-a-service. Augmented by support and professional services, HP Software solutions allow large IT organizations to manage infrastructure, operations, application life cycles, application quality and security, IT services, business processes, and structured and unstructured data. In addition, these solutions help businesses proactively safeguard digital assets, comply with corporate and regulatory policies, and control internal and external security risks.

- *HP Financial Services* supports and enhances HP's global product and services solutions, providing a broad range of value-added financial life cycle management services. HPFS enables HP's worldwide customers to acquire complete IT solutions, including hardware, software and services. HPFS offers leasing, financing, utility programs, and asset recovery services, as well as financial asset management services, for large global and enterprise customers. HPFS also provides an array of specialized financial services to SMBs and educational and governmental entities. HPFS offers innovative, customized and flexible alternatives to balance unique customer cash flow, technology obsolescence and capacity needs.

- *Corporate Investments* includes business intelligence solutions, HP Labs, webOS software, and certain business incubation projects. Business intelligence solutions enable businesses to standardize on consistent data management schemes, connect and share data across the enterprise and apply analytics. This segment also derives revenue from licensing specific HP technology to third parties.

Segment Data

HP derives the results of the business segments directly from its internal management reporting system. The accounting policies HP uses to derive business segment results are substantially the same as those the consolidated company uses. Management measures the performance of each business segment based on several metrics, including earnings from operations. Management uses these results, in part, to evaluate the performance of, and to assign resources to, each of the business segments. HP does not allocate to its business segments certain operating expenses, which it manages separately at the corporate level. These unallocated costs include primarily restructuring charges and any associated adjustments related to restructuring actions, amortization of purchased intangible assets, impairment of goodwill and purchased intangible assets, stock-based compensation expense related to HP-granted employee stock options, PRUs, restricted stock awards and the employee stock purchase plan, certain acquisition-related charges and charges for purchased IPR&D, as well as certain corporate governance costs.

Selected operating results information for each business segment was as follows for the following fiscal years ended October 31:

(In millions)	Total Net Revenue			Earnings (Loss) from Operations		
	2011	2010[1]	2009[1]	2011	2010[1]	2009[1]
Personal Systems Group	$ 39,574	$ 40,741	$ 35,305	$ 2,350	$ 2,032	$ 1,661
Services	35,954	35,529	35,380	5,149	5,661	5,102
Imaging and Printing Group	25,783	25,764	24,011	3,973	4,412	4,310
Enterprise Servers, Storage and Networking[2]	22,241	20,356	16,121	3,026	2,825	1,657
HP Software[3]	3,217	2,729	2,655	698	782	731
HP Financial Services	3,596	3,047	2,673	348	281	206
Corporate Investments[4]	322	346	191	(1,616)	(366)	(300)
Segment total	$130,687	$128,512	$116,336	$13,928	$15,627	$13,367

[1] Certain fiscal 2011 organizational reclassifications have been reflected retroactively to provide improved visibility and comparability. In fiscal 2010 and fiscal 2009, the reclassifications resulted in the transfer of revenue and operating profit among ESSN, HP Software, Services and Corporate Investments. Reclassifications between segments included the transfer of the networking business from Corporate Investments to ESSN, the transfer of the communications and media solutions business from HP Software to Services, and the transfer of the business intelligence business from HP Software to Corporate Investments. There was no impact on the previously reported financial results for PSG, HPFS or IPG.

[2] Includes the results of 3Com and 3PAR from the dates of acquisition in April 2010 and September 2010, respectively.

[3] Includes the results of ArcSight from the date of acquisition in October 2010.

[4] Includes the results of Palm from the date of acquisition in July 2010 and the impact of the decision to wind down the webOS device business during the quarter ended October 31, 2011.

The reconciliation of segment operating results information to HP consolidated totals was as follows for the following fiscal years ended October 31:

(In millions)	2011	2010	2009
Net revenue:			
Segment total	$130,687	$128,512	$116,336
Elimination of intersegment net revenue and other	(3,442)	(2,479)	(1,784)
Total HP consolidated net revenue	$127,245	$126,033	$114,552
Earnings before taxes:			
Total segment earnings from operations	$ 13,928	$ 15,627	$ 13,367
Corporate and unallocated costs and eliminations	(314)	(614)	(219)
Unallocated costs related to certain stock-based compensation expense	(618)	(613)	(552)
Amortization of purchased intangible assets	(1,607)	(1,484)	(1,578)
Impairment of goodwill and purchased intangible assets	(885)	—	—
Acquisition-related charges	(182)	(293)	(242)
Restructuring charges	(645)	(1,144)	(640)
Interest and other, net	(695)	(505)	(721)
Total HP consolidated earnings before taxes	$ 8,982	$ 10,974	$ 9,415

HP allocates its assets to its business segments based on the primary segments benefiting from the assets. Total assets by segment and the reconciliation of segment assets to HP consolidated total assets were as follows at October 31:

(In millions)	2011	2010	2009
Personal Systems Group	$ 15,781	$ 16,548	$ 15,767
Services	40,614	41,989	41,189
Imaging and Printing Group	11,939	12,514	12,173
Enterprise Servers, Storage and Networking	17,539	18,262	12,185
HP Software	21,028	9,979	8,546
HP Financial Services	13,543	12,123	10,842
Corporate Investments	517	1,619	391
Corporate and unallocated assets	8,556	11,469	13,706
Total HP consolidated assets	$129,517	$124,503	$114,799

The total assets allocated to the Corporate Investments segment decreased 68% in fiscal 2011 mostly due to an impairment charge to goodwill and certain purchased intangible assets associated with the Palm acquisition following the decision to wind down the webOS device business. Assets allocated to HP software increased by 111% in fiscal 2011 due to the acquisition of Autonomy. In addition, in connection with certain fiscal 2011 organizational realignments, HP reclassified total assets of its networking business from Corporate Investments to ESSN and total assets of the communications and media solutions business from HP Software to Services. There have been no other material changes to the total assets of HP's segments since October 31, 2010.

Major Customers

No single customer represented 10% or more of HP's total net revenue in any fiscal year presented.

Geographic Information

Net revenue, classified by the major geographic areas in which HP operates, was as follows for the following fiscal years ended October 31:

(In millions)	2011	2010	2009
Net revenue:			
U.S.	$ 44,111	$ 44,542	$ 41,314
Non-U.S.	83,134	81,491	73,238
Total HP consolidated net revenue	$127,245	$126,033	$114,552

Net revenue by geographic area is based upon the sales location that predominately represents the customer location. For each of the years ended October 31, 2011, 2010 and 2009, other than the United States, no country represented more than 10% of HP's total consolidated net revenue. HP reports revenue net of sales taxes, use taxes and value-added taxes directly imposed by governmental authorities on HP's revenue producing transactions with its customers.

At October 31, 2011, the United States and the Netherlands had 10% or more of HP's total consolidated net assets. At October 31, 2010, no single country other than the United States had 10% or more of HP's total consolidated net assets. At October 31, 2009, Belgium and the United States held 10% or more of HP's total consolidated net assets.

No single country other than the United States had more than 10% of HP's total consolidated net property, plant and equipment in any period presented. HP's long-lived assets other than goodwill and purchased intangible assets are composed principally of net property, plant and equipment.

Net property, plant and equipment, classified by major geographic areas in which HP operates, was as follows for the following fiscal years ended October 31:

(In millions)	2011	2010
Net Property, Plant and Equipment:		
U.S.	$ 6,126	$ 6,479
Non-U.S.	6,166	5,284
Total HP consolidated net property, plant and equipment	$12,292	$11,763

Net Revenue by Segment and Business Unit

The following table provides net revenue by segment and business unit for the following fiscal years ended October 31:

(In millions)	2011	2010[1]	2009[1]
Net revenue:			
Notebooks	$21,319	$22,602	$20,223
Desktops	15,260	15,519	12,892
Workstations	2,216	1,786	1,261
Other[2]	779	834	929
Personal Systems Group	39,574	40,741	35,305
Infrastructure Technology Outsourcing	15,189	14,942	14,563
Technology Services	10,879	10,627	10,665
Application Services	6,852	6,792	6,926
Business Process Outsourcing	2,672	2,872	2,977
Other	362	296	249
Services	35,954	35,529	35,380
Supplies	17,154	17,249	16,532
Commercial Hardware	5,790	5,569	4,778
Consumer Hardware	2,839	2,946	2,701
Imaging and Printing Group	25,783	25,764	24,011
Industry Standard Servers	13,521	12,574	9,296
Storage[3]	4,056	3,785	3,473
Business Critical Systems	2,095	2,292	2,590
HP Networking[4]	2,569	1,705	762
Enterprise Servers, Storage and Networking	$22,241	$20,356	$16,121

(continued)

(In millions)	2011	2010[1]	2009[1]
HP Software[5]	$ 3,217	$ 2,729	$ 2,655
HP Financial Services	3,596	3,047	2,673
Corporate Investments[6]	322	346	191
Total segments	130,687	128,512	116,336
Eliminations of inter-segment net revenue and other	(3,442)	(2,479)	(1,784)
Total HP consolidated net revenue	$127,245	$126,033	$114,552

[1] Certain fiscal 2011 organizational reclassifications have been reflected retroactively to provide improved visibility and comparability. In fiscal 2010 and fiscal 2009, the reclassifications resulted in the transfer of revenue and operating profit among ESSN, HP Software, Services and Corporate Investments. Reclassifications between segments included the transfer of the networking business from Corporate Investments to ESSN, the transfer of the communications and media solutions business from HP Software to Services, and the transfer of the business intelligence business from HP Software to Corporate Investments. Revenue was also transferred among the business units within Services and within PSG. In addition, net revenue reported for the Infrastructure Technology Outsourcing business unit and eliminations of inter-segment net revenue have both been reduced to reflect a change in inter-segment reporting model. There was no impact on the previously reported financial results for HPFS and IPG or for the business units within IPG.

[2] The Handhelds business unit, which includes devices that run on Windows Mobile software, was realigned into the Other business unit within PSG in fiscal 2011.

[3] Includes the results of 3PAR from the date of acquisition in September 2010.

[4] The networking business was added to ESSN in fiscal 2011. Also includes the results of 3Com from the date of acquisition in April 2010.

[5] The Business Technology Optimization and Other Software business units were consolidated into a single business unit within the HP Software segment in fiscal 2011. Also includes the results of ArcSight from the date of acquisition in October 2010.

[6] Includes the results of Palm from the date of acquisition in July 2010 and the impact of the decision to wind down the webOS device business during the quarter ended October 31, 2011.

1.48

APPLIED MATERIALS, INC. (OCT)

NOTES TO CONSOLIDATED FINANCIAL STATEMENTS

Note 16—Industry Segment Operations

Applied's four reportable segments are: Silicon Systems Group, Applied Global Services, Display, and Energy and Environmental Solutions. Applied's chief operating decision-maker has been identified as the President and Chief Executive Officer, who reviews operating results to make decisions about allocating resources and assessing performance for the entire company. Segment information is presented based upon Applied's management organization structure as of October 30, 2011 and the distinctive nature of each segment. Future changes to this internal financial structure may result in changes to Applied's reportable segments.

Each reportable segment is separately managed and has separate financial results that are reviewed by Applied's chief operating decision-maker. Each reportable segment contains closely related products that are unique to the particular segment. Segment operating income is determined based upon internal performance measures used by Applied's chief operating decision-maker.

Applied derives the segment results directly from its internal management reporting system. The accounting policies Applied uses to derive reportable segment results are substantially the same as those used for external reporting purposes. Management measures the performance of each reportable segment based upon several metrics including orders, net sales and operating income. Management uses these results to evaluate the performance of, and to assign resources to, each of the reportable segments. Applied does not allocate to its reportable segments certain operating expenses that it manages separately at the corporate level, which include costs related to share-based compensation; certain management, finance, legal, human resources, and research, development and engineering functions provided at the corporate level; and unabsorbed information technology and occupancy. In addition, Applied does not allocate to its reportable segments restructuring and asset impairment charges and any associated adjustments related to restructuring actions, unless these charges or adjustments pertain to a specific reportable segment. Segment operating income excludes interest income/expense and other financial charges and income taxes. Management does not consider the unallocated costs in measuring the performance of the reportable segments.

In fiscal 2010, as part of the restructuring of the Energy and Environmental Solutions segment, Applied discontinued marketing of its fully-integrated SunFab production lines but continued to offer individual tools for thin film solar manufacturing. Applied is supporting existing SunFab customers with services, upgrades and capacity increases through its Applied Global Services segment as these products are considered to have reached a particular stage in the product lifecycle. Effective in the first quarter of fiscal 2011, Applied accounts for thin film products under its Applied Global Services segment.

The Silicon Systems Group segment includes semiconductor capital equipment for etch, rapid thermal processing, deposition, chemical mechanical planarization, metrology and inspection, and wafer packaging.

The Applied Global Services segment includes technically differentiated products and services to improve operating efficiency, reduce operating costs and lessen the environmental impact of semiconductor, display and solar customers' factories. Applied Global Services' products consist of spares, services, certain earlier generation products, remanufactured equipment, and products that have reached a particular stage in the product lifecycle. Customer demand for these products and services is fulfilled through a global distribution system with trained service engineers located in close proximity to customer sites.

The Display segment includes products for manufacturing LCDs for TVs, personal computers, video-enabled devices and touch panel applications.

The Energy and Environmental Solutions segment includes products for fabricating crystalline-silicon (c-Si) solar photovoltaic cells and modules, high throughput roll-to-roll coating systems for flexible electronics and web products, and systems used in the manufacture of energy-efficient glass.

Information for each reportable segment as of October 30, 2011, October 31, 2010 and October 25, 2009 and for the fiscal years then ended, is as follows:

(In millions)	Net Sales	Operating Income (Loss)	Depreciation/ Amortization	Capital Expenditures	Segment Assets
2011:					
Silicon Systems Group	$ 5,415	$1,764	$ 52	$ 59	$2,036
Applied Global Services	2,413	482	13	7	1,337
Display	699	147	7	31	459
Energy and Environmental Solutions	1,990	453	34	16	1,438
Total Segment	$10,517	$2,846	$106	$113	$5,270
2010:					
Silicon Systems Group	$ 5,304	$1,892	$ 66	$ 39	$2,317
Applied Global Services	1,865	337	25	5	1,285
Display	899	267	8	5	419
Energy and Environmental Solutions	1,481	(466)	57	41	1,402
Total Segment	$ 9,549	$2,030	$156	$ 90	$5,423
2009:					
Silicon Systems Group	$ 1,960	$ 201	$ 53	$ 23	$1,195
Applied Global Services	1,397	115	34	15	1,043
Display	502	51	12	15	445
Energy and Environmental Solutions	1,155	(234)	80	51	1,853
Total Segment	$ 5,014	$ 133	$179	$104	$4,536

In fiscal 2011, Applied entered into an agreement to divest certain assets held in the Applied Global Services segment and determined certain identified intangible assets and purchased technology to be impaired. Operating results for fiscal 2011 included impairment charges of $24 million, which were reported in the Applied Global Services segment.

In fiscal 2010, Applied recorded charges related to a plan to restructure its Energy and Environmental Solutions segment totaling $405 million, which included inventory related charges of $247 million related to SunFab thin film solar equipment, asset impairment charges of $110 million, employee severance charges of $45 million, and other costs of $3 million. These charges were reported in the Energy and Environmental Solutions segment. Operating results in the Energy and Environmental Solutions segment for fiscal 2011 included favorable adjustments of $36 million related to this restructuring program.

Reconciliations of segment operating results to Applied consolidated totals for fiscal 2011, 2010 and 2009 are as follows:

(In millions)	2011	2010	2009
Total segment operating income	$2,846	$2,030	$133
Corporate and unallocated costs	(496)	(553)	(371)
Restructuring charges and asset impairments	21	(93)	(156)
Gain on sale of facility	27	—	—
Income (loss) from operations	$2,398	$1,384	$(394)

Reconciliations of depreciation and amortization expense to Applied consolidated totals for fiscal 2011, 2010 and 2009 are as follows:

(In millions)	2011	2010	2009
Total segment depreciation and amortization	$106	$156	$179
Depreciation on shared facilities and information technology assets	140	149	112
Consolidated depreciation and amortization	$246	$305	$291

Reconciliations of capital expenditures to Applied consolidated totals for fiscal 2011, 2010 and 2009 are as follows:

(In millions)	2011	2010	2009
Total segment capital expenditures	$113	$ 90	$104
Shared facilities and information technology assets	96	79	145
Consolidated capital expenditures	$209	$169	$249

Reconciliations of segment assets to Applied consolidated totals as of October 30, 2011, October 31, 2010 and October 25, 2009 are as follows:

(In millions)	October 30, 2011	October 31, 2010	October 25, 2009
Total segment assets	$ 5,270	$ 5,423	$4,536
Cash and investments	7,174	3,892	3,267
Allowance for bad debts	(73)	(74)	(68)
Deferred income taxes	658	625	455
Other current assets	90	93	337
Common property, plant and equipment	620	740	821
Other assets	122	244	226
Consolidated total assets	$13,861	$10,943	$9,574

For geographical reporting, revenue is attributed to the geographic location in which the customers' facilities are located. Long-lived assets consist primarily of property, plant and equipment and equity-method investments, and are attributed to the geographic location in which they are located.

Net sales and long-lived assets by geographic region were as follows:

(In millions)	Net Sales	Long-Lived Assets
2011:		
North America[1]	$ 1,963	$ 623
China	2,574	81
Taiwan	2,093	33
Korea	1,263	8
Europe	1,120	128
Japan	912	7
Southeast Asia	592	71
Total outside North America	8,554	328
Consolidated total	$10,517	$ 951
2010:		
North America[1]	$ 1,147	$ 715
China	1,557	78
Taiwan	2,750	32
Korea	1,768	5
Europe	981	95
Japan	768	5
Southeast Asia	578	65
Total outside North America	8,402	280
Consolidated total	$ 9,549	$ 995
2009:		
North America[1]	$ 966	$ 803
China	635	98
Taiwan	1,026	33
Korea	664	5
Europe	753	115
Japan	718	7
Southeast Asia	252	57
Total outside North America	4,048	315
Consolidated total	$ 5,014	$1,118

[1] Primarily the United States.

The following companies accounted for at least 10 percent of Applied's net sales in fiscal 2011, 2010, and/or 2009, which were for products in multiple reportable segments.

	2011	2010	2009
Samsung Electronics Co., Ltd.	12%	14%	10%
Taiwan Semiconductor Manufacturing Company Limited	10%	11%	*
Intel Corporation	10%	*	12%

* Less than 10%.

1.49

AIR PRODUCTS AND CHEMICALS, INC. (SEP)

NOTES TO THE CONSOLIDATED FINANCIAL STATEMENTS

(Millions of dollars, except for share data)

24. Business Segment and Geographic Information

Our segments are organized based on differences in product and/or type of customer. We have four business segments consisting of Merchant Gases, Tonnage Gases, Electronics and Performance Materials, and Equipment and Energy.

Merchant Gases

The Merchant Gases segment sells atmospheric gases such as oxygen, nitrogen, and argon (primarily recovered by the cryogenic distillation of air); process gases such as hydrogen and helium (purchased or refined from crude helium); and medical and specialty gases, along with certain services and equipment, throughout the world to customers in many industries, including those in metals, glass, chemical processing, food processing, healthcare, steel, general manufacturing, and petroleum and natural gas industries. There are four principal types of products: liquid bulk, packaged gases, small on-site plants, and healthcare products. Most merchant product is delivered via bulk supply, in liquid or gaseous form, by tanker or tube trailer. Smaller quantities of industrial, specialty, and medical gases are delivered in cylinders and dewars as "packaged gases," or through small on-sites (cryogenic or noncryogenic generators). Through our healthcare business, we offer respiratory therapies, home medical equipment, and infusion services, primarily in Europe. Electricity is the largest cost component in the production of atmospheric gases. Natural gas is also an energy source at a number of our Merchant Gases facilities. We mitigate energy and natural gas prices through pricing formulas and surcharges. The Merchant Gases segment also includes our share of the results of several joint ventures accounted for by the equity method. The largest of these joint ventures operate in Mexico, Italy, South Africa, India and Thailand. Merchant Gases competes worldwide against global industrial gas companies and several regional sellers. Competition in industrial gases is based primarily on price, reliability of supply, and the development of industrial gas applications. Competition in the healthcare business involves price, quality, service, and reliability of supply.

Tonnage Gases

Tonnage Gases provides hydrogen, carbon monoxide, nitrogen, oxygen, and syngas principally to the energy production and refining, chemical, and metallurgical industries worldwide. The Tonnage Gases segment also includes our Polyurethane Intermediates (PUI) business. The PUI business markets toluene diamine to customers under long-term contracts. For large-volume, or "tonnage" industrial gas users, we either construct a gas plant adjacent to or near the customer's facility—hence the term "on-site"—or deliver product through a pipeline from a nearby location. We are the world's largest provider of hydrogen, which is used by refiners to lower the sulfur content of gasoline and diesel fuels to reduce smog and ozone depletion. Electricity is the largest cost component in the production of atmospheric gases, and natural gas is the principal raw material for hydrogen, carbon monoxide, and syngas production. We mitigate energy and natural gas price changes through our long-term cost pass-through type contracts. Tonnage Gases competes against global industrial gas companies, as well as regional competitors. Competition is based primarily on price, reliability of supply, the development of applications that use industrial gases and, in some cases, provision of other services or products such as power and steam generation. We also derive a competitive advantage in regions where we have pipeline networks, which enable us to provide reliable and economic supply of products to customers.

Electronics and Performance Materials

The Electronics and Performance Materials segment employs applications technology to provide solutions to a broad range of global industries through expertise in chemical synthesis, analytical technology, process engineering, and surface science. This segment provides specialty and tonnage gases, specialty chemicals, services, and equipment to the electronics industry for the manufacture of silicon and compound semiconductors, LCD and other displays, and photovoltaic devices. The segment also provides performance chemical solutions for the coatings, inks, adhesives, civil engineering, personal care, institutional and industrial cleaning, mining, oil field, polyurethane, and other industries. The Electronics and Performance Materials segment faces competition on a product-by-product basis against competitors ranging from niche suppliers with a single product to larger and more vertically integrated companies. Competition is principally conducted on the basis of price, quality, product performance, reliability of product supply, technical innovation, service, and global infrastructure.

Equipment and Energy

The Equipment and Energy segment designs and manufactures cryogenic and gas processing equipment for air separation, hydrocarbon recovery and purification, natural gas liquefaction (LNG), and helium distribution, and serves energy markets in a variety of ways. Equipment is sold worldwide to customers in a variety of industries, including chemical and petrochemical manufacturing, oil and gas recovery and processing, and steel and primary metals processing. Energy markets are served through our operation and partial ownership of cogeneration and flue gas desulfurization facilities. In addition, we are developing hydrogen as an energy carrier, waste-to-energy facilities to produce electricity, carbon capture technologies for a variety of industrial and power applications, and oxygen-based technologies to serve energy markets in the future. Equipment and Energy competes with a great number of firms for all of its offerings except LNG heat exchangers, for which there are fewer competitors due to the limited market size and proprietary technologies. Competition is based primarily on technological performance, service, technical know-how, price, and performance guarantees.

Other

Other operating income (loss) includes other expense and income that cannot be directly associated with the business segments, including foreign exchange gains and losses, and costs previously allocated to businesses now reported as discontinued operations. Also included are LIFO inventory adjustments, as the business segments use FIFO and the LIFO pool adjustments are not allocated to the business segments. Corporate general and administrative costs and research and development costs are fully allocated to the business segments.

Other assets include cash, restricted cash, deferred tax assets, pension assets, financial instruments, and corporate assets previously allocated to businesses now reported as discontinued operations.

Customers

We do not have a homogeneous customer base or end market, and no single customer accounts for more than 10% of our consolidated revenues.

Accounting Policies

The accounting policies of the segments are the same as those described in Note 1, Major Accounting Policies. We evaluate the performance of segments based upon reported segment operating income. Operating income of the business segments includes general corporate expenses. Intersegment sales are not material and are recorded at selling prices that approximate market prices. Equipment manufactured for our industrial gas business is generally transferred at cost and not reflected as an intersegment sale.

Business Segments

Sales to External Customers	2011	2010	2009
Merchant Gases	$ 4,073.2	$3,718.3	$3,610.6
Tonnage Gases	3,316.7	2,930.8	2,573.6
Electronics and Performance Materials	2,291.5	1,904.7	1,582.2
Equipment and Energy	400.6	472.2	489.8
Segment and Consolidated Totals	$10,082.0	$9,026.0	$8,256.2

Operating Income	2011	2010	2009
Merchant Gases	$ 759.8	$ 729.4	$ 661.2
Tonnage Gases	503.1	444.2	399.6
Electronics and Performance Materials	361.1	251.8	101.6
Equipment and Energy	62.8	67.3	42.2
Segment total	$ 1,686.8	$1,492.7	$1,204.6
Global cost reduction plan[A]	—	—	(298.2)
Net loss on Airgas transaction	(48.5)	(96.0)	—
Customer bankruptcy and asset actions	—	6.4	(32.1)
Pension settlement	—	(11.5)	(10.7)
Other	(16.1)	(2.6)	(17.3)
Consolidated Total	$ 1,622.2	$1,389.0	$ 846.3

[A] Information about how this charge related to the businesses at the segment level is discussed in Note 5, Global Cost Reduction Plan.

Depreciation and Amortization	2011	2010	2009
Merchant Gases	$ 396.6	$ 377.9	$ 372.3
Tonnage Gases	310.9	303.0	272.2
Electronics and Performance Materials	154.9	169.0	178.2
Equipment and Energy	11.0	12.7	15.9
Segment total	$ 873.4	$ 862.6	$ 838.6
Other	.5	.8	1.7
Consolidated Total	$ 873.9	$ 863.4	$ 840.3

Equity Affiliates' Income	2011	2010	2009
Merchant Gases	$ 134.6	$ 104.3	$ 98.3
Other segments	19.7	22.6	13.9
Segment and Consolidated Totals	$ 154.3	$ 126.9	$ 112.2

Total Assets	2011	2010	2009
Merchant Gases	$ 5,892.1	$ 5,824.7	$ 5,630.8
Tonnage Gases	4,581.8	3,958.1	3,672.0
Electronics and Performance Materials	2,560.7	2,336.1	2,299.1
Equipment and Energy	357.5	362.7	333.8
Segment total	$13,392.1	$12,481.6	$11,935.7
Other	898.6	1,024.3	1,093.4
Consolidated Total	$14,290.7	$13,505.9	$13,029.1

Investment in and Advances to Equity Affiliates	2011	2010	2009
Merchant Gases	$ 800.4	$ 749.4	$ 713.8
Other segments	211.2	163.4	154.3
Segment and Consolidated Totals	$ 1,011.6	$ 912.8	$ 868.1

Identifiable Assets	2011	2010	2009
Merchant Gases	$ 5,091.7	$ 5,075.3	$ 4,917.0
Tonnage Gases	4,464.3	3,876.4	3,597.8
Electronics and Performance Materials	2,488.9	2,275.8	2,249.5
Equipment and Energy	335.6	341.3	303.3
Segment total	$12,380.5	$11,568.8	$11,067.6
Other	898.6	1,024.3	1,093.4
Consolidated Total	$13,279.1	$12,593.1	$12,161.0

Expenditures for Long Lived Assets[A]	2011	2010	2009
Merchant Gases	$ 432.9	$ 311.5	$ 510.8
Tonnage Gases	669.9	557.2	532.1
Electronics and Performance Materials	196.0	139.0	125.4
Equipment and Energy	45.9	22.4	9.8
Segment total	$ 1,344.7	$ 1,030.1	$ 1,178.1
Other	7.0	.8	1.0
Consolidated Total	$ 1,351.7	$ 1,030.9	$ 1,179.1

[A] Includes plant and equipment.

Geographic Information

Sales to External Customers	2011	2010	2009
United States	$ 4,423.8	$4,110.2	$3,779.8
Canada	297.0	260.3	238.6
Europe	3,002.1	2,819.7	2,765.1
Asia	2,122.1	1,621.0	1,294.2
Latin America/other	237.0	214.8	178.5
	$10,082.0	$9,026.0	$8,256.2

Long Lived Assets[A]	2011	2010	2009
United States	$ 3,099.2	$2,968.0	$2,987.1
Canada	566.1	608.8	535.2
Europe	1,833.7	1,711.1	1,766.8
Asia	1,786.2	1,658.4	1,462.3
Latin America/other	126.8	105.0	108.2
	$ 7,412.0	$7,051.3	$6,859.6

[A] Long lived assets include plant and equipment, net.

Geographic information is based on country of origin. Included in United States revenues are export sales to third party customers of $589.7 in 2011, $570.5 in 2010, and $510.2 in 2009. The Europe segment operates principally in Belgium, France, Germany, the Netherlands, Poland, the U.K., and Spain. The Asia segment operates principally in China, Japan, Korea, and Taiwan.

ACCOUNTING CHANGES AND ERROR CORRECTIONS

PRESENTATION

1.50 FASB ASC 250 defines various types of accounting changes, including a change in accounting principle, and provides guidance on the manner of reporting each type of change.

1.51 Paragraphs 1–2 of FASB ASC 250-10-45 include the presumption that, once adopted, an entity should not change an accounting principle (policy) to account for events and transactions of a similar type. FASB ASC 250-10-45-2 permits an entity to change an accounting principle in certain circumstances, such as when required to do so by new authoritative accounting guidance that mandates the use of a new accounting principle, interprets an existing principle, expresses a preference for an accounting principle, or rejects a specific principle. This paragraph also permits an entity to change an accounting principle if it can justify the use of an allowable alternative accounting principle on the basis that it is preferable.

1.52 FASB ASC 250-10-45-1 does not consider the following to be changes in accounting principle:

- Initial adoption of an accounting principle for new events or transactions
- Initial adoption of an accounting principle for new events or transactions that previously were immaterial in their effect
- Adoption or modification of an accounting principle for substantively different transactions or events from those occurring previously

1.53 FASB ASC 250-10-45-5 requires an entity to apply a change in accounting principle retrospectively to all prior periods, unless it is impracticable to do so. Retrospective application requires cumulative adjustments to the carrying amounts of assets and liabilities at the beginning of the earliest period presented; an adjustment, if any, to the opening balance of retained earnings or other relevant equity account; and adjusted financial statements for each individual prior period presented to reflect the period-specific effects of applying the new accounting principle. FASB ASC 250-10-45-7 provides an impracticability exception for period-specific effects or all periods. However, FASB ASC 250-10-45-8 permits only direct effects of the change, including any related income tax effects, to be included in the retrospective adjustment and prohibits an entity from including indirect effects that would have been recognized if the newly adopted accounting principle had been followed in prior periods. If indirect effects are actually incurred and recognized, an entity should only report for those indirect effects in the period in which the accounting change is made.

1.54 FASB ASC 250-10-45-17 requires an entity to account for a change in accounting estimate prospectively in the period of change if the change affects that period only or in the period of change and future periods if the change affects both.

1.55 Paragraphs 18–19 of FASB ASC 250-10-45 recognize that it may be difficult to distinguish between a change in an accounting principle and a change in an accounting estimate. Additional guidance is provided for those circumstances when an entity's change in estimate is affected by a change in accounting principle, recognizing that the effect of a change in accounting principle or the method of applying it may be inseparable from the effect of the change in accounting estimate. An example of such change is a change in the method of depreciation, amortization, or depletion for long-lived nonfinancial assets. Although an entity is permitted to apply this change prospectively as a change in accounting estimate, an entity should only make a change in accounting estimate affected by a change in accounting principle if the entity can justify the new accounting principle on the basis that it is preferable.

1.56 Paragraphs 23–24 of FASB ASC 250-10-45 require an entity to correct any error in the financial statements of a prior period discovered after the financial statements are issued or available to be issued by restating the prior-period financial

statements. Such errors are required to be reported as an error correction by restating the prior-period financial statements retrospectively with adjustments to the financial statements.

DISCLOSURE

1.57 As discussed in FASB ASC 250-10-50, among the required disclosures for a change in accounting principle, the reason should be disclosed, including an explanation about why the new method is preferable. Specific disclosures are also required for a change in accounting estimate, a change in reporting entity, correction of an error in previously-issued financial statements, and error corrections related to prior interim periods of the current fiscal year. As indicated in Table 1-7, most of the accounting changes disclosed by the survey entities were changes made to conform to requirements stated in new ASUs.

1.58

TABLE 1-7: ACCOUNTING CHANGES AND ERROR CORRECTIONS

Table 1-7 lists the accounting changes and error corrections disclosed by the survey entities.

	Number of Entities	
	2011	2010
Change in Accounting Principle		
Depreciation method	—	2
Stock-based compensation	—	2
Defined benefit pension and other postretirement	7	14
Business combinations	6	43
Fair value measurements	2	30
Derivatives and hedging activities	—	1
Noncontrolling interests	3	35
Financial instruments with debt and equity characteristics	2	16
Earnings per share	—	6
Inventory	3	N/C*
Revenue recognition	9	N/C*
Transfers of financial assets and variable interest entities	12	N/C*
Other, described	15	53
Change in Accounting Estimate		
Impairment or disposal of long-lived assets	2	1
Depreciable lives	3	3
Income tax (uncertainties)	3	5
Fair value measurements	2	3
Derivatives and hedging activities	1	—
Other, described	9	6
Correction of an Error		
Prior-period financial statement misstatements	22	6
Other, described	3	5

* N/C = Not compiled. Line item was not included in the table for the year shown.

PRESENTATION AND DISCLOSURE EXCERPTS

Change in Accounting Principle: Pension and Other Postretirement Benefits

1.59

PERKINELMER, INC. (DEC)

NOTES TO CONSOLIDATED FINANCIAL STATEMENTS

(In thousands, except share and per share data)

Note 1: Nature of Operations and Accounting Policies (in part)

Change in Accounting for Pension and Other Postretirement Benefits: During the fourth quarter of fiscal year 2011 the Company changed its method of recognizing defined benefit pension and other postretirement benefit costs. Historically the Company recognized the actuarial gains and losses as a component of stockholders' equity on the consolidated balance sheets. These gains and losses were amortized into results of operations over the average future service period of the active employees, to the extent such gains and losses were outside of a corridor. Additionally, for the Company's principal U.S. defined benefit pension plan, the Company used a calculated value of plan assets reflecting changes in the fair value of plan assets over a five year period. Under the Company's new method of accounting, the Company immediately recognizes actuarial gains and losses in operating results in the year in which the gains and losses occur. This change is intended to recognize the effects of current economic and interest rate trends on plan investments and assumptions as they occur. Actuarial gains and losses are measured annually as of fiscal year end and accordingly will be recorded in the fourth quarter, unless the Company is required to perform an interim remeasurement. Additionally, the Company now uses actual fair value of plan assets for the principal U.S. defined benefit pension plan that had not previously utilized this method. Accordingly, the financial data for all periods presented has been retrospectively adjusted to reflect the effect of these accounting changes. The Company believes that the new policies are preferable as they eliminate the delay in the recognition of actuarial gains and losses, and changes to the fair value of plan assets.

The cumulative effect of the change on retained earnings as of December 28, 2008 was a decrease of approximately $108.5 million, with offsetting adjustments to accumulated other comprehensive income and inventory. The significant effects of the change in accounting for pension and other postretirement benefits on the Company's consolidated statements of operations, consolidated statements of comprehensive income, consolidated balance sheets, and consolidated statements of cash flows for the periods presented were as follows:

	January 1, 2012		January 2, 2011		January 3, 2010	
	As Computed Under Prior Method	As Reported Under New Method	As Previously Reported	As Adjusted	As Previously Reported	As Adjusted
Statement of Operations Information:						
Cost of product and service revenue	$1,068,995	$1,070,708	$945,715	$943,112	$851,784	$849,521
Selling, general and administrative expenses	569,028	627,172	490,658	489,892	468,292	476,821
Research and development expenses	115,580	115,821	95,409	94,811	90,781	90,491
Operating income from continuing operations	151,226	91,128	153,601	157,568	121,922	115,946
Income from continuing operations before income taxes	124,452	64,354	161,984	165,951	106,135	100,159
Provision for income taxes	83,938	63,182	26,062	27,043	31,800	26,698
Net income from continuing operations	40,514	1,172	135,922	138,908	74,335	73,461
Income from discontinued operations before income taxes	—	—	24,138	30,772	18,883	14,919
(Benefit from) provision for income taxes on discontinued operations and dispositions	(4,484)	(4,484)	94,037	96,593	4,628	3,308
Net income from discontinued operations and dispositions	6,483	6,483	247,997	252,075	11,264	8,620
Net income	46,997	7,655	383,919	390,983	85,599	82,081

	January 1, 2012		January 2, 2011		January 3, 2010	
	As Computed Under Prior Method	As Reported Under New Method	As Previously Reported	As Adjusted	As Previously Reported	As Adjusted
Basic Earnings per Share:						
Continuing operations	$ 0.36	$ 0.01	$ 1.16	$ 1.19	$ 0.64	$ 0.63
Discontinued operations	0.06	0.06	2.12	2.15	0.10	0.07
Net income	$ 0.42	$ 0.07	$ 3.28	$ 3.34	$ 0.74	$ 0.71
Diluted Earnings per Share:						
Continuing operations	$ 0.36	$ 0.01	$ 1.15	$ 1.18	$ 0.64	$ 0.63
Discontinued operations	0.06	0.06	2.10	2.14	0.10	0.07
Net income	$ 0.41	$ 0.07	$ 3.25	$ 3.31	$ 0.73	$ 0.70
Statement of Comprehensive Income Information:						
Other comprehensive (loss) income	$ (37,273)	$ 3,058	$ (26,240)	$ (33,445)	$ 3,988	$ 6,064
Balance Sheet Information:						
Inventories, net	$ 240,201	$ 240,763	$ 207,278	$ 206,851		
Retained earnings	1,654,972	1,510,683	1,639,581	1,534,635		
Accumulated other comprehensive (loss) income	(90,764)	54,086	(53,491)	51,028		
Statement of Cash Flows Information:						
Operating activities:						
Net income	$ 46,997	$ 7,655	$ 383,919	$ 390,983	$ 85,599	$ 82,081
Net income from discontinued operations and dispositions	(6,483)	(6,483)	(247,997)	(252,075)	(11,264)	(8,620)
Income from continuing operations	40,514	1,172	135,922	138,908	74,335	73,461
Pension and other postretirement benefit expense[1]	—	74,974	—	3,832	—	21,348
Deferred taxes	20,467	(289)	(25,476)	(24,495)	27,495	22,393
Inventories, net	(1,454)	(2,200)	(22,630)	(22,535)	(4,474)	(3,675)
Accrued expenses and other	47,971	33,841	754	(7,140)	(45,858)	(62,029)

[1] In conjunction with the retrospective application of the Company's changes in accounting methods related to pension and other postretirement benefit costs, the Company has reclassified pension and other postretirement benefit expense into a separate line item within operating activities on the statement of cash flows. Previously this expense had been included within accrued expenses and other on the statement of cash flows.

The Company's funding policy provides that payments to the U.S. pension trusts shall at least be equal to the minimum funding requirements of the Employee Retirement Income Security Act of 1974. Non-U.S. plans are accrued for, but generally not fully funded, and benefits are paid from operating funds.

Change in Accounting Principle: Business Combinations

1.60

HUNTSMAN CORPORATION (DEC)

NOTES TO CONSOLIDATED FINANCIAL STATEMENTS

2. Summary of Significant Accounting Policies (in part)

Recently Issued Accounting Pronouncements (in part)

Accounting Pronouncements Adopted During 2011 (in part)

In December 2010, the FASB Emerging Issues Task Force issued ASU No. 2010-29, *Business Combinations (Topic 805)—Disclosure of Supplementary Pro Forma Information for Business Combinations*, which requires public entities that present comparative financial statements to disclose revenue and earnings of the combined entity as though the business combination(s) that occurred during the current year had occurred at the beginning of the comparable prior annual reporting period only. The amendments in this ASU also expand the supplemental pro forma disclosures under Topic 805 to include a description of the nature and amount of material, nonrecurring pro forma adjustments directly attributable to the business combination included in the reported pro forma revenue and earnings. The amendments in this ASU are effective for business combinations for which the acquisition date is on or after the beginning of the first annual reporting period beginning on or after December 15, 2010. We complied with the disclosure requirements of this standard in connection with our April 2, 2011 Laffans Acquisition and in connection with our April 1, 2011 consolidation of the Sasol-Huntsman joint venture. See "Note 3. Business Combinations and Dispositions" and "Note 7. Variable Interest Entities."

3. Business Combinations and Dispositions (in part)

Laffans Acquisition

On April 2, 2011, we completed the acquisition of the chemical business of Laffans Petrochemicals Limited, an amines and surfactants manufacturer located in Ankleshwar, India at an acquisition cost of approximately $23 million. The acquired business has been integrated into our Performance

Products segment. Transaction costs charged to expense related to this acquisition were not significant.

We have accounted for the Laffans Acquisition using the acquisition method. As such, we analyzed the fair value of tangible and intangible assets acquired and liabilities assumed. The preliminary allocation of acquisition cost to the assets acquired and liabilities assumed is summarized as follows (dollars in millions):

Acquisition cost	$23
Fair value of assets acquired and liabilities assumed:	
Accounts receivable	$10
Inventories	2
Other current assets	2
Property, plant and equipment	14
Accounts payable	(3)
Accrued liabilities	(1)
Other noncurrent liabilities	(1)
Total fair value of net assets acquired	$23

The acquisition cost allocation is preliminary pending final determination of the fair value of assets acquired and liabilities assumed, including final valuation of property, plant and equipment, intangible assets and the determination of related deferred taxes. For purposes of this preliminary allocation of fair value, we have assigned any excess of the acquisition cost over historical carrying values to property, plant and equipment and no amounts have been allocated to goodwill. It is possible that changes to this allocation could occur.

If this acquisition were to have occurred on January 1, 2010 the following estimated pro forma revenues and net income attributable to Huntsman Corporation and Huntsman International would have been reported (dollars in millions):

Huntsman Corporation

	Pro Forma Year Ended (Unaudited)	
	2011	2010
Revenues	$11,235	$9,301
Net income attributable to Huntsman Corporation	248	28

Huntsman International

	Pro Forma Year Ended (Unaudited)	
	2011	2010
Revenues	$11,235	$9,301
Net income attributable to Huntsman International	254	181

7. Variable Interest Entities (in part)

Sasol-Huntsman is our 50/50 joint venture with Sasol that owns and operates a maleic anhydride facility in Moers, Germany. This joint venture manufactures products for our Performance Products segment. Prior to April 1, 2011, we accounted for Sasol-Huntsman using the equity method. In April 2011, an expansion at this facility began production, which triggered the reconsideration of this joint venture as a VIE. The joint venture uses our technology and expertise, and we bear a disproportionate amount of risk of loss due to a related-party loan to Sasol-Huntsman for which we bear the default risk. As a result, we concluded that we were the primary beneficiary and began consolidating Sasol-Huntsman beginning April 1, 2011.

The following table summarizes the fair value of Sasol-Huntsman's assets and liabilities as of April 1, 2011 recorded upon initial consolidation in our consolidated balance sheet and the carrying amounts of such assets and liabilities as of December 31, 2011, before intercompany eliminations (dollars in millions):

	December 31, 2011	April 1, 2011
Current assets	$ 54	$ 61
Property, plant and equipment, net	141	155
Intangible assets	17	16
Goodwill	15	17
Total assets	$227	$249
Current liabilities	$ 30	$ 23
Long-term debt	87	93
Deferred income taxes	8	8
Other noncurrent liabilities	2	7
Total liabilities	$127	$131

Goodwill of $17 million was recognized upon consolidation of Sasol-Huntsman, of which approximately $12 million is deductible for income tax purposes. The total amount of goodwill changed approximately $2 million from the date of consolidation to December 31, 2011, due to a change in the foreign currency exchange rate. All other intangible assets are being amortized over an average useful life of 18 years.

Sasol-Huntsman had revenues and earnings of $116 million and $7 million, respectively, for the period from the date of consolidation to December 31, 2011. If this consolidation had occurred on January 1, 2010, the approximate pro forma revenues attributable to both our Company and Huntsman International would have been $11,259 million and $9,337 million for 2011 and 2010, respectively. There would have been no impact to the combined earnings attributable to us or Huntsman International excluding a one-time noncash gain of approximately $12 million recognized upon consolidation included in other operating income in the consolidated statements of operations and comprehensive (loss) income. Upon consolidation we also recognized a one-time noncash income tax expense of approximately $2 million. The fair value of the noncontrolling interest was estimated to be $61 million at April 1, 2011. The noncontrolling interest was valued at 50% of the fair value of the net assets as of April 1, 2011, as dictated by the ownership interest percentages, adjusted for certain tax consequences only applicable to one parent.

Change in Accounting Principle: Interest and Penalties for Uncertain Tax Positions

1.61

COACH, INC. (JUN)

NOTES TO CONSOLIDATED FINANCIAL STATEMENTS

(Dollars and shares in thousands, except per share data)

2. Significant Accounting Policies (in part)

Income Taxes

The Company accounts for income taxes in accordance with Accounting Standards Codification ("ASC") 740, "Income Taxes." Under ASC 740, a deferred tax liability or asset is recognized for the estimated future tax consequences of temporary differences between the carrying amounts of assets and liabilities in the financial statements and their respective tax bases. In evaluating the unrecognized tax benefits associated with the Company's various tax filing positions, management records these positions using a more-likely-than-not recognition threshold for income tax positions taken or expected to be taken in accordance with ASC 740. The Company classifies interest and penalties, if present, on un-

certain tax positions in the Provision for income taxes. See the note on Change in Accounting Principle.

16. Change in Accounting Principle

Coach adopted the FASB's guidance for accounting for uncertainty in income taxes, codified within ASC 740 "Income Taxes," on July 1, 2007, the first day of fiscal 2008. At adoption, Coach elected to classify interest and penalties related to uncertain tax positions as a component of interest expense included within Interest income, net. On July 4, 2010, the Company changed its method of accounting to include such amounts as a component of the provision for income taxes. The Company believes this change is preferable because: it will improve Coach's comparability with its industry peers; it is more consistent with the way in which the Company manages the settlement of uncertain tax positions as one overall amount inclusive of interest and penalties; and it will provide more meaningful information to investors by including only interest expense related to revolving credit facilities and long-term debt financing activities within Interest income, net.

The change in accounting method for presentation of interest and penalties for uncertain tax positions was completed in accordance with ASC 250, "Accounting Changes and Error Corrections." Accordingly, the change in accounting principle has been applied retrospectively by adjusting the financial statement amounts for the prior periods presented. The change to current or historical periods presented herein due to the change in accounting principle was limited to income statement classification, with no effect on net income.

The following tables detail the retrospective application impact on previously reported amounts:

For the Year Ended July 3, 2010	As Previously Reported	Effect of Accounting Principle Change	Adjusted
Interest income, net	$ 1,757	$6,204	$ 7,961
Provision for income taxes	416,988	6,204	423,192

For the Year Ended June 27, 2009			
Interest income, net	$ 5,168	$5,611	$ 10,779
Provision for income taxes	353,712	5,611	359,323

The following table shows the impact of the accounting principle change on reported balances for the year ended July 2, 2011:

For the Year Ended July 2, 2011	As Computed Under Prior Method	Effect of Accounting Principle Change	As Reported Under Current Method
Interest income, net	$ 4,226	(3,195)	$ 1,031
Provision for income taxes	423,614	(3,195)	420,419

Change in Accounting Principle: Inventory

1.62

THE STANDARD REGISTER COMPANY (DEC)

NOTES TO CONSOLIDATED FINANCIAL STATEMENTS

(Dollars in thousands, except per share amounts)

Note 1—Summary of Significant Accounting Policies (in part)

Inventories

Our inventories are stated at the lower of cost or market using the first-in, first-out (FIFO) method.

In the fourth quarter of 2011, we changed our method of accounting for inventory from using a combination of the last-in, last-out (LIFO) method and the FIFO method to using the FIFO method for all of our inventories. We believe the new method of accounting for inventory is preferable because the FIFO method better reflects the current value of inventories, is used by key users of our financial statements including our lenders which use FIFO to value the collateral and to calculate our borrowing capacity and compliance with debt covenants, enhances comparability with our peers, and

provides consistency across all of our operations regarding the method of accounting used for financial reporting.

In accordance with Accounting Standards Codification (ASC) 250 "Accounting Changes and Error Corrections," all prior periods presented have been retrospectively adjusted to apply the new method of accounting. As a result of the change in accounting principle, beginning retained earnings as of January 3, 2010 increased by $20,198 which represents the cumulative effect of the change on periods prior to fiscal 2009. For a summary of the retrospective adjustments, see Note 7 to the financial statements.

Note 7—Inventories

Inventories consist of the following:

	January 1, 2012	January 2, 2011
Materials and supplies	$ 6,468	$ 6,007
Jobs in process	1,787	1,433
Finished products	40,567	46,621
Total	$48,822	$54,061

In the fourth quarter of 2011, we changed our method of accounting for inventory from a combination of the LIFO method and the FIFO method to the FIFO method for all inventories. As a result of the retrospective application of this change in accounting principle, certain amounts in our consolidated statements of income for 2010 and 2009 were adjusted as follows:

	52 Weeks Ended January 2, 2011		53 Weeks Ended January 3, 2010	
	As Originally Reported	As Adjusted	As Originally Reported	As Adjusted
Cost of sales	$454,796	$458,569	$473,446	$478,367
Gross margin	213,581	209,808	220,570	215,649
Income (loss) from operations	7,668	3,895	(20,314)	(25,235)
Income tax expense (benefit)	2,503	1,005	(8,724)	(10,678)
Net income (loss)	2,643	368	(12,397)	(15,364)
Basic and diluted income (loss) per share	$ 0.09	$ 0.01	$ (0.43)	$ (0.53)

Our consolidated statement of financial position for 2010 was adjusted as follows:

	January 2, 2011	
	As Originally Reported	As Adjusted
Inventories	$ 29,253	$ 54,061
Deferred income taxes	11,991	2,139
Retained earnings	143,562	158,518

Our consolidated statements of cash flows for 2010 and 2009 were adjusted as follows:

	52 Weeks Ended January 2, 2011		53 Weeks Ended January 3, 2010	
	As Originally Reported	As Adjusted	As Originally Reported	As Adjusted
Net income (loss)	$2,643	$ 368	$(12,397)	$(15,364)
Deferred tax expense (benefit)	1,560	62	(8,724)	(10,678)
Inventories	4,480	8,253	5,093	10,014

Our consolidated statements of income for the interim quarters of 2011 were adjusted as follows:

	13 Weeks Ended April 3, 2011		13 Weeks Ended July 3, 2011		13 Weeks Ended October 2, 2011	
	As Originally Reported	As Adjusted	As Originally Reported	As Adjusted	As Originally Reported	As Adjusted
Cost of sales	$111,257	$111,435	$113,381	$113,524	$111,284	$111,392
Gross margin	53,632	53,454	50,904	50,761	46,259	46,151
Income (loss) from operations	1,255	1,077	(1,328)	(1,471)	15,246	15,138
Income tax expense (benefit)	153	82	(497)	(554)	6,257	6,214
Net income (loss)	535	428	(910)	(996)	8,419	8,354
Basic and diluted income (loss) per share	$ 0.02	$ 0.01	$ (0.03)	$ (0.03)	$ 0.29	$ 0.29

Our segment results are reported on the FIFO basis; therefore, segment information for prior periods was not impacted by the change in accounting principle.

Change in Accounting Principle: Revenue Recognition

1.63

JDS UNIPHASE CORPORATION (JUN)

NOTES TO CONSOLIDATED FINANCIAL STATEMENTS

Note 1. Description of Business and Summary of Significant Accounting Policies (in part)

Revenue Recognition (in part)

The Company recognizes revenue when it is realized or realizable and earned. The Company considers revenue realized or realizable and earned when it has persuasive evidence of an arrangement, delivery has occurred, the sales price is fixed or determinable, and collectability is reasonably assured. Delivery does not occur until products have been shipped or services have been provided, risk of loss has transferred and in cases where formal acceptance is required, customer acceptance has been obtained or customer acceptance provisions have lapsed. In situations where a formal acceptance is required but the acceptance only relates to whether the product meets its published specifications, revenue is recognized upon shipment provided all other revenue recognition criteria are met. The sales price is not considered to be fixed or determinable until all contingencies related to the sale have been resolved.

The Company reduces revenue for rebates and other similar allowances. Revenue is recognized only if these estimates can be reliably determined. The Company's estimates are based on its historical results taking into consideration the type of customer, the type of transaction and the specifics of each arrangement.

In addition to the aforementioned general policies, the following are the specific revenue recognition policies for multiple-element arrangements and for each major category of revenue.

Multiple-Element Arrangements

In October 2009, the FASB issued authoritative guidance that applies to arrangements with multiple deliverables. The guidance eliminates the residual method of revenue recognition, on non-software arrangements, and allows the use of management's best estimate of selling price ("BESP") for individual elements of an arrangement when vendor-specific objective evidence ("VSOE") or third-party evidence ("TPE") is unavailable. In addition, the FASB issued authoritative guidance which removes non-software components of tangible products and certain software components of tangible products from the scope of existing software revenue guidance, resulting in the recognition of revenue similar to that for other tangible products. The Company adopted these standards at the beginning of its first quarter of fiscal year 2011 on a prospective basis for applicable transactions originating or materially modified on or after July 3, 2010.

When a sales arrangement contains multiple deliverables, such as sales of products that include services, the multiple deliverables are evaluated to determine the units of accounting, and the entire fee from the arrangement is allocated to each unit of accounting based on the relative selling price. Under this approach, the selling price of a unit of accounting is determined by using a selling price hierarchy which requires the use of VSOE of fair value if available, TPE if VSOE is not available, or BESP if neither VSOE nor TPE is available. Revenue is recognized when the revenue recognition criteria for each unit of accounting are met.

The Company establishes VSOE of selling price using the price charged for a deliverable when sold separately and, in remote circumstances, using the price established by management having the relevant authority. TPE of selling price is established by evaluating similar and interchangeable competitor goods or services in sales to similarly situated customers. When VSOE or TPE are not available the Company then use BESP. Generally, the Company is not able to determine TPE because its product strategy differs from that of others in our markets, and the extent of customization varies among comparable products or services from its peers. The Company establishes BESP using historical selling price trends and considering multiple factors including, but not limited to geographies, market conditions, competitive landscape, internal costs, gross margin objectives, and pricing practices. When determining BESP, the Company applies significant judgment in establishing pricing strategies and evaluating market conditions and product lifecycles.

The determination of BESP is made through consultation with and approval by the segment management. Segment management may modify or develop new pricing practices and strategies in the future. As these pricing strategies evolve, we may modify our pricing practices in the future, which may result in changes in BESP. The aforementioned factors may result in a different allocation of revenue to the deliverables in multiple element arrangements from fiscal 2011, which may change the pattern and timing of revenue recognition for these elements but will not change the total revenue recognized for the arrangement.

To the extent that a deliverable(s) in a multiple-element arrangement is subject to specific guidance (for example, software that is subject to the authoritative guidance on software revenue recognition) the Company allocates the fair value of the units of accounting using relative selling price and that unit of accounting is accounted for in accordance with the specific guidance. Some product offerings include hardware that are integrated with or sold with software that delivers the functionality of the equipment. The Company believes that this equipment is not considered software related and would therefore be excluded from the scope of the authoritative guidance on software revenue recognition.

If the transactions entered into or materially modified on or after July 3, 2010 were subject to the previous accounting guidance, the reported net revenue amount during the year ended July 2, 2011, would decrease by approximately $7 million.

Software

The Company's software arrangements generally consist of a perpetual license fee and PCS. Generally the Company has established VSOE of fair value for PCS contracts based on the renewal rate or the bell curve methodology. Revenue from maintenance, unspecified upgrades and technical support is recognized over the period such items are delivered. In multiple-element revenue arrangements that include software, software related and non software-related elements are accounted for in accordance with the following policies.

- Non software and software related products are bifurcated based on a relative selling price
- Software related products are separated into units of accounting if all of the following criteria are met:
- The functionality of the delivered element(s) is not dependent on the undelivered element(s).
- There is VSOE of fair value of the undelivered element(s).
- Delivery of the delivered element(s) represents the culmination of the earnings process for that element(s).

If these criteria are not met, the software revenue is deferred until the earlier of when such criteria are met or when the last undelivered element is delivered. If there is VSOE of the undelivered item(s) but no such evidence for the delivered item(s), the residual method is used to allocate the arrangement consideration. Under the residual method, the amount of consideration allocated to the delivered item(s) equals the total arrangement consideration less the aggregate VSOE of the undelivered elements. In cases where VSOE is not established for PCS, revenue is recognized ratably over the PCS period after all software deliverables have been made and the only undelivered item is PCS.

Change in Accounting Principle: Transfers of Financial Assets and Variable Interest Entities

1.64

JABIL CIRCUIT, INC. (AUG)

NOTES TO CONSOLIDATED FINANCIAL STATEMENTS

2. Trade Accounts Receivable Securitization and Sale Programs

The Company regularly sells designated pools of trade accounts receivable under two asset-backed securitization programs, two trade accounts receivable sale programs and a factoring program.

a. Asset-Backed Securitization Program

In connection with the asset-backed securitization program, the Company regularly sells a designated pool of trade accounts receivable to a wholly-owned subsidiary, which in turn sells 100% of the eligible receivables to conduits, administered by unaffiliated financial institutions. This wholly-owned subsidiary is a separate bankruptcy-remote entity and its assets would be available first to satisfy the creditor claims of the conduits. As the receivables sold are collected, the wholly-owned subsidiary is able to sell additional receivables up to the maximum permitted amount under the program. Net cash proceeds of $300.0 million are available at any one time under the securitization program.

Prior to September 1, 2010, the transactions in this program were accounted for as sales under applicable accounting guidance. Effective September 1, 2010, the Company adopted new accounting guidance that resulted in more stringent conditions for reporting the transfer of a financial asset as a sale. As a result of the adoption of this new guidance, the accounts receivable transferred under this program no longer qualified for sale treatment and as such were accounted for as secured borrowings. During the first quarter of fiscal year 2011, this program was amended which resulted in the transfers of the applicable accounts receivable again being accounted for as sales. Under the amended program the Company sells 100% of the eligible receivables to conduits and any portion of the purchase price for the receivables which is not paid in cash upon the sale taking place is recorded as a deferred purchase price receivable, which is paid by the conduits from available cash as payments on the receivables are collected. The securitization program requires compliance with several financial covenants including an interest coverage ratio and debt to EBITDA ratio, as defined in the securitization agreements. The securitization agreement, as amended on November 5, 2010, expires on November 4, 2011.

Net receivables sold under this program are excluded from trade accounts receivable on the Consolidated Balance Sheets and are reflected as cash provided by operating activities on the Consolidated Statements of Cash Flows. The wholly-owned subsidiary is assessed (i) a fee on the unused portion of the program of 0.50% per annum based on the average daily unused aggregate receivables sold during the period, (ii) a usage fee on the utilized portion of the program equal to 0.95% per annum (inclusive of the unused fee) on the average daily outstanding aggregate receivables sold during the immediately preceding calendar month and (iii) a fee on the weighted average amount outstanding under the program during the period multiplied by the applicable rate in effect for the period (i.e. Commercial Paper rate). The securitization conduits and the investors in the conduits have no recourse to the Company's assets for failure of debtors to pay when due.

The Company continues servicing the receivables sold and in exchange receives a servicing fee. Servicing fees recognized during fiscal years 2011, 2010 and 2009 were not material and are included in other expense within the Consolidated Statements of Operations. The Company does not record a servicing asset or liability as the Company estimates the fee it receives in return for its obligation to service these receivables is at fair value.

The Company sold $5.8 billion, $5.3 billion and $4.7 billion of eligible trade accounts receivable during fiscal years 2011, 2010 and 2009, respectively. In exchange, the Company received cash proceeds of $5.5 billion, $5.1 billion and $4.5 billion during fiscal years 2011, 2010 and 2009, respectively, and a net deferred purchase price receivable (at August 31, 2011) or a retained interest (at August 31, 2010 and 2009). At August 31, 2011, the deferred purchase price receivable totaled approximately $295.6 million, which was recorded initially at fair value as prepaid expenses and other current assets on the Consolidated Balance Sheets. At August 31, 2010 and 2009, the Company retained an interest in the receivables of $225.1 million and $222.3 million, respectively. The deferred purchase price receivable was valued using unobservable inputs (Level 3 inputs), primarily discounted cash flows, and due to its credit quality and short-term maturity, the fair value approximated book value.

The Company recognized pretax losses on the sales of receivables of approximately $2.7 million, $3.6 million and $5.3 million during fiscal years 2011, 2010 and 2009, respectively, which are recorded to other expense within the Consolidated Statements of Operations. Prior to execution of the previously discussed amendment, the Company recognized interest expense of approximately $0.5 million during the first quarter of fiscal year 2011 associated with the secured borrowings. See Note 15—"New Accounting Guidance" to the Consolidated Financial Statements.

b. Foreign Asset-Backed Securitization Program

In connection with the foreign asset-backed securitization program, prior to the amendment in the third quarter of fiscal year 2011, certain of the Company's foreign subsidiaries sold, on an ongoing basis, an undivided interest in designated pools of trade accounts receivable to a special purpose entity, which in turn borrowed up to $100.0 million from an unaffiliated financial institution and granted a security interest in the accounts receivable as collateral for the borrowings. The securitization program was accounted for as a borrowing. The loan balance was calculated based on the terms of the securitization program agreements.

In the third quarter of fiscal year 2011, the securitization program was amended to provide for the sale of 100% of the designated trade accounts receivable of the Company's foreign subsidiaries to the special purpose entity which in turn sells 100% of the receivables to an unaffiliated financial institution. The special purpose entity is a separate bankruptcy-remote entity and its assets would be available first to satisfy the creditor claims of the unaffiliated financial institution. Net cash proceeds of $200.0 million are available at any one time under the amended securitization program. Transfers of the receivables to the unaffiliated financial institution are accounted for as sales. Under the amended program, any portion of the purchase price for the receivables which is not paid in cash to the special purpose entity upon the sale taking place is recorded as a deferred purchase price receivable, which is paid to the special purpose entity as payments on the receivables are collected. The foreign asset-backed securitization program requires compliance with several covenants including limitations on certain corporate actions such as mergers and consolidations. The securitization agreement, as amended during the third quarter of fiscal year 2011, expires on May 10, 2012.

As the Company has the power to direct the activities of the special purpose entity and the obligation to absorb the majority of the expected losses or the right to receive benefits from the transfer of trade accounts receivable into the special purpose entity it is deemed the primary beneficiary. Accordingly, the Company consolidates the special purpose entity (which was also the case prior to the amendment in the third quarter of fiscal year 2011).

Net receivables sold under this program are excluded from trade accounts receivable on the Consolidated Balance Sheets and are reflected as cash provided by operating activities on the Consolidated Statements of Cash Flows. The special purpose entity is assessed (i) a fee in an amount equal to 0.45% per annum multiplied by the maximum aggregate invested amount during the period and (ii) a fee on the average amount outstanding under the program during the period multiplied by the applicable rate in effect for the period (i.e. LIBOR for U.S. dollars, EURIBOR for euros and WIBOR for Polish zlotys) plus a 0.45% per annum margin. The unaffiliated financial institution has no recourse to the Company's assets for failure of debtors to pay when due.

The Company continues servicing the receivables in the program and in exchange receives a servicing fee. Servicing fees recognized during fiscal years 2011, 2010 and 2009 were not material and are included in interest expense up through the amendment that occurred in the third quarter of fiscal year 2011, and are included in other expense within the Consolidated Statements of Operations subsequent to the amendment. The Company does not record a servicing asset or liability on the Consolidated Balance Sheets as the Company estimates the fee it receives in return for its obligation to service these receivables is at fair value.

Subsequent to the amendment that occurred in the third quarter of fiscal year 2011, the Company sold (including amounts transferred into the program on the amendment date) $928.0 million of eligible trade accounts receivable during fiscal year 2011. In exchange, the Company received cash proceeds of $783.9 million during the same period, and a net deferred purchase price receivable. At August 31, 2011, the deferred purchase price receivable totaled approximately $143.5 million, which was recorded initially at fair value as prepaid expenses and other current assets on the Consolidated Balance Sheets. The deferred purchase price receivable was valued using unobservable inputs (Level 3 inputs), primarily discounted cash flows, and due to its credit quality and short-term maturity the fair value approximated book value. The resulting losses on the sales of the receivables subsequent to the amendment that occurred in the third quarter of fiscal year 2011 were $0.7 million during fiscal year 2011 and were recorded to other expense within the Consolidated Statements of Operations. Prior to execution of the previously discussed amendment, the Company recognized interest expense of approximately $0.9 million during fiscal year 2011 associated with the secured borrowings.

At August 31, 2010, the Company had $71.4 million of secured borrowings outstanding under the program. In addition, the Company incurred interest expense of $2.1 million and $3.9 million recorded in the Consolidated Statements of Operations during fiscal years 2010 and 2009, respectively.

c. Trade Accounts Receivable Factoring Agreement

In connection with a factoring agreement, the Company transfers ownership of eligible trade accounts receivable of a foreign subsidiary without recourse to a third party purchaser in exchange for cash. The factoring of trade accounts receivable under this agreement is accounted for as a sale. Proceeds from the transfer reflect the face value of the account less a discount. The discount is recorded as a loss to other expense within the Consolidated Statements of Operations in the period of the sale. In April 2011, the factoring agreement was extended through September 30, 2011, at which time it automatically renewed for an additional six-month period.

The receivables sold pursuant to this factoring agreement are excluded from trade accounts receivable on the Consolidated Balance Sheets and are reflected as cash provided by operating activities on the Consolidated Statements of Cash Flows. The Company continues to service, administer and collect the receivables sold under this program. Servicing fees recognized during fiscal years 2011, 2010 and 2009 were not material, and were recorded to other expense within the Consolidated Statements of Operations. The Company does not record a servicing asset or liability on the Consolidated Balance Sheets as the Company estimates the fee it receives in return for its obligation to service these receivables is at fair value. The third party purchaser has no recourse to the Company's assets for failure of debtors to pay when due.

The Company sold $68.5 million, $90.9 million and $137.3 million of trade accounts receivable during fiscal years 2011, 2010 and 2009, respectively, and in exchange, received cash proceeds of $68.4 million, $90.8 million and $137.2 million, respectively. The resulting losses on the sales of trade accounts receivables sold under this factoring agreement for fiscal years 2011, 2010 and 2009 were not material, and were recorded to other expense within the Consolidated Statements of Operations.

d. Trade Accounts Receivable Sale Programs

In fiscal year 2010, the Company entered into two separate uncommitted accounts receivable sale agreements with banks which originally allowed the Company and certain of its subsidiaries to elect to sell and the banks to elect to purchase at a discount, on an ongoing basis, up to a maximum of $150.0 million and $75.0 million of specific trade accounts receivable at any one time. The sale programs have been amended to increase the facility limits from $150.0 million to $200.0 million and from $75.0 million to $175.0 million of specific trade accounts receivable at any one time. The programs are accounted for as sales. Net receivables sold under the programs are excluded from trade accounts receivable on the Consolidated Balance Sheets and are reflected as cash provided by operating activities on the Consolidated Statements of Cash Flows. The $200.0 million and $175.0 million sale programs were amended during the third quarter of fiscal year 2011 and the fourth quarter of fiscal year 2011, respectively, such that the programs no longer have defined termination dates and either party can elect to cancel the agreements by giving prior written notification to the other party of no less than 30 days.

The Company continues servicing the receivables in the program. Servicing fees recognized during fiscal years 2011 and 2010 were not material and are included in other expense within the Consolidated Statements of Operations. The Company does not record a servicing asset or liability on the Consolidated Balance Sheets as the Company estimates the fee it receives in return for its obligation to service these receivables is at fair value.

During fiscal years 2011 and 2010, the Company sold $2.4 billion and $0.3 billion of trade accounts receivable under these programs, respectively. In exchange, the Company received cash proceeds of $2.4 billion and $0.3 billion, respectively. The resulting losses on the sales of trade accounts receivable during fiscal years 2011 and 2010 were not material and were recorded to other expense within the Consolidated Statements of Operations.

15. New Accounting Guidance (in part)

a. Recently Adopted Accounting Guidance (in part):

During the fourth quarter of fiscal year 2009, the FASB issued new accounting guidance on accounting for transfers of financial assets. This new guidance became effective for the Company on September 1, 2010. This guidance amends previous guidance by eliminating the concept of a qualifying special-purpose entity, creating more stringent conditions for reporting a transfer of a portion of a financial asset as a sale, clarifying other sale-accounting criteria and changing the initial measurement of a transferor's interest in transferred financial assets. Additionally, the guidance requires extensive new disclosure regarding an entity's involvement in a transfer of financial assets. As a result of the adoption of this new guidance, the accounts receivable transferred under the asset-backed securitization program, prior to amendment on November 5, 2010, no longer qualified for sale treatment and as such were accounted for as secured borrowings. During the first quarter of fiscal year 2011, the program was amended resulting in the transfers of receivables again being accounted for as a sale. The amended program allows the Company to regularly sell a designated pool of trade accounts receivable to a wholly-owned subsidiary, which in turn sells 100% of the eligible receivables to conduits, administered by unaffiliated financial institutions. Refer to Note 2—"Trade Accounts Receivable Securitization and Sale Programs."

1.65

MONSANTO COMPANY (AUG)

NOTES TO THE CONSOLIDATED FINANCIAL STATEMENTS

Note 2. Significant Accounting Policies (in part)

Basis of Consolidation (in part)

On September 1, 2010, Monsanto prospectively adopted the accounting standard update regarding improvements to financial reporting by enterprises involving variable interest entities (VIEs). This accounting standard codification (ASC) requires former qualifying Special Purpose Entities (SPE) to be evaluated for consolidation and also changed the approach to determining a VIEs primary beneficiary and requires companies to more frequently reassess whether they must consolidate VIEs. Arrangements with business enterprises are evaluated, and those in which Monsanto is determined to be the primary beneficiary are consolidated. See Note 8—Variable Interest Entities—for a description of consolidated and non-consolidated VIEs.

Note 8. Variable Interest Entities

Effective Sept. 1, 2010, Monsanto prospectively adopted the accounting standard update regarding improvements to financial reporting by enterprises involving variable interest entities (VIEs). A VIE is a legal entity that lacks sufficient equity to finance its activities, or the equity investors of the entity as a group lack any of the characteristics of a controlling interest. Monsanto is involved with various special purpose entities and other entities that are deemed to be VIEs. Monsanto has determined that the company holds variable interests in entities that are established as revolving financing programs. These programs allow the company to transfer a limited amount of customer receivables to a VIE. One program is in Brazil and the other is in Argentina. In addition, Monsanto has various variable interests in biotechnology companies that focus on plant gene research, development and commercialization. These variable interests have also been determined to be VIEs.

If a company is considered the primary beneficiary of a VIE, the company is required to consolidate the entity. The primary beneficiary of a VIE is the enterprise that has both the power to direct the activities most significant to the economic performance of the VIE and the obligation to absorb losses or receive benefits that could potentially be significant to the VIE. For all VIEs in which the company has a variable interest, the company performs ongoing qualitative assessments to determine whether it is the primary beneficiary. In determining whether Monsanto is the primary beneficiary, a number of factors are considered, including the structure of the entity, contractual provisions that grant any additional rights to influence or control the economic performance of the VIE, and the company's obligation to absorb significant losses. In addition, the company determines which activities most significantly impact the economic performance of the VIE and whether the company has any rights that would allow it to direct those activities. If Monsanto is determined to be the primary beneficiary, the assets, liabilities and operations of the VIE are consolidated.

As a result of the adoption of the updated accounting guidance, Monsanto was required to consolidate certain VIEs that are established as revolving financing programs including the special purpose entity referred to in Note 7—Customer Financing Programs. As of the date of the initial consolidation of these VIEs, the company measured the assets and liabilities of the newly consolidated VIEs at their carrying value. The company was not required to deconsolidate any VIEs as of Sept. 1, 2010. The cumulative effect of the adoption of this guidance was insignificant to additional contributed capital, retained earnings and accumulated other comprehensive loss and, therefore, not identified separately on the Statement of Consolidated Shareowners' Equity and Comprehensive Income but is recorded within the Statement of Consolidated Operations.

Consolidated VIEs

Under the accounting guidance effective prior to Sept. 1, 2010, none of the interests in VIEs held were consolidated by Monsanto. For the most part, the VIEs involving the revolving financing programs are funded by investments from the company and other third parties, primarily investment funds, and have been established to service Monsanto's customer receivables. Creditors have no recourse against Monsanto in the event of default by these VIEs nor does the company have any implied or unfunded commitments to these VIEs. The company's financial or other support provided to these VIEs is limited to its original investment. Even though Monsanto holds a subordinate interest in the VIEs, the VIEs were established to service transactions involving the company and the company determines the receivables that are included in the revolving financing programs. Therefore, the determination is that Monsanto has the power to direct the activities most significant to the economic performance of the VIEs. As a result, the company is the primary beneficiary of these VIEs and, effective Sept. 1, 2010, these VIEs have been consolidated in Monsanto's Consolidated Financial Statements. The assets of these VIEs may only be used to settle the obligations of the respective entity. Third-party investors in the VIEs do not have recourse to the general assets of Monsanto other than the maximum exposure to loss relating to the VIE. The following table presents the carrying value of assets and liabilities, which are identified as restricted assets and liabilities on the company's Condensed Statement of Consolidated Financial Position, and the maximum exposure to loss relating to the VIEs for which Monsanto is the primary beneficiary.

(Dollars in millions)	As of Aug. 31, 2011 Financing Programs VIEs
Cash and cash equivalents	$ 96
Trade receivables, net	51
Total Assets	$147
Total Liabilities	—
Maximum Exposure to Loss	$ 11

Non-Consolidated VIEs

Monsanto has variable interests through investments and arrangements with biotechnology companies that focus on plant gene research, development, and commercialization. The company has not provided financial or other support with respect to these investments or arrangements other than its original interest. The company also has no implied or unfunded commitments to these VIEs. The company determined that it was not the primary beneficiary due to the relative size of Monsanto's investment in comparison to the total equity of the VIEs, the level of the company's obligation to absorb losses or right to receive benefits from the VIEs, and the company's inability to direct the activities that most significantly impact the economic performance of the VIEs. Monsanto's maximum exposure to loss on these variable interests is limited to the amount of the company's investment in the entity. The following table presents the carrying value of assets and liabilities and the maximum exposure to loss relating to VIEs that the company does not consolidate:

(Dollars in millions)	As of Aug. 31, 2011 Biotechnology VIEs
Property, plant, and equipment, net	$ 5
Other intangible assets, net	9
Other assets	15
Total Non-Current Assets	$29
Total Liabilities	—
Maximum Exposure to Loss	$15

Change in Accounting Principle: Multiemployer Pension Plans

1.66

AUTONATION, INC. (DEC)

NOTES TO CONSOLIDATED FINANCIAL STATEMENTS

(All tables in millions, except per share data)

1. Description of Business and Summary of Significant Accounting Policies (in part)

New Accounting Pronouncements (in part)

Multiemployer Pension Plan Disclosures

In September 2011, the FASB issued an accounting standard update that requires employers that participate in multiemployer pension plans to provide additional quantitative and qualitative disclosures. The amended disclosures provide users with more detailed information about an employer's involvement in multiemployer pension plans and are effective for annual periods ending after December 15, 2011. Five of our 215 stores participate in multiemployer pension plans. We adopted this standard effective December 31, 2011, and have included the required disclosures in Note 21 of the Notes to Consolidated Financial Statements.

21. Multiemployer Pension Plans

Five of our 215 stores participate in multiemployer pension plans. We contribute to these multiemployer defined benefit pension plans under the terms of collective-bargaining agreements that cover certain of our union-represented employees. The risks of participating in these multiemployer plans are different from single-employer plans in the following aspects:

a. Assets contributed to the multiemployer plan by one employer may be used to provide benefits to employees of other participating employers.

b. If a participating employer stops contributing to the plan, the unfunded obligations of the plan may be assumed by the remaining participating employers.

c. If we choose to stop participating in a multiemployer plan, we may be required to pay the plan an amount based on the underfunded status of the plan, referred to as a withdrawal liability.

One of the multiemployer pension plans in which we participate is designated as being in "red zone" status, as defined by the Pension Protection Act (PPA) of 2006. Our participation in this plan for the year ended December 31, 2011, is outlined in the table below. The "EIN/Pension Plan Number" column provides the Employer Identification Number (EIN) and the three-digit plan number. The most recent PPA zone status available in 2011 and 2010 is for the plan's year end at December 31, 2010, and December 31, 2009, respectively. The zone status is based on information that we received from the plan and is certified by the plan's actuary. Among other factors, plans in the red zone are generally less than 65 percent funded. The last column lists the expiration date of the collective-bargaining agreements to which the plan is subject. A rehabilitation plan has been implemented for this plan. There have been no significant changes that affect the comparability of 2011, 2010, and 2009 contributions.

Pension Fund	EIN/Pension Plan Number	Pension Protection Act Zone Status 2011	2010	Contributions of autoNation ($ in Millions) 2011	2010	2009	Surcharge Imposed	Expiration Date of Collective-Bargaining Agreement
Automotive Industries Pension Plan	94-1133245-001	Red	Red	$0.5	$0.5	$0.5	No	[1]
Other funds				0.2	0.2	0.2		
Total contributions				$0.7	$0.7	$0.7		

[1] We are party to two collective-bargaining agreements that require contributions to the Automotive Industries Pension Plan. One expired May 31, 2011, and one expired June 30, 2011, and both are currently extended during collective bargaining for new agreements.

In the event that we decide to cease participating in this plan, we could be assessed a withdrawal liability. We currently do not have any plans that would trigger the withdrawal liability under this multiemployer pension plan.

1.67

EMCOR GROUP, INC. (DEC)

NOTES TO CONSOLIDATED FINANCIAL STATEMENTS

Note 2—Summary of Significant Accounting Policies (in part)

In September 2011, an accounting pronouncement was issued by the FASB to update the disclosure requirements of an employer who participates in multiemployer pension plans. This new pronouncement requires the disclosure of: (a) the amount of employer contributions made to each significant plan and to all plans in the aggregate; (b) an indication of whether the employer's contributions represent more than five percent of the total contributions to the plan; (c) an indication of which plans, if any, are subject to a funding improvement plan; (d) the expiration date(s) of collective bargaining agreement(s) and any minimum funding arrangements; (e) the most recent funded status of the plan; and (f) a description of the nature and effect of any changes affecting comparability for each period in which a statement of operations is presented. The enhanced disclosures are required for fiscal years ending after December 15, 2011. The adoption of this pronouncement did not have any effect on our financial condition or results of operations, though it will require enhanced disclosures in our notes to consolidated financial statements. See Note 16—Retirement Plans for additional information regarding multiemployer pension plans.

Note 16—Retirement Plans (in part)

Multiemployer Plans

We participate in over 175 multiemployer pension plans ("MEPPs") that provide retirement benefits to certain union employees in accordance with various collective bargaining agreements ("CBAs"). As one of many participating employers in these MEPPs, we are responsible with the other participating employers for any plan underfunding. Our contributions to a particular MEPP are established by the applicable CBAs; however, our required contributions may increase based on the funded status of an MEPP and legal requirements of the Pension Protection Act of 2006 (the "PPA"), which requires substantially underfunded MEPPs to implement a funding improvement plan ("FIP") or a rehabilitation

plan ("RP") to improve their funded status. Factors that could impact funded status of an MEPP include, without limitation, investment performance, changes in the participant demographics, decline in the number of contributing employers, changes in actuarial assumptions and the utilization of extended amortization provisions.

An FIP or RP requires a particular MEPP to adopt measures to correct its underfunding status. These measures may include, but are not limited to: (a) an increase in our contribution rate as a signatory to the applicable CBA, (b) a reallocation of the contributions already being made by participating employers for various benefits to individuals participating in the MEPP and/or (c) a reduction in the benefits to be paid to future and/or current retirees. In addition, the PPA requires that a 5% surcharge be levied on employer contributions for the first year commencing shortly after the date the employer receives notice that the MEPP is in critical status and a 10% surcharge on each succeeding year until a CBA is in place with terms and conditions consistent with the RP.

We could also be obligated to make payments to MEPPs if we either cease to have an obligation to contribute to the MEPP or significantly reduce our contributions to the MEPP because we reduce our number of employees who are covered by the relevant MEPP for various reasons, including, but not limited to, layoffs or closure of a subsidiary assuming the MEPP has unfunded vested benefits. The amount of such payments (known as a complete or partial withdrawal liability) would equal our proportionate share of the MEPPs' unfunded vested benefits. We believe that certain of the MEPPs in which we participate may have unfunded vested benefits. Due to uncertainty regarding future factors that could trigger withdrawal liability, as well as the absence of specific information regarding the MEPP's current financial situation, we are unable to determine (a) the amount and timing of any future withdrawal liability, if any, and (b) whether our participation in these MEPPs could have a material adverse impact on our financial condition, results of operations or liquidity. We did not record any withdrawal liability for the years ended December 31, 2011 and 2010. We recorded approximately $1.0 million for withdrawal liabilities for the year ended December 31, 2009.

The following table lists all domestic MEPPs to which our contributions exceeded $2.0 million in 2011. Additionally, this table also lists all domestic MEPPs to which we contributed in 2011 in excess of $0.5 million for MEPPs in the critical status, "red zone" and $1.0 million in the endangered status, "orange or yellow zones", as defined by the PPA (in thousands):

Pension Fund	EIN/Pension Plan Number	PPA Zone Status		FIP/RP Status	Contributions			Contributions Greater Than 5% of Total Plan Contributions[1]	Expiration Date of CBA
		2011	2010		2011	2010	2009		
Plumbers & Pipefitters National Pension Fund	52-6152779 001	Yellow	Yellow	Implemented	$12,279	$9,392	$9,717	No	April 2012 to April 2015
Sheet Metal Workers National Pension Fund	52-6112463 001	Red	Red	Implemented	9,665	7,688	7,474	No	May 2012 to June 2015
National Electrical Benefit Fund	53-0181657 001	Green	Green	N/A	8,541	8,100	7,035	No	February 2012 to September 2015
National Automatic Sprinkler Industry Pension Fund	52-6054620 001	Red[3]	Red[3]	Implemented	5,452	4,825	3,963	No	April 2012 to June 2014
Central Pension Fund of the International Union of Operating Engineers and Participating Employers	36-6052390 001	Green	Green	N/A	5,392	3,847	3,702	No	February 2012 to December 2015
Pension, Hospitalization & Benefit Plan of the Electrical Industry-Pension Trust Account	13-6123601 001	Green	Green	N/A	5,364	5,291	6,118	No	January 2012 to May 2013
Southern California IBEW-NECA Pension Trust Fund	95-6392774 001	Green	Red	N/A	3,345	2,541	3,155	No	May 2012 to November 2014
Plumbers Pipefitters & Mechanical Equipment Service Local Union #392 Pension Plan	31-0655223 001	Red	Red	Implemented	3,332	3,174	2,730	Yes	June 2014
Electrical Contractors Association of the City of Chicago Local Union 134, IBEW Joint Pension Trust of Chicago Pension Plan 2	51-6030753 002	Green	Green	N/A	3,019	1,780	1,556	No	June 2014
Southern California Pipe Trades Retirement Fund	51-6108443 001	Green[3]	Yellow[3]	N/A	2,903	2,944	2,186	No	June 2012 to June 2014
Arizona Pipe Trades Pension Plan	86-6025734 001	Green	Green	N/A	2,877	2,874	1,633	Yes	June 2012 to June 2014
Sheet Metal Workers Pension Plan of Northern California	51-6115939 001	Red[3]	Green[3]	Implemented	2,604	1,831	2,309	No	June 2013
Northern California Pipe Trades Pension Plan	94-3190386 001	Green[3]	Green[3]	N/A	2,596	2,464	3,986	No	June 2012 to June 2013
Electrical Workers Local No. 26 Pension Trust Fund	52-6117919 001	Green	Green	N/A	2,244	2,007	1,647	No	May 2012 to July 2012
Eighth District Electrical Pension Fund	84-6100393 001	Green	Green	N/A	2,159	2,267	1,899	No	February 2014 to May 2015
Heating, Piping & Refrigeration Pension Fund	52-1058013 001	Orange	Green	Implemented	2,143	1,578	1,460	No	July 2013
Pipefitters Union Local 537 Pension Fund	51-6030859 001	Green	Green	Implemented	2,140	2,576	3,421	Yes	July 2012 to August 2013
CT Plumbers and Pipefitters Pension Fund	06-6050353 001	Green	Red	N/A	1,690	1,695	1,245	Yes	May 2012
Boilermaker-Blacksmith National Pension Trust	48-6168020 001	Yellow	Yellow	Implemented	1,635	1,881	1,170	No	August 2012 to September 2014
Local No. 697 IBEW and Electrical Industry Pension Fund	51-6133048 001	Yellow[3]	Yellow[3]	Implemented	1,557	1,383	1,100	Yes	May 2012
Sheet Metal Workers Pension Plan of Southern California, Arizona & Nevada	95-6052257 001	Red[3]	Red[3]	Pending[2]	1,396	1,731	1,906	No	June 2014 to June 2016

SEC 1.67

Pension Fund	EIN/Pension Plan Number	PPA Zone Status		FIP/RP Status	Contributions			Contributions Greater Than 5% of Total Plan Contributions[1]	Expiration Date of CBA
		2011	2010		2011	2010	2009		
IBEW Local 531 & NECA Pension Plan	35-6068417 001	Yellow[3]	Yellow[3]	Implemented	1,263	581	175	Yes	September 2012
Pipefitters Retirement Fund, Local 597	62-6105084 001	Yellow	Yellow	Implemented	1,210	875	810	No	May 2012 to May 2014
IBEW Local 456 Pension Plan	22-6238995 001	Yellow	Yellow	Implemented	1,175	2,047	764	Yes	May 2014
Construction Industry Laborers Pension Fund	43-6060737 001	Red[3]	Red[3]	Implemented	1,148	1,165	1,290	Yes	August 2016
Steamfitters Local Union No. 420 Pension Plan	23-2004424 001	Yellow	Red	Implemented	1,138	1,234	1,235	No	April 2013 to April 2014
Pension Fund of Local Union No. 274	22-1665268 001	Yellow[3]	Red[3]	Implemented	1,094	583	801	Yes	April 2013
Plumbers Local 9 Pension Plan	51-0219541 001	Red	Yellow	Implemented	944	483	127	No	June 2013
Plumbers and Steamfitters Local No. 166 AFL—CIO Pension Plan	51-6132690 001	Red	Red	Implemented	901	930	354	Yes	May 2012
Carpenters Pension Trust Fund For Northern California	94-6050970 001	Red	Red	Implemented	512	313	344	No	July 2015
Other Multiemployer Pension Plans					37,944	40,203	42,682		Various
Total Contributions					$129,662	$120,283	$117,994		

[1] This information was obtained from the respective plans' Form 5500 for the most current available filing. These dates may not correspond with our fiscal year contributions. The above noted percentages of contributions are based upon disclosures contained in the plans' Form 5500 filing ("Forms"). Those Forms, among other things, disclose the names of individual participating employers whose annual contributions account for more than 5% of the aggregate annual amount contributed by all participating employers for a plan year. Accordingly, if the annual contribution of two or more of our subsidiaries each accounted for less than 5% of such contributions, but in the aggregate accounted for in excess of 5% of such contributions, that greater percentage is not available and accordingly is not disclosed.

[2] For these respective plans, a funding surcharge is currently in effect for 2011.

[3] This zone status represents the most recent available information for the respective MEPP, which is 2010 for the 2011 year and 2009 for the 2010 year.

The nature and diversity of our business may result in volatility of the amount of our contributions to a particular MEPP for any given period. That is because, in any given market, we could be working on a significant project and/or projects, which could result in an increase in our direct labor force and a corresponding increase in our contributions to the MEPP(s) dictated by the applicable CBA. When that particular project(s) finishes and is not replaced, the level of direct labor would also decrease, as would our level of contributions to the particular MEPP(s). Additionally, the level of contributions to a particular MEPP could also be affected by the terms of the CBA, which could require at a particular time, an increase in the contribution rate and/or surcharges. We have also acquired various companies since 2009, some of which participate in MEPPs, and as a result, our level of contributions have increased as a result of including the acquired companies' contributions with respect to a particular MEPP in our consolidated information. As a result of these acquisitions, our contributions to various MEPPs increased by $10.1 million, $3.4 million and $0.9 million in the years ended December 31, 2011, 2010 and 2009, respectively.

We also participate in two MEPPs that are located within the United Kingdom for which we have contributed $0.3 million for each of the years ended December 31, 2011, 2010 and 2009. The information that we have obtained relating to these plans is not as readily available and/or comparable as the information that has been ascertained in the United States. Based upon the most recently available information, one of the plans is at least 80% funded, and the other plan is between 65% and 80% funded. A recovery plan has been put in place for the plan that is between 65% and 80% funded, which required higher contribution amounts to be paid by our UK operations.

Additionally, we contribute to certain multiemployer plans that provide post retirement benefits such as health and welfare benefits and/or defined contribution/annuity plans, among others. Our contributions to these plans approximated $64.2 million, $54.1 million and $52.5 million for the years ended December 31, 2011, 2010 and 2009, respectively. Acquisitions during the period of 2009 to 2011 account for an increase in our contributions to these types of plans of $2.9 million, $0.2 million and $0.1 million in the years ended December 31, 2011, 2010 and 2009, respectively. The level of funding for these plans is also subject for the most part to the factors discussed above in conjunction with the MEPPs.

Change in Accounting Principle: Comprehensive Income

1.68

CONOCOPHILLIPS (DEC)

CONSOLIDATED STATEMENT OF COMPREHENSIVE INCOME

	Millions of Dollars		
Years Ended December 31	**2011**	**2010**	**2009**
Net Income	$12,502	11,417	4,492
Other comprehensive income (loss)			
Defined benefit plans			
Prior service cost (credit) arising during the period	19	(13)	—
Reclassification adjustment for amortization of prior service cost included in net income	2	15	21
Net change	21	2	21
Net actuarial loss arising during the period	(1,185)	(9)	(388)
Reclassification adjustment for amortization of prior net losses included in net income	226	215	206
Net change	(959)	206	(182)
Nonsponsored plans*	(50)	5	39
Income taxes on defined benefit plans	375	(67)	52
Defined benefit plans, net of tax	(613)	146	(70)
Unrealized holding gain on securities**	8	631	—
Reclassification adjustment for gain included in net income	(255)	(384)	—
Income taxes on unrealized holding gain on securities	89	(89)	—
Unrealized gain on securities, net of tax	(158)	158	—
Foreign currency translation adjustments	(387)	1,417	5,092
Reclassification adjustment for gain included in net income	(516)	—	—
Income taxes on foreign currency translation adjustments	(14)	(13)	(85)
Foreign currency translation adjustments, net of tax	(917)	1,404	5,007
Hedging activities	1	—	(2)
Income taxes on hedging activities	—	—	5
Hedging activities, net of tax	1	—	3
Other comprehensive income (loss), net of tax	(1,687)	1,708	4,940
Comprehensive income	10,815	13,125	9,432
Less: comprehensive income attributable to noncontrolling interests	(66)	(59)	(78)
Comprehensive Income Attributable to ConocoPhillips	$10,749	13,066	9,354

* Plans for which ConocoPhillips is not the primary obligor—primarily those administered by equity affiliates.
* Available-for-sale securities of LUKOIL.
See Notes to Consolidated Financial Statements.

NOTES TO CONSOLIDATED FINANCIAL STATEMENTS

Note 2—Changes in Accounting Principles

Comprehensive Income

Effective December 31, 2011, we early adopted Financial Accounting Standards Board (FASB) Accounting Standards Update (ASU) No. 2011-05, "Presentation of Comprehensive Income." This ASU amends FASB Accounting Standards Codification (ASC) Topic 220, "Comprehensive Income," by requiring a more prominent presentation of the components of other comprehensive income. We elected the two-statement approach presenting other comprehensive income in a separate statement immediately following the income statement. On December 23, 2011, the FASB issued ASU 2011-12, "Deferral of the Effective Date for Amendments to the Presentation of Reclassifications of Items Out of Accumulated Other Comprehensive Income in ASU No. 2011-05." ASU 2011-12 defers the ASU 2011-05 requirement to present items reclassified into net income from other comprehensive income. This deferral only impacted the presentation requirement on the consolidated income statement.

Change in Accounting Principle: Goodwill

1.69

FIRST SOLAR, INC. (DEC)

NOTES TO CONSOLIDATED FINANCIAL STATEMENTS

Note 2. Summary of Significant Accounting Policies (in part)

Goodwill. Goodwill represents the excess of the purchase price of acquired businesses over the estimated fair value assigned to the individual assets acquired and liabilities assumed. We do not amortize goodwill, but instead are required to test goodwill for impairment at least annually in the fourth quarter and, if necessary, we would record any impairment in accordance with ASC 350, *Intangibles—Goodwill and Other.* We will perform an impairment test between scheduled annual tests if facts and circumstances indicate that it is more-likely-than-not that the fair value of a reporting unit that has goodwill is less than its carrying value.

In accordance with ASC 350, as amended by ASU 2011-08, the provisions of which we elected to adopt on October 1, 2011, we may first make a qualitative assessment of whether it is more-likely-than-not that a reporting unit's fair value is less than its carrying value to determine whether it is necessary to perform the two-step goodwill impairment test. The qualitative impairment test includes considering various factors including macroeconomic conditions, industry and market conditions, cost factors, a sustained share price or market capitalization decrease, and any reporting unit specific events. If it is determined through the qualitative assessment that a reporting unit's fair value is more-likely-than-not greater than its carrying value, the two-step impairment test is not required. If the qualitative assessment indicates it is more-likely-than-not that a reporting unit's fair value is not greater than its carrying value, we must perform the two-step impairment test. We may also elect to proceed directly to the two-step impairment test without considering such qualitative factors.

The first step in a two-step impairment test is the comparison of the fair value of a reporting unit with its carrying amount, including goodwill. Our two reporting units are the components and systems reporting units, which are the same as our reportable segments as described in Note 24. "Segment and Geographical Information," to our consolidated financial statements. In accordance with the authoritative guidance over fair value measurements, we define the fair value of a reporting unit as the price that would be received to sell the unit as a whole in an orderly transaction between market participants at the measurement date. We primarily use the income approach methodology of valuation, which includes the discounted cash flow method, and the market approach methodology of valuation, which considers values of comparable businesses to estimate the fair values of our reporting units. We do not believe that a cost approach is relevant to measuring the fair values of our reporting units.

Significant management judgment is required when estimating the fair value of our reporting units including the forecasting of future operating results, the discount rates and expected future growth rates that we use in the discounted cash flow method of valuation, and in the selection of comparable businesses that we use in the market approach. If the estimated fair value of the reporting unit exceeds the carrying value assigned to that unit, goodwill is not impaired and no further analysis is required.

If the carrying value assigned to a reporting unit exceeds its estimated fair value in the first step, then we are required to perform the second step of the impairment test. In this step, we assign the fair value of the reporting unit calculated in step one to all of the assets and liabilities of that reporting unit, as if a market participant just acquired the reporting unit in a business combination. The excess of the fair value of the reporting unit determined in the first step of the impairment test over the total amount assigned to the assets and liabilities in the second step of the impairment test represents the implied fair value of goodwill. If the carrying value of a reporting unit's goodwill exceeds the implied fair value of goodwill, we would record an impairment loss equal to the difference. If there is no such excess then all goodwill for a reporting unit is considered impaired.

See Note 5. "Goodwill and Intangible Assets," to our consolidated financial statements for additional information on our goodwill impairment tests.

Note 3. Recent Accounting Pronouncements (in part)

In December 2010, the Financial Accounting Standards Board (FASB) issued Accounting Standards Update (ASU) 2010-28, *When to Perform Step 2 of the Goodwill Impairment Test for Reporting Units with Zero or Negative Carrying Amounts.* This ASU amends guidance for Step 1 of the goodwill impairment test for reporting units with zero or negative carrying amounts. For those reporting units, an entity is required to perform Step 2 of the goodwill impairment test if it is more likely than not that a goodwill impairment exists. ASU 2010-28 is effective for fiscal years and interim periods beginning after December 15, 2010, with early adoption not permitted. The adoption of ASU 2010-28 did not have a material impact on our financial position, results of operations, or cash flows.

In September 2011, the FASB issued ASU 2011-08, *Intangibles—Goodwill and Other (Topic 350): Testing Goodwill for Impairment.* ASU 2011-08 permits an entity to make a qualitative assessment of whether it is more-likely-than-not that a reporting unit's fair value is less than its carrying value to determine whether it is necessary to perform the two-step goodwill impairment test. If it is determined through the qualitative assessment that a reporting unit's fair value is more-likely-than-not greater than its carrying value, the two-step impairment tests are not required. The qualitative assessment is optional, allowing entities to go directly to the two-step impairment test. ASU 2011-08 is effective for annual and interim goodwill impairment tests performed in fiscal years beginning after December 15, 2011, with early adoption permitted. We elected to adopt the guidance effective October 1, 2011. The adoption of ASU 2011-08 did not have an impact on our financial position, results of operations, or cash flows.

Note 5. Goodwill and Intangible Assets (in part)

Goodwill

The changes in the carrying amount of goodwill for the years ended December 31, 2011 and December 31, 2010 were as follows (in thousands):

	Components	Systems	Consolidated
Ending balance, December 26, 2009	$ 251,275	$35,240	$ 286,515
Goodwill from acquisition	142,090	4,683	146,773
Ending balance, December 31, 2010	393,365	39,923	433,288
Goodwill from acquisition	—	25,521	25,521
Goodwill impairment	(393,365)	—	(393,365)
Ending balance, December 31, 2011	$ —	$65,444	$ 65,444

Goodwill represents the excess of the purchase price of acquired businesses over the estimated fair value assigned to the individual assets acquired and liabilities assumed. We do not amortize goodwill, but instead are required to test goodwill for impairment at least annually in the fourth quarter and, if necessary, we would record any impairment in accordance with ASC 350, *Intangibles—Goodwill and Other*. We will perform an impairment test between scheduled annual tests if facts and circumstances indicate that it is more-likely-than-not that the fair value of a reporting unit that has goodwill is less than its carrying value. See Note 2. "Summary of Significant Accounting Policies," for details on our policy on goodwill impairment testing.

As of December 31, 2010, the $393.4 million in goodwill related to our components reporting unit primarily represented goodwill allocated from the acquisitions of OptiSolar in 2009 and NextLight in 2010. The allocation of substantially all the goodwill from these acquisitions to our components reporting unit represented the expected synergies, economies of scale and vertical integration our components business would realize from using our solar modules in the project pipelines obtained from these acquisitions. The goodwill allocation to our components business was consistent with our historical view that the systems business has functioned as an "enabler" for the components business to drive module throughput. Once goodwill has been assigned to a reporting unit, for accounting purposes, the goodwill is no longer directly associated with the underlying acquisitions that the goodwill originated from, but rather the reporting unit to which it has been allocated.

We commenced our annual goodwill impairment test in the fourth quarter of 2011 (as of October 1, 2011). However, considering qualitative factors including the continuing reduction in our market capitalization during December 2011 and our new business strategy and 2012 outlook announced in December 2011, we concluded that a two-step goodwill impairment test was required for both of our reporting units.

In estimating the fair value of our reporting units in the first step of the impairment test, significant management judgment was required. In using the income approach methodology of valuation, our estimates to determine the fair value of our reporting units included management judgment related to forecasts of future operating results, discount rates, and expected future growth rates that are used in the discounted cash flow method of valuation. In using the market approach methodology of valuation, we must make judgments related to the selection of comparable businesses. The sum of the fair values of our reporting units is also compared to our external market capitalization in order for us to assess the appropriateness of such estimates. The underlying assumptions used in the first step of the impairment test considered our market capitalization as of December 31, 2011 and the current industry environment and its expected impact on the fair value of our reporting units. We determined that the fair value of our systems reporting unit exceeded the carrying value by a significant amount indicating no impairment was necessary for the systems reporting unit. We determined the fair value of the components reporting unit was less than the carrying value, which required us to perform the second step of the impairment test for the components reporting unit.

We performed the second step of the impairment test to determine the implied fair value of goodwill for the components reporting unit, which requires us to allocate the fair value of the components reporting unit determined in step one to all of the assets and liabilities including any unrecognized intangible assets of the components reporting unit. We determined the implied fair value of goodwill in the components reporting unit to be zero. As a result, we impaired all of the goodwill in the components reporting unit and recorded $393.4 million of impairment expense, which also represents our accumulated goodwill impairment losses.

We recorded no goodwill impairment charges for the years ended December 31, 2010, and December 26, 2009.

Change in Accounting Principle: Troubled Debt Restructuring

1.70

GENERAL ELECTRIC COMPANY (DEC)

NOTES TO CONSOLIDATED FINANCIAL STATEMENTS

Note 1. Summary of Significant Accounting Policies (in part)

Accounting Changes (in part)

On July 1, 2011, we adopted FASB ASU 2011-02, an amendment to ASC 310, *Receivables*. ASU 2011-02 provides guidance for determining whether a restructuring of a debt constitutes a TDR. ASU 2011-02 requires that a restructuring be classified as a TDR when it is both a concession and the debtor is experiencing financial difficulties. The amendment also clarifies the guidance on a creditor's evaluation of whether it has granted a concession. The amendment applies to restructurings that have occurred subsequent to January 1, 2011. As a result of adopting these amendments on July 1, 2011, we have classified an additional $271 million of financing receivables as TDRs and have recorded an increase of $77 million to our allowance for losses on financing receivables. See Note 23.

Note 23. Supplemental Information About the Credit Quality of Financing Receivables and Allowance for Losses on Financing Receivables

We provide further detailed information about the credit quality of our Commercial, Real Estate and Consumer financing receivables portfolios. For each portfolio, we describe the characteristics of the financing receivables and provide information about collateral, payment performance, credit quality indicators, and impairment. We manage these portfolios using delinquency and nonearning data as key performance indicators. The categories used within this section such as impaired loans, TDR and nonaccrual financing receivables are defined by the authoritative guidance and we base our categorization on the related scope and definitions contained in the related standards. The categories of nonearning and delinquent are defined by us and are used in our process for managing our financing receivables. Definitions of these categories are provided in Note 1.

Commercial

Financing Receivables and Allowance for Losses

The following table provides further information about general and specific reserves related to Commercial financing receivables.

Commercial (In millions)	Financing Receivables at	
	December 31, 2011	December 31, 2010
CLL		
Americas[a]	$ 80,505	$ 88,558
Europe	36,899	37,498
Asia	11,635	11,943
Other[a]	436	664
Total CLL	129,475	138,663
Energy Financial Services	5,912	7,011
GECAS	11,901	12,615
Other	1,282	1,788
Total Commercial financing receivables, before allowance for losses	$148,570	$160,077
Non-impaired financing receivables	$142,908	$154,257
General reserves	718	1,014
Impaired loans	5,662	5,820
Specific reserves	812	1,031

[a] During 2011, we transferred our Railcar lending and leasing portfolio from CLL Other to CLL Americas. Prior-period amounts were reclassified to conform to the current-period presentation.

Past Due Financing Receivables

The following table displays payment performance of Commercial financing receivables.

	At			
	December 31, 2011		December 31, 2010	
Commercial	Over 30 Days Past Due	Over 90 Days Past Due	Over 30 Days Past Due	Over 90 Days Past Due
CLL				
Americas	1.3%	0.8%	1.2%	0.8%
Europe	3.8	2.1	4.2	2.3
Asia	1.3	1.0	2.2	1.4
Other	2.0	0.1	2.4	1.2
Total CLL	2.0	1.2	2.1	1.3
Energy Financial Services	0.3	0.3	0.9	0.8
GECAS	—	—	—	—
Other	3.7	3.5	5.8	5.5
Total	2.0	1.1	2.0	1.2

Nonaccrual Financing Receivables

The following table provides further information about Commercial financing receivables that are classified as nonaccrual. Of our $4,718 million and $5,463 million of nonaccrual

financing receivables at December 31, 2011 and December 31, 2010, respectively, $1,227 million and $1,016 million are currently paying in accordance with their contractual terms, respectively.

Commercial (In millions)	Nonaccrual Financing Receivables at		Nonearning Financing Receivables at	
	December 31, 2011	December 31, 2010	December 31, 2011	December 31, 2010
CLL				
Americas	$2,417	$3,208	$1,862	$2,573
Europe	1,599	1,415	1,167	1,241
Asia	428	616	269	406
Other	68	7	11	6
Total CLL	4,512	5,246	3,309	4,226
Energy Financial Services	22	78	22	62
GECAS	69	—	55	—
Other	115	139	65	102
Total	$4,718	$5,463	$3,451	$4,390
Allowance for losses percentage	32.4%	37.4%	44.3%	46.6%

Impaired Loans

The following table provides information about loans classified as impaired and specific reserves related to Commercial.

Commercial[a] (In millions)	With No Specific Allowance			With a Specific Allowance			
	Recorded Investment in Loans	Unpaid Principal Balance	Average Investment in Loans	Recorded Investment in Loans	Unpaid Principal Balance	Associated Allowance	Average Investment in Loans
December 31, 2011							
CLL							
Americas	$2,136	$2,219	$2,128	$1,367	$1,415	$ 425	$1,468
Europe	936	1,060	1,001	730	717	263	602
Asia	85	83	94	156	128	84	214
Other	54	58	13	11	11	2	5
Total CLL	3,211	3,420	3,236	2,264	2,271	774	$2,289
Energy Financial Services	4	4	20	18	18	9	87
GECAS	28	28	59	—	—	—	11
Other	62	63	67	75	75	29	97
Total	$3,305	$3,515	$3,382	$2,357	$2,364	$ 812	$2,484
December 31, 2010							
CLL							
Americas	$2,030	$2,127	$1,547	$1,699	$1,744	$ 589	$1,754
Europe	802	674	629	566	566	267	563
Asia	119	117	117	338	303	132	334
Other	—	—	9	—	—	—	—
Total CLL	2,951	2,918	2,302	2,603	2,613	988	2,651
Energy Financial Services	54	61	76	24	24	6	70
GECAS	24	24	50	—	—	—	31
Other	58	57	30	106	99	37	82
Total	$3,087	$3,060	$2,458	$2,733	$2,736	$1,031	$2,834

[a] We recognized $193 million and $88 million of interest income, including $59 million and $39 million on a cash basis, for the years ended December 31, 2011 and 2010, respectively, principally in our CLL Americas business. The total average investment in impaired loans for the years ended December 31, 2011 and 2010 was $5,866 million and $5,292 million, respectively.

Impaired loans classified as TDRs in our CLL business were $3,642 million and $2,911 million at December 31, 2011 and 2010, respectively, and were primarily attributable to CLL Americas ($2,746 million and $2,347 million, respectively). For the year ended December 31, 2011, we modified $1,856 million of loans classified as TDRs, primarily in CLL Americas ($1,105 million) and CLL EMEA ($646 million). Changes to these loans primarily included debt to equity exchange, extensions, interest only payment periods and forbearance or other actions, which are in addition to, or sometimes in lieu of, fees and rate increases. Of our modifications classified as TDRs in the last year, $101 million have subsequently experienced a payment default.

Credit Quality Indicators

Substantially all of our Commercial financing receivables portfolio is secured lending and we assess the overall quality of the portfolio based on the potential risk of loss measure. The metric incorporates both the borrower's credit quality along with any related collateral protection.

Our internal risk ratings process is an important source of information in determining our allowance for losses and represents a comprehensive, statistically validated approach to evaluate risk in our financing receivables portfolios. In deriving our internal risk ratings, we stratify our Commercial portfolios into twenty-one categories of default risk and/or six categories of loss given default to group into three categories: A, B and C. Our process starts by developing an internal risk rating for our borrowers, which are based upon our proprietary models using data derived from borrower financial statements, agency ratings, payment history information, equity prices and other commercial borrower characteristics. We then evaluate the potential risk of loss for the specific lending transaction in the event of borrower default, which takes into account such factors as applicable collateral value, historical loss and recovery rates for similar transactions, and our collection capabilities. Our internal risk ratings process and the models we use are subject to regular monitoring and validation controls. The frequency of rating updates is set by our credit risk policy, which requires annual Audit Committee approval. The models are updated on a regular basis and statistically validated annually, or more frequently as circumstances warrant.

The table below summarizes our Commercial financing receivables by risk category. As described above, financing receivables are assigned one of twenty-one risk ratings based on our process and then these are grouped by similar characteristics into three categories in the table below. Category A is characterized by either high credit quality borrowers or transactions with significant collateral coverage which substantially reduces or eliminates the risk of loss in the event of borrower default. Category B is characterized by borrowers with weaker credit quality than those in Category A, or transactions with moderately strong collateral coverage which minimizes but may not fully mitigate the risk of loss in the event of default. Category C is characterized by borrowers with higher levels of default risk relative to our overall portfolio or transactions where collateral coverage may not fully mitigate a loss in the event of default.

Commercial	Secured			
(In millions)	A	B	C	Total
December 31, 2011				
CLL				
Americas[a]	$ 73,103	$2,816	$4,586	$ 80,505
Europe	33,481	1,080	1,002	35,563
Asia	10,644	116	685	11,445
Other[a]	345	—	91	436
Total CLL	117,573	4,012	6,364	127,949
Energy Financial Services	5,727	24	18	5,769
GECAS	10,881	970	50	11,901
Other	1,282	—	—	1,282
Total	$135,463	$5,006	$6,432	$146,901
December 31, 2010				
CLL				
Americas[a]	$ 78,939	$4,103	$5,516	$ 88,558
Europe	33,642	840	1,262	35,744
Asia	10,777	199	766	11,742
Other[a]	544	66	54	664
Total CLL	123,902	5,208	7,598	136,708
Energy Financial Services	6,775	183	53	7,011
GECAS	11,034	1,193	388	12,615
Other	1,788	—	—	1,788
Total	$143,499	$6,584	$8,039	$158,122

[a] During 2011, we transferred our Railcar lending and leasing portfolio from CLL Other to CLL Americas. Prior-period amounts were reclassified to conform to the current-period presentation.

For our secured financing receivables portfolio, our collateral position and ability to work out problem accounts mitigates our losses. Our asset managers have deep industry expertise that enables us to identify the optimum approach to default situations. We price risk premiums for weaker credits at origination, closely monitor changes in creditworthiness through our risk ratings and watch list process, and are engaged early with deteriorating credits to minimize economic loss. Secured financing receivables within risk Category C are predominantly in our CLL businesses and are primarily composed of senior term lending facilities and factoring programs secured by various asset types including inventory, accounts receivable, cash, equipment and related business facilities as well as franchise finance activities secured by underlying equipment.

Loans within Category C are reviewed and monitored regularly, and classified as impaired when it is probable that they will not pay in accordance with contractual terms. Our internal risk rating process identifies credits warranting closer monitoring; and as such, these loans are not necessarily classified as nonearning or impaired.

Substantially all of our unsecured Commercial financing receivables portfolio is attributable to our Interbanca S.p.A. and GE Sanyo Credit acquisitions in Europe and Asia, respectively. At December 31, 2011 and December 31, 2010,

these financing receivables included $325 million and $208 million rated A, $748 million and $964 million rated B, and $596 million and $783 million rated C, respectively.

Real Estate

Financing Receivables and Allowance for Losses

The following table provides further information about general and specific reserves related to Real Estate financing receivables.

Real Estate	Financing Receivables at	
(In millions)	December 31, 2011	December 31, 2010
Debt	$24,501	$30,249
Business Properties	8,248	9,962
Total Real Estate financing receivables, before allowance for losses	$32,749	$40,211
Non-impaired financing receivables	$24,002	$30,394
General reserves	267	338
Impaired loans	8,747	9,817
Specific reserves	822	1,150

Past Due Financing Receivables

The following table displays payment performance of Real Estate financing receivables.

	At			
	December 31, 2011		December 31, 2010	
Real Estate	Over 30 Days Past Due	Over 90 Days Past Due	Over 30 Days Past Due	Over 90 Days Past Due
Debt	2.4%	2.3%	4.3%	4.1%
Business Properties	3.9	3.0	4.6	3.9
Total	2.8	2.5	4.4	4.0

Nonaccrual Financing Receivables

The following table provides further information about Real Estate financing receivables that are classified as nonaccrual. Of our $6,949 million and $9,719 million of nonaccrual financing receivables at December 31, 2011 and December 31, 2010, respectively, $6,061 million and $7,888 million are currently paying in accordance with their contractual terms, respectively.

Real Estate	Nonaccrual Financing Receivables at		Nonearning Financing Receivables at	
(Dollars in millions)	December 31, 2011	December 31, 2010	December 31, 2011	December 31, 2010
Debt	$6,351	$9,039	$541	$ 961
Business Properties	598	680	249	386
Total	$6,949	$9,719	$790	$1,347
Allowance for losses percentage	15.7%	15.3%	137.8%	110.5%

Impaired Loans

The following table provides information about loans classified as impaired and specific reserves related to Real Estate.

Real Estate[a] (In millions)	With No Specific Allowance			With a Specific Allowance			
	Recorded Investment in Loans	Unpaid Principal Balance	Average Investment in Loans	Recorded Investment in Loans	Unpaid Principal Balance	Associated Allowance	Average Investment in Loans
December 31, 2011							
Debt	$3,558	$3,614	$3,568	$4,560	$4,652	$ 717	$5,435
Business Properties	232	232	215	397	397	105	460
Total	$3,790	$3,846	$3,783	$4,957	$5,049	$ 822	$5,895
December 31, 2010							
Debt	$2,814	$2,873	$1,598	$6,323	$6,498	$1,007	$6,116
Business Properties	191	213	141	489	476	143	382
Total	$3,005	$3,086	$1,739	$6,812	$6,974	$1,150	$6,498

[a] We recognized $399 million and $189 million of interest income, including $339 million and $189 million on a cash basis, for the years ended December 31, 2011 and 2010, respectively, principally in our Real Estate-Debt portfolio. The total average investment in impaired loans for the years ended December 31, 2011 and 2010 was $9,678 million and $8,237 million, respectively.

Real Estate TDRs increased from $4,866 million at December 31, 2010 to $7,006 million at December 31, 2011, primarily driven by loans scheduled to mature during 2011, some of which were modified during 2011 and classified as TDRs upon modification. We deem loan modifications to be TDRs when we have granted a concession to a borrower experiencing financial difficulty and we do not receive adequate compensation in the form of an effective interest rate that is at current market rates of interest given the risk characteristics of the loan or other consideration that compensates us for the value of the concession. The limited liquidity and higher return requirements in the real estate market for loans with higher loan-to-value (LTV) ratios has typically resulted in the conclusion that the modified terms are not at current market rates of interest, even if the modified loans are ex-

pected to be fully recoverable. For the year ended December 31, 2011, we modified $3,965 million of loans classified as TDRs, substantially all in our Debt portfolio. Changes to these loans primarily included maturity extensions, principal payment acceleration, changes to collateral or covenant terms and cash sweeps, which are in addition to, or sometimes in lieu of, fees and rate increases. Of our modifications classified as TDRs in the last year, $140 million have subsequently experienced a payment default.

Credit Quality Indicators

Due to the primarily non-recourse nature of our Debt portfolio, loan-to-value ratios provide the best indicators of the credit quality of the portfolio. By contrast, the credit quality of the Business Properties portfolio is primarily influenced by the strength of the borrower's general credit quality, which is reflected in our internal risk rating process, consistent with the process we use for our Commercial portfolio.

(In millions)	Loan-to-Value Ratio at					
	December 31, 2011			December 31, 2010		
	Less Than 80%	80% to 95%	Greater Than 95%	Less Than 80%	80% to 95%	Greater Than 95%
Debt	$14,454	$4,593	$5,454	$12,362	$9,392	$8,495

(In millions)	Internal Risk Rating at					
	December 31, 2011			December 31, 2010		
	A	B	C	A	B	C
Business Properties	$7,628	$110	$510	$8,746	$437	$779

Within Real Estate-Debt, these financing receivables are primarily concentrated in our North American and European Lending platforms and are secured by various property types. A substantial majority of the Real Estate-Debt financing receivables with loan-to-value ratios greater than

95% are paying in accordance with contractual terms. Substantially all of these loans and substantially all of the Real Estate-Business Properties financing receivables included in Category C are impaired loans which are subject to the specific reserve evaluation process described in Note 1. The ultimate recoverability of impaired loans is driven by collection strategies that do not necessarily depend on the sale of the underlying collateral and include full or partial repayments through third-party refinancing and restructurings.

Consumer

At December 31, 2011, our U.S. consumer financing receivables included private-label credit card and sales financing for approximately 56 million customers across the U.S. with no metropolitan area accounting for more than 5% of the portfolio. Of the total U.S. consumer financing receivables, approximately 65% relate to credit card loans, which are often subject to profit and loss sharing arrangements with the retailer (which are recorded in revenues), and the remaining 35% are sales finance receivables, which provide financing to customers in areas such as electronics, recreation, medical and home improvement.

Financing Receivables and Allowance for Losses

The following table provides further information about general and specific reserves related to Consumer financing receivables.

	Financing Receivables at	
Consumer (In millions)	December 31, 2011	December 31, 2010
Non-U.S. residential mortgages	$ 36,170	$ 40,011
Non-U.S. installment and revolving credit	18,544	20,132
U.S. installment and revolving credit	46,689	43,974
Non-U.S. auto	5,691	7,558
Other	7,244	8,304
Total Consumer financing receivables, before allowance for losses	$114,338	$119,979
Non-impaired financing receivables	$111,233	$117,431
General reserves	3,014	3,945
Impaired loans	3,105	2,548
Specific reserves	717	555

Past Due Financing Receivables

The following table displays payment performance of Consumer financing receivables.

	At			
	December 31, 2011		December 31, 2010	
Consumer	Over 30 Days Past Due	Over 90 Days Past Due[a]	Over 30 Days Past Due	Over 90 Days Past Due[a]
Non-U.S. residential mortgages	13.4%	8.8%	13.7%	8.8%
Non-U.S. installment and revolving credit	4.1	1.2	4.5	1.3
U.S. installment and revolving credit	5.0	2.2	6.2	2.8
Non-U.S. auto	3.1	0.5	3.3	0.6
Other	3.5	2.0	4.2	2.3
Total	7.3	4.0	8.1	4.4

[a] Included $45 million and $65 million of loans at December 31, 2011 and December 31, 2010, respectively, which are over 90 days past due and accruing interest, mainly representing accretion on loans acquired at a discount.

Nonaccrual Financing Receivables

The following table provides further information about Consumer financing receivables that are classified as nonaccrual.

	Nonaccrual Financing Receivables at		Nonearning Financing Receivables at	
Consumer (Dollars in millions)	December 31, 2011	December 31, 2010	December 31, 2011	December 31, 2010
Non-U.S. residential mortgages	$3,475	$3,986	$3,349	$3,738
Non-U.S. installment and revolving credit	321	302	263	289
U.S. installment and revolving credit	990	1,201	990	1,201
Non-U.S. auto	43	46	43	46
Other	487	600	419	478
Total	$5,316	$6,135	$5,064	$5,752
Allowance for losses percentage	70.2%	73.3%	73.7%	78.2%

SEC 1.70

Impaired Loans

The vast majority of our Consumer nonaccrual financing receivables are smaller balance homogeneous loans evaluated collectively, by portfolio, for impairment and therefore are outside the scope of the disclosure requirement for impaired loans. Accordingly, impaired loans in our Consumer business represent restructured smaller balance homogeneous loans meeting the definition of a TDR, and are therefore subject to the disclosure requirement for impaired loans, and commercial loans in our Consumer—Other portfolio. The recorded investment of these impaired loans totaled $3,105 million (with an unpaid principal balance of $2,679 million) and comprised $69 million with no specific allowance, primarily all in our Consumer—Other portfolio, and $3,036 million with a specific allowance of $717 million at December 31, 2011. The impaired loans with a specific allowance included $369 million with a specific allowance of $102 million in our Consumer—Other portfolio and $2,667 million with a specific allowance of $615 million across the remaining Consumer business and had an unpaid principal balance and average investment of $2,244 million and $2,343 million, respectively, at December 31, 2011. We recognized $141 million and $114 million of interest income, including $15 million and $30 million on a cash basis, for the years ended December 31, 2011 and 2010, respectively, principally in our Consumer—Non-U.S. and U.S. installment and revolving credit portfolios. The total average investment in impaired loans for the years ended December 31, 2011 and 2010 was $2,840 million and $2,009 million, respectively.

Impaired loans classified as TDRs in our Consumer business were $2,935 million and $2,256 million at December 31, 2011 and 2010, respectively. We utilize certain loan modification programs for borrowers experiencing financial difficulties in our Consumer loan portfolio. These loan modification programs primarily include interest rate reductions and payment deferrals in excess of three months, which were not part of the terms of the original contract, and are primarily concen-

trated in our non-U.S. residential mortgage and U.S. credit card portfolios. For the year ended December 31, 2011, we modified $1,970 million of consumer loans for borrowers experiencing financial difficulties, which are classified as TDRs, and included $1,020 million of non-U.S. consumer loans, primarily residential mortgages, credit cards and personal loans and approximately $950 million of credit card loans in the U.S. We expect borrowers whose loans have been modified under these programs to continue to be able to meet their contractual obligations upon the conclusion of the modification. For loans modified as TDRs in the last year, $251 million have subsequently experienced a payment default, primarily in our U.S. credit card and non-U.S. residential mortgage portfolios.

Credit Quality Indicators

Our Consumer financing receivables portfolio comprises both secured and unsecured lending. Secured financing receivables comprise residential loans and lending to small and medium-sized enterprises predominantly secured by auto and equipment, inventory finance and cash flow loans. Unsecured financing receivables include private-label credit card financing. A substantial majority of these cards are not for general use and are limited to the products and services sold by the retailer. The private label portfolio is diverse with no metropolitan area accounting for more than 5% of the related portfolio.

Non-U.S. Residential Mortgages

For our secured non-U.S. residential mortgage book, we assess the overall credit quality of the portfolio through loan-to-value ratios (the ratio of the outstanding debt on a property to the value of that property at origination). In the event of default and repossession of the underlying collateral, we have the ability to remarket and sell the properties to eliminate or mitigate the potential risk of loss. The table below provides additional information about our non-U.S. residential mortgages based on loan-to-value ratios.

| | Loan-to-Value Ratio at | | | | | |
| | December 31, 2011 | | | December 31, 2010 | | |
(In millions)	80% or Less	Greater Than 80% to 90%	Greater Than 90%	80% or Less	Greater Than 80% to 90%	Greater Than 90%
Non-U.S.residential mortgages	$20,379	$6,145	$9,646	$22,403	$7,023	$10,585

The majority of these financing receivables are in our U.K. and France portfolios and have re-indexed loan-to-value ratios of 84% and 56%, respectively. We have third-party mortgage insurance for approximately 68% of the balance of Consumer non-U.S. residential mortgage loans with loan-to-value ratios greater than 90% at December 31, 2011. Such loans were primarily originated in the U.K. and France.

Installment and Revolving Credit

For our unsecured lending products, including the non-U.S. and U.S. installment and revolving credit and non-U.S. auto portfolios, we assess overall credit quality using internal and external credit scores. Our internal credit scores imply a probability of default which we consistently translate into three approximate credit bureau equivalent credit score categories, including (a) 681 or higher, which are considered the strongest credits; (b) 615 to 680, considered moderate credit risk; and (c) 614 or less, which are considered weaker credits.

| | Internal Ratings Translated to Approximate Credit Bureau Equivalent Score at | | | | | |
| | December 31, 2011 | | | December 31, 2010 | | |
(In millions)	681 or Higher	615 to 680	614 or Less	681 or Higher	615 to 680	614 or Less
Non-U.S. installment and revolving credit	$ 9,913	$4,838	$3,793	$10,192	$5,749	$4,191
U.S. installment and revolving credit	28,918	9,398	8,373	25,940	8,846	9,188
Non-U.S. auto	3,927	1,092	672	5,379	1,330	849

Of those financing receivable accounts with credit bureau equivalent scores of 614 or less at December 31, 2011, 95% relate to installment and revolving credit accounts. These smaller balance accounts have an average outstanding balance less than one thousand U.S. dollars and are primarily concentrated in our retail card and sales finance receivables in the U.S. (which are often subject to profit and loss sharing arrangements), and closed-end loans outside the U.S., which minimizes the potential for loss in the event of default. For lower credit scores, we adequately price for the incremental risk at origination and monitor credit migration through our risk ratings process. We continuously adjust our credit line underwriting management and collection strategies based on customer behavior and risk profile changes.

Consumer—Other

Secured lending in Consumer—Other comprises loans to small and medium-sized enterprises predominantly secured by auto and equipment, inventory finance and cash flow loans. We develop our internal risk ratings for this portfolio in a manner consistent with the process used to develop our Commercial credit quality indicators, described above. We use the borrower's credit quality and underlying collateral strength to determine the potential risk of loss from these activities.

At December 31, 2011, Consumer—Other financing receivables of $5,580 million, $757 million and $907 million were rated A, B, and C, respectively. At December 31, 2010, Consumer—Other financing receivables of $6,415 million, $822 million and $1,067 million were rated A, B, and C, respectively.

Change in Accounting Principle: Consolidation

1.71

KRAFT FOODS INC. (DEC)

NOTES TO CONSOLIDATED FINANCIAL STATEMENTS

Note 1. Summary of Significant Accounting Policies (in part)

Principles of Consolidation (in part):

The consolidated financial statements include Kraft Foods, as well as our wholly owned and majority owned subsidiaries.

The majority of our operating subsidiaries report results as of the last Saturday of the year. A portion of our international operating subsidiaries report results as of the last calendar day or the last Saturday of the year. Because a significant number of our operating subsidiaries report results on the last Saturday of the year and this year, that day fell on December 31, our results included an extra week ("53rd week") of operating results than in the prior two years which had 52-weeks.

In 2011, we changed the consolidation date for certain operations of our Kraft Foods Europe segment and in the Latin America and Central and Eastern Europe, Middle East and Africa ("CEEMA") regions within our Kraft Foods Developing Markets segment. Previously, these operations primarily reported results two weeks prior to the end of the period. Now, our Kraft Foods Europe segment reports results as of the last Saturday of each period. Our operations in Latin America and certain operations in CEEMA now report results as of the last calendar day of the period or the last Saturday of the period. These changes and the 53rd week in 2011 resulted in a favorable impact to net revenues of approximately $920 million and a favorable impact of approximately $150 million to operating income in 2011.

In 2010, we changed the consolidation date for certain European biscuits operations, which are included within our Kraft Foods Europe segment, and certain operations in Asia Pacific and Latin America within our Kraft Foods Developing Markets segment. Previously, these operations primarily reported period-end results one month or two weeks prior to the end of the period. Kraft Foods Europe moved the reporting of these operations to two weeks prior to the end of the period, and Asia Pacific and Latin America moved the reporting of these operations to the last day of the period. These changes resulted in a favorable impact to net revenues of approximately $200 million and had an insignificant impact on operating income in 2010.

We believe these changes are preferable and will improve business planning and financial reporting by better matching the close dates of the operating subsidiaries within our Kraft Foods Europe segment and Kraft Foods Developing Markets segment and by bringing the reporting date closer to the period-end date. As the effect to prior-period results was not material, we have not revised prior-period results.

Change in Accounting Estimates

1.72

ARCHER DANIELS MIDLAND COMPANY (JUN)

SELECTED FINANCIAL DATA

(In millions, except ratio and per share data)

Selected Financial Data

	2011	2010	2009	2008	2007
Net sales and other operating income	$80,676	$61,682	$69,207	$69,816	$44,018
Depreciation	827	857	730	721	701
Net earnings attributable to controlling interests	2,036	1,930	1,684	1,780	2,154
Basic earnings per common share	3.17	3.00	2.62	2.76	3.31
Diluted earnings per common share	3.13	3.00	2.62	2.75	3.28
Cash dividends	395	372	347	316	281
Per common share	0.62	0.58	0.54	0.49	0.43
Working capital	$14,286	$ 9,561	$10,523	$10,833	$ 7,254
Current ratio	2.1	2.1	2.2	1.7	1.9
Inventories	12,055	7,871	7,782	10,160	6,060
Net property, plant, and equipment	9,500	8,712	7,950	7,125	6,010
Gross additions to property, plant, and equipment	1,512	1,788	2,059	1,789	1,404
Total assets	42,193	31,808	31,582	37,052	25,114
Long-term debt, excluding current maturities	8,266	6,830	7,592	7,443	4,468
Shareholders' equity	18,838	14,631	13,653	13,666	11,446
Per common share	27.87	22.89	21.27	21.22	17.80
Weighted average shares outstanding-basic	642	643	643	644	651
Weighted average shares outstanding-diluted	654	644	644	646	656

Significant items affecting the comparability of the financial data shown above are as follows (in part):

- Net earnings attributable to controlling interests for 2011 include a gain of $71 million ($44 million after tax, equal to $0.07 per share) related to the acquisition of the remaining interest in Golden Peanut, start up costs for the Company's significant new greenfield plants of $94 million ($59 million after tax, equal to $0.09 per share), charges on early extinguishment of debt of $15 million ($9 million after tax, equal to $0.01 per share), gains on interest rate swaps of $30 million ($19 million after tax, equal to $0.03 per share) and a gain of $78 million ($49 million after tax, equal to $0.07 per share) related to the sale of bank securities held by the Company's equity investee, Gruma S.A.B de C.V. During the second quarter of fiscal year 2011, the Company updated its estimates for service lives of certain of its machinery and equipment assets. The effect of this change in accounting estimate on pre-tax earnings for the year ended June 30, 2011 was an increase of $133 million ($83 million after tax, equal to $0.13 per share). Basic and diluted weighted average shares outstanding for 2011 include 44 million shares issued on June 1, 2011 related to the Equity Unit conversion. Diluted weighted average shares outstanding for 2011 include 44 million shares assumed issued on January 1, 2011 as required using the "if-converted" method of calculating diluted earnings per share for the quarter ended March 31, 2011. See Note 9 in Item 8, Financial Statements and Supplementary Data (Item 8), for earnings per share calculation.

NOTES TO CONSOLIDATED FINANCIAL STATEMENTS

Note 1. Summary of Significant Accounting Policies (in part)

Use of Estimates

The preparation of consolidated financial statements in conformity with generally accepted accounting principles requires management to make estimates and assumptions that affect amounts reported in its consolidated financial statements and accompanying notes. Actual results could differ from those estimates.

During the second quarter of fiscal year 2011, the Company updated its estimates for service lives of certain of its machinery and equipment assets in order to better match the Company's depreciation expense with the periods these assets are expected to generate revenue based on planned and historical service periods. The new estimated service lives were established based on manufacturing engineering data, external benchmark data and on new information obtained as a result of the Company's recent major construction projects. These new estimated service lives are also supported by biofuels legislation and mandates in many countries that are driving requirements over time for greater future usage and higher blend rates of biofuels.

The Company accounted for this service life update as a change in accounting estimate as of October 1, 2010 in accordance with the guidance of ASC Topic 250, *Accounting Changes and Error Corrections*, thereby impacting the quarter in which the change occurred and future quarters. The effect of this change on after-tax earnings and diluted earnings per share was an increase of $83 million and $0.13, respectively, for the year ended June 30, 2011.

1.73

SEALY CORPORATION (NOV)

NOTES TO CONSOLIDATED FINANCIAL STATEMENTS

Note 3: Change in Estimate

During fiscal 2011, the Company reviewed its computation of reserves for warrantable and other product returns and refined the calculations of these reserves in order to better predict the Company's future liability related to these claims. The effect of this change in estimate for warranty claims was to reduce other accrued liabilities and cost of sales by approximately $3.1 million. The change in estimate for other product returns decreased accounts receivable balances by approximately $4.7 million, with a corresponding decrease in net sales. For the year ended November 27, 2011, the change in estimate decreased operating income by $1.6 million and increased net loss by $0.9 million. This change in estimate also increased net loss per basic and diluted share by $0.01 for the year ended November 27, 2011.

Correction of Errors

1.74

KOHL'S CORPORATION (JAN)

NOTES TO CONSOLIDATED FINANCIAL STATEMENTS

2. Restatement

We are restating our previously issued consolidated financial statements for the year ended January 29, 2011 to correct various errors in our accounting for leases.

The most significant of the corrections resulted from improper application of the sale-leaseback provisions of ASC 840, Leases. We are often involved extensively in the construction of leased stores. In many cases, we are responsible for construction cost over runs or construct non-standard tenant improvements (e.g. roof or HVAC systems). As a result of this involvement, we are deemed the "owner" for accounting purposes during the construction period, so are required to capitalize the construction costs on our Balance Sheet. Upon completion of the project, we must perform a sale-leaseback analysis pursuant to ASC 840 to determine if we can remove the assets from our Balance Sheet. In many of our leases, we are reimbursed a portion of the construction costs via adjusted rental and/or cash payments or have terms which fix the rental payments for a significant percentage of the leased asset's economic life. These items are generally considered "continuing involvement" which preclude us from derecognizing the constructed assets from our Balance Sheet when construction is complete.

Additionally, certain store and equipment leases were improperly recorded as operating leases, rather than capital leases.

To correct the accounting errors, we have recorded additional property and the related capital lease and financing obligations on our Balance Sheets. In our Statements of Income, lease payments related to these properties are now recognized as depreciation and interest expense, rather than rent expense (which we record in Selling, General and Administrative Expense). The corrections impact the classification of cash flows from operations, financing activities and investing activities, but have no impact on the net increase or decrease in cash and cash equivalents reported in our Statements of Cash Flows. As part of the restatement, we also reversed a $31 million cumulative lease accounting correction to net income which was recorded in the quarterly period ended October 30, 2010 (as disclosed in our quarterly report on Form 10-Q which was filed on December 9, 2010) and recorded the adjustment in the proper accounting periods.

The following tables summarize the corrections by financial statement line item.

(In millions)	January 29, 2011		
	Previously Reported[1]	Adjustments	Restated
Assets			
Current assets:			
Cash and cash equivalents	$ 2,277	$ —	$ 2,277
Merchandise inventories	3,036	—	3,036
Deferred income taxes	77	—	77
Other	255	(3)	252
Total current assets	5,645	(3)	5,642
Property and equipment, net	7,256	1,436	8,692
Long-term investments	277	—	277
Other assets	386	(218)	168
Total assets	$13,564	$1,215	$14,779
Liabilities and Shareholders' Equity			
Current liabilities:			
Accounts payable	$ 1,138	$ —	$ 1,138
Accrued liabilities	1,027	3	1,030
Income taxes payable	127	—	127
Current portion of long-term debt	400	—	400
Current portion of capital lease and financing obligations	18	68	86
Total current liabilities	2,710	71	2,781
Long-term debt	1,494	—	1,494
Capital lease and financing obligations	184	1,834	2,018
Deferred income taxes	418	(162)	256
Other long-term liabilities	656	(276)	380
Shareholders' equity	8,102	(252)	7,850
Total liabilities and shareholders' equity	$13,564	$1,215	$14,779

[1] Includes certain reclassifications to conform to the current presentation.

(In millions)	January 30, 2010		
	Previously Reported[1]	Adjustments	Restated
Assets			
Current assets:			
Cash and cash equivalents	$ 2,267	$ —	$ 2,267
Merchandise inventories	2,923	—	2,923
Deferred income taxes	73	—	73
Other	222	—	222
Total current assets	5,485	—	5,485
Property and equipment, net	7,018	1,488	8,506
Long-term investments	321	—	321
Other assets	336	(183)	153
Total assets	$13,160	$1,305	$14,465
Liabilities and Shareholders' Equity			
Current liabilities:			
Accounts payable	$ 1,188	$ —	$ 1,188
Accrued liabilities	1,002	3	1,005
Income taxes payable	184	—	184
Current portion of capital lease and financing obligations	16	62	78
Total current liabilities	2,390	65	2,455
Long-term debt	1,894	—	1,894
Capital lease and financing obligations	158	1,810	1,968
Deferred income taxes	377	(163)	214
Other long-term liabilities	488	(149)	339
Shareholders' equity	7,853	(258)	7,595
Total liabilities and shareholders' equity	$13,160	$1,305	$14,465

[1] Includes certain reclassifications to conform to the current presentation.

(In millions, except per share data)	2010		
	Previously Reported	**Adjustments**	**Restated**
Sales	$18,391	$ —	$18,391
Cost of merchandise sold	11,359	—	11,359
Gross margin	7,032	—	7,032
Operating expenses:			
Selling, general, and administrative	4,462	(272)	4,190
Depreciation and amortization	656	94	750
Operating income	1,914	178	2,092
Interest expense, net	132	172	304
Income before income taxes	1,782	6	1,788
Provision for income taxes	668	—	668
Net income	$ 1,114	$ 6	$ 1,120
Net income per share:			
Basic	$ 3.67	$0.02	$ 3.69
Diluted	$ 3.65	$0.01	$ 3.66

(In millions, except per share data)	2009		
	Previously Reported	**Adjustments**	**Restated**
Sales	$17,178	$ —	$17,178
Cost of merchandise sold	10,680	—	10,680
Gross margin	6,498	—	6,498
Operating expenses:			
Selling, general, and administrative	4,196	(245)	3,951
Depreciation and amortization	590	98	688
Operating income	1,712	147	1,859
Interest expense, net	124	177	301
Income before income taxes	1,588	(30)	1,558
Provision for income taxes	597	(12)	585
Net income	$ 991	$ (18)	$ 973
Net income per share:			
Basic	$ 3.25	$(0.06)	$ 3.19
Diluted	$ 3.23	$(0.06)	$ 3.17

(In millions, except per share data)	2008		
	Previously Reported	**Adjustments**	**Restated**
Sales	$16,389	$ —	$16,389
Cost of merchandise sold	10,334	—	10,334
Gross margin	6,055	—	6,055
Operating expenses:			
Selling, general, and administrative	3,978	(209)	3,769
Depreciation and amortization	541	91	632
Operating income	1,536	118	1,654
Interest expense, net	111	164	275
Income before income taxes	1,425	(46)	1,379
Provision for income taxes	540	(18)	522
Net income	$ 885	$ (28)	$ 857
Net income per share:			
Basic	$ 2.89	$(0.09)	$ 2.80
Diluted	$ 2.89	$(0.09)	$ 2.80

SEC 1.74

The cumulative effect of the restatement on retained earnings for all periods prior to February 2, 2008 was $212 million.

(In millions)	2010 Previously Reported	Adjustments	Restated
Operating Activities			
Net income	$1,114	$ 6	$1,120
Adjustments to reconcile net income to net cash provided by operating activites:			
Depreciation and amortization	656	94	750
Share-based compensation	66	—	66
Excess tax benefits from share-based compensation	3	—	3
Deferred income taxes	38	1	39
Other non-cash revenues and expenses	66	(31)	35
Changes in operating assets and liabilities:			
Merchandise inventories	(107)	—	(107)
Other current and long-term assets	(50)	—	(50)
Accounts payable	(50)	—	(50)
Accrued and other long-term liabilities	3	10	13
Income taxes	(63)	—	(63)
Net cash provided by operating activities	1,676	80	1,756
Investing Activities			
Acquisition of property and equipment	(761)	(40)	(801)
Sales of investments in auction rate securities	42	—	42
Other	2	—	2
Net cash used in investing activities	(717)	(40)	(757)
Financing Activities			
Treasury stock purchases	(1,004)	—	(1,004)
Capital lease and financing obligation payments	(17)	(67)	(84)
Proceeds from financing obligations	—	27	27
Proceeds from stock option exercises	75	—	75
Excess tax benefits from share-based compensation	(3)	—	(3)
Net cash used in financing activities	(949)	(40)	(989)
Net increase in cash and cash equivalents	10	—	10
Cash and cash equivalents at beginning of period	2,267	—	2,267
Cash and cash equivalents at end of period	$2,277	$ —	$2,277

(In millions)	2009 Previously Reported	Adjustments	Restated
Operating Activities			
Net income	$ 991	$(18)	$ 973
Adjustments to reconcile net income to net cash provided by operating activites:			
Depreciation and amortization	590	98	688
Share-based compensation	64	—	64
Excess tax benefits from share-based compensation	3	—	3
Deferred income taxes	52	(12)	40
Other non-cash revenues and expenses	52	(17)	35
Changes in operating assets and liabilities:			
Merchandise inventories	(119)	—	(119)
Other current and long-term assets	(13)	—	(13)
Accounts payable	306	—	306
Accrued and other long-term liabilities	234	1	235
Income taxes	74	—	74
Net cash provided by operating activities	2,234	52	2,286
Investing Activities			
Acquisition of property and equipment	(666)	(9)	(675)
Sales of investments in auction rate securities	28	—	28
Other	(2)	—	(2)
Net cash used in investing activities	$ (640)	$ (9)	$ (649)

(continued)

	2009		
	Previously Reported	**Adjustments**	**Restated**
Financing Activities			
Treasury stock purchases	$ (1)	$ —	$ (1)
Capital lease and financing obligation payments	(17)	(53)	(70)
Proceeds from financing obligations	—	10	10
Proceeds from stock option exercises	51	—	51
Excess tax benefits from share-based compensation	(3)	—	(3)
Net cash provided by (used in) financing activities	30	(43)	(13)
Net increase in cash and cash equivalents	1,624	—	1,624
Cash and cash equivalents at beginning of period	643	—	643
Cash and cash equivalents at end of period	$2,267	$ —	$2,267

	2008		
(In Millions)	**Previously Reported**	**Adjustments**	**Restated**
Operating Activities			
Net income	$ 885	$(28)	$ 857
Adjustments to reconcile net income to net cash provided by operating activites:			
Depreciation and amortization	541	91	632
Share-based compensation	55	—	55
Deferred income taxes	84	(18)	66
Other non-cash revenues and expenses	49	8	57
Changes in operating assets and liabilities:			
Merchandise inventories	60	—	60
Other current and long-term assets	(40)	—	(40)
Accounts payable	48	—	48
Accrued and other long-term liabilities	42	1	43
Income taxes	(26)	—	(26)
Net cash provided by operating activities	1,698	54	1,752
Investing Activities			
Acquisition of property and equipment	(1,014)	(52)	(1,066)
Purchases of investments in auction rate securities	(53)	—	(53)
Sales of investments in auction rate securities	93	—	93
Other	11	—	11
Net cash used in investing activities	(963)	(52)	(1,015)
Financing Activities			
Treasury stock purchases	(262)	—	(262)
Capital lease and financing obligation payments	(16)	(46)	(62)
Proceeds from financing obligations	—	44	44
Proceeds from stock option exercises	5	—	5
Net cash used in financing activities	(273)	(2)	(275)
Net increase in cash and cash equivalents	462	—	462
Cash and cash equivalents at beginning of period	181	—	181
Cash and cash equivalents at end of period	$ 643	$ —	$ 643

SEC 1.74

1.75

COMPUTER SCIENCES CORPORATION (MAR)

NOTES TO CONSOLIDATED FINANCIAL STATEMENTS

Note 2—Out of Period Adjustments

During fiscal 2011, the Company recorded various pre-tax adjustments reducing income from continuing operations before taxes by $51 million ($34 million, net of taxes), that should have been recorded in prior fiscal years. As discussed below, these recorded adjustments comprised $91 million of charges reducing income from continuing operations before taxes originating out of the Company's MSS operations in the Nordic region, and $40 million of adjustments increasing income from continuing operations before taxes, principally out of other MSS businesses with $36 million of the $40 million within MSS. These adjustments reduced MSS operating income (a non-GAAP measure) by $53 million as discussed in Note 15, Segment and Geographic Information. The Company also recorded out of period income tax benefits in fiscal 2011 of $17 million, consisting of $12 million of income tax benefits related to the net out of period adjustments and $5 million of unrelated income tax benefit adjustments.

The out of period recorded adjustments are attributable to the following prior fiscal years (in millions):

	MSS	Non-MSS	Income From Continuing Operations Before Taxes	Taxes on Income	Net Income Attributable to CSC Common Shareholders
Fiscal 2010	$(52)	$4	$(48)	$(18)	$(30)
Fiscal 2009	(2)	—	(2)	—	(2)
Prior fiscal years	(1)	—	(1)	1	(2)
Total	$(55)	$4	$(51)	$(17)	$(34)

Nordic Region Adjustments

As part of closing the Company's financial statements for the first quarter of fiscal 2011, management identified and recorded out of period charges totaling $21 million in its Nordic operations. In response to these errors, the Company made changes in operational and financial management and utilized experienced finance personnel from other business units and internal audit to assist with the closing of the Nordic financial statements for the second, third, and fourth quarters of fiscal 2011. As part of the quarterly closing procedures, the Company performed a detailed review of account reconciliations, customer contractual arrangements, labor agreements and employee benefit plans. As a result of these procedures, the Company recognized additional out of period pre-tax charges totaling $39 million, $25 million, and $6 million in the second, third, and fourth quarters, respectively. The $91 million of out-of-period adjustments recorded in fiscal 2011 were attributable to:

(Amounts in millions)	Pre-Tax Nordic Region Adjustments
Operating costs inappropriately capitalized	$66
Misapplication of US GAAP	13
Miscellaneous errors	12
Total	$91

Based upon the Company's review of the underlying documentation for certain transactions and balances, review of contract documentation and discussions with Nordic personnel, the Company has attributed the majority of the $91 million of adjustments to accounting irregularities arising from suspected intentional misconduct by certain former employees in our Danish subsidiaries.

The $66 million of out-of-period adjustments for inappropriately capitalized costs are related to the following consolidated balance sheet line items:
- Prepaid expenses and other current assets ($35 million)
- Outsourcing contract costs ($12 million)
- Property and equipment ($15 million)
- Receivables ($4 million)

Other Adjustments

As noted above, the Company also identified out of period adjustments of $40 million that increased income from continuing operations before taxes, of which $36 million relates to other MSS operations. The adjustments attributable to the MSS segment are related to the following consolidated balance sheet line items:
- Accounts payable ($13 million)
- Other accrued expenses ($8 million)
- Deferred revenue ($5 million)
- Accounts receivable and other current assets ($8 million)
- Property and equipment ($2 million)

The remaining $4 million of out-of-period adjustments consist of reductions of other accrued expenses related to non-MSS segments with $2 million from an adjustment to corporate general and administrative expense, and $2 million adjustment to costs of services. The Company also identified $5 million of net out of period adjustments related to income tax benefits associated with complex tax positions.

The following table summarizes the effect on net income attributable to CSC common shareholders of the consolidated out-of-period adjustments recorded in each quarter of fiscal 2011 (in millions):

(Amounts in millions)	Quarter Ended July 2, 2010	Quarter Ended October 1, 2010	Quarter Ended December 31, 2010	Quarter Ended April 1, 2011	Total
Operating costs inappropriately capitalized	$16	$36	$ 8	$ 6	$66
Misapplication of US GAAP	3	3	7	—	13
Miscellaneous errors	2	—	10	—	12
Total Nordic adjustments	21	39	25	6	91
Other adjustments	(15)	(11)	(4)	(10)	(40)
Effect on income from continuing operations before taxes	6	28	21	(4)	51
Income tax benefit	(4)	(4)	(4)	—	(12)
Other income tax adjustments	(1)	(13)	(6)	15	(5)
Effect on net income attributable to CSC common shareholders	$ 1	$11	$11	$11	$34

As previously disclosed, in fiscal year 2011, the Company initiated an investigation into certain accounting errors in our MSS segment, primarily involving accounting irregularities in the Nordic region. Initially, the investigation was conducted by Company personnel, but outside Company counsel and forensic accountants retained by such counsel later assisted in the Company's investigation. On January 28, 2011, the Company was notified by the Division of Enforcement of the SEC that it had commenced a formal civil investigation relating to these matters and other matters subsequently identified by the SEC, with which the Company is cooperating. On May 2, 2011, the Audit Committee of the Board of Directors commenced an independent investigation into matters relating to MSS and the Nordic region, matters identified by subpoenas issued by the SEC's Division of Enforcement and certain other accounting matters identified by the Audit Committee and retained independent counsel to represent CSC on behalf of, and under the exclusive direction of, the Audit Committee in connection with such independent investigation. Independent counsel has retained forensic accountants to assist their work. Independent counsel also represents CSC on behalf of, and under the exclusive direction of, the Audit Committee in connection with the investigation by the SEC's Division of Enforcement.

In addition, the SEC's Division of Corporation Finance has issued comment letters to the Company requesting additional information regarding its previously disclosed adjustments in connection with the above-referenced accounting errors, the Company's conclusions regarding the materiality of such adjustments and the Company's analysis of the effectiveness of its disclosure controls and procedures and its internal control over financial reporting. The Division of Corporation Finance's comment letter process is ongoing, and the Company is continuing to cooperate with that process.

The investigations being conducted by the Division of Enforcement and the Audit Committee as well as the review of our financial disclosures by the Division of Corporation Finance are continuing and could identify other accounting errors. As a result, we have incurred and will continue to incur significant legal and accounting expenditures, and a significant amount of time of our senior management has been focused on these matters. We are unable to predict how long the Division of Enforcement's and Audit Committee's investigations will continue or whether, at the conclusion of its investigation, the SEC will seek to impose fines or take other actions against us. In addition, we are unable to predict the timing of the completion of the Division of Corporation Finance's review of our financial disclosures or the outcome of such review. Publicity surrounding the foregoing or any enforcement action as a result of the SEC's investigation, even if ultimately resolved favorably for us, could have an adverse impact on our reputation, business, financial condition or results of operations.

The net impact of the out of period adjustments was immaterial to the consolidated results, financial position and cash flows for each fiscal year affected by the adjustments. Consequently, in the accompanying consolidated financial statements, the cumulative effect is recorded in fiscal 2011. The primary Consolidated Statement of Income line items affected by the adjustments in fiscal 2011 and 2010 are shown below. The effect of the adjustments on 2009 and prior fiscal years Consolidated Statements of Income are not presented since the amounts were less than 1% for each of the line items shown below. There was no change to discontinued operations amounts in any of the reported years. The impact on the Consolidated Balance Sheet was less than 1% for any line item for all fiscal years. The effect on the Consolidated Cash Flow Statement was less than 0.5% for cash provided by operating and investing activities and there was no impact to cash from financing activities.

The following schedules show the effect on selected line items in the preliminary fiscal 2011 and fiscal 2010 Consolidated Statements of Income under the rollover method.

Twelve Months Ended April 1, 2011 (Amounts in millions, except per share amounts)	As Reported	Adjustments Increase/(Decrease)	Amount Adjusted for Removal of Errors
Revenue	$16,042	$ 35	$16,077
Costs of services (excludes depreciation and amortization)	12,925	(19)	12,906
Selling, general and administrative	965	1	966
Depreciation and amortization	1,073	3	1,076
Interest expense	168	(1)	167
Other (income) expense	(20)	—	(20)
Income from continuing operations before taxes	968	51	1,019
Taxes on income	243	17	260
Income from continuing operations	725	34	759
Income from discontinued operations, net of taxes	34	—	34
Net income attributable to CSC common shareholders	740	34	774
EPS—Diluted			
Continuing operations	$ 4.51	$0.22	$ 4.73
Discontinued operations	0.22	—	0.22
Total	4.73	0.22	4.95

Twelve Months Ended April 2, 2010 (Amounts in millions, except per share amounts)	As Reported	Adjustments Increase/(Decrease)	Amount Adjusted for Removal of Errors
Revenue	$15,921	$ (19)	$15,902
Costs of services (excludes depreciation and amortization)	12,618	33	12,651
Selling, general and administrative	981	(2)	979
Depreciation and amortization	1,095	(2)	1,093
Interest expense	252	—	252
Other (income) expense	(20)	—	(20)
Income from continuing operations before taxes	1,022	(48)	974
Taxes on income	192	(18)	174
Income from continuing operations	830	(30)	800
Income from discontinued operations, net of taxes	4	—	4
Net income attributable to CSC common shareholders	817	(30)	787
EPS—Diluted			
Continuing operations	$ 5.27	$(0.20)	$ 5.07
Discontinued operations	0.01	—	0.01
Total	5.28	(0.20)	5.08

1.76

THE MANITOWOC COMPANY, INC. (DEC)

NOTES TO CONSOLIDATED FINANCIAL STATEMENTS

1. Company and Basis of Presentation (in part)

Revision of Prior Period Financial Statements

During the quarter ended December 31, 2011, the company identified a $28.5 million error related to its income taxes payable and goodwill accounts that originated during 2008, resulting in the overstatement of these accounts in its previously filed financial statements. This $28.5 million error also overstated the goodwill impairment charge included in the company's Consolidated Statement of Operations for the year ended December 31, 2009. The impact of the error on the 2009 goodwill impairment charge is non-deductible for tax purposes. In addition, the company had previously identified an error related to the understatement of the 2009 tax benefit by $6.6 million that had been corrected as an out-of-period adjustment in the third quarter of 2010. The company does not believe these errors to be material to the company's results of operations, financial position, or cash flows for any of the company's previously filed annual or quarterly financial statements. Accordingly, the Consolidated Statement of Operations for the years ended December 31, 2010 and 2009, and the Consolidated Balance Sheet as of December 31, 2010, included herein have been revised to correct these errors. The company has also revised the prior period financial statements to correct immaterial errors related to overstated intercompany profit elimination and understated foreign exchange transaction gains. The correction of the overstated intercompany profit elimination decreased cost of sales

$0.7 million for the year ended December 31, 2010, increased costs of sales $0.2 million for the year ended December 31, 2009 and increased inventory $1.1 million at December 31, 2010. The correction of the understated foreign exchange transaction gains increased other income $0.2 million and $0.2 million for the years ended December 31, 2010 and 2009, respectively, and decreased accounts payable $0.4 million at December 31, 2010. In addition, the quarterly infor-

mation for 2010 has been revised. See Note 24, "Quarterly Financial Data (Unaudited)" for further discussion of the quarterly revisions. The impacts of these revisions are as follows:

	As of December 31, 2010	
Consolidated Balance Sheets:	As Reported	As Revised
Accounts payable and accrued expenses	$ 776.1	$748.0
Total current liabilities	1,025.5	997.4
Total equity	$ 478.5	$508.5

	For the Years Ended December 31			
	2010		2009	
Consolidated Statements of Operations:	As Reported	As Revised	As Reported	As Revised
Goodwill impairment	$ —	$ —	$ 548.8	$ 520.3
Total costs and expenses	—	—	4,132.2	4,103.9
Operating earnings (loss) from continuing operations	—	—	(512.4)	(484.1)
Earnings (loss) from continuing operations before taxes on earnings	—	—	(707.3)	(678.8)
Provision (benefit) for taxes on earnings	23.9	30.9	(58.9)	(65.5)
Loss from continuing operations	(68.5)	(74.6)	(648.4)	(613.3)
Net loss	(76.1)	(82.2)	(706.7)	(671.6)
Net loss attributable to Manitowoc	$(73.4)	$(79.5)	$ (704.2)	$ (669.1)
Basic and diluted earnings (loss) per share from continuing operations	$(0.50)	$(0.55)	$ (4.96)	$ (4.69)
Basic and diluted earnings (loss) per share	$(0.56)	$(0.61)	$ (5.41)	$ (5.14)

24. Quarterly Financial Data (Unaudited)

The following table presents quarterly financial data for 2011 and 2010:

	2011				2010			
(In millions, except per share data)	First	Second	Third	Fourth	First	Second	Third	Fourth
Net sales	$732.2	$949.8	$935.4	$1,034.5	$684.4	$819.3	$807.1	$830.9
Gross profit	180.5	225.0	223.4	209.1	166.0	207.2	199.9	193.0
Earnings (loss) from continuing operations	(15.8)	3.0	34.9	15.3	(37.9)	17.7	1.1	(24.6)
Discontinued operations:								
Earnings (loss) from discontinued operations, net of income taxes	(2.7)	(0.3)	(0.1)	(0.8)	0.1	0.4	1.9	(10.0)
Gain (loss) on sale of discontinued operations, net of income taxes	(33.4)	(0.2)	—	(1.0)	—	—	—	—
Net earnings (loss)	(53.3)	1.7	21.5	13.1	(23.8)	13.9	(6.2)	(66.1)
Less: Net earnings (loss) attributable to noncontrolling interest, net of tax	(0.9)	(1.1)	(2.1)	(2.4)	(0.4)	(0.8)	(0.9)	(0.6)
Net earnings (loss) attributable to Manitowoc	$(52.4)	$ 2.8	$ 23.6	$ 15.5	$(23.4)	$ 14.7	$ (5.3)	$ (65.5)
Basic earnings per share:								
Earnings (loss) from continuing operations attributable to Manitowoc common shareholders	$(0.12)	$ 0.03	$ 0.18	$ 0.13	$(0.18)	$ 0.11	$(0.06)	$ (0.42)
Discontinued operations:								
Earnings (loss) from discontinued operations attributable to Manitowoc common shareholders	(0.02)	—	—	(0.01)	—	—	0.01	(0.08)
Gain (loss) on sale of discontinued operations, net of income taxes	(0.26)	—	—	(0.01)	—	—	—	—
Earnings (loss) per share attributable to Manitowoc common shareholders	$(0.40)	$ 0.02	$ 0.18	$ 0.12	$(0.18)	$ 0.11	$(0.04)	$ (0.50)
Diluted earnings per share:								
Earnings (loss) from continuing operations attributable to Manitowoc common shareholders	$(0.12)	$ 0.02	$ 0.18	$ 0.13	$(0.18)	$ 0.11	$(0.06)	$ (0.42)
Discontinued operations:								
Earnings (loss) from discontinued operations attributable to Manitowoc common shareholders	(0.02)	—	—	(0.01)	—	—	0.01	(0.08)
Gain (loss) on sale of discontinued operations, net of income taxes	(0.26)	—	—	(0.01)	—	—	—	—
Earnings (loss) per share attributable to Manitowoc common shareholders	$(0.40)	$ 0.02	$ 0.18	$ 0.12	$(0.18)	$ 0.11	(0.04)	$ (0.50)
Dividends per common share	$ —	$ —	$ —	$ 0.08	$ —	$ —	$ —	$ 0.08

SEC 1.76

During the fourth quarter of 2011, the company revised previously issued financial statements. See Note 1, "Company and Basis of Presentation" for further discussion of these revisions. Items (1)–(5) describe the impact of these revisions on the quarterly results.

1. Gross profit was impacted as follows, increase/(decrease)
   a. 2011: Q1—$0.1 million; Q2—$0.4 million; Q3—$(0.1) million
   b. 2010: Q1—$(0.4) million; Q2—$1.0 million; Q3—$(0.3) million; Q4—$0.4 million
2. Earnings (loss) from continuing operations was impacted as follows, increase/(decrease)
   a. 2011: Q1—$0.1 million; Q2—$0.4 million; Q3—$(0.1) million
   b. 2010: Q1—$(0.4) million; Q2—$0.9 million; Q3—$(0.2) million; Q4—$0.6 million
3. Net earnings (loss) was impacted as follows, increase/(decrease)
   a. 2011: Q2—$0.1 million; Q3—$(0.1) million
   b. 2010: Q1—$(0.2) million; Q2—$0.6 million; Q3—$(6.7) million; Q4—$(0.2) million
4. Net earnings (loss) attributable to Manitowoc was impacted as follows, increase/(decrease)
   a. 2011: Q2—$0.1 million; Q3—$(0.1) million
   b. 2010: Q1—$(0.2) million; Q2—$0.6 million; Q3—$(6.7) million; Q4—$(0.2) million
5. Basic and diluted earnings per share from continuing operations were impacted as follows, increase/(decrease)
   a. 2011: Q2—$0.01
   b. 2010: Q2—$0.01; Q3—$(0.06)

CONSOLIDATION

RECOGNITION AND MEASUREMENT

1.77 FASB ASC 810-10-10 states that the purpose of consolidated financial statements is to present, primarily for the benefit of the owners and creditors of the parent, the results of operations and the financial position of a parent and all its subsidiaries as if the consolidated group were a single economic entity. It is presumed that consolidated financial statements are more meaningful than separate financial statements and are usually necessary for a fair presentation when one of the entities in the consolidated group directly or indirectly has a controlling financial interest in the other entities.

1.78 As explained by FASB ASC 810-10-05-8, the "General" subsections of FASB ASC 810, *Consolidation*, apply to certain legal entities in which equity investors do not have sufficient equity at risk for the legal entity to finance its activities without additional subordinated financial support, or as a group, the holders of the equity investment at risk lack any of the following three characteristics:

- The power, through voting or similar rights, to direct the activities of a legal entity that most significantly affect the entity's economic performance
- The obligation to absorb the expected losses of the legal entity

- The right to receive the expected residual returns of the legal entity

Consolidated financial statements are usually necessary for a fair presentation if one of the entities in the consolidated group directly or indirectly has a controlling financial interest, typically a majority voting interest. Application of the majority voting interest requirement to certain types of entities may not identify the party with a controlling financial interest because that interest may be achieved through other arrangements. FASB ASC 810-10-25-38A explains that a reporting entity with a variable interest in a variable interest entity (VIE) should assess whether the reporting entity has a controlling financial interest in the VIE and, thus, is the VIE's primary beneficiary. The reporting enterprise with a variable interest(s) that provides the reporting entity with a controlling financial interest in a VIE will have both the following characteristics: (*a*) the power to direct the activities of a VIE that most significantly affect the VIE's performance and (*b*) the obligation to absorb losses of the VIE that could potentially be significant to the VIE or the right to receive benefits from the VIE that could potentially be significant to the VIE. Only one reporting entity, if any, is expected to be identified as the primary beneficiary of a VIE. Although more than one reporting entity could have the obligation to absorb losses previously mentioned, only one reporting entity (if any) will have the power to direct the activities of a VIE that most significantly affect the VIE's economic performance. Further, the concept of a qualifying special-purpose entity no longer exists in FASB ASC.

1.79 FASB ASC 810 also establishes accounting and reporting standards for the noncontrolling interest in a subsidiary and the deconsolidation of a subsidiary. A *noncontrolling interest* is the portion of equity (net assets) in a subsidiary not directly or indirectly attributable to a parent. A noncontrolling interest is sometimes called a minority interest.

PRESENTATION

1.80 FASB ASC 810-10-45-23 requires that a change in a parent's ownership interest while the parent retains its controlling financial interest in its subsidiary should be accounted for as equity transactions (investments by owners and distributions to owners acting in their capacity as owners). Therefore, no gain or loss shall be recognized in consolidated net income or comprehensive income. The carrying amount of the noncontrolling interest should be adjusted to reflect the change in its ownership interest in the subsidiary. Any difference between the fair value of the consideration received or paid and the amount by which the noncontrolling interest is adjusted should be recognized in equity attributable to the parent.

1.81 Paragraphs 4–5 of FASB ASC 810-10-40 state that a parent should deconsolidate a subsidiary or derecognize a group of assets specified in FASB ASC 810-10-40-3A as of the date the parent ceases to have a controlling financial interest in that subsidiary or group of assets. If a parent deconsolidates a subsidiary or derecognizes a group of assets through a nonreciprocal transfer to owners, such as a spinoff, the applicable guidance is in FASB ASC 845-10. Otherwise, a parent should account for the deconsolidation of a subsidiary or derecognition of a group of assets by recognizing a gain or loss in net income attributable to the parent. This gain or loss is measured as the difference between (*a*) the aggregate of the fair value of any consideration received; the fair value of any retained noncontrolling interest in the former subsidiary of the group of assets at the date the subsidiary is deconsolidated or the group of assets is derecognized, and the carrying amount of any noncontrolling interest in the former subsidiary, including any accumulated other comprehensive income attributable to the noncontrolling interest, at the date the subsidiary is deconsolidated and (*b*) the carrying amount of the former subsidiary's assets and liabilities or the carrying amount of the group of assets.

DISCLOSURE

1.82 FASB ASC 810-10-50 states in part that consolidated financial statements should disclose the consolidation policy that is being followed. In most cases, this can be made apparent by the headings or other information in the financial statements, but in other cases, a footnote is required.

1.83 FASB ASC 810-10-50-1A also requires disclosure on the face of the consolidated financial statements of the amounts of consolidated net income and consolidated comprehensive income attributable to the parent and noncontrolling interest. Disclosures in the consolidated financial statements should clearly identify and distinguish between the interests of the parent's owners and the interests of the noncontrolling owners of a subsidiary. Those disclosures include a reconciliation of the beginning and ending balances of the equity attributable to the parent and noncontrolling owners and a schedule showing the effects of changes in a parent's ownership interest in a subsidiary on the equity attributable to the parent.

PRESENTATION AND DISCLOSURE EXCERPTS

Consolidation

1.84

CONAGRA FOODS, INC. (MAY)

NOTES TO CONSOLIDATED FINANCIAL STATEMENTS

(Columnar amounts in millions except per share amounts)

7. Variable Interest Entities

Variable Interest Entities Consolidated

We own a 49.99% interest in Lamb Weston BSW, LLC ("Lamb Weston BSW"), a potato processing venture with Ochoa Ag Unlimited Foods, Inc. ("Ochoa"). We provide all sales and marketing services to Lamb Weston BSW. Under certain circumstances, we could be required to compensate the other equity owner of Lamb Weston BSW for lost profits resulting from significant production shortfalls ("production shortfalls"). Commencing on June 1, 2018, or on an earlier date under certain circumstances, we have a contractual right

to purchase the remaining equity interest in Lamb Weston BSW from Ochoa (the "call option"). Commencing on July 30, 2011, or on an earlier date under certain circumstances, we are subject to a contractual obligation to purchase all of Ochoa's equity investment in Lamb Weston BSW at the option of Ochoa (the "put option"). The purchase prices under the call option and the put option (the "options") are based on the book value of Ochoa's equity interest at the date of exercise, as modified by an agreed-upon rate of return for the holding period of the investment balance. The agreed-upon rate of return varies depending on the circumstances under which any of the options are exercised. We have determined that Lamb Weston BSW is a variable interest entity and that we are the primary beneficiary of the entity. Accordingly, we consolidate the financial statements of Lamb Weston BSW.

As of May 29, 2011, we provided lines of credit of up to $15.0 million to Lamb Weston BSW. Borrowings under the lines of credit bear interest at a rate of LIBOR plus 200 basis points with a floor of 3.25%. In the first quarter of fiscal 2011, we repaid $35.4 million of bank borrowings of Lamb Weston BSW and took assignment of a promissory note from the joint venture, the balance of which was $36.1 million at May 29, 2011. The promissory note is due in December 2015. The promissory note is currently accruing interest at a rate of LIBOR plus 200 basis points with a floor of 3.25%. The amounts owed by Lamb Weston BSW to the Company are not reflected in our balance sheets, as they are eliminated in consolidation.

Our variable interests in Lamb Weston BSW include an equity investment in the venture, the options, the promissory note, certain fees paid to us by Lamb Weston BSW for sales and marketing services, the contingent obligation related to production shortfalls, and the lines of credit advanced to Lamb Weston BSW. Our maximum exposure to loss as a result of our involvement with this venture is equal to our equity investment in the venture, the balance of the promissory note extended to the venture, the amount, if any, advanced under the lines of credit, and the amount, if any, by which the put option exercise price exceeds the fair value of the noncontrolling interest in Lamb Weston BSW on, or after, the put option exercise date. Also, in the event of a production shortfall, we could be required to compensate the other equity owner of Lamb Weston BSW for lost profits. It is not possible to determine the maximum exposure to losses from the potential exercise of the put option or from potential production shortfalls. However, we do not expect to incur material losses resulting from these exposures.

We also consolidate the assets and liabilities of several entities from which we lease corporate aircraft. Each of these entities has been determined to be a variable interest entity and we have been determined to be the primary beneficiary of each of these entities. Under the terms of the aircraft leases, we provide guarantees to the owners of these entities of a minimum residual value of the aircraft at the end of the lease term. We also have fixed price purchase options on the aircraft leased from these entities. Our maximum exposure to loss from our involvement with these entities is limited to the difference between the fair value of the leased aircraft and the amount of the residual value guarantees at the time we terminate the leases (the leases expire between December 2011 and October 2012). The total amount of the residual value guarantees for these aircraft at the end of the respective lease terms is $38.4 million.

Due to the consolidation of these variable interest entities, we reflected in our consolidated balance sheets:

	May 29, 2011	May 30, 2010
Cash and cash equivalents	$ 5.3	$ —
Receivables, less allowance for doubtful accounts	18.9	16.9
Inventories	1.5	1.4
Prepaid expenses and other current assets	0.3	0.3
Property, plant and equipment, net	91.8	96.5
Goodwill	18.8	18.8
Brands, trademarks and other intangibles, net	9.0	9.8
Total assets	$145.6	$143.7
Current installments of long-term debt	$ 13.4	$ 6.4
Accounts payable	13.1	12.2
Accrued payroll	0.4	0.3
Other accrued liabilities	0.7	0.7
Senior long-term debt, excluding current installments	30.1	76.8
Other noncurrent liabilities (minority interest)	26.7	24.8
Total liabilities	$ 84.4	$121.2

The liabilities recognized as a result of consolidating the Lamb Weston BSW entity do not represent additional claims on our general assets. The creditors of Lamb Weston BSW have claims only on the assets of Lamb Weston BSW. The assets recognized as a result of consolidating Lamb Weston BSW are the property of the venture and are not available to us for any other purpose, other than as a secured lender under the promissory note and lines of credit.

Variable Interest Entities Not Consolidated

We also have variable interests in certain other entities that we have determined to be variable interest entities, but for which we are not the primary beneficiary. We do not consolidate the financial statements of these entities.

We hold a 50% interest in Lamb Weston RDO, a potato processing venture. We provide all sales and marketing services to Lamb Weston RDO. We receive a fee for these services based on a percentage of the net sales of the venture. We reflect the value of our ownership interest in this venture in other assets in our consolidated balance sheets, based upon the equity method of accounting. The balance of our investment was $13.6 million and $13.8 million at May 29, 2011 and May 30, 2010, respectively, representing our maximum exposure to loss as a result of our involvement with this venture. The capital structure of Lamb Weston RDO includes owners' equity of $27.3 million and term borrowings from banks of $49.5 million as of May 29, 2011. We have determined that we do not have the power to direct the activities that most significantly impact the economic performance of this venture.

We lease certain office buildings from entities that we have determined to be variable interest entities. The lease agreements with these entities include fixed-price purchase options for the assets being leased, representing our only variable interest in these lessor entities. These leases are accounted for as operating leases, and accordingly, there are no material assets or liabilities associated with these entities included in our balance sheets. We have no material exposure to loss from our variable interests in these entities.

We have determined that we do not have the power to direct the activities that most significantly impact the economic performance of these entities. In making this determination, we have considered, among other items, the terms of the lease agreements, the expected remaining useful lives of the assets leased, and the capital structure of the lessor entities.

1.85

JOHNSON CONTROLS, INC. (SEP)

NOTES TO CONSOLIDATED FINANCIAL STATEMENTS

1. Summary of Significant Accounting Policies (in part)

Principles of Consolidation

The consolidated financial statements include the accounts of Johnson Controls, Inc. and its domestic and non-U.S. subsidiaries that are consolidated in conformity with accounting principles generally accepted in the United States of America (U.S. GAAP). All significant intercompany transactions have been eliminated. Investments in partially-owned affiliates are accounted for by the equity method when the Company's interest exceeds 20% and the Company does not have a controlling interest. The financial results for the year ended September 30, 2009 include an out of period adjustment of $62 million made in the first and second quarters of fiscal 2009 to correct an error related to the power solutions segment. The correction of the error, which reduces segment income, primarily originated in fiscal 2007 and 2008 and resulted in the overstatement of inventory and understatement of cost of sales in prior periods. The Company determined that the impact of the error on the originating periods was immaterial, and accordingly a restatement of prior period amounts was not considered necessary. The Company also determined the impact of correcting the error in fiscal 2009 was not material.

On October 1, 2010, the Company adopted Accounting Standards Update (ASU) No. 2009-17, "Consolidations (Topic 810): Improvements to Financial Reporting by Enterprises Involved with Variable Interest Entities." ASU No. 2009-17 amends the consolidation guidance applicable to variable interest entities ("VIEs") and requires additional disclosures concerning an enterprise's continuing involvement with VIEs. Under certain criteria as provided for in Financial Accounting Standards Board (FASB) Accounting Standards Codification (ASC) 810, "Consolidation," the Company may consolidate a partially-owned affiliate. To determine whether to consolidate a partially-owned affiliate, the Company first determines if the entity is a VIE. An entity is considered to be a VIE if it has one of the following characteristics: 1) the entity is thinly capitalized; 2) residual equity holders do not control the entity; 3) equity holders are shielded from economic losses or do not participate fully in the entity's residual economics; or 4) the entity was established with non-substantive voting. If the entity meets one of these characteristics, the Company then determines if it is the primary beneficiary of the VIE. The party with the power to direct activities of the VIE that most significantly impact the VIE's economic performance and the potential to absorb benefits or losses that could be significant to the VIE is considered the primary beneficiary and consolidates the VIE. The Company evaluated the impact of this guidance and determined that the adoption did not result in consolidation of additional entities or deconsolidation of existing VIEs. As such, the adoption of this guidance had no impact on the Company's consolidated financial condition and results of operations, and appropriate disclosures have been included herein.

Consolidated VIEs

Based upon the criteria set forth in ASC 810, the Company has determined that for the reporting periods ended September 30, 2011 and 2010 it was the primary beneficiary in two VIEs in which it holds less than 50% ownership as the Company absorbs significant economics of the entities and has the power to direct the activities that are considered most significant to the entities. The Company funds the entities' short term liquidity needs through revolving credit facilities and has the power to direct the activities that are considered most significant to the entities through its key customer supply relationships. These two VIEs manufacture products in North America for the automotive industry. The carrying amounts and classification of assets (none of which are restricted) and liabilities included in the Company's consolidated statements of financial position for the consolidated VIEs are as follows (in millions):

	September 30	
	2011	2010
Current assets	$207	$215
Noncurrent assets	55	69
Total assets	$262	$284
Current liabilities	$144	$174
Noncurrent liabilities	—	—
Total liabilities	$144	$174

Nonconsolidated VIEs

During the three month period ended June 30, 2011, the Company acquired a 40% interest in an equity method investee. The investee produces and sells lead-acid batteries of which the Company will both purchase and supply certain batteries to complement each investment partners' portfolio. Commencing on the third anniversary of the closing date, the Company has a contractual right to purchase the remaining 60% equity interest in the investee (the "call option"). If the Company does not exercise the call option on or before the fifth anniversary of the closing date and for a period of six months thereafter, the Company is subject to a contractual obligation at the counterparty's option to sell the Company's equity investment in the investee to the counterparty (the "repurchase option"). The purchase price is fixed under both the call option and the repurchase option. Based upon the criteria set forth in ASC 810, the Company has determined that the investee is a VIE as the equity holders, through their equity investments, may not participate fully in the entity's residual economics. The Company is not the primary beneficiary as the Company does not have the power to make

key operating decisions considered to be most significant to the VIE. Therefore, the investee is accounted for under the equity method of accounting as the Company's interest exceeds 20% and the Company does not have a controlling interest. The investment balance included within investments in partially-owned affiliates in the consolidated statement of financial position at September 30, 2011 was $49 million, which represents the Company's maximum exposure to loss. Current assets and liabilities related to the VIE are immaterial and represent normal course of business trade receivables and payables for all presented periods.

Based upon the criteria set forth in ASC 810, the Company has determined that it holds a variable interest in an equity method investee that was considered thinly capitalized at the time of its initial investment. The entity has been primarily financed with third party debt. During the three month period ended March 31, 2011, the owners of the remaining interest exercised their option to put their interest to the Company. The Company has twelve months from the date the notice was received to set the date of the put closing, reorganize the ownership structure or secure a third party buyer. The value of the put will be at a price that approximates fair value. The Company is not the primary beneficiary as the Company cannot make key operating decisions considered to be most significant to the VIE prior to the put closing. Therefore, the entity is accounted for under the equity method of accounting as the Company's interest exceeds 20% and the Company does not have a controlling interest. The Company's maximum exposure to loss, which includes the partially-owned affiliate investment balance and a note receivable, approximates $43 million at September 30, 2011 and $41 million at September 30, 2010. Current liabilities due to the VIE are immaterial and represent normal course of business trade payables for all presented periods. Additionally, the Company consumes a significant amount of the investee's manufacturing output.

The Company did not have a significant variable interest in any other nonconsolidated VIEs for the presented reporting periods.

New Accounting Pronouncements (in part)

In December 2009, the FASB issued ASU No. 2009-17, "Consolidations (Topic 810): Improvements to Financial Reporting by Enterprises Involved with Variable Interest Entities." ASU No. 2009-17 changes how a company determines when an entity that is insufficiently capitalized or is not controlled through voting should be consolidated. The determination of whether a company is required to consolidate an entity is based on, among other things, an entity's purpose and design and a company's ability to direct the activities of the entity that most significantly impact the entity's economic performance. This statement was effective for the Company beginning in the first quarter of fiscal 2011 (October 1, 2010). The adoption of this guidance had no impact on the Company's consolidated financial condition and results of operations. Refer to the "Principles of Consolidation" section of Note 1, "Summary of Significant Accounting Policies," of the notes to consolidated financial statements for further discussion.

SEC 1.85

BUSINESS COMBINATIONS

RECOGNITION AND MEASUREMENT

1.86 FASB ASC 805, *Business Combinations*, requires that the acquisition method be used for all business combinations. An acquirer is required to recognize the identifiable acquired assets, the liabilities assumed, and any noncontrolling interest in the acquiree at the acquisition date, measured at their fair values as of that date. Additionally, FASB ASC 805 requires costs incurred to affect the acquisition to be recognized as expenses as incurred, rather than included in the cost allocated to the acquired assets and assumed liabilities. However, the costs to issue debt or equity securities should be recognized in accordance with other applicable GAAP. In a business combination achieved in stages, FASB ASC 805 also requires the acquirer to remeasure its previously-held equity interest in the acquiree at its acquisition date fair value and recognize the resulting gain or loss, if any, in earnings. For all business combinations, the guidance requires the acquirer to recognize goodwill as of the acquisition date, measured as the excess of (a) over (b):

a. The aggregate of the following:
 i. The transferred consideration measured in accordance with FASB ASC 805-30, which generally requires acquisition-date fair value
 ii. The fair value of any noncontrolling interest in the acquire
 iii. In a business combination achieved in stages, the acquisition-date fair value of the acquirer's previously-held equity interest in the acquiree
b. The net of the acquisition-date amounts of the identifiable acquired assets and the assumed liabilities, measured in accordance with FASB ASC 805

If the amounts in (b) are in excess of those in (a), a bargain purchase has occurred. Before recognizing a gain on a bargain purchase, the acquirer shall reassess whether it has correctly identified all the acquired assets and assumed liabilities and should recognize any additional assets or liabilities identified in that review. If an excess still remains, the acquirer should recognize the resulting gain in earnings on the acquisition date.

DISCLOSURE

1.87 FASB ASC 805-10-50 requires the acquirer to disclose information that enables financial statement users to evaluate the nature and financial statement effect of a business combination that occurs during the current reporting period or after the reporting date but before the financial statements are issued or available to be issued. To meet this objective, the following items should be disclosed:

- The name and a description of the acquiree
- The acquisition date
- The percentage of voting equity interests acquired
- The primary reasons for the business combination and a description of how control was obtained
- For public business entities
  - The amounts of revenue and earnings of the acquiree since the acquisition date included in the consolidated income statement for the reporting period
  - Pro forma information that differs depending upon whether the entity presents comparative financial statements. If an entity presents comparative financial statements, it should provide pro forma disclosures for the comparative prior period for revenue and earnings of the combined entity
  - Nature and amount of any material, nonrecurring pro forma adjustments directly attributable to the business combination, that are included in the reported pro forma revenue and earnings
- For a business combination achieved in stages:
  - Acquisition date fair value of the equity interest in the acquiree held by the acquirer immediately before the acquisition
  - Amount of any gain or loss recognized as a result of remeasuring to fair value the equity interest that the acquirer held immediately before the business combination
  - Line item in the income statement in which that gain or loss is recognized
  - Valuation technique(s) used to measure the acquisition date fair value of the equity interest the acquirer held immediately before the business combination
  - Other information helpful to users in assessing the inputs used to develop the fair value measurement of the equity interest in the acquiree held by the acquirer immediately before the business combination.

If any of the preceding disclosures for public business entities are impracticable, the acquirer should disclose that fact and explain why. Additional disclosures are required for transactions that are recognized separately from the acquisition of assets and assumptions of liabilities in the business combination.

1.88

TABLE 1-8: BUSINESS COMBINATION DISCLOSURES

The nature of information commonly disclosed for business combinations is listed in Table 1-8.

	2011	2010	2009
Method of Payment			
Cash only	242	171	147
Cash and stock	21	20	13
Stock only	3	2	8
Other, described	8	9	5
Intangible assets not subject to amortization	96	72	156
Intangible assets subject to amortization	177	151	114
Preliminary allocation of acquisition cost	159	96	81
Contingent payments	39	30	26
Purchased research and development costs	16	16	25
Fair value of noncontrolling interest	7	9	4
Bargain purchase gain (negative goodwill)	6	3	2
Other, described	23	19	N/C*

* N/C = Not compiled. Line item was not included in the table for the year shown.

PRESENTATION AND DISCLOSURE EXCERPTS

Business Combinations

1.89

HARRIS CORPORATION (JUN)

NOTES TO CONSOLIDATED FINANCIAL STATEMENTS

Note 4: Business Combinations (in part)

During fiscal 2011 we made the following significant acquisitions:

- *Acquisition of CapRock.* On July 30, 2010, we acquired privately held CapRock Holdings, Inc. and its subsidiaries, including CapRock Communications, Inc. (collectively, "CapRock"), a global provider of mission-critical, managed satellite communications services for the government, energy and maritime industries. CapRock's solutions include broadband Internet access, voice over Internet Protocol ("VOIP") telephony, wideband networking and real-time video, delivered to nearly 2,000 customer sites around the world. The acquisition of CapRock increased the breadth of our *assured communications®* capabilities, while enabling us to enter new vertical markets and increase our international presence. The total net purchase price for CapRock was $517.5 million. Our fiscal 2011 results of operations included revenue of $357.0 million and a pre-tax loss of $16.3 million (including $21.9 million of acquisition-related charges) associated with CapRock for the eleven-month period following the date of acquisition. We report CapRock as part of Managed Satellite

and Terrestrial Communications Solutions under our Integrated Network Solutions segment.

- *Acquisition of Schlumberger GCS.* On April 4, 2011, we acquired from Schlumberger B.V. and its affiliates ("Schlumberger") substantially all of the assets of the Schlumberger group's Global Connectivity Services business ("Schlumberger GCS"), a provider of satellite and terrestrial communications services for the worldwide energy industry. The total net purchase price for Schlumberger GCS was $380.6 million, subject to post-closing adjustments. Our fiscal 2011 results of operations include revenue of $34.6 million and a pre-tax loss of $12.5 million (including $17.0 million of acquisition-related charges) associated with Schlumberger GCS for the three-month period following the date of acquisition. We report Schlumberger GCS as part of Managed Satellite and Terrestrial Communications Solutions under our Integrated Network Solutions segment.

- *Acquisition of Carefx.* Also on April 4, 2011, we acquired privately held Carefx Corporation ("Carefx"), a provider of interoperability workflow solutions for government and commercial healthcare providers. Carefx's solution suite is used by more than 800 hospitals, healthcare systems and health information exchanges across North America, Europe and Asia. The acquisition expanded our presence in government healthcare, provided entry into the commercial healthcare market and is expected to leverage the healthcare interoperability workflow products offered by Carefx and the broader scale of enterprise intelligence solutions and services that we provide. The total net purchase price for Carefx was $152.6 million, subject to post-closing adjustments. We report Carefx as part of Healthcare Solutions under our Integrated Network Solutions segment.

The following tables provide further detail of these acquisitions in fiscal 2011:

(In millions)	CapRock	Schlumberger GCS	Carefx
Date of acquisition	7/30/10	4/4/11	4/4/11
Reporting business segment	Integrated Network Solutions	Integrated Network Solutions	Integrated Network Solutions
Cash consideration paid to former owners	$540.2	$384.6	$153.8
Less cash acquired	(22.7)	(4.0)	(1.2)
Total net purchase price paid as of July 1, 2011	517.5	380.6	152.6
Estimated post-closing acquired cash true-up	—	—	0.7
Total estimated net purchase price	$517.5	$380.6	$153.3
Allocation of purchase price:			
Accounts and notes receivable	$ 41.3	$ 4.8	$ 5.8
Inventories	36.6	3.9	4.4
Other current assets	4.3	4.2	0.3
Current deferred income taxes	14.3	—	1.5
Property, plant and equipment	59.1	33.7	—
Goodwill	381.9	268.3	118.8
Identifiable intangible assets	131.5	75.4	31.4
Other assets	—	—	0.1
Total assets acquired	669.0	390.3	162.3
Accounts payable and accrued expenses	88.6	5.4	4.7
Advance payments and unearned income	3.3	—	2.8
Non-current deferred income taxes	50.1	4.3	0.6
Other liabilities	9.5	—	0.9
Total liabilities acquired	151.5	9.7	9.0
Net assets acquired	$517.5	$380.6	$153.3

SEC 1.89

	CapRock		Schlumberger GCS		Carefx	
	Weighted Average Amortization Period	Total	Weighted Average Amortization Period	Total	Weighted Average Amortization Period	Total
	(In years)	(In millions)	(In years)	(In millions)	(In years)	(In millions)
Identifiable Intangible Assets:						
Customer relationships	16.0	$ 68.0	13.0	$66.7	11.0	$ 7.1
Contract backlog	5.0	49.0	2.0	7.2	4.5	10.6
Trade names	5.0	14.0	6.0	0.2	3.5	2.9
Developed technology			6.0	1.3	4.5	10.8
Other	15.0	0.5				
Weighted average amortization period and total	10.7	$131.5	11.8	$75.4	5.9	$31.4

The purchase price for the CapRock acquisition gives effect to post-closing adjustments while the purchase prices for the Schlumberger GCS and Carefx acquisitions remain subject to post-closing adjustments. The purchase price allocations for all of these acquisitions are preliminary and subject to changes in the fair value of working capital and other assets and liabilities on the effective dates, completion of an appraisal of assets acquired and liabilities assumed, and final valuation of intangible assets.

Pro Forma Results (Unaudited)

The following summary, prepared on a pro forma basis, presents our unaudited consolidated results of operations as if the acquisitions of CapRock and Schlumberger GCS had been completed as of the beginning of fiscal 2010, after including in fiscal 2010 integration and other costs associated with these acquisitions, and after including the impact of adjustments such as amortization of intangible assets and interest expense on related borrowings and, in each case, the related income tax effects. This pro forma presentation does not include any impact of transaction synergies. In the following table, "income from continuing operations" refers to income from continuing operations attributable to Harris Corporation common shareholders.

(In millions, except per share amounts)	2011	2010
Revenue from product sales and services—as reported	$5,924.6	$5,206.1
Revenue from product sales and services—pro forma	$6,082.4	$5,750.8
Income from continuing operations—as reported	$ 588.0	$ 561.6
Income from continuing operations—pro forma	$ 595.8	$ 539.3
Income from continuing operations per diluted common share—as reported	$ 4.60	$ 4.28
Income from continuing operations per diluted common share—pro forma	$ 4.66	$ 4.11

The pro forma results are not necessarily indicative of our results of operations had we owned CapRock and Schlumberger GCS for the entire periods presented.

1.90

ROBBINS & MYERS, INC. (AUG)

NOTES TO CONSOLIDATED FINANCIAL STATEMENTS

Note 1—Summary of Significant Accounting Policies (in part)

Acquisition and Disposition (in part)

On January 10, 2011 ("the acquisition date"), we completed our acquisition of T-3 Energy Services, Inc. ("T-3"), such that T-3 became a wholly-owned subsidiary of Robbins & Myers, Inc. The operating results of T-3 are included in our consolidated financial statements since the acquisition date within our Fluid Management segment. See Note 3—Acquisition. The merger was accounted for under the acquisition method of accounting in accordance with Accounting Standards Codification ("ASC") 805, "Business Combinations." Accordingly, we made an allocation of the purchase price at the acquisition date based upon our estimates of the fair value of the acquired assets and assumed liabilities obtained during our due diligence process and through other sources, including through tangible and intangible asset appraisals. Additionally, as required by ASC 805, all integration-related costs, including professional fees and severance, were expensed as incurred. See Note 3—Acquisition.

Note 3—Acquisition

On January 10, 2011, we acquired 100% of the outstanding common stock and voting interests of T-3. T-3 designs, manufactures, repairs and services products used in the drilling, completion and production of new oil and gas wells, the workover of existing wells, and the production and transportation of oil and gas. Its products are used in both onshore and offshore applications throughout the world. We believe the acquisition will significantly expand and complement our energy business within our Fluid Management segment and create a stronger strategic platform with better scale to support our future growth.

The purchase price for acquiring all of the outstanding common stock of T-3 was approximately $618.4 million, which consisted of approximately $106.3 million in cash, $492.1 million as the fair value of our common shares and

$20.0 million as the fair value of options and warrants issued to replace T-3 grants for pre-merger services and warrants, based on the weighted average Black-Scholes valuation of $20.41 per R&M share. The fair value of R&M common shares issued of $41.18 per common share was based on the closing price of R&M shares on the New York Stock Exchange ("NYSE") on January 7, 2011 (opening price on January 10, 2011). We funded the cash portion of the purchase price from our available cash on hand. Transaction expenses were funded with available cash of the Company. We issued approximately 12.0 million shares as part of the purchase price to T-3 stockholders. T-3 had annual revenues of approximately $206.7 million (unaudited) for its last completed fiscal year ended December 31, 2010.

We have finalized third party valuations of certain nonmonetary tangible assets, intangible assets and contingencies. The following table summarizes the estimated fair values of the assets acquired and liabilities assumed at the acquisition date (in thousands):

Cash	$ 15,863
Accounts receivable	41,618
Inventories	60,740
Other current assets	13,257
Property, plant and equipment, net	54,392
Other long-term assets	12,296
Intangible assets	214,120
Total identifiable assets acquired excluding goodwill	412,286
Current liabilities	45,287
Long-term liabilities	78,980
Total liabilities assumed	124,267
Net identifiable assets acquired excluding goodwill	288,019
Goodwill	330,377
Net assets acquired	$618,396

The purchase price allocation resulted in the recognition of $330.4 million in goodwill (approximately $25.0 million of which is deductible for tax purposes) and $214.1 million of definite-lived intangible assets with no residual value, including $156.5 million of customer relationships, $17.8 million of trademarks and trade names, $32.6 million of technology and $7.2 million of backlog. The amounts assigned to customer relationships, trademarks and trade names, technology and backlog are amortized over the estimated useful life of 10-20 years, 20 years, 15 years and up to 1 year, respectively. The weighted average life over which these acquired intangibles will be amortized is approximately 18 years. Goodwill recognized from the acquisition primarily relates to the expected contributions of the entity to the overall corporate strategy in addition to synergies and acquired workforce, which are not separable from goodwill. The total purchase price adjustment to goodwill since the acquisition date was approximately $11.4 million and related primarily to intangible assets and deferred taxes.

Net customer sales and EBIT of T-3 included in our operating results in fiscal 2011 from the acquisition date were $179.0 million and $15.9 million, respectively. In fiscal 2011, the Company incurred merger-related costs of $7.2 million for amortization of intangible assets related to customer backlog at the time of acquisition, $3.0 million related to severance costs, $5.9 million related to professional fees and ac-

celerated stock compensation expense (included in "Other expense" line in our consolidated condensed statement of income) and $9.5 million related to the inventory write-up values in cost of sales (included in the "Cost of sales" line in our consolidated statement of income). No further costs relating to backlog or the write-up of inventory will be incurred.

The unaudited pro forma information for the periods set forth below gives effect to the acquisition as if it had occurred at the beginning of each respective fiscal year. These amounts have been calculated after applying our accounting policies and adjusting the results of T-3 to reflect the additional cost of sales, depreciation and amortization that would have been charged assuming the fair value adjustments to inventory, property, plant and equipment and intangible assets had been applied as at the beginning of each respective year, together with the consequential tax effects, as applicable. The pro forma information is presented for informational purposes only and is not necessarily indicative of the results of operations that actually would have been achieved had the acquisition been consummated as of that time or that may result in the future:

(In thousands, except per share data)	2011	2010
Net sales from continuing operations:		
As reported	$820,640	$478,193
Pro forma	899,088	674,067
Net income attributable to Robbins & Myers, Inc. from continuing operations:		
As reported	$ 80,375	$ 29,338
Pro forma	85,381	21,161
Basic net income per share from continuing operations:		
As reported	$ 1.96	$ 0.89
Pro forma	1.88	0.47
Diluted net income per share from continuing operations:		
As reported	$ 1.94	$ 0.89
Pro forma	1.86	0.47

Each fiscal year pro forma period reflects the expense due to the inventory write-up values and amortization of backlog of $16.7 million ($10.8 million after tax and $0.24 per share based on the Company's marginal tax rate) which had lives of three months or less. Therefore, these assets were fully amortized in the first three months of each respective year.

1.91

MCKESSON CORPORATION (MAR)

FINANCIAL NOTES

1. Significant Accounting Policies (in part)

Business Combinations: We account for acquired businesses using the acquisition method of accounting, which requires that the assets acquired and liabilities assumed be recorded at the date of acquisition at their respective fair values. Any excess of the purchase price over the estimated fair values of the net assets acquired is recorded as goodwill. Effective April 1, 2009, acquisition-related expenses and restructuring costs are recognized separately from the business combinations and are expensed as incurred. Acquisition-related expenses totaled $52 million in 2011 and were not material in 2010.

2. Business Combinations

On December 30, 2010, we acquired all of the outstanding shares of US Oncology Holdings, Inc. ("US Oncology") of The Woodlands, Texas for approximately $2.1 billion, consisting of cash consideration of $0.2 billion, net of cash acquired, and the assumption of liabilities with a fair value of $1.9 billion. As an integrated oncology company, US Oncology is affiliated with community-based oncologists, and works with patients, hospitals, payers and the medical industry across all phases of the cancer research and delivery continuum. The acquisition of US Oncology expands our existing specialty pharmaceutical distribution business and adds practice management services for oncologists. The cash paid at acquisition was funded from cash on hand.

The following table summarizes the preliminary recording of the fair values of the assets acquired and liabilities assumed as of the acquisition date:

(In millions)	Amounts Previously Recognized as of Acquisition Date (Provisional)[1]	Measurement Period Adjustments	Amounts Recognized as of Acquisition Date (Provisional as Adjusted)
Current assets, net of cash acquired	$ 546	$116	$ 662
Goodwill	774	34	808
Intangible assets	1,099	(92)	1,007
Other long-term assets	396	(42)	354
Current liabilities	(535)	46	(489)
Current portion of long-term debt	(1,751)	16	(1,735)
Other long-term liabilities	(270)	(68)	(338)
Other stockholders' equity	(15)	(10)	(25)
Net assets acquired, less cash and cash equivalents	$ 244	$ —	$ 244

[1] Represents amounts reported in our Form 10-Q for the quarter ended December 31, 2010.

During the fourth quarter of 2011, the fair value measurements of assets acquired and liabilities assumed as of the acquisition date were revised. Due to the recent timing of the acquisition, these amounts are subject to change within the measurement period as our fair value assessments are finalized.

Included in the purchase price allocation are acquired identifiable intangibles of $1.0 billion, the fair value of which was determined by using Level 3 inputs, which are estimated using significant unobservable inputs. Acquired intangibles primarily consist of $0.7 billion of service agreements and $0.2 billion of customer lists. The estimated weighted average lives of the service agreements, customer lists and total acquired intangibles are 18 years, 10 years and 16 years. The fair value of the debt acquired was determined primarily by using Level 3 inputs, which are estimated using significant unobservable inputs. Refer to Financial Note 11, "Debt and Financing Activities," for additional information on the assumption and funding of acquired debt. The excess of the purchase price over the net tangible and intangible assets of approximately $808 million was recorded as goodwill, which primarily reflects the expected future benefits to be realized upon integrating the business.

Financial results for US Oncology have been included in the results of operations within our Distribution Solutions segment beginning in the fourth quarter of 2011. We recorded $52 million of net acquisition-related expenses in 2011 as follows:

(In millions)	Distribution Solutions	Corporate & Interest Expense	Total
Operating expenses:			
Transaction closing expenses	$22	$ —	$ 22
Severance and relocation	9	—	9
Other integration expenses	10	2	12
Total operating expenses	41	2	43
Other income: reimbursement of post-acquisition interest expense from former shareholders	—	(16)	(16)
Interest expense: bridge loan fees	—	25	25
Total acquisition-related expenses	$41	$ 11	$ 52

On May 21, 2008, we acquired McQueary Brothers Drug Company ("McQueary Brothers") of Springfield, Missouri for approximately $190 million. McQueary Brothers is a regional distributor of pharmaceutical, health and beauty products to independent and regional chain pharmacies in the Midwestern U.S. This acquisition expanded our existing U.S. pharmaceutical distribution business. The acquisition was funded with cash on hand. Financial results for McQueary Brothers have been included within our Distribution Solutions segment since the date of acquisition.

The following table summarizes the fair values of the assets acquired and liabilities assumed as of the acquisition date:

(In millions)	
Goodwill	$126
Intangible assets	67
Other assets	89
Accounts payable and other liabilities	(92)
Net assets acquired, less cash and cash equivalents	$190

During the first quarter of 2010, the fair value measurements of assets acquired and liabilities assumed as of the acquisition date were completed. The excess of the purchase price over the net tangible and intangible assets of approximately $126 million was recorded as goodwill, which primarily reflected the expected future benefits from synergies to be realized upon integrating the business. Included in the purchase price allocation were acquired identifiable intangibles of $61 million primarily representing a customer relationship with a useful life of 7 years, a trade name of $2 million with a useful life of less than one year and a not-to-compete agreement of $4 million with a useful life of 4 years.

During the last three years, we also completed a number of other smaller acquisitions within both of our operating segments. Financial results for our business acquisitions have been included in our consolidated financial statements since their respective acquisition dates. Purchase prices for our business acquisitions have been allocated based on estimated fair values at the date of acquisition.

Goodwill recognized for our business acquisitions is generally not expected to be deductible for tax purposes. Pro forma results of operations for our business acquisitions have not been presented because the effects were not material to the consolidated financial statements on either an individual or an aggregate basis.

11. Debt and Financing Activities (in part)

Senior Bridge Term Loan Facility

In connection with our execution of an agreement to acquire US Oncology, in November 2010 we entered into a $2.0 billion unsecured Senior Bridge Term Loan Agreement ("Bridge Loan"). In December 2010, we reduced the Bridge Loan commitment to $1.0 billion. On January 31, 2011, we borrowed $1.0 billion under the Bridge Loan. On February 28, 2011, we repaid the funds obtained under the Bridge Loan with long-term debt, as further described below, and the Senior Bridge Term Loan Agreement was terminated. During the time it was outstanding, the Bridge Loan bore interest of 1.76%, which was based on the London Interbank Offered Rate plus a margin based on the Company's credit rating. Bridge Loan fees of $25 million were included in interest expense.

US Oncology Debt Acquired

Upon our purchase of US Oncology in December 2010, we assumed the outstanding debt of US Oncology Holdings, Inc. and its wholly-owned subsidiary US Oncology, Inc. Immediately prior to our acquisition, US Oncology Holdings, Inc. called for redemption all of its outstanding Senior Unsecured Floating Rate Toggle Notes due 2012 and US Oncology, Inc. called for redemption all of its outstanding 9.125% Senior Secured Notes due 2017 and 10.75% Senior Subordinated Notes due 2014. In the fourth quarter of 2011, we paid interest of $50 million and redeemed these notes, including the remaining accrued interest for $1,738 million using cash on hand and borrowings under our Bridge Loan.

1.92

CENTURYLINK, INC. (DEC)

NOTES TO CONSOLIDATED FINANCIAL STATEMENTS

(1) Basis of Presentation and Summary of Significant Accounting Policies (in part)

The accompanying consolidated financial statements include our accounts and the accounts of our subsidiaries over which we exercise control. These subsidiaries include our acquisition of SAVVIS, Inc. ("Savvis") on July 15, 2011, Qwest Communications International Inc. ("Qwest") on April 1, 2011 and Embarq Corporation ("Embarq") on July 1, 2009 (See Note 2—Acquisitions). All intercompany amounts and transactions with our consolidated subsidiaries have been eliminated.

(2) Acquisitions

Acquisition of Savvis

On July 15, 2011, we acquired all of the outstanding common stock of Savvis, a provider of cloud hosting, managed hosting, colocation and network services in domestic and foreign markets. We believe this acquisition enhances our ability to be an information technology partner with our existing business customers and strengthens our opportunities to attract new business customers in the future. Each share of Savvis common stock outstanding immediately prior to the acquisition converted into the right to receive $30 per share in cash and 0.2479 shares of CenturyLink common stock. The aggregate consideration of $2.382 billion consisted of:
- cash payments of $1.732 billion;
- the 14.313 million shares of CenturyLink common stock issued to consummate the acquisition;
- the closing stock price of CenturyLink common stock at July 14, 2011 of $38.54; and
- the estimated net value of the pre-combination portion of certain share-based compensation awards assumed by CenturyLink of $98 million, of which $33 million was paid in cash.

Upon completing the acquisition, we also paid $547 million to retire certain pre-existing Savvis debt and accrued interest, and paid related transaction expenses totaling $15 million. The cash payments required on or about the closing date were funded using existing cash balances, which included the net proceeds from the June 2011 issuance of senior notes with an aggregate principal amount of $2.0 billion. See Note 4—Long-term Debt and Credit Facilities, for additional information about our senior notes.

We have recognized the assets and liabilities of Savvis based on our preliminary estimates of their acquisition date fair values. The determination of the fair values of the acquired assets and assumed liabilities (and the related determination of estimated lives of depreciable tangible and identifiable intangible assets) requires significant judgment. As such, we have not completed our valuation analysis and calculations in sufficient detail necessary to arrive at the final estimates of the fair value of Savvis' assets acquired and liabilities assumed, along with the related allocations to goodwill and intangible assets. The fair values of certain tangible assets, intangible assets, certain contingent liabilities and residual goodwill are the most significant areas not yet finalized and therefore are subject to change. We expect to complete our final fair value determinations no later than the second quarter of 2012. Our final fair value determinations may be significantly different than those reflected in our consolidated financial statements at December 31, 2011.

Based on our preliminary estimate, the aggregate consideration exceeds the aggregate estimated fair value of the acquired assets and assumed liabilities by $1.357 billion, which has been recognized as goodwill. This goodwill is attributable to strategic benefits, including enhanced financial and operational scale and product and market diversification that we expect to realize. None of the goodwill associated with this acquisition is deductible for income tax purposes.

The following is our preliminary assignment of the aggregate consideration:

(Dollars in millions)	July 15, 2011
Cash, accounts receivable and other current assets	$ 213
Property, plant and equipment	1,335
Identifiable intangible assets	
Customer relationships	794
Other	51
Other noncurrent assets	27
Current liabilities, excluding current maturities of long-term debt	(129)
Current maturities of long-term debt	(38)
Long-term debt	(840)
Deferred credits and other liabilities	(388)
Goodwill	1,357
Aggregate consideration	$2,382

Acquisition of Qwest

On April 1, 2011, we acquired all of the outstanding common stock of Qwest, a provider of data, Internet, video and voice services nationwide and globally. We entered into this acquisition, among other things, to realize certain strategic benefits, including enhanced financial and operational scale, market diversification and leveraged combined networks. As of the acquisition date, Qwest served approximately 9.0 million access lines and approximately 3.0 million broadband subscribers across 14 states. Each share of Qwest common stock outstanding immediately prior to the acquisition converted into the right to receive 0.1664 shares of CenturyLink common stock, with cash paid in lieu of fractional shares. The aggregate consideration was $12.273 billion based on:

- the 294 million shares of CenturyLink common stock issued to consummate the acquisition;
- the closing stock price of CenturyLink common stock at March 31, 2011 of $41.55;
- the estimated net value of the pre-combination portion of share-based compensation awards assumed by CenturyLink of $52 million (excluding the value of restricted stock included in the number of issued shares specified above); and
- cash paid in lieu of the issuance of fractional shares of $5 million.

We assumed approximately $12.7 billion of long-term debt in connection with our acquisition of Qwest.

We have recognized the assets and liabilities of Qwest based on our preliminary estimates of their acquisition date fair values. The determination of the fair values of the acquired assets and assumed liabilities (and the related determination of estimated lives of depreciable tangible and identifiable intangible assets) requires significant judgment. As such, we have not completed our valuation analysis and calculations in sufficient detail necessary to arrive at the final estimates of the fair value of Qwest's assets acquired and liabilities assumed, along with the related allocations to goodwill and intangible assets. The fair values of certain tangible assets, intangible assets, certain contingent liabilities and residual goodwill are the most significant areas not yet finalized and therefore are subject to change. We expect to complete our final fair value determinations no later than the first quarter of 2012. Our final fair value determinations may be significantly different than those reflected in our consolidated financial statements at December 31, 2011.

Based on our preliminary estimate, the aggregate consideration exceeds the aggregate estimated fair value of the acquired assets and assumed liabilities by $10.106 billion, which amount has been recognized as goodwill. This goodwill is attributable to strategic benefits, including enhanced financial and operational scale, market diversification and leveraged combined networks that we expect to realize. None of the goodwill associated with this acquisition is deductible for income tax purposes.

The following is our preliminary assignment of the aggregate consideration:

(Dollars in millions)	April 1, 2011
Cash, accounts receivable and other current assets	$ 2,128
Property, plant and equipment	9,554
Identifiable intangible assets	
Customer relationships	7,625
Capitalized software	1,702
Other	189
Other noncurrent assets	373
Current liabilities, excluding current maturities of long-term debt	(2,428)
Current maturities of long-term debt	(2,422)
Long-term debt	(10,253)
Deferred credits and other liabilities	(4,301)
Goodwill	10,106
Aggregate consideration	$12,273

Acquisition of Embarq

On July 1, 2009, we acquired all of the outstanding common stock of Embarq Corporation ("Embarq"), a provider of data, Internet, video and voice services. We entered into this acquisition, among other things, to realize certain strategic benefits, including enhanced financial and operational scale, market diversification and leveraged combined networks. As of the acquisition date, Embarq served approximately 5.4 million access lines and approximately 1.5 million broadband subscribers across 18 states. Each share of Embarq common stock outstanding immediately prior to the acquisition converted into the right to receive 1.37 shares of CenturyLink common stock, with cash paid in lieu of fractional shares. The aggregate consideration of $6.070 billion was based on:

- the 196 million shares of CenturyLink common stock issued to consummate the acquisition;
- the closing stock price of CenturyLink common stock at June 30, 2009 of $30.70; and
- the estimated net value of the pre-combination portion of share-based compensation awards assumed by CenturyLink of approximately $50 million (excluding the value of restricted stock included in the number of issued shares specified above).

We assumed approximately $4.9 billion of long-term debt in connection with our acquisition of Embarq.

In connection with the Embarq acquisition, we amended our charter to eliminate our time-phase voting structure, which previously entitled persons who beneficially owned shares of our common stock continuously since May 30, 1987 to ten votes per share.

We have recognized the assets and liabilities of Embarq based on their acquisition date fair values. Based on our final determination of fair value in June 2010, the aggregate consideration exceeds the aggregate estimated fair value of the acquired assets and assumed liabilities by $6.245 billion, which amount has been recognized as goodwill. This goodwill is attributable to strategic benefits, including enhanced financial and operational scale, market diversification and leveraged combined networks that we expect to realize. None of the goodwill associated with this acquisition is deductible for income tax purposes.

The following is our assignment of the aggregate consideration:

(Dollars in millions)	July 1, 2009
Cash, accounts receivable and other current assets	$ 676
Property, plant and equipment	6,078
Identifiable intangible assets	
Customer relationships	1,098
Right of way	268
Other	27
Other noncurrent assets	24
Current liabilities, excluding current maturities of long-term debt	(837)
Current maturities of long-term debt	(2)
Long-term debt	(4,885)
Deferred credits and other liabilities	(2,622)
Goodwill	6,245
Aggregate consideration	$6,070

In connection with consummating the Embarq acquisition, we amended our charter to (i) eliminate our time-phase voting structure, which previously entitled persons who beneficially owned shares of our common stock continuously since May 30, 1987 to ten votes per share, and (ii) increase the authorized number of shares of our common stock from 350 million to 800 million. As so amended and restated, our charter provides that each share of our common stock is entitled to one vote per share with respect to each matter properly submitted to shareholders for their vote, consent, waiver, release or other action.

References to Acquired Businesses

In the discussion that follows, we refer to the business that we operated prior to the Qwest acquisition (including Embarq's business) as "Legacy CenturyLink" and refer to the incremental business activities that we now operate as a result of the Savvis acquisition and the Qwest acquisition as "Legacy Savvis" and "Legacy Qwest," respectively.

Combined Pro Forma Operating Results (Unaudited)

For the year ended December 31, 2011, CenturyLink's results of operations included operating revenues (net of intercompany eliminations) attributable to Qwest and Savvis of $8.2 billion and $483 million, respectively. The addition of Qwest and Savvis post-acquisition operations did not contribute significantly to our consolidated net income.

The following unaudited pro forma financial information presents the combined results of CenturyLink as if the Qwest and Savvis acquisitions had been consummated as of January 1, 2010.

	Years Ended December 31	
(Dollars in millions)	2011	2010
Operating revenues	$18,692	19,431
Net income	601	293
Basic earnings per common share	.97	.48
Diluted earnings per common share	.97	.48

This pro forma information reflects certain adjustments to previously reported operating results, consisting of primarily:

- decreased operating revenues and expenses due to the elimination of deferred revenues and deferred expenses associated with installation activities and capacity leases that were assigned no value at the acquisition date and the elimination of transactions among CenturyLink, Qwest and Savvis that are now subject to intercompany elimination;
- increased amortization expense related to identifiable intangible assets, net of decreased depreciation expense to reflect the fair value of property, plant and equipment;
- decreased recognition of retiree benefit expenses for Qwest due to the elimination of unrecognized actuarial losses;
- decreased interest expense primarily due to the amortization of an adjustment to reflect the increased fair value of long-term debt of Qwest recognized on the acquisition date; and
- the related income tax effects.

The pro forma information does not necessarily reflect the actual results of operations had the Qwest and Savvis acquisitions been consummated at January 1, 2010, nor is it necessarily indicative of future operating results. The pro forma information does not give effect to any potential revenue enhancements, cost synergies or other operating efficiencies that could result from the acquisitions (other than those realized in our historical financial statements after the respective acquisition dates).

At December 31, 2011, we had incurred cumulative acquisition related expenses, consisting primarily of integration and severance related expenses, of $41 million for Savvis, $393 million for Qwest, and $459 million for Embarq. The total amount of these expenses recognized in our costs of services and products and selling, general and administrative expenses for years ended December 31, 2011, 2010 and 2009 was $467 million, $145 million and $271 million, respectively. An additional $16 million consists of transaction expenses incurred in connection with terminating an unused loan financing commitment related to our Savvis acquisition. This amount was not considered an operating activity and therefore not included as an operating expense.

Qwest incurred cumulative pre-acquisition related expenses of $71 million, including $36 million in periods prior to being acquired and $35 million on the date of acquisition. Savvis incurred cumulative pre-acquisition related expenses of $22 million, including $3 million in periods prior to being acquired and $19 million on the date of acquisition. These amounts are not included in our results of operations.

COMMITMENTS

DISCLOSURE

1.93 FASB ASC 440, *Commitments*, requires the disclosure of commitments such as those for unused letters of credit; long-term leases; assets pledged as security for loans; pension plans; cumulative preferred stock dividends in arrears; plant acquisition, obligations to reduce debts, maintain working capital, and restrict dividends; and unconditional purchase obligations.

PRESENTATION AND DISCLOSURE EXCERPTS

Restrictive Covenants

1.94

LEAR CORPORATION (DEC)

NOTES TO CONSOLIDATED FINANCIAL STATEMENTS

(8) Long-Term Debt (in part)

A summary of long-term debt and the related weighted average interest rates is shown below (in millions):

December 31	2011		2010	
Debt Instrument	Long-Term Debt	Weighted Average Interest Rate	Long-Term Debt	Weighted Average Interest Rate
7.875% Senior Notes due 2018	$347.9	8.00%	$347.7	8.00%
8.125% Senior Notes due 2020	347.5	8.25%	347.2	8.25%
Long-term debt	$695.4		$694.9	

Senior Notes

On March 26, 2010, the Company issued $350 million in aggregate principal amount at maturity of senior unsecured notes due 2018 at a stated coupon rate of 7.875% (the "2018 Notes") and $350 million in aggregate principal amount at maturity of senior unsecured notes due 2020 at a stated coupon rate of 8.125% (the "2020 Notes" and together with the 2018 Notes, the "Notes"). The 2018 Notes were priced at 99.276% of par, resulting in a yield to maturity of 8.00%, and the 2020 Notes were priced at 99.164% of par, resulting in a yield to maturity of 8.25%. The net proceeds from the issuance of the Notes, together with existing cash on hand, were used to repay in full an aggregate amount of $925.0 million of term loans provided under the Company's first and second lien credit agreements (described below).

Interest is payable on the Notes on March 15 and September 15 of each year. The 2018 Notes mature on March 15, 2018, and the 2020 Notes mature on March 15, 2020.

The Company may redeem all or part of the Notes, at its option, at any time on or after March 15, 2014, in the case of the 2018 Notes, and March 15, 2015, in the case of the 2020 Notes, at the redemption prices set forth below, plus accrued and unpaid interest to the redemption date.

Twelve-Month Period Commencing March 15	2018 Notes	2020 Notes
2014	103.938%	N/A
2015	101.969%	104.063%
2016	100.0%	102.708%
2017	100.0%	101.354%
2018 and thereafter	100.0%	100.0%

Prior to March 15, 2013, the Company may redeem up to 35% of the original aggregate principal amount of the 2018 Notes and the 2020 Notes at a price equal to 107.875% and 108.125%, respectively, of the principal amount thereof, plus accrued and unpaid interest to the redemption date, with the net cash proceeds of one or more equity offerings, provided that at least 65% of the original aggregate principal amount of each series of Notes remains outstanding after the redemption. The Company may also redeem all or part of the Notes at any time prior to March 15, 2014, in the case of the 2018 Notes, and March 15, 2015, in the case of the 2020 Notes, at a price equal to 100% of the principal amount thereof, plus accrued and unpaid interest to the redemption date and a "make-whole" premium. In addition, the Company may redeem up to 10% of the original aggregate principal amount of each series of Notes during any 12-month period prior to March 15, 2014, in the case of the 2018 Notes, and March 15, 2015, in the case of the 2020 Notes, at a price equal to 103% of the principal amount thereof, plus accrued and unpaid interest to the redemption date.

Subject to certain limitations, in the event of a change of control of the Company, the Company will be required to make an offer to purchase the Notes at a purchase price equal to 101% of the principal amount of the Notes, plus accrued and unpaid interest to the date of purchase.

The Notes are senior unsecured obligations. The Company's obligations under the Notes are fully and unconditionally guaranteed, jointly and severally, on a senior unsecured basis by certain domestic subsidiaries, which are directly or indirectly 100% owned by Lear. See Note 18, "Supplemental Guarantor Condensed Consolidating Financial Statements."

The indenture governing the Notes contains restrictive covenants that, among other things, limit the ability of the Company and its subsidiaries to: (i) incur additional debt, (ii) pay dividends and make other restricted payments, (iii) create or permit certain liens, (iv) issue or sell capital stock of the Company's restricted subsidiaries, (v) use the proceeds from sales of assets and subsidiary stock, (vi) create or permit restrictions on the ability of the Company's restricted subsidiaries to pay dividends or make other distributions to the Company, (vii) enter into transactions with affiliates, (viii) enter into sale and leaseback transactions and (ix) consolidate or merge or sell all or substantially all of the Company's assets. The foregoing limitations are subject to exceptions as set forth in the Notes. In addition, if in the future the Notes have an investment grade credit rating from both Moody's Investors Service and Standard & Poor's Ratings Services and no default has occurred and is continuing, certain of these covenants will, thereafter, no longer apply to the Notes for so long as the Notes have an investment grade credit rating by both rating agencies.

As of December 31, 2011, the Company was in compliance with all covenants under the indenture governing the Notes.

Revolving Credit Facility

On June 17, 2011, the Company entered into an amendment and restatement of its senior secured credit agreement (the "Amended and Restated Credit Agreement") to, among other things, (i) extend the maturity of the Company's existing revolving credit facility from March 18, 2013 to June 17, 2016, (ii) increase the amount available under its existing revolving credit facility from $110 million to $500 million, (iii) adjust the interest rates payable on outstanding borrowings, as described below, and (iv) modify the covenants under the existing credit agreement to provide the Company with significant flexibility with respect to certain actions. In connection with this amendment and restatement, the Company paid debt issuance costs of $4.8 million in the second quarter of 2011. The revolving credit facility permits borrowings for general corporate and working capital purposes and the issuance of letters of credit. As of December 31, 2011, there were no borrowings outstanding under the revolving credit facility.

Advances under the revolving credit facility generally bear interest at a variable rate per annum equal to (i) the Eurocurrency Rate (as defined in the Amended and Restated Credit Agreement) plus an adjustable margin of 1.375% to 3.0%

based on the Company's corporate rating (2.25% as of December 31, 2011), payable on the last day of each applicable interest period but in no event less frequently than quarterly, or (ii) the Adjusted Base Rate (as defined in the Amended and Restated Credit Agreement) plus an adjustable margin of 0.375% to 2.0% based on the Company's corporate rating (1.25% as of December 31, 2011), payable quarterly. A facility fee is payable which ranges from 0.375% to 0.50% of the total amount committed under the revolving credit facility.

The Company's obligations under the Amended and Restated Credit Agreement are secured on a first priority basis by a lien on substantially all of the U.S. assets of the Company and its domestic subsidiaries, as well as 100% of the stock of the Company's domestic subsidiaries and 65% of the stock of certain of the Company's foreign subsidiaries. In addition, obligations under the Amended and Restated Credit Agreement are guaranteed, jointly and severally, on a first priority basis, by certain domestic subsidiaries, which are directly or indirectly 100% owned by Lear. See Note 18, "Supplemental Guarantor Condensed Consolidating Financial Statements."

The Amended and Restated Credit Agreement contains various customary representations, warranties and covenants by the Company, including, without limitation, (i) covenants regarding maximum leverage and minimum interest coverage, (ii) limitations on fundamental changes involving the Company or its subsidiaries and (iii) limitations on indebtedness, liens, investments and restricted payments. As of December 31, 2011, the Company was in compliance with all covenants under the agreement governing the Amended and Restated Credit Agreement.

1.95

STEEL DYNAMICS, INC. (DEC)

NOTES TO CONSOLIDATED FINANCIAL STATEMENTS

Note 2. Long-Term Debt (in part)

The Facility contains financial covenants and other covenants that limit or restrict our ability to make capital expenditures; incur indebtedness; permit liens on property; enter into transactions with affiliates; make restricted payments or investments; enter into mergers, acquisitions or consolidations; conduct asset sales; pay dividends or distributions and enter into other specified transactions and activities. Our ability to borrow funds within the terms of the Revolver is dependent upon our continued compliance with the financial and other covenants. The Facility also contains a borrowing base requirement regarding the maximum availability of the Revolver. The company's Revolver must be the lesser of:

I. $1.1 billion less other applicable commitments, such as letters of credit and other secured debt, as defined within the credit agreement, or;

II. The sum of 85% of the company's eligible accounts receivable and 65% of the company's eligible inventories, less other applicable commitments, such as letters of credit and other secured debt, as defined within the credit agreement.

At December 31, 2011, the company had $1.1 billion of availability on the Revolver, $16.5 million of outstanding letters of credit and other obligations which reduce availability, and there were no borrowings outstanding.

The Facility's financial covenants are as follows:

I. Minimum Liquidity—Liquidity is defined as unrestricted cash and Revolver availability, each as defined in the credit agreement. The company must maintain minimum liquidity of $150.0 million plus any outstanding amount of the $700.0 million senior notes due 2012, which requirement was $850 million at December 31, 2011. At December 31, 2011, the company's liquidity was almost $1.6 billion.

II. Interest Coverage—Interest coverage is defined as the ratio of the company's consolidated LTM adjusted EBITDA to the company's consolidated LTM gross interest expense. The company must maintain an interest coverage ratio of not less than 2.50 to 1.00. At December 31, 2011, the company's interest coverage ratio was 4.92 to 1.00.

III. Net Debt Leverage—Net debt leverage is defined as the ratio of the company's consolidated net debt, as defined within the credit agreement, to consolidated LTM adjusted EBITDA. The company must maintain a net debt leverage ratio of less than 5.00 to 1.00. In addition, if the total debt to consolidated LTM adjusted EBITDA ratio exceeds 3.50 to 1.00 at any time, then the ability of the company to make restricted payments as defined in the credit agreement (which includes cash dividends to stockholders and share purchases, among other things), could be limited. At December 31, 2011, the company's net debt leverage ratio was 2.36 to 1.00.

The company was in compliance with its financial covenants at December 31, 2011 and anticipates remaining in compliance during the next twelve months.

1.96

EL PASO CORPORATION (DEC)

NOTES TO CONSOLIDATED FINANCIAL STATEMENTS

1. Basis of Presentation and Significant Accounting Policies (in part)

Proposed Merger with Kinder Morgan, Inc. (in part)

On October 16, 2011, we announced a definitive merger agreement with Kinder Morgan, Inc. (KMI) whereby KMI will acquire El Paso Corporation (El Paso) in a transaction that valued El Paso at approximately $38 billion (based on the KMI stock price at that date), including the assumption of debt. The merger agreement has been approved by each of our and KMI's board of directors. The completion of the merger is subject to satisfaction or waiver of certain closing conditions including, among others, customary regulatory approvals, approval by our stockholders and approval of the issuance of KMI stock and warrants by KMI's stockholders. A voting agreement has been executed by certain stockholders of KMI, holding approximately 75 percent of the vot-

ing power of KMI, in which such stockholders have agreed to vote in favor of the merger and issuance of KMI stock and warrants. The completion of the merger will constitute a change of control for El Paso that may trigger provisions in certain agreements including those related to (i) debt and other financing agreements, (ii) severance agreements and (iii) incentive compensation plan agreements that will result in an immediate acceleration of all unvested stock based compensation awards upon closing of the merger. For our debt and other financing agreements containing covenants related to change in control events and that will not be terminated pursuant to the merger, we have either amended the agreements or obtained waivers of those covenants. However, if there was a downgrade of our credit ratings upon completion of the merger with KMI, it could trigger certain other change of control provisions to certain agreements to which we are a party.

Upon the merger, El Paso shareholders will receive a combination of Class P shares of common stock of KMI, common stock purchase warrants of KMI and cash. Each share of El Paso common stock (excluding any shares held by KMI or its subsidiaries or by El Paso and dissenting shares in accordance with Delaware law), will, at the effective time of the merger, be converted into the right to receive, at the election of the holder but subject to pro-ration with respect to the stock and cash portion such that approximately 57 percent of the aggregate merger consideration (excluding the warrants) is paid in cash and approximately 43 percent (excluding the warrants) is paid in Class P common stock of KMI, par value $0.01 per share (the "KMI Class P Common Stock"): (i) 0.9635 of a share of KMI Class P Common Stock and 0.640 of a common stock purchase warrant of KMI (a "KMI Warrant"), (ii) $25.91 in cash without interest and 0.640 of a KMI Warrant or (iii) 0.4187 of a share of KMI Class P Common Stock, $14.65 in cash without interest and 0.640 of a KMI Warrant. Each KMI Warrant will entitle its holder to purchase one share of KMI Class P Common Stock at an exercise price of $40.00 per share, subject to certain adjustments, at any time during the five-year period following the closing of the merger.

The merger agreement includes customary representations, warranties and covenants, and specific agreements relating to (i) the conduct of each of El Paso's and KMI's respective businesses between the date of the signing of the merger agreement and the closing of the merger transactions and (ii) the efforts of the parties to cause the merger transactions to be completed. In addition to certain other covenants, we have agreed not to encourage, solicit, initiate or facilitate any takeover proposal from a third party or enter into any agreement, arrangement or understanding requiring us to abandon, terminate or fail to consummate the merger and related transactions. The merger agreement contains certain termination rights for both El Paso and KMI and further provides that, upon termination of the merger agreement, under certain circumstances, El Paso may be required to pay KMI a termination fee equal to $650 million or, in certain other circumstances, El Paso may be required to reimburse KMI for its expenses up to $20 million and certain financing related expenses.

Under the terms of the merger agreement, we have agreed to conduct our business in the ordinary course and in all material respects in substantially the same manner as conducted prior to the date of the merger agreement, subject to certain conditions, restrictions and thresholds including, but not limited to, our ability to (i) commit to capital expenditures above our current capital budgets (ii) acquire, invest in, or dispose of any material properties, assets, or equity interests as defined in the merger agreement (iii) incur new debt, refinance, or guarantee any debt or borrowed money, (iv) enter into, terminate, or amend certain material contracts, (v) issue, grant, sell, or redeem new El Paso capital stock or stock-based compensation awards and/or pay dividends in excess of $0.01/share, among other limitations.

In conjunction with the merger, KMI announced that they intend to sell our exploration and production assets. On February 24, 2012, we entered into a purchase and sale agreement to sell all of our exploration and production assets to an affiliate of Apollo Global Management, LLC ("Apollo") and certain other parties for $7.15 billion subject to certain adjustments for items such as contributions or distributions, incurrence of debt and title defects. The sale is contemplated by the merger agreement with KMI. The closing of the sale is conditioned upon the closing of the transactions contemplated by the merger agreement with KMI. Both transactions are expected to be completed in the second quarter of 2012. The purchase and sale agreement contains customary representations and warranties relating to the exploration and production assets and operations. Additionally, El Paso has entered into a performance guarantee in favor of Apollo, under which we guarantee the performance of all of our seller subsidiaries' obligations under the purchase and sale agreement. Pursuant to the merger agreement with KMI, KMI is required to indemnify us from any and all cost incurred by us arising from or relating to the sale of the exploration and production assets. Upon completion of the sale, the exploration and production business will be reflected as a discontinued operation in our financial statements.

11. Debt, Other Financing Obligations and Other Credit Facilities (in part)

Restrictive Covenants and Collateral Provisions

$1.25 Billion Revolving Credit Agreement. El Paso and certain of its subsidiaries have guaranteed this facility, which is collateralized by our general partnership interests in EPB and by our stock ownership in EPNG and TGP who are also eligible borrowers. During 2011 our collateral restrictions were modified providing us the ability to sell up to 100 percent of our ownership interests in either EPNG or TGP, or a combination thereof, to EPB. Upon achieving investment grade status (with stable outlook) by either of the two rating agencies, Standard & Poors and Moody's, collateral support on this facility will be eliminated. Our covenants under the $1.25 billion revolving credit facility include restrictions on debt levels, restrictions on liens securing debt and guarantees, restrictions on mergers (e.g. our proposed merger with KMI) and on the sales of assets, dividend restrictions, cross default and cross-acceleration provisions. A breach of any of these covenants could result in acceleration of our debt and other financial obligations and that of our subsidiaries upon such event unless our agreement is amended or these covenants are waived. Under our credit agreement, the most restrictive debt covenants and cross default provisions are:

(a) Our ratio of Debt to Consolidated earnings before interest, income taxes, depreciation and amortization (EBITDA), each as defined in the credit agreement, shall not exceed 5.25 to 1 until maturity;

(b) Our ratio of Consolidated EBITDA, as defined in the credit agreement, to interest expense plus dividends paid shall not be less than 2.0 to 1 until maturity;

(c) EPNG and TGP cannot incur incremental debt if the incurrence of this incremental debt would cause their Debt to Consolidated EBITDA ratio, each as defined in the credit agreement, for that particular company to exceed 5.0 to 1; and

(d) The occurrence of an event of default after the expiration of any applicable grace period, with respect to debt in an aggregate principal amount of $200 million or more.

EPE $1.0 Billion Revolving Credit Agreement. This facility is collateralized by certain of our oil and natural gas properties. The credit agreement is subject to a borrowing base redetermination on a semi-annual basis. In November 2011, the latest revaluation, our borrowing base capacity was reaffirmed at $1.0 billion by the lenders in the facility. EPE's borrowings under this facility are also subject to other conditions. The financial coverage ratio under the facility requires that EPE's debt to EBITDA, as defined in the credit agreement, must not exceed 4.0 to 1.0 and that EPE's EBITDA to interest expense not be less than 2.0 to 1.0.

EPPOC $1.0 Billion Revolving Credit Facility. This facility requires that EPB and Wyoming Interstate (WIC) maintain a consolidated leverage ratio (consolidated indebtedness to consolidated EBITDA) as defined in the credit agreement as of the end of each quarter of less than 5.0 to 1.0 for any trailing four consecutive quarter period; and 5.5 to 1.0 for any such four quarter period during the three full fiscal quarters subsequent to the consummation of specified permitted acquisitions. Borrowings under this facility are restricted for use by EPPOC and its subsidiaries.

Other Restrictions and Provisions. In addition to the above restrictions and provisions, we and/or our subsidiaries are subject to various financial and non-financial covenants and restrictions. These covenants and restrictions include change in control provisions; limitations of additional debt at some of our subsidiaries; limitations on the use of proceeds from borrowing at some of our subsidiaries; limitations, in some cases, on transactions with our affiliates; limitations on the incurrence of liens; limitations on some of our subsidiaries to participate in our cash management program and potential limitations on the ability of some of our subsidiaries to declare and pay dividends. Our most restrictive cross-acceleration provision is associated with the indenture of one of our subsidiaries. This indenture states that should an event of default occur resulting in the acceleration of other debt obligations of that subsidiary in excess of $10 million, the long-term debt obligation containing that provision could be accelerated. The acceleration of our debt would adversely affect our liquidity position and in turn, our financial condition. As of December 31, 2011, we were in compliance with the debt covenants and restrictions in each of the credit agreements and facilities noted above.

We have also issued various guarantees securing financial obligations of our subsidiaries and affiliates with similar covenants as the above facilities.

1.97

UNIFI, INC. (JUN)

*NOTES TO CONSOLIDATED FINANCIAL
STATEMENTS*

(Amounts in thousands, except per share amounts)

12. Long-Term Debt (in part)

Revolving Credit Facility (in part)

Concurrent with the issuance of the 2014 notes, the Company amended its senior secured asset-based revolving credit facility ("Amended Credit Agreement") which, along with revising certain terms and covenants, extended its maturity date to May 15, 2011. On September 9, 2010, the Company and the Subsidiary Guarantors (as co-borrowers) entered into the First Amendment to the Amended and Restated Credit Agreement ("First Amended Credit Agreement") with Bank of America, N.A. (as both Administrative Agent and Lender). The First Amended Credit Agreement provides for a revolving credit facility of $100,000 (with the ability of the Company to request that the borrowing capacity be increased up to $150,000) that matures on September 9, 2015. However, if the 2014 notes have not been paid in full on or before February 15, 2014, the maturity date of the Company's revolving credit facility will be automatically adjusted to February 15, 2014.

The First Amended Credit Agreement contains customary affirmative and negative covenants for asset-based loans that restrict future borrowings and certain transactions. Such covenants include restrictions and limitations on (i) sales of assets, consolidation, merger, dissolution and the issuance of the Company's capital stock, (ii) permitted encumbrances on the Company's property, (iii) the incurrence of indebtedness by the Company, (iv) the making of loans or investments by the Company, (v) the declaration of dividends and redemptions by the Company and (vi) transactions with affiliates by the Company. So long as pro forma excess availability is at least 27.5% of the total credit facility or, if applicable, other specific conditions are met, the Company can make certain distributions and investments including (i) the payment or making of any dividend, (ii) the redemption or other acquisition of any of the Company's capital stock, (iii) cash investments in joint ventures, (iv) acquisition of the property and assets or capital stock or a business unit of another entity and (v) loans or other investments to a non-borrower subsidiary. The First Amended Credit Agreement requires the Company to maintain a trailing twelve month fixed charge coverage ratio of at least 1.0 to 1.0 should borrowing availability decrease below 15% of the total credit facility. There are no capital expenditure limitations under the First Amended Credit Agreement. The Company was in compliance with all covenants at June 26, 2011.

1.98

ENERGIZER HOLDINGS, INC. (SEP)

*NOTES TO CONSOLIDATED FINANCIAL
STATEMENTS*

(Dollars in millions, except per share and percentage data)

(12) Debt (in part)

Under the terms of the Company's credit agreements, the ratio of the Company's indebtedness to its EBITDA, as defined in the agreements and detailed below, cannot be greater than 4.00 to 1, and may not remain above 3.50 to 1 for more than four consecutive quarters. If and so long as the ratio is above 3.50 to 1 for any period, the Company is required to pay additional interest expense for the period in which the ratio exceeds 3.50 to 1. The interest rate margin and certain fees vary depending on the indebtedness to EBITDA ratio. Under the Company's private placement note agreements, the ratio of indebtedness to EBITDA may not exceed 4.00 to 1. However, if the ratio is above 3.50 to 1, the Company is required to pay an additional 75 basis points in interest for the period in which the ratio exceeds 3.50 to 1. In addition, under the credit agreements, the ratio of its current year EBIT, as defined in the agreements, to total interest expense must exceed 3.00 to 1. The Company's ratio of indebtedness to its proforma EBITDA was 2.92 to 1, and the ratio of its proforma EBIT to total interest expense was 4.33 to 1, as of September 30, 2011. These ratios were negatively impacted by a significant portion of the pre-tax charges associated with the Household Products restructuring activities in fiscal 2011 as such charges reduced EBITDA as defined in the agreements. If the Company fails to comply with the financial covenants referred to above or with other requirements of the credit agreements or private placement note agreements, the lenders would have the right to accelerate the maturity of the debt. Acceleration under one of these facilities would trigger cross defaults on other borrowings.

Under the credit agreements, EBITDA is defined as net earnings, as adjusted to add-back interest expense, income taxes, depreciation and amortization, all of which are determined in accordance with GAAP. In addition, the credit agreement allows certain non-cash charges such as stock award amortization and asset write-offs or impairments to be "added-back" in determining EBITDA for purposes of the indebtedness ratio. Severance and other cash charges incurred as a result of restructuring and realignment activities as well as expenses incurred in acquisition integration activities are included as reductions in EBITDA for calculation of the indebtedness ratio. In the event of an acquisition, such as ASR in fiscal 2011, the EBITDA is calculated on a proforma basis to include the trailing twelve-month EBITDA of the acquired company or brands. Total debt is calculated in accordance with GAAP, but excludes outstanding borrowings under the receivable securitization program. EBIT is calculated in a fashion identical to EBITDA except that depreciation and amortization are not "added-back." Total interest expense is calculated in accordance with GAAP.

On May 2, 2011, the Company amended and renewed, for a three year term, its existing receivables securitization program. Borrowings under this program, which may not exceed $200, receive favorable treatment in the Company's debt compliance covenants. At September 30, 2011, $35.0 was outstanding under this facility.

Leasing Commitments

1.99

FIDELITY NATIONAL INFORMATION SERVICES, INC. (DEC)

NOTES TO CONSOLIDATED FINANCIAL STATEMENTS

Leases (in part)

The Company leases certain of its property under leases which expire at various dates. Several of these agreements include escalation clauses and provide for purchases and renewal options for periods ranging from one to five years.

Future minimum operating lease payments for leases with remaining terms greater than one year for each of the years in the five years ending December 31, 2016, and thereafter in the aggregate, are as follows (in millions):

2012	$69.9
2013	55.6
2014	42.3
2015	31.3
2016	22.5
Thereafter	63.7
Total	$285.3

In addition, the Company has operating lease commitments relating to office equipment and computer hardware with annual lease payments of approximately $12.2 million per year that renew on a short-term basis.

Rent expense incurred under all operating leases during the years ended December 31, 2011, 2010 and 2009 was $93.6 million, $116.1 million and $100.2 million, respectively. Included in discontinued operations in the Consolidated Statements of Earnings was rent expense of $0.5 million, $2.0 million and $1.8 million for the years ended December 31, 2011, 2010 and 2009, respectively.

During the year ended December 31, 2011, the Company entered into capital lease obligations of $31.4 million for certain computer hardware and software. The assets are included in property and equipment and computer software and the remaining capital lease obligation is classified as long-term debt on our Consolidated Balance Sheet as of December 31, 2011. Periodic payments are included in Repayment of borrowings on the Consolidated Statements of Cash Flows.

Sales/Marketing Agreements

1.100

THE SCOTTS MIRACLE-GRO COMPANY (SEP)

NOTES TO CONSOLIDATED FINANCIAL STATEMENTS

Note 7. Marketing Agreement

The Company is Monsanto's exclusive agent for the marketing and distribution of consumer Roundup® herbicide products (with additional rights to new products containing glyphosate or other similar non-selective herbicides) in the consumer lawn and garden market within the United States and other specified countries, including Australia, Austria, Belgium, Canada, France, Germany, the Netherlands and the United Kingdom. Under the terms of the Marketing Agreement, the Company is entitled to receive an annual commission from Monsanto as consideration for the performance of the Company's duties as agent. The annual gross commission under the Marketing Agreement is calculated as a percentage of the actual earnings before interest and income taxes (EBIT) of the consumer Roundup® business in the markets covered by the Marketing Agreement and is based on the achievement of two earnings thresholds, as defined in the Marketing Agreement. The Marketing Agreement also requires the Company to make annual payments to Monsanto as a contribution against the overall expenses of the consumer Roundup® business. The annual contribution payment is defined in the Marketing Agreement as $20 million.

In consideration for the rights granted to the Company under the Marketing Agreement for North America, the Company was required to pay a marketing fee of $32 million to Monsanto. The Company has deferred this amount on the basis that the payment will provide a future benefit through commissions that will be earned under the Marketing Agreement. The economic useful life over which the marketing fee is being amortized is 20 years, with a remaining amortization period of seven years as of September 30, 2011.

Under the terms of the Marketing Agreement, the Company performs certain functions, primarily manufacturing conversion, distribution and logistics, and selling and marketing support, on behalf of Monsanto in the conduct of the consumer Roundup® business. The actual costs incurred for these activities are charged to and reimbursed by Monsanto. The Company records costs incurred under the Marketing Agreement for which the Company is the primary obligor on a gross basis, recognizing such costs in "Cost of sales" and the reimbursement of these costs in "Net sales," with no effect on gross profit or net income. The related net sales and cost of sales were $63.7 million, $65.0 million and $67.8 million for fiscal 2011, fiscal 2010 and fiscal 2009, respectively.

The gross commission earned under the Marketing Agreement, the contribution payments to Monsanto and the amortization of the initial marketing fee paid to Monsanto are included in the calculation of net sales in the Company's Consolidated Statements of Operations. For fiscal 2011, fiscal 2010 and fiscal 2009, the net amount earned under the Marketing Agreement was $57.1 million, $70.0 million and $51.4 million, respectively. The elements of the net commission earned under the Marketing Agreement and included in

"Net sales" for each of the three years in the period ended September 30, 2011 were as follows (in millions):

	2011	2010	2009
Gross commission	$ 77.9	$ 90.8	$ 72.2
Contribution expenses	(20.0)	(20.0)	(20.0)
Amortization of marketing fee	(0.8)	(0.8)	(0.8)
Net commission income	57.1	70.0	51.4
Reimbursements associated with Marketing Agreement	63.7	65.0	67.8
Total net sales associated with Marketing Agreement	$120.8	$135.0	$119.2

The Marketing Agreement has no definite term except as it relates to the European Union countries (the "EU term"). The current EU term extends through September 30, 2013, with an automatic renewal period of two years, subject to non-renewal only upon the occurrence of certain performance defaults. Thereafter, the Marketing Agreement provides that the parties may agree to renew the EU term for an additional three years.

The Marketing Agreement provides Monsanto with the right to terminate the Marketing Agreement upon an event of default (as defined in the Marketing Agreement) by the Company, a change in control of Monsanto or the sale of the consumer Roundup® business. The Marketing Agreement provides the Company with the right to terminate the Marketing Agreement in certain circumstances, including an event of default by Monsanto or the sale of the consumer Roundup® business. Unless Monsanto terminates the Marketing Agreement due to an event of default by the Company, Monsanto is required to pay a termination fee to the Company that varies by program year. The termination fee is calculated as a percentage of the value of the Roundup® business exceeding a certain threshold, but in no event will the termination fee be less than $16 million. If Monsanto were to terminate the Marketing Agreement for cause, the Company would not be entitled to any termination fee. Monsanto may also be able to terminate the Marketing Agreement within a given region, including North America, without paying a termination fee if unit volume sales to consumers in that region decline: (1) over a cumulative three-fiscal-year period; or (2) by more than 5% for each of two consecutive years. If the Marketing Agreement was terminated for any reason, the Company would also lose all, or a substantial portion, of the significant source of earnings and overhead expense absorption the Marketing Agreement provides.

Under the Marketing Agreement, Monsanto must provide the Company with notice of any proposed sale of the consumer Roundup® business, allow the Company to participate in the sale process and negotiate in good faith with the Company with respect to any such proposed sale. In the event the Company acquires the consumer Roundup® business in such a sale, the Company would receive as a credit against the purchase price the amount of the termination fee that would have been paid to the Company if Monsanto had exercised its right to terminate the Marketing Agreement in connection with a sale to another party. If Monsanto decides to sell the consumer Roundup® business to another party, the Company must let Monsanto know whether the Company intends to terminate the Marketing Agreement and forfeit any right to a termination fee or whether it will agree to continue to perform under the Marketing Agreement on behalf of the purchaser.

Royalty, Licensing, and Marketing Obligations

1.101

ELECTRONIC ARTS INC. (MAR)

NOTES TO CONSOLIDATED FINANCIAL STATEMENTS

(7) Restructuring and Other Charges (in part)

Fiscal 2011 Restructuring

In fiscal year 2011, we announced a plan focused on the restructuring of certain licensing and developer agreements in an effort to improve the long-term profitability of our packaged goods business. Under this plan, we amended certain licensing and developer agreements. To a much lesser extent, as part of this restructuring we had workforce reductions and facilities closures through March 31, 2011. Substantially all of these exit activities were completed by March 31, 2011.

As part of our fiscal 2011 restructuring plan, we amended certain license agreements to terminate certain rights we previously had to use the licensors' intellectual property. However, under these agreements we continue to be obligated to pay the contractual minimum royalty-based commitments set forth in the original agreements. Accordingly, we recognized losses and impairments of $102 million representing (1) the net present value of the estimated payments related to terminating these rights and (2) writing down assets associated with these agreements to their approximate fair value. In addition, for one agreement, the actual amount of the loss is variable and subject to periodic adjustments as it is dependent upon the actual revenue we generate from the games. Because the loss for one agreement will be paid in installments through June 2016, our accrued loss was computed using the effective interest method. We currently estimate recognizing in future periods through June 2016, approximately $21 million for the accretion of interest expense related to this obligation. This interest expense will be included in restructuring and other charges in our Consolidated Statement of Operations.

In addition, for the development of certain games, we previously entered into publishing agreements with independent software developers. Under these agreements, we were obligated to pay the independent software developers a predetermined amount (a "Minimum Guarantee") upon delivery of a completed product. The independent software developers were thinly capitalized and they financed the development of products through bank borrowings. During fiscal year 2011, in order to more directly influence the development, product quality and product completion, we amended these agreements whereby we agreed to advance a portion of the Minimum Guarantee prior to completion of the product which were used by the independent software developers to repay their bank loans. In addition, we are now committed to advance the remaining portion of the Minimum Guarantee during the remaining development period. As a result, we have now assumed development risk of the products.

Because the independent software developers are thinly capitalized, our sole ability to recover the Minimum Guarantee is effectively through publishing the software product in development. We also have exclusive rights to exploit the software product once completed. Therefore, we concluded that the substance of the arrangement is the purchase of research and development that has no alternative future use and was expensed upon acquisition. Accordingly, we recognized a $31 million charge in our Consolidated Statement of Operations during the fiscal year ended March 31, 2011. In addition, we will recognize the remaining portion of the Minimum Guarantee to be advanced during the development period as research and development expense as the services are incurred.

Since the inception of the fiscal 2011 restructuring plan through March 31, 2011, we have incurred charges of $148 million, consisting of (1) $104 million related to the amendment of certain licensing agreements and other intangible asset impairment costs, (2) $31 million related to the amendment of certain developer agreements, and (3) $13 million in employee-related expenses. The $104 million restructuring accrual as of March 31, 2011 related to the fiscal 2011 restructuring is expected to be settled by June 2016. In fiscal year 2012, we anticipate incurring less than $10 million of restructuring and other charges related to the fiscal 2011 restructuring (primarily interest expense accretion).

(11) Commitments and Contingencies (in part)

Development, Celebrity, League and Content Licenses: Payments and Commitments (in part)

The products we produce in our studios are designed and created by our employee designers, artists, software programmers and by non-employee software developers ("independent artists" or "third-party developers"). We typically advance development funds to the independent artists and third-party developers during development of our games,

usually in installment payments made upon the completion of specified development milestones. Contractually, these payments are generally considered advances against subsequent royalties on the sales of the products. These terms are set forth in written agreements entered into with the independent artists and third-party developers.

In addition, we have certain celebrity, league and content license contracts that contain minimum guarantee payments and marketing commitments that may not be dependent on any deliverables. Celebrities and organizations with whom we have contracts include: FIFA, FIFPRO Foundation, FAPL (Football Association Premier League Limited), and DFL Deutsche Fußball Liga GmbH (German Soccer League) (professional soccer); National Basketball Association (professional basketball); PGA TOUR and Tiger Woods (professional golf); National Hockey League and NHL Players' Association (professional hockey); Warner Bros. (Harry Potter); National Football League Properties, PLAYERS Inc., and Red Bear Inc. (professional football); Collegiate Licensing Company (collegiate football); ESPN (content in EA SPORTS games); Hasbro, Inc. (most of Hasbro's toy and game intellectual properties); LucasArts and Lucas Licensing (Star Wars: The Old Republic), and the Estate of Robert Ludlum (Robert Ludlum novels and films). These developer and content license commitments represent the sum of (1) the cash payments due under non-royalty-bearing licenses and services agreements and (2) the minimum guaranteed payments and advances against royalties due under royalty-bearing licenses and services agreements, the majority of which are conditional upon performance by the counterparty. These minimum guarantee payments and any related marketing commitments are included in the table below.

The following table summarizes our unrecognized minimum contractual obligations as of March 31, 2011 (in millions):

		Contractual Obligations			
Fiscal Year Ending March 31	**Leases[a]**	**Developer/Licensor Commitments**	**Marketing**	**Other Purchase Obligations**	**Total**
2012	$ 44	$ 331	$ 90	$ 8	$ 473
2013	36	199	37	3	275
2014	26	124	66	3	219
2015	21	114	32	2	169
2016	15	83	33	—	131
Thereafter	9	366	95	—	470
Total	$151	$1,217	$353	$16	$1,737

[a] Lease commitments have not been reduced by minimum sub-lease rentals for unutilized office space resulting from our reorganization activities of approximately $12 million due in the future under non-cancelable sub-leases.

The amounts represented in the table above reflect our unrecognized minimum cash obligations for the respective fiscal years, but do not necessarily represent the periods in which they will be recognized and expensed in our Consolidated Financial Statements. In addition, the amounts in the table above are presented based on the dates the amounts are contractually due; however, certain payment obligations may be accelerated depending on the performance of our operating results.

In addition to what is included in the table above as of March 31, 2011, in connection with our acquisitions, we may be required to pay an additional $110 million of cash consideration through March 31, 2014, that is contingent upon the achievement of certain performance milestones. As of March 31, 2011, we have accrued $51 million of contingent consideration on our Consolidated Balance Sheet.

Purchase Agreements

1.102

JDS UNIPHASE CORPORATION (JUN)

MANAGEMENT'S DISCUSSION AND ANALYSIS OF FINANCIAL CONDITION AND RESULTS OF OPERATIONS

Contractual Obligations (in part)

The following summarizes our contractual obligations at July 2, 2011, and the effect such obligations are expected to have on our liquidity and cash flow over the next five years (*in millions*):

		Payments Due by Period			
	Total	Less Than 1 Year	1–3 Years	3–5 Years	More Than 5 Years
Contractual Obligations					
Asset retirement obligations—expected cash payments	$ 10.3	$ 0.9	$ 2.6	$ 4.1	$ 2.7
Long-Term Debt:[1]					
1% Senior convertible notes	325.0	—	325.0	—	—
Estimated interest payments	6.1	3.3	2.8	—	—
Purchase obligations[2]	146.2	145.1	1.1	—	—
Operating lease obligations[2]	148.4	25.4	40.4	28.6	54.0
Software lease obligations[2]	15.3	11.4	3.9	—	—
Pension and postretirement benefit payments[3]	86.2	5.7	11.2	12.0	57.3
Other non-current liabilities	1.3	—	0.2	—	1.1
Total	$738.8	$191.8	$387.2	$44.7	$115.1

[1] See "Note 11. Convertible Debt and Letters of Credit" for more information.
[2] See "Note 18. Commitments and Contingencies" for more information.
[3] See "Note 16. Employee Benefit Plans" for more information.

As of July 2, 2011, operating lease obligations of $3.0 million in connection with our restructuring program were accrued in our Consolidated Balance Sheet. Operating lease obligations of $1.7 million were included in "Other current liabilities" and $1.3 million was accrued in "Other non-current liabilities."

Purchase obligations represent legally-binding commitments to purchase inventory and other commitments made in the normal course of business to meet operational requirements. Of the $146.2 million of purchase obligations as of July 2, 2011, $58.4 million are related to inventory and the $87.8 million are non-inventory items.

NOTES TO CONSOLIDATED FINANCIAL STATEMENTS

Note 18. Commitments and Contingencies (in part)

Purchase Obligations

Purchase obligations of $146.2 million as of July 2, 2011, represent legally-binding commitments to purchase inventory and other commitments made in the normal course of business to meet operational requirements. Although open purchase orders are considered enforceable and legally binding, the terms generally allow the option to cancel, reschedule and adjust the requirements based on the Company's business needs prior to the delivery of goods or performance of services. Obligations to purchase inventory and other commitments are generally expected to be fulfilled within one year.

The Company depends on a limited number of contract manufacturers, subcontractors, and suppliers for raw materials, packages and standard components. The Company generally purchases these single or limited source products through standard purchase orders or one-year supply agreements and has no significant long-term guaranteed supply agreements with such vendors. While the Company seeks to maintain a sufficient safety stock of such products and maintains ongoing communications with its suppliers to guard against interruptions or cessation of supply, the Company's business and results of operations could be adversely affected by a stoppage or delay of supply, substitution of more expensive or less reliable products, receipt of defective parts or contaminated materials, increases in the price of such supplies, or the Company's inability to obtain reduced pricing from its suppliers in response to competitive pressures.

CONTINGENCIES

RECOGNITION AND MEASUREMENT

1.103 The FASB ASC glossary defines a *contingency* as an existing condition, situation, or set of circumstances involving uncertainty about possible gain (gain contingency) or loss (loss contingency) to an entity that will ultimately be resolved when one or more future events occur or fail to occur. FASB ASC 450-20 sets forth guidance for the recognition and disclosure of loss contingencies. An estimated loss from a loss contingency should be accrued by a charge to income if both of the following conditions are met:

- Information available before the financial statements are issued or available to be issued indicates that it is probable that an asset had been impaired or a liability had been incurred at the date of the financial statements. It is implicit in this condition that it must be probable that one or more future events will occur confirming the fact of the loss.
- The amount of loss can be reasonably estimated.

1.104 Disclosure is preferable to accrual when a reasonable estimate of loss cannot be made. Even losses that are reasonably estimable should not be accrued if it is not probable that an asset has been impaired or a liability has been incurred at the date of the entity's financial statements because those losses relate to a future period, rather than the current period. If some amount within a range of loss appears at the time to be a better estimate than any other amount within the range, that amount should be accrued. When no amount within the range is a better estimate than any other amount, however, the minimum amount in that range should be accrued. Select loss contingency disclosures do not apply to loss contingencies arising from an entity's recurring estimation of its allowance for credit losses. FASB ASC 450-30 states the guidance for the recognition and disclosure for gain contingencies and explains that a contingency that might result in a gain usually should not be reflected in the financial statements because to do so might be to recognize revenue before its realization. When contingency disclosures exist, public companies generally present a balance sheet caption for contingencies, in accordance with Rule 5-02 of Regulation S-X.

1.105

TABLE 1-9: CONTINGENCIES

Table 1-9 lists the loss and gain contingencies disclosed in the annual reports of the survey entities.

	Number of Entities		
	2011	2010	2009
Loss Contingencies			
Litigation	355	344	379
Environmental	195	193	203
Possible tax assessments	124	133	145
Insurance	154	101	132
Government investigations	101	107	95
Warranties	30	25	N/C*
Other, described	41	33	63
Gain Contingencies			
Operating loss carryforward	367	262	429
Tax credits and other tax credit carryforwards	263	212	273
Capital loss carryforward	46	60	69
Alternative minimum tax carryforward	12	22	44
Plaintiff litigation	10	13	42
Asset sale receivable	—	—	8
Investment credit carryforward	2	3	7
Potential tax refund	7	7	7
Charitable contribution carryforward	2	3	4
Other, described	11	6	6

* N/C = Not compiled. Line item was not included in the table for the year shown.

PRESENTATION AND DISCLOSURE EXCERPTS

Legal Matters

1.106

AMERICAN INTERNATIONAL GROUP, INC. (DEC)

NOTES TO CONSOLIDATED FINANCIAL STATEMENTS

16. Commitments, Contingencies and Guarantees (in part)

In the normal course of business, various commitments and contingent liabilities are entered into by AIG and certain of its subsidiaries. In addition, AIG guarantees various obligations of certain subsidiaries.

Although AIG cannot currently quantify its ultimate liability for unresolved litigation and investigation matters, including those referred to below, it is possible that such liability could have a material adverse effect on AIG's consolidated financial condition or its consolidated results of operations or consolidated cash flows for an individual reporting period.

(A) Litigation and Investigations

Overview. AIG and its subsidiaries, in common with the insurance and financial services industries in general, are subject to litigation, including claims for punitive damages, in the normal course of their business. In AIG's insurance operations (including UGC), litigation arising from claims settlement activities is generally considered in the establishment of AIG's liability for unpaid claims and claims adjustment expense. However, the potential for increasing jury awards and settlements makes it difficult to assess the ultimate outcome of such litigation. AIG is also subject to derivative, class action and other claims asserted by its shareholders and others alleging, among other things, breach of fiduciary duties by its directors and officers and violations of insurance laws and regulations, as well as federal and state securities laws. In the case of any derivative action brought on behalf of AIG, any recovery would accrue to the benefit of AIG.

Various regulatory and governmental agencies have been reviewing certain public disclosures, transactions and practices of AIG and its subsidiaries in connection with industry-wide and other inquiries into, among other matters, AIG's liquidity, compensation paid to certain employees, payments made to counterparties, and certain business practices and valuations of current and former operating insurance subsidiaries. AIG has cooperated, and will continue to cooperate, in producing documents and other information in response to subpoenas and other requests.

AIG's life insurance companies have received industry-wide regulatory inquiries, including a multi-state audit covering compliance with unclaimed property laws and a directive from the New York Insurance Department (the New York Directive) regarding claims settlement practices. In particular, the above referenced multi-state audit seeks to require insurers to use the Social Security Death Master File (SSDMF) to identify potential deceased insureds, notwithstanding that the beneficiary or other payee has not presented the company with a valid claim, to determine whether a claim is payable and to take appropriate action. The multi-state audit covers certain policies in force at any time since 1992. The New York Directive generally requires a similar review and action although the time frame under review is different.

AIG recorded an increase of $202 million in the estimated reserves for incurred but not reported death claims in 2011 in conjunction with the use of the SSDMF to identify potential claims not yet presented. Although AIG has enhanced its claims practices to include use of the SSDMF, it is possible that the inquiries, audits and other regulatory activity could result in the payment of additional death claims, additional escheatment of funds deemed abandoned under state laws, administrative penalties and interest. AIG believes it is adequately reserved for such claims, but there can be no assurance that the ultimate cost will not vary, perhaps materially, from its estimate. Additionally, state regulators are considering a variety of proposals that would require life insurance companies to take additional steps to identify unreported deceased policy holders.

The National Association of Insurance Commissioners Market Analysis Working Group, led by the states of Ohio and Iowa, is conducting a multi-state examination of certain accident and health products, including travel products, issued by National Union Fire Insurance Company of Pittsburgh, Pa. (National Union). The examination formally commenced in September 2010 after National Union, based on the identification of certain regulatory issues related to the conduct of its accident and health insurance business, including rate and form issues, producer licensing and appointment, and vendor management, requested that state regulators collectively conduct an examination of the regulatory issues in its

accident and health business. In addition to Ohio and Iowa, the lead states in the multi-state examination are Minnesota, New Jersey and Pennsylvania, and currently a total of 38 states have agreed to participate in the multi-state examination. As part of the multi-state examination, the following Interim Consent Orders were entered into with Ohio: (a) on January 7, 2011, in which National Union agreed, on a nationwide basis, to cease marketing directly to individual bank customers accident/sickness policy forms that had been approved to be sold only as policies providing blanket coverage, and to certain related remediation and audit procedures and (b) on February 14, 2012, in which National Union agreed, on a nationwide basis, to limit outbound telemarketing to certain forms and rates. A Consent Order was entered into with Minnesota on February 10, 2012, in which National Union and Travel Guard Group Inc., an AIG subsidiary, agreed to (i) cease automatically enrolling Minnesota residents in certain insurance relating to air travel, (ii) pay a civil penalty to Minnesota of $250,000 and (iii) refund premium to Minnesota residents who were automatically enrolled in certain insurance relating to air travel. In early 2012, Chartis U.S., Inc., on behalf of itself, National Union, and certain of Chartis U.S., Inc.'s insurance companies (collectively, Chartis U.S.) and the lead regulators agreed in principle upon certain terms to resolve the multi-state examination. The terms include Chartis U.S.'s (i) payment of a civil penalty of up to $51 million, (ii) agreement to enter into a corrective action plan describing agreed-upon specific steps and standards for evaluating Chartis U.S.'s ongoing compliance with laws and regulations governing the regulatory issues identified in the examination, and (iii) agreement to pay a contingent fine in the event that Chartis U.S. fails to substantially comply with the steps and standards agreed to in the corrective action plan. As of December 31, 2011, AIG has an accrued liability equal to the amount of the civil penalty under the proposed agreement. As the terms outlined above are subject to agreement by the lead and participating states and appropriate agreements or orders, AIG (i) can give no assurance that these terms will not change prior to a final resolution of the multi-state examination that is binding on all parties and (ii) cannot predict what other regulatory action, if any, will result from resolving the multi-state examination. There can be no assurance that any regulatory action resulting from the issues identified will not have a material adverse effect on AIG's consolidated results of operations for an individual reporting period, the ongoing operations of the business being examined, or on similar business written by other AIG carriers. National Union and other AIG companies are also currently subject to civil litigation relating to the conduct of their accident and health business, and may be subject to additional litigation relating to the conduct of such business from time to time in the ordinary course.

Industry-wide examinations conducted by the Minnesota Department of Insurance and the Department of Housing and Urban Development (HUD) on captive reinsurance practices by lenders and mortgage insurance companies, including UGC, have been ongoing for several years. Recently, the newly formed Consumer Financial Protection Bureau assumed responsibility for violations of the Real Estate Settlement Procedures Act from HUD, and assumed HUD's aforementioned ongoing investigation. UGC recently received a proposed consent order from the Minnesota Commissioner of Commerce (the MN Commissioner) which alleges that UGC violated the Real Estate Settlement Procedures Act, the Fair Credit Reporting Act and other state and federal laws in connection with its practices with captive reinsurance companies owned by lenders. UGC is currently engaged in discussions with the MN Commissioner with respect to the terms of the proposed consent order. UGC cannot predict if or when a consent order may be entered into or, if entered into, what the terms of the final consent order will be. UGC is also currently subject to civil litigation relating to its placement of reinsurance with captives owned by lenders, and may be subject to additional litigation relating to the conduct of such business from time to time in the ordinary course.

AIG's Subprime Exposure, AIGFP Credit Default Swap Portfolio and Related Matters

AIG, AIGFP and certain directors and officers of AIG, AIGFP and other AIG subsidiaries have been named in various actions relating to AIG's exposure to the U.S. residential subprime mortgage market, unrealized market valuation losses on AIGFP's super senior credit default swap portfolio, losses and liquidity constraints relating to AIG's securities lending program and related disclosure and other matters (Subprime Exposure Issues).

Consolidated 2008 Securities Litigation. Between May 21, 2008 and January 15, 2009, eight purported securities class action complaints were filed against AIG and certain directors and officers of AIG and AIGFP, AIG's outside auditors, and the underwriters of various securities offerings in the United States District Court for the Southern District of New York (the Southern District of New York), alleging claims under the Securities Exchange Act of 1934 (the Exchange Act) or claims under the Securities Act of 1933 (the Securities Act). On March 20, 2009, the Court consolidated all eight of the purported securities class actions as In re American International Group, Inc. 2008 Securities Litigation (the Consolidated 2008 Securities Litigation). Subsequently, on November 18, 2011 and January 20, 2012, two separate, though similar, securities actions were brought against AIG and certain directors and officers of AIG and AIGFP by the Kuwait Investment Office and various Oppenheimer Funds, respectively.

On May 19, 2009, lead plaintiff in the Consolidated 2008 Securities Litigation filed a consolidated complaint on behalf of purchasers of AIG Common Stock during the alleged class period of March 16, 2006 through September 16, 2008, and on behalf of purchasers of various AIG securities offered pursuant to AIG's shelf registration statements. The consolidated complaint alleges that defendants made statements during the class period in press releases, AIG's quarterly and year-end filings, during conference calls, and in various registration statements and prospectuses in connection with the various offerings that were materially false and misleading and that artificially inflated the price of AIG Common Stock. The alleged false and misleading statements relate to, among other things, the Subprime Exposure Issues. The consolidated complaint alleges violations of Sections 10(b) and 20(a) of the Exchange Act and Sections 11, 12(a)(2), and 15 of the Securities Act. On August 5, 2009, defendants filed motions to dismiss the consolidated complaint, and on September 27, 2010, the Court denied the motions to dismiss.

On November 24, 2010 and December 10, 2010, AIG and all other defendants filed answers to the consolidated complaint denying the material allegations therein and asserting their defenses.

On April 1, 2011, the lead plaintiff in the Consolidated 2008 Securities Litigation filed a motion to certify a class of plaintiffs. On November 2, 2011, the Court terminated the motion without prejudice to an application for restoration.

As of February 23, 2012, plaintiffs in the Consolidated 2008 Securities Litigation have not specified an amount of alleged damages, discovery is ongoing and the Court has not determined if a class action is appropriate or the size or scope of any class. As a result, AIG is unable to reasonably estimate the possible loss or range of losses, if any, arising from the litigation.

As of February 23, 2012, the actions initiated by the Kuwait Investment Office and various Oppenheimer Funds are in their early stages, no discussions concerning potential damages have occurred and the plaintiffs have not specified an amount of alleged damages in their respective actions. As a result, AIG is unable to reasonably estimate the possible loss or range of losses, if any, arising from these litigations.

ERISA Actions—Southern District of New York. Between June 25, 2008, and November 25, 2008, AIG, certain directors and officers of AIG, and members of AIG's Retirement Board and Investment Committee were named as defendants in eight purported class action complaints asserting claims on behalf of participants in certain pension plans sponsored by AIG or its subsidiaries. On March 19, 2009, the Court consolidated these eight actions as In re American International Group, Inc. ERISA Litigation II. On June 26, 2009, lead plaintiffs' counsel filed a consolidated amended complaint. The action purports to be brought as a class action under the Employee Retirement Income Security Act of 1974, as amended (ERISA), on behalf of all participants in or beneficiaries of certain benefit plans of AIG and its subsidiaries that offered shares of AIG Common Stock. In the consolidated amended complaint, plaintiffs allege, among other things, that the defendants breached their fiduciary responsibilities to plan participants and their beneficiaries under ERISA, by continuing to offer the AIG Stock Fund as an investment option in the plans after it allegedly became imprudent to do so. The alleged ERISA violations relate to, among other things, the defendants' purported failure to monitor and/or disclose certain matters, including the Subprime Exposure Issues. On September 18, 2009, defendants filed motions to dismiss the consolidated amended complaint.

On March 31, 2011, the Court granted defendants' motions to dismiss with respect to one plan at issue, and denied defendants' motions to dismiss with respect to the other two plans at issue.

On August 5, 2011, AIG and all other defendants filed answers to the consolidated complaint denying the material allegations therein and asserting their defenses.

As of February 23, 2012, plaintiffs have not specified an amount of alleged damages, discovery is ongoing, and the Court has not determined if a class action is appropriate or the size or scope of any class. As a result, AIG is unable to reasonably estimate the possible loss or range of losses, if any, arising from the litigation.

Consolidated 2007 Derivative Litigation. On November 20, 2007 and August 6, 2008, purported shareholder derivative actions were filed in the Southern District of New York naming as defendants directors and officers of AIG and its subsidiaries and asserting claims on behalf of nominal defendant AIG. The actions have been consolidated as In re American International Group, Inc. 2007 Derivative Litigation (the Consolidated 2007 Derivative Litigation). On June 3, 2009, lead plaintiff filed a consolidated amended complaint naming additional directors and officers of AIG and its subsidiaries as defendants. As amended, the factual allegations include the Subprime Exposure Issues and AIG and AIGFP employee retention payments and related compensation issues. The claims asserted on behalf of nominal defendant AIG include breach of fiduciary duty, waste of corporate assets, unjust enrichment, contribution and violations of Sections 10(b) and 20(a) of the Exchange Act. On August 5 and 26, 2009, AIG and defendants filed motions to dismiss the consolidated amended complaint. On December 18, 2009, a separate action, previously commenced in the United States District Court for the Central District of California (Central District of California) and transferred to the Southern District of New York on June 5, 2009, was consolidated into the Consolidated 2007 Derivative Litigation and dismissed without prejudice to the pursuit of the claims in the Consolidated 2007 Derivative Litigation.

On March 30, 2010, the Court dismissed the action due to plaintiff's failure to make a pre-suit demand on AIG's Board of Directors. On March 17, 2011, the United States Court of Appeals for the Second Circuit (the Second Circuit) affirmed the Southern District of New York's dismissal of the Consolidated 2007 Derivative Litigation due to plaintiff's failure to make a pre-suit demand.

On August 10, 2011 and August 15, 2011, the plaintiff that brought the Consolidated 2007 Derivative Litigation sent letters to AIG's Board of Directors (the Board) demanding that the Board cause AIG to pursue the claims asserted in the Consolidated 2007 Derivative Litigation. On September 13, 2011, the Board rejected the demand.

Other Derivative Actions. Separate purported derivative actions, alleging similar claims as the Consolidated 2007 Derivative Litigation, have been brought asserting claims on behalf of the nominal defendant AIG in various jurisdictions. These actions are described below:

- *Supreme Court of New York, Nassau County.* On February 29, 2008, a purported shareholder derivative complaint was filed in the Supreme Court of Nassau County, naming as defendants certain directors and officers of AIG and its subsidiaries. On March 9, 2009, this action was stayed.

- *Supreme Court of New York, New York County.* On March 20, 2009, a purported shareholder derivative complaint was filed in the Supreme Court of New York County naming as defendants certain directors and officers of AIG and recipients of AIGFP retention payments. The complaint has not been served on any defendant.

- *Delaware Court of Chancery.* On September 17, 2008, a purported shareholder derivative complaint was filed in the Delaware Court of Chancery, naming as defendants certain directors and officers of AIG and its subsidiaries. On July 17, 2009 the case was stayed. On May 4, 2011, the parties filed a stipulation with the court agreeing to lift the stay, and granting plaintiff leave to file an amended complaint. On June 17, 2011, AIG filed a motion to dismiss the second amended complaint due to plaintiff's failure to make a pre-suit demand on the Board. On February 1, 2012, the Court approved a stipulation between the parties, dismissing the second amended complaint with prejudice.

- *Superior Court for the State of California, Los Angeles County.* On November 20, 2009, a purported shareholder derivative complaint was filed in the Superior Court for the State of California, Los Angeles County,

naming as defendants certain directors and officers of AIG and its subsidiaries. On February 9, 2010, the case was stayed.

Southern District of New York. On January 4, 2011, Wanda Mimms, a participant in the AIG Incentive Savings Plan (the Plan), filed a purported derivative action on behalf of the Plan in the United States District Court for the Southern District of New York against PricewaterhouseCoopers, LLP (PwC) and asserting a claim for professional malpractice in conducting audits of AIG's 2007 financial statements. The complaint, as amended on April 20, 2011, also asserts a claim for breach of fiduciary duty under ERISA against members of the Plan's Retirement Board for failing to pursue a claim for professional malpractice on behalf of the Plan against PwC. On July 6, 2011, the Plan and defendants filed motions to dismiss the amended complaint. On February 16, 2012, the Court granted the motions to dismiss and dismissed the amended complaint without leave to replead.

Canadian Securities Class Action—Ontario Superior Court of Justice. On November 12, 2008, an application was filed in the Ontario Superior Court of Justice for leave to bring a purported class action against AIG, AIGFP, certain directors and officers of AIG and Joseph Cassano, the former Chief Executive Officer of AIGFP, pursuant to the Ontario Securities Act. If the Court grants the application, a class plaintiff will be permitted to file a statement of claim against defendants. The proposed statement of claim would assert a class period of November 10, 2006 through September 16, 2008 (later amended to March 16, 2006 through September 16, 2008) and would allege that during this period defendants made false and misleading statements and omissions in quarterly and annual reports and during oral presentations in violation of the Ontario Securities Act.

On April 17, 2009, defendants filed a motion record in support of their motion to stay or dismiss for lack of jurisdiction and forum non conveniens. On July 12, 2010, the Court adjourned a hearing on the motion pending a decision by the Supreme Court of Canada in another action with respect to similar issues raised in the action pending against AIG.

In plaintiff's proposed statement of claim, plaintiff alleged general and special damages of $500 million, and punitive damages of $50 million plus prejudgment interest or such other sums as the Court finds appropriate. As of February 23, 2012, the Court has not determined whether it has jurisdiction or granted plaintiff's application to file a statement of claim and no merits discovery has occurred. As a result, AIG is unable to reasonably estimate the possible loss or range of losses, if any, arising from the litigation.

*Starr International Litigation—*On November 21, 2011, Starr International Company, Inc. (SICO) filed a complaint against the Department of the Treasury in the United States Court of Federal Claims, bringing claims, both individually and on behalf of all others similarly situated and derivatively on behalf of AIG (the Starr Treasury Action). The complaint challenges the government's assistance of AIG, pursuant to which AIG entered into the FRBNY Credit Facility and the Department of the Treasury received an approximately 80 percent ownership in AIG. The complaint alleges that the interest rate imposed on AIG and the appropriation of approximately 80 percent of AIG's equity was discriminatory, unprecedented, and inconsistent with liquidity assistance offered by the Government to other comparable firms at the time and violated the Equal Protection, Due Process, and Takings Clauses of the U.S. Constitution.

On the same day that SICO commenced the Starr Treasury Action, SICO also filed a second complaint in the United States District Court in the Southern District of New York, this one against the FRBNY bringing claims, both individually and on behalf of all others similarly situated and derivatively on behalf of AIG. This complaint also challenges the Government's assistance of AIG, pursuant to which AIG entered into the FRBNY Credit Facility and the Department of the Treasury received an approximately 80 percent ownership in AIG. The complaint alleges that the FRBNY owed fiduciary duties to AIG as a controlling shareholder of AIG, and that the FRBNY breached these fiduciary duties by "divert[ing] the rights and assets of AIG and its shareholders to itself and favored third parties" through transactions involving ML III, an entity controlled by FRBNY, and by "participating in, and causing AIG's officers and directors to participate in, the evasion of AIG's existing Common Stock shareholders' right to approve the massive issuance of the new Common Shares required to complete the Government's taking of a nearly 80 percent interest in the Common Stock of AIG." SICO also alleges that the "FRBNY has asserted that in exercising its control over, and acting on behalf of, AIG it did not act in an official, governmental capacity or at the direction of the Department of the Treasury," but that "[t]o the extent the proof at or prior to trial shows that the FRBNY did in fact act in a governmental capacity, or at the direction of the Department of the Treasury, the improper conduct . . . constitutes the discriminatory takings of the property and property rights of AIG without due process or just compensation."

In both of the actions commenced by SICO, the only claims naming AIG as a party are derivative claims on behalf of AIG, and AIG thus faces no potential damages. The FRBNY has requested indemnification under the FRBNY Credit Facility from AIG in connection with the action against it and AIG is discussing the request and its scope with the FRBNY. On January 31, 2012 and February 1, 2012, amended complaints were filed in the Court of Claims and the Southern District of New York, respectively. These amended complaints contain additional factual allegations, but do not contain any new claims against the Department of Treasury, the FRBNY or AIG.

Other Litigation Related to AIGFP

On September 30, 2009, Brookfield Asset Management, Inc. and Brysons International, Ltd. (together, Brookfield) filed a complaint against AIG and AIGFP in the Southern District of New York. Brookfield seeks a declaration that a 1990 interest rate swap agreement between Brookfield and AIGFP (guaranteed by AIG) terminated upon the occurrence of certain alleged events that Brookfield contends constituted defaults under the swap agreement's standard "bankruptcy" default provision. Brookfield claims that it is excused from all future payment obligations under the swap agreement on the basis of the purported termination. At December 31, 2011, the estimated present value of expected future cash flows discounted at LIBOR was $1.5 billion, which represents AIG's maximum contractual loss from the alleged termination of the contract. It is AIG's position that no termination event has occurred and that the swap agreement remains in effect. A determination that a termination event has occurred could result in AIG losing its entitlement to all future payments under the swap agreement and result in a loss to AIG of the full value at which AIG is carrying the swap agreement.

Additionally, a determination that AIG triggered a "bankruptcy" event of default under the swap agreement could also, depending on the Court's precise holding, affect other AIG or AIGFP agreements that contain the same or similar default provisions. Such a determination could also affect derivative agreements or other contracts between third parties, such as credit default swaps under which AIG is a reference credit, which could affect the trading price of AIG securities. During the third quarter of 2011, beneficiaries of certain previously repaid AIGFP guaranteed investment agreements brought an action against AIG Parent and AIGFP making "bankruptcy" event of default allegations similar to those made by Brookfield. AIG has moved to dismiss that complaint.

On December 17, 2009, AIG and AIGFP filed a motion to dismiss Brookfield's complaint. On September 28, 2010, the Court issued a decision granting defendants' motion in part and denying it in part, holding that the complaint: (i) failed to allege that an event of default had occurred based upon defendants' failure to pay or inability to pay debts as they became due; but, (ii) sufficiently alleged that an event of default had occurred based upon other sections of the swap agreement's "bankruptcy" default provision. On January 26, 2011, Brookfield filed an amended complaint that sought to reassert, on the basis of additional factual allegations, the claims that were dismissed from the initial complaint. While AIG initially moved to dismiss the claim that Brookfield sought to reassert in its amended complaint, after Brookfield filed a second amended complaint on September 15, 2011, AIG informed the Court that, in light of the advanced stage of fact discovery in the case, it intends to defer seeking to dismiss Brookfield's claims until motions for summary judgment have been filed, when the discovery record can be considered. AIG and AIGFP filed an answer to the second amended complaint on November 8, 2011. Fact discovery is currently scheduled to conclude on May 15, 2012.

Securities Lending Dispute with Transatlantic Holdings Inc.

On May 24, 2010, Transatlantic Holdings, Inc. (Transatlantic) and two of its subsidiaries, Transatlantic Reinsurance Company and Trans Re Zurich Reinsurance Company Ltd. (collectively, Claimants), commenced an arbitration proceeding before the American Arbitration Association in New York against AIG and two of its subsidiaries (the AIG Respondents). Claimants allege breach of contract, breach of fiduciary duty, and common law fraud in connection with certain securities lending agency agreements between AIG's subsidiaries and Claimants. Claimants allege that AIG and its subsidiaries should be liable for the losses that Claimants purport to have suffered in connection with securities lending and investment activities, and seek damages of $350 million and other unspecified damages.

On June 29, 2010, AIG brought a petition in the Supreme Court of the State of New York, seeking to enjoin the arbitration on the ground that AIG is not a party to the securities lending agency agreements with Claimants. On July 29, 2010, the parties agreed to resolve that petition by consolidating the arbitration commenced by Claimants with a separate arbitration, commenced by AIG on June 29, 2010, in which AIG is seeking damages of Euro 17.6 million ($22.8 million at the December 31, 2011 exchange rate) from Transatlantic for breach of a Master Separation Agreement among Transatlantic, AIG and one of its subsidiary companies.

On September 13, 2010, the AIG Respondents submitted an answer to Claimants' claims asserting, among other things, that there was no breach of the securities lending agency agreements, and that Claimants' other allegations including purported breach of fiduciary duty and fraud are not meritorious. Transatlantic submitted an answer denying liability with respect to AIG's claim on September 13, 2010. Claimants recently increased its claimed damages to an amount of approximately $500 million.

On January 26, 2012, AIG Respondents and Claimants reached a binding agreement to terminate the arbitration proceedings and to dismiss all claims between the parties without any admission of liability by any of the parties. Pursuant to the agreement, the parties will first seek to reach an overall mediated settlement of the claims in the arbitration proceeding along with various other business matters that were not at issue in the arbitration. If a mediated resolution including all claims and outstanding business issues cannot be reached by April 30, 2012, then the parties will try to reach a mediated resolution of the securities lending claims only, including a settlement payment to Transatlantic between $45 million and $125 million. If the parties cannot reach such resolution, the parties have agreed that the mediator will, by June 1, 2012, determine the amount of a settlement payment to Transatlantic with respect to the securities lending claims in a range between $45 million and $125 million. Accordingly, AIG has accrued an amount it believes is reasonable for this settlement.

Employment Litigation against AIG and AIG Global Real Estate Investment Corporation

Fitzpatrick matter. On December 9, 2009, AIG Global Real Estate Investment Corporation's (AIGGRE) former President, Kevin P. Fitzpatrick, several entities he controls, and various other single purpose entities (the SPEs) filed a complaint in the Supreme Court of the State of New York, New York County against AIG and AIGGRE (the Defendants). The case was removed to the Southern District of New York, and an amended complaint was filed on March 8, 2010. The amended complaint asserts that the Defendants violated fiduciary duties to Fitzpatrick and his controlled entities and breached Fitzpatrick's employment agreement and agreements of SPEs that purportedly entitled him to carried interest fees arising out of the sale or disposition of certain real estate. Fitzpatrick has also brought derivative claims on behalf of the SPEs, purporting to allege that the Defendants breached contractual and fiduciary duties in failing to fund the SPEs with various amounts allegedly due under the SPE agreements. Fitzpatrick has also requested injunctive relief, an accounting, and that a receiver be appointed to manage the affairs of the SPEs. He has further alleged that the SPEs are subject to a constructive trust. Fitzpatrick also has alleged a violation of ERISA relating to retirement benefits purportedly due. Fitzpatrick has claimed that he is currently owed damages totaling approximately $196 million, and that potential future amounts owed to him are approximately $78 million, for a total of approximately $274 million. Fitzpatrick further claims unspecified amounts of carried interest on certain additional real estate assets of AIG and its affiliates. He also seeks punitive damages for the alleged breaches of fiduciary duties. Defendants assert that Fitzpatrick has been paid all amounts currently due and owing pursuant to the various agreements through which he seeks recovery. As set forth above, the possible range of loss to AIG is $0 to $274 million, although Fitzpatrick claims that he is also entitled to additional unspecified amounts of carried interest and punitive damages.

Defendants filed counterclaims against Fitzpatrick and a motion to dismiss. On September 28, 2010, the Court dismissed the Defendants' counterclaims, and denied Defendants' motion to dismiss. On March 14, 2011, both plaintiffs and defendants filed motions for partial summary judgment. Those motions are still pending, and no trial date has been set.

Behm matter. Frank Behm, former President of AIG Global Real Estate Asia Pacific, Inc. ("AIGGREAP"), has filed two actions in connection with the termination of his employment. Behm filed an action on or about October 1, 2010 in Delaware Superior Court in which he asserts claims of breach of implied covenant of good faith and fair dealing for termination in violation of public policy, deprivation of compensation, and breach of contract. Additionally, on or about March 29, 2011, Behm filed an arbitration proceeding before the American Arbitration Association alleging wrongful termination, in which he seeks the payment of carried interest or "promote" distributed through the SPEs, based on the sales of certain real estate assets. Behm also contends that he is entitled to promote as a third-party beneficiary of Kevin Fitzpatrick's employment agreement, which, Behm claims, defines broadly a class of individuals, allegedly including himself, who, with the approval of AIG's Chief Investment Officer, became eligible to receive promote payments. Behm is claiming approximately $33 million in carried interest. Multiple AIG entities (the AIG Entities) are named as parties in each of the Behm matters. The AIG Entities have filed a counterclaim in the Delaware case, contending that Behm owes them approximately $3.6 million (before pre-judgment interest) in tax equalization payments made by the AIG Entities on Behm's behalf.

Both matters filed by Behm are premised on the same key allegations. Behm claims that the AIG Entities wrongfully terminated him from AIGGREAP in an effort to silence him for voicing opposition to allegedly improper practices concerning the amount of AIG reserves for carried interest that Behm contends is due to him and others. The AIG Entities contend that their reserves are appropriate, as Behm's claim for additional carried interest are without merit. Behm claims that, when he refused to accede to the AIG Entities' position as to the amount of carried interest due, he was targeted for investigation and subsequently terminated, purportedly for providing confidential AIG information to a competitor, and its executive search firm. Behm argues that he did not disclose any confidential information; instead, he met with several of the competitor's representatives in order to foster interest in purchasing AIGGREAP.

The parties have finalized the selection of the arbitration panel and the arbitration hearing dates have been set for May 2012. No trial date has been set in the Delaware action. As set forth above, the possible range of loss to AIG is $0 to $33 million, although Behm claims that he is also entitled to additional unspecified amounts of carried interest and punitive damages.

False Claims Act Complaint

On February 25, 2010, a complaint was filed in the United States District Court for the Southern District of California by two individuals (Relators) seeking to assert claims on behalf of the United States against AIG and certain other defendants, including Goldman Sachs and Deutsche Bank, under the False Claims Act. Relators filed a First Amended Complaint on September 30, 2010, adding certain additional defendants, including Bank of America and Société Générale. The amended complaint alleges that defendants engaged in fraudulent business practices in respect of their activities in the over-the-counter market for collateralized debt obligations, and submitted false claims to the United States in connection with the FRBNY Credit Facility and the Maiden Lane Interests through, among other things, misrepresenting AIG's ability and intent to repay amounts drawn on the FRBNY Credit Facility, and misrepresenting the value of the securities that the Maiden Lane Interests acquired from AIG and certain of its counterparties. The complaint seeks unspecified damages pursuant to the False Claims Act in the amount of three times the damages allegedly sustained by the United States as well as interest, attorneys' fees, costs and expenses. The complaint and amended complaints were initially filed and maintained under seal while the United States considered whether to intervene in the action. On or about April 28, 2011, after the United States declined to intervene, the District Court lifted the seal, and Relators served the amended complaint on AIG on July 11, 2011.

On October 14, 2011, the defendants that had been served filed motions to dismiss the amended complaint, which are currently pending. The Court will hear oral argument on those motions on April 23, 2012. The Relators have not specified in their amended complaint an amount of alleged damages. As a result, AIG is unable to reasonably estimate the possible loss or range of losses, if any, arising from the litigation.

2006 Regulatory Settlements and Related Regulatory Matters

2006 Regulatory Settlements. In February 2006, AIG reached a resolution of claims and matters under investigation with the United States Department of Justice (DOJ), the Securities and Exchange Commission (SEC), the Office of the New York Attorney General (NYAG) and the New York State Department of Insurance (DOI). The settlements resolved investigations conducted by the SEC, NYAG and DOI in connection with the accounting, financial reporting and insurance brokerage practices of AIG and its subsidiaries, as well as claims relating to the underpayment of certain workers' compensation premium taxes and other assessments. These settlements did not, however, resolve investigations by regulators from other states into insurance brokerage practices related to contingent commissions and other broker-related conduct, such as alleged bid rigging. Nor did the settlements resolve any obligations that AIG may have to state guarantee funds in connection with any of these matters.

As a result of these settlements, AIG made payments or placed amounts in escrow in 2006 totaling approximately $1.64 billion, $225 million of which represented fines and penalties.

In addition to the escrowed funds, $800 million was deposited into, and subsequently disbursed by, a fund under the supervision of the SEC, to resolve claims asserted against AIG by investors, including the securities class action and shareholder lawsuits described below. Additional amounts held in escrow totaling approximately $597 million, including interest thereon, are included in Other assets at December 31, 2011, and, as discussed below, are specifically designated to satisfy regulatory and class-action liabilities related to workers' compensation premium reporting issues. Approximately $338 million of the $597 million of the current total workers' compensation related escrow amount was originally held in an account established as part of the 2006 New York regulatory settlement and referred to as the Workers' Compensation Fund.

On February 1, 2012, AIG was informed by the SEC that AIG had complied with the terms of the settlement order under which AIG had agreed to retain an independent consultant, and as of that date, was no longer subject to such order.

Other Regulatory Settlements. AIG's 2006 regulatory settlements with the SEC, DOJ, NYAG and DOI did not resolve investigations by regulators from other states into insurance brokerage practices. AIG entered into agreements effective in early 2008 with the Attorneys General of the States of Florida, Hawaii, Maryland, Michigan, Oregon, Texas and West Virginia; the Commonwealths of Massachusetts and Pennsylvania; and the District of Columbia; as well as the Florida Department of Financial Services and the Florida Office of Insurance Regulation, relating to their respective industry-wide investigations into producer compensation and insurance placement practices. The settlements called for total payments of $26 million by AIG, of which $4.4 million was paid under previous settlement agreements. During the term of the settlement agreements, which run through early 2018, AIG will continue to maintain certain producer compensation disclosure and ongoing compliance initiatives. AIG will also continue to cooperate with the industry-wide investigations. On April 7, 2010, it was announced that AIG and the Ohio Attorney General entered into a settlement agreement to resolve the Ohio Attorney General's claim concerning producer compensation and insurance placement practices. AIG paid the Ohio Attorney General $9 million as part of that settlement.

NAIC Examination of Workers' Compensation Premium Reporting. During 2006, the Settlement Review Working Group of the National Association of Insurance Commissioners (NAIC), under the direction of the States of Indiana, Minnesota and Rhode Island, began an investigation into AIG's reporting of workers' compensation premiums. In late 2007, the Settlement Review Working Group recommended that a multi-state targeted market conduct examination focusing on workers' compensation insurance be commenced under the direction of the NAIC's Market Analysis Working Group. AIG was informed of the multi-state targeted market conduct examination in January 2008. The lead states in the multi-state examination are Delaware, Florida, Indiana, Massachusetts, Minnesota, New York, Pennsylvania, and Rhode Island. All other states (and the District of Columbia) have agreed to participate in the multi-state examination. The examination focused on legacy issues related to AIG's writing and reporting of workers' compensation insurance prior to 1996 and current compliance with legal requirements applicable to such business.

On December 17, 2010, AIG and the lead states reached an agreement to settle all regulatory liabilities arising out of the subjects of the multistate examination. The regulatory settlement agreement, which has been agreed to by all 50 states and the District of Columbia, includes, among other terms, (i) AIG's payment of $100 million in regulatory fines and penalties; (ii) AIG's payment of $46.5 million in outstanding premium taxes; (iii) AIG's agreement to enter into a compliance plan describing agreed-upon specific steps and standards for evaluating AIG's ongoing compliance with state regulations governing the setting of workers' compensation insurance premium rates and the reporting of workers' compensation premiums; and (iv) AIG's agreement to pay up to $150 million in contingent fines in the event that AIG fails to comply substantially with the compliance plan requirements. The $146.5 million in fines, penalties and premium taxes have been funded out of the $338 million originally held in the Workers' Compensation Fund and placed into an escrow account pursuant to the terms of the regulatory settlement agreement. The regulatory settlement is contingent upon and will not become effective until, among other events: (i) a final, court-approved settlement is reached in all the lawsuits that comprise the Workers' Compensation Premium Reporting Litigation, discussed below, including the putative class action, except that such settlement need not resolve claims between AIG and the Liberty Mutual Group in order for the regulatory settlement to become effective and (ii) a settlement is reached and consummated between AIG and certain state insurance guaranty funds that may assert claims against AIG for underpayment of guaranty-fund assessments.

As of December 31, 2011, AIG has an accrued liability for the amounts payable under the proposed settlement.

Litigation Related to the Matters Underlying the 2006 Regulatory Settlements

AIG and certain present and former directors and officers of AIG have been named in various actions related to the matters underlying the 2006 Regulatory Settlements. These actions are described below.

The Consolidated 2004 Securities Litigation. Beginning in October 2004, a number of putative securities fraud class action suits were filed in the Southern District of New York against AIG and consolidated as In re American International Group, Inc. Securities Litigation (the Consolidated 2004 Securities Litigation). Subsequently, a separate, though similar, securities fraud action was also brought against AIG by certain Florida pension funds. The lead plaintiff in the Consolidated 2004 Securities Litigation is a group of public retirement systems and pension funds benefiting Ohio state employees, suing on behalf of themselves and all purchasers of AIG's publicly traded securities between October 28, 1999 and April 1, 2005. The named defendants are AIG and a number of present and former AIG officers and directors, as well as C.V. Starr & Co., Inc. (Starr), Starr International Company, Inc. (SICO), General Reinsurance Corporation (General Re), and PwC, among others. The lead plaintiff alleges, among other things, that AIG: (i) concealed that it engaged in anti-competitive conduct through alleged payment of contingent commissions to brokers and participation in illegal bid-rigging; (ii) concealed that it used "income smoothing" products and other techniques to inflate its earnings; (iii) concealed that it marketed and sold "income smoothing" insurance products to other companies; and (iv) misled investors about the scope of government investigations. In addition, the lead plaintiff alleges that Maurice R. Greenberg, AIG's former Chief Executive Officer, manipulated AIG's stock price. The lead plaintiff asserts claims for violations of Sections 11 and 15 of the Securities Act, Section 10(b) of the Exchange Act and Rule 10b-5 promulgated thereunder, and Sections 20(a) and Section 20A of the Exchange Act.

On July 14, 2010, AIG approved the terms of a settlement (the Settlement) with lead plaintiffs. The Settlement is conditioned on, among other things, court approval and a minimum level of shareholder participation. Under the terms of the Settlement, if consummated, AIG would pay an aggregate of $725 million.

On July 20, 2010, at the joint request of AIG and lead plaintiffs, the District Court entered an order staying all deadlines in the case. On November 30, 2010, AIG and lead plaintiffs executed their agreement of settlement and compromise. On November 30, 2010, lead plaintiffs filed a motion for preliminary approval of the settlement with AIG.

On October 5, 2011, the District Court granted lead plaintiffs' motion for preliminary approval of the settlement between AIG and lead plaintiffs. Notices to class members of the settlement were mailed on October 14, 2011. On December 2, 2011, Lead Plaintiff filed a motion for final approval of the settlement and for attorneys' fees. Objections to the settlement and requests to be excluded from the settlement were due to the District Court by December 30, 2011. Only two shareholders objected to the settlement, and 25 shareholders claiming to hold less than 1.5 percent of AIG's outstanding shares at the end of the class period submitted timely and valid requests to opt out of the class. Of those 25 shareholders, seven are investment funds controlled by the same investment group, and that investment group is the only opt-out who held more than 1,000 shares at the end of the class period. By order dated February 2, 2012, the District Court granted lead plaintiffs' motion for final approval of the Settlement between AIG and lead plaintiffs. AIG has fully funded the amount of the Settlement into an escrow account. On February 17, 2012, one of the objectors filed a notice to appeal the District Court's February 2, 2012 order to the Court of Appeals for the Second Circuit.

On January 23, 2012, AIG and the Florida pension funds, who had brought a separate securities fraud action, executed a settlement agreement. Under the terms of the settlement agreement, AIG paid $4 million.

The Multi-District Litigation. Commencing in 2004, policyholders brought multiple federal antitrust and Racketeer Influenced and Corrupt Organizations Act (RICO) class actions in jurisdictions across the nation against insurers and brokers, including AIG and a number of its subsidiaries, alleging that the insurers and brokers engaged in one or more broad conspiracies to allocate customers, steer business, and rig bids. These actions, including 24 complaints filed in different federal courts naming AIG or an AIG subsidiary as a defendant, were consolidated by the judicial panel on multi-district litigation and transferred to the United States District Court for the District of New Jersey (District of New Jersey) for coordinated pretrial proceedings. The consolidated actions have proceeded in that Court in two parallel actions, In re Insurance Brokerage Antitrust Litigation (the Commercial Complaint) and In re Employee Benefits Insurance Brokerage Antitrust Litigation (the Employee Benefits Complaint, and, together with the Commercial Complaint, the Multi-District Litigation).

The plaintiffs in the Commercial Complaint are a group of corporations, individuals and public entities that contracted with the broker defendants for the provision of insurance brokerage services for a variety of insurance needs. The broker defendants are alleged to have placed insurance coverage on the plaintiffs' behalf with a number of insurance companies named as defendants, including AIG subsidiaries. The Commercial Complaint also named various brokers and other insurers as defendants (three of which have since settled). The Commercial Complaint alleges that defendants engaged in a number of overlapping "broker-centered" conspiracies to allocate customers through the payment of contingent commissions to brokers and through purported "bid-rigging" practices. It also alleges that the insurer and broker defendants participated in a "global" conspiracy not to disclose to policyholders the payment of contingent commissions. Plaintiffs assert that the defendants violated the Sherman Antitrust Act, RICO, and the antitrust laws of 48 states and the District of Columbia, and are liable under common law breach of fiduciary duty and unjust enrichment theories. Plaintiffs seek treble damages plus interest and attorneys' fees as a result of the alleged RICO and Sherman Antitrust Act violations.

The plaintiffs in the Employee Benefits Complaint are a group of individual employees and corporate and municipal employers alleging claims on behalf of two separate nationwide purported classes: an employee class and an employer class that acquired insurance products from the defendants from January 1, 1998 to December 31, 2004. The Employee Benefits Complaint names AIG, as well as various other brokers and insurers, as defendants. The activities alleged in the Employee Benefits Complaint, with certain exceptions, track the allegations of customer allocation through steering and bid-rigging made in the Commercial Complaint.

The District Court, in connection with the Commercial and Employee Benefits Complaints, granted (without leave to amend) defendants' motions to dismiss the federal antitrust and RICO claims on August 31, 2007 and September 28, 2007, respectively. The Court declined to exercise supplemental jurisdiction over the state law claims in the Commercial Complaint and therefore dismissed it in its entirety. Plaintiffs appealed the dismissal of the Commercial Complaint to the United States Court of Appeals for the Third Circuit (the Third Circuit) on October 10, 2007. On January 14, 2008, the District Court granted summary judgment to defendants on plaintiffs' ERISA claims in the Employee Benefits Complaint. On February 12, 2008, plaintiffs filed a notice of appeal to the Third Circuit with respect to the dismissal of the antitrust and RICO claims in the Employee Benefits Complaint.

On August 16, 2010, the Third Circuit affirmed the dismissal of the Employee Benefits Complaint in its entirety, affirmed in part and vacated in part the District Court's dismissal of the Commercial Complaint, and remanded the case for further proceedings consistent with the opinion. Specifically, the Third Circuit affirmed the dismissal of plaintiffs' broader antitrust and RICO claims, but the Court reversed the District Court's dismissal of alleged "Marsh-centered" antitrust and RICO claims based on allegations of bid-rigging involving excess casualty insurance. The Court remanded these Marsh-centered claims to the District Court for consideration as to whether plaintiffs had adequately pleaded them. Because the Third Circuit vacated in part the judgment dismissing the federal claims in the Commercial Complaint, the Third Circuit also vacated the District Court's dismissal of the state-law claims in the Commercial Complaint.

On October 1, 2010, defendants named in the Commercial Complaint filed motions to dismiss the remaining remanded claims in the District of New Jersey. On March 18, 2011, AIG and certain other defendants announced that they had entered into a memorandum of understanding (MOU) with class plaintiffs to settle the claims asserted against them in the Commercial Complaint. As of May 20, 2011, the parties to the MOU and certain other defendants entered into a Stipulation of Settlement. Under the terms of the settlement, it is anticipated that AIG will pay $6.75 million of a total aggregate settlement amount of approximately $37 million. The settlement is conditioned on final court approval. Plaintiffs'

attorneys' fees and litigation expenses, and the aggregate costs of notice and claims administration in connection with the settlement, would be paid from the settlement fund.

On June 20, 2011, the Court "administratively terminated" without prejudice the various Defendants' pending motions to dismiss the proposed class plaintiffs' operative pleading indicating that those motions may be re-filed after adjudication of all issues related to the proposed class settlement and subject to the approval of the Magistrate Judge. On June 27, 2011, the Court preliminarily approved the class settlement. On June 30, 2011, AIG placed its portion of the total settlement payment into escrow. If the settlement does not receive final court approval, those funds will revert to AIG. A final fairness hearing was held on September 14, 2011. The Court has not yet ruled on the motion for final approval of the class settlement.

A number of complaints making allegations similar to those in the Multi-District Litigation have been filed against AIG and other defendants in state and federal courts around the country. The defendants have thus far been successful in having the federal actions transferred to the District of New Jersey and consolidated into the Multi-District Litigation. These additional consolidated actions are still pending in the District of New Jersey, but are currently stayed. In one of those consolidated actions, *Palm Tree Computer Systems, Inc. v. Ace USA (Palm Tree)*, which is brought by two named plaintiffs on behalf of a proposed class of insurance purchasers, the plaintiffs allege specifically with respect to their claim for breach of fiduciary duty against the insurer defendants that neither named plaintiff nor any member of the proposed class suffered damages "exceeding $74,999 each." Plaintiffs do not specify damages as to other claims against the insurer defendants in the complaint. The plaintiffs in *Palm Tree* have not yet sought certification of the class, as that case has been stayed by the District Court of New Jersey. Because discovery has not been completed and the District Court has not determined if a class action is appropriate or the size or scope of any class, AIG is unable to reasonably estimate the possible loss or range of losses, if any, arising from the *Palm Tree* litigation. In another consolidated action, *The Heritage Corp. of South Florida v. National Union Fire Ins. Co. (Heritage)*, an individual plaintiff alleges damages "in excess of $75,000." Because discovery has not been completed and a precise amount of damages has not been specified, AIG is unable to reasonably estimate the possible loss or range of losses, if any, arising from the *Heritage* litigation. For the remaining consolidated actions, as of February, 2012, plaintiffs have not specified an amount of alleged damages arising from these actions. AIG is therefore unable to reasonably estimate the possible loss or range of losses, if any, arising from these matters.

In June 2011, the Court ordered counsel for each of the tag-along actions in the Multi-District Litigation (including the following cases where AIG is a defendant: *Avery Dennison Corp. v. Marsh & McLennan Companies, Inc.; Henley Management Co. v. Marsh Inc.; Heritage; and Palm Tree*) to submit a letter to the Court within 30 days of the date of that order that outlines the effect the current proposed class settlement will have on their respective cases if finalized in due course. In July 2011, several plaintiffs submitted letters to the Court. Defendants submitted an omnibus response to the Court on August 19, 2011.

On October 17, 2011, the Court conducted a conference and subsequently ordered that discovery and motion practice may proceed in all tag-along actions. The parties were ordered to submit a proposed scheduling order for discovery and any additional motion practice to the Court by October 31, 2011. The Court has not yet issued a scheduling order.

The AIG defendants have also sought to have state court actions making similar allegations stayed pending resolution of the Multi-District Litigation proceeding. These efforts have generally been successful, although four cases have proceeded; one each in Florida and New Jersey state courts that have settled, and one each in Texas and Kansas state courts have proceeded (although discovery is stayed in both actions). In the Texas action, plaintiff filed its Fourth Amended Petition on July 13, 2009 and on August 14, 2009, defendants filed renewed special exceptions. Plaintiff in the Texas action alleges a "maximum" of $125 million in total damages (after trebling). Because the Court has not rendered a decision on defendants' renewed special exceptions and discovery has not been completed, AIG is unable to reasonably estimate the possible loss or range of losses, if any, arising from the Texas action. In the Kansas action, defendants are appealing to the Kansas Supreme Court the trial court's denial of defendants' motion to dismiss on statute of limitations grounds. In the Kansas action, the plaintiff alleges damages in an amount "greater than $75,000" for each of the three claims directed against AIG in the complaint. Because the Kansas Supreme Court has not decided the appeal of the trial court's denial of defendants' motion to dismiss, a precise amount of damages has not been specified and discovery has not been completed, AIG is unable to reasonably estimate the possible loss or range of losses, if any, from the Kansas action.

Workers' Compensation Premium Reporting. On May 24, 2007, the National Council on Compensation Insurance (NCCI), on behalf of the participating members of the National Workers' Compensation Reinsurance Pool (the NWCRP), filed a lawsuit in the United States District Court for the Northern District of Illinois (Northern District of Illinois) against AIG with respect to the underpayment by AIG of its residual market assessments for workers' compensation insurance. The complaint alleged claims for violations of RICO, breach of contract, fraud and related state law claims arising out of AIG's alleged underpayment of these assessments between 1970 and the present and sought damages purportedly in excess of $1 billion. On August 6, 2007, the Court denied AIG's motion seeking to dismiss or stay the complaint or, in the alternative, to transfer to the Southern District of New York. On December 26, 2007, the Court denied AIG's motion to dismiss the complaint.

On March 17, 2008, AIG filed an amended answer, counterclaims and third-party claims against NCCI (in its capacity as attorney-in-fact for the NWCRP), the NWCRP, its board members, and certain of the other insurance companies that are members of the NWCRP alleging violations of RICO, as well as claims for conspiracy, fraud, and other state law claims. The counterclaim-defendants and third-party defendants filed motions to dismiss on June 9, 2008. On January 26, 2009, AIG filed a motion to dismiss all claims in the complaint for lack of subject-matter jurisdiction. On February 23, 2009, the Court issued a decision and order sustaining AIG's counterclaims and sustaining, in part, AIG's third-party claims. The Court also dismissed certain of AIG's third-party claims without prejudice.

On April 13, 2009, third-party defendant Liberty Mutual Group (Liberty Mutual) filed third-party counterclaims against AIG, certain of its subsidiaries, and former AIG executives. On August 23, 2009, the Court granted AIG's motion to dismiss the NCCI complaint for lack of standing. On September

25, 2009, AIG filed its First Amended Complaint, reasserting its RICO claims against certain insurance companies that both underreported their workers' compensation premium and served on the NWCRP Board, and repleading its fraud and other state law claims. Defendants filed a motion to dismiss the First Amended Complaint on October 30, 2009. On October 8, 2009, Liberty Mutual filed an amended counterclaim against AIG. The amended counterclaim is substantially similar to the complaint initially filed by NCCI, but also seeks damages related to non-NWCRP states, guaranty funds, and special assessments, in addition to asserting claims for other violations of state law. The amended counterclaim also removes as defendants the former AIG executives. On October 30, 2009, AIG filed a motion to dismiss the Liberty amended counterclaim.

On April 1, 2009, Safeco Insurance Company of America (Safeco) and Ohio Casualty Insurance Company (Ohio Casualty) filed a complaint in the Northern District of Illinois, on behalf of a purported class of all NWCRP participant members, against AIG and certain of its subsidiaries with respect to the underpayment by AIG of its residual market assessments for workers' compensation insurance. The complaint was styled as an "alternative complaint," should the Court grant AIG's motion to dismiss the NCCI lawsuit for lack of subject-matter jurisdiction. The allegations in the class action complaint are substantially similar to those filed by the NWCRP, but the complaint names former AIG executives as defendants and asserts a RICO claim against those executives. On August 28, 2009, the class action plaintiffs filed an amended complaint, removing the AIG executives as defendants. On October 30, 2009, AIG filed a motion to dismiss the amended complaint. On July 16, 2010, Safeco and Ohio Casualty filed their motion for class certification, which AIG opposed on October 8, 2010.

On July 1, 2010, the Court ruled on the pending motions to dismiss that were directed at all parties' claims. With respect to the underreporting NWCRP companies' and board members' motion to dismiss AIG's first amended complaint, the Court denied the motion to dismiss all counts except AIG's claim for unjust enrichment, which it found to be precluded by the surviving claims for breach of contract. With respect to NCCI and the NWCRP's motion to dismiss AIG's first amended complaint, the Court denied the NCCI and the NWCRP's motions to dismiss AIG's claims for an equitable accounting and an action on an open, mutual, and current account. With respect to AIG's motions to dismiss Liberty's counterclaims and the class action complaint, the Court denied both motions, except that it dismissed the class claim for promissory estoppel. On July 30, 2010, the NWCRP filed a motion for reconsideration of the Court's ruling denying its motion to dismiss AIG's claims for an equitable accounting and an action on an open, mutual, and current account. The Court denied the NWCRP's motion for reconsideration on September 16, 2010. The plaintiffs filed a motion for class certification on July 16, 2010. AIG opposed the motion.

On January 5, 2011, AIG executed a term sheet with a group of intervening plaintiffs, made up of seven participating members of the NWCRP that filed a motion to intervene in the class action for the purpose of settling the claims at issue on behalf of a settlement class. The proposed class-action settlement would require AIG to pay $450 million to satisfy all liabilities to the class members arising out of the workers' compensation premium reporting issues, a portion of which would be funded out of the remaining amount held in the Workers' Compensation Fund less any amounts previously withdrawn to satisfy AIG's regulatory settlement obligations, as addressed above. On January 13, 2011, their motion to intervene was granted. On January 19, 2011, the intervening class plaintiffs filed their Complaint in Intervention. On January 28, 2011, AIG and the intervening class plaintiffs entered into a settlement agreement embodying the terms set forth in the January 5, 2011 term sheet and filed a joint motion for certification of the settlement class and preliminary approval of the settlement. If approved by the Court (and such approval becomes final), the settlement agreement will resolve and dismiss with prejudice all claims that have been made or that could have been made in the consolidated litigations pending in the Northern District of Illinois arising out of workers' compensation premium reporting, including the class action, other than claims that are brought by any class member that opts out of the settlement. On April 29, 2011, Liberty Mutual filed papers in opposition to preliminary approval of the proposed settlement and in opposition to certification of a settlement class, in which it alleged AIG's actual exposure, should the class action continue through judgment, to be in excess of $3 billion. AIG disputes and will defend against this allegation. The Court held a hearing on the motions for class certification and preliminary approval of the proposed class-action settlement on June 21 and July 25, 2011.

On August 1, 2011, the Court issued an opinion and order granting the motion for class certification and preliminarily approving the proposed class-action settlement, subject to certain minor modifications that the Court noted the parties already had agreed to make. The opinion and order became effective upon the entry of a separate Findings and Order Preliminarily Certifying a Settlement Class and Preliminarily Approving Proposed Settlement on August 5, 2011. Liberty Mutual sought leave from the United States Court of Appeals for the Seventh Circuit to appeal the August 5, 2011 class certification decision, which was denied on August 19, 2011. Notice of the settlement was issued to the class members on August 19, 2011 advising that any class member wishing to opt out of or object to the class-action settlement was required to do so by October 3, 2011. RLI Insurance Company and its affiliates, which were to receive less than one thousand dollars under the proposed settlement, sent the only purported opt-out notice. Liberty Mutual, including its subsidiaries Safeco and Ohio Casualty, and the Kemper group of insurance companies, through their affiliate Lumbermens Mutual Casualty, were the only two objectors. AIG and the settling class plaintiffs filed responses to the objectors' submissions on October 28, 2011. The Court conducted a final fairness hearing on November 29, 2011. On December 21, 2011, the Court issued an order granting final approval of the settlement, but staying that ruling pending a forthcoming opinion. On January 19, 2012, Liberty Mutual and Safeco and Ohio Casualty filed notices of their intent to appeal the Court's order granting class-action settlement approval.

The $450 million settlement amount, which is currently held in escrow pending final resolution of the class-action settlement, was funded in part from the approximately $191.5 million remaining in the Workers' Compensation Fund, after the transfer of the $146.5 million in fines, penalties, and premium taxes discussed in the NAIC Examination of Workers' Compensation Premium Reporting matter above into a separate escrow account pursuant to the regulatory settlement agreement. In the event that the proposed class action settlement is not approved, the litigation will resume. As of December 31, 2011, AIG has an accrued liability equal to the amounts payable under the settlement.

Litigation Matters Relating to AIG's Insurance Operations

Caremark. AIG and certain of its subsidiaries have been named defendants in two putative class actions in state court in Alabama that arise out of the 1999 settlement of class and derivative litigation involving Caremark Rx, Inc. (Caremark). The plaintiffs in the second-filed action intervened in the first-filed action, and the second-filed action was dismissed. An excess policy issued by a subsidiary of AIG with respect to the 1999 litigation was expressly stated to be without limit of liability. In the current actions, plaintiffs allege that the judge approving the 1999 settlement was misled as to the extent of available insurance coverage and would not have approved the settlement had he known of the existence and/or unlimited nature of the excess policy. They further allege that AIG, its subsidiaries, and Caremark are liable for fraud and suppression for misrepresenting and/or concealing the nature and extent of coverage. In addition, the intervenors originally alleged that various lawyers and law firms who represented parties in the underlying class and derivative litigation (the Lawyer Defendants) were also liable for fraud and suppression, misrepresentation, and breach of fiduciary duty.

The complaints filed by the plaintiffs and the intervenors request compensatory damages for the 1999 class in the amount of $3.2 billion, plus punitive damages. AIG and its subsidiaries deny the allegations of fraud and suppression, assert that information concerning the excess policy was publicly disclosed months prior to the approval of the settlement, that the claims are barred by the statute of limitations, and that the statute cannot be tolled in light of the public disclosure of the excess coverage. The plaintiffs and intervenors, in turn, have asserted that the disclosure was insufficient to inform them of the nature of the coverage and did not start the running of the statute of limitations.

In November 2007, the trial court dismissed the intervenors' complaint against the Lawyer Defendants, and the Alabama Supreme Court affirmed that dismissal in September 2008. After the case was sent back down to the trial court, the intervenors retained additional counsel and filed an Amended Complaint in Intervention that named only Caremark and AIG and various subsidiaries as defendants, purported to bring claims against all defendants for deceit and conspiracy to deceive, and purported to bring a claim against AIG and its subsidiaries for aiding and abetting Caremark's alleged deception. The defendants moved to dismiss the Amended Complaint in Intervention, and the plaintiffs moved to disqualify all of the lawyers for the intervenors because, among other things, the newly retained firm had previously represented Caremark. The intervenors, in turn, moved to disqualify the lawyers for the plaintiffs in the first-filed action. The cross-motions to disqualify were withdrawn after the two sets of plaintiffs agreed that counsel for the original plaintiffs would act as lead counsel, and intervenors also withdrew their Amended Complaint in Intervention. The trial court approved all of the foregoing steps and, in April 2009, established a schedule for class action discovery that was to lead to a hearing on class certification in March 2010. The Court has since appointed a special master to oversee class action discovery and has directed the parties to submit a new discovery schedule after certain discovery disputes are resolved. Class discovery is ongoing. A class certification hearing has been set for March 2012, but it is expected to be adjourned until later in the Spring.

As of February 23, 2012, the parties have not completed class action discovery, general discovery has not commenced, and the court has not determined if a class action is appropriate or the size or scope of any class. As a result, AIG is unable to reasonably estimate the possible loss or range of losses, if any, arising from the litigation.

Tax Contingencies

1.107

ALTRIA GROUP, INC. (DEC)

NOTES TO CONSOLIDATED FINANCIAL STATEMENTS

Note 15—Income Taxes (in part)

Altria Group, Inc.'s U.S. subsidiaries join in the filing of a U.S. federal consolidated income tax return. The U.S. federal statute of limitations remains open for the year 2004 and forward, with years 2004 to 2006 currently under examination by the Internal Revenue Service ("IRS") as part of a routine audit conducted in the ordinary course of business. State jurisdictions have statutes of limitations generally ranging from 3 to 4 years. Certain of Altria Group, Inc.'s state tax returns are currently under examination by various states as part of routine audits conducted in the ordinary course of business.

A reconciliation of the beginning and ending amount of unrecognized tax benefits for the years ended December 31, 2011, 2010 and 2009 was as follows:

(In millions)	2011	2010	2009
Balance at beginning of year	$399	$601	$669
Additions based on tax positions related to the current year	22	21	15
Additions for tax positions of prior years	71	30	34
Reductions for tax positions due to lapse of statutes of limitations	(39)	(58)	(22)
Reductions for tax positions of prior years	(67)	(164)	(87)
Settlements	(5)	(31)	(8)
Balance at end of year	$381	$399	$601

Unrecognized tax benefits and Altria Group, Inc.'s consolidated liability for tax contingencies at December 31, 2011 and 2010, were as follows:

(In millions)	2011	2010
Unrecognized tax benefits—Altria Group, Inc.	$191	$220
Unrecognized tax benefits—Kraft	112	101
Unrecognized tax benefits—PMI	78	78
Unrecognized tax benefits	381	399
Accrued interest and penalties	618	261
Tax credits and other indirect benefits	(211)	(85)
Liability for tax contingencies	$788	$575

The amount of unrecognized tax benefits that, if recognized, would impact the effective tax rate at December 31, 2011 was $350 million, along with $31 million affecting deferred taxes. However, the impact on net earnings at December 31,

2011 would be $160 million, as a result of receivables from Altria Group, Inc.'s former subsidiaries Kraft Foods Inc. ("Kraft") and Philip Morris International Inc. ("PMI") of $112 million and $78 million, respectively, discussed below. The amount of unrecognized tax benefits that, if recognized, would impact the effective tax rate at December 31, 2010 was $360 million, along with $39 million affecting deferred taxes. However, the impact on net earnings at December 31, 2010 would be $181 million, as a result of receivables from Kraft and PMI of $101 million and $78 million, respectively, discussed below.

Under tax sharing agreements entered into in connection with the 2007 and 2008 spin-offs between Altria Group, Inc. and its former subsidiaries Kraft and PMI, respectively, Kraft and PMI are responsible for their respective pre-spin-off tax obligations. Altria Group, Inc., however, remains severally liable for Kraft's and PMI's pre-spin-off federal tax obligations pursuant to regulations governing federal consolidated income tax returns. As a result, at December 31, 2011, Altria Group, Inc. continues to include the pre-spin-off federal income tax reserves of Kraft and PMI of $112 million and $78 million, respectively, in its liability for uncertain tax positions, and also includes corresponding receivables from Kraft and PMI of $112 million and $78 million, respectively, in its assets.

In the fourth quarter of 2011, the IRS, Kraft and Altria Group, Inc. executed a closing agreement that resolved certain Kraft tax matters arising out of the IRS's examination of Altria Group, Inc.'s consolidated federal income tax returns for the years ended 2004-2006. As a result of this closing agreement in the fourth quarter of 2011, Altria Group, Inc. recorded an income tax benefit of $12 million attributable to the reversal of federal income tax reserves and associated interest related to the resolution of certain Kraft tax matters.

As discussed in Note 19. *Contingencies*, Altria Group, Inc. and the IRS executed a closing agreement during the second quarter of 2010 in connection with the IRS's examination of Altria Group, Inc.'s consolidated federal income tax returns for the years 2000-2003, which resolved various tax matters for Altria Group, Inc. and its subsidiaries, including its former subsidiaries—Kraft and PMI. As a result of the closing agreement, Altria Group, Inc. paid the IRS approximately $945 million of tax and associated interest during the third quarter of 2010 with respect to certain PMCC leveraged lease transactions referred to by the IRS as lease-in/lease-out ("LILO") and sale-in/lease-out ("SILO") transactions, entered into during the 1996-2003 years. During the first quarter of 2011, Altria Group, Inc. filed claims for a refund of the approximately $945 million paid to the IRS. The IRS disallowed the claims during the third quarter of 2011. In addition, as a result of this closing agreement, in the second quarter of 2010, Altria Group, Inc. recorded (i) a $47 million income tax benefit primarily attributable to the reversal of tax reserves and associated interest related to Altria Group, Inc. and its current subsidiaries; and (ii) an income tax benefit of $169 million attributable to the reversal of federal income tax reserves and associated interest related to the resolution of certain Kraft and PMI tax matters.

In the third quarter of 2009, the IRS, Kraft, and Altria Group, Inc. executed a closing agreement that resolved certain Kraft tax matters arising out of the 2000-2003 IRS audit of Altria Group, Inc. As a result of this closing agreement, in the third quarter of 2009, Altria Group, Inc. recorded an income tax benefit of $88 million attributable to the reversal of federal income tax reserves and associated interest related to the resolution of certain Kraft tax matters.

The tax benefits of $12 million, $169 million and $88 million, for the years ended December 31, 2011, 2010 and 2009, respectively, were offset by a reduction to the corresponding receivables from Kraft and PMI, which were recorded as reductions to operating income on Altria Group, Inc.'s consolidated statements of earnings for the years ended December 31, 2011, 2010, and 2009, respectively. In addition, during 2011, Altria Group, Inc. recorded an additional tax provision and associated interest of $26 million related to various tax matters for Kraft. This additional tax provision was offset by an increase to the corresponding receivable from Kraft, which was recorded as an increase to operating income on Altria Group, Inc.'s consolidated statement of earnings for the year ended December 31, 2011. For the years ended December 31, 2011, 2010 and 2009, there was no impact on Altria Group, Inc.'s net earnings associated with the Kraft and PMI tax matters discussed above.

Altria Group, Inc. recognizes accrued interest and penalties associated with uncertain tax positions as part of the tax provision. As of December 31, 2011, Altria Group, Inc. had $618 million of accrued interest and penalties, of which approximately $39 million and $21 million related to Kraft and PMI, respectively, for which Kraft and PMI are responsible under their respective tax sharing agreements. As of December 31, 2010, Altria Group, Inc. had $261 million of accrued interest and penalties, of which approximately $32 million and $19 million related to Kraft and PMI, respectively. The corresponding receivables from Kraft and PMI are included in assets on Altria Group, Inc.'s consolidated balance sheets at December 31, 2011 and 2010.

For the years ended December 31, 2011, 2010 and 2009, Altria Group, Inc. recognized in its consolidated statements of earnings $496 million, $(69) million and $3 million, respectively, of gross interest expense (income) associated with uncertain tax positions, which in 2011 primarily relates to the PMCC Leveraged Lease Charge.

Altria Group, Inc. is subject to income taxation in many jurisdictions. Uncertain tax positions reflect the difference between tax positions taken or expected to be taken on income tax returns and the amounts recognized in the financial statements. Resolution of the related tax positions with the relevant tax authorities may take many years to complete, since such timing is not entirely within the control of Altria Group, Inc. It is reasonably possible that within the next 12 months certain examinations will be resolved, which could result in a decrease in unrecognized tax benefits of approximately $250 million, the majority of which would relate to the unrecognized tax benefits of Kraft and PMI, for which Altria Group, Inc. is indemnified.

The effective income tax rate on pre-tax earnings differed from the U.S. federal statutory rate for the following reasons for the years ended December 31, 2011, 2010 and 2009:

	2011	2010	2009
U.S. federal statutory rate	35.0%	35.0%	35.0%
Increase (decrease) resulting from:			
State and local income taxes, net of federal tax benefit	3.8	3.7	2.4
Uncertain tax positions	5.5	(2.3)	(0.6)
SABMiller dividend benefit	(2.0)	(2.3)	(2.4)
Domestic manufacturing deduction	(2.4)	(2.4)	(1.5)
Other	(0.7)		1.3
Effective tax rate	39.2%	31.7%	34.2%

The tax provision in 2011 includes a $312 million charge that primarily represents a permanent charge for interest, net of income tax benefit, on tax underpayments, associated with the previously discussed PMCC Leveraged Lease Charge which was recorded during the second quarter of 2011 and is reflected in uncertain tax positions above. The tax provision in 2011 also includes tax benefits of $77 million primarily attributable to the reversal of tax reserves and associated interest related to the expiration of statutes of limitations, closure of tax audits and the reversal of tax accruals no longer required. The tax provision in 2010 includes tax benefits of $216 million from the reversal of tax reserves and associated interest resulting from the execution of the 2010 closing agreement with the IRS discussed above. The tax provision in 2010 also includes tax benefits of $64 million from the reversal of tax reserves and associated interest following the resolution of several state audits and the expiration of statutes of limitations. The tax provision in 2009 includes tax benefits of $88 million from the reversal of tax reserves and associated interest resulting from the execution of the 2009 closing agreement with the IRS discussed above. The tax provision in 2009 also includes a tax benefit of $53 million from the utilization of net operating losses in the third quarter.

1.108

INGRAM MICRO INC. (DEC)

NOTES TO CONSOLIDATED FINANCIAL STATEMENTS

(In 000s, except per share data)

Note 10—Commitments and Contingencies (in part)

Our Brazilian subsidiary has received a number of tax assessments including: (1) a 2005 Federal import tax assessment claiming certain commercial taxes totaling Brazilian Reais 12,714 ($6,777 at December 31, 2011 exchange rates) were due on the import of software acquired from international vendors for the period January through September of 2002; (2) a 2007 Sao Paulo Municipal tax assessment claiming Brazilian Reais 29,111 ($15,518 at December 31, 2011 exchange rates) of service taxes were due on the resale of acquired software covering years 2002 through 2006, plus Brazilian Reais 25,972 ($13,844 at December 31, 2011 exchange rates) of associated penalties; and (3) a 2011 Federal income tax assessment, a portion of which claims statutory penalties totaling Brazilian Reais 15,900 ($8,475 at December 31, 2011 exchange rates) for delays in providing certain electronic files during the audit of tax years 2008 and 2009, which was conducted through the course of 2011. After working with our advisor in evaluating the 2011 Federal income tax assessment, we believe the matters raised in the assessment, other than the one noted above, represent a remote risk of loss.

In addition to the amounts assessed, it is possible that we could also be assessed up to Brazilian Reais 26,217 ($13,975 at December 31, 2011 exchange rates) for penalties and interest on the 2005 assessment and up to Brazilian Reais

101,353 ($54,026 at December 31, 2011 exchange rates) for interest and inflationary adjustments on the 2007 assessment. After working with our advisors on these matters, we believe we have good defenses against each matter and do not believe it is probable that we will suffer a material loss for amounts in the 2007 and the 2011 assessments or any other unassessed amounts noted above. While we will continue to vigorously pursue administrative and, if applicable, judicial action in defending against the 2005 Federal import tax assessment, we continue to maintain a reserve for the full amount assessed at December 31, 2011.

There are various other claims, lawsuits and pending actions against us incidental to our operations. It is the opinion of management that the ultimate resolution of these matters will not have a material adverse effect on our consolidated financial position, results of operations or cash flows. However, we can make no assurances that we will ultimately be successful in our defense of any of these matters.

Environmental Matters

1.109

ALCOA INC. (DEC)

NOTES TO THE CONSOLIDATED FINANCIAL STATEMENTS

(Dollars in millions, except per-share amounts)

A. Summary of Significant Accounting Policies (in part)

Environmental Matters. Expenditures for current operations are expensed or capitalized, as appropriate. Expenditures relating to existing conditions caused by past operations, which will not contribute to future revenues, are expensed. Liabilities are recorded when remediation costs are probable and can be reasonably estimated. The liability may include costs such as site investigations, consultant fees, feasibility studies, outside contractors, and monitoring expenses. Estimates are generally not discounted or reduced by potential claims for recovery. Claims for recovery are recognized as agreements are reached with third parties. The estimates also include costs related to other potentially responsible parties to the extent that Alcoa has reason to believe such parties will not fully pay their proportionate share. The liability is continuously reviewed and adjusted to reflect current remediation progress, prospective estimates of required activity, and other factors that may be relevant, including changes in technology or regulations.

N. Contingencies and Commitments (in part)

Contingencies (in part)

Environmental Matters. Alcoa continues to participate in environmental assessments and cleanups at a number of locations (more than 100). These include owned or operating facilities and adjoining properties, previously owned or operating facilities and adjoining properties, and waste sites, including Superfund (Comprehensive Environmental Response, Compensation and Liability Act (CERCLA)) sites.

A liability is recorded for environmental remediation when a cleanup program becomes probable and the costs or damages can be reasonably estimated.

As assessments and cleanups proceed, the liability is adjusted based on progress made in determining the extent of remedial actions and related costs and damages. The liability can change substantially due to factors such as the nature and extent of contamination, changes in remedial requirements, and technological changes, among others.

Alcoa's remediation reserve balance was $347 and $333 at December 31, 2011 and 2010 (of which $58 and $31 was classified as a current liability), respectively, and reflects the most probable costs to remediate identified environmental conditions for which costs can be reasonably estimated. In 2011, the remediation reserve was increased by $31 due to charges of $18 related to the decision to permanently shut down and demolish a U.S. smelter (see Note D) and a net increase of $13 associated with a number of other sites. In 2010, the remediation reserve was increased by $46 due to charges of $19 related to the Massena West, NY site discussed below, $14 related to the decision to permanently shut down and demolish two U.S. smelters (see Note D), and $11 related to a settlement offer made in late 2010 for outstanding claims resulting from historical discharges into nearby rivers from both smelters in Massena, NY (separate from matter below); a reversal of $9 for previous charges related to a facility located in Russia due to new information; and a net increase of $11 associated with a number of other sites. In both periods, the changes to the remediation reserve, except for the aforementioned $18 in 2011 and $14 in 2010, were recorded in Cost of goods sold on the accompanying Statement of Consolidated Operations. Payments related to remediation expenses applied against the reserve were $19 and $17 in 2011 and 2010, respectively. These amounts include expenditures currently mandated, as well as those not required by any regulatory authority or third party. In 2011 and 2010, the change in the reserve also reflects a decrease of $1 and $3, respectively, due to the effects of foreign currency translation. Also, the change in the 2011 reserve reflects an increase of $3 related to the acquisition of an aerospace fasteners business (see Note F).

Included in annual operating expenses are the recurring costs of managing hazardous substances and environmental programs. These costs are estimated to be approximately 2% of cost of goods sold.

The following discussion provides details regarding the current status of certain significant reserves related to current or former Alcoa sites.

Massena West, NY—Alcoa has been conducting investigations and studies of the Grasse River, adjacent to Alcoa's Massena plant site, under a 1989 order from the U.S. Environmental Protection Agency (EPA) issued under CERCLA. Sediments and fish in the river contain varying levels of polychlorinated biphenyls (PCBs).

Alcoa submitted various Analysis of Alternatives Reports to the EPA starting in 1998 through 2002 that reported the results of river and sediment studies, potential alternatives for remedial actions related to the PCB contamination, and additional information requested by the EPA.

In June 2003, the EPA requested that Alcoa gather additional field data to assess the potential for sediment erosion from winter river ice formation and breakup. The results of these additional studies, submitted in a report to the EPA in April 2004, suggest that this phenomenon has the potential to occur approximately every 10 years and may impact sediments in certain portions of the river under all remedial scenarios. The EPA informed Alcoa that a final remedial decision for the river could not be made without substantially more information, including river pilot studies on the effects of ice formation and breakup on each of the remedial techniques. Alcoa submitted to the EPA, and the EPA approved, a Remedial Options Pilot Study (ROPS) to gather this information. The scope of this study included sediment removal and capping, the installation of an ice control structure, and significant monitoring.

From 2004 through 2008, Alcoa completed the work outlined in the ROPS. In November 2008, Alcoa submitted an update to the EPA incorporating the new information obtained from the ROPS related to the feasibility and costs associated with various capping and dredging alternatives, including options for ice control. As a result, Alcoa increased the reserve associated with the Grasse River by $40 for the estimated costs of a proposed ice control remedy and for partial settlement of potential damages of natural resources.

In late 2009, the EPA requested that Alcoa submit a complete revised Analysis of Alternatives Report in March 2010 to address questions and comments from the EPA and various stakeholders. On March 24, 2010, Alcoa submitted the revised report, which included an expanded list of proposed remedial alternatives, as directed by the EPA. Alcoa increased the reserve associated with the Grasse River by $17 to reflect an increase in the estimated costs of the Company's recommended capping alternative as a result of changes in scope that occurred due to the questions and comments from the EPA and various stakeholders. While the EPA reviews the revised report, Alcoa will continue with its on-going monitoring and field studies activities. In late 2010, Alcoa increased the reserve by $2 based on the most recent estimate of costs expected to be incurred for on-going monitoring and field studies activities. In late 2011, the EPA and various stakeholders completed their review of the March 2010 revised report and submitted questions and comments to Alcoa. As a result, Alcoa increased the reserve by $1 to reflect a revision in the estimate of costs expected to be incurred for on-going monitoring and field studies activities.

The ultimate selection of a remedy may result in additional liability. Alternatives analyzed in the most recent Analysis of Alternatives report that are equally effective as the recommended capping remedy range in additional estimated costs between $20 and $100. Alcoa may be required to record a subsequent reserve adjustment at the time the EPA's Record of Decision is issued that may exceed the estimated range.

Sherwin, TX—In connection with the sale of the Sherwin alumina refinery, which was required to be divested as part of the Reynolds merger in 2000, Alcoa agreed to retain responsibility for the remediation of the then existing environmental conditions, as well as a pro rata share of the final closure of the active waste disposal areas, which remain in use. Alcoa's share of the closure costs is proportional to the total period of operation of the active waste disposal areas. Alcoa estimated its liability for the active disposal areas by making certain assumptions about the period of operation, the amount of material placed in the area prior to closure, and the appropriate technology, engineering, and regulatory status applicable to final closure. The most probable cost for remediation was reserved.

East St. Louis, IL—In response to questions regarding environmental conditions at the former East St. Louis operations, Alcoa and the City of East St. Louis, the owner of the site, entered into an administrative order with the EPA

in December 2002 to perform a remedial investigation and feasibility study of an area used for the disposal of bauxite residue from historic alumina refining operations. A draft feasibility study was submitted to the EPA in April 2005. The feasibility study included remedial alternatives that ranged from no further action to significant grading, stabilization, and water management of the bauxite residue disposal areas. As a result, Alcoa increased the environmental reserve for this location by $15 in 2005. The EPA's ultimate selection of a remedy could result in additional liability. Alcoa may be required to record a subsequent reserve adjustment at the time the EPA's Record of Decision is issued.

Vancouver, WA—In 1987, Alcoa sold its Vancouver smelter to a company that is now known as Evergreen Aluminum (Evergreen). The purchase and sale agreement contained a provision that Alcoa retain liability for any environmental issues that arise subsequent to the sale that pre-date 1987. As a result of this obligation, Alcoa recorded a reserve for the Vancouver location at that time. Evergreen decommissioned the smelter and cleaned up its portion of the site under a consent order with the Washington Department of Ecology (WDE). In February 2008, Evergreen notified Alcoa that it had identified numerous areas containing contamination that predated 1987.

Separately, in September 2008, Alcoa completed a Remedial Investigation/Feasibility Study (RI/FS) under the Washington State Model Toxics Control Act and negotiated a consent decree with the WDE, which requires Alcoa to complete cleanup of PCB contaminated sediments in the Columbia River as well as remediate soil contamination in upland portions of the Vancouver property.

In late 2008, Alcoa started cleanup work on the Columbia River and discovered additional contamination and waste materials along the shoreline area and in upland areas. In addition, Evergreen presented additional cost estimates for contaminated areas that were discovered since March 2008.

As a result of all of the above items related to the former Vancouver site, Alcoa increased the environmental reserve by $16 in 2008.

While continuing the cleanup work on the Columbia River in early 2009, Alcoa discovered more contamination and waste materials, resulting in a $2 increase to the environmental reserve. Later in 2009, cleanup work was completed related to the Evergreen property, the Columbia River, and the upland portions of the Vancouver property. Alcoa submitted a final report on this cleanup work to the WDE near the end of 2009 satisfying the remediation requirements of the consent decree.

On March 17, 2010, Alcoa received a letter from the WDE stating that the work performed by Alcoa related to the Columbia River and the upland portions of the Vancouver property met all of the requirements of the consent decree, as well as the industrial cleanup standards under the Washington State Model Toxics Control Act. No additional reserve adjustment was necessary.

Fusina and Portovesme, Italy—In 1996, Alcoa acquired the Fusina smelter and rolling operations and the Portovesme smelter, both of which are owned by Alcoa's subsidiary Alcoa Trasformazioni S.r.l., from Alumix, an entity owned by the Italian Government. At the time of the acquisition, Alumix indemnified Alcoa for pre-existing environmental contamination at the sites. In 2004, the Italian Ministry of Environment (MOE) issued orders to Alcoa Trasformazioni S.r.l. and Alumix for the development of a clean-up plan related to soil contamination in excess of allowable limits under legislative decree and to institute emergency actions and pay natural resource damages. Alcoa Trasformazioni S.r.l. appealed the orders and filed suit against Alumix, among others, seeking indemnification for these liabilities under the provisions of the acquisition agreement. In 2009, Ligestra S.r.l., Alumix's successor, and Alcoa Trasformazioni S.r.l. agreed to a stay on the court proceedings while investigations were conducted and negotiations advanced towards a possible settlement. In December 2009, Alcoa Trasformazioni S.r.l. and Ligestra S.r.l. reached an agreement for settlement of the liabilities related to Fusina while negotiations continue related to Portovesme. The agreement outlines an allocation of payments to the MOE for emergency action and natural resource damages and the scope and costs for a proposed soil remediation project, which was formally presented to the MOE in mid-2010. The agreement is contingent upon final acceptance of the remediation project by the MOE. As a result of entering into this agreement, Alcoa increased the reserve by $12 for Fusina. Additionally, due to new information derived from the site investigations conducted at Portovesme in 2009, Alcoa increased the reserve by $3 in 2009.

Other. In addition to the matters discussed above, various other lawsuits, claims, and proceedings have been or may be instituted or asserted against Alcoa, including those pertaining to environmental, product liability, and safety and health matters. While the amounts claimed in these other matters may be substantial, the ultimate liability cannot now be determined because of the considerable uncertainties that exist. Therefore, it is possible that the Company's liquidity or results of operations in a particular period could be materially affected by one or more of these other matters. However, based on facts currently available, management believes that the disposition of these other matters that are pending or asserted will not have a material adverse effect, individually or in the aggregate, on the financial position of the Company.

1.110

THE DOW CHEMICAL COMPANY (DEC)

NOTES TO THE CONSOLIDATED FINANCIAL STATEMENTS

Note A—Summary of Significant Accounting Policies (in part)

Environmental Matters

Accruals for environmental matters are recorded when it is probable that a liability has been incurred and the amount of the liability can be reasonably estimated based on current law and existing technologies. These accruals are adjusted periodically as assessment and remediation efforts progress or as additional technical or legal information becomes available. Accruals for environmental liabilities are included in the consolidated balance sheets in "Accrued and other current liabilities" and "Other noncurrent obligations" at undiscounted amounts. Accruals for related insurance or other third-party recoveries for environmental liabilities are recorded when it is probable that a recovery will be realized and are included in the consolidated balance sheets as "Accounts and notes receivable—Other."

Environmental costs are capitalized if the costs extend the life of the property, increase its capacity, and/or mitigate or prevent contamination from future operations. Environmental costs are also capitalized in recognition of legal asset retirement obligations resulting from the acquisition, construction and/or normal operation of a long-lived asset. Costs related to environmental contamination treatment and cleanup are charged to expense. Estimated future incremental operations, maintenance and management costs directly related to remediation are accrued when such costs are probable and reasonably estimable.

Note N—Commitments and Contingent Liabilities (in part)

Environmental Matters

Accruals for environmental matters are recorded when it is probable that a liability has been incurred and the amount of the liability can be reasonably estimated based on current law and existing technologies. At December 31, 2011, the Company had accrued obligations of $733 million for probable environmental remediation and restoration costs, including $69 million for the remediation of Superfund sites and $50 million for environmental liabilities recognized in the fourth quarter of 2011 related to the Camaçari, Brazil site. This is management's best estimate of the costs for remediation and restoration with respect to environmental matters for which the Company has accrued liabilities, although it is reasonably possible that the ultimate cost with respect to these particular matters could range up to approximately twice that amount. Consequently, it is reasonably possible that environmental remediation and restoration costs in excess of amounts accrued could have a material impact on the Company's results of operations, financial condition and cash flows. It is the opinion of the Company's management, however, that the possibility is remote that costs in excess of the range disclosed will have a material impact on the Company's results of operations, financial condition and cash flows. Inherent uncertainties exist in these estimates primarily due to unknown conditions, changing governmental regulations and legal standards regarding liability, and emerging remediation technologies for handling site remediation and restoration. At December 31, 2010, the Company had accrued obligations of $607 million for probable environmental remediation and restoration costs, including $59 million for the remediation of Superfund sites.

The following table summarizes the activity in the Company's accrued obligations for environmental matters for the years ended December 31, 2011 and 2010:

Accrued Obligations for Environmental Matters In millions	2011	2010
Balance at January 1	$ 607	$ 619
Additional accruals	286	159
Charges against reserve	(149)	(171)
Foreign currency impact	(11)	—
Balance at December 31	$ 733	$ 607

The amounts charged to income on a pretax basis related to environmental remediation totaled $261 million in 2011, $158 million in 2010 and $269 million in 2009. Capital expenditures for environmental protection were $170 million in 2011, $173 million in 2010 and $219 million in 2009.

Midland Off-Site Environmental Matters

On June 12, 2003, the Michigan Department of Environmental Quality ("MDEQ") issued a Hazardous Waste Operating License (the "License") to the Company's Midland, Michigan manufacturing site (the "Midland site"), which included provisions requiring the Company to conduct an investigation to determine the nature and extent of off-site contamination in the City of Midland soils, the Tittabawassee River and Saginaw River sediment and floodplain soils, and the Saginaw Bay, and, if necessary, undertake remedial action.

City of Midland

Matters related to the City of Midland remain under the primary oversight of the State of Michigan (the "State") under the License, and the Company and the State are in ongoing discussions regarding the implementation of the requirements of the License.

Tittabawassee and Saginaw Rivers, Saginaw Bay

The Company, the U.S. Environmental Protection Agency ("EPA") and the State entered into an administrative order on consent ("AOC"), effective January 21, 2010, that requires the Company to conduct a remedial investigation, a feasibility study and a remedial design for the Tittabawassee River, the Saginaw River and the Saginaw Bay, and pay the oversight costs of the EPA and the State under the authority of the Comprehensive Environmental Response, Compensation, and Liability Act ("CERCLA"). These actions, to be conducted under the lead oversight of the EPA, will build upon the investigative work completed under the State Resource Conservation Recovery Act ("RCRA") program from 2005 through 2009. The Tittabawassee River, beginning at the Midland Site and extending down to the first six miles of the Saginaw River, are designated as the first Operable Unit for purposes of conducting the remedial investigation, feasibility study and remedial design work. This work will be performed in a largely upriver to downriver sequence for eight geographic segments of the Tittabawassee and upper Saginaw Rivers. The remainder of the Saginaw River and the Saginaw Bay are designated as a second Operable Unit and the work associated with that unit may also be geographically segmented. The AOC does not obligate the Company to perform removal or remedial action; that action can only be required by a separate order. The Company and the EPA will be negotiating orders separate from the AOC that will obligate the Company to perform remedial actions under the scope of work of the AOC. The Company and the EPA have entered into three separate orders to perform limited remedial actions to implement early actions. In addition, the Company and the EPA have entered into the first order to address remedial actions in the first of the eight geographic segments in the first Operable Unit.

Alternative Dispute Resolution Process

The Company, the EPA, the U.S. Department of Justice, and the natural resource damage trustees (which include the Michigan Office of the Attorney General, the MDEQ, the U.S. Fish and Wildlife Service, the U.S. Bureau of Indian Affairs, and the Saginaw-Chippewa tribe) have been engaged in negotiations to seek to resolve potential governmental claims against the Company related to historical off-site contamination associated with the City of Midland, the Tittabawassee

and Saginaw Rivers and the Saginaw Bay. The Company and the governmental parties started meeting in the fall of 2005 and entered into a Confidentiality Agreement in December 2005. The Company continues to conduct negotiations under the Federal Alternative Dispute Resolution Act with all of the governmental parties, except the EPA which withdrew from the alternative dispute resolution process on September 12, 2007.

On September 28, 2007, the Company and the natural resource damage trustees entered into a Funding and Participation Agreement that addressed the Company's payment of past costs incurred by the natural resource damage trustees, payment of the costs of a trustee coordinator and a process to review additional cooperative studies that the Company might agree to fund or conduct with the natural resource damage trustees. On March 18, 2008, the Company and the natural resource damage trustees entered into a Memorandum of Understanding to provide a mechanism for the Company to fund cooperative studies related to the assessment of natural resource damages. This Memorandum of Understanding has been amended and extended until March 2013. On April 7, 2008, the natural resource damage trustees released their "Natural Resource Damage Assessment Plan for the Tittabawassee River System Assessment Area."

At December 31, 2011, the accrual for these off-site matters was $40 million (included in the total accrued obligation of $733 million). At December 31, 2010, the Company had an accrual for these off-site matters of $32 million (included in the total accrued obligation of $607 million).

Environmental Matters Summary

It is the opinion of the Company's management that the possibility is remote that costs in excess of those disclosed will have a material impact on the Company's results of operations, financial condition and cash flows.

Self-Insurance

1.111

PULTEGROUP, INC. (DEC)

NOTES TO CONSOLIDATED FINANCIAL STATEMENTS

15. Commitments and Contingencies (in part)

Self-Insured Risks

We maintain, and require our subcontractors to maintain, general liability insurance coverage. We also maintain builders' risk, property, errors and omissions, workers compensation, and other business insurance coverage. These insurance policies protect us against a portion of the risk of loss from claims. However, we retain a significant portion of the overall risk for such claims either through policies issued by our captive insurance subsidiaries or through our own self-insured per occurrence and aggregate retentions, deductibles, and claims in excess of available insurance policy limits.

Our general liability insurance includes coverage for certain construction defects. While construction defect claims can relate to a variety of circumstances, the majority of our claims relate to alleged problems with siding, plumbing, foundations and other concrete work, windows, roofing, and heating, ventilation and air conditioning systems. The availability of general liability insurance for the homebuilding industry and its subcontractors has become increasingly limited, and the insurance policies available require companies to maintain higher per occurrence and aggregate retention levels. In certain instances, we may offer our subcontractors the opportunity to purchase insurance through one of our captive insurance subsidiaries or to participate in a project-specific insurance program provided by the Company. Policies issued by the captive insurance subsidiaries represent self-insurance of these risks by the Company. This self-insured exposure is limited by reinsurance policies that we purchase. General liability coverage for the homebuilding industry is complex, and our coverage varies from policy year to policy year. We are self-insured for a per occurrence deductible, which is capped at an overall aggregate retention level. Beginning with the first dollar, amounts paid on insured claims satisfy our per occurrence and aggregate retention obligations. Any amounts incurred in excess of the occurrence or aggregate retention levels are covered by insurance up to our purchased coverage levels. Our insurance policies, including the captive insurance subsidiaries' reinsurance policies, are maintained with highly-rated underwriters for whom we believe counterparty default risk is not significant.

At any point in time, we are managing over 1,000 individual claims related to general liability, property, errors and omission, workers compensation, and other business insurance coverage. We reserve for costs associated with such claims (including expected claims management expenses relating to legal fees, expert fees, and claims handling expenses) on an undiscounted basis at the time product revenue is recognized for each home closing and evaluate the recorded liabilities based on actuarial analyses of our historical claims. The actuarial analyses calculate an estimate of the ultimate net cost of all unpaid losses, including estimates for incurred but not reported losses ("IBNR"). IBNR represents losses related to claims incurred but not yet reported plus development on reported claims. These estimates make up a significant portion of our liability and are subject to a high degree of uncertainty due to a variety of factors, including changes in claims reporting and resolution patterns, third party recoveries, insurance industry practices, the regulatory environment, and legal precedent. State regulations vary, but construction defect claims are reported and resolved over an extended period often exceeding ten years. In certain instances, we have the ability to recover a portion of our costs under various insurance policies or from subcontractors or other third parties. Estimates of such amounts are recorded when recovery is considered probable.

Our recorded reserves for all such claims totaled $741.4 million and $785.6 million at December 31, 2011 and 2010, respectively, the vast majority of which relate to general liability claims. The recorded reserves include loss estimates related to both (i) existing claims and related claim expenses and (ii) IBNR and related claim expenses. Liabilities related to IBNR and related claim expenses represented approximately 78% of the total general liability reserves at both December

31, 2011 and 2010. The actuarial analyses that determine the IBNR portion of reserves consider a variety of factors, including the frequency and severity of losses, which are based on our historical claims experience supplemented by industry data. The actuarial analyses of the reserves also consider historical third party recovery rates and claims management expenses.

Adjustments to estimated reserves are recorded in the period in which the change in estimate occurs. Because the majority of our recorded reserves relates to IBNR, adjustments to reserve amounts for individual existing claims generally do not impact the recorded reserves materially. However, changes in the frequency and timing of reported claims and the estimates of specific claim values can impact the underlying inputs and trends utilized in the actuarial analyses, which could have a material impact on the recorded reserves. Because of the inherent uncertainty in estimating future losses related to these claims, actual costs could differ significantly from estimated costs.

We have experienced a high level of insurance-related expenses in recent years, primarily due to the adverse development of general liability claims, the frequency and severity of which have increased significantly over historical levels. During 2010, we experienced a greater than anticipated frequency of newly reported claims and a significant increase in specific case reserves related to certain known claims. The general nature of these claims was not out of the ordinary, but the frequency and severity of the claims were in excess of our historical experience. As a result of these unfavorable trends, we recorded additional reserves totaling $ 280.4 million ($ 0.74 per basic and diluted share) within selling, general, and administrative expenses. Substantially all of this additional reserve related to general liability exposures, a large portion of which resulted from revising our actuarial assumptions surrounding the long-term frequency, severity, and development of claims. During the industry downturn over the last several years, and especially in 2010, we experienced adverse claim frequency and severity compared with longer term averages. In 2010, we deemed it appropriate to assume that the long-term future frequency, severity, and development of claims will most closely resemble the claims activity experienced in recent years.

Changes in these liabilities were as follows ($000's omitted):

	2011	2010	2009
Balance, beginning of period	$785,562	$551,020	$323,227
Reserves provided	53,068	313,606	34,939
Liabilities assumed with Centex merger	—	2,514	271,071
Payments	(97,247)	(81,578)	(78,217)
Balance, end of period	$741,383	$785,562	$551,020

As reflected in the above table, we assumed insurance-related liabilities of $ 271.1 million effective with the Centex merger, which were increased by $ 2.5 million upon completion of a final valuation in 2010. The reserves provided reflected in the above table are classified within selling, general, and administrative expenses.

Investigations and Regulatory Action

1.112

JOHNSON & JOHNSON (DEC)

NOTES TO CONSOLIDATED FINANCIAL STATEMENTS

21. Legal Proceedings (in part)

Government Proceedings

Like other companies in the pharmaceutical and medical devices and diagnostics industries, Johnson & Johnson and certain of its subsidiaries are subject to extensive regulation by national, state and local government agencies in the United States and other countries in which they operate. As a result, interaction with government agencies is ongoing. The most significant litigation brought by, and investigations conducted by, government agencies are listed below. It is possible that criminal charges and substantial fines and/or civil penalties or damages could result from government investigations or litigation.

Average Wholesale Price (Awp) Litigation

Johnson & Johnson and several of its pharmaceutical subsidiaries (the J&J AWP Defendants), along with numerous other pharmaceutical companies, are defendants in a series of lawsuits in state and federal courts involving allegations that the pricing and marketing of certain pharmaceutical products amounted to fraudulent and otherwise actionable conduct because, among other things, the companies allegedly reported an inflated Average Wholesale Price (AWP) for the drugs at issue. Payors alleged that they used those AWPs in calculating provider reimbursement levels. Many of these cases, both federal actions and state actions removed to federal court, were consolidated for pre-trial purposes in a Multi-District Litigation (MDL) in the United States District Court for the District of Massachusetts.

The plaintiffs in these cases included three classes of private persons or entities that paid for any portion of the purchase of the drugs at issue based on AWP, and state government entities that made Medicaid payments for the drugs at issue based on AWP. In June 2007, after a trial on the merits, the MDL Court dismissed the claims of two of the plaintiff classes against the J&J AWP Defendants. In March 2011, the Court dismissed the claims of the third class against the J&J AWP Defendants without prejudice.

AWP cases brought by various Attorneys General have proceeded to trial against other manufacturers. Several state cases against certain of Johnson & Johnson's subsidiaries have been settled, including Kentucky, which had been set for trial in January 2012. Kansas is set for trial in March 2013, and other state cases are likely to be set for trial. In addition, an AWP case against the J&J AWP Defendants brought by the Commonwealth of Pennsylvania was tried in Commonwealth Court in October and November 2010. The Court found in the Commonwealth's favor with regard to certain of its claims under the Pennsylvania Unfair Trade Practices and Consumer Protection Law ("UTPL"), entered an injunction, and awarded $45 million in restitution and $6.5 million in civil penalties. The Court found in the J&J AWP Defendants' favor on the Commonwealth's claims of unjust enrichment,

misrepresentation/fraud, civil conspiracy, and on certain of the Commonwealth's claims under the UTPL. The J&J AWP Defendants have appealed the Commonwealth Court's UTPL ruling to the Pennsylvania Supreme Court. The Company believes that the J&J AWP Defendants have strong arguments supporting their appeal. Because the Company believes that the potential for an unfavorable outcome is not probable, it has not established an accrual with respect to the verdict.

Risperdal®

In January 2004, Janssen Pharmaceutica Inc. (Janssen) (now Janssen Pharmaceuticals, Inc. (JPI)) received a subpoena from the Office of the Inspector General of the United States Office of Personnel Management seeking documents concerning sales and marketing of, any and all payments to physicians in connection with sales and marketing of, and clinical trials for, RISPERDAL® from 1997 to 2002. Documents subsequent to 2002 have also been requested by the Department of Justice. An additional subpoena seeking information about marketing of, and adverse reactions to, RISPERDAL® was received from the United States Attorney's Office for the Eastern District of Pennsylvania in November 2005. Numerous subpoenas seeking testimony from various witnesses before a grand jury were also received. JPI cooperated in responding to these requests for documents and witnesses. The United States Department of Justice and the United States Attorney's Office for the Eastern District of Pennsylvania (the Government) are continuing to actively pursue both criminal and civil actions. In February 2010, the Government served Civil Investigative Demands seeking additional information relating to sales and marketing of RISPERDAL® and sales and marketing of INVEGA®. The focus of these matters is the alleged promotion of RISPERDAL® and INVEGA® for off-label uses. The Government has notified JPI that there are also pending qui tam actions alleging off-label promotion of RISPERDAL®. The Government informed JPI that it will intervene in these qui tam actions and file a superseding complaint.

Discussions have been ongoing in an effort to resolve criminal penalties under the Food Drug and Cosmetic Act related to the promotion of RISPERDAL®. An agreement in principle on key issues relevant to a disposition of criminal charges pursuant to a single misdemeanor violation of the Food Drug and Cosmetic Act has been reached, but certain issues remain open before a settlement can be finalized. During 2011, the Company accrued amounts to cover the financial component of the proposed criminal settlement.

In addition, discussions with state and federal government representatives to resolve the separate civil claims related to the marketing of RISPERDAL® and INVEGA®, including those under the False Claims Act (the qui tam actions), are still ongoing. Although it still remains unclear whether a settlement can be reached with respect to the federal and state civil claims, there has been a substantial narrowing of the issues and potential liability, and in 2011, the Company established an accrual to cover the estimated financial component of the potential federal civil settlement. If a negotiated resolution cannot be reached, civil litigation relating to the allegations of off-label promotion of RISPERDAL® and/or INVEGA® is likely.

The Attorneys General of multiple states, including Alaska, Arkansas, Louisiana, Massachusetts, Mississippi, Montana, New Mexico, Pennsylvania, South Carolina, Texas and Utah, have pending actions against Janssen (now JPI) seeking one or more of the following remedies: reimbursement of Medicaid or other public funds for RISPERDAL® prescriptions written for off-label use, compensation for treating their citizens for alleged adverse reactions to RISPERDAL®, civil fines or penalties, damages for "overpayments" by the state and others, violations of state consumer fraud statutes, punitive damages, or other relief relating to alleged unfair business practices. Certain of these actions also seek injunctive relief relating to the promotion of RISPERDAL®. In January 2012, JPI agreed to settle a lawsuit filed by the Attorney General of Texas. Trial in the lawsuit brought by the Attorney General of Arkansas is scheduled to commence in March 2012; JPI has filed motions for summary judgment in the Arkansas matter.

The Attorney General of West Virginia commenced suit in 2004 against Janssen (now JPI) based on claims of alleged consumer fraud as to DURAGESIC®, as well as RISPERDAL®. JPI was found liable and damages were assessed at $4.5 million. JPI filed an appeal, and in November 2010, the West Virginia Supreme Court reversed the trial court's decision. In December 2010, the Attorney General of West Virginia dismissed the case as it related to RISPERDAL® without any payment. Thereafter, JPI settled the case insofar as it related to DURAGESIC®.

In 2004, the Attorney General of Louisiana filed a multi-count Complaint against Janssen (now JPI). Johnson & Johnson was later added as a defendant. The case was tried in October 2010. The issue tried to the jury was whether Johnson & Johnson or JPI had violated the State's Medicaid Fraud Act (the Act) through misrepresentations allegedly made in the mailing of a November 2003 Dear Health Care Professional letter regarding RISPERDAL®. The jury returned a verdict that JPI and Johnson & Johnson had violated the Act and awarded $257.7 million in damages. The trial judge subsequently awarded the Attorney General counsel fees and expenses in the amount of $73 million. Johnson & Johnson's and JPI's motion for a new trial was denied. Johnson & Johnson and JPI have filed an appeal and believe that they have strong arguments supporting the appeal. The Company believes that the potential for an unfavorable outcome is not probable, and therefore, the Company has not established an accrual with respect to the verdict.

In 2007, the Office of General Counsel of the Commonwealth of Pennsylvania filed a lawsuit against Janssen (now JPI) on a multi-Count Complaint related to Janssen's sale of RISPERDAL® to the Commonwealth's Medicaid program. The trial occurred in June 2010. The trial judge dismissed the case after the close of the plaintiff's evidence. The Commonwealth's post-trial motions were denied. The Commonwealth filed an appeal in April 2011. The oral argument is scheduled to take place in May 2012.

In 2007, the Attorney General of South Carolina filed a lawsuit against Johnson & Johnson and Janssen (now JPI) on several counts. In March 2011, the matter was tried on liability only, at which time the lawsuit was limited to claims of violation of the South Carolina Unfair Trade Practice Act, including, among others, questions of whether Johnson & Johnson or JPI engaged in unfair or deceptive acts or practices in the conduct of any trade or commerce by distributing the November 2003 Dear Health Care Professional letter regarding RISPERDAL® or in their use of the product's FDA-approved label. The jury found in favor of Johnson & Johnson and against JPI. In June 2011, the Court awarded civil penalties of approximately $327.1 million. JPI has appealed this judgment. The Company believes that JPI has strong arguments supporting an appeal and that the potential for an unfavorable outcome is not probable. Therefore, the Company has not established an accrual with respect to the verdict.

The Attorneys General of approximately 40 other states have indicated a potential interest in pursuing similar litigation against JPI, and have obtained a tolling agreement staying the running of the statute of limitations while they pursue a coordinated civil investigation of JPI regarding potential consumer fraud actions in connection with the marketing of RISPERDAL®.

In 2011, the Company established an accrual with respect to the above state matters.

In the Company's opinion, the ultimate resolution of any of the above RISPERDAL® matters is not expected to have a material adverse effect on the Company's financial position, although the resolution in any reporting period could have a material impact on the Company's results of operations and cash flows for that period.

McNeil Consumer Healthcare

Starting in June 2010, McNeil Consumer Healthcare Division of McNEIL-PPC, Inc. (McNeil Consumer Healthcare) and certain affiliates, including Johnson & Johnson (the Companies), received grand jury subpoenas from the United States Attorney's Office for the Eastern District of Pennsylvania requesting documents broadly relating to recent recalls of various products of McNeil Consumer Healthcare, and the FDA inspections of the Fort Washington, Pennsylvania and Lancaster, Pennsylvania manufacturing facilities, as well as certain documents relating to recent recalls of a small number of products of other subsidiaries. In addition, in February 2011, the government served McNEIL-PPC, Inc. (McNEIL-PPC) with a Civil Investigative Demand seeking records relevant to its investigation to determine if there was a violation of the Federal False Claims Act. The Companies are cooperating with the United States Attorney's Office in responding to these subpoenas.

The Companies have also received Civil Investigative Demands from multiple State Attorneys General Offices broadly relating to the McNeil recall issues. The Companies continue to cooperate with these inquiries. In January 2011, the Oregon Attorney General filed a civil complaint against Johnson & Johnson, McNEIL-PPC and McNeil Healthcare LLC in state court alleging civil violations of the Oregon Unlawful Trade Practices Act relating to an earlier recall of a McNeil OTC product. After a removal to federal court, the case was remanded back to state court in Oregon. The Companies filed a motion to dismiss in February 2012.

In March 2011, the United States filed a complaint for injunctive relief in the United States District Court for the Eastern District of Pennsylvania against McNEIL-PPC and two of its employees, alleging that McNEIL-PPC is in violation of FDA regulations regarding the manufacture of drugs at the facilities it operates in Lancaster, Pennsylvania, Fort Washington, Pennsylvania, and Las Piedras, Puerto Rico. On the same day, the parties filed a consent decree of permanent injunction resolving the claims set forth in the complaint. The Court approved and entered the consent decree on March 16, 2011.

The consent decree, which is subject to ongoing enforcement by the court, requires McNEIL-PPC to take enhanced measures to remediate the three facilities. The Fort Washington facility, which was voluntarily shut down in April 2010, will remain shut down until a third-party consultant certifies that its operations will be in compliance with applicable law, and the FDA concurs with the third-party certification. The Lancaster and Las Piedras facilities may continue to manufacture and distribute drugs, provided that a third party reviews manufacturing records for selected batches of drugs released from the facilities, and certifies that any deviations reviewed do not adversely affect the quality of the selected batches. McNEIL-PPC has submitted a workplan to the FDA for remediation of the Lancaster and Las Piedras facilities; that plan is subject to FDA approval. Third-party batch record review may cease if the FDA has stated that the facilities appear to be in compliance with applicable law. Each facility is subject to a five-year audit period by a third party after the facility has been deemed by the FDA to be in apparent compliance with applicable law.

Omnicare

In September 2005, Johnson & Johnson received a subpoena from the United States Attorney's Office for the District of Massachusetts, seeking documents related to the sales and marketing of eight drugs to Omnicare, Inc. (Omnicare), a manager of pharmaceutical benefits for long-term care facilities. In April 2009, Johnson & Johnson and certain of its pharmaceutical subsidiaries were served in two civil qui tam cases asserting claims under the Federal False Claims Act and related state law claims alleging that the defendants provided Omnicare with rebates and other alleged kickbacks, causing Omnicare to file false claims with Medicaid and other government programs. In January 2010, the government intervened in both of these cases, naming Johnson & Johnson, Ortho-McNeil-Janssen Pharmaceuticals, Inc. (now Janssen Pharmaceuticals, Inc. (JPI)), and Johnson & Johnson Health Care Systems Inc. as defendants. Subsequently, the Commonwealth of Massachusetts, Virginia, and Kentucky, and the States of California and Indiana intervened in the action. The defendants moved to dismiss the complaints, and in February 2011, the United States District Court for the District of Massachusetts dismissed one qui tam case entirely and dismissed the other case in part, rejecting allegations that the defendants had violated their obligation to report its "best price" to health care program officials. The defendants subsequently moved the Court to reconsider its decision not to dismiss the second case in its entirety, which the Court denied in May 2011. The claims of the United States and individual states remain pending.

In November 2005, a lawsuit was filed under seal by Scott Bartz, a former employee, in the United States District Court for the Eastern District of Pennsylvania against Johnson & Johnson and certain of its pharmaceutical subsidiaries (the J&J Defendants), along with co-defendants McKesson Corporation (McKesson) and Omnicare, Inc. The Bartz complaint raises many issues in common with the Omnicare-related litigation discussed above already pending before the United States District Court for the District of Massachusetts, such as best price and a number of kickback allegations. After investigation, the United States declined to intervene. The case was subsequently unsealed in January 2011. In February 2011, the plaintiff filed an amended complaint, which was placed under seal. Thereafter, on the J&J Defendants' motion, the case was transferred to the United States District Court for the District of Massachusetts, where it is currently pending. In April 2011, the amended complaint was ordered unsealed and alleges a variety of causes of action under the Federal False Claims Act and corresponding state and local statutes, including that the J&J Defendants engaged in various improper transactions that were allegedly designed to report false prescription drug prices to the federal government in order to reduce the J&J Defendants' Medicaid rebate obligations. The complaint further alleges that the J&J Defendants improperly retaliated against the plaintiff for having raised these allegations internally. Bartz seeks multiple forms of relief, including damages and reinstatement to a position with the same seniority status.

The J&J Defendants subsequently moved to dismiss the complaint in May 2011, and oral argument was held in August 2011. In June 2011, Bartz filed a notice of intent to voluntarily dismiss McKesson and Omnicare from the case and added McKesson Specialty Pharmaceuticals, LLC, as a co-defendant. The parties are awaiting a ruling on the motion to dismiss.

Other

In July 2005, Scios Inc. (Scios) received a subpoena from the United States Attorney's Office for the District of Massachusetts, seeking documents related to the sales and marketing of NATRECOR®. In August 2005, Scios was advised that the investigation would be handled by the United States Attorney's Office for the Northern District of California in San Francisco. In February 2009, two qui tam complaints were unsealed in the United States District Court for the Northern District of California, alleging, among other things, improper activities in the promotion of NATRECOR®. In June 2009, the United States government intervened in one of the qui tam actions, and filed a complaint against Scios and Johnson & Johnson seeking relief under the Federal False Claims Act and asserting a claim of unjust enrichment. The civil case is proceeding and discovery is ongoing. In October 2011, the Court approved a settlement of the criminal case in which Scios pled guilty to a single misdemeanor violation of the Food, Drug & Cosmetic Act and paid a fine of $85 million.

In February 2007, Johnson & Johnson voluntarily disclosed to the United States Department of Justice (DOJ) and the United States Securities & Exchange Commission (SEC) that subsidiaries outside the United States are believed to have made improper payments in connection with the sale of medical devices in two small-market countries, which payments may fall within the jurisdiction of the Foreign Corrupt Practices Act (FCPA). In the course of continuing dialogues with the agencies, other issues potentially rising to the level of FCPA violations in additional markets were brought to the attention of the agencies by Johnson & Johnson. In addition, in February 2006, Johnson & Johnson received a subpoena from the SEC requesting documents relating to the participation by several of its subsidiaries in the United Nations Iraq Oil for Food Program. In April 2011, Johnson & Johnson resolved the FCPA and Oil for Food matters through settlements with the DOJ, SEC and United Kingdom Serious Fraud Office. These settlements required payments of approximately $78 million in financial penalties. As part of the settlement with the DOJ, Johnson & Johnson entered into a Deferred Prosecution Agreement that requires Johnson & Johnson to complete a three-year term of enhanced compliance practices.

In June 2008, Johnson & Johnson received a subpoena from the United States Attorney's Office for the District of Massachusetts relating to the marketing of biliary stents by Cordis Corporation (Cordis). Cordis is currently cooperating in responding to the subpoena. In addition, in January 2010, a complaint was unsealed in the United States District Court for the Northern District of Texas seeking damages against Cordis for alleged violations of the Federal False Claims Act and several similar state laws in connection with the marketing of biliary stents. The United States Department of Justice and several states have declined to intervene at this time. In April 2011, the United States District Court for the Northern District of Texas dismissed the complaint without prejudice.

In October 2011, the European Commission announced that it opened an investigation concerning an agreement between Janssen-Cilag B.V. and Sandoz B.V. relating to the supply of fentanyl patches in The Netherlands. The investigation seeks to determine whether the agreement infringes European competition law.

In recent years Johnson & Johnson has received numerous requests from a variety of United States Congressional Committees to produce information relevant to ongoing congressional inquiries. It is Johnson & Johnson's policy to cooperate with these inquiries by producing the requested information.

Warranties

1.113

APPLE INC. (SEP)

NOTES TO CONSOLIDATED FINANCIAL STATEMENTS

Note 7—Commitments and Contingencies (in part)

Accrued Warranty and Indemnification

The Company offers a basic limited parts and labor warranty on its hardware products. The basic warranty period for hardware products is typically one year from the date of purchase by the end-user. The Company also offers a 90-day basic warranty for its service parts used to repair the Company's hardware products. The Company provides currently for the estimated cost that may be incurred under its basic limited product warranties at the time related revenue is recognized. Factors considered in determining appropriate accruals for product warranty obligations include the size of the installed base of products subject to warranty protection, historical and projected warranty claim rates, historical and projected cost-per-claim, and knowledge of specific product failures that are outside of the Company's typical experience. The Company assesses the adequacy of its pre-existing warranty liabilities and adjusts the amounts as necessary based on actual experience and changes in future estimates.

The following table reconciles changes in the Company's accrued warranty and related costs for the three years ended September 24, 2011 (in millions):

	2011	2010	2009
Beginning accrued warranty and related costs	$ 761	$ 577	$ 671
Cost of warranty claims	(1,147)	(713)	(534)
Accruals for product warranty	1,626	897	440
Ending accrued warranty and related costs	$ 1,240	$ 761	$ 577

The Company generally does not indemnify end-users of its operating system and application software against legal claims that the software infringes third-party intellectual property rights. Other agreements entered into by the Company sometimes include indemnification provisions under which the Company could be subject to costs and/or damages in the event of an infringement claim against the Company or an indemnified third-party. However, the Company has not been required to make any significant payments resulting from such an infringement claim asserted against it or an indemnified third-party. In the opinion of management, there was not at least a reasonable possibility the Company may have incurred a material loss with respect to indemnification of end-users of its operating system or application software for infringement of third-party intellectual property rights. The Company did not record a liability for infringement costs related to indemnification as of either September 24, 2011 or September 25, 2010.

The Company has entered into indemnification agreements with its directors and executive officers. Under these agreements, the Company has agreed to indemnify such individuals to the fullest extent permitted by law against liabilities that arise by reason of their status as directors or officers and to advance expenses incurred by such individuals in connection with related legal proceedings. It is not possible to determine the maximum potential amount of payments the Company could be required to make under these agreements due to the limited history of prior indemnification claims and the unique facts and circumstances involved in each claim. However, the Company maintains directors and officers liability insurance coverage to reduce its exposure to such obligations, and payments made under these agreements historically have not been material.

Tax Credits and Other Tax Carryforwards

1.114

CRANE CO. (DEC)

NOTES TO CONSOLIDATED FINANCIAL STATEMENTS

Note 2—Income Taxes (in part)

Deferred Taxes and Valuation Allowances

The components of deferred tax assets and liabilities included on the Company's Consolidated Balance Sheets are as follows:

(In thousands)

December 31	2011	2010
Deferred tax assets:		
Asbestos-related liabilities	$ 260,969	$ 199,009
Tax loss and credit carryforwards	93,337	78,289
Environmental reserves	20,042	11,333
Inventories	15,858	14,737
Accrued bonus and stock-based compensation	12,488	15,105
Pension and post-retirement benefits	50,623	13,074
Other	35,362	19,879
Total	488,679	351,426
Less: valuation allowance	107,511	62,830
Total deferred tax assets, net of valuation allowance	381,168	288,596
Deferred tax liabilities:		
Basis difference in fixed assets	(35,341)	(36,479)
Basis difference in intangible assets	(75,127)	(74,132)
Total deferred tax liabilities	(110,468)	(110,611)
Net deferred tax asset	$ 270,700	$ 177,985
Balance sheet classification:		
Current deferred tax assets	46,664	$ 44,956
Long-term deferred tax assets	265,849	182,832
Accrued liabilities	(145)	(951)
Long-term deferred tax liability	(41,668)	(48,852)
Net deferred tax asset	$ 270,700	$ 177,985

As of December 31, 2011, the Company had U.S. federal, U.S. state and non-U.S. tax loss and credit carryforwards that will expire, if unused, as follows:

(In thousands)

Year of Expiration	U.S. Federal Tax Credits	U.S. Federal Tax Losses	U.S. State Tax Credits	U.S. State Tax Losses	Non-U.S. Tax Losses	Total
2012–2016	$ 105	$ —	$ 1,624	$136,179	$ 10,470	
After 2016	34,430	505	3,253	342,590	24,963	
Indefinite	—	—	13,969	—	29,748	
Total tax carryforwards	$34,535	$505	$ 18,846	$478,769	$ 65,181	
Deferred tax asset on tax carryforwards	$34,535	$177	$ 12,250	$ 27,880	$ 18,495	$ 93,337
Valuation allowance on tax carryforwards	(105)	—	(11,587)	(27,880)	(18,490)	(58,062)
Net deferred tax asset on tax carryforwards	$34,430	$177	$ 663	$ —	$ 5	$ 35,275

As of December 31, 2011, the Company has determined that it is more likely than not that $58.1 million of its deferred tax assets related to tax loss and credit carryforwards will not be realized. As a result, the Company has recorded a valuation allowance against these deferred tax assets as shown in the table above. The Company has also determined that it is more likely than not that a portion of the benefit related to U.S. state and non-U.S. deferred tax assets other than tax loss and credit carryforwards will be not realized. Accordingly, a $49.4 million valuation allowance has been established against these U.S. state and non-U.S. deferred tax assets. The Company's total valuation allowance at December 31, 2011 is $107.5 million.

Net Operating Loss and Tax Credit Carryforwards

1.115

KLA-TENCOR CORPORATION (JUN)

NOTES TO CONSOLIDATED FINANCIAL STATEMENTS

Note 12—Income Taxes (in part)

The significant components of deferred income tax assets and liabilities are as follows:

	As of June 30	
(In thousands)	2011	2010
Deferred tax assets:		
Tax credits and net operating losses	$ 62,173	$ 83,480
Employee benefits accrual	86,741	70,845
Stock-based compensation	66,638	88,078
Capitalized R&D expenses	84,283	110,286
Inventory reserves	55,451	67,141
Non-deductible reserves	50,304	54,038
Deferred profit	95,157	83,700
Unearned revenue	27,723	19,648
Other	36,853	43,352
Gross deferred tax assets	565,323	620,568
Valuation allowance	(30,722)	(44,184)
Net deferred tax assets	$534,601	$576,384
Deferred tax liabilities:		
Unremitted earnings of foreign subsidiaries not permanently reinvested	$ (25,293)	$ (19,863)
Depreciation and amortization	(21,047)	(6,148)
Unrealized gain on investments	(2,215)	(1,409)
Total deferred tax liabilities	(48,555)	(27,420)
Total net deferred tax assets	$486,046	$548,964

As of June 30, 2011, the Company had U.S. federal, state and foreign net operating loss ("NOL") carry-forwards of approximately $45.5 million, $117.6 million and $43.9 million, respectively. The U.S. net operating loss and tax credit carry-forwards will expire at various dates beginning in 2023 through 2029. The utilization of NOLs created by acquired companies is subject to annual limitations under Section

382 of the Internal Revenue Code. However, it is not expected that such annual limitation will impair the realization of these NOLs. The state NOLs will begin to expire in 2013. State credits of $42.7 million will be carried over indefinitely. The foreign net operating loss carry-forwards will begin to expire in 2013.

The net deferred tax asset valuation allowance was $30.7 million as of June 30, 2011 and $44.2 million as of June 30, 2010. The valuation allowance is based on the Company's assessment that it is more likely than not that certain deferred tax assets will not be realized in the foreseeable future. Of the valuation allowance as of June 30, 2011, $26.8 million relates to state credit carry-forwards. The remainder of the valuation allowance relates primarily to foreign net operating loss carry-forwards.

As of June 30, 2011, U.S. income taxes were not provided for on a cumulative total of approximately $599.0 million of undistributed earnings for certain non-U.S. subsidiaries. If these undistributed earnings were repatriated to the United States, they would generate foreign tax credits to reduce the federal tax liability associated with the foreign dividend. Assuming a full utilization of the foreign tax credits, the potential deferred tax liability associated with undistributed earnings would be approximately $198.0 million.

KLA-Tencor benefits from several tax holidays in Israel and Singapore where it manufactures certain of its products. These tax holidays are on approved investments and are scheduled to expire at varying times within the next three to ten years. The Company was in compliance with all the terms and conditions of the tax holidays as of June 30, 2011. The net impact of these tax holidays was to decrease the Company's tax expense by approximately $30.4 million, $12.7 million and $8.9 million in the fiscal years ended June 30, 2011, 2010 and 2009, respectively. The benefits of the tax holidays on diluted net income per share were $0.18, $0.07 and $0.05 for the fiscal years ended June 30, 2011, 2010, 2009, respectively.

Value-Added Tax Credits

1.116

UNIVERSAL CORPORATION (MAR)

NOTES TO CONSOLIDATED FINANCIAL STATEMENTS

Note 1. Nature of Operations and Significant Accounting Policies (in part)

Recoverable Value-Added Tax Credits

In many foreign countries, the Company's local operating subsidiaries pay significant amounts of value-added tax ("VAT") on purchases of unprocessed and processed tobacco, crop inputs, packing materials, and various other goods and services. In some countries, VAT is a national tax, and in other countries it is assessed at the state level. Items subject to VAT vary from jurisdiction to jurisdiction, as do the rates at which the tax is assessed. When tobacco is sold to customers in the country of origin, the operating subsidiaries generally collect VAT on those sales. The subsidiaries are normally permitted to offset those VAT payments against the collections and remit only the incremental VAT collections to the tax authorities. When tobacco is sold for export, VAT is normally not assessed. In countries where tobacco sales are predominately for export markets, VAT collections generated on downstream sales are often not sufficient to fully offset the subsidiaries' VAT payments. In those situations, unused VAT credits can accumulate. Some jurisdictions have procedures that allow companies to apply for refunds of unused VAT credits from the tax authorities, but the refund process often takes an extended period of time and it is not uncommon for refund applications to be challenged or rejected in part on technical grounds. Other jurisdictions may permit companies to sell or transfer unused VAT credits to third parties in private transactions, although approval for such transactions must normally be obtained from the tax authorities, limits on the amounts that can be transferred are usually imposed, and the proceeds realized may be heavily discounted from the face value of the credits. Due to these factors, local operating subsidiaries in some countries can accumulate significant balances of VAT credits over time. The Company reviews these balances on a regular basis and records valuation allowances on the credits to reflect amounts that are not expected to be recovered, as well as discounts anticipated on credits that are expected to be sold or transferred. At March 31, 2011, the aggregate balance of recoverable tax credits held by the Company's subsidiaries totaled approximately $75 million, and the related valuation allowance totaled approximately $22 million.

FINANCIAL INSTRUMENTS

RECOGNITION AND MEASUREMENT

1.117 FASB ASC 815 establishes accounting and reporting standards for derivative instruments, including certain derivative instruments embedded in other contracts (collectively referred to as derivatives), and hedging activities. FASB ASC 815 requires that an entity recognize all derivatives as either assets or liabilities in the statement of financial position and measure those instruments at fair value. In addition, paragraphs 4–6 of FASB ASC 815-15-25 simplify the accounting for certain hybrid financial instruments by permitting an entity to irrevocably elect to initially and subsequently measure that hybrid financial instrument in its entirety at fair value, with changes recognized in earnings. This election is also available when a previously-recognized financial instrument is subject to a re-measurement (new basis) event and the separate recognition of an embedded derivative.

1.118 FASB ASC 825, *Financial Instruments*, permits entities to choose to measure at fair value many financial instruments and certain other items that are not currently required to be measured at fair value. Further, under FASB ASC 825, a business entity should report unrealized gains and losses on eligible items for which the fair value option has been elected in earnings at each subsequent reporting date. The irrevocable election of the fair value option is made on an instrument-by-instrument basis, with certain exceptions, and applied to the entire instrument, not only to specified risks, specific cash flows, or portions of that instrument.

DISCLOSURE

1.119 The disclosures required by FASB ASC 815 for entities with derivative instruments or nonderivative instruments that are designated and qualify as hedging instruments are intended to enable users of financial statements to understand
- How and why an entity uses derivative or nonderivative instruments.
- How derivative instruments or such nonderivative instruments and related hedged items are accounted for under FASB ASC 815.
- How derivative instruments or such nonderivative instruments and related hedged items affect an entity's financial position, financial performance, and cash flows.

1.120 To meet those objectives, FASB ASC 815 requires qualitative disclosures about an entity's objectives and strategies for using derivatives and such nonderivative instruments. An entity that holds or issues derivative instruments or such nonderivative instruments should disclose all of the following for each interim and annual reporting period for which a statement of financial position and statement of financial performance are presented:
- Its objectives for holding or issuing those instruments.
- The context needed to understand those objectives. This should be disclosed in the context of each instrument's primary underlying risk exposure.
- Its strategies for achieving those objectives. This should be disclosed in the context of each instrument's primary underlying risk exposure.

1.121 These instruments should be disclosed in the context of each instrument's primary underlying risk exposure and should be distinguished among those used for risk management purposes, those used as economic hedges and other purposes related to risk exposure, and those used for other purposes. Those used for risk management purposes should be distinguished between those designated as hedging instruments and, further, whether they are fair value hedges, cash flow hedges, or foreign currency hedges. Information that would enable users of its financial statements to understand the volume of its activity in those instruments should also be disclosed for the same periods. An entity should select the format and specifics for this that are most relevant and practicable for its individual facts and circumstances. For any derivatives not designated as hedging instruments under FASB ASC 815-20, the description should include the purpose of the derivative activity.

1.122 FASB ASC 815 also requires quantitative disclosures about derivatives and such nonderivative instruments. For every annual and interim reporting period for which a statement of financial position and statement of financial performance are presented, an entity that holds or issues derivative instruments is required to disclose the location and fair value amounts of derivative instruments and such nonderivative instruments reported in the statement of financial position. The fair value of those instruments should be presented on a gross basis, even when those instruments are subject to master netting arrangements and qualify for net presentation in the statement of financial position. Cash collateral payables and receivables associated with these instruments should not be added to, or netted against, the fair value amounts.

1.123 Fair value amounts should be presented as separate asset and liability values segregated between derivatives that are designated and qualifying as hedging instruments presented separately by type of contract and those that are not. The disclosure should also identify the line item(s) in the statement of financial position in which the fair value amounts for these categories of derivative instruments are included. Also, disclosure of the location and amount of the gains and losses on derivative instruments and such nonderivative instruments and related hedged items in the statement of financial performance or statement of financial position (for example, in other comprehensive income) is required. These gain and loss disclosures should be presented separately by type of contract. These quantitative disclosures are required to be presented in tabular format, except for disclosures regarding hedged items that can be presented in either tabular or nontabular format.

1.124 For derivative instruments not designated or qualifying as hedging instruments under FASB ASC 815-20, if the entity's policy is to include them in its trading activities, the entity can elect not to separately disclose gains and losses, provided that the entity discloses certain other information. Additionally, FASB ASC 815 requires specific disclosures for derivative instruments that contain credit-risk-related features and credit derivatives.

1.125 FASB ASC 825 requires certain reporting entities to disclose the fair value of financial instruments and disclosure requirements of credit risk concentrations of all financial instruments, and it provides guidance on the fair value option. FASB ASC 825 also establishes presentation and disclosure requirements designed to facilitate comparison between entities that choose different measurement attributes for similar types of assets and liabilities.

1.126

TABLE 1-10: FINANCIAL INSTRUMENTS—FINANCIAL GUARANTEES/INDEMNIFICATIONS

Table 1-10 lists the frequencies of financial guarantees/indemnifications for the survey entities.

	Number of Entities		
	2011	2010	2009
Debt or line of credit	173	194	172
Lease payments	311	170	90
Contract performance	72	53	95
Employee related	27	19	53
Environmental	31	30	60
Tax	27	15	51
Intellectual property related	26	27	41
Product/service related	119	58	61
Letters of credit	225	359	314
Other	59	28	47

1.127

TABLE 1-11: FINANCIAL INSTRUMENTS—INTEREST RATE CONTRACTS

Table 1-11 lists the frequencies of interest rate contracts for the survey entities.

	Number of Entities		
	2011	2010	2009
Swaps	257	247	N/C*
Futures	15	3	N/C*
Forward contracts	28	31	N/C*
Caps	16	10	N/C*
Floors	4	N/C*	N/C*
Collars	3	4	N/C*
Swaption	3	2	N/C*
Locks	18	23	N/C*
Options	21	9	N/C*
Other, described	3	3	N/C*

* N/C = Not compiled. Line item was not included in the table for the year shown.

1.128

TABLE 1-12: FINANCIAL INSTRUMENTS—FOREIGN CURRENCY CONTRACTS

Table 1-12 lists the frequencies of foreign currency contracts for the survey entities.

	Number of Entities		
	2011	2010	2009
Forward contracts, foreign exchange contracts, or similar	312	302	N/C*
Options	58	60	N/C*
Swaps	51	43	N/C*
Futures	8	7	N/C*
Collars	6	7	N/C*
Other, described	2	4	N/C*

* N/C = Not compiled. Line item was not included in the table for the year shown.

1.129

TABLE 1-13: FINANCIAL INSTRUMENTS—COMMODITY CONTRACTS

Table 1-13 lists the frequencies of commodity contracts for the survey entities.

	Number of Entities		
	2011	2010	2009
Swaps	55	50	N/C*
Futures	53	36	N/C*
Forward contracts	68	85	N/C*
Options	43	33	N/C*
Collars	6	9	N/C*
Other, described	9	4	N/C*

* N/C = Not compiled. Line item was not included in the table for the year shown.

1.130

TABLE 1-14: FINANCIAL INSTRUMENTS—OTHER FINANCIAL INSTRUMENTS

Table 1-14 lists the frequencies of other financial instruments for the survey entities.

	Number of Entities		
	2011	2010	2009
Sale of receivables with recourse	30	12	11
Equity derivatives, put options, warrants, and forward contracts on stock.............................	46	40	N/C*
Other, described..	22	11	N/C*

* N/C = Not compiled. Line item was not included in the table for the year shown.

PRESENTATION AND DISCLOSURE EXCERPTS

Financial Guarantees and Indemnifications—Line of Credit

1.131

PLUM CREEK TIMBER COMPANY, INC. (DEC)

NOTES TO CONSOLIDATED FINANCIAL STATEMENTS

Note 8. Borrowings (in part)

All of our borrowings, except the Note Payable to Timberland Venture, are made by Plum Creek Timberlands, L.P., the company's wholly-owned operating partnership ("the Partnership"). Furthermore, all of the outstanding indebtedness of the Partnership is unsecured. Outstanding borrowings consist of the following (in millions):

	December 31, 2011	December 31, 2010
Line of Credit maturing 2015, 1.71% at 12/31/11, based on LIBOR plus 1.50%	$ 348	$ 166
Term Credit Agreement due 2012, 0.65% at 12/31/11, based on LIBOR plus 0.375%	350	350
Senior Notes due 2011, 7.83%	—	49
Senior Notes due 2013, 6.18%	174	174
Senior Notes due 2013, 7.76% less unamortized discount of $0.3 at 12/31/11, effective rate of 8.05%	72	111
Senior Notes due 2015, 5.875% less unamortized discount of $3.4 at 12/31/11, effective rate of 6.10%	454	454
Senior Notes due 2016, mature serially 2012 to 2016, 8.05%	17	24
Senior Notes due 2021, 4.70% less unamortized discount of $0.3 at 12/31/11, effective rate of 4.71%	575	575
Note Payable to Timberland Venture due 2018, 7.375%	783	783
Total Long-Term Debt	2,773	2,686
Less: Current Portion of Long-Term Debt	352	94
Less: Line of Credit	348	166
Long-Term Portion	$2,073	$2,426

Line of Credit. The company has a $600 million revolving line of credit agreement that matures January 30, 2015. The weighted-average interest rate for the borrowings on the line of credit was 1.71% and 1.95% as of December 31, 2011 and December 31, 2010, respectively. The interest rate on the line of credit is based on LIBOR plus 1.50%. This rate can range from LIBOR plus 1.275% to LIBOR plus 2% depending on our debt ratings. In addition to interest, the line has an annual facility fee of 0.25% that can vary depending on debt rating. Subject to customary covenants, the line of credit allows for borrowings from time to time up to $600 million, including up to $100 million of standby letters of credit. Borrowings on the line of credit fluctuate daily based on cash needs. As of December 31, 2011, we had $348 million of borrowings and $2 million of standby letters of credit outstanding; $250 million remained available for borrowing under our line of credit. As of January 3, 2012, $251 million of the borrowings under our line of credit was repaid. The line of credit has been classified as a current liability in our Consolidated Balance Sheet as of December 31, 2011, because the company used its cash as of December 31, 2011 to repay a portion of the line.

1.132

MCKESSON CORPORATION (MAR)

FINANCIAL NOTES

16. Financial Guarantees and Warranties (in part)

Financial Guarantees

We have agreements with certain of our Canadian customers' financial institutions under which we have guaranteed the repurchase of our customers' inventory or our customers' debt in the event these customers are unable to meet their obligations to those financial institutions. For our inventory repurchase agreement, among other requirements, inventories must be in resalable condition and any repurchase would be at a discount. The inventory repurchase agreements mostly range from one to two years. Customers' debt guarantees range from one to five years and were primarily provided to facilitate financing for certain customers. The majority of our customers' debt guarantees are secured by certain assets of the customer. We also have an agreement with one software customer that, under limited circumstances, may require us to secure standby financing. Because the amount of the standby financing is not explicitly stated, the overall amount of this guarantee cannot reasonably be estimated. At March 31, 2011, the maximum amounts of inventory repurchase guarantees and customers' debt guarantees were $138 million and $38 million, none of which had been accrued.

The expirations of the above noted financial guarantees are as follows: $119 million, $21 million, $3 million, $4 and $1 million from 2012 through 2016 and $28 million thereafter.

In addition, at March 31, 2011, our banks and insurance companies have issued $128 million of standby letters of credit and surety bonds, which were issued on our behalf mostly related to our customer contracts and in order to meet the security requirements for statutory licenses and permits, court and fiduciary obligations and our workers' compensation and automotive liability programs.

Our software license agreements generally include certain provisions for indemnifying customers against liabilities if our software products infringe a third party's intellectual property rights. To date, we have not incurred any material costs as a result of such indemnification agreements and have not accrued any liabilities related to such obligations.

In conjunction with certain transactions, primarily divestitures, we may provide routine indemnification agreements (such as retention of previously existing environmental, tax and employee liabilities) whose terms vary in duration and often are not explicitly defined. Where appropriate, obligations for such indemnifications are recorded as liabilities. Because the amounts of these indemnification obligations often are not explicitly stated, the overall maximum amount of these commitments cannot be reasonably estimated. Other than obligations recorded as liabilities at the time of divestiture, we have historically not made significant payments as a result of these indemnification provisions.

Derivative Financial Instruments—Interest Rate Hedging Instruments

1.133

DARDEN RESTAURANTS, INC. (MAY)

NOTES TO CONSOLIDATED FINANCIAL STATEMENTS

Note 10—Derivative Instruments and Hedging Activities (in part)

We use financial and commodities derivatives to manage interest rate, equity-based compensation and commodities pricing and foreign currency exchange rate risks inherent in our business operations. By using these instruments, we expose ourselves, from time to time, to credit risk and market risk. Credit risk is the failure of the counterparty to perform under the terms of the derivative contract. When the fair value of a derivative contract is positive, the counterparty owes us, which creates credit risk for us. We minimize

this credit risk by entering into transactions with high quality counterparties. We currently do not have any provisions in our agreements with counterparties that would require either party to hold or post collateral in the event that the market value of the related derivative instrument exceeds a certain limit. As such, the maximum amount of loss due to counterparty credit risk we would incur at May 29, 2011, if counterparties to the derivative instruments failed completely to perform, would approximate the values of derivative instruments currently recognized as assets in our consolidated balance sheet. Market risk is the adverse effect on the value of a financial instrument that results from a change in interest rates, commodity prices, or the market price of our common stock. We minimize this market risk by establishing and monitoring parameters that limit the types and degree of market risk that may be undertaken.

The notional values of our derivative contracts designated as hedging instruments and derivative contracts not designated as hedging instruments are as follows:

(In millions)	May 29, 2011	May 30, 2010
Derivative contracts designated as hedging instruments:		
Natural gas	$ 3.8	$ 3.2
Foreign currency	20.7	18.9
Interest rate locks	150.0	150.0
Interest rate swaps	350.0	375.0
Equity forwards	18.0	12.6
Derivative contracts not designated as hedging instruments:		
Natural gas	$ 7.7	$ 0.6
Other commodities	12.7	4.2
Equity forwards	24.0	12.8

At various times during fiscal 2008 and 2009, we entered into treasury-lock derivative instruments with $150.0 million of notional value to hedge a portion of the risk of changes in the benchmark interest rate associated with the expected issuance of long-term debt in fiscal 2012, as changes in the benchmark interest rate will cause variability in our forecasted interest payments. Subsequent to our fiscal 2011 year end, we entered into an additional $50.0 million of treasury-lock instruments. These derivative instruments are designated as cash flow hedges.

During the quarter ended August 29, 2010, we entered into forward-starting interest rate swap agreements with $200.0 million of notional value to hedge a portion of the risk of changes in the benchmark interest rate associated with the expected issuance of long-term debt to refinance our $350.0 million 5.625 percent senior notes due October 2012, as changes in the benchmark interest rate will cause variability in our forecasted interest payments. These derivative instruments are designated as cash flow hedges.

During fiscal 2010, we entered into interest rate swap agreements with $375.0 million of notional value to limit the risk of changes in fair value of our $150.0 million 4.875 percent notes due August 2010, $75.0 million 7.450 percent notes due April 2011, and a portion of the $350 million 5.625 percent notes due October 2012 attributable to changes in the benchmark interest rate, between fiscal 2010 and maturity of the related debt. Concurrent with the maturity of the $150.0 million notes due August 2010 and $75.0 million notes due April 2011, interest rate swap agreements with a notional value of $150.0 million and $75.0 million, respectively, expired during fiscal 2011. Accordingly, as of May 29,

2011, the remaining notional value of these swap agreements was $150.0 million. The swap agreements effectively swap the fixed rate obligations for floating rate obligations, thereby mitigating changes in fair value of the related debt prior to maturity. The swap agreements were designated as fair value hedges of the related debt and met the requirements to be accounted for under the short-cut method, resulting in no ineffectiveness in the hedging relationship. During the fiscal years ended May 29, 2011 and May 30, 2010, $3.6 million and $3.4 million, respectively, was recorded as a reduction to interest expense related to the net swap settlements.

The fair value of our derivative contracts designated as hedging instruments and derivative contracts that are not designated as hedging instruments are as follows:

(In millions)	Balance Sheet Location	Derivative Assets		Derivative Liabilities	
		May 29, 2011	May 30, 2010	May 29, 2011	May 30, 2010
Derivative contracts designated as hedging instruments					
Commodity contracts	(1)	$0.1	$ —	$ —	$ (0.6)
Equity forwards	(1)	0.4	—	—	(0.4)
Interest rate related	(1)	3.6	3.4	(23.2)	(10.5)
Foreign currency forwards	(1)	0.6	1.1	—	—
		$4.7	$4.5	$(23.2)	$(11.5)
Derivative contracts not designated as hedging instruments					
Commodity contracts	(1)	$0.6	$ —	$ —	$ —
Equity forwards	(1)	0.5	—	—	(0.6)
		$1.1	$ —	$ —	$ (0.6)
Total derivative contracts		$5.8	$4.5	$(23.2)	$(12.1)

(1) Derivative assets and liabilities are included in Receivables, net, Prepaid expenses and other current assets, and Other current liabilities, as applicable, on our consolidated balance sheets.

The effects of derivative instruments in cash flow hedging relationships on the consolidated statements of earnings are as follows:

(In millions)	Amount of Gain (Loss) Recognized in AOCI (Effective Portion) Fiscal Year			Location of Gain (Loss) Reclassified from AOCI to Earnings	Amount of Gain (Loss) Reclassified from AOCI to Earnings (Effective Portion) Fiscal Year			Location of Gain (Loss) Recognized in Earnings (Ineffective Portion)	Amount of Gain (Loss) Recognized In Earnings (Ineffective Portion)(1) Fiscal Year		
	2011	2010	2009		2011	2010	2009		2011	2010	2009
Commodity	$ (0.2)	$(2.1)	$ (8.7)	(2)	$(0.9)	$(3.8)	$(6.1)	(2)	$ —	$ —	$—
Equity	2.6	3.9	1.2	(3)	—	—	—	(3)	0.2	0.3	—
Interest rate	(12.2)	(7.7)	(6.9)	Interest, net	0.7	0.5	(1.3)	Interest, net	(0.5)	—	—
Foreign currency	(0.1)	1.3	0.8	(4)	0.4	1.1	—	(4)	—	—	—
	$ (9.9)	$(4.6)	$(13.6)		$0.2	$(2.2)	$(7.4)		$(0.3)	$0.3	$—

(1) Generally, all of our derivative instruments designated as cash flow hedges have some level of ineffectiveness, which is recognized currently in earnings. However, as these amounts are generally nominal and our consolidated financial statements are presented "in millions," these amounts may appear as zero in this tabular presentation.

(2) Location of the gain (loss) reclassified from AOCI to earnings as well as the gain (loss) recognized in earnings for the ineffective portion of the hedge is food and beverage costs and restaurant expenses, which are components of cost of sales.

(3) Location of the gain (loss) reclassified from AOCI to earnings as well as the gain (loss) recognized in earnings for the ineffective portion of the hedge is restaurant labor expenses, which is a component of cost of sales, and selling, general and administrative expenses.

(4) Location of the gain (loss) reclassified from AOCI to earnings as well as the gain (loss) recognized in earnings for the ineffective portion of the hedge is food and beverage costs, which is a component of cost of sales, and selling, general and administrative expenses.

SEC 1.133

The effects of derivative instruments in fair value hedging relationships on the consolidated statements of earnings are as follows:

(In millions)	Amount of Gain (Loss) Recognized in Earnings on Derivatives			Location of Gain (Loss) Recognized in Earnings on Derivatives	Hedged Item in Fair Value Hedge Relationship	Amount of Gain (Loss) Recognized in Earnings on Related Hedged Item			Location of Gain (Loss) Recognized in Earnings on Related Hedged Item
	Fiscal Year					Fiscal Year			
	2011	2010	2009			2011	2010	2009	
Interest rate	$0.2	$3.4	$—	Interest, net	Debt	$(0.2)	$(3.4)	$—	Interest, net

Derivative Financial Instruments—Forward Contracts

1.134

TIFFANY & CO. (JAN)

NOTES TO CONSOLIDATED FINANCIAL STATEMENTS

J. Hedging Instruments (in part)

Background Information

The Company uses derivative financial instruments, including interest rate swap agreements, forward contracts, put option contracts and net-zero-cost collar arrangements (combination of call and put option contracts) to mitigate its exposures to changes in interest rates, foreign currency and precious metal prices. Derivative instruments are recorded on the consolidated balance sheet at their fair values, as either assets or liabilities, with an offset to current or comprehensive earnings, depending on whether the derivative is designated as part of an effective hedge transaction and, if it is, the type of hedge transaction. If a derivative instrument meets certain hedge accounting criteria, the derivative instrument is designated as one of the following on the date the derivative is entered into:

- Fair Value Hedge—A hedge of the exposure to changes in the fair value of a recognized asset or liability or an unrecognized firm commitment. For fair value hedge transactions, both the effective and ineffective portions of the changes in the fair value of the derivative and changes in the fair value of the item being hedged are recorded in current earnings.
- Cash Flow Hedge—A hedge of the exposure to variability in the cash flows of a recognized asset, liability or a forecasted transaction. For cash flow hedge transactions, the effective portion of the changes in fair value of derivatives are reported as other comprehensive income ("OCI") and are recognized in current earnings in the period or periods during which the hedged transaction affects current earnings. Amounts excluded from the effectiveness calculation and any ineffective portions of the change in fair value of the derivative are recognized in current earnings.

The Company formally documents the nature and relationships between the hedging instruments and hedged items for a derivative to qualify as a hedge at inception and throughout the hedged period. The Company also documents its risk management objectives, strategies for undertaking the various hedge transactions and method of assessing hedge effectiveness. Additionally, for hedges of forecasted transactions, the significant characteristics and expected terms of a forecasted transaction must be specifically identified, and it must be probable that each forecasted transaction will occur. If it were deemed probable that the forecasted transaction would not occur, the gain or loss on the derivative financial instrument would be recognized in current earnings. Derivative financial instruments qualifying for hedge accounting must maintain a specified level of effectiveness between the hedge instrument and the item being hedged, both at inception and throughout the hedged period.

The Company does not use derivative financial instruments for trading or speculative purposes.

Types of Derivative Instruments (in part)

Foreign Exchange Forward and Put Option Contracts—The Company uses foreign exchange forward contracts or put option contracts to offset the foreign currency exchange risks associated with foreign currency-denominated liabilities, intercompany transactions and forecasted purchases of merchandise between entities with differing functional currencies. For put option contracts, if the market exchange rate at the time of the put option contract's expiration is stronger than the contracted exchange rate, the Company allows the put option contract to expire, limiting its loss to the cost of the put option contract. The Company assesses hedge effectiveness based on the total changes in the put option contracts' cash flows. These foreign exchange forward contracts and put option contracts are designated and accounted for as either cash flow hedges or economic hedges that are not designated as hedging instruments.

As of October 31, 2010, the Company de-designated all of its outstanding put option contracts (notional amount of $64,100,000 outstanding at January 31, 2011) and entered into offsetting call option contracts. These put and call option contracts are accounted for as undesignated hedges. Any gains or losses on these de-designated put option contracts are substantially offset by losses or gains on the call option contracts.

As of January 31, 2011, the notional amount of foreign exchange forward contracts accounted for as cash flow hedges was $179,200,000 and the notional amount of foreign exchange forward contracts accounted for as undesignated hedges was $19,258,000. The term of all outstanding foreign exchange forward contracts as of January 31, 2011 ranged from less than one month to 16 months.

Precious Metal Collars & Forward Contracts—The Company periodically hedges a portion of its forecasted purchases of precious metals for use in its internal manufacturing operations in order to minimize the effect of volatility in precious metal prices. The Company may use a combination of call and put option contracts in net-zero-cost collar arrangements ("precious metal collars") or forward contracts.

For precious metal collars, if the price of the precious metal at the time of the expiration of the precious metal collar is within the call and put price, the precious metal collar would expire at no cost to the Company. The Company accounts for its precious metal collars and forward contracts as cash flow hedges. The Company assesses hedge effectiveness based on the total changes in the precious metal collars and forward contracts' cash flows. The maximum term over which the Company is hedging its exposure to the variability of future cash flows for all forecasted transactions is 12 months. As of January 31, 2011, there were approximately 2,700 ounces of platinum and no silver precious metal derivative instruments outstanding.

Information on the location and amounts of derivative gains and losses in the Consolidated Statements of Earnings is as follows:

| | Years Ended January 31 | | | |
| | 2011 | | 2010 | |
(In thousands)	Pre-Tax Gain Recognized in Earnings on Derivatives	Pre-Tax Loss Recognized in Earnings on Hedged Item	Pre-Tax Gain Recognized in Earnings on Derivatives	Pre-Tax Loss Recognized in Earnings on Hedged Item
Derivatives in Fair Value Hedging Relationships:				
Interest rate swap agreements[a]	$4,159	$(3,655)	$1,996	$(1,913)

| | Years Ended January 31 | | | |
| | 2011 | | 2010 | |
(In thousands)	Pre-Tax (Loss) Gain Recognized in OCI (Effective Portion)	(Loss) Gain Reclassified from Accumulated OCI to Earnings (Effective Portion)	Pre-Tax (Loss) Gain Recognized in OCI (Effective Portion)	(Loss) Gain Reclassified from Accumulated OCI to Earnings (Effective Portion)
Derivatives in Cash Flow Hedging Relationships:				
Foreign exchange forward contracts[c]	$(2,596)	$ (885)	$(3,029)	$(1,675)
Put option contracts[c]	(2,236)	(2,711)	(754)	(3,840)
Precious metal collars[c]	824	(1,036)	2,996	(3,126)
Precious metal forward contracts[c]	3,550	1,728	1,937	28
	$ (458)	$(2,904)	$ 1,150	$(8,613)

| | Pre-Tax (Loss) Gain Recognized in Earnings on Derivatives | |
(In thousands)	Year Ended January 31, 2011	Year Ended January 31, 2010
Derivatives Not Designated as Hedging Instruments:		
Foreign exchange forward contracts[b]	$(918)[d]	$ (928)[d]
Call option contracts[c]	413	360
Put option contracts[c]	(454)	(436)
	$(959)	$(1,004)

[a] The gain or loss recognized in earnings is included within Interest expense and financing costs on the Company's Consolidated Statement of Earnings.

[b] The gain or loss recognized in earnings is included within Other income, net on the Company's Consolidated Statement of Earnings.

[c] The gain or loss recognized in earnings is included within Cost of Sales on the Company's Consolidated Statement of Earnings.

[d] Gains or losses on the undesignated foreign exchange forward contracts substantially offset foreign exchange losses or gains on the liabilities and transactions being hedged.

Hedging activity affected accumulated other comprehensive loss, net of tax, as follows:

(In thousands)	Years Ended January 31	
	2011	2010
Balance at beginning of period	$(2,607)	$(8,984)
Losses transferred to earnings, net of tax	1,921	5,511
Change in fair value, net of tax	(506)	866
	$(1,192)	$(2,607)

There was no material ineffectiveness related to the Company's hedging instruments for the periods ended January 31, 2011 and 2010. The Company expects approximately $861,000 of net pre-tax derivative losses included in accumulated other comprehensive income at January 31, 2011 will be reclassified into earnings within the next 12 months. This amount will vary due to fluctuations in foreign currency exchange rates and precious metal prices.

Standby Letters of Credit

1.135

THE PNC FINANCIAL SERVICES GROUP, INC. (DEC)

NOTES TO CONSOLIDATED FINANCIAL STATEMENTS

Note 23. Commitments and Guarantees (in part)

Standby Letters of Credit

We issue standby letters of credit and have risk participations in standby letters of credit and bankers' acceptances issued by other financial institutions, in each case to support obligations of our customers to third parties, such as remarketing programs for customers' variable rate demand notes. Net outstanding standby letters of credit and internal credit ratings were as follows:

Net Outstanding Standby Letters of Credit

(Dollars in billions)	December 31, 2011	December 31, 2010
Net outstanding standby letters of credit	$10.8	$10.1
Internal credit ratings (as a percentage of portfolio):		
Pass[a]	94%	90%
Below pass[b]	6%	10%

[a] Indicates that expected risk of loss is currently low.
[b] Indicates a higher degree of risk of default.

If the customer fails to meet its financial or performance obligation to the third party under the terms of the contract or there is a need to support a remarketing program, then upon the request of the guaranteed party, we would be obligated to make payment to them. The standby letters of credit and risk participations in standby letters of credit and bankers' acceptances outstanding on December 31, 2011 had terms ranging from less than 1 year to 7 years. The aggregate maximum amount of future payments PNC could be required to make under outstanding standby letters of credit and risk participations in standby letters of credit and bankers' acceptances was $14.4 billion at December 31, 2011, of which $7.4 billion support remarketing programs.

As of December 31, 2011, assets of $2.0 billion secured certain specifically identified standby letters of credit. Recourse provisions from third parties of $3.6 billion were also available for this purpose as of December 31, 2011. In addition, a portion of the remaining standby letters of credit and letter of credit risk participations issued on behalf of specific customers is also secured by collateral or guarantees that secure the customers' other obligations to us. The carrying amount of the liability for our obligations related to standby letters of credit and risk participations in standby letters of credit and bankers' acceptances was $247 million at December 31, 2011.

FAIR VALUE

Author's Note

In May 2011, FASB issued ASU No. 2011-04, *Fair Value Measurement (Topic 820): Amendments to Achieve Common Fair Value Measurement and Disclosure Requirements in GAAP and IFRSs*, in an effort to improve comparability of fair value measurements in financial statements prepared in accordance with GAAP and IFRSs. The wording used to describe many of the requirements for measuring and disclosing fair value measurements under GAAP was changed to clarify FASB's intent about the application of existing fair value measurement and disclosure requirements. In addition, the amendments serve to change a particular principle or requirement for measuring fair value or disclosing information about fair value measurements. This ASU is effective during interim and annual periods beginning after December 15, 2011; as such, the excerpts below may not reflect the amendments of this ASU.

RECOGNITION AND MEASUREMENT

1.136 FASB ASC 820, *Fair Value Measurements and Disclosures*, defines fair value, establishes a framework for measuring fair value, and requires certain disclosures about fair value measurements. *Fair value* is defined as an exit price (that is, a price that would be received to sell, versus acquire, an asset or transfer a liability). Further, fair value is a market-based measurement. It establishes a fair value hierarchy that distinguishes between assumptions developed based on market data obtained from independent external sources and the reporting entity's own assumptions. Further, fair value measurement should consider adjustment for risk, such as the risk inherent in a valuation technique or its inputs.

1.137 FASB ASC 820-10-35-10 provides that a fair value measurement of an asset assumes the highest and best use of the asset by market participants, considering the use of the asset that is physically possible, legally permissible, and financially feasible at the measurement date. Highest and best use is determined based on the use of the asset by market participants, even if the intended use of the asset by the reporting entity is different. FASB ASC 820-10-35-10 states that the highest and best use for an asset is established by one of two valuation premises: value in use or value in exchange. The highest and best use of the asset is in use if the asset would provide maximum value to market participants principally through its use in combination with other assets as a group (as installed or otherwise configured for use). For example, value in use might be appropriate for certain nonfinancial assets. The highest and best use of the asset is in exchange if the asset would provide maximum value to market participants principally on a stand-alone basis. For example, value in exchange might be appropriate for a financial asset. According to paragraphs 12–13 of FASB ASC 820-10-35, an asset's value in use should be based on the price that would be received in a current transaction to sell the asset, assuming that the asset would be used with other assets as a group and that those other assets would be available to market participants. An asset's value in exchange is determined based on the price that would be received in a current transaction to sell the asset on a stand-alone basis.

1.138 According to paragraphs 16–16A of FASB ASC 820-10-35, a fair value measurement of a liability assumes that both (*a*) the liability is transferred to a market participant at the measurement date (the liability to the counterparty continues; it is not settled), and (*b*) the nonperformance risk relating to that liability is the same before and after its transfer. Certain liabilities, such as debt obligations, are traded in the marketplace as assets. However, liabilities are rarely transferred in the marketplace due to contractual or other legal restrictions. A reporting entity is permitted, as a practical expedient, to estimate the fair value of an investment within the scope of paragraphs 4–5 of FASB ASC 820-10-15 using the net asset value per share (or its equivalent) of the investment if the net asset value per share or its equivalent is calculated in a manner consistent with the measurement principles of FASB ASC 946, *Financial Services— Investment Companies*, as of the reporting entity's measurement date.

DISCLOSURE

1.139 For assets and liabilities measured at fair value, whether on a recurring or nonrecurring basis, FASB ASC 820-10-50 specifies the required disclosures concerning the inputs used to measure fair value. "Pending Content" in FASB ASC 820-10-50-1 explains that the reporting entity should disclose information that enables users of its financial statements to assess the following: (*a*) for assets and liabilities measured at fair value on a recurring basis in periods subsequent to initial recognition or measured on a nonrecurring basis in periods subsequent to initial recognition, the valuation techniques and inputs used to develop those measurements and (*b*) for recurring fair value measurements using significant unobservable inputs (level 3), the effect of the measurements on earnings for the period.

PRESENTATION AND DISCLOSURE EXCERPTS

Fair Value Measurements

1.140

GENERAL ELECTRIC COMPANY (DEC)

NOTES TO CONSOLIDATED FINANCIAL STATEMENTS

Note 1. Summary of Significant Accounting Policies (in part)

Fair Value Measurements

For financial assets and liabilities measured at fair value on a recurring basis, fair value is the price we would receive to sell an asset or pay to transfer a liability in an orderly transaction with a market participant at the measurement date. In the absence of active markets for the identical assets or liabilities, such measurements involve developing assumptions based on market observable data and, in the absence of such data, internal information that is consistent with what market participants would use in a hypothetical transaction that occurs at the measurement date.

Observable inputs reflect market data obtained from independent sources, while unobservable inputs reflect our market assumptions. Preference is given to observable inputs. These two types of inputs create the following fair value hierarchy:

Level 1—Quoted prices for identical instruments in active markets.

Level 2—Quoted prices for similar instruments in active markets; quoted prices for identical or similar instruments in markets that are not active; and model-derived valuations whose inputs are observable or whose significant value drivers are observable.

Level 3—Significant inputs to the valuation model are unobservable.

We maintain policies and procedures to value instruments using the best and most relevant data available. In addition, we have risk management teams that review valuation, including independent price validation for certain instruments. With regards to Level 3 valuations (including instruments valued by third parties), we perform a variety of procedures to assess the reasonableness of the valuations. Such reviews, which may be performed quarterly, monthly or weekly, include an evaluation of instruments whose fair value change exceeds predefined thresholds (and/or does not change) and consider the current interest rate, currency and credit environment, as well as other published data, such as rating agency market reports and current appraisals. These reviews are performed within each business by the asset and risk managers, pricing committees and valuation committees. A detailed review of methodologies and assumptions is performed by individuals independent of the business for individual measurements with a fair value exceeding predefined thresholds. This detailed review may include the use of a third-party valuation firm.

The following section describes the valuation methodologies we use to measure different financial instruments at fair value on a recurring basis.

Investments in Debt and Equity Securities. When available, we use quoted market prices to determine the fair value of investment securities, and they are included in Level 1. Level 1 securities primarily include publicly-traded equity securities.

For large numbers of investment securities for which market prices are observable for identical or similar investment securities but not readily accessible for each of those investments individually (that is, it is difficult to obtain pricing information for each individual investment security at the measurement date), we obtain pricing information from an independent pricing vendor. The pricing vendor uses various pricing models for each asset class that are consistent with what other market participants would use. The inputs and assumptions to the model of the pricing vendor are derived from market observable sources including: benchmark yields, reported trades, broker/dealer quotes, issuer spreads, benchmark securities, bids, offers, and other market-related data. Since many fixed income securities do not trade on a daily basis, the methodology of the pricing vendor uses available information as applicable such as benchmark curves, benchmarking of like securities, sector groupings, and matrix pricing. The pricing vendor considers available market observable inputs in determining the evaluation for a security. Thus, certain securities may not be priced using quoted prices, but rather determined from market observable information. These investments are included in Level 2 and primarily comprise our portfolio of corporate fixed income, and government, mortgage and asset-backed securities. In infrequent circumstances, our pricing vendors may provide us with valuations that are based on significant unobservable inputs, and in those circumstances we classify the investment securities in Level 3.

Annually, we conduct reviews of our primary pricing vendor to validate that the inputs used in that vendor's pricing process are deemed to be market observable as defined in the standard. While we are not provided access to proprietary models of the vendor, our reviews have included on-site walk-throughs of the pricing process, methodologies and control procedures for each asset class and level for which prices are provided. Our reviews also include an examination of the underlying inputs and assumptions for a sample of individual securities across asset classes, credit rating levels and various durations, a process we perform each reporting period. In addition, the pricing vendor has an established challenge process in place for all security valuations, which facilitates identification and resolution of potentially erroneous prices. We believe that the prices received from our pricing vendor are representative of prices that would be received to sell the assets at the measurement date (exit prices) and are classified appropriately in the hierarchy.

We use non-binding broker quotes and other third-party pricing services as our primary basis for valuation when there is limited, or no, relevant market activity for a specific instrument or for other instruments that share similar characteristics. We have not adjusted the prices we have obtained. Investment securities priced using non-binding broker quotes and other third-party pricing services are included in Level 3. As is the case with our primary pricing vendor, third-party brokers and other third-party pricing services do not provide access to their proprietary valuation models, inputs and assumptions. Accordingly, our risk management personnel conduct reviews of vendors, as applicable, similar to the reviews performed of our primary pricing vendor. In addition, we conduct internal reviews of pricing for all such investment securities quarterly to ensure reasonableness of valuations used in our financial statements. These reviews are designed to identify prices that appear stale, those that have changed significantly from prior valuations, and other anomalies that may indicate that a price may not be accurate. Based on the information available, we believe that the fair values provided by the brokers and other third-party pricing services are representative of prices that would be received to sell the assets at the measurement date (exit prices).

Derivatives. We use closing prices for derivatives included in Level 1, which are traded either on exchanges or liquid over-the-counter markets.

The majority of our derivatives are valued using internal models. The models maximize the use of market observable inputs including interest rate curves and both forward and spot prices for currencies and commodities. Derivative assets and liabilities included in Level 2 primarily represent interest rate swaps, cross-currency swaps and foreign currency and commodity forward and option contracts.

Derivative assets and liabilities included in Level 3 primarily represent equity derivatives and interest rate products that contain embedded optionality or prepayment features.

Non-Recurring Fair Value Measurements. Certain assets are measured at fair value on a non-recurring basis. These assets are not measured at fair value on an ongoing basis, but are subject to fair value adjustments only in certain circumstances. These assets can include loans and long-lived assets that have been reduced to fair value when they are held for sale, impaired loans that have been reduced based on the fair value of the underlying collateral, cost and equity method investments and long-lived assets that are written down to fair value when they are impaired and the remeasurement of retained investments in formerly consolidated subsidiaries upon a change in control that results in deconsolidation of a subsidiary, if we sell a controlling interest and retain a noncontrolling stake in the entity. Assets that are written down to fair value when impaired and retained investments are not subsequently adjusted to fair value unless further impairment occurs.

The following describes the valuation methodologies we use to measure financial and non-financial instruments accounted for at fair value on a non-recurring basis and for certain assets within our pension plans and retiree benefit plans at each reporting period, as applicable.

Loans. When available, we use observable market data, including pricing on recent closed market transactions, to value loans that are included in Level 2. When this data is unobservable, we use valuation methodologies using current market interest rate data adjusted for inherent credit risk, and such loans are included in Level 3. When appropriate, loans may be valued using collateral values as a practical expedient (see Long-Lived Assets below).

Cost and Equity Method Investments. Cost and equity method investments are valued using market observable data such as quoted prices when available. When market observable data is unavailable, investments are valued using a discounted cash flow model, comparative market multiples or a combination of both approaches as appropriate and other third-party pricing sources. These investments are generally included in Level 3.

Investments in private equity, real estate and collective funds are valued using net asset values. The net asset values are determined based on the fair values of the underlying investments in the funds. Investments in private equity and real estate funds are generally included in Level 3 because they are not redeemable at the measurement date. Investments in collective funds are included in Level 2.

Long-lived Assets. Fair values of long-lived assets, including aircraft and real estate, are primarily derived internally and are based on observed sales transactions for similar assets. In other instances, for example, collateral types for which we do not have comparable observed sales transaction data, collateral values are developed internally and corroborated by external appraisal information. Adjustments to third-party valuations may be performed in circumstances where market comparables are not specific to the attributes of the specific collateral or appraisal information may not be reflective of current market conditions due to the passage of time and the occurrence of market events since receipt of the information. For real estate, fair values are based on discounted cash flow estimates which reflect current and projected lease profiles and available industry information about capitalization rates and expected trends in rents and occupancy and are corroborated by external appraisals. These investments are generally included in Level 3.

Retained Investments in Formerly Consolidated Subsidiaries. Upon a change in control that results in deconsolidation of a subsidiary, the fair value measurement of our retained noncontrolling stake in the former subsidiary is valued using an income approach, a market approach, or a combination of both approaches as appropriate. In applying these methodologies, we rely on a number of factors, including actual operating results, future business plans, economic projections, market observable pricing multiples of similar businesses and comparable transactions, and possible control premium. These investments are included in Level 1 or Level 3, as appropriate, determined at the time of the transaction.

Note 21. Fair Value Measurements

For a description of how we estimate fair value, see Note 1.

The following tables present our assets and liabilities measured at fair value on a recurring basis. Included in the tables are investment securities primarily supporting obligations to annuitants and policyholders in our run-off insurance operations, supporting obligations to holders of GICs in Trinity (which ceased issuing new investment contracts beginning in the first quarter of 2010) and investment securities held at our treasury operations and investments held in our CLL business collateralized by senior secured loans of high-quality, middle-market companies in a variety of industries. Such securities are mainly investment grade.

(In millions)	Level 1[a]	Level 2[a]	Level 3[b]	Netting Adjustment[c]	Net Balance
December 31, 2011					
Assets					
Investment securities					
Debt					
U.S. corporate	$ —	$20,535	$3,235	$ —	$23,770
State and municipal	—	3,157	77	—	3,234
Residential mortgage-backed	—	2,568	41	—	2,609
Commercial mortgage-backed	—	2,824	4	—	2,828
Asset-backed[d]	—	930	4,040	—	4,970
Corporate—non-U.S.	71	1,058	1,204	—	2,333
Government—non-U.S.	1,003	1,444	84	—	2,531
U.S. government and federal agency	—	3,805	253	—	4,058
Retained interests	—	—	35	—	35
Equity					
Available-for-sale	730	18	17	—	765
Trading	241	—	—	—	241
Derivatives[e]	—	15,252	393	(5,604)	10,041
Other[f]	—	—	817	—	817
Total	$2,045	$51,591	$10,200	$(5,604)	$58,232

(continued)

(In millions)	Level 1[a]	Level 2[a]	Level 3[b]	Netting Adjustment[c]	Net Balance
Liabilities					
Derivatives	$ —	$ 5,010	$ 27	$(4,308)	$ 729
Other[g]	—	863	—	—	863
Total	$ —	$ 5,873	$ 27	$(4,308)	$ 1,592
December 31, 2010					
Assets					
Investment securities					
Debt					
U.S. corporate	$ —	$18,956	$3,199	$ —	$22,155
State and municipal	—	2,499	225	—	2,724
Residential mortgage-backed	47	2,696	66	—	2,809
Commercial mortgage-backed	—	2,875	49	—	2,924
Asset-backed	—	690	2,540	—	3,230
Corporate—non-U.S.	89	1,292	1,486	—	2,867
Government—non-U.S.	777	1,333	156	—	2,266
U.S. government and federal agency	—	3,576	210	—	3,786
Retained interests	—	—	39	—	39
Equity					
Available-for-sale	677	20	24	—	721
Trading	417	—	—	—	417
Derivatives[e]	—	10,997	359	(5,910)	5,446
Other[f]	—	—	906	—	906
Total	$2,007	$44,934	$9,259	$(5,910)	$50,290
Liabilities					
Derivatives	$ —	$ 6,553	$ 103	$(5,242)	$ 1,414
Other[g]	—	920	—	—	920
Total	$ —	$ 7,473	$ 103	$(5,242)	$ 2,334

[a] The fair value of securities transferred between Level 1 and Level 2 was $67 million in 2011.

[b] Level 3 investment securities valued using non-binding broker quotes and other third parties totaled $2,386 million and $1,054 million at December 31, 2011 and 2010, respectively, and were classified as available-for-sale securities.

[c] The netting of derivative receivables and payables is permitted when a legally enforceable master netting agreement exists and when collateral is posted to us.

[d] Includes investments in our CLL business in asset-backed securities collateralized by senior secured loans of high-quality, middle-market companies in a variety of industries.

[e] The fair value of derivatives included an adjustment for non-performance risk. The cumulative adjustment was a loss of $13 million at December 31, 2011 and $10 million at December 31, 2010. See Note 22 for additional information on the composition of our derivative portfolio.

[f] Included private equity investments and loans designated under the fair value option.

[g] Primarily represented the liability associated with certain of our deferred incentive compensation plans.

The following tables present the changes in Level 3 instruments measured on a recurring basis for the years ended December 31, 2011 and 2010, respectively. The majority of our Level 3 balances consist of investment securities classified as available-for-sale with changes in fair value recorded in shareowners' equity.

(In millions)	Balance at January 1, 2011	Net Realized/ Unrealized Gains (Losses) Included in Earnings[a]	Net Realized/ Unrealized Gains (Losses) Included in Accumulated Other Comprehensive Income	Purchases	Sales	Settle-ments	Transfers Into Level 3[b]	Transfers Out of Level 3[b]	Balance at December 31, 2011	Net Change in Unrealized Gains (Losses) Relating to Instruments Still Held at December 31, 2011[c]
Investment securities										
Debt										
U.S. corporate	$3,199	$ 78	$(157)	$ 235	$(183)	$(112)	$182	$ (7)	$3,235	$ —
State and municipal	225	—	—	12	—	(8)	—	(152)	77	—
Residential mortgage-backed	66	(3)	1	2	(5)	(1)	71	(90)	41	—
Commercial mortgage-backed	49	—	—	6	—	(4)	3	(50)	4	—
Asset-backed	2,540	(10)	61	2,157	(185)	(11)	1	(513)	4,040	—
Corporate—non-U.S.	1,486	(47)	(91)	25	(55)	(118)	85	(81)	1,204	—
Government—non-U.S.	156	(100)	48	41	(1)	(27)	107	(140)	84	—
U.S. government and federal agency	210	—	43	500	—	—	—	(500)	253	—
Retained interests	39	(28)	26	8	(5)	(5)	—	—	35	—
Equity										
Available-for-sale	24	—	—	—	—	—	4	(11)	17	—
Trading	—	—	—	—	—	—	—	—	—	—
Derivatives[d][e]	265	151	2	(2)	—	(207)	150	10	369	130
Other	906	95	(9)	152	(266)	(6)	—	(55)	817	34
Total	$9,165	$136	$(76)	$3,136	$(700)	$(499)	$603	$(1,589)	$10,176	$164

[a] Earnings effects are primarily included in the "GECS revenues from services" and "Interest and other financial charges" captions in the Statement of Earnings.

[b] Transfers in and out of Level 3 are considered to occur at the beginning of the period. Transfers out of Level 3 were a result of increased use of quotes from independent pricing vendors based on recent trading activity.

[c] Represented the amount of unrealized gains or losses for the period included in earnings.

[d] Represented derivative assets net of derivative liabilities and included cash accruals of $3 million not reflected in the fair value hierarchy table.

[e] Gains (losses) included in net realized/unrealized gains (losses) included in earnings were offset by the earnings effects from the underlying items that were economically hedged. See Note 22.

SEC 1.140

Changes in Level 3 Instruments for the Year Ended December 31, 2010

(In millions)	Balance at January 1, 2010(a)	Net Realized/ Unrealized Gains (Losses) Included in Earnings(b)	Net Realized/ Unrealized Gains (Losses) Included in Accumulated Other Comprehensive Income	Purchases, Issuances and Settlements	Transfers in and/or Out of Level 3(c)	Balance at December 31, 2010	Net Change in Unrealized Gains (Losses) Relating to Instruments Still Held at December 31, 2010(d)
Investment securities							
Debt							
U.S. corporate	$3,068	$ 79	$276	$ (215)	$ (9)	$3,199	$—
State and municipal	205	—	25	(5)	—	225	—
Residential mortgage-backed	123	(1)	13	2	(71)	66	—
Commercial mortgage-backed	1,041	30	(2)	(1,017)	(3)	49	—
Asset-backed	1,872	25	14	733	(104)	2,540	—
Corporate—non-U.S.	1,331	(38)	(39)	250	(18)	1,486	—
Government—non-U.S.	163	—	(8)	—	1	156	—
U.S. government and federal agency	256	—	(44)	(2)	—	210	—
Retained interests	45	(1)	3	(8)	—	39	—
Equity							
Available-for-sale	19	—	3	—	2	24	1
Trading	—	—	—	—	—	—	—
Derivatives(e)(f)	236	220	15	(79)	(127)	265	41
Other	891	5	(30)	40	—	906	3
Total	$9,250	$319	$226	$ (301)	$(329)	$9,165	$45

(a) Included $1,015 million in debt securities, a reduction in retained interests of $8,782 million and a reduction in derivatives of $365 million related to adoption of ASU 2009-16 & 17.

(b) Earnings effects are primarily included in the "GECS revenues from services" and "Interest and other financial charges" captions in the Statement of Earnings.

(c) Transfers in and out of Level 3 are considered to occur at the beginning of the period. Transfers out of Level 3 were a result of increased use of quotes from independent pricing vendors based on recent trading activity.

(d) Represented the amount of unrealized gains or losses for the period included in earnings.

(e) Represented derivative assets net of derivative liabilities and included cash accruals of $9 million not reflected in the fair value hierarchy table.

(f) Gains (losses) included in net realized/unrealized gains (losses) included in earnings were offset by the earnings effects from the underlying items that were economically hedged. See Note 22.

Non-Recurring Fair Value Measurements

The following table represents non-recurring fair value amounts (as measured at the time of the adjustment) for those assets remeasured to fair value on a non-recurring basis during the fiscal year and still held at December 31, 2011 and 2010. These assets can include loans and long-lived assets that have been reduced to fair value when they are held for sale, impaired loans that have been reduced based on the fair value of the underlying collateral, cost and equity method investments and long-lived assets that are written down to fair value when they are impaired and the remeasurement of retained investments in formerly consolidated subsidiaries upon a change in control that results in deconsolidation of a subsidiary, if we sell a controlling interest and retain a non-controlling stake in the entity. Assets that are written down to fair value when impaired and retained investments are not subsequently adjusted to fair value unless further impairment occurs.

| (In millions) | Remeasured During the Year Ended December 31 | | | |
| | 2011 | | 2010 | |
	Level 2	Level 3	Level 2	Level 3
Financing receivables and loans held for sale	$ 158	$5,348	$ 54	$ 6,833
Cost and equity method investments[a]	—	403	—	510
Long-lived assets, including real estate	1,343	3,288	1,025	5,811
Retained investments in formerly consolidated subsidiaries[b]	—	—	—	113
Total	$1,501	$9,039	$1,079	$13,267

[a] Includes the fair value of private equity and real estate funds included in Level 3 of $123 million and $296 million at December 31, 2011 and 2010, respectively.

[b] Excluded our retained investment in Regency, a formerly consolidated subsidiary, that was remeasured to a Level 1 fair value of $549 million in 2010.

The following table represents the fair value adjustments to assets measured at fair value on a non-recurring basis and still held at December 31, 2011 and 2010.

| (In millions) | Year Ended December 31 | |
	2011	2010
Financing receivables and loans held for sale	$ (925)	$(1,745)
Cost and equity method investments[a]	(274)	(274)
Long-lived assets, including real estate[b]	(1,431)	(2,958)
Retained investments in formerly consolidated subsidiaries	—	184
Total	$(2,630)	$(4,793)

[a] Includes fair value adjustments associated with private equity and real estate funds of $(24) million and $(198) million during 2011 and 2010, respectively.

[b] Includes impairments related to real estate equity properties and investments recorded in other costs and expenses of $976 million and $2,089 million during 2011 and 2010, respectively.

SUBSEQUENT EVENTS

RECOGNITION AND MEASUREMENT

1.141 The FASB ASC glossary defines *subsequent events* as events or transactions that occur subsequent to the balance sheet date but before financial statements are issued or available to be issued. The following are the two types of subsequent events: the first type existed at the balance sheet date and includes the estimates inherent in the process of preparing financial statements (recognized subsequent events); the second type did not exist at the balance sheet date but arose subsequent to that date (nonrecognized subsequent events). The first type of subsequent event should be recognized in the entity's financial statements. An entity that is either an SEC filer or a conduit bond obligor for conduit debt securities that are traded in a public market must evaluate subsequent events through the date the financial statements are issued. The SEC has indicated that issuance of financial statements generally is the earlier of when the annual or quarterly financial statements are widely distributed to all shareholders and other financial statement users or filed with the SEC.

DISCLOSURE

1.142 Some nonrecognized subsequent events may be of such a nature that they must be disclosed in order to keep the financial statements from being misleading. In that case, the entity should disclose the nature of the event and estimate of its financial effect or a statement that such an estimate cannot be made. For entities that are not SEC filers, the date through which subsequent events have been evaluated and whether that date is when the financial statements were issued or available to be issued must be disclosed. An entity that is an SEC filer is not required to disclose the date through which subsequent events have been evaluated.

1.143

TABLE 1-15: SUBSEQUENT EVENTS

Table 1-15 lists the subsequent events disclosed in the financial statements of the survey entities.

| | Number of Entities | | |
	2011	2010	2009
Debt incurred, reduced, or refinanced	31	24	56
Business combinations pending or consummated	29	66	44
Litigation	14	9	37
Discontinued operations or asset disposals	15	28	33
Employee benefit plan adopted, amended, or terminated	3	2	N/C*
Capital stock issued or purchased	18	17	17
Reorganization, restructuring, realignment, recapitalization, or bankruptcy	13	13	16
Credit agreements, revolving credit/accounts receivable securitization entered into/terminated/amended	9	11	N/C*
Tax matter resolution	—	3	N/C*
Acquisition	32	N/C*	N/C*
Other, described	30	33	51

* N/C = Not compiled. Line item was not included in the table for the year shown.

PRESENTATION AND DISCLOSURE EXCERPTS

Notes

1.144

HOVNANIAN ENTERPRISES, INC. (OCT)

NOTES TO CONSOLIDATED FINANCIAL STATEMENTS

24. Subsequent Events

On November 1, 2011, K. Hovnanian issued $141.8 million aggregate principal amount of 5.0% Senior Secured Notes due 2021 and $53.2 million aggregate principal amount of 2.0% Senior Secured Notes due 2021 in exchange for $195.0 million of K. Hovnanian's unsecured senior notes as follows: $16.7 million in aggregate principal amount of 6 1/2% Senior Notes due 2014, $26.2 million in aggregate principal amount of 6 3/8% Senior Notes due 2014, $67.6 million in aggregate principal amount of 11 7/8% Senior Notes due 2015, $31.3 million in aggregate principal amount of 6 1/4% Senior Notes due 2015, $13.3 million in aggregate principal amount of 6 1/4% Senior Notes due 2016, $20.7 million in aggregate principal amount of 7 1/2% Senior Notes due 2016 and $19.2 million in aggregate principal amount of 8 5/8% Senior Notes due 2017. Holders of the senior notes due 2014 and 2015 that were exchanged in the exchange offer also received an aggregate of approximately $14.2 million in cash payments and all holders of senior notes that were exchanged in the exchange received accrued and unpaid interest (in the aggregate amount of approximately $3.3 million). The 5.0% Senior Secured Notes and the 2.0% Senior Secured Notes were issued as separate series under an indenture, but have substantially the same terms other than with respect to interest rate and related redemption provisions, and will vote together as a single class. These secured notes are guaranteed by each of Hovnanian's subsidiaries, except for its home mortgage subsidiaries, certain of its joint ventures, joint venture holding companies (other than members of the "Secured Group" (as defined below)), and certain of its title insurance subsidiaries. The guarantees of K. Hovnanian JV Holdings, L.L.C. and its subsidiaries other than certain joint ventures and joint venture holding companies (collectively, the "Secured Group"), are secured, subject to permitted liens and other exceptions, by a first-priority lien on substantially all of the assets of the members of the Secured Group. As of October 31, 2011, the collateral securing the guarantees primarily includes $135.9 million of cash and cash equivalents and equity interest in guarantors that are members of the Secured Group. Subsequent to such date, cash uses include general business operations and real estate and other investments. Members of the Secured Group also own equity in joint ventures, either directly or indirectly through ownership of joint venture holding companies, with a book value of $47.8 million as of October 31, 2011; this equity is not pledged to secure, and is not collateral for, these senior secured notes. Members of the Secured Group are "unrestricted subsidiaries" under K. Hovnanian's other senior and senior secured notes and Amortizing Notes, and thus have not guaranteed such

indebtedness. These senior secured notes are redeemable in whole or in part at our option at any time, at 100.0% of the principal amount plus the greater of 1% of the principal amount and an applicable "Make-Whole Amount." In addition, we may redeem up to 35% of the aggregate principal amount of the notes before November 1, 2014 with the net cash proceeds from certain equity offerings at 105.0% (in the case of the 5.0% Secured Notes) and 102.0% (in the case of the 2.0% Secured Notes) of principal. The accounting for the exchange is being treated as a Troubled Debt Restructuring. Under this accounting, the Company would not recognize any gain or loss on extinguishment of debt.

The Indenture under which the 5.0% Senior Secured Notes and the 2.0% Senior Secured Notes were issued contains restrictive covenants that limit among other things, the ability of Hovnanian and certain of its subsidiaries, including K. Hovnanian, to incur additional indebtedness, pay dividends and make distributions on common and preferred stock, repurchase common and preferred stock, make other restricted payments, make investments, sell certain assets, incur liens, consolidate, merge, sell or otherwise dispose of all or substantially all of its assets and enter into certain transactions with affiliates. The indenture also contains customary events of default which would permit the holders of the 5.00% secured notes and 2.00% Secured Notes to declare those notes to be immediately due and payable if not cured within applicable grace periods, including the failure to make timely payments on the notes or other material indebtedness, the failure to satisfy covenants, the failure of the documents granting security for the notes to be in full force and effect, the failure of the liens on any material portion of the collateral securing the notes to be valid and perfected and specified events of bankruptcy and insolvency.

In addition, on November 1, 2011, K. Hovnanian entered into a Second Supplemental Indenture (the "11 7/8% Notes Supplemental Indenture"), among K. Hovnanian, Hovnanian, as guarantor, the other guarantors party thereto and Wilmington Trust Company, as trustee, amending and supplementing that certain Indenture dated February 14, 2011 (the "Base Indenture") by and among K. Hovnanian, Hovnanian, as guarantor, and Wilmington Trust Company, as trustee, as amended by the First Supplemental Indenture dated as of February 14, 2011 (the "First Supplemental Indenture"), by and among K. Hovnanian, Hovnanian, as guarantor, the other guarantors party thereto and Wilmington Trust Company, as trustee (the Base Indenture as amended by the First Supplemental Indenture, the "Existing Indenture"). The 11 7/8% Notes Supplemental Indenture was executed and delivered following the receipt by K. Hovnanian of consents from a majority of the holders of K. Hovnanian's 11 7/8/% Senior Notes due 2015. The 11 7/8% Notes Supplemental Indenture provides for the elimination of substantially all of the restrictive covenants and certain of the default provisions contained in the Existing Indenture and the 11 7/8% Senior Notes due 2015.

Separate from the above, in the first quarter of fiscal 2012, we repurchased approximately $44 million principal amount of our unsecured senior notes for an aggregate purchase price of approximately $19 million in cash, excluding cash paid for interest, resulting in an approximate gain on extinguishment of debt of $25 million.

Term Loan & Credit Facilities

1.145

THE BON-TON STORES, INC. (JAN)

NOTES TO CONSOLIDATED FINANCIAL STATEMENTS

(In thousands except share and per share data)

20. Subsequent Events (in part)

On January 31, 2011, the Company voluntarily prepaid its outstanding indebtedness under the Term Loan Facility that provided for $75,000 of term loans expiring November 18, 2013 (see Note 9). As a result of such prepayment, the Term Loan Facility was terminated. As provided in the Term Loan Facility, the Company paid an early termination fee of $3,750 (5.0% of the principal amount repaid) simultaneously with the prepayment of the outstanding indebtedness. In addition, $4,415 of unamortized deferred financing fees related to the facility was accelerated on the date of termination.

On March 21, 2011, the Company entered into a $625,000 senior secured asset-based Second Amended Revolving Credit Facility, which will expire on March 21, 2016, subject to the maturity of the senior unsecured notes and certain other debt of the Company. The Second Amended Revolving Credit Facility replaced the Company's pre-existing $675,000 2009 Revolving Credit Facility, which was scheduled to mature on June 4, 2013. The proceeds of the Second Amended Revolving Credit Facility were used to pay the outstanding balance under the 2009 Revolving Credit Facility and will be used for other general corporate purposes. Unamortized deferred financing fees of $1,271 related to the facility were accelerated on the date of the agreement.

The financial covenant contained in the Second Amended Revolving Credit Facility requires that the minimum excess availability be an amount greater than or equal to the greater of (1) 10% of the lesser of: (a) the aggregate commitments, as defined in the agreement, at such time and (b) the aggregate borrowing base, as defined in the agreement, at such time and (2) $50,000. Other covenants continue the requirements of the 2009 Revolving Credit Facility and require that the Company provide the lenders with certain financial statements, forecasts and other reports, borrowing base certificates and notices and comply with various federal, state and local rules and regulations.

Borrowings under the Second Amended Revolving Credit Facility will be at either (1) Adjusted LIBOR (based on the British Bankers Association per annum LIBOR Rate based on an interest period selected by the Company) plus an applicable margin or (2) a base rate (based on the highest of (a) the Federal Funds Rate plus 0.5%, (b) the Bank of America prime rate, and (c) Adjusted LIBOR based on an interest period of one month plus 1.0%) plus the applicable margin. The applicable margin is determined based upon the excess availability under the Second Amended Revolving Credit Facility.

The Second Amended Revolving Credit Facility is secured by a first priority security position on substantially all of the current and future assets of the Company, including, but not limited to, inventory, general intangibles, trademarks, equipment, certain real estate and proceeds from any of the foregoing, subject to certain exceptions and liens.

Litigation

1.146

JPMORGAN CHASE & CO. (DEC)

NOTES TO CONSOLIDATED FINANCIAL STATEMENTS

Note 2—Business Changes and Developments (in part)

Subsequent Events (in part)

Global Settlement on Servicing and Origination of Mortgages

On February 9, 2012, the Firm announced that it agreed to a settlement in principle (the "global settlement") with a number of federal and state government agencies, including the U.S. Department of Justice, the U.S. Department of Housing and Urban Development, the Consumer Financial Protection Bureau and the State Attorneys General, relating to the servicing and origination of mortgages. The global settlement, which is subject to the execution of a definitive agreement and court approval, calls for the Firm to, among other things: (i) make cash payments of approximately $1.1 billion (a portion of which will be set aside for payments to borrowers); (ii) provide approximately $500 million of refinancing relief to certain "underwater" borrowers whose loans are owned by the Firm; and (iii) provide approximately $3.7 billion of additional relief for certain borrowers, including reductions of principal on first and second liens, payments to assist with short sales, deficiency balance waivers on past foreclosures and short sales, and forbearance assistance for unemployed homeowners. (If the Firm does not meet certain targets for provision of the refinancing or other borrower relief within certain prescribed time periods, the Firm will instead make cash payments.) In addition, under the global settlement the Firm will be required to adhere to certain enhanced mortgage servicing standards.

The global settlement releases the Firm from further claims related to servicing activities, including foreclosures and loss mitigation activities; certain origination activities; and certain bankruptcy-related activities. Not included in the global settlement are any claims arising out of securitization activities, including representations made to investors respecting mortgage-backed securities; criminal claims; and repurchase demands from the GSEs, among other items.

Also on February 9, 2012, the Firm entered into agreements in principle with the Federal Reserve and the Office of the Comptroller of the Currency for the payment of civil money penalties related to conduct that was the subject of consent orders entered into with the banking regulators in April 2011. The Firm's payment obligations under those agreements will be deemed satisfied by the Firm's payments and provisions of relief under the global settlement.

While the Firm expects to incur additional operating costs to comply with portions of the global settlement, including the enhanced servicing standards, the Firm's prior period results of operations have reflected the estimated costs of the global settlement. Accordingly, the Firm expects that the financial impact of the global settlement on the Firm's financial condition and results of operations for the first quarter of 2012 and future periods will not be material. For further information on this settlement, see "Mortgage Foreclosure

Investigations and Litigation" in Note 31 on pages 290–299 of this Annual Report.

Discontinued Operations

1.147

COMMERCIAL METALS COMPANY (AUG)

NOTES TO CONSOLIDATED FINANCIAL STATEMENTS

Note 22. Subsequent Events

On October 7, 2011, The Company announced its decision to exit the business in CMCS by way of sale and/or closure. During 2011, the Company made operational improvements in the business but not to a level which would restore profitability for the long run. Additionally, delayed entry in the European Union, cyclical demand for tubular products, unsustainable losses and increased demand for capital resources resulted in the decision to exit the business. The operation will service any existing customer commitments and the Company expects to wind down operations and liquidate inventory over the next several months. In connection with this decision, the Company expects to incur severance and other closure costs between $25 million and $40 million in fiscal 2012.

1.148

CENVEO, INC. (DEC)

NOTES TO CONSOLIDATED FINANCIAL STATEMENTS

3. Discontinued Operations

Subsequent Events

On February 10, 2012, the Company completed the sale of its documents and forms business ("Documents Group"), which was included in the Company's envelopes and labels segment, for cash proceeds of approximately $40.0 million, of which $4.0 million will remain in escrow for a certain period of time. In the fourth quarter of 2011, the Company recorded a non-cash goodwill impairment charge of $12.5 million that was allocated to the Documents Group. The operating results of the Documents Group, as well as the non-cash allocated goodwill impairment charge, are reported in discontinued operations in the Company's consolidated financial statements for all periods presented herein.

On January 27, 2012, the Company completed the sale of its wide format business, which was included in the Company's envelopes and labels segment, for cash proceeds of approximately $4.7 million. In the fourth quarter of 2011, the

Company recorded a non-cash goodwill impairment charge of $1.0 million that was allocated to its wide-format business. For all periods presented herein, the operating results of the wide-format business, as well as the non-cash allocated goodwill impairment charge, are reported in discontinued operations in the Company's consolidated financial statements for all periods presented herein.

The following table shows the components of assets and liabilities that are classified as discontinued operations in the Company's consolidated balance sheets as of the years ended 2011 and 2010.

	Years Ended	
	2011	**2010**
Accounts receivable, net	$ 7,647	$ 8,912
Inventories	14,356	14,080
Prepaid and other current assets	953	526
Assets of discontinued operations—current	22,956	23,518
Property, plant and equipment, net	10,273	11,926
Other assets, net[1]	17,143	31,659
Assets of discontinued operations—long-term	27,416	43,585
Accounts payable	4,352	3,129
Accrued compensation and related liabilities	548	412
Other current liabilities	446	675
Liabilities of discontinued operations—current	5,346	4,216
Liabilities of discontinued operations—long-term	8,474	9,247
Net assets	$36,552	$53,640

[1] Includes $2.8 million and $16.3 million of goodwill and $14.3 million and $15.1 million of intangible assets for 2011 and 2010, respectively.

The following table summarizes certain statement of operations information for discontinued operations (in thousands):

	Years Ended		
	2011	**2010**	**2009**
Net sales	$99,611	$106,187	$100,035
Income (loss) from discontinued operations before income taxes[1][2][3]	(3,697)	14,184	15,040
Income tax (benefit) expense	3,840	2,863	(3,057)
(Loss) income from discontinued operations, net of taxes[1][2][3]	$ (7,537)	$11,321	$ 18,097
Income (loss) per share	$ (0.12)	$ 0.18	$ 0.32

[1] Includes $13.5 million of allocated non-cash goodwill impairment charges in 2011.

[2] Income from discontinued operations for 2010 also includes the reduction of our liability for uncertain tax positions of $4.4 million, net of deferred tax assets of $1.6 million, as a result of the expiration of certain statute of limitations on uncertain tax positions related to the Supremex Income Fund (the "Fund").

[3] Income from discontinued operations for 2009 also includes the reduction of our liability for uncertain tax positions of $12.1 million, net of deferred tax assets of $2.6 million, as a result of the expiration of certain statute of limitations on uncertain tax positions related to the Fund.

Restructuring

1.149

FIRST SOLAR, INC. (DEC)

NOTES TO CONSOLIDATED FINANCIAL STATEMENTS

Note 4. Restructuring and Acquisitions (in part)

February 2012 Manufacturing Restructuring

In February 2012, executive management completed an evaluation of and approved a set of manufacturing capacity and other initiatives primarily intended to adjust our previously planned manufacturing capacity expansions and global manufacturing footprint. The primary goal of these initiatives is to better align production capacity and geographic location of such capacity with expected geographic market requirements and demand. In connection with these initiatives, we expect to incur total charges to operating expense of up to $135 million during the first half of 2012 and up to $140 million in total by the time such initiatives are complete, which is expected to be by the end of 2012. These expected charges consist primarily of (i) between $60 million to $100 million of asset impairment and related charges due to our decision in February 2012 not to proceed with our 4-line manufacturing plant under construction in Vietnam (carrying value of $134.4 million as of December 31, 2011), (ii) between $20 million and $30 million of asset impairment and related charges due to our decision in February 2012 to cease the use of certain manufacturing machinery and equipment intended for use in the production of certain components of our solar modules (carrying value of $28.5 million as of December 31, 2011), and (iii) between $5 million to $10 million of asset impairment and related charges primarily due to our decision in February 2012 to cease use of certain other long-lived assets (carrying value of $7.2 million as of December 31, 2011).

Based upon expected future market demand and our focus on providing utility-scale PV generation solutions primarily to sustainable geographic markets, we have decided not to proceed with our previously announced 4-line plant in Vietnam. We expect to actively market the plant for sale after all necessary construction has been completed, which is currently expected to occur in the first half of 2012. Once certain criteria are met including the completion of all necessary construction activities and active marketing of the Vietnam plant, we expect to meet the "held for sale" criteria, at which time we expect to record an impairment charge based primarily upon the then-current fair value of the Vietnam plant.

We evaluated the asset group that includes our manufacturing plant under construction in Vietnam, which is considered "held and used," for potential impairment as of December 31, 2011 in accordance with ASC 360. In performing the recoverability test, we concluded that the long-lived asset group was recoverable after comparing the undiscounted future cash flows, including the eventual disposition of the asset group at market value, to the asset group's carrying value.

We also evaluated the asset group that includes certain manufacturing machinery and equipment intended for use in the production of certain components of our solar modules, which is considered "held and used," for potential impairment as of December 31, 2011 in accordance with ASC 360. In performing the recoverability test, we concluded that the long-lived asset group was recoverable after comparing the undiscounted future cash flows, including the eventual disposition of the asset group at market value, to the asset group's carrying value. In connection with the decision in February 2012 to cease use of such machinery and equipment, the assets are considered abandoned for accounting purposes. As a result, we expect to record an impairment charge in the first quarter of 2012.

Acquisitions

1.150

NETAPP, INC. (APR)

NOTES TO CONSOLIDATED FINANCIAL STATEMENTS

20. Subsequent Event

On May 6, 2011, we completed the acquisition of certain assets related to the Engenio external storage systems business (ESG) of LSI Corporation (LSI). We paid LSI $480 million in cash and also assumed certain assets and liabilities related to ESG. Over the next three years, LSI will pay us between $13.0 million and $14.5 million to service certain LSI customer warranties. This acquisition will enable us to address emerging and fast-growing market segments such as video, including full-motion video capture and digital video surveillance, as well as high performance computing applications, such as genomics sequencing and scientific research.

We are in the process of completing a purchase price allocation for this acquisition. We currently expect between $250.0 million and $350.0 million of the purchase price to be allocated to identifiable intangible assets other than goodwill in the final purchase price allocation. A preliminary purchase price allocation is currently expected to be included in our consolidated financial statements for the quarter ending July 29, 2011.

The following unaudited pro forma condensed combined financial information gives effect to the acquisition of ESG as if it were consummated on April 25, 2009. Due to differing fiscal year ends of NetApp and ESG, the unaudited pro forma condensed combined financial information is based on the historical results of NetApp for fiscal 2011 and fiscal 2010, respectively and the historical results of ESG for the twelve month periods ended April 3, 2011 and April 4, 2010, respectively. The unaudited pro forma condensed combined financial information is presented for informational purposes only and is not intended to represent or be indicative of the results of operations of the Company that would have been reported had the acquisition occurred on April 25, 2009 (the beginning of the earliest period presented) and should not be taken as representative of future consolidated results of operations of the combined company (in millions).

	Year Ended	
	April 29, 2011	April 30, 2010
Net revenues	$5,823.8	$4,605.7
Net income	$ 606.8	$ 366.9

An adjustment of $2.5 million has been reflected in the unaudited pro forma condensed combined information to exclude acquisition related costs directly attributable to the acquisition because they will not have a continuing impact on the combined results.

Restricted Stock and Performance Share Grants

1.151

REGAL ENTERTAINMENT GROUP (DEC)

NOTES TO CONSOLIDATED FINANCIAL STATEMENTS

14. Subsequent Events (in part)

Restricted Stock and Performance Share Grants (in part)

On January 11, 2012, 327,287 restricted shares were granted under the Incentive Plan at nominal cost to officers, directors and key employees. Under the Incentive Plan, Class A common stock of the Company may be granted at nominal cost to officers, directors and key employees, subject to a continued employment restriction (typically one to four years after the award date). The awards vest 25% at the end of each year for four years in the case of officers and key employees and vest 100% at the end of one year in the case of directors. The plan participants are entitled to cash dividends and to vote their respective shares, although the sale and transfer of such shares is prohibited during the restricted period. The shares are subject to the terms and conditions of the Incentive Plan. The closing price of our Class A common stock on the date of this grant was $12.30 per share.

Also on January 11, 2012, 326,072 performance shares were granted under our Incentive Plan at nominal cost to officers and key employees. Each performance share represents the right to receive from 0% to 150% of the target numbers of shares of restricted Class A common stock. The number of shares of restricted common stock earned will be determined based on the attainment of specified performance goals by January 11, 2015 (the third anniversary of the grant date) set forth in the 2009 Performance Agreement. The shares are subject to the terms and conditions of the Incentive Plan. The closing price of our Class A common stock on the date of this grant was $12.30 per share.

RELATED PARTY TRANSACTIONS

DISCLOSURE

1.152 FASB ASC 850, *Related Party Disclosures*, specifies the nature of information that should be disclosed in financial statements about related-party transactions and certain common control relationships. Financial statements should include disclosures of material related-party transactions, other than compensation arrangements, expense allowances, and other similar items in the ordinary course of business. The disclosures should include the nature of the relationship(s) involved, a description of the transactions, the dollar amounts of the transactions, and amounts due to or from related parties. For entities with separately-issued financial statements that are members of a consolidated tax return, additional disclosures are required. Further, if the reporting entity and one or more other companies are under common ownership or management control, and the existence of that control could result in operating results or a financial position of the reporting entity significantly different from those that would have been obtained if the companies were autonomous, the nature of the control relationship should be disclosed, even though there are no transactions between the entities.

PRESENTATION AND DISCLOSURE EXCERPTS

Transaction Between Reporting Entity & Investee

1.153

MARRIOTT INTERNATIONAL, INC. (DEC)

NOTES TO CONSOLIDATED FINANCIAL STATEMENTS

22. Related Party Transactions

Equity Method Investments

We have equity method investments in entities that own properties for which we provide management and/or franchise services and receive fees. In addition, in some cases we provide loans, preferred equity or guarantees to these entities. We generally own between 10 and 49 percent of these equity method investments. Undistributed earnings attributable to our equity method investments represented approximately $4 million of our consolidated retained earnings at year-end 2011.

The following tables present financial data resulting from transactions with these related parties:

Income Statement Data

($ in millions)	2011	2010	2009
Base management fees	$ 37	$ 35	$ 44
Franchise fees	—	—	—
Incentive management fees	—	3	2
Cost reimbursements	383	328	321
Owned, leased, corporate housing, and other	8	4	—
Total revenue	$ 428	$ 370	$ 367
General, administrative, and other	$ (5)	$ (1)	$ (1)
Reimbursed costs	(383)	(328)	(321)
Gains and other income	4	6	6
Interest expense-capitalized	2	5	4
Interest income	3	3	8
Equity in (losses) earnings	(13)	(18)	(66)
Timeshare strategy-impairment charges (non-operating)	—	—	(138)
Provision for income taxes	—	—	—

Balance Sheet Data

($ in millions)	At Year-End 2011	At Year-End 2010
Current assets-accounts and notes receivable	$ 12	$ 9
Contract acquisition costs and other	28	30
Equity and cost method investments	234	190
Notes receivable	2	2
Deferred taxes, net asset	16	22
Other	13	—
Current liabilities:		
Other	(6)	(25)
Other long-term liabilities	(30)	(34)

Summarized information for the entities in which we have equity method investments is as follows:

Income Statement Data

($ in millions)	2011	2010	2009
Sales	$1,215	$914	$ 850
Net (loss) income	$ (39)	$ (77)	$(241)

Balance Sheet Summary

($ in millions)	At Year-End 2011	At Year-End 2010
Assets (primarily comprised of hotel real estate managed by us)	$3,159	$3,186
Liabilities	$2,532	$2,446

Major Stockholder Transactions

1.154

THE MOSAIC COMPANY (MAY)

NOTES TO CONSOLIDATED FINANCIAL STATEMENTS

(Tables in millions, except per share amounts)

2. Cargill Transaction

On May 25, 2011, we consummated the first in a series of transactions intended to result in the split-off and orderly distribution of Cargill's approximately 64% equity interest in us through a series of public offerings (the "*Cargill Transaction*"). These transactions include the following:

- A Merger (the "*Merger*") between a subsidiary of GNS II (U.S.) Corp. ("*GNS*") and MOS Holdings Inc. ("*MOS Holdings*") that had the effect of recapitalizing our prior Common Stock into three classes: Common Stock, Class A Common Stock and Class B Common Stock. The Common Stock is substantially identical to our prior Common Stock, and all three new classes have the same economic rights as our prior Common Stock. Holders of the Common Stock and the Class A Common Stock have one vote per share on all matters on which they are entitled to vote, whereas holders of the Class B Common Stock have ten votes per share solely for the election of directors and one vote per share on all other matters on which they are entitled to vote. The Class A—Common Stock and the Class B Common Stock are subject to transfer restrictions, have conversion rights and class voting rights, and are not publicly traded. Following the Merger, our Common Stock continues to trade under the ticker symbol MOS.

- Prior to the Merger, GNS was a wholly-owned subsidiary of the company then known as The Mosaic Company. The Merger made GNS the parent company of MOS Holdings. In connection with the Merger, the company formerly known as The Mosaic Company was renamed MOS Holdings Inc. and GNS was renamed The Mosaic Company.

- In the Merger, a portion of our Common Stock held by Cargill was converted, on a one-for-one basis, into the right to receive Class A Common Stock and Class B Common Stock. Each other outstanding share of our prior Common Stock (including a portion of the shares of our prior Common Stock held by Cargill) was converted into the right to receive a share of our Common Stock.

- Cargill conducted a split-off (the "*Split-off*") in which it exchanged 178.3 million of our shares that it received in the Merger for shares of Cargill stock held by certain Cargill stockholders (the "*Exchanging Cargill Stockholders*"). Immediately after the Split-off, the Exchanging Cargill Stockholders held approximately 40% of our total outstanding shares that represented approximately 82% of the total voting power with respect to the election of our directors.

- Cargill also exchanged the remaining 107.5 million of our shares that it received in the Merger with certain holders of Cargill debt (the "*Exchanging Cargill Debt Holders*") for such Cargill debt (the "*Debt Exchange*").

- Certain of the Exchanging Cargill Stockholders (the "*MAC Trusts*") and the Exchanging Cargill Debt Holders (collectively, the "*Selling Stockholders*") then sold an aggregate of 115.0 million shares of our Common Stock that they received in the Split-off and the Debt Exchange in an underwritten secondary public offering (the initial "*Formation Offering*").

Pursuant to a ruling from the U.S. Internal Revenue Service, the Merger, Split-off and Debt Exchange are expected to be tax-free to Cargill, Mosaic and their respective stockholders.

Cargill is required to reimburse us for $18.5 million in the aggregate of fees and expenses we incurred in connection with the matters described above and negotiation of the Cargill Transaction; such reimbursement was recorded as a capital contribution in stockholders' equity.

We have agreed to conduct a series of additional Formation Offerings, if necessary, within 15 months after the Split-off to provide for the sale by the MAC Trusts of an additional 42.0 million of the shares of our stock that they received in the Split-off.

All other shares of our stock received by the Exchanging Cargill Stockholders and not sold in the Formation Offerings (approximately 128.8 million shares in the aggregate) are generally subject to transfer restrictions and are to be released in three equal annual installments beginning on the two and one-half year anniversary of the Split-off. We would, at the request of the MAC Trusts or at our own election, register certain of our shares for sale in a secondary offering that could occur each year after the second anniversary of the Split-off, with the first such offering occurring not earlier than twelve months after the last of the Formation Offerings and certain other primary or secondary offerings.

Following 180 days after the four-and-a-half year anniversary of the Split-off, the MAC Trusts would have two rights to request that we file a registration statement under the Securities Act of 1933, pursuant to which the MAC Trusts could sell any remaining shares they received in the Split-off.

Our agreements with Cargill and the Exchanging Cargill Stockholders also contain additional provisions relating to private and market sales under specified conditions.

We have agreed that, among other things, and subject to certain exceptions:

- For a period ending two years after the Merger, we will not engage in certain prohibited acts ("*Prohibited Acts*"), unless we receive an opinion, satisfactory to Cargill, that such action will not result in the Merger, Split-off or Debt Exchange being treated as taxable transactions. Our ability to obtain such an opinion would potentially give us the flexibility to take such actions based on the then-present facts and circumstances. Receipt of any such opinion does not relieve us of our potential indemnification obligations, described below, for engaging in a Prohibited Act.
- We will indemnify Cargill for certain taxes and tax-related losses imposed on Cargill if we engage in a Prohibited Act or in the event we are in breach of representations or warranties made in support of the tax-free nature of the Merger, Split-off and Debt Exchange, if our Prohibited Act or breach causes the Merger, Split-off and/or Debt Exchange to fail to qualify as tax-free transactions.

Generally speaking, Prohibited Acts include:

- Entering into any agreements, understandings, arrangements or substantial negotiations pursuant to which any person would acquire, increase or have the right to acquire or increase such person's ownership interest in us, provided that equity issuances, redemptions from the MAC Trusts and approvals of transfers within an agreed-upon "basket" of up to approximately 40.6 million shares (subject to reductions in the event of redemptions) are not Prohibited Acts.
- Approving or recommending a third-party tender offer or exchange offer for our stock or causing or permitting any merger, reorganization, combination or consolidation of Mosaic or MOS Holdings.
- Causing our "separate affiliated group" (as defined in the Internal Revenue Code) to fail to be engaged in the fertilizer business.
- Reclassifying, exchanging or converting any shares of our stock into another class or series, or changing the voting rights of any shares of our stock (other than a conversion of Class B Common Stock to either Class A Common Stock or Common Stock with stockholder approval in accordance with the applicable provisions of the agreements relating to the Cargill Transaction) or declaring or paying a stock dividend in respect of our common stock.
- Facilitating the acquisition of Mosaic's stock by any person or coordinating group (as defined in IRS regulations) (other than Cargill and its subsidiaries), if such acquisition would result in any person or coordinating group beneficially owning 10% or more of our outstanding Common Stock.
- Facilitating participation in management or operation of the Company (including by becoming a director) by a person or coordinating group (as defined in IRS regulations) (other than Cargill and its subsidiaries) who beneficially owns 5% or more of our outstanding Common Stock.

The Cargill Transaction resulted in no change to our total outstanding shares, the economic rights of our shares or earnings per share. In addition, these transactions did not result in any changes to our accounting policies applied to our Consolidated Financial Statements.

23. Related Party Transactions

On May 25, 2011, Cargill, our former majority stockholder, exchanged its 64% stake in our company with certain Cargill stockholders and debt holders. For further discussion of these exchanges as part of the Cargill Transaction, see Note 2 of the Notes to Consolidated Financial Statements. Until these exchanges, Cargill was considered a related party due to its ownership interest in us.

We engage in various transactions, arrangements and agreements with Cargill, which are described below. The Cargill transactions subcommittee of the corporate governance and nominating committee of our board of directors, comprised solely of independent directors, is responsible for reviewing and approving these transactions, arrangements and agreements. Our related person transactions approval policy provides for the delegation of approval authority for certain transactions with Cargill, other than those of the type described in such related person transactions approval policy, to an internal committee comprised of senior managers. The internal management committee is required to report its activities to the Cargill transactions subcommittee on a periodic basis.

We negotiated each of the following transactions, arrangements and agreements with Cargill on the basis of what we believe to be competitive market practices.

- *Supply Agreement.* We sell fertilizer to Cargill or its subsidiaries under supply agreements for resale through their retail stores in the United States and Western Canada. We sell phosphate fertilizer under a supply agreement with Cargill's subsidiary in Argentina. We also have an agreement to sell untreated white muriate of potash to Cargill's salt business in the United States. In addition, we have various agreements relating to the supply of feed grade phosphate, potash and urea products to Cargill's animal nutrition, grain and oilseeds, and poultry businesses.
- *Spot Fertilizer Sales.* From time to time, we make spot fertilizer sales to Cargill's subsidiary in Paraguay and Bolivia.
- *Ocean Transportation Agreement.* We have a nonexclusive agreement with Cargill's Ocean Transportation Division to perform various freight related service for us.
- *Barter Agreements.* We have barter relationships with Cargill's grain and oilseeds businesses in Brazil and Argentina. The number of barter transactions varies from year to year.
- *Miscellaneous Co-Location Agreements*. We have various office sharing and sublease arrangements with Cargill in various geographic locations, including with respect to certain offices in China and the United States.
- *Miscellaneous.* There are various other agreements between us and Cargill which we believe are not significant to us.

Cargill made net equity contributions (distributions) of $18.5 million to us in fiscal 2011, $0 in fiscal 2010, and ($0.6) million to us during fiscal 2009. As of May 31, 2011, accounts receivable include $18.5 million related to the fiscal 2011 contribution.

In summary, the Consolidated Statements of Earnings included the following transactions with Cargill:

(In millions)	Years Ended May 31		
	2011	2010	2009
Transactions with Cargill included in net sales	$238.1	$127.9	$286.3
Transactions with Cargill included in cost of goods sold	146.8	96.4	173.1
Transactions with Cargill included in selling, general and administrative expenses	6.1	8.2	11.6
Interest income received from Cargill	0.2	—	0.8

We have also entered into transactions and agreements with certain of our non-consolidated companies. As of May 31, 2011 and 2010, the net amount due from our non-consolidated companies totaled $145.7 million and $140.8 million, respectively.

The Consolidated Statements of Earnings included the following transactions with our non-consolidated companies:

(In millions)	Years Ended May 31		
	2011	2010	2009
Transactions with non-consolidated companies included in net sales	$1,015.7	$624.0	$1,315.9
Transactions with non-consolidated companies included in cost of goods sold	511.3	273.0	384.8

Transaction Between Reporting Entity and Officer/Director

1.155

NEWS CORPORATION (JUN)

NOTES TO THE CONSOLIDATED FINANCIAL STATEMENTS

Note 15. Related Parties (in part)

Director Transactions

The Company had engaged, prior to May 2010, Mrs. Wendi Murdoch, the wife of Mr. K.R. Murdoch, the Company's Chairman and Chief Executive Officer, to provide strategic advice for the development of the Myspace business in China. No amounts were paid to Mrs. Murdoch in the fiscal year ended June 30, 2011. The fees paid to Mrs. Murdoch pursuant to this arrangement were $92,000, and $100,000 in fiscal 2010 and 2009, respectively. Mrs. Murdoch is a Director of Myspace China Holdings Limited ("Myspace China"), a joint venture in which the Company owns a 51.5% interest on a fully diluted basis, which licenses the technology and brand to the local company in China that operates the Myspace China website. Similar to other Directors of Myspace China, Mrs. Murdoch received options over 2.5% of the fully diluted shares of Myspace China that will vest over four years under the Myspace China option plan.

Freud Communications, which is controlled by Matthew Freud, Mr. K.R. Murdoch's son-in-law, provided external support to the press and publicity activities of the Company during fiscal years 2011, 2010 and 2009. The fees paid by the Company to Freud Communications were approximately $202,000, $350,000 and $473,000 in fiscal years ended June 30, 2011, 2010 and 2009, respectively. At June 30, 2011, there were no outstanding amounts due to or from Freud Communications.

Shine was controlled by Ms. Elisabeth Murdoch, the daughter of Mr. K.R. Murdoch through April 2011. In April 2011, the Company acquired Shine (See Note 3—Acquisitions, Disposals and Other Transactions for further discussion). Prior to the acquisition, through the normal course of business, certain subsidiaries of the Company entered into various production and distribution arrangements with Shine. Pursuant to these arrangements, the Company paid Shine an aggregate of approximately $4.1 million in the period from July 1, 2010 through the date of acquisition and approximately $11.9 million in the fiscal year ended June 30, 2010. No amounts were paid to Shine in fiscal year 2009. As of the acquisition date, transactions with Shine are eliminated in consolidation.

Mr. Mark Hurd was a Director of the Company until October 2010 and was Chief Executive Officer of Hewlett-Packard Company ("HP") until August 6, 2010. Through the normal course of business, HP sells certain equipment and provides services to the Company and its subsidiaries pursuant to a worldwide agreement entered into by the Company and HP in August 2007. Pursuant to this agreement, the Company paid HP approximately $55 million and $47 million in the fiscal years ended June 30, 2010 and 2009, respectively.

Mr. Stanley Shuman, Director Emeritus, and Mr. Kenneth Siskind, son of Mr. Arthur M. Siskind, who is a Director and senior advisor to the Chairman, are Managing Directors of Allen & Company LLC, a U.S. based investment bank, which provided investment advisory services to the Company. Total fees paid to Allen & Company LLC were $13.6 million, nil and $17.5 million in fiscal 2011, 2010 and 2009, respectively.

The Company acquired an approximate 23% equity stake in Beyond Oblivion, a digital music start-up company, for approximately $9.2 million in April 2010. In April 2010, Mr. Shuman had an approximate 18% interest in Beyond Oblivion. Mr. Shuman also serves as a member of its board of directors. Mr. Shuman does not receive compensation for his Beyond Oblivion board service. In fiscal 2011, the Company contributed an additional $2 million to Beyond Oblivion. As of June 30, 2011, the Company and Mr. Shuman own approximately 20% and 14%, respectively, of Beyond Oblivion.

Transaction Between Reporting Entity and Variable Interest Entity

1.156

NACCO INDUSTRIES, INC. (DEC)

NOTES TO CONSOLIDATED FINANCIAL STATEMENTS

(Tabular amounts in millions, except per share and percentage data)

NOTE 22—Related Party Transactions

Nine of NACoal's wholly owned subsidiaries, Coteau, Falkirk, Sabine, Demery, Caddo Creek, Camino Real, Liberty, NoDak and NACC India each meet the definition of a variable interest entity. See Note 1 for a discussion of these entities. The taxes resulting from the earnings of the unconsolidated mines and NoDak are solely the responsibility of the Company. The pre-tax income from the seven unconsolidated mines is reported on the line "Earnings of unconsolidated mines" in the Consolidated Statements of Operations, with related taxes included in the provision for income taxes. The Company has included the pre-tax earnings of the unconsolidated mines above operating profit as they are an integral component of the Company's business and operating results. The pre-tax income from NoDak is reported on the line "Other" in the "Other (income) expense" section of the Consolidated Statement of Operations, with the related income

taxes included in the provision for income taxes. The net income from NACC India is reported on the line "Other" in the "Other (income) expense" section of the Consolidated Statements of Operations. The investment in the unconsolidated mines and related tax asset was $22.0 million and $21.6 million at December 31, 2011 and 2010, respectively, and is included on the line "Other Non-current Assets" in the Consolidated Balance Sheets. The Company's maximum risk of loss relating to these entities is limited to its invested capital, which was $6.3 million, $5.0 million and $3.5 million at December 31, 2011, 2010 and 2009, respectively.

Summarized financial information for the unconsolidated mines is as follows:

	2011	2010	2009
Statement of Operations			
Revenues	$502.6	$461.7	$421.1
Gross profit	$ 71.7	$ 71.7	$ 63.7
Income before income taxes	$ 47.0	$ 43.4	$ 38.6
Income from continuing operations	$ 36.5	$ 33.1	$ 29.8
Net income	$ 36.5	$ 33.1	$ 29.8
Balance Sheet			
Current assets	$144.1	$130.9	
Non-current assets	$685.2	$633.6	
Current liabilities	$162.1	$115.2	
Non-current liabilities	$660.9	$644.3	

NACoal received dividends of $35.2 million and $31.6 million from the unconsolidated mines in 2011 and 2010, respectively.

In addition, NMHG maintains an interest in one variable interest entity, NFS. NFS is a joint venture with GECC formed primarily for the purpose of providing financial services to independent Hyster® and Yale® lift truck dealers and National Account customers in the United States. NMHG does not have a controlling financial interest or have the power to direct the activities that most significantly affect the economic performance of NFS. Therefore, the Company has concluded that NMHG is not the primary beneficiary and will continue to use the equity method to account for its 20% interest in NFS. NMHG does not consider its variable interest in NFS to be significant.

Generally, NMHG sells lift trucks through its independent dealer network or directly to customers. These dealers and customers may enter into a financing transaction with NFS or other unrelated third-parties. NFS provides debt financing to dealers and lease financing to both dealers and customers. NFS' total purchases of Hyster® and Yale® lift trucks from dealers, customers and directly from NMHG, such that NFS could provide lease financing to dealers and customers, for the years ended December 31, 2011, 2010 and 2009 were $337.3 million, $243.9 million and $266.7 million, respectively. Of these amounts, $38.7 million, $23.7 million and $38.0 million for the years ended December 31, 2011, 2010 and 2009, respectively, were invoiced directly from NMHG to NFS so that the dealer or customer could obtain operating lease financing from NFS. Amounts receivable from NFS were $4.9 million and $3.2 million at December 31, 2011 and 2010, respectively.

Under the terms of the joint venture agreement with GECC, NMHG provides recourse for financing provided by NFS to NMHG dealers. Additionally, the credit quality of a customer or concentration issues within GECC may necessitate providing recourse or repurchase obligations of the lift trucks purchased by customers and financed through NFS. At December 31, 2011, approximately $112.9 million of the Company's total recourse or repurchase obligations related to transactions with NFS. NMHG has reserved for losses under the terms of the recourse or repurchase obligations in its consolidated financial statements. Historically, NMHG has not had significant losses with respect to these obligations. During 2011, 2010 and 2009, the net losses resulting from customer defaults did not have a material impact on NMHG's results of operations or financial position.

In connection with the joint venture agreement, NMHG also provides a guarantee to GECC for 20% of NFS' debt with GECC, such that NMHG would become liable under the terms of NFS' debt agreements with GECC in the case of default by NFS. At December 31, 2011, loans from GECC to NFS totaled $684.7 million. Although NMHG's contractual guarantee was $136.9 million, the loans by GECC to NFS are secured by NFS' customer receivables, of which NMHG guarantees $112.9 million. Excluding the $112.9 million of NFS receivables guaranteed by NMHG from NFS' loans to GECC, NMHG's incremental obligation as a result of this guarantee to GECC is $114.4 million. NFS has not defaulted under the terms of this debt financing in the past and although there can be no assurances, NMHG is not aware of any circumstances that would cause NFS to default in future periods.

In addition to providing financing to NMHG's dealers, NFS provides operating lease financing to NMHG. Operating lease obligations primarily relate to specific sale-leaseback-sublease transactions for certain NMHG customers whereby NMHG sells lift trucks to NFS, NMHG leases these lift trucks back under an operating lease agreement and NMHG subleases those lift trucks to customers under an operating lease agreement. Total obligations to NFS under the operating lease agreements were $6.0 million and $7.3 million at December 31, 2011 and 2010, respectively. In addition, NMHG provides certain subsidies to its customers that are paid directly to NFS. Total subsidies were $1.4 million, $4.0 million and $5.4 million for 2011, 2010 and 2009, respectively.

NMHG provides certain services to NFS for which it receives compensation under the terms of the joint venture agreement. These services consist primarily of administrative functions and remarketing services. Total income recorded by NMHG related to these services was $7.3 million in 2011, $5.0 million in 2010 and $7.6 million in 2009.

NMHG has a 50% ownership interest in SN, a limited liability company that was formed primarily to manufacture and distribute Sumitomo-Yale branded lift trucks in Japan and export Hyster®-and Yale®-branded lift trucks and related components and service parts outside of Japan. NMHG purchases products from SN under normal trade terms based on current market prices. In 2011, 2010 and 2009, purchases from SN were $105.5 million, $66.9 million and $44.7 million, respectively. Amounts payable to SN at December 31, 2011 and 2010 were $21.6 million and $30.7 million, respectively.

During 2010 and 2009, NMHG recognized $1.1 million and $1.8 million, respectively, in expenses related to payments to SN for engineering design services. These expenses were included in "Selling, general and administrative expenses" in the Consolidated Statement of Operations. No expenses were recognized for these services in 2011. Additionally, NMHG recognized income of $1.6 million, $1.2 million and $0.4 million for payments from SN for use of technology developed by NMHG that are included in "Revenues" in the

Consolidated Statement of Operations for the years ended December 31, 2011, 2010 and 2009, respectively.

Summarized financial information for both equity investments is as follows:

	2011	2010	2009
Statement of Operations			
Revenues	$444.3	$ 358.6	$310.6
Gross profit	$126.9	$ 106.7	$ 88.5
Income from continuing operations	$ 23.7	$ 7.1	$ 1.5
Net income	$ 23.7	$ 7.1	$ 1.5
Balance Sheet			
Current assets	$138.8	$ 128.6	
Non-current assets	$997.2	$1,038.0	
Current liabilities	$122.8	$ 119.0	
Non-current liabilities	$875.7	$ 925.9	

The Company's percentage share of the net income or loss from its equity investments is reported on the line "(Income) loss from other unconsolidated affiliates" in the "Other (income) expense" portion of the Consolidated Statements of Operations.

At December 31, 2011 and 2010, NMHG's investment in NFS was $13.6 million and $12.1 million, respectively, and NMHG's investment in SN was $34.2 million and $30.3 million, respectively. NMHG received dividends of $2.3 million and $2.9 million from NFS in 2011 and 2010, respectively. No dividends were received from SN in 2011 and 2010.

Legal services rendered by Jones Day approximated $4.9 million, $14.3 million and $2.7 million for the years ended December 31, 2011, 2010 and 2009, respectively. The significant increase in services rendered during 2010 related to the Applica litigation discussed further in Note 5. A director of the Company is also a partner of this law firm.

Transactions With Related Parties

1.157

CABLEVISION SYSTEMS CORPORATION (DEC)

NOTES TO CONSOLIDATED FINANCIAL STATEMENTS

(Dollars in thousands, except per share amounts)

Note 17. Related Party Transactions

In connection with the AMC Networks Distribution and the MSG Distribution, the Company entered into various agreements with AMC Networks and Madison Square Garden, including distribution agreements, tax disaffiliation agreements, transition services agreements, employee matters agreements and certain related party arrangements. These agreements govern the Company's relationship with AMC Networks and Madison Square Garden subsequent to the AMC Networks Distribution and the MSG Distribution and provide for the allocation of employee benefits, taxes and certain other liabilities and obligations attributable to periods prior to the AMC Networks Distribution and the MSG Distribution. These agreements also include arrangements with respect to transition services and a number of on-going relationships. The distribution agreements include agreements that the Company and AMC Networks and the Company and Madison Square Garden agree to provide each other with indemnities with respect to liabilities arising out of the businesses the Company transferred to AMC Networks and Madison Square Garden.

The following table summarizes the revenue and charges (credits) related to services provided to or received from AMC Networks reflected in continuing operations not discussed elsewhere in the accompanying combined notes to the consolidated financial statements:

	Years Ending December 31		
	2011[a]	2010[a]	2009[a]
Revenues, net	$ 2,746	$ 2,455	$ 1,780
Operating expenses (credits):			
Technical expenses, net of credits	$ 23,037	$ 18,753	$ 21,351
Selling, general and administrative expenses (credits):			
Corporate general and administrative expense allocations	(4,797)	(5,661)	(5,445)
Health and welfare plan allocations	(9,719)	(8,209)	(8,601)
Risk management and general insurance allocations	(836)	(1,626)	(1,619)
Other	(1,901)	(1,627)	(1,223)
Selling, general and administrative expenses (credits), subtotal	(17,253)	(17,123)	(16,888)
Operating expenses, net	5,784	1,630	4,463
Net charges (credits)	$ 3,038	$ (825)	$ 2,683

[a] Amounts relating to AMC Networks for the period prior to the AMC Networks Distribution are eliminated in consolidation. Operating results of AMC Networks are reported in discontinued operations for all periods presented prior to the AMC Networks Distribution. Corporate overhead costs previously allocated to AMC Networks that were not eliminated as a result of the AMC Networks Distribution have been reclassified to continuing operations and are not reflected in the table above.

The following table summarizes the revenue and charges (credits) related to services provided to or received from Madison Square Garden reflected in continuing operations not discussed elsewhere in the accompanying combined notes to the consolidated financial statements:

	Years Ending December 31		
	2011[a]	2010[a]	2009[a]
Revenues, net	$ 2,476	$ 1,926	$ 2,403
Operating expenses (credits):			
Technical expenses, net of credits	$155,794	$152,889	$123,191
Selling, general and administrative expenses (credits):			
Corporate general and administrative expense allocations	(3,170)	(8,135)	(5,626)
Health and welfare plan allocations	—	—	(12,682)
Risk management and general insurance allocations	—	(713)	(6,161)
Other	3,429	2,888	4,805
Selling, general and administrative expenses (credits), subtotal	259	(5,960)	(19,664)
Operating expenses, net	156,053	146,929	103,527
Net charges	$153,577	$145,003	$101,124

[a] Amounts relating to Madison Square Garden for the period prior to the MSG Distribution are eliminated in consolidation. Operating results of Madison Square Garden are reported in discontinued operations for all periods presented prior to the MSG Distribution. Corporate overhead costs previously allocated to Madison Square Garden that were not eliminated as a result of the MSG Distribution have been reclassified to continuing operations and are not reflected in the table above.

Revenues, Net

The Company recognizes revenue in connection with television advertisements and print advertising, as well as certain telecommunication services charged by its subsidiaries to AMC Networks and Madison Square Garden.

The Company and its subsidiaries, together with AMC Networks and Madison Square Garden, may enter into agreements with third parties in which the amounts paid/received by AMC Networks and Madison Square Garden, their subsidiaries, or the Company may differ from the amounts that would have been paid/received if such arrangements were negotiated separately. Where subsidiaries of the Company have incurred a cost incremental to fair value and Madison Square Garden or AMC Networks have received a benefit incremental to fair value from these negotiations, the Company and its subsidiaries will charge Madison Square Garden or AMC Networks for the incremental amount.

Technical Expenses, Net of Credits

Technical expenses include costs incurred by the Company for the carriage of the MSG networks and Fuse program services, as well as for AMC, WE tv, IFC and Sundance Channel on Cablevision's cable systems. The Company also purchases certain programming signal transmission and production services from AMC Networks.

Effective January 1, 2010, a new long-term affiliation agreement was entered into between Cablevision and the MSG networks, which are owned by Madison Square Garden. This new long-term affiliation agreement resulted in incremental programming costs to the Company of approximately $29,000 for the year ended December 31, 2010, as compared to the amount of programming costs recognized by the Company pursuant to the Company's arrangement with Madison Square Garden in 2009. This new affiliation agreement provides for the carriage of the MSG Network and MSG Plus program services on the Company's cable television systems in the tri-state area. This agreement has a term of 10 years, obligates the Company to carry the MSG networks program services on its cable television systems and provides for the payment by the Company to the MSG networks of a per subscriber license fee, which fee is increased each year during the term of the agreement.

Selling, General and Administrative Expenses (Credits)

Corporate General and Administrative Expense Allocations

General and administrative costs, primarily costs of maintaining common support functions such as executive management, human resources, legal, finance, tax, accounting, audit, treasury, strategic planning, information technology, transportation services, creative and production services, etc., were allocated to Madison Square Garden through December 31, 2009 and to AMC Networks through June 30, 2011. Subsequent to January 1, 2010 and July 1, 2011, amounts allocated to Madison Square Garden and AMC Networks, respectively, represent charges pursuant to transition services agreements. Corporate overhead costs previously allocated to AMC Networks and Madison Square Garden that were not eliminated as a result of the AMC Networks Distribution and MSG Distribution have been reclassified to continuing operations.

Health and Welfare Plan Allocations

Employees of Madison Square Garden and AMC Networks participated in health and welfare plans sponsored by the Company through December 31, 2009 and December 31, 2011, respectively. Health and welfare benefit costs have generally been charged to AMC Networks and Madison Square Garden based upon the proportionate number of participants in the plans.

Risk Management and General Insurance Allocations

The Company provided AMC Networks and Madison Square Garden with risk management and general insurance related services through the dates of the AMC Networks Distribution and the MSG Distribution.

Other

The Company, AMC Networks and Madison Square Garden routinely enter into transactions with each other in the ordinary course of business. Such transactions may include, but are not limited to, sponsorship agreements and cross-promotion arrangements.

Transactions with Other Affiliates

During 2011, 2010 and 2009, the Company provided services to or incurred costs on behalf of certain related parties, including from time to time, members of the Dolan family or to entities owned by members of the Dolan family. All costs incurred on behalf of these related parties are reimbursed to the Company.

Aggregate amounts due from and due to AMC Networks, Madison Square Garden and other affiliates at December 31, 2011 and 2010 are summarized below:

	December 31	
Cablevision	**2011**	**2010**
Amounts due from affiliates	$ 6,818	$ 25,127
Amounts due to affiliates	32,682	31,517

	December 31	
CSC Holdings	**2011**	**2010**
Amounts due from affiliates (principally Cablevision)	$503,576	$515,698
Amounts due to affiliates	30,065	31,200

Merger Agreement and Exchange Agreement

1.158

SPECTRUM BRANDS HOLDINGS, INC. (SEP)

NOTES TO CONSOLIDATED FINANCIAL STATEMENTS

(In thousands, except per share figures)

(13) Related Party Transactions

Merger Agreement and Exchange Agreement

On June 16, 2010 (the "Closing Date"), SB Holdings completed the Merger pursuant to the Agreement and Plan of Merger, dated as of February 9, 2010, as amended on March 1, 2010, March 26, 2010 and April 30, 2010, by and among SB Holdings, Russell Hobbs, Spectrum Brands, Battery Merger Corp., and Grill Merger Corp. (the "Merger Agreement"). As a result of the Merger, each of Spectrum Brands and Russell Hobbs became a wholly-owned subsidiary of SB Holdings. At the effective time of the Merger, (i) the outstanding shares of Spectrum Brands common stock were canceled and converted into the right to receive shares of SB Holdings common stock, and (ii) the outstanding shares of Russell Hobbs common stock and preferred stock were canceled and converted into the right to receive shares of SB Holdings common stock.

Pursuant to the terms of the Merger Agreement, on February 9, 2010, Spectrum Brands entered into support agreements with the Harbinger Parties and Avenue International

Master, L.P. and certain of its affiliates (the "Avenue Parties"), in which the Harbinger Parties and the Avenue Parties agreed to vote their shares of Spectrum Brands common stock acquired before the date of the Merger Agreement in favor of the Merger and against any alternative proposal that would impede the Merger.

Immediately following the consummation of the Merger, the Harbinger Parties owned approximately 64% of the outstanding SB Holdings common stock and the stockholders of Spectrum Brands (other than the Harbinger Parties) owned approximately 36% of the outstanding SB Holdings common stock.

On January 7, 2011, the Harbinger Parties contributed 27,757 shares of SB Holdings common stock to Harbinger Group Inc. ("HRG") and received in exchange for such shares an aggregate of 119,910 shares of HRG common stock (such transaction, the "Share Exchange"), pursuant to a Contribution and Exchange Agreement (the "Exchange Agreement"). Immediately following the Share Exchange, (i) HRG owned approximately 54.4% of the outstanding shares of SB Holding's common stock and the Harbinger Parties owned approximately 12.7% of the outstanding shares of SB Holdings common stock, and (ii) the Harbinger Parties owned 129,860 shares of HRG common stock, or approximately 93.3% of the outstanding HRG common stock.

On June 28, 2011 the Company filed a Form S-3 registration statement with the SEC under which 1,150 shares of its common stock and 6,320 shares of the Company's common stock held by Harbinger Capital Partners Master Fund I, Ltd. were offered to the public.

In connection with the Merger, the Harbinger Parties and SB Holdings entered into a stockholder agreement, dated February 9, 2010 (the "Stockholder Agreement"), which provides for certain protective provisions in favor of minority stockholders and provides certain rights and imposes certain obligations on the Harbinger Parties, including:

- for so long as the Harbinger Parties and their affiliates beneficially own 40% or more of the outstanding voting securities of SB Holdings, the Harbinger Parties and the Company will cooperate to ensure, to the greatest extent possible, the continuation of the structure of the SB Holdings board of directors as described in the Stockholder Agreement;
- the Harbinger Parties will not effect any transfer of equity securities of SB Holdings to any person that would result in such person and its affiliates owning 40% or more of the outstanding voting securities of SB Holdings, unless specified conditions are met; and
- the Harbinger Parties will be granted certain access and informational rights with respect to SB Holdings and its subsidiaries.

Pursuant to a joinder to the Stockholder Agreement entered into by the Harbinger Parties and HRG, upon consummation of the Share Exchange, HRG became a party to the Stockholder Agreement, and is subject to all of the covenants, terms and conditions of the Stockholder Agreement to the same extent as the Harbinger Parties were bound thereunder prior to giving effect to the Share Exchange.

Certain provisions of the Stockholder Agreement terminate on the date on which the Harbinger Parties or HRG no longer constitutes a Significant Stockholder (as defined in the Stockholder Agreement). The Stockholder Agreement terminates when any person (including the Harbinger Parties or HRG) acquires 90% or more of the outstanding voting securities of SB Holdings.

Also in connection with the Merger, the Harbinger Parties and SB Holdings entered into a registration rights agreement, dated as of February 9, 2010 (the "SB Holdings Registration Rights Agreement"), pursuant to which the Harbinger Parties have, among other things and subject to the terms and conditions set forth therein, certain demand and so-called "piggy back" registration rights with respect to their shares of SB Holdings common stock. On September 10, 2010, the Harbinger Parties and HRG entered into a joinder to the SB Holdings Registration Rights Agreement, pursuant to which, effective upon the consummation of the Share Exchange, HRG will become a party to the SB Holdings Registration Rights Agreement, entitled to the rights and subject to the obligations of a holder thereunder.

INFLATIONARY ACCOUNTING

DISCLOSURE

1.159 FASB ASC 255, *Changing Prices*, states that entities are encouraged to disclose supplementary information on the effects of changing prices (inflation). Entities are not discouraged from experimenting with other forms of disclosure.

1.160 However, the Item 303 of the SEC's Regulation S-K requires that registrants discuss in "Management's Discussion and Analysis of Financial Condition and Results of Operations" the effects of inflation and other changes in prices when considered material. The SEC also encourages experimentation with these disclosures in order to provide the most meaningful presentation of the impact of price changes on the registrant's financial statements. Accordingly, many of the survey entities include comments about inflation in MD&A.

PRESENTATION AND DISCLOSURE EXCERPT

Inflationary Accounting

1.161

ENERGIZER HOLDINGS, INC. (SEP)

NOTES TO CONSOLIDATED FINANCIAL STATEMENTS

(Dollars in millions, except per share and percentage data)

(2) Summary of Significant Accounting Policies (in part)

Foreign Currency Translation—Financial statements of foreign operations where the local currency is the functional currency are translated using end-of-period exchange rates for assets and liabilities, and average exchange rates during the period for results of operations. Related translation adjustments are reported as a component within accumulated other comprehensive income in the shareholders' equity section of the Consolidated Balance Sheets.

For foreign operations that are considered highly inflationary, translation practices differ in that inventories, properties, accumulated depreciation and depreciation expense are translated at historical rates of exchange, and translation adjustments for monetary assets and liabilities are included in earnings. Gains and losses from foreign currency transactions are generally included in earnings.

Effective January 1, 2010, the financial statements for our Venezuela subsidiary are consolidated under the rules governing the translation of financial information in a highly inflationary economy based on the use of the blended National Consumer Price Index in Venezuela. Under GAAP, an economy is considered highly inflationary if the cumulative inflation rate for a three year period meets or exceeds 100 percent. If a subsidiary is considered to be in a highly inflationary economy, the financial statements of the subsidiary must be re-measured into our reporting currency (U.S. dollar) and future exchange gains and losses from the re-measurement of monetary assets and liabilities are reflected in current earnings, rather than exclusively in the equity section of the balance sheet, until such time as the economy is no longer considered highly inflationary. For further information regarding the Company's Venezuela affiliate, see Note 5 of the Notes to Consolidated Financial Statements.

(5) Venezuela

For fiscal 2011, the Company recorded pre-tax expense of $1.8 related to the change in the carrying value of the net monetary assets of its Venezuelan affiliate under highly inflationary accounting. This charge was included in other financing expense, net on the Consolidated Statements of Earnings and Comprehensive Income.

At December 31, 2009, which is the end of our first fiscal quarter of 2010, the Company determined that the exchange rate available in the parallel rate market was the appropriate rate to use for the translation of our Venezuela affiliates' financial statements for the purpose of consolidation based on the facts and circumstances of our business, including the fact that, at the time, the parallel rate market was the then current method used to settle U.S. dollar invoices for newly imported product. As a result, the Company recorded a pre-tax loss, net of the impact of certain settlements and adjustments, primarily as a result of devaluing its U.S. dollar based intercompany payable of approximately $18 in fiscal 2010, which was included in other financing expense, net on the Consolidated Statements of Earnings and Comprehensive Income. The pre-tax loss reflects the higher local currency expected to be required to settle this U.S. dollar based obligation due to the use of the parallel market rate at that time, which was substantially unfavorable to the then official exchange rate. This U.S. dollar intercompany payable was an obligation of our Venezuela affiliate to other Energizer affiliates for costs associated with the importing of goods for resale in Venezuela.

Effective January 1, 2010 and continuing through fiscal 2011, the financial statements for our Venezuela subsidiary are consolidated under the rules governing the translation of financial information in a highly inflationary economy based on the use of the blended National Consumer Price Index

in Venezuela. Under GAAP, an economy is considered highly inflationary if the cumulative inflation rate for a three year period meets or exceeds 100 percent. If a subsidiary is considered to be in a highly inflationary economy, the financial statements of the subsidiary must be re-measured into our reporting currency (U.S. dollar) and future exchange gains and losses from the re-measurement of monetary assets and liabilities are reflected in current earnings, rather than exclusively in the equity section of the balance sheet, until such time as the economy is no longer considered highly inflationary. At September 30, 2011, the U.S. dollar value of monetary assets, net of monetary liabilities, which would be subject to an earnings impact from translation rate movements for our Venezuela affiliate under highly inflationary accounting was approximately $39.

On January 8, 2010, the Venezuelan government announced its intention to devalue the Bolivar Fuerte relative to the U.S. dollar. The revised official exchange rate for imported goods considered non-essential moved to an exchange rate of 4.30 to 1 U.S. dollar, which was twice the previous official rate prior to the devaluation. As noted above, the Company determined, prior to this official devaluation, that exchange rates available in the then existing parallel rate market were the appropriate rates to use for the translation of our Venezuela affiliates' financial statements, so this official devaluation action did not result in any further devaluation charges.

In May 2010, the Venezuela government introduced additional exchange controls over securities transactions in the previously mentioned parallel rate market. It established the Central Bank of Venezuela as the only legal intermediary through which parallel rate market transactions can be executed and established government control over the parallel exchange rate, which was set at approximately 5.60 to 1 U.S. dollar at September 30, 2011. At the same time, it significantly reduced the notional amount of transactions that run through this Central Bank controlled, parallel rate market mechanism.

Since foreign exchange is no longer available in the historical parallel rate market, the Company is now using the exchange rate available in the Central Bank-controlled parallel rate market as the translation rate for our Venezuela affiliates' financial statements for the purposes of consolidation, rather than the official exchange rate, as this is the rate at which the Company is obtaining U.S. dollars for the settlement of invoices on new imports. Due to the level of uncertainty in Venezuela, we cannot predict the exchange rate that will ultimately be used to convert our local currency monetary assets to U.S. dollars in the future. As a result, further charges reflecting a less favorable exchange rate outcome are possible.

Our ability to effectively manage sales and profit levels in Venezuela will be impacted by several factors, including the Company's ability to mitigate the effect of any potential future devaluation, further actions of the Venezuelan government, economic conditions in Venezuela, such as inflation and consumer spending, the availability of raw materials, utilities and energy and the future state of exchange controls in Venezuela including the availability of U.S. dollars at the official foreign exchange rate or the Central Bank-controlled parallel rate.

Section 2: Balance Sheet and Related Disclosures

GENERAL BALANCE SHEET CONSIDERATIONS

PRESENTATION

2.01 Financial Accounting Standards Board (FASB) *Accounting Standards Codification*™ (ASC) describes the benefits of presenting comparative financial statements instead of single-period financial statements and addresses the required disclosures and how the comparative information should be presented. Securities and Exchange Commission (SEC) Regulation S-X, together with Financial Reporting Releases and Staff Accounting Bulletins, prescribe the form and content of, and requirements for, financial statements filed with the SEC. However, those requirements are modified for smaller reporting companies, as defined by SEC Regulation S-K, in Article 8 of Regulation S-X.

2.02 FASB ASC 810, *Consolidation*, and Rule 3A-02 of Regulation S-X state that a presumption exists that consolidated financial statements are more meaningful than separate financial statements and that they are usually necessary for a fair presentation when one of the entities in the consolidated group directly or indirectly has a controlling financial interest in the other entities. Rule 3-01(a) of Regulation S-X requires an entity to present consolidated balance sheets as of the end of each of the two most recent fiscal years, unless the entity has been in existence for less than one year.

2.03 FASB ASC does not require an entity to present a classified balance sheet or mandate any particular ordering of balance sheet accounts. However, FASB ASC 210-10-05-4 states that entities usually present a classified balance sheet to facilitate calculation of working capital. FASB ASC 210-10-05-5 indicates that in the statements of manufacturing, trading, and service entities, assets and liabilities are generally classified and segregated. Financial institutions generally present unclassified balance sheets. The FASB ASC glossary includes definitions of *current assets* and *current liabilities* for when an entity presents a classified balance sheet. FASB ASC 210-10-45 provides additional guidance for determining these classifications.

DISCLOSURE

Author's Note

In December 2011, FASB issued Accounting Standards Update (ASU) No. 2011-11, *Balance Sheet (Topic 210): Disclosures about Offsetting Assets and Liabilities*, to enhance comparability of financial statements prepared in accordance with GAAP and IFRS. The amendments in this update will enhance disclosures by requiring improved information about financial instruments and derivative instruments that are either (*a*) offset in accordance with either FASB ASC 210-20-45 or 815-10-45 or (*b*) subject to an enforceable master netting arrangement or similar agreement, irrespective of whether they are offset in accordance with either of the aforementioned FASB ASC sections. The additional disclosures will enable financial statement users to better understand the effect of such arrangements on their financial position. Entities are required to apply the amendments in this Update for annual reporting periods beginning on or after January 1, 2013, and interim periods within those annual periods. Given the effective date of this Update, no survey entity will have adopted these requirements in its 2011 financial statements.

2.04 FASB ASC sets forth disclosure guidelines regarding capital structure and other balance sheet items. SEC regulations also contain additional requirements for disclosures that registrants should provide outside the financial statements.

2.05 FASB ASC 205-10-50 states that reclassifications or other changes in the manner of, or basis for, presenting corresponding items for two or more periods should be explained. This conforms with the well-recognized principle that any change that affects comparability of financial statements should be disclosed.

2.06

TABLE 2-1: BALANCE SHEET CLASSIFICATION*

	Number of Entities		
	2011	2010	2009
Classified balance sheet...........................	470	480	N/C^
Unclassified balance sheet.......................	30	18	N/C^
Other, described......................................	—	2	N/C^
Total Entities.......................................	**500**	**500**	**500**

* Appearing in the balance sheet or notes to financial statements, or both.
^ N/C = Not compiled. Line item was not included in the table for the year shown.

PRESENTATION AND DISCLOSURE EXCERPTS

Reclassifications

2.07

JPMORGAN CHASE & CO. (DEC)

NOTES TO CONSOLIDATED FINANCIAL STATEMENTS

Note 1—Basis of Presentation (in part)

Certain amounts reported in prior periods have been reclassified to conform to the current presentation.

Note 3—Fair Value Measurement (in part)

The following table presents the carrying values and estimated fair values of financial assets and liabilities.

December 31 (In billions)	2011		2010	
	Carrying Value	Estimated Fair Value	Carrying Value	Estimated Fair Value
Financial Assets				
Assets for which fair value approximates carrying value	$ 144.9	$ 144.9	$ 49.2	$ 49.2
Accrued interest and accounts receivable	61.5	61.5	70.1	70.1
Federal funds sold and securities purchased under resale agreements (included $24.9 and $20.3 at fair value)	235.3	235.3	222.6	222.6
Securities borrowed (included $15.3 and $14.0 at fair value)	142.5	142.5	123.6	123.6
Trading assets	444.0	444.0	489.9	489.9
Securities (included $364.8 and $316.3 at fair value)	364.8	364.8	316.3	316.3
Loans (included $2.1 and $2.0 at fair value)[a]	696.1	695.8	660.7	663.5
Mortgage servicing rights at fair value	7.2	7.2	13.6	13.6
Other (included $16.5 and $18.2 at fair value)	66.3	66.8	64.9	65.0
Financial Liabilities				
Deposits (included $4.9 and $4.4 at fair value)	$1,127.8	$1,128.3	$930.4	$931.5
Federal funds purchased and securities loaned or sold under repurchase agreements (included $9.5 and $4.1 at fair value)	213.5	213.5	276.6	276.6
Commercial paper	51.6	51.6	35.4	35.4
Other borrowed funds (included $9.6 and $9.9 at fair value)[b]	21.9	21.9	34.3	34.3
Trading liabilities	141.7	141.7	146.2	146.2
Accounts payable and other liabilities (included $0.1 and $0.2 at fair value)	167.0	166.9	138.2	138.2
Beneficial interests issued by consolidated VIEs (included $1.3 and $1.5 at fair value)	66.0	66.2	77.6	77.9
Long-term debt and junior subordinated deferrable interest debentures (included $34.7 and $38.8 at fair value)[b]	256.8	254.2	270.7	271.9

[a] Fair value is typically estimated using a discounted cash flow model that incorporates the characteristics of the underlying loans (including principal, contractual interest rate and contractual fees) and other key inputs, including expected lifetime credit losses, interest rates, prepayment rates, and primary origination or secondary market spreads. For certain loans, the fair value is measured based on the value of the underlying collateral. The difference between the estimated fair value and carrying value of a financial asset or liability is the result of the different methodologies used to determine fair value as compared with carrying value. For example, credit losses are estimated for a financial asset's remaining life in a fair value calculation but are estimated for a loss emergence period in a loan loss reserve calculation; future loan income (interest and fees) is incorporated in a fair value calculation but is generally not considered in a loan loss reserve calculation. For a further discussion of the Firm's methodologies for estimating the fair value of loans and lending-related commitments, see pages 186–188 of this Note.

[b] Effective January 1, 2011, $23.0 billion of long-term advances from FHLBs were reclassified from other borrowed funds to long-term debt. The prior-year period has been revised to conform with the current presentation.

SEC 2.07

Note 14—Loans (in part)

Loan Portfolio (in part)

The following table summarizes the Firm's loan balances by portfolio segment.

December 31, 2011 (In millions)	Wholesale	Consumer, Excluding Credit Card	Credit Card	Total
Retained	$278,395	$308,427	$132,175	$718,997[a]
Held-for-sale	2,524	—	102	2,626
At fair value	2,097	—	—	2,097
Total	$283,016	$308,427	$132,277	$723,720

December 31, 2010 (In millions)	Wholesale	Consumer, Excluding Credit Card	Credit Card	Total
Retained	$222,510	$327,464	$135,524	$685,498[a]
Held-for-sale	3,147	154	2,152	5,453
At fair value	1,976	—	—	1,976
Total	$227,633	$327,618	$137,676	$692,927

[a] Loans (other than PCI loans and those for which the fair value option has been selected) are presented net of unearned income, unamortized discounts and premiums, and net deferred loan costs of $2.7 billion and $1.9 billion at December 31, 2011 and 2010, respectively.

The following table provides information about the carrying value of retained loans purchased, retained loans sold and retained loans reclassified to held-for-sale during the periods indicated. These tables exclude loans recorded at fair value. On an ongoing basis, the Firm manages its exposure to credit risk. Selling loans is one way that the Firm reduces its credit exposures.

Year Ended December 31, 2011 (In millions)	Wholesale	Consumer, Excluding Credit Card	Credit Card	Total
Purchases	$ 906	$7,525	$ —	$8,431
Sales	3,289	1,384	—	4,673
Retained loans reclassified to held-for-sale	538	—	2,006	2,544

CASH AND CASH EQUIVALENTS

PRESENTATION

2.08 Cash is commonly considered to consist of currency and demand deposits. The FASB ASC glossary defines *cash equivalents* as short-term, highly liquid investments that are both readily convertible into known amounts of cash and so near their maturity that they present an insignificant risk of changes in value because of changes in interest rates. Generally, only investments with original maturities of three months or less qualify under that definition.

DISCLOSURE

2.09 Rule 5-02.1 of Regulation S-X states that separate disclosure should be made of the cash and cash items that are restricted regarding withdrawal or usage. The provisions of any restrictions should be described in a note to the financial statements. Restrictions may include legally restricted deposits held as compensating balances against short-term borrowing arrangements, contracts entered into with others, or company statements of intention with regard to particular deposits; however, time deposits and short-term certificates of deposit are not generally included in legally restricted deposits. Compensating balance arrangements that do not legally restrict the use of cash should be described in the notes to the financial statements; the amount involved, if determinable, for the most recent audited balance sheet and any subsequent unaudited balance sheet should be disclosed. Compensating balances maintained under an agreement to assure future credit availability should be disclosed, along with the amount and terms of such agreement.

PRESENTATION AND DISCLOSURE EXCERPTS

Reclassifications

2.10

THE CLOROX COMPANY (JUN)

CONSOLIDATED BALANCE SHEETS (in part)

	As of June 30	
Dollars in millions, except share amounts	**2011**	**2010**
Assets		
Current assets		
Cash and cash equivalents	$ 259	$ 87
Receivables, net	525	540
Inventories, net	382	332
Assets held for sale, net	—	405
Other current assets	113	125
Total current assets	1,279	1,489

NOTES TO CONSOLIDATED FINANCIAL STATEMENTS

(Dollars in millions, except per share amounts)

Note 1. Summary of Significant Accounting Policies (in part)

Cash and Cash Equivalents

Cash equivalents consist of highly liquid instruments, time deposits and money market funds with an initial maturity at purchase of three months or less. The fair value of cash and cash equivalents approximates the carrying amount.

The Company's cash position includes amounts held by foreign subsidiaries, and, as a result, the repatriation of certain cash balances from some of the Company's foreign subsidiaries could result in additional tax costs. However, these cash balances are generally available without legal restriction to fund local business operations. In addition, a portion of the Company's cash balances is held in U.S. dollars by foreign subsidiaries, whose functional currency is their local currency. Such U.S. dollar balances are reported on the foreign subsidiaries books, in their functional currency, with the impact from foreign currency exchange rate differences recorded in other (income) expense, net. The Company's cash holdings as of the end of fiscal years 2011 and 2010 were as follows:

	2011	2010
Non-U.S. dollar balances held by non-U.S. dollar functional currency subsidiaries	$ 98	$42
U.S. dollar balances held by non-U.S. dollar functional currency subsidiaries	15	13
Non-U.S. dollar balances held by U.S. dollar functional currency subsidiaries	26	7
U.S. dollar balances held by U.S. dollar functional currency subsidiaries	120	25
Total	$259	$87

MARKETABLE SECURITIES

RECOGNITION AND MEASUREMENT

2.11 FASB ASC 320, *Investments—Debt and Equity Securities*, provides guidance on accounting for and reporting investments in equity securities that have readily determinable fair values and all investments in debt securities.

2.12 FASB ASC 320-10-25 requires that at acquisition, entities classify certain debt and equity securities into one of three categories: held to maturity, trading, or available for sale. Investments in debt securities that the entity has the positive intent and ability to hold to maturity are classified as held to maturity and reported at amortized cost in the statement of financial position. Securities that are bought and held principally for the purpose of selling them in the near term (thus held for only a short period of time) are classified as trading securities and reported at fair value. Trading generally reflects active and frequent buying and selling, and trading securities are generally used to generate profit on short-term differences in price. Investments not classified as either held-to-maturity or trading securities are classified as available-for-sale securities and reported at fair value. Unrealized holding gains and losses are included in earnings for trading securities and other comprehensive income for available-for-sale securities.

2.13 FASB ASC 320 indicates when certain investments are considered impaired, whether that impairment is other than temporary, and the measurement and recognition of an impairment loss. FASB ASC 320 also provides guidance on accounting considerations for debt securities subsequent to the recognition of an other-than-temporary impairment and requires certain disclosures about unrealized losses that have not been recognized as other-than-temporary impairments.

PRESENTATION

2.14 Under FASB ASC 320-10-45-2, an entity that presents a classified balance sheet should report individual held-to-maturity securities, individual available-for-sale securities, and individual trading securities as either current or noncurrent.

DISCLOSURE

2.15 FASB ASC 320-10-50 includes detailed disclosure requirements for various marketable securities, including matters such as the nature and risks of the securities; cost, fair value, and transaction information; contractual maturities; impairment of securities; and certain transaction information.

2.16 By definition, investments in debt and equity securities are financial instruments. FASB ASC 825, *Financial Instruments*, requires disclosure of the fair value of those investments for which it is practicable to estimate that value, the methods and assumptions used in estimating the fair value of marketable securities, and a description of any changes in the methods and assumptions during the period. Under FASB ASC 825-10-50-3, the fair value disclosures are optional for certain nonpublic entities with assets less than $100 million.

2.17 FASB ASC 820, *Fair Value Measurement*, defines *fair value*, sets out a framework for measuring fair value, and requires certain disclosures about fair value measurements. FASB ASC 820 clarifies the definition of fair value as an exit price (that is, a price that would be received to sell, versus acquire, an asset or paid to transfer a liability). FASB ASC 820 emphasizes that fair value is a market-based measurement. It establishes a fair value hierarchy that distinguishes between assumptions developed based on market data obtained from independent external sources and the reporting entity's own assumptions. Further, FASB ASC 820 specifies that fair value measurement should consider adjustment for risk, such as the risk inherent in a valuation technique or its inputs. For assets measured at fair value, whether on a recurring or nonrecurring basis, FASB ASC 820 specifies the required disclosures concerning the inputs used to measure fair value.

2.18 FASB ASC 820-10-50 requires robust disclosures about different classes of assets and liabilities measured at fair value; the valuation techniques and inputs used; the activity in level 3 fair value measurements; and the transfers between levels 1, 2, and 3. "Pending Content" in FASB ASC 820-10-50-1 states that the reporting entity should disclose information that helps users of its financial statements assess both of the following:

a. For assets and liabilities that are measured at fair value on a recurring or nonrecurring basis in the statement of financial position after initial recognition, the valuation techniques and inputs used to develop those measurements

b. For recurring fair value measurements using significant unobservable inputs (Level 3), the effect of the measurements on earnings (or changes in net assets) or other comprehensive income for the period.

2.19 "Pending Content" in FASB ASC 820-10-5-2 states that the reporting entity should disclose all of the following information for each interim and annual period separately for each class of assets and liabilities:

a. the fair value measurement at the reporting date

b. the level within the fair value hierarchy in which the fair value measurement in its entirety falls (quoted prices in active markets for identical assets or liabilities—Level 1; significant other observable inputs—Level 2; significant unobservable inputs—Level 3)

c. the amounts of significant transfers between Level 1 and Level 2 and the reasons for the transfers

d. for Level 3 measurements, a reconciliation of beginning and ending balances showing gains and losses for the period, purchases, sales, issuances, and settlements, and transfers in and/or out of Level 3 and reasons for those transfers.

e. the amount of total gains or losses for the period that are attributable to the change in unrealized gains or losses relating to those assets and liabilities still held at the reporting date and a description of where those unrealized gains or losses are reported in the statement of income (or activities).

f. for Level 2 and Level 3 measurements, a description of the valuation technique and the inputs used in determining the fair values of each class of assets or liabilities.

Author's Note

In May 2011, FASB issued ASU No. 2011-04, *Fair Value Measurement (Topic 820): Amendments to Achieve Common Fair Value Measurement and Disclosure Requirements in U.S. GAAP and IFRSs.* According to FASB, the objective of this update is to improve the comparability of fair value measurements presented and disclosed in financial statements prepared in accordance with GAAP and IFRSs by changing the wording used to describe many of the requirements in GAAP for measuring fair value and disclosing information about fair value measurements. The amendments include those that clarify FASB's intent about the application of existing fair value measurement and disclosure requirements and those that change a particular principle or requirement for measuring fair value or disclosing information about fair value measurements. This Update, which is to be applied prospectively, is effective for public entities during interim and annual periods beginning after December 15, 2011 (early application is not permitted). For nonpublic entities, the amendments are effective for annual periods beginning after December 15, 2011. Nonpublic entities may early implement during interim periods beginning after December 15, 2011. Given the effective date of this Update, no survey entity will have adopted these requirements in its 2011 financial statements.

2.20 FASB ASC 825 permits entities to choose to measure many financial instruments and certain other items at fair value that are not currently required to be measured at fair value. Further, under FASB ASC 825, a business entity shall report unrealized gains and losses on eligible items for which the fair value option has been elected in earnings at each subsequent reporting date. The irrevocable election of the fair value option is made on an instrument-by-instrument basis and applied to the entire instrument, not just a portion of it. FASB ASC 825 also establishes presentation and disclosure requirements designed to facilitate comparison between entities that choose different measurement attributes for similar types of assets and liabilities. The required disclosures are optional for certain nonpublic entities.

2.21

TABLE 2-2: FAIR VALUE INPUTS FOR DEBT AND EQUITY SECURITIES

Table 2-2 lists the level of input for the fair value of marketable securities.

	Number of Entities		
	2011	2010	2009
Available for Sale Securities			
No available for sale securities.....................	249	245	N/C*
Debt securities: fair value level 1 inputs.........	128	109	N/C*
Debt securities: fair value level 2 inputs.........	136	107	N/C*
Debt securities: fair value level 3 inputs.........	50	39	N/C*
Debt securities: other, described...................	2	2	N/C*
Equity securities: fair value level 1 inputs......	133	155	N/C*
Equity securities: fair value level 2 inputs......	57	67	N/C*
Equity securities: fair value level 3 inputs......	16	19	N/C*
Equity securities: other, described................	—	2	N/C*
Held to Maturity Securities			
No held to maturity securities........................	467	461	N/C*
Debt securities: amortized cost.....................	11	9	N/C*
Debt securities: fair value level 1 inputs.........	9	12	N/C*
Debt securities: fair value level 2 inputs.........	10	6	N/C*
Debt securities: fair value level 3 inputs.........	5	2	N/C*
Debt securities: other, described...................	2	1	N/C*
Trading Securities			
No trading securities....................................	445	448	N/C*
Debt securities: fair value level 1 inputs.........	21	10	N/C*
Debt securities: fair value level 2 inputs.........	11	9	N/C*
Debt securities: fair value level 3 inputs.........	7	2	N/C*
Debt securities: other, described...................	—	1	N/C*
Equity securities: fair value level 1 inputs......	34	31	N/C*
Equity securities: fair value level 2 inputs......	17	11	N/C*
Equity securities: fair value level 3 inputs......	7	2	N/C*
Equity securities: other, described................	1	1	N/C*

* N/C = Not compiled. Line item was not included in the table for the year shown.

PRESENTATION AND DISCLOSURE EXCERPTS

Marketable Securities—Available-for-Sale Securities

2.22

CISCO SYSTEMS, INC. (JUL)

CONSOLIDATED BALANCE SHEETS (in part)

(In millions, except par value)

	July 30, 2011	July 31, 2010
Assets		
Current assets:		
Cash and cash equivalents	$ 7,662	$ 4,581
Investments	36,923	35,280
Accounts receivable, net of allowance for doubtful accounts of $204 at July 30, 2011 and $235 at July 31, 2010	4,698	4,929
Inventories	1,486	1,327
Financing receivables, net	3,111	2,303
Deferred tax assets	2,410	2,126
Other current assets	941	875
Total current assets	57,231	51,421

NOTES TO CONSOLIDATED FINANCIAL STATEMENTS

2. Summary of Significant Accounting Policies (in part)

(b) Available-for-Sale Investments. The Company classifies its investments in both fixed income securities and publicly traded equity securities as available-for-sale investments. Fixed income securities primarily consist of U.S. government securities, U.S. government agency securities, non-U.S. government and agency securities, corporate debt securities, and asset-backed securities. These available-for-sale investments are primarily held in the custody of a major financial institution. The specific identification method is used to determine the cost basis of fixed income securities sold. The weighted-average method is used to determine the cost basis of publicly traded equity securities sold. These investments are recorded in the Consolidated Balance Sheets at fair value. Unrealized gains and losses on these investments, to the extent the investments are unhedged, are included as a separate component of accumulated other comprehensive income (AOCI), net of tax. The Company classifies its investments as current based on the nature of the investments and their availability for use in current operations.

8. Investments (in part)

(a) Summary of Available-for-Sale Investments

The following tables summarize the Company's available-for-sale investments (in millions):

July 30, 2011	Amortized Cost	Gross Unrealized Gains	Gross Unrealized Losses	Fair Value
Fixed income securities:				
U.S. government securities	$19,087	$ 52	$ —	$19,139
U.S. government agency securities[1]	8,742	35	(1)	8,776
Non-U.S. government and agency securities[2]	3,119	14	(1)	3,132
Corporate debt securities	4,333	65	(4)	4,394
Asset-backed securities	120	5	(4)	121
Total fixed income securities	35,401	171	(10)	35,562
Publicly traded equity securities	734	639	(12)	1,361
Total	$36,135	$810	$(22)	$36,923

July 31, 2010	Amortized Cost	Gross Unrealized Gains	Gross Unrealized Losses	Fair Value
Fixed income securities:				
U.S. government securities	$16,570	$ 42	$ —	$16,612
U.S. government agency securities[1]	13,511	68	—	13,579
Non-U.S. government and agency securities[2]	1,452	15	—	1,467
Corporate debt securities	2,179	64	(21)	2,222
Asset-backed securities	145	9	(5)	149
Total fixed income securities	33,857	198	(26)	34,029
Publicly traded equity securities	889	411	(49)	1,251
Total	$34,746	$609	$(75)	$35,280

[1] Includes corporate securities that are guaranteed by the Federal Deposit Insurance Corporation (FDIC).
[2] Includes agency and corporate securities that are guaranteed by non-U.S. governments.

(b) Gains and Losses on Available-for-Sale Investments

The following tables present the gross and net realized gains (losses) related to the Company's available-for-sale investments (in millions):

Years Ended	July 30, 2011	July 31, 2010	July 25, 2009
Gross realized gains	$ 348	$ 279	$ 435
Gross realized losses	(169)	(110)	(459)
Total	$ 179	$ 169	$ (24)

Years Ended	July 30, 2011	July 31, 2010	July 25, 2009
Realized gains (losses) net:			
Publicly traded equity securities	$ 88	$ 66	$ 86
Fixed income securities	91	103	(110)
Total	$179	$169	$ (24)

There were no significant impairment charges on available-for-sale investments for the year ended July 30, 2011. There was no impairment charge for the year ended July 31, 2010 while for the year ended July 25, 2009, net losses on fixed income securities and net gains on publicly traded equity securities included impairment charges of $219 million and $39 million, respectively. The impairment charges for fiscal 2009 were due to a decline in the fair value of the investments below their cost basis that were judged to be other than temporary and were recorded as a reduction to the amortized cost of the respective investments.

The following table summarizes the activity related to credit losses for fixed income securities (in millions):

	July 30, 2011	July 31, 2010
Balance at beginning of fiscal year	$(95)	$(153)
Sales of other-than-temporarily impaired fixed income securities	72	58
Balance at end of fiscal year	$(23)	$ (95)

The following tables present the breakdown of the available-for-sale investments with gross unrealized losses and the duration that those losses had been unrealized at July 30, 2011 and July 31, 2010 (in millions):

July 30, 2011	Unrealized Losses Less Than 12 Months Fair Value	Gross Unrealized Losses	Unrealized Losses 12 Months or Greater Fair Value	Gross Unrealized Losses	Total Fair Value	Gross Unrealized Losses
Fixed income securities:						
U.S. government agency securities[1]	$2,310	$ (1)	$ —	$—	$2,310	$ (1)
Non-U.S. government and agency securities[2]	875	(1)	—	—	875	(1)
Corporate debt securities	548	(2)	56	(2)	604	(4)
Asset-backed securities	—	—	105	(4)	105	(4)
Total fixed income securities	3,733	(4)	161	(6)	3,894	(10)
Publicly traded equity securities	112	(12)	—	—	112	(12)
Total	$3,845	$(16)	$161	$(6)	$4,006	$(22)

July 30, 2010	Unrealized Losses Less Than 12 Months Fair Value	Gross Unrealized Losses	Unrealized Losses 12 Months or Greater Fair Value	Gross Unrealized Losses	Total Fair Value	Gross Unrealized Losses
Fixed income securities:						
Corporate debt securities	$140	$ (1)	$304	$(20)	$ 444	$(21)
Asset-backed securities	2	—	115	(5)	117	(5)
Total fixed income securities	142	(1)	419	(25)	561	(26)
Publicly traded equity securities	168	(12)	393	(37)	561	(49)
Total	$310	$(13)	$812	$(62)	$1,122	$(75)

[1] Includes corporate securities that are guaranteed by the FDIC.
[2] Includes agency and corporate securities that are guaranteed by non-U.S. governments.

For fixed income securities that have unrealized losses as of July 30, 2011, the Company has determined that (i) it does not have the intent to sell any of these investments and (ii) it is not more likely than not that it will be required to sell any of these investments before recovery of the entire amortized cost basis. In addition, as of July 30, 2011, the Company anticipates that it will recover the entire amortized cost basis of such fixed income securities and has determined that no other-than-temporary impairments associated with credit losses were required to be recognized during the year ended July 30, 2011.

The Company has evaluated its publicly traded equity securities as of July 30, 2011 and has determined that there was no indication of other-than-temporary impairments in the respective categories of unrealized losses. This determination was based on several factors, which include the length of time and extent to which fair value has been less than the cost basis, the financial condition and near-term prospects of the issuer, and the Company's intent and ability to hold the publicly traded equity securities for a period of time sufficient to allow for any anticipated recovery in market value.

Marketable Securities—Held-to-Maturity Securities

2.23

CITIGROUP INC. (DEC)

CONSOLIDATED BALANCE SHEET (in part)

	December 31	
(In millions of dollars, except shares)	2011	2010
Assets		
Cash and due from banks (including segregated cash and other deposits)	$ 28,701	$ 27,972
Deposits with banks	155,784	162,437
Federal funds sold and securities borrowed or purchased under agreements to resell (including $142,862 and $87,512 as of December 31, 2011 and 2010, respectively, at fair value)	275,849	246,717
Brokerage receivables	27,777	31,213
Trading account assets (including $109,719 and $117,554 pledged to creditors at December 31, 2011 and 2010, respectively)	291,734	317,272
Investments (including $14,940 and $12,546 pledged to creditors at December 31, 2011 and 2010, respectively, and $274,040 and $281,174 at December 31, 2011 and 2010, respectively, at fair value)	293,413	318,164
Loans, net of unearned income		
Consumer (including $1,326 and $1,745 as of December 31, 2011 and 2010, respectively, at fair value)	423,731	455,732
Corporate (including $3,939 and $2,627 at December 31, 2011 and 2010, respectively, at fair value)	223,511	193,062
Loans, net of unearned income	$ 647,242	$ 648,794
Allowance for loan losses	(30,115)	(40,655)
Total loans, net	$ 617,127	$ 608,139
Goodwill	25,413	26,152
Intangible assets (other than MSRs)	6,600	7,504
Mortgage servicing rights (MSRs)	2,569	4,554
Other assets (including $11,241 and $19,530 as of December 31, 2011 and 2010, respectively, at fair value)	148,911	163,778
Total assets	$1,873,878	$1,913,902

NOTES TO CONSOLIDATED FINANCIAL STATEMENTS

15. Investments (in part)

Overview

(In millions of dollars)	2011	2010
Securities available-for-sale	$265,204	$274,079
Debt securities held-to-maturity[1]	11,483	29,107
Non-marketable equity securities carried at fair value[2]	8,836	7,095
Non-marketable equity securities carried at cost[3]	7,890	7,883
Total investments	$293,413	$318,164

[1] Recorded at amortized cost less impairment for securities that have credit-related impairment.

[2] Unrealized gains and losses for non-marketable equity securities carried at fair value are recognized in earnings.

[3] Non-marketable equity securities carried at cost primarily consist of shares issued by the Federal Reserve Bank, Federal Home Loan Banks, foreign central banks and various clearing houses of which Citigroup is a member.

Debt Securities Held-to-Maturity

The carrying value and fair value of debt securities held-to-maturity (HTM) at December 31, 2011 and December 31, 2010 were as follows:

(In millions of dollars)	Amortized cost[1]	Net Unrealized Loss Recognized in AOCI	Carrying Value[2]	Gross Unrealized Gains	Gross Unrealized Losses	Fair Value
December 31, 2011						
Debt securities held-to-maturity						
Mortgage-backed securities[3]						
Prime	$ 360	$ 73	$ 287	$ 21	$ 20	$ 288
Alt-A	4,732	1,404	3,328	20	319	3,029
Subprime	383	47	336	1	71	266
Non-U.S. residential	3,487	520	2,967	59	290	2,736
Commercial	513	1	512	4	52	464
Total mortgage-backed securities	$ 9,475	$2,045	$ 7,430	$ 105	$ 752	$ 6,783
State and municipal	$ 1,422	$ 95	$ 1,327	$ 68	$ 72	$ 1,323
Corporate	1,862	113	1,749	—	254	1,495
Asset-backed securities[3]	1,000	23	977	9	87	899
Total debt securities held-to-maturity	$13,759	$2,276	$11,483	$ 182	$1,165	$10,500
December 31, 2010						
Debt securities held-to-maturity						
Mortgage-backed securities[3]						
Prime	$ 4,748	$ 794	$ 3,954	$ 379	$ 11	$ 4,322
Alt-A	11,816	3,008	8,808	536	166	9,178
Subprime	708	75	633	9	72	570
Non-U.S. residential	5,010	793	4,217	259	72	4,404
Commercial	908	21	887	18	96	809
Total mortgage-backed securities	$23,190	$4,691	$18,499	$1,201	$ 417	$19,283
State and municipal	$ 2,523	$ 127	$ 2,396	$ 11	$ 104	$ 2,303
Corporate	6,569	145	6,424	447	267	6,604
Asset-backed securities[3]	1,855	67	1,788	57	54	1,791
Total debt securities held-to-maturity	$34,137	$5,030	$29,107	$1,716	$ 842	$29,981

[1] For securities transferred to HTM from *Trading account assets* in 2008, amortized cost is defined as the fair value of the securities at the date of transfer plus any accretion income and less any impairments recognized in earnings subsequent to transfer. For securities transferred to HTM from AFS in 2008, amortized cost is defined as the original purchase cost, plus or minus any accretion or amortization of a purchase discount or premium, less any impairment recognized in earnings.

[2] HTM securities are carried on the Consolidated Balance Sheet at amortized cost less any unrealized gains and losses recognized in AOCI. The changes in the values of these securities are not reported in the financial statements, except for other-than-temporary impairments. For HTM securities, only the credit loss component of the impairment is recognized in earnings, while the remainder of the impairment is recognized in AOCI.

[3] The Company invests in mortgage-backed and asset-backed securities. These securitizations are generally considered VIEs. The Company's maximum exposure to loss from these VIEs is equal to the carrying amount of the securities, which is reflected in the table above. For mortgage-backed and asset-backed securitizations in which the Company has other involvement, see Note 22 to the Consolidated Financial Statements.

The Company has the positive intent and ability to hold these securities to maturity absent any unforeseen further significant changes in circumstances, including deterioration in credit or with regard to regulatory capital requirements. The net unrealized losses classified in AOCI relate to debt securities reclassified from AFS investments to HTM investments in a prior year. Additionally, for HTM securities that have suffered credit impairment, declines in fair value for reasons other than credit losses are recorded in AOCI. The AOCI balance was $2.3 billion as of December 31, 2011, compared to $5.0 billion as of December 31, 2010. The AOCI balance for HTM securities is amortized over the remaining life of

the related securities as an adjustment of yield in a manner consistent with the accretion of discount on the same debt securities. This will have no impact on the Company's net income because the amortization of the unrealized holding loss reported in equity will offset the effect on interest income of the accretion of the discount on these securities.

For any credit-related impairment on HTM securities, the credit loss component is recognized in earnings.

During the first quarter of 2011, the Company determined that it no longer had the intent to hold $12.7 billion of HTM securities to maturity. As a result, the Company reclassified $10.0 billion carrying value of mortgage-backed, other asset-backed, state and municipal, and corporate debt securities from *Investments* held-to-maturity to *Trading account assets*. The Company also sold an additional $2.7 billion of such HTM securities, recognizing a corresponding receivable from the unsettled sales as of March 31, 2011. As a result of these actions, a net pretax loss of $709 million ($427 million after tax) was recognized in the Consolidated Statement of Income for the three months ended March 31, 2011, composed of gross unrealized gains of $311 million included in *Other revenue*, gross unrealized losses of $1,387 million included in *Other-than-temporary-impairment losses on investments*, and net realized gains of $367 million included in *Realized gains (losses) on sales of investments*. Prior to the reclassification, unrealized losses totalling $1,656 million pretax ($1,012 million after tax) had been reflected in AOCI (see table below) and have now been reflected in the Consolidated Statement of Income, as detailed above.

Citigroup reclassified and sold the securities as part of its overall efforts to mitigate its risk-weighted assets (RWA) in order to comply with significant new regulatory capital requirements which, although not yet implemented or formally adopted, are nonetheless currently being used to assess the forecasted capital adequacy of the Company and other large U.S. banking organizations. These regulatory capital changes, which were largely unforeseen when the Company initially reclassified the debt securities from *Trading account assets* and *Investments* available-for-sale to *Investments* held-to-maturity in the fourth quarter of 2008 (see note 1 to the table below), include: (i) the U.S. Basel II credit and operational risk capital standards; (ii) the Basel Committee's agreed-upon, and the U.S.-proposed, revisions to the market risk capital rules, which significantly increased the risk weightings for certain trading book positions; (iii) the Basel Committee's substantial issuance of Basel III, which raised the quantity and quality of required regulatory capital and materially increased RWA for securitization exposures; and (iv) certain regulatory capital-related provisions in The Dodd-Frank Wall Street Reform and Consumer Protection Act of 2010.

Through December 31, 2011, the Company has sold substantially all of the $12.7 billion of HTM securities that were reclassified to *Trading account assets* in the first quarter of 2011. The carrying value and fair value of debt securities at the date of reclassification or sale were as follows:

(In millions of dollars)	Amortized Cost[2]	Net Unrealized Loss Recognized in AOCI	Carrying Value[3]	Gross Gains	Gross Losses	Fair Value
Held-to-maturity debt securities transferred to *Trading account assets* or sold[1]						
Mortgage-backed securities						
Prime	$ 3,410	$ 528	$ 2,882	$ 131	$131	$ 2,882
Alt-A	5,357	896	4,461	605	188	4,878
Subprime	240	7	233	5	36	202
Non-U.S. residential	317	75	242	76	2	316
Commercial	117	18	99	22	—	121
Total mortgage-backed securities	$ 9,441	$1,524	$ 7,917	$ 839	$357	$ 8,399
State and municipal	$ 900	$ 8	$ 892	$ 68	$ 7	$ 953
Corporate	3,569	115	3,454	396	41	3,809
Asset-backed securities	456	9	447	50	2	495
Total held-to-maturity debt securities transferred to *Trading account assets* or sold[1]	$14,366	$1,656	$12,710	$1,353	$407	$13,656

[1] During the fourth quarter of 2008, $6.647 billion and $6.063 billion carrying value of these debt securities were transferred from *Trading account assets* and *Investments* available-for-sale to *Investments* held-to-maturity, respectively. The transfer of these debt securities from *Trading account assets* was in response to the significant deterioration in market conditions, which was especially acute during the fourth quarter of 2008.

[2] For securities transferred to held-to-maturity from *Trading account assets* in 2008, amortized cost is defined as the fair value amount of the securities at the date of transfer plus any accretion income and less any impairments recognized in earnings subsequent to transfer. For securities transferred to held-to-maturity from available-for-sale in 2008, amortized cost is defined as the original purchase cost, plus or minus any accretion or amortization of a purchase discount or premium, less any impairment recognized in earnings.

[3] Held-to-maturity securities are carried on the Consolidated Balance Sheet at amortized cost and the changes in the value of these securities other than impairment charges are not reported in the financial statements.

The table below shows the fair value of debt securities in HTM that have been in an unrecognized loss position for less than 12 months or for 12 months or longer as of December 31, 2011 and December 31, 2010:

(In millions of dollars)	Less Than 12 Months		12 Months or Longer		Total	
	Fair Value	Gross Unrecognized Losses	Fair Value	Gross Unrecognized Losses	Fair Value	Gross Unrecognized Losses
December 31, 2011						
Debt securities held-to-maturity						
Mortgage-backed securities	$ 735	$ 63	$ 4,827	$ 689	$ 5,562	$ 752
State and municipal	—	—	682	72	682	72
Corporate	—	—	1,427	254	1,427	254
Asset-backed securities	480	71	306	16	786	87
Total debt securities held-to-maturity	$1,215	$134	$ 7,242	$1,031	$ 8,457	$1,165
December 31, 2010						
Debt securities held-to-maturity						
Mortgage-backed securities	$ 339	$ 30	$14,410	$ 387	$14,749	$ 417
State and municipal	24	—	1,273	104	1,297	104
Corporate	1,584	143	1,579	124	3,163	267
Asset-backed securities	159	11	494	43	653	54
Total debt securities held-to-maturity	$2,106	$184	$17,756	$ 658	$19,862	$ 842

Excluded from the gross unrecognized losses presented in the above table are the $2.3 billion and $5.0 billion of gross unrealized losses recorded in AOCI as of December 31, 2011 and December 31, 2010, respectively, mainly related to the HTM securities that were reclassified from AFS investments.

Virtually all of these unrecognized losses relate to securities that have been in a loss position for 12 months or longer at both December 31, 2011 and December 31, 2010.

The following table presents the carrying value and fair value of HTM debt securities by contractual maturity dates as of December 31, 2011 and December 31, 2010:

(In millions of dollars)	December 31, 2011		December 31, 2010	
	Carrying Value	Fair Value	Carrying Value	Fair Value
Mortgage-backed securities				
Due within 1 year	$ —	$ —	$ 21	$ 23
After 1 but within 5 years	275	239	321	309
After 5 but within 10 years	238	224	493	434
After 10 years[1]	6,917	6,320	17,664	18,517
Total	$ 7,430	$ 6,783	$18,499	$19,283
State and municipal				
Due within 1 year	$ 4	$ 4	$ 12	$ 12
After 1 but within 5 years	43	46	55	55
After 5 but within 10 years	31	30	86	85
After 10 years[1]	1,249	1,243	2,243	2,151
Total	$ 1,327	$ 1,323	$ 2,396	$ 2,303
All other[2]				
Due within 1 year	$ 21	$ 21	$ 351	$ 357
After 1 but within 5 years	470	438	1,344	1,621
After 5 but within 10 years	1,404	1,182	4,885	4,765
After 10 years[1]	831	753	1,632	1,652
Total	$ 2,726	$ 2,394	$ 8,212	$ 8,395
Total debt securities held-to-maturity	$11,483	$10,500	$29,107	$29,981

[1] Investments with no stated maturities are included as contractual maturities of greater than 10 years. Actual maturities may differ due to call or prepayment rights.
[2] Includes corporate and asset-backed securities.

SEC 2.23

Marketable Securities—Trading Securities

2.24

JPMORGAN CHASE & CO. (DEC)

CONSOLIDATED BALANCE SHEETS (in part)

December 31

(In millions, except share data)	2011	2010
Assets		
Cash and due from banks	$ 59,602	$ 27,567
Deposits with banks	85,279	21,673
Federal funds sold and securities purchased under resale agreements (included $24,891 and $20,299 at fair value)	235,314	222,554
Securities borrowed (included $15,308 and $13,961 at fair value)	142,462	123,587
Trading assets (included assets pledged of $89,856 and $73,056)	443,963	489,892
Securities (included $364,781 and $316,318 at fair value and assets pledged of $94,691 and $86,891)	364,793	316,336
Loans (included $2,097 and $1,976 at fair value)	723,720	692,927
Allowance for loan losses	(27,609)	(32,266)
Loans, net of allowance for loan losses	696,111	660,661
Accrued interest and accounts receivable	61,478	70,147
Premises and equipment	14,041	13,355
Goodwill	48,188	48,854
Mortgage servicing rights	7,223	13,649
Other intangible assets	3,207	4,039
Other assets (included $16,499 and $18,201 at fair value and assets pledged of $1,316 and $1,485)	104,131	105,291
Total assets[a]	$2,265,792	$2,117,605
Liabilities		
Deposits (included $4,933 and $4,369 at fair value)	$1,127,806	$ 930,369
Federal funds purchased and securities loaned or sold under repurchase agreements (included $9,517 and $4,060 at fair value)	213,532	276,644
Commercial paper	51,631	35,363
Other borrowed funds (included $9,576 and $9,931 at fair value)	21,908	34,325
Trading liabilities	141,695	146,166
Accounts payable and other liabilities (included $51 and $236 at fair value)	202,895	170,330
Beneficial interests issued by consolidated variable interest entities (included $1,250 and $1,495 at fair value)	65,977	77,649
Long-term debt (included $34,720 and $38,839 at fair value)	256,775	270,653
Total liabilities[a]	2,082,219	1,941,499

NOTES TO CONSOLIDATED FINANCIAL STATEMENTS

Note 3—Fair Value Measurement (in part)

The following table presents the asset and liabilities measured at fair value as of December 31, 2011 and 2010 by major product category and fair value hierarchy.

Assets and Liabilities Measured at Fair Value on a Recurring Basis

December 31, 2011 (In millions)	Fair Value Hierarchy Level 1[h]	Level 2[h]	Level 3[h]	Netting Adjustments	Total Fair Value
Federal funds sold and securities purchased under resale agreements	$ —	$ 24,891	$ —	$ —	$ 24,891
Securities borrowed	—	15,308	—	—	15,308
Trading assets:					
Debt instruments:					
Mortgage-backed securities:					
U.S. government agencies[a]	27,082	7,801	86	—	34,969
Residential—nonagency	—	2,956	796	—	3,752
Commercial—nonagency	—	870	1,758	—	2,628
Total mortgage-backed securities	27,082	11,627	2,640	—	41,349
U.S. Treasury and government agencies[a]	11,508	8,391	—	—	19,899
Obligations of U.S. states and municipalities	—	15,117	1,619	—	16,736
Certificates of deposit, bankers' acceptances and commercial paper	—	2,615	—	—	2,615
Non-U.S. government debt securities	18,618	40,080	104	—	58,802
Corporate debt securities	—	33,938	6,373	—	40,311
Loans[b]	—	21,589	12,209	—	33,798
Asset-backed securities	—	2,406	7,965	—	10,371
Total debt instruments	57,208	135,763	30,910	—	223,881
Equity securities	93,799	3,502	1,177	—	98,478
Physical commodities[c]	21,066	4,898	—	—	25,964
Other	—	2,283	880	—	3,163
Total debt and equity instruments[d]	172,073	146,446	32,967	—	351,486
Derivative receivables:					
Interest rate	1,324	1,433,469	6,728	(1,395,152)	46,369
Credit	—	152,569	17,081	(162,966)	6,684
Foreign exchange	833	162,689	4,641	(150,273)	17,890
Equity	—	43,604	4,132	(40,943)	6,793
Commodity	4,561	50,409	2,459	(42,688)	14,741
Total derivative receivables[e]	6,718	1,842,740	35,041	(1,792,022)	92,477
Total trading assets	178,791	1,989,186	68,008	(1,792,022)	443,963
Available-for-sale securities:					
Mortgage-backed securities:					
U.S. government agencies[a]	92,426	14,681	—	—	107,107
Residential—nonagency	—	67,554	3	—	67,557
Commercial—nonagency	—	10,962	267	—	11,229
Total mortgage-backed securities	92,426	93,197	270	—	185,893
U.S. Treasury and government agencies[a]	3,837	4,514	—	—	8,351
Obligations of U.S. states and municipalities	36	16,246	258	—	16,540
Certificates of deposit	—	3,017	—	—	3,017
Non-U.S. government debt securities	25,381	19,884	—	—	45,265
Corporate debt securities	—	62,176	—	—	62,176
Asset-backed securities:					
Credit card receivables	—	4,655	—	—	4,655
Collateralized loan obligations	—	116	24,745	—	24,861
Other	—	11,105	213	—	11,318
Equity securities	2,667	38	—	—	2,705
Total available-for-sale securities	124,347	214,948	25,486	—	364,781
Loans	—	450	1,647	—	2,097
Mortgage servicing rights	—	—	7,223	—	7,223
Other assets:					
Private equity investments[f]	99	706	6,751	—	7,556
All other	4,336	233	4,374	—	8,943
Total other assets	4,435	939	11,125	—	16,499
Total assets measured at fair value on a recurring basis[g]	$307,573	$2,245,722	$113,489	$(1,792,022)	$874,762

(continued)

SEC 2.24

| December 31, 2011 | Fair Value Hierarchy | | | Netting | Total |
(In millions)	Level 1[h]	Level 2[h]	Level 3[h]	Adjustments	Fair Value
Deposits	$ —	$ 3,515	$ 1,418	$ —	$ 4,933
Federal funds purchased and securities loaned or sold under repurchase agreements	—	9,517	—	—	9,517
Other borrowed funds	—	8,069	1,507	—	9,576
Trading liabilities:					
Debt and equity instruments[d]	50,830	15,677	211	—	66,718
Derivative payables:					
Interest rate	1,537	1,395,113	3,167	(1,371,807)	28,010
Credit	—	155,772	9,349	(159,511)	5,610
Foreign exchange	846	159,258	5,904	(148,573)	17,435
Equity	—	39,129	7,237	(36,711)	9,655
Commodity	3,114	53,684	3,146	(45,677)	14,267
Total derivative payables[e]	5,497	1,802,956	28,803	(1,762,279)	74,977
Total trading liabilities	56,327	1,818,633	29,014	(1,762,279)	141,695
Accounts payable and other liabilities	—	—	51	—	51
Beneficial interests issued by consolidated VIEs	—	459	791	—	1,250
Long-term debt	—	24,410	10,310	—	34,720
Total liabilities measured at fair value on a recurring basis	$ 56,327	$1,864,603	$ 43,091	$(1,762,279)	$201,742

| December 31, 2010 | Fair Value Hierarchy | | | Netting | Total |
(In millions)	Level 1[h]	Level 2[h]	Level 3[h]	Adjustments	Fair Value
Federal funds sold and securities purchased under resale agreements	$ —	$ 20,299	$ —	$ —	$ 20,299
Securities borrowed	—	13,961	—	—	13,961
Trading assets:					
Debt instruments:					
Mortgage-backed securities:					
U.S. government agencies[a]	36,813	10,738	174	—	47,725
Residential—nonagency	—	2,807	687	—	3,494
Commercial—nonagency	—	1,093	2,069	—	3,162
Total mortgage-backed securities	36,813	14,638	2,930	—	54,381
U.S. Treasury and government agencies[a]	12,863	9,026	—	—	21,889
Obligations of U.S. states and municipalities	—	11,715	2,257	—	13,972
Certificates of deposit, bankers' acceptances and commercial paper	—	3,248	—	—	3,248
Non-U.S. government debt securities	31,127	38,482	202	—	69,811
Corporate debt securities	—	42,280	4,946	—	47,226
Loans[b]	—	21,736	13,144	—	34,880
Asset-backed securities	—	2,743	8,460	—	11,203
Total debt instruments	80,803	143,868	31,939	—	256,610
Equity securities	124,400	3,153	1,685	—	129,238
Physical commodities[c]	18,327	2,708	—	—	21,035
Other	—	1,598	930	—	2,528
Total debt and equity instruments[d]	223,530	151,327	34,554	—	409,411
Derivative receivables:					
Interest rate	2,278	1,120,282	5,422	(1,095,427)	32,555
Credit	—	111,827	17,902	(122,004)	7,725
Foreign exchange	1,121	163,114	4,236	(142,613)	25,858
Equity	30	38,718	4,885	(39,429)	4,204
Commodity	1,324	56,076	2,197	(49,458)	10,139
Total derivative receivables[e]	4,753	1,490,017	34,642	(1,448,931)	80,481
Total trading assets	228,283	1,641,344	69,196	(1,448,931)	489,892
Available-for-sale securities:					
Mortgage-backed securities:					
U.S. government agencies[a]	104,736	15,490	—	—	120,226
Residential—nonagency	1	48,969	5	—	48,975
Commercial—nonagency	—	5,403	251	—	5,654
Total mortgage-backed securities	104,737	69,862	256	—	174,855

(continued)

December 31, 2010 (In millions)	Fair Value Hierarchy			Netting Adjustments	Total Fair Value
	Level 1[h]	Level 2[h]	Level 3[h]		
U.S. Treasury and government agencies[a]	$ 522	$ 10,826	$ —	$ —	$ 11,348
Obligations of U.S. states and municipalities	31	11,272	256	—	11,559
Certificates of deposit	6	3,641	—	—	3,647
Non-U.S. government debt securities	13,107	7,670	—	—	20,777
Corporate debt securities	—	61,793			61,793
Asset-backed securities:					
Credit card receivables	—	7,608	—	—	7,608
Collateralized loan obligations	—	128	13,470	—	13,598
Other	—	8,777	305	—	9,082
Equity securities	1,998	53	—	—	2,051
Total available-for-sale securities	120,401	181,630	14,287	—	316,318
Loans	—	510	1,466	—	1,976
Mortgage servicing rights	—	—	13,649	—	13,649
Other assets:					
Private equity investments[f]	49	826	7,862	—	8,737
All other	5,093	192	4,179	—	9,464
Total other assets	5,142	1,018	12,041	—	18,201
Total assets measured at fair value on a recurring basis[g]	$353,826	$1,858,762	$110,639	$(1,448,931)	$874,296
Deposits	$ —	$ 3,596	$ 773	$ —	$ 4,369
Federal funds purchased and securities loaned or sold under repurchase agreements	—	4,060	—	—	4,060
Other borrowed funds	—	8,547	1,384	—	9,931
Trading liabilities:					
Debt and equity instruments[d]	58,468	18,425	54	—	76,947
Derivative payables:					
Interest rate	2,625	1,085,233	2,586	(1,070,057)	20,387
Credit	—	112,545	12,516	(119,923)	5,138
Foreign exchange	972	158,908	4,850	(139,715)	25,015
Equity	22	39,046	7,331	(35,949)	10,450
Commodity	862	54,611	3,002	(50,246)	8,229
Total derivative payables[e]	4,481	1,450,343	30,285	(1,415,890)	69,219
Total trading liabilities	62,949	1,468,768	30,339	(1,415,890)	146,166
Accounts payable and other liabilities	—	—	236	—	236
Beneficial interests issued by consolidated VIEs	—	622	873	—	1,495
Long-term debt	—	25,795	13,044	—	38,839
Total liabilities measured at fair value on a recurring basis	$ 62,949	$1,511,388	$ 46,649	$(1,415,890)	$205,096

[a] At December 31, 2011 and 2010, included total U.S. government-sponsored enterprise obligations of $122.4 billion and $137.3 billion respectively, which were predominantly mortgage-related.

[b] At December 31, 2011 and 2010, included within trading loans were $20.1 billion and $22.7 billion, respectively, of residential first-lien mortgages, and $2.0 billion and $2.6 billion, respectively, of commercial first-lien mortgages. Residential mortgage loans include conforming mortgage loans originated with the intent to sell to U.S. government agencies of $11.0 billion and $13.1 billion, respectively, and reverse mortgages of $4.0 billion and $4.0 billion, respectively.

[c] Physical commodities inventories are generally accounted for at the lower of cost or fair value.

[d] Balances reflect the reduction of securities owned (long positions) by the amount of securities sold but not yet purchased (short positions) when the long and short positions have identical Committee on Uniform Security Identification Procedures numbers ("CUSIPs").

[e] As permitted under U.S. GAAP, the Firm has elected to net derivative receivables and derivative payables and the related cash collateral received and paid when a legally enforceable master netting agreement exists. For purposes of the tables above, the Firm does not reduce derivative receivables and derivative payables balances for this netting adjustment, either within or across the levels of the fair value hierarchy, as such netting is not relevant to a presentation based on the transparency of inputs to the valuation of an asset or liability. Therefore, the balances reported in the fair value hierarchy table are gross of any counterparty netting adjustments. However, if the Firm were to net such balances within level 3, the reduction in the level 3 derivative receivable and payable balances would be $11.7 billion and $12.7 billion at December 31, 2011 and 2010, respectively; this is exclusive of the netting benefit associated with cash collateral, which would further reduce the level 3 balances.

[f] Private equity instruments represent investments within the Corporate/Private Equity line of business. The cost basis of the private equity investment portfolio totaled $9.5 billion and $10.0 billion at December 31, 2011 and 2010, respectively.

[g] At December 31, 2011 and 2010, balances included investments valued at net asset values of $10.8 billion and $12.1 billion, respectively, of which $5.3 billion and $5.9 billion, respectively, were classified in level 1, $1.2 billion and $2.0 billion, respectively, in level 2, and $4.3 billion and $4.2 billion, respectively, in level 3.

[h] For the years ended December 31, 2011 and 2010, there were no significant transfers between levels 1 and 2. For the year ended December 31, 2011, transfers from level 3 into level 2 included $2.6 billion of long-term debt due to a decrease in valuation uncertainty of certain structured notes. For the year ended December 31, 2010, transfers from level 3 into level 2 included $1.2 billion of trading loans due to increased price transparency. There were no significant transfers into level 3 for the years ended December 31, 2011 and 2010. All transfers are assumed to occur at the beginning of the reporting period.

SEC 2.24

Trading Assets and Liabilities

Trading assets include debt and equity instruments owned by JPMorgan Chase ("long" positions) that are held for client market-making and client-driven activities, as well as for certain risk management activities, certain loans managed on a fair value basis and for which the Firm has elected the fair value option, and physical commodities inventories that are generally accounted for at the lower of cost or fair value. Trading liabilities include debt and equity instruments that the Firm has sold to other parties but does not own ("short" positions). The Firm is obligated to purchase instruments at a future date to cover the short positions. Included in trading assets and trading liabilities are the reported receivables (unrealized gains) and payables (unrealized losses) related to derivatives. Trading assets and liabilities are carried at fair value on the Consolidated Balance Sheets. Balances reflect the reduction of securities owned (long positions) by the amount of securities sold but not yet purchased (short positions) when the long and short positions have identical Committee on Uniform Security Identification Procedures numbers ("CUSIPs").

Trading Assets and Liabilities—Average Balances

Average trading assets and liabilities were as follows for the periods indicated.

Year Ended December 31

(In millions)	2011	2010	2009
Trading assets—debt and equity instruments[a]	$393,890	$354,441	$318,063
Trading assets—derivative receivables	90,003	84,676	110,457
Trading liabilities—debt and equity instruments[a][b]	81,916	78,159	60,224
Trading liabilities—derivative payables	71,539	65,714	77,901

[a] Balances reflect the reduction of securities owned (long positions) by the amount of securities sold, but not yet purchased (short positions) when the long and short positions have identical CUSIP numbers.
[b] Primarily represent securities sold, not yet purchased.

CURRENT RECEIVABLES

PRESENTATION

2.25 FASB ASC 310, *Receivables*, indicates that loans or trade receivables may be presented on the balance sheet as aggregate amounts. However, major categories of loans or trade receivables should be presented separately either in the balance sheet or notes to the financial statements. Also, any such receivables held for sale should be a separate balance sheet category. Receivables from officers, employees, or affiliated companies should be shown separately and not included under a general heading, such as "Accounts Receivable." Valuation allowance for credit losses or doubtful accounts and any unearned income included in the face amount of receivables should be shown as a deduction from the related receivables.

DISCLOSURE

2.26 FASB ASC 310 states that allowances for doubtful accounts should be deducted from the related receivables and appropriately disclosed. FASB ASC 310-10-50-4 requires, as applicable, any unearned income, unamortized premiums and discounts, and net unamortized deferred fees and costs be disclosed in the financial statements. Under FASB ASC 825, fair value disclosure is not required for trade receivables when the carrying amount of the trade receivable approximates its fair value.

PRESENTATION AND DISCLOSURE EXCERPTS

Receivables from Related Parties

2.27

CHESAPEAKE ENERGY CORPORATION (DEC)

CONSOLIDATED BALANCE SHEETS (in part)

($ in millions)	December 31 2011	2010
Current assets:		
Cash and cash equivalents ($1 and $0 attributable to our VIE)	$ 351	$ 102
Restricted cash	44	—
Accounts receivable	2,505	1,974
Short-term derivative assets	13	947
Deferred income tax asset	139	139
Other current assets	125	104
Total current assets	3,177	3,266

NOTES TO CONSOLIDATED FINANCIAL STATEMENTS

1. Basis of Presentation and Summary of Significant Accounting Policies (in part)

Accounts Receivable

Our accounts receivable are primarily from purchasers of natural gas and oil and exploration and production companies which own interests in properties we operate. This industry concentration has the potential to impact our overall exposure to credit risk, either positively or negatively, in that our customers and joint working interest owners may be similarly affected by changes in economic, industry or other conditions. We monitor the creditworthiness of all our counterparties and we generally require letters of credit or parent guarantees for receivables from parties which are judged to have sub-standard credit, unless the credit risk can otherwise be mitigated. During 2011 and 2010, we recognized nominal amounts and during 2009, we recognized $13 million of bad debt expense related to potentially uncollectible receivables. Accounts receivable as of December 31, 2011 and 2010 are detailed below.

($ in millions)	December 31	
	2011	2010
Natural gas and oil sales	$1,089	$ 821
Joint interest	1,171	977
Oilfield services	43	10
Related parties[a]	45	30
Other	176	154
Allowance for doubtful accounts	(19)	(18)
Total accounts receivable	$2,505	$1,974

[a] See Note 6 for discussion of related party transactions.

6. Related Party Transactions (in part)

Chief Executive Officer

As of December 31, 2011 and 2010, we had accrued accounts receivable from our Chief Executive Officer, Aubrey K. McClendon, of $45 million and $30 million, respectively, representing joint interest billings from December 2011 and 2010. These amounts were invoiced and timely paid in the following month. Since Chesapeake was founded in 1989, Mr. McClendon has acquired working interests in virtually all of our natural gas and oil properties by participating in our drilling activities under the terms of the Founder Well Participation Program (FWPP) and predecessor participation arrangements provided for in Mr. McClendon's employment agreements. Under the FWPP, approved by our shareholders in June 2005, Mr. McClendon may elect to participate in all or none of the wells drilled by or on behalf of Chesapeake during a calendar year, but he is not allowed to participate only in selected wells. A participation election is required to be received by the Compensation Committee of Chesapeake's Board of Directors not less than 30 days prior to the start of each calendar year. His participation is permitted only under the terms outlined in the FWPP, which, among other things, limits his individual participation to a maximum working interest of 2.5% in a well and prohibits participation in situations where Chesapeake's working interest would be reduced below 12.5% as a result of his participation. In addition, the Company is reimbursed for costs associated with leasehold acquired by Mr. McClendon as a result of his well participation. From time to time, Mr. McClendon has sold his FWPP interests in conjunction with sales by the Company of its interests in the same properties, and the proceeds related to those sales have been allocated between Mr. McClendon

and the Company based on their respective ownership interests and on the same terms as those that applied to the Company's properties included in the sale.

On December 31, 2008, we entered into a new five-year employment agreement with Mr. McClendon that contained a one-time well cost incentive award to him. The total cost of the award to Chesapeake was $75 million plus employment taxes in the amount of approximately $1 million. The incentive award is subject to a clawback equal to any unvested portion of the award if during the initial five-year term of the employment agreement, Mr. McClendon resigns from the Company or is terminated for cause by the Company. We are recognizing the incentive award as general and administrative expense over the five-year vesting period for the clawback resulting in an expense of approximately $15 million per year beginning in 2009. The net incentive award, after deduction of applicable withholding and employment taxes, of approximately $44 million was fully applied against costs attributable to interests in company wells acquired by Mr. McClendon or his affiliates under the FWPP.

In 2011, Chesapeake entered into a license and naming rights agreement with The Professional Basketball Club, LLC (PBC) for the arena in downtown Oklahoma City. The PBC is the owner of the Oklahoma City Thunder basketball team, a National Basketball Association franchise and the arena's primary tenant. Mr. McClendon has a 19.2% equity interest in PBC. Under the terms of the agreement, Chesapeake has committed to pay fees ranging from $3 million to $4 million per year through 2023 for the arena naming rights and other associated benefits. The naming rights provide Chesapeake with an enhanced public awareness and recognition both locally and nationally. Since 2008, Chesapeake has been a founding sponsor of the Oklahoma City Thunder under successive one-year contracts. In 2011, it entered into a 12-year sponsorship agreement, committing to pay an average annual fee of $3 million for advertising, use of an arena suite and other benefits. In 2011, the Company also agreed to purchase Oklahoma City Thunder game tickets for the 2011-2012 regular season home games for approximately $3 million and committed to purchase tickets for any 2012 home playoff games.

Pursuant to a court-approved litigation settlement with certain plaintiff shareholders described in Note 4, the sale of an antique map collection that occurred in December 2008 between Mr. McClendon and the Company will be rescinded. Mr. McClendon will pay the Company approximately $12 million plus interest, and the Company will reconvey the map collection to Mr. McClendon. The transaction is scheduled to be completed not later than 30 days after entry of a final non-appealable judgment.

Finance Receivables

2.28

CISCO SYSTEMS, INC. (JUL)

CONSOLIDATED BALANCE SHEETS (in part)

(In millions, except par value)

	July 30, 2011	July 31, 2010
Assets		
Current assets:		
Cash and cash equivalents	$ 7,662	$ 4,581
Investments	36,923	35,280
Accounts receivable, net of allowance for doubtful accounts of $204 at July 30, 2011 and $235 at July 31, 2010	4,698	4,929
Inventories	1,486	1,327
Financing receivables, net	3,111	2,303
Deferred tax assets	2,410	2,126
Other current assets	941	875
Total current assets	57,231	51,421
Property and equipment, net	3,916	3,941
Financing receivables, net	3,488	2,614
Goodwill	16,818	16,674
Purchased intangible assets, net	2,541	3,274
Other assets	3,101	3,206
Total assets	$87,095	$81,130

NOTES TO CONSOLIDATED FINANCIAL STATEMENTS

1. Basis of Presentation

(f) Financing Receivables—The Company provides financing arrangements, including leases, financed service contracts, and loans, for certain qualified end-user customers to build, maintain, and upgrade their networks. Lease receivables primarily represent sales-type and direct-financing leases. Leases have on average a four-year term and are usually collateralized by a security interest in the underlying assets while loan receivables generally have terms of up to three years. Financed service contracts typically have terms of one to three years and primarily relate to technical support services.

The Company determines the adequacy of its allowance for credit loss by assessing the risks and losses inherent in its financing receivables that are disaggregated by portfolio segment and class. The portfolio segment is based on the financing transactions offered by the Company: lease receivables, loan receivables, and financed service contracts and other. The financing receivables are further disaggregated by class based on their risk characteristics. The two classes of receivables that the Company has identified are Established Markets and Growth Markets. The Growth Markets class consists of countries in the Company's Emerging Markets segment as well as China and India, and the Established Markets class consists of the remaining geographies in which the Company has financing receivables. See Note 7.

The Company determines the allowance for credit loss for each class of financing receivables by applying the loss factor based on a given internal credit risk rating assigned to each financing receivables class. The loss factor is developed using external data as benchmarks, such as the external long-term historical loss rates and expected default rates that are published annually by a major third party credit-rating agency. Internal credit risk rating is derived by taking into consideration various customer-specific factors and macroeconomic conditions. These factors include the strength of the customer's business and financial performance, the quality of the customer's banking relationships, the Company's specific historical experience with the customer, the performance and outlook of the customer's industry, the customer's legal and regulatory environment, the potential sovereign risk of the geographic locations in which the customer is operating, and independent third-party evaluations. Such factors are updated regularly or when facts and circumstances indicate that an update is deemed necessary. The Company's internal credit risk ratings are categorized as 1 through 10 with the lowest credit risk rating representing the highest quality financing receivables.

Receivables with a risk rating of 8 or higher are deemed to be impaired and are subject to impairment evaluation. When evaluating lease and loan receivables and the earned portion of financed service contracts for possible impairment, the Company considers historical experience, credit quality, age of the receivable balances, and economic conditions that may affect a customer's ability to pay. When the Company, based on current information and events, determines that it is probable that all amounts due, including scheduled interest payments, pursuant to the contractual terms of the financing agreement are unable to be collected, the financing receivable is considered impaired. All such outstanding amounts, including any accrued interest, are assessed at the customer level and will be fully reserved. Financing receivables are written off at the point when they are considered uncollectible and all outstanding balances, including any previously earned but uncollected interest income, will be reversed and charged against earnings. The Company does not typically have any partially written-off financing receivables.

Outstanding financing receivables that are aged 31 days or more from the contractual payment date are considered past due. The Company does not accrue interest on financing receivables that are considered impaired or more than 90 days past due unless either the receivable has not been collected due to administrative reasons or the receivable is well secured. Financing receivables may be placed on non-accrual status earlier if, in management's opinion, a timely collection of the full principal and interest becomes uncertain. After a financing receivable has been categorized as non-accrual, interest will be recognized when cash is received. A financing receivable may be returned to accrual status after all of the customer's delinquent balances of principal and interest have been settled and the customer remains current for an appropriate period.

The Company facilitates third-party financing arrangements for channel partners, consisting of revolving short-term financing, generally with payment terms ranging from 60 to 90 days. In certain instances, these financing arrangements result in a transfer of the Company's receivables to the third party. The receivables are derecognized upon transfer, as these transfers qualify as true sales, and the Company receives a payment for the receivables from the third party based on the Company's standard payment terms. These financing arrangements facilitate the working capital requirements of the channel partners and, in some cases, the Company guarantees a portion of these arrangements. The Company also provides financing guarantees for third-party financing arrangements extended to end-user customers related to leases and loans, which typically have terms of up to three years. The Company could be called upon to make payments under these guarantees in the event of nonpayment by the channel partners or end-user customers. Deferred revenue relating to these financing arrangements is recorded in accordance with revenue recognition policies or for the fair value of the financing guarantees.

7. Financing Receivables and Guarantees (in part)

(a) Financing Receivables

Financing receivables primarily consist of lease receivables, loan receivables, and financed service contracts and other. Lease receivables represent sales-type and direct-financing leases resulting from the sale of the Company's and complementary third-party products and are typically collateralized by a security interest in the underlying assets. Lease receivables consist of arrangements with terms of four years on average while loan receivables generally have terms of up to three years. The financed service contracts and other category includes financing receivables related to technical support and other services, as well as an insignificant amount of receivables related to financing of certain indirect costs associated with leases. Revenue related to the technical support services is typically deferred and included in deferred service revenue and is recognized ratably over the period during which the related services are to be performed, which typically ranges from one to three years.

A summary of the Company's financing receivables is presented as follows (in millions):

July 30, 2011	Lease Receivables	Loan Receivables	Financed Service Contracts & Other[1]	Total Financing Receivables
Gross	$3,111	$1,468	$2,637	$7,216
Unearned income	(250)	—	—	(250)
Allowance for credit loss	(237)	(103)	(27)	(367)
Total, net	$2,624	$1,365	$2,610	$6,599
Reported as:				
Current	$1,087	$ 673	$1,351	$3,111
Noncurrent	1,537	692	1,259	3,488
Total, net	$2,624	$1,365	$2,610	$6,599

[1] As of July 30, 2011, the deferred service revenue related to financed service contracts and other was $2,044 million.

July 31, 2010	Lease Receivables	Loan Receivables	Financed Service Contracts & Other	Total Financing Receivables
Gross	$2,411	$1,249	$1,773	$5,433
Unearned income	(215)	—	—	(215)
Allowance for credit loss	(207)	(73)	(21)	(301)
Total, net	$1,989	$1,176	$1,752	$4,917
Reported as:				
Current	$ 813	$ 501	$ 989	$2,303
Noncurrent	1,176	675	763	2,614
Total, net	$1,989	$1,176	$1,752	$4,917

SEC 2.28

Contractual maturities of the gross lease receivables at July 30, 2011 are summarized as follows (in millions):

Fiscal Year	Amount
2012	$1,269
2013	919
2014	572
2015	270
2016	76
Thereafter	5
Total	$3,111

Actual cash collections may differ from the contractual maturities due to early customer buyouts, refinancings, or defaults.

(b) Credit Quality of Financing Receivables

Financing receivables categorized by the Company's internal credit risk rating for each portfolio segment and class as of July 30, 2011 are summarized as follows (in millions):

	Internal Credit Risk Rating					Gross Receivables, Net of Unearned Income
	1 to 4	5 to 6	7 and Higher	Total	Residual Value	
Established Markets						
Lease receivables	$1,214	$1,182	$ 23	$2,419	$292	$2,711
Loan receivables	204	187	4	395	—	395
Financed service contracts & other	1,622	939	52	2,613	—	2,613
Total Established Markets	$3,040	$2,308	$ 79	$5,427	$292	$5,719
Growth Markets						
Lease receivables	$ 35	$ 93	$ 18	$ 146	$ 4	$ 150
Loan receivables	458	580	35	1,073	—	1,073
Financed service contracts & other	1	19	4	24	—	24
Total Growth Markets	$ 494	$ 692	$ 57	$1,243	$ 4	$1,247
Total	$3,534	$3,000	$136	$6,670	$296	$6,966

Credit risk ratings of 1 through 4 correspond to investment-grade ratings, while credit risk ratings of 5 and 6 correspond to non-investment-grade ratings. Credit risk ratings of 7 and higher correspond to substandard ratings and constitute a relatively small portion of the Company's financing receivables. The credit risk profile of the Company's financing receivables as of July 30, 2011 is not materially different than the credit risk profile as of July 31, 2010.

In circumstances when collectability is not deemed reasonably assured, the associated revenue is deferred in accordance with the Company's revenue recognition policies, and the related allowance for credit loss, if any, is included in deferred revenue. The Company also records deferred revenue associated with financing receivables when there are remaining performance obligations, as it does for financed service contracts. The total of the allowances for credit loss and the deferred revenue associated with total financing receivables as of July 30, 2011 was $2,793 million, compared with a gross financing receivables balance (net of unearned income) of $6,966 million as of July 30, 2011. The losses that the Company has incurred historically with respect to its financing receivables have been immaterial and consistent with the performance of an investment-grade portfolio.

As of July 30, 2011, the portion of the portfolio that was deemed to be impaired, generally with a credit risk rating of 8 or higher, was immaterial. The total net write-offs of financing receivables were not material for fiscal 2011. During fiscal 2011, the Company did not modify any financing receivables.

The following table presents the aging analysis of financing receivables by portfolio segment and class as of July 30, 2011 (in millions):

Established Markets	31–60 Days Past Due[1]	61–90 Days Past Due[1]	Greater Than 90 Days Past Due[1][2]	Total Past Due	Current	Gross Receivables, Net of Unearned Income	Non-Accrual Financing Receivables	Impaired Financing Receivables
Lease receivables	$ 85	$ 33	$139	$257	$2,454	$2,711	$16	$ 6
Loan receivables	6	1	9	16	379	395	1	1
Financed service contracts & other	68	33	265	366	2,247	2,613	17	6
Total Established Markets	$159	$ 67	$413	$639	$5,080	$5,719	$34	$13
Growth Markets								
Lease receivables	$ 4	$ 2	$ 13	$ 19	$ 131	$ 150	$18	$18
Loan receivables	2	6	12	20	1,053	1,073	3	3
Financed service contracts & other	—	—	—	—	24	24	—	—
Total Growth Markets	$ 6	$ 8	$ 25	$ 39	$1,208	$1,247	$21	$21
Total	$165	$ 75	$438	$678	$6,288	$6,966	$55	$34

[1] Past due financing receivables are those that are 31 days or more past due according to their contractual payment terms. The data in the preceding table are presented by contract and the aging classification of each contract is based on the oldest outstanding receivable, and therefore past due amounts also include unbilled and current receivables within the same contract. Effective in the fourth quarter of fiscal 2011, the presentation of the aging table excludes pending adjustments on billed tax assessment in certain international markets.

[2] The balance of either unbilled or current financing receivables included in the greater-than-90 days past due category for lease receivables, loan receivables, and financed service contracts and other was $116 million, $15 million, and $230 million as of July 30, 2011, respectively.

The aging profile of the Company's financing receivables as of July 30, 2011 is not materially different than that of July 31, 2010. As of July 30, 2011, the Company had financing receivables of $50 million, net of unbilled or current receivables from the same contract, that were in the greater than 90 days past due category but remained on accrual status. A financing receivable may be placed on non-accrual status earlier if, in management's opinion, a timely collection of the full principal and interest becomes uncertain.

(c) Allowance for Credit Loss Rollforward

The activity for fiscal 2011 related to the allowances for credit loss and the related financing receivables as of July 30, 2011 are summarized as follows (in millions):

| | Credit Loss Allowances | | | |
	Lease Receivables	Loan Receivables	Financed Service Contracts & Other	Total
Allowance for credit loss as of July 31, 2010	$ 207	$ 73	$ 21	$ 301
Provisions	31	43	8	82
Write-offs, net	(13)	(18)	(2)	(33)
Foreign exchange and other	12	5	—	17
Allowance for credit loss as of July 30, 2011	$ 237	$ 103	$ 27	$ 367
Gross receivables as of July 30, 2011, net of unearned income	$2,861	$1,468	$2,637	$6,966

Financing receivables that were individually evaluated for impairment during fiscal 2011 were not material and therefore are not presented separately in the preceding table.

SEC 2.28

Insurance Claims

2.29

THE DOW CHEMICAL COMPANY (DEC)

CONSOLIDATED BALANCE SHEETS (in part)

(In millions, except share amounts)

At December 31	2011	2010
Assets		
Current assets		
Cash and cash equivalents (variable interest entities restricted—2011: $170; 2010: $145)	$ 5,444	$ 7,039
Marketable securities and interest-bearing deposits	2	—
Accounts and notes receivable:		
Trade (net of allowance for doubtful receivables—2011: $121; 2010: $128)	4,900	4,616
Other	4,726	4,428
Inventories	7,577	7,087
Deferred income tax assets—current	471	611
Other current assets	302	349
Total current assets	23,422	24,130

NOTES TO THE CONSOLIDATED FINANCIAL STATEMENTS

Note N—Commitments and Contingent Liabilities (in part)

Asbestos-Related Matters of Union Carbide Corporation (in part)

Insurance Receivables

At December 31, 2002, Union Carbide increased the receivable for insurance recoveries related to its asbestos liability to $1.35 billion, substantially exhausting its asbestos product liability coverage. The insurance receivable related to the asbestos liability was determined by Union Carbide after a thorough review of applicable insurance policies and the 1985 Wellington Agreement, to which Union Carbide and many of its liability insurers are signatory parties, as well as other insurance settlements, with due consideration given to applicable deductibles, retentions and policy limits, and taking into account the solvency and historical payment experience of various insurance carriers. The Wellington Agreement and other agreements with insurers are designed to facilitate an orderly resolution and collection of Union Carbide's insurance policies and to resolve issues that the insurance carriers may raise.

In September 2003, Union Carbide filed a comprehensive insurance coverage case, now proceeding in the Supreme Court of the State of New York, County of New York, seeking to confirm its rights to insurance for various asbestos claims and to facilitate an orderly and timely collection of insurance proceeds (the "Insurance Litigation"). The Insurance Litigation was filed against insurers that are not signatories to the Wellington Agreement and/or do not otherwise have agreements in place with Union Carbide regarding their asbestos-related insurance coverage, in order to facilitate an orderly resolution and collection of such insurance policies and to resolve issues that the insurance carriers may raise. Since the filing of the case, Union Carbide has reached settlements with several of the carriers involved in the Insurance Litigation, including settlements reached with two significant carriers in the fourth quarter of 2009. The Insurance Litigation is ongoing.

Union Carbide's receivable for insurance recoveries related to its asbestos liability was $40 million at December 31, 2011 and $50 million at December 31, 2010. At December 31, 2011 and December 31, 2010, all of the receivable for insurance recoveries was related to insurers that are not signatories to the Wellington Agreement and/or do not otherwise have agreements in place regarding their asbestos-related insurance coverage.

In addition to the receivable for insurance recoveries related to its asbestos liability, Union Carbide had receivables for defense and resolution costs submitted to insurance carriers that have settlement agreements in place regarding their asbestos-related insurance coverage.

The following table summarizes Union Carbide's receivables related to its asbestos-related liability:

Receivables for Asbestos-Related Costs at December 31

(In millions)	2011	2010
Receivables for defense costs—carriers with settlement agreements	$ 20	$ 12
Receivables for resolution costs—carriers with settlement agreements	158	236
Receivables for insurance recoveries—carriers without settlement agreements	40	50
Total	$218	$298

Union Carbide expenses defense costs as incurred. The pre-tax impact for defense and resolution costs, net of insurance, was $88 million in 2011, $73 million in 2010 and $58 million in 2009, and was reflected in "Cost of sales" in the consolidated statements of income.

After a review of its insurance policies, with due consideration given to applicable deductibles, retentions and policy limits, after taking into account the solvency and historical payment experience of various insurance carriers; existing insurance settlements; and the advice of outside counsel with respect to the applicable insurance coverage law relating to the terms and conditions of its insurance policies, Union Carbide continues to believe that its recorded receivable for insurance recoveries from all insurance carriers is probable of collection.

Summary

The amounts recorded by Union Carbide for the asbestos-related liability and related insurance receivable described above were based upon current, known facts. However, future events, such as the number of new claims to be filed and/or received each year, the average cost of disposing of each such claim, coverage issues among insurers, and the continuing solvency of various insurance companies, as well as the numerous uncertainties surrounding asbestos litigation in the United States, could cause the actual costs and insurance recoveries for Union Carbide to be higher or lower than those projected or those recorded.

Because of the uncertainties described above, Union Carbide's management cannot estimate the full range of the cost of resolving pending and future asbestos-related claims facing Union Carbide and Amchem. Union Carbide's management believes that it is reasonably possible that the cost of disposing of Union Carbide's asbestos-related claims, including future defense costs, could have a material impact on Union Carbide's results of operations and cash flows for a particular period and on the consolidated financial position of Union Carbide.

It is the opinion of Dow's management that it is reasonably possible that the cost of Union Carbide disposing of its asbestos-related claims, including future defense costs, could have a material impact on the Company's results of operations and cash flows for a particular period and on the consolidated financial position of the Company.

Sale of Assets—Escrow Receivable

2.30

BASSETT FURNITURE INDUSTRIES, INCORPORATED (NOV)

CONSOLIDATED BALANCE SHEETS (in part)

November 26, 2011 and November 27, 2010

(In thousands, except share and per share data)

	2011	2010
Assets		
Current assets		
Cash and cash equivalents	$ 69,601	$11,071
Accounts receivable, net of allowance for doubtful accounts of $2,092 and $7,366 as of November 26, 2011 and November 27, 2010, respectively	14,756	31,621
Marketable securities	2,939	—
Inventories	45,129	41,810
Other current assets	7,778	6,969
Total current assets	140,203	91,471

NOTES TO CONSOLIDATED FINANCIAL STATEMENTS

(In thousands, except share and per share data)

11. Unconsolidated Affiliated Companies (in part)

International Home Furnishings Center (in part)

On May 2, 2011 we sold our 46.9% interest in International Home Furnishings Center, Inc. ("IHFC") to International Market Centers, L.P. ("IMC"). Consideration received, the balance of our investment in IHFC at the time of sale, and the resulting gain from the sale are as follows:

Gain of Sale on Affiliate:	
Consideration received:	
Cash	$69,152
Tax escrow receivable[1]	1,413
Indemnification escrow receivable[2]	4,695
Investment in IMC[3]	1,000
Total consideration received	$76,260
Investment in IHFC:	
Distributions in excess of affiliate earnings	9,282
Gain on sale of affiliate	$85,542

[1] Included in other current assets in the accompanying consolidated balance sheet at November 26, 2011.

[2] $2,348 included in other current assets in the accompanying consolidated balance sheet at November 26, 2011, with the remainder included in other assets.

[3] Included in other assets in the accompanying consolidated balance sheet at November 26, 2011.

The tax escrow receivable represents the portion of escrowed sales proceeds expected to be released to us after the settlement of certain outstanding IHFC tax obligations. In addition, $4,695 of proceeds was placed in escrow to indemnify the purchaser with respect to various contingencies. Any unused portions of these escrowed funds will be released to us over a three year period. Also in connection with the sale, we acquired a minority equity stake in IMC in exchange for $1,000. IMC is majority owned by funds managed by Bain Capital Partners and a subsidiary of certain investment funds managed by Oaktree Capital Management, L.P. Our investment in IMC is accounted for using the cost method as we do not have significant influence over IMC.

RECEIVABLES SOLD OR COLLATERALIZED

RECOGNITION AND MEASUREMENT

2.31 FASB ASC 860, *Transfers and Servicing*, establishes criteria for determining whether a transfer of financial assets in exchange for cash or other consideration should be accounted for as a sale or pledge of collateral in a secured borrowing. FASB ASC 860 also establishes the criteria for accounting for securitizations and other transfers of financial assets and collateral and requires certain disclosures.

2.32 FASB ASC 860 requires that all separately recognized servicing assets and liabilities be initially measured at fair value. Further, FASB ASC 860 permits, but does not require, the subsequent measurement of servicing assets and liabilities at fair value.

2.33 ASU No. 2009-16, *Transfers and Servicing (Topic 860): Accounting for Transfers of Financial Assets*, eliminated the exceptions for qualifying special-purpose entities from the consolidation guidance. Further, ASU No. 2009-16 provides clarifications of the requirements for isolation and limitations on portions of financial assets that are eligible for sale accounting. ASU No. 2009-16 was effective for fiscal years beginning after November 15, 2009.

Author's Note

In April 2011, FASB issued ASU No. 2011-03, *Transfers and Servicing (Topic 860): Reconsideration of Effective Control for Repurchase Agreements*. The main objective of FASB ASU No. 2011-03 is to improve the accounting for repurchase agreements and other arrangements that both entitle and obligate a transferor to repurchase or redeem financial assets before their maturity. The amendments in FASB ASU No. 2011-03 remove from the assessment of effective control the criterion requiring the transferor to have the ability to repurchase or redeem the financial assets on substantially the agreed terms, even in the event of default by the transferee, and the collateral maintenance implementation guidance related to that criterion. FASB ASU No. 2011-03 is effective for years beginning on or after December 15, 2011. Given the effective date of FASB ASU No. 2011-03, no survey entity will have adopted these requirements in its 2011 financial statements.

DISCLOSURE

2.34 FASB ASC 860 requires additional disclosures and separate balance sheet presentation of the carrying amounts of servicing assets and liabilities that are subsequently measured at fair value. FASB ASC 860-50-50-2 requires disclosures including (*a*) a description of the risks inherent in servicing assets and servicing liabilities, (*b*) the amount of contractually specified servicing fees, late fees, and ancillary fees earned for each period, including a description of where each amount is reported in the statement of income, and (c) quantitative and qualitative information about the assumptions used to estimate fair value.

PRESENTATION AND DISCLOSURE EXCERPTS

Receivables Sold or Collateralized

2.35

TENNECO INC. (DEC)

CONSOLIDATED BALANCE SHEETS (in part)

	December 31	
	2011	**2010**
	(Millions)	
Assets		
Current assets:		
Cash and cash equivalents	$ 214	$ 233
Receivables—		
Customer notes and accounts, net	936	796
Other	44	30
Inventories	592	547
Deferred income taxes	40	38
Prepayments and other	153	146
Total current assets	1,979	1,790

NOTES TO CONSOLIDATED FINANCIAL STATEMENTS

5. Long-Term Debt, Short-Term Debt, and Financing Arrangements (in part)

Accounts Receivable Securitization. We securitize some of our accounts receivable on a limited recourse basis in North America and Europe. As servicer under these accounts receivable securitization programs, we are responsible for performing all accounts receivable administration functions for these securitized financial assets including collections and processing of customer invoice adjustments. In North America, we have an accounts receivable securitization program with three commercial banks comprised of a first priority facility and a second priority facility. We securitize original equipment and aftermarket receivables on a daily basis under the bank program. In March 2011, the North American program was amended and extended to March 23, 2012. The first priority facility continues to provide financing of up to $110 million and the second priority facility, which is subordinated to the first priority facility, continues to provide up to an additional $40 million of financing. Both facilities monetize accounts receivable generated in the U.S. and Canada that meet certain eligibility requirements, and the second priority facility also monetizes certain accounts receivable generated in the U.S. or Canada that would otherwise be ineligible under the first priority securitization facility. The amendments to the North American program expand the trade receivables that are eligible for purchase under the program and decrease the margin we pay to our banks. We had no outstanding third party investments in our securitized accounts receivable under the North American program at December 31, 2011 and 2010, respectively.

Each facility contains customary covenants for financings of this type, including restrictions related to liens, payments, mergers or consolidation and amendments to the agreements underlying the receivables pool. Further, each facility may be terminated upon the occurrence of customary events (with customary grace periods, if applicable), including breaches of covenants, failure to maintain certain financial ratios, inaccuracies of representations and warranties, bankruptcy and insolvency events, certain changes in the rate of default or delinquency of the receivables, a change of control and the entry or other enforcement of material judgments. In addition, each facility contains cross-default provisions, where the facility could be terminated in the event of non-payment of other material indebtedness when due and any other event which permits the acceleration of the maturity of material indebtedness.

We also securitize receivables in our European operations with regional banks in Europe. The arrangements to securitize receivables in Europe are provided under seven separate facilities provided by various financial institutions in each of the foreign jurisdictions. The commitments for these arrangements are generally for one year, but some may be cancelled with notice 90 days prior to renewal. In some instances, the arrangement provides for cancellation by the applicable financial institution at any time upon 15 days, or less, notification. The amount of outstanding third party investments in our securitized accounts receivable in Europe was $121 million and $91 million at December 31, 2011 and 2010, respectively.

If we were not able to securitize receivables under either the North American or European securitization programs, our borrowings under our revolving credit agreements might increase. These accounts receivable securitization programs provide us with access to cash at costs that are generally favorable to alternative sources of financing, and allow us to reduce borrowings under our revolving credit agreements.

We adopted the amended accounting guidance under ASC Topic 860, Accounting for Transfers of Financial Assets effective January 1, 2010. Prior to the adoption of this new guidance, we accounted for activities under our North American and European accounts receivable securitization programs as sales of financial assets to our banks. The new accounting guidance changed the condition that must be met for the transfer of financial assets to be accounted for as a sale. The new guidance adds additional conditions that must be satisfied for transfers of financial assets to be accounted for as sales when the transferor has not transferred the entire original financial asset, including the requirement that no partial interest holder have rights in the transferred asset that are subordinate to the rights of other partial interest holders.

In our North American accounts receivable securitization programs, we transfer a partial interest in a pool of receivables and the interest that we retain is subordinate to the transferred interest. Accordingly, beginning January 1, 2010, we account for our North American securitization program as a secured borrowing. In our European programs, we transfer accounts receivables in their entirety to the acquiring entities and satisfy all of the conditions established under ASC Topic 860 to report the transfer of financial assets in their entirety as a sale. The fair value of assets received as proceeds in exchange for the transfer of accounts receivable under our European securitization programs approximates the fair value of such receivables. We recognized $3 million and $4 million in interest expense for the years ended 2011 and 2010, respectively, relating to our North American securitization program, which effective January 1, 2010, is accounted for as a secured borrowing under the amended accounting guidance for transfers of financial assets. In addition, we recognized

a loss of $5 million, $3 million and $9 million for the years ended 2011, 2010 and 2009, respectively, on the sale of trade accounts receivable in our European and North American accounts receivable securitization programs, representing the discount from book values at which these receivables were sold to our banks. The discount rate varies based on funding costs incurred by our banks, which averaged approximately three percent, four percent and five percent for the years ended 2011, 2010 and 2009, respectively.

2.36

GREIF, INC. (OCT)

CONSOLIDATED BALANCE SHEETS (in part)

(Dollars in thousands)

As of October 31	2011	2010
		(As Restated)
Assets		
Current assets		
Cash and cash equivalents	$ 127,413	$ 106,957
Trade accounts receivable, less allowance of $13,754 in 2011 and $13,311 in 2010	568,624	480,158
Inventories	432,518	396,572
Deferred tax assets	23,654	19,526
Net assets held for sale	11,381	11,742
Current portion related party notes receivable	1,714	—
Prepaid expenses and other current assets	140,033	134,269
	1,305,337	1,149,224

NOTES TO CONSOLIDATED FINANCIAL STATEMENTS

Note 3—Sale of Non-United States Accounts Receivable

Pursuant to the terms of a Receivable Purchase Agreement (the "RPA") between Greif Coordination Center BVBA, an indirect wholly-owned subsidiary of Greif, Inc., and a major international bank, the seller agreed to sell trade receivables meeting certain eligibility requirements that seller had purchased from other indirect wholly-owned subsidiaries of Greif, Inc., including Greif Belgium BVBA, Greif Germany GmbH, Greif Nederland BV, Greif Packaging Belgium NV, Greif Spain SA, Greif Sweden AB, Greif Packaging Norway AS, Greif Packaging France, SAS, Greif Packaging Spain SA, Greif Portugal Lda and Greif UK Ltd, under discounted receivables purchase agreements and from Greif France SAS under a factoring agreement. This agreement is amended from time to time to add additional Greif entities. In addition, Greif Italia S.P.A., also an indirect wholly-owned subsidiary of Greif, Inc., entered into the Italian Receivables Purchase Agreement with the Italian branch of the major international bank (the "Italian RPA") agreeing to sell trade receivables that meet certain eligibility criteria to the Italian branch of the major international bank. The Italian RPA is similar in structure and terms as the RPA. The maximum amount of receivables that may be financed under the RPA and the Italian RPA is €115 million ($162.7 million) as of October 31, 2011.

In October 2007, Greif Singapore Pte. Ltd., an indirect wholly-owned subsidiary of Greif, Inc., entered into the Singapore Receivable Purchase Agreement (the "Singapore RPA") with a major international bank. The maximum amount of aggregate receivables that may be sold under the Singapore RPA is 15.0 million Singapore Dollars ($12.0 million) as of October 31, 2011.

In October 2008, Greif Embalagens Industrialis Do Brasil Ltda., an indirect wholly-owned subsidiary of Greif, Inc., entered into agreements (the "Brazil Agreements") with Brazilian banks. As of October 31, 2011, there were no more sales of trade receivables under this agreement.

In May 2009, Greif Malaysia Sdn Bhd., an indirect wholly-owned Malaysian subsidiary of Greif, Inc., entered into the Malaysian Receivables Purchase Agreement (the "Malaysian Agreement") with Malaysian banks. The maximum amount of the aggregate receivables that may be sold under the Malaysian Agreement is 15.0 million Malaysian Ringgits ($4.8 million) as of October 31, 2011.

The structure of the transactions provide for a legal true sale, on a revolving basis, of the receivables transferred from the various Greif, Inc. subsidiaries to the respective banks. The bank funds an initial purchase price of a certain percentage of eligible receivables based on a formula with the initial purchase price approximating 75 percent to 90 percent of eligible receivables. The remaining deferred purchase price is settled upon collection of the receivables. At the balance sheet reporting dates, the Company removes from accounts receivable the amount of proceeds received from the initial purchase price since they meet the applicable criteria of ASC 860, "Transfers and Servicing," and continues to recognize the deferred purchase price in its accounts receivable. The receivables are sold on a non-recourse basis with the total funds in the servicing collection accounts pledged to the banks between settlement dates.

As of October 31, 2011 and October 31, 2010, €105.4 million ($149.2 million) and €117.6 million ($162.9 million), respectively, of accounts receivable were sold under the RPA and Italian RPA.

As of October 31, 2011 and October 31, 2010, 12.2 million Singapore Dollars ($9.8 million) and 6.7 million Singapore Dollars ($5.4 million), respectively, of accounts receivable were sold under the Singapore RPA.

As of October 31, 2011 there were no accounts receivable sold and, 11.7 million Brazilian Reais ($6.9 million) of accounts receivable were sold under the Brazil Agreements as of October 31, 2010.

As of October 31, 2011 and October 31, 2010, 12.6 million Malaysian Ringgits ($4.1million) and 6.3 million Malaysian Ringgits ($2.0 million), respectively, of accounts receivable were sold under the Malaysian Agreement.

Expenses associated with the RPA and Italian RPA totaled €3.1 million ($4.3 million), €2.9 million ($3.9 million) and €3.7 million ($5.5 million) for the year ended October 31, 2011, 2010 and 2009, respectively.

Expenses associated with the Singapore RPA totaled 0.4 million Singapore Dollars ($0.3 million), 0.4 million Singapore Dollars ($0.3 million) and 0.3 million Singapore Dollars ($0.2 million) for the year ended October 31, 2011, 2010 and 2009, respectively.

Expenses associated with the Brazil Agreements totaled 2.8 million Brazilian Reais ($1.7 million), 4.4 million Brazilian Reais ($2.5 million) and 1.3 million Brazilian Reais ($0.8 million) for the year ended October 31, 2011, 2010 and 2009, respectively.

Expenses associated with the Malaysian Agreement totaled 0.7 million Malaysian Ringgits ($0.2 million), 0.4 million Malaysian Ringgits ($0.1 million) and 0.2 million Malaysian Ringgits ($0.1 million) for the year ended October 31, 2011, 2010 and 2009, respectively.

Additionally, the Company performs collections and administrative functions on the receivables sold similar to the procedures it uses for collecting all of its receivables, including receivables that are not sold under the RPA, the Italian RPA, the Singapore RPA, the Brazil Agreements, and the Malaysian Agreement. The servicing liability for these receivables is not material to the consolidated financial statements.

2.37

JARDEN CORPORATION (DEC)

CONSOLIDATED BALANCE SHEETS (in part)

(In millions, except per share amounts)

	As of December 31	
	2011	2010
Assets		
Cash and cash equivalents	$ 808.3	$ 695.4
Accounts receivable, net of allowances of $83.9 in 2011, $64.7 in 2010	1,080.5	1,067.7
Inventories	1,274.4	1,294.6
Deferred taxes on income	181.6	166.5
Prepaid expenses and other current assets	148.7	146.6
Total current assets	3,493.5	3,370.8

NOTES TO CONSOLIDATED FINANCIAL STATEMENTS

(Dollars in millions, except per share data and unless otherwise indicated)

9. Debt (in part)

Debt is comprised of the following at December 31, 2011 and 2010:

(In millions)	2011	2010
Senior Secured Credit Facility Term Loans	$1,001.6	$1,059.8
8% Senior Notes due 2016[1]	294.6	293.6
6 1 / 8% Senior Notes due 2022[1]	300.0	300.0
7 1 / 2% Senior Subordinated Notes due 2017[2]	656.5	639.8
7 1 / 2% Senior Subordinated Notes due 2020[2]	464.0	470.2
Securitization Facility	300.0	300.0
Revolving Credit Facility	—	—
2% Subordinated Note due 2012	99.7	98.4
Non-U.S. borrowings	35.6	62.0
Other	7.4	16.8
Total debt	3,159.4	3,240.6
Less: current portion	(269.3)	(434.6)
Total long-term debt	$2,890.1	$2,806.0

[1] Collectively, the "Senior Notes."
[2] Collectively, the "Senior Subordinated Notes."

Securitization Facility

The Company maintains a receivables purchase agreement (the "Securitization Facility") that bears interest at a margin over the commercial paper rate. Under the Securitization Facility, substantially all of the Company's Outdoor Solutions, Consumer Solutions and Branded Consumables domestic accounts receivable are sold to a special purpose entity, Jarden Receivables, LLC ("JRLLC"), which is a wholly-owned consolidated subsidiary of the Company. JRLLC funds these purchases with borrowings under a loan agreement, which are secured by the accounts receivable. There is no recourse to the Company for the unpaid portion of any loans under this loan agreement. To the extent there is availability, the Securitization Facility will be drawn upon and repaid as needed to fund general corporate purposes. At December 31, 2011, the borrowing rate margin and the unused line fee on the securitization were 1.25% and 0.625% per annum, respectively.

In February 2012, the Company entered into an amendment to the Securitization Facility that, in part, increased maximum borrowings from $300 to $400 and extended the term from May 2014 until February 2015. Following the renewal, the borrowing rate margin is 0.90% and the unused line fee is 0.45% per annum.

Non-U.S. Borrowings

As of December 31, 2011 and 2010, non-U.S. borrowings consisted of the foreign senior debt of none and $26.5, respectively; and amounts borrowed under various foreign credit lines and facilities totaling $35.6 and $35.5, respectively. Certain of these foreign credit lines are secured by certain non-U.S. subsidiaries' inventory and/or accounts receivable.

INVENTORY

RECOGNITION AND MEASUREMENT

2.38 FASB ASC 330, *Inventory*, states that the primary basis of accounting for inventories is cost, but a departure from the cost basis of pricing the inventory is required when the utility of the goods is no longer as great as their cost.

2.39 FASB ASC 330-10-35-14 states that if inventories are written down below cost at the close of a fiscal year, such reduced amount is to be considered the cost for subsequent accounting purposes. Similarly, the Topic 5(BB), "Inventory Valuation Allowances," of the SEC's *Codification of Staff Accounting Bulletins* indicates that a write-down of inventory creates a new cost basis that subsequently cannot be marked up.

PRESENTATION

2.40 Rule 5-02.6 of Regulation S-X requires separate presentation in the balance sheet or notes of the amounts of major classes of inventory, such as finished goods, work in process, raw materials, and supplies. Additional disclosures are required for amounts related to long-term contracts or programs.

DISCLOSURE

2.41 FASB ASC 330 requires disclosure of the basis for stating inventories. Rule 5-02.6 of Regulation S-X requires disclosure of the method by which amounts are removed from inventory (for example, average cost; first in, first out (FIFO); last in, first out (LIFO); estimated average cost per unit).

2.42 Rule 5-02.6c of Regulation S-X requires that registrants using LIFO disclose the excess of replacement or current cost over stated LIFO value, if material. 325 survey entities disclosed the effect of income from using LIFO, rather than FIFO or average cost, to determine inventory cost.

2.43

TABLE 2-3: INVENTORY COST DETERMINATION

Table 2-3 summarizes the methods used by the survey entities to determine inventory costs.

	Number of Entities		
	2011	2010	2009
Not disclosed	5	55	N/C*
First in, first out (FIFO)	312	316	325
Last in, first out (LIFO)	163	166	176
Average cost	133	113	147
Standard costs	16	15	N/C*
Retail method	18	21	N/C*
Other	22	74	18

* N/C = Not compiled. Line item was not included in the table for the year shown.

2.44

TABLE 2-4: INVENTORY COST DETERMINATION—USE OF LIFO

Table 2-4 indicates the portion of inventory cost determined by LIFO.

	Number of Entities		
	2011	2010	2009
Use of LIFO			
All inventories..	4	4	4
50% or more of inventories..............................	66	83	82
Less than 50% of inventories...........................	71	54	78
Not determinable...	22	25	12
Additional LIFO Information			
LIFO discontinued for all or portion of			
inventories..	1	1	N/C*
LIFO liquidation..	22	28	N/C*
Effect on income from using LIFO instead of			
FIFO or average cost..................................	56	50	N/C*
Dollar value LIFO used to calculate LIFO			
inventory cost...	1	1	N/C*

* N/C = Not compiled. Line item was not included in the table for the year shown.

PRESENTATION AND DISCLOSURE EXCERPTS

First-In First-Out

2.45

GOODRICH CORPORATION (DEC)

CONSOLIDATED BALANCE SHEET (in part)

(As of December 31, 2011 and 2010)

	December 31	
(Dollars in millions, except share amounts)	2011	2010
Current assets		
Cash and cash equivalents	$ 987.0	$ 798.9
Accounts and notes receivable—net	1,343.2	1,102.7
Inventories—net	2,876.6	2,449.4
Deferred income taxes	197.8	158.3
Prepaid expenses and other assets	60.0	68.1
Income taxes receivable	—	93.7
Total current assets	5,464.6	4,671.1

NOTES TO CONSOLIDATED FINANCIAL STATEMENTS

Note 2. Significant Accounting Policies (in part)

Inventories. Inventories are stated at the lower of cost or market. The costs of certain U.S. inventories were determined by the last-in, first-out (LIFO) cost method. Costs for the re-maining inventories were determined by the first-in, first-out (FIFO) cost method. See Note 9, "Inventories."

Inventoried costs on long-term contracts include certain pre-production costs, consisting primarily of tooling and engineering design and production costs, including applicable overhead. The costs attributed to units delivered under long-term commercial contracts are based on the estimated average cost of all units expected to be produced and are determined under the learning curve concept, which anticipates a predictable decrease in unit costs as tasks and production techniques become more efficient through repetition. This usually results in an increase in inventory (referred to as "excess-over average") during the early years of a contract. If in-process inventory plus estimated costs to complete a specific contract exceed the anticipated remaining sales value of such contract, the excess is charged to cost of sales in the period identified.

In accordance with industry practice, costs in inventory include amounts relating to contracts with long production cycles, some of which are not expected to be realized within one year.

Note 9. Inventories

Inventories consist of the following:

	December 31	
(Dollars in millions)	2011	2010
Average or Actual Cost (Which Approximates Current Costs):		
Finished products	$ 220.8	$ 224.4
In-process	2,360.6	1,866.1
Raw materials and supplies	753.7	692.8
	3,335.1	2,783.3
Less:		
Reserve to reduce certain inventories to LIFO basis	(54.2)	(52.7)
Progress payments and advances	(404.3)	(281.2)
Total	$2,876.6	$2,449.4

Approximately 6% of the inventory costs were determined under the LIFO method of accounting at December 31, 2011 and 2010. All other inventory costs were determined under the FIFO method of accounting. LIFO reserve adjustments, recorded as costs of sales, were a $1.5 million loss, $1 million loss and $5 million gain for 2011, 2010 and 2009, respectively. The Company uses the LIFO method of valuing inventory for certain of the Company's legacy aerospace manufacturing businesses, primarily the aircraft wheels and brakes business unit in the Actuation and Landing Systems segment.

Progress payments and advances represent (1) non-refundable payments for work-in-process and (2) cash received from government customers where the government has legal title to the work-in-process.

At December 31, 2011 and 2010, the amount of inventory consigned to customers and suppliers was approximately $61 million and $65 million, respectively.

In-process inventories which include pre-production and excess-over-average inventory accounted for under long-term contract accounting and engineering costs with a guaranteed right of recovery, are summarized by platform as follows (dollars in millions, except quantities which are number of aircraft or number of engines if the engine is used on multiple aircraft platforms):

December 31, 2011

	Aircraft Order Status[1] (Unaudited)			Company Order Status (Unaudited)				In-Process Inventory		
	Delivered To Airlines	Unfilled Orders	Unfilled Options	Contract Quantity[2]	Delivered	Firm Unfilled Orders[3]	Year Complete[4]	Production	Pre-Production and Excess-Over-Average	Total
Aircraft Platforms—Number of Aircraft										
787	3	857	232	2,818	29	29	2030	$257.9	$ 755.6	$1,013.5
A350 XWB	—	555	185	1,884	—	—	2030	7.1	303.8	310.9
7Q7	—	—	—	19	2	—	2018	0.1	27.1	27.2
Engine Type—Number of Engines (Engines are Used on Multiple Aircraft Platforms)										
CF34-10	954	394	766	1,316	1,052	190	2013	10.3	11.8	22.1
Trent 900	144	272	88	945	227	161	2025	32.7	17.3	50.0
PW 1000G—MRJ	—	130	120	678	—	—	2029	—	113.9	113.9
PW 1000G—C Series	—	266	238	2,476	—	—	2028	0.3	197.2	197.5
Other								115.1	80.3	195.4
Total in-process inventory related to long-term contracts under the contract accounting method of accounting								423.5	1,507.0	1,930.5
A380 engineering costs recoverable under long-term contractual arrangements								27.1	21.8	48.9
Other in-process inventory								348.3	32.9	381.2
Total								375.4	54.7	430.1
Balance at December 31, 2011								$798.9	$1,561.7	$2,360.6

December 31, 2010

	Aircraft Order Status[1] (Unaudited)			Company Order Status (Unaudited)				In-Process Inventory		
	Delivered To Airlines	Unfilled Orders	Unfilled Options	Contract Quantity[2]	Delivered	Firm Unfilled Orders[3]	Year Complete[4]	Production	Pre-Production and Excess-Over-Average	Total
Aircraft Platforms—Number of Aircraft										
787	—	848	229	1,882	9	21	2023	$249.6	$ 579.2	$ 828.8
A350 XWB	—	573	183	1,884	—	—	2030	4.1	234.6	238.7
7Q7	—	—	—	19	1	1	2018	1.7	28.5	30.2
Engine Type—Number of Engines (Engines are Used on Multiple Aircraft Platforms)										
CF34-10	794	418	654	1,316	842	52	2013	7.4	24.7	32.1
Trent 900	88	224	60	945	154	217	2025	25.7	18.6	44.3
PW 1000G—MRJ	—	30	20	678	—	—	2029	—	53.9	53.9
PW 1000G—C Series	—	180	180	2,476	—	—	2028	0.1	104.7	104.8
Other								104.9	52.8	157.7
Total in-process inventory related to long-term contracts under the contract accounting method of accounting								393.5	1,097.0	1,490.5
A380 engineering costs recoverable under long-term contractual arrangements								16.8	28.9	45.7
Other in-process inventory								301.6	28.3	329.9
Total								318.4	57.2	375.6
Balance at December 31, 2010								$711.9	$1,154.2	$1,866.1

[1] Represents the aircraft order status as reported by independent sources of the related number of aircraft or the number of engines as noted.
[2] Represents the number of aircraft or the number of engines as noted used to obtain average unit cost.
[3] Represents the number of aircraft or the number of engines as noted for which the Company has firm unfilled orders.
[4] The year presented represents the year in which the final production units included in the contract quantity are expected to be delivered. The contract may continue in effect beyond this date.

Last-In First-Out

2.46

FRED'S, INC. (JAN)

CONSOLIDATED BALANCE SHEETS (in part)

(In thousands, except for number of shares)

	January 29, 2011	January 30, 2010
Assets		
Current assets:		
Cash and cash equivalents	$ 49,182	$ 54,742
Receivables, less allowance for doubtful accounts of $1,218 and $764, respectively	28,146	28,893
Inventories	313,384	294,024
Other non-trade receivables	26,378	25,193
Prepaid expenses and other current assets	12,723	10,945
Total current assets	429,813	413,797

NOTES TO CONSOLIDATED FINANCIAL STATEMENTS

Note 1—Description of Business and Summary of Significant Accounting Policies

Inventories. Merchandise inventories are valued at the lower of cost or market using the retail first-in, first-out (FIFO) method for goods in our stores and the cost first-in, first-out (FIFO) method for goods in our distribution centers. The retail inventory method is a reverse mark-up, averaging method which has been widely used in the retail industry for many years. This method calculates a cost-to-retail ratio that is applied to the retail value of inventory to determine the cost value of inventory and the resulting cost of goods sold and gross margin. The assumption that the retail inventory method provides for valuation at lower of cost or market and the inherent uncertainties therein are discussed in the following paragraphs. In order to assure valuation at the lower of cost or market, the retail value of our inventory is adjusted on a consistent basis to reflect current market conditions. These adjustments include increases to the retail value of inventory for initial markups to set the selling price of goods or additional markups to adjust pricing for inflation and decreases to the retail value of inventory for markdowns associated with promotional, seasonal or other declines in the market value. Because these adjustments are made on a consistent basis and are based on current prevailing market conditions, they approximate the carrying value of the inventory at net realizable value (market value). Therefore, after applying the cost to retail ratio, the cost value of our inventory is stated at the lower of cost or market as is prescribed by U.S. GAAP.

Because the approximation of net realizable value (market value) under the retail inventory method is based on estimates such as markups, markdowns and inventory losses (shrink), there exists an inherent uncertainty in the final determination of inventory cost and gross margin. In order to mitigate that uncertainty, the Company has a formal review by product class which considers such variables as current market trends, seasonality, weather patterns and age of merchandise to ensure that markdowns are taken currently, or a markdown reserve is established to cover future anticipated markdowns. This review also considers current pricing trends and inflation to ensure that markups are taken if necessary. The estimation of inventory losses (shrink) is a significant element in approximating the carrying value of inventory at net realizable value, and as such the following paragraph describes our estimation method as well as the steps we take to mitigate the risk that this estimate has in the determination of the cost value of inventory.

The Company calculates inventory losses (shrink) based on actual inventory losses occurring as a result of physical inventory counts during each fiscal period and estimated inventory losses occurring between yearly physical inventory counts. The estimate for shrink occurring in the interim period between physical counts is calculated on a store-specific basis and is based on history, as well as performance on the most recent physical count. It is calculated by multiplying each store's shrink rate, which is based on the previously mentioned factors, by the interim period's sales for each store. Additionally, the overall estimate for shrink is adjusted at the corporate level to a three-year historical average to ensure that the overall shrink estimate is the most accurate approximation of shrink based on the Company's overall history of shrink. The three-year historical estimate is calculated by dividing the "book to physical" inventory adjustments for the trailing 36 months by the related sales for the same period. In order to reduce the uncertainty inherent in the shrink calculation, the Company first performs the calculation at the lowest practical level (by store) using the most current performance indicators. This ensures a more reliable number, as opposed to using a higher level aggregation or percentage method. The second portion of the calculation ensures that the extreme negative or positive performance of any particular store or group of stores does not skew the overall estimation of shrink. This portion of the calculation removes additional uncertainty by eliminating short-term peaks and valleys that could otherwise cause the underlying carrying cost of inventory to fluctuate unnecessarily. The Company has experienced improvement in reducing shrink as a percentage of sales from year to year due to improved inventory control measures, which includes the chain-wide utilization of the NEX/DEX technology.

Management believes that the Company's Retail Inventory Method provides an inventory valuation which reasonably approximates cost and results in carrying inventory at the lower of cost or market. For pharmacy inventories, which were approximately $32.5 million and $30.2 million at January 29, 2011 and January 30, 2010, respectively, cost was determined using the retail LIFO (last-in, first-out) method in which inventory cost is maintained using the Retail Inventory Method, then adjusted by application of the Producer Price Index published by the U.S. Department of Labor for the cumulative annual periods. The current cost of inventories exceeded the LIFO cost by approximately $24.0 million at January 29, 2011 and $21.5 million at January 30, 2010. The LIFO reserve increased by approximately $2.4 million during 2010, $2.4 million during 2009 and $3.7 million during 2008.

The Company has historically included an estimate of inbound freight and certain general and administrative costs in merchandise inventory as prescribed by GAAP. These costs include activities surrounding the procurement and storage of merchandise inventory such as merchandise planning and buying, warehousing, accounting, information technology and human resources, as well as inbound freight.

The total amount of procurement and storage costs and inbound freight included in merchandise inventory at January 29, 2011 is $19.5 million, with the corresponding amount of $17.4 million at January 30, 2010.

The Company did not record any below-cost inventory adjustments during the years ended January 29, 2011 and January 30, 2010 in connection with planned store closures (see Note 11 Exit and Disposal Activity).

Average Cost

2.47

GENERAL CABLE CORPORATION (DEC)

CONSOLIDATED BALANCE SHEETS (in part)

(In millions, except share data)

	Dec 31, 2011	Dec 31, 2010
Assets		
Current assets:		
Cash and cash equivalents	$ 434.1	$ 458.7
Receivables, net of allowances of $17.2 million in 2011 and $21.1 million in 2010	1,080.9	1,067.0
Inventories	1,228.7	1,118.9
Deferred income taxes	43.4	39.8
Prepaid expenses and other	100.0	121.3
Total current assets	2,887.1	2,805.7

NOTES TO CONSOLIDATED FINANCIAL STATEMENTS

2. Summary of Significant Accounting Policies (in part)

Inventories

Effective January 1, 2010, the Company changed its method of accounting for its North American inventories and non-North American metal inventories from the LIFO method to the average cost method. Inventories valued using the LIFO method represented approximately 57% of total inventories as of December 31, 2009 prior to the change in method. The Company believes the change is preferable because the average cost method improves financial reporting by better matching sales and expenses, particularly during periods of metal and petrochemical price volatility or reductions in inventory quantities and enhances comparability with industry peers. The Company applied this change in accounting principle retrospectively to all prior periods presented herein in accordance with ASC 250—*Accounting Changes and Error Corrections*. The Company converted its accounting systems on January 1, 2010, which effectively eliminated its LIFO pools prospectively.

As a result of the retrospective application of this change in accounting principle, certain amounts in the Company's year ended December 31, 2009 consolidated statement of operations were adjusted as presented below:

(In millions, except per share data)	Year Ended December 31, 2009		
	As Originally Reported	Adjustments	As Adjusted
Cost of sales	$3,787.9	$ 77.8	$3,865.7
Operating income	257.7	(77.8)	179.9
Provision for income taxes	(58.4)	25.7	(32.7)
Net income including noncontrolling interest	116.6	(52.1)	64.5
Net income attributable to Company common shareholders	108.4	(52.1)	56.3
Earnings per common share—basic	2.08	(1.00)	1.08
Earnings per common share—assuming dilution	2.06	(0.99)	1.07

The consolidated statement of cash flows for the year ended December 31, 2009 was adjusted as presented below:

(In millions)	Year Ended December 31, 2009		
	As Originally Reported	Adjustments	As Adjusted
Net income including noncontrolling interests	$116.6	$(52.1)	$ 64.5
Deferred income taxes	(29.9)	(25.7)	(55.6)
Inventory impairment charges	(34.6)	34.6	—
Increase in inventories	192.8	43.2	236.0
Net cash flows of operating activities	546.3	—	546.3

There was no impact to net cash flows of operating activities as a result of this change in accounting policy.

Approximately 82% of the Company's inventories are valued using the average cost method and all remaining inventories are valued using the first-in, first-out (FIFO) method. All inventories are stated at the lower of cost or market value.

The Company has consignment inventory at certain of its customer locations for purchase and use by the customer or other parties. General Cable retains title to the inventory and records no sale until it is ultimately sold either to the customer storing the inventory or to another party. In general, the value and quantity of the consignment inventory is verified by General Cable through either cycle counting or annual physical inventory counting procedures.

5. Inventories

Approximately 82% of the Company's inventories are valued using the average cost method and all remaining inventories are valued using the first-in, first-out (FIFO) method. All inventories are stated at the lower of cost or market value.

(In millions)	Dec 31, 2011	Dec 31, 2010
Raw materials	$ 298.2	$ 206.9
Work in process	199.3	215.5
Finished goods	731.2	696.5
Total	$1,228.7	$1,118.9

As of December 31, 2009, inventories have been retrospectively adjusted for the change from the LIFO method of inventory accounting to the average cost method. Refer to Footnote 2—Summary of Significant Accounting Policies for information on this change in accounting principle.

At December 31, 2011 and 2010, the Company had approximately $26.4 million and $32.5 million, respectively of consignment inventory at locations not operated by the Company with approximately 85% and 82%, respectively, of the consignment inventory located throughout the United States and Canada.

OTHER CURRENT ASSETS

PRESENTATION

2.48 Rule 5-02.8 of Regulation S-X requires that any amounts in excess of 5 percent of total current assets be stated separately on the balance sheet or disclosed in the notes.

2.49

TABLE 2-5: OTHER CURRENT ASSETS*

	Number of Entities		
	2011	2010	2009
Nature of Asset			
Deferred and prepaid income taxes.............	360	331	381
Derivatives....................................	188	142	232
Property held for sale.....................	54	56	79
Advances or deposits.....................	32	25	8
Current assets of discontinued operations......	26	22	N/C^
Unbilled costs or costs in excess of related billings..................................	18	16	N/C^
Program/broadcast rights............................	6	7	N/C^

* Other than cash, marketable securities, inventories, and prepaid expenses and appearing in the balance sheet or notes to financial statements, or both.

^ N/C = Not compiled. Line item was not included in the table for the year shown.

PRESENTATION AND DISCLOSURE EXCERPTS

Deferred Taxes

2.50

ROCKWELL COLLINS, INC. (SEP)

CONSOLIDATED STATEMENT OF FINANCIAL POSITION (in part)

(In millions, except per share amounts)

	September 30	
	2011	2010
Assets		
Current assets:		
Cash and cash equivalents	$ 530	$ 435
Receivables, net	969	1,024
Inventories, net	1,195	1,004
Current deferred income taxes	106	129
Other current assets	89	97
Total current assets	2,889	2,689

NOTES TO CONSOLIDATED FINANCIAL STATEMENTS

17. Income Taxes

The components of income tax expense from continuing operations are as follows:

(In millions)	2011	2010	2009
Current:			
U.S. federal	$128	$144	$171
Non-U.S.	16	11	6
U.S. state and local	3	(2)	4
Total current	147	153	181
Deferred:			
U.S. federal	83	74	72
Non-U.S.	—	5	10
U.S. state and local	10	7	6
Total deferred	93	86	88
Income tax expense	$240	$239	$269

Net current deferred income tax benefits (liabilities) consist of the tax effects of temporary differences related to the following:

	September 30	
(In millions)	2011	2010
Inventory	$ (49)	$ (31)
Product warranty costs	46	58
Customer incentives	31	35
Contract reserves	14	15
Compensation and benefits	42	28
Valuation allowance	(1)	—
Other	21	20
Current deferred income taxes, net	$104	$125

Net long-term deferred income tax benefits (liabilities) consist of the tax effects of temporary differences related to the following:

(In millions)	September 30	
	2011	2010
Retirement benefits	$537	$459
Intangibles	(45)	(45)
Property	(114)	(98)
Stock-based compensation	27	24
Valuation allowance	(13)	(15)
Other	44	50
Long-term deferred income taxes, net	$436	$375

Current deferred income tax assets and liabilities and long-term deferred income tax assets and liabilities are included in the Consolidated Statement of Financial Position as follows:

(In millions)	September 30	
	2011	2010
Current deferred income taxes	$106	$129
Other current liabilities	(2)	(4)
Current deferred income taxes, net	$104	$125
Long-term deferred income taxes	$448	$389
Other liabilities	(12)	(14)
Long-term deferred income taxes, net	$436	$375

Management believes it is more likely than not that the current and long-term deferred tax assets will be realized through the reduction of future taxable income, except for $14 million of deferred tax assets which have been fully reserved and relate to foreign net operating losses in Sweden and the United Kingdom which are not subject to expirations. Significant factors considered by management in its determination of the probability of the realization of the deferred tax assets include: (a) the historical operating results of the Company ($1,482 million of U.S. taxable income over the past three years), (b) expectations of future earnings, and (c) the extended period of time over which the retirement benefit liabilities will be paid.

The effective income tax rate from continuing operations differed from the U.S. statutory tax rate as detailed below:

	2011	2010	2009
Statutory tax rate	35.0%	35.0%	35.0%
State and local income taxes	1.1	0.8	0.7
Research and development credit	(4.7)	(1.2)	(2.2)
Domestic manufacturing deduction	(1.9)	(1.1)	(1.3)
Tax settlements	(0.4)	(2.4)	—
Other	(1.0)	(1.1)	(0.8)
Effective income tax rate	28.1%	30.0%	31.4%

Income tax expense from continuing operations was calculated based on the following components of income before income taxes:

(In millions)	2011	2010	2009
U.S. income	$778	$723	$790
Non-U.S. income	77	73	68
Total	$855	$796	$858

The Company's U.S. Federal income tax returns for the tax years ended September 30, 2007 and prior have been audited by the IRS and are closed to further adjustments by the IRS except for refund claims the Company filed for the tax years ended September 30, 2006 and 2007. The IRS is currently auditing the Company's tax returns for the years ended September 30, 2008 and 2009 as well as refund claims for prior years. The Company is also currently under audit in various U.S. states and non-U.S. jurisdictions. The U.S. state and non-U.S. jurisdictions have statutes of limitations generally ranging from 3 to 5 years. The Company believes it has adequately provided for any tax adjustments that may result from the various audits.

No provision has been made as of September 30, 2011 for U.S. federal or state, or additional non-U.S. income taxes related to approximately $345 million of undistributed earnings of non-U.S. subsidiaries which have been or are intended to be permanently reinvested. It is not practicable to estimate the amount of tax that might be payable on the undistributed earnings.

The Company had net income tax payments of $96 million, $125 million and $157 million in 2011, 2010 and 2009, respectively.

A reconciliation of the beginning and ending amount of unrecognized tax benefits for the years ended September 30 is as follows:

(In millions)	2011	2010	2009
Beginning balance	$ 78	$98	$73
Additions for tax positions related to the current year	22	14	24
Additions for tax positions of prior years	6	5	1
Additions for tax positions related to acquisitions	—	2	—
Reductions for tax positions of prior years	(4)	(21)	—
Reductions for tax positions of prior years related to lapse of statute of limitations	(1)	(2)	—
Reductions for tax positions related to settlements with taxing authorities	(1)	(18)	—
Ending balance	$100	$78	$98

The total amounts of unrecognized tax benefits that, if recognized, would affect the effective income tax rate were $57 million, $52 million and $56 million as of September 30, 2011, 2010 and 2009, respectively. Although the timing and outcome of tax settlements are uncertain, it is reasonably possible that during the next 12 months, a reduction in unrecognized tax benefits may occur in the range of $0 to $35 million based on the outcome of tax examinations or as a result of the expiration of various statutes of limitations.

The Company includes interest and penalties related to unrecognized tax benefits in income tax expense. The total amount of interest and penalties recognized within Other Liabilities in the Consolidated Statement of Financial Position was $6 million and $5 million as of September 30, 2011 and 2010, respectively. The total amount of interest and penalties recorded as an expense or (income) within Income tax expense in the Consolidated Statement of Operations was $1 million, $(3) million and $3 million for the years ended September 30, 2011, 2010 and 2009, respectively.

SEC 2.50

Advances

2.51

UNIVERSAL CORPORATION (MAR)

CONSOLIDATED BALANCE SHEETS (in part)

	March 31	
(In thousands of dollars)	**2011**	**2010**
Assets		
Current assets		
Cash and cash equivalents	$ 141,007	$ 245,953
Accounts receivable, net	335,575	266,960
Advances to suppliers, net	160,616	167,400
Accounts receivable—unconsolidated affiliates	10,433	11,670
Inventories—at lower of cost or market:		
Tobacco	742,422	812,186
Other	48,647	52,952
Prepaid income taxes	18,661	13,514
Deferred income taxes	47,009	47,074
Other current assets	73,864	75,367
Total current assets	1,578,234	1,693,076

NOTES TO CONSOLIDATED FINANCIAL STATEMENTS

(All dollar amounts are in thousands, except per share amounts or as otherwise noted.)

Note 1. Nature of Operations and Significant Accounting Policies (in part)

Advances to Suppliers

In some regions where the Company operates, it provides agronomy services and seasonal advances of seed, fertilizer, and other supplies to tobacco farmers for crop production, or makes seasonal cash advances to farmers for the procurement of those inputs. These advances are short term, are repaid upon delivery of tobacco to the Company, and are reported in advances to suppliers in the consolidated balance sheet. Primarily in Brazil, the Company has made long-term advances to tobacco farmers to finance curing barns and other farm infrastructure. In addition, due to low crop yields and other factors, in some years individual farmers may not deliver sufficient volumes of tobacco to fully repay their seasonal advances, and the Company may extend repayment of those advances into the following crop year. The long-term portion of advances is included in other noncurrent assets in the consolidated balance sheet. Both the current and the long-term portions of advances to suppliers are reported net of allowances recorded when the Company determines that amounts outstanding are not likely to be collected. Total allowances were $74.9 million at March 31, 2011, and $56.2 million at March 31, 2010, and were estimated based on the Company's historical loss information and crop projections. The allowances were increased by provisions for estimated uncollectible amounts of approximately $18.7 million in fiscal year 2011, $18.5 million in fiscal year 2010, and $26.9 million in fiscal year 2009. These provisions are included in selling, general, and administrative expenses in the consolidated statements of income. Interest on advances is recognized in earnings upon the farmers' delivery of tobacco in payment of principal and interest. Recognition of interest is discontinued when an advance is not expected to be fully collected. Advances on which interest accrual had been discontinued totaled approximately $76 million at March 31, 2011, and $64.2 million at March 31, 2010.

Note 14. Commitments and Other Matters (in part)

Commitments

The Company enters into contracts to purchase tobacco from farmers in a number of the countries in which it operates. The majority of these contracts are with farmers in Brazil and several African countries. Most contracts cover one annual growing season, but some contracts with a small number of commercial farmers in Africa cover multiple years. Primarily with the farmer contracts in Brazil, the Company provides seasonal financing to support the farmers' production of their crops or guarantees their financing from third-party banks. At March 31, 2011, the Company had contracts to purchase approximately $650 million of tobacco, $560 million of which represented volumes to be delivered during the coming fiscal year. These amounts are estimates since actual quantities purchased will depend on crop yields, and prices will depend on the quality of the tobacco delivered and other market factors. Tobacco purchase obligations have been partially funded by advances to farmers and other suppliers, which totaled approximately $160 million at March 31, 2011. The Company withholds payments due to farmers on delivery of the tobacco to satisfy repayment of the seasonal or long-term financing it provided to the farmers. As discussed in more detail below, the Company also has arrangements to guarantee bank loans to farmers, primarily in Brazil, and payments are also withheld on delivery of tobacco to satisfy repayment of those loans. In addition to its contractual obligations to purchase tobacco, the Company has commitments related to agricultural materials, approved capital expenditures, and various other requirements that approximated $55 million at March 31, 2011.

Assets Held for Sale

2.52

QUALCOMM INCORPORATED (SEP)

CONSOLIDATED BALANCE SHEETS (in part)

(In millions, except per share data)

	September 25, 2011	September 26, 2010
Assets		
Current assets:		
Cash and cash equivalents	$ 5,462	$ 3,547
Marketable securities	6,190	6,732
Accounts receivable, net	993	730
Inventories	765	528
Deferred tax assets	537	321
Other current assets	346	275
Total current assets	14,293	12,133
Marketable securities	9,261	8,123
Deferred tax assets	1,703	1,922
Assets held for sale	746	—
Property, plant and equipment, net	2,414	2,373
Goodwill	3,432	1,488
Other intangible assets, net	3,099	3,022
Other assets	1,474	1,511
Total assets	$36,422	$30,572

Note 11. Discontinued Operations (in part)

On December 20, 2010, the Company agreed to sell substantially all of its 700 MHz spectrum for $1.9 billion, subject to the satisfaction of customary closing conditions, including approval by the U.S. Federal Communications Commission (FCC). The agreement terminates on January 13, 2013; however, either party can extend the agreement for another 90 days thereafter if the FCC approval has not been received by then. The agreement followed the Company's previously announced plan to restructure and evaluate strategic options related to the FLO TV business and network. The FLO TV business and network were shut down on March 27, 2011. Since then, the Company has been working to sell the remaining assets and exit contracts. The 700 MHz spectrum with a carrying value of $746 million that the Company has agreed to sell was classified as held for sale, and all other assets were considered disposed of at September 25, 2011. Accordingly, the results of operations of the FLO TV business were presented as discontinued operations at September 25, 2011. Loss from discontinued operations includes share-based payments and excludes certain general corporate expenses allocated to the FLO TV business during the periods presented. The Company's consolidated statements of operations for all prior periods presented have been adjusted to conform.

Summarized results from discontinued operations were as follows (in millions):

	Year Ended		
	September 25, 2011	September 26, 2010	September 27, 2009
Revenues	$ 5	$ 9	$ 29
Loss from discontinued operations	(507)	(459)	(327)
Income tax benefit	194	186	127
Discontinued operations, net of income taxes	$(313)	$(273)	$(200)

The carrying amounts of the major classes of assets and liabilities of discontinued operations in the consolidated balance sheet were as follows (in millions):

	September 25, 2011
Assets	
Current assets	$ 10
Property, plant and equipment, net	156
Assets held for sale	746
Other assets	1
	$913
Liabilities	
Trade accounts payable	$ 2
Payroll and other benefits related liabilities	2
Other current liabilities	75
Other noncurrent liabilities	183
	$262

The Company has a significant number of site leases, and the Company has corresponding capital lease assets, capital lease liabilities and asset retirement obligations (Note 9). The capital lease assets, included in property, plant and equipment, net, were considered disposed of at March 27, 2011 when the Company shut down the FLO TV business.

Current Assets of Discontinued Operations

2.53

PRECISION CASTPARTS CORP. (MAR)

CONSOLIDATED BALANCE SHEETS (in part)

(In millions, except share data)	April 3, 2011	March 28, 2010
Assets		
Current assets:		
Cash and cash equivalents	$1,159.0	$ 112.4
Receivables, net of allowance of $2.5 in		
2011 and $4.2 in 2010	978.7	846.6
Inventories	1,459.4	1,435.3
Prepaid expenses and other current assets	21.0	21.7
Income tax receivable	20.0	78.7
Deferred income taxes	—	3.4
Discontinued operations	12.5	24.0
Total current assets	3,650.6	2,522.1

NOTES TO CONSOLIDATED STATEMENTS

(In millions, except option share and per share data)

4. Discontinued Operations (in part)

Fiscal 2011

During the second quarter of fiscal 2011, we sold an automotive fastener business. The transaction resulted in a gain of approximately $6.4 million (net of tax).

During the first quarter of fiscal 2011, we decided to divest a small non-core business in the Fastener Products segment and reclassified it to discontinued operations.

Fiscal 2010

In the fourth quarter of fiscal 2010, we decided to dispose of a small non-core business in the Fasteners Products' segment and reclassified it to discontinued operations. The sale of the business was completed in the second quarter of fiscal 2011.

In the third quarter of fiscal 2010, we decided to divest a small non-core business in the Investment Cast Products segment and reclassified it to discontinued operations. The sale of the business was completed in the fourth quarter of fiscal 2010. The transaction resulted in a gain of approximately $11.4 million (net of tax) in fiscal 2010.

Fiscal 2009

In the third quarter of fiscal 2009, we decided to dispose of two automotive fastener operations. The decision to discontinue these automotive fastener operations resulted from their non-core nature coupled with further erosion in the automotive market. These operations were reclassified from the Fasteners Products segment to discontinued operations in the third quarter of fiscal 2009. We recognized an impairment loss of approximately $8.7 million (net of tax) in the second quarter of fiscal 2010 related to these automotive fastener businesses held for sale due to continued erosion in the automotive market. The sale of these businesses was completed in the second quarter of fiscal 2011.

In the first quarter of fiscal 2009, we sold the stock of several small entities, a group of foreign operations held for sale and previously recorded as discontinued from our former Flow Technologies pumps and valves business. The transaction resulted in a net gain of approximately $3.0 million in fiscal 2009.

These businesses each meet the criteria as a component of an entity under accounting guidance for the disposal of long-lived assets. Accordingly, any operating results of these businesses are presented in the Consolidated Statements of Income as discontinued operations, net of income tax, and all prior periods have been reclassified.

Included in the Consolidated Balance Sheets are the following major classes of assets and liabilities associated with the discontinued operations after adjustment for write-downs to fair value less cost to sell:

	April 3, 2011	March 28, 2010
Assets of discontinued operations:		
Current assets	$12.5	$24.0
Net property, plant and equipment	31.1	37.0
Other assets	14.2	14.8
	$57.8	$75.8
Liabilities of discontinued operations:		
Other current liabilities	$ 6.2	$11.1
Other long-term liabilities	—	6.1
	$ 6.2	$17.2

Costs and Estimated Earnings in Excess of Billings

2.54

EMCOR GROUP, INC. (DEC)

CONSOLIDATED BALANCE SHEETS (in part)

(In thousands, except share and per share data)

	December 31	
	2011	2010
Assets		
Current assets:		
Cash and cash equivalents	$ 511,322	$ 710,836
Accounts receivable, less allowance for doubtful accounts of $16,685 and $17,287, respectively	1,187,832	1,090,927
Costs and estimated earnings in excess of billings on uncompleted contracts	114,836	88,253
Inventories	44,914	32,778
Prepaid expenses and other	77,749	57,373
Total current assets	1,936,653	1,980,167

NOTES TO CONSOLIDATED FINANCIAL STATEMENTS

Note 2—Summary of Significant Accounting Policies (in part)

Costs and Estimated Earnings on Uncompleted Contracts

Costs and estimated earnings in excess of billings on uncompleted contracts arise in the consolidated balance sheets when revenues have been recognized but the amounts cannot be billed under the terms of the contracts. Such amounts are recoverable from customers upon various measures of performance, including achievement of certain milestones, completion of specified units, or completion of a contract. Also included in costs and estimated earnings on uncompleted contracts are amounts we seek or will seek to collect from customers or others for errors or changes in contract specifications or design, contract change orders in dispute or unapproved as to both scope and/or price or other customer-related causes of unanticipated additional contract costs (claims and unapproved change orders). Such amounts are recorded at estimated net realizable value when realization is probable and can be reasonably estimated. No profit is recognized on construction costs incurred in connection with claim amounts. Claims and unapproved change orders made by us involve negotiation and, in certain cases, litigation. In the event litigation costs are incurred by us in connection with claims or unapproved change orders, such litigation costs are expensed as incurred, although we may seek to recover these costs. We believe that we have established legal bases for pursuing recovery of our recorded unapproved change orders and claims, and it is management's intention to pursue and litigate such claims, if necessary, until a decision or settlement is reached. Unapproved change orders and claims also involve the use of estimates, and it is reasonably possible that revisions to the estimated recoverable amounts of recorded claims and unapproved change orders may be made in the near term. If we do not successfully resolve these matters, a net expense (recorded as a reduction in revenues) may be required, in addition to amounts that may have been previously provided for. We record the profit associated with the settlement of claims upon receipt of final payment. Claims against us are recognized when a loss is considered probable and amounts are reasonably determinable.

Costs and estimated earnings on uncompleted contracts and related amounts billed as of December 31, 2011 and 2010 were as follows (in thousands):

	2011	2010
Costs incurred on uncompleted contracts	$7,598,325	$7,274,211
Estimated earnings, thereon	830,622	811,651
	8,428,947	8,085,862
Less: billings to date	8,755,806	8,454,299
	$ (326,859)	$ (368,437)

Such amounts were included in the accompanying Consolidated Balance Sheets at December 31, 2011 and 2010 under the following captions (in thousands):

	2011	2010
Costs and estimated earnings in excess of billings on uncompleted contracts	$ 114,836	$ 88,253
Billings in excess of costs and estimated earnings on uncompleted contracts	(441,695)	(456,690)
	$(326,859)	$(368,437)

As of December 31, 2011 and 2010, costs and estimated earnings in excess of billings on uncompleted contracts included unbilled revenues for unapproved change orders of approximately $14.5 million and $9.3 million, respectively, and claims of approximately $1.6 million and $6.3 million, respectively. In addition, accounts receivable as of December 31, 2011 and 2010 included claims of approximately $0.2 million and $1.8 million, respectively, plus contractually billed amounts related to such contracts of $40.4 million and $42.7 million, respectively. Generally, contractually billed amounts will not be paid by the customer to us until final resolution of related claims.

Derivatives

2.55

THE J. M. SMUCKER COMPANY (APR)

CONSOLIDATED BALANCE SHEETS (in part)

	April 30	
(Dollars in thousands)	2011	2010
Assets		
Current assets		
Cash and cash equivalents	$ 319,845	$ 283,570
Trade receivables, less allowance for doubtful accounts	344,410	238,867
Inventories:		
Finished products	518,243	413,269
Raw materials	345,336	241,670
	863,579	654,939
Other current assets	109,165	46,254
Total current assets	1,636,999	1,223,630

NOTES TO CONSOLIDATED FINANCIAL STATEMENTS

(Dollars in thousands, unless otherwise noted, except per share data)

Note A: Accounting Policies (in part)

Derivative Financial Instruments: The Company utilizes derivative instruments such as basis contracts, commodity futures and options contracts, foreign currency forwards and options, and an interest rate swap to manage exposures in commodity prices, foreign currency exchange rates, and interest rates. The Company accounts for these derivative instruments in accordance with Financial Accounting Standards Board ("FASB") Accounting Standards Codification ("ASC") 815, *Derivatives and Hedging*. FASB ASC 815 requires that all derivative instruments be recognized in the financial statements and measured at fair value regardless of the purpose or intent for holding them. For derivatives designated as a cash flow hedge that are used to hedge an anticipated transaction, changes in fair value are deferred and recognized in shareholders' equity as a component of accumulated other comprehensive income (loss) to the extent the hedge is effective and then recognized in the Statements of Consolidated Income in the period during which the hedged transaction affects earnings. Hedge effectiveness is measured at inception and on a monthly basis. Any ineffectiveness associated with the hedge or changes in fair value of derivatives that are nonqualifying are recognized immediately in the Statements of Consolidated Income. The Company's interest rate swap is designated as a fair value hedge and is used to hedge against changes in the fair value of the underlying long-term debt. The interest rate swap is recognized at fair value in the Consolidated Balance Sheet at April 30, 2011, and changes in the fair value are recognized in the Statement of Consolidated Income for the year ended April 30, 2011. The change in the fair value of the interest rate swap is offset by the change in the fair value of the underlying long-term debt. By policy, the Company historically has not entered into derivative financial instruments for trading purposes or for speculation. For additional information, see Note M: Derivative Financial Instruments.

Note M: Derivative Financial Instruments (in part)

The Company is exposed to market risks, such as changes in commodity prices, foreign currency exchange rates, and interest rates. To manage the volatility relating to these exposures, the Company enters into various derivative transactions. By policy, the Company historically has not entered into derivative financial instruments for trading purposes or for speculation.

Commodity Price Management: The Company enters into commodity futures and options contracts to manage the price volatility and reduce the variability of future cash flows related to anticipated inventory purchases of green coffee, edible oils, flour, milk, corn, and corn sweetener. The Company also enters into commodity futures and options contracts to manage price risk for energy input costs, including natural gas and diesel fuel. The derivative instruments generally have maturities of less than one year.

Certain of the derivative instruments associated with the Company's U.S. Retail Oils and Baking Market and U.S. Retail Coffee Market segments meet the hedge criteria according to FASB ASC 815 and are accounted for as cash flow hedges. The mark-to-market gains or losses on qualifying hedges are deferred and included as a component of accumulated other comprehensive income (loss) to the extent effective, and reclassified to cost of products sold in the period during which the hedged transaction affects earnings. Cash flows related to qualifying hedges are classified consistently with the cash flows from the hedged item in the Statements of Consolidated Cash Flows. In order to qualify as a hedge of commodity price risk, it must be demonstrated that the changes in the fair value of the commodity's futures contracts are highly effective in hedging price risks associated with the commodity purchased. Hedge effectiveness is measured at inception and on a monthly basis.

The mark-to-market gains or losses on nonqualifying and ineffective portions of hedges are recognized in cost of products sold immediately.

Foreign Currency Exchange Rate Hedging: The Company utilizes foreign currency forwards and options contracts to manage the effect of foreign currency exchange fluctuations on future cash payments primarily related to purchases of certain raw materials, finished goods, and fixed assets. The contracts generally have maturities of less than one year. At the inception of the contract, the derivative is evaluated and documented for hedge accounting treatment. Instruments currently used to manage foreign currency exchange exposures do not meet the requirements for hedge accounting treatment and the change in value of these instruments is immediately recognized in cost of products sold. If the contract qualifies for hedge accounting treatment, to the extent the hedge is deemed effective, the associated mark-to-market gains and losses are deferred and included as a component of accumulated other comprehensive income (loss). These gains or losses are reclassified to earnings in the period the contract is executed. The ineffective portion of these contracts is immediately recognized in earnings.

Interest Rate Hedging: The Company utilizes derivative instruments to manage changes in the fair value of its debt. Interest rate swaps mitigate the risk associated with the underlying hedged item. At the inception of the contract, the instrument is evaluated and documented for hedge accounting treatment. The Company's interest rate swap met the criteria to be designated as a fair value hedge. The Company receives a fixed rate and pays variable rates, hedging the underlying debt and the associated changes in the fair value of the debt. The interest rate swap is recognized at fair value in the Consolidated Balance Sheet at April 30, 2011, and changes in the fair value are recognized in interest expense. Gains and losses recognized in interest expense on the instrument have no net impact to earnings as the change in the fair value of the derivative is equal to the change in fair value of the underlying debt.

The following table sets forth the fair value of derivative instruments as recognized in the Consolidated Balance Sheets at April 30, 2011 and 2010.

	April 30, 2011			April 30, 2010	
	Other Current Assets	Other Current Liabilities	Other Noncurrent Liabilities	Other Current Assets	Other Current Liabilities
Derivatives designated as hedging instruments:					
Commodity contracts	$ 3,408	$ —	$ —	$1,874	$ 9
Interest rate contract	5,423	—	1,384	—	—
Total derivatives designated as hedging instruments	$ 8,831	$ —	$1,384	$1,874	$ 9
Derivatives not designated as hedging instruments:					
Commodity contracts	$ 9,887	$5,432	$ —	$2,414	$ 599
Foreign currency exchange contracts	317	3,204	—	—	830
Total derivatives not designated as hedging instruments	$10,204	$8,636	$ —	$2,414	$1,429
Total derivative instruments	$19,035	$8,636	$1,384	$4,288	$1,438

The Company has elected to not offset fair value amounts recognized for commodity derivative instruments and its cash margin accounts executed with the same counterparty. The Company maintained cash margin accounts of $12,292 and $5,714 at April 30, 2011 and 2010, respectively, that are included in other current assets in the Consolidated Balance Sheets.

Content Rights

2.56

DISCOVERY COMMUNICATIONS, INC. (DEC)

CONSOLIDATED BALANCE SHEETS (in part)

(in millions, except par value)

	As of December 31	
	2011	2010
Assets		
Current assets:		
Cash and cash equivalents	$1,048	$ 466
Receivables, net	1,042	880
Content rights, net	93	83
Deferred income taxes	73	81
Prepaid expenses and other current assets	175	225
Total current assets	2,431	1,735

NOTES TO CONSOLIDATED FINANCIAL STATEMENTS

Note 2. Summary of Significant Accounting Policies (in part)

Content Rights

Content rights principally consist of television series and television specials. Content aired on the Company's television networks is primarily obtained through third-party production companies and is classified either as produced, coproduced or licensed. Substantially all produced content includes programming for which the Company has engaged third parties to develop and produce, and it owns most or all rights. Coproduced content refers to programs for which the Company collaborates with third parties to finance and develop, and it retains significant rights to exploit the programs. Licensed content is comprised of films or series that have been previously produced by third parties and the Company retains limited airing rights over a contractual term. Capitalized content costs are stated at the lower of cost less accumulated amortization or net realizable value.

Costs of produced and coproduced content consist of development costs, acquired production costs, direct production costs, certain production overhead costs and participation costs. Costs incurred for produced and coproduced content are capitalized if the Company has previously generated revenues from similar content in established markets and the content will be used and revenues will be generated for a period of at least one year. The Company's coproduction arrangements generally provide for the sharing of production cost. The Company records its costs, but does not record the costs borne by the other party as the Company does not share any associated economics of exploitation. Program licenses typically have fixed terms and require payments during the term of the license. The cost of licensed content is capitalized when the programs are delivered or the Company has paid for the programs. Development costs for programs that the Company has determined will not be produced are written off. Additionally, distribution, advertising, marketing, general and administrative costs are expensed as incurred.

Amortization of content rights is recognized based on the proportion that current estimated revenues bear to the estimated remaining total lifetime revenues, which results in either an accelerated method or a straight-line method over the estimated useful lives of up to five years. Amortization of capitalized costs for produced and coproduced content begins when a program has been aired. Amortization of capitalized costs for licensed content commences when the license period begins and the program is available for use.

The Company periodically evaluates the net realizable value of content by considering expected future revenue generation. Estimates of future revenues consider historical airing patterns and future plans for airing content, including any changes in strategy.

Estimated future revenues may differ from actual revenues based on changes in expectations related to market acceptance, network affiliate fee rates, advertising demand, the number of cable and satellite television subscribers receiving the Company's networks, and program usage. Accordingly, the Company continually reviews revenue estimates and planned usage and revises its assumptions if necessary. Given the significant estimates and judgments involved, actual demand or market conditions may be less favorable than those projected, requiring a write-down to net realizable value.

All produced and coproduced content is classified as long-term. The portion of the unamortized licensed content balance that will be amortized within one year is classified as a current asset.

Note 7. Content Rights

The following table presents a summary of the components of content rights (in millions).

	As of December 31	
	2011	2010
Produced content rights:		
Completed	$ 2,257	$ 1,963
In-production	221	229
Coproduced content rights:		
Completed	491	446
In-production	80	76
Licensed content rights:		
Acquired	346	297
Prepaid	21	19
Content rights, at cost	3,416	3,030
Accumulated amortization	(2,021)	(1,702)
Total content rights, net	1,395	1,328
Current portion	(93)	(83)
Noncurrent portion	$ 1,302	$ 1,245

Content expense, which consists of content amortization, impairments and other production charges included in the cost of revenues on the consolidated statements of operations, was $968 million, $833 million and $828 million for 2011, 2010 and 2009, respectively. Content impairments were $62 million, $51 million and $75 million for 2011, 2010 and 2009, respectively. As of December 31, 2011, the Company estimates that approximately 96% of unamortized costs of content rights, excluding content in-production and prepaid licenses, will be amortized within the next three years. As of December 31, 2011, the Company expects to amortize $574 million of unamortized content rights, excluding content in-production and prepaid licenses, during the next twelve months.

The Company enters into arrangements whereby it collaborates with third parties to finance and develop programming ("coproduced content"). The Company capitalizes the net cost of coproduced content and amortizes such cost in accordance with its content amortization policy. The Company's policy is to record cash receipts for distribution, advertising and royalty revenue that result from coproduced content as gross revenue. The Company generally does not allocate revenue to specific content rights, and there were no royalty revenues or expenses associated with coproduction partners during 2011, 2010 and 2009. Content costs of $151 million, $122 million and $123 million were capitalized as part of coproduction arrangements during 2011, 2010 and 2009, respectively.

Prepaid Expenses

2.57

WILLIAMS-SONOMA, INC. (JAN)

CONSOLIDATED BALANCE SHEETS *(in part)*

Dollars and shares in thousands, except per share amounts	Jan. 30, 2011	Jan. 31, 2010
Assets		
Current assets		
Cash and cash equivalents	$ 628,403	$ 513,943
Restricted cash	12,512	0
Accounts receivable, net	41,565	44,187
Merchandise inventories, net	513,381	466,124
Prepaid catalog expenses	36,825	32,777
Prepaid expenses	21,120	22,109
Deferred income taxes	85,612	92,195
Other assets	8,176	8,858
Total current assets	1,347,594	1,180,193

NOTES TO CONSOLIDATED FINANCIAL STATEMENTS

Note A: Summary of Significant Accounting Policies (in part)

Advertising and Prepaid Catalog Expenses

Advertising expenses consist of media and production costs related to catalog mailings, e-commerce advertising and other direct marketing activities. All advertising costs are expensed as incurred, or upon the release of the initial advertisement, with the exception of prepaid catalog expenses. Prepaid catalog expenses consist primarily of third party incremental direct costs, including creative design, paper, printing, postage and mailing costs for all of our direct response catalogs. Such costs are capitalized as prepaid catalog expenses and are amortized over their expected period of future benefit. Such amortization is based upon the ratio of actual revenues to the total of actual and estimated future revenues on an individual catalog basis. Estimated future revenues are based upon various factors such as the total number of catalogs and pages circulated, the probability and magnitude of consumer response and the assortment of merchandise offered. Each catalog is generally fully amortized over a six to nine month period, with the majority of the amortization occurring within the first four to five months. Prepaid catalog expenses are evaluated for realizability on a monthly basis by comparing the carrying amount associated with each catalog to the estimated probable remaining future profitability (remaining net revenues less merchandise cost of goods sold, selling expenses and catalog-related costs) associated with that catalog. If the catalog is not expected to be profitable, the carrying amount of the catalog is impaired accordingly.

Total advertising expenses (including catalog advertising, e-commerce advertising and all other advertising costs) were approximately $293,623,000, $264,963,000 and $328,019,000 in fiscal 2010, fiscal 2009 and fiscal 2008, respectively.

PROPERTY, PLANT, AND EQUIPMENT

RECOGNITION AND MEASUREMENT

Author's Note

In December 2011, FASB issued ASU No. 2011-10, *Property, Plant, and Equipment (Topic 360): Derecognition of in Substance Real Estate—a Scope Clarification (a consensus of the FASB Emerging Issues Task Force)*. FASB ASU 2011-10 addresses the accounting for situations in which a parent company ceases to have a controlling financial interest (as described in FASB ASC 810-10) in a subsidiary that is in-substance real estate as a result of default on the subsidiary's nonrecourse debt. The amendments in this update state that the parent company should apply the guidance in FASB ASC 360-20 to determine whether it should derecognize the in-substance real estate. This guidance is effective for public entities for fiscal years, and interim periods within those years, beginning on or after June 15, 2012, and after December 15, 2013, for nonpublic entities. Early adoption is permitted. Given the effective dates of FASB ASU 2011-10, no survey entity will have adopted these requirements in its 2011 financial statements.

2.58 *Property, plant, and equipment* are the long-lived, physical assets of the entity acquired for use in the entity's normal business operations and not intended for resale by the entity. FASB ASC 360, *Property, Plant, and Equipment*, states that these assets are initially recorded at historical cost, which includes the costs necessarily incurred to bring them to the condition and location necessary for their intended use. FASB ASC 835-20 establishes standards for capitalizing interest cost as part of the historical cost of acquiring assets constructed by an entity for its own use or produced for the entity by others for which deposits or progress payments have been made.

2.59 An entity may acquire or develop computer software either for internal use or for sale or lease to others. If for internal use, FASB ASC 350-40 provides guidance on accounting for the costs of computer software and for determining whether the software is for internal use. Under FASB ASC 350-40, internal and external costs incurred to develop internal-use software during the application development stage should be capitalized and amortized over the software's estimated useful life. Accounting for software acquired or developed for sale or lease is addressed by FASB ASC 985-20. Whether for internal use or sale or lease, FASB ASC refers to capitalized software costs as amortizable intangible assets.

PRESENTATION

2.60 FASB ASC 210-10-45-4 indicates that property, plant, and equipment should be classified as noncurrent when a classified balance sheet is presented. Under FASB ASC 805-20-55-37, some use rights acquired in a business combination may have characteristics of tangible, rather than intangible, assets. An example is mineral rights.

2.61 Under FASB ASC 985-20-45-2, capitalized costs related to software for sale or lease having a life of more than one year or one operating cycle should be presented as an other asset. Under FASB ASC 985-20, amortization expense should be on a product-by-product basis and charged to cost of sales or a similar expense category because it relates to a software product that is marketed to others. Presentations of capitalized computer software costs by survey entities vary.

DISCLOSURE

2.62 FASB ASC 360-10-50 requires the following disclosures in the financial statements or notes thereto:
a. Depreciation expense for the period
b. Balance of major classes of depreciable assets, by nature or function, at the balance sheet date
c. Accumulated depreciation, either by major classes of depreciable assets or in total, at the balance sheet date
d. A general description of the method(s) used in computing depreciation with respect to major classes of depreciable assets.

FASB ASC 360 also provides accounting and disclosure guidance for the long-lived assets that are impaired or held for disposal. Rule 5-02 of Regulation S-X requires that registrants state the basis of determining the amounts of property, plant, and equipment.

PRESENTATION AND DISCLOSURE EXCERPTS

Property, Plant, and Equipment

2.63

AUTONATION, INC. (DEC)

CONSOLIDATED BALANCE SHEETS (in part)

As of December 31,

(In millions, except share and per share data)

	2011	2010
Assets		
Current assets:		
Cash and cash equivalents	$ 86.6	$ 95.1
Receivables, net	587.4	462.0
Inventory	1,809.2	1,867.0
Other current assets	193.0	204.7
Total current assets	2,676.2	2,628.8
Property and equipment, net	1,950.7	1,838.0
Goodwill, net	1,172.2	1,142.4
Other intangible assets, net	217.8	202.0
Other assets	181.9	163.0
Total assets	$6,198.8	$5,974.2

NOTES TO CONSOLIDATED FINANCIAL STATEMENTS

(All tables in millions, except per share data)

1. Description of Business and Summary of Significant Accounting Policies (in part)

Property and Equipment, Net

Property and equipment are recorded at cost less accumulated depreciation. Expenditures for major additions and improvements are capitalized, while minor replacements, maintenance, and repairs are charged to expense as incurred. Leased property meeting certain criteria is capitalized and the present value of the related lease payments is recorded as a liability and included in current and/or long-term debt based on the lease term. When property is retired or otherwise disposed of, the cost and accumulated depreciation are removed from the accounts and any resulting gain or loss is reflected in Other Expenses (Income), Net in the Consolidated Income Statements. See Note 4 of the Notes to Consolidated Financial Statements for detailed information about our property and equipment.

Depreciation is provided over the estimated useful lives of the assets involved using the straight-line method. Leasehold improvements and capitalized lease assets are amortized over the estimated useful life of the asset or the respective lease term used in determining lease classification, whichever is shorter. The range of estimated useful lives is as follows:

Buildings and improvements	5 to 40 years
Furniture, fixtures, and equipment	3 to 12 years

We continually evaluate property and equipment, including leasehold improvements, to determine whether events or changes in circumstances have occurred that may warrant revision of the estimated useful life or whether the remaining balance should be evaluated for possible impairment. We use an estimate of the related undiscounted cash flows over the remaining life of the property and equipment in assessing whether an asset has been impaired. We measure impairment losses based upon the amount by which the carrying amount of the asset exceeds the fair value. See Note 17 of the Notes to Consolidated Financial Statements for information about our fair value measurements.

We recorded $0.6 million during 2010 of non-cash impairment charges related to our property and equipment held and used in continuing operations to reduce the carrying value of these assets to fair market value. These charges are recorded as a component of Other Expenses (Income), Net in the Consolidated Income Statements, of which $0.4 million was reflected as a component of Import Segment Income and $0.2 million was reflected as a component of Domestic Segment Income of our segment information.

When property and equipment is identified as held for sale, we reclassify the held for sale assets to Other Current Assets and cease recording depreciation. Assets held for sale in both continuing operations and discontinued operations are reported in the "Corporate and other" category of our segment information.

We had assets held for sale of $70.1 million at December 31, 2011, and $62.5 million at December 31, 2010, included in continuing operations. We recorded $1.1 million during 2011 and $2.5 million during 2010 of non-cash impairment charges related to our continuing operations assets held for sale to reduce the carrying value of these assets to fair value less cost to sell. We also recorded $1.1 million during 2011 of non-cash impairment charges related to a valuation adjustment for the cumulative depreciation not recorded during the held for sale period for continuing operations assets that were reclassified from held for sale to held and used during 2011. The 2011 and 2010 charges are recorded as a component of Other Expenses (Income), Net in the Consolidated Income Statements and are reported in the "Corporate and other" category of our segment information.

We had assets held for sale of $49.5 million at December 31, 2011, and $53.8 million at December 31, 2010, included in discontinued operations. We recorded $0.5 million during 2011 and $3.4 million during 2010 of non-cash net impairment charges related to our discontinued operations assets held for sale to reduce the carrying value of these assets to fair value less cost to sell. These charges are recorded as a component of Loss from Discontinued Operations in the Consolidated Income Statements.

4. Property and Equipment, Net

A summary of property and equipment, net, at December 31 is as follows:

	2011	2010
Land	$ 867.1	$ 837.7
Buildings and improvements	1,321.8	1,210.3
Furniture, fixtures, and equipment	518.6	479.6
	2,707.5	2,527.6
Less: accumulated depreciation and amortization	(756.8)	(689.6)
Property and equipment, net	$1,950.7	$1,838.0

2.64

CABLEVISION SYSTEMS CORPORATION (DEC)

CONSOLIDATED BALANCE SHEETS (in part)

December 31, 2011 and 2010

(Dollars in thousands)

	2011	2010
Assets		
Current assets:		
Cash and cash equivalents	$ 611,947	$ 313,991
Restricted cash	29,068	1,149
Accounts receivable, trade (less allowance for doubtful accounts of $14,907 and $17,786)	295,277	295,149
Prepaid expenses and other current assets	135,579	127,058
Amounts due from affiliates	6,818	25,127
Deferred tax asset	84,925	103,645
Investment securities pledged as collateral	191,338	235,932
Assets distributed to stockholders in 2011	—	564,231
Total current assets	1,354,952	1,666,282
Property, plant and equipment, net of accumulated depreciation of $9,221,694 and $8,564,884	3,269,232	3,361,590
Other receivables	3,279	4,843
Investment securities pledged as collateral	317,896	235,932
Derivative contracts	18,617	—
Other assets	53,871	44,086
Deferred tax asset	—	99,287
Amortizable intangible assets, net of accumulated amortization of $115,043 and $60,028	252,871	292,144
Indefinite-lived cable television franchises	1,240,228	1,240,228
Other indefinite-lived intangible assets	55,895	66,895
Goodwill	442,773	442,067
Deferred financing and other costs, net of accumulated amortization of $81,269 and $72,642	133,711	140,064
Assets distributed to stockholders in 2011	—	1,273,674
	$7,143,325	$8,867,092

See accompanying notes to consolidated financial statements.

COMBINED NOTES TO CONSOLIDATED FINANCIAL STATEMENTS

(Dollars in thousands, except per share amounts)

Note 2. Summary of Significant Accounting Policies (in part)

Summary of Significant Accounting Policies (in part)

Long-Lived and Indefinite-Lived Assets (in part)

Property, plant and equipment, including construction materials, are carried at cost, and include all direct costs and certain indirect costs associated with the construction of cable television transmission and distribution systems, and the costs of new product and subscriber installations. Equipment under capital leases is recorded at the present value of the total minimum lease payments. Depreciation on equipment is calculated on the straight-line basis over the estimated useful lives of the assets or, with respect to equipment under capital leases and leasehold improvements, amortized over the shorter of the lease term or the assets' useful lives and reported in depreciation and amortization (including impairments) in the consolidated statements of income.

The Company capitalizes certain internal and external costs incurred to acquire or develop internal-use software. Capitalized software costs are amortized over the estimated useful life of the software and reported in depreciation and amortization.

The Company reviews its long-lived assets (property, plant and equipment, and intangible assets subject to amortization that arose from acquisitions) for impairment whenever events or circumstances indicate that the carrying amount of an asset may not be recoverable. If the sum of the expected cash flows, undiscounted and without interest, is less than the carrying amount of the asset, an impairment loss is recognized as the amount by which the carrying amount of the asset exceeds its fair value.

Note 8. Property, Plant and Equipment

Costs incurred in the construction of the Company's cable television system, including line extensions to, and upgrade of, the Company's hybrid fiber-coaxial infrastructure and headend facilities are capitalized. These costs consist of materials, subcontractor labor, direct consulting fees, and internal labor and related costs associated with the construction activities. The internal costs that are capitalized consist of salaries and benefits of the Company's employees and the portion of facility costs, including rent, taxes, insurance and utilities, that supports the construction activities. These costs are depreciated over the estimated life of the plant (10 to 25 years), and headend facilities (4 to 25 years). Costs of operating the plant and the technical facilities, including repairs and maintenance, are expensed as incurred.

Costs incurred to connect businesses or residences that have not been previously connected to the infrastructure or digital platform are also capitalized. These costs include materials, subcontractor labor, internal labor to connect, provision and provide on-site and remote technical assistance and other related costs associated with the connection activities. In addition, on-site and remote technical assistance during the provisioning process for new digital product offerings are capitalized. The departmental activities supporting the connection process are tracked through specific metrics, and the portion of departmental costs that is capitalized is determined through a time weighted activity allocation of costs incurred based on time studies used to estimate the average time spent on each activity. New connections are amortized over the estimated useful lives of 5 years or 12 years for residence wiring and feeder cable to the home, respectively. The portion of departmental costs related to reconnection, programming service up- and down-grade, repair and maintenance, and disconnection activities are expensed as incurred.

Property, plant and equipment (including equipment under capital leases) consist of the following assets, which are depreciated or amortized on a straight-line basis over the estimated useful lives shown below:

| | December 31 | | Estimated |
	2011	2010	Useful Lives
Customer equipment	$ 2,371,584	$ 2,293,637	2 to 5 years
Headends and related equipment	1,194,608	1,024,480	3 to 25 years
Central office equipment	695,424	655,953	3 to 10 years
Infrastructure	5,682,079	5,558,949	3 to 25 years
Equipment and software	1,373,891	1,255,762	2 to 10 years
Construction in progress (including materials and supplies)	109,617	68,138	
Furniture and fixtures	156,944	160,221	3 to 12 years
Transportation equipment	210,238	196,485	3 to 20 years
Buildings and building improvements	264,543	246,393	10 to 40 years
Leasehold improvements	404,071	438,554	Term of lease
Land	27,927	27,902	
	12,490,926	11,926,474	
Less accumulated depreciation and amortization	(9,221,694)	(8,564,884)	
	$ 3,269,232	$ 3,361,590	

Depreciation expense on property, plant and equipment (including capital leases) for the years ended December 31, 2011, 2010 and 2009 amounted to $945,403, $859,750 and $897,539 (including impairments of $2,506, $1,803 and $1,436 in 2011, 2010 and 2009), respectively. In addition, the Company acquired $78,073 and $54,414 of property and equipment that was accrued but unpaid at December 31, 2011 and 2010, respectively.

At December 31, 2011 and 2010, the gross amount of equipment and related accumulated amortization recorded under capital leases were as follows:

| | December 31 | |
	2011	2010
Equipment	$ 57,271	$ 42,790
Less accumulated amortization	(27,409)	(21,325)
	$ 29,862	$ 21,465

EQUITY METHOD AND JOINT VENTURES

RECOGNITION AND MEASUREMENT

2.65 FASB ASC 323, *Investments—Equity Method and Joint Ventures*, stipulates that the equity method should be used to account for investments in corporate joint ventures and certain other noncontrolled entities when an investor has the ability to exercise significant influence over operating and financial policies of an investee, even though the investor holds 50 percent or less of the common stock. FASB ASC 323 considers an investor to have the ability to exercise significant influence when it owns 20 percent or more of the voting stock of an investee. FASB ASC 323 specifies the criteria for applying the equity method of accounting to 50 percent or less owned entities and lists circumstances under which, despite 20 percent ownership, an investor may not be able to exercise significant influence.

PRESENTATION

2.66 Under the equity method, FASB ASC 323-10-45-1 requires that an investment in common stock be shown in the balance sheet of an investor as a single amount.

DISCLOSURE

2.67 Under FASB ASC 323-10-50-2, the significance of an equity method investment to the investor's financial position and results of operations should be considered in evaluating the extent of disclosures of the financial position and results of operations of an investee. If the investor has more than one investment in common stock, disclosures wholly or partly on a combined basis may be appropriate. FASB ASC 323-10-50-3 details disclosures required for equity method investments, including name and percentage of ownership of the investee, investor accounting policies, any difference between the amount at which an investment is carried and the amount of underlying equity in net assets, and the accounting treatment of the difference.

2.68

TABLE 2-6: NONCURRENT INVESTMENTS—CARRYING BASES*

| | Number of Entities | | |
	2011	2010	2009
Equity method	170	111	237
Valued at cost	86	36	88
Fair value	136	135	131
Other, described	1	7	2

* Appearing in the balance sheet or notes to financial statements, or both.

PRESENTATION AND DISCLOSURE EXCERPTS

Equity Method

2.69

CONSTELLATION BRANDS, INC. (FEB)

CONSOLIDATED BALANCE SHEETS (in part)

(In millions, except share and per share data)

	February 28, 2011	February 28, 2010
Assets		
Current assets:		
Cash and cash investments	$ 9.2	$ 43.5
Accounts receivable, net	417.4	514.7
Inventories	1,369.3	1,879.9
Prepaid expenses and other	287.1	151.0
Total current assets	2,083.0	2,589.1
Property, plant and equipment, net	1,219.6	1,567.2
Goodwill	2,619.8	2,570.6
Intangible assets, net	886.3	925.0
Other assets, net	358.9	442.4
Total assets	$7,167.6	$8,094.3

NOTES TO CONSOLIDATED FINANCIAL STATEMENTS

February 28, 2011

1. Summary of Significant Accounting Policies (in part)

Equity Investments

If the Company is not required to consolidate its investment in another entity, the Company uses the equity method if

the Company (i) can exercise significant influence over the other entity and (ii) holds common stock and/or in-substance common stock of the other entity. Under the equity method, investments are carried at cost, plus or minus the Company's equity in the increases and decreases in the investee's net assets after the date of acquisition and certain other adjustments. The Company's share of the net income or loss of the investee is included in equity in earnings of equity method investees on the Company's Consolidated Statements of Operations. Dividends received from the investee reduce the carrying amount of the investment.

Equity method investments are also reviewed for impairment whenever events or changes in circumstances indicate that the carrying amount of the investments may not be recoverable. No instances of impairment were noted on the Company's equity method investments for the year ended February 28, 2011. During the third quarter of fiscal 2010, the Company determined that its CWNA segment's international equity method investment, Ruffino S.r.l. ("Ruffino") was impaired primarily due to a decline in revenue and profit forecasts for this equity method investee combined with an unfavorable foreign exchange movement between the Euro and the U.S. Dollar. The Company measured the amount of impairment by calculating the amount by which the carrying value of its investment exceeded its estimated fair value, based on projected discounted cash flows of this equity method investee (Level 3 fair value measurement—see Note 6). As a result of this review, the Company recorded an impairment loss of $25.4 million in equity in earnings of equity method investees on the Company's Consolidated Statements of Operations. For the year ended February 28, 2009, the Company recorded impairment losses of $79.2 million primarily associated with Ruffino ($48.6 million) and its CWAE segment's international equity method investment, Matthew Clark ($30.1 million). These impairment losses resulted primarily from a decline in revenue and profit forecasts for these two equity method investees reflecting significant market deterioration during the fourth quarter of fiscal 2009. The Company measured the amount of impairment for each investment by calculating the amount by which the carrying value of its investment exceeded its estimated fair value, based on projected discounted cash flows of each equity method investee. These impairment losses are included in equity in earnings of equity method investees on the Company's Consolidated Statements of Operations.

6. Fair Value of Financial Instruments (in part)

Investment in Equity Method Investee

For the year ended February 28, 2010, in connection with the Company's review of its equity method investments for other-than-temporary impairment in the third quarter of fiscal 2010, the Company's CWNA segment's international equity method investment, Ruffino, with a carrying value of $29.8 million was written down to its fair value of $4.2 million, resulting in a loss of $25.4 million. This loss is included in equity in earnings of equity method investees on the Company's Consolidated Statements of Operations. The Company measured the amount of impairment by calculating the amount by which the carrying value of its investment exceeded its estimated fair value, which was based on projected discounted cash flows of this equity method investee.

9. Other Assets (in part)

The major components of other assets are as follows:

(In millions)	February 28, 2011	February 28, 2010
Investments in equity method investees	$262.9	$278.5
Investment in Accolade	49.6	—
Deferred financing costs	47.3	47.1
Notes receivable	4.8	65.7
Other	22.4	70.2
	387.0	461.5
Less—Accumulated amortization	(28.1)	(19.1)
	$358.9	$442.4

Investments in Equity Method Investees—

Crown Imports:

Constellation Beers Ltd. ("Constellation Beers") (previously known as Barton Beers, Ltd.), an indirect wholly-owned subsidiary of the Company, and Diblo, S.A. de C.V. ("Diblo"), an entity owned 76.75% by Grupo Modelo, S.A.B. de C.V. ("Modelo") and 23.25% by Anheuser-Busch Companies, Inc., each have, directly or indirectly, equal interests in a joint venture, Crown Imports LLC ("Crown Imports"). Crown Imports has the exclusive right to import, market and sell Modelo's Mexican beer portfolio (the "Modelo Brands") in the U.S. and Guam. In addition, Crown Imports also has the exclusive rights to import, market and sell the Tsingtao and St. Pauli Girl brands in the U.S.

The Company accounts for the investment in Crown Imports under the equity method. Accordingly, the results of operations of Crown Imports are included in equity in earnings of equity method investees on the Company's Consolidated Statements of Operations. As of February 28, 2011, and February 28, 2010, the Company's investment in Crown Imports was $183.3 million and $167.2 million, respectively. The carrying amount of the investment is greater than the Company's equity in the underlying assets of Crown Imports by $13.6 million due to the difference in the carrying amounts of the indefinite lived intangible assets contributed to Crown Imports by each party. The Company received $210.0 million, $191.7 million and $265.9 million of cash distributions from Crown Imports for the years ended February 28, 2011, February 28, 2010, and February 28, 2009, respectively, all of which represent distributions of earnings.

Constellation Beers provides certain administrative services to Crown Imports. Amounts related to the performance of these services for the years ended February 28, 2011, February 28, 2010, and February 28, 2009, were not material. In addition, as of February 28, 2011, and February 28, 2010, amounts receivable from Crown Imports were not material.

Ruffino:

The Company has a 49.9% interest in Ruffino, the well-known Italian fine wine company. The Company does not have a controlling interest in Ruffino or exert any managerial control. The Company accounts for the investment in Ruffino under the equity method; accordingly, the results of operations of Ruffino are included in equity in earnings of equity method investees on the Company's Consolidated Statements of Operations.

In connection with the Company's December 2004 investment in Ruffino, the Company granted separate irrevocable and unconditional options to the two other shareholders of Ruffino to put to the Company all of the ownership interests held by these shareholders for a price as calculated in the joint venture agreement. Each option was exercisable during the period starting from January 1, 2010, and ending on December 31, 2010. For the year ended February 28, 2010, in connection with the notification by the 9.9% shareholder of Ruffino to exercise its option to put its entire equity interest in Ruffino to the Company for the specified minimum value of €23.5 million, the Company recognized a loss of $34.3 million for the third quarter of fiscal 2010 on the contractual obligation created by this notification. This loss was included in selling, general and administrative expenses on the Company's Consolidated Statements of Operations. In May 2010, the Company settled this put option through a cash payment of €23.5 million ($29.6 million) to the 9.9% shareholder of Ruffino, thereby increasing the Company's equity interest in Ruffino from 40.0% to 49.9%. In December 2010, the Company received notification from the 50.1% shareholder of Ruffino that it was exercising its option to put its entire equity interest in Ruffino to the Company for €55.9 million. Prior to this notification, the Company had initiated arbitration proceedings against the 50.1% shareholder alleging various matters which should affect the validity of the put option. However, subsequent to the initiation of the arbitration proceedings, the Company began discussions with the 50.1% shareholder on a framework for settlement of all legal actions. The framework of the settlement would include the Company's purchase of the 50.1% shareholder's entire equity interest in Ruffino on revised terms to be agreed upon by both parties. As a result, the Company recognized a loss for the fourth quarter of fiscal 2011 of €43.4 million ($60.0 million) on the contingent obligation. This loss is included in selling, general and administrative expenses on the Company's Consolidated Statements of Operations. As of February 28, 2011, and February 28, 2010, the Company's investment in Ruffino was $7.4 million and $4.1 million, respectively.

The Company's CWNA segment distributes Ruffino's products, primarily in the U.S. Amounts purchased from Ruffino under this arrangement for the years ended February 28, 2011, February 28, 2010, and February 28, 2009, were not material. As of February 28, 2011, and February 28, 2010, amounts payable to Ruffino were not material.

Other:

In connection with prior acquisitions, the Company acquired several investments which are being accounted for under the equity method. The primary investment consists of Opus One Winery LLC ("Opus One"), a 50% owned joint venture arrangement. As of February 28, 2011, and February 28, 2010, the Company's investment in Opus One was $57.2 million and $57.4 million, respectively. The percentage of ownership of the remaining investments ranges from 20% to 50%.

The following table presents summarized financial information for the Company's Crown Imports equity method investment and the other material equity method investments discussed above. The amounts shown represent 100% of these equity method investments' financial position and results of operations.

| (In millions) | February 28, 2011 | | | February 28, 2010 | | |
	Crown Imports	Other	Total	Crown Imports	Other	Total
Current assets	$ 386.9	$ 110.1	$ 497.0	$ 336.6	$ 255.7	$ 592.3
Noncurrent assets	$ 32.1	$ 120.9	$ 153.0	$ 32.3	$ 177.6	$ 209.9
Current liabilities	$(147.5)	$(100.7)	$(248.2)	$(161.7)	$(198.1)	$(359.8)
Noncurrent liabilities	$ (0.1)	$ (76.3)	$ (76.4)	$ (0.1)	$(122.4)	$(122.5)

2.70

MICRON TECHNOLOGY, INC. (AUG)

CONSOLIDATED BALANCE SHEETS (in part)

(In millions except par value amounts)

As of	September 1, 2011	September 2, 2010
Assets		
Cash and equivalents	$ 2,160	$ 2,913
Receivables	1,497	1,531
Inventories	2,080	1,770
Other current assets	95	119
Total current assets	5,832	6,333
Intangible assets, net	414	323
Property, plant and equipment, net	7,555	6,601
Equity method investments	483	582
Restricted cash	8	335
Other noncurrent assets	460	519
Total assets	$14,752	$14,693

NOTES TO CONSOLIDATED FINANCIAL STATEMENTS

(All tabular amounts in millions except per share amounts)

Variable Interest Entities (in part)

We have interests in joint venture entities that are VIEs. If we are the primary beneficiary of the VIE, we are required to consolidate it. To determine if we are the primary beneficiary, we evaluate whether we have the power to direct the activities that most significantly impact the VIE's economic performance and the obligation to absorb losses or the right to receive benefits of the VIE that could potentially be significant to the VIE. Our evaluation includes identification of significant activities and an assessment of our ability to direct those activities based on governance provisions and arrangements to provide or receive product and process technology, product supply, operations services, equity funding, financing and other applicable agreements and circumstances. Our assessments of whether we are the primary beneficiary of our VIEs require significant assumptions and judgment. For further information regarding our VIEs that we

account for under the equity method, see "Equity Method Investments" note. For further information regarding our consolidated VIEs, see "Consolidated Variable Interest Entities" note.

Unconsolidated Variable Interest Entities (in part)

Inotera and MeiYa—Inotera Memories, Inc. ("Inotera") and MeiYa Technology Corporation ("MeiYa") are VIEs because of the terms of their supply agreements with us and our partner, Nanya Technology Corporation ("Nanya"). We have determined that we do not have power to direct the activities of Inotera and MeiYa that most significantly impact their economic performance, primarily due to (1) limitations on our governance rights that require the consent of other parties for key operating decisions and (2) our dependence on our joint venture partner for financing and the ability to operate in Taiwan. Therefore, we account for our interests in these entities under the equity method.

Transform—Transform Solar Pty Ltd. ("Transform") is a VIE because its equity is not sufficient to permit Transform to finance its activities without additional subordinated financial support from us and our partner, Origin Energy Limited ("Origin"). We have determined that we do not have power to direct the activities of Transform that most significantly impacts its economic performance, primarily due to limitations on our governance rights that require the consent of Origin for key operating decisions. Therefore, we account for our interest in Transform under the equity method.

Equity Method Investments (in part)

| As of | 2011 | | 2010 | |
	Investment Balance	Ownership Percentage	Investment Balance	Ownership Percentage
Inotera	$388	29.7%	$434	29.9%
MeiYa	1	50.0%	44	50.0%
Transform	87	50.0%	82	50.0%
Aptina	7	35.0%	22	35.0%
	$483		$582	

The summarized financial information in the tables below include the aggregate of all of our equity method investees on a stand-alone basis. The tables below include the respective years and periods through which we recorded our proportionate share of each of their results of operations, generally on a two-month lag. The summarized results of operations in the table below include the operating results of Inotera, Transform and Aptina only for the periods subsequent to our acquisition of our ownership interests.

As of	2011	2010
Current assets	$ 942	$ 898
Noncurrent assets (primarily property, plant and equipment)	4,189	3,537
Current liabilities	3,201	1,479
Noncurrent liabilities	173	900

For the Years Ended	2011	2010	2009
Net sales	$1,839	$1,927	$ 670
Gross margin	(268)	73	(370)
Operating loss	(559)	(181)	(473)
Net loss	(594)	(237)	(553)

Cost Method

2.71

ST. JUDE MEDICAL, INC. (DEC)

CONSOLIDATED BALANCE SHEETS (in part)

(In thousands, except share amounts)

	December 31, 2011	January 1, 2011
Assets		
Current assets		
Cash and cash equivalents	$ 985,807	$ 500,336
Accounts receivable, less allowances for doubtful accounts	1,366,877	1,331,210
Inventories	624,476	667,545
Deferred income taxes, net	231,907	196,599
Other current assets	181,499	216,458
Total current assets	3,390,566	2,912,148
Property, Plant and Equipment		
Land, buildings and improvements	528,346	493,992
Machinery and equipment	1,546,439	1,377,768
Diagnostic equipment	379,570	352,589
Property, plant and equipment at cost	2,454,355	2,224,349
Less accumulated depreciation	(1,065,946)	(900,418)
Net property, plant and equipment	1,388,409	1,323,931
Goodwill	2,952,937	2,955,602
Intangible assets, net	856,013	987,060
Other assets	417,268	387,707
Total assets	$ 9,005,193	$ 8,566,448

NOTES TO THE CONSOLIDATED FINANCIAL STATEMENTS

Note 12—Fair Value Measurements and Financial Instruments (in part)

Assets and Liabilities That are Measured at Fair Value on a Nonrecurring Basis (in part)

Cost method investments: The Company also holds investments in equity securities that are accounted for as cost method investments, which are classified as other assets and measured at fair value on a nonrecurring basis. The carrying value of these investments approximated $128 million and $124 million at December 31, 2011 and January 1, 2011, respectively. The fair value of the Company's cost method investments is not estimated if there are no identified events or changes in circumstances that may have a significant adverse effect on the fair value of these investments. When measured on a nonrecurring basis, the Company's cost method investments are considered Level 3 in the fair value hierarchy due to the use of unobservable inputs to measure fair value. During 2009, the Company determined that the fair value of a cost method investment was below its carrying value and that the carrying value of the investment would not be recoverable within a reasonable period of time. As a result, the Company measured the fair value of the investment using market participant valuations from recent and proposed equity offerings for this company (Level 3) and recognized an $8.3 million impairment charge in other expense (see Note 9), reducing the $13.5 million carrying value of the investment to $5.2 million. During 2010, the Company further determined that this cost method investment was fully impaired as it did not believe that any of the investment carrying value would be recovered due to the company's substantial inability to operate as a going concern given its financial condition. As a result, the Company recognized a $5.2 million impairment charge in other expense during 2010.

Fair Value

2.72

KOHL'S CORPORATION (JAN)

CONSOLIDATED BALANCE SHEETS (in part)

(Dollars in Millions, Except Per Share Data)

(Restated)

	January 29, 2011	January 30, 2010
Assets		
Current assets:		
Cash and cash equivalents	$ 2,277	$ 2,267
Merchandise inventories	3,036	2,923
Deferred income taxes	77	73
Other	252	222
Total current assets	5,642	5,485
Property and equipment, net	8,692	8,506
Long-term investments	277	321
Other assets	168	153
Total assets	$14,779	$14,465

NOTES TO CONSOLIDATED FINANCIAL STATEMENTS

1. Business and Summary of Accounting Policies (in part)

Long-Term Investments

Long-term investments consist primarily of investments in auction rate securities ("ARS") which are classified as available-for-sale securities and recorded at market.

3. Long-Term Investments

As of January 29, 2011, the par value of our long-term investments was $338 million and the estimated fair value was $277 million. Our auction rate securities ("ARS") portfolio consists entirely of highly-rated, insured student loan backed securities. Substantially all of the principal and interest is insured by the federal government and the remainder is insured by highly-rated insurance companies. Approximately $145 million of our ARS (at fair value) are rated "AAA" by Moody's, Standard & Poor's and/or Fitch Ratings.

Beginning in February 2008, liquidity issues in the global credit markets resulted in the failure of auctions for all of our ARS. A "failed" auction occurs when the amount of securities submitted for sale in the auction exceeds the amount of purchase bids. As a result, holders are unable to liquidate their investment through the auction. A failed auction is not a default of the debt instrument, but does set a new interest rate in accordance with the terms of the debt instrument. A failed auction limits liquidity for holders until there is a successful auction or until such time as another market for ARS develops. ARS are generally callable by the issuer at any time. Scheduled auctions continue to be held until the ARS matures or is called.

To date, we have collected all interest payable on outstanding ARS when due and expect to continue to do so in the future. At this time, we have no reason to believe that any of the underlying issuers of our ARS or their insurers are presently at risk or that the reduced liquidity has had a significant impact on the underlying credit quality of the assets backing our ARS. While the auction failures limit our ability to liquidate these investments, we do not believe these failures will have any significant impact on our ability to fund ongoing operations and growth initiatives.

We intend to hold these ARS until maturity or until we can liquidate them at par value. Based on our other sources of liquidity, we do not believe we will be required to sell them before recovery of par value. Therefore, impairment charges are considered temporary and have been included in Accumulated Other Comprehensive Loss within our Consolidated Balance Sheet. In certain cases, holding the investments until recovery may mean until maturity, which ranges from 2015 to 2056. The weighted-average maturity date is 2035. As a result of the persistent failed auctions and the uncertainty of when these investments could be successfully liquidated at par, we have recorded all of our ARS as Long-term Investments within the Consolidated Balance Sheet.

ASC No. 820, "Fair Value Measurements and Disclosures," requires fair value measurements be classified and disclosed in one of the following three categories:

Level 1: Financial instruments with unadjusted, quoted prices listed on active market exchanges.

Level 2: Financial instruments lacking unadjusted, quoted prices from active market exchanges, including over-the-counter traded financial instruments. The prices for the financial instruments are determined using prices for recently traded financial instruments with similar underlying terms as well as directly or indirectly observable inputs, such as interest rates and yield curves that are observable at commonly quoted intervals.

Level 3: Financial instruments that are not actively traded on a market exchange. This category includes situations where there is little, if any, market activity for the financial instrument. The prices are determined using significant unobservable inputs or valuation techniques.

The fair value for our ARS is based on third-party pricing models and is classified as a Level 3 pricing category. We utilized a discounted cash flow model to estimate the current fair market value for each of the securities we owned as there was no recent activity in the secondary markets in these types of securities. This model used unique inputs for each security including discount rate, interest rate currently being paid and maturity. The discount rate was calculated using the closest match available for other insured asset backed securities. A market failure scenario was employed as recent successful auctions of these securities were very limited.

The following table presents a rollforward of our long-term ARS, all of which are measured at fair value on a recurring basis using unobservable inputs (Level 3):

(In millions)	2010	2009
Balance at beginning of year	$320	$332
Sales	(42)	(28)
Unrealized gains/(losses)	(2)	16
Balance at end of year	$276	$320

Unrealized gains/(losses) are reported net of deferred taxes of $1 million at January 29, 2011 and $6 million at January 30, 2010 as a component of Accumulated Other Comprehensive Gain (Loss) in the Consolidated Statements of Changes in Shareholders' Equity.

NONCURRENT RECEIVABLES

PRESENTATION

2.73 FASB ASC 210, *Balance Sheet*, states that the concept of current assets excludes receivables arising from unusual transactions that are not expected to be collected within 12 months, such as the sale of capital assets or loans or advances to affiliates, officers, or employees.

2.74 FASB ASC 825 includes noncurrent receivables as financial instruments. FASB ASC 820 requires disclosure of both the fair value and bases for estimating the fair value of noncurrent receivables, unless it is not practicable to estimate that value. However, FASB ASC 825-10-50-14 indicates that for trade receivables and payables, fair value disclosure is not required if the carrying amount approximates fair value.

PRESENTATION AND DISCLOSURE EXCERPTS

Long-Term Receivables

2.75

AUTOMATIC DATA PROCESSING, INC. (JUN)

CONSOLIDATED BALANCE SHEETS (in part)

(In millions, except per share amounts)

June 30	2011	2010
Assets		
Current assets:		
Cash and cash equivalents	$ 1,389.4	$ 1,643.3
Short-term marketable securities	36.3	27.9
Accounts receivable, net	1,364.8	1,127.7
Other current assets	648.3	673.4
Assets held for sale	9.1	11.8
Total current assets before funds held for clients	3,447.9	3,484.1
Funds held for clients	25,135.6	18,832.6
Total current assets	28,583.5	22,316.7
Long-term marketable securities	98.0	104.3
Long-term receivables, net	128.7	129.4
Property, plant and equipment, net	716.2	673.8
Other assets	922.6	712.3
Goodwill	3,073.6	2,383.3
Intangible assets, net	715.7	542.4
Total assets	$34,238.3	$26,862.2

NOTES TO CONSOLIDATED FINANCIAL STATEMENTS

(Tabular dollars in millions, except per share amounts)

Note 1. Summary of Significant Accounting Policies (in part)

F. Long-term Receivables. Long-term receivables relate to notes receivable from the sale of computer systems, primarily to auto, truck, motorcycle, marine, recreational vehicle and heavy equipment dealers. Unearned income from finance receivables represents the excess of gross receivables over the sales price of the computer systems financed. Unearned income is amortized using the effective-interest method to maintain a constant rate of return over the term of each contract.

The allowance for doubtful accounts on long-term receivables is the Company's best estimate of the amount of probable credit losses related to the Company's existing note receivables.

Note 7. Receivables

Accounts receivable, net, includes the Company's trade receivables, which are recorded based upon the amount the Company expects to receive from its clients, net of an allowance for doubtful accounts. The Company's receivables also include notes receivable for the financing of the sale of computer systems, primarily from auto, truck, motorcycle, marine, recreational vehicle and heavy equipment dealers. Notes receivable are recorded based upon the amount the Company expects to receive from its clients, net of an allowance for doubtful accounts and unearned income. The allowance for doubtful accounts is the Company's best estimate of probable credit losses related to trade receivables and notes receivable based upon the aging of the receivables, historical collection data, internal assessments of credit quality and the economic conditions in the automobile industry, as well as in the economy as a whole. The Company charges off uncollectable amounts against the reserve in the period in which it determines they are uncollectable. Unearned income on notes receivable is amortized using the effective interest method.

The Company's receivables, whose carrying value approximates fair value, are as follows:

	June 30, 2011		June 30, 2010	
	Current	Long-Term	Current	Long-Term
Trade receivables	$1,333.2	$ —	$1,076.3	$ —
Notes receivable	90.5	146.4	110.3	155.0
Less:				
Allowance for doubtful accounts—trade receivables	(44.8)	—	(39.6)	—
Allowance for doubtful accounts—notes receivable	(5.7)	(9.4)	(9.4)	(16.1)
Unearned income-notes receivable	(8.4)	(8.3)	(9.9)	(9.5)
Total	$1,364.8	$128.7	$1,127.7	$129.4

Long-term receivables at June 30, 2011 mature as follows:

2013	$ 67.5
2014	45.4
2015	24.5
2016	9.0
2017	—
	$146.4

The Company determines the allowance for doubtful accounts related to notes receivable based upon a specific reserve for known collection issues, as well as a non-specific reserve based upon aging, both of which are based upon history of such losses and current economic conditions. Based upon our methodology, the notes receivable balances with specific and non-specific reserves and the specific and non-specific reserves associated with those balances are as follows:

	June 30, 2011			
	Notes Receivable		Reserve	
	Current	Long-Term	Current	Long-Term
Specific Reserve	$ 0.6	$ 0.9	$0.6	$0.9
Non-specific Reserve	89.9	145.5	5.1	8.5
Total	$90.5	$146.4	$5.7	$9.4

	June 30, 2010			
	Notes Receivable		Reserve	
	Current	Long-Term	Current	Long-Term
Specific Reserve	$ 3.8	$ 6.6	$3.8	$ 6.6
Non-specific Reserve	106.5	148.4	5.6	9.5
Total	$110.3	$155.0	$9.4	$16.1

The rollforward of the allowance for doubtful accounts related to notes receivable is as follows:

	Current	Long-Term
Balance at June 30, 2010	$ 9.4	$16.1
Incremental provision	1.8	3.0
Recoveries	(3.7)	(6.8)
Chargeoffs	(1.8)	(2.9)
Balance at June 30, 2011	$ 5.7	$ 9.4

As of June 30, 2011 and June 30, 2010, the allowance for doubtful accounts as a percentage of notes receivable is approximately 6% and 10%, respectively.

Notes receivable aged over 30 days past due are considered delinquent. Notes receivable aged over 60 days past due and notes receivable with known collection issues are placed on non-accrual status. Interest revenue is not recognized on notes receivable while on non-accrual status. Cash payments received on non-accrual receivables is applied towards principal. When notes receivable on non-accrual status are again less than 60 days past due, recognition of interest revenue for notes receivable is resumed. At June 30, 2011, the Company had $2.2 million in notes receivable on non-accrual status, including $0.1 million of notes receivable aged over 60 days past due.

On an ongoing basis, the Company evaluates the credit quality of its financing receivables, utilizing aging of receivables, collection experience and charge-offs. In addition, the Company evaluates economic conditions in the auto industry and specific dealership matters, such as bankruptcy. As events related to a specific client dictate, the credit quality of a client is reevaluated.

The aging of the notes receivable past due at June 30, 2011 is as follows:

	Over 30 Days to 60 Days	Over 60 Days
Notes Receivables	$1.2	$0.1

At June 30, 2011, approximately 99% of notes receivable are current. During the twelve months ended June 30, 2011, the charge-offs as a percentage of notes receivable were 1.9%.

Notes Receivable

2.76

BASSETT FURNITURE INDUSTRIES, INCORPORATED (NOV)

CONSOLIDATED BALANCE SHEETS (in part)

November 26, 2011 and November 27, 2010
(In thousands, except share and per share data)

	2011	2010
Assets		
Current assets		
Cash and cash equivalents	$ 69,601	$ 11,071
Accounts receivable, net of allowance for doubtful accounts of $2,092 and $7,366 as of November 26, 2011 and November 27, 2010, respectively	14,756	31,621
Marketable securities	2,939	—
Inventories	45,129	41,810
Other current assets	7,778	6,969
Total current assets	140,203	91,471
Property and equipment, net	49,946	46,250
Long-term assets		
Investments	806	15,111
Retail real estate	16,257	27,513
Notes receivable, net of allowance for doubtful accounts and discounts of $4,140 and $6,748 as of November 26, 2011 and November 27, 2010, respectively	1,802	7,508
Other	14,160	9,464
Total long-term assets	33,025	59,596
Total assets	$223,174	$197,317

NOTES TO CONSOLIDATED FINANCIAL STATEMENTS

(In thousands, except share and per share data)

6. Notes Receivable (in part)

Notes receivable consists of the following:

	November 26, 2011	November 27, 2010
Notes receivable	$ 6,017	$14,914
Allowance for doubtful accounts and discounts on notes receivable	(4,140)	(6,748)
Notes receivable, net	1,877	8,166
Less: current portion of notes receivable	(75)	(658)
Long term notes receivable	$ 1,802	$ 7,508

Our notes receivable, which bear interest at rates ranging from 2% to 6%, consist primarily of amounts due from our licensees from loans made by the Company to help licensees fund their operations. Approximately 43% and 61% of our notes receivable represent conversions of past due accounts receivable at November 26, 2011 and November 27, 2010, respectively. We have discontinued these conversions and have no plans to resume this practice. At the inception of the note receivable, we determined whether the note carried a market rate of interest. A discount on the note was recorded if we determined that the note carried an interest rate below the market rate. We amortize the related note discount over the contractual term of the note and cease amortizing the discount to interest income when the present value of expected future cash flows is less than the carrying value of the note. Interest income on the notes receivable, which is included in other income (loss), net, was as follows:

	2011	2010	2009
Interest income	$129	$463	$681

The initial carrying value of the notes receivable was determined using present value techniques which consider the fair market rate of interest based on the licensee's risk profile and estimated cash flows to be received. The estimated fair value of our notes receivable portfolio was $1,877 at November 26, 2011 and $8,212 at November 27, 2010. The inputs into these fair value calculations reflect our market assumptions and are not observable. Consequently, the inputs are considered to be Level 3 as specified in the fair value hierarchy in ASC Topic 820, *Fair Value Measurements and Disclosures*. See Note 8.

Substantially all of our notes receivable comprise a single portfolio segment of financing receivables consisting of notes receivable from current and former licensees. These notes receivable are evaluated in three classes—those due from current licensees, those due from former licensees which are secured by real estate, and those due from former licensees which are unsecured. On a quarterly basis, we examine these notes receivable for evidence of impairment. With respect to current licensees, we consider factors such as licensee capitalization, projected operating performance, the viability of the market in which the licensee operates and the licensee's operating history, including our cash receipts from the licensee, licensee sales and any underlying collateral. Our evaluation of former licensees is primarily based upon payment history and an evaluation of the underlying collateral. After considering these factors, should we believe that all or a portion of the expected cash flows attributable to the note receivable will not be received, we record an impairment charge on the note by estimating future cash flows and discounting them at the effective interest rate. Any difference between the estimated discounted cash flows and the carrying value of the note is recorded as an increase to the allowance for doubtful accounts. Notes receivable are charged off if they are deemed to be uncollectible with no recoverable collateral value. Each note within a class is evaluated individually using the criteria described above as applicable to its respective class.

These notes receivable, as well as our accounts receivable, are generally secured by the filing of security statements in accordance with the Uniform Commercial Code and/or real estate owned by the maker of the note and in some cases, personal guarantees by our licensees.

INTANGIBLE ASSETS

RECOGNITION AND MEASUREMENT

2.77 FASB ASC 350, *Intangibles—Goodwill and Other*, specifies that goodwill and intangible assets that have indefinite lives are not subject to amortization but, rather, should be tested at least annually for impairment. In addition, FASB ASC 350 provides specific guidance on how to determine and measure impairment of goodwill and intangible assets not subject to amortization. Intangible assets that have finite useful lives should be amortized over their useful lives.

2.78 FASB ASC 350-20-35 delineates a comprehensive two-step approach to impairment testing of a reporting unit that includes goodwill. First, the goodwill impairment test compares the fair value of a reporting unit with its carrying amount, including goodwill. When the carrying amount is greater than zero and its fair value exceeds its carrying amount, the entity should not consider the goodwill impaired and the second step is unnecessary. When the carrying amount of the reporting unit exceeds its fair value, an entity should proceed to step two to measure the loss by comparing the implied fair value of the goodwill with its carrying value. When the carrying amount of the reporting unit is zero or negative, an entity should proceed to step two to measure an impairment loss, if any, when it is more likely than not that a goodwill impairment exists. An entity should evaluate whether there are adverse qualitative factors in making that "more likely than not" assessment. FASB ASC 350-20-35-30 (a)–(g) provide examples of such qualitative factors.

Author's Note

In September 2011, FASB issued ASU No. 2011-08, *Intangibles—Goodwill and Other (Topic 350): Testing Goodwill for Impairment*, to simplify how entities test goodwill for impairment. Previously, an annual quantitative assessment was required by comparing the fair value of a reporting unit with its carrying amount, including goodwill (step 1), but FASB now permits an entity to first assess qualitative factors to determine whether it is more likely than not that the fair value of a reporting unit is less than its carrying amount as a basis for determining whether it is necessary to perform the two-step goodwill impairment test described in FASB ASC 350. The more-likely-than-not threshold is defined as having a likelihood of more than 50 percent. This guidance is effective for annual and interim goodwill impairment tests performed for fiscal years beginning after December 15, 2011. Given the effective date of FASB ASU No. 2011-08, no survey entity will have adopted these requirements in its 2011 financial statements.

2.79 FASB ASC 350 also provides guidance on accounting for the cost of computer software developed or obtained for internal use and website development costs.

PRESENTATION

2.80 FASB ASC 350-20-45-1 requires that the aggregate amount of goodwill be presented as a separate line item in the balance sheet. Under FASB ASC 350-30-45-1, at minimum, all intangible assets should be aggregated and presented as a separate line item in the balance sheet. However, that requirement does not preclude the presentation of individual intangible assets or classes of intangible assets as separate line items. Rule 5-02 of Regulation S-X also calls for separately stating each class of intangible assets in excess of 5 percent of total assets and for separate presentation of the amount of accumulated amortization of intangible assets.

DISCLOSURE

2.81 FASB ASC 350 requires additional disclosures for each period for which a balance sheet is presented, including information about gross carrying amounts and changes therein of goodwill and other intangible assets, accumulated amortization for amortizable assets, and estimates about intangible asset amortization expense for each of the five succeeding fiscal years. For intangibles, the balance sheet disclosures should be in total and by major intangible asset class.

2.82

TABLE 2-7: INTANGIBLE ASSETS*

Table 2-7 lists those intangible assets, amortized or not, which are most frequently disclosed by the survey entities.

	Number of Entities		
	2011	2010	2009
Goodwill recognized in a business combination	435	443	434
Trademarks, brand names, copyrights	302	300	307
Customer lists/relationships	320	288	277
Technology	156	156	148
Licenses, franchises, memberships	73	104	96
Research and development acquired in a business combination	26	19	12
Software (described as intangible)	49	N/C^	N/C^
Patents	134	N/C^	N/C^
Noncompete covenants	89	N/C^	N/C^
Contracts, agreements, leasehold	81	N/C^	N/C^
Other, described	109	267	380

* Appearing in the balance sheet or notes to financial statements, or both.
^ N/C = Not compiled. Line item was not included in the table for the year shown.

2.83

TABLE 2-8: INTANGIBLE ASSETS AMORTIZATION PERIOD*

Table 2-8 lists the amortization periods for categories of intangible assets.

	Number of Entities 2011
Trademarks/Copyrights/Brand Names	
More than 40	5
31–40	4
21–30	18
11–20	60
Up to 10	79
Estimated/legal/contractual life	20
Customer Lists/Relationships	
More than 40	—
31–40	1
21–30	12
11–20	96
Up to 10	114
Estimated/legal/contractual life	20
Technology	
More than 40	—
31–40	—
21–30	3
11–20	41
Up to 10	71
Estimated/legal/contractual life	7
Software	
More than 40	—
31–40	—
21–30	—
11–20	5
Up to 10	24
Estimated/legal/contractual life	6
Licenses/Franchises/Memberships	
More than 40	1
31–40	3
21–30	9
11–20	16
Up to 10	14
Estimated/legal/contractual life	4

2.83

TABLE 2-8: INTANGIBLE ASSETS AMORTIZATION PERIOD—(continued)

	Number of Entities 2011
Research and Development Acquired in a Business Combination	
More than 40	—
31–40	—
21–30	—
11–20	—
Up to 10	5
Estimated/legal/contractual life	2
Patents	
More than 40	—
31–40	—
21–30	4
11–20	40
Up to 10	37
Estimated/legal/contractual life	10
Noncompete Covenants	
More than 40	—
31–40	—
21–30	1
11–20	9
Up to 10	47
Estimated/legal/contractual life	4
Contracts/Agreements/Leasehold	
More than 40	1
31–40	1
21–30	4
11–20	20
Up to 10	25
Estimated/legal/contractual life	8
Other, Described	
More than 40	4
31–40	2
21–30	4
11–20	21
Up to 10	38
Estimated/legal/contractual life	7

* This is the first year these data were compiled, so no prior year data exist.

PRESENTATION AND DISCLOSURE EXCERPTS

Goodwill

2.84

SUPERMEDIA INC. (DEC)

CONSOLIDATED BALANCE SHEETS (in part)

	At December 31	
(In millions, except share amounts)	2011	2010
Assets		
Current assets:		
Cash and cash equivalents	$ 90	$ 174
Accounts receivable, net of allowances of		
$59 and $89	147	210
Accrued taxes receivable	27	—
Deferred directory costs	155	199
Prepaid expenses and other	12	13
Total current assets	431	596
Property, plant and equipment	127	122
Less: accumulated depreciation	53	28
	74	94
Goodwill	704	1,707
Intangible assets, net	345	481
Pension assets	75	42
Other non-current assets	4	6
Total assets	$1,633	$2,926

NOTES TO CONSOLIDATED FINANCIAL STATEMENTS

Note 1 Description of Business and Summary of Significant Accounting Policies (in part)

Goodwill and Intangible Assets (in part)

The Company has goodwill of $704 million and intangible assets of $345 million on the consolidated balance sheet as of December 31, 2011.

Goodwill

In accordance with U.S. GAAP, impairment testing for goodwill is performed at least annually unless indicators of impairment exist in interim periods. The impairment test for goodwill uses a two-step approach, which is performed at the entity level (the reporting unit). Step one compares the fair value of the reporting unit (calculated using the enterprise value-market capitalization approach) to its carrying value. If the carrying value exceeds the fair value, there is a potential impairment and step two must be performed. Step two compares the carrying value of the reporting unit's goodwill to its implied fair value (i.e., the fair value of the reporting unit less the fair value of the unit's assets and liabilities, including identifiable intangible assets). If the carrying value of goodwill exceeds its implied fair value, the excess is required to be recorded as an impairment.

In September 2011, the Company recorded a non-cash, goodwill impairment charge of $1,003 million ($997 million after-tax). For additional information related to goodwill impairment, see Note 2.

The Company also performed its annual impairment test of goodwill as of October 1, 2011. The Company determined the fair value of the reporting unit exceeded the carrying value of the reporting unit; therefore there was no additional impairment of goodwill.

Recent Accounting Pronouncements (in part)

In December 2010, the FASB issued Accounting Standards Update No. 2010-28 ("ASU 2010-28"), *"When to Perform Step 2 of the Goodwill Impairment Test for Reporting Units with Zero or Negative Carrying Amounts (Topic 350)—Intangibles—Goodwill and Other,"* which amends the criteria for performing Step 2 of the goodwill impairment test for reporting units with zero or negative carrying amounts and requires performing Step 2 if qualitative factors indicate that it is more likely than not that a goodwill impairment exists. The Company adopted ASU 2010-28 on January 1, 2011 and it did not have an impact on our consolidated financial statements.

Note 2 Goodwill Impairment

In accordance with U.S. GAAP, impairment testing for goodwill is performed at least annually. The Company performs its annual impairment test as of October 1. Goodwill is tested for impairment between annual tests if an event occurs or circumstances change that would more likely than not reduce the fair value of a reporting unit below its carrying value.

The impairment test for goodwill uses a two-step approach, which is performed at the entity level as the Company has one reporting unit. Step 1 compares the fair value of the reporting unit to its carrying value including goodwill. If the carrying value exceeds the fair value, there is a potential impairment and Step 2 must be performed. Step 2 compares the carrying value of the reporting unit's goodwill to its implied fair value (i.e., the fair value of the reporting unit less the fair value of the unit's assets and liabilities, including identifiable intangible assets). If the carrying value of goodwill exceeds its implied fair value, the excess is recorded as an impairment.

The Company performed its annual test of goodwill as of October 1, 2011. The Company determined the fair value of the reporting unit exceeded the carrying value of the reporting unit.

For the quarter ended September 30, 2011, the Company concluded there were indicators of potential goodwill impairment, including the decline in the value of the Company's debt and equity securities and the impact of current economic and market conditions on our business. As a result of identifying indicators of impairment, the Company performed an impairment test of goodwill as of August 31, 2011.

In performing Step 1 of the impairment test, the Company estimated the fair value of the reporting unit using a combination of the income and market approaches with greater emphasis placed on the income approach, for purposes of estimating the total enterprise value for the Company.

The income approach is based on a discounted cash flow analysis and calculates the fair value of the reporting unit by estimating the after-tax cash flows attributable to the reporting unit and then discounting the after-tax cash flows to a present value, using a weighted average cost of capital ("WACC"). The WACC utilized in the Company's analysis using the income approach was 20%. The WACC is an estimate of the overall after-tax rate of return required for equity and debt holders of a business enterprise. The reporting unit's cost of equity and debt was developed based on data and factors relevant to the economy, the industry and the reporting unit. The cost of equity was estimated using the capital asset pricing model ("CAPM"). The CAPM uses a risk-free rate of return and an appropriate market risk premium for equity investments and the specific risks of the investment. The analysis also included comparisons to a group of guideline companies engaged in the same or similar businesses. The cost of debt was estimated using the current after-tax average borrowing cost that a market participant would expect to pay to obtain its debt financing assuming a target capital structure.

The market approach is based on the guideline publicly traded company method to determine the fair value of the reporting unit. Under this method, market multiples ratios were applied to the reporting unit's earnings with consideration given to the Company's size, product offerings, growth, and other relevant factors compared to those of the guideline companies. The guideline companies selected were engaged in the same or a similar line of business as the Company. Market multiples were then selected based on consideration of risk, growth, and profitability differences between the Company and the guideline companies. The selected market multiples were then multiplied by the Company's earnings streams for the twelve months ended June 30, 2011, an annual 2011 forecast, and an annual 2012 forecast, with each given equal weighting, to arrive at an estimate of fair value for the Company.

Based on the above analysis, it was determined that the carrying value of the reporting unit including goodwill exceeded the fair value of the reporting unit, requiring the Company to perform Step 2 of the goodwill impairment test to measure the amount of impairment loss, if any.

In performing Step 2 of the goodwill impairment test, the Company compared the implied fair value of the reporting unit's goodwill to its carrying value of goodwill. This test resulted in a non-cash, goodwill impairment charge of $1,003 million ($997 million after-tax), which was recognized during the three months ended September 30, 2011. This charge had no impact on our cash flows or our compliance with debt covenants.

The following table sets forth the balance of the Company's goodwill as of December 31, 2010 and 2011:

(In millions)	December 31, 2010	Additions	Impairments	December 31, 2011
Goodwill, gross	$1,707	$—	$ —	$1,707
Accumulated impairment losses	—	—	(1,003)	(1,003)
Total goodwill, net	$1,707	$—	$(1,003)	$704

The fair value estimates used in the goodwill impairment analysis required significant judgment. The Company's fair value estimates for purposes of determining the goodwill impairment charge are considered Level 3 fair value measurements. We based our fair value estimates on assumptions that we believe to be reasonable but that are inherently uncertain, including estimates of future revenues and operating margins and assumptions about the overall economic climate and the competitive environment for our business. Our estimates assume that revenues will decline into the foreseeable future. There can be no assurance that our estimates and assumptions will prove to be accurate predictions of the future. If our assumptions regarding business plans, competitive environments or anticipated operating results are not correct, we may be required to record goodwill impairment charges in future periods.

2.85

BOSTON SCIENTIFIC CORPORATION (DEC)

CONSOLIDATED BALANCE SHEETS (in part)

	As of December 31	
(In millions, except share and per share data)	2011	2010
Assets		
Current assets:		
Cash and cash equivalents	$ 267	$ 213
Trade accounts receivable, net	1,246	1,320
Inventories	931	894
Deferred income taxes	458	429
Assets held for sale		576
Prepaid expenses and other current assets	203	183
Total current assets	3,105	3,615
Property, plant and equipment, net	1,670	1,697
Goodwill	9,761	10,186
Other intangible assets, net	6,473	6,343
Other long-term assets	281	287
Total assets	$21,290	$22,128

NOTES TO THE CONSOLIDATED FINANCIAL STATEMENTS

Note A—Significant Accounting Policies (in part)

Goodwill Valuation

We allocate any excess purchase price over the fair value of the net tangible and identifiable intangible assets acquired in a business combination to goodwill. We test our April 1 goodwill balances during the second quarter of each year for impairment, or more frequently if indicators are present or changes in circumstances suggest that impairment may exist. In performing the assessment, we utilize the two-step approach prescribed under ASC Topic 350, *Intangibles—Goodwill and Other*. The first step requires a comparison of the carrying value of the reporting units, as defined, to the fair value of these units. We assess goodwill for impairment at the reporting unit level, which is defined as an operating segment or one level below an operating segment, referred to as a component. We determine our reporting units by first identifying our operating segments, and then assess whether any components of these segments constitute a business for which discrete financial information is available and where segment management regularly reviews the operating results of that component. We aggregate components within an operating segment that have similar economic characteristics. For our April 1, 2011 annual impairment assessment, we identified six reporting units within the U.S., including our CRM, Neuromodulation, Endoscopy, Urology/Women's Health, Electrophysiology, and Cardiovascular (consisting of Interventional Cardiology and Peripheral Interventions) franchises, which in aggregate make up the U.S. reportable segment. In addition, we identified four international reporting units, including EMEA, Japan, Asia Pacific and the Americas. When allocating goodwill from business combinations to our reporting units, we assign goodwill to the reporting units that we expect to benefit from the respective business combination at the time of acquisition. In addition, for purposes of performing our annual goodwill impairment test, assets and liabilities, including corporate assets, which relate to a reporting unit's operations and would be considered in determining its fair value, are allocated to the individual reporting units. We allocate assets and liabilities not directly related to a specific reporting unit, but from which the reporting unit benefits, based primarily on the respective revenue contribution of each reporting unit.

During 2011, 2010, and 2009, we used only the income approach, specifically the discounted cash flow (DCF) method, to derive the fair value of each of our reporting units in preparing our goodwill impairment assessment. This approach calculates fair value by estimating the after-tax cash flows attributable to a reporting unit and then discounting these after-tax cash flows to a present value using a risk-adjusted discount rate. We selected this method as being the most meaningful in preparing our goodwill assessments because we believe the income approach most appropriately measures our income producing assets. We have considered using the market approach and cost approach but concluded they are not appropriate in valuing our reporting units given the lack of relevant market comparisons available for application of the market approach and the inability to replicate the value of the specific technology-based assets within our reporting units for application of the cost approach. Therefore, we believe that the income approach represents the most appropriate valuation technique for which sufficient data is available to determine the fair value of our reporting units.

In applying the income approach to our accounting for goodwill, we make assumptions about the amount and timing of future expected cash flows, terminal value growth rates and appropriate discount rates. The amount and timing of future cash flows within our DCF analysis is based on our most recent operational budgets, long range strategic plans and other estimates. The terminal value growth rate is used to calculate the value of cash flows beyond the last projected period in our DCF analysis and reflects our best estimates for stable, perpetual growth of our reporting units. We use estimates of market-participant risk-adjusted weighted-average costs of capital (WACC) as a basis for determining the discount rates to apply to our reporting units' future expected cash flows.

If the carrying value of a reporting unit exceeds its fair value, we then perform the second step of the goodwill impairment test to measure the amount of impairment loss, if any. The second step of the goodwill impairment test compares the estimated fair value of a reporting unit's goodwill to its carrying value. If we were unable to complete the second step of the test prior to the issuance of our financial statements and an impairment loss was probable and could be reasonably estimated, we would recognize our best estimate of the loss in our current period financial statements and disclose that the amount is an estimate. We would then recognize any adjustment to that estimate in subsequent reporting periods, once we have finalized the second step of the impairment test. See *Note D—Goodwill and Other Intangible Assets* for discussion of our 2011 and 2010 goodwill impairment charges.

Note D—Goodwill and Other Intangible Assets (in part)

The gross carrying amount of goodwill and other intangible assets and the related accumulated amortization for intangible assets subject to amortization and accumulated write-offs of goodwill as of December 31, 2011 and 2010 is as follows:

(In millions)	As of December 31, 2011		As of December 31, 2010	
	Gross Carrying Amount	Accumulated Amortization/ Write-Offs	Gross Carrying Amount	Accumulated Amortization/ Write-Offs
Amortizable intangible assets				
Technology—core	$ 6,786	$(1,722)	$ 6,658	$(1,424)
Technology—developed	1,037	(1,012)	1,026	(966)
Patents	539	(331)	527	(309)
Other intangible assets	808	(376)	808	(325)
	$ 9,170	$(3,441)	$ 9,019	$(3,024)
Unamortizable intangible assets				
Goodwill	$14,888	$(5,127)	$14,616	$(4,430)
Technology—core	242		291	
Purchased research and development	502		57	
	$15,632	$(5,127)	$14,964	$(4,430)

Goodwill Impairment Charges

2011 Charge

We test our April 1 goodwill balances during the second quarter of each year for impairment, or more frequently if indicators are present or changes in circumstances suggest that impairment may exist. Based on market information that became available to us toward the end of the first quarter of 2011, we concluded that there was a reduction in the estimated size of the U.S. implantable cardioverter defibrillator (ICD) market, which led to lower projected U.S. Cardiac Rhythm Management (CRM) results compared to prior forecasts and created an indication of potential impairment of the goodwill balance attributable to our U.S. CRM business unit. Therefore, we performed an interim impairment test in accordance with U.S. GAAP and our accounting policies and recorded a non-deductible goodwill impairment charge of $697 million, on both a pre-tax and after-tax basis, associated with this business unit during the first quarter of 2011.

We used the income approach, specifically the discounted cash flow (DCF) method, to derive the fair value of the U.S. CRM reporting unit. We updated all aspects of the DCF model associated with the U.S. CRM business, including the amount and timing of future expected cash flows, terminal value growth rate and the appropriate market-participant risk-adjusted weighted average cost of capital (WACC) to apply.

As a result of physician reaction to study results published by the Journal of the American Medical Association regarding evidence-based guidelines for ICD implants and U.S. Department of Justice (DOJ) investigations into hospitals' ICD implant practices and the expansion of Medicare recovery audits, among other factors, we estimated the U.S. CRM market would experience negative growth rates in 2011, as compared to 2010. Due to these estimated near-term market reductions, as well as the economic impact of physician alignment to hospitals, recent demographic information released by the American Heart Association indicating a lower prevalence of heart failure, and increased competitive and other pricing pressures, we lowered our estimated average U.S. CRM net sales growth rates within our 15-year DCF model from the mid-single digits to the low-single digits. Partially offsetting these factors are increased levels of prof-

itability as a result of cost-reduction initiatives and process efficiencies within the U.S. CRM business. The impact of the reduction in the size of the U.S. ICD market, and the related reduction in our forecasted 2011 U.S. CRM net sales, as well as the change in our expected sales growth rates thereafter as a result of the trends noted above were the key factors contributing to the first quarter 2011 goodwill impairment charge.

In the second quarter of 2011, we performed our annual goodwill impairment test for all of our reporting units. In conjunction with our annual test, the fair value of each reporting unit exceeded its carrying value, with the exception of our U.S. CRM reporting unit. Based on the remaining book value of our U.S. CRM reporting unit following the goodwill impairment charge recorded during the first quarter of 2011, the carrying value of our U.S. CRM reporting unit exceeded its fair value, due primarily to the value of amortizable intangible assets allocated to this reporting unit. The remaining book value of our U.S. CRM amortizable intangible assets was approximately $3.3 billion as of December 31, 2011. In accordance with ASC Topic 350, *Intangibles—Goodwill and Other* and our accounting policies, we tested our U.S. CRM amortizable intangible assets for impairment on an undiscounted cash flow basis as of March 31, 2011, in conjunction with the goodwill impairment charge, and determined that these assets were not impaired. The assumptions used in our annual goodwill impairment test performed during the second quarter of 2011 related to our U.S. CRM reporting unit were substantially consistent with those used in our first quarter interim impairment test; therefore, it was not deemed necessary to proceed to the second step of the impairment test.

We continue to identify four reporting units with a material amount of goodwill that are at higher risk of potential failure of the first step of the impairment test in future reporting periods. These reporting units include our U.S. CRM reporting unit, which holds $780 million of allocated goodwill; our U.S. Cardiovascular reporting unit, which holds $2.4 billion of allocated goodwill; our U.S. Neuromodulation reporting unit, which holds $1.3 billion of allocated goodwill; and our EMEA region, which holds $4.0 billion of allocated goodwill, each as of December 31, 2011. As of the most recent annual assessment as of April 1, the level of excess fair value over carrying value for these reporting units identified as being at higher risk (with the exception of the U.S. CRM reporting unit, whose carrying value continues to exceed its fair value) ranged from approximately eight percent to 15 percent. On a quarterly basis, we monitor the key drivers of fair value for these reporting units to detect events or other changes that would warrant an interim impairment test. The key variables that drive the cash flows of our reporting units are estimated revenue growth rates, levels of profitability and terminal value growth rate assumptions, as well as the WACC rate applied. These assumptions are subject to uncertainty, including our ability to grow revenue and improve profitability levels. For each of these reporting units, relatively small declines in the future performance and cash flows of the reporting unit or small changes in other key assumptions, including increases to the reporting unit carrying value, may result in the recognition of significant goodwill impairment charges. For example, keeping all other variables constant, a 50 basis point increase in the WACC applied to the reporting units, excluding acquisitions, would require that we perform the second step of the goodwill impairment test for our U.S. CRM reporting unit, and a 100 basis point increase would require that we perform the second step of the goodwill impairment test for our U.S. Neuromodulation, U.S. Cardiovascular and EMEA reporting units. In addition, keeping all other variables constant, a 100 basis point decrease in terminal value growth rates would require that we perform the second step of the goodwill impairment test for our U.S. CRM reporting unit, and a 200 basis point decrease in terminal value growth rates would require that we perform the second step of the goodwill impairment test for our U.S. Neuromodulation and EMEA reporting units. During the third and fourth quarters of 2011, we closely monitored these key variables and other factors and determined that we were not required to perform an interim impairment test. The estimates used for our future cash flows and discount rates represent management's best estimates, which we believe to be reasonable, but future declines in the business performance of our reporting units may impair the recoverability of our goodwill balance. Future events that could have a negative impact on the levels of excess fair value over carrying value of the reporting units include, but are not limited to:

- decreases in estimated market sizes or market growth rates due to greater-than-expected declines in procedural volumes, pricing pressures, product actions, and/or disruptive technology developments;
- declines in our market share and penetration assumptions due to increased competition, an inability to develop or launch new products, and market and/or regulatory conditions that may cause significant launch delays or product recalls;
- the impacts of the European sovereign debt crisis, including greater-than-expected declines in pricing, reductions in procedural volumes, fluctuations in foreign exchange rates, or an inability to collect or factor our EMEA accounts receivable;
- decreases in our profitability due to an inability to successfully implement and achieve timely and sustainable cost improvement measures consistent with our expectations, increases in our market-participant tax rate, and/or changes in tax laws;
- negative developments in intellectual property litigation that may impact our ability to market certain products or increase our costs to sell certain products;

- the level of success of on-going and future research and development efforts, including those related to recent acquisitions, and increases in the research and development costs necessary to obtain regulatory approvals and launch new products;
- the level of success in managing the growth of acquired companies, achieving sustained profitability consistent with our expectations, and establishing government and third-party payer reimbursement, and increases in the costs and time necessary to integrate acquired businesses into our operations successfully;
- declines in revenue as a result of loss of key members of our sales force and other key personnel;
- increases in our market-participant risk-adjusted WACC; and
- changes in the structure of our business as a result of future reorganizations or divestitures of assets or businesses.

Negative changes in one or more of these factors could result in additional impairment charges.

2010 Charge

The ship hold and product removal actions associated with our U.S. ICD and cardiac resynchronization therapy defibrillator (CRT-D) products, which we announced on March 15, 2010, and the forecasted corresponding financial impact on our operations created an indication of potential impairment of the goodwill balance attributable to our U.S. CRM reporting unit during the first quarter of 2010. Therefore, we performed an interim impairment test in accordance with U.S. GAAP and our accounting policies and recorded an estimated non-deductible goodwill impairment charge of $1.817 billion, on both a pre-tax and after-tax basis, associated with our U.S. CRM reporting unit.

At the time we performed our 2010 interim goodwill impairment test, we estimated that our U.S. defibrillator market share would decrease approximately 400 basis points exiting 2010 as a result of the ship hold and product removal actions, as compared to our market share exiting 2009, and that these actions would negatively impact our 2010 U.S. CRM revenues by approximately $300 million. In addition, we expected that, our on-going U.S. CRM net sales and profitability would likely continue to be adversely impacted as a result of the ship hold and product removal actions. Therefore, as a result of these product actions, as well as lower expectations of market growth in new areas and increased competitive and other pricing pressures, we lowered our estimated average U.S. CRM net sales growth rates within our 15-year discounted cash flow (DCF) model, as well as our terminal value growth rate, by approximately a couple of hundred basis points to derive the fair value of the U.S. CRM reporting unit. The reduction in our forecasted 2010 U.S. CRM net sales, the change in our expected sales growth rates thereafter and the reduction in profitability as a result of the recently enacted excise tax on medical device manufacturers were several key factors contributing to the impairment charge. Partially offsetting these factors was a 50 basis point reduction in our estimated market-participant risk-adjusted weighted-average cost of capital (WACC) used in determining our discount rate.

Trademarks and Other Intangibles

2.86

AGCO CORPORATION (DEC)

CONSOLIDATED BALANCE SHEETS (in part)

(In millions, except share amounts)

	December 31, 2011	December 31, 2010
Assets		
Current assets:		
Cash and cash equivalents	$ 724.4	$ 719.9
Accounts and notes receivable, net	994.2	908.5
Inventories, net	1,559.6	1,233.5
Deferred tax assets	142.7	52.6
Other current assets	241.9	206.5
Total current assets	3,662.8	3,121.0
Property, plant and equipment, net	1,222.6	924.8
Investment in affiliates	346.3	398.0
Deferred tax assets	37.6	58.0
Other assets	126.9	130.8
Intangible assets, net	666.5	171.6
Goodwill	1,194.5	632.7
Total assets	$7,257.2	$5,436.9

NOTES TO CONSOLIDATED FINANCIAL STATEMENTS

1. Operations and Summary of Significant Accounting Policies (in part)

Goodwill and Other Intangible Assets (in part)

The Company amortizes certain acquired identifiable intangible assets primarily on a straight-line basis over their estimated useful lives, which range from five to 45 years. The acquired intangible assets have a weighted average useful life as follows:

Intangible Asset	Weighted-Average Useful Life
Customer relationships	13 years
Technology and patents	13 years
Trademarks and tradenames	21 years
Land use rights	45 years

For the years ended December 31, 2011, 2010 and 2009, acquired intangible asset amortization was $21.6 million, $18.4 million and $18.0 million, respectively. The Company estimates amortization of existing intangible assets will be $48.7 million for 2012, $48.7 million for 2013, $40.2 million for 2014, $40.2 million for 2015, and $39.0 million for 2016.

The Company has previously determined that two of its trademarks have an indefinite useful life. The Massey Ferguson trademark has been in existence since 1952 and was formed from the merger of Massey-Harris (established in the 1890's) and Ferguson (established in the 1930's). The Massey Ferguson brand is currently sold in over 140 countries worldwide, making it one of the most widely sold tractor brands in the world. The Company has also identified the Valtra trademark as an indefinite-lived asset. The Valtra trademark has been in existence since the late 1990's, but is a derivative of the Valmet trademark which has been in existence since 1951. Valtra and Valmet are used interchangeably in the marketplace today, and Valtra is recognized to be the tractor line of the Valmet name. The Valtra brand is currently sold in approximately 50 countries around the world. Both the Massey Ferguson brand and the Valtra brand are primary product lines of the Company's business, and the Company plans to use these trademarks for an indefinite period of time. The Company plans to continue to make investments in product development to enhance the value of these brands into the future. There are no legal, regulatory, contractual, competitive, economic or other factors that the Company is aware of or that the Company believes would limit the useful lives of the trademarks. The Massey Ferguson and Valtra trademark registrations can be renewed at a nominal cost in the countries in which the Company operates.

Changes in the carrying amount of acquired intangible assets during 2011 and 2010 are summarized as follows (in millions):

	Trademarks and Tradenames	Customer Relationships	Patents and Technology	Land Use Rights	Total
Gross carrying amounts:					
Balance as of December 31, 2009	$ 33.4	$103.3	$54.3	$ —	$191.0
Acquisition	4.8	21.9	—	—	26.7
Foreign currency translation	0.2	(0.3)	(3.5)	—	(3.6)
Balance as of December 31, 2010	38.4	124.9	50.8	—	214.1
Acquisitions	79.7	396.1	36.5	8.5	520.8
Foreign currency translation	—	(9.6)	(1.6)	0.1	(11.1)
Balance as of December 31, 2011	$118.1	$511.4	$85.7	$8.6	$723.8

	Trademarks and Tradenames	Customer Relationships	Patents and Technology	Land Use Rights	Total
Accumulated amortization:					
Balance as of December 31, 2009	$ 9.9	$63.1	$46.5	$—	$119.5
Amortization expense	1.1	10.7	6.6	—	18.4
Foreign currency translation	—	(0.1)	(2.7)	—	(2.8)
Balance as of December 31, 2010	11.0	73.7	50.4	—	135.1
Amortization expense	2.1	18.2	1.3	—	21.6
Foreign currency translation	—	(6.6)	(1.4)	—	(8.0)
Balance as of December 31, 2011	$13.1	$85.3	$50.3	$—	$148.7

	Trademarks and Tradenames
Indefinite-lived intangible assets:	
Balance as of December 31, 2009	$95.3
Foreign currency translation	(2.7)
Balance as of December 31, 2010	92.6
Foreign currency translation	(1.2)
Balance as of December 31, 2011	$91.4

Merchandising Rights and Other Intangibles

2.87

LIZ CLAIBORNE, INC. (DEC)

CONSOLIDATED BALANCE SHEETS (in part)

In thousands, except share data	December 31, 2011	January 1, 2011
Assets		
Current assets:		
Cash and cash equivalents	$179,936	$ 22,714
Accounts receivable—trade, net	119,551	208,081
Inventories, net	193,343	289,439
Deferred income taxes	165	3,916
Other current assets	58,750	87,773
Total current assets	551,745	611,923
Property and equipment, net	238,664	375,529
Goodwill and intangibles, net	118,873	228,110
Deferred Income taxes	—	3,217
Other assets	40,722	38,880
Total assets	$950,004	$1,257,659

NOTES TO CONSOLIDATED FINANCIAL STATEMENTS

Note 1: Basis of Presentation and Significant Accounting Policies (in part)

Use of Estimates and Critical Accounting Policies (in part)

Intangibles, Net

Intangible assets with indefinite lives are not amortized, but rather tested for impairment at least annually. The Company's annual impairment test is performed as of the first day of the third fiscal quarter.

The fair values of purchased intangible assets with indefinite lives, primarily trademarks and tradenames, are estimated and compared to their carrying values. The Company estimates the fair value of these intangible assets based on an income approach using the relief-from-royalty method. This methodology assumes that, in lieu of ownership, a third party would be willing to pay a royalty in order to exploit the related benefits of these types of assets. This approach is dependent on a number of factors, including estimates of future growth and trends, royalty rates in the category of intellectual property, discount rates and other variables. The Company bases its fair value estimates on assumptions it believes to be reasonable, but which are unpredictable and inherently uncertain. Actual future results may differ from those estimates. The Company recognizes an impairment loss when the estimated fair value of the intangible asset is less than the carrying value.

The recoverability of the carrying values of all intangible assets with finite lives is re-evaluated when events or changes in circumstances indicate an asset's value may be impaired. Impairment testing is based on a review of forecasted operating cash flows and the profitability of the related brand. If such analysis indicates that the carrying value of these assets is not recoverable, the carrying value of such assets is reduced to fair value through a charge to the Consolidated Statement of Operations.

Intangible assets with finite lives are amortized over their respective lives to their estimated residual values. Trademarks with finite lives are amortized over their estimated useful lives. Intangible merchandising rights are amortized over a period of 3 to 4 years. Customer relationships are amortized assuming gradual attrition over periods ranging from 12 to 14 years.

The Company classifies gains and losses on the sales of trademarks as Other income (expense), net.

As a result of the impairment analysis performed in connection with the Company's purchased trademarks with indefinite lives, no impairment charges were recorded during 2011, 2010 or 2009.

During 2011, the Company recorded non-cash impairment charges of $1.0 million primarily within its Adelington Design Group & Other segment principally related to merchandising rights of its MONET and former licensed DKNY® Jeans brands due to decreased use of such intangible assets.

During 2010, the Company recorded non-cash impairment charges of $2.6 million primarily within its Adelington Design Group & Other segment principally related to merchandising rights of its LIZ CLAIBORNE and former licensed DKNY®

Jeans brands due to decreased use of such intangible assets.

Also, as a result of the decline in actual and projected performance and cash flows of the former licensed DKNY® Jeans and DKNY® Active brands during 2009, the Company determined the carrying value of the related licensed trademark intangible asset exceeded its estimated fair value and recorded a non-cash impairment charge of $9.5 million.

In addition, as a result of the Company's entering into the 2009 license agreements with JCPenney and QVC (see Note 16—Additional Financial Information), the Company performed an impairment analysis of its LIZ CLAIBORNE merchandising rights. The decreased use of such intangible assets resulted in the recognition of a non-cash impairment charge of $4.5 million to reduce the carrying value of the merchandising rights to their estimated fair value.

Note 5: Goodwill and Intangibles, Net (in part)

The following tables disclose the carrying value of all the intangible assets:

(In thousands)	Weighted Average Amortization Period	December 31, 2011	January 1, 2011
Amortized intangible assets:			
Gross carrying amount:			
Owned trademarks	4 years	$ 1,479	$ 1,479
Customer relationships(a)	13 years	9,478	12,319
Merchandising rights(b)	4 years	17,742	29,048
Other	4 years	2,322	2,322
Subtotal	7 years	31,021	45,168
Accumulated amortization:			
Owned trademarks		(1,112)	(753)
Customer relationships		(5,426)	(4,453)
Merchandising rights		(12,837)	(21,744)
Other		(1,792)	(1,643)
Subtotal		(21,167)	(28,593)
Net:			
Owned trademarks		367	726
Customer relationships		4,052	7,866
Merchandising rights		4,905	7,304
Other		530	679
Total amortized intangible assets, net		9,854	16,575
Unamortized intangible assets:			
Owned trademarks (c)		107,500	210,127
Total intangible assets		117,354	226,702
Goodwill		1,519	1,408
Total goodwill and intangibles, net		$118,873	$228,110

(a) The decrease in the balance compared to January 1, 2011 primarily reflected the sale of the customer relationships associated with the Company's former KENSIE and MAC & JAC brands.

(b) The decrease in the balance compared to January 1, 2011 primarily reflected the sale of an 81.25% interest in the global MEXX business and included non-cash impairment charges of $1.0 million primarily within the Company's Adelington Design Group & Other segment related to the merchandising rights of its former MONET and former licensed DKNY® Jeans brands (see Note 1—Basis of Presentation and Significant Accounting Policies).

(c) The decrease in the balance compared to January 1, 2011 primarily reflected the sale of an 81.25% interest in the global MEXX business, the sale of the MONET trademark rights in the US and Puerto Rico and the sale of the KENSIE, KENSIE GIRL and MAC & JAC trademarks (see Note 1—Basis of Presentation and Significant Accounting Policies).

Amortization expense of intangible assets was $4.4 million, $5.6 million and $14.7 million for the years ended December 31, 2011, January 1, 2011 and January 2, 2010, respectively.

The estimated amortization expense of intangible assets for the next five years is as follows:

Fiscal Year	Amortization Expense
(In millions)	
2012	$2.9
2013	2.0
2014	1.6
2015	0.9
2016	0.5

Customer Contracts and Related Customer Relationships

2.88

CACI INTERNATIONAL INC (JUN)

CONSOLIDATED BALANCE SHEETS (in part)

(amounts in thousands, except per share data)

	June 30 2011	2010
Assets		
Current assets:		
Cash and cash equivalents	$ 164,817	$ 254,543
Accounts receivable, net	573,042	531,033
Deferred income taxes	16,080	12,641
Prepaid expenses and other current assets	28,139	42,529
Total current assets	782,078	840,746
Goodwill	1,266,285	1,161,861
Intangible assets, net	108,102	108,298
Property and equipment, net	62,755	58,666
Supplemental retirement savings plan assets	66,880	51,736
Accounts receivable, long-term	8,657	9,291
Other long-term assets	25,374	14,168
Total assets	$2,320,131	$2,244,766

NOTES TO CONSOLIDATED FINANCIAL STATEMENTS

Note 8. Intangible Assets

Intangible assets consisted of the following (in thousands):

	June 30 2011	2010
Customer contracts and related customer relationships	$ 291,174	$ 253,031
Acquired technologies	27,177	27,177
Covenants not to compete	3,070	2,373
Other	1,637	1,631
Intangible assets	323,058	284,212
Less accumulated amortization	(214,956)	(175,914)
Total intangible assets, net	$ 108,102	$ 108,298

Intangible assets are primarily amortized on an accelerated basis over periods ranging from 12 to 120 months. The weighted-average period of amortization for customer contracts and related customer relationships as of June 30, 2011 is 8.5 years, and the weighted-average remaining period of amortization is 6.8 years. The weighted-average period of amortization for acquired technologies as of June 30, 2011 is 6.7 years, and the weighted-average remaining period of amortization is 6.0 years.

Amortization expense for the years ended June 30, 2011, 2010 and 2009 was $38.8 million, $37.2 million, and $32.1 million, respectively. Accumulated amortization as of June 30, 2011 for customer contracts and related customer relationships and for acquired technologies was $198.7 million

and $13.0 million, respectively. Expected amortization expense for each of the fiscal years through June 30, 2016 and for periods thereafter is as follows (in thousands):

	Amount
Year ending June 30, 2012	$ 29,261
Year ending June 30, 2013	21,677
Year ending June 30, 2014	17,859
Year ending June 30, 2015	13,296
Year ending June 30, 2016	8,606
Thereafter	17,403
Total intangible assets, net	$108,102

Technology

2.89

INTEL CORPORATION (DEC)

CONSOLIDATED BALANCE SHEETS (in part)

(In Millions, Except Par Value)	December 31, 2011 and December 25, 2010 2011	2010
Assets		
Current assets:		
Cash and cash equivalents	$ 5,065	$ 5,498
Short-term investments	5,181	11,294
Trading assets	4,591	5,093
Accounts receivable, net of allowance for doubtful accounts of $36 ($28 in 2010)	3,650	2,867
Inventories	4,096	3,757
Deferred tax assets	1,700	1,488
Other current assets	1,589	1,614
Total current assets	25,872	31,611
Property, plant and equipment, net	23,627	17,899
Marketable equity securities	562	1,008
Other long-term investments	889	3,026
Goodwill	9,254	4,531
Identified intangible assets, net	6,267	860
Other long-term assets	4,648	4,251
Total assets	$71,119	$63,186

NOTES TO CONSOLIDATED FINANCIAL STATEMENTS

Note 2: Accounting Policies (in part)

Identified Intangible Assets

Licensed technology assets are generally amortized on a straight-line basis over the periods of benefit. We amortize all acquisition-related intangible assets that are subject to amortization over the estimated useful life based on economic benefit. Acquisition-related in-process research and development assets represent the fair value of incomplete research and development projects that had not reached technological feasibility as of the date of acquisition and are initially classified as "other intangible assets" that are not subject to amortization. Assets related to projects that have been completed are transferred from "other intangible assets" to "acquisition-related developed technology," and are subject to amortization, while assets related to projects that have been abandoned are impaired. In the quarter following the period in which identified intangible assets become fully amortized, the fully amortized balances are removed from the gross asset and accumulated amortization amounts.

The estimated useful life ranges for identified intangible assets that are subject to amortization as of December 31, 2011 are as follows:

	Estimated Useful Life (In Years)
Acquisition-related developed technology	3–9
Acquisition-related customer relationships	2–8
Acquisition-related trade names	5–7
Licensed technology	5–17

We perform a quarterly review of identified intangible assets to determine if facts and circumstances indicate that the useful life is shorter than we had originally estimated or that the carrying amount of assets may not be recoverable. If such facts and circumstances exist, we assess recoverability by comparing the projected undiscounted net cash flows associated with the related asset or group of assets over their remaining lives against their respective carrying amounts. Impairments, if any, are based on the excess of the carrying amount over the fair value of those assets. If the useful life is shorter than originally estimated, we accelerate the rate of amortization and amortize the remaining carrying value over the new shorter useful life.

For further discussion of identified intangible assets, see "Note 17: Identified Intangible Assets."

Note 17: Identified Intangible Assets

Identified intangible assets consisted of the following as of December 31, 2011 and December 25, 2010:

(In Millions)	December 31, 2011 Gross Assets	Accumulated Amortization	Net
Acquisition-related developed technology	$2,615	$ (570)	$2,045
Acquisition-related customer relationships	1,714	(254)	1,460
Acquisition-related trade names	68	(21)	47
Licensed technology	2,395	(707)	1,688
Identified intangible assets subject to amortization	$6,792	$(1,552)	$5,240
Acquisition-related trade names	806	—	806
Other intangible assets	221	—	221
Identified intangible assets not subject to amortization	$1,027	$ —	$1,027
Total identified intangible assets	$7,819	$(1,552)	$6,267

(In Millions)	December 25, 2010 Gross Assets	Accumulated Amortization	Net
Acquisition-related developed technology	$ 235	$ (97)	$138
Acquisition-related customer relationships	152	(10)	142
Acquisition-related trade names	46	(10)	36
Licensed technology	1,204	(765)	439
Identified intangible assets subject to amortization	$1,637	$(882)	$755
Other intangible assets	105	—	105
Total identified intangible assets	$1,742	$(882)	$860

As a result of our acquisition of McAfee during the first quarter of 2011, we recorded $3.6 billion of identified intangible assets. In addition, as a result of our other acquisitions during 2011, we recorded $1.4 billion of identified intangible assets, the substantial majority of which was from the acquisition of the WLS business of Infineon. For further information about identified intangible assets recorded as a result of acquisitions during 2011, see "Note 14: Acquisitions."

In January 2011, we entered into a long-term patent cross-license agreement with NVIDIA. Under the agreement, we received a license to all of NVIDIA's patents with a capture period that runs through March 2017 while NVIDIA products are licensed to our patents, subject to exclusions for x86 products, certain chipsets, and certain flash memory technology products. The agreement also included settlement of the existing litigation between the companies as well as broad mutual general releases. We agreed to make payments

totaling $1.5 billion to NVIDIA over six years ($300 million in each of January 2011, 2012, and 2013; and $200 million in each of January 2014, 2015, and 2016), which resulted in a liability totaling approximately $1.4 billion, on a discounted basis. In the fourth quarter of 2010, we recognized an expense of $100 million related to the litigation settlement. In the first quarter of 2011, we recognized the remaining amount of $1.3 billion as licensed technology, which will be amortized into cost of sales over its estimated useful life of 17 years. The initial recognition of the intangible asset and associated liability for future payments to NVIDIA is treated as a non-cash transaction and, therefore, has no impact on our consolidated statements of cash flows. Future payments will be treated as cash used for financing activities. As of December 31, 2011, the remaining liability of $1.2 billion is classified within other accrued liabilities and other long-term liabilities, based on the expected timing of the underlying payments.

As a result of our acquisitions in 2010, we recorded acquisition-related developed technology for $37 million with lives of four years, and additions to acquisition-related customer relationships of $58 million with a weighted average life of seven years. In addition, we acquired other intangible assets for $104 million in 2010 that are not subject to amortization.

We recorded amortization expense on the consolidated statements of income as follows: acquisition-related developed technology and licensed technology substantially all are in cost of sales, and acquisition-related customer relationships and trade names in amortization of acquisition-related intangibles.

Amortization expenses for the three years ended December 31, 2011 were as follows:

(In Millions)	2011	2010	2009
Acquisition-related developed technology	$482	$ 65	$ 30
Acquisition-related customer relationships	$250	$ 10	$ —
Acquisition-related trade names	$ 10	$ 8	$ 3
Licensed technology	$181	$157	$149
Other intangible assets	$ —	$ —	$126

Based on identified intangible assets that are subject to amortization as of December 31, 2011, we expect future amortization expense to be as follows:

(In Millions)	2012	2013	2014	2015	2016
Acquisition-related developed technology	$541	$526	$504	$235	$154
Acquisition-related customer relationships	$283	$265	$260	$252	$234
Acquisition-related trade names	$ 11	$ 11	$ 10	$ 10	$ 4
Licensed technology	$181	$164	$154	$135	$120

Software

2.90

THE DUN & BRADSTREET CORPORATION (DEC)

CONSOLIDATED BALANCE SHEETS (in part)

	December 31	
(Amounts in millions, except per share data)	2011	2010
Assets		
Current Assets		
Cash and cash equivalents	$ 84.4	$ 78.5
Accounts receivable, net of allowance of $17.1 at December 31, 2011 and $17.5 at December 31, 2010	507.5	504.3
Other receivables	5.7	8.3
Prepaid taxes	1.5	1.5
Deferred income tax	32.1	31.8
Other prepaids	55.1	36.6
Assets held for sale	32.7	0.0
Other current assets	7.9	7.3
Total current assets	726.9	668.3
Non-current assets		
Property, plant and equipment, net of accumulated depreciation of $83.1 at December 31, 2011 and $81.5 at December 31, 2010	45.7	53.1
Computer software, net of accumulated amortization of $409.9 at December 31, 2011 and $372.0 at December 31, 2010	127.6	127.9
Goodwill	598.4	599.7
Deferred income tax	243.1	181.7
Other receivables	58.4	66.3
Other intangibles (Note 15)	116.1	139.8
Other non-current assets	60.9	82.7
Total non-current assets	1,250.2	1,251.2
Total assets	$1,977.1	$1,919.5

NOTES TO CONSOLIDATED FINANCIAL STATEMENTS

(Tabular dollar amounts in millions, except per share data)

Note 1. Description of Business and Summary of Significant Accounting Policies (in part)

Computer Software. We develop various computer software applications for internal use including systems which support our databases and common business services and processes (back-end systems), our financial and administrative systems (backoffice systems) and systems which we use to deliver our information solutions to customers (customer-facing systems).

We expense costs as incurred during the preliminary development stage which includes conceptual formulation and review of alternatives. Once that stage is complete, we begin the application development stage which includes design, coding and testing. Direct internal and external costs incurred during this stage are capitalized. Capitalization of costs cease when the software is ready for its intended use and all substantial testing is completed. Upgrades and enhancements which provide added functionality are accounted for in the same manner. Maintenance costs incurred solely to extend the life of the software are expensed as incurred.

We periodically reassess the estimated useful lives of our computer software considering our overall technology strategy, the effects of obsolescence, technology, competition and other economic factors on the useful life of these assets. Effective April 1, 2009, we increased the lives of our back-end and back-office software from three to five years to five to eight years. Customer-facing software will continue to have lives of three to five years. The impact of this change for the year ended December 31, 2009 was a reduction in software amortization expense by approximately $7 million after-tax ($0.14 per diluted share), respectively.

Internal-use software is tested for impairment along with other long-lived assets (See Impairment of Long-Lived Assets).

We also develop software for sale to customers. Costs are expensed until technological feasibility is established after which costs are capitalized until the software is ready for general release to customers. Costs of enhancements that extend the life or improve the marketability of the software are capitalized once technological feasibility is reached. Maintenance and customer support are expensed as incurred.

Capitalized costs of software for sale are amortized on a straight-line basis over the estimated economic life of the software of three years. We continually evaluate recoverability of the unamortized costs, which are reported at the lower of unamortized cost or net realizable value.

The computer software amortization expense for the years ended December 31, 2011, 2010 and 2009 were $46.0 million, $40.1 million and $35.0 million, respectively. As of December 31, 2011 and 2010, we acquired $7.8 million and $4.6 million, respectively, of computer software, which was included in accounts payable and accrued liabilities on the accompanying consolidated balance sheet as of December 31, 2011 and 2010, and was therefore excluded from the consolidated statement of cash flows for the years ended December 31, 2011 and 2010, respectively.

Licenses

2.91

AT&T INC. (DEC)

CONSOLIDATED BALANCE SHEETS (in part)

	December 31	
Dollars in millions except per share amounts	**2011**	**2010**
Assets		
Current assets		
Cash and cash equivalents	$ 3,185	$ 1,437
Accounts receivable—net of allowances for doubtful accounts of $878 and $957	13,606	13,610
Prepaid expenses	1,155	1,458
Deferred income taxes	1,470	1,170
Other current assets	3,611	3,179
Total current assets	23,027	20,854
Property, plant and equipment—net	107,087	103,196
Goodwill	70,842	73,601
Licenses	51,374	50,372
Customer lists and relationships—net	2,757	4,708
Other intangible assets—net	5,212	5,440
Investments in equity affiliates	3,718	4,515
Other assets	6,327	6,705
Total assets	$270,344	$269,391

NOTES TO CONSOLIDATED FINANCIAL STATEMENTS

Dollars in millions except per share amounts

Note 1. Summary of Significant Accounting Policies (in part)

Goodwill and Other Intangible Assets—AT&T has four major classes of intangible assets: goodwill, Federal Communications Commission (FCC) licenses, other indefinite-lived intangible assets, made up predominately of the AT&T brand, and various other finite-lived intangible assets.

Goodwill represents the excess of consideration paid over the fair value of net assets acquired in business combinations. FCC licenses provide us with the exclusive right to utilize certain radio frequency spectrum to provide wireless communications services. While FCC licenses are issued for a fixed period of time (generally 10 years), renewals of FCC licenses have occurred routinely and at nominal cost. Moreover, we have determined that there are currently no legal, regulatory, contractual, competitive, economic or other factors that limit the useful lives of our FCC licenses. We acquired the rights to the AT&T and other brand names in previous acquisitions. We have the effective ability to retain these exclusive rights permanently at a nominal cost.

Goodwill, FCC licenses and other indefinite-lived intangible assets are not amortized but are tested at least annually for impairment. The testing is performed on the value as of October 1 each year, and is generally composed of comparing the book value of the assets to their fair value. Goodwill is tested by comparing the book value of each reporting unit, deemed to be our principal operating segments (Wireless, Wireline and Advertising Solutions), to the fair value of those reporting units calculated under a market multiple approach as well as a discounted cash flow approach. FCC licenses are tested for impairment on an aggregate basis, consistent with the management of the business on a national scope. We perform our test of the fair values of FCC licenses using a discounted cash flow model. Brand names are tested by comparing the book value to a fair value calculated using a discounted cash flow approach on a presumed royalty rate derived from the revenues related to the brand name. The fair value measurements used are considered Level 3 under the Fair Value and Disclosure framework (see Note 9).

Intangible assets that have finite useful lives are amortized over their useful lives, a weighted average of 8.3 years (7.9 years for customer lists and relationships and 11.2 years for other). Customer lists and relationships are amortized using primarily the sum-of-the-months-digits method of amortization over the expected period in which those relationships are expected to contribute to our future cash flows. The remaining finite-lived intangible assets are generally amortized using the straight-line method of amortization.

Note 2. Acquisitions, Dispositions and Other Adjustments (in part)

Acquisitions (in part)

Qualcomm Spectrum Purchase—In December 2011, we completed our purchase of spectrum licenses in the Lower 700 MHz frequency band from Qualcomm Incorporated (Qualcomm) for approximately $1,925 in cash. The spectrum covers more than 300 million people total nationwide, including 12 MHz of Lower 700 MHz D and E block spectrum covering more than 70 million people in five of the top 15 metropolitan areas and 6 MHz of Lower 700 MHz D block spectrum covering more than 230 million people across the rest of the United States. We plan to deploy this spectrum as supplemental downlink capacity, using carrier aggregation technology once compatible handsets and network equipment are developed.

Wireless Properties Transactions—In June 2010, we acquired certain wireless properties, including FCC licenses and network assets, from Verizon Wireless for $2,376 in cash. The assets primarily represent former Alltel Wireless assets and served approximately 1.6 million subscribers in 79 service areas across 18 states. The fair value of the acquired net assets of $1,439 included $368 of property, plant and equipment, $937 of goodwill, $765 of FCC licenses, and $224 of customer lists and other intangible assets.

Centennial—In December 2010, we completed our acquisition accounting of Centennial Communications Corporation (Centennial), which included net assets of $1,518 in goodwill, $655 in FCC licenses, and $449 in customer lists and other intangible assets.

Note 6. Goodwill and Other Intangible Assets (in part)

Our other intangible assets are summarized as follows:

	December 31, 2011		December 31, 2010	
Other Intangible Assets	**Gross Carrying Amount**	**Accumulated Amortization**	**Gross Carrying Amount**	**Accumulated Amortization**
Amortized intangible assets:				
Customer lists and relationships:				
AT&T Mobility LLC	$ 6,845	$ 5,906	$ 6,987	$ 5,240
BellSouth	9,205	7,686	9,215	6,807
AT&T Corp.	2,483	2,205	3,134	2,647
Other	350	329	350	284
Subtotal	18,883	16,126	19,686	14,978
Other	485	258	525	239
Total	$19,368	$16,384	$20,211	$15,217
Indefinite-lived intangible assets not subject to amortization:				
Licenses	$51,374		$50,372	
Trade names	4,985		5,154	
Total	$56,359		$55,526	

Amortized intangible assets are definite-life assets, and as such, we record amortization expense based on a method that most appropriately reflects our expected cash flows from these assets. Amortization expense for definite-life intangible assets was $2,009 for the year ended December 31, 2011, $2,977 for the year ended December 31, 2010, and $3,666 for the year ended December 31, 2009. Amortization expense is estimated to be $1,335 in 2012, $744 in 2013, $347 in 2014, $217 in 2015, and $123 in 2016. In 2011, we wrote off approximately $1,130 in fully amortized intangible assets (primarily customer lists). We review other amortizing intangible assets for impairment whenever events or circumstances indicate that the carrying amount may not be recoverable over the remaining life of the asset or asset group.

We review indefinite-lived intangible assets for impairment annually (see Note 1). Licenses include wireless FCC licenses of $51,358 at December 31, 2011 and $50,356 at December 31, 2010, that provide us with the exclusive right to utilize certain radio frequency spectrum to provide wireless communications services. In 2011, we completed our acquisition of spectrum from Qualcomm of $1,925, and recorded the intended transfer upon regulatory approval of $962 of spectrum licenses to Deutsche Telekom in conjunction with the termination of the T-Mobile merger agreement (see Note 2).

We recorded a $165 impairment in 2011 and an $85 impairment in 2010 for a trade name.

In-Process Research and Development (IPR&D)

2.92

MEDTRONIC, INC. (APR)

CONSOLIDATED BALANCE SHEETS (in part)

(In millions, except per share data)	April 29, 2011	April 30, 2010
Assets		
Current assets:		
Cash and cash equivalents	$ 1,382	$ 1,400
Short-term investments	1,046	2,375
Accounts receivable, less allowances of $97 and $67, respectively	3,822	3,335
Inventories	1,695	1,481
Deferred tax assets, net	605	544
Prepaid expenses and other current assets	567	704
Total current assets	9,117	9,839
Property, plant, and equipment, net	2,511	2,421
Goodwill	9,537	8,391
Other intangible assets, net	2,777	2,559
Long-term investments	6,120	4,632
Other assets	362	248
Total assets	$30,424	$28,090

NOTES TO CONSOLIDATED FINANCIAL STATEMENTS

1. Summary of Significant Accounting Policies (in part)

Intangible Assets—Intangible assets include patents, trademarks, purchased technology, and in-process research and development (IPR&D) (since April 25, 2009). Intangible assets with a definite life are amortized on a straight-line or accelerated basis, as appropriate, with estimated useful lives ranging from three to 20 years. Intangible assets are tested for impairment annually or whenever events or circumstances indicate that a carrying amount of an asset (asset group) may not be recoverable. Impairment is calculated as the excess of the asset's carrying value over its fair value. Fair value is generally determined using a discounted future cash flow analysis.

IPR&D—When the Company acquires another entity, the purchase price is allocated, as applicable, between IPR&D, other identifiable intangible assets, and net tangible assets, with the remainder recognized as goodwill. During fiscal year 2010, the Company adopted authoritative guidance related to business combinations. Under this guidance, IPR&D is capitalized. Prior to the adoption of this guidance, IPR&D was immediately expensed. The adoption of the authoritative guidance did not change the requirement to expense IPR&D immediately with respect to asset acquisitions. These IPR&D charges are included within *acquisition-related items* in the Company's consolidated statements of earnings. IPR&D has an indefinite life and is not amortized until completion and development of the project at which time the IPR&D becomes an amortizable asset. If the related project is not completed in a timely manner, the Company may have an impairment related to the IPR&D, calculated as the excess of the asset's carrying value over its fair value.

The Company's policy defines IPR&D as the value assigned to those projects for which the related products have not received regulatory approval and have no alternative future use. Determining the portion of the purchase price allocated to IPR&D requires the Company to make significant estimates. The amount of the purchase price allocated to IPR&D is determined by estimating the future cash flows of each project or technology and discounting the net cash flows back to their present values. The discount rate used is determined at the time of acquisition in accordance with accepted valuation methods. These methodologies include consideration of the risk of the project not achieving commercial feasibility.

At the time of acquisition, the Company expects all acquired IPR&D will reach technological feasibility, but there can be no assurance that the commercial viability of these products will actually be achieved. The nature of the efforts to develop the acquired technologies into commercially viable products consists principally of planning, designing, and conducting clinical trials necessary to obtain regulatory approvals. The risks associated with achieving commercialization include, but are not limited to, delay or failure to obtain regulatory approvals to conduct clinical trials, delay or failure to obtain required market clearances, and patent issuance, and validity and litigation, if any. If commercial viability were not achieved, the Company would likely look to other alternatives to provide these therapies.

6. Fair Value Measurements (in part)

Assets and Liabilities That Are Measured at Fair Value on a Nonrecurring Basis (in part)

The Company assesses the impairment of intangible assets annually or whenever events or changes in circumstances indicate that the carrying amount of an intangible asset may not be recoverable. The aggregate carrying amount of intangible assets approximated $2.777 billion as of April 29, 2011 and $2.559 billion as of April 30, 2010. These assets are measured at fair value on a nonrecurring basis. The fair value of the Company's intangible assets is not estimated if there is no change in events or circumstances that indicate the carrying amount of an intangible asset may not be recoverable. During fiscal year 2011, the Company determined that changes in events and circumstances indicated that the carrying amounts of certain intangible assets may not be fully recoverable. To determine the impairment, the Company calculated the excess of the intangible asset's carrying value over its fair value utilizing a discounted future cash flow analysis. As a result of the analysis performed in fiscal year 2011, the fair values of the intangible assets were deemed to be less than the carrying values, resulting in pre-tax impairment losses of $28 million of which $19 million is related to the fiscal year 2011 restructuring initiative and was recorded in *restructuring charges* and $9 million was recorded in *other expense, net* in the Company's consolidated statement of earnings. The Company did not record any intangible asset impairments during fiscal years 2010 or 2009. The inputs used in the fair value analysis fall within Level 3 of the fair value hierarchy due to the use of significant unobservable inputs to determine fair value.

7. Goodwill and Other Intangible Assets (in part)

Balances of intangible assets, excluding goodwill, are as follows:

(In millions)	Purchased Technology and Patents	Trademarks and Tradenames	Acquired IPR&D	Other	Total
Amortizable intangible assets as of April 29, 2011:					
Original cost	$ 3,565	$ 373	$338	$ 150	$ 4,426
Accumulated amortization	(1,265)	(290)	—	(94)	(1,649)
Carrying value	$ 2,300	$ 83	$338	$ 56	$ 2,777
Weighted average original life (in years)	12.3	10.3	N/A	8.5	
Amortizable intangible assets as of April 30, 2010:					
Original cost	$ 3,300	$ 373	$114	$ 252	$ 4,039
Accumulated amortization	(1,040)	(254)	—	(186)	(1,480)
Carrying value	$ 2,260	$ 119	$114	$ 66	$ 2,559
Weighted average original life (in years)	12.6	10.3	N/A	8.6	

Amortization expense for fiscal years 2011, 2010, and 2009 was $340 million, $318 million, and $281 million, respectively.

OTHER NONCURRENT ASSETS

RECOGNITION AND MEASUREMENT

2.93 FASB ASC 210 indicates that the concept of current assets excludes resources such as the following:
- Cash restricted regarding withdrawal or use for other than current operations, designated for expenditure in the acquisition or construction of noncurrent assets, or segregated for the liquidation of long-term debts
- Investments or advances for the purposes of control, affiliation, or other continuing business advantage
- Certain receivables (see the "Noncurrent Receivables" section)
- Cash surrender value of life insurance
- Land and other natural resources
- Long-term prepayments chargeable to operations over several years

DISCLOSURE

2.94 Rule 5-02 of Regulation S-X requires that any item not classed in another Regulation S-X caption and in excess of 5 percent of total assets be stated separately on the balance sheet or disclosed in the notes.

2.95

TABLE 2-9: OTHER NONCURRENT ASSETS*

Table 2-9 summarizes the nature of assets (other than property, investments, noncurrent receivables, and intangible assets) classified as noncurrent assets on the balance sheet of the survey entities.

	Number of Entities		
	2011	2010	2009
Deferred income taxes	258	232	277
Pension asset	159	106	160
Derivatives	131	95	150
Advances/deposits/prepayments	31	40	N/C^
Segregated cash or securities	62	41	103
Software	28	25	87
Debt issue costs	68	70	68
Property held for sale	37	33	43
Cash surrender value of life insurance	30	37	42
Assets of nonhomogeneous operations	3	5	9
Contracts	9	7	8
Estimated insurance recoveries	13	12	5
Assets leased to others	6	4	5
Property held for future development	4	6	N/C^
Other	187	177	58

* Appearing in the balance sheet or notes to financial statements, or both.

^ N/C = Not compiled. Line item was not included in the table for the year shown.

PRESENTATION AND DISCLOSURE EXCERPTS

Assets of Discontinued Operations

2.96

CAREER EDUCATION CORPORATION (DEC)

CONSOLIDATED BALANCE SHEETS (in part)

(In thousands, except share and per share amounts)

	As of December 31	
	2011	**2010**
Assets		
Current assets:		
Cash and cash equivalents	$ 280,592	$ 260,644
Short-term investments	160,607	159,671
Total cash and cash equivalents and short-term investments	441,199	420,315
Student receivables, net of allowance for doubtful accounts of $43,891 and $50,099 as of December 31, 2011 and 2010, respectively	60,573	62,091
Receivables, other, net	2,914	1,861
Prepaid expenses	62,399	51,380
Inventories	11,356	13,142
Deferred income tax assets, net	10,940	31,665
Other current assets	17,769	6,089
Assets of discontinued operations	3,328	39,982
Total current assets	610,478	626,525
Non-current assets:		
Property and equipment, net	349,788	363,516
Goodwill	212,626	374,587
Intangible assets, net	77,186	110,222
Student receivables, net of allowance for doubtful accounts of $21,062 and $40,840 as of December 31, 2011 and 2010, respectively	9,297	12,522
Deferred income tax assets, net	9,522	6,793
Other assets, net	30,122	38,923
Assets of discontinued operations	17,101	39,872
Total assets	$1,316,120	$1,572,960

NOTES TO CONSOLIDATED FINANCIAL STATEMENTS

December 31, 2011, 2010 and 2009

2. Summary of Significant Accounting Policies (in part)

j. Discontinued Operations

Discontinued operations are accounted for in accordance with the provisions of FASB ASC Section 360-10-35 Property, Plant, and Equipment. In accordance with FASB ASC Section 360-10-35, the net assets of discontinued operations are recorded on our consolidated balance sheet at estimated fair value. The results of operations of discontinued operations are segregated from operations and reported separately as discontinued operations in our consolidated statement of operations. See Note 5 "Discontinued Operations" of the notes to our consolidated financial statements for further discussion.

5. Discontinued Operations (in part)

On November 14, 2011, we completed the sale of our Istituto Marangoni schools in Milan, Paris and London. As a result of that transaction, we recorded a pretax gain of approximately $27.1 million, which represented the difference between the proceeds of $49.8 million received and the book value of the net assets sold. Included in the net assets of the business was a $2.8 million cumulative translation loss resulting from the effects of foreign currency on Istituto Marangoni's balance sheet. This loss had been included within other comprehensive income (loss) within the audited consolidated balance sheets. As a result of the sale, the cumulative translation loss, along with the remaining net assets of the business were written off. Excluded from the net assets of the business was $20.2 million of goodwill which was allocated to the remainder of the International reporting unit in accordance with FASB ASC Topic 350 *Intangibles—Goodwill and Other*. See Note 10 "Goodwill and Other Intangible Assets" of the notes to our consolidated financial statements for further discussion. All current and prior period financial statements have been recast to include the results of operations and financial position of Istituto Marangoni as a component of discontinued operations. In addition, discontinued operations include the results of operations for schools that have previously ceased operations or were sold.

Assets and Liabilities of Discontinued Operations

Assets and liabilities of discontinued operations on our consolidated balance sheets as of December 31, 2011 and 2010 include the following:

	As of December 31	
(Dollars in thousands)	2011	2010
Assets:		
Current assets:		
Cash and cash equivalents	$ —	$28,838
Receivables, net	104	2,556
Prepaid expenses	—	3,071
Deferred income tax assets	3,224	4,786
Other current assets	—	731
Total current assets	3,328	39,982
Non-current assets:		
Property and equipment, net	—	3,259
Goodwill	—	6,889
Intangible assets, net	—	8,541
Deferred income tax assets	15,421	15,342
Other assets, net	1,680	5,841
Total assets of discontinued operations	$20,429	$79,854
Liabilities:		
Current liabilities:		
Accounts payable	$ 3	$ 3,227
Accrued payroll and related benefits	—	1,168
Accrued expenses	498	4,281
Deferred tuition revenue	—	23,512
Remaining lease obligations	7,902	12,802
Total current liabilities	8,403	44,990
Non-current liabilities:		
Remaining lease obligations	37,935	37,576
Other long-term liabilities	—	931
Total liabilities of discontinued operations	$46,338	$83,497

Pension Asset

2.97

H.J. HEINZ COMPANY (APR)

CONSOLIDATED BALANCE SHEETS (in part)

(In thousands)	April 27, 2011	April 28, 2010
Assets		
Current assets:		
Cash and cash equivalents	$ 724,311	$ 483,253
Trade receivables (net of allowances: 2011—$10,909 and 2010—$10,196)	1,039,064	794,845
Other receivables (net of allowances: 2011—$503 and 2010—$268)	225,968	250,493
Inventories:		
Finished goods and work-in-process	1,165,069	979,543
Packaging material and ingredients	286,477	269,584
Total inventories	1,451,546	1,249,127
Prepaid expenses	159,521	130,819
Other current assets	153,132	142,588
Total current assets	3,753,542	3,051,125
Property, plant and equipment:		
Land	85,457	77,248
Buildings and leasehold improvements	1,019,311	842,346
Equipment, furniture and other	4,119,947	3,546,046
	5,224,715	4,465,640
Less accumulated depreciation	2,719,632	2,373,844
Total property, plant and equipment, net	2,505,083	2,091,796
Other non-current assets:		
Goodwill	3,298,441	2,770,918
Trademarks, net	1,156,221	895,138
Other intangibles, net	442,563	402,576
Other non-current assets	1,074,795	864,158
Total other non-current assets	5,972,020	4,932,790
Total assets	$12,230,645	$10,075,711

NOTES TO CONSOLIDATED FINANCIAL STATEMENTS

11. Pension and Other Postretirement Benefit Plans (in part)

Obligations and Funded Status:

The following table sets forth the changes in benefit obligation, plan assets and funded status of the Company's principal defined benefit plans and other postretirement benefit plans at April 27, 2011 and April 28, 2010.

(Dollars in thousands)	Pension Benefits		Other Retiree Benefits	
	2011	2010	2011	2010
Change in benefit obligation:				
Benefit obligation at the beginning of the year	$2,585,984	$2,230,102	$ 235,297	$ 234,175
Service cost	32,329	30,486	6,311	5,999
Interest cost	142,133	149,640	12,712	15,093
Participants' contributions	2,444	2,674	822	905
Amendments	377	5,807	(3,710)	(21,115)
Actuarial (gain)/loss	(8,457)	238,168	(3,786)	9,672
Divestitures	—	(413)	—	—
Settlement	(3,275)	(4,663)	—	—
Curtailment	—	(3,959)	—	—
Benefits paid	(159,307)	(156,807)	(16,986)	(18,395)
Exchange/other	173,088	94,949	3,770	8,963
Benefit obligation at the end of the year	$2,765,316	$2,585,984	$ 234,430	$ 235,297
Change in plan assets:				
Fair value of plan assets at the beginning of the year	$2,869,971	$1,874,702	$ —	$ —
Actual return on plan assets	318,494	561,997	—	—
Divestitures	—	(413)	—	—
Settlement	(3,275)	(4,663)	—	—
Employer contribution	22,411	539,939	16,164	17,490
Participants' contributions	2,444	2,674	822	905
Benefits paid	(159,307)	(156,807)	(16,986)	(18,395)
Exchange	211,143	52,542	—	—
Fair value of plan assets at the end of the year	3,261,881	2,869,971	—	—
Funded status	$ 496,565	$ 283,987	$(234,430)	$(235,297)

Amounts recognized in the consolidated balance sheets consist of the following:

(Dollars in thousands)	Pension Benefits		Other Retiree Benefits	
	2011	2010	2011	2010
Other non-current assets	$ 644,598	$ 424,554	$ —	$ —
Other accrued liabilities	(31,589)	(12,842)	(18,259)	(18,874)
Other non-current liabilities	(116,444)	(127,725)	(216,171)	(216,423)
Net amount recognized	$ 496,565	$ 283,987	$(234,430)	$(235,297)

Certain of the Company's pension plans have projected benefit obligations in excess of the fair value of plan assets. For these plans, the projected benefit obligations and the fair value of plan assets at April 27, 2011 were $175.0 million and $27.0 million, respectively. For pension plans having projected benefit obligations in excess of the fair value of plan assets at April 28, 2010, the projected benefit obligations and the fair value of plan assets were $160.9 million and $20.3 million, respectively.

The accumulated benefit obligation for all defined benefit pension plans was $2,602.0 million at April 27, 2011 and $2,414.3 million at April 28, 2010.

Certain of the Company's pension plans have accumulated benefit obligations in excess of the fair value of plan assets. For these plans, the accumulated benefit obligations, projected benefit obligations and the fair value of plan assets at April 27, 2011 were $154.3 million, $175.0 million and $27.0 million, respectively. For pension plans having accumulated benefit obligations in excess of the fair value of plan

assets at April 28, 2010, the accumulated benefit obligations, projected benefit obligations and the fair value of plan assets were $137.0 million, $160.9 million and $20.3 million, respectively.

Pension Plan Assets:

The underlying basis of the investment strategy of the Company's defined benefit plans is to ensure that pension funds are available to meet the plans' benefit obligations when they are due. The Company's investment objectives include: investing plan assets in a high-quality, diversified manner in order to maintain the security of the funds; achieving an optimal return on plan assets within specified risk tolerances; and investing according to local regulations and requirements specific to each country in which a defined benefit plan operates. The investment strategy expects equity investments to yield a higher return over the long term than fixed income securities, while fixed income securities are expected to provide certain matching characteristics to the plans' benefit payment cash flow requirements. Company common stock held as part of the equity securities amounted to less than one percent of plan assets at April 27, 2011 and April 28, 2010. The Company's investment policy specifies the type of investment vehicles appropriate for the Plan, asset allocation guidelines, criteria for the selection of investment managers, procedures to monitor overall investment performance as well as investment manager performance. It also provides guidelines enabling Plan fiduciaries to fulfill their responsibilities.

The Company's defined benefit pension plans' weighted average asset allocation at April 27, 2011 and April 28, 2010 and weighted average target allocation were as follows:

Asset Category	Plan Assets at		Target Allocation at	
	2011	2010	2011	2010
Equity securities	62%	58%	58%	63%
Debt securities	32%	29%	32%	35%
Real estate	3%	1%	9%	1%
Other(1)	3%	12%	1%	1%
	100%	100%	100%	100%

(1) Plan assets at April 28, 2010 in the Other asset category include 11% of cash which reflects significant cash contributions to the pension plans prior to the end of fiscal year 2010.

In Fiscal 2010, the Company adopted a new accounting standard requiring additional disclosures for Plan assets of defined benefit pension and other post-retirement plans. As required by the standard, the Company categorized Plan assets within a three level fair value hierarchy. The following section describes the valuation methodologies used to measure the fair value of pension plan assets, including an indication of the level in the fair value hierarchy in which each type of asset is generally classified.

Equity Securities. These securities consist of direct investments in the stock of publicly traded companies. Such investments are valued based on the closing price reported in an active market on which the individual securities are traded. As such, the direct investments are classified as Level 1.

Equity Securities (mutual and pooled funds). Mutual funds are valued at the net asset value of shares held by the Plan at year end. As such, these mutual fund investments are classified as Level 1. Pooled funds are similar in nature to retail mutual funds, but are more efficient for institutional investors than retail mutual funds. As pooled funds are only accessible by institutional investors, the net asset value is not readily observable by non-institutional investors; therefore, pooled funds are classified as Level 2.

Fixed Income Securities. These securities consist of publicly traded U.S. and non-U.S. fixed interest obligations (principally corporate bonds and debentures). Such investments are valued through consultation and evaluation with brokers in the institutional market using quoted prices and other observable market data. As such, a portion of these securities are included in Levels 1, 2 and 3.

Other Investments. Primarily consist of real estate, private equity holdings and interest rate swaps. Direct investments of real estate and private equity are valued by investment managers based on the most recent financial information available, which typically represents significant observable data. As such, these investments are generally classified as Level 3. The fair value of interest rate swaps is determined through use of observable market swap rates and are classified as Level 2.

Cash and Cash Equivalents. This consists of direct cash holdings and institutional short-term investment vehicles. Direct cash holdings are valued based on cost, which approximates fair value and are classified as Level 1. Institutional short-term investment vehicles are valued daily and are classified as Level 2.

Asset Category (Dollars in thousands)	April 27, 2011			
	Level 1	Level 2	Level 3	Total
Equity securities	$ 863,404	$ —	$ —	$ 863,404
Equity securities (mutual and pooled funds)	157,296	1,005,678	—	1,162,974
Fixed income securities	53,381	966,157	9,649	1,029,187
Other investments	—	—	131,095	131,095
Cash and cash equivalents	16,270	58,951	—	75,221
Total	$1,090,351	$2,030,786	$140,744	$3,261,881

Asset Category (Dollars in thousands)	April 28, 2010			
	Level 1	Level 2	Level 3	Total
Equity securities	$ 894,684	$ —	$ —	$ 894,684
Equity securities (mutual and pooled funds)	122,753	641,727	—	764,480
Fixed income securities	49,951	785,924	8,646	844,521
Other investments	—	7,491	35,569	43,060
Cash and cash equivalents	14,260	308,966	—	323,226
Total	$1,081,648	$1,744,108	$44,215	$2,869,971

SEC 2.97

Deferred Compensation Arrangements

2.98

LAM RESEARCH CORPORATION (JUN)

CONSOLIDATED BALANCE SHEETS (in part)

(In thousands, except per share data)

	June 26, 2011	June 27, 2010
Assets		
Cash and cash equivalents	$1,492,132	$ 545,767
Short-term investments	630,115	280,690
Accounts receivable, less allowance for doubtful accounts of $4,720 as of June 26, 2011 and $10,609 as of June 27, 2010	590,568	499,890
Inventories	396,607	318,479
Deferred income taxes	78,435	46,158
Prepaid expenses and other current assets	88,935	65,677
Total current assets	3,276,792	1,756,661
Property and equipment, net	270,458	200,336
Restricted cash and investments	165,256	165,234
Deferred income taxes	3,892	26,218
Goodwill	169,182	169,182
Intangible assets, net	47,434	67,724
Other assets	124,380	102,037
Total assets	$4,057,394	$2,487,392

NOTES TO CONSOLIDATED FINANCIAL STATEMENTS

June 26, 2011

Note 12: Retirement and Deferred Compensation Plans (in part)

Deferred Compensation Arrangements

The Company has an unfunded, non-qualified deferred compensation plan whereby certain executives may defer a portion of their compensation. Participants earn a return on their deferred compensation based on their allocation of their account balance among measurement funds. The Company controls the investment of these funds and the participants remain general creditors of the Company. Participants are able to elect the payment of benefits on a specified date at least three years after the opening of a deferral subaccount or upon retirement. Distributions are made in the form of lump sum or annual installments over a period of up to 20 years as elected by the participant. If no alternate election has been made, a lump sum payment will be made upon termination of a participant's employment with the Company. As of June 26, 2011 and June 27, 2010 the liability of the Company to the plan participants was $62.5 million and $55.1 million, respectively, which was recorded in accrued expenses and other current liabilities on the Consolidated Balance Sheets. As of June 26, 2011 and June 27, 2010 the Company had investments in the aggregate amount of $64.7 million and $53.0 million respectively that correlate to the deferred compensation obligations, which were recorded in other assets on the consolidated balance sheets.

Deposits

2.99

INSPERITY, INC. (DEC)

CONSOLIDATED BALANCE SHEETS (in part)

(In thousands)

	December 31, 2011	December 31, 2010
Assets		
Current assets:		
Cash and cash equivalents	$211,208	$234,829
Restricted cash	44,737	41,204
Marketable securities	56,987	43,367
Accounts receivable, net:		
Trade	7,893	1,194
Unbilled	158,508	134,187
Other	4,532	6,726
Prepaid insurance	21,300	24,978
Other current assets	11,488	8,528
Income taxes receivable	2,902	1,808
Deferred income taxes	3,233	1,267
Total current assets	522,788	498,088
Property and equipment:		
Land	3,653	3,260
Buildings and improvements	67,496	64,953
Computer hardware and software	76,105	67,714
Software development costs	32,699	27,482
Furniture and fixtures	36,133	35,164
Aircraft	35,866	31,524
	251,952	230,097
Accumulated depreciation and amortization	(159,008)	(154,070)
Total property and equipment, net	92,944	76,027
Other assets:		
Prepaid health insurance	9,000	9,000
Deposits—health insurance	2,640	2,640
Deposits—workers' compensation	52,320	51,731
Goodwill and other intangible assets, net	28,433	21,251
Other assets	4,134	1,108
Total other assets	96,527	85,730
Total assets	$712,259	$659,845

NOTES TO CONSOLIDATED FINANCIAL STATEMENTS

December 31, 2011

1. Accounting Policies (in part)

Workers' Compensation Costs (in part)

At the beginning of each policy period, the insurance carrier establishes monthly funding requirements comprised of premium costs and funds to be set aside for payment of future claims ("claim funds"). The level of claim funds is primarily based upon anticipated worksite employee payroll levels and expected workers' compensation loss rates, as determined by the insurance carrier. Monies funded into the program for incurred claims expected to be paid within one year are recorded as restricted cash, a short-term asset, while the remainder of claim funds are included in deposits, a long-term asset in our Consolidated Balance Sheets. In 2011, we received $10.0 million for the return of excess claim funds related to the ACE program, which reduced deposits. As of December 31, 2011, we had restricted cash of $44.7 million and deposits of $52.3 million.

4. Deposits

The contractual arrangement with United for health insurance coverage requires Insperity to maintain an accumulated cash surplus in the plan of $9.0 million, which is reported as long-term prepaid health insurance. Please read Note 1 "Accounting Policies" for a discussion of our accounting policies for health insurance costs.

As of December 31, 2011, we had $52.3 million of workers' compensation long-term deposits. Please read Note 1 "Accounting Policies" for a discussion of our accounting policies for workers' compensation costs.

Long-Term Deferred Income Tax Asset

2.100

THE L.S. STARRETT COMPANY (JUN)

CONSOLIDATED BALANCE SHEETS (in part)

(In thousands except share data)

	June 30, 2011	June 26, 2010 (As Adjusted)
Assets		
Current assets:		
Cash	$ 21,572	$ 20,478
Investments	6,421	1,250
Accounts receivable (less allowance for doubtful accounts of $416 and $607, respectively)	45,567	33,707
Inventories	58,789	46,156
Current deferred income tax asset	6,100	3,300
Prepaid expenses and other current assets	5,494	5,510
Total current assets	143,943	110,401
Property, plant and equipment, net	56,265	56,529
Property held for sale	788	2,699
Intangible assets, net	231	1,303
Other assets	951	280
Long-term taxes receivable	3,594	2,807
Long-term deferred income tax asset, net	21,407	26,115
Total assets	$227,179	$200,134

NOTES TO CONSOLIDATED FINANCIAL STATEMENTS

10. Income Taxes (in part)

Deferred income taxes at June 30, 2011 and June 26, 2010 are attributable to the following (in thousands):

	2011	2010
Deferred assets (current):		
Inventories	$ 4,598	$ 1,816
Employee benefits (other than pension)	548	276
Book reserves	954	1,208
	$ 6,100	$ 3,300
Deferred assets (long-term):		
Federal NOL, carried forward	$ 7,438	$ 9,820
State NOL, various carryforward periods	1,039	962
Foreign NOL, various carried forward periods	1,583	914
Foreign tax credit carryforward, expiring 2012–2016	1,117	1,194
Pension benefit	3,980	5,589
Retiree medical benefits	4,615	4,562
Intangibles	3,813	3,553
Other	651	1,389
	$24,236	$27,983
Valuation reserve for state NOL, foreign NOL and foreign tax credits	$ (2,829)	$ (1,868)
Long-term deferred assets	$21,407	$26,115
Deferred liabilities (long-term):		
Depreciation	(2,806)	(2,436)
	$ (2,806)	$ (2,436)
Net deferred tax assets	$24,701	$26,979

As of June 30, 2011 and June 26, 2010, the net long-term deferred tax asset and deferred tax liability respectively, on the balance sheet are as follows:

	2011	2010
Long-term liabilities	$ (2,806)	$ (2,436)
Long-term assets	21,407	26,115
	$18,601	$23,679

Foreign operations deferred assets (current) relate primarily to book reserves.

Foreign operations net deferred assets (long-term) relate primarily to pension benefits.

Amounts related to foreign operations included in the long-term portion of deferred liabilities relate primarily to depreciation.

Cash Surrender Value of Life Insurance

2.101

INTERNATIONAL FLAVORS & FRAGRANCES INC. (DEC)

CONSOLIDATED BALANCE SHEET (in part)

	December 31	
(Dollars in thousands)	2011	2010
Assets		
Current assets:		
Cash and cash equivalents	$ 88,279	$ 131,332
Receivables:		
Trade	476,031	458,128
Allowance for doubtful accounts	(3,685)	(6,324)
Inventories	544,439	531,675
Deferred income taxes	54,054	74,160
Prepaid expenses and other current assets	158,102	136,224
Total current assets	1,317,220	1,325,195
Property, plant and equipment, net	608,065	538,118
Goodwill	665,582	665,582
Other intangible assets, net	42,763	48,834
Deferred income taxes	152,118	122,800
Other assets	179,833	171,926
Total assets	$2,965,581	$2,872,455

NOTES TO CONSOLIDATED FINANCIAL STATEMENTS

Note 5. Other Assets

Other assets consist of the following amounts:

	December 31	
(Dollars in thousands)	2011	2010
Overfunded pension plans	$ 67,518	$ 66,274
Cash surrender value of life insurance contracts	56,177	54,046
Other	56,138	51,606
Total	$179,833	$171,926

Note 13. Employee Benefits (in part)

We offer a non-qualified Deferred Compensation Plan (DCP) for certain key employees and non-employee directors. Eligible employees and non-employee directors may elect to defer receipt of salary, incentive payments and Board of Directors' fees into participant directed investments, which are generally invested by the Company in individual variable life insurance contracts we own that are designed to informally fund savings plans of this nature. The cash surrender value of life insurance is based on the net asset values of the underlying funds available to plan participants. At December 31, 2011 and December 31, 2010, the Consolidated Balance Sheet reflects liabilities of $27.0 million and $27.0 million, respectively, related to the DCP in Other liabilities and $12.0 million and $11.5 million, respectively, included in Capital in excess of par value related to the portion of the DCP that will be paid out in IFF shares.

The total cash surrender value of life insurance contracts the Company owns in relation to the DCP and post-retirement life insurance benefits amounted to $56.2 million and $54.0 million at December 31, 2011 and 2010, respectively, and are recorded in Other assets in the Consolidated Balance Sheet.

Derivatives

2.102

MERCK & CO., INC. (DEC)

CONSOLIDATED BALANCE SHEET (in part)

December 31

($ in millions except per share amounts)

	2011	2010
Assets		
Current assets		
Cash and cash equivalents	$ 13,531	$ 10,900
Short-term investments	1,441	1,301
Accounts receivable (net of allowance for doubtful accounts of $131 in 2011 and $104 in 2010)	8,261	7,344
Inventories (excludes inventories of $1,379 in 2011 and $1,194 in 2010 classified in Other assets—see Note 8)	6,254	5,868
Deferred income taxes and other current assets	3,694	3,651
Total current assets	33,181	29,064
Investments	3,458	2,175
Property, Plant and Equipment (at cost)		
Land	623	658
Buildings	12,733	11,945
Machinery, equipment and office furnishings	16,919	15,894
Construction in progress	2,198	2,066
	32,473	30,563
Less: accumulated depreciation	16,176	13,481
	16,297	17,082
Goodwill	12,155	12,378
Other intangibles, net	34,302	39,456
Other assets	5,735	5,626
	$105,128	$105,781

NOTES TO CONSOLIDATED FINANCIAL STATEMENTS

($ in millions except per share amounts)

7. Financial Instruments (in part)

Derivative Instruments and Hedging Activities (in part)

The Company manages the impact of foreign exchange rate movements and interest rate movements on its earnings, cash flows and fair values of assets and liabilities through operational means and through the use of various financial instruments, including derivative instruments.

A significant portion of the Company's revenues and earnings in foreign affiliates is exposed to changes in foreign exchange rates. The objectives and accounting related to the Company's foreign currency risk management program, as well as its interest rate risk management activities are discussed below.

Foreign Currency Risk Management

A significant portion of the Company's revenues are denominated in foreign currencies. The Company has established revenue hedging, balance sheet risk management, and net investment hedging programs to protect against volatility of future foreign currency cash flows and changes in fair value caused by volatility in foreign exchange rates.

The objective of the revenue hedging program is to reduce the potential for longer-term unfavorable changes in foreign exchange rates to decrease the U.S. dollar value of future cash flows derived from foreign currency denominated sales, primarily the euro and Japanese yen. To achieve this objective, the Company will hedge a portion of its forecasted foreign currency denominated third-party and intercompany distributor entity sales that are expected to occur over its planning cycle, typically no more than three years into the future. The Company will layer in hedges over time, increasing the portion of third-party and intercompany distributor entity sales hedged as it gets closer to the expected date of the forecasted foreign currency denominated sales, such that it is probable the hedged transaction will occur. The portion of sales hedged is based on assessments of cost-benefit profiles that consider natural offsetting exposures, revenue and exchange rate volatilities and correlations, and the cost of hedging instruments. The hedged anticipated sales are a specified component of a portfolio of similarly denominated foreign currency-based sales transactions, each of which responds to the hedged currency risk in the same manner. The Company manages its anticipated transaction exposure principally with purchased local currency put options, which provide the Company with a right, but not an obligation, to sell foreign currencies in the future at a predetermined price. If the U.S. dollar strengthens relative to the currency of the hedged anticipated sales, total changes in the options' cash flows offset the decline in the expected future U.S. dollar equivalent cash flows of the hedged foreign currency sales. Conversely, if the U.S. dollar weakens, the options' value reduces to zero, but the Company benefits from the increase in the U.S. dollar equivalent value of the anticipated foreign currency cash flows.

In connection with the Company's revenue hedging program, a purchased collar option strategy may be utilized. With a purchased collar option strategy, the Company writes a local currency call option and purchases a local currency put option. As compared to a purchased put option strategy alone, a purchased collar strategy reduces the upfront costs associated with purchasing puts through the collection of premium by writing call options. If the U.S. dollar weakens relative to the currency of the hedged anticipated sales, the purchased put option value of the collar strategy reduces to zero and the Company benefits from the increase in the U.S. dollar equivalent value of its anticipated foreign currency cash flows, however this benefit would be capped at the strike level of the written call. If the U.S. dollar strengthens relative to the currency of the hedged anticipated sales, the written call option value of the collar strategy reduces to zero and the changes in the purchased put cash flows of the collar strategy would offset the decline in the expected future U.S. dollar equivalent cash flows of the hedged foreign currency sales.

The Company may also utilize forward contracts in its revenue hedging program. If the U.S. dollar strengthens relative to the currency of the hedged anticipated sales, the increase in the fair value of the forward contracts offsets the decrease in the expected future U.S. dollar cash flows of the hedged foreign currency sales. Conversely, if the U.S. dollar weakens, the decrease in the fair value of the forward contracts offsets the increase in the value of the anticipated foreign currency cash flows.

The fair values of these derivative contracts are recorded as either assets (gain positions) or liabilities (loss positions) in the Consolidated Balance Sheet. Changes in the fair value of derivative contracts are recorded each period in either current earnings or *OCI*, depending on whether the derivative is designated as part of a hedge transaction and, if so, the type of hedge transaction. For derivatives that are designated as cash flow hedges, the effective portion of the unrealized gains or losses on these contracts is recorded in *AOCI* and reclassified into *Sales* when the hedged anticipated revenue is recognized. The hedge relationship is highly effective and hedge ineffectiveness has been *de minimis*. For those derivatives which are not designated as cash flow hedges, unrealized gains or losses are recorded to *Sales* each period. The cash flows from these contracts are reported as operating activities in the Consolidated Statement of Cash Flows. The Company does not enter into derivatives for trading or speculative purposes.

The primary objective of the balance sheet risk management program is to mitigate the exposure of foreign currency denominated net monetary assets of foreign subsidiaries where the U.S. dollar is the functional currency from the effects of volatility in foreign exchange. In these instances, Merck principally utilizes forward exchange contracts, which enable the Company to buy and sell foreign currencies in the future at fixed exchange rates and economically offset the consequences of changes in foreign exchange from the monetary assets. Merck routinely enters into contracts to offset the effects of exchange on exposures denominated in developed country currencies, primarily the euro and Japanese yen. For exposures in developing country currencies, the Company will enter into forward contracts to partially offset the effects of exchange on exposures when it is deemed economical to do so based on a cost-benefit analysis that considers the magnitude of the exposure, the volatility of the exchange rate and the cost of the hedging instrument. The Company will also minimize the effect of exchange on monetary assets and liabilities by managing operating activities and net asset positions at the local level.

Monetary assets and liabilities denominated in a currency other than the functional currency of a given subsidiary are remeasured at spot rates in effect on the balance sheet date with the effects of changes in spot rates reported in *Other (income) expense, net*. The forward contracts are not designated as hedges and are marked to market through *Other (income) expense, net*. Accordingly, fair value changes in the forward contracts help mitigate the changes in the value of the remeasured assets and liabilities attributable to changes in foreign currency exchange rates, except to the extent of the spot-forward differences. These differences are not significant due to the short-term nature of the contracts, which typically have average maturities at inception of less than one year.

During 2009, the Company used, and may in the future use, forward contracts to hedge the changes in fair value of certain foreign currency denominated available-for-sale securities attributable to fluctuations in foreign currency exchange rates. These derivative contracts are designated as fair value hedges. Accordingly, changes in the fair value of the hedged securities due to fluctuations in spot rates are recorded in *Other (income) expense, net*, and are offset by the fair value changes in the forward contracts attributable to spot rate fluctuations. Changes in the contracts' fair value due to spot-forward differences are excluded from the designated hedge relationship and recognized in *Other (income) expense, net*. These amounts, as well as hedge ineffectiveness, were not significant for 2009. The cash flows from these contracts are reported as operating activities in the Consolidated Statement of Cash Flows.

The Company also uses forward exchange contracts to hedge its net investment in foreign operations against movements in exchange rates. The forward contracts are designated as hedges of the net investment in a foreign operation. The Company hedges a portion of the net investment in certain of its foreign operations and measures ineffectiveness based upon changes in spot foreign exchange rates. The effective portion of the unrealized gains or losses on these contracts is recorded in foreign currency translation adjustment within *OCI*, and remains in *AOCI* until either the sale or complete or substantially complete liquidation of the subsidiary. The cash flows from these contracts are reported as investing activities in the Consolidated Statement of Cash Flows.

Foreign exchange risk is also managed through the use of foreign currency debt. The Company's senior unsecured euro-denominated notes have been designated as, and are effective as, economic hedges of the net investment in a foreign operation. Accordingly, foreign currency transaction gains or losses due to spot rate fluctuations on the euro-denominated debt instruments are included in foreign currency translation adjustment within *OCI*. Included in the cumulative translation adjustment are pretax gains of $6 million in 2011, $277 million in 2010 and $78 million for the post-Merger period in 2009 from euro-denominated notes which have been designated as, and are effective as, economic hedges of the net investment in a foreign operation.

Interest Rate Risk Management

The Company may use interest rate swap contracts on certain investing and borrowing transactions to manage its net exposure to interest rate changes and to reduce its overall cost of borrowing. The Company does not use leveraged swaps and, in general, does not leverage any of its investment activities that would put principal capital at risk.

In February 2011, the Company entered into nine pay-floating, receive-fixed interest rate swap contracts with notional amounts of $3.5 billion in the aggregate designated as fair value hedges for fixed-rate notes in which the notional amounts matched the amount of the hedged fixed-rate notes.

Two interest rate swap contracts designated as fair value hedges of fixed-rate notes matured in 2011 with notional amounts of $125 million each that effectively converted the Company's $250 million, 5.125% fixed-rate notes due 2011 to floating rate instruments. The interest rate swap contracts were designated hedges of the fair value changes in the notes attributable to changes in the benchmark London Interbank Offered Rate ("LIBOR") swap rate. The fair value changes in the notes attributable to changes in the bench-

mark interest rate were recorded in interest expense and offset by the fair value changes in the swap contracts. Also during 2011, the Company terminated pay-floating, receive-fixed interest rate swap contracts designated as fair value hedges of fixed-rate notes in which the notional amounts match the amount of the hedged fixed-rate notes. These swaps effectively converted $5.1 billion of its fixed-rate notes, with maturity dates varying from March 2015 to June 2019, to floating rate instruments. The interest rate swap contracts were designated hedges of the fair value changes in the notes attributable to changes in the benchmark LIBOR swap rate. As a result of the swap terminations, the Company received $288 million in cash, which included $43 million in accrued interest. The unamortized adjustment to the carrying value of the debt associated with the interest rate swap contracts of $245 million is being amortized as a reduction of interest expense over the respective term of the notes. The cash flows from these contracts are reported as operating activities in the Consolidated Statement of Cash Flows.

Presented in the table below is the fair value of derivatives segregated between those derivatives that are designated as hedging instruments and those that are not designated as hedging instruments as of December 31:

($ in millions)	Balance Sheet Caption	2011 Fair Value of Derivative		U.S. Dollar Notional	2010 Fair Value of Derivative		U.S. Dollar Notional
		Asset	Liability		Asset	Liability	
Derivatives Designated as Hedging Instruments							
Foreign exchange contracts (current)	Deferred income taxes and other current assets	$196	$ —	$ 3,727	$167	$—	$ 2,344
Foreign exchange contracts (non-current)	Other assets	420	—	4,956	310	—	3,720
Foreign exchange contracts (current)	Accrued and other current liabilities	—	53	1,718	—	18	1,505
Foreign exchange contracts (non-current)	Deferred income taxes and noncurrent liabilities	—	1	104	—	6	503
Interest rate swaps (non-current)	Other assets	—	—	—	56	—	1,000
Interest rate swaps (non-current)	Deferred income taxes and noncurrent liabilities	—	—	—	—	7	850
		$616	$ 54	$10,505	$533	$31	$ 9,922
Derivatives Not Designated as Hedging Instruments							
Foreign exchange contracts (current)	Deferred income taxes and other current assets	$139	$ —	$ 5,306	$ 95	—	$ 6,295
Foreign exchange contracts (current)	Accrued and other current liabilities	—	54	5,013	—	30	4,229
		$139	$ 54	$10,319	$ 95	$30	$10,524
		$755	$108	$20,824	$628	$61	$20,446

SEC 2.102

Retail Real Estate

2.103

BASSETT FURNITURE INDUSTRIES,
INCORPORATED (NOV)

CONSOLIDATED BALANCE SHEET (in part)

November 26, 2011 and November 27, 2010
(In thousands, except share and per share data)

	2011	2010
Assets		
Current assets		
Cash and cash equivalents	$ 69,601	$ 11,071
Accounts receivable, net of allowance for doubtful accounts of $2,092 and $7,366 as of November 26, 2011 and November 27, 2010, respectively	14,756	31,621
Marketable Securities	2,939	—
Inventories	45,129	41,810
Other current assets	7,778	6,969
Total current assets	140,203	91,471
Property and equipment, net	49,946	46,250
Long-term assets		
Investments	806	15,111
Retail real estate	16,257	27,513
Notes receivable, net of allowance for doubtful accounts and discounts of $4,140 and $6,748 as of November 26, 2011 and November 27, 2010, respectively	1,802	7,508
Other	14,160	9,464
Total long-term assets	33,025	59,596
Total assets	$223,174	$197,317

NOTES TO CONSOLIDATED FINANCIAL STATEMENTS

(In thousands, except share and per share data)

2. Significant Accounting Policies (in part)

Retail Real Estate

Retail real estate is comprised of owned and leased properties utilized by licensee operated BHF stores. These properties are located in high traffic, upscale locations that are normally occupied by large successful national retailers. This real estate is stated at cost less accumulated depreciation and is depreciated over the useful lives of the respective assets utilizing the straight line method. Buildings and improvements are generally depreciated over a period of 10 to 39 years. Leasehold improvements are amortized based on the underlying lease term, or the asset's estimated useful life, whichever is shorter. As of November 26, 2011 and November 27, 2010, the cost of retail real estate included land totaling $5,731 and $8,011, respectively, and building and leasehold improvements of $15,431 and $27,843, respectively. As of November 26, 2011 and November 27, 2010, accumulated depreciation of retail real estate was $4,905 and $8,341, respectively. Depreciation expense was $876, $1,306, and $1,353 in fiscal 2011, 2010, and 2009, respectively. Impairment charges related to retail real estate totaled $3,953 for 2011 and are included in retail real estate impairment charges in other income, a component of non-operating expense in our Consolidated Statements of Operations. There were no retail real estate impairment charges in 2009 and 2010.

Software

2.104

COMPUTER SCIENCES CORPORATION (MAR)

CONSOLIDATED BALANCE SHEETS (in part)

(Amounts in millions)	April 1, 2011	April 2, 2010
Current assets:		
Cash and cash equivalents	$ 1,837	$ 2,784
Receivables, net of allowance for doubtful accounts of $46 (2011) and $47 (2010)	3,719	3,849
Prepaid expenses and other current assets	2,001	1,789
Total current assets	7,557	8,422
Intangible and other assets:		
Software, net of accumulated amortization of $1,291 (2011) and $1,205 (2010)	562	511
Outsourcing contract costs, net of accumulated amortization of $1,324 (2011) and $1,233 (2010)	647	642
Goodwill	4,038	3,866
Other assets	820	773
Total intangible and other assets	6,067	5,792
Property and equipment—at cost:		
Land, buildings and leasehold improvements	1,281	1,191
Computers and related equipment	4,565	4,301
Furniture and other equipment	503	480
	6,349	5,972
Less: accumulated depreciation and amortization	3,853	3,731
Property and equipment, net	2,496	2,241
Total assets	$16,120	$16,455

NOTES TO CONSOLIDATED FINANCIAL STATEMENTS

Note 1—Summary of Significant Accounting Policies (in part)

Software Development Costs

The Company capitalizes costs incurred to develop commercial software products after technological feasibility has been established. Costs incurred to establish technological feasibility are charged to expense as incurred. Enhancements to software products are capitalized where such enhancements extend the life or significantly expand the marketability of the products. Amortization of capitalized software development costs is determined separately for each software product. Annual amortization expense is calculated based on the greater of (a) the ratio of current gross revenues for each product to the total of current anticipated future gross revenues for the product or (b) the straight-line method over the estimated economic life of the product.

Unamortized capitalized software costs associated with commercial software products are regularly evaluated for impairment on a product-by-product basis by a comparison of the unamortized balance to the product's net realizable value. The net realizable value is the estimated future gross revenues from that product reduced by the related estimated future costs. When the unamortized balance exceeds the net realizable value, the unamortized balance is written down to the net realizable value and an impairment charge is recorded.

The Company capitalizes costs incurred to develop internal-use computer software. Internal and external costs incurred in connection with development of upgrades or enhancements that result in additional functionality are also capitalized. These capitalized costs are amortized on a straight-line basis over the estimated useful life of the software. Purchased software is capitalized and amortized over the estimated useful life of the software.

Note 8—Intangible Assets (in part)

A summary of amortizable intangible assets as of April 1, 2011, and April 2, 2010, is as follows:

	April 1, 2011		
(Amounts in millions)	Gross Carrying Value	Accumulated Amortization	Net Carrying Value
Outsourcing contract costs	$1,971	$1,324	$ 647
Software	1,853	1,291	562
Customer and other intangible assets	436	265	171
Total intangible assets	$4,260	$2,880	$1,380

(Amounts in millions)	April 2, 2010		
	Gross Carrying Value	Accumulated Amortization	Net Carrying Value
Outsourcing contract costs	$1,875	$1,233	$ 642
Software	1,716	1,205	511
Customer and other intangible assets	397	234	163
Total intangible assets	$3,988	$2,672	$1,316

Amortization expense for the years ended April 1, 2011, April 2, 2010, and April 3, 2009, was $381 million, $375 million and $404 million, respectively. In addition, the amortization of outsourcing contract cost premium, which is recorded as a reduction of revenue, was $63 million, $59 million, and $84 million, respectively (see Note 1).

Estimated amortization related to intangible assets, including amortization of contract cost premium, at April 1, 2011, for each of the subsequent five years, fiscal 2012 through fiscal 2016, is $367 million, $288 million, $233 million, $160 million and $88 million, respectively.

Purchased and internally developed software, net of accumulated amortization, consisted of the following:

(Amounts in millions)	April 1, 2011	April 2, 2010
Purchased software	$363	$322
Internally developed commercial software	191	178
Internally developed internal-use software	8	11
Total	$562	$511

Amortization expense related to purchased software was $135 million, $117 million, and $130 million for the years ended April 1, 2011, April 2, 2010, and April 3, 2009, respectively. Amortization expense related to internally developed commercial software was $34 million, $31 million, and $35 million, for the years ended April 1, 2011, April 2, 2010, and April 3, 2009, respectively. Amortization expense related to internally developed internal-use software was $6 million, $9 million, and $9 million for the years ended April 1, 2011, April 2, 2010, and April 3, 2009, respectively.

Debt Issuance Costs

2.105

SPECTRUM BRANDS HOLDINGS, INC. (SEP)

CONSOLIDATED STATEMENTS OF FINANCIAL POSITION (in part)

September 30, 2011 and September 30, 2010
  (In thousands)

	Successor Company	
	2011	2010
Assets		
Current assets:		
Cash and cash equivalents	$ 142,414	$ 170,614
Receivables:		
Trade accounts receivable, net of allowances of $14,128 and $4,351, respectively	356,605	365,002
Other	33,235	41,548
Inventories	434,630	530,342
Deferred income taxes	28,170	35,735
Prepaid expenses and other	48,792	56,574
Total current assets	1,043,846	1,199,815
Property, plant and equipment, net	206,389	201,164
Deferred charges and other	36,824	46,352
Goodwill	610,338	600,055
Intangible assets, net	1,683,909	1,769,360
Debt issuance costs	40,957	56,961
Total assets	$3,622,263	$3,873,707

NOTES TO CONSOLIDATED FINANCIAL STATEMENTS

(In thousands, except per share amounts)

(2) Significant Accounting Policies and Practices (in part)

(j) Debt Issuance Costs

Debt issuance costs are capitalized and amortized to interest expense using the effective interest method over the lives of the related debt agreements.

(6) Debt

Senior Term Credit Facility (in part)

The Company recorded $10,545 of fees in connection with the Term Loan during Fiscal 2011. The fees are classified as Debt issuance costs within the accompanying Consolidated Statements of Financial Position and are amortized as an adjustment to interest expense over the remaining life of the Term Loan. In connection with the refinancing, included in Fiscal 2011 Interest expense are cash charges of $4,954 and accelerated amortization of portions of the unamortized discount and unamortized Debt issuance costs totaling $24,370. In connection with voluntary prepayments of $220,000 of the Term Loan during Fiscal 2011, the Company recorded cash charges of $700 and accelerated amortization of portions of the unamortized discount and unamortized Debt issuance costs totaling $7,521 as an adjustment to increase interest expense. At September 30, 2011 and September 30, 2010, the aggregate amount outstanding under the Term Loan totaled $525,237 and $750,000, respectively.

9.5% Notes (in part)

The 9.5% Notes were issued at a 1.37% discount and were recorded net of the $10,245 amount incurred. The discount is reflected as an adjustment to the carrying value of principal, and is being amortized with a corresponding charge to interest expense over the remaining life of the 9.5% Notes. During Fiscal 2010, the Company recorded $20,823 of fees in connection with the issuance of the 9.5% Notes. The fees are classified as Debt issuance costs within the accompanying Consolidated Statements of Financial Position and are amortized as an adjustment to interest expense over the remaining life of the 9.5% Notes.

12% Notes (in part)

In connection with the Merger, the Company obtained the consent of the note holders to certain amendments to the 2019 Indenture (the "Supplemental Indenture"). The Supplemental Indenture became effective upon the closing of the Merger. Among other things, the Supplemental Indenture amended the definition of change in control to exclude the Harbinger Capital Partners Master Fund I, Ltd. ("Harbinger Master Fund"), Harbinger Capital Partners Special Situations Fund, L.P. ("Harbinger Special Fund") and, together with Harbinger Master Fund, the "HCP Funds"), Global Opportunities Breakaway Ltd. (together with the HCP Funds, the "Harbinger Parties"), and their respective affiliates and increased the Company's ability to incur indebtedness up to $1,850,000.

During Fiscal 2010, the Company recorded $2,966 of fees in connection with the consent. The fees are classified as Debt issuance costs within the accompanying Consolidated Statements of Financial Position and are amortized as an adjustment to interest expense over the remaining life of the 12% Notes effective with the closing of the Merger.

ABL Revolving Credit Facility (in part)

During Fiscal 2010, the Company recorded $9,839 of fees in connection with the ABL Revolving Credit Facility. During Fiscal 2011, the Company recorded $2,071 of fees in connection with the amendment. The fees are classified as Debt issuance costs within the accompanying Consolidated Statements of Financial Position and are amortized as an adjustment to interest expense over the remaining life of the ABL Revolving Credit Facility. Pursuant to the credit and se-

curity agreement, the obligations under the ABL credit agreement are secured by certain current assets of the guarantors, including, but not limited to, deposit accounts, trade receivables and inventory.

Contracts

2.106

THE BOEING COMPANY (DEC)

CONSOLIDATED STATEMENTS OF FINANCIAL POSITION (in part)

	December 31	
(Dollars in millions, except per share data)	**2011**	**2010**
Assets		
Cash and cash equivalents	$10,049	$ 5,359
Short-term and other investments	1,223	5,158
Accounts receivable, net	5,793	5,422
Current portion of customer financing, net	476	285
Deferred income taxes	29	31
Inventories, net of advances and progress billings	32,240	24,317
Total current assets	49,810	40,572
Customer financing, net	4,296	4,395
Property, plant and equipment, net	9,313	8,931
Goodwill	4,945	4,937
Acquired intangible assets, net	3,044	2,979
Deferred income taxes	5,892	4,031
Investments	1,043	1,111
Other assets, net of accumulated amortization of $717 and $630	1,643	1,609
Total assets	$79,986	$68,565

NOTES TO THE CONSOLIDATED FINANCIAL STATEMENTS

Years ended December 31, 2011, 2010 and 2009

(Dollars in millions, except per share data)

Note 6—Accounts Receivable

Accounts receivable at December 31 consisted of the following:

	2011	2010
U.S. government contracts	$2,950	$2,969
Commercial customers	1,390	1,241
Reinsurance receivables	585	487
Non-U.S. military contracts	553	514
Other	368	253
Less valuation allowance	(53)	(42)
Total	$5,793	$5,422

The following table summarizes our accounts receivable under long-term contracts that were not billable or related to outstanding claims as of December 31:

	Unbillable		Claims	
	2011	2010	2011	2010
Current	$1,174	$ 994	$ 49	$ 30
Expected to be collected after one year	498	507	209	194
Total	$1,672	$1,501	$258	$224

Under contract accounting unbillable receivables on long-term contracts arise when the sales or revenues based on performance attainment, though appropriately recognized, cannot be billed yet under terms of the contract as of the balance sheet date. Any adjustment for the credit quality of unbillable receivables, if required, would be recorded as a direct reduction of revenue. Factors considered in assessing the collectability of unbillable receivables include, but are not limited to, a customer's extended delinquency, requests for restructuring and filings for bankruptcy. Unbillable receivables related to commercial customers expected to be collected after one year were $192 and $213 at December 31, 2011 and 2010. Accounts receivable related to claims are items that we believe are earned, but are subject to uncertainty concerning their determination or ultimate realization. Accounts receivable, other than those described above, expected to be collected after one year are not material.

Note 7—Inventories (in part)

Inventories at December 31 consisted of the following:

	2011	2010
Long-term contracts in progress	$ 13,587	$ 14,400
Commercial aircraft programs	35,080	26,550
Commercial spare parts, used aircraft, general stock materials and other	7,832	5,788
Inventory before advances and progress billings	56,499	46,738
Less advances and progress billings	(24,259)	(22,421)
Total	$ 32,240	$ 24,317

Long-Term Contracts in Progress

Long-term contracts in progress included Delta launch program inventory that will be sold at cost to United Launch Alliance (ULA) under an inventory supply agreement that terminates on March 31, 2021. At December 31, 2011 and 2010, the inventory balance was $1,085 and $1,385. As of December 31, 2011, $739 of this inventory relates to yet unsold launches. ULA is continuing to assess the future of the Delta II program. In the event ULA is unable to sell additional Delta II inventory, our earnings could be reduced by up to $58. See Note 13.

Inventory balances included $236 subject to claims or other uncertainties relating to the A-12 program as of December 31, 2011 and 2010. See Note 21.

Capitalized precontract costs of $1,728 and $527 at December 31, 2011 and 2010, are included in long-term contracts in progress inventories.

SHORT-TERM DEBT

PRESENTATION

2.107 FASB ASC 470, *Debt*, addresses classification determination for specific debt obligations, such as the following:
- Short-term obligations expected to be refinanced on a long-term basis
- Due-on-demand loan arrangements
- Callable debt
- Sales of future revenue
- Increasing-rate debt
- Debt that includes covenants
- Revolving credit agreements subject to lock-box arrangements and subjective acceleration clauses

DISCLOSURE

2.108 Rule 5-02 of Regulation S-X calls for disclosure of the amount and terms of unused lines of credit for short-term financing, if significant. The weighted average interest rate on short-term borrowings outstanding as of the date of each balance sheet presented should be furnished. Further, the amount of these lines of credit that support commercial paper or similar borrowing arrangements should be separately identified.

2.109 By definition, *short-term notes payable*, *loans payable*, and *commercial paper* are financial instruments. FASB ASC 825 requires disclosure of both the fair value and bases for estimating the fair value of short-term notes payable, loans payable, and commercial paper, unless it is not practicable to estimate that value.

PRESENTATION AND DISCLOSURE EXCERPTS

Short-Term Debt

2.110

ALLIANCE ONE INTERNATIONAL, INC. (MAR)

CONSOLIDATED BALANCE SHEETS (in part)

(In thousands)	March 31, 2011	March 31, 2010
Liabilities and stockholders' equity		
Current liabilities		
Notes payable to banks	$231,407	$188,981
Accounts payable	86,103	146,395
Due to related parties	38,937	20,275
Advances from customers	17,576	102,286
Accrued expenses and other current liabilities	78,459	113,048
Income taxes	17,149	16,281
Long-term debt current	784	457
Total current liabilities	$470,415	$587,723

NOTES TO CONSOLIDATED FINANCIAL STATEMENTS

(In thousands)

Note 7—Short-Term Borrowing Arrangements

Excluding all long-term credit agreements, the Company has lines of credit arrangements with a number of banks under which the Company may borrow up to a total of $798,599 and $619,294 at March 31, 2011 and 2010, respectively. The weighted average variable interest rate for the twelve months ending March 31, 2011 was 3.5%. At March 31, 2011 and 2010, amounts outstanding under the lines were $231,407 and $188,981, respectively. Unused lines of credit at March 31, 2011 amounted to $553,211 ($416,131 at March 31, 2010), net of $13,981 of letters of credit lines. Certain non-U.S. borrowings of approximately $2,818 and $1,349 have inventories of approximately $2,849 and $1,353 as collateral at March 31, 2011 and 2010, respectively. At March 31, 2011 and 2010, respectively, $296 and $294 were held on deposit as a compensating balance.

Subsequent to year end, the Company has entered into a $30,000 limited recourse receivable purchase program with one of its lenders. Under the program, the lender takes the receivable payment risk of the customer subject to usual and customary covenants, while the Company fulfills contractual obligations. Funding of the purchased receivable is 80% of the face value, and the Company retains an interest in the remaining 20%, which is paid at collection.

2.111

DEERE & COMPANY (OCT)

CONSOLIDATED BALANCE SHEET (in part)

As of October 31, 2011 and 2010

(In millions of dollars except per share amounts)

	2011	2010
Liabilities		
Short-term borrowings	$ 6,852.3	$ 5,325.7
Short-term securitization borrowings	2,777.4	2,208.8
Payables to unconsolidated affiliates	117.7	203.5
Accounts payable and accrued expenses	7,804.8	6,481.7
Deferred income taxes	168.3	144.3
Long-term borrowings	16,959.9	16,814.5
Retirement benefits and other liabilities	6,712.1	5,784.9
Total liabilities	$41,392.5	$36,963.4

NOTES TO CONSOLIDATED FINANCIAL STATEMENTS

1. Organization and Consolidation (in part)

Reclassifications

Certain items previously reported in specific financial statement captions have been reclassified to conform to the 2011 financial statement presentation. Short-term securitization borrowings have been shown separately from other short-term borrowings on the Consolidated Balance Sheet as a result of the adoption of Financial Accounting Standards Board (FASB) Accounting Standards Update (ASU) No. 2009-17 (see Note 3). In the Supplemental Consolidating Data in Note 31, the costs and collections of trade receivables and wholesale notes for the financial services statement of cash flows investing activities have been presented on a net basis. These receivables have short durations with a high turnover rate. The total cash flows for the financial services investing activities have not changed. The presentation of these receivables on the Statement of Consolidated Cash Flows has also not changed and continues to be shown as an adjustment to net income in the operating activities since they are related to sales.

13. Securitization of Financing Receivables (in part)

The company, as a part of its overall funding strategy, periodically transfers certain financing receivables (retail notes) into variable interest entities (VIEs) that are special purpose entities (SPEs), or a non-VIE banking operation, as part of its asset-backed securities programs (securitizations). The structure of these transactions is such that the transfer of the retail notes did not meet the criteria of sales of receivables, and is, therefore, accounted for as a secured borrowing. SPEs utilized in securitizations of retail notes differ from other entities included in the company's consolidated statements because the assets they hold are legally isolated. Use of the assets held by the SPEs or the non-VIE is restricted by terms of the documents governing the securitization transactions.

In securitizations of retail notes related to secured borrowings, the retail notes are transferred to certain SPEs or to a non-VIE banking operation, which in turn issue debt to investors. The resulting secured borrowings are recorded as "Short-term securitization borrowings" on the balance sheet. The securitized retail notes are recorded as "Financing receivables securitized—net" on the balance sheet. The total restricted assets on the balance sheet related to these securitizations include the financing receivables securitized less an allowance for credit losses, and other assets primarily representing restricted cash. For those securitizations in which retail notes are transferred into SPEs, the SPEs supporting the secured borrowings are consolidated unless the company does not have both the power to direct the activities that most significantly impact the SPEs' economic performance and the obligation to absorb losses or the right to receive benefits that could potentially be significant to the SPEs. No additional support to these SPEs beyond what was previously contractually required has been provided during the reporting periods.

In certain securitizations, the company consolidates the SPEs since it has both the power to direct the activities that most significantly impact the SPEs' economic performance through its role as servicer of all the receivables held by the SPEs, and the obligation through variable interests in the SPEs to absorb losses or receive benefits that could potentially be significant to the SPEs. The restricted assets (retail notes securitized, allowance for credit losses and other assets) of the consolidated SPEs totaled $1,523 million and $1,739 million at October 31, 2011 and 2010, respectively. The liabilities (short-term securitization borrowings and accrued interest) of these SPEs totaled $1,395 million and $1,654 million at October 31, 2011 and 2010, respectively. The credit holders of these SPEs do not have legal recourse to the company's general credit.

In certain securitizations, the company transfers retail notes to a non-VIE banking operation, which is not consolidated since the company does not have a controlling interest in the entity. The company's carrying values and interests related to the securitizations with the unconsolidated non-VIE were restricted assets (retail notes securitized, allowance for credit losses and other assets) of $369 million and liabilities (short-term securitization borrowings and accrued interest) of $346 million at October 31, 2011.

In certain securitizations, the company transfers retail notes into bank-sponsored, multi-seller, commercial paper conduits, which are SPEs that are not consolidated. The company does not service a significant portion of the conduits' receivables, and therefore, does not have the power to direct the activities that most significantly impact the conduits' economic performance. These conduits provide a funding source to the company (as well as other transferors into the conduit) as they fund the retail notes through the issuance of commercial paper. The company's carrying values and variable interest related to these conduits were restricted assets (retail notes securitized, allowance for credit losses and other assets) of $1,109 million and $589 million at October 31, 2011 and 2010, respectively. The liabilities (short-term securitization borrowings and accrued interest) related to these conduits were $1,038 million and $557 million at October 31, 2011 and 2010, respectively.

The company's carrying amount of the liabilities to the unconsolidated conduits, compared to the maximum exposure to loss related to these conduits, which would only be incurred in the event of a complete loss on the restricted assets, was as follows at October 31 in millions of dollars:

	2011
Carrying value of liabilities	$1,038
Maximum exposure to loss	1,109

The total assets of unconsolidated VIEs related to securitizations were approximately $23 billion at October 31, 2011.

The components of consolidated restricted assets related to secured borrowings in securitization transactions at October 31 were as follows in millions of dollars:

	2011	2010
Financing receivables securitized (retail notes)	$2,923	$2,265
Allowance for credit losses	(18)	(27)
Other assets	96	90
Total restricted securitized assets	$3,001	$2,328

The components of consolidated secured borrowings and other liabilities related to securitizations at October 31 were as follows in millions of dollars:

	2011	2010
Short-term securitization borrowings	$2,777	$2,209
Accrued interest on borrowings	2	2
Total liabilities related to restricted securitized assets	$ 2,779	$ 2,211

The secured borrowings related to these restricted securitized retail notes are obligations that are payable as the retail notes are liquidated. Repayment of the secured borrowings depends primarily on cash flows generated by the restricted assets. Due to the company's short-term credit rating, cash collections from these restricted assets are not required to be placed into a segregated collection account until immediately prior to the time payment is required to the secured creditors. At October 31, 2011, the maximum remaining term of all securitized retail notes was approximately seven years.

18. Total Short-Term Borrowings

Total short-term borrowings at October 31 consisted of the following in millions of dollars:

	2011	2010
Equipment Operations		
Commercial paper	$ 265	$ 37
Notes payable to banks	19	8
Long-term borrowings due within one year	244	40
Total	528	85
Financial Services		
Commercial paper	1,014	1,991
Notes payable to banks	61	36
Long-term borrowings due within one year	5,249*	3,214*
Total	6,324	5,241
Short-term borrowings	6,852	5,326
Financial Services		
Short-term securitization borrowings	2,777	2,209
Total short-term borrowings	$9,629	$7,535

* Includes unamortized fair value adjustments related to interest rate swaps.

The notes payable related to short-term securitization borrowings for financial services are secured by financing receivables (retail notes) on the balance sheet (see Note 13). Although these notes payable are classified as short-term since payment is required if the retail notes are liquidated early, the payment schedule for these borrowings of $2,777 million at October 31, 2011 based on the expected liquidation of the retail notes in millions of dollars is as follows: 2012—$1,447, 2013—$775, 2014—$358, 2015—$150, 2016—$44 and 2017—$3.

The weighted-average interest rates on total short-term borrowings, excluding current maturities of long-term borrowings, at October 31, 2011 and 2010 were 1.1 percent and 1.0 percent, respectively.

Lines of credit available from U.S. and foreign banks were $5,080 million at October 31, 2011. At October 31, 2011, $3,721 million of these worldwide lines of credit were unused. For the purpose of computing the unused credit lines, commercial paper and short-term bank borrowings, excluding secured borrowings and the current portion of long-term borrowings, were primarily considered to constitute utilization. Included in the above lines of credit were long-term credit facility agreements for $2,750 million, expiring in April 2015, and $1,500 million, expiring in April 2013. The agreements are mutually extendable and the annual facility fees are not significant. These credit agreements require Capital Corporation to maintain its consolidated ratio of earnings to fixed charges at not less than 1.05 to 1 for each fiscal quarter and the ratio of senior debt, excluding securitization indebtedness, to capital base (total subordinated debt and stockholder's equity excluding accumulated other comprehensive income (loss)) at not more than 11 to 1 at the end of any fiscal quarter. The credit agreements also require the equipment operations to maintain a ratio of total debt to total capital (total debt and stockholders' equity excluding accumulated other comprehensive income (loss)) of 65 percent or less at the end of each fiscal quarter. Under this provision, the company's excess equity capacity and retained earnings balance free of restriction at October 31, 2011 was $8,503 million. Alternatively under this provision, the equipment operations had the capacity to incur additional debt of $15,791 million at October 31, 2011. All of these requirements of the credit agreements have been met during the periods included in the consolidated financial statements.

Deere & Company has an agreement with Capital Corporation pursuant to which it has agreed to continue to own at least 51 percent of the voting shares of capital stock of Capital Corporation and to maintain Capital Corporation's consolidated tangible net worth at not less than $50 million. This agreement also obligates Deere & Company to make payments to Capital Corporation such that its consolidated ratio of earnings to fixed charges is not less than 1.05 to 1 for each fiscal quarter. Deere & Company's obligations to make payments to Capital Corporation under the agreement are independent of whether Capital Corporation is in default on its indebtedness, obligations or other liabilities. Further, Deere & Company's obligations under the agreement are not measured by the amount of Capital Corporation's indebtedness, obligations or other liabilities. Deere & Company's obligations to make payments under this agreement are expressly stated not to be a guaranty of any specific indebtedness, obligation or liability of Capital Corporation and are enforceable only by or in the name of Capital Corporation. No payments were required under this agreement during the periods included in the consolidated financial statements.

TRADE ACCOUNTS PAYABLE

RECOGNITION AND MEASUREMENT

2.112 FASB ASC 210 states that current liabilities generally include obligations for items that have entered into the operating cycle, such as payables incurred in the acquisition of materials and supplies to be used in the production of goods or in providing services to be offered for sale.

PRESENTATION

2.113 Rule 5.02 of Regulation S-X requires that amounts payable to trade creditors be separately stated.

DISCLOSURE

2.114 Under FASB ASC 825, fair value disclosure is not required for trade payables when the carrying amount of the trade payable approximates its fair value.

EMPLOYEE-RELATED LIABILITIES

PRESENTATION

2.115 FASB ASC 715, *Compensation—Retirement Benefits*, requires that an entity recognize the overfunded or underfunded status of a single-employer defined benefit postretirement plan as an asset or a liability in its statement of financial position. FASB ASC 715 also requires that an employer that presents a classified balance sheet should classify the liability for an underfunded plan as a current liability, a noncurrent liability, or a combination of both. The current portion (determined on a plan-by-plan basis) is the amount by which the actuarial present value of benefits included in the benefit obligation that is payable in the next 12 months, or operating cycle if longer, exceeds the fair value of plan assets. The asset for an overfunded plan shall be classified as a noncurrent asset in a classified balance sheet. The amount classified as a current liability is limited to the amount of the plan's unfunded status recognized in the employer's balance sheet.

DISCLOSURE

2.116 FASB ASC 715 requires that employers recognize changes in that funded status in comprehensive income and disclose in the notes to financial statements additional information about plan assets, the benefit obligation, reconciliations of beginning and ending balances of both plan assets and obligations, and net periodic benefit cost.

2.117 In September 2011, FASB issued ASU No. 2011-09, *Compensation—Retirement Benefits—Multiemployer Plans (Subtopic 715-80): Disclosures about an Employer's Participation in a Multiemployer Plan*, to improve transparency about such plans by requiring employers to provide additional disclosures. An entity should include additional details in these disclosures including plan names and identifying numbers for significant multiemployer plans, the level of employers' participation in the plans, the financial health of the plans, and the nature of the employer commitments to the plans. The amendments in this Update are effective for fiscal years ending after December 15, 2011, for public entities and December 15, 2012, for nonpublic entities.

PRESENTATION AND DISCLOSURE EXCERPTS

Employee-Related Liabilities

2.118

MERITOR, INC. (SEP)

CONSOLIDATED BALANCE SHEET (in part)

(In millions)

	September 30	
	2011	**2010**
Liabilities and Equity (Deficit) *(in part)*		
Current liabilities:		
Short-term debt	$ 84	$ —
Accounts payable	841	670
Other current liabilities	327	358
Liabilities of discontinued operations	1	362
Total current liabilities	1,253	1,390
Long-term debt	950	1,029
Retirement benefits	1,096	1,162
Other liabilities	325	321

NOTES TO CONSOLIDATED FINANCIAL STATEMENTS

19. Retirement Medical Plans (in part)

The company has retirement medical plans that cover certain of its U.S. and non-U.S. employees, including certain employees of divested businesses, and provide for medical payments to eligible employees and dependents upon retirement. These plans are unfunded.

The company approved amendments to certain retiree medical plans in fiscal years 2002 and 2004. The cumulative effect of these amendments was a reduction in the accumulated postretirement benefit obligation (APBO) of $293 million, which was being amortized as a reduction of retiree medical expense over the average remaining service period of approximately 12 years. These plan amendments have been challenged in three separate class action lawsuits that have been filed in the United States District Court for the Eastern District of Michigan (District Court). The lawsuits allege that the changes breach the terms of various collective bargaining agreements entered into with the United Auto Workers (the UAW lawsuit) and the United Steel Workers (the USW lawsuit) at facilities that have either been closed or sold. The complaints also allege a companion claim under the Employee Retirement Income Security Act of 1974 (ERISA) essentially restating the alleged collective bargaining breach claims and seeking to bring them under ERISA. Plaintiffs sought injunctive relief requiring the company to provide lifetime retiree health care benefits under the applicable collective bargaining agreements.

On December 22, 2005, the District Court issued an order granting a motion by the UAW for a preliminary injunction. The order enjoined the company from implementing the changes to retiree health benefits that had been scheduled to become effective on January 1, 2006, and ordered the company to reinstate and resume paying the full cost of health benefits for the UAW retirees at the levels existing prior to the changes approved in 2002 and 2004. On August 17, 2006, the District Court denied a motion by the company and the other defendants for summary judgment; granted a motion by the UAW for summary judgment; and granted the UAW's request to make the terms of the preliminary injunction permanent (the injunction). Due to the uncertainty related to the ongoing lawsuits and because the injunction has the impact of at least temporarily changing the benefits provided under the existing postretirement medical plans, the company has accounted for the injunction as a rescission of the 2002 and 2004 plan amendments that modified UAW retiree healthcare benefits. The company recalculated the APBO as of December 22, 2005, which resulted in an increase in the APBO of $168 million. The company began recording the impact of the injunction in March 2006. In addition, the injunction ordered the defendants to reimburse the plaintiffs for out-of-pocket expenses incurred since the date of the earlier benefit modifications. The company has recorded a $5 million reserve at September 30, 2011 and 2010 as the best estimate of its liability for these retroactive benefits. The company continues to believe it has meritorious defenses to these actions and has appealed the District Court's order to the U.S. Court of Appeals for the Sixth Circuit. The ultimate outcome of the UAW lawsuit may result in future plan amendments. The impact of any future plan amendments cannot be currently estimated.

On November 12, 2008, the company settled the USW lawsuit with the United Steel Workers with respect to certain retiree medical plan amendments for approximately $28 million. This settlement was paid in November 2008 and increased the accumulated postretirement benefit obligation (APBO) by approximately $23 million. The increase in APBO has been reflected in the company's actuarial valuations as an increase in actuarial losses and is being amortized into periodic retiree medical expense over an average expected remaining service life of approximately 10 years.

The company's retiree medical obligations were measured as of September 30, 2011 and 2009. The following are the assumptions used in the measurement of the APBO and retiree medical expense:

	2011	2010	2009
Discount rate	4.60%	4.60%	5.60%
Health care cost trend rate (weighted average)	7.50%	7.75%	7.85%
Ultimate health care trend rate	5.00%	5.00%	5.00%
Year ultimate rate is reached	2023	2023	2021

The assumptions noted above are used to calculate the APBO for each fiscal year end and retiree medical expense for the subsequent fiscal year.

The discount rate is used to calculate the present value of the APBO. This rate is determined based on high-quality fixed income investments that match the duration of expected retiree medical benefits. The company has used the corporate AA/Aa bond rate for this assumption. The health care cost trend rate represents the company's expected annual rates of change in the cost of health care benefits. The company's projection for fiscal year 2012 is an increase in health care costs of 7.50 percent.

The APBO as of the September 30, 2011 and 2010 measurement dates are summarized as follows (in millions):

	2011	2010
Retirees	$521	$564
Employees eligible to retire	9	10
Employees not eligible to retire	15	15
Total	$545	$589

The following reconciles the change in APBO and the amounts included in the consolidated balance sheet for years ended September 30, 2011 and 2010, respectively (in millions):

	2011	2010
APBO—beginning of year	$589	$633
Service cost	1	1
Interest cost	26	32
Participant contributions	3	3
Actuarial loss (gain)	(32)	14
Divestitures[1]	—	(49)
Foreign currency rate changes	1	2
Benefit payments	(43)	(47)
APBO—end of year	545	589
Other[2]	5	5
Retiree medical liability	$550	$594

[1] The decrease in APBO represents retiree medical liabilities of MSSC which were assumed by the buyer as part of the sale transaction that closed in the first quarter of fiscal year 2010 (see Note 3).

[2] The company recorded a $5 million reserve for retiree medical liabilities at September 30, 2011 and 2010 as its best estimate for retroactive benefits related to the previously mentioned injunction.

Actuarial losses relate to changes in the discount rate and earlier than expected retirements due to certain plant closings and restructuring actions. In accordance with FASB ASC Topic 715, "Compensation—Retirement Benefits," a portion of the actuarial losses is not subject to amortization. The actuarial losses that are subject to amortization are generally amortized over the average expected remaining service life, which is approximately 10 years. Union plan amendments are generally amortized over the contract period, or three years.

The Medicare Prescription Drug Improvement and Modernization Act of 2003 provides for a federal subsidy to sponsors of retiree health care benefit plans that provide a benefit at least actuarially equivalent to the benefit established by the law. The company provides retiree medical benefits for certain plans that exceed the value of the benefits that are provided by the Medicare Part D plan. Therefore, management concluded that these plans are at least actuarially equivalent to the Medicare Part D plan and the company is eligible for the federal subsidy. The impact of the subsidy was a reduction in the fiscal year 2011 and 2010 retiree medical expense of $6 million. In September 2011, in connection with the Health Care and Education Reconciliation Act of 2010, the company converted its current prescription drug program for certain retirees to a group-based company sponsored Medicare Part D program, or Employer Group Waiver Plan (EGWP). Beginning in 2013, the company will use the Part D subsidies delivered through EGWP each year to reduce its net retiree medical costs. As a result of this change in assumption, the company reduced its APBO by approximately $35 million, which will be amortized over an average expected remaining service life of approximately 10 years.

The retiree medical liability is included in the consolidated balance sheet as follows (in millions):

	September 30	
	2011	2010
Current—included in compensation and benefits	$ 44	$ 45
Long-term—included in retirement benefits	506	549
Retiree medical liability	$550	$594

20. Retirement Pension Plans (in part)

The company sponsors defined benefit pension plans that cover the majority of its U.S. employees and certain non-U.S. employees. Pension benefits for salaried employees are based on years of credited service and compensation. Pension benefits for hourly employees are based on years of service and specified benefit amounts. The company's funding policy provides that annual contributions to the pension trusts will be at least equal to the minimum amounts required by ERISA in the U.S. and the actuarial recommendations or statutory requirements in other countries.

On August 1, 2010, Meritor amended its defined benefit pension plan in the United Kingdom to cease the accrual of future benefits for all of its active plan participants. Subsequent to the freeze date, the company began making contributions to its defined contribution savings plan on behalf of the affected employees. The amount of the savings plan contribution will be based on a percentage of the employees' pay. These changes do not affect current retirees. The company began recording the impact of the plan freeze in the fourth quarter of fiscal year 2010. The amendment to freeze the plan triggered a curtailment in the fourth quarter of fiscal year 2010 reducing pension expense by $7 million. The reduction in expense was primarily attributable to the required immediate recognition of negative prior service costs which were previously being amortized into net periodic pension expense over the active participants remaining average service life. Subsequent to the plan freeze, accumulated actuarial losses are being amortized into net periodic pension expense over the average life expectancy of inactive plan participants of approximately 28 years rather than over their remaining average service life.

On February 24, 2009, the company announced the closure of its commercial truck brakes plant in Tilbury, Ontario, Canada. All salaried and hourly employees at this facility participate in both a salaried or hourly pension plan and a retiree medical plan. The expected closure of this facility triggered plan curtailments requiring the remeasurement of each plan. The measurement date of these valuations was February 28, 2009. The FASB's retirement benefits guidance requires a plan curtailment loss to be recognized in earnings when it is probable that a curtailment will occur and the effects are reasonably estimable. Including pension termination benefits of approximately $14 million required to be paid under the terms of the plans, the company recognized plan curtailment losses of approximately $16 million, which include $2 million of retiree medical benefits, recorded in restructuring costs (see Note 5) in the consolidated statement of operations.

On March 5, 2009, the company announced its plans to close its coil spring operations in Milton, Ontario, Canada, which is part of MSSC. As noted in Note 3, the company sold its 57 percent interest in MSSC in October 2009. The company recognized an $8 million curtailment charge, primarily related to pension termination benefits, which is included in loss from discontinued operations in the consolidated statement of operations.

In April 2007, the company announced a freeze of its defined benefit pension plan for salaried and non-represented employees in the United States, effective January 1, 2008. The change affected approximately 3,800 employees including certain employees who continued to accrue benefits for an additional transition period, ending June 30, 2011. After these freeze dates, the company is instead making additional contributions to its defined contribution savings plan on behalf of the affected employees. The amount of the savings plan contribution is based on a percentage of the employees' pay, with the contribution percentage increasing as a function of employees' age. These changes do not affect current retirees or represented employees. Subsequent to the June 30, 2011 freeze date, accumulated actuarial losses are being amortized into net periodic pension expense over the average life expectancy of inactive plan participants of approximately 28 years. Prior to June 30, 2011, accumulated actuarial losses were being amortized over the remaining average service life of approximately 9 years.

The company's pension obligations were measured as of September 30, 2011, 2010 and 2009. The U.S. plans include a qualified and non-qualified pension plans. The company's significant non-U.S. plan is located in the United Kingdom. Other non-U.S. plans include plans primarily in Canada, Germany and Switzerland.

The following table reconciles the change in the PBO, the change in plan assets and amounts included in the consolidated balance sheet for the years ended September 30, 2011 and 2010, respectively (in millions):

	2011			2010		
	U.S.	Non-U.S.	Total	U.S.	Non-U.S.	Total
PBO—beginning of year	$1,201	$ 762	$1,963	$1,047	$ 806	$1,853
Service cost	5	2	7	6	10	16
Interest cost	57	36	93	58	37	95
Participant contributions	—	1	1	—	2	2
Actuarial loss (gain)	19	(27)	(8)	154	42	196
Divestitures[1]	—	(38)	(38)	—	(78)	(78)
Benefit payments	(64)	(36)	(100)	(64)	(45)	(109)
Foreign currency rate changes	—	(2)	(2)	—	(12)	(12)
PBO—end of year	1,218	698	1,916	1,201	762	1,963
Change in plan assets						
Fair value of assets—beginning of year	765	589	1,354	726	610	1,336
Actual return on plan assets	57	15	72	60	45	105
Employer contributions	5	30	35	43	37	80
Participant contributions	—	1	1	—	2	2
Divestitures[1]	—	—	—	—	(57)	(57)
Benefit payments	(64)	(36)	(100)	(64)	(45)	(109)
Foreign currency rate changes	—	(3)	(3)	—	(3)	(3)
Fair value of assets—end of year	763	596	1,359	765	589	1,354
Funded status	$ (455)	$(102)	$ (557)	$ (436)	$(173)	$ (609)

[1] The decrease in PBO and fair value of assets represents the net pension liabilities of Body Systems and MSSC which were assumed by the buyers as part of the sale transactions that closed in fiscal years 2011 and 2010, respectively (see Note 3).

Amounts included in the consolidated balance sheet at September 30 are comprised of the following (in millions):

	2011			2010		
	U.S.	Non-U.S.	Total	U.S.	Non-U.S.	Total
Non-current assets	$ —	$ 10	$ 10	$ —	$ 9	$ 9
Current liabilities	(5)	(3)	(8)	(5)	(3)	(8)
Retirement benefits-non-current	(450)	(109)	(559)	(431)	(179)	(610)
Net amount recognized	$(455)	$(102)	$(557)	$(436)	$(173)	$(609)

2.119

INSPERITY, INC. (DEC)

CONSOLIDATED BALANCE SHEETS (in part)

(In thousands)

Liabilities and Stockholders' Equity (in part)

	December 31, 2011	December 31, 2010
Current liabilities:		
Accounts payable	$ 5,085	$ 3,309
Payroll taxes and other payroll deductions payable	168,652	145,096
Accrued worksite employee payroll cost	130,317	109,697
Accrued health insurance costs	9,427	15,419
Accrued workers' compensation costs	46,548	42,081
Accrued corporate payroll and commissions	22,383	23,743
Other accrued liabilities	13,814	14,264
Total current liabilities	396,226	353,609
Noncurrent liabilities:		
Accrued workers' compensation costs	60,054	55,730
Other accrued liabilities	—	1,261
Deferred income taxes	10,772	8,850
Total noncurrent liabilities	70,826	65,841

NOTES TO CONSOLIDATED FINANCIAL STATEMENTS

December 31, 2011

1. Accounting Policies (in part)

Description of Business (in part)

Health Insurance Costs

Insperity provides group health insurance coverage to its worksite employees through a national network of carriers including UnitedHealthcare ("United"), Kaiser Permanente, Blue Shield of California, HMSA BlueCross BlueShield, Unity Health Plan and Tufts, all of which provide fully insured policies or service contracts.

The policy with United provides the majority of our health insurance coverage. As a result of certain contractual terms, Insperity has accounted for this plan since its inception using a partially self-funded insurance accounting model. Accordingly, Insperity records the costs of the United plan, including an estimate of the incurred claims, taxes and administrative fees (collectively the "Plan Costs") as benefits expense in the Consolidated Statements of Operations. The estimated incurred claims are based upon: (i) the level of claims processed during each quarter; (ii) estimated completion rates based upon recent claim development patterns under the plan; and (iii) the number of participants in the plan, including both active and COBRA enrollees. Each reporting period, changes in the estimated ultimate costs resulting from claim trends, plan design and migration, participant demographics and other factors are incorporated into the benefits costs.

Additionally, since the plan's inception, under the terms of the contract, United establishes cash funding rates 90 days in advance of the beginning of a reporting quarter. If the Plan Costs for a reporting quarter are greater than the premiums paid and owed to United, a deficit in the plan would be incurred and a liability for the excess costs would be accrued in our Consolidated Balance Sheets. On the other hand, if the Plan Costs for the reporting quarter are less than the premiums paid and owed to United, a surplus in the plan would be incurred and we would record an asset for the excess premiums in its Consolidated Balance Sheets. The terms of the arrangement require Insperity to maintain an accumulated cash surplus in the plan of $9.0 million, which is reported as long-term prepaid insurance. As of December 31, 2011, Plan Costs were less than the net premiums paid and owed to United by $24.0 million. As this amount is in excess of the agreed-upon $9.0 million surplus maintenance level, the $15.0 million balance is included in prepaid insurance, a current asset, in our Consolidated Balance Sheets. The premiums owed to United at December 31, 2011, were $6.1 million, which is included in accrued health insurance costs, a current liability in our Consolidated Balance Sheets.

Workers' Compensation Costs

Insperity's workers' compensation coverage has been provided through an arrangement with the ACE Group of Companies ("the ACE Program") since 2007. The ACE Program is fully insured in that ACE has the responsibility to pay all claims incurred regardless of whether Insperity satisfies its responsibilities. Through September 30, 2010, Insperity bore the economic burden for the first $1 million layer of claims per occurrence and the insurance carrier was and remains responsible for the economic burden for all claims in excess of such first $1 million layer.

Effective October 1, 2010, in addition to Insperity bearing the economic burden for the first $1 million layer of claims per occurrence, we also bear the economic burden for those claims exceeding $1 million, up to a maximum aggregate amount of $5 million per policy year.

Because Insperity bears the economic burden for claims up to the levels noted above, such claims, which are the primary component of our workers' compensation costs, are recorded in the period incurred. Workers' compensation insurance includes ongoing health care and indemnity coverage whereby claims are paid over numerous years following the date of injury. Accordingly, the accrual of related incurred costs in each reporting period includes estimates, which take into account the ongoing development of claims and therefore requires a significant level of judgment.

Insperity employs a third party actuary to estimate its loss development rate, which is primarily based upon the nature of worksite employees' job responsibilities, the location of worksite employees, the historical frequency and severity of workers compensation claims, and an estimate of future cost trends. Each reporting period, changes in the actuarial assumptions resulting from changes in actual claims experience and other trends are incorporated into our workers' compensation claims cost estimates. During the years ended December 31, 2011 and 2010, Insperity reduced accrued workers' compensation costs by $11.4 million and $6.2 million, respectively, for changes in estimated losses related to prior reporting periods. Workers' compensation cost estimates are discounted to present value at a rate based upon the U.S. Treasury rates that correspond with the weighted average estimated claim payout period (the average discount rates utilized in 2011 and 2010 were 1.1% and 1.4%, respectively) and are accreted over the estimated claim payment period and included as a component of direct costs in our Consolidated Statements of Operations.

The following table provides the activity and balances related to incurred but not reported workers' compensation claims:

| (In thousands) | Year Ended December 31 | |
	2011	2010
Beginning balance	$ 96,934	$ 88,450
Accrued claims	36,845	34,345
Present value discount	(1,513)	(1,675)
Paid claims	(27,475)	(24,186)
Ending balance	$104,791	$ 96,934
Current portion of accrued claims	$ 44,737	$ 41,204
Long-term portion of accrued claims	60,054	55,730
	$104,791	$ 96,934

The current portion of accrued workers' compensation costs at December 31, 2011 and 2010, includes $1.8 million and $877,000, respectively, of workers' compensation administrative fees.

As of December 31, the undiscounted accrued workers' compensation costs were $118.3 million in 2011 and $111.5 million in 2010.

At the beginning of each policy period, the insurance carrier establishes monthly funding requirements comprised of premium costs and funds to be set aside for payment of future claims ("claim funds"). The level of claim funds is primarily based upon anticipated worksite employee payroll levels and expected workers' compensation loss rates, as determined by the insurance carrier. Monies funded into the program for incurred claims expected to be paid within one year are recorded as restricted cash, a short-term asset, while the remainder of claim funds are included in deposits,

a long-term asset in our Consolidated Balance Sheets. In 2011, we received $10.0 million for the return of excess claim funds related to the ACE program, which reduced deposits. As of December 31, 2011, we had restricted cash of $44.7 million and deposits of $52.3 million.

Insperity's estimate of incurred claim costs expected to be paid within one year are recorded as accrued workers' compensation costs and included in short-term liabilities, while its estimate of incurred claim costs expected to be paid beyond one year are included in long-term liabilities on our Consolidated Balance Sheets.

2.120

ROCK-TENN COMPANY (SEP)

CONSOLIDATED BALANCE SHEETS (in part)

| (In millions, except share and per share data) | September 30 | |
	2011	2010
Liabilities and Equity (in part)		
Current liabilities:		
Current portion of debt	$ 143.3	$231.6
Accounts payable	780.7	252.3
Accrued compensation and benefits	220.0	90.7
Other current liabilities	174.3	56.6
Total current liabilities	1,318.3	631.2
Long-term debt due after one year	3,302.5	897.3
Pension liabilities, net of current portion	1,431.0	165.3
Postretirement benefit liabilities, net of current portion	155.2	0.8
Deferred income taxes	827.1	166.4
Other long-term liabilities	153.3	29.2

NOTES TO CONSOLIDATED FINANCIAL STATEMENTS

Note 14. Retirement Plans (in part)

We have defined benefit pension plans for certain U.S. and Canadian employees. In addition, under several labor contracts, we make payments based on hours worked into multiemployer pension plan trusts established for the benefit of certain collective bargaining employees in facilities both inside and outside the United States. We also have a Supplemental Executive Retirement Plan ("SERP") and other nonqualified defined benefit pension plans that provide unfunded supplemental retirement benefits to certain of our executives and former executives. The SERP provides for incremental pension benefits in excess of those offered in our principal pension plan.

Salaried and nonunion hourly employees hired on or after January 1, 2005 are not eligible to participate in RockTenn benefit plans in effect prior to the Smurfit-Stone Acquisition. However, we provide an enhanced 401(k) plan match for such employees. The defined benefit pension plans acquired in connection with the Smurfit-Stone Acquisition cover substantially all hourly employees, as well as salaried employees hired prior to January 1, 2006. These plans were frozen for salaried employees at various stages prior to the acquisition. The postretirement plans that were acquired in connection with the Smurfit-Stone Acquisition provide certain health care and life insurance benefits for certain salaried and hourly employees who meet specified age and service requirements as defined by the plans. The references in the tables that follow to Canadian pension plans and U.S. and Canadian postretirement plans are plans acquired in the Smurfit-Stone acquisition.

The benefits under our defined benefit pension plans are based on either compensation or a combination of years of service and negotiated benefit levels, depending upon the plan. We allocate our pension assets to several investment management firms across a variety of investment styles. Our

Defined Benefit Investment Committee meets at least four times a year with an investment advisor to review each management firm's performance and monitor their compliance with their stated goals, our investment policy and applicable regulatory requirements in the U.S. and Canada.

We understand that investment returns are volatile. We believe that, by investing in a variety of asset classes and utilizing multiple investment management firms, we can create a portfolio that yields adequate returns with reduced volatility. After we consulted with our actuary and investment advisor, we adopted the target allocations in the table that follows for our pension plans to produce the desired performance. These target allocations are guidelines, not limitations, and occasionally plan fiduciaries will approve allocations above or below target ranges.

The assumptions used to measure the benefit plan obligations at September 30 were:

	Pension Plans		Postretirement Plans
	2011	2010	2011
Discount rate—U.S. Plans	5.27%	5.41%	5.27%
Rate of compensation increase–U.S. Plans	3.22%	0.4–3.50%	N/A
Discount rate–Canadian Plans	4.90%	N/A	4.90%
Rate of compensation increase–Canadian Plans	3.13%	N/A	N/A
Discount rate—SERP and Other Executive Plans	0.87–4.61%	3.21%	N/A
Rate of compensation increase–SERP and Other Executive Plans	0–6.00%	6.00%	N/A

We determine the discount rate with the assistance of actuaries. At September 30, 2011, the discount rate for the U.S. pension and postretirement plans was determined based on the yield on a theoretical portfolio of high-grade corporate bonds, and the discount rate for the Canadian pension, postretirement plans, SERP and the other executive plans was determined based on a yield curve developed by our actuary.

The theoretical portfolio of high-grade corporate bonds used to select the September 30, 2011 discount rate for the U.S. pension plans includes bonds generally rated Aa- or better with at least $100 million outstanding par value and bonds that are non-callable (unless the bonds possess a "make whole" feature). The theoretical portfolio of bonds

has cash flows that generally match our expected benefit payments in future years.

Our assumption regarding the increase in compensation levels is reviewed periodically and the assumption is based on both our internal planning projections and recent history of actual compensation increases. We typically review our expected long-term rate of return on plan assets periodically through an asset allocation study with either our actuary or investment advisor. For fiscal 2012, we are changing our expected rate of return to 8.0% for our U.S. plans and remain at 6.0% for our Canadian plans based on an updated analysis of our long-term expected rate of return and our current asset allocation.

Changes in benefit obligation for the years ended September 30 (in millions):

	Pension Plans		Postretirement Plans
	2011	2010	2011
Benefit obligation at beginning of year	$ 472.1	$438.9	$ 0.8
Service cost	17.2	11.1	0.6
Interest cost	95.1	23.8	3.2
Amendments	0.6	0.3	(1.0)
Actuarial loss	127.4	14.3	2.0
Plan participant contributions	1.2	—	2.3
Benefits paid	(101.6)	(16.3)	(6.4)
Business combinations	3,823.3	—	169.7
Foreign currency rate changes	(71.8)	—	(3.7)
Benefit obligation at end of year	$4,363.5	$472.1	$167.5

The accumulated benefit obligation of the pension plans was $4,318.8 million and $458.3 million at September 30, 2011 and 2010, respectively. At September 30, 2011 and 2010, no plans had a fair value of plan assets which exceeded their accumulated benefit obligation. Changes in plan assets for the years ended September 30 (in millions):

	Pension Plans		Postretirement Plans
	2011	2010	2011
Fair value of plan assets at beginning of year	$ 306.3	$277.3	$—
Actual gain (loss) on plan assets	(114.8)	24.6	—
Employer contributions	62.4	20.7	4.1
Plan participant contributions	1.2	—	2.3
Benefits paid	(101.6)	(16.3)	(6.4)
Business combinations	2,823.8	—	—
Foreign currency rate changes	(57.9)	—	—
Fair value of assets at end of year	$2,919.4	$306.3	$—

The table below sets forth the under funded status recognized in the consolidated balance sheets at September 30 (in millions):

	Pension Plans		Postretirement Plans
	2011	2010	2011
Other current liability	$ (13.1)	$ (0.5)	$ (12.3)
Accrued pension and other long-term benefits	(1,431.0)	(165.3)	(155.2)
Net amount recognized	$(1,444.1)	$(165.8)	$(167.5)

The assumed health care cost trend rates used in measuring the accumulated postretirement benefit obligation ("APBO") are as follows at September 30:

	2011
U.S. Plans	
Health care cost trend rate assumed for next year	9.63%
Rate to which the cost trend rate is assumed to decline (the ultimate trend rate)	5.00%
Year the rate reaches the ultimate trend rate	2030
Canadian Plans	
Health care cost trend rate assumed for next year	7.90%
Rate to which the cost trend rate is assumed to decline (the ultimate trend rate)	4.70%
Year the rate reaches the ultimate trend rate	2029

The effect of a 1% change in the assumed health care cost trend rate would increase and decrease the APBO as of September 30, 2011 by approximately $10 million and would increase and decrease the annual net periodic postretirement benefit cost for 2011 by an immaterial amount.

Defined Contribution Plans

We have 401(k) and other defined contribution plans that cover all of our salaried and nonunion hourly employees as well as certain employees covered by union collective bargaining agreements, subject to an initial waiting period. The 401(k) plans permit participants to make contributions by salary reduction pursuant to Section 401(k) of the Code. Due primarily to acquisitions, we have plans with varied terms with company contributions ranging from 0% to 7%. During fiscal 2011, 2010, and 2009, we recorded expense of $20.3

million, $12.3 million, and $11.2 million, respectively, related to the 401(k) plans and defined contribution plans.

Supplemental Retirement Plans

We have supplemental retirement savings plans (the "Supplemental Plans") that are nonqualified deferred compensation plans. We intend to provide participants with an opportunity to supplement their retirement income through deferral of current compensation. These plans are divided into a broad based section and the senior executive section. The broad based section was put into effect on January 1, 2006 for certain highly compensated employees whose 401(k) contributions were capped at a maximum deferral rate in certain 401(k) plans in an effort to pass the nondiscrimination tests in those plans. Participants in the broad based section of the plan can contribute base pay up to a certain maximum dollar amount determined annually. In addition, amounts are contributed for certain executives whose participation in our pension plans is limited or excluded. Contributions in the broad based section of the plan are not matched. Amounts deferred and payable under the Supplemental Plans are our unsecured obligations (the "Obligations"), and rank equally with our other unsecured and unsubordinated indebtedness outstanding. Each participant in the senior executive portion of the plan elects the amount of eligible base salary and/or eligible bonus to be deferred to a maximum deferral of 6% of base salary and eligible bonus. We match $0.50 on the dollar of the amount contributed by participants in the senior executive section. Each Obligation will be payable on a date selected by us pursuant to the terms of the Supplemental Plans. Generally, we are obligated to pay the Obligations after termination of the participant's employment or in certain emergency situations. We will adjust each participant's account for investment gains and losses as if the credits to the participant's account had been invested in the benchmark investment alternatives available under the Supplemental Plans in accordance with the participant's investment election or elections (or default election or elections) as in effect from time to time. We will make all such adjustments at the same time and in accordance with the same procedures followed under our 401(k) plans for crediting investment gains and losses to a participant's account under our 401(k) plans. The Obligations are denominated and payable in United States dollars. The amount recorded for both the asset and liability was approximately $5.0 million at September 30, 2011. The benchmark investment alternatives available under the Supplemental Plans are the same as the investment alternatives available under our 401(k) plans or are, in our view, comparable to the investment alternatives available under our 401(k) plans. The recorded expense for the current fiscal year and the preceding two fiscal years was not significant.

INCOME TAX LIABILITY

PRESENTATION

2.121 FASB ASC 210 provides general guidance for classification of accounts in balance sheets. FASB 740-10-45 addresses classification matters applicable to income tax accounts and is incremental to the general guidance.

DISCLOSURE

2.122 FASB 740-10-50 provides detailed disclosures for income taxes, including the components of the net deferred tax liability or asset recognized in an entity's balance sheet.

PRESENTATION AND DISCLOSURE EXCERPTS

Income Taxes Payable

2.123

IAC/INTERACTIVE CORP (DEC)

CONSOLIDATED BALANCE SHEET (in part)

	December 31	
(In thousands, except share data)	2011	2010
Liabilities and Shareholders' Equity *(in part)*		
Liabilities:		
Accounts payable, trade	$ 64,398	$ 56,375
Deferred revenue	126,297	78,175
Accrued expenses and other current liabilities	343,490	222,323
Total current liabilities	534,185	356,873
Long-term debt	95,844	95,844
Income taxes payable	450,533	475,685
Deferred income taxes	302,213	270,501
Other long-term liabilities	16,601	20,239
Redeemable noncontrolling interests	50,349	59,869
Commitments and contingencies		

NOTES TO CONSOLIDATED FINANCIAL STATEMENTS

Note 4—Income Taxes (in part)

The current income tax payable was reduced by $18.0 million, $5.2 million and $0.8 million for the years ended December 31, 2011, 2010 and 2009, respectively, for excess tax deductions attributable to stock-based compensation. The related income tax benefits were recorded as amounts credited to additional paid-in capital or a reduction in goodwill. In addition, the current income tax payable was reduced by $4.1 million, $4.8 million and $4.3 million for the years ended December 31, 2011, 2010 and 2009, respectively, for excess tax deductions attributable to settlements of vested stock-based awards denominated in subsidiaries' equity. The related income tax benefits were recorded as amounts credited to additional paid-in-capital.

The tax effects of cumulative temporary differences that give rise to significant portions of the deferred tax assets and deferred tax liabilities are presented below. The valuation allowance is related to items for which it is more likely than not that the tax benefit will not be realized.

(In thousands)	December 31	
	2011	**2010**
Deferred tax assets:		
Accrued expenses	$ 25,130	$ 18,361
Net operating loss carryforwards	31,000	35,298
Tax credit carryforwards	10,518	12,765
Stock-based compensation	84,543	68,633
Income tax reserves, including related interest	57,016	64,191
Intangible and other assets	—	10,339
Equity method investments	12,850	—
Other	22,490	32,103
Total deferred tax assets	243,547	241,690
Less valuation allowance	(45,084)	(40,266)
Net deferred tax assets	198,463	201,424
Deferred tax liabilities:		
Property and equipment	(16,264)	(16,648)
Investment in subsidiaries	(374,282)	(378,704)
Intangible and other assets	(56,597)	—
Equity method investments	—	(32,601)
Other	(11,437)	(8,124)
Total deferred tax liabilities	(458,580)	(436,077)
Net deferred tax liability	$(260,117)	$(234,653)

Included in "Other current assets" in the accompanying consolidated balance sheet at December 31, 2011 and 2010 is a current deferred tax asset of $41.0 million and $34.9 million, respectively and included in "Other non-current assets" in the accompanying consolidated balance sheet at December 31, 2011 and 2010 is a non-current deferred tax asset of $1.4 million and $0.9 million, respectively. In addition, included in "Accrued expenses and other current liabilities" in the accompanying consolidated balance sheet at December 31, 2011 is a current deferred tax liability of $0.4 million.

At December 31, 2011, the Company had federal and state net operating losses ("NOLs") of $35.1 million and $115.6 million, respectively. If not utilized, the federal NOLs will expire at various times between 2023 and 2031, and the state NOLs will expire at various times between 2012 and 2031. Utilization of federal NOLs will be subject to limitations under Section 382 of the Internal Revenue Code of 1986, as amended. In addition, utilization of certain state NOLs may be subject to limitations under state laws similar to Section 382 of the Internal Revenue Code of 1986. At December 31, 2011, the Company had foreign NOLs of $48.2 million available to offset future income. Of these foreign NOLs, $42.1 million can be carried forward indefinitely and $6.1 million will expire at various times between 2012 and 2031. During 2011, the Company recognized tax benefits related to NOLs of $2.7 million. Included in this amount was $1.1 million of tax benefits of acquired attributes which was recorded as a reduction in goodwill. At December 31, 2011, the Company had $3.1 million of federal capital losses and $267.4 million of state capital losses. If not utilized, the federal capital losses will expire in 2015, and the state capital losses will expire between 2013 and 2015. Utilization of capital losses will be limited to the Company's ability to generate future capital gains.

At December 31, 2011, the Company had tax credit carryforwards of $12.1 million. Of this amount, $6.2 million related to federal credits for foreign taxes, $4.9 million related to state tax credits for research activities, and $1.0 million related to various state and local tax credits. Of these credit carryforwards, $5.9 million can be carried forward indefinitely and $6.2 million will expire within ten years.

During 2011, the Company's valuation allowance increased by $4.8 million primarily due to losses from equity method investments. Of this amount, $1.8 million relates to a change in judgment about the realizability of beginning of the year deferred tax assets. At December 31, 2011, the Company had a valuation allowance of $45.1 million related to the portion of tax loss carryforwards and other items for which it is more likely than not that the tax benefit will not be realized.

A reconciliation of the beginning and ending amount of unrecognized tax benefits, excluding interest, is as follows:

(In thousands)	December 31		
	2011	**2010**	**2009**
Balance at January 1	$389,909	$394,294	$372,633
Additions based on tax positions related to the current year	1,749	3,060	2,333
Additions for tax positions of prior years	9,560	9,897	35,432
Reductions for tax positions of prior years	(26,595)	(13,164)	(14,991)
Settlements	(16,810)	(1,025)	(1,113)
Expiration of applicable statute of limitations	(6,252)	(3,153)	—
Balance at December 31	$351,561	$389,909	$394,294

At December 31, 2011 and 2010, unrecognized tax benefits, including interest, were $462.8 million and $487.6 million, respectively. The total unrecognized tax benefits as of December 31, 2011 include $12.3 million that have been netted against the related deferred tax assets. The remaining balance of $450.5 million is reflected in "non-current income taxes payable" in the accompanying consolidated balance sheet at December 31, 2011. Unrecognized tax benefits for the year ended December 31, 2011 decreased by $38.3 million due principally to the expiration of statutes of limitations, the effective settlement of audits and a net decrease in deductible temporary differences. Included in unrecognized tax benefits at December 31, 2011 is $88.5 million relating to tax positions for which the ultimate deductibility is highly certain but for which there is uncertainty about the timing of such deductibility. If unrecognized tax benefits as of December 31, 2011 are subsequently recognized, $89.5 million and $213.6 million, net of related deferred tax assets and interest, would reduce income tax expense from continuing operations and discontinued operations, respectively. If unrecognized tax benefits as of December 31, 2010 are subsequently recognized, $103.1 million and $206.9 million, net of related deferred tax assets and interest, would reduce income tax expense from continuing operations and discontinued operations, respectively. In addition, a continuing operations tax provision of $5.1 million would be required upon the subsequent recognition of unrecognized tax benefits for an increase in the Company's valuation allowance against certain deferred tax assets.

The Company is routinely under audit by federal, state, local and foreign authorities in the area of income tax. These audits include questioning the timing and the amount of income and deductions and the allocation of income and deductions among various tax jurisdictions. The Internal Revenue Service ("IRS") has substantially completed its review of the Company's tax returns for the years ended December 31, 2001 through 2006. The settlement has not yet been submitted to the Joint Committee of Taxation for approval. The IRS began its review of the Company's tax returns for the years ended December 31, 2007 through 2009 in July 2011. The statute of limitations for the years 2001 through 2008 has currently been extended to December 31, 2012. Various state and local jurisdictions are currently under examination, the most significant of which are California, New York and New York City for various tax years beginning with 2005. Income taxes payable include reserves considered sufficient to pay assessments that may result from examination of prior year tax returns. Changes to reserves from period to period and differences between amounts paid, if any, upon resolution of issues raised in audits and amounts previously provided may be material. Differences between the reserves for income tax contingencies and the amounts owed by the Company are recorded in the period they become known. The Company believes that it is reasonably possible that its unrecognized tax benefits could decrease by $60.3 million within twelve months of the current reporting date, of which approximately $13.1 million could decrease income tax provision, primarily due to settlements, expirations of statutes of limitations, and the reversal of deductible temporary differences that will primarily result in a corresponding decrease in net deferred tax assets. An estimate of other changes in unrecognized tax benefits, while potentially significant, cannot be made.

2.124

KELLOGG COMPANY (DEC)

NOTES TO CONSOLIDATED FINANCIAL STATEMENTS

Note 11

Income Taxes

The components of income before income taxes and the provision for income taxes were as follows:

(Millions)	2011	2010	2009
Income before income taxes			
United States	$1,267	$1,271	$1,207
Foreign	465	471	477
	1,732	1,742	1,684
Income taxes			
Currently payable			
Federal	285	97	331
State	26	10	39
Foreign	108	129	146
	419	236	516
Deferred			
Federal	56	239	(8)
State	13	26	(3)
Foreign	15	1	(29)
	84	266	(40)
Total income taxes	$ 503	$ 502	$ 476

The difference between the U.S. federal statutory tax rate and the Company's effective income tax rate was:

	2011	2010	2009
U.S. statutory income tax rate	35.0%	35.0%	35.0%
Foreign rates varying from 35%	(4.2)	(4.1)	(4.2)
State income taxes, net of federal benefit	1.5	1.4	1.4
Cost (benefit) of remitted and unremitted foreign earnings	(1.3)	0.9	(0.8)
Tax audit activity	(0.4)	(1.6)	(0.9)
Net change in valuation allowances	0.6	0.5	0.4
Statutory rate changes, deferred tax impact	(0.4)	—	—
U.S. deduction for qualified production activities	(1.3)	(1.1)	(1.6)
Other	(0.5)	(2.2)	(1.1)
Effective income tax rate	29.0%	28.8%	28.2%

As presented in the preceding table, the Company's 2011 consolidated effective tax rate was 29.0%, as compared to 28.8% in 2010 and 28.2% in 2009. The 2011 effective income tax rate benefited from an international legal restructuring reflected in the cost (benefit) of remitted and unremitted foreign earnings. During the third quarter of 2011, the Company recorded a benefit of $7 million from the decrease in the statutory rate in the United Kingdom.

As of December 31, 2011, the Company had recorded a deferred tax liability of $25 million related to $325 million of earnings. Accumulated foreign earnings of approximately $1.7 billion, primarily in Europe, were considered indefinitely reinvested. Accordingly, deferred income taxes have not been provided on these earnings and it is not practical to estimate the deferred tax impact of those earnings.

The 2010 effective income tax rate was impacted primarily by the remeasurement of liabilities for uncertain tax positions. Authoritative guidance related to liabilities for uncertain tax positions requires the Company to remeasure its liabilities for uncertain tax positions based on information obtained during the period, including interactions with tax authorities. Based on these interactions with tax authorities in various state and foreign jurisdictions, we reduced certain liabilities for uncertain tax positions by $42 million and increased others by $13 million in 2010. The other line item contains the benefit from an immaterial correction of an item related to prior years that was booked in the first quarter of 2010, as well as the U.S. research and development tax credit.

The 2009 effective tax rate reflected the favorable impact of various audit settlements as well as a U.S. deduction for qualified production activities as defined by the Internal Revenue Code. The deduction is based on U.S. manufacturing activities. During 2009, the Company finalized its assessment of foreign earnings and capital to be repatriated under the prior year repatriation plan resulting in a favorable impact to the cost of remitted and unremitted foreign earnings.

Changes in valuation allowances on deferred tax assets and the corresponding impacts on the effective income tax rate result from management's assessment of the Company's ability to utilize certain future tax deductions, operating losses and tax credit carryforwards prior to expiration. Valuation allowances were recorded to reduce deferred tax assets to an amount that will, more likely than not, be realized in the future. The total tax benefit of carryforwards at year-end 2011 and 2010 were $41 million and $60 million, respectively, with related valuation allowances at year-end 2011 and 2010 of $38 and $35 million. Of the total carryforwards at year-end 2011, $4 million expire in 2014; $2 million in 2015; $4 million in 2016 and the remainder expiring thereafter.

The following table provides an analysis of the Company's deferred tax assets and liabilities as of year-end 2011 and 2010. Operating loss and credit carryforwards decreased in 2011 due to the utilization of net operating losses and tax credit carryforwards. Deferred tax assets on employee benefits increased in 2011 due to losses on plan assets and discount rate reductions associated with the Company's pension and postretirement plans recorded in Other Comprehensive Income, net of tax. Additionally, the deferred tax liability for unremitted foreign earnings decreased by $32 million; $24 million of this change is attributable to the benefit recorded in 2011's consolidated effective income tax rate, while $8 million relates to remeasurement for foreign currency changes.

(Millions)	Deferred Tax Assets		Deferred Tax Liabilities	
	2011	2010	2011	2010
U.S. state income taxes	$ 8	$ 7	$ 85	$ 77
Advertising and promotion-related	22	24	—	3
Wages and payroll taxes	29	25	—	—
Inventory valuation	26	28	—	—
Employee benefits	312	187	—	65
Operating loss and credit carryforwards	41	60	—	—
Hedging transactions	3	1	—	16
Depreciation and asset disposals	—	25	365	311
Capitalized interest	—	7	2	9
Trademarks and other intangibles	—	—	477	472
Deferred compensation	39	48	—	—
Stock options	48	52	—	—
Unremitted foreign earnings	—	—	25	57
Other	53	51	—	8
	581	515	954	1,018
Less valuation allowance	(46)	(36)	—	—
Total deferred taxes	$ 535	$ 479	$954	$1,018
Net deferred tax asset (liability)	$(419)	$(539)		
Classified in balance sheet as:				
Other current assets	$ 149	$ 110		
Other current liabilities	(7)	(13)		
Other assets	76	61		
Other liabilities	(637)	(697)		
Net deferred tax asset (liability)	$(419)	$(539)		

The change in valuation allowance reducing deferred tax assets was:

(Millions)	2011	2010	2009
Balance at beginning of year	$36	$28	$22
Additions charged to income tax expense	12	11	14
Reductions credited to income tax expense	(1)	(2)	(7)
Currency translation adjustments	(1)	(1)	(1)
Balance at end of year	$46	$36	$28

Cash paid for income taxes was (in millions): 2011–$271; 2010–$409; 2009–$409. Income tax benefits realized from stock option exercises and deductibility of other equity-based awards are presented in Note 7.

Uncertain Tax Positions

The Company is subject to federal income taxes in the U.S. as well as various state, local, and foreign jurisdictions. The Company's annual provision for U.S. federal income taxes represents approximately 70% of the Company's consolidated income tax provision. The Company was chosen to participate in the Internal Revenue Service (IRS) Compliance Assurance Program (CAP) beginning with the 2008 tax year. As a result, with limited exceptions, the Company is no longer subject to U.S. federal examinations by the IRS for years prior to 2011. The Company is under examination for income and non-income tax filings in various state and foreign jurisdictions, most notably Spain for years 2005 to 2006.

As of December 31, 2011, the Company has classified $15 million of unrecognized tax benefits as a current liability. Management's estimate of reasonably possible changes in unrecognized tax benefits during the next twelve months is comprised of the current liability balance expected to be settled within one year, offset by approximately $7 million of projected additions related primarily to ongoing intercompany transfer pricing activity. Management is currently unaware of any issues under review that could result in significant additional payments, accruals, or other material deviation in this estimate.

Following is a reconciliation of the Company's total gross unrecognized tax benefits as of the years ended December 31, 2011, January 1, 2011 and January 2, 2010. For the 2011 year, approximately $49 million represents the amount that, if recognized, would affect the Company's effective income tax rate in future periods.

(Millions)	2011	2010	2009
Balance at beginning of year	$104	$130	$132
Tax positions related to current year:			
Additions	7	12	17
Tax positions related to prior years:			
Additions	8	13	4
Reductions	(19)	(42)	(9)
Settlements	(27)	(6)	(8)
Lapses in statutes of limitation	(7)	(3)	(6)
Balance at end of year	$ 66	$104	$130

For the year ended December 31, 2011, the Company recognized a decrease of $3 million of tax-related interest and penalties and had $16 million accrued at year end. For the year ended January 1, 2011, the Company recognized an increase of $2 million of tax-related interest and penalties

and had approximately $26 million accrued at January 1, 2011. For the year ended January 2, 2010, the Company recognized a reduction of $1 million of tax-related interest and penalties and had approximately $25 million accrued at January 2, 2010.

CURRENT AMOUNT OF LONG-TERM DEBT

PRESENTATION

2.125 FASB ASC 470 addresses classification determination for specific debt obligations, such as the following:
- Short-term obligations expected to be refinanced on a long-term basis
- 'Due-on-demand loan arrangements
- Callable debt
- Sales of future revenue
- Increasing rate debt
- Debt that includes covenants
- Revolving credit agreements subject to lock-box arrangements and subjective acceleration clauses

DISCLOSURE

2.126 FASB ASC 470 includes disclosures required for long-term debt (see the "Long-Term Debt" section). FASB ASC 825 requires disclosure of both the fair value and bases for estimating the fair value of the current amount of long-term debt, unless it is not practicable to estimate that value.

PRESENTATION AND DISCLOSURE EXCERPTS

Current Amount of Long-Term Debt

2.127

ARMSTRONG WORLD INDUSTRIES, INC. (DEC)

CONSOLIDATED BALANCE SHEETS (in part)

(Amounts in millions, except share data)

	December 31, 2011	December 31, 2010
Liabilities and Shareholders' Equity *(in part)*		
Current liabilities:		
Short-term debt	$ 2.0	$ 25.0
Current installments of long-term debt	18.1	10.3
Accounts payable and accrued expenses	359.6	340.3
Income tax payable	4.0	4.9
Deferred income taxes	2.4	2.4
Total current liabilities	386.1	382.9

*NOTES TO CONSOLIDATED FINANCIAL
STATEMENTS*

(Dollar amounts in millions)

Note 17. Debt (in part)

	December 31, 2011	Average Year-End Interest Rate	December 31, 2010	Average Year-End Interest Rate
Term loan A due 2015	$250.0	3.30%	$250.0	3.28%
Term loan B due 2018	545.9	4.25%	550.0	5.00%
Revolver due 2015	—	—	25.0	5.25%
Other	2.1	1.98%	4.9	3.85%
Tax exempt bonds due 2025–2041	45.0	0.99%	45.0	2.00%
Subtotal	843.0	3.79%	874.9	4.36%
Less current portion and short-term debt	20.1	3.42%	35.3	5.02%
Total long-term debt, less current portion	$822.9	3.80%	$839.6	4.33%

On November 23, 2010, we refinanced our $1.1 billion credit facility and executed a $1.05 billion senior credit facility arranged by Merrill Lynch, Pierce, Fenner & Smith, Inc., J.P. Morgan Securities, Inc., and Barclays Capital. This facility consists of a $250 million revolving credit facility (with a $150 million sublimit for letters of credit), a $250 million Term Loan A and a $550 million Term Loan B. This $1.05 billion senior credit facility is secured by U.S. personal property, the capital stock of material U.S. subsidiaries, and a pledge of 65% of the stock of our material first tier foreign subsidiaries. In 2010, in connection with the refinancing, we repaid amounts owed under the previous credit facility and wrote off $3.8 million of unamortized debt financing costs related to our previous credit facility to interest expense.

On March 10, 2011, we amended our $1.05 billion senior credit facility. The amended terms of Term Loan B resulted in a lower LIBOR floor (1.0% vs. 1.5%) and interest rate spread (3.0% vs. 3.5%). We also extended its maturity from May 2017 to March 2018. All other terms, conditions and covenants were unchanged from the November 23, 2010 agreement. In connection with the amendment to Term Loan B, we paid a $5.5 million prepayment premium (representing one percent of the principal amount of Term Loan B). The premium was capitalized and is being amortized into interest expense over the life of the loan. Additionally, we paid approximately $1.6 million of fees to third parties (banks, attorneys, etc.), which is reflected in interest expense.

The senior credit facility includes two financial covenants which require the ratio of consolidated earnings before interest, taxes, depreciation and amortization ("EBITDA") to consolidated cash interest expense minus cash consolidated interest income ("consolidated interest coverage ratio") to be greater than or equal to 3.0 to 1.0 and require the ratio of consolidated funded indebtedness minus AWI and domestic subsidiary unrestricted cash and cash equivalents up to

$100 million to consolidated EBITDA ("consolidated leverage ratio") to be less than or equal to 4.5 to 1.0 through June 30, 2012, 4.0 to 1.0 after June 30, 2012 through September 30, 2013 and 3.75 to 1.0 after September 30, 2013. Our debt agreements include other restrictions, including restrictions pertaining to the acquisition of additional debt, the redemption, repurchase or retirement of our capital stock, payment of dividends, and certain financial transactions as it relates to specified assets. As of December 31, 2011 we were in compliance with these covenants. We believe that default under these covenants is unlikely. Fully borrowing under our revolving credit facility would not violate these covenants.

The Revolving Credit and Term Loan A portions are currently priced at a spread of 3.00% over LIBOR and the Term Loan B portion is priced at 3.00% over LIBOR with a 1.00% LIBOR floor for its entire term. The Term Loan A and Term Loan B were both fully drawn and are currently priced on a variable interest rate basis. The unpaid balances of Term Loan A ($250 million), Revolving Credit ($0 million) and Term Loan B ($545.9 million) of the credit facility may be prepaid without penalty at the maturity of their respective interest reset periods. Any amounts prepaid on the Term Loan A or Term Loan B may not be re-borrowed.

Mandatory prepayments are required under the senior credit facility pursuant to an annual leverage test starting with the year ending December 31, 2011 under which, if our consolidated leverage ratio is greater than 2.0 to1.0 but less than 2.5 to 1.0, we would be required to make a prepayment of 25% of fiscal year Consolidated Excess Cash Flow as defined by the credit agreement. If our Consolidated Leverage Ratio is greater than 2.5 to 1.0, the prepayment amount would be 50% of fiscal year Consolidated Excess Cash Flow. As of December 31, 2011, we were not required to make a mandatory prepayment on our loan obligations.

2.128

EASTMAN KODAK COMPANY (DEC)

CONSOLIDATED STATEMENT OF FINANCIAL POSITION (in part)

	As of December 31	
(In millions, except share and per share data)	**2011**	**2010**
Liabilities and Equity *(in part)*		
Current liabilities		
Accounts payable, trade	$ 706	$ 959
Short-term borrowings and current portion of long-term debt	152	50
Accrued income taxes	40	343
Other current liabilities	1,252	1,468
Total current liabilities	2,150	2,820
Long-term debt, net of current portion	1,363	1,195
Pension and other postretirement liabilities	3,053	2,661
Other long-term liabilities	462	625
Total liabilities	7,028	7,301

NOTES TO FINANCIAL STATEMENTS

Note 9: Short-Term Borrowings and Long-Term Debt (in part)

Short-Term Borrowings and Current Portion of Long-Term Debt

The Company's current portion of long-term debt was $152

million and $50 million as of December 31, 2011 and 2010, respectively. There was $100 million outstanding under short-term bank borrowings as of December 31, 2011.

Long-Term Debt, Including Lines of Credit (in part)

Long-term debt and related maturities and interest rates were as follows:

			As of December 31			
			2011		**2010**	
(In millions) Country	Type	Maturity	Weighted-Average Effective Interest Rate	Amount Outstanding	Weighted-Average Effective Interest Rate	Amount Outstanding
U.S.	Term note	2011–2013	6.16%	$ 19	6.16%	$ 27
Germany	Term note	2011–2013	6.16%	75	6.16%	109
Brazil	Term note	2012–2013	19.80%	5	—	—
U.S.	Term note	2013	7.25%	250	7.25%	300
U.S.	Revolver	2013	4.75%	100	—	—
U.S.	Convertible	2017	12.75%	315	12.75%	305
U.S.	Secured term note	2018	10.11%	491	10.11%	491
U.S.	Term note	2018	9.95%	3	9.95%	3
U.S.	Secured term note	2019	10.87%	247	—	—
U.S.	Term note	2021	9.20%	10	9.20%	10
				1,515		1,245
Current portion of long-term debt				(152)		(50)
Long-term debt, net of current portion				$1,363		$1,195

Annual maturities (in millions) of long-term debt outstanding at December 31, 2011 were as follows:

	Carrying Value	Principal Amount
2012	$ 52	$ 52
2013	397	402
2014	—	—
2015	—	—
2016	—	—
2017 and thereafter	1,066	1,164
Total	$1,515	$1,618

OTHER CURRENT LIABILITIES

PRESENTATION

2.129 Rule 5-02 of Regulation S-X requires that any items in excess of 5 percent of total current liabilities be stated separately on the balance sheet or disclosed in the notes. In addition, registrants should state separately amounts payable to the following:
- Banks for borrowings
- Factors or other financial institutions for borrowings
- Holders of commercial paper
- Trade creditors
- Related parties
- Underwriters, promoters, and employees (other than related parties)
- Others

Amounts applicable to the first three categories may be stated separately in the balance sheet or in a note thereto.

2.130

TABLE 2-10: OTHER CURRENT LIABILITIES*

Table 2-10 summarizes other identified current liabilities. The most common types of other current liabilities are liabilities related to derivatives, discontinued operations, deferred revenue, accrued interest, and deferred taxes.

	Number of Entities		
	2011	2010	2009
Derivatives	193	129	253
Costs related to discontinued operations/restructuring	123	116	158
Deferred revenue	161	150	140
Interest	106	96	123
Deferred taxes	150	138	118
Taxes other than federal income taxes	153	138	116
Guarantees or warranties	98	83	99
Insurance	90	87	86
Advertising	49	59	64
Dividends	57	54	59
Environmental costs	55	48	59
Rebates/discounts/incentives	80	63	55
Customer advances, deposits	71	54	54
Litigation	47	30	43
Tax uncertainties	9	38	33
Billings on uncompleted contracts	20	18	26
Due to affiliated companies	10	4	23
Royalties	17	15	19
Asset retirement obligations	16	15	15
Unrecognized tax (benefit) liability	11	37	N/C^
Outstanding checks	29	18	N/C^
Merger/acquisition	5	8	N/C^
Professional fees	16	11	N/C^
Accrued rent/lease payments	20	13	N/C^
Other—described	305	193	135

* Appearing in the balance sheet or notes to financial statements, or both.
^ N/C = Not compiled. Line item was not included in the table for the year shown.

PRESENTATION AND DISCLOSURE EXCERPTS

Dividends

2.131

INTERNATIONAL FLAVORS & FRAGRANCES INC. (DEC)

CONSOLIDATED BALANCE SHEET (in part)

	December 31	
(Dollars in thousands)	2011	2010
Liabilities and Shareholders' Equity *(in part)*		
Current liabilities:		
Bank borrowings, overdrafts and current portion of long-term debt	$116,688	$133,899
Accounts payable	208,759	200,153
Dividends payable	25,086	21,657
Restructuring and other charges	10,198	3,977
Other current liabilities	203,835	301,265
Total current liabilities	564,566	660,951

NOTES TO CONSOLIDATED FINANCIAL STATEMENTS

Note 10. Shareholders' Equity

On March 9, 2000, we adopted a shareholder protection rights agreement (the "Rights Agreement") and declared a dividend of one right on each share of common stock outstanding on March 24, 2000 or issued thereafter. The Rights Agreement expired in March 2010.

Cash dividends declared per share were $1.16, $1.04 and $1.00 in 2011, 2010 and 2009, respectively. The Consolidated Balance Sheet reflects $25.1 million of dividends payable at December 31, 2011. This amount relates to a cash dividend of $0.31 per share declared in December 2011 and paid in January 2012. Dividends declared, but not paid at December 31, 2010 and 2009 were $21.7 million ($0.27 per share) and $19.8 million ($0.25 per share), respectively.

Advance Payments from Customers

2.132

VARIAN MEDICAL SYSTEMS, INC. (SEP)

CONSOLIDATED BALANCE SHEETS (in part)

(In thousands, except par values)	September 30, 2011	October 1, 2010
Liabilities and Stockholders' Equity *(in part)*		
Current liabilities:		
Accounts payable	$ 154,946	$ 119,018
Accrued expenses	290,009	287,851
Product warranty	50,128	53,233
Deferred revenues	140,173	141,916
Advance payments from customers	299,380	275,998
Short-term borrowings	181,400	20,000
Current maturities of long-term debt	9,876	5,525
Total current liabilities	1,125,912	903,541
Long-term debt	6,250	17,869
Other long-term liabilities	122,708	127,175
Total liabilities	1,254,870	1,048,585

NOTES TO CONSOLIDATED FINANCIAL STATEMENTS

1. Summary of Significant Accounting Policies (in part)

Contracts for Customized Equipment

Revenues related to certain highly customized image detection systems, proton therapy systems and proton therapy system commissioning contracts are recognized in accordance with contract accounting. For contracts in which the Company can estimate contract costs with reasonable dependability, the Company recognizes contract revenues under the percentage-of-completion method. Revenues recognized under the percentage-of-completion method are based on contract costs incurred to date compared with total estimated contract costs. Changes in estimates of total contract revenue, total contract cost or the extent of progress towards completion are recognized in the period in which the changes in estimates are identified. Estimated losses on contracts are recognized in the period in which the loss is identified. In circumstances in which the final outcome of a contract cannot be precisely estimated but a loss on the contract is not expected, the Company recognizes revenues under the percentage-of-completion method based on a zero profit margin until more precise estimates can be made. If and when the Company can make more precise estimates, revenues and costs of sales are adjusted in the same period.

Costs incurred and revenues recognized under the percentage-of-completion method in excess of customer billings are included in "Accounts receivable" in the Consolidated Balance Sheets. Customer billings in excess of costs incurred and revenue recognized under the percentage-of-completion method are included in "Advance payments from customers" in the Consolidated Balance Sheets. The Company did not have material balances of i) costs incurred and revenues recognized in excess of customer billings and ii) customer billings in excess of costs incurred and revenue recognized as of September 30, 2011 and October 1, 2010.

Advance Payments from Customers

Except for government tenders, group purchases and orders with letters of credit, the Company typically requires its Oncology Systems, SIP and VPT customers to provide a down payment prior to transfer of risk of loss of ordered products or an advance payment prior to performance under service contracts. These payments are recorded as "Advance payments from customers" in the Consolidated Balance Sheets.

Deferred Income Taxes

2.133

CA, INC. (MAR)

CONSOLIDATED BALANCE SHEETS (in part)

	March 31	
(In millions, except share amounts)	2011	2010
Assets		
Current assets		
Cash and cash equivalents	$ 3,049	$ 2,583
Marketable securities—current	75	—
Trade and installment accounts receivable, net	849	931
Deferred income taxes—current	246	360
Other current assets	152	116
Total current assets	4,371	3,990
Marketable securities—noncurrent	104	—
Installment accounts receivable, due after one year, net	—	46
Property and equipment, net of accumulated depreciation of $632 and $538, respectively	437	452
Goodwill	5,688	5,605
Capitalized software and other intangible assets, net	1,284	1,215
Deferred income taxes—noncurrent	284	348
Other noncurrent assets, net	246	232
Total assets	$12,414	$11,888
Liabilities and Stockholders' Equity (in part)		
Current liabilities		
Current portion of long-term debt and loans payable	$ 269	$ 15
Accounts payable	100	81
Accrued salaries, wages, and commissions	293	348
Accrued expenses and other current liabilities	395	469
Deferred revenue (billed or collected)—current	2,600	2,504
Taxes payable, other than income taxes payable—current	75	82
Federal, state, and foreign income taxes payable—current	124	31
Deferred income taxes—current	68	51
Total current liabilities	3,924	3,581
Long-term debt, net of current portion	1,282	1,530
Federal, state, and foreign income taxes payable—noncurrent	414	450
Deferred income taxes—noncurrent	64	137
Deferred revenue (billed or collected)—noncurrent	969	1,052
Other noncurrent liabilities	141	151
Total liabilities	6,794	6,901

NOTES TO THE CONSOLIDATED FINANCIAL STATEMENTS

Note 1—Significant Accounting Policies (in part)

(p) Income taxes: Income taxes are accounted for under the asset and liability method. Deferred tax assets and liabilities are recognized for the future tax consequences attributable to differences between the financial statement carrying amounts of existing assets and liabilities and their respective tax bases and operating loss and tax credit carryforwards. Deferred tax assets and liabilities are measured using enacted tax rates expected to apply to taxable income in the years in which those temporary differences are expected to be recovered or settled. The effect on deferred tax assets and liabilities from a change in tax rates is recognized in income in the period that includes the enactment date.

The Company recognizes the effect of income tax positions only if those positions are more likely than not to be sustained. Changes in recognition or measurement are reflected in the period in which the change in judgment occurs. The Company records interest and penalties related to uncertain tax positions in income tax expense. See Note 16, "Income Taxes," for additional information.

Note 16—Income Taxes (in part)

Deferred income taxes reflect the effect of temporary differences between the carrying amounts of assets and liabilities recognized for financial reporting purposes and the amounts recognized for tax purposes. The tax effects of the temporary differences from continuing operations are as follows:

	March 31	
(In millions)	2011	2010
Deferred tax assets:		
Modified accrual basis accounting for revenue	$445	$442
Share-based compensation	50	76
Accrued expenses	53	76
Net operating losses	154	157
Intangible assets amortizable for tax purposes	16	17
Deductible state tax and interest benefits	43	37
Other	51	83
Total deferred tax assets	812	888
Valuation allowances	(63)	(73)
Total deferred tax assets, net of valuation allowances	749	815
Deferred tax liabilities:		
Purchased software	73	41
Depreciation	17	1
Other intangible assets	70	81
Capitalized development costs	191	172
Total deferred tax liabilities	351	295
Net deferred tax asset	$398	$520

In management's judgment, it is more likely than not that the total deferred tax assets, net of valuation allowance, of approximately $749 million will be realized as reductions to future taxable income or by utilizing available tax planning strategies. Worldwide net operating loss carryforwards (NOLs) totaled approximately $586 million and $574 million at March 31, 2011 and 2010, respectively. The NOLs will expire as follows: $434 million between 2012 and 2032 and $152 million may be carried forward indefinitely.

A valuation allowance has been provided for deferred tax assets related to NOLs that are not expected to be realized. The valuation allowance decreased approximately $10 million and $3 million at March 31, 2011 and 2010, respectively. The decrease in the valuation allowance at March 31, 2011 and March 31, 2010 primarily relates to the likelihood of utilization of NOLs.

No provision has been made for U.S. federal income taxes on approximately $1,198 million and $1,067 million at March 31, 2011 and 2010, respectively, of unremitted earnings of the Company's foreign subsidiaries since the Company plans to permanently reinvest all such earnings outside the U.S. It is not practicable to determine the amount of tax associated with such unremitted earnings.

Warranties

2.134

WINNEBAGO INDUSTRIES, INC. (AUG)

CONSOLIDATED BALANCE SHEETS (in part)

(In thousands, except per share data)	August 27, 2011	August 28, 2010
Liabilities and Stockholders' Equity (in part)		
Current liabilities:		
Accounts payable	$21,610	$19,725
Income taxes payable	104	99
Accrued expenses:		
Accrued compensation	10,841	10,529
Product warranties	7,335	7,634
Self-insurance	3,203	4,409
Accrued loss on repurchases	1,174	1,362
Promotional	2,177	1,817
Other	4,874	4,797
Total current liabilities	51,318	50,372

NOTES TO CONSOLIDATED FINANCIAL STATEMENTS

Note 9: Warranty

We provide our motor home customers a comprehensive 12-month/15,000-mile warranty on our Class A, B and C motor homes, and a 3-year/36,000-mile structural warranty on Class A and C sidewalls and floors. We provide a comprehensive 12-month warranty on all towable products. We have also incurred costs for certain warranty-type expenses which occurred after the normal warranty period. We have voluntarily agreed to pay such costs to help protect the reputation of our products and the goodwill of our customers. Estimated costs related to product warranty are accrued at the time of sale and are based upon past warranty claims and unit sales history and adjusted as required to reflect actual costs incurred, as information becomes available. A significant increase in dealership labor rates, the cost of parts or the frequency of claims could have a material adverse impact on our operating results for the period or periods in which

such claims or additional costs materialize. We also incur costs as a result of additional service actions not covered by our warranties, including product recalls and customer satisfaction actions. Estimated costs are accrued at the time the service action is implemented and are based upon past claim rate experiences and the estimated cost of the repairs.

Changes in our product warranty liability during Fiscal 2011, Fiscal 2010 and Fiscal 2009 are as follows:

(In thousands)	August 27, 2011	August 28, 2010	August 29, 2009
Balance at beginning of year	$ 7,634	$ 6,408	$ 9,859
Provision	5,566	6,209	3,843
Claims paid	(5,865)	(4,983)	(7,294)
Balance at end of year	$ 7,335	$ 7,634	$ 6,408

Billings in Excess of Costs and Estimated Earnings

2.135

TUTOR PERINI CORPORATION (DEC)

CONSOLIDATED BALANCE SHEETS (in part)

December 31, 2011 and 2010

(In thousands, except share data)

Liabilities and Stockholders' Equity (in part)

	2011	2010
Current liabilities:		
Current maturities of long-term debt	$ 59,959	$ 21,334
Accounts payable, including retainage of $151,907 and $280,867	785,725	653,542
Billings in excess of costs and estimated earnings	384,282	199,750
Accrued expenses and other current liabilities	163,268	93,488
Total current liabilities	1,393,234	968,114

NOTES TO CONSOLIDATED FINANCIAL STATEMENTS

For the Years Ended December 31, 2011, 2010 and 2009

[1] Summary of Significant Accounting Policies (in part)

(d) Method of Accounting for Contracts (in part)

The Company includes in current assets and current liabilities amounts related to construction contracts realizable and payable over a period in excess of one year. Billings in excess of costs and estimated earnings represents the excess of contract billings to date over the amount of contract costs and profits (or contract revenue) recognized to date on the percentage of completion accounting method on certain contracts. Costs and estimated earnings in excess of billings represents the excess of contract costs and profits (or contract revenue) recognized to date on the percentage of completion accounting method over the amount of contract billings to date on the remaining contracts. Costs and estimated earnings in excess of billings results when (1) the appropriate contract revenue amount has been recognized in accordance with the percentage of completion accounting method, but a portion of the revenue recorded cannot be billed currently due to the billing terms defined in the contract and/or (2) costs, recorded at estimated realizable value, related to unapproved change orders or claims are incurred.

Restructuring

2.136

HEWLETT-PACKARD COMPANY (OCT)

CONSOLIDATED BALANCE SHEETS (in part)

	October 31	
(In millions, except par value)	**2011**	**2010**
Liabilities and Stockholders' Equity *(in part)*		
Current liabilities:		
Notes payable and short-term borrowings	$ 8,083	$ 7,046
Accounts payable	14,750	14,365
Employee compensation and benefits	3,999	4,256
Taxes on earnings	1,048	802
Deferred revenue	7,449	6,727
Accrued restructuring	654	911
Other accrued liabilities	14,459	15,296
Total current liabilities	50,442	49,403

NOTES TO CONSOLIDATED FINANCIAL STATEMENTS

Note 8: Restructuring Charges

HP records restructuring charges associated with management-approved restructuring plans to either reorganize one or more of HP's business segments, or to remove duplicative headcount and infrastructure associated with one or more business acquisitions. Restructuring charges can include severance costs to eliminate a specified number of employee positions, infrastructure charges to vacate facilities and consolidate operations, and contract cancellation cost. Restructuring charges are recorded based upon planned employee termination dates and site closure and consolidation plans. The timing of associated cash payments is dependent upon the type of restructuring charge and can extend over a multi-year period. HP records the short-term portion of the restructuring liability in Accrued restructuring and the long-term portion in Other liabilities in the Consolidated Balance Sheets.

Fiscal 2010 Acquisitions

In connection with the acquisitions of Palm and 3Com in fiscal 2010, HP's management approved and initiated plans to restructure the operations of the acquired companies, including severance for employees, contract cancellation costs, costs to vacate duplicative facilities and other items. The total expected combined cost of the plans is $121 million, which includes $33 million of additional restructuring costs recorded in the fourth quarter of fiscal 2011 in connection with HP's decision to wind down the webOS device business. As of October 31, 2011, HP had recorded the majority of the costs of the plans based upon the anticipated timing of planned terminations and facility closure costs. With respect to the Palm plan, no further restructuring charges are anticipated, and the majority of the remaining costs are expected to be paid out through fiscal 2012. The remaining costs pertaining to the 3Com plan are expected to be paid out through fiscal 2016 as fixed lease payments are made.

Fiscal 2010 ES Restructuring Plan

On June 1, 2010, HP's management announced a plan to restructure its enterprise services business, which includes its Infrastructure Technology Outsourcing, Business Process Outsourcing and Application Services business units. The multi-year restructuring program includes plans to consolidate commercial data centers, tools and applications. The total expected cost of the plan that will be recorded as restructuring charges is approximately $1.0 billion, and includes severance costs to eliminate approximately 9,000 positions and infrastructure charges. As of October 31, 2011, HP had recorded the majority of the severance costs. HP expects to record the majority of the infrastructure charges through fiscal 2012. The timing of the charges is based upon planned termination dates and site closure and consolidation plans. The majority of the associated cash payments are expected to be paid out through the fourth quarter of fiscal 2012. As of October 31, 2011, approximately 5,700 positions have been eliminated with the remaining anticipated over the next 12 months.

Fiscal 2009 Restructuring Plan

In May 2009, HP's management approved and initiated a restructuring plan to structurally change and improve the effectiveness of the Imaging and Printing Group ("IPG"), the Personal Systems Group ("PSG"), and Enterprise Servers, Storage and Networking ("ESSN") businesses. The total expected cost of the plan was $294 million in severance-related costs associated with the planned elimination of approximately 4,400 positions. As of October 31, 2011, all planned eliminations had occurred and the majority of the restructuring costs have been paid out.

Fiscal 2008 HP/EDS Restructuring Plan

In connection with the acquisition of EDS on August 26, 2008, HP's management approved and initiated a restructuring plan to combine and align HP's services businesses, eliminate duplicative overhead functions and consolidate and vacate duplicative facilities. The restructuring plan is expected to be implemented over four years from the acquisition date at a total expected cost of $3.4 billion. Approximately $1.5 billion of the expected costs were associated with pre-acquisition EDS and were reflected in the fair value of purchase consideration of EDS. These costs are subject to change based on the actual costs incurred. The remaining costs are primarily associated with HP and will be recorded as a restructuring charge.

The restructuring plan includes severance costs related to eliminating approximately 25,000 positions. As of October 31, 2011, all planned eliminations had occurred and the vast majority of the associated severance costs had been paid out. The infrastructure charges in the restructuring plan include facility closure and consolidation costs and the costs associated with early termination of certain contractual obligations. HP has recorded the majority of these costs based upon the execution of site closure and consolidation plans. The associated cash payments are expected to be paid out through fiscal 2016.

Summary of Restructuring Plans

The adjustments to the accrued restructuring expenses related to all of HP's restructuring plans described above for the twelve months ended October 31, 2011 were as follows:

| | | | | | | As of October 31, 2011 | |
(In millions)	Balance, October 31, 2010	Fiscal Year 2011 Charges	Cash Payments	Non-Cash Settlements and Other Adjustments	Balance, October 31, 2011	Total Costs and Adjustments to Date	Total Expected Costs and Adjustments
Fiscal 2010 acquisitions	$ 44	$ 51	$ (36)	$ —	$ 59	$ 114	$ 121
Fiscal 2010 ES Plan:							
Severance	$ 620	$ 93	$ (229)	$ 9	$493	$ 723	$ 724
Infrastructure	4	173	(170)	(4)	3	193	268
Total ES Plan	$ 624	$266	$ (399)	$ 5	$496	$ 916	$ 992
Fiscal 2009 Plan	$ 57	$ 2	$ (54)	$ (5)	$ —	$ 294	$ 294
Fiscal 2008 HP/EDS Plan:							
Severance	$ 75	$ 45	$ (110)	$(10)	$ —	$2,190	$2,190
Infrastructure	408	281	(404)	(27)	258	974	1,167
Total HP/EDS Plan	$ 483	$326	$ (514)	$(37)	$258	$3,164	$3,357
Total restructuring plans	$1,208	$645	$(1,003)	$(37)	$813	$4,488	$4,764

At October 31, 2011 and October 31, 2010, HP included the long-term portion of the restructuring liability of $159 million and $297 million, respectively, in Other liabilities, and the short-term portion of $654 million and $911 million, respectively, in Accrued restructuring in the accompanying Consolidated Balance Sheets.

Self-Insurance Reserves

2.137

THE KROGER CO. (JAN)

CONSOLIDATED BALANCE SHEETS (in part)

(In millions, except par values)	January 29, 2011	January 30, 2010
Liabilities *(in part)*		
Current liabilities		
Current portion of long-term debt including obligations under capital leases and financing obligations	$ 588	$ 579
Trade accounts payable	4,227	3,890
Accrued salaries and wages	888	786
Deferred income taxes	220	354
Other current liabilities	2,147	2,118
Total current liabilities	8,070	7,727

NOTES TO CONSOLIDATED FINANCIAL STATEMENTS

All dollar amounts are in millions except share and per share amounts.

Certain prior-year amounts have been reclassified to conform to current year presentation.

1. Accounting Policies (in part)

Self-Insurance Costs

The Company is primarily self-insured for costs related to workers' compensation and general liability claims. Liabilities are actuarially determined and are recognized based on claims filed and an estimate of claims incurred but not reported. The liabilities for workers' compensation claims are accounted for on a present value basis. The Company has purchased stop-loss coverage to limit its exposure to any significant exposure on a per claim basis. The Company is insured for covered costs in excess of these per claim limits.

The following table summarizes the changes in the Company's self-insurance liability through January 29, 2011.

	2010	2009	2008
Beginning balance	$ 485	$ 468	$ 470
Expense	210	202	189
Claim payments	(181)	(185)	(191)
Ending balance	514	485	468
Less current portion	(181)	(182)	(192)
Long-term portion	$ 333	$ 303	$ 276

The current portion of the self-insured liability is included in "Other current liabilities," and the long-term portion is included in "Other long-term liabilities" in the Consolidated Balance Sheets.

The Company is also similarly self-insured for property-related losses. The Company has purchased stop-loss coverage to limit its exposure to losses in excess of $25 on a per claim basis, except in the case of an earthquake, for which stop-loss coverage is in excess of $50 per claim, up to $200 per claim in California and $300 outside of California.

Deferred Net Revenue

2.138

ELECTRONIC ARTS INC. (MAR)

CONSOLIDATED BALANCE SHEETS (in part)

(In millions, except par value data)	March 31, 2011	March 31, 2010
Liabilities and Stockholders' Equity (in part)		
Current liabilities:		
Accounts payable	$ 228	$ 91
Accrued and other current liabilities	768	717
Deferred net revenue (packaged goods and digital content)	1,005	766
Total current liabilities	2,001	1,574

NOTES TO CONSOLIDATED FINANCIAL STATEMENTS

(9) Balance Sheet Details (in part)

Accrued and Other Current Liabilities

Accrued and other current liabilities as of March 31, 2011 and 2010 consisted of (in millions):

	As of March 31	
	2011	2010
Other accrued expenses	$359	$293
Accrued compensation and benefits	232	177
Accrued royalties	96	144
Deferred net revenue (other)	81	103
Accrued and other current liabilities	$768	$717

Deferred net revenue (other) includes the deferral of subscription revenue, deferrals related to our Switzerland distribution business, advertising revenue, licensing arrangements and other revenue for which revenue recognition criteria has not been met.

Deferred Net Revenue (Packaged Goods and Digital Content)

Deferred net revenue (packaged goods and digital content) was $1,005 million and $766 million as of March 31, 2011 and 2010, respectively. Deferred net revenue (packaged goods

and digital content) includes the unrecognized revenue from (1) bundled sales of certain online-enabled packaged goods and digital content for which either we do not have vendor-specific objective evidence of fair value ("VSOE") for the on-line service that we provide in connection with the sale of the software or we have an obligation to provide future incremental unspecified digital content, (2) certain packaged goods sales of massively-multiplayer online role-playing games, and (3) sales of certain incremental content associated with our core subscription services that can only be played online, which are types of "micro-transactions." We recognize revenue from sales of online-enabled packaged goods and digital content for which (1) we do not have VSOE for the online service that we provided in connection with the sale and (2) we have an obligation to deliver incremental unspecified digital content in the future without an additional fee on a straight-line basis generally over an estimated six-month period beginning in the month after shipment. However, we expense the cost of goods sold related to these transactions during the period in which the product is delivered (rather than on a deferred basis).

Environment

2.139

OWENS-ILLINOIS, INC. (DEC)

CONSOLIDATED BALANCE SHEETS (in part)

Dollars in millions, except per share amounts

December 31	2011	2010
Liabilities and Share Owners' Equity		
Current liabilities:		
Short-term loans	$ 330	$ 257
Accounts payable	1,038	878
Salaries and wages	149	160
U.S. and foreign income taxes	38	32
Current portion of asbestos-related liabilities	165	170
Other accrued liabilities	449	485
Long-term debt due within one year	76	97
Total current liabilities	2,245	2,079

NOTES TO CONSOLIDATED FINANCIAL STATEMENTS

Tabular data dollars in millions, except per share amounts

17. Contingencies

The Company is a defendant in numerous lawsuits alleging bodily injury and death as a result of exposure to asbestos dust. From 1948 to 1958, one of the Company's former business units commercially produced and sold approximately $40 million of a high-temperature, calcium-silicate based pipe and block insulation material containing asbestos. The Company exited the pipe and block insulation business in April 1958. The typical asbestos personal injury lawsuit alleges various theories of liability, including negligence, gross negligence and strict liability and seeks compensatory and in some cases, punitive damages in various amounts (herein referred to as "asbestos claims").

The following table shows the approximate number of plaintiffs and claimants who had asbestos claims pending against the Company at the beginning of each listed year, the number of claims disposed of during that year, the year's filings and the claims pending at the end of each listed year (eliminating duplicate filings):

	2011	2010	2009
Pending at beginning of year	5,900	6,900	11,500
Disposed	4,500	4,200	10,700
Filed	3,200	3,200	6,100
Pending at end of year	4,600	5,900	6,900

Based on an analysis of the lawsuits pending as of December 31, 2011, approximately 71% of plaintiffs either do not specify the monetary damages sought, or in the case of court filings, claim an amount sufficient to invoke the jurisdictional minimum of the trial court. Approximately 27% of plaintiffs specifically plead damages of $15 million or less, and 2% of plaintiffs specifically plead damages greater than $15 million but less than $100 million. Fewer than 1% of plaintiffs specifically plead damages $100 million or greater but less than $122 million.

As indicated by the foregoing summary, current pleading practice permits considerable variation in the assertion of monetary damages. The Company's experience resolving hundreds of thousands of asbestos claims and lawsuits over an extended period demonstrates that the monetary relief that may be alleged in a complaint bears little relevance to a claim's merits or disposition value. Rather, the amount potentially recoverable is determined by such factors as the severity of the plaintiff's asbestos disease, the product identification evidence against the Company and other defendants, the defenses available to the Company and other defendants, the specific jurisdiction in which the claim is made, and the plaintiff's medical history and exposure to other disease-causing agents.

In addition to the pending claims set forth above, the Company has claims-handling agreements in place with many plaintiffs' counsel throughout the country. These agreements require evaluation and negotiation regarding whether particular claimants qualify under the criteria established by such agreements. The criteria for such claims include verification of a compensable illness and a reasonable probability of exposure to a product manufactured by the Company's former business unit during its manufacturing period ending in 1958. Some plaintiffs' counsel have historically withheld claims under these agreements for later presentation while focusing their attention on active litigation in the tort system. The Company believes that as of December 31, 2011 there are approximately 400 claims against other defendants which are likely to be asserted sometime in the future against the Company. These claims are not included in the pending "lawsuits and claims" totals set forth above.

The Company is also a defendant in other asbestos-related lawsuits or claims involving maritime workers, medical monitoring claimants, co-defendants and property damage claimants. Based upon its past experience, the Company believes that these categories of lawsuits and claims will not involve any material liability and they are not included in the above description of pending matters or in the following description of disposed matters.

Since receiving its first asbestos claim, the Company as of December 31, 2011, has disposed of the asbestos claims of approximately 387,000 plaintiffs and claimants at an average indemnity payment per claim of approximately $8,100. Certain of these dispositions have included deferred amounts payable over a number of years. Deferred amounts payable totaled approximately $18 million at December 31, 2011 ($26 million at December 31, 2010) and are included in the foregoing average indemnity payment per claim. The Company's asbestos indemnity payments have varied on a per claim basis, and are expected to continue to vary considerably over time. As discussed above, a part of the Company's objective is to achieve, where possible, resolution of asbestos claims pursuant to claims-handling agreements. Failure of claimants to meet certain medical and product exposure criteria in the Company's administrative claims handling agreements has generally reduced the number of marginal or suspect claims that would otherwise have been received. In addition, certain courts and legislatures have reduced or eliminated the number of marginal or suspect claims that the Company otherwise would have received. These developments generally have had the effect of increasing the Company's per-claim average indemnity payment over time.

The Company believes that its ultimate asbestos-related liability (i.e., its indemnity payments or other claim disposition costs plus related legal fees) cannot reasonably be estimated. Beginning with the initial liability of $975 million established in 1993, the Company has accrued a total of approximately $4.0 billion through 2011, before insurance recoveries, for its asbestos-related liability. The Company's ability to reasonably estimate its liability has been significantly affected by, among other factors, the volatility of asbestos-related litigation in the United States, the significant number of co-defendants that have filed for bankruptcy, the magnitude and timing of co-defendant bankruptcy trust payments, the inherent uncertainty of future disease incidence and claiming patterns, the expanding list of non-traditional defendants that have been sued in this litigation, and the use of mass litigation screenings to generate large numbers of claims by parties who allege exposure to asbestos dust but have no present physical asbestos impairment.

The Company has continued to monitor trends that may affect its ultimate liability and has continued to analyze the developments and variables affecting or likely to affect the resolution of pending and future asbestos claims against the Company. The material components of the Company's accrued liability are based on amounts determined by the Company in connection with its annual comprehensive review and consist of the following estimates, to the extent it is probable that such liabilities have been incurred and can be reasonably estimated: (i) the liability for asbestos claims already asserted against the Company; (ii) the liability for preexisting but unasserted asbestos claims for prior periods arising under its administrative claims-handling agreements with various plaintiffs' counsel; (iii) the liability for asbestos claims not yet asserted against the Company, but which the Company believes will be asserted in the next several years; and (iv) the legal defense costs likely to be incurred in connection with the foregoing types of claims.

The significant assumptions underlying the material components of the Company's accrual are:

a. the extent to which settlements are limited to claimants who were exposed to the Company's asbestos-containing insulation prior to its exit from that business in 1958;

b. the extent to which claims are resolved under the Company's administrative claims agreements or on terms comparable to those set forth in those agreements;

c. the extent of decrease or increase in the incidence of serious disease cases and claiming patterns for such cases;

d. the extent to which the Company is able to defend itself successfully at trial;

e. the extent to which courts and legislatures eliminate, reduce or permit the diversion of financial resources for unimpaired claimants;

f. the number and timing of additional co-defendant bankruptcies;

g. the extent to which bankruptcy trusts direct resources to resolve claims that are also presented to the Company and the timing of the payments made by the bankruptcy trusts; and

h. the extent to which co-defendants with substantial resources and assets continue to participate significantly in the resolution of future asbestos lawsuits and claims.

As noted above, the Company conducts a comprehensive review of its asbestos-related liabilities and costs annually in connection with finalizing and reporting its annual results of operations, unless significant changes in trends or new developments warrant an earlier review. If the results of an annual comprehensive review indicate that the existing amount of the accrued liability is insufficient to cover its estimated future asbestos-related costs, then the Company will record an appropriate charge to increase the accrued liability. The Company believes that a reasonable estimation of the probable amount of the liability for claims not yet asserted against the Company is not possible beyond a period of several years. Therefore, while the results of future annual comprehensive reviews cannot be determined, the Company expects the addition of one year to the estimation period will result in an annual charge.

On March 11, 2011, the Company received a verdict in an asbestos case in which conspiracy claims had been asserted against the Company. Of the total nearly $90 million awarded by the jury against the four defendants in the case, almost $10 million in compensatory damages were assessed against all four defendants, and $40 million in punitive damages were assessed against the Company.

The Company continues to deny the conspiracy allegations in this case and will vigorously challenge this verdict, if necessary, in the appellate courts, and, therefore, has made no change to its asbestos-related liability as of December 31, 2011. While the Company cannot predict the ultimate outcome of this lawsuit, the Company and other conspiracy defendants have successfully challenged jury verdicts in similar cases.

The Company's reported results of operations for 2011 were materially affected by the $165 million fourth quarter charge for asbestos-related costs and asbestos-related payments continue to be substantial. Any future additional charge would likewise materially affect the Company's results of operations for the period in which it is recorded. Also, the continued use of significant amounts of cash for asbestos-related costs has affected and may continue to affect the Company's cost of borrowing and its ability to pursue global or domestic acquisitions. However, the Company believes that its operating cash flows and other sources of liquidity will be sufficient to pay its obligations for asbestos-related costs and to fund its working capital and capital expenditure requirements on a short-term and long-term basis.

Other litigation is pending against the Company, in many cases involving ordinary and routine claims incidental to the business of the Company and in others presenting allegations that are non-routine and involve compensatory, punitive or treble damage claims as well as other types of relief. The Company records a liability for such matters when it is both probable that the liability has been incurred and the amount of the liability can be reasonably estimated. Recorded amounts are reviewed and adjusted to reflect changes in the factors upon which the estimates are based, including additional information, negotiations, settlements and other events.

Acquisition-Related Items

2.140

MEDTRONIC, INC. (APR)

CONSOLIDATED BALANCE SHEETS (in part)

(In millions, except per share data)	April 29, 2011	April 30, 2010
Liabilities and Shareholders' Equity (in part)		
Current liabilities:		
Short-term borrowings	$1,723	$2,575
Accounts payable	511	420
Accrued compensation	896	1,001
Accrued income taxes	50	235
Other accrued expenses	1,534	890
Total current liabilities	4,714	5,121

NOTES TO CONSOLIDATED FINANCIAL STATEMENTS

1. Summary of Significant Accounting Policies (in part)

Contingent Consideration—During fiscal year 2010, as mentioned above, the Company adopted authoritative guidance related to business combinations. Under this guidance, the Company must recognize contingent purchase price consideration at fair value at the acquisition date. Prior to the adoption of this guidance, contingent consideration was not included on the balance sheet and was recorded as incurred. The acquisition date fair value is measured based on the consideration expected to be transferred (probability-weighted), discounted back to present value. The discount rate used is determined at the time of the acquisition in accordance with accepted valuation methods. The fair value of the contingent milestone consideration is remeasured at the estimated fair value at each reporting period with the change in fair value recognized as income or expense within acquisition-related items in the Company's consolidated statements of earnings. Therefore, any changes in the fair value will impact the Company's earnings in such reporting period thereby resulting in potential variability in the Company's earnings until contingencies are resolved.

4. Acquisitions and Acquisition-Related Items (in part)

Contingent Consideration

Certain of the Company's business combinations or purchases of intellectual property involve the potential for the payment of future contingent consideration upon the achievement of certain product development milestones and/or various other favorable operating conditions. Payment of the additional consideration is generally contingent on the acquired company reaching certain performance milestones, including attaining specified revenue levels, achieving product development targets, or obtaining regulatory approvals. As a result of the Company adopting new authoritative guidance in fiscal year 2010 related to business combinations, contingent consideration is recorded at the acquisition date estimated fair value of the contingent milestone payments for all acquisitions subsequent to April 24, 2009. The fair value of the contingent milestone consideration is remeasured at the estimated fair value at each reporting period with the change in fair value recognized as income or expense within *acquisition-related items* in the consolidated statements of earnings. The Company measures the initial liability and remeasures the liability on a recurring basis using Level 3 inputs as defined under authoritative guidance for fair value measurements. See Note 6 for further information regarding fair value measurements.

During the third quarter of fiscal year 2011, the Company decreased the undiscounted future contingent consideration by $81 million to reflect the achievement and subsequent payment of a revenue milestone to the former shareholders of CoreValve in accordance with the fiscal year 2009 acquisition agreement. At April 29, 2011, the estimated maximum potential amount of undiscounted future contingent consideration that the Company is expected to make associated with all completed business combinations or purchases of intellectual property prior to April 24, 2009 was approximately $240 million. The milestones associated with the contingent consideration must be reached in future periods ranging from fiscal years 2012 to 2016 in order for the consideration to be paid.

The fair value of contingent milestone payments associated with acquisitions subsequent to April 24, 2009 was remeasured as of April 29, 2011 and April 30, 2010 at $335 million and $118 million, respectively. As of April 29, 2011, $269 million was reflected in *other long-term liabilities* and $66 million was reflected in *other accrued expenses* in the consolidated balance sheet. As of April 30, 2010, $118 million was reflected in *other long-term liabilities*. The following table provides a reconciliation of the beginning and ending balances of contingent milestone payments associated with acquisitions subsequent to April 24, 2009 measured at fair value that used significant unobservable inputs (Level 3):

	Fiscal Year	
(In millions)	2011	2010
Beginning balance	$118	$ —
Purchase price contingent consideration	203	118
Change in fair value of contingent consideration	14	—
Ending balance	$335	$118

Litigation

2.141

MOLEX INCORPORATED (JUN)

CONSOLIDATED BALANCE SHEETS (in part)

(In thousands)

	June 30	
	2011	2010
Liabilities and Stockholders' Equity (in part)		
Current liabilities:		
Current portion of long-term debt and short-term borrowings	$119,764	$110,070
Accounts payable	359,812	395,474
Accrued expenses:		
Salaries, commissions and bonuses	90,913	96,403
Restructuring	14,049	26,898
Accrual for unauthorized activities in Japan	182,460	165,815
Other	112,666	96,531
Income taxes payable	2,383	21,505
Total current liabilities	882,047	912,696

NOTES TO CONSOLIDATED FINANCIAL STATEMENTS

3. Unauthorized Activities in Japan

As we previously reported in our fiscal 2010 Annual Report on Form 10-K, we launched an investigation into unauthorized activities at Molex Japan Co., Ltd. in April 2010. We learned that an individual working in Molex Japan's finance group obtained unauthorized loans from third-party lenders, that included in at least one instance the attempted unauthorized pledge of Molex Japan facilities as security, in Molex Japan's name that were used to cover losses resulting from unauthorized trading, including margin trading, in Molex Japan's name. We also learned that the individual misappropriated funds from Molex Japan's accounts to cover losses from unauthorized trading. The individual admitted to forging documentation in arranging and concealing the transactions. We retained outside legal counsel, and they retained forensic accountants, to investigate the matter. The investigation has been completed. Based on our consultation with legal counsel in Japan and the information learned from the investigation, we intend to vigorously contest the enforceability of the outstanding unauthorized loans and any attempt by the lender to obtain payment.

As previously reported in our Annual Report on Form 10-K for the year ended June 30, 2010, based on the results of the completed investigation, we recorded for accounting purposes an accrued liability for the effect of unauthorized activities pending the resolution of these matters including the legal proceedings reported in Note 20.

We believe these unauthorized activities and related losses occurred from at least as early as 1988 through 2010, with approximately $167.4 million of losses occurring prior to June 30, 2007. The accrued liability for these potential net losses was $182.5 million as of June 30, 2011, including $16.6 million in cumulative foreign currency translation, which was recorded as a component of accumulated other comprehensive income. To the extent we prevail in not having to pay all or any portion of the outstanding unauthorized loans, we would recognize a gain in that amount. In addition, we have a contingent liability of $31.2 million for other loan-related expenses, interest expense and delay damages on the outstanding unauthorized loans.

20. Contingencies (in part)

We are currently a party to various legal proceedings, claims and investigations including those disclosed in this note. While management presently believes that the ultimate outcome of these proceedings, individually and in the aggregate, will not materially adversely impact our financial position or overall trends in operations, legal proceedings are subject to inherent uncertainties, and unfavorable rulings or other events could occur. If unfavorable final outcomes were to occur, then there exists the possibility of a material adverse impact.

Molex Japan Co., Ltd

As we previously reported in our fiscal 2010 Annual Report on Form 10-K, we launched an investigation into unauthorized activities at Molex Japan Co., Ltd. in April 2010. We learned that an individual working in Molex Japan's finance group obtained unauthorized loans from third party lenders, that included in at least one instance the attempted unauthorized pledge of Molex Japan facilities as security, in Molex Japan's name that were used to cover losses resulting from unauthorized trading, including margin trading, in Molex Japan's name. We also learned that the individual misappropriated funds from Molex Japan's accounts to cover losses from unauthorized trading. The individual admitted to forging documentation in arranging and concealing the transactions. We retained outside legal counsel, and they retained forensic accountants, to investigate the matter. The investigation has been completed.

On August 31, 2010, Mizuho Bank (Mizuho), which holds the unauthorized loans, filed a complaint in Tokyo District Court requesting the court to find Molex Japan liable for the payment of the outstanding unauthorized loans and to enter a judgment for such payment. Mizuho is claiming payment of outstanding principal borrowings of ¥3 billion ($37.2 million), ¥5 billion ($62.1 million), ¥5 billion ($62.1 million) and ¥2 billion ($24.8 million), other loan-related expenses of approximately ¥106 million ($1.3 million) and interest and delay damages of approximately ¥2.5 billion ($31.2 million) as of June 30, 2011. On October 13, 2010, Molex Japan filed a written answer requesting the court to dismiss the complaint, Mizuho filed plaintiff's brief no. 1 on December 15, 2010, Molex Japan filed defendant's brief no. 1 on February 16, 2011 and Mizuho filed plaintiff's brief no. 2 on April 20, 2011. Molex Japan filed defendant's brief no. 2 on June 28, 2011 and the court instructed Mizuho to file a reply brief by the end of August. We intend to vigorously contest the enforceability of the outstanding unauthorized loans and any attempt by the lender to obtain payment. See Note 3 for accounting treatment of the accrual for unauthorized activities in Japan.

As we reported on April 29, 2011, the Securities and Exchange Commission informed us that the SEC has issued a formal order of private investigation in connection with the activities in Molex Japan Co., Ltd. We are fully cooperating with the SEC's investigation.

Derivatives

2.142

REGAL BELOIT CORPORATION (DEC)

CONSOLIDATED BALANCE SHEETS (in part)

(Dollars in thousands, except per share data)

	December 31, 2011	January 1, 2011
Liabilities and Equity (in part)		
Current liabilities:		
Accounts payable	$249,400	$231,705
Dividends payable	7,484	6,562
Accrued compensation and employee benefits	81,656	63,842
Other accrued expenses	149,853	88,297
Hedging obligations	26,073	299
Current maturities of debt	10,030	8,637
Total current liabilities	524,496	399,342

NOTES TO THE CONSOLIDATED FINANCIAL STATEMENTS

For The Three Years Ended December 31, 2011

(3) Accounting Policies (in part)

Derivative Financial Instruments

Derivative instruments are recorded on the consolidated balance sheet at fair value. Any fair value changes are recorded in net earnings or Accumulated Other Comprehensive Income ("AOCI") as determined under accounting guidance that establishes criteria for designation and effectiveness of the hedging relationships.

The Company uses derivative instruments to manage its exposure to fluctuations in certain raw material commodity pricing, fluctuations in the cost of forecasted foreign currency transactions, and variability in interest rate exposure on floating rate borrowings. These derivative instruments have been designated as cash flow hedges (see Note 13 to the Consolidated Financial Statements).

(13) Derivative Financial Instruments (in part)

The Company is exposed to certain risks relating to its ongoing business operations. The primary risks managed using derivative instruments are commodity price risk, currency exchange risk, and interest rate risk. Forward contracts on certain commodities are entered into to manage the price risk associated with forecasted purchases of materials used in the Company's manufacturing process. Forward contracts on certain currencies are entered into to manage forecasted cash flows in certain foreign currencies. Interest rate swaps are entered into to manage interest rate risk associated with the Company's floating rate borrowings.

The Company is exposed to credit losses in the event of non-performance by the counterparties to various financial agreements, including its commodity hedging transactions, foreign currency exchange contracts and interest rate swap agreements. Exposure to counterparty credit risk is managed by limiting counterparties to major international banks and financial institutions meeting established credit guidelines and continually monitoring their compliance with the credit guidelines. The Company does not obtain collateral or other security to support financial instruments subject to credit risk. The Company does not anticipate non-performance by its counterparties, but cannot provide assurances.

The Company recognizes all derivative instruments as either assets or liabilities at fair value in the statement of financial position. Accordingly, the Company designates commodity forward contracts as cash flow hedges of forecasted purchases of commodities, currency forward contracts as cash flow hedges of forecasted foreign currency cash flows and interest rate swaps as cash flow hedges of forecasted LIBOR-based interest payments. There were no significant collateral deposits on derivative financial instruments as of December 31, 2011.

Fair values of derivative instruments were (in millions):

	December 31, 2011			
	Prepaid Expenses	Other Noncurrent Assets	Hedging Obligations (current)	Hedging Obligations
Designated as hedging instruments:				
Interest rate swap contracts	$ —	$ —	$ —	$42.0
Foreign exchange contracts	0.4	0.1	13.6	11.7
Commodity contracts	2.1	1.0	12.2	1.4
Not designated as hedging instruments:				
Foreign exchange contracts	0.1	—	—	—
Commodity contracts	0.2	—	0.3	—
Total derivatives:	$2.8	$1.1	$26.1	$55.1

	January 1, 2011			
	Prepaid Expenses	Other Noncurrent Assets	Hedging Obligations (Current)	Hedging Obligations
Designated as hedging instruments:				
Interest rate swap contracts	$ —	$ —	$ —	$39.1
Foreign exchange contracts	7.1	1.4	0.2	0.1
Commodity contracts	24.7	4.2	0.1	—
Not designated as hedging instruments:				
Foreign exchange contracts	0.2	—	—	—
Commodity contracts	0.2	—	—	—
Total derivatives:	$32.2	$5.6	$0.3	$39.2

Returns, Rebates and Incentives

2.143

ROCKWELL AUTOMATION, INC. (SEP)

MANAGEMENT'S DISCUSSION AND ANALYSIS OF FINANCIAL CONDITION AND RESULTS OF OPERATIONS

Revenue Recognition (in part)

Returns, Rebates and Incentives

Our primary incentive program provides distributors with cash rebates or account credits based on agreed amounts that vary depending on the customer to whom our distributor ultimately sells the product. We also offer various other incentive programs that provide distributors and direct sale customers with cash rebates, account credits or additional products and services based on meeting specified program criteria. Certain distributors are offered a right to return product, subject to contractual limitations.

We record accruals for customer returns, rebates and incentives at the time of revenue recognition based primarily on historical experience. Adjustments to the accrual may be required if actual returns, rebates and incentives differ from historical experience or if there are changes to other assumptions used to estimate the accrual. A critical assumption used in estimating the accrual for our primary distributor rebate program is the time period from when revenue is recognized to when the rebate is processed. If the time period were to change by 10 percent, the effect would be an adjustment to the accrual of approximately $8.5 million.

Returns, rebates and incentives are recognized as a reduction of sales if distributed in cash or customer account credits. Rebates and incentives are recognized in cost of sales for additional products and services to be provided. Accruals are reported as a current liability in our balance sheet or, where a right of offset exists, as a reduction of accounts receivable. The accrual for customer returns, rebates and incentives was $162.0 million at September 30, 2011 and $135.9 million at September 30, 2010, of which $8.0 million at September 30, 2011 and $16.4 million at September 30, 2010 was included as an offset to accounts receivable.

CONSOLIDATED BALANCE SHEET (in part)

	September 30	
(In millions)	2011	2010
Liabilities and Shareowners' Equity *(in part)*		
Current liabilities		
Accounts payable	$ 455.1	$ 435.7
Compensation and benefits	319.6	300.1
Advance payments from customers and deferred revenue	189.0	184.9
Customer returns, rebates and incentives	154.0	119.5
Other current liabilities	212.2	182.1
Total current liabilities	1,329.9	1,222.3

Asset Retirement Obligation

2.144

THE MOSAIC COMPANY (MAY)

NOTES TO CONSOLIDATED FINANCIAL STATEMENTS

Tables in millions, except per share amounts

15. Accounting for Asset Retirement Obligations

We recognize AROs in the period in which we have an existing legal obligation associated with the retirement of a tangible long-lived asset, and the amount of the liability can be reasonably estimated. The ARO is recognized at fair value when the liability is incurred with a corresponding increase in the carrying amount of the related long lived asset. We depreciate the tangible asset over its estimated useful life. Our legal obligations related to asset retirement require us to: (i) reclaim lands disturbed by mining as a condition to receive permits to mine phosphate ore reserves; (ii) treat low pH process water in phosphogypsum management systems to neutralize acidity; (iii) close and monitor phosphogypsum management systems at our Florida and Louisiana facilities at the end of their useful lives; (iv) remediate certain other conditional obligations; and (v) remove all surface structures and equipment, plug and abandon mine shafts, contour and revegetate, as necessary, and monitor for five years after closing our Carlsbad, New Mexico facility. The estimated liability for these legal obligations is based on the estimated cost to satisfy the above obligations which is discounted using a credit-adjusted risk-free rate.

A reconciliation of our AROs is as follows:

	May 31	
(In millions)	2011	2010
Asset retirement obligations, beginning of year	$525.9	$530.7
Liabilities incurred	35.0	27.1
Liabilities settled	(73.1)	(67.6)
Accretion expense	31.6	29.6
Revisions in estimated cash flows	53.7	6.1
Asset retirement obligations, end of year	573.1	525.9
Less current portion	90.6	83.1
	$482.5	$442.8

We also have unrecorded AROs that are conditional upon a certain event. These AROs generally include the removal and disposition of non-friable asbestos. The most recent estimate of the aggregate cost of these AROs, expressed in 2011 dollars, is approximately $26.0 million. We have not recorded a liability for these conditional AROs as of May 31, 2011 because we do not currently believe there is a reasonable basis for estimating a date or range of dates for demolition of these facilities. In reaching this conclusion, we considered the historical performance of each facility and have taken into account factors such as planned maintenance, asset replacements and upgrades which, if conducted as in the past, can extend the physical lives of our facilities indefinitely. We also considered the possibility of changes in technology, risk of obsolescence, and availability of raw materials in arriving at our conclusion.

LONG-TERM DEBT

PRESENTATION

2.145 FASB ASC 470 addresses classification determination for specific debt obligations. FASB ASC 470-10-45-11 states that the current liability classification is intended to include long-term obligations that are or will be callable by the creditor either because the debtors' violation of a provision of the debt agreement at the balance sheet date makes the obligation callable, or the violation, if not cured within a specified grace period, will make the obligation callable. Accordingly, such callable obligations should be classified as current liabilities, unless one of the following conditions is met:

- The creditor has waived or subsequently lost the right to demand payment for more than one year, or operating cycle if longer, from the balance sheet date. For example, the debtor may have cured the violation after the balance sheet date, and the obligation is not callable at the time the financial statements are issued or available to be issued.
- For long-term obligations containing a grace period within which the debtor may cure the violation, it is probable that the violation will be cured within that period, thus preventing the obligation from becoming callable.

DISCLOSURE

2.146 FASB ASC 470 requires, for each of the five years following the date of the latest balance sheet presented, disclosure of the combined aggregate amount of maturities and sinking fund requirements for all long-term borrowings. In addition, FASB ASC 440, *Commitments*, requires disclosure of terms and conditions provided in loan agreements, such as assets pledged as collateral and covenants to limit additional debt, maintain working capital, and restrict dividends. Regulation S-X has similar or expanded requirements for matters such as debt details, assets subject to lien, defaults, dividend restrictions, and changes in long-term debt.

2.147 FASB ASC 825 requires disclosure of both the fair value and bases for estimating the fair value of long-term debt, unless it is not practicable to estimate the value.

2.148

TABLE 2-11: LONG-TERM DEBT*

Table 2-11 summarizes the types of long-term debt most frequently disclosed by the survey companies.

	Number of Entities	
	2011	2010
Unsecured		
Notes	384	360
Credit agreement/revolving credit	207	180
Debentures	110	91
Loans	82	77
Foreign borrowing	18	30
Commercial paper	43	24
Bonds	19	31
Employee stock ownership plan loans	2	4
Other, described	13	26
Collateralized		
Notes	61	70
Credit agreements	54	62
Loans	27	32
Mortgages	35	24
Industrial revenue/development bonds	43	31
Pollution control bonds	2	3
Leases	143	101
Receivable financing/securitization	36	24
Other, described	13	6
Convertible		
Debentures	14	19
Notes	67	64
Debt exchangeable into stock of another company	1	2
Other, described	1	3

* Appearing in the balance sheet or notes to financial statements, or both.
Note: Classification of long-term debt changed for the 2011 edition, so no 2009 data are available.

PRESENTATION AND DISCLOSURE EXCERPTS

Unsecured

2.149

ARCHER DANIELS MIDLAND COMPANY (JUN)

CONSOLIDATED BALANCE SHEETS (in part)

(In millions)	June 30	
	2011	**2010**
Liabilities and Shareholders' Equity *(in part)*		
Current liabilities		
Short-term debt	$ 1,875	$ 374
Accounts payable	7,550	5,538
Accrued expenses	3,615	2,577
Current maturities of long-term debt	178	344
Total current liabilities	13,218	8,833
Long-term liabilities		
Long-term debt	8,266	6,830
Deferred income taxes	859	439
Other	1,012	1,075
Total long-term liabilities	10,137	8,344

NOTES TO CONSOLIDATED FINANCIAL STATEMENTS

Note 8. Debt and Financing Arrangements (in part)

(In millions)	2011	2010
Floating Rate Notes $1.5 billion face amount, due in 2012	$1,500	$ —
0.875% Convertible Senior Notes $1.15 billion face amount, due in 2014	1,026	982
5.765% Debentures $1.0 billion face amount, due in 2041	1,008	—
4.479% Debentures $750 million face amount, due in 2021	756	—
5.45% Notes $700 million face amount, due in 2018	700	700
5.375% Debentures $600 million face amount, due in 2035	587	587
5.935% Debentures $500 million face amount, due in 2032	495	495
6.625% Debentures $298 million face amount, due in 2029	296	296
8.375% Debentures $295 million face amount, due in 2017	292	292
7.5% Debentures $282 million face amount, due in 2027	281	281
6.95% Debentures $250 million face amount, due in 2097	246	246
7.0% Debentures $246 million face amount, due in 2031	244	244
7.125% Debentures $243 million face amount, due in 2013	243	243
6.45% Debentures $215 million face amount, due in 2038	215	215
6.75% Debentures $200 million face amount, due in 2027	197	197
8.125% Debentures $103 million face amount, due in 2012	103	103
4.70% Debentures $1.75 billion face amount, due in 2041	—	1,750
5.87% Debentures $196 million face amount, due in 2010	—	191
8.875% Debentures $102 million face amount, due in 2011	—	102
Other	255	250
Total long-term debt including current maturities	8,444	7,174
Current maturities	(178)	(344)
Total long-term debt	$8,266	$6,830

In June 2008, the Company issued $1.75 billion of Equity Units, which were a combination of debt and a forward contract for the holder to purchase the Company's common stock. The debt and equity instruments were deemed to be separate instruments as the investor may transfer or settle the equity instrument separately from the debt instrument.

On March 30, 2011, the Company initiated a remarketing of the $1.75 billion 4.7% debentures underlying the Equity Units into two tranches: $0.75 billion principal amount of 4.479% notes due in 2021 and $1.0 billion principal amount of 5.765% debentures due in 2041. As a result of the remarketing, the Company was required to use the "if-converted" method of calculating diluted earnings per share with respect to the forward contracts for the quarter ended March 31, 2011 (see Note 9). The Company incurred early extinguishment of debt charges of $8 million as a result of the debt remarketing.

The forward purchase contracts underlying the Equity Units were settled on June 1, 2011, for 44 million shares of the Company's common stock in exchange for receipt of $1.75 billion in cash.

On February 11, 2011, the Company issued $1.5 billion in aggregate principal amount of floating rate notes due on August 13, 2012. Interest on the notes accrues at a floating rate of three-month LIBOR reset quarterly plus 0.16% and is paid quarterly. As of June 30, 2011, the interest rate on the notes was 0.42%.

In March 2010, the Company repurchased an aggregate principal amount of $500 million of its outstanding debentures in accordance with its announced tender offers, resulting in charges on early extinguishment of debt of $75 million, which consisted of $71 million in premium and other related expenses and $4 million in write-off of debt issuance costs.

In February 2007, the Company issued $1.15 billion principal amount of convertible senior notes due in 2014 (the Notes) in a private placement. The Notes were issued at par and bear interest at a rate of 0.875% per year, payable semiannually. The Notes are convertible based on an initial conversion rate of 22.8423 shares per $1,000 principal amount of Notes (which is equal to a conversion price of approximately $43.78 per share). The Notes may be converted, subject to adjustment, only under the following circumstances: 1) during any calendar quarter beginning after March 31, 2007, if the closing price of the Company's common stock for at least 20 trading days in the 30 consecutive trading days ending on the last trading day of the immediately preceding quarter is more than 140% of the applicable conversion price per share, which is $1,000 divided by the then applicable conversion rate, 2) during the five consecutive business day period immediately after any five consecutive trading day period (the note measurement period) in which the average of the trading price per $1,000 principal amount of Notes was equal to or less than 98% of the average of the product of the closing price of the Company's common stock and the conversion rate at each date during the note measurement period, 3) if the Company makes specified distributions to its common stockholders or specified corporate transactions occur, or 4) at any time on or after January 15, 2014, through the business day preceding the maturity date. Upon conversion, a holder would receive an amount in cash equal to the lesser of 1) $1,000 and 2) the conversion value, as defined. If the conversion value exceeds $1,000, the Company will deliver, at the Company's election, cash or common stock or a combination of cash and common stock for the conversion value in excess of $1,000. If the Notes are converted in connection with a change in control, as defined, the Company may be required to provide a make-whole premium in the form of an increase in the conversion rate, subject to a stated maximum amount. In addition, in the event of a change in control, the holders may require the Company to purchase all or a portion of their Notes at a purchase price equal to 100% of the principal amount of the Notes, plus accrued and unpaid interest, if any. In accordance with ASC Topic 470-20, the Company recognized the Notes proceeds received in 2007 as long-term debt of $853 million and equity of $297 million. The discount on the long-term debt is being amortized over the life of the Notes using the effective interest method. Discount amortization expense of $43 million, $40 million, and $39 million for 2011, 2010, and 2009, respectively, were included in interest expense related to the Notes.

Concurrent with the issuance of the Notes, the Company purchased call options in private transactions at a cost of $300 million. The purchased call options allow the Company to receive shares of its common stock and/or cash from the counterparties equal to the amounts of common stock and/or cash related to the excess of the current market price of the Company's common stock over the exercise price of the purchased call options. In addition, the Company sold warrants in private transactions to acquire, subject to customary anti-dilution adjustments, 26.3 million shares of its common stock at an exercise price of $62.56 per share and received proceeds of $170 million. If the average price of the Company's common stock during a defined period ending on or about the respective settlement dates exceeds the exercise price of the warrants, the warrants will be settled, at the Company's option, in cash or shares of common stock. The purchased call options and warrants are intended to reduce the potential dilution upon future conversions of the Notes by effectively increasing the initial conversion price to $62.56 per share. The net cost of the purchased call options and warrant transactions of $130 million was recorded as a reduction of shareholders' equity.

As of June 30, 2011, none of the conditions permitting conversion of the Notes had been satisfied. In addition, as of June 30, 2011, the market price of the Company's common stock was not greater than the exercise price of the purchased call options or warrants. As of June 30, 2011, no share amounts related to the conversion of the Notes or exercise of the warrants are included in diluted average shares outstanding.

At June 30, 2011, the fair value of the Company's long-term debt exceeded the carrying value by $842 million, as estimated using quoted market prices or discounted future cash flows based on the Company's current incremental borrowing rates for similar types of borrowing arrangements.

The aggregate maturities of long-term debt for the five years after June 30, 2011, are $178 million, $1.8 billion, $1.1 billion, $28 million, and $17 million, respectively.

At June 30, 2011, the Company had pledged certain property, plant, and equipment with a carrying value of $344 million as security for certain long-term debt obligations.

At June 30, 2011, the Company had lines of credit totaling $6.9 billion, of which $5.7 billion were unused. The weighted average interest rates on short-term borrowings outstanding at June 30, 2011 and 2010, were 0.65% and 2.29%, respectively. Of the Company's total lines of credit, $4.6 billion support a commercial paper borrowing facility, against which there was $620 million of commercial paper outstanding at June 30, 2011.

The Company's credit facilities and certain debentures require the Company to comply with specified financial and non-financial covenants including maintenance of minimum tangible net worth as well as limitations related to incurring liens, secured debt, and certain other financing arrangements. The Company is in compliance with these covenants as of June 30, 2011.

The Company has outstanding standby letters of credit and surety bonds at June 30, 2011 and 2010, totaling $620 million and $459 million, respectively.

Collateralized

2.150

RITE AID CORPORATION (FEB)

CONSOLIDATED BALANCE SHEETS (in part)

(In thousands, except per share amounts)

	February 26, 2011	February 27, 2010
Liabilities and Stockholders' Deficit *(in part)*		
Current liabilities:		
Current maturities of long-term debt and lease financing obligations	$ 63,045	$ 51,502
Accounts payable	1,307,872	1,159,069
Accrued salaries, wages and other current liabilities	1,049,406	965,121
Total current liabilities	2,420,323	2,175,692
Long-term debt, less current maturities	6,034,525	6,185,633
Lease financing obligations, less current maturities	122,295	133,764
Other noncurrent liabilities	1,190,074	1,228,373
Total liabilities	9,767,217	9,723,462

NOTES TO CONSOLIDATED FINANCIAL STATEMENTS

For the Years Ended February 26, 2011, February 27, 2010 and February 28, 2009

(In thousands, except per share amounts)

10. Indebtedness and Credit Agreement (in part)

Following is a summary of indebtedness and lease financing obligations at February 26, 2011 and February 27, 2010:

	2011	2010
Secured Debt:		
Senior secured revolving credit facility due September 2012	$ —	$ 80,000
Senior secured revolving credit facility due August 2015 (or April 2014, see *Credit Facility* below)	28,000	—
Senior secured credit facility term loan due June 2014	1,074,613	1,085,663
Senior secured credit facility term loan due June 2014 ($342,125 and $345,625 face value less unamortized discount of $19,718 and $25,634)	322,407	319,991
Senior secured credit facility term loan due June 2015 ($650,000 face value less unamortized net discount of $15,036)	—	634,964
9.75% senior secured notes (first lien) due June 2016 ($410,000 face value less unamortized discount of $5,635 and $6,692)	404,365	403,308
8.00% senior secured notes (first lien) due August 2020	650,000	—
10.375% senior secured notes (second lien) due July 2016 ($470,000 face value less unamortized discount of $29,952 and $35,481)	440,048	434,519
7.5% senior secured notes (second lien) due March 2017	500,000	500,000
10.25% senior secured notes (second lien) due October 2019 ($270,000 face value less unamortized discount of $1,774 and $1,978)	268,226	268,022
Other secured	5,408	2,316
	$3,693,067	$3,728,783

(continued)

	2011	2010
Guaranteed Unsecured Debt:		
8.625% senior notes due March 2015	$ 500,000	$ 500,000
9.375% senior notes due December 2015 ($410,000 face value less unamortized discount of $3,345 and $4,049)	406,655	405,951
9.5% senior notes due June 2017 ($810,000 face value less unamortized discount of $8,130 and $9,431)	801,870	800,569
	1,708,525	1,706,520
Unsecured Unguaranteed Debt:		
8.125% notes due May 2010	—	11,117
9.25% senior notes due June 2013	6,015	6,015
6.875% senior debentures due August 2013	184,773	184,773
8.5% convertible notes due May 2015	64,188	158,000
7.7% notes due February 2027	295,000	295,000
6.875% fixed-rate senior notes due December 2028	128,000	128,000
	677,976	782,905
Lease financing obligations	140,297	152,691
Total debt	6,219,865	6,370,899
Current maturities of long-term debt and lease financing obligations	(63,045)	(51,502)
Long-term debt and lease financing obligations, less current maturities	$6,156,820	$6,319,397

Credit Facility

The Company has a senior secured credit facility that consists of a $1,175,000 revolving credit facility and two term loans. Borrowings under the revolving credit facility bear interest at a rate per annum between LIBOR plus 3.25% and LIBOR plus 3.75% if the Company chooses to make LIBOR borrowings, or between Citibank's base rate plus 2.25% and Citibank's base rate plus 2.75%, in each case based upon the amount of revolver availability, as defined in the senior secured credit facility. The Company is required to pay fees between 0.50% and 0.75% per annum on the daily unused amount of the revolver depending on the amount of revolver availability. Amounts drawn under the revolver become due and payable on August 19, 2015, provided that such maturity date shall instead be April 18, 2014 in the event that on or prior to April 18, 2014 the Company does not repay, refinance or otherwise extend the maturity date of its Tranche 2 Term Loan (as defined below) to a date that is at least 90 days after August 19, 2015 and, in the case of a repayment or refinancing, the Company must have at least $500,000 of availability under the revolver.

The Company's ability to borrow under the revolver is based upon a specified borrowing base consisting of accounts receivable, inventory and prescription files. At February 26, 2011, the Company had $28,000 of borrowings outstanding under the revolver and had letters of credit outstanding thereunder of $142,686 which gave the Company additional borrowing capacity of $1,004,314.

The credit facility also includes a $1,105,000 senior secured term loan (the "Tranche 2 Term Loan"). The Tranche 2 Term Loan will mature on June 4, 2014 and currently bears interest at a rate per annum equal to LIBOR plus 1.75%, if the Company elects LIBOR borrowings, or at Citibank's base rate plus 0.75%. Mandatory prepayments are required to be made from proceeds of asset dispositions and casualty events (subject to certain limitations), a portion of excess cash flows (as defined in the senior secured credit facility) and proceeds from certain issuances of equity or debt (subject to certain exceptions). If at any time there is a shortfall in the borrowing base under the senior credit facility, prepayment of the Tranche 2 Term Loan may also be required.

The senior secured credit facility also restricts the Company and the subsidiary guarantors from accumulating cash on hand in excess of $200,000 at any time when revolving loans are outstanding (not including cash located in the Company's store deposit accounts, cash necessary to cover the Company's current liabilities and certain other exceptions) and from accumulating cash on hand with revolver borrowings in excess of $100,000 over three consecutive business days. The senior secured credit facility also states that if at any time (other than following the exercise of remedies or acceleration of any senior obligations or second priority debt and receipt of a triggering notice by the senior collateral agent from a representative of the senior obligations or the second priority debt) either (a) an event of default exists under the Company's senior secured credit facility or (b) the sum of revolver availability under the Company's senior secured credit facility and certain amounts held on deposit with the senior collateral agent in a concentration account is less than $100,000 for three consecutive business days (a "cash sweep period"), the funds in the Company's deposit accounts will be swept to a concentration account with the senior collateral agent and will be applied first to repay outstanding revolving loans under the senior secured credit facility, and then held as Collateral for the senior obligations until such cash sweep period is rescinded pursuant to the terms of the Company's senior secured credit facility.

The senior secured credit facility allows the Company to have outstanding, at any time, up to $1,500,000 in secured second priority debt and unsecured debt in addition to borrowings under the senior secured credit facility and existing indebtedness, provided that not in excess of $750,000 of such secured second priority debt and unsecured debt shall mature or require scheduled payments of principal prior to three months after June 4, 2014. The senior secured credit facility allows the Company to incur an unlimited amount of unsecured debt with a maturity beyond three months after June 4, 2014; however, other debentures limit the amount of unsecured debt that can be incurred if certain interest coverage levels are not met at the time of incurrence of said debt. The senior secured facility also allows, so long as the senior secured credit facility is not in default, for the repurchase of any debt with a maturity on or before June 4, 2014, for the voluntary repurchase of debt with a maturity after June 4, 2014, and the mandatory repurchase of the Company's 8.5% convertible notes due 2015 if the Company maintains availability on the revolving credit facility of at least $100,000.

The senior secured credit facility contains covenants, which place restrictions on the incurrence of debt beyond the restrictions described above, the payments of dividends, sale of assets, mergers and acquisitions and the granting of liens. The credit facility has a financial covenant, which is the maintenance of a fixed charge coverage ratio. The covenant requires that, if availability on the revolving credit facility is less than $150.0 million, the Company must maintain a minimum fixed charge coverage ratio of 1.00 to 1.00 for the quarter ending February 26, 2011 and for the three subsequent quarters. This ratio increases to 1.05 to 1.00 in the last quarter of Fiscal 2012 and remains at that level for the remaining term of the facility. As of February 26, 2011, the Company was in compliance with this financial covenant.

The senior secured credit facility provides for events of default including nonpayment, misrepresentation, breach of covenants and bankruptcy. It is also an event of default if the Company fails to make any required payment on debt having a principal amount in excess of $50,000 or any event occurs that enables, or which with the giving of notice or the lapse of time would enable, the holder of such debt to accelerate the maturity or require the repurchase of such debt. The August 2010 amendments to the senior secured credit facility exclude the mandatory repurchase of the 8.5% convertible notes due 2015 from this event of default.

Substantially all of Rite Aid Corporation's wholly-owned subsidiaries guarantee the obligations under the senior secured credit facility. The subsidiary guarantees of the senior secured credit facility; the 9.75% senior secured notes due 2016 and the 8.00% senior secured notes due 2020 are secured by a senior lien on, among other things, accounts receivable, inventory and prescription files of the subsidiary guarantors. Rite Aid Corporation is a holding company with no direct operations and is dependent upon dividends, distributions and other payments from its subsidiaries to service payments due under the senior secured credit facility. The Company's 10.375% senior secured notes due 2016, the 7.5% senior secured notes due 2017 and the 10.25% senior secured notes due 2019 are guaranteed by substantially all of the Company's wholly-owned subsidiaries, which are the same subsidiaries that guarantee the senior secured credit facility, the 9.75% senior secured notes due 2016 and the 8.00% senior secured notes due 2020, and are secured on a second priority basis by the same collateral as the senior secured credit facility, the 9.75% senior secured notes due 2016 and the 8.00% senior secured notes due 2020. The 8.625% senior notes due 2015, the 9.375% senior notes due 2015 and the 9.5% senior notes due 2017 are also guaranteed by all of the same subsidiaries on an unsecured basis.

The subsidiary guarantees related to the Company's senior secured credit facility and secured notes and on an unsecured basis the guaranteed indentures are full and unconditional and joint and several, and there are no restrictions on the ability of the parent to obtain funds from its subsidiaries. Also, the parent company has no independent assets or operations, and subsidiaries not guaranteeing the credit facility and applicable indentures are minor. Accordingly, condensed consolidating financial information for the parent and subsidiaries is not presented.

The indentures that govern the Company's secured and guaranteed unsecured notes contain restrictions on the amount of additional secured and unsecured debt that can be incurred by the Company. As of February 26, 2011, the amount of additional secured and unsecured debt that could be incurred under these indentures was $1,075,262 (which does not include the ability to enter into certain sale and leaseback transactions.) However, the Company could not incur any additional secured debt assuming a fully drawn revolver and the outstanding letters of credit. The ability to issue additional unsecured debt under these indentures is governed by an interest coverage ratio test.

The Company has an excess cash flow payment requirement under the senior secured credit facility. Included in these payments above is a repayment of $39.8 million of the Tranche 2 Term Loan and the Tranche 5 Term Loan, as required under the Company's senior secured credit facility. This excess cash flow will be in lieu of scheduled amortization payments for the next three fiscal years.

Convertible

2.151

HARMAN INTERNATIONAL INDUSTRIES, INCORPORATED (JUN)

CONSOLIDATED BALANCE SHEETS (in part)

	June 30	
(In thousands)	2011	2010
Liabilities and Shareholders' Equity		
(in part)		
Current liabilities		
Current portion of long-term debt	$ 386	$ 463
Short-term debt	1,785	13,472
Accounts payable	473,486	382,985
Accrued liabilities	436,537	363,261
Accrued warranties	122,396	99,329
Income taxes payable	12,991	3,941
Total current liabilities	1,047,581	863,451
Convertible senior notes	378,401	362,693
Other senior debt	0	1,209
Other non-current liabilities	208,855	193,970
Total liabilities	1,634,837	1,421,323

NOTES TO THE CONSOLIDATED FINANCIAL STATEMENTS

(Dollars in thousands, except per-share data and unless otherwise indicated)

Note 7—Earnings (Loss) Per Share (in part)

The conversion terms of our $400 million of 1.25 percent convertible senior notes ("Convertible Senior Notes") will affect the calculation of diluted earnings per share if the price of our common stock exceeds the conversion price of the Convertible Senior Notes. The initial conversion price of the Convertible Senior Notes was approximately $104 per share, subject to adjustment in specified circumstances as described in the indenture governing the Convertible Senior Notes (the

"Indenture"). Upon conversion, a holder of the Convertible Senior Notes will receive an amount per Convertible Senior Note in cash equal to the lesser of $1,000 or the conversion value of the Convertible Senior Notes, determined in the manner set forth in the Indenture. If the conversion value exceeds $1,000, we will deliver $1,000 in cash and at our option, cash or common stock or a combination of cash and common stock for the conversion price in excess of $1,000. The conversion option is indexed to our common stock and therefore is classified as equity. The conversion option will not result in an adjustment to net income in cal-culating diluted earnings per share. The dilutive effect of the conversion option will be calculated using the treasury stock method. Therefore, conversion settlement shares will be included in diluted shares outstanding if the price of our common stock exceeds the conversion price of the Convertible Senior Notes. Refer to Note 9—*Debt* for further information.

Note 9—Debt (in part)

Long-Term Debt and Current Portion of Long-Term-Debt (in part)

At June 30, 2011 and 2010, long-term debt consisted of the following:

	Face Value at June 30, 2011	Book Value at June 30, 2011	Face Value at June 30, 2010	Book Value at June 30, 2010
Convertible senior notes due 2012, interest due semi-annually at 1.25 percent[1]	$400,000	$378,401	$400,000	$362,693
Obligations under capital leases	442	442	741	741
Other unsubordinated loans	386	386	931	931
Total long-term debt	400,828	379,229	401,672	364,365
Less: current portion of long-term debt	(828)	(828)	(463)	(463)
Total long-term debt	$400,000	$378,401	$401,209	$363,902

[1] Book values as of June 30, 2011 and 2010 are presented net of unamortized discounts of $21.6 million and $37.3 million, respectively, resulting from the adoption of new accounting guidance in fiscal year 2010. The fair value of the Convertible Senior Notes at June 30, 2011 and 2010 was $383.9 million and $351.2 million, respectively.

Interest expense is reported net of interest income in our Consolidated Statements of Operations. Interest expense, net was $22.6 million, $30.2 million and $20.6 million for the fiscal years ended June 30, 2011, 2010 and 2009, respectively. Gross interest expense was $32.5 million, $33.8 million and $28.7 million for the fiscal years ended June 30, 2011, 2010 and 2009, respectively, of which $19.3 million, $17.4 million and $14.8 million, respectively, was non-cash interest expense associated with the amortization of the debt discount on the Convertible Senior Notes and the amortization of debt issuance costs on the Convertible Senior Notes and our existing and prior revolving credit facilities, and $13.2 million, $16.4 million and $13.9 million, for the fiscal years ended June 30, 2011, 2010 and 2009 respectively, was cash interest expense. Interest income was $9.9 million, $3.6 million and $8.1 million for the fiscal years ended June 30, 2011, 2010 and 2009, respectively. Refer to the heading "New Revolving Credit Facility" below for further information on our revolving credit facility.

Convertible Senior Notes

We had $400 million of Convertible Senior Notes outstanding at June 30 2011 and 2010 which were issued on October 23, 2007 (the "Issuance Date") and are due on October 15, 2012. The Convertible Senior Notes were issued at par and we pay interest at a rate of 1.25 percent per annum on a semiannual basis. The initial conversion rate on the Convertible Senior Notes is 9.6154 shares of our common stock per $1,000 principal amount of the Convertible Senior Notes (which is equal to an initial conversion price of approximately $104 per share). The conversion rate is subject to adjustment in specified circumstances described in the Indenture.

Accounting guidance issued by the FASB requires the issuer of convertible debt instruments with cash settlement features to account separately for the liability and equity components of the instrument. Under this guidance, the debt is recognized at the present value of its cash flows discounted using the issuer's nonconvertible debt borrowing rate at the time of issuance and the equity component is recognized as the difference between the proceeds from the issuance of the note and the fair value of the liability, net of taxes. The reduced carrying value on the convertible debt results in a debt discount that is accreted back to the convertible debt's principal amount through the recognition of noncash interest expense over the expected life of the debt, which results in recognizing interest expense on these borrowings at effective rates approximating what we would have incurred had nonconvertible debt with otherwise similar terms been issued.

In accordance with this guidance, we measured the fair value of the debt components of the Convertible Senior Notes at the Issuance Date using an effective interest rate of 5.6 percent. As a result, we attributed $75.7 million of the proceeds received to the conversion feature of the Convertible Senior Notes at the Issuance Date, which is netted against the face value of the Convertible Senior Notes as a debt discount. This amount represents the excess proceeds received over the fair value of the Convertible Senior Notes at the Issuance Date and is being accreted back to the principal amount of the Convertible Senior Notes through the recognition of noncash interest expense over the expected life of the Convertible Senior Notes. In addition, we recorded $48.3 million within additional paid-in capital in our Consolidated Balance Sheets representing the equity component of the Convertible Senior Notes, which is net of deferred taxes. The effect of this guidance has resulted in a decrease to net income and earnings per share for all periods presented; however, there is no effect on our cash interest payments.

The principal amounts, unamortized discount and net carrying amounts of the liability components and the equity components for the Convertible Senior Notes as of June 30, 2011 and 2010 are as follows:

	Principal Balance	Unamortized Discount	Net Carrying Amount	Equity Component
June 30, 2011	$400,000	$(21,599)	$378,401	$48,323
June 30, 2010	$400,000	$(37,307)	$362,693	$48,323

At June 30, 2011, the unamortized discount is recognized as a reduction in the carrying value of the Convertible Senior Notes in the Consolidated Balance Sheets and is being amortized to Interest expense, net in our Consolidated Statement of Operations over the expected remaining term of the Convertible Senior Notes of 16 months.

Debt issuance costs of $4.8 million were recorded in connection with this transaction and are included in Other assets in our Consolidated Balance Sheets and are also being amortized to Interest expense, net in our Consolidated Statements of Operations over the expected remaining term of the Convertible Senior Notes. The unamortized balance of debt issuance costs at June 30, 2011 and 2010 was $1.1 million and $1.8 million, respectively.

Total interest expense related to the Convertible Senior Notes for the fiscal years ended June 30, 2011, 2010 and 2009, includes $5.0 million in all fiscal years of contractual cash interest expense and an additional $15.7 million, $14.8 million and $13.9 million of noncash interest expense, respectively, related to the amortization of the discount and $0.8 million, $0.8 million and $0.2 million, respectively, related to the amortization of debt issuance costs.

The Indenture contains covenants, one of which required us to calculate the ratio of Consolidated Total Debt to Consolidated EBITDA, as defined in the Indenture, each time we incurred additional indebtedness, for the most recently ended four quarter period (the "Incurrence of Debt Covenant"). On January 12, 2010, we entered into a supplemental indenture to the Indenture (the "Supplemental Indenture") which amended the Incurrence of Debt Covenant. Under the Supplemental Indenture, we were permitted to, without complying with the ratio of Consolidated Total Debt to Consolidated EBITDA of 3.25 to 1.00: (a) incur revolving extensions of credit under the 2009 Credit Agreement, up to a maximum amount of $231.6 million, and (b) incur additional indebtedness, subject to a requirement to make a pro rata offer to purchase a principal face amount of the Convertible Senior Notes equal to 50 percent of the aggregate amount of such indebtedness so incurred, plus accrued and unpaid interest thereon. The Incurrence of Debt Covenant lapsed on October 23, 2010, and was no longer applicable to us after this date. At June 30, 2011, we were in compliance with all covenants under the Indenture, as amended.

Covenants

2.152

BOYD GAMING CORPORATION (DEC)

CONSOLIDATED BALANCE SHEETS (in part)

As of December 31, 2011 and 2010

	December 31	
(In thousands, except share and per share data)	2011	2010
Liabilities and Stockholders' Equity *(in part)*		
Current liabilities		
Current maturities of long-term debt	$ 43,230	$ 25,690
Accounts payable	98,015	57,183
Accrued liabilities	295,459	278,469
Tax liabilities	5,630	6,506
Non-recourse obligations of variable interest entity	29,686	22,487
Total current liabilities	472,020	390,335
Long-term debt, net of current maturities	3,347,226	3,193,065
Deferred income taxes	379,958	362,174
Other long-term tax liabilities	45,598	44,813
Other liabilities	71,193	84,533
Non-recourse obligations of variable interest entity	192,980	220,572

NOTES TO CONSOLIDATED FINANCIAL STATEMENTS

As of December 31, 2011 and 2010 and for the years ended December 31, 2011, 2010 and 2009

Note 10. Long-Term Debt, Net of Current Maturities (in part)

Long-term debt, net of current maturities consists of the following:

	December 31, 2011			
(In thousands)	Outstanding Principal	Unamortized Discount	Unamortized Origination Fees	Long-Term Debt, Net
Boyd Gaming Corporation Debt:				
Bank credit facility	$1,632,750	$(4,318)	$ (6,717)	$1,621,715
9.125% senior notes due 2018	500,000	—	(8,556)	491,444
6.75% senior subordinated notes due 2014	215,668	—	—	215,668
7.125% senior subordinated notes due 2016	240,750	—	—	240,750
Other	11,071	—	—	11,071
	$2,600,239	$(4,318)	$(15,273)	$2,580,648
Borgata Debt:				
Bank credit facility	40,200	—	—	40,200
9.50% senior secured notes due 2015	398,000	(3,271)	(7,680)	387,049
9.875% senior secured notes due 2018	393,500	(2,366)	(8,575)	382,559
	$ 831,700	$(5,637)	$(16,255)	$ 809,808
Less current maturities	43,230	—	—	43,230
Long-term debt, net	$3,388,709	$(9,955)	$(31,528)	$3,347,226

	December 31, 2010			
(In thousands)	Outstanding Principal	Unamortized Discount	Unamortized Origination Fees	Long-Term Debt, Net
Boyd Gaming Corporation Debt:				
Bank credit facility	$1,425,000	$ —	$ —	$1,425,000
9.125% senior notes due 2018	500,000	—	(9,794)	490,206
6.75% senior subordinated notes due 2014	215,668	—	—	215,668
7.125% senior subordinated notes due 2016	240,750	—	—	240,750
Other	11,761	—	—	11,761
	$2,393,179	$ —	$ (9,794)	$2,383,385
Borgata Debt:				
Bank credit facility	60,900	—	—	60,900
9.50% senior secured notes due 2015	400,000	(3,969)	(9,319)	386,712
9.875% senior secured notes due 2018	400,000	(2,648)	(9,594)	387,758
	$ 860,900	$(6,617)	$(18,913)	$ 835,370
Less current maturities	25,690	—	—	25,690
Long-term debt, net	$3,228,389	$(6,617)	$(28,707)	$3,193,065

Boyd Gaming Corporation Debt (in part)

Bank Credit Facility

On December 3, 2010, we entered into an Amendment and Restatement Agreement among certain financial institutions (each a "Lender"), Bank of America, N.A., as administrative agent and letter of credit issuer and Wells Fargo Bank, National Association, as swing line lender (the "Amendment and Restatement Agreement"). Pursuant to the terms of the Amendment and Restatement Agreement, our First Amended and Restated Credit Agreement, dated as of May 24, 2007, as amended by the First Amendment and Consent to First Amended Credit Agreement, dated as of December 21, 2009 (as amended, the "Amended Credit Facility"), was amended and restated to, among other things, (i) reduce the aggregate commitments under the former credit facility and (ii) permit consenting Lenders to extend the maturity date of their commitments, new Lenders to issue revolving commitments and term loans and existing Lenders to increase their commitments (each, an "Extending Lender") in each case with a maturity date five years from the effective date.

The blended interest rate for outstanding borrowings under our Amended Credit Facility was 4.2% and 3.8% at December 31, 2011 and 2010, respectively. At December 31, 2011, approximately $1.63 billion was outstanding under our Amended Credit Facility, with $15.5 million allocated to support various letters of credit, leaving remaining contractual availability of approximately $136.8 million.

The amounts outstanding under the Amended Credit Facility are comprised of the following:

(In thousands)	December 31 2011	2010
Extended Revolving Facility	$ 807,000	$ 572,636
Non-Extended Revolving Facility	—	327,364
Initial Term Loan	475,000	500,000
Incremental Term Loan	338,965	—
Swing Loan	750	25,000
	$1,621,715	$1,425,000

Extended Revolving Facility

Each of the Extending Lenders permanently reduced their commitments under the former credit facility by up to 50% of the amount thereof. As a result, the aggregate commitments under the Amended Credit Facility were reduced from $3 billion to approximately $1.5 billion (excluding the non-extending amounts), which commitments may be increased from time to time by up to $500 million through additional revolving credit or term loans under the Amended Credit Facility. The applicable margin on the outstanding balance on the Extended Revolving Facility ranges from 2.50% to 3.50% (if using LIBOR), and from 1.50% to 2.50% (if using the base rate). The applicable margin on the outstanding balance of the loans and commitments of the non-extending lenders continues to range from 0.625% to 1.625% (if using LIBOR), and from 0.0% to 0.375% (if using the base rate). A fee of a percentage per annum (which ranges from 0.250% to 0.500%) determined by the level of the total leverage ratio is payable on the unused portions of the Amended Credit Facility. The "base rate" under the Amended Credit Facility is the highest of (x) Bank of America's publicly-announced prime rate, (y) the federal funds rate plus 0.50%, or (z) the Eurodollar rate for a one month period plus 1.00%.

The letter of credit fees under the Amended Credit Facility remain the same as those under the Credit Facility; however, the margins payable to Extending Lenders are based on the margins applicable to the Extended Revolving Facility. Subject to certain conditions, amounts outstanding under the Amended Credit Facility may be prepaid without premium or penalty, and the unutilized portion of any of the commitments may be terminated without penalty.

Initial Term Loan

The Amended Credit Facility included the conversion of certain outstanding revolving commitments to a term loan in the amount of $500 million (the "Initial Term Loan"). Pursuant to the terms of the Amended Credit Facility, the Initial Term Loan amortizes in an annual amount equal to 5% of the original principal amount thereof, commencing March 31, 2011,

payable on a quarterly basis. The interest rate per annum applicable to term loans under the Amended Credit Facility are based upon, at the option of the Company, LIBOR or the "base rate," plus an applicable margin in either case. The applicable margin is a percentage per annum determined in accordance with a specified pricing grid based on the total leverage ratio.

Incremental Term Loan

On November 2, 2011, the Company entered into the "Lender Joinder Agreement," which increases the term loan commitments under the Amended Credit Facility by an aggregate amount of $350 million (the "Incremental Term Loan").

The Incremental Term Loan was funded on November 10, 2011, with proceeds being used to repay the outstanding Non-Extended Revolving Facility. The Non-Extended Revolving Facility was terminated in full on November 10, 2011 by borrowing under the Extended Revolving Facility, which augmented the proceeds from the Incremental Term Loan in an amount sufficient to repay the outstanding balance of the Non-Extended Revolving Facility in full.

Pursuant to its terms, the Incremental Term Loan amortizes in an annual amount equal to 5.0% of the original principal amount thereof, commencing in March 2012 and payable on a quarterly basis. At any time and to the extent that the Incremental Term Loan is a Eurodollar Rate Loan, the Incremental Term Loan shall bear interest on the outstanding principal amount thereof for each quarterly interest period at a rate per annual equal to the "effective Eurodollar Rate" for such period plus 4.75%, and at any time and to the extent that the Incremental Term Loan bears interest at the base rate, the outstanding principal amount thereof at a rate per annum equal to the base rate for such Interest Period plus 3.75%.

Guarantees

The Company's obligations under the Amended Credit Facility, subject to certain exceptions, are guaranteed by certain of the Company's subsidiaries and are secured by the capital stock of certain subsidiaries. In addition, subject to certain exceptions, the Company and each of the guarantors granted the administrative agent first priority liens and security interests on substantially all of their real and personal property (other than gaming licenses and subject to certain other exceptions) as additional security for the performance of the secured obligations under the Amended Credit Facility.

Financial and Other Covenants

The Amended Credit Facility contains certain financial and other covenants, including, without limitation, various covenants (i) requiring the maintenance of a minimum consolidated interest coverage ratio of 2.00 to 1.00, (ii) establishing a maximum permitted consolidated total leverage ratio (discussed below), (iii) establishing a maximum permitted secured leverage ratio (discussed below), (iv) imposing limitations on the incurrence of indebtedness, (v) imposing limitations on transfers, sales and other dispositions and (vi) imposing restrictions on investments, dividends and certain other payments. Subject to certain exceptions, the Company may be required to repay the amounts outstanding under the Amended Credit Facility in connection with certain asset sales and issuances of certain additional secured indebtedness.

The minimum consolidated Interest Coverage Ratio (as defined in our Amended Credit Facility) is calculated as (a) twelve-month trailing Consolidated EBITDA (as defined in our Amended Credit Facility) to (b) consolidated interest expense (as also defined in our Amended Credit Facility).

The maximum permitted consolidated Total Leverage Ratio (as defined in our Amended Credit Facility) is calculated as Consolidated Funded Indebtedness to twelve-month trailing Consolidated EBITDA (all capitalized terms are defined in the Amended Credit Facility). The following table provides our maximum Total Leverage Ratio during the remaining term of the Amended Credit Facility.

For the Trailing Four Quarters Ending	Maximum Total Leverage Ratio
December 31, 2010 through and including December 31, 2011	7.75 to 1.00
March 31, 2012 through and including September 30, 2012	7.50 to 1.00
December 31, 2012 and March 31, 2013	7.25 to 1.00
June 30, 2013	7.00 to 1.00
September 30, 2013 and December 31, 2013	6.75 to 1.00
March 31, 2014	6.50 to 1.00
June 30, 2014	6.25 to 1.00
September 30, 2014	6.00 to 1.00
December 31, 2014	5.75 to 1.00
March 31, 2015 and thereafter	5.50 to 1.00

The maximum permitted Secured Leverage Ratio (as defined in our Amended Credit Facility) is calculated as Secured Indebtedness to twelve-month trailing Consolidated EBITDA (all capitalized terms are defined in the Amended Credit Facility). The following table provides our maximum Secured Leverage Ratio during the remaining term of the Amended Credit Facility.

For the Trailing Four Quarters Ending	Minimum Secured Leverage Ratio
December 31, 2010 through and including March 31, 2012	4.50 to 1.00
June 30, 2012 and September 30, 2012	4.25 to 1.00
December 31, 2012 and March 31, 2013	4.00 to 1.00
June 30, 2013 and September 30, 2013	3.75 to 1.00
December 31, 2013 and March 31, 2014	3.50 to 1.00
June 30, 2014 and thereafter	3.25 to 1.00

Compliance with Financial Covenants

We believe that, at December 31, 2011, we were in compliance with the Amended Credit Facility covenants, including the minimum consolidated Interest Coverage Ratio, the maximum permitted consolidated Total Leverage Ratio and the maximum permitted Secured Leverage Ratio, which, at December 31, 2011, were 2.50 to 1.00, 6.80 to 1.00 and 4.27 to 1.00, respectively.

At December 31, 2011, assuming our current level of Consolidated Funded Indebtedness remains constant, we estimate that a 12.3% or greater decline in our twelve-month trailing Consolidated EBITDA, as compared to December 31, 2011, would cause us to exceed our maximum permitted consolidated Total Leverage Ratio covenant for that period. In addition, at December 31, 2011, assuming our current level of Secured Indebtedness remains constant, we estimate that

5.3% or greater decline in our twelve-month trailing Consolidated EBITDA, as compared to December 31, 2011, would cause us to exceed our maximum permitted Secured Leverage Ratio covenant for that period. Additionally, at December 31, 2011, assuming our current level of interest expense remains constant, we estimate that a 20.1% or greater decline in our twelve-month trailing Consolidated EBITDA, as compared to December 31, 2011, would cause us to go below our minimum consolidated Interest Coverage Ratio covenant for that period.

CREDIT AGREEMENTS

DISCLOSURE

2.153 Regulation S-X requires disclosure of the amounts and terms, including commitment fees and conditions for drawdowns, of unused commitments for short-term and long-term financing.

PRESENTATION AND DISCLOSURE EXCERPTS

Credit Agreements

2.154

GAMESTOP CORP. (JAN)

NOTES TO CONSOLIDATED FINANCIAL STATEMENTS

9. Debt (in part)

On January 4, 2011, the Company entered into a $400 million credit agreement (the "Revolver"), which amends and restates, in its entirety, the Company's prior credit agreement entered into on October 11, 2005 (the "Credit Agreement"). The Revolver provides for a five-year, $400 million asset-based facility, including a $50 million letter of credit sublimit, secured by substantially all of the Company's and its domestic subsidiaries' assets. The Company has the ability to increase the facility, which matures in January 2016, by $150 million under certain circumstances. The extension of the Revolver to 2016 reduces our exposure to potential tightening in the credit markets.

The availability under the Revolver is limited to a borrowing base which allows the Company to borrow up to 90% of the appraisal value of the inventory, in each case plus 90% of eligible credit card receivables, net of certain reserves. Letters of credit reduce the amount available to borrow by their face value. The Company's ability to pay cash dividends, redeem options and repurchase shares is generally permitted, except under certain circumstances, including if Revolver excess availability is less than 20%, or is projected to be within 12 months after such payment. In addition, if Revolver usage is projected to be equal to or greater than 25% of the borrowing base during the prospective 12-month period, the

Company is subject to meeting a fixed charge coverage ratio of 1.1:1.0 prior to making such payments. In the event that excess availability under the Revolver is at any time less than the greater of (1) $40.0 million or (2) 12.5% of the lesser of the total commitment or the borrowing base, the Company will be subject to a fixed charge coverage ratio covenant of 1.1:1.0.

The Revolver places certain restrictions on the Company and its subsidiaries, including limitations on asset sales, additional liens, investments, loans, guarantees, acquisitions and the incurrence of additional indebtedness. The per annum interest rate under the Revolver is variable and is calculated by applying a margin (1) for prime rate loans of 1.25% to 1.50% above the highest of (a) the prime rate of the administrative agent, (b) the federal funds effective rate plus 0.50% and (c) the LIBO rate for a 30-day interest period as determined on such day plus 1.00%, and (2) for LIBO rate loans of 2.25% to 2.50% above the LIBO rate. The applicable margin is determined quarterly as a function of the Company's average daily excess availability under the facility and is set at 1.25% for prime rate loans and 2.25% for LIBO rate loans until the first day of the fiscal quarter of the borrowers commencing on May 1, 2011. In addition, the Company is required to pay a commitment fee of 0.375% or 0.50%, depending on facility usage, for any unused portion of the total commitment under the Revolver. As of January 29, 2011 the applicable margin was 1.25% for prime rate loans and 2.25%

for LIBO rate loans while the required commitment fee was 0.50% for the unused portion of the Revolver.

The Revolver provides for customary events of default with corresponding grace periods, including failure to pay any principal or interest when due, failure to comply with covenants, any material representation or warranty made by the Company or the Borrowers proving to be false in any material respect, certain bankruptcy, insolvency or receivership events affecting the Company or its subsidiaries, defaults relating to certain other indebtedness, imposition of certain judgments and mergers or the liquidation of the Company or certain of its subsidiaries.

During fiscal 2010, the Company borrowed and repaid $120.0 million under the prior Credit Agreement. During fiscal 2009, the Company borrowed and repaid $115.0 million under the prior Credit Agreement.

As of January 29, 2011, there were no borrowings outstanding under the Revolver and letters of credit outstanding totaled $8.2 million.

2.155

THE GREAT ATLANTIC & PACIFIC TEA COMPANY, INC. (FEB)

Note 9—Indebtedness and Other Financial Liabilities (in part)

Our debt consists of the following:

	At Feb. 26, 2011			At Feb. 27, 2010
	Indebtedness and Other Financial Liabilities Prior to Financial Statement Classification	Amounts Classified as Subject to Compromise[1]	Indebtedness and Other Financial Liabilities	Indebtedness and Other Financial Liabilities
Debtor-in-Possession Credit Agreement, due June 14, 2012	$ 350,000	$ —	$350,000	$ —
Related Party Promissory Note, due August 18, 2011	10,000	(10,000)	—	10,000
5.125% Convertible Senior Notes, due June 15, 2011	165,000	(165,000)	—	155,333
9.125% Senior Notes, due December 15, 2011	12,840	(12,840)	—	12,840
6.750% Convertible Senior Notes, due December 15, 2012	255,000	(255,000)	—	223,838
11.375% Senior Secured Notes, due August 4, 2015	260,000	(260,000)	—	253,668
9.375% Notes, due August 1, 2039	200,000	(200,000)	—	200,000
Borrowings under Credit Agreement	—	—	—	132,900
Other	2,544	(2,544)	—	1,971
Subtotal	1,255,384	(905,384)	350,000	990,550
Less current portion of long-term debt	(159)	159	—	(191)
Long-term debt	$1,255,225	$(905,225)	$350,000	$990,359

[1] Refer to Note 10—Liabilities subject to compromise for additional information.

Debtor-In-Possession Credit Agreement

In connection with the Bankruptcy Filing, on December 13, 2010, the Bankruptcy Court entered its interim financing order, among other things, permitting us to enter into a Superpriority Debtor-in-Possession Credit Agreement (as amended and restated by that certain Amended and Restated Superpriority Debtor-in-Possession Credit Agreement dated as of December 21, 2010 and further amended by that certain First Amendment thereto dated January 10, 2011,

the "DIP Credit Agreement") with JPMorgan Chase Bank, N.A., as administrative agent and as collateral agent (in such capacity, the "Agent"), the lenders from time to time party thereto (collectively, the "DIP Lenders") and our Company and certain subsidiaries as borrowers thereunder. On December 14, 2010, we satisfied all of the conditions to the effectiveness of the DIP Credit Agreement and consummated the transactions contemplated thereunder including the refinancing in full of our Company's and its applicable subsidiaries' obligations under the pre-existing first lien credit facility. Pursuant to the terms of the DIP Credit Agreement:

- the DIP Lenders agreed to lend up to $800.0 million in the form of a $350.0 million term loan and a $450.0 million revolving credit facility with a $250.0 million sublimit for letters of credit, in each case subject to the terms and conditions therein;
- our Company's and the Subsidiary Borrower's obligations under the DIP Credit Agreement and the other specified loan documents are guaranteed by our Company's certain other subsidiaries that are Debtors ("Subsidiary Guarantors" and, together with our Company and the Subsidiary Borrowers, the "Loan Parties"); and
- the Loan Parties' obligations under the DIP Credit Agreement and such other specified loan documents are secured by a security interest in, and lien upon, substantially all of the Loan Parties' existing and after-acquired personal and real property, having the priority and subject to the terms therein and in the order(s) entered into by the Bankruptcy Court, as applicable.

Our Company will have the option to have interest on the revolving loans under the revolving credit facility provided under the DIP Credit Agreement accrue at an alternate base rate plus 200 basis points or at adjusted LIBOR plus 300 basis points. Our Company will have the option to have interest on the term loan provided under the DIP Credit Agreement accrue at an alternate base rate plus 600 basis points or at adjusted LIBOR (with a floor of 175 basis points) plus 700 basis points. The DIP Credit Agreement limits, among other things, our Company's and the other Loan Parties' ability to (i) incur indebtedness, (ii) incur or create liens, (iii) dispose of assets, (iv) prepay certain indebtedness and make other restricted payments, (v) enter into sale and leaseback transactions and (vi) modify the terms of certain indebtedness and certain material contracts.

The DIP Credit Agreement also contains certain financial covenants, including a minimum excess availability covenant of $100.0 million, minimum liquidity covenant of $100.0 million and minimum cumulative EBITDA covenant as defined in the DIP Credit Agreement. Minimum cumulative EBITDA measured beginning on April 24, 2011 is as follows (in millions):

Date	Minimum Cumulative EBITDA
August 13, 2011	$ —
September 10, 2011	10.0
October 8, 2011	20.0
November 5, 2011	35.0
December 3, 2011	50.0
December 31, 2011	65.0
January 28, 2012	90.0
February 25, 2012	100.0
March 24, 2012	110.0
April 21, 2012	125.0
May 19, 2012	150.0
June 16, 2012	175.0

We are currently in compliance with all covenants. Meeting our EBITDA covenant requires increasing levels of performance throughout the year. Achieving this improving performance will require our Company to successfully implement our business improvement initiatives beginning as early as June 2011 with the benefits reflected in our results shortly thereafter. The DIP Credit Agreement matures upon the earliest to occur of (a) June 14, 2012, (b) the acceleration of the loans and the termination of the commitment thereunder, and (c) the substantial consummation (as defined in Section 1101(2) of the Bankruptcy Code, which for purposes hereof shall be no later than the effective date thereof) of a plan of reorganization that is confirmed pursuant to an order entered by the Bankruptcy Court. The Bankruptcy Court entered a final order approving the DIP Credit Agreement on January 11, 2011.

LONG-TERM LEASES

RECOGNITION AND MEASUREMENT

2.156 FASB ASC 840 establishes standards of financial accounting and reporting for leases on the financial statements of lessees and lessors. FASB ASC 840 classifies leases as capital or operating. Capital leases are accounted for as the acquisition of an asset and the incurrence of an obligation by the lessee and as a sale or financing by the lessor. All other leases are accounted for as operating leases.

PRESENTATION

2.157 Under FASB ASC 840-30, lessees should separately identify on the balance sheet or notes thereto assets recorded under capital leases, the accumulated amortization thereon, and obligations. Capital lease obligations are subject to the same considerations as other obligations in classifying them with current and noncurrent liabilities in classified balance sheets. Similarly, a lessor's net investment in a sales-type or direct financing lease is also subject to the same considerations as other assets in classification as current or noncurrent assets.

2.158 FASB ASC 840-20 requires that lessors include property subject to operating leases with or near property, plant, and equipment in the balance sheet. Accumulated depreciation should be deducted by lessors from the investments in the leased property.

DISCLOSURE

2.159 FASB ASC 840-20-50 and 840-30-50 contain detailed disclosure requirements for lessors and lessees under operating and capital leases, respectively.

PRESENTATION AND DISCLOSURE EXCERPTS

Lessee Leases

2.160

GRIFFON CORPORATION (SEP)

CONSOLIDATED BALANCE SHEETS (in part)

(In thousands, except per share data)

	At September 30, 2011	At September 30, 2010
Current Assets		
Cash and equivalents	$ 243,029	$ 169,802
Accounts receivable, net of allowances of $6,072 and $6,581	268,026	252,852
Contract costs and recognized income not yet billed, net of progress payments of $9,697 and $1,423	74,737	63,155
Inventories, net	263,809	268,801
Prepaid and other current assets	48,828	55,782
Assets of discontinued operations	1,381	1,079
Total current assets	899,810	811,471
Property, plant and equipment, net	350,050	314,760
Goodwill	357,333	360,749
Intangible assets, net	223,189	233,011
Other assets	31,197	27,907
Assets of discontinued operations	3,675	5,803
Total assets	$1,865,254	$1,753,701

NOTES TO CONSOLIDATED FINANCIAL STATEMENTS

(Dollars in thousands, except per share data)

(Unless otherwise indicated, all references to years or year-end refer to Griffon's fiscal period ending September 30)

Note 1—Description of Business and Summary of Significant Accounting Policies (in part)

Property, Plant and Equipment (in part)

Property, plant and equipment includes the historical cost of land, buildings, equipment and significant improvements to existing plant and equipment. Expenditures for maintenance, repairs and minor renewals are expensed as incurred. When property or equipment is sold or otherwise disposed of, the related cost and accumulated depreciation is removed from the respective accounts and the gain or loss is realized in income.

Depreciation expense, which includes amortization of assets under capital leases, was $52,844, $38,456 and $40,919 for the years ended September 30, 2011, 2010 and 2009, respectively, and was calculated on a straight-line basis over the estimated useful lives of the assets. Estimated useful lives for property, plant and equipment are as follows: buildings and building improvements, 25 to 40 years; machinery and equipment, 2 to 15 years and leasehold improvements, over the term of the lease or life of the improvement, whichever is shorter.

Note 10—Notes Payable, Capitalized Leases and Long-Term Debt (in part)

The present value of the net minimum payments on capitalized leases as of September 30, 2011 is as follows:

	At September 30, 2011
Total minimum lease payments	$15,126
Less amount representing interest	(3,230)
Present value of net minimum lease payments	11,896
Current portion	(1,046)
Capitalized lease obligation, less current portion	$10,850

Minimum payments under current capital leases for the next five years are as follows: $1,598 in 2012, $1,610 in 2013, $1,560 in 2014, $1,532 in 2015 and $1,497 in 2016.

Included in the consolidated balance sheet at September 30, 2011 under property, plant and equipment are cost and accumulated depreciation subject to capitalized leases of $10,501 and $1,197, respectively, and included in other assets are deferred interest charges of $257. At September 30, 2010, the amounts subject to capitalized leases were $10,046 and $647, respectively, and included in other assets were deferred interest charges of $283 and restricted cash, for investment in the Troy, Ohio facility, of $4,629. The capitalized leases carry interest rates from 5% to 10% and mature from 2012 through 2022.

In October 2006, a subsidiary of Griffon entered into a capital lease totaling $14,290 for real estate it occupies in Troy, Ohio. Approximately $10,000 was used to acquire the building and the remaining amount is restricted for improvements. The lease matures in 2021, bears interest at a fixed rate of 5.1%, is secured by a mortgage on the real estate and is guaranteed by Griffon.

2.161

CAREER EDUCATION CORPORATION (DEC)

CONSOLIDATED BALANCE SHEETS (in part)

(In thousands, except share and per share amounts)

	As of December 31	
	2011	2010
Liabilities and Stockholders' Equity		
(in part)		
Current liabilities:		
Current maturities of capital lease obligations	$ 844	$ 783
Accounts payable	48,408	53,115
Accrued expenses:		
Payroll and related benefits	41,853	72,657
Advertising and production costs	17,717	18,846
Earnout payments	5,735	17,439
Other	61,536	96,664
Deferred tuition revenue	144,947	152,590
Liabilities of discontinued operations	8,403	44,990
Total current liabilities	329,443	457,084
Non-current liabilities:		
Capital lease obligations, net of current maturities	207	1,223
Deferred rent obligations	102,079	103,872
Earnout payments	—	7,690
Other liabilities	40,365	30,047
Liabilities of discontinued operations	37,935	38,507
Total non-current liabilities	180,586	181,339

NOTES TO CONSOLIDATED FINANCIAL STATEMENTS

December 31, 2011, 2010 and 2009

9. Leases (in part)

We lease most of our administrative and educational facilities and certain equipment under non-cancelable operating leases expiring at various dates through 2028. Lease terms generally range from five to ten years with one to two renewal options for extended terms. In most cases, we are required to make additional payments under facility operating leases for taxes, insurance and other operating expenses incurred during the operating lease period.

Certain of our leases contain rent escalation clauses or lease incentives, including rent abatements and tenant improvement allowances. Rent escalation clauses and lease incentives are taken into account in determining total rent expense to be recognized during the term of the lease, which begins on the date we take control of the leased space. Renewal options are taken into account in evaluating the overall term of the lease. In accordance with FASB ASC Topic 840—*Leases*, differences between periodic rent expense and periodic cash rental payments, caused primarily by the recognition of rent expense on a straight-line basis and tenant improvement allowances due or received from lessors, are recorded as deferred rent obligations on our consolidated balance sheets.

In addition, we have financed the acquisition of certain property and equipment through capital lease arrangements and have assumed capital lease obligations in connection with certain acquisitions. The current portion of our capital lease obligations for continuing operations is included within current maturities of capital lease obligations on our consolidated balance sheets, and the non-current portion of our capital lease obligations is included within capital lease obligations, net of current maturities on our consolidated balance sheets. The cost basis and accumulated depreciation of assets recorded under capital leases from continuing operating activities, which are included in property and equipment, are as follows as of December 31, 2011 and 2010:

	December 31	
(Dollars in thousands)	2011	2010
Cost	$ 9,143	$ 9,320
Accumulated depreciation	(6,691)	(5,910)
Net book value	$ 2,452	$ 3,410

Depreciation expense for continuing operations recorded in connection with assets recorded under capital leases was $0.9 million, $0.6 million, and $1.2 million for the years ended December 31, 2011, 2010 and 2009, respectively.

Remaining Lease Obligations (in part)

We have recorded lease exit costs over the past three years associated with our exit of space within Corporate & Other, Culinary Arts, AIU, Art & Design and Health Education. These costs are recorded within educational services and facilities expense on our consolidated statements of operations. The current portion of the liability for these charges is reflected within other accrued expenses under current liabilities and the long-term portion of these charges are included in other liabilities under the non-current liabilities section of our consolidated balance sheets. Changes in our future minimum lease obligations for the years ended December 31, 2011, 2010 and 2009 were as follows:

(Dollars in thousands)	Balance, Beginning of Period	Charges Incurred[1]	Net Cash Payments	Other[2]	Balance, End of Period
For the twelve months ended December 31, 2011	$18,219	$ 1,291	$(6,847)	$292	$12,955
For the twelve months ended December 31, 2010	$20,160	$ 4,557	$(6,414)	$ (84)	$18,219
For the twelve months ended December 31, 2009	$ 8,603	$15,837	$(4,505)	$225	$20,160

[1] Includes charges for newly vacated spaces and subsequent adjustments for accretion, revised estimates and variances between estimated and actual charges, net of any reversals for terminated lease obligations.

[2] Includes existing deferred rent liability balances for newly vacated spaces that offset the losses incurred in the period recorded.

As of December 31, 2011, future minimum lease payments under capital leases and operating leases for continuing and discontinued operations are as follows:

(Dollars in thousands)	Capital Leases	Operating Leases Continuing Operations	Operating Leases Discontinued Operations	Total
2012	$1,049	$101,656	$13,388	$116,093
2013	212	98,596	13,738	$112,546
2014	—	93,552	13,893	$107,445
2015	—	81,762	12,750	$ 94,512
2016	—	67,718	9,909	$ 77,627
2017 and thereafter	—	195,750	13,710	$209,460
Total	$1,261	$639,034	$77,388	$717,683
Less—Portion representing interest at annual rates ranging from 5.21% to 6.25%	(210)			
Principal	1,051			
Less—Current portion	(844)			
	$ 207			

2.162

FRED'S, INC. (JAN)

MANAGEMENT'S DISCUSSION AND ANALYSIS OF FINANCIAL CONDITION AND RESULTS OF OPERATIONS

Contractual Obligations and Commercial Commitments (in part)

As discussed in Note 5 to the Consolidated Financial Statements, the Company leases certain of its store locations under noncancelable operating leases expiring at various dates through 2029. Many of these leases contain renewal options and require the Company to pay contingent rent based upon a percentage of sales, taxes, maintenance, insurance and certain other operating expenses applicable to the leased properties. In addition, the Company leases various equipment under noncancelable operating leases.

The following table summarizes the Company's significant contractual obligations as of January 29, 2011, which excludes the effect of imputed interest:

(Dollars in thousands)	2011	2012	2013	2014	2015	Thereafter	Total
Operating leases[1]	$ 46,266	$39,852	$29,073	$19,981	$14,032	$25,561	$174,765
Inventory purchase obligations[2]	105,966						105,966
Equipment leases[3]	2,487	1,469	1,066	945	710	916	7,593
Mortgage loans on land & buildings and other[4]	201	170	1,109	525	520	1,645	4,170
Postretirement benefits[5]	41	41	44	46	44	241	457
Total contractual obligations	$154,961	$41,532	$31,292	$21,497	$15,306	$28,363	$292,951

[1] Operating leases are described in Note 5 to the Consolidated Financial Statements.
[2] Inventory purchase obligations represent open purchase orders and any outstanding purchase commitments as of January 29, 2011.
[3] Equipment leases represent the cooler program and other equipment operating leases.
[4] Mortgage loans for purchased land and buildings and other debt.
[5] Postretirement benefits are described in Note 9 to the Consolidated Financial Statements.

NOTES TO CONSOLIDATED FINANCIAL STATEMENTS

Note 1—Description of Business and Summary of Significant Accounting Policies (in part)

Property and equipment. Property and equipment are carried at cost. Depreciation is recorded using the straight-line method over the estimated useful lives of the assets. Improvements to leased premises are depreciated using the straight-line method over the shorter of the initial term of the lease or the useful life of the improvement. Leasehold improvements added late in the lease term are depreciated over the shorter of the remaining term of the lease (including the upcoming renewal option, if the renewal is reasonably assured) or the useful life of the improvement, whichever is lesser. Gains or losses on the sale of assets are recorded at disposal. The following average estimated useful lives are generally applied:

	Estimated Useful Lives
Building and building improvements	8–31.5 years
Furniture, fixtures and equipment	3–10 years
Leasehold improvements	3–10 years or term of lease, if shorter
Automobiles and vehicles	3–6 years
Airplane	9 years

Assets under capital lease are depreciated in accordance with the Company's normal depreciation policy for owned assets or over the lease term (regardless of renewal options), if shorter, and the charge to earnings is included in depreciation expense in the Consolidated Financial Statements. We did not incur any depreciation expense on assets under capital lease for 2010 as the assets were fully depreciated.

Leases. Certain operating leases include rent increases during the initial lease term. For these leases, the Company recognizes the related rental expense on a straight-line basis over the term of the lease (which includes the pre-opening period of construction, renovation, fixturing and merchandise placement) and records the difference between the amounts charged to operations and amounts paid as a rent liability. Rent is recognized on a straight-line basis over the lease term, which includes any rent holiday period.

The Company recognizes contingent rental expense when the achievement of specified sales targets are considered probable in accordance with FASB ASC 840 "Leases." The amount expensed but not paid was $1.0 million and $1.1 million at January 29, 2011 and January 30, 2010 respectively, and is included in "Accrued expenses and other" in the consolidated balance sheet (See Note 2).

The Company occasionally receives reimbursements from landlords to be used towards construction of the store the Company intends to lease. The reimbursement is primarily for the purpose of performing work required to divide a much larger location into smaller segments, one of which the Company will use for its store. This work could include the addition or demolition of walls, separation of plumbing, utilities, electrical work, entrances (front and back) and other work as required. Leasehold improvements are recorded at their gross costs including items reimbursed by landlords. The reimbursements are initially recorded as a deferred credit and then amortized as a reduction of rent expense over the initial lease term.

Based upon an overall analysis of store performance and expected trends, we periodically evaluate the need to close underperforming stores. When we determine that an underperforming store should be closed and a lease obligation still exists, we record the estimated future liability associated with the rental obligation on the date the store is closed in accordance with FASB ASC 420, "Exit or Disposal Cost Obligations." Liabilities are computed based at the point of closure for the present value of any remaining operating lease obligations, net of estimated sublease income, and at the communication date for severance and other exit costs, as prescribed by FASB ASC 420. The assumptions in calculating the liability include the timeframe expected to terminate the lease agreement, estimates related to the sublease of potential closed locations, and estimation of other related exit costs. If the actual timing and the potential termination costs or realization of sublease income differ from our estimates, the resulting liabilities could vary from recorded amounts. We periodically review the liability for closed stores and make adjustments when necessary.

Note 5—Long-Term Leases (in part)

The Company leases certain of its store locations under noncancelable operating leases that require monthly rental payments primarily at fixed rates (although a number of the leases provide for additional rent based upon sales) expiring at various dates through fiscal 2029. None of our operating leases contain residual value guarantees. Many of these leases contain renewal options and require the Company to pay taxes, maintenance, insurance and certain other operating expenses applicable to the leased properties. In addition, the Company leases various equipment under noncancelable operating leases. Total rent expense under operating leases was $53.4 million, $53.2 million and $54.1 million, for 2010, 2009 and 2008, respectively. Total contingent rentals included in operating leases above was $1.0 million for 2010 and $1.1 million for 2009 and 2008.

Future minimum rental payments under all operating leases as of January 29, 2011 are as follows:

(In thousands)	Operating Leases
2011	$ 46,266
2012	39,852
2013	29,073
2014	19,981
2015	14,032
Thereafter	25,561
Total minimum lease payments	$174,765

The gross amount of property and equipment under capital leases was $5.0 million at January 29, 2011 and $5.0 million at January 30, 2010. Accumulated depreciation on property and equipment under capital leases was $5.0 million at January 29, 2011 and January 30, 2010, respectively. We did not incur any depreciation expense on assets under capital lease for 2010 as the assets were fully depreciated. Depreciation expense on assets under capital lease for 2009 and 2008 was $39 thousand and $92 thousand, respectively.

Note 11—Exit and Disposal Activity (in part)

Lease Termination

For store closures where a lease obligation still exists, we record the estimated future liability associated with the rental obligation on the cease use date (when the store is closed) in accordance with FASB ASC 420, "Exit or Disposal Cost Obligations." Liabilities are established at the cease use date for the present value of any remaining operating lease obligations, net of estimated sublease income, and at the communication date for severance and other exit costs, as prescribed by FASB ASC 420. Key assumptions in calculating the liability include the timeframe expected to terminate lease agreements, estimates related to the sublease potential of closed locations, and estimation of other related exit costs. If actual timing and potential termination costs or realization of sublease income differ from our estimates, the resulting liabilities could vary from recorded amounts. These liabilities are reviewed periodically and adjusted when necessary.

During fiscal 2007, we closed 17 underperforming stores and recorded lease contract termination costs of $1.6 million in rent expense in conjunction with those closings, of which $1.0 million was utilized during fiscal 2007, leaving $.6 million in the reserve at the beginning of fiscal year 2008.

During fiscal 2008, we closed 74 underperforming stores and recorded lease contract termination costs of $10.5 million, of which $9.6 million was charged to rent expense and $.9 million reduced the liability for deferred rent. We utilized

$7.7 million during the period, leaving $3.4 million in the reserve at January 31, 2009.

During fiscal 2009, we reserved an additional $0.1 million in rent expense related to the 9 store closings. We utilized $2.4 million during the period, leaving $1.1 million in the reserve at January 30, 2010.

During fiscal 2010, we reserved an additional $0.6 million in rent expense related to the revision of the estimated amount of the remaining lease liability for the fiscal 2008 and 2009 store closures. We also utilized $1.0 million, leaving $.7 million in the reserve at January 29, 2011.

The following table illustrates the exit and disposal activity related to the store closures discussed in the previous paragraphs (in millions):

	Beginning Balance January 30, 2010	Additions FY10	Utilized FY10	Ending Balance January 29, 2011
Lease contract termination liability	$1.1	$0.6	$(1.0)	$0.7

Lessor Leases

2.163

JACK IN THE BOX INC. (SEP)

CONSOLIDATED BALANCE SHEETS (in part)

(Dollars in thousands, except per share data)

	October 2, 2011	October 3, 2010
Assets (in part)		
Current assets:		
Cash and cash equivalents	$ 11,424	$ 10,607
Accounts and other receivables, net	86,213	81,150
Inventories	38,931	37,391
Prepaid expenses	18,737	36,100
Deferred income taxes	45,520	46,185
Assets held for sale and leaseback	51,793	59,897
Other current assets	1,793	3,592
Total current assets	254,411	274,922

NOTES TO CONSOLIDATED FINANCIAL STATEMENTS

1. Nature of Operations and Summary of Significant Accounting Policies (in part)

Accounts and other receivables, net is primarily comprised of receivables from franchisees, tenants and credit card processors. Franchisee receivables primarily include rents, royalties, and marketing fees associated with the franchise agreements, and receivables arising from distribution services provided to most franchisees. Tenant receivables relate to subleased properties where we are on the master lease agreement. We charge interest on past due accounts receivable and accrue interest on notes receivable based on the contractual terms. The allowance for doubtful accounts is based on historical experience and a review of existing receivables. Changes in accounts and other receivables are classified as an operating activity in the consolidated statements of cash flows.

8. Leases (in part)

As lessor—We lease or sublease restaurants to certain franchisees and others under agreements that generally provide for the payment of percentage rentals in excess of stipulated minimum rentals, usually for a period of 20 years. Most of our leases have rent escalation clauses and renewal clauses of 5 to 20 years. Total rental income was $166.9 million, $133.8 million and $105.5 million, including contingent rentals of $10.4 million, $7.7 million and $13.0 million, in 2011, 2010 and 2009, respectively.

The minimum rents receivable expected to be received under these non-cancelable operating leases, excluding contingent rentals, as of October 2, 2011 are as follows *(in thousands)*:

Fiscal Year

2012	$ 160,795
2013	172,879
2014	171,848
2015	170,502
2016	184,239
Thereafter	1,711,989
Total minimum future rentals	$2,572,252

Assets held for lease consisted of the following at each year-end *(in thousands)*:

	2011	2010
Land	$ 63,839	$ 49,913
Buildings	583,168	410,823
Equipment	3,244	373
	650,251	461,109
Less accumulated depreciation	(298,801)	(207,616)
	$351,450	$253,493

OTHER NONCURRENT LIABILITIES

PRESENTATION

2.164 FASB ASC 210 indicates that liabilities classified as noncurrent (that is, beyond the operating cycle) include long-term deferments of the delivery of goods or services, such as the issuance of a long-term warranty or the advance receipt by a lessor of rental for the final period of a 10-year lease. Similarly, a loan on a life insurance policy with the intent that it will not be paid but will be liquidated by deduction from the proceeds of the policy upon maturity or cancellation should be excluded from current liabilities.

2.165 FASB ASC 480, *Distinguishing Liabilities from Equity*, requires that an issuer classify certain financial instruments with characteristics of both liabilities and equity as liabilities. Some issuances of stock, such as mandatorily redeemable preferred stock, impose unconditional obligations requiring the issuer to transfer assets or issue its equity shares. FASB ASC 480 requires an issuer to classify such financial instruments as liabilities, not present them between the "Liabilities" and "Equity" sections of the balance sheet. Rule 5-02 of Regulation S-X includes matters related to redeemable preferred stocks to be stated on the face of the balance sheet or included in the notes.

2.166 Rule 5-02 of Regulation S-X requires that any item not classed in another Regulation S-X liability caption and in excess of 5 percent of total liabilities be stated separately on the balance sheet or disclosed in the notes. Regulation S-X also requires that deferred income taxes, deferred tax credits, and deferred income be stated separately in the balance sheet.

2.167 Rule 5-02 of Regulation S-X includes a balance sheet caption for commitments and contingent liabilities. When commitments or contingent liabilities exist and are disclosed in footnotes, registrants customarily include a caption on the balance sheet without an amount but with a reference to the related footnote.

2.168

TABLE 2-12: OTHER NONCURRENT LIABILITIES—RELATED TO EMPLOYEES*

Table 2-12 shows other noncurrent liabilities related to employees.

	Number of Entities		
	2011	2010	2009
Pension accruals	326	295	311
Benefits	264	255	268
Deferred compensation	100	77	65
Workers' compensation	39	22	N/C^
Other, described	35	32	24

* Appearing in the balance sheet or notes to financial statements, or both.

^ N/C = Not compiled. Line item was not included in the table for the year shown.

2.169

TABLE 2-13: OTHER NONCURRENT LIABILITIES—DEFERRED CREDITS*

Table 2-13 shows the entities' deferred credits.

	Number of Entities		
	2011	2010	2009
Deferred profit, income, gain, revenue from sale of assets	28	14	N/C^
Described deferred profit, income, gain, revenue—other than sale of assets	45	36	N/C^
Deferred profit/credit/income/revenue—nature not disclosed	25	40	N/C^
Deferred subscription revenue	6	4	N/C^
Deferred service contract income	12	9	N/C^
Grants	—	2	N/C^
Deferred rent revenue	21	22	N/C^
Other, described	17	9	N/C^

* Appearing in the balance sheet or notes to financial statements, or both.
^ N/C = Not compiled. Line item was not included in the table for the year shown.

2.170

TABLE 2-14: OTHER NONCURRENT LIABILITIES—OTHER THAN EMPLOYEE RELATED AND DEFERRED CREDITS*

Table 2-14 shows all other noncurrent liabilities besides those related to employees and deferred credits.

	Number of Entities		
	2011	2010	2009
Redeemable noncontrolling/minority interest	20	15	65
Deferred income taxes	350	314	340
Tax uncertainties	144	120	155
Interest/penalties on tax uncertainties	66	34	33
Insurance	55	46	46
Discontinued operations/restructuring	49	52	58
Preferred stock	2	2	13
Warranties	45	30	28
Guarantees	15	9	N/C^
Environmental	62	62	70
Asset retirement obligations	40	37	43
Litigation	23	16	23
Derivatives	107	87	152
Other, described	96	87	72

* Appearing in the balance sheet or notes to financial statements, or both.
^ N/C = Not compiled. Line item was not included in the table for the year shown.

PRESENTATION AND DISCLOSURE EXCERPTS

Deferred Income Taxes

2.171

WORTHINGTON INDUSTRIES, INC. (MAY)

CONSOLIDATED BALANCE SHEETS (in part)

(Dollars in thousands)

	May 31	
	2011	2010
Liabilities and Equity *(in part)*		
Current liabilities:		
Accounts payable	$253,404	$258,730
Short-term borrowings	132,956	—
Accrued compensation, contributions to employee benefit plans and related taxes	72,312	62,413
Dividends payable	7,175	7,932
Other accrued items	52,023	41,635
Income taxes payable	7,132	9,092
Total current liabilities	525,002	379,802
Other liabilities	67,309	68,380
Long-term debt	250,254	250,238
Deferred income taxes	83,981	71,893
Total liabilities	926,546	770,313

NOTES TO CONSOLIDATED FINANCIAL STATEMENTS

Fiscal Years Ended May 31, 2011, 2010 and 2009

Note K—Income Taxes

Earnings (loss) before income taxes for the years ended May 31 include the following components:

(In thousands)	2011	2010	2009
United States based operations	$166,137	$73,122	$(170,405)
Non—United States based operations	16,393	5,035	28,966
Earnings (loss) before income taxes	182,530	78,157	(141,439)
Less: Net earnings attributable to noncontrolling interests*	8,968	6,266	4,529
Earnings (loss) before income taxes attributable to controlling interest	$173,562	$71,891	$(145,968)

* Net earnings attributable to noncontrolling interests are not taxable to Worthington.

Significant components of income tax expense (benefit) for the years ended May 31 were as follows:

(In thousands)	2011	2010	2009
Current:			
Federal	$47,698	$30,080	$(21,609)
State and local	1,246	1,333	3,146
Foreign	2,070	1,347	6,188
	51,014	32,760	(12,275)
Deferred:			
Federal	3,950	(6,804)	(19,393)
State	3,599	1,399	(4,359)
Foreign	(67)	(705)	(1,727)
	7,482	(6,110)	(25,479)
	$58,496	$26,650	$(37,754)

Tax benefits related to stock-based compensation that were credited to additional paid-in capital were $835,000, $6,000, and $433,000 for fiscal 2011, fiscal 2010 and fiscal 2009, respectively. Tax benefits (expenses) related to defined benefit pension liability that were credited to (deducted from) other comprehensive income (loss) ("OCI") were ($760,000), $1,163,000, and $14,000 for fiscal 2011, fiscal 2010 and fiscal 2009, respectively. Tax benefits (expenses) related to cash flow hedges that were credited to (deducted from) OCI were $563,000, $854,000, and $3,187,000 for fiscal 2011, fiscal 2010 and fiscal 2009, respectively.

A reconciliation of the 35% federal statutory tax rate to total tax provision (benefit) follows:

	2011	2010	2009
Federal statutory rate	35.0%	35.0%	35.0%
State and local income taxes, net of federal tax benefit	1.8	(1.5)	2.3
Change in state and local valuation allowances	1.0	5.0	(0.7)
Change in income tax accruals for resolution of tax audits and change in estimate of deferred tax	0.2	1.6	(0.1)
Non-U.S. income taxes at other than 35%	(2.2)	(1.6)	3.9
Qualified production activities deduction	(1.9)	(2.1)	—
Goodwill impairment non-deductible	—	—	(13.9)
Other	(0.2)	0.7	(0.6)
Effective tax rate attributable to controlling interest	33.7%	37.1%	25.9%

The above effective tax rate attributable to controlling interest excludes any impact from the inclusion of net earnings attributable to noncontrolling interests in our consolidated statements of earnings. The effective tax rates upon inclusion of net earnings attributable to noncontrolling interests were 32.0%, 34.1% and 26.7% for fiscal 2011, fiscal 2010 and fiscal 2009, respectively. The change in effective income tax rates, upon inclusion of net earnings attributable to noncontrolling interests, is primarily a result of our Spartan consolidated joint venture. The earnings attributable to the noncontrolling interest in Spartan do not generate tax expense to Worthington since the investors in Spartan are taxed directly based on the earnings attributable to them.

Under applicable accounting guidance, a tax benefit may be recognized from an uncertain tax position only if it is more likely than not that the tax position will be sustained on examination by the taxing authorities, including resolution of any related appeals or litigation processes, based on the technical merits of the position. Any tax benefits recognized in our financial statements from such a position were measured based on the largest benefit that has a greater than fifty percent likelihood of being realized upon ultimate settlement.

The total amount of unrecognized tax benefits were $5,381,000, $5,933,000, and $3,897,000 as of May 31, 2011, May 31, 2010 and May 31, 2009, respectively. The total amount of unrecognized tax benefits that, if recognized, would affect the effective tax rate attributable to controlling interest was $3,361,000 as of May 31, 2011. Unrecognized tax benefits are the differences between a tax position taken, or expected to be taken in a tax return, and the benefit recognized for accounting purposes. Accrued amounts of interest and penalties related to unrecognized tax benefits are recognized as part of income tax expense within our consolidated statements of earnings. As of May 31, 2011, May 31, 2010 and May 31, 2009, we had accrued liabilities of $1,184,000, $1,232,000 and $1,143,000, respectively, for interest and penalties related to unrecognized tax benefits.

A tabular reconciliation of unrecognized tax benefits follows:

(In thousands)	
Balance at June 1, 2010	$5,933
Increases—tax positions taken in prior years	584
Decreases—tax positions taken in prior years	(505)
Increases—current tax positions	745
Settlements	(934)
Lapse of statutes of limitations	(442)
Balance at May 31, 2011	$5,381

Approximately $620,000 of the liability for unrecognized tax benefits is expected to be settled in the next twelve months due to the expiration of statutes of limitations in various tax jurisdictions and as a result of expected settlements with various tax jurisdictions. While it is expected that the amount of unrecognized tax benefits will change in the next twelve months, any change is not expected to have a material impact on our consolidated financial position, results of operations or cash flows.

Following is a summary of the tax years open to examination by major tax jurisdiction:

U.S. Federal—2007 and forward
U.S. State and Local—2003 and forward
Austria—2004 and forward
Canada—2007 and forward

Earnings before income taxes attributable to foreign sources for fiscal 2011, fiscal 2010 and fiscal 2009 were as noted above. As of May 31, 2011, and based on the tax laws in effect at that time, it remains our intention to continue to indefinitely reinvest our undistributed foreign earnings, except for the foreign earnings of our TWB joint venture. Accordingly, no deferred tax liability has been recorded for those foreign earnings. Undistributed earnings of our consolidated foreign subsidiaries at May 31, 2011 were approximately $265,000,000. If such earnings were not permanently reinvested, a deferred tax liability of approximately $23,000,000 would have been required.

The components of our deferred tax assets and liabilities as of May 31 were as follows:

(In thousands)	2011	2010
Deferred tax assets:		
Accounts receivable	$ 1,870	$ 2,938
Inventories	5,932	4,005
Accrued expenses	29,227	21,712
Net operating and capital loss carryforwards	22,501	22,418
Tax credit carryforwards	1,265	2,127
Stock-based compensation	7,187	5,761
Derivative contracts	3,761	3,410
Other	7	58
Total deferred tax assets	71,750	62,429
Valuation allowance for deferred tax assets	(22,292)	(19,629)
Net deferred tax assets	49,458	42,800
Deferred tax liabilities:		
Property, plant and equipment	(58,606)	(67,317)
Undistributed earnings of unconsolidated affiliates	(43,947)	(20,893)
Other	(583)	(1,243)
Total deferred tax liabilities	(103,136)	(89,453)
Net deferred tax liabilities	$ (53,678)	$(46,653)

The above amounts are classified in the consolidated balance sheets as of May 31 as follows:

(In thousands)	2011	2010
Current assets:		
Deferred income taxes	$ 28,297	$ 21,964
Other assets:		
Deferred income taxes	2,006	3,276
Noncurrent liabilities:		
Deferred income taxes	(83,981)	(71,893)
Net deferred tax liabilities	$(53,678)	$(46,653)

At May 31, 2011, we had tax benefits for federal net operating loss carryforwards of $205,000 that expire from fiscal 2012 to the fiscal year ending May 31, 2020. These net operating loss carryforwards are subject to utilization limitations. At May 31, 2011, we had tax benefits for state net operating loss carryforwards of $18,184,000 that expire from fiscal 2012 to the fiscal year ending May 31, 2031. At May 31, 2011, we had tax benefits for foreign net operating loss carryforwards of $2,728,000 for income tax purposes that expire from fiscal 2012 to the fiscal year ending May 31, 2031. At May 31, 2011, we had a tax benefit for a foreign capital loss carryforward of $1,384,000 with no future expiration date. At May 31, 2011,

we had tax benefits for foreign tax credit carryforwards of $1,265,000 that expire in the fiscal year ending May 31, 2021.

The valuation allowance for deferred tax assets of $22,292,000 is associated primarily with the net operating and capital loss carryforwards and foreign tax credit carryforwards. The valuation allowance includes $1,470,000 for federal, $17,404,000 for state and $3,418,000 for foreign. The majority of the federal valuation allowance relates to foreign tax credits with the remainder relating to the net operating loss carryforwards. The majority of the state valuation allowance relates to Metal Framing operations in various states and our Decatur, Alabama facility, while the foreign valuation allowance relates to operations in China, Canada, and the Czech Republic. Based on our history of profitability and taxable income projections, we have determined that it is more likely than not that the remaining net deferred tax assets are otherwise realizable.

Taxes Payable

2.172

QUANEX BUILDING PRODUCTS CORPORATION (OCT)

CONSOLIDATED BALANCE SHEETS (in part)

(In thousands, except share data)	October 31	
	2011	2010
Liabilities and Stockholders' Equity (in part)		
Current liabilities:		
Accounts payable	$ 66,339	$ 70,986
Accrued liabilities	38,058	43,447
Current maturities of long-term debt	352	327
Current liabilities of discontinued operations	—	30
Total current liabilities	104,749	114,790
Long-term debt	1,314	1,616
Deferred pension and postretirement benefits	7,784	3,667
Liability for uncertain tax positions	8,412	6,327
Non-current environmental reserves	11,221	12,027
Other liabilities	14,223	11,391
Total liabilities	147,703	149,818

NOTES TO CONSOLIDATED FINANCIAL STATEMENTS

9. Income Taxes (in part)

A reconciliation of the change in the unrecognized income tax benefit balance from November 1, 2008 to October 31, 2011 is as follows (in thousands):

	Accrued Interest and Penalties	Unrecognized Income Tax Benefits
Balance at November 1, 2008	$ 43	$16,999
Additions for tax positions related to the current year	—	9
Additions for tax positions related to the prior year	166	1,324
Balance at October 31, 2009	$209	$18,332
Additions for tax positions related to the current year	—	13
Additions for tax positions related to the prior year	227	270
Balance at October 31, 2010	$436	$18,615
Additions for tax positions related to the current year	—	13
Additions for tax positions related to the prior year	301	414
Balance at October 31, 2011	$737	$19,042

The Company's unrecognized tax benefit (UTB) is related to the Separation as discussed in Note 1 and state tax items regarding the interpretations of tax laws and regulations. The total UTB as of October 31, 2011 is $19.0 million. Of this, $8.4 million is recorded in Liability for uncertain tax positions and $10.6 million is recorded in Deferred income taxes (non-current assets). The UTB includes $1.1 million for which the disallowance of such items would not affect the annual effective tax rate. As of October 31, 2010 the total UTB was $18.6 million with $6.3 million recorded in Liabilities for uncertain tax positions and $12.3 million recorded in Deferred income taxes (non-current assets). For the years ended October 31, 2011 and 2010, the Company recognized $0.3 million and $0.2 million, respectively in interest and penalties, which are reported as Income tax expense in the Consolidated Statements of Income consistent with past practice.

The Company and its subsidiaries file income tax returns in the U.S. federal and various state jurisdictions as well as in the U.K., Germany and Canada. The Company is not currently under a tax examination, but in certain jurisdictions the statute of limitations has not yet expired. The Company generally remains subject to examination of its U.S. federal income tax returns for 2008 and subsequent years. The Company generally remains subject to examination of its various state income tax returns for a period of four to five years from the date the return was filed. The state impact of any federal changes remains subject to examination by various states for a period of up to one year after formal notification to the state of the federal change.

Judgment is required in assessing the future tax consequences of events that have been recognized in the Company's financial statements or income tax returns. The final outcome of the future tax consequences of legal proceedings, if any, as well as the outcome of competent authority proceedings, changes in regulatory tax laws, or interpretation of those tax laws could impact the Company's financial statements. The Company is subject to the effects of these matters occurring in various jurisdictions. The Company believes that it is reasonably possible that a decrease of approximately $3.5 million in the UTB may be recognized within the next twelve months as a result of a lapse in the statute of limitations.

Tax Uncertainties

2.173

POLO RALPH LAUREN CORPORATION (MAR)

CONSOLIDATED BALANCE SHEETS (in part)

(Millions)	April 2, 2011	April 3, 2010
Liabilities and Equity *(in part)*		
Current liabilities:		
Accounts payable	$ 214.7	$ 149.8
Income tax payable	8.9	37.8
Accrued expenses and other	608.4	559.7
Total current liabilities	832.0	747.3
Long-term debt	291.9	282.1
Non-current liability for unrecognized tax benefits	156.4	126.0
Other non-current liabilities	396.1	376.9
Commitments and contingencies (Note 17)		
Total liabilities	1,676.4	1,532.3

NOTES TO CONSOLIDATED FINANCIAL
STATEMENTS

13. Income Taxes (in part)

Uncertain Income Tax Benefits

Fiscal 2011, Fiscal 2010 and Fiscal 2009 Activity

A reconciliation of the beginning and ending amounts of unrecognized tax benefits, excluding interest and penalties, for Fiscal 2011, Fiscal 2010 and Fiscal 2009 is presented below:

	Fiscal Years Ended		
(Millions)	**April 2, 2011**	**April 3, 2010**	**March 28, 2009**
Unrecognized tax benefits beginning balance	$ 96.2	113.7	$117.5
Additions related to current period tax positions	2.2	6.1	5.4
Additions related to prior period tax positions	45.6	5.1	19.4
Reductions related to prior period tax positions	(18.0)	(13.4)	(17.8)
Reductions related to expiration of statutes of limitations	(1.4)	—	—
Reductions related to settlements with taxing authorities	(2.4)	(15.5)	(5.8)
Additions (reductions) charged to foreign currency translation	2.8	0.2	(5.0
Unrecognized tax benefits ending balance	$125.0	96.2	$113.7

The Company classifies interest and penalties related to unrecognized tax benefits as part of its provision for income taxes. A reconciliation of the beginning and ending amounts of accrued interest and penalties related to unrecognized tax benefits for Fiscal 2011, Fiscal 2010 and Fiscal 2009 is presented below:

	Fiscal Years Ended		
(Millions)	**April 2, 2011**	**April 3, 2010**	**March 28, 2009**
Accrued interest and penalties beginning balance	$29.8	$41.1	$48.0
Additions (reductions) charged to expense	1.2	(3.3)	(0.8)
Reductions related to settlements with taxing authorities	—	(8.0)	(5.1)
Additions (reductions) charged to foreign currency translation	0.4	—	(1.0)
Accrued interest and penalties ending balance	$31.4	$29.8	$41.1

The total amount of unrecognized tax benefits, including interest and penalties, was $156.4 million as of April 2, 2011 and $126.0 million as of April 3, 2010 and was included within non-current liability for unrecognized tax benefits in the consolidated balance sheets. The total amount of unrecognized tax benefits that, if recognized, would affect the Company's effective tax rate was $110.8 million as of April 2, 2011 and $99.6 million as of April 3, 2010.

Future Changes in Unrecognized Tax Benefits

The total amount of unrecognized tax benefits relating to the Company's tax positions is subject to change based on future events including, but not limited to, the settlements of ongoing audits and/or the expiration of applicable statutes of limitations. Although the outcomes and timing of such events are highly uncertain, the Company does not anticipate that the balance of gross unrecognized tax benefits, excluding interest and penalties, will change significantly during the next 12 months. However, changes in the occurrence, expected outcomes and timing of those events could cause the Company's current estimate to change materially in the future.

The Company files tax returns in the U.S. federal and various state, local and foreign jurisdictions. With few exceptions for those tax returns, the Company is no longer subject to examinations by the relevant tax authorities for years prior to Fiscal 2004.

Insurance

2.174

REPUBLIC SERVICES, INC. (DEC)

CONSOLIDATED BALANCE SHEETS (in part)

(In millions, except per share data)

	December 31, 2011	December 31, 2010
Liabilities and Stockholders' Equity *(in part)*		
Current liabilities:		
Accounts payable	$ 563.6	$ 606.5
Notes payable and current maturities of long-term debt	34.8	878.5
Deferred revenue	290.2	295.1
Accrued landfill and environmental costs, current portion	184.2	182.0
Accrued interest	72.2	93.1
Other accrued liabilities	752.5	621.3
Total current liabilities	1,897.5	2,676.5
Long-term debt, net of current maturities	6,887.0	5,865.1
Accrued landfill and environmental costs, net of current portion	1,396.5	1,416.6
Deferred income taxes and other long-term tax liabilities	1,161.1	1,044.8
Self-insurance reserves, net of current portion	303.9	304.5
Other long-term liabilities	222.1	305.5

NOTES TO CONSOLIDATED FINANCIAL STATEMENTS

2. Summary of Significant Accounting Policies (in part)

Self-Insurance Reserves

Our insurance programs for workers' compensation, general liability, vehicle liability and employee-related health care benefits are effectively self-insured. Accruals for self-insurance reserves are based on claims filed and estimates of claims incurred but not reported. We consider our past claims experience, including both frequency and settlement amount of claims, in determining these estimates. It is possible that recorded reserves may not be adequate to cover the future payment of claims. Adjustments, if any, to estimates recorded resulting from ultimate claim payments will be reflected in the consolidated statements of income in the periods in which such adjustments are known. In general, our self-insurance reserves are recorded on an undiscounted basis. However, the self-insurance liabilities we acquired in the Allied acquisition have been recorded at estimated fair value, and, therefore, have been discounted to present value based on our estimate of the timing of the related cash flows.

As we are the primary obligor for payment of all claims, we report our insurance claim liabilities on a gross basis in other current and long-term liabilities and any associated recoveries from our insurers are recorded in other assets.

7. Other Liabilities (in part)

Other Accrued Liabilities (in part)

A summary of other accrued liabilities as of December 31 is as follows:

	2011	2010
Accrued payroll and benefits	$168.9	$158.4
Accrued fees and taxes	115.3	111.8
Self-insurance reserves, current portion	114.4	112.7
Accrued dividends	81.4	76.7
Synergy incentive plan	68.1	—
Current tax liabilities	29.4	—
Restructuring liabilities	0.3	3.9
Accrued professional fees and contingent legal liabilities	81.3	53.1
Other	93.4	104.7
Total	$752.5	$621.3

Other accrued liabilities include the fair value of fuel and recycling commodity hedges of $5.4 million and $8.4 million at December 31, 2011 and 2010, respectively.

We expect to pay amounts earned under the synergy incentive plan during the first quarter of 2012. The synergy incentive plan was fully accrued and was included in other long-term liabilities as of December 31, 2010.

Other Long-Term Liabilities

A summary of other long-term liabilities as of December 31 is as follows:

	2011	2010
Deferred compensation plan liability	$ 31.4	$ 27.7
Pension and other postretirement liabilities	46.8	14.4
Contingent legal liabilities	59.3	105.8
Ceded insurance reserves	58.0	54.5
Synergy incentive plan	—	68.1
Other	26.6	35.0
Total	$222.1	$305.5

Self-Insurance Reserves

In general, our self-insurance reserves are recorded on an undiscounted basis. However, our estimate of the self-insurance liabilities assumed in the Allied acquisition have been recorded at fair value, and, therefore, have been discounted to present value using a rate of 9.75%. Discounted reserves are accreted to non-cash interest expense through the period that they are paid.

Our liabilities for unpaid and incurred but not reported claims at December 31, 2011 (which includes claims for workers' compensation, general liability, vehicle liability and employee health care benefits) were $418.3 million under our current risk management program and are included in other accrued liabilities and self-insurance reserves, net of current portion in our consolidated balance sheets. While the ultimate amount of claims incurred is dependent on future developments, we believe recorded reserves are adequate to cover the future payment of claims. However, it is possible that recorded reserves may not be adequate to cover the future payment of claims. Adjustments, if any, to estimates recorded resulting from ultimate claim payments will be reflected in our consolidated statements of income in the periods in which such adjustments are known. The following table summarizes the activity in our self-insurance reserves for the years ended December 31:

	2011	2010	2009
Balance at beginning of year	$ 417.2	$ 412.9	$ 408.1
Additions charged to expense	367.3	364.9	481.3
Payments	(372.1)	(368.9)	(489.7)
Accretion expense	5.9	8.3	13.2
Balance at end of year	418.3	417.2	412.9
Less: Current portion	(114.4)	(112.7)	(110.9)
Long-term portion	$ 303.9	$ 304.5	$ 302.0

Discontinued Operations

2.175

GRIFFON CORPORATION (SEP)

CONSOLIDATED BALANCE SHEETS (in part)

(In thousands, except per share data)

	At September 30, 2011	At September 30, 2010
Current liabilities		
Notes payable and current portion of long-term debt	$ 25,164	$ 20,901
Accounts payable	183,136	185,165
Accrued liabilities	102,785	130,006
Liabilities of discontinued operations	3,794	4,289
Total current liabilities	314,879	340,361
Long-term debt, net of debt discount of $19,693 and $30,650	688,247	503,935
Other liabilities	204,434	190,244
Liabilities of discontinued operations	5,786	8,446
Total liabilities	1,213,346	1,042,986

NOTES TO CONSOLIDATED FINANCIAL STATEMENTS

(Dollars in thousands, except per share data)

(Unless otherwise indicated, all references to years or year-end refer to Griffon's fiscal period ending September 30)

Note 6—Discontinued Operations

In 2008, as a result of the downturn in the residential housing market, Griffon exited substantially all operating activities of its Installation Services segment which sold, installed and serviced garage doors and openers, fireplaces, floor cov-

erings, cabinetry and a range of related building products, primarily for the new residential housing market. Operating results of substantially all this segment has been reported as discontinued operations in the Consolidated Statements of Operations for all periods presented; the Installation Services segment is excluded from segment reporting.

In May 2008, Griffon's Board of Directors approved a plan to exit substantially all operating activities of the Installation Services segment in 2008. In the third quarter of 2008, Griffon sold nine units to one buyer, closed one unit and merged two units into CBP. In the fourth quarter of 2008, Griffon sold its two remaining units in Phoenix and Las Vegas.

Griffon substantially concluded its remaining disposal activities in the second quarter of 2009. There was no reported revenue in 2011, 2010 and 2009.

The following amounts related primarily to the Installation Services segment have been segregated from Griffon's continuing operations and are reported as assets and liabilities of discontinued operations in the consolidated balance sheets:

	At September 30, 2011		At September 30, 2010	
	Current	Long-Term	Current	Long-Term
Assets of discontinued operations:				
Prepaid and other current assets	$1,381	$ —	$1,079	$ —
Other long-term assets	—	3,675	—	5,803
Total assets of discontinued operations	$1,381	$3,675	$1,079	$5,803
Liabilities of discontinued operations:				
Accounts payable	$ 6	$ —	$ 8	$ —
Accrued liabilities	3,788	—	4,281	—
Other long-term liabilities	—	5,786	—	8,446
Total liabilities of discontinued operations	$3,794	$5,786	$4,289	$8,446

Warranty

2.176

CUMMINS INC. (DEC)

CONSOLIDATED BALANCE SHEETS (in part)

	December 31	
In millions, except par value	2011	2010
Liabilities		
Current liabilities		
Loans payable (Note 10)	$ 28	$ 82
Accounts payable (principally trade)	1,546	1,362
Current portion of accrued product warranty (Note 11)	422	421
Accrued compensation, benefits and retirement costs	511	468
Deferred revenue	208	182
Taxes payable (including taxes on income)	282	202
Other accrued expenses	660	543
Total current liabilities	3,657	3,260
Long-term liabilities		
Long-term debt (Note 10)	658	709
Pensions (Note 12)	205	195
Postretirement benefits other than pensions (Note 12)	432	439
Other liabilities and deferred revenue (Note 13)	885	803
Total liabilities	5,837	5,406

NOTES TO CONSOLIDATED FINANCIAL STATEMENTS

Note 1. Summary of Significant Accounting Policies (in part)

Warranty

We charge the estimated costs of warranty programs, other than product recalls, to income at the time products are shipped to customers. We use historical experience of war-ranty programs to develop the estimated liability for our various warranty programs. As a result of the uncertainty surrounding the nature and frequency of product recall programs, the liability for such programs is recorded when we commit to a recall action or when a recall becomes probable and estimable, which generally occurs when it is announced. The liability for these programs is reflected in the provision for warranties issued line item. We review and assess the liability for these programs on a quarterly basis. We also assess our ability to recover certain costs from our suppliers and record a receivable from the supplier when we believe a recovery is probable. At December 31, 2011, we had $14 million of receivables related to estimated supplier recoveries of which $7 million was included in "Trade and other receivables, net" and $7 million was included in "Other assets" on our *Consolidated Balance Sheets*. At December 31, 2010, we had $12 million of receivables related to estimated supplier recoveries of which $7 million was included in "Trade and other receivables, net" and $5 million was included in "Other assets" on our *Consolidated Balance Sheets*.

In addition, we sell extended warranty coverage on most of our engines. The revenue collected is initially deferred and is recognized as revenue in proportion to the costs expected to be incurred in performing services over the contract period. We compare the remaining deferred revenue balance quarterly to the estimated amount of future claims under extended warranty programs and provide an additional accrual when the deferred revenue balance is less than expected future costs.

Note 11. Product Warranty Liability

We charge the estimated costs of warranty programs, other than product recalls, to income at the time products are shipped to customers. We use historical claims experience to develop the estimated liability. We review product recall programs on a quarterly basis and, if necessary, record a liability when we commit to an action or when they become probable and estimable, which is reflected in the provision for warranties issued line. We also sell extended warranty coverage on several engines. The following is a tabular reconciliation of the product warranty liability, including the deferred revenue related to our extended warranty coverage and accrued recall programs:

(In millions)	December 31 2011	2010
Balance, beginning of year	$ 980	$ 989
Provision for warranties issued	428	401
Deferred revenue on extended warranty contracts sold	124	105
Payments	(409)	(421)
Amortization of deferred revenue on extended warranty contracts	(95)	(86)
Changes in estimates for pre-existing warranties	(7)	(7)
Foreign currency translation	(7)	(1)
Balance, end of year	$1,014	$ 980

Warranty related deferred revenue, supplier recovery receivables and the long-term portion of the warranty liability on our *Consolidated Balance Sheets* were as follows:

(In millions)	December 31 2011	2010	Balance Sheet Locations
Deferred revenue related to extended coverage programs:			
Current portion	$103	$ 91	Deferred revenue
Long-term portion	210	193	Other liabilities and deferred revenue
Total	$313	$284	
Receivables related to estimated supplier recoveries:			
Current portion	$ 7	$ 7	Trade and other receivables
Long-term portion	7	5	Other assets
Total	$ 14	$ 12	
Long-term portion of warranty liability	$279	$275	Other liabilities and deferred revenue

Note 13. Other Liabilities and Deferred Revenue

Other liabilities and deferred revenue include the following:

(In millions)	December 31 2011	2010
Accrued warranty	$279	$275
Deferred revenue	252	231
Accrued compensation	165	149
Other long-term liabilities	189	148
Other liabilities and deferred revenue	$885	$803

Environmental

2.177

SCHNITZER STEEL INDUSTRIES, INC. (AUG)

CONSOLIDATED BALANCE SHEETS (in part)

(In thousands)

	August 31 2011	2010
Liabilities and Equity *(in part)*		
Current liabilities:		
Short-term borrowings and capital lease obligations, current	$ 643	$ 1,189
Accounts payable	141,011	91,879
Accrued payroll and related liabilities	36,475	34,162
Environmental liabilities	2,983	2,588
Accrued income taxes	13,833	1,816
Other accrued liabilities	38,368	28,479
Total current liabilities	233,313	160,113
Deferred income taxes	85,378	58,630
Long-term debt and capital lease obligations, net of current maturities	403,287	99,240
Environmental liabilities, net of current portion	37,872	37,286
Other long-term liabilities	10,030	8,517
Total liabilities	769,880	363,786

NOTES TO THE CONSOLIDATED FINANCIAL STATEMENTS

Note 2—Summary of Significant Accounting Policies (in part)

Environmental Liabilities

The Company estimates future costs for known environmental remediation requirements and accrues for them on an undiscounted basis when it is probable that the Company has incurred a liability and the related costs can be reasonably estimated but the timing of incurring the estimated costs is unknown. The Company considers various factors when estimating its environmental liabilities. Adjustments to the liabilities are made when additional information becomes available that affects the estimated costs to study or remediate any environmental issues or when expenditures are made for which reserves were established. Legal costs incurred in connection with environmental contingencies are expensed as incurred.

When only a wide range of estimated amounts can be reasonably established and no other amount within the range is a better estimate than another, the low end of the range is recorded in the financial statements. In a number of cases, it is possible that the Company may receive reimbursement through insurance or from other potentially responsible parties for a site. In these situations, recoveries of environmental remediation costs from other parties are recognized when the claim for recovery is actually realized. The amounts recorded for environmental liabilities are reviewed periodically as site assessment and remediation progresses at individual sites and adjusted to reflect additional information that becomes available. Due to evolving remediation technology, changing regulations, possible third party contributions, the subjective nature of the assumptions used and other factors, amounts accrued could vary significantly from amounts paid.

Note 11—Commitments and Contingencies (in part)

Contingencies—Environmental

The Company evaluates the adequacy of its reserves for environmental liabilities on a quarterly basis in accordance with Company policy and adjustments are made when additional information becomes available that affects the estimated costs to study or remediate any environmental issues or expenditures are made for which reserves were established.

Changes in the Company's reserves for environmental liabilities for the years ended August 31, 2011 and 2010 were as follows (in thousands):

Reporting Segment	Balance 9/1/2009	Reserves Established (Released), Net[1]	Payments	Ending Balance 8/31/2010	Reserves Established (Released), Net[2]	Payments	Ending Balance 8/31/2011	Short-Term	Long-Term
Metals Recycling Business	$25,608	$ 710	$(944)	$25,374	$1,040	$(759)	$25,655	$2,429	$23,226
Auto Parts Business	16,300	(1,800)	—	14,500	700	—	15,200	554	14,646
Total	$41,908	$(1,090)	$(944)	$39,874	$1,740	$(759)	$40,855	$2,983	$37,872

[1] During fiscal 2010, the Company released $2 million in environmental reserves through discontinued operations related to the full-service auto parts operation, which was partially offset by $1 million in environmental liabilities recorded in purchase accounting.

[2] During fiscal 2011, the Company recorded $1 million in environmental liabilities in purchase accounting related to acquisitions completed in fiscal 2011.

Metals Recycling Business

As of August 31, 2011, MRB had environmental reserves of $26 million for the potential remediation of locations where it has conducted business or has environmental liabilities from historical or recent activities.

Portland Harbor

In December 2000, the Company was notified by the United States Environmental Protection Agency ("EPA") under the Comprehensive Environmental Response, Compensation and Liability Act ("CERCLA") that it is one of the potentially responsible parties ("PRPs") that own or operate or formerly owned or operated sites which are part of or adjacent to the Portland Harbor Superfund site (the "Site"). The precise nature and extent of any cleanup of the Site, the parties to be involved, the process to be followed for any cleanup and the allocation of the costs for any cleanup among responsible parties have not yet been determined, but the process of identifying additional PRPs and beginning allocation of costs is underway. The EPA has indicated that it expects to issue a record of decision that will discuss remedial alternatives for the Site sometime in 2013. It is unclear to what extent the Company will be liable for environmental costs or natural resource damage claims or third party contribution or damage claims with respect to the Site. While the Company participated in certain preliminary Site study efforts, it is not party to the consent order entered into by the EPA with certain other PRPs, referred to as the "Lower Willamette Group" ("LWG"), for a remedial investigation/feasibility study ("RI/FS").

During fiscal 2007, the Company and certain other parties agreed to an interim settlement with the LWG under which the Company made a cash contribution to the LWG RI/FS. The Company has also joined with more than 80 other PRPs, including the LWG, in a voluntary process to establish an allocation of costs at the Site. These parties have selected an allocation team and finalized an allocation process design agreement. The LWG has also commenced federal court litigation, which has been stayed, seeking to bring additional parties into the allocation process.

In January 2008, the Natural Resource Damages Trustee Council ("Trustees") for Portland Harbor invited the Company and other PRPs to participate in funding and implementing the Natural Resource Injury Assessment for the Site.

Following meetings among the Trustees and the PRPs, a funding and participation agreement was negotiated under which the participating PRPs agreed to fund the first phase of the natural resource damage assessment. The Company joined in that agreement and paid a portion of those costs. The Company did not participate in funding the second phase of the natural resource damage assessment.

The cost of the investigations and any remediation associated with the Site will not be reasonably estimable until completion of the data review and further investigations now being conducted by the LWG and the Trustees and the selection and approval of a remedy by the EPA. However, given the size of the Site and the nature of the conditions identified to date, the total cost of the investigations and remediation is likely to be substantial. In addition, because there has not been a determination of the total cost of the investigations, the remediation that will be required, the amount of natural resource damages or how the costs of the ongoing investigations and any remedy and natural resource damages will be allocated among the PRPs, it is not possible to estimate the costs which the Company might incur in connection with the Site, although such costs could be material to the Company's financial position, results of operations, cash flows or liquidity. The Company has insurance policies that it believes will provide reimbursement for costs it incurs for defense and remediation in connection with the Site, although there is no assurance that those policies will cover all of the costs which the Company may incur. In fiscal 2006, the Company recorded a liability for its then estimated share of the costs of the investigation incurred by the LWG to date. As of August 31, 2011 and 2010, the Company's reserve for third party investigation costs of the Site was $1 million.

The Oregon Department of Environmental Quality is separately providing oversight of voluntary investigations by the Company involving the Company's sites adjacent to the Portland Harbor which are focused on controlling any current "uplands" releases of contaminants into the Willamette River. No reserves have been established in connection with these investigations because the extent of contamination (if any) and the Company's responsibility for the contamination (if any) has not yet been determined.

Other Metals Recycling Business Sites

As of August 31, 2011, the Company had environmental reserves related to various MRB sites other than Portland Harbor of $25 million. The reserves, which range up to $2 million per site, relate to the potential future remediation of soil contamination, groundwater contamination and storm water runoff issues. No material environmental compliance enforcement proceedings are currently pending related to these sites.

Auto Parts Business

As of August 31, 2011, the Company had environmental reserves related to various APB sites of $15 million. The reserves, which range up to $2 million per site, relate to the potential future remediation of soil contamination, groundwater contamination and storm water runoff issues. No material environmental compliance enforcement proceedings are currently pending related to these sites.

Steel Manufacturing Business

SMB's electric arc furnace generates dust ("EAF dust") that is classified as hazardous waste by the EPA because of its zinc and lead content. As a result, the Company captures the EAF dust and ships it in specialized rail cars to a domestic firm that applies a treatment that allows the EAF dust to be delisted as hazardous waste so it can be disposed of as a non-hazardous solid waste.

SMB has an operating permit issued under Title V of the Clean Air Act Amendments of 1990, which governs certain air quality standards. The permit was first issued in 1998, has since been renewed through March 1, 2012 and is expected to be renewed again prior to its expiration. The permit is based upon an annual production capacity of 950 thousand tons.

SMB had no environmental reserves as of August 31, 2011.

Other than the Portland Harbor Superfund site, which is discussed above, management currently believes that adequate provision has been made in the Consolidated Financial Statements for the potential impact of these issues and that the ultimate outcomes will not have a material adverse effect on the Consolidated Financial Statements of the Company as a whole. Historically, the amounts the Company has ultimately paid for such remediation activities have not been material in any given period.

Asset Retirement Obligations

2.178

APACHE CORPORATION (DEC)

CONSOLIDATED BALANCE SHEET (in part)

	December 31	
(In millions)	2011	2010
Liabilities and Shareholders' Equity		
(in part)		
Current liabilities:		
Accounts payable	$ 1,048	$ 779
Accrued liabilities	2,648	1,816
Current debt	431	46
Asset retirement obligation	447	407
Derivative instruments	113	194
Other	276	282
	4,963	3,524
Long-term debt	6,785	8,095
Deferred credits and other noncurrent liabilities:		
Income taxes	7,197	4,249
Asset retirement obligation	3,440	2,465
Other	673	715
	11,310	7,429

NOTES TO CONSOLIDATED FINANCIAL STATEMENTS

1. Summary of Significant Accounting Policies (in part)

Asset Retirement Obligation

The initial estimated asset retirement obligation related to property and equipment is recorded as a liability at its fair value, with an offsetting asset retirement cost recorded as an increase to the associated property and equipment on the consolidated balance sheet. If the fair value of the recorded asset retirement obligation changes, a revision is recorded to both the asset retirement obligation and the asset retirement cost. Revisions in estimated liabilities can result from changes in estimated inflation rates, changes in service and equipment costs and changes in the estimated timing of an asset's retirement. Asset retirement costs are depreciated using a systematic and rational method similar to that used for the associated property and equipment. Accretion expense on the liability is recognized over the estimated productive life of the related assets.

5. Asset Retirement Obligation

The following table describes changes to the Company's ARO liability for the years ended December 31, 2011 and 2010:

(In millions)	2011	2010
Asset retirement obligation at beginning of year	$2,872	$1,784
Liabilities incurred	419	270
Liabilities acquired	592	847
Liabilities settled	(549)	(329)
Accretion expense	154	111
Revisions in estimated liabilities	399	189
Asset retirement obligation at end of year	3,887	2,872
Less current portion	(447)	(407)
Asset retirement obligation, long-term	$3,440	$2,465

The ARO liability reflects the estimated present value of the amount of dismantlement, removal, site reclamation, and similar activities associated with Apache's oil and gas properties. The Company utilizes current retirement costs to estimate the expected cash outflows for retirement obligations. The Company estimates the ultimate productive life of the properties, a risk-adjusted discount rate, and an inflation factor in order to determine the current present value of this obligation. To the extent future revisions to these assumptions impact the present value of the existing ARO liability, a corresponding adjustment is made to the oil and gas property balance.

During 2011, the Company recorded $592 million in additional abandonment liabilities on properties acquired, primarily related to the Mobil North Sea acquisition. An additional $419 million in abandonment liabilities was recognized on our current year drilling and development program. Increases in offshore abandonment costs, particularly in our international jurisdictions, resulted in a $399 million revision.

Liabilities settled in 2011 relate to individual properties, platforms and facilities plugged and abandoned during the period. The Company continues to have an active ongoing abandonment program, particularly in the Gulf of Mexico and Canada. Additionally, our 2011 abandonment program included the retirement of our offshore facilities in Australia's Legendre field.

Litigation

2.179

CRANE CO. (DEC)

CONSOLIDATED BALANCE SHEETS (in part)

(In thousands, except shares and per share data)	Balance at December 31	
	2011	2010
Liabilities and Equity (in part)		
Current liabilities:		
Short-term borrowings	$ 1,112	$ 984
Accounts payable	194,158	157,051
Current asbestos liability	100,943	100,000
Accrued liabilities	226,717	229,462
U.S. and foreign taxes on income	10,165	11,057
Total current liabilities	533,095	498,554
Long-term debt	398,914	398,736
Accrued pension and postretirement benefits	178,382	98,324
Long-term deferred tax liability	41,668	48,852
Long-term asbestos liability	792,701	619,666
Other liabilities	76,715	49,535
Commitments and Contingencies (Note 10)		

NOTES TO CONSOLIDATED FINANCIAL STATEMENTS

Note 10—Commitments and Contingencies (in part)

Asbestos Liability

Information Regarding Claims and Costs in the Tort System

As of December 31, 2011, the Company was a defendant in cases filed in numerous state and federal courts alleging injury or death as a result of exposure to asbestos. Activity related to asbestos claims during the periods indicated was as follows:

	Year Ended December 31		
	2011	2010	2009
Beginning claims	64,839	66,341	74,872
New claims	3,748	5,032	3,664
Settlements*	(1,117)	(1,127)	(1,024)
Dismissals	(11,059)	(6,363)	(11,171)
MARDOC claims**	2,247	956	—
Ending claims	58,658	64,839	66,341

* Includes *Earl Haupt* judgment.

** As of January 1, 2010, the Company was named in 36,448 maritime actions which had been administratively dismissed by the United States District Court for the Eastern District of Pennsylvania ("MARDOC claims"), and therefore were not included in "Beginning claims". As of December 31, 2011, pursuant to an ongoing review process initiated by the Court, 26,605 claims were permanently dismissed, 3,200 claims were restored to active status and 3 new filings in 2011 were added to active status (and have been added to "Ending claims"). In addition, the Company was named in 8 new maritime actions in 2010 (not included in "Beginning claims") which had been administratively dismissed upon filing in 2010. The Company expects that more of the remaining 6,648 maritime actions will be activated, or permanently dismissed, as the Court's review process continues.

Of the 58,658 pending claims as of December 31, 2011, approximately 20,800 claims were pending in New York, approximately 10,000 claims were pending in Texas, approximately 5,500 claims were pending in Mississippi, and approximately 5,300 claims were pending in Ohio, all jurisdictions in which legislation or judicial orders restrict the types of claims that can proceed to trial on the merits.

Substantially all of the claims the Company resolves are either dismissed or concluded through settlements. To date, the Company has paid two judgments arising from adverse jury verdicts in asbestos matters. The first payment, in the amount of $2.54 million, was made on July 14, 2008, approximately two years after the adverse verdict in the *Joseph Norris* matter in California, after the Company had exhausted all post-trial and appellate remedies. The second payment, in the amount of $0.02 million, was made in June 2009 after an adverse verdict in the *Earl Haupt* case in Los Angeles, California on April 21, 2009.

During the fourth quarter of 2007 and the first quarter of 2008, the Company tried several cases resulting in defense verdicts by the jury or directed verdicts for the defense by the court, one of which, the *Patrick O'Neil* claim in Los Angeles, was reversed on appeal. In an opinion dated January 12, 2012, the California Supreme Court reversed the decision of the Court of Appeal and instructed the trial court to enter a judgment of nonsuit in favor of the defendants.

On March 14, 2008, the Company received an adverse verdict in the *James Baccus* claim in Philadelphia, Pennsylvania, with compensatory damages of $2.45 million and additional damages of $11.9 million. The Company's post-trial motions were denied by order dated January 5, 2009. The case was concluded by settlement in the fourth quarter of 2010 during the pendency of the Company's appeal to the Superior Court of Pennsylvania. The settlement is reflected in the settled claims for 2010.

On May 16, 2008, the Company received an adverse verdict in the *Chief Brewer* claim in Los Angeles, California. The amount of the judgment entered was $0.68 million plus in-

terest and costs. The Company is pursuing an appeal in this matter.

On February 2, 2009, the Company received an adverse verdict in the *Dennis Woodard* claim in Los Angeles, California. The jury found that the Company was responsible for one-half of one percent (0.5%) of plaintiffs' damages of $16.93 million; however, based on California court rules regarding allocation of damages, judgment was entered against the Company in the amount of $1.65 million, plus costs. Following entry of judgment, the Company filed a motion with the trial court requesting judgment in the Company's favor notwithstanding the jury's verdict, and on June 30, 2009, the court advised that the Company's motion was granted and judgment was entered in favor of the Company. The trial court's ruling was affirmed on appeal by order dated August 25, 2011. The plaintiffs have appealed that ruling to the Supreme Court of California, which has accepted review of the matter.

On March 23, 2010, a Philadelphia County, Pennsylvania, state court jury found the Company responsible for a 1/11th share of a $14.5 million verdict in the *James Nelson* claim, and for a 1/20th share of a $3.5 million verdict in the *Larry Bell* claim. On February 23, 2011, the court entered judgment on the verdicts in the amount of $0.2 million against the Company, only, in Bell, and in the amount of $4.0 million, jointly, against the Company and two other defendants in Nelson, with additional interest in the amount of $0.01 million being assessed against the Company, only, in Nelson. All defendants, including the Company, and the plaintiffs have taken timely appeals of certain aspects of those judgments. Those appeals are pending.

On August 17, 2011, a New York City state court jury found the Company responsible for a 99% share of a $32 million verdict on the *Ronald Dummitt* claim. The Company has filed post-trial motions seeking to overturn the verdict, to grant a new trial, or to reduce the damages, which the Company argues are excessive under New York appellate case law governing awards for non-economic losses. The Court held oral argument on these motions on October 18, 2011, and a written decision is expected to be issued. The Company anticipates that it will likely appeal any judgment that may be entered on the verdict.

Such judgment amounts are not included in the Company's incurred costs until all available appeals are exhausted and the final payment amount is determined.

The gross settlement and defense costs incurred (before insurance recoveries and tax effects) for the Company for the years ended December 31, 2011, 2010 and 2009 totaled $105.5 million, $106.6 million and $110.1 million, respectively. In contrast to the recognition of settlement and defense costs, which reflect the current level of activity in the tort system, cash payments and receipts generally lag the tort system activity by several months or more, and may show some fluctuation from quarter to quarter. Cash payments of settlement amounts are not made until all releases and other required documentation are received by the Company, and reimbursements of both settlement amounts and defense costs by insurers may be uneven due to insurer payment practices, transitions from one insurance layer to the next excess layer and the payment terms of certain reimbursement agreements. The Company's total pre-tax payments for settlement and defense costs, net of funds received from insurers, for the years ended December 31, 2011, 2010 and 2009 totaled a $79.3 million net payment, $66.7 million net payment and a $55.8 million net payment (reflecting the receipt of $14.5 million in 2009 for full policy buyout from Highlands Insurance Company ("Highlands"), respectively. Detailed below are the comparable amounts for the periods indicated.

(In millions)	Year Ended December 31		
	2011	2010	2009
Settlement/indemnity costs incurred[1]	$ 50.2	$ 52.7	$ 58.3
Defense costs incurred[1]	55.3	53.9	51.8
Total costs incurred	$105.5	$106.6	$110.1
Settlement/indemnity payments	$ 55.0	$ 46.9	$ 57.3
Defense payments	56.5	54.4	52.2
Insurance receipts[2]	(32.2)	(34.6)	(53.7)
Pre-tax cash payments[2]	$ 79.3	$ 66.7	$ 55.8

[1] Before insurance recoveries and tax effects.
[2] The year ended December 31, 2009 includes a $14.5 million payment from Highlands in January 2009.

The amounts shown for settlement and defense costs incurred, and cash payments, are not necessarily indicative of future period amounts, which may be higher or lower than those reported.

Cumulatively through December 31, 2011, the Company has resolved (by settlement or dismissal) approximately 84,000 claims, not including the MARDOC claims referred to above. The related settlement cost incurred by the Company and its insurance carriers is approximately $330 million, for an average settlement cost per resolved claim of approximately $4,000. The average settlement cost per claim resolved during the years ended December 31, 2011, 2010 and 2009 was $4,123, $7,036 and $4,781 respectively. Because claims are sometimes dismissed in large groups, the average cost per resolved claim, as well as the number of open claims, can fluctuate significantly from period to period. In addition to large group dismissals, the nature of the disease and corresponding settlement amounts for each claim resolved will also drive changes from period to period in the average settlement cost per claim. Accordingly, the average cost per resolved claim is not considered in the Company's periodic review of its estimated asbestos liability. For a discussion regarding the four most significant factors affecting the liability estimate, see "Effects on the Condensed Consolidated Financial Statements."

Effects on the Consolidated Financial Statements

The Company has retained the firm of Hamilton, Rabinovitz & Associates, Inc. ("HR&A"), a nationally recognized expert in the field, to assist management in estimating the Company's asbestos liability in the tort system. HR&A reviews information provided by the Company concerning claims filed, settled and dismissed, amounts paid in settlements and relevant claim information such as the nature of the asbestos-related disease asserted by the claimant, the jurisdiction where filed and the time lag from filing to disposition of the claim. The methodology used by HR&A to project future asbestos costs is based largely on the Company's experience during a base reference period of eleven quarterly periods (consisting of the two full preceding calendar years and three additional quarterly periods to the estimate date) for claims filed, settled and dismissed. The Company's experience is then compared to the results of previously conducted epidemiological studies estimating the number of individuals likely to

develop asbestos-related diseases. Those studies were undertaken in connection with national analyses of the population of workers believed to have been exposed to asbestos. Using that information, HR&A estimates the number of future claims that would be filed against the Company and estimates the aggregate settlement or indemnity costs that would be incurred to resolve both pending and future claims based upon the average settlement costs by disease during the reference period. This methodology has been accepted by numerous courts. After discussions with the Company, HR&A augments its liability estimate for the costs of defending asbestos claims in the tort system using a forecast from the Company which is based upon discussions with its defense counsel. Based on this information, HR&A compiles an estimate of the Company's asbestos liability for pending and future claims, based on claim experience during the reference period and covering claims expected to be filed through the indicated forecast period. The most significant factors affecting the liability estimate are (1) the number of new mesothelioma claims filed against the Company, (2) the average settlement costs for mesothelioma claims, (3) the percentage of mesothelioma claims dismissed against the Company and (4) the aggregate defense costs incurred by the Company. These factors are interdependent, and no one factor predominates in determining the liability estimate. Although the methodology used by HR&A will also show claims and costs for periods subsequent to the indicated period (up to and including the endpoint of the asbestos studies referred to above), management believes that the level of uncertainty regarding the various factors used in estimating future asbestos costs is too great to provide for reasonable estimation of the number of future claims, the nature of such claims or the cost to resolve them for years beyond the indicated estimate.

In the Company's view, the forecast period used to provide the best estimate for asbestos claims and related liabilities and costs is a judgment based upon a number of trend factors, including the number and type of claims being filed each year; the jurisdictions where such claims are filed, and the effect of any legislation or judicial orders in such jurisdictions restricting the types of claims that can proceed to trial on the merits; and the likelihood of any comprehensive asbestos legislation at the federal level. In addition, the dynamics of asbestos litigation in the tort system have been significantly affected over the past five to ten years by the substantial number of companies that have filed for bankruptcy protection, thereby staying any asbestos claims against them until the conclusion of such proceedings, and the establishment of a number of post-bankruptcy trusts for asbestos claimants, which are estimated to provide $30 billion for payments to current and future claimants. These trend factors have both positive and negative effects on the dynamics of asbestos litigation in the tort system and the related best estimate of the Company's asbestos liability, and these effects do not move in a linear fashion but rather change over multi-year periods. Accordingly, the Company's management continues to monitor these trend factors over time and periodically assesses whether an alternative forecast period is appropriate.

Each quarter, HR&A compiles an update based upon the Company's experience in claims filed, settled and dismissed during the updated reference period (consisting of the preceding eleven quarterly periods) as well as average settlement costs by disease category (mesothelioma, lung cancer, other cancer, asbestosis and other non-malignant conditions) during that period. In addition to this claims experience, the Company also considers additional quantitative and qualitative factors such as the nature of the aging of pending claims, significant appellate rulings and legislative developments, and their respective effects on expected future settlement values. As part of this process, the Company also takes into account trends in the tort system such as those enumerated above. Management considers all these factors in conjunction with the liability estimate of HR&A and determines whether a change in the estimate is warranted.

Updating the Liability Estimate. With the assistance of HR&A, effective as of December 31, 2011, the Company updated and extended its estimate of the asbestos liability, including the costs of settlement or indemnity payments and defense costs relating to currently pending claims and future claims projected to be filed against the Company through 2021. The Company's previous estimate was for asbestos claims filed or projected to be filed through 2017. As a result of this updated estimate, the Company recorded an additional liability of $285 million as of December 31, 2011. The Company's decision to take this action at such date was based on several factors which contribute to the Company's ability to reasonably estimate this liability for the additional period noted. First, the number of mesothelioma claims (which although constituting approximately 8% of the Company's total pending asbestos claims, have accounted for approximately 90% of the Company's aggregate settlement and defense costs) being filed against the Company and associated settlement costs have recently stabilized. In the Company's opinion, the outlook for mesothelioma claims expected to be filed and resolved in the forecast period is reasonably stable. Second, there have been favorable developments in the trend of case law which has been a contributing factor in stabilizing the asbestos claims activity and related settlement costs. Third, there have been significant actions taken by certain state legislatures and courts over the past several years that have reduced the number and types of claims that can proceed to trial, which has been a significant factor in stabilizing the asbestos claims activity. Fourth, the Company has now entered into coverage-in-place agreements with almost all of its excess insurers, which enables the Company to project a more stable relationship between settlement and defense costs paid by the Company and reimbursements from its insurers.

Taking all of these factors into account, the Company believes that it can reasonably estimate the asbestos liability for pending claims and future claims to be filed through 2021. While it is probable that the Company will incur additional charges for asbestos liabilities and defense costs in excess of the amounts currently provided, the Company does not believe that any such amount can be reasonably estimated beyond 2021. Accordingly, no accrual has been recorded for any costs which may be incurred for claims which may be made subsequent to 2021.

Management has made its best estimate of the costs through 2021 based on the analysis by HR&A completed in January 2012. A liability of $894 million was recorded as of December 31, 2011 to cover the estimated cost of asbestos claims now pending or subsequently asserted through 2021, of which approximately 80% is attributable to settlement and defense costs for future claims projected to be filed through 2021. The liability is reduced when cash payments are made in respect of settled claims and defense costs. It is not possible to forecast when cash payments related to the asbestos liability will be fully expended; however, it is expected such cash payments will continue for a number of years past 2021,

due to the significant proportion of future claims included in the estimated asbestos liability and the lag time between the date a claim is filed and when it is resolved. None of these estimated costs have been discounted to present value due to the inability to reliably forecast the timing of payments. The current portion of the total estimated liability at December 31, 2011 was $101 million and represents the Company's best estimate of total asbestos costs expected to be paid during the twelve-month period. Such amount is based upon the HR&A model together with the Company's prior year payment experience for both settlement and defense costs.

Insurance Coverage and Receivables. Prior to 2005, a significant portion of the Company's settlement and defense costs were paid by its primary insurers. With the exhaustion of that primary coverage, the Company began negotiations with its excess insurers to reimburse the Company for a portion of its settlement and/or defense costs as incurred. To date, the Company has entered into agreements providing for such reimbursements, known as "coverage-in-place," with eleven of its excess insurer groups. Under such coverage-in-place agreements, an insurer's policies remain in force and the insurer undertakes to provide coverage for the Company's present and future asbestos claims on specified terms and conditions that address, among other things, the share of asbestos claims costs to be paid by the insurer, payment terms, claims handling procedures and the expiration of the insurer's obligations. Similarly, under a variant of coverage-in-place, the Company has entered into an agreement with a group of insurers confirming the aggregate amount of available coverage under the subject policies and setting forth a schedule for future reimbursement payments to the Company based on aggregate indemnity and defense payments made. In addition, with six of its excess insurer groups, the Company entered into policy buyout agreements, settling all asbestos and other coverage obligations for an agreed sum, totaling $79.5 million in aggregate. Reimbursements from insurers for past and ongoing settlement and defense costs allocable to their policies have been made in accordance with these coverage-in-place and other agreements. All of these agreements include provisions for mutual releases, indemnification of the insurer and, for coverage-in-place, claims handling procedures. With the agreements referenced above, the Company has concluded settlements with all but one of its solvent excess insurers whose policies are expected to respond to the aggregate costs included in the updated liability estimate. That insurer, which issued a single applicable policy, has been paying the shares of defense and indemnity costs the Company has allocated to it, subject to a reservation of rights. There are no pending legal proceedings between the Company and any insurer contesting the Company's asbestos claims under its insurance policies.

In conjunction with developing the aggregate liability estimate referenced above, the Company also developed an estimate of probable insurance recoveries for its asbestos liabilities. In developing this estimate, the Company considered its coverage-in-place and other settlement agreements described above, as well as a number of additional factors. These additional factors include the financial viability of the insurance companies, the method by which losses will be allocated to the various insurance policies and the years covered by those policies, how settlement and defense costs will be covered by the insurance policies and interpretation of the effect on coverage of various policy terms and limits and their interrelationships. In addition, the timing and amount of reimbursements will vary because the Company's insurance coverage for asbestos claims involves multiple insurers, with different policy terms and certain gaps in coverage. In addition to consulting with legal counsel on these insurance matters, the Company retained insurance consultants to assist management in the estimation of probable insurance recoveries based upon the aggregate liability estimate described above and assuming the continued viability of all solvent insurance carriers. Based upon the analysis of policy terms and other factors noted above by the Company's legal counsel, and incorporating risk mitigation judgments by the Company where policy terms or other factors were not certain, the Company's insurance consultants compiled a model indicating how the Company's historical insurance policies would respond to varying levels of asbestos settlement and defense costs and the allocation of such costs between such insurers and the Company. Using the estimated liability as of December 31, 2011 (for claims filed or expected to be filed through 2021), the insurance consultant's model forecasted that approximately 25% of the liability would be reimbursed by the Company's insurers, although actual insurance reimbursements vary from period to period, and will decline over time, for the reasons cited above. While there are overall limits on the aggregate amount of insurance available to the Company with respect to asbestos claims, those overall limits were not reached by the total estimated liability currently recorded by the Company, and such overall limits did not influence the Company in its determination of the asset amount to record. The proportion of the asbestos liability that is allocated to certain insurance coverage years, however, exceeds the limits of available insurance in those years. The Company allocates to itself the amount of the asbestos liability (for claims filed or expected to be filed through 2021) that is in excess of available insurance coverage allocated to such years. An asset of $225 million was recorded as of December 31, 2011 representing the probable insurance reimbursement for such claims expected through 2021. The asset is reduced as reimbursements and other payments from insurers are received.

The Company reviews the aforementioned estimated reimbursement rate with its insurance consultants on a periodic basis in order to confirm its overall consistency with the Company's established reserves. The reviews encompass consideration of the performance of the insurers under coverage-in-place agreements and, the effect of any additional lump-sum payments under policy buyout agreements.

Uncertainties. Estimation of the Company's ultimate exposure for asbestos-related claims is subject to significant uncertainties, as there are multiple variables that can affect the timing, severity and quantity of claims. The Company cautions that its estimated liability is based on assumptions with respect to future claims, settlement and defense costs based on past experience that may not prove reliable as predictors. A significant upward or downward trend in the number of claims filed, depending on the nature of the alleged injury, the jurisdiction where filed and the quality of the product identification, or a significant upward or downward trend in the costs of defending claims, could change the estimated liability, as would substantial adverse verdicts at trial that withstand appeal. A legislative solution, structured settlement transaction, or significant change in relevant case law could also change the estimated liability.

The same factors that affect developing estimates of probable settlement and defense costs for asbestos-related liabilities also affect estimates of the probable insurance reim-

bursements, as do a number of additional factors. These additional factors include the financial viability of the insurance companies, the method by which losses will be allocated to the various insurance policies and the years covered by those policies, how settlement and defense costs will be covered by the insurance policies and interpretation of the effect on coverage of various policy terms and limits and their interrelationships. In addition, due to the uncertainties inherent in litigation matters, no assurances can be given regarding the outcome of any litigation, if necessary, to enforce the Company's rights under its insurance policies or settlement agreements.

Many uncertainties exist surrounding asbestos litigation, and the Company will continue to evaluate its estimated asbestos-related liability and corresponding estimated insurance reimbursement as well as the underlying assumptions and process used to derive these amounts. These uncertainties may result in the Company incurring future charges or increases to income to adjust the carrying value of recorded liabilities and assets, particularly if the number of claims and settlement and defense costs change significantly, or if there are significant developments in the trend of case law or court procedures, or if legislation or another alternative solution is implemented; however, the Company is currently unable to estimate such future changes and, accordingly, while it is probable that the Company will incur additional charges for asbestos liabilities and defense costs in excess of the amounts currently provided, the Company does not believe that any such amount can be reasonably determined beyond 2021. Although the resolution of these claims may take many years, the effect on the results of operations, financial position and cash flow in any given period from a revision to these estimates could be material.

Derivatives

2.180

ALCOA INC. (DEC)

CONSOLIDATED BALANCE SHEET (in part)

(In millions)

December 31	2011	2010
Liabilities		
Current liabilities:		
Short-term borrowings (K & X)	$ 62	$ 92
Commercial paper (K & X)	224	—
Accounts payable, trade	2,692	2,331
Accrued compensation and retirement costs	985	932
Taxes, including income taxes	438	461
Other current liabilities	1,167	1,204
Long-term debt due within one year (K & X)	445	231
Total current liabilities	6,013	5,251
Long-term debt, less amount due within one year (K & X)	8,640	8,842
Accrued pension benefits (W)	3,261	2,923
Accrued other postretirement benefits (W)	2,583	2,615
Other noncurrent liabilities and deferred credits (L)	2,428	2,576
Total liabilities	22,925	22,207

NOTES TO THE CONSOLIDATED FINANCIAL STATEMENTS

(Dollars in millions, except per-share amounts)

A. Summary of Significant Accounting Policies (in part)

Derivatives and Hedging. Derivatives are held for purposes other than trading and are part of a formally documented risk management program. For derivatives designated as fair value hedges, Alcoa measures hedge effectiveness by formally assessing, at least quarterly, the historical high correlation of changes in the fair value of the hedged item and the derivative hedging instrument. For derivatives designated as cash flow hedges, Alcoa measures hedge effectiveness by formally assessing, at least quarterly, the probable high correlation of the expected future cash flows of the hedged item and the derivative hedging instrument. The ineffective portions of both types of hedges are recorded in sales or other income or expense in the current period. If the hedging relationship ceases to be highly effective or it becomes probable that an expected transaction will no longer occur, future gains or losses on the derivative instrument are recorded in other income or expense.

Alcoa accounts for interest rate swaps related to its existing long-term debt and hedges of firm customer commitments for aluminum as fair value hedges. As a result, the fair values of the derivatives and changes in the fair values of the underlying hedged items are reported in other current and noncurrent assets and liabilities in the Consolidated Balance Sheet. Changes in the fair values of these derivatives and underlying hedged items generally offset and are recorded each period in sales or interest expense, consistent with the underlying hedged item.

Alcoa accounts for hedges of foreign currency exposures and certain forecasted transactions as cash flow hedges. The fair values of the derivatives are recorded in other current and noncurrent assets and liabilities in the Consolidated Balance Sheet. The effective portions of the changes in the fair values of these derivatives are recorded in other comprehensive income and are reclassified to sales, cost of goods sold, or other income or expense in the period in which earnings are impacted by the hedged items or in the period that the transaction no longer qualifies as a cash flow hedge. These contracts cover the same periods as known or expected exposures, generally not exceeding five years.

If no hedging relationship is designated, the derivative is marked to market through earnings.

Cash flows from derivatives are recognized in the Statement of Consolidated Cash Flows in a manner consistent with the underlying transactions.

Fair Value Accounting (in part)—On January 1, 2011, Alcoa adopted changes issued by the FASB to disclosure requirements for fair value measurements. Specifically, the changes require a reporting entity to disclose, in the reconciliation of fair value measurements using significant unobservable inputs (Level 3), separate information about purchases, sales, issuances, and settlements (that is, on a gross basis rather than as one net number). These changes were applied to the disclosures in Note W and the Derivatives section of Note X to the Consolidated Financial Statements.

Derivative Instruments and Hedging Activities—On July 1, 2010, Alcoa adopted changes to existing accounting requirements for embedded credit derivatives. Specifically, the changes clarify the scope exception regarding when embedded credit derivative features are not considered embedded derivatives subject to potential bifurcation and separate accounting. The adoption of these changes had no impact on the Consolidated Financial Statements.

On January 1, 2009, Alcoa adopted changes issued by the FASB to disclosures about derivative instruments and hedging activities. These changes require enhanced disclosures about an entity's derivative and hedging activities, including (i) how and why an entity uses derivative instruments, (ii) how derivative instruments and related hedged items are accounted for, and (iii) how derivative instruments and related hedged items affect an entity's financial position, financial performance, and cash flows. Other than the required disclosures (see the Derivatives section of Note X), the adoption of these changes had no impact on the Consolidated Financial Statements.

L. Other Noncurrent Liabilities and Deferred Credits

December 31	2011	2010
Fair value of derivative contracts (X)	$ 624	$ 703
Asset retirement obligations (C)	503	442
Deferred income taxes (T)	395	388
Accrued compensation and retirement costs	304	314
Environmental remediation (N)	289	302
Deferred alumina sales revenue	116	125
Other	197	302
	$2,428	$2,576

X. Derivatives and Other Financial Instruments (in part)

Derivatives (in part). Alcoa is exposed to certain risks relating to its ongoing business operations, including financial, market, political, and economic risks. The following discussion provides information regarding Alcoa's exposure to the risks of changing commodity prices, interest rates, and foreign currency exchange rates.

Alcoa's commodity and derivative activities are subject to the management, direction, and control of the Strategic Risk Management Committee (SRMC). The SRMC is composed of the chief executive officer, the chief financial officer, and other officers and employees that the chief executive officer selects. The SRMC reports to the Board of Directors on the scope of its activities.

The aluminum, energy, interest rate, and foreign exchange contracts are held for purposes other than trading. They are used primarily to mitigate uncertainty and volatility, and to cover underlying exposures. Alcoa is not involved in trading activities for energy, weather derivatives, or other nonexchange commodity trading activities.

The fair values of outstanding derivative contracts recorded as assets in the accompanying Consolidated Balance Sheet were as follows:

Asset Derivatives	December 31, 2011	December 31, 2010
Derivatives designated as hedging instruments:		
Prepaid expenses and other current assets:		
Aluminum contracts	$ 56	$ 48
Foreign exchange contracts	—	2
Interest rate contracts	8	19
Other noncurrent assets:		
Aluminum contracts	6	22
Energy contracts	2	9
Interest rate contracts	37	62
Total derivatives designated as hedging instruments	$109	$162
Derivatives not designated as hedging instruments*:		
Prepaid expenses and other current assets:		
Aluminum contracts	$ 1	$ 3
Other noncurrent assets:		
Aluminum contracts	5	—
Foreign exchange contracts	1	1
Total derivatives not designated as hedging instruments	$ 7	$ 4
Less margin held:		
Prepaid expenses and other current assets:		
Aluminum contracts	$ 7	$ 4
Interest rate contracts	8	13
Other noncurrent assets:		
Interest rate contracts	7	2
Sub-total	$ 22	$ 19
Total asset derivatives	$ 94	$147

* See the "Other" section within Note X for additional information on Alcoa's purpose for entering into derivatives not designated as hedging instruments and its overall risk management strategies.

The fair values of outstanding derivative contracts recorded as liabilities in the accompanying Consolidated Balance Sheet were as follows:

Liability Derivatives	December 31, 2011	December 31, 2010
Derivatives designated as hedging instruments:		
Other current liabilities:		
Aluminum contracts	$ 79	$ 89
Other noncurrent liabilities and deferred credits:		
Aluminum contracts	574	647
Total derivatives designated as hedging instruments	$653	$736
Derivatives not designated as hedging instruments*:		
Other current liabilities:		
Aluminum contracts	$ 35	$ 52
Energy contracts	—	62
Other noncurrent liabilities and deferred credits:		
Aluminum contracts	22	33
Embedded credit derivative	28	23
Total derivatives not designated as hedging instruments	$ 85	$170
Less margin posted:		
Other current liabilities:		
Aluminum contracts	$ 1	$ 4
Energy contracts	—	37
Sub-total	$ 1	$ 41
Total liability derivatives	$737	$865

* See the "Other" section within Note X for additional information on Alcoa's purpose for entering into derivatives not designated as hedging instruments and its overall risk management strategies.

The following table shows the net fair values of outstanding derivative contracts at December 31, 2011 and the effect on these amounts of a hypothetical change (increase or decrease of 10%) in the market prices or rates that existed at December 31, 2011:

	Fair Value Asset/ (Liability)	Index Change of + / – 10%
Aluminum contracts	$(648)	$137
Embedded credit derivative	(28)	9
Energy contracts	2	375
Foreign exchange contracts	1	—
Interest rate contracts	30	2

Fair value is defined as the price that would be received to sell an asset or paid to transfer a liability in an orderly transaction between market participants at the measurement date. The fair value hierarchy distinguishes between (1) market participant assumptions developed based on market data obtained from independent sources (observable inputs) and (2) an entity's own assumptions about market participant assumptions developed based on the best information available in the circumstances (unobservable inputs). The fair value hierarchy consists of three broad levels, which gives the highest priority to unadjusted quoted prices in active markets for identical assets or liabilities (Level 1) and the lowest priority to unobservable inputs (Level 3). The three levels of the fair value hierarchy are described below:

- Level 1—Unadjusted quoted prices in active markets that are accessible at the measurement date for identical, unrestricted assets or liabilities.
- Level 2—Inputs other than quoted prices included within Level 1 that are observable for the asset or liability, either directly or indirectly, including quoted prices for similar assets or liabilities in active markets; quoted prices for identical or similar assets or liabilities in markets that are not active; inputs other than quoted prices that are observable for the asset or liability (e.g., interest rates); and inputs that are derived principally from or corroborated by observable market data by correlation or other means.
- Level 3—Inputs that are both significant to the fair value measurement and unobservable.

Deferred Credits

2.181

SERVICE CORPORATION INTERNATIONAL (DEC)

CONSOLIDATED BALANCE SHEET

	December 31	
(In thousands, except share amounts)	2011	2010
Liabilities & Equity *(in part)*		
Current liabilities:		
Accounts payable and accrued liabilities	$ 358,904	$ 342,651
Current maturities of long-term debt	23,554	22,502
Income taxes	3,150	1,474
Total current liabilities	385,608	366,627
Long-term debt	1,861,116	1,832,380
Deferred preneed funeral revenues	575,546	580,223
Deferred preneed cemetery revenues	833,303	813,493
Deferred tax liability	405,615	323,303
Other liabilities	414,773	399,620
Deferred preneed funeral and cemetery receipts held in trust	2,424,356	2,408,074
Care trusts' corpus	1,015,300	986,872
Commitments and contingencies (Note 12)		

NOTES TO CONSOLIDATED FINANCIAL STATEMENTS

2. Summary of Significant Accounting Policies (in part)

Funeral Operations

Revenue is recognized when funeral services are performed or funeral merchandise is delivered. We sell price-guaranteed preneed funeral contracts through various programs providing for future funeral services at prices prevailing when the agreements are signed. Revenue associated with sales of preneed funeral contracts is deferred until such time that the funeral services are performed or funeral merchandise is delivered. Sales taxes collected are recognized on a net basis in our consolidated financial statements.

Pursuant to state or provincial law, all or a portion of the proceeds from funeral merchandise or services sold on a preneed basis may be required to be paid into trust funds. We defer investment earnings related to these merchandise and service trusts until the associated merchandise is delivered or services are performed. Costs related to sales of merchandise and services are charged to expense when merchandise is delivered or services are performed. See Note 4 for more information regarding preneed funeral activities.

Cemetery Operations

Revenue associated with sales of cemetery merchandise and services is recognized when the service is performed or merchandise is delivered. Revenue associated with sales of preneed cemetery interment rights is recognized in accordance with the Revenue Recognition Topic of the ASC. Under this guidance, revenue related to the preneed sale of unconstructed cemetery property is deferred until it is constructed and 10% of the sales price is collected. For services and non-personalized merchandise (such as vaults), we defer the revenues until the services are performed or the merchandise is delivered. For personalized marker merchandise, with the customer's direction generally obtained at the time of sale, we can choose to order, store, and transfer title to the customer. In situations in which we have no further obligation or involvement related to the merchandise, we recognize revenues and record the cost of sales in accordance with the Revenue Recognition Topic of the ASC upon the earlier of vendor storage of these items or delivery in our cemetery. Sales taxes collected are recognized on a net basis in our consolidated financial statements.

Pursuant to state or provincial law, all or a portion of the proceeds from cemetery merchandise or services sold on a preneed basis may be required to be paid into trust funds. We defer investment earnings related to these merchandise and services trusts until the associated merchandise is delivered or services are performed.

A portion of the proceeds from the sale of cemetery property interment rights is required by state or provincial law to be paid into perpetual care trust funds. Investment earnings from these trusts are distributed to us regularly, are recognized in current cemetery revenues, and are intended to defray cemetery maintenance costs, which are expensed as incurred. The principal of such perpetual care trust funds generally cannot be withdrawn.

Costs related to the sale of property interment rights include the property and construction costs specifically identified by project. At the completion of the project, construction costs are charged to expense in the same period revenue is recognized. Costs related to sales of merchandise and services are charged to expense when merchandise is delivered or when services are performed.

See Notes 5 and 6 for more information regarding preneed cemetery activities.

Preneed Funeral and Cemetery Receivables

We sell preneed funeral and cemetery contracts whereby the customer enters into arrangements for future merchandise and services prior to the time of need. As these contracts are prior to the delivery of the related goods and services, the preneed funeral and cemetery receivables are offset by a comparable deferred revenue amount. These receivables have an interest component for which interest income is recorded when the interest amount is considered collectible and realizable, which typically coincides with cash payment. We do not accrue interest on financing receivables that are not paid in accordance with the contractual payment date given the nature of our goods and services, the nature of our contracts with customers, and the timing of the delivery of our services. We do not consider receivables to be past due until the service or goods are required to be delivered at which time the preneed receivable is paid or reclassified as a trade receivable with payment terms of less than 30 days. As the preneed funeral and cemetery receivables are offset by comparable deferred revenue amount, we have no risk of loss related to these receivables.

If a preneed contract is cancelled prior to delivery, state or provincial law determines the amount of the refund owed to the customer, if any, including the amount of the attributed investment earnings. Upon cancellation, we receive the amount of principal deposited to the trust and previously undistributed net investment earnings and, where required, issue a refund to the customer. We retain excess funds, if any, and recognize the attributed investment earnings (net of any investment earnings payable to the customer) as revenue in the consolidated statement of operations. In certain jurisdictions, we may be obligated to fund any shortfall if the amount deposited by the customers exceed the funds in trust. Based on our historical experience, we have provided an allowance for cancellation of these receivables, which is recorded as a reduction in receivables with a corresponding offset to deferred revenue.

4. Preneed Funeral Activities (in part)

Deferred Preneed Funeral Revenues

At December 31, 2011 and 2010, *Deferred preneed funeral revenues*, net of allowance for cancellation, represent future funeral revenues, including distributed trust investment earnings associated with unperformed trust-funded preneed funeral contracts that are not held in trust accounts. *Deferred preneed funeral revenues* are recognized in current funeral revenues when the service is performed or merchandise is delivered. Future funeral service revenues and net trust investment earnings that are held in trust accounts are included in *Deferred preneed funeral receipts held in trust*.

The following table summarizes the activity in *Deferred preneed funeral revenues* for the years ended December 31 were as follows:

(In thousands)	2011	2010	2009
Beginning balance—Deferred preneed funeral revenues, net	$ 580,223	$ 596,966	$ 588,198
Net preneed contract sales	105,866	112,678	141,752
Acquisitions (dispositions) of businesses, net	142,026	26,816	(794)
Net investment (losses) earnings[1]	(12,164)	83,605	135,842
Recognized deferred preneed revenues	(182,408)	(151,484)	(153,382)
Change in cancellation allowance	(1,526)	(761)	(2,972)
Change in deferred preneed funeral receipts held in trust	(57,936)	(69,694)	(117,181)
Effect of foreign currency and other	1,465	(17,903)	5,503
Ending balance—Deferred preneed funeral revenues, net	$ 575,546	$ 580,223	$ 596,966

[1] Includes both realized and unrealized investment earnings (losses).

5. Preneed Cemetery Activities (in part)

Deferred Preneed Cemetery Revenues

At December 31, 2011 and 2010, *Deferred preneed cemetery revenues*, net of allowance for cancellation, represent future cemetery revenues, including distributed trust investment earnings associated with unperformed trust-funded preneed cemetery contracts that are not held in trust accounts. *Deferred preneed cemetery revenues* are recognized in current cemetery revenues when the service is performed or merchandise is delivered. Future cemetery revenues and net trust investment earnings that are held in trust accounts are included in *Deferred preneed cemetery receipts held in trust*.

The following table summarizes the activity in *Deferred preneed cemetery revenues* for the years ended December 31:

(In thousands)	2011	2010	2009
Beginning balance—Deferred preneed cemetery revenues	$ 813,493	$ 817,543	$ 771,117
Net preneed and atneed deferred sales	363,523	349,786	342,984
(Dispositions) acquisitions of businesses, net	(10,861)	1,090	5,461
Net investment (losses) earnings[1]	(26,431)	117,331	242,483
Recognized deferred preneed revenues	(350,356)	(347,996)	(325,036)
Change in cancellation allowance	802	(2,457)	10,855
Change in deferred preneed cemetery receipts held in trust	37,173	(125,974)	(235,031)
Effect of foreign currency and other	5,960	4,170	4,710
Ending balance—Deferred preneed cemetery revenues	$ 833,303	$ 813,493	$ 817,543

[1] Includes both realized and unrealized investment earnings (losses).

7. Deferred Preneed Funeral and Cemetery Receipts Held in Trust and Care Trusts' Corpus (in part)

Deferred Preneed Funeral and Cemetery Receipts Held in Trust

We consolidate the merchandise and service trusts associated with our preneed funeral and cemetery activities in accordance with the Consolidation Topic of the ASC. Al-though the guidance requires the consolidation of the merchandise and service trusts, it does not change the legal relationships among the trusts, us, or our customers. The customers are the legal beneficiaries of these merchandise and service trusts; therefore, their interests in these trusts represent a liability to us.

The components of *Deferred preneed funeral and cemetery receipts held in trust* in our consolidated balance sheet at December 31, 2011 and 2010 are detailed below.

	December 31, 2011			December 31, 2010		
	Preneed Funeral	Preneed Cemetery	Total	Preneed Funeral	Preneed Cemetery	Total
	(In thousands)			(In thousands)		
Trust investments	$1,271,446	$1,156,023	$2,427,469	$1,216,542	$1,194,795	$2,411,337
Accrued trust operating payables and other	(1,261)	(1,852)	(3,113)	(975)	(2,288)	(3,263)
Deferred preneed funeral and cemetery receipts held in trust	$1,270,185	$1,154,171	$2,424,356	$1,215,567	$1,192,507	$2,408,074

ACCUMULATED OTHER COMPREHENSIVE INCOME

PRESENTATION

2.182 FASB ASC 220, *Comprehensive Income*, requires that a separate caption for accumulated other comprehensive income be presented in the "Equity" section of a balance sheet. An entity should disclose accumulated balances for each classification in that separate component of equity on the face of a balance sheet, in a statement of changes in equity, or in notes to the financial statements.

Author's Note

In June 2011, FASB issued ASU No. 2011-05, *Comprehensive Income (Topic 220): Presentation of Comprehensive Income*, which amends FASB ASC by eliminating the option to present the components of OCI as part of the statement of changes in stockholders' equity. Going forward, an entity will present the total of comprehensive income, the components of net income, and the components of OCI either in a single continuous statement of comprehensive income or in two separate but consecutive statements. In either option, an entity should present each component of net income together with total net income, each component of OCI together with a total for OCI, and a total amount for comprehensive income. The amendments to FASB ASC 220, *Comprehensive Income*, in FASB ASU No. 2011-05 do not change which items an entity should present in OCI or when an entity should reclassify an item of OCI to net income. FASB ASU No. 2011-05 is effective for fiscal years, and interim periods within those years, beginning after December 15, 2011. For nonpublic entities, the amendments are effective for fiscal years ending after December 15, 2012, and interim and annual periods thereafter. Early adoption is permitted because the remaining options are already permitted by FASB ASC 220. The amendments do not require any transition disclosures.

In December 2011, FASB issued ASU No. 2011-12, *Comprehensive Income (Topic 220): Deferral of the Effective Date for Amendments to the Presentation of Reclassifications of Items Out of Accumulated Other Comprehensive Income in ASU No. 2011-05*. ASU No. 2011-12 defers the changes in ASU No. 2011-05 related only to the presentation of reclassification adjustments. Preparers had argued that these reclassification adjustments would be difficult for preparers and might add unnecessary complexity to the financial statements. FASB issued ASU No. 2011-12 to allow sufficient time for it to redeliberate whether an entity should present the effects of reclassification adjustments on the face of the financial statements for all periods presented. While FASB is considering preparers' concerns, entities should continue to report reclassification adjustments in accordance with the requirements of FASB ASC 220 in effect before issuance of FASB ASU No. 2011-05. The amendments in FASB ASU No. 2011-12 are effective at the same time as the amendments in FASB ASU No. 2011-05.

2.183

TABLE 2-15: ACCUMULATED OTHER COMPREHENSIVE INCOME— PRESENTATION OF COMPONENT BALANCES

Table 2-15 shows where accumulated component balances are presented.

	2011	2010	2009
Notes to financial statements................................	106	105	298
Statement of changes in stockholders' equity.....	220	232	90
"Stockholders' Equity" section of the balance sheet..	132	123	27
Statement of comprehensive income..................	24	12	1
Component balances not presented....................	11	19	73
	493	491	489
No accumulated other comprehensive income ...	7	9	11
Total Entities...	**500**	**500**	**500**

PRESENTATION AND DISCLOSURE EXCERPTS

Accumulated Other Comprehensive Income—Equity Section of Balance Sheet

2.184

PALL CORPORATION (JUL)

CONSOLIDATED BALANCE SHEETS

(In thousands, except per share data)

	July 31, 2011	July 31, 2010
Stockholders' equity:		
Common stock, par value $.10 per share; 500,000 shares authorized; 127,958 shares issued	12,796	12,796
Capital in excess of par value	246,665	217,696
Retained earnings	1,619,051	1,394,321
Treasury stock, at cost (2011–12,963 shares, 2010–12,490 shares)	(483,705)	(412,335)
Stock option loans	(133)	(224)
Accumulated other comprehensive income/(loss):		
Foreign currency translation	207,478	97,249
Pension liability adjustment	(121,831)	(132,577)
Unrealized investment gains	9,500	5,424
	95,147	(29,904)
Total stockholders' equity	1,489,821	1,182,350

2.185

BRUNSWICK CORPORATION (DEC)

CONSOLIDATED BALANCE SHEETS (in part)

	As of December 31	
(In millions, except share data)	2011	2010
Shareholders' equity		
Common stock; authorized: 200,000,000 shares, $0.75 par value; issued: 102,538,000 shares	76.9	76.9
Additional paid-in capital	434.6	424.6
Retained earnings	457.7	390.3
Treasury stock, at cost: 13,434,000 and 13,877,000 shares	(397.5)	(405.9)
Accumulated other comprehensive income (loss), net of tax:		
Foreign currency translation	12.0	32.4
Defined benefit plans:		
Prior service credits	11.7	11.5
Net actuarial losses	(560.1)	(459.8)
Unrealized investment gains (losses)	(0.1)	0.7
Unrealized losses on derivatives	(4.3)	(0.3)
Total accumulated other comprehensive loss	(540.8)	(415.5)
Shareholders' equity	30.9	70.4

Accumulated Other Comprehensive Income—Statement of Changes in Equity

2.186

ROCK-TENN COMPANY (SEP)

CONSOLIDATED STATEMENTS OF EQUITY (in part)

	Year Ended September 30		
(In millions, except share and per share data)	2011	2010	2009
Number of Shares of Class A Common Stock Outstanding:			
Balance at beginning of year	38,903,036	38,707,695	38,228,523
Shares issued under restricted stock plan	537,078	182,800	194,885
Restricted stock grants forfeited	(7,675)	(15,926)	(26,499)
Issuance of Class A common stock, net of stock received for minimum tax withholdings[1]	31,035,465	103,368	310,786
Purchases of Class A common stock	—	(74,901)	—
Balance at end of year	70,467,904	38,903,036	38,707,695
Class A Common Stock:			
Balance at beginning of year	$ 0.4	$ 0.4	$ 0.4
Issuance of Class A common stock, net of stock received for minimum tax withholdings[1]	0.3	—	—
Balance at end of year	$ 0.7	$ 0.4	$ 0.4
Capital in Excess of Par Value:			
Balance at beginning of year	290.5	264.5	238.8
Income tax benefit from share-based plans	—	4.3	5.5
Compensation expense under share-based plans	21.4	16.0	11.9
Issuance of Class A common stock, net of stock received for minimum tax withholdings[1]	2,412.4	6.2	8.3
Fair value of share-based awards issued in the Smurfit-Stone Acquisition	56.4	—	—
Purchase of subsidiary shares from noncontrolling interest	(18.0)	—	—
Purchases of Class A common stock	—	(0.5)	—
Balance at end of year	2,762.7	290.5	264.5
Retained Earnings:			
Balance at beginning of year	812.6	620.3	421.7
Net income attributable to Rock-Tenn Company shareholders	141.1	225.6	222.3
Cash dividends (per share—$0.80, $0.60 and $0.40)	(37.6)	(23.4)	(15.3)
Issuance of Class A common stock, net of stock received for minimum tax withholdings[1]	(8.7)	(6.8)	(8.4)
Purchases of Class A common stock	—	(3.1)	—
Balance at end of year	907.4	812.6	620.3
Accumulated Other Comprehensive (Loss) Income:			
Balance at beginning of year	(92.2)	(108.4)	(20.4)
Foreign currency translation gain (loss)	(12.9)	6.7	(2.1)
Net deferred loss on cash flow hedges	(0.3)	(3.5)	(16.7)
Reclassification adjustment of net loss on cash flow hedges included in earnings	4.0	6.0	5.2
Net actuarial loss arising during period	(210.3)	(7.9)	(78.6)
Amortization of net actuarial loss	11.8	11.6	4.5
Prior service (cost) credit arising during period	0.3	(0.1)	(1.0)
Amortization of prior service cost	0.4	0.5	0.7
Other adjustments	—	2.9	—
Net other comprehensive income (loss) adjustments, net of tax	(207.0)	16.2	(88.0)
Balance at end of year	(299.2)	(92.2)	(108.4)
Total Rock-Tenn Company Shareholders' equity	3,371.6	1,011.3	776.8
Noncontrolling Interests:[2]			
Balance at beginning of year	6.1	6.3	8.2
Purchase of subsidiary shares from noncontrolling interest	(5.3)	—	—
Net income	2.0	2.8	1.9
Distributions	(2.5)	(3.2)	(3.5)
Foreign currency translation gain (loss)	0.4	0.2	(0.3)
Balance at end of year	0.7	6.1	6.3
Total equity	$ 3,372.3	$ 1,017.4	$ 783.1

[1] Included in the Issuance of Class A common stock is the issuance of approximately 31.0 million shares of Common Stock valued at $2,378.8 million in connection with the Smurfit-Stone Acquisition, including approximately 0.7 million shares reserved but unissued at September 30, 2011 for the resolution of Smurfit-Stone bankruptcy claims.

[2] Excludes amounts related to contingently redeemable noncontrolling interests which are separately classified outside of permanent equity in the mezzanine section of the Consolidated Balance Sheets.

2.187

EMERSON ELECTRIC CO. (SEP)

CONSOLIDATED STATEMENTS OF EQUITY (in part)

Years ended September 30 | Dollars in millions, except per share amounts

	2009	2010	2011
Common stock	$ 477	477	477
Additional paid-in capital			
Beginning balance	146	157	192
Stock plans and other	11	35	125
Ending balance	157	192	317
Retained earnings			
Beginning balance	14,002	14,714	15,869
Net earnings common stockholders	1,724	2,164	2,480
Cash dividends (per share: 2009, $1.32; 2010, $1.34; 2011, $1.38)	(998)	(1,009)	(1,039)
Adoption of ASC 715 measurement date provision, net of tax: 2009, $7	(14)	—	—
Ending balance	14,714	15,869	17,310
Accumulated other comprehensive income			
Beginning balance	141	(496)	(426)
Foreign currency translation	(104)	55	22
Pension and postretirement, net of tax: 2009, $334; 2010, $(6); 2011, $47	(568)	(12)	(56)
Cash flow hedges and other, net of tax: 2009, $(29); 2010, $(16); 2011, $60	35	27	(102)
Ending balance	(496)	(426)	(562)
Treasury stock			
Beginning balance	(5,653)	(6,297)	(6,320)
Purchases	(695)	(100)	(958)
Issued under stock plans and other	51	77	135
Ending balance	(6,297)	(6,320)	(7,143)
Common stockholders' equity	8,555	9,792	10,399
Noncontrolling interests in subsidiaries			
Beginning balance	188	151	160
Net earnings	47	53	50
Other comprehensive income	2	—	4
Cash dividends	(80)	(57)	(61)
Other	(6)	13	(1)
Ending balance	151	160	152
Total equity	$ 8,706	9,952	10,551

Accumulated Other Comprehensive Income—Notes to Consolidated Financial Statements

2.188

ARCHER DANIELS MIDLAND COMPANY (JUN)

NOTES TO CONSOLIDATED FINANCIAL STATEMENTS

Note 11. Accumulated Other Comprehensive Income (Loss)

The following table sets forth information with respect to accumulated other comprehensive income:

	Foreign Currency Translation Adjustment	Deferred Gain (Loss) on Hedging Activities	Pension Liability Adjustment	Unrealized Gain (Loss) on Investments	Accumulated Other Comprehensive Income (Loss)
			(In millions)		
Balance at June 30, 2008	$1,026	$ 90	$(179)	$ 20	$ 957
Unrealized gains (losses)	(819)	(24)	(591)	(26)	(1,460)
(Gains) losses reclassified to earnings	—	(126)	8	6	(112)
Tax effect	—	47	206	7	260
Net of tax amount	(819)	(103)	(377)	(13)	(1,312)
Balance at June 30, 2009	207	(13)	(556)	7	(355)
Unrealized gains (losses)	(557)	46	(123)	37	(597)
(Gains) losses reclassified to earnings	—	24	41	6	71
Tax effect	—	(27)	25	(16)	(18)
Net of tax amount	(557)	43	(57)	27	(544)
Balance at June 30, 2010	(350)	30	(613)	34	(899)
Unrealized gains (losses)	859	43	230	49	1,181
(Gains) losses reclassified to earnings	—	(46)	70	(13)	11
Tax effect	—	2	(106)	(13)	(117)
Net of tax amount	859	(1)	194	23	1,075
Balance at June 30, 2011	$ 509	$ 29	$(419)	$ 57	$ 176

2.189

THE ESTEE LAUDER COMPANIES INC. (JUN)

*NOTES TO CONSOLIDATED FINANCIAL
STATEMENTS*

*Note 18—Accumulated Other Comprehensive Income
(Loss)*

The components of Accumulated OCI ("AOCI") included in
the accompanying consolidated balance sheets consist of
the following:

(In millions)	Year Ended June 30		
	2011	**2010**	**2009**
Net unrealized investment gains, beginning of year	$ 0.2	$ (0.2)	$ 0.3
Unrealized investment gains (losses)	0.4	0.6	(0.8)
Benefit (provision) for deferred income taxes	(0.1)	(0.2)	0.3
Net unrealized investment gains, end of year	0.5	0.2	(0.2)
Net derivative instruments, beginning of year	14.3	1.5	7.9
Gain (loss) on derivative instruments	(38.0)	(0.2)	16.5
Benefit (provision) for deferred income taxes on derivative instruments	13.4	(0.1)	(5.8)
Reclassification to earnings during the year:			
Foreign currency forward and option contracts	15.1	20.3	(26.1)
Settled interest rate-related derivatives	(0.3)	(0.2)	(0.3)
Benefit (provision) for deferred income taxes on reclassification	(5.2)	(7.0)	9.3
Net derivative instruments, end of year	(0.7)	14.3	1.5
Net pension and post-retirement adjustments, beginning of year	(217.6)	(190.7)	(108.8)
Changes in plan assets and benefit obligations:			
Net actuarial gains (losses) recognized	30.7	(65.6)	(138.5)
Net prior service credit (cost) recognized	(10.6)	2.6	(0.7)
Translation adjustments	(16.4)	6.5	8.7
Amortization of amounts included in net periodic benefit cost:			
Net actuarial (gains) losses	26.3	9.3	4.1
Net prior service cost (credit)	3.1	3.1	3.0
Net transition asset (obligation)	—	—	—
Benefit (provision) for deferred income taxes	(14.5)	17.2	41.5
Net pension and post-retirement adjustments, end of year	(199.0)	(217.6)	(190.7)
Cumulative translation adjustments, beginning of year	6.4	72.3	211.4
Translation adjustments	213.2	(65.5)	(138.4)
Benefit (provision) for deferred income taxes	(2.7)	(0.4)	(0.7)
Cumulative translation adjustments, end of year	216.9	6.4	72.3
Accumulated other comprehensive income (loss)	$ 17.7	$(196.7)	$(117.1)

Of the $0.7 million, net of tax, derivative instrument loss
recorded in AOCI at June 30, 2011, $8.5 million in losses, net
of tax, related to foreign currency forward contracts which
the Company will reclassify to earnings through March 2013.
Also included in the net derivative instrument loss recorded
in OCI was $0.6 million, net of tax, related to a loss from the
settlement of a series of forward-starting interest rate swap
agreements upon the issuance of the Company's 6.00% Senior Notes due May 2037, which will be reclassified to earnings as an addition to interest expense over the life of the

debt. These losses were partially offset by $8.4 million, net
of tax, related to the October 2003 gain from the settlement
of the treasury lock agreements upon the issuance of the
Company's 5.75% Senior Notes due October 2033, which is
being reclassified to earnings as an offset to interest expense
over the life of the debt.

Refer to Note 13—Pension, Deferred Compensation and
Post-retirement Benefit Plans for the discussion regarding
the net pension and post-retirement adjustments.

Section 3: Income Statement

INCOME STATEMENT FORMAT

PRESENTATION

3.01 Either a single-step or multistep form is acceptable for preparing a statement of income. In a single-step format, income tax is shown as a separate last item. In a multistep format, either costs are deducted from sales to show the gross margin, or costs and expenses are deducted from sales to show operating income. Further, net income should reflect all items of profit and loss recognized during the period, except for certain entities (investment companies, insurance entities, and certain not-for-profit entities) and with the sole exception of error corrections, as discussed in Financial Accounting Standards Board (FASB) *Accounting Standards Codification* (ASC) 250, *Accounting Changes and Error Corrections*.

3.02 FASB ASC 220, *Comprehensive Income*, requires that comprehensive income and its components be reported in a financial statement. Comprehensive income and its components can be reported in an income statement, a separate statement of comprehensive income, or a statement of changes in stockholders' equity.

Author's Note

In June 2011, FASB issued Accounting Standards Update (ASU) No. 2011-05, *Comprehensive Income (Topic 220): Presentation of Comprehensive Income*, which amends the FASB ASC by eliminating the option to present the components of other comprehensive income as part of the statement of changes in stockholders' equity. Going forward, an entity will present the total of comprehensive income, the components of net income, and the components of other comprehensive income either in a single continuous statement of comprehensive income or in two separate but consecutive statements. In either option, an entity should present each component of net income together with total net income, each component of other comprehensive income together with a total for other comprehensive income, and a total amount for comprehensive income. The amendments to Topic 220 in this update do not change which items an entity should present in other comprehensive income or when an entity should reclassify an item of other comprehensive income to net income.

This update is effective for fiscal years, and interim periods within those years, beginning after December 31, 2011. For nonpublic entities, the amendments are effective for fiscal years ending after December 15, 2012, and interim and annual periods thereafter. Early adoption is permitted because the remaining options are already permitted by Topic 220. The amendments do not require any transition disclosures.

In December 2011, FASB issued ASU No. 2011-12, *Comprehensive Income (Topic 220): Deferral of the Effective Date for Amendments to the Presentation of Reclassifications of Items Out of Accumulated Other Comprehensive Income*

in *Accounting Standards Update No. 2011-05*. This udpate defers the changes in ASU No. 2011-05 related only to the presentation of reclassification adjustments. Preparers had argued that these reclassification adjustments would be difficult for preparers and might add unnecessary complexity to the financial statements. FASB issued this ASU to allow sufficient time for it to redeliberate whether an entity should present the effects of reclassification adjustments on the face of the financial statements for all periods presented. While FASB is considering preparers' concerns, entities should continue to report reclassification adjustments in accordance with the requirements of Topic 220 in effect before issuance of ASU No. 2011-05. The amendments ASU No. 2011-12 are effective at the same time as the amendments in ASU No. 2011-05.

PRESENTATION AND DISCLOSURE EXCERPTS

Reclassifications

3.03

BEAM INC. (DEC)

NOTES TO CONSOLIDATED FINANCIAL STATEMENTS

1. Description of Business, Basis of Presentation, and Summary of Significant Accounting Policies (in part)

Reclassifications

Reclassifications have been made to the prior year financial information to conform to the current year presentation, for the presentation of revenue net of excise tax (as discussed below in *Changes in Basis of Presentation and Accounting*), the presentation of advertising and marketing expenses separate from selling, general, and administrative expenses ("SG&A"), and the presentation of the Home & Security and Golf businesses as discontinued operations (as discussed below in *Changes in Basis of Presentation and Accounting*).

Changes in Basis of Presentation and Accounting

The results of operations of the Home & Security and Golf businesses were reclassified to discontinued operations in the accompanying statement of income for the years ended December 31, 2011, 2010, and 2009. The assets and liabilities of the Home & Security and Golf businesses were reclassified to discontinued operations in the accompanying consolidated balance sheet as of December 31, 2010. The cash flows from discontinued operations for the years ended December 31, 2011, 2010, and 2009 are not separately stated and classified in the accompanying consolidated statement of cash flows. Footnote disclosures only relate to continuing operations except where noted otherwise. Information on business segments does not include discontinued operations. In accordance with authoritative accounting guidance, the Company has not allocated any corporate overhead to the discontinued operations; however, it has allocated interest expense.

In accordance with GAAP, taxes collected from customers and remitted to governmental authorities may be presented either on a gross basis (included in sales and costs) or a net basis (excluded from sales). In 2011, we changed our presentation of excise taxes from the gross method to the net method. We refer to the presentation of excise tax on a net basis as "net sales" in our financial statements. The change in presentation to the net method is preferable for consistency in comparison to internal Beam financial statements reviewed by management to evaluate the business and also to the external financial statements of other standalone spirits companies. Historical periods have been reclassified to conform to the new presentation.

13. Derivative Instruments (in part)

The effects of derivative financial instruments on the statement of income and OCI for the years ended December 31, 2011 and 2010 were (in millions):

| | Gain (Loss) | | | | |
| | Recognized in OCI (Effective Portion) | | Recognized in Income | | |
Type of Hedge	2011	2010	Location of Gain (Loss) Recognized in Income	2011	2010
Cash flow—foreign exchange contracts	$(4.3)	$(8.5)	Net sales	$(10.6)	$(11.6)
Fair value—interest rate contracts[a]	n/a	n/a	Interest expense	13.2	19.6
Fair value—foreign exchange contracts	n/a	n/a	Other income	(24.6)	(1.5)
Total	$(4.3)	$(8.5)		$(22.0)	$ 6.5

[a] Represents the gain recorded prior to the third quarter 2011 termination of the interest rate swaps with a notional amount of $900.0 million that hedged the fair value of certain fixed rate debt. The amounts recorded for the swap were offset by corresponding debt fair value adjustments that were also recorded to interest expense. We received cash proceeds of approximately $45 million upon termination of the swaps, which was performed in conjunction with planned debt retirements (see Note 15, Debt). The adjustment to the fair value of the debt is being recognized over the term of the debt, including accelerated amortization related to early debt extinguishments. There were no interest rate swaps outstanding as of December 31, 2011.

We estimate that less than $1 million of net derivative gains included in OCI as of December 31, 2011 will be reclassified to earnings within the next twelve months.

21. Other Comprehensive Income (Loss) (in part)

Other comprehensive income (loss) includes activity relating to discontinued operations prior to the Spin-Off. The components of other comprehensive income (loss) for the years ended December 31, 2011, 2010, and 2009 are as follows (in millions):

	2011	2010	2009
Foreign currency translation (losses) gains	$(189.7)	$42.0	$293.3
Reclassifications adjustments included in earnings	(39.6)	1.3	—
Tax benefit (expense)	3.8	(17.3)	(5.2)
Foreign currency translation adjustments, net	(225.5)	26.0	288.1
Derivative instruments losses	(12.4)	(9.3)	(19.0)
Reclassifications adjustments included in earnings	21.2	10.6	(22.0)
Tax (expense) benefit	(2.1)	1.5	1.8
Derivative instruments, net	6.7	2.8	(39.2)
Current year actuarial loss—pension plans	(112.7)	(1.8)	(23.6)
Current year actuarial gain (loss)—other postretirement benefit plans	1.8	(0.3)	10.8
Current year prior service cost—other postretirement benefit plans	—	—	10.8
Reclassification adjustments included in earnings	73.9	21.2	32.4
Tax benefit (expense)	15.9	(8.1)	(12.7)
Pension and other postretirement benefit adjustments, net	(21.1)	11.0	17.7
Other comprehensive (loss) income attributable to Beam Inc. stockholders	$(239.9)	$39.8	$266.6

Reclassification adjustments included in earnings related to pension and other postretirement benefits includes amortization of actuarial gains (losses) and prior service credits (costs) and the recognition of actuarial gains and prior service cost related to curtailments and settlements. Reclassification adjustments in 2011 include amounts recorded to earnings due to the sale of the Golf business. See Note 17, Pension and Other Postretirement Benefits, for more information.

REVENUES AND GAINS

RECOGNITION AND MEASUREMENT

3.04 As explained by FASB ASC 605-10-25-1, the recognition of revenue and gains of an entity during a period involves consideration of the following two factors, with sometimes one and sometimes the other being the more important consideration:

- *Being realized or realizable.* Revenue and gains generally are not recognized until realized or realizable. Paragraph 83(a) of FASB Concepts Statement No. 5, *Recognition and Measurement in Financial Statements of Business Enterprises,* states that revenue and gains are realized when products (goods or services), merchandise, or other assets are exchanged for cash or claims to cash. That paragraph states that revenue and gains are realizable when related assets received or held are readily convertible to known amounts of cash or claims to cash.
- *Being earned.* Paragraph 83(b) of FASB Concepts Statement No. 5 states that revenue is not recognized until earned. That paragraph states that an entity's revenue-earning activities involve delivering or producing goods, rendering services, or other activities that constitute its ongoing major or central operations, and revenues are considered to have been earned when the entity has substantially accomplished what it must do to be entitled to the benefits represented by the revenues. That paragraph states that gains commonly result from transactions and other events that involve no earning process, and for recognizing gains, being earned is generally less significant than being realized or realizable.

3.05 FASB ASC 605-25 contains guidance on segmenting of transactions, referred to as *multiple element arrangements,* for both recognition and measurement. FASB ASC 605-25-25-2 requires that an entity should divide revenue arrangements with multiple deliverables into separate units of accounting if both the delivered item(s) have value to the customer on a standalone basis and, if the arrangement includes a general right of return, delivery and performance of the undelivered item(s) is probable and substantially in the vendor's control. FASB ASC 605-25-30-2 requires an entity to allocate the arrangement consideration at the inception of the arrangement to all deliverables based on their relative selling price (relative selling price method), except when another Topic in the FASB ASC requires a unit of accounting in the arrangement to be recorded at fair value or the amount that can be allocated to a unit of accounting is limited to an amount that is not contingent on delivery of additional deliverables or specified performance conditions. When a vendor applies the relative selling price method, an entity should determine the selling price using vendor-specific objective evidence of selling price, if it exists. Otherwise, the vendor should use its best estimate of selling price for that deliverable. Vendors should not ignore information that is reasonably available without undue cost or effort.

3.06

TABLE 3-1: FREQUENTLY DISCLOSED GAINS AND OTHER INCOME*

Gains and other income most frequently shown on the face of the income statement or disclosed by the survey entities are listed in Table 3-1. Excluded from Table 3-1 are credits shown after the income tax caption, segment disposals, and extraordinary credits.

	Number of Entities		
	2011	**2010**	**2009**
Interest	330	285	318
Change in fair value of derivatives	98	77	202
Sale of assets	139	121	149
Equity in earnings of investees	122	107	108
Dividends	37	28	60
Liability accruals reduced	26	19	60
Foreign currency transactions	55	51	59
Debt extinguishments	18	14	33
Royalty, franchise and license fees	27	31	32
Litigation settlements	14	16	26
Insurance recoveries	18	13	15
Change in fair value of financial assets/liabilities	24	29	12
Employee benefit/pension related	15	16	8
Rentals	16	5	6
Noncontrolling interest in investee loss	12	13	6
Business combination adjustment gain	15	16	6
Other	110	95	N/C^

* Appearing in the income statement or notes to the financial statements, or both.

^ N/C = Not compiled. The line item was not included in the table for the year shown.

PRESENTATION AND DISCLOSURE EXCERPTS

Revenues

3.07

CISCO SYSTEMS, INC. (JUL)

CONSOLIDATED STATEMENTS OF OPERATIONS (in part)

(In millions, except per-share amounts)

Years Ended	July 30, 2011	July 31, 2010	July 25, 2009
Net Sales:			
Product	$34,526	$32,420	$29,131
Service	8,692	7,620	6,986
Total net sales	43,218	40,040	36,117
Cost of Sales:			
Product	13,647	11,620	10,481
Service	3,035	2,777	2,542
Total cost of sales	16,682	14,397	13,023
Gross Margin	26,536	25,643	23,094

NOTES TO CONSOLIDATED FINANCIAL STATEMENTS

2. Summary of Significant Accounting Policies (in part)

<u>(n) Revenue Recognition</u> The Company recognizes revenue when persuasive evidence of an arrangement exists, delivery has occurred, the fee is fixed or determinable, and collectibility is reasonably assured. In instances where final acceptance of the product, system, or solution is specified by the customer, revenue is deferred until all acceptance criteria have been met. For hosting arrangements, the Company recognizes subscription revenue ratably over the subscription period, while usage revenue is recognized based on utilization. Technical support services revenue is deferred and recognized ratably over the period during which the services are to be performed, which is typically from one to three years. Advanced services revenue is recognized upon delivery or completion of performance.

The Company uses distributors that stock inventory and typically sell to systems integrators, service providers, and other resellers. In addition, certain products are sold through retail partners. The Company refers to this as its two-tier system of sales to the end customer. Revenue from distributors and retail partners generally is recognized based on a sell-through method using information provided by them. Distributors and retail partners participate in various cooperative marketing and other programs, and the Company maintains estimated accruals and allowances for these programs. The Company accrues for warranty costs, sales returns, and other allowances based on its historical experience. Shipping and handling fees billed to customers are included in net sales, with the associated costs included in cost of sales.

In October 2009, the FASB amended the accounting standards for revenue recognition to remove from the scope of industry-specific software revenue recognition guidance tangible products containing software components and nonsoftware components that function together to deliver the product's essential functionality. In October 2009, the FASB also amended the accounting standards for multiple-deliverable revenue arrangements to:

i. provide updated guidance on whether multiple deliverables exist, how the deliverables in an arrangement should be separated, and how consideration should be allocated;

ii. require an entity to allocate revenue in an arrangement using estimated selling prices (ESP) of deliverables if a vendor does not have vendor-specific objective evidence of selling price (VSOE) or third-party evidence of selling price (TPE); and

iii. eliminate the use of the residual method and require an entity to allocate revenue using the relative selling price method.

The Company elected to early adopt this accounting guidance at the beginning of its first quarter of fiscal 2010 on a prospective basis for applicable transactions originating or materially modified after July 25, 2009. This guidance does not generally change the units of accounting for the Company's revenue transactions. Most products and services qualify as separate units of accounting and the revenue is recognized when the applicable revenue recognition criteria are met. The Company's arrangements generally do not include any provisions for cancellation, termination, or refunds that would significantly impact recognized revenue.

Many of the Company's products have both software and nonsoftware components that function together to deliver the products' essential functionality. The Company's product offerings fall into the following categories: Routers, Switches, New Products, and Other Products. The Other Products category includes optical networking and emerging technology items. The Company also provides technical support and advanced services. The Company has a broad customer base that encompasses virtually all types of public and private entities, including enterprise businesses, service providers, commercial customers, and consumers. The Company and its salesforce are not organized by product divisions and the Company's products and services can be sold standalone or together in various combinations across the Company's geographic segments or customer markets. For example, service provider arrangements are typically larger in scale with longer deployment schedules and involve the delivery of a variety of product technologies, including high-end routing, video and network management software, and other product technologies along with technical support and advanced services. The Company's enterprise and commercial arrangements are typically unique for each customer and smaller in scale and may include network infrastructure products such as routers and switches or collaboration technologies such as unified communications and Cisco TelePresence systems products along with technical support services. Consumer products, which constitute a small portion of the Company's overall business, are sold in standalone arrangements directly to distributors and retailers without support, as customers generally only require repair or replacement of defective products or parts under warranty.

The Company enters into revenue arrangements that may consist of multiple deliverables of its product and service offerings due to the needs of its customers. For example, a customer may purchase routing products along with a contract for technical support services. This arrangement would consist of multiple elements, with the products delivered in one reporting period and the technical support services delivered across multiple reporting periods. Another customer may purchase networking products along with advanced service offerings, in which all the elements are delivered within the same reporting period. In addition, distributors and retail partners purchase products or technical support services on a standalone basis for resale to an end user or for purposes of stocking certain products, and these transactions would not result in a multiple element arrangement. For transactions entered into prior to the first quarter of fiscal 2010, the Company primarily recognized revenue based on software revenue recognition guidance. For the vast majority of the Company's arrangements involving multiple deliverables, such as sales of products with services, the entire fee from the arrangement was allocated to each respective element based on its relative selling price, using VSOE. In the limited circumstances when the Company was not able to determine VSOE for all of the deliverables of the arrangement, but was able to obtain VSOE for any undelivered elements, revenue was allocated using the residual method. Under the residual method, the amount of revenue allocated to delivered elements equaled the total arrangement consideration less the aggregate selling price of any undelivered elements, and no revenue was recognized until all elements without VSOE had been delivered. If VSOE of any undelivered items did not exist, revenue from the entire arrangement was initially deferred and recognized at the earlier of (i) delivery of those elements for which VSOE did not exist or (ii) when VSOE could be established. However, in limited cases where technical support services were the only undelivered element without VSOE, the entire arrangement fee was recognized ratably as a single unit of accounting over the technical services contractual period. The residual and ratable revenue recognition methods were generally used in a limited number of arrangements containing products within the New Products category, such as Cisco TelePresence systems. Several of these technologies are sold as solution offerings, whereas products or services are not sold on a standalone basis.

In many instances, products are sold separately in standalone arrangements as customers may support the products themselves or purchase support on a time-and-materials basis. Advanced services are sometimes sold in standalone engagements such as general consulting, network management, or security advisory projects and technical support services are sold separately through renewals of annual contracts. As a result, for substantially all of the arrangements with multiple deliverables pertaining to routing and switching products and related services, as well as most arrangements containing products within the New Products and Other Products categories, the Company has used and intends to continue using VSOE to allocate the selling price to each deliverable. Consistent with its methodology under previous accounting guidance, the Company determines VSOE based on its normal pricing and discounting practices for the specific product or service when sold separately. In determining VSOE, the Company requires that a substantial majority of the selling prices for a product or service fall within a reasonably narrow pricing range, generally evidenced by approximately 80% of such historical standalone transactions falling within plus or minus 15% of the median rates. In addition, the Company considers the geographies in which the products or services are sold, major product and service groups and customer classifications, and other environmental or marketing variables in determining VSOE.

In certain limited instances, the Company is not able to establish VSOE for all deliverables in an arrangement with multiple elements. This may be due to the Company infrequently selling each element separately, not pricing products within a narrow range, or only having a limited sales history, such as in the case of certain products within the New Products and Other Products categories. When VSOE cannot be established, the Company attempts to establish selling price of each element based on TPE. TPE is determined based on competitor prices for similar deliverables when sold separately. Generally, the Company's go-to-market strategy typically differs from that of its peers and its offerings contain a significant level of customization and differentiation such that the comparable pricing of products with similar functionality cannot be obtained. Furthermore, the Company is unable to reliably determine what similar competitor products' selling prices are on a standalone basis. Therefore, the Company is typically not able to determine TPE.

When the Company is unable to establish selling price using VSOE or TPE, the Company uses ESP in its allocation of arrangement consideration. The objective of ESP is to determine the price at which the Company would transact a sale if the product or service were sold on a standalone basis. ESP is generally used for new or highly customized offerings and solutions or offerings not priced within a narrow range, and it applies to a small proportion of the Company's arrangements with multiple deliverables.

The Company determines ESP for a product or service by considering multiple factors, including, but not limited to, geographies, market conditions, competitive landscape, internal costs, gross margin objectives, and pricing practices. The determination of ESP is made through consultation with and formal approval by the Company's management, taking into consideration the go-to-market strategy.

The Company regularly reviews VSOE, TPE and ESP, and maintains internal controls over the establishment and updates of these estimates. There were no material impacts during the fiscal year nor does the Company currently expect a material impact in the near term from changes in VSOE, TPE or ESP.

The Company's arrangements with multiple deliverables may have a standalone software deliverable that is subject to the existing software revenue recognition guidance. In these cases, revenue for the software is generally recognized upon shipment or electronic delivery. The revenue for these multiple-element arrangements is allocated to the software deliverable and the nonsoftware deliverables based on the relative selling prices of all of the deliverables in the arrangement using the hierarchy in the new revenue accounting guidance. In the limited circumstances where the Company cannot determine VSOE or TPE of the selling price for all of the deliverables in the arrangement, including the software deliverable, ESP is used for the purposes of performing this allocation.

Interest

3.08

CITIGROUP INC. (DEC)

CONSOLIDATED STATEMENT OF INCOME (in part)

(In millions of dollars, except per-share amounts)	Citigroup Inc. and Subsidiaries Year Ended December 31		
	2011	**2010**	**2009**
Revenues			
Interest revenue	$72,681	$79,282	$76,398
Interest expense	24,234	25,096	27,902
Net interest revenue	$48,447	$54,186	$48,496

NOTES TO CONSOLIDATED FINANCIAL STATEMENTS

1. Summary of Significant Accounting Policies (in part)

Investment Securities (in part)

Investments include fixed income and equity securities. Fixed income instruments include bonds, notes and redeemable preferred stocks, as well as certain loan-backed and structured securities that are subject to prepayment risk. Equity securities include common and nonredeemable preferred stock.

Investment securities are classified and accounted for as follows:

- Fixed income securities classified as "held-to-maturity" represent securities that the Company has both the ability and the intent to hold until maturity, and are carried at amortized cost. Interest income on such securities is included in *Interest revenue*.

- Fixed income securities and marketable equity securities classified as "available-for-sale" are carried at fair value with changes in fair value reported in a separate component of *Stockholders' equity*, net of applicable income taxes. As described in more detail in Note 15 to the Consolidated Financial Statements, credit-related declines in fair value that are determined to be other–than-temporary are recorded in earnings immediately. Realized gains and losses on sales are included in income primarily on a specific identification cost basis. Interest and dividend income on such securities is included in *Interest revenue*.
- Venture capital investments held by Citigroup's private equity subsidiaries that are considered investment companies are carried at fair value with changes in fair value reported in *Other revenue*. These subsidiaries include entities registered as Small Business Investment Companies and engage exclusively in venture capital activities.
- Certain investments in non-marketable equity securities and certain investments that would otherwise have been accounted for using the equity method are carried at fair value, since the Company has elected to apply fair value accounting. Changes in fair value of such investments are recorded in earnings.
- Certain non-marketable equity securities are carried at cost and periodically assessed for other-than-temporary impairment, as set out in Note 15 to the Consolidated Financial Statements.

Trading Account Assets and Liabilities (in part)

Other than physical commodities inventory, all trading account assets and liabilities are carried at fair value. Revenues generated from trading assets and trading liabilities are generally reported in *Principal transactions* and include realized gains and losses as well as unrealized gains and losses resulting from changes in the fair value of such instruments. Interest income on trading assets is recorded in *Interest revenue* reduced by interest expense on trading liabilities.

Securities Borrowed and Securities Loaned (in part)

Securities borrowing and lending transactions generally do not constitute a sale of the underlying securities for accounting purposes, and so are treated as collateralized financing transactions when the transaction involves the exchange of cash. Such transactions are recorded at the amount of cash advanced or received plus accrued interest. As described in Note 26 to the Consolidated Financial Statements, the Company has elected to apply fair value accounting to a number of securities borrowing and lending transactions. Irrespective of whether the Company has elected fair value accounting, fees paid or received for all securities lending and borrowing transactions are recorded in *Interest expense* or *Interest revenue* at the contractually specified rate.

Repurchase and Resale Agreements (in part)

Securities sold under agreements to repurchase (repos) and securities purchased under agreements to resell (reverse repos) generally do not constitute a sale for accounting purposes of the underlying securities and so are treated as collateralized financing transactions. As set out in Note 26 to

the Consolidated Financial Statements, the Company has elected to apply fair value accounting to a majority of such transactions, with changes in fair value reported in earnings. Any transactions for which fair value accounting has not been elected are recorded at the amount of cash advanced or received plus accrued interest. Irrespective of whether the Company has elected fair value accounting, interest paid or received on all repo and reverse repo transactions is recorded in *Interest expense* or *Interest revenue* at the contractually specified rate.

Loans (in part)

Loans are reported at their outstanding principal balances net of any unearned income and unamortized deferred fees and costs except that credit card receivable balances also include accrued interest and fees. Loan origination fees and certain direct origination costs are generally deferred and recognized as adjustments to income over the lives of the related loans.

As described in Note 26 to the Consolidated Financial Statements, Citi has elected fair value accounting for certain loans. Such loans are carried at fair value with changes in fair value reported in earnings. Interest income on such loans is recorded in *Interest revenue* at the contractually specified rate.

5. Interest Revenue and Expense

For the years ended December 31, 2011, 2010 and 2009, respectively, interest revenue and expense consisted of the following:

(In millions of dollars)	2011	2010	2009
Interest revenue			
Loan interest, including fees	$50,281	$55,056	$47,457
Deposits with banks	1,750	1,252	1,478
Federal funds sold and securities borrowed or purchased under agreements to resell	3,631	3,156	3,084
Investments, including dividends	8,320	11,004	12,882
Trading account assets[1]	8,186	8,079	10,723
Other interest	513	735	774
Total interest revenue	$72,681	$79,282	$76,398
Interest expense			
Deposits[2]	$ 8,556	$ 8,371	$10,146
Federal funds purchased and securities loaned or sold under agreements to repurchase	3,197	2,808	3,433
Trading account liabilities[1]	408	379	289
Short-term borrowings	650	917	1,425
Long-term debt	11,423	12,621	12,609
Total interest expense	$24,234	$25,096	$27,902
Net interest revenue	$48,447	$54,186	$48,496
Provision for loan losses	11,773	25,194	38,760
Net interest revenue after provision for loan losses	$36,674	$28,992	$ 9,736

[1] Interest expense on *Trading account liabilities* of ICG is reported as a reduction of interest revenue from *Trading account assets*.

[2] Includes deposit insurance fees and charges of $1.3 billion, $981 million and $1.5 billion for the 12 months ended December 31, 2011, 2010 and 2009, respectively. The 12-month period ended December 31, 2009 includes the one-time FDIC special assessment.

Dividends

3.09

DIRECTV (DEC)

NOTES TO THE CONSOLIDATED FINANCIAL STATEMENTS

Note 8: Investments

Equity Method Investments (in part)

Other (in part)

The following table sets forth the book value of our investments which we account for under the equity method of accounting:

	As of December 31	
(Dollars in millions)	2011	2010
Sky Mexico	$ 490	$ 501
GSN	420	446
Other equity method investments	131	139
Total investments accounted for the equity method of accounting	$1,041	$1,086

The following table sets forth equity in earnings and losses of our investments accounted for under the equity method of accounting for the periods presented:

	Years Ended December 31		
(Dollars in millions)	2011	2010	2009
Sky Mexico	$ 52	$33	$32
GSN	29	33	—
Other	28	24	19
Total equity earnings for investments accounted for under the equity method of accounting	$109	$90	$51

We received cash dividends of $104 million in 2011, $78 million in 2010 and $94 million in 2009 from companies that we account for under the equity method. Undistributed earnings from equity method investments were $256 million as of December 31, 2011 and $219 million as of December 31, 2010.

Royalty Revenue

3.10

PHILLIPS-VAN HEUSEN CORPORATION (JAN)

CONSOLIDATED INCOME STATEMENTS (in part)

(In thousands, except per share data)

	2010	2009	2008
Net sales	$4,219,739	$2,070,754	$2,160,716
Royalty revenue	309,642	242,026	236,552
Advertising and other revenue	107,467	85,951	94,667
Total revenue	4,636,848	2,398,731	2,491,935
Cost of goods sold	2,214,897	1,216,128	1,291,267
Gross profit	2,421,951	1,182,603	1,200,668

NOTES TO CONSOLIDATED FINANCIAL STATEMENTS

(Currency and share amounts in thousands, except per share data)

1. Summary of Significant Accounting Policies (in part)

Revenue Recognition—Revenue from the Company's wholesale operations is recognized at the time title to the goods passes and the risk of loss is transferred to customers. For sales by the Company's retail stores, revenue is recognized when goods are sold to consumers. Allowances for estimated returns and discounts are provided when sales are recorded. Revenue from gift cards is recognized at the time of redemption. Royalty revenue for licensees whose sales exceed contractual sales minimums, including licensee contributions toward advertising, is recognized when licensed products are sold as reported by the Company's licensees. For licensees whose sales do not exceed contractual sales minimums, royalty revenue is recognized ratably based on contractual requirements for the timing of minimum payments.

18. Segment Data (in part)

The following tables present summarized information by segment *(in part)*:

	2010	2009	2008
Revenue—Heritage Brand Wholesale Dress Furnishings			
Net sales	$ 523,901	$ 489,845	$ 480,881
Royalty revenue	5,815	5,859	7,064
Advertising and other revenue	2,689	1,681	2,613
Total	532,405	497,385	490,558
Revenue—Heritage Brand Wholesale Sportswear			
Net sales	568,447	473,101	501,675
Royalty revenue	10,731	10,133	11,355
Advertising and other revenue	1,764	1,931	3,254
Total	580,942	485,165	516,284
Revenue—Heritage Brand Retail			
Net sales	638,902	610,337	692,936[1]
Royalty revenue	5,023	4,361	4,878
Advertising and other revenue	842	795	1,307
Total	644,767	615,493	699,121
Revenue—Calvin Klein Licensing			
Net sales	38,326	32,696	33,411
Royalty revenue	247,825	221,673	213,255
Advertising and other revenue	94,596	81,544	87,493
Total	380,747	335,913	334,159
Revenue—Tommy Hilfiger North America			
Net sales	889,630	—	—
Royalty revenue	11,558	—	—
Advertising and other revenue	3,257	—	—
Total	904,445	—	—
Revenue—Tommy Hilfiger International			
Net sales	1,007,776	—	—
Royalty revenue	28,690	—	—
Advertising and other revenue	4,319	—	—
Total	1,040,785	—	—
Revenue—Other (Calvin Klein Apparel)			
Net sales	552,757	464,775	451,813
Total	552,757	464,775	451,813
Total Revenue			
Net sales	4,219,739	2,070,754	2,160,716
Royalty revenue	309,642	242,026	236,552
Advertising and other revenue	107,467	85,951	94,667
Total[2]	$4,636,848	$2,398,731	$2,491,935

[1] Revenue for the Heritage Brand Retail segment for 2008 includes $94,885 associated with the Company's Geoffrey Beene outlet retail division, which was closed during 2008.

[2] Macy's, Inc. accounted for 10.1%, 11.9% and 11.5% of the Company's revenue in 2010, 2009 and 2008, respectively. This revenue is reported in the Heritage Brand Wholesale Dress Furnishings, Heritage Brand Wholesale Sportswear, Other (Calvin Klein Apparel) and Tommy Hilfiger North America segments.

SEC 3.10

Equity in Earnings of Affiliates

3.11

HORMEL FOODS CORPORATION (OCT)

CONSOLIDATED STATEMENTS OF OPERATIONS
(in part)

	Fiscal Year Ended		
(In thousands, except per share amounts)	October 30, 2011	October 31, 2010	October 25, 2009
Net sales	$7,895,089	$7,220,719	$6,533,671
Cost of products sold	6,560,976	5,981,977	5,434,800
Gross Profit	1,334,113	1,238,742	1,098,871
Selling, general and administrative	618,586	605,293	567,085
Equity in earnings of affiliates	26,757	13,126	4,793
Operating Income	742,284	646,575	536,579

NOTES TO CONSOLIDATED FINANCIAL STATEMENTS

October 30, 2011

Note A—Summary of Significant Accounting Policies (in part)

Equity Method Investments: The Company has a number of investments in joint ventures where its voting interests are in excess of 20 percent but not greater than 50 percent. The Company accounts for such investments under the equity method of accounting, and its underlying share of each investee's equity is reported in the Consolidated Statements of Financial Position as part of investments in and receivables from affiliates.

The Company regularly monitors and evaluates the fair value of our equity investments. If events and circumstances indicate that a decline in the fair value of these assets has occurred and is other than temporary, the Company will record a charge in equity in earnings of affiliates in the Consolidated Statements of Operations. The Company's equity invest-

ments do not have a readily determinable fair value as none of them are publicly traded. The fair values of the Company's private equity investments are determined by discounting the estimated future cash flows of each entity. These cash flow estimates include assumptions on growth rates and future currency exchange rates (Level 3). The Company did not record an impairment charge on any of its equity investments in fiscal years 2011, 2010, or 2009.

See additional discussion regarding the Company's equity method investments in Note G.

Note G—Investments in and Receivables from Affiliates

The Company accounts for its majority-owned operations under the consolidation method. Investments in which the Company owns a minority interest, and for which there are no other indicators of control, are accounted for under the equity or cost method. These investments, along with any related receivables from affiliates, are included in the Consolidated Statements of Financial Position as investments in and receivables from affiliates.

Investments in and receivables from affiliates consists of the following:

(In thousands)	Segment	% Owned	October 30, 2011	October 31, 2010
MegaMex Foods, LLC	Grocery Products	50%	$205,523	$122,447
Purefoods-Hormel Company	All Other	40%	65,140	63,894
San Miguel Purefoods (Vietnam) Co. Ltd.	All Other	49%	17,442	20,501
Other	Various	Various	7,593	7,547
Total			$295,698	$214,389

Equity in earnings of affiliates consists of the following:

(In thousands)	Segment	2011	2010	2009
MegaMex Foods, LLC	Grocery Products	$24,532	$11,996	$ N/A
Purefoods-Hormel Company	All Other	5,182	3,523	1,561
San Miguel Purefoods (Vietnam) Co. Ltd.	All Other	(3,059)	(1,315)	(210)
Other	Various	102	(1,078)	3,442
Total		$26,757	$13,126	$4,793

MegaMex Foods, LLC

On October 26, 2009, the Company completed the formation of MegaMex Foods, LLC (MegaMex), a 50/50 joint venture formed by the Company and Herdez Del Fuerte, S.A. de C.V. to market Mexican foods in the United States. On October 6, 2010, MegaMex acquired 100 percent of the stock of Don Miguel Foods Corp. (Don Miguel). Don Miguel is a leading provider of branded frozen and fresh authentic Mexican appetizers, snacks, and hand held items. On August 22, 2011, MegaMex acquired 100 percent of Fresherized Foods, which produces *Wholly Guacamole,*® *Wholly Salsa,*® and *Wholly Queso*® products.

The Company recognized a basis difference of $21.3 million associated with the formation of MegaMex, which is being amortized through equity in earnings of affiliates.

Gain on Asset Disposals

3.12

GREIF, INC. (OCT)

CONSOLIDATED STATEMENTS OF INCOME (in part)

(Dollars in thousands, except per share amounts)

For the Years Ended October 31	2011	2010	2009
Net sales	$4,247,954	$3,461,537	$2,792,217
Costs of products sold	3,446,829	2,757,875	2,292,573
Gross profit	801,125	703,662	499,644
Selling, general and administrative expenses	448,399	362,935	267,589
Restructuring charges	30,496	26,746	66,590
(Gain) on disposal of properties, plants and equipment, net	(14,855)	(11,434)	(34,432)
Operating profit	337,085	325,415	199,897

NOTES TO CONSOLIDATED FINANCIAL STATEMENTS

Note 1—Basis of Presentation and Summary of Significant Accounting Policies (in part)

Properties, Plants and Equipment (in part)

For 2011, the Company recorded a gain of $14.9 million, primarily consisting of $3.2 million gain on the sale of specific Rigid Industrial Packaging & Services segment assets, $0.9 million gain on the sale of a Paper Packaging segment property, $11.4 million in net gains from the sale of surplus and higher and better use ("HBU") timber properties and other miscellaneous losses of $0.6 million. The Company also recognized an impairment loss on machinery in our Rigid Industrial Packaging and Services segment of $1.3 million as well as several smaller impairment charges of $0.2 million.

Revenue Recognition (in part)

The Company reports the sale of surplus and HBU property in our consolidated statements of income under "gain on disposals of properties, plants and equipment, net" and reports the sale of development property under "net sales" and "cost of products sold." All HBU and development property, together with surplus property, is used by the Company to productively grow and sell timber until the property is sold.

Note 5—Net Assets Held for Sale

As of October 31, 2011 there were seven locations in the Rigid Industrial Packaging & Services segment with assets held for sale. During 2011, the Company sold seven locations, added four locations and placed six locations back in service for purposes of GAAP and resumed depreciation. As a result of placing six locations back in service in 2011, the 2010 consolidated balance sheet has been reclassified for such locations to conform to the current year presentation. The net assets held for sale are being marketed for sale and it is the Company's intention to complete the facility sales within the upcoming year. In 2011, there were sales in the Rigid Industrial Packaging & Services segment which resulted in a $3.2 million gain, sales in the Paper Packaging segment which resulted in a $0.9 million gain, sales in the Land Management segment of HBU and surplus properties which resulted in a $11.4 million gain and sales of other miscellaneous equipment which resulted in a $0.6 million loss.

Bargain Purchase Gain

3.13

BOYD GAMING CORPORATION (DEC)

CONSOLIDATED STATEMENTS OF OPERATIONS
(in part)

For the years ended December 31, 2011, 2010 and 2009

(In thousands, except per share data)	Year Ended December 31		
	2011	**2010**	**2009**
Revenues			
Operating revenues:			
Gaming	$1,986,644	$1,812,487	$1,372,091
Food and beverage	388,148	347,588	229,374
Room	246,209	211,046	122,305
Other	135,176	123,603	100,396
Gross revenues	2,756,177	2,494,724	1,824,166
Less promotional allowances	419,939	353,825	183,180
Net revenues	2,336,238	2,140,899	1,640,986
Cost and Expenses			
Operating costs and expenses:			
Gaming	924,451	859,818	664,739
Food and beverage	200,165	180,840	125,830
Room	56,111	49,323	39,655
Other	108,907	99,458	77,840
Selling, general and administrative	394,991	369,217	284,937
Maintenance and utilities	153,512	140,722	92,296
Depreciation and amortization	195,343	199,275	164,427
Corporate expense	48,962	48,861	47,617
Preopening expenses	6,634	7,459	17,798
Other operating charges, net	14,058	4,713	41,780
Total operating costs and expenses	2,103,134	1,959,686	1,556,919
Operating income from Borgata	—	8,146	72,126
Operating income	233,104	189,359	156,193
Other expense (income):			
Interest income	(46)	(5)	(6)
Interest expense, net of amounts capitalized	250,731	180,558	146,830
Fair value adjustment of derivative instruments	265	480	—
(Gain) loss on early retirements of debt	14	(2,758)	(15,284)
Gain on equity distribution	—	(2,535)	—
Other income	(11,582)	(10,000)	—
Other non-operating expenses	—	—	33
Other non-operating expenses from Borgata, net	—	3,133	19,303
Total other expense, net	239,382	168,873	150,876
Income (loss) before income taxes	(6,278)	20,486	5,317
Income taxes	(1,721)	(8,236)	(1,076)
Net income (loss)	(7,999)	12,250	4,241
Net (income) loss attributable to noncontrolling interests	4,145	(1,940)	—
Net income (loss) attributable to Boyd Gaming Corporation	$ (3,854)	$ 10,310	$ 4,241

*NOTES TO CONSOLIDATED FINANCIAL
STATEMENTS*

*As of December 31, 2011 and 2010 and for the years ended
December 31, 2011, 2010 and 2009*

Note 2. Acquisitions (in part)

IP Casino Resort Spa (in part)

Acquisition Method Accounting

The Company has applied the acquisition method of accounting to this business combination, which promulgates
the following:

- Identifying the acquirer
  The Company did not acquire the equity interests of
  the sellers, but rather acquired certain assets and assumed certain liabilities. However, the assets acquired
  and liabilities assumed by the Company constitute a
  business, as all associated processes and productive
  outputs were obtained in the transaction. The Company created a wholly-owned subsidiary to record the
  activities of this business.
- Determining the acquisition date
  Title to all acquired assets, transfer of licensing requirements and the assumption of certain liabilities occurred
  upon closing, at midnight on October 4, 2011.
- Recognizing and measuring the identifiable assets acquired and the liabilities assumed
  The Company has completed its valuation procedures,
  and the resulting fair value of the acquired assets and
  assumed liabilities has been recorded based upon our
  consideration of an independent valuation of the business enterprise and IP's tangible and intangible assets.
- Recognizing and measuring goodwill or a gain from a
  bargain purchase
  The Company has recorded a bargain purchase in this
  business combination, as further discussed below, because the fair values of the identifiable net assets acquired and liabilities assumed exceeded the consideration transferred.

The application of the acquisition method accounting guidance had the following effects on our consolidated financial statements: (i) we measured the fair value of identifiable
assets and liabilities in accordance with promulgated valuation recognition and measurement provisions and recognized such in our consolidated balance sheet as of October
4, 2011; and (ii) we have reported the operating results of IP
in our consolidated statements of operations and cash flows

for the period from October 4, 2011 through December 31,
2011 (the "Stub Period").

Consideration Transferred

The fair value of the consideration transferred on the acquisition date, and as retrospectively adjusted, included the
purchase price of the net assets transferred and certain liabilities incurred on behalf of the sellers. Total consideration
was comprised of the following:

(In thousands)	Total Consideration
Cash paid directly to or on behalf of sellers:	
Purchase price pursuant to the Agreement for Purchase and Sale	$277,000
Donation to charitable foundation at direction of seller	10,000
Liabilities assumed on behalf of sellers:	
Certain employee obligations assumed on behalf of seller	1,881
Adjustment for value of current assets acquired and current liabilities assumed:	
Working capital adjustments	(8,252)
Total consideration	$280,629

In addition to this total consideration, the Company intends
to perform certain capital improvement projects with respect to the property at an estimated cost of $44 million. Pur-
suant to the terms of the agreement, to the extent that the
costs of the capital improvements exceed the original cost
estimate, the Company will be solely responsible for the additional costs; however, to the extent that costs are less than
the original cost estimate, the Company is obligated to pay
the seller an amount equal to one-half of the difference between the actual costs and the original estimated costs. The
Company has not recorded any contingent consideration as
a result; however, as it is presently likely that these capital
improvements will require the entire $44 million spend.

Acquisition Expenses

Acquisition-related costs were not included as part of the
consideration transferred, but rather expensed as incurred.
The Company incurred and expensed the following acquisition costs associated with this acquisition:

Consolidated Balance Sheet Impact

The following table summarizes the recognized fair values of the assets acquired and liabilities assumed as of October 4, 2011.

(In thousands)	As Recorded, at Fair Value
Current Assets	
Cash and cash equivalents	$ 2,173
Accounts receivable, net	1,230
Inventories	1,579
Prepaid expenses and other current assets	6,638
Tangible Assets	
Property and equipment, net	264,703
Identified Intangible Assets	
Trademark	25,300
Customer relationships	3,300
Total acquired assets	304,923
Current liabilities	
Accounts payable	3,018
Accrued liabilities	14,182
Other liabilities	
Deferred tax liability	2,512
Total liabilities assumed	19,712
Net identifiable assets	$285,211

The fair value of the current assets acquired and current liabilities assumed was presumed to be historical acquired value, based on the relatively short term nature of these assets and liabilities. The $1.2 million of acquired accounts receivable is net of a $2.1 million reserve, reducing the gross amount of $3.3 million to an amount reflecting the expected cash flows from such outstanding balances.

The fair value of the tangible assets utilized a combination of the income, market or cost approaches, depending on the characteristics of the asset classification. With respect to certain personal property components of these assets (slot machines, furniture, fixtures and equipment, resort sign, vehicles and computer equipment) the cost approach was used, which is based on replacement or reproduction costs of the asset. The fair value of the barge, as well as land was determined using the market approach, which considers sales of comparable assets and applies compensating factors for any differences specific to the particular assets. Building and site improvements were valued using the cost approach using a direct cost model built on estimates of replacement cost.

The fair value of the identified intangible assets was determined using a cash flow model following the income approach. Specifically, the identified intangible assets include the value of the IP trademark and customer relationships. The value of the trademark relied upon a relief from royalty method, which discounts a stream of payments associated with the right to use such name. The value of customer relationships followed a multi-period excess earnings method, which is an application of the discounted cash flow method and computes the present value of after-tax cash flows attributable to the associated future income stream.

Bargain Purchase Gain

The business combination resulted in the recording of a bargain purchase gain, due to the excess fair value of net identifiable assets over the total consideration. The gain was computed as follows:

(In thousands)	Bargain Purchase Gain
Fair value of net identifiable assets	$285,211
Total consideration	280,629
Bargain purchase gain	$ 4,582

The bargain purchase gain was reported in other income in our consolidated statement of operations during the year ended December 31, 2011.

Upon the initial determination that the fair value of the acquired net assets would result in a gain representing a bargain purchase, the Company reassessed the valuation assumptions utilized to determine these fair values as part of the acquisition method accounting. The reassessment performed focused on whether the Company had: (i) correctly identified all of the assets acquired and all of the liabilities assumed; and (ii) critically reviewed the procedures used to measure the relative fair values of such amounts. As a result of this reassessment, certain adjustments to the valuation assumptions were identified and modified; however, the effect of such was a significant reduction, but not a full elimination of the bargain purchase gain. The Company believes the reassessment appropriately reflects its consideration of all available information as of the acquisition date.

The events and circumstances resulting in a bargain purchase of IP were primarily related to the acceptance of the property in an "as-is" condition, coupled with the facts that there was not a competitive bidding process, and the representations and warranties received from the seller were not conventional or conforming for this size or type of transaction.

During our preliminary due diligence process, we identified certain deferred maintenance issues regarding the property, after initial negotiations had commenced. As previously disclosed, the Company intends to immediately begin capital improvements to the property at an estimated cost of $44 million. These improvements are necessary to extend the useful life of the hull on which the gaming barge sits, and perform other deferred maintenance projects related to the back of house areas. Additionally, and as importantly, the improvements to the hull will preserve compliance with specific building codes.

The sellers of the IP did not run a competitive bidding process, and the Company's purchase was on an "as-is" basis. While the negotiations were relatively confined prior to the discovery of these required improvements, we believe it was advantageous to our overall negotiations to deal directly with the sellers on these issues, as such were identified. The Company's willingness to accept, and ultimately fund the significant cost to pay for these improvements provided an advantageous position to renegotiate the original purchase price.

Litigation

3.14

NEWMARKET CORPORATION (DEC)

CONSOLIDATED STATEMENTS OF INCOME (in part)

	Years Ended December 31		
(In thousands, except per-share amounts)	2011	2010	2009
Revenue:			
Net sales—product	$2,138,127	$1,786,076	$1,530,122
Rental revenue	11,431	11,316	0
	2,149,558	1,797,392	1,530,122
Costs:			
Cost of goods sold—product	1,586,145	1,277,505	1,066,862
Cost of rental	4,386	4,428	0
	1,590,531	1,281,933	1,066,862
Gross profit	559,027	515,459	463,260
Selling, general, and administrative expenses	151,602	136,967	114,900
Research, development, and testing expenses	105,496	91,188	86,072
Gain on legal settlement, net	38,656	0	0
Operating profit	340,585	287,304	262,288

NOTES TO CONSOLIDATED FINANCIAL STATEMENTS

(Tabular amounts in thousands, except per-share amounts)

18. Commitments and Contingencies (in part)

Litigation (in part)

As previously disclosed, NewMarket Corporation and Afton Chemical Corporation (collectively, NewMarket) brought two civil actions against Innospec Inc. and its subsidiaries Alcor Chemie Vertriebs GmbH and Innospec Ltd. (collectively, Innospec) in July 2010.

NewMarket and Innospec have agreed to settle these actions pursuant to the terms of a settlement agreement between them signed on September 13, 2011 which provides for mutual releases of the parties and dismissal of the actions with prejudice. Under the settlement agreement, Innospec will pay NewMarket an aggregate amount of approximately $45 million, payable in a combination of cash, a promissory note, and stock, of which $25 million was paid in cash on September 20, 2011 and approximately $5 million was paid in the form of 195,313 shares of unregistered Innospec Inc. common stock. Fifteen million dollars is payable in three equal annual installments of $5 million under the promissory note, which bears interest at 1% per year. The first installment is due on September 10, 2012.

Derivatives

3.15

FORD MOTOR COMPANY (DEC)

NOTES TO THE FINANCIAL STATEMENTS

Note 25. Derivative Financial Instruments and Hedging Activities (in part)

In the normal course of business, our operations are exposed to global market risks, including the effect of changes in foreign currency exchange rates, certain commodity prices, and interest rates. To manage these risks, we enter into various derivatives contracts:

- Foreign currency exchange contracts, including forwards and options, that are used to manage foreign exchange exposure;
- Commodity contracts, including forwards and options, that are used to manage commodity price risk;
- Interest rate contracts including swaps, caps, and floors that are used to manage the effects of interest rate fluctuations; and
- Cross-currency interest rate swap contracts that are used to manage foreign currency and interest rate exposures on foreign-denominated debt.

Our derivatives are over-the-counter customized derivative transactions and are not exchange-traded. We review our hedging program, derivative positions, and overall risk management strategy on a regular basis.

Derivative Financial Instruments and Hedge Accounting. All derivatives are recognized on the balance sheet at fair value. We do not net our derivative position by counterparty for purposes of balance sheet presentation and disclosure. We do, however, consider our net position for determining fair value.

We have elected to apply hedge accounting to certain derivatives. Derivatives that are designated in hedging relationships are evaluated for effectiveness using regression analysis at the time they are designated and throughout the hedge period. Cash flows and the profit impact associated with designated hedges are reported in the same category as the underlying hedged item.

Some derivatives do not qualify for hedge accounting; for others, we elect not to apply hedge accounting. Regardless, we only enter into transactions that we believe will be highly effective at offsetting the underlying economic risk. We report changes in the fair value of derivatives not designated as hedging instruments through *Automotive cost of sales*, *Automotive interest income and other non-operating income/(expense), net*, or *Financial Services other income/(loss), net* depending on the sector and underlying exposure. Cash flows associated with non-designated or de-designated derivatives are reported in *Net cash (used in)/provided by investing activities* in our statements of cash flows.

Cash Flow Hedges. Our Automotive sector has designated certain forward contracts as cash flow hedges of forecasted transactions with exposure to foreign currency exchange risk.

The effective portion of changes in the fair value of cash flow hedges is deferred in *Accumulated other comprehensive income/(loss)* and is recognized in *Automotive cost of sales* when the hedged item affects earnings. The ineffective portion is reported in *Automotive cost of sales*. Our policy is to de-designate cash flow hedges prior to the time forecasted transactions are recognized as assets or liabilities on the balance sheet and report subsequent changes in fair value through *Automotive cost of sales*. If it becomes probable that the originally-forecasted transaction will not occur, the related amount also is reclassified from *Accumulated other comprehensive income/(loss)* and recognized in earnings. Our cash flow hedges mature in two years or less.

Fair Value Hedges. Our Financial Services sector uses derivatives to reduce the risk of changes in the fair value of liabilities. We have designated certain receive-fixed, pay-float interest rate swaps as fair value hedges of fixed-rate debt. The risk being hedged is the risk of changes in the fair value of the hedged debt attributable to changes in the benchmark interest rate. If the hedge relationship is deemed to be highly effective, we record the changes in the fair value of the hedged debt related to the risk being hedged in

Financial Services debt with the offset in *Financial Services other income/(loss), net*. The change in fair value of the related derivative (excluding accrued interest) also is recorded in *Financial Services other income/(loss), net*. Hedge ineffectiveness, recorded directly in earnings, is the difference between the change in fair value of the derivative and the change in the value of the hedged debt that is attributable to the changes in the benchmark interest rate.

For our Financial Services sector, net interest settlements and accruals on fair value hedges are excluded from the assessment of hedge effectiveness. We report net interest settlements and accruals on fair value hedges in *Interest expense*, with the exception of foreign currency revaluation on accrued interest, which is reported in *Selling, administrative, and other expenses*. Ineffectiveness on fair value hedges and gains and losses on interest rate contracts not designated as hedging instruments are reported in *Financial Services other income/(loss), net*. Gains and losses on foreign exchange and cross-currency interest rate swap contracts not designated as hedging instruments are reported in *Selling, administrative, and other expenses*.

When a fair value hedge is de-designated, or when the derivative is terminated before maturity, the fair value adjustment to the hedged debt continues to be reported as part of the carrying value of the debt and is amortized over its remaining life.

Net Investment Hedges. We have used foreign currency exchange derivatives to hedge the net assets of certain foreign entities to offset the translation and economic exposures related to our investment in these entities. The effective portion of changes in the value of designated instruments is included in *Accumulated other comprehensive income/(loss)* as a foreign currency translation adjustment until the hedged investment is sold or liquidated. When the investment is sold or liquidated, the hedge gains and losses previously reported in *Accumulated other comprehensive income/(loss)* are recognized in *Automotive interest income and other non-operating income/(expense), net* as part of the gain or loss on sale. Presently, we have had no derivative instruments in an active net investment hedging relationship. We have elected the spot to spot method.

Normal Purchases and Normal Sales Classification. We have elected to apply the normal purchases and normal sales classification for physical supply contracts that are entered into for the purpose of procuring commodities to be used in production over a reasonable period in the normal course of our business.

Income Effect of Derivative Instruments

The following tables summarize by hedge designation the pre-tax gains/(losses) recorded in Other comprehensive income/(loss) ("OCI"), reclassified from *Accumulated other comprehensive income/(loss)* ("AOCI") to income and/or recognized directly in income (in millions):

	2011			2010			2009		
	Gain/ (Loss) Recorded in OCI	Gain/(Loss) Reclassified from AOCI to Income	Gain/ (Loss) Recognized in Income	Gain/ (Loss) Recorded in OCI	Gain/(Loss) Reclassified from AOCI to Income	Gain/ (Loss) Recognized in Income	Gain/ (Loss) Recorded in OCI	Gain/(Loss) Reclassified from AOCI to Income	Gain/(Loss) Recognized in Income
Automotive Sector									
Cash flow hedges:									
Foreign currency exchange contracts	$(100)	$119[a]	$ (3)	$(7)	$17	$ —	$(86)	$37[b]	$ (1)
Commodity contracts	—	—		—	—	—	—	4	—
Total	$(100)	$119	$ (3)	$(7)	$17	$ —	$(86)	$41	$ (1)
Derivatives not designated as hedging instruments:									
Foreign currency exchange contracts—operating exposures		$ 20			$(183)			$(120)	
Foreign currency exchange contracts—investment portfolios		—			—			(11)	
Commodity contracts		(423)			68			(4)	
Other—warrants		(1)			2			(12)	
Total		$(404)			$(113)			$(147)	
Financial Services Sector									
Fair value hedges:									
Interest rate contracts									
Net interest settlements and accruals excluded from the assessment of hedge effectiveness		$ 217			$ 225			$ 164	
Ineffectiveness[c]		(30)			(6)			(13)	
Total		$ 187			$ 219			$ 151	
Derivatives not designated as hedging instruments:									
Interest rate contracts		$ (5)			$ 38			$ (63)	
Foreign currency exchange contracts		(48)			(88)			(268)	
Cross-currency interest rate swap contracts		(3)			(1)			12	
Other[d]		65			—			—	
Total		$ 9			$ (51)			$(319)	

[a] Includes $3 million loss reclassified from AOCI to income in fourth quarter 2011 attributable to transactions no longer probable to occur, related to Ford of Thailand.

[b] Includes $4 million gain reclassified from AOCI to income in first quarter 2009 attributable to transactions no longer probable to occur, primarily related to Volvo.

[c] For 2011, 2010 and 2009, hedge ineffectiveness reflects change in fair value on derivatives of $433 million gain, $117 million gain, and $46 million loss, respectively, and change in fair value on hedged debt of $463 million loss, $123 million loss, and $33 million gain, respectively.

[d] Reflects gains/(losses) for derivative features included in the FUEL notes (see Note 4).

In 2010, a net gain of $7 million of foreign currency translation on net investment hedges was transferred from *Accumulated other comprehensive income/(loss)* to earnings due to the sale of investments in foreign affiliates.

SEC 3.15

Investment Gains

3.16

BERKSHIRE HATHAWAY INC. (DEC)

CONSOLIDATED STATEMENTS OF EARNINGS
(in part)

(Dollars in millions except per-share amounts)

	Year Ended December 31		
	2011	2010	2009
Revenues:			
Insurance and Other:			
Insurance premiums earned	$32,075	$30,749	$27,884
Sales and service revenues	72,803	67,225	62,555
Interest, dividend and other investment income	4,792	5,215	5,531
Investment gains/losses	1,973	4,044	358
Other-than-temporary impairment losses on investments	(908)	(1,973)	(3,155)
	110,735	105,260	93,173
Railroad, Utilities and Energy:			
Operating revenues	30,721	26,186	11,204
Other	118	178	239
	30,839	26,364	11,443
Finance and Financial Products:			
Interest, dividend and other investment income	1,618	1,683	1,600
Investment gains/losses	209	14	(40)
Derivative gains/losses	(2,104)	261	3,624
Other	2,391	2,603	2,693
	2,114	4,561	7,877
	143,688	136,185	112,493

NOTES TO CONSOLIDATED FINANCIAL STATEMENTS

December 31, 2011

(6) Investment Gains/Losses and Other-Than-Temporary Investment Losses (in part)

Investment gains/losses for each of the three years ending December 31, 2011 are summarized below (in millions).

	2011	2010	2009
Fixed maturity securities			
Gross gains from sales and other disposals	$ 310	$ 720	$357
Gross losses from sales and other disposals	(10)	(16)	(54)
Equity securities and other investments			
Gross gains from sales and other disposals	1,889	2,603	701
Gross losses from sales and other disposals	(36)	(266)	(617)
Other	29	1,017	(69)
	$2,182	$4,058	$318

Investment gains from equity securities and other investments in 2011 included $1,775 million with respect to the redemptions of our GS and GE Preferred investments and $1.3 billion in 2010 from the redemption of the Swiss Re perpetual capital instrument. In 2010, other gains included a one-time holding gain of $979 million related to our BNSF acquisition.

Net investment gains/losses for each of the three years ending December 31, 2011 are reflected in our Consolidated Statements of Earnings as follows (in millions).

	2011	2010	2009
Insurance and other	$1,973	$4,044	$358
Finance and financial products	209	14	(40)
	$2,182	$4,058	$318

Insurance Recoveries

3.17

CONAGRA FOODS, INC. (MAY)

CONSOLIDATED STATEMENTS OF EARNINGS (in part)

Dollars in millions except per share amounts

	For the Fiscal Years Ended May		
	2011	2010	2009
Net sales	$12,303.1	$12,014.9	$12,348.6
Costs and expenses:			
Cost of goods sold	9,389.6	8,953.7	9,571.1
Selling, general and administrative expenses	1,511.1	1,819.4	1,683.2
Interest expense, net	177.5	160.4	186.0
Income from continuing operations before income taxes and equity method investment earnings	1,224.9	1,081.4	908.3
Income tax expense	421.0	360.9	317.1
Equity method investment earnings	26.4	22.1	24.0
Income from continuing operations	830.3	742.6	615.2
Income (loss) from discontinued operations, net of tax	(11.5)	(19.3)	363.8
Net income	$ 818.8	$ 723.3	$ 979.0

NOTES TO CONSOLIDATED FINANCIAL STATEMENTS

Fiscal years ended May 29, 2011, May 30, 2010, and May 31, 2009

Columnar Amounts in Millions Except Per Share Amounts

5. Garner, North Carolina Accident

On June 9, 2009, an accidental explosion occurred at our manufacturing facility in Garner, North Carolina (the "Garner accident"). This facility was the primary production facility for our *Slim Jim®* branded meat snacks. On June 13, 2009, the U.S. Bureau of Alcohol, Tobacco, Firearms and Explosives announced its determination that the explosion was the result of an accidental natural gas release, and not a deliberate act.

The costs incurred and insurance recoveries recognized, for fiscal 2011 and 2010, were reflected in our consolidated financial statements as follows:

	Fiscal Year Ended May 29, 2011			Fiscal Year Ended May 30, 2010		
	Consumer Foods	Corporate	Total	Consumer Foods	Corporate	Total
Cost of goods sold:						
Inventory write-downs and other costs	$ 0.9	$ —	$ 0.9	$ 11.9	$ —	$11.9
Selling, general and administrative expenses:						
Fixed asset impairments, clean-up costs, etc.	$ 2.6	$0.6	$ 3.2	$ 47.5	$2.6	$50.1
Insurance recoveries recognized	(109.4)	—	(109.4)	(58.1)	—	(58.1)
Total selling, general and administrative expenses	$(106.8)	$0.6	$(106.2)	$(10.6)	$2.6	$ (8.0)
Net loss (gain)	$(105.9)	$0.6	$(105.3)	$ 1.3	$2.6	$ 3.9

The amounts in the table above exclude actual lost profits due to the interruption of the meat snacks business in the periods presented, but do reflect the recovery of the related business interruption insurance claim in the fourth quarter of fiscal 2011.

During the fourth quarter of fiscal 2011, the Company settled its property and business interruption claims related to the accident with our insurance providers. Through May 29, 2011, the total payments received from the insurers was $167.5 million and all previously deferred balances have now been recognized. The insurance recoveries recognized in fiscal 2011, included in selling, general and administrative ex-

penses, totaled $109.4 million, representing $84.0 million of reimbursement for business interruption, a $21.3 million gain on involuntary conversion of property, plant and equipment, and recovery of other expenses incurred of $4.1 million.

Gains on Extinguishment of Debt

3.18

HOVNANIAN ENTERPRISES, INC. (OCT)

CONSOLIDATED STATEMENTS OF OPERATIONS
(in part)

	Year Ended		
(In thousands except per share data)	October 31, 2011	October 31, 2010	October 31, 2009
Revenues:			
Homebuilding:			
Sale of homes	$1,072,474	$1,327,499	$1,522,469
Land sales and other revenues	32,952	12,370	38,271
Total homebuilding	1,105,426	1,339,869	1,560,740
Financial services	29,481	31,973	35,550
Total revenues	1,134,907	1,371,842	1,596,290
Expenses:			
Homebuilding:			
Cost of sales, excluding interest	913,901	1,104,049	1,398,087
Cost of sales interest	74,676	84,440	105,814
Inventory impairment loss and land option write-offs (Note 14)	101,749	135,699	659,475
Total cost of sales	1,090,326	1,324,188	2,163,376
Selling, general and administrative	161,456	178,331	239,606
Total homebuilding expenses	1,251,782	1,502,519	2,402,982
Financial services	21,371	23,074	29,295
Corporate general and administrative	49,938	59,900	81,980
Other interest	97,169	97,919	94,655
Other operations	4,805	9,715	23,541
Total expenses	1,425,065	1,693,127	2,632,453
Gain on extinguishment of debt (Note 9)	7,528	25,047	410,185
(Loss) income from unconsolidated joint ventures (Note 20)	(8,958)	956	(46,041)
Loss before income taxes	(291,588)	(295,282)	(672,019)

NOTES TO CONSOLIDATED FINANCIAL STATEMENTS

9. Senior Secured, Senior and Senior Subordinated Notes (in part)

On December 3, 2008, K. Hovnanian issued $29.3 million of 18.0% Senior Secured Notes due 2017 in exchange for $71.4 million of various series of our unsecured senior notes. This exchange resulted in a recognized gain on extinguishment of debt of $41.3 million, net of the write-off of unamortized discounts and fees. The notes were secured, subject to permitted liens and other exceptions, by a third-priority lien on substantially all of the assets owned by us, K. Hovnanian, and the guarantors to the extent such assets secured obligations under our first-priority and second-priority secured

notes. The notes were redeemable in whole or in part at our option at 102% of principal commencing May 1, 2011, 101% of principal commencing November 1, 2011, and 100% of principal commencing November 1, 2012. These third lien notes were the subject of tender offers, and notes that remained outstanding following such tender offers were subsequently redeemed, as discussed below.

On July 21, 2009, we completed cash tender offers whereby we purchased (1) in a fixed-price tender offer, approximately $17.8 million principal amount of 6% Senior Subordinated Notes due 2010 for approximately $17.5 million, plus accrued and unpaid interest, (2) in a modified "Dutch Auction," a total of approximately $49.5 million principal amount of 8% Senior Notes due 2012, 8 7/8% Senior Subordinated Notes due 2012 and 7 3/4% Senior Subordinated Notes due 2013 for approximately $36.1 million, plus accrued and unpaid interest and (3) in a modified "Dutch Auction," a total of approximately $51.9 million of 6 1/2% Senior Notes due 2014, 6 3/8% Senior Notes due 2014, 6 1/4% Senior Notes due 2015, 6 1/4% Senior Notes due 2016, 7 1/2% Senior Notes due 2016 and 8 5/8% Senior Notes due 2017 for approximately $26.9 million, plus accrued and unpaid interest. These tender offers resulted in a gain on extinguishment of debt of $37.0 million, net of the write-off of unamortized discounts and fees.

On October 20, 2009, we completed cash tender offers and consent solicitations whereby we purchased (1) in a fixed-price tender offer approximately $599.5 million principal amount of 11 1/2% Senior Secured Notes due 2013 for approximately $635.5 million, plus accrued and unpaid interest, (2) in a fixed-price tender offer approximately $17.6 million principal amount of 18.0% Senior Secured Notes due 2017 for approximately $17.6 million, plus accrued and unpaid interest, and (3) in a fixed price tender offer for certain series of our unsecured notes, a total of approximately $125.4 million principal amount of 8% Senior Notes due 2012, 6 1/2% Senior Notes due 2014, 6 3/8% Senior Notes due 2014, 6 1/4% Senior Notes due 2015, and 7 1/2% Senior Notes due 2016 for approximately $100.0 million, plus accrued and unpaid interest. These tender offers resulted in a loss on extinguishment of debt of $36.4 million, net of the write-off of unamortized discounts and fees.

During the year ended October 31, 2009, we repurchased in open market transactions $11.3 million principal amount of 8% Senior Notes due 2012, $64.4 million principal amount of 6 1/2% Senior Notes due 2014, $40.6 million principal amount of 6 3/8% Senior Notes due 2014, $71.7 million principal amount of 6 1/4% Senior Notes due 2015, $88.9 million principal amount of 6 1/4% Senior Notes due 2016, $78.5 million principal amount of 7 1/2% Senior Notes due 2016, $41.8 million principal amount of 8 5/8% Senior Notes due 2017, $68.6 million principal amount of 6% Senior Subordinated Notes due 2010, $80.1 million principal amount of 8 7/8% Senior Subordinated Notes due 2012, and $82.6 million principal amount of 7 3/4% Senior Subordinated Notes due 2013. The aggregate purchase price for these repurchases was $255.4 million, plus accrued and unpaid interest. These repurchases resulted in a gain on extinguishment of debt of $368.0 million for the year ended October 31, 2009, net of the write-off of unamortized discounts and fees. The gains from the exchange and repurchases are included in the Consolidated Statement of Operations as "Gain of extinguishment of debt."

On January 15, 2010, the remaining $13.6 million of our 6% Senior Subordinated Notes due 2010 matured and was paid. During the year ended October 31, 2010, we repurchased in open market transactions $27.0 million principal amount of 6 1/2% Senior Notes due 2014, $54.5 million principal amount of 6 3/8% Senior Notes due 2014, $29.5 million principal amount of 6 1/4% Senior Notes due 2015, $1.4 mil-

lion principal amount of 8 7/8% Senior Subordinated Notes due 2012, and $11.1 million principal amount of 7 3/4% Senior Subordinated Notes due 2013. The aggregate purchase price for these repurchases was $97.9 million, plus accrued and unpaid interest. These repurchases resulted in a gain on extinguishment of debt of $25.0 million during the year ended October 31, 2010, net of the write-off of unamortized discounts and fees.

During the three months ended October 31, 2011 we completed a number of open market repurchases. These included $24.6 million principal amount of 11 7/8% Senior Notes due 2015, and $1.0 million principal amount of 6 1/2% Senior Notes due 2014. The aggregate purchase price for these repurchases was $14.0 million, plus accrued and unpaid interest. These repurchases resulted in a gain on extinguishment of debt of $10.6 million, net of the write-off of unamortized discounts and fees. The gains from the repurchases are included in the Consolidated Statement of Operations as "Gain on extinguishment of debt."

Separate from the above, in the first quarter of fiscal 2012, we repurchased approximately $44 million principal amount of our unsecured senior notes for an aggregate purchase price of approximately $19 million in cash, excluding cash paid for interest, resulting in an approximate gain on extinguishment of debt of $25 million.

EXPENSES AND LOSSES

PRESENTATION

3.19 Paragraphs 80 and 83 of FASB Concepts Statement No. 6, *Elements of Financial Statements—a replacement of FASB Concepts Statement No. 3 (incorporating an amendment of FASB Concepts Statement No. 2)*, define expenses and losses as follows:

80. Expenses are outflows or other using up of assets or incurrences of liabilities (or a combination of both) from delivering or producing goods, rendering services, or carrying out other activities that constitute the entity's ongoing major or central operations.

83. Losses are decreases in equity (net assets) from peripheral or incidental transactions of an entity and from all other transactions and other events and circumstances affecting the entity except those that result from expenses or distributions to owners.

3.20

TABLE 3-2: EXPENSES AND LOSSES—OTHER THAN COST OF GOODS SOLD*

Table 3-2 summarizes the nature of expenses and losses most frequently disclosed by the survey entities, other than cost of goods sold. Excluded from Table 3-2 are rent, employee benefits, depreciation, income taxes, losses shown after the caption for income taxes, segment disposals, and extraordinary losses.

	Number of Entities		
	2011	2010	2009
Selling, general and administrative................	307	296	300
Selling and administrative.............................	67	56	70
General and/or administrative........................	82	71	98
Selling...	39	15	40
Interest..	377	265	453
Interest and penalty on income taxes............	4	14	24
Research, development, engineering, and so on..	176	170	229
Advertising..	109	99	173
Provision for doubtful accounts.....................	68	39	122
Warranty..	52	15	99
Shipping...	40	41	62
Asset retirement obligation accretion............	21	9	43
Taxes other than income taxes......................	14	18	17
Maintenance and repairs................................	22	25	14
Exploration, dry holes, abandonments...........	8	10	7
Intangible asset amortization.........................	184	168	276
Write-down of assets......................................	106	139	248
Restructuring of operations............................	202	205	242
Change in fair value of derivatives................	95	78	239
Impairment of intangibles...............................	123	93	166
Foreign currency transactions.......................	61	88	101
Sale of assets..	44	41	84
Debt extinguishment.......................................	62	70	68
Litigation...	46	27	49
Equity in losses of investees.........................	25	27	47
Environmental cleanup....................................	37	25	37
Sale of receivables...	8	8	33
Merger costs..	36	29	33
Software amortization......................................	18	29	32
Fair value adjustments....................................	23	18	23
Minority interests...	61	6	14
Start-up costs...	3	1	11
Purchased research and development...........	1	3	10
Royalties...	2	5	10
Business combination adjustment loss..........	9	3	4
Other, described..	224	N/C^	N/C^

* Appearing in the income statement or notes to the financial statements, or both.

^ N/C = Not compiled. The line item was not included in the table for the year shown.

PRESENTATION AND DISCLOSURE EXCERPTS

Selling, General, and Administrative

3.21

KOHL'S CORPORATION (JAN)

CONSOLIDATED STATEMENTS OF INCOME (in part)

(In Millions, Except Per Share Data)

(Restated)

	2010	2009	2008
Net sales	$18,391	$17,178	$16,389
Cost of merchandise sold (exclusive of depreciation shown separately below)	11,359	10,680	10,334
Gross margin	7,032	6,498	6,055
Operating expenses:			
Selling, general, and administrative	4,190	3,951	3,769
Depreciation and amortization	750	688	632
Operating income	2,092	1,859	1,654

NOTES TO CONSOLIDATED FINANCIAL STATEMENTS

1. Business and Summary of Accounting Policies (in part)

Cost of Merchandise Sold and Selling, General and Administrative Expenses

The following table illustrates the primary costs classified in Cost of Merchandise Sold and Selling, General and Administrative Expenses:

Cost of Merchandise Sold	Selling, General and Administrative Expenses

• Total cost of products sold including product development costs, net of vendor payments other than reimbursement of specific, incremental and identifiable costs
• Inventory shrink
• Markdowns
• Freight expenses associated with moving merchandise from our vendors to our distribution centers
• Shipping and handling expenses of E-Commerce sales
• Terms cash discount
	• Compensation and benefit costs including:
	  • Stores
	  • Corporate headquarters, including buying and merchandising
	  • Distribution centers
	• Rent expense and other occupancy and operating costs of our retail, distribution and corporate facilities
	• Net revenues from the Kohl's credit card agreement with JPMorgan Chase
	• Freight expenses associated with moving merchandise from our distribution centers to our retail stores, and among distribution and retail facilities
	• Advertising expenses, offset by vendor payments for reimbursement of specific, incremental and identifiable costs
	• Costs incurred prior to new store openings, such as advertising, hiring and training costs for new employees, processing and transporting initial merchandise, and rent expense
	• Other administrative costs

The classification of these expenses varies across the retail industry.

Research, Development, and Engineering

3.22

GENERAL DYNAMICS CORPORATION (DEC)

CONSOLIDATED STATEMENT OF EARNINGS (in part)

(Dollars in millions, except per-share amounts)	Year Ended December 31		
	2009	**2010**	**2011**
Revenues:			
Products	$21,977	$21,723	$21,440
Services	10,004	10,743	11,237
	31,981	32,466	32,677
Operating Costs and Expenses:			
Products	17,808	17,359	17,230
Services	8,544	9,198	9,591
General and administrative	1,954	1,964	2,030
	28,306	28,521	28,851
Operating earnings	3,675	3,945	3,826
Interest, net	(160)	(157)	(141)
Other, net	(2)	2	33
Earnings from continuing operations before income taxes	3,513	3,790	3,718
Provision for income taxes, net	1,106	1,162	1,166
Earnings from continuing operations	2,407	2,628	2,552
Discontinued operations, net of tax	(13)	(4)	(26)
Net earnings	$ 2,394	$ 2,624	$ 2,526

(Dollars in millions, except per-share amounts or unless otherwise noted).

NOTES TO CONSOLIDATED FINANCIAL STATEMENTS

A. Summary of Significant Accounting Policies (in part)

Research and Development Expenses. Research and development (R&D) expenses consisted of the following:

Year Ended December 31	2009	2010	2011
Company-sponsored R&D, including product development costs	$360	$ 325	$ 372
Bid and proposal costs	160	183	173
Total company-sponsored R&D	520	508	545
Customer-sponsored R&D	405	548	667
Total R&D	$925	$1,056	$1,212

R&D expenses are included in operating costs and expenses in the Consolidated Statement of Earnings in the period in which they are incurred. Customer-sponsored R&D expenses are charged directly to the related contract.

The Aerospace group has cost-sharing arrangements with some of its suppliers that enhance the group's internal development capabilities and offset a portion of the financial risk associated with the group's product development efforts. These arrangements explicitly state that supplier contributions are for reimbursements of costs we incur in the development of new aircraft models and technologies, and we retain substantial rights in the products developed under these arrangements. We record amounts received from these cost-sharing arrangements as a reduction of R&D expenses. We have no obligation to refund any amounts received under the agreement regardless of the outcome of the development effort. Under the terms of each agreement, payments received from suppliers for their share of the costs are based typically on milestones and are recognized as earned when we achieve a milestone event.

Exploration

3.23

HESS CORPORATION (DEC)

STATEMENT OF CONSOLIDATED INCOME (in part)

	Years Ended December 31		
(Millions of dollars, except per share data)	**2011**	**2010**	**2009**
Revenues and Non-Operating Income			
Sales (excluding excise taxes) and other operating revenues	$38,466	$33,862	$29,614
Income (loss) from equity investment in HOVENSA L.L.C.	(1,073)	(522)	(229)
Gains on asset sales	446	1,208	—
Other, net	32	65	184
Total revenues and non-operating income	37,871	34,613	29,569
Costs and Expenses			
Cost of products sold (excluding items shown separately below)	26,774	23,407	20,961
Production expenses	2,352	1,924	1,805
Marketing expenses	1,069	1,021	1,008
Exploration expenses, including dry holes and lease impairment	1,195	865	829
Other operating expenses	171	213	183
General and administrative expenses	702	662	647
Interest expense	383	361	360
Depreciation, depletion and amortization	2,406	2,317	2,200
Asset impairments	358	532	54
Total costs and expenses	35,410	31,302	28,047
Income before income taxes	2,461	3,311	1,522
Provision for income taxes	785	1,173	715
Net income	$ 1,676	$ 2,138	$ 807

NOTES TO CONSOLIDATED FINANCIAL STATEMENTS

1. Summary of Significant Accounting Policies (in part)

Exploration and Development Costs: E&P activities are accounted for using the successful efforts method. Costs of acquiring unproved and proved oil and gas leasehold acreage, including lease bonuses, brokers' fees and other related costs, are capitalized. Annual lease rentals, exploration expenses and exploratory dry hole costs are expensed as incurred. Costs of drilling and equipping productive wells, including development dry holes, and related production facilities are capitalized. In production operations, costs of injected CO 2 for tertiary recovery are expensed as incurred.

The costs of exploratory wells that find oil and gas reserves are capitalized pending determination of whether proved reserves have been found. Exploratory drilling costs remain capitalized after drilling is completed if (1) the well has found a sufficient quantity of reserves to justify completion as a producing well and (2) sufficient progress is being made in assessing the reserves and the economic and operational viability of the project. If either of those criteria is not met, or if there is substantial doubt about the economic or operational viability of a project, the capitalized well costs are charged to expense. Indicators of sufficient progress in assessing reserves and the economic and operating viability of a project include commitment of project personnel, active negotiations for sales contracts with customers, negotiations with governments, operators and contractors, firm plans for additional drilling and other factors.

6. Property, Plant and Equipment

Property, plant and equipment at December 31 consist of the following:

(Millions of dollars)	2011	2010
Exploration and Production		
Unproved properties	$ 4,064	$ 3,796
Proved properties	3,975	3,496
Wells, equipment and related facilities	29,239	26,064
	37,278	33,356
Marketing, Refining and Corporate	2,432	2,347
Total—at cost	39,710	35,703
Less: reserves for depreciation, depletion, amortization and lease impairment	14,998	14,576
Property, plant and equipment—net	$24,712	$21,127

In the fourth quarter of 2011, the Corporation agreed to sell its interests in the Snohvit Field in Norway (Hess 3%) for approximately $135 million, after normal closing adjustments. At December 31, 2011, the Corporation classified this property and another property as assets held for sale. At December 31, 2011, the total carrying amount of these assets of $764 million was reported in Other current assets, including goodwill of $62 million. In addition, related asset retirement obligations and deferred income taxes totaling $556 million were reported in Accrued liabilities. In accordance with GAAP, properties classified as held for sale are not depreciated but are subject to impairment testing.

The following table discloses the amount of capitalized exploratory well costs pending determination of proved reserves at December 31, and the changes therein during the respective years:

(Millions of dollars)	2011	2010	2009
Beginning balance at January 1	$1,783	$1,437	$1,094
Additions to capitalized exploratory well costs pending the determination of proved reserves	512	675	433
Reclassifications to wells, facilities, and equipment based on the determination of proved reserves	(171)	(87)	(16)
Capitalized exploratory well costs charged to expense	(90)	(110)	(74)
Dispositions	(12)	(132)	—
Ending balance at December 31	$2,022	$1,783	$1,437
Number of wells at end of year	59	77	53

The preceding table excludes exploratory dry hole costs of $348 million, $127 million and $193 million in 2011, 2010 and 2009, respectively, which were incurred and subsequently expensed in the same year. In 2011, capitalized well costs reclassified based on the determination of proved reserves primarily related to the Tubular Bells project in the deepwater Gulf of Mexico, which was sanctioned during the year.

At December 31, 2011, exploratory drilling costs capitalized in excess of one year past completion of drilling were incurred as follows (in millions of dollars):

2010	$ 423
2009	448
2008	392
2007	72
2006	168
	$1,503

The capitalized well costs in excess of one year relate to 11 projects. Approximately 43% of the capitalized well costs in excess of one year relates to the Pony prospect in the deepwater Gulf of Mexico. The Corporation has signed a nonbinding agreement with the owners of the adjacent Knotty Head prospect on Green Canyon Block 512 that outlines a proposal to jointly develop the field. Negotiation of a joint operating agreement, including working interest percentages for the partners, and planning for the field development are progressing. The project is now targeted for sanction in 2013. Approximately 30% relates to Block WA-390-P, offshore Western Australia, where further drilling and other appraisal and commercial activities are ongoing. Approximately 18% relates to Area 54, offshore Libya, where force majeure was declared in 2011 following the civil unrest in Libya, see Note 3, Libyan Operations in the notes to the Consolidated Financial Statements. The Corporation expects the force majeure to be lifted in 2012 and commercial negotiations with the Libyan government to resume. The remainder of the capitalized well costs in excess of one year relates to projects where further drilling is planned or development planning and other assessment activities are ongoing to determine the economic and operating viability of the projects.

Advertising

3.24

DOMINO'S PIZZA, INC. (DEC)

CONSOLIDATED STATEMENTS OF INCOME (in part)

	For the Years Ended		
(In thousands, except per share amounts)	January 3, 2010	January 2, 2011	January 1, 2012
Revenues:			
Domestic Company-owned stores	$ 335,779	$ 345,636	$ 336,349
Domestic franchise	157,780	173,345	187,007
Domestic supply chain	763,733	875,517	927,904
International	146,765	176,396	200,933
Total revenues	1,404,057	1,570,894	1,652,193
Cost of Sales:			
Domestic Company-owned stores	274,474	278,297	267,066
Domestic supply chain	680,427	778,510	831,665
International	62,180	75,498	82,946
Total cost of sales	1,017,081	1,132,305	1,181,677
Operating Margin	386,976	438,589	470,516

NOTES TO CONSOLIDATED FINANCIAL STATEMENTS

(1) Description of Business and Summary of Significant Accounting Policies (in part)

Advertising

Advertising costs are expensed as incurred. Advertising expense, which relates primarily to Company-owned stores, was approximately $33.0 million, $30.2 million and $28.5 million during 2009, 2010 and 2011, respectively.

Domestic Stores are required to contribute a certain percentage of sales to the Domino's National Advertising Fund Inc. (DNAF), a not-for-profit subsidiary that administers the Domino's Pizza system's national and market level advertising activities. Included in advertising expense were national advertising contributions from Company-owned stores to DNAF of approximately $16.4 million, $19.5 million and $18.5 million in 2009, 2010 and 2011, respectively. DNAF also received national advertising contributions from franchisees of approximately $131.2 million, $161.4 million and $165.8 million during 2009, 2010 and 2011, respectively. Franchisee contributions to DNAF and offsetting disbursements are presented net in the accompanying statements of income.

DNAF assets, consisting primarily of cash received from franchisees and accounts receivable from franchisees, can only be used for activities that promote the Domino's Pizza brand. Accordingly, all assets held by the DNAF are considered restricted.

$1.60 to $4.35 per pack. Between the end of 1998 and February 13, 2012, the weighted-average state and certain local cigarette excise taxes increased from $0.36 to $1.37 per pack. During 2011, Connecticut, Hawaii and Vermont increased their cigarette excise taxes and New Hampshire decreased its cigarette excise tax. As of February 13, 2012, no state has increased its cigarette excise tax in 2012.

Tax increases are expected to continue to have an adverse impact on sales of tobacco products by our tobacco subsidiaries, due to lower consumption levels and to a potential shift in adult consumer purchases from the premium to the non-premium or discount segments or to other low-priced or low-taxed tobacco products or to counterfeit and contraband products. Such shifts may have an impact on the reported share performance of tobacco products of Altria Group, Inc.'s tobacco subsidiaries.

A majority of states currently tax smokeless tobacco products using an *ad valorem* method, which is calculated as a percentage of the price of the product, typically the wholesale price. This *ad valorem* method results in more tax being paid on premium products than is paid on lower-priced products of equal weight. Altria Group, Inc.'s subsidiaries support legislation to convert *ad valorem* taxes on smokeless tobacco to a weight-based methodology because, unlike the *ad valorem* tax, a weight-based tax subjects cans of equal weight to the same tax. As of February 13, 2012, twenty-one states, Washington, D.C. and Philadelphia, Pennsylvania have adopted a weight-based tax methodology for smokeless tobacco.

Taxes Other Than Income Taxes

3.25

ALTRIA GROUP, INC. (DEC)

CONSOLIDATED STATEMENTS OF EARNINGS (in part)

(In millions of dollars, except per share data)

For the Years Ended December 31	2011	2010	2009
Net revenues	$23,800	$24,363	$23,556
Cost of sales	7,680	7,704	7,990
Excise taxes on products	7,181	7,471	6,732
Gross profit	8,939	9,188	8,834

MANAGEMENT'S DISCUSSION AND ANALYSIS OF FINANCIAL CONDITION AND RESULTS OF OPERATIONS

Excise Taxes

Tobacco products are subject to substantial excise taxes in the United States. Significant increases in tobacco-related taxes or fees have been proposed or enacted and are likely to continue to be proposed or enacted at the federal, state and local levels within the United States.

Federal, state and local excise taxes have increased substantially over the past decade, far outpacing the rate of inflation. For example, in 2009, the FET on cigarettes increased from 39 cents per pack to approximately $1.01 per pack and on July 1, 2010, the New York state excise tax increased

Provision for Losses

3.26

GENERAL ELECTRIC COMPANY (DEC)

STATEMENT OF EARNINGS (in part)

For the Years Ended December 31 (In millions; per-share amounts in dollars)	General Electric Company and Consolidated Affiliates		
	2011	2010	2009
Revenues			
Sales of goods	$ 66,875	$ 60,812	$ 65,067
Sales of services	27,648	39,625	38,710
Other income (Note 17)	5,063	1,151	1,006
GECS earnings from continuing operations	—	—	—
GECS revenues from services (Note 18)	47,714	48,005	49,655
Total revenues	147,300	149,593	154,438
Costs and Expenses (Note 19)			
Cost of goods sold	51,455	46,005	50,580
Cost of services sold	16,823	25,708	25,341
Interest and other financial charges	14,545	15,553	17,697
Investment contracts, insurance losses and insurance annuity benefits	2,912	3,012	3,017
Provision for losses on financing receivables (Notes 6 and 23)	4,083	7,176	10,585
Other costs and expenses	37,384	38,054	37,354
Total costs and expenses	127,202	135,508	144,574
Earnings (loss) from continuing operations before income taxes	20,098	14,085	9,864

For the Years Ended December 31	GE(a)			GECS		
(In millions; per-share amounts in dollars)	2011	2010	2009	2011	2010	2009
Revenues						
Sales of goods	$ 67,012	$ 60,345	$ 64,211	$ 148	$ 533	$ 970
Sales of services	28,024	39,875	39,246	—	—	—
Other income (Note 17)	5,269	1,285	1,179	—	—	—
GECS earnings from continuing operations	6,432	3,023	1,177	—	—	—
GECS revenues from services (Note 18)	—	—	—	48,933	49,348	50,848
Total revenues	106,737	104,528	105,813	49,081	49,881	51,818
Costs and Expenses (Note 19)						
Cost of goods sold	51,605	45,570	49,886	135	501	808
Cost of services sold	17,199	25,958	25,878	—	—	—
Interest and other financial charges	1,299	1,600	1,478	13,883	14,526	16,870
Investment contracts, insurance losses and insurance annuity benefits	—	—	—	3,059	3,197	3,193
Provision for losses on financing receivables (Notes 6 and 23)	—	—	—	4,083	7,176	10,585
Other costs and expenses	17,556	16,340	14,841	20,469	22,433	23,051
Total costs and expenses	87,659	89,468	92,083	41,629	47,833	54,507
Earnings (loss) from continuing operations before income taxes	19,078	15,060	13,730	7,452	2,048	(2,689)

NOTES TO CONSOLIDATED FINANCIAL STATEMENTS

Note 6. Gecs Financing Receivables and Allowance for Losses on Financing Receivables (in part)

	At	
(In millions)	December 31, 2011	December 31, 2010
Loans, net of deferred income[a]	$257,515	$275,877
Investment in financing leases, net of deferred income	38,142	44,390
	295,657	320,267
Less allowance for losses	(6,350)	(8,033)
Financing receivables—net[b]	$289,307	$312,234

[a] Deferred income was $2,319 million and $2,351 million at December 31, 2011 and December 31, 2010, respectively.

[b] Financing receivables at December 31, 2011 and December 31, 2010 included $1,062 million and $1,503 million, respectively, relating to loans that had been acquired in a transfer but have been subject to credit deterioration since origination per ASC 310, *Receivables*.

GECS financing receivables include both loans and financing leases. Loans represent transactions in a variety of forms, including revolving charge and credit, mortgages, installment loans, intermediate-term loans and revolving loans secured by business assets. The portfolio includes loans carried at the principal amount on which finance charges are billed periodically, and loans carried at gross book value, which includes finance charges.

Investment in financing leases consists of direct financing and leveraged leases of aircraft, railroad rolling stock, autos, other transportation equipment, data processing equipment, medical equipment, commercial real estate and other manufacturing, power generation, and commercial equipment and facilities.

For federal income tax purposes, the leveraged leases and the majority of the direct financing leases are leases in which GECS depreciates the leased assets and is taxed upon the accrual of rental income. Certain direct financing leases are loans for federal income tax purposes. For these transactions, GECS is taxed only on the portion of each payment that constitutes interest, unless the interest is tax-exempt (e.g., certain obligations of state governments).

Investment in direct financing and leveraged leases represents net unpaid rentals and estimated unguaranteed residual values of leased equipment, less related deferred income. GECS has no general obligation for principal and interest on notes and other instruments representing third-party participation related to leveraged leases; such notes and other instruments have not been included in liabilities but have been offset against the related rentals receivable. The GECS share of rentals receivable on leveraged leases is subordinate to the share of other participants who also have security interests in the leased equipment. For federal income tax purposes, GECS is entitled to deduct the interest expense accruing on non-recourse financing related to leveraged leases.

Net Investment in Financing Leases

December 31 (In millions)	Total Financing Leases 2011	Total Financing Leases 2010	Direct Financing Leases[a] 2011	Direct Financing Leases[a] 2010	Leveraged Leases[b] 2011	Leveraged Leases[b] 2010
Total minimum lease payments receivable	$44,157	$52,180	$33,667	$40,037	$10,490	$12,143
Less principal and interest on third-party non-recourse debt	(6,812)	(8,110)	—	—	(6,812)	(8,110)
Net rentals receivables	37,345	44,070	33,667	40,037	3,678	4,033
Estimated unguaranteed residual value of leased assets	7,592	8,495	5,140	5,991	2,452	2,504
Less deferred income	(6,795)	(8,175)	(5,219)	(6,438)	(1,576)	(1,737)
Investment in financing leases, net of deferred income	38,142	44,390	33,588	39,590	4,554	4,800
Less amounts to arrive at net investment						
Allowance for losses	(294)	(396)	(281)	(378)	(13)	(18)
Deferred taxes	(6,718)	(6,168)	(2,938)	(2,266)	(3,780)	(3,902)
Net investment in financing leases	$31,130	$37,826	$30,369	$36,946	$ 761	$ 880

[a] Included $413 million and $452 million of initial direct costs on direct financing leases at December 31, 2011 and 2010, respectively.

[b] Included pre-tax income of $116 million and $133 million and income tax of $35 million and $51 million during 2011 and 2010, respectively. Net investment credits recognized on leveraged leases during 2011 and 2010 were insignificant.

The following tables provide additional information about our financing receivables and related activity in the allowance for losses for our Commercial, Real Estate and Consumer portfolios.

Financing Receivables—Net

The following table displays our financing receivables balances.

(In millions)	At December 31, 2011	At December 31, 2010
Commercial		
CLL		
Americas[a]	$ 80,505	$ 88,558
Europe	36,899	37,498
Asia	11,635	11,943
Other[a]	436	664
Total CLL	129,475	138,663
Energy Financial Services	5,912	7,011
GE Capital Aviation Services (GECAS)	11,901	12,615
Other	1,282	1,788
Total Commercial financing receivables	148,570	160,077
Real Estate		
Debt	24,501	30,249
Business Properties	8,248	9,962
Total Real Estate financing receivables	32,749	40,211
Consumer		
Non-U.S. residential mortgages	36,170	40,011
Non-U.S. installment and revolving credit	18,544	20,132
U.S. installment and revolving credit	46,689	43,974
Non-U.S. auto	5,691	7,558
Other	7,244	8,304
Total Consumer financing receivables	114,338	119,979
Total financing receivables	295,657	320,267
Less allowance for losses	(6,350)	(8,033)
Total financing receivables—net	$289,307	$312,234

[a] During 2011, we transferred our Railcar lending and leasing portfolio from CLL Other to CLL Americas. Prior-period amounts were reclassified to conform to the current-period presentation.

Allowance for Losses on Financing Receivables

The following tables provide a roll-forward of our allowance for losses on financing receivables.

(In millions)	Balance at January 1, 2011	Provision Charged to Operations[a]	Other[b]	Gross Write-Offs[c]	Recoveries[c]	Balance at December 31, 2011
Commercial						
CLL						
Americas	$1,288	$ 281	$ (96)	$ (700)	$ 116	$ 889
Europe	429	195	(5)	(286)	67	400
Asia	222	105	13	(214)	31	157
Other	6	3	(3)	(2)	—	4
Total CLL	1,945	584	(91)	(1,202)	214	1,450
Energy Financial Services	22	—	(1)	(4)	9	26
GECAS	20	—	—	(3)	—	17
Other	58	23	—	(47)	3	37
Total Commercial	2,045	607	(92)	(1,256)	226	1,530
Real Estate						
Debt	1,292	242	2	(603)	16	949
Business Properties	196	82	—	(144)	6	140
Total Real Estate	1,488	324	2	(747)	22	1,089
Consumer						
Non-U.S. residential mortgages	803	249	(20)	(381)	55	706
Non-U.S. installment and revolving credit	937	490	(30)	(1,257)	577	717
U.S. installment and revolving credit	2,333	2,241	1	(3,095)	528	2,008
Non-U.S. auto	168	30	(4)	(216)	123	101
Other	259	142	(20)	(272)	90	199
Total Consumer	4,500	3,152	(73)	(5,221)	1,373	3,731
Total	$8,033	$4,083	$(163)	$(7,224)	$1,621	$6,350

[a] Included a provision of $77 million at Consumer related to the July 1, 2011 adoption of ASU 2011-02. See Note 23.
[b] Other primarily included transfers to held for sale and the effects of currency exchange.
[c] Net write-offs (write-offs less recoveries) in certain portfolios may exceed the beginning allowance for losses as our revolving credit portfolios turn over more than once per year or, in all portfolios, can reflect losses that are incurred subsequent to the beginning of the fiscal year due to information becoming available during the current year, which may identify further deterioration on existing financing receivables.

(In millions)	Balance at December 31, 2009	Adoption of ASU 2009 16 & 17[a]	Balance at January 1, 2010	Provision Charged to Operations	Other[b]	Gross Write-Offs[c]	Recoveries[c]	Balance at December 31, 2010
Commercial								
CLL								
Americas	$1,180	$ 66	$1,246	$1,059	$ (11)	$ (1,136)	$ 130	$1,288
Europe	575	—	575	269	(37)	(440)	62	429
Asia	244	(10)	234	153	(6)	(181)	22	222
Other	10	—	10	(2)	(1)	(1)	—	6
Total CLL	2,009	56	2,065	1,479	(55)	(1,758)	214	1,945
Energy Financial Services	28	—	28	65	—	(72)	1	22
GECAS	104	—	104	12	—	(96)	—	20
Other	34	—	34	33	—	(9)	—	58
Total Commercial	2,175	56	2,231	1,589	(55)	(1,935)	215	2,045
Real Estate								
Debt	1,358	(3)	1,355	764	10	(838)	1	1,292
Business Properties	136	45	181	146	(8)	(126)	3	196
Total Real Estate	1,494	42	1,536	910	2	(964)	4	1,488
Consumer								
Non-U.S. residential mortgages	892	—	892	256	(41)	(381)	77	803
Non-U.S. installment and revolving credit	1,106	—	1,106	1,047	(68)	(1,733)	585	937
U.S. installment and revolving credit	1,551	1,602	3,153	3,018	(6)	(4,300)	468	2,333
Non-U.S. auto	292	—	292	91	(61)	(313)	159	168
Other	292	—	292	265	5	(394)	91	259
Total Consumer	4,133	1,602	5,735	4,677	(171)	(7,121)	1,380	4,500
Total	$7,802	$1,700	$9,502	$7,176	$(224)	$(10,020)	$1,599	$8,033

[a] Reflects the effects of our adoption of ASU 2009-16 & 17 on January 1, 2010.
[b] Other primarily included the effects of currency exchange.
[c] Net write-offs (write-offs less recoveries) in certain portfolios may exceed the beginning allowance for losses as our revolving credit portfolios turn over more than once per year or, in all portfolios, can reflect losses that are incurred subsequent to the beginning of the fiscal year due to information becoming available during the current year, which may identify further deterioration on existing financing receivables.

(In millions)	Balance at January 1, 2009	Provision Charged to Operations	Other[a]	Gross Write-Offs[b]	Recoveries[b]	Balance at December 31, 2009
Commercial						
CLL						
Americas	$ 846	$ 1,400	$ (42)	$(1,117)	$ 93	$1,180
Europe	311	625	(14)	(431)	84	575
Asia	163	257	3	(203)	24	244
Other	1	8	5	(4)	—	10
Total CLL	1,321	2,290	(48)	(1,755)	201	2,009
Energy Financial Services	58	33	4	(67)	—	28
GECAS	58	65	(3)	(16)	—	104
Other	28	29	—	(24)	1	34
Total Commercial	1,465	2,417	(47)	(1,862)	202	2,175
Real Estate						
Debt	282	1,295	13	(232)	—	1,358
Business Properties	19	147	—	(32)	2	136
Total Real Estate	301	1,442	13	(264)	2	1,494
Consumer						
Non-U.S. residential mortgages	328	883	69	(469)	81	892
Non-U.S. installment and revolving credit	1,000	1,741	39	(2,235)	561	1,106
U.S. installment and revolving credit	1,616	3,367	(975)	(2,612)	155	1,551
Non-U.S. auto	187	389	30	(510)	196	292
Other	225	346	45	(389)	65	292
Total Consumer	3,356	6,726	(792)	(6,215)	1,058	4,133
Total	$5,122	$10,585	$(826)	$(8,341)	$1,262	$7,802

[a] Other primarily included the effects of securitization activity and currency exchange.

[b] Net write-offs (write-offs less recoveries) in certain portfolios may exceed the beginning allowance for losses as our revolving credit portfolios turn over more than once per year or, in all portfolios, can reflect losses that are incurred subsequent to the beginning of the fiscal year due to information becoming available during the current year, which may identify further deterioration on existing financing receivables.

See Note 23 for supplemental information about the credit quality of financing receivables and allowance for losses on financing receivables.

Note 23. Supplemental Information about the Credit Quality of Financing Receivables and Allowance for Losses on Financing Receivables (in part)

We provide further detailed information about the credit quality of our Commercial, Real Estate and Consumer financing receivables portfolios. For each portfolio, we describe the characteristics of the financing receivables and provide information about collateral, payment performance, credit quality indicators, and impairment. We manage these portfolios using delinquency and nonearning data as key performance indicators. The categories used within this section such as impaired loans, TDR and nonaccrual financing receivables are defined by the authoritative guidance and we base our categorization on the related scope and definitions contained in the related standards. The categories of nonearning and delinquent are defined by us and are used in our process for managing our financing receivables. Definitions of these categories are provided in Note 1.

Commercial

Financing Receivables and Allowance for Losses

The following table provides further information about general and specific reserves related to Commercial financing receivables.

Commercial (In millions)	Financing Receivables at	
	December 31, 2011	December 31, 2010
CLL		
Americas[a]	$ 80,505	$ 88,558
Europe	36,899	37,498
Asia	11,635	11,943
Other[a]	436	664
Total CLL	129,475	138,663
Energy Financial Services	5,912	7,011
GECAS	11,901	12,615
Other	1,282	1,788
Total Commercial financing receivables, before allowance for losses	$148,570	160,077
Non-impaired financing receivables	$142,908	$154,257
General reserves	718	1,014
Impaired loans	5,662	5,820
Specific reserves	812	1,031

[a] During 2011, we transferred our Railcar lending and leasing portfolio from CLL Other to CLL Americas. Prior-period amounts were reclassified to conform to the current-period presentation.

Past Due Financing Receivables

The following table displays payment performance of Commercial financing receivables.

	At			
	December 31, 2011		December 31, 2010	
Commercial	Over 30 Days Past Due	Over 90 Days Past Due	Over 30 Days Past Due	Over 90 Days Past Due
CLL				
Americas	1.3%	0.8%	1.2%	0.8%
Europe	3.8	2.1	4.2	2.3
Asia	1.3	1.0	2.2	1.4
Other	2.0	0.1	2.4	1.2
Total CLL	2.0	1.2	2.1	1.3
Energy Financial Services	0.3	0.3	0.9	0.8
GECAS	—	—	—	—
Other	3.7	3.5	5.8	5.5
Total	2.0	1.1	2.0	1.2

Nonaccrual Financing Receivables

The following table provides further information about Commercial financing receivables that are classified as nonaccrual. Of our $4,718 million and $5,463 million of nonaccrual financing receivables at December 31, 2011 and December 31, 2010, respectively, $1,227 million and $1,016 million are currently paying in accordance with their contractual terms, respectively.

	Nonaccrual Financing Receivables at		Nonearning Financing Receivables at	
Commercial (Dollars in millions)	December 31, 2011	December 31, 2010	December 31, 2011	December 31, 2010
CLL				
Americas	$2,417	$3,208	$1,862	$2,573
Europe	1,599	1,415	1,167	1,241
Asia	428	616	269	406
Other	68	7	11	6
Total CLL	4,512	5,246	3,309	4,226
Energy Financial Services	22	78	22	62
GECAS	69	—	55	—
Other	115	139	65	102
Total	$4,718	$5,463	$3,451	$4,390
Allowance for losses percentage	32.4%	37.4%	44.3%	46.6%

Impaired Loans

The following table provides information about loans classified as impaired and specific reserves related to Commercial.

Commercial[a] (In millions)	With No Specific Allowance			With a Specific Allowance			
	Recorded Investment in Loans	Unpaid Principal Balance	Average Investment in Loans	Recorded Investment in Loans	Unpaid Principal Balance	Associated Allowance	Average Investment in Loans
December 31, 2011							
CLL							
Americas	$2,136	$2,219	$2,128	$1,367	$1,415	$ 425	$1,468
Europe	936	1,060	1,001	730	717	263	602
Asia	85	83	94	156	128	84	214
Other	54	58	13	11	11	2	5
Total CLL	3,211	3,420	3,236	2,264	2,271	774	2,289
Energy Financial Services	4	4	20	18	18	9	87
GECAS	28	28	59	—	—	—	11
Other	62	63	67	75	75	29	97
Total	$3,305	$3,515	$3,382	$2,357	$2,364	$ 812	$2,484
December 31, 2010							
CLL							
Americas	$2,030	$2,127	$1,547	$1,699	$1,744	$ 589	$1,754
Europe	802	674	629	566	566	267	563
Asia	119	117	117	338	303	132	334
Other	—	—	9	—	—	—	—
Total CLL	2,951	2,918	2,302	2,603	2,613	988	2,651
Energy Financial Services	54	61	76	24	24	6	70
GECAS	24	24	50	—	—	—	31
Other	58	57	30	106	99	37	82
Total	$3,087	$3,060	$2,458	$2,733	$2,736	$1,031	$2,834

[a] We recognized $193 million and $88 million of interest income, including $59 million and $39 million on a cash basis, for the years ended December 31, 2011 and 2010, respectively, principally in our CLL Americas business. The total average investment in impaired loans for the years ended December 31, 2011 and 2010 was $5,866 million and $5,292 million, respectively.

Impaired loans classified as TDRs in our CLL business were $3,642 million and $2,911 million at December 31, 2011 and 2010, respectively, and were primarily attributable to CLL Americas ($2,746 million and $2,347 million, respectively). For the year ended December 31, 2011, we modified $1,856 million of loans classified as TDRs, primarily in CLL Americas ($1,105 million) and CLL EMEA ($646 million). Changes to these loans primarily included debt to equity exchange, extensions, interest only payment periods and forbearance or other actions, which are in addition to, or sometimes in lieu of, fees and rate increases. Of our modifications classified as TDRs in the last year, $101 million have subsequently experienced a payment default.

Credit Quality Indicators

Substantially all of our Commercial financing receivables portfolio is secured lending and we assess the overall quality of the portfolio based on the potential risk of loss measure. The metric incorporates both the borrower's credit quality along with any related collateral protection.

Our internal risk ratings process is an important source of information in determining our allowance for losses and represents a comprehensive, statistically validated approach to evaluate risk in our financing receivables portfolios. In deriving our internal risk ratings, we stratify our Commercial portfolios into twenty-one categories of default risk and/or six categories of loss given default to group into three categories: A, B and C. Our process starts by developing an internal risk rating for our borrowers, which are based upon our proprietary models using data derived from borrower financial statements, agency ratings, payment history information, equity prices and other commercial borrower characteristics. We then evaluate the potential risk of loss for the specific lending transaction in the event of borrower default, which takes into account such factors as applicable collateral value, historical loss and recovery rates for similar transactions, and our collection capabilities. Our internal risk ratings process and the models we use are subject to regular monitoring and validation controls. The frequency of rating updates is set by our credit risk policy, which requires annual Audit Committee approval. The models are updated on a regular basis and statistically validated annually, or more frequently as circumstances warrant.

The table below summarizes our Commercial financing receivables by risk category. As described above, financing receivables are assigned one of twenty-one risk ratings based on our process and then these are grouped by similar characteristics into three categories in the table below. Category A is characterized by either high credit quality borrowers or transactions with significant collateral coverage which substantially reduces or eliminates the risk of loss in the event of borrower default. Category B is characterized by borrowers with weaker credit quality than those in Category

A, or transactions with moderately strong collateral coverage which minimizes but may not fully mitigate the risk of loss in the event of default. Category C is characterized by borrowers with higher levels of default risk relative to our overall portfolio or transactions where collateral coverage may not fully mitigate a loss in the event of default.

Commercial (In millions)	Secured			
	A	B	C	Total
December 31, 2011				
CLL				
Americas[a]	$ 73,103	$2,816	$4,586	$ 80,505
Europe	33,481	1,080	1,002	35,563
Asia	10,644	116	685	11,445
Other[a]	345	—	91	436
Total CLL	117,573	4,012	6,364	127,949
Energy Financial Services	5,727	24	18	5,769
GECAS	10,881	970	50	11,901
Other	1,282	—	—	1,282
Total	$135,463	$5,006	$6,432	$146,901
December 31, 2010				
CLL				
Americas[a]	$ 78,939	$4,103	$5,516	$ 88,558
Europe	33,642	840	1,262	35,744
Asia	10,777	199	766	11,742
Other[a]	544	66	54	664
Total CLL	123,902	5,208	7,598	136,708
Energy Financial Services	6,775	183	53	7,011
GECAS	11,034	1,193	388	12,615
Other	1,788	—	—	1,788
Total	$143,499	$6,584	$8,039	$158,122

[a] During 2011, we transferred our Railcar lending and leasing portfolio from CLL Other to CLL Americas. Prior-period amounts were reclassified to conform to the current-period presentation.

For our secured financing receivables portfolio, our collateral position and ability to work out problem accounts mitigates our losses. Our asset managers have deep industry expertise that enables us to identify the optimum approach to default situations. We price risk premiums for weaker credits at origination, closely monitor changes in creditworthiness through our risk ratings and watch list process, and are engaged early with deteriorating credits to minimize economic loss. Secured financing receivables within risk Category C are predominantly in our CLL businesses and are primarily composed of senior term lending facilities and factoring programs secured by various asset types including inventory, accounts receivable, cash, equipment and related business facilities as well as franchise finance activities secured by underlying equipment.

Loans within Category C are reviewed and monitored regularly, and classified as impaired when it is probable that they will not pay in accordance with contractual terms. Our internal risk rating process identifies credits warranting closer monitoring; and as such, these loans are not necessarily classified as nonearning or impaired.

Substantially all of our unsecured Commercial financing receivables portfolio is attributable to our Interbanca S.p.A. and GE Sanyo Credit acquisitions in Europe and Asia, respectively. At December 31, 2011 and December 31, 2010, these financing receivables included $325 million and $208 million rated A, $748 million and $964 million rated B, and $596 million and $783 million rated C, respectively.

Real Estate

Financing Receivables and Allowance for Losses

The following table provides further information about general and specific reserves related to Real Estate financing receivables.

Real Estate (In millions)	Financing receivables at	
	December 31, 2011	December 31, 2010
Debt	$24,501	$30,249
Business Properties	8,248	9,962
Total Real Estate financing receivables, before allowance for losses	$32,749	$40,211
Non-impaired financing receivables	$24,002	$30,394
General reserves	267	338
Impaired loans	8,747	9,817
Specific reserves	822	1,150

Past Due Financing Receivables

The following table displays payment performance of Real Estate financing receivables.

| | At | | | |
| | December 31, 2011 | | December 31, 2010 | |
Real Estate	Over 30 Days Past Due	Over 90 Days Past Due	Over 30 Days Past Due	Over 90 Days Past Due
Debt	2.4%	2.3%	4.3%	4.1%
Business Properties	3.9	3.0	4.6	3.9
Total	2.8	2.5	4.4	4.0

Nonaccrual Financing Receivables

The following table provides further information about Real Estate financing receivables that are classified as nonaccrual. Of our $6,949 million and $9,719 million of nonaccrual financing receivables at December 31, 2011 and December 31, 2010, respectively, $6,061 million and $7,888 million are currently paying in accordance with their contractual terms, respectively.

| | Nonaccrual Financing Receivables at | | Nonearning Financing Receivables at | |
Real Estate (Dollars in millions)	December 31, 2011	December 31, 2010	December 31, 2011	December 31, 2010
Debt	$6,351	$9,039	$541	$ 961
Business Properties	598	680	249	386
Total	$6,949	$9,719	$790	$1,347
Allowance for losses percentage	15.7%	15.3%	137.8%	110.5%

Impaired Loans

The following table provides information about loans classified as impaired and specific reserves related to Real Estate.

| | With No Specific Allowance | | | With a Specific Allowance | | | |
Real Estate[a] (In millions)	Recorded Investment in Loans	Unpaid Principal Balance	Average Investment in Loans	Recorded Investment in Loans	Unpaid Principal Balance	Associated Allowance	Average Investment in Loans
December 31, 2011							
Debt	$3,558	$3,614	$3,568	$4,560	$4,652	$ 717	$5,435
Business Properties	232	232	215	397	397	105	460
Total	$3,790	$3,846	$3,783	$4,957	$5,049	$ 822	$5,895
December 31, 2010							
Debt	$2,814	$2,873	$1,598	$6,323	$6,498	$1,007	$6,116
Business Properties	191	213	141	489	476	143	382
Total	$3,005	$3,086	$1,739	$6,812	$6,974	$1,150	$6,498

[a] We recognized $399 million and $189 million of interest income, including $339 million and $189 million on a cash basis, for the years ended December 31, 2011 and 2010, respectively, principally in our Real Estate-Debt portfolio. The total average investment in impaired loans for the years ended December 31, 2011 and 2010 was $9,678 million and $8,237 million, respectively.

Real Estate TDRs increased from $4,866 million at December 31, 2010 to $7,006 million at December 31, 2011, primarily driven by loans scheduled to mature during 2011, some of which were modified during 2011 and classified as TDRs upon modification. We deem loan modifications to be TDRs when we have granted a concession to a borrower experiencing financial difficulty and we do not receive adequate compensation in the form of an effective interest rate that is at current market rates of interest given the risk characteristics of the loan or other consideration that compensates us for the value of the concession. The limited liquidity and higher return requirements in the real estate market for loans with higher loan-to-value (LTV) ratios has typically resulted in the conclusion that the modified terms are not at current market rates of interest, even if the modified loans are expected to be fully recoverable. For the year ended December 31, 2011, we modified $3,965 million of loans classified as TDRs, substantially all in our Debt portfolio. Changes to these loans primarily included maturity extensions, principal payment acceleration, changes to collateral or covenant terms and cash sweeps, which are in addition to, or sometimes in lieu of, fees and rate increases. Of our modifications classi-fied as TDRs in the last year, $140 million have subsequently experienced a payment default.

Credit Quality Indicators

Due to the primarily non-recourse nature of our Debt port-folio, loan-to-value ratios provide the best indicators of the credit quality of the portfolio. By contrast, the credit quality of the Business Properties portfolio is primarily influenced by the strength of the borrower's general credit quality, which is reflected in our internal risk rating process, consistent with the process we use for our Commercial portfolio.

| | Loan-to-Value Ratio at | | | | | |
| | December 31, 2011 | | | December 31, 2010 | | |
(In millions)	Less Than 80%	80% to 95%	Greater Than 95%	Less Than 80%	80% to 95%	Greater Than 95%
Debt	$14,454	$4,593	$5,454	$12,362	$9,392	$8,495

| | Internal Risk Rating at | | | | | |
| | December 31, 2011 | | | December 31, 2010 | | |
(In millions)	A	B	C	A	B	C
Business Properties	$7,628	$110	$510	$8,746	$437	$779

Within Real Estate-Debt, these financing receivables are primarily concentrated in our North American and European Lending platforms and are secured by various property types. A substantial majority of the Real Estate-Debt financing receivables with loan-to-value ratios greater than 95% are paying in accordance with contractual terms. Substantially all of these loans and substantially all of the Real Estate-Business Properties financing receivables included in Category C are impaired loans which are subject to the specific reserve evaluation process described in Note 1. The ultimate recoverability of impaired loans is driven by collection strategies that do not necessarily depend on the sale of the underlying collateral and include full or partial repayments through third-party refinancing and restructurings.

Consumer

At December 31, 2011, our U.S. consumer financing receivables included private-label credit card and sales financing for approximately 56 million customers across the U.S. with no metropolitan area accounting for more than 5% of the portfolio. Of the total U.S. consumer financing receivables, approximately 65% relate to credit card loans, which are often subject to profit and loss sharing arrangements with the retailer (which are recorded in revenues), and the remaining 35% are sales finance receivables, which provide financing to customers in areas such as electronics, recreation, medical and home improvement.

Financing Receivables and Allowance for Losses

The following table provides further information about general and specific reserves related to Consumer financing receivables.

| Consumer (In millions) | Financing Receivables at | |
	December 31, 2011	December 31, 2010
Non-U.S. residential mortgages	$ 36,170	$ 40,011
Non-U.S. installment and revolving credit	18,544	20,132
U.S. installment and revolving credit	46,689	43,974
Non-U.S. auto	5,691	7,558
Other	7,244	8,304
Total consumer financing receivables, before allowance for losses	$114,338	$119,979
Non-impaired financing receivables	$111,233	$117,431
General reserves	3,014	3,945
Impaired loans	3,105	2,548
Specific reserves	717	555

Past Due Financing Receivables

The following table displays payment performance of Consumer financing receivables.

	At			
	December 31, 2011		December 31, 2010	
Consumer	Over 30 Days Past Due	Over 90 Days Past Due[a]	Over 30 Days Past Due	Over 90 Days Past Due[a]
Non-U.S. residential mortgages	13.4%	8.8%	13.7%	8.8%
Non-U.S. installment and revolving credit	4.1	1.2	4.5	1.3
U.S. installment and revolving credit	5.0	2.2	6.2	2.8
Non-U.S. auto	3.1	0.5	3.3	0.6
Other	3.5	2.0	4.2	2.3
Total	7.3	4.0	8.1	4.4

[a] Included $45 million and $65 million of loans at December 31, 2011 and December 31, 2010, respectively, which are over 90 days past due and accruing interest, mainly representing accretion on loans acquired at a discount.

Nonaccrual Financing Receivables

The following table provides further information about Consumer financing receivables that are classified as nonaccrual.

	Nonaccrual Financing Receivables at		Nonearning Financing Receivables at	
Consumer (Dollars in millions)	December 31, 2011	December 31, 2010	December 31, 2011	December 31, 2010
Non-U.S. residential mortgages	$3,475	$3,986	$3,349	$3,738
Non-U.S. installment and revolving credit	321	302	263	289
U.S. installment and revolving credit	990	1,201	990	1,201
Non-U.S. auto	43	46	43	46
Other	487	600	419	478
Total	$5,316	$6,135	$5,064	$5,752
Allowance for losses percentage	70.2%	73.3%	73.7%	78.2%

Impaired Loans

The vast majority of our Consumer nonaccrual financing receivables are smaller balance homogeneous loans evaluated collectively, by portfolio, for impairment and therefore are outside the scope of the disclosure requirement for impaired loans. Accordingly, impaired loans in our Consumer business represent restructured smaller balance homogeneous loans meeting the definition of a TDR, and are therefore subject to the disclosure requirement for impaired loans, and commercial loans in our Consumer–Other portfolio. The recorded investment of these impaired loans totaled $3,105 million (with an unpaid principal balance of $2,679 million) and comprised $69 million with no specific allowance, primarily all in our Consumer–Other portfolio, and $3,036 million with a specific allowance of $717 million at December 31, 2011. The impaired loans with a specific allowance included $369 million with a specific allowance of $102 million in our Consumer–Other portfolio and $2,667 million with a specific allowance of $615 million across the remaining Consumer business and had an unpaid principal balance and average investment of $2,244 million and $2,343 million, respectively, at December 31, 2011. We recognized $141 million and $114 million of interest income, including $15 million and $30 million on a cash basis, for the years ended December 31, 2011 and 2010, respectively, principally in our Consumer –Non-U.S. and U.S.

installment and revolving credit portfolios. The total average investment in impaired loans for the years ended December 31, 2011 and 2010 was $2,840 million and $2,009 million, respectively.

Impaired loans classified as TDRs in our Consumer business were $2,935 million and $2,256 million at December 31, 2011 and 2010, respectively. We utilize certain loan modification programs for borrowers experiencing financial difficulties in our Consumer loan portfolio. These loan modification programs primarily include interest rate reductions and payment deferrals in excess of three months, which were not part of the terms of the original contract, and are primarily concentrated in our non-U.S. residential mortgage and U.S. credit card portfolios. For the year ended December 31, 2011, we modified $1,970 million of consumer loans for borrowers experiencing financial difficulties, which are classified as TDRs, and included $1,020 million of non-U.S. consumer loans, primarily residential mortgages, credit cards and personal loans and approximately $950 million of credit card loans in the U.S. We expect borrowers whose loans have been modified under these programs to continue to be able to meet their contractual obligations upon the conclusion of the modification. For loans modified as TDRs in the last year, $251 million have subsequently experienced a payment default, primarily in our U.S. credit card and non-U.S. residential mortgage portfolios.

Credit Quality Indicators

Our Consumer financing receivables portfolio comprises both secured and unsecured lending. Secured financing receivables comprise residential loans and lending to small and medium-sized enterprises predominantly secured by auto and equipment, inventory finance and cash flow loans. Unsecured financing receivables include private-label credit card financing. A substantial majority of these cards are not for general use and are limited to the products and services sold by the retailer. The private label portfolio is diverse with no metropolitan area accounting for more than 5% of the related portfolio.

Non-U.S. Residential Mortgages

For our secured non-U.S. residential mortgage book, we assess the overall credit quality of the portfolio through loan-to-value ratios (the ratio of the outstanding debt on a property to the value of that property at origination). In the event of default and repossession of the underlying collateral, we have the ability to remarket and sell the properties to eliminate or mitigate the potential risk of loss. The table below provides additional information about our non-U.S. residential mortgages based on loan-to-value ratios.

| | Loan-to-Value Ratio at | | | | | |
| | December 31, 2011 | | | December 31, 2010 | | |
(In millions)	80% or less	Greater Than 80% to 90%	Greater Than 90%	80% or less	Greater Than 80% to 90%	Greater Than 90%
Non-U.S. residential mortgages	$20,379	$6,145	$9,646	$22,403	$7,023	$10,585

The majority of these financing receivables are in our U.K. and France portfolios and have re-indexed loan-to-value ratios of 84% and 56%, respectively. We have third-party mortgage insurance for approximately 68% of the balance of Consumer non-U.S. residential mortgage loans with loan-to-value ratios greater than 90% at December 31, 2011. Such loans were primarily originated in the U.K. and France.

Installment and Revolving Credit

For our unsecured lending products, including the non-U.S. and U.S. installment and revolving credit and non-U.S. auto portfolios, we assess overall credit quality using internal and external credit scores. Our internal credit scores imply a probability of default which we consistently translate into three approximate credit bureau equivalent credit score categories, including (a) 681 or higher, which are considered the strongest credits; (b) 615 to 680, considered moderate credit risk; and (c) 614 or less, which are considered weaker credits.

| | Internal Ratings Translated to Approximate Credit Bureau Equivalent Score at | | | | | |
| | December 31, 2011 | | | December 31, 2010 | | |
(In millions)	681 or Higher	615 to 680	614 or Less	681 or Higher	615 to 680	614 or Less
Non-U.S. installment and revolving credit	$ 9,913	$4,838	$3,793	$10,192	$5,749	$4,191
U.S. installment and revolving credit	28,918	9,398	8,373	25,940	8,846	9,188
Non-U.S. auto	3,927	1,092	672	5,379	1,330	849

Of those financing receivable accounts with credit bureau equivalent scores of 614 or less at December 31, 2011, 95% relate to installment and revolving credit accounts. These smaller balance accounts have an average outstanding balance less than one thousand U.S. dollars and are primarily concentrated in our retail card and sales finance receivables in the U.S. (which are often subject to profit and loss sharing arrangements), and closed-end loans outside the U.S., which minimizes the potential for loss in the event of default. For lower credit scores, we adequately price for the incremental risk at origination and monitor credit migration through our risk ratings process. We continuously adjust our credit line underwriting management and collection strategies based on customer behavior and risk profile changes.

Consumer—Other

Secured lending in Consumer—Other comprises loans to small and medium-sized enterprises predominantly secured by auto and equipment, inventory finance and cash flow loans. We develop our internal risk ratings for this portfolio in a manner consistent with the process used to develop our Commercial credit quality indicators, described above. We use the borrower's credit quality and underlying collateral strength to determine the potential risk of loss from these activities.

At December 31, 2011, Consumer—Other financing receivables of $5,580 million, $757 million and $907 million were rated A, B, and C, respectively. At December 31, 2010, Consumer—Other financing receivables of $6,415 million, $822 million and $1,067 million were rated A, B, and C, respectively.

Warranty

3.27

KB HOME (NOV)

MANAGEMENT'S DISCUSSION AND ANALYSIS OF FINANCIAL CONDITION AND RESULTS OF OPERATIONS

Critical Accounting Policies (in part)

Warranty Costs. As discussed in Note 13. Commitments and Contingencies in the Notes to Consolidated Financial Statements in this report, we provide a limited warranty on all of our homes. The specific terms and conditions of these limited warranties vary depending upon the market in which we do business. We generally provide a structural warranty of 10 years, a warranty on electrical, heating, cooling, plumbing and other building systems each varying from two to five years based on geographic market and state law, and a warranty of one year for other components of the home. We estimate the costs that may be incurred under each limited warranty and record a liability in the amount of such costs at the time the revenue associated with the sale of each home is recognized. Our expense associated with the issuance of these warranties totaled $4.9 million in 2011, $5.2 million in 2010 and $6.8 million in 2009.

Factors that affect our warranty liability include the number of homes delivered, historical and anticipated rates of warranty claims, and cost per claim. Our primary assumption in estimating the amounts we accrue for warranty costs is that historical claims experience is a strong indicator of future claims experience. We periodically assess the adequacy of our recorded warranty liabilities, which are included in accrued expenses and other liabilities in the consolidated balance sheets, and adjust the amounts as necessary based on our assessment. Our assessment includes the review of our actual warranty costs incurred to identify trends and changes in our warranty claims experience, and considers our construction quality and customer service initiatives and outside events. Based on the trends in our actual warranty costs incurred, our assessments in 2011 resulted in the recording of warranty adjustments of $7.4 million as reductions to construction and land costs. In 2009, we incurred a charge of $5.7 million associated with the repair of allegedly defective drywall. While we believe the warranty liability reflected in our consolidated balance sheets to be adequate, unanticipated changes in the legal environment, local weather, land or environmental conditions, quality of materials or methods used in the construction of homes, or customer service practices could have a significant impact on our actual warranty costs in the future and such amounts could differ from our estimates. A 10% change in the historical warranty rates used to estimate our warranty accrual would not result in a material change in our accrual.

NOTES TO CONSOLIDATED FINANCIAL STATEMENTS

Note 1. Summary of Significant Accounting Policies (in part)

Warranty Costs. The Company provides a limited warranty on all of its homes. The Company estimates the costs that may be incurred under each limited warranty and records a liability in the amount of such costs at the time the revenue associated with the sale of each home is recognized. Factors that affect the Company's warranty liability include the number of homes delivered, historical and anticipated rates of warranty claims, and cost per claim. The Company's primary assumption in estimating the amounts it accrues for warranty costs is that historical claims experience is a strong indicator of future claims experience. The Company periodically assesses the adequacy of its recorded warranty liabilities and adjusts the amounts as necessary based on its assessment.

Note 13. Commitments and Contingencies (in part)

Commitments and contingencies include typical obligations of homebuilders for the completion of contracts and those incurred in the ordinary course of business.

Warranty. The Company provides a limited warranty on all of its homes. The specific terms and conditions of these limited warranties vary depending upon the market in which the Company does business. The Company generally provides a structural warranty of 10 years, a warranty on electrical, heating, cooling, plumbing and other building systems each varying from two to five years based on geographic market and state law, and a warranty of one year for other components of the home. The Company estimates the costs that may be incurred under each limited warranty and records a liability in the amount of such costs at the time the revenue associated with the sale of each home is recognized. Factors that affect the Company's warranty liability include the number of homes delivered, historical and anticipated rates of warranty claims, and cost per claim. The Company's primary assumption in estimating the amounts it accrues for warranty costs is that historical claims experience is a strong indicator of future claims experience. The Company periodically assesses the adequacy of its recorded warranty liabilities, which are included in accrued expenses and other liabilities in the consolidated balance sheets, and adjusts the amounts as necessary based on its assessment. The Company's assessment includes the review of its actual warranty costs incurred to identify trends and changes in its warranty claims experience, and considers the Company's construction quality and customer service initiatives and outside events. While the Company believes the warranty liability reflected in its consolidated balance sheets to be adequate, unanticipated changes in the legal environment, local weather, land or environmental conditions, quality of materials or methods used in the construction of homes, or customer service practices could have a significant impact on its actual warranty costs in the future and such amounts could differ from the Company's estimates.

The changes in the Company's warranty liability are as follows (in thousands):

	Years Ended November 30		
	2011	**2010**	**2009**
Balance at beginning of year	$ 93,988	$135,749	$145,369
Warranties issued	4,852	5,173	6,846
Payments	(25,024)	(44,973)	(24,690)
Adjustments	(6,123)	(1,961)	8,224
Balance at end of year	$ 67,693	$ 93,988	$135,749

The Company's warranty adjustments for the year ended November 30, 2011 include $7.4 million of adjustments that were recorded as reductions to construction and land costs in the consolidated statements of operations, and mainly resulted from the Company's assessment of trends in its overall warranty claims experience on homes previously delivered. In addition, for the year ended November 30, 2009, the Company incurred a charge of $5.7 million associated with the repair of allegedly defective drywall.

The Company's overall warranty liability of $67.7 million at November 30, 2011 included $4.8 million for estimated remaining repair costs associated with 87 homes that have been identified as containing or suspected of containing allegedly defective drywall manufactured in China. These homes are located in Florida and were primarily delivered in 2006 and 2007. The Company's overall warranty liability of $94.0 million at November 30, 2010 included $11.3 million for estimated remaining repair costs associated with 296 such identified affected homes, and its overall warranty liability of $135.7 million at November 30, 2009 included $14.4 million for estimated remaining repair costs associated with 229 such identified affected homes. The decreases in the liability for estimated repair costs associated with identified affected homes during the years ended November 30, 2011 and 2010 reflected the lower number of identified affected homes with unresolved repairs at each date compared to the previous year. During the years ended November 30, 2011, 2010 and 2009, repairs were resolved on 239, 141 and zero identified affected homes, respectively, and the Company identified 30, 208 and 229 additional affected homes, respectively. For these purposes, the Company considers repairs for identified affected homes to be "resolved" when all repairs are complete and all repair costs are fully paid. Repairs for identified affected homes are considered "unresolved" if repairs are not complete and/or there are repair costs remaining to be paid.

The drywall used in the construction of the Company's homes is purchased and installed by subcontractors. The Company's subcontractors obtained drywall material from multiple domestic and foreign sources through late 2008. In late 2008, the Company directed its subcontractors to obtain only domestically sourced drywall. The Company has identified homes that contain or may contain allegedly defective drywall manufactured in China primarily by responding to homeowner-initiated warranty claims or customer service questions regarding such material or regarding conditions or items in a home that may be affected by such material. Additionally, in certain communities where there had been a high number of affected homes identified through the warranty/customer service process, the Company proactively undertook community-wide reviews that identified more affected homes. The Company completed all such community-wide reviews at the end of May 2011. The Company's customer service personnel or, in some instances, third-party consultants handled these matters. Because of the testing process required to determine the origin of drywall material obtained before December 2008, the source of drywall for homes that have not been the subject of a customer service/warranty request or community-wide review is unknown. As a result, the Company is unable to readily identify the total number of homes that may contain the allegedly defective drywall material manufactured in China.

While the Company continues to respond to individual warranty/customer service requests as they are made, the number of additional affected homes newly identified each quarter has fallen significantly since the third quarter of 2009 to a nominal amount. Based on the significantly reduced individual warranty/customer service request rate, the completion of its community-wide reviews and the domestic sourcing of drywall material since late 2008, the Company anticipates that it has identified substantially all potentially affected homes and will receive at most only nominal additional claims in future periods.

During the years ended November 30, 2011, 2010 and 2009, the Company paid $13.7 million, $25.5 million and $1.3 million, respectively, to repair identified affected homes, and estimated its additional repair costs with respect to the newly identified affected homes to be $7.1 million, $22.4 million and $15.7 million, respectively. Since first identifying affected homes in 2009, the Company has identified a total of 467 affected homes and has resolved repairs on 380 of those homes through November 30, 2011. As of November 30, 2011, the Company has paid $40.5 million of the total estimated repair costs of $45.3 million associated with the identified affected homes.

In assessing its overall warranty liability, the Company evaluates the costs related to identified homes affected by the allegedly defective drywall material and other home warranty-related items on a combined basis. While the Company has considered the repair costs related to the identified affected homes in conjunction with its quarterly assessments of its overall warranty liability since the third quarter of 2009, the Company has experienced favorable trends in its actual warranty costs incurred with respect to other home warranty-related items. These favorable trends reflect the Company's ongoing focus on construction quality and customer service, among other things. Based on its assessments, the Company determined that its overall warranty liability at each reporting date was sufficient with respect to the Company's then-estimated remaining repair costs associated with identified affected homes and its overall warranty obligations on homes delivered. In light of these assessments, the Company did not incur charges in its consolidated statements of operations for the years ended November 30, 2011 or 2010 with respect to repair costs associated with the identified affected homes. Additionally, based on the trends in the Company's actual warranty costs incurred, the Company's assessments in 2011 resulted in the recording of warranty adjustments of $7.4 million as reductions to construction and land costs. The overall warranty liability has decreased since 2009 in part because of the payments the Company has made to resolve repairs on identified affected homes and in part due to the decrease in the number of homes the Company has delivered over the past several years.

Depending on the number of additional affected homes identified, if any, and the actual costs the Company incurs to repair identified affected homes in future periods, including costs to provide affected homeowners with temporary housing, the Company may revise the estimated amount of its liability with respect to this issue, which could result in an increase or decrease in the Company's overall warranty liability.

As of November 30, 2011, the Company has been named as a defendant in 11 lawsuits relating to the allegedly defective drywall material, and it may in the future be subject to other similar litigation or claims that could cause the Company to incur significant costs. Given the preliminary stages of the proceedings, the Company has not concluded whether the outcome of any of these lawsuits will be material to its consolidated financial statements.

SEC 3.27

The Company intends to seek and is undertaking efforts, including legal proceedings, to obtain reimbursement from various sources for the costs it has incurred or expects to incur to investigate and complete repairs and to defend itself in litigation associated with this drywall material. The Company has not recorded any amounts for potential future recoveries as of November 30, 2011.

Interest

3.28

THE GREAT ATLANTIC & PACIFIC TEA COMPANY, INC. (FEB)

(Debtors-in-Possession)

CONSOLIDATED STATEMENTS OF OPERATIONS

(Dollars in thousands, except per share amounts)

	Fiscal 2010	Fiscal 2009	Fiscal 2008
Sales	$ 8,078,455	$ 8,813,568	$ 9,516,186
Cost of merchandise sold	(5,677,800)	(6,146,808)	(6,613,150)
Gross margin	2,400,655	2,666,760	2,903,036
Store operating, general and administrative expense	(2,737,093)	(2,790,154)	(2,978,099)
Goodwill, trademark and long-lived asset impairment	(114,183)	(477,180)	—
Loss from continuing operations before nonoperating income (loss), interest expense, net, and reorganization items, net	(450,621)	(600,574)	(75,063)
Nonoperating income (loss)	13,777	(9,181)	116,864
Interest expense, net	(218,369)	(192,889)	(157,000)
Reorganization items, net	(21,985)	—	—
Loss from continuing operations before income taxes	(677,198)	(802,644)	(115,199)

Note 15—Interest Expense, Net

Interest expense, net is comprised of the following:

	Fiscal 2010	Fiscal 2009	Fiscal 2008
$655 million Credit Agreement	$ 11,873	$ 15,411	$ 21,139
$800 million Debtor-in-Possession Credit Agreement	7,804	—	—
Related Party Promissory Note, due Aug. 18, 2011	480	607	300
11.375% Senior Secured Notes, due Aug. 1, 2015	29,493	16,665	—
9.125% Senior Notes, due Dec. 15, 2011	924	1,168	1,188
5.125% Convertible Senior Notes, due June 15, 2011	6,668	8,433	8,553
6.750% Convertible Senior Notes, due Dec. 15, 2012	13,572	17,165	17,409
9.375% Notes, due August 1, 2039	14,782	18,729	19,011
Capital lease obligations and Real estate liabilities	50,795	52,552	53,970
Dividends on Preferred Stock Liability	—	3,505	—
Self-insurance and GHI interest	17,148	14,792	10,859
GHI discount rate adjustment and COLI non-cash interest	6,070	15,906	1,375
Amortization of deferred financing fees and discounts	58,471	26,619	23,030
Other	329	1,506	757
Subtotal	218,409	193,058	157,591
Interest and dividend income	(40)	(169)	(591)
Interest Expense, net	$218,369	$192,889	$157,000

We recorded $35.7 million in financing fees and $7.8 million in contractual interest from the DIP Credit Agreement in fiscal 2010. We continued to record contractual interest for our $260 million 11.375% Senior Secured Notes due 2015 that were issued in August 2009. We did not record contractual interest expense of approximately $9.6 million for our Related Party Promissory Note, due August 18, 2011, 9.125% Senior Notes, due December 15, 2011, 5.125% Convertible Senior Notes, due June 15, 2011, 6.750% Convertible Senior Notes, due December 15, 2012, and 9.375% Notes, due August 1, 2039, all of which are unsecured obligations for which we ceased accruing interest during the fourth quarter 2010 as a result of the Bankruptcy Filing. Debt discounts and deferred financing fees for all debt which is subject to compromise were reclassified into the carrying value of the respective indebtedness upon the Bankruptcy Filing and the balances were then adjusted to the face value of the debt. As a result of this reclassification, we ceased amortization of deferred financing fees and discounts effective as of the Bankruptcy Filing date. Although we have recorded interest accretion expense on capital leases and real estate liabilities, self-insurance reserves, GHI and corporate owned life insurance obligations, we have not made a final determination as to the value of any underlying assets or the rejection/assumption of any of the obligations. Once a determination is made, the accretion of the interest expense may change.

Interest and Penalties Related to Unrecognized Tax Benefits

3.29

GENUINE PARTS COMPANY (DEC)

CONSOLIDATED STATEMENTS OF INCOME (in part)

(In thousands, except per share amounts)	Year Ended December 31		
	2011	2010	2009
Net sales	$12,458,877	$11,207,589	$10,057,512
Cost of goods sold	8,852,837	7,954,645	7,047,750
Gross margin	3,606,040	3,252,944	3,009,762
Operating expenses:			
Selling, administrative, and other expenses	2,594,372	2,366,667	2,219,935
Depreciation and amortization	88,936	89,332	90,411
Provision for doubtful accounts	13,248	10,597	28,463
Total operating expenses	2,696,556	2,466,596	2,338,809
Non-operating expenses (income):			
Interest expense	27,036	28,061	27,885
Other	(8,358)	(3,496)	(1,097)
Total non-operating expenses	18,678	24,565	26,788
Income before income taxes	890,806	761,783	644,165
Income taxes	325,690	286,272	244,590
Net income	$ 565,116	$ 475,511	$ 399,575

NOTES TO CONSOLIDATED FINANCIAL STATEMENTS

December 31, 2011

6. Income Taxes (in part)

The components of income tax expense are as follows:

(In thousands)	2011	2010	2009
Current:			
Federal	$260,222	$221,770	$171,691
State	41,511	36,291	28,591
Foreign	26,294	16,217	16,409
Deferred	(2,337)	11,994	27,899
	$325,690	$286,272	$244,590

The reasons for the difference between total tax expense and the amount computed by applying the statutory Federal income tax rate to income before income taxes are as follows:

(In thousands)	2011	2010	2009
Statutory rate applied to income	$311,782	$266,624	$225,458
Plus state income taxes, net of Federal tax benefit	26,790	24,621	20,977
Other	(12,882)	(4,973)	(1,845)
	$325,690	$286,272	$244,590

The Company or one of its subsidiaries files income tax returns in the U.S. federal jurisdiction, various states, and foreign jurisdictions. With few exceptions, the Company is no longer subject to federal, state and local tax examinations by tax authorities for years before 2008 or subject to non-United States income tax examinations for years ended prior to 2002. The Company is currently under audit in the United States and Canada. Some audits may conclude in the next 12 months and the unrecognized tax benefits recorded in relation to the audits may differ from actual settlement amounts. It is not possible to estimate the effect, if any, of the amount of such change during the next twelve months to previously recorded uncertain tax positions in connection with the audits. However, the Company does not anticipate total unrecognized tax benefits will significantly change during the year due to the settlement of audits and the expiration of statutes of limitations.

A reconciliation of the beginning and ending amount of unrecognized tax benefits is as follows:

(In thousands)	2011	2010	2009
Balance at beginning of year	$39,425	$33,322	$30,453
Additions based on tax positions related to the current year	6,035	4,243	5,648
Additions for tax positions of prior years	7,966	3,493	993
Reductions for tax positions for prior years	(481)	(624)	—
Reduction for lapse in statute of limitations	(4,563)	(451)	(2,779)
Settlements	(1,537)	(558)	(993)
Balance at end of year	$46,845	$39,425	$33,322

The amount of gross tax effected unrecognized tax benefits, including interest and penalties, as of December 31, 2011 and 2010 was approximately $59,532,000 and $50,216,000, respectively, of which approximately $18,966,000 and $18,189,000, respectively, if recognized, would affect the effective tax rate. During the years ended December 31, 2011, 2010, and 2009, the Company paid interest and penalties of approximately $759,000, $272,000, and $363,000, respectively. The Company had approximately $12,687,000 and $10,791,000 of accrued interest and penalties at December 31, 2011 and 2010, respectively. The Company recognizes potential interest and penalties related to unrecognized tax benefits as a component of income tax expense.

Accretion on Asset Retirement Obligation

3.30

FREEPORT-MCMORAN COPPER & GOLD INC. (DEC)

CONSOLIDATED STATEMENTS OF INCOME (in part)

(In millions, except per share amounts)	Years Ended December 31		
	2011	**2010**	**2009**
Revenues	$20,880	$18,982	$15,040
Cost of sales:			
Production and delivery	9,898	8,335	7,006
Depreciation, depletion and amortization	1,022	1,036	1,014
Total cost of sales	10,920	9,371	8,020

NOTES TO CONSOLIDATED FINANCIAL STATEMENTS

Note 1. Summary of Significant Accounting Policies (in part)

Asset Retirement Obligations. FCX records the fair value of estimated asset retirement obligations (AROs) associated with tangible long-lived assets in the period incurred. Retirement obligations associated with long-lived assets are those for which there is a legal obligation to settle under existing or enacted law, statute, written or oral contract or by legal construction. These obligations, which are initially estimated based on discounted cash flow estimates, are accreted to full value over time through charges to cost of sales. In addition, asset retirement costs (ARCs) are capitalized as part of the related asset's carrying value and are depreciated (primarily on a unit-of-production basis) over the asset's respective useful life. Reclamation costs for future disturbances are recognized as an ARO and as a related ARC in the period of the disturbance. FCX's AROs consist primarily of costs associated with mine reclamation and closure activities. These activities, which are site specific, generally include costs for earthwork, revegetation, water treatment and demolition (refer to Note 13 for further discussion).

Note 13. Contingencies (in part)

Asset Retirement Obligations (AROs) (in part). FCX's ARO cost estimates are reflected on a third-party cost basis and comply with FCX's legal obligation to retire tangible, long-lived assets.

A summary of changes in FCX's AROs for the years ended December 31 follows:

	2011	**2010**	**2009**
Balance at beginning of year	$856	$731	$712
Liabilities incurred	9	5	12
Revisions to cash flow estimates	48	105	(17)
Accretion expense	58	54	52
Spending	(49)	(38)	(28)
Foreign currency translation adjustment	(1)	(1)	—
Balance at end of year	921	856	731
Less current portion	(31)	(69)	(46)
Long-term portion	$890	$787	$685

ARO costs may increase or decrease significantly in the future as a result of changes in regulations, changes in engineering designs and technology, permit modifications or updates, changes in mine plans, inflation or other factors and as actual reclamation spending occurs. ARO activities and expenditures generally are made over an extended period of time commencing near the end of the mine life; however, certain reclamation activities may be accelerated if legally required or if determined to be economically beneficial.

During 2011 and 2010, the revisions to cash flow estimates are primarily related to increased costs of near-term closure activities at the Chino mine in New Mexico. Additionally, accelerated timing of closure activities at the Chino mine resulted in revisions to cash flow estimates during 2010.

Legal requirements in New Mexico, Arizona and Colorado require financial assurance to be provided for the estimated costs of reclamation and closure, including groundwater quality protection programs. FCX has satisfied financial assurance requirements by using a variety of mechanisms, such as performance guarantees, financial capability demonstrations, trust funds, surety bonds, letters of credit and collateral. The applicable regulations specify financial strength tests that are designed to confirm a company's or guarantor's financial capability to fund estimated reclamation and closure costs. The amount of financial assurance FCX is required to provide will vary with changes in laws, regulations and reclamation and closure requirements and cost estimates. At December 31, 2011, FCX's financial assurance obligations associated with these closure and reclamation costs totaled $899 million, of which approximately $565 million was in the form of parent company guarantees and financial capability demonstrations. At December 31, 2011, FCX had trust assets totaling $151 million, which are legally restricted to fund a portion of its AROs for the Chino, Tyrone and Cobre mines as required by New Mexico regulatory authorities.

Write-down of Assets

3.31

COMMERCIAL METALS COMPANY (AUG)

CONSOLIDATED STATEMENTS OF OPERATIONS
(in part)

	Year Ended August 31		
(In thousands, except per share data)	2011	2010	2009
Net sales	$7,918,430	$6,306,102	$6,409,376
Costs and expenses:			
Cost of goods sold	7,301,815	5,911,065	5,712,347
Selling, general and administrative expenses	537,113	520,369	612,563
Impairment of assets	118,795	3,766	5,568
Interest expense	70,806	75,508	76,964
	8,028,529	6,510,708	6,407,442

NOTES TO CONSOLIDATED FINANCIAL STATEMENTS

Note 7. Impairment and Facility Closure Costs

The Company evaluates the carrying value of property, plant and equipment and finite-lived intangible assets whenever a change in circumstances indicates that the carrying value may not be recoverable. Facility closures and changes in market conditions and economic environment could impact future operating results and cash flows.

During the fourth quarter of 2011, the Company prepared an impairment analysis on its steel pipe manufacturing operation at CMCS based on the following impairment indicators: management determined that improvements in key operating areas could not be achieved and maintained without additional capital expenditures; CMCS could not achieve adequate market share for billets as the mill is currently designed; the down-turn in global economy, especially debt issues in Europe, further delayed recovery and will likely result in continued losses in future years; accession of Croatia to the European Union which is required to allow the operation to be competitive was further delayed until 2013 or mid-2014; and uncertainties in the Middle East and North Africa, the primary markets for CMCS. As a result, the Company recorded impairment charges to impair the CMCS operation. The operations of CMCS are included as part of the International Mills segment.

Additionally, the Company decided to close certain rebar fabrication and construction services ("CRP") locations and the Company's fabrication operation in Germany during the fourth quarter of 2011. As a result, the Company recorded impairment charges for these locations. Additionally, the Company determined that based on current market conditions and operating results as part of the Company's annual budget process, one of the Company's rebar fabrication customer base intangible assets was not recoverable. As a result, the Company recorded an impairment charge to reduce the customer base intangible to its estimated fair value. The rebar and CRP operations are included as part of the Americas Fabrication segment and the German fabrication operation is included as part of the International Mills segment.

The impairment of property, plant and equipment was based on the fair values calculated by independent appraisals. The fair values include estimated cost to sell the assets. The CRP locations are leased properties. Lease termination costs represent the estimated fair value of future lease payments less any sub-lease income which the Company recorded at the cease use date of the leased property.

In connection with these actions, the following pre-tax charges were recorded in 2011:

	(In thousands)
Impairment of property, plant and equipment and other assets	$106,655
Impairment of customer list intangible asset	12,140
Write-down of inventory	8,500
Severance costs	5,051
Lease termination costs	2,196
Other closure costs	7,700

Restructuring

3.32

CAMPBELL SOUP COMPANY (JUL)

CONSOLIDATED STATEMENTS OF EARNINGS
(in part)

(Millions, except per share amounts)	**2011**	**2010**	**2009**
Net sales	$7,719	$7,676	$7,586
Costs and expenses			
Cost of products sold	4,616	4,526	4,558
Marketing and selling expenses	1,007	1,058	1,077
Administrative expenses	612	605	591
Research and development expenses	129	123	114
Other expenses/(income)	13	4	61
Restructuring charges	63	12	—
Total costs and expenses	6,440	6,328	6,401
Earnings before interest and taxes	1,279	1,348	1,185

NOTES TO CONSOLIDATED FINANCIAL STATEMENTS

(Currency in millions, except per share amounts)

7. Restructuring Charges (in part)

2011 Initiatives

On June 28, 2011, the company announced a series of initiatives to improve supply chain efficiency and reduce overhead costs across the organization to help fund plans to drive the growth of the business. The company also announced its intent to exit the Russian market. The company expects to eliminate approximately 750 positions in connection with these initiatives. Details of the plans include:

- In Australia, the company will invest in a new system to automate packing operations at its biscuit plant in Virginia. This investment will occur over an 18-month period and will result in the elimination of approximately 190 positions, subject to union and employee consultations. Further, the company will improve asset utilization in the U.S. by shifting production of ready-to-serve soups from Paris, Texas, to other facilities in 2012. In addition, the manufacturing facility in Marshall, Michigan, was closed in 2011, and manufacturing of *Campbell's Soup at Hand* microwavable products will be consolidated at the Maxton, North Carolina, plant in 2012.
- The company streamlined its salaried workforce by approximately 510 positions around the world, including approximately 130 positions at its world headquarters in Camden, New Jersey. These actions were substan-

tially completed in 2011. As part of this initiative, the company outsourced a larger portion of its U.S. retail merchandising activities to its current retail sales agent, Acosta Sales and Marketing, and eliminated approximately 190 positions. The company expects that this action will enhance merchandising effectiveness and coverage for its U.S. customers.
- In connection with exiting the Russian market, the company will eliminate approximately 50 positions. The exit process commenced in 2011 and is expected to be completed in fiscal 2012.

In 2011, the company recorded a restructuring charge of $63 ($41 after tax or $.12 per share) related to these initiatives. A summary of the pre-tax charge and remaining costs associated with the initiatives is as follows:

	Total Program	Recognized as of July 31, 2011	Remaining Costs to be Recognized
Severance pay and benefits	$40	$(37)	$ 3
Asset impairment/ accelerated depreciation	25	(22)	3
Other exit costs	10	(4)	6
Total	$75	$(63)	$12

Of the aggregate $75 of pre-tax costs, the company expects approximately $50 will be cash expenditures, the majority of which will be spent in 2012. In addition, the company expects to invest approximately $40 in capital expenditures in connection with the actions. The initiatives are expected to be completed by the end of fiscal 2013.

A summary of restructuring activity and related reserves associated with these initiatives at July 31, 2011 is as follows:

	Accrued Balance at August 1, 2010	2011 Charges	2011 Cash Payments	Accrued Balance at July 31, 2011
Severance pay and benefits	$—	$37	$(2)	$35
Asset impairment/accelerated depreciation	—	22		
Other exit costs	—	4	—	4
Total	$—	$63	$(2)	$39

A summary of restructuring charges associated with each segment is as follows:

	U.S. Simple Meals	U.S. Beverages	Global Baking and Snacking	International Simple Meals and Beverages	North America Foodservice	Corporate	Total
Severance pay and benefits	$10	$3	$12	$10	$1	$1	$37
Asset impairment/accelerated depreciation	20	—	—	2	—	—	22
Other exit costs	1	—	—	—	—	3	4
	$31	$3	$12	$12	$1	$4	$63

The company expects to incur additional pre-tax costs of approximately $12 by segment as follows: U.S. Simple Meals—$2, Global Baking and Snacking—$3, International Simple Meals and Beverages—$6 and Corporate—$1. Segment operating results do not include restructuring charges as segment performance is evaluated excluding such charges.

Intangible Asset Amortization

3.33

SPRINT NEXTEL CORPORATION (DEC)

CONSOLIDATED STATEMENTS OF COMPREHENSIVE LOSS (in part)

	Year Ended December 31		
(In millions, except per share amounts)	2011	2010	2009
Net operating revenues	$33,679	$32,563	$32,260
Net operating expenses			
Cost of services and products (exclusive of depreciation and amortization included below)	19,015	17,492	16,435
Selling, general and administrative	9,592	9,438	9,453
Severance, exit costs and asset impairments	106	133	447
Depreciation	4,455	5,074	5,827
Amortization	403	1,174	1,589
Other, net	—	(153)	(93)
	33,571	33,158	33,658
Operating income (loss)	108	(595)	(1,398)

NOTES TO THE CONSOLIDATED FINANCIAL STATEMENTS

Note 2. Summary of Significant Accounting Policies and Other Information (in part)

Long-Lived Asset Impairment

Sprint evaluates long-lived assets, including intangible assets subject to amortization, for impairment whenever events or changes in circumstances indicate that the carrying amount of an asset group may not be recoverable. Asset groups are determined at the lowest level for which identifiable cash flows are largely independent of cash flows of other groups of assets and liabilities. When it is probable that undiscounted future cash flows will not be sufficient to recover an asset group's carrying amount, an impairment is determined by the excess of the asset group's net carrying value over the estimated fair value. Refer to note 8 for additional information on asset impairments.

Certain assets that have not yet been deployed in the business, including network equipment, cell site development costs and software in development, are periodically assessed to determine recoverability. Network equipment and cell site development costs are expensed whenever events or changes in circumstances cause the Company to conclude the assets are no longer needed to meet management's strategic network plans and will not be deployed. Software development costs are expensed when it is no longer probable that the software project will be deployed. Network equipment that has been removed from the network is also periodically assessed to determine recoverability. If we continue to have operational challenges, including retaining and attracting subscribers, future cash flows of the Company may not be sufficient to recover the carrying value of our wireless asset group, and we could record asset impairments that are material to Sprint's consolidated results of operations and financial condition.

During 2011, we assessed the recoverability of the wireless asset group, which includes tangible and intangible long-lived assets subject to amortization as well as indefinite-lived intangible assets. We included cash flow projections from wireless operations along with cash flows associated with the eventual disposition of the long-lived assets, which included estimated proceeds from the assumed sale of

Federal Communications Commission (FCC) licenses and other intangible assets.

Indefinite-Lived Intangible Assets

Our indefinite-lived intangible assets primarily consists of goodwill, FCC licenses acquired primarily through FCC auctions and business combinations to deploy our wireless services, and certain of our trademarks. Goodwill represents the excess of consideration paid over the estimated fair value of the net tangible and identifiable intangible assets acquired in business combinations. In determining whether an intangible asset, other than goodwill, is indefinite-lived, we consider the expected use of the assets, the regulatory and economic environment within which they are being used, and the effects of obsolescence on their use. We assess our indefinite-lived intangible assets for impairment at least annually or, if necessary, more frequently, whenever events or changes in circumstances indicate the asset may be impaired. Such indicators may include a sustained, significant decline in our market capitalization since our previous impairment assessment, a significant decline in our expected future cash flows, a significant adverse change in legal factors or in the business climate, unanticipated competition, and/or slower growth rates, among others.

Note 6. Intangible Assets (in part)

Indefinite-Lived Intangible Assets

(In millions)	December 31, 2009	Net Additions/ (Reductions)	December 31, 2010	Net Additions/ (Reductions)	December 31, 2011
FCC licenses	$19,502	$425	$19,927	$117	$20,044
Trademarks	409	—	409	—	409
Goodwill[1]	373	(14)	359	—	359
	$20,284	$411	$20,695	$117	$20,812

[1] The net reduction to goodwill of $14 million was a result of purchase price allocation adjustments recognized in the first quarter of 2010 associated with the 2009 acquisitions of Virgin Mobile and iPCS primarily related to deferred tax assets and liabilities.

We hold 1.9 gigahertz (GHz), 800 megahertz (MHz), and 900 MHz FCC licenses authorizing the use of radio frequency spectrum to deploy our wireless services. We also hold FCC licenses that are not yet placed in service but that we intend to use in accordance with FCC requirements. As long as the Company acts within the requirements and constraints of the regulatory authorities, the renewal and extension of these licenses is reasonably certain at minimal cost. We are not aware of any technology being developed that would render this spectrum obsolete and have concluded that these licenses are indefinite-lived intangible assets. Our Sprint and Boost Mobile trademarks have also been identified as indefinite-lived intangible assets. During 2011, we conducted our annual assessment of the estimated fair value of indefinite-lived intangible assets other than goodwill and determined that no adjustment was necessary.

Intangible Assets Subject to Amortization

Sprint's customer relationships are amortized using the sum of the years' digits method. We reduce the gross carrying value and associated accumulated amortization when specified intangible assets become fully amortized. During 2011, we reduced the gross carrying value and accumulated amortization by approximately $1.6 billion associated with fully amortized intangible assets primarily related to customer relationships in connection with the acquisitions of Nextel Partners, Inc. and Virgin Mobile. Other intangible assets primarily include certain rights under affiliation agreements that were reacquired in connection with the acquisitions of Affiliates and Nextel Partners, Inc., which are being amortized over the remaining terms of those affiliation agreements on a straight-line basis, and the Nextel, Direct Connect and Virgin Mobile trade names, which are being amortized on a straight-line basis. During 2011, we conducted our annual assessment of the recoverability of intangible assets subject to amortization and determined that no adjustment was necessary.

(In millions)	Useful Lives	December 31, 2011			December 31, 2010		
		Gross Carrying Value	Accumulated Amortization	Net Carrying Value	Gross Carrying Value	Accumulated Amortization	Net Carrying Value
Customer relationships	4 to 5 years	$ 341	$ (297)	$ 44	$1,925	$(1,717)	$ 208
Other intangible assets							
Trademarks	10 to 37 years	1,169	(585)	584	1,169	(490)	679
Reacquired rights	9 to 14 years	1,571	(652)	919	1,571	(519)	1,052
Other	9 to 16 years	126	(57)	69	116	(46)	70
Total other intangible assets		2,866	(1,294)	1,572	2,856	(1,055)	1,801
Total definite-lived intangible assets		$3,207	$(1,591)	$1,616	$4,781	$(2,772)	$2,009

(In millions)	2012	2013	2014	2015	2016
Estimated amortization expense	$280	$243	$239	$198	$137

Foreign Currency

3.34

GAMESTOP CORP. (JAN)

CONSOLIDATED STATEMENTS OF OPERATIONS
(in part)

(In millions, except per share data)	52 Weeks Ended January 29, 2011	52 Weeks Ended January 30, 2010	52 Weeks Ended January 31, 2009
Sales	$9,473.7	$9,078.0	$8,805.9
Cost of sales	6,936.1	6,643.3	6,535.8
Gross profit	2,537.6	2,434.7	2,270.1
Selling, general and administrative expenses	1,700.3	1,635.1	1,445.4
Depreciation and amortization	174.7	162.6	145.0
Merger-related expenses	—	—	4.6
Operating earnings	662.6	637.0	675.1

NOTES TO CONSOLIDATED FINANCIAL STATEMENTS

1. Summary of Significant Accounting Policies (in part)

Foreign Currency Translation

GameStop has determined that the functional currencies of its foreign subsidiaries are the subsidiaries' local currencies. The assets and liabilities of the subsidiaries are translated at the applicable exchange rate as of the end of the balance sheet date and revenue and expenses are translated at an average rate over the period. Currency translation adjustments are recorded as a component of other comprehensive income. Transaction gains and (losses) are included in selling, general and administrative expenses and amounted to $2.5 million, $3.9 million and ($10.0) million for the 52 weeks ended January 29, 2011, January 30, 2010 and January 31, 2009, respectively. The foreign currency transaction gains and losses are primarily due to the decrease or increase in the value of the U.S. dollar compared to the functional currencies in the countries the Company operates in internationally. In fiscal 2010, the foreign currency transaction gains are primarily due to the decrease in the value of the U.S. dollar compared to the Canadian dollar and the Australian dollar. In fiscal 2009, the foreign currency transaction gains are primarily due to the decrease in the value of the U.S. dollar compared to the euro, the Canadian dollar and the Australian dollar. The foreign currency transaction losses in fiscal 2008 are primarily related to the increase in the value of the U.S. dollar compared to the euro, the Canadian dollar and the Australian dollar. The net foreign currency transaction loss in the 52 weeks ended January 31, 2009 included a $3.5 million net loss related to the change in foreign exchange rates related to the funding of the Micromania acquisition recorded in merger-related expenses.

The Company uses forward exchange contracts, foreign currency options and cross-currency swaps, (together, the "Foreign Currency Contracts") to manage currency risk primarily related to intercompany loans denominated in non-functional currencies and certain foreign currency assets and liabilities. These Foreign Currency Contracts are not designated as hedges and, therefore, changes in the fair values of these derivatives are recognized in earnings, thereby offsetting the current earnings effect of the re-measurement of related intercompany loans and foreign currency assets and liabilities (see Note 5).

5. Fair Value Measurements and Financial Instruments (in part)

The Company defines fair value as the price that would be received from selling an asset or paid to transfer a liability in an orderly transaction between market participants at the measurement date. Fair value accounting guidance applies to our Foreign Currency Contracts, Company-owned life insurance policies with a cash surrender value and certain nonqualified deferred compensation liabilities that are measured at fair value on a recurring basis in periods subsequent to initial recognition.

Fair value accounting guidance requires disclosures that categorize assets and liabilities measured at fair value into one of three different levels depending on the observability of the inputs employed in the measurement. Level 1 inputs are quoted prices in active markets for identical assets or liabilities. Level 2 inputs are observable inputs other than quoted prices included within Level 1 for the asset or liability, either directly or indirectly through market-corroborated inputs. Level 3 inputs are unobservable inputs for the asset or liability reflecting our assumptions about pricing by market participants.

We value our Foreign Currency Contracts, Company-owned life insurance policies with cash surrender values and certain nonqualified deferred compensation liabilities based on Level 2 inputs using quotations provided by major market news services, such as Bloomberg and The Wall Street Journal, and industry-standard models that consider various assumptions, including quoted forward prices, time value, volatility factors, and contractual prices for the underlying instruments, as well as other relevant economic measures. When appropriate, valuations are adjusted to reflect credit considerations, generally based on available market evidence.

The Company uses Foreign Currency Contracts to manage currency risk primarily related to intercompany loans denominated in non-functional currencies and certain foreign currency assets and liabilities. These Foreign Currency Contracts are not designated as hedges and, therefore, changes in the fair values of these derivatives are recognized in earnings, thereby offsetting the current earnings effect of the re-measurement of related intercompany loans and foreign currency assets and liabilities. We do not use derivative financial instruments for trading or speculative purposes. We are exposed to counterparty credit risk on all of our derivative financial instruments and cash equivalent investments. The Company manages counterparty risk according to the guidelines and controls established under comprehensive risk management and investment policies. We continuously monitor our counterparty credit risk and utilize a number of different counterparties to minimize our exposure to potential defaults. We do not require collateral under derivative or investment agreements.

As of January 29, 2011, the Company had a series of Foreign Currency Contracts outstanding, with a gross notional value of $495.2 million and a net notional value of $201.3 million. For the 52 weeks ended January 29, 2011, the Company recognized losses of $7.1 million in selling, general and administrative expenses related to the trading of derivative instruments. As of January 30, 2010, the Company had a series of Foreign Currency Contracts outstanding, with a gross notional value of $643.5 million and a net notional value of $356.6 million. For the 52 weeks ended January 30, 2010, the Company recognized gains of $8.7 million in selling, general and administrative expenses related to the trading of derivative instruments.

The Company's carrying value of financial instruments approximates their fair value, except for differences with respect to the senior notes. The fair value of the Company's senior notes payable in the accompanying consolidated balance sheets is estimated based on recent quotes from brokers. As of January 29, 2011, the senior notes payable had a carrying value of $249.0 million and a fair value of $256.6 million. As of January 30, 2010, the senior notes payable had a carrying value of $447.3 million and a fair value of $466.0 million.

Software Amortization

3.35

FIDELITY NATIONAL INFORMATION SERVICES, INC. (DEC)

CONSOLIDATED STATEMENTS OF EARNINGS (in part)

Years Ended December 31, 2011, 2010 and 2009. (In millions, except per share amounts)

	2011	2010	2009
Processing and services revenues (for related party activity, see note 4)	$5,745.7	$5,269.5	$3,711.1
Cost of revenues (for related party activity, see note 4)	3,998.0	3,637.7	2,741.5
Gross profit	1,747.7	1,631.8	969.6
Selling, general, and administrative expenses (for related party activity, see note 4)	671.8	675.8	547.1
Impairment charges	9.1	154.9	136.9
Operating income	1,066.8	801.1	285.6

NOTES TO CONSOLIDATED FINANCIAL STATEMENTS

(2) Summary of Significant Accounting Policies (in part)

(i) Computer Software

Computer software includes software acquired in business combinations, purchased software and capitalized software development costs. Purchased software is recorded at cost and amortized using the straight-line method over its estimated useful life and software acquired in business combinations is recorded at its fair value and amortized using straight-line or accelerated methods over its estimated useful life, ranging from five to ten years.

The capitalization of software development costs is governed by FASB ASC Subtopic 985-20 if the software is to be sold, leased or otherwise marketed, or by FASB ASC Subtopic 350-40 if the software is for internal use. After the technological feasibility of the software has been established (for software to be marketed), or at the beginning of application development (for internal-use software), software development costs, which include salaries and related payroll costs and costs of independent contractors incurred during development, are capitalized. Research and development costs incurred prior to the establishment of technological feasibility (for software to be marketed), or prior to application development (for internal-use software), are expensed as incurred. Software development costs are amortized on a product by product basis commencing on the date of general release of the products (for software to be marketed) or the date placed in service (for internal-use software). Software development costs for software to be marketed are amortized using the greater of (1) the straight-line method over its estimated useful life, which ranges from three to ten years, or (2) the ratio of current revenues to total anticipated revenue over its useful life.

(n) Cost of Revenue and Selling, General and Administrative Expenses

Cost of revenue includes payroll, employee benefits, occupancy costs and other costs associated with personnel employed in customer service roles, including program design and development and professional services. Cost of revenue also includes data processing costs, amortization of software, customer relationship intangible assets and depreciation on operating assets.

Selling, general and administrative expenses include payroll, employee benefits, occupancy and other costs associated with personnel employed in sales, marketing, human resources, finance and other administrative roles. Selling, general and administrative expenses also include depreciation on non-operating corporate assets, advertising costs and other marketing-related programs.

(10) Computer Software

Computer software as of December 31, 2011 and 2010 consisted of the following (in millions):

	2011	2010
Software from business acquisitions	$ 654.9	$ 653.7
Capitalized software development costs	772.1	690.9
Purchased software	90.0	76.5
Computer software	1,517.0	1,421.1
Accumulated amortization	(635.5)	(512.1)
Computer software, net of accumulated amortization	$ 881.5	$ 909.0

Amortization expense for computer software was $209.4 million, $195.1 million and $149.8 million for the years ended December 31, 2011, 2010 and 2009, respectively. Included

in discontinued operations in the Consolidated Statements of Earnings was amortization expense on computer software of $0.0 million, $3.3 million and $0.7 million for the years ended December 31, 2011, 2010 and 2009, respectively. During the year ended December 31, 2010, as a result of Banco Santander's exit from the Brazilian Venture, we recorded a $14.6 million charge pertaining to capitalized software development costs incurred exclusively for use in processing Banco Santander's card activity. The write-off was included in the ISG segment. During the year ended December 31, 2009, we recorded a $12.9 million charge to write-off the carrying value of impaired software resulting from the rationalization of FIS and Metavante product lines. Of this total, $6.8 million related to FSG and $6.1 million related to PSG. The impairment was recorded in the Corporate and Other Segment.

Litigation

3.36

HILL-ROM HOLDINGS, INC. (SEP)

STATEMENTS OF CONSOLIDATED INCOME (LOSS) (in part)

(Dollars in millions except per share data)

	Years Ended September 30		
	2011	2010	2009
Net Revenues			
Capital sales	$1,119.0	$ 996.6	$ 921.5
Rental revenues	472.7	473.0	465.4
Total revenues	1,591.7	1,469.6	1,386.9
Cost of Revenues			
Cost of goods sold	606.8	548.6	555.7
Rental expenses	203.6	204.4	203.3
Total cost of revenues	810.4	753.0	759.0
Gross Profit	781.3	716.6	627.9
Research and development expenses	63.8	58.3	55.7
Selling and administrative expenses	502.0	474.6	461.6
Litigation charge (credit) (Note 14)	47.3	(21.2)	—
Impairment of goodwill and other intangibles (Note 4)	—	—	472.8
Special charges (Note 9)	1.4	13.2	20.5
Operating Profit (Loss)	166.8	191.7	(382.7)

NOTES TO CONSOLIDATED FINANCIAL STATEMENTS

(Dollars in millions except per share data)

Note 14. Commitments and Contingencies (in part)

Legal Proceedings

Batesville Casket Antitrust Litigation

In 2005 the Funeral Consumers Alliance, Inc. and a number of individual consumer casket purchasers filed a purported class action antitrust lawsuit on behalf of certain consumer purchasers of Batesville® caskets against us and our former Batesville Casket Company, Inc. subsidiary (now wholly-owned by Hillenbrand, Inc.), and three national funeral home businesses.

The district court has dismissed the claims and denied class certification, but in October 2010, the plaintiffs appealed these decisions to the United States Court of Appeals for the Fifth Circuit. If the plaintiffs were to succeed in reversing the district court's dismissal of the claims, but not the denial of class certification, then the plaintiffs would be able to pursue individual damages claims: the alleged overcharges on the plaintiffs' individual casket purchases, which would be trebled as a matter of law, plus reasonable attorneys fees and costs.

If the plaintiffs were to (1) succeed in reversing the district court's dismissal of the claims, (2) succeed in reversing the district court order denying class certification and certify a class, and (3) prevail at trial, then the damages awarded to the plaintiffs, which would be trebled as a matter of law, could have a significant material adverse effect on our results of operations, financial condition and/or liquidity. The plaintiffs filed a report indicating that they are seeking damages ranging from approximately $947.0 million to approximately $1.5 billion before trebling on behalf of the purported class of consumers they seek to represent.

We and Hillenbrand, Inc. have entered into a judgment sharing agreement that apportions the costs and any potential liabilities associated with this litigation between us and Hillenbrand, Inc. We believe that we have committed no wrongdoing as alleged by the plaintiffs and that we have meritorious defenses to class certification and to plaintiffs' underlying allegations and damage theories.

Office of Inspector General Investigation

In February 2008, we were served with an Administrative Investigative Demand subpoena by the United States Attorney's Office for the Eastern District of Tennessee pursuant to a Health and Human Services' Office of Inspector General investigation. In September 2008, we were informed that the investigation was precipitated by the 2005 filing of a *qui tam* complaint under the False Claims Act in the United States District Court for the Eastern District of Tennessee. In June 2011, we reached agreement with respect to a tentative financial settlement and recognized a charge in the third quarter of $42.3 million. This settlement was finalized and paid in September 2011. Concurrently with this settlement, we entered into a five year Corporate Integrity Agreement, which provides for certain other compliance-related activities during the five year term of the agreement, including specific written standards, monitoring, training, education, independent review, disclosure and reporting requirements. We did not admit any wrongdoing as part of the settlement.

Freedom Medical Antitrust Litigation

On October 19, 2009, Freedom Medical, Inc. filed a complaint against us, another manufacturer and two group purchasing organizations in the United States District Court for the Eastern District of Texas. The plaintiff alleged, among

other things, that we and the other defendants conspired to exclude it from the biomedical equipment rental market and to maintain our market share by engaging in a variety of conduct in violation of state and federal antitrust laws. In September 2011, we settled this matter in exchange for a payment of $5.0 million. We did not admit any wrongdoing as part of the settlement.

Stryker Litigation

On April 4, 2011, we filed two separate actions against Stryker Corporation alleging infringement of certain Hill-Rom patents covering proprietary communications networks, status information systems and powered wheels used in our beds or stretchers. One suit was filed in the Southern District of Indiana and the other was filed in the Western District of Wisconsin. Both suits seek monetary damages and injunctions against Stryker for selling or distributing any beds, stretchers or ancillary products that infringe Hill-Rom's patents. Stryker responded in the Wisconsin litigation with counterclaims seeking declaratory judgment for non-infringement and invalidity for the patents at issue. In the Indiana litigation, Stryker has counterclaimed for non-infringement and invalidity for several of the patents at issue, and has filed counterclaims alleging infringement of three of their patents. In August 2011 the Wisconsin litigation was transferred to the Southern District of Indiana. No trial dates have been set. Because the litigation is in a preliminary stage, we cannot assess the likelihood of a positive or negative outcome or determine an estimate, or a range of estimates, of potential damages, nor can we give any assurances that this matter will not have a material adverse impact on our financial condition, results of operations or cash flows.

Antitrust Settlement

In fiscal 2005, we entered into a definitive, court approved agreement with Spartanburg Regional Healthcare Systems and its attorneys to settle a purported antitrust class action lawsuit. A number of potential plaintiffs, including the United States government, opted out of the settlement, and we retained a reserve of $21.2 million against these potential claims. However, no individual claims were filed prior to the August 2010 statute of limitations deadline, and we therefore reversed this reserve into income as of September 30, 2010.

General

We are subject to various other claims and contingencies arising out of the normal course of business, including those relating to governmental investigations and proceedings, commercial transactions, product liability, employee related matters, antitrust, safety, health, taxes, environmental and other matters. Litigation is subject to many uncertainties and the outcome of individual litigated matters is not predictable with assurance. It is possible that some litigation matters for which reserves have not been established could be decided unfavorably to us, and that any such unfavorable decisions could have a material adverse effect on our financial condition, results of operations and cash flows.

Equity in Losses of Investees

3.37

INTEL CORPORATION (DEC)

NOTES TO CONSOLIDATED FINANCIAL STATEMENTS

Note 11: Equity Method and Cost Method Investments (in part)

Equity Method Investments

Equity method investments as of December 31, 2011 and December 25, 2010 were as follows:

	2011		2010	
(In millions, except percentages)	Carrying Value	Ownership Percentage	Carrying Value	Ownership Percentage
IM Flash Technologies, LLC	$ 863	49%	$1,126	49%
IM Flash Singapore, LLP	466	18%	335	22%
Intel-GE Care Innovations, LLC	167	50%	—	—
SMART Technologies, Inc.	37	14%	31	14%
Clearwire Communications, LLC	—	7%	145	7%
Other equity method investments	136		154	
Total	$1,669		$1,791	

IMFT/IMFS

Micron and Intel formed IM Flash Technologies, LLC (IMFT) and IM Flash Singapore, LLP (IMFS) to manufacture NAND flash memory products for Micron and Intel. The carrying value of our investment in IMFT/IMFS was $1.3 billion as of December 31, 2011 ($1.5 billion as of December 25, 2010) and is classified within other long-term assets. In the third quarter of 2011, we made an additional investment of $131 million in IMFS. The IMFS fabrication facility began initial production in the second quarter of 2011. IMFT and IMFS are each governed by a Board of Managers, with Micron and Intel initially appointing an equal number of managers to each of the boards. The number of managers appointed by each party adjusts depending on the parties' ownership interests. As a result of our overall net reduction of our ownership interest in IMFS, Micron now appoints the majority of the managers on the IMFS board. Through our remaining managers on the IMFS board, we continue to have significant influence over the operations of IMFS, and therefore continue to account for our interests using the equity method of accounting. These ventures are expected to operate until 2016 but are subject to earlier termination under certain terms and conditions.

These joint ventures are variable interest entities. All costs of the joint ventures will be passed on to Micron and Intel through our purchase agreements. IMFT and IMFS are dependent upon Micron and Intel for any additional cash requirements. Our known maximum exposure to loss approximated the carrying value of our investment balance in IMFT/IMFS as of December 31, 2011. Except for the amount due to IMFT/IMFS for product purchases and services, we did not have any additional liabilities recognized on our consolidated balance sheets in connection with our interests in these joint ventures as of December 31, 2011. Future cash calls could increase our investment balance and the related

exposure to loss. Potential future losses could be higher than the carrying amount of our investment, as Intel and Micron are liable for other future operating costs or obligations of IMFT/IMFS. Finally, as we are currently committed to purchasing 49% of IMFT's and 22% of IMFS's production output and production-related services, we may be required to purchase products at a cost in excess of realizable value. As of December 31, 2011, our contractual commitment to purchase product output and fund production-related services from IMFS adjusts to changes in our ownership percentage on an eight-month lag.

Our portion of IMFT/IMFS costs, primarily related to product purchases and production-related services, was approximately $985 million during 2011 (approximately $795 million during 2010 and approximately $755 million during 2009). The amount due to IMFT/IMFS for product purchases and services provided was approximately $125 million as of December 31, 2011 (approximately $105 million as of December 25, 2010). During 2011, $263 million was returned to Intel by IMFT/IMFS, which is reflected as a return of equity method investment within investing activities on the consolidated statements of cash flows ($199 million during 2010 and $449 million during 2009). In 2010, IMFT increased its capital expenditures compared to 2009. The cash used for those capital expenditures reduced the amount of cash provided by IMFT to us as a return of equity method investment in 2010. Costs that Intel and Micron have incurred for product development and process development related to IMFT/IMFS are generally split evenly between Intel and Micron and are generally classified in research and development.

Under the accounting standards for consolidating variable interest entities, the consolidating investor is the entity with the power to direct the activities of the venture that most significantly impact the venture's economic performance and with the obligation to absorb losses or the right to receive benefits from the venture that could potentially be significant to the venture. We have determined that we do not have both of these characteristics and, therefore, we account for our interests using the equity method of accounting.

Intel-GE Care Innovations, LLC

In the first quarter of 2011, Intel and General Electric Company (GE) formed an equally owned joint venture, Intel-GE Care Innovations, LLC (Care Innovations), in the healthcare industry that focuses on independent living and delivery of health-related services via telecommunications. The company was formed by combining assets of GE Healthcare's Home Health division and Intel's Digital Health Group. As a result of the formation of Care Innovations, we recognized a gain of $164 million in the first quarter of 2011 that is recorded in interest and other, net.

Care Innovations is dependent upon Intel and GE for any additional cash requirements and, therefore, is a variable interest entity. Our known maximum exposure to loss approximated the carrying value of our investment balance in Care Innovations as of December 31, 2011. In addition to the potential loss of our existing investment, our actual losses could be higher, as we are liable to contribute additional future funding up to $38 million if Care Innovations meets established milestones.

Intel and GE equally share the power to direct all of Care Innovations' activities that most significantly impact its economic performance. As a result, we account for our interests in Care Innovations under the equity method of accounting.

SMART Technologies, Inc.

We hold an equity interest in SMART and account for our interest using the equity method of accounting. In 2010, SMART completed an initial public offering of shares approved for listing on The NASDAQ Global Select Market*. We sold approximately 10 million of our 27.5 million shares in the secondary offering. We recognized a gain of $181 million on the initial public offering and subsequent sale of our shares in the secondary offering, which is included in gains (losses) on equity investments, net.

Clearwire Communications, LLC

In 2008, we invested in Clearwire Communications, LLC (Clearwire LLC), a wholly owned subsidiary of Clearwire Corporation. Our investment in Clearwire LLC is accounted for under the equity method of accounting, and our proportionate share of the income or loss is recognized on a one-quarter lag. We recognize our proportionate share of losses to the extent that our investment has a positive carrying value. During 2011, we recognized $145 million of equity method losses ($116 million in 2010). During 2009, we recorded $27 million of equity method losses, which was net of a gain of $37 million as a result of a dilution of our ownership interest from an additional investment. These equity method losses are included in gains (losses) on equity investments, net.

Numonyx B.V.

In 2008, we divested our NOR flash memory business in exchange for an ownership interest in Numonyx. Our investment was accounted for under the equity method of accounting, and our proportionate share of the income or loss was recognized on a one-quarter lag. During 2010, we rec-

ognized $42 million of equity method gains ($31 million of equity method losses in 2009) within gains (losses) on equity investments, net.

During the second quarter of 2010, we sold our ownership interest in Numonyx to Micron and recognized a gain on the sale of $91 million, which is included in gains (losses) on equity investments, net. In exchange for our investment in Numonyx, we received 57.9 million shares of Micron common stock, with an additional 8.6 million shares held in escrow for 12 months after the sale, and we issued a $72 million short-term note payable, which was subsequently paid.

In the fourth quarter of 2010, we sold 21.5 million shares of Micron common stock, which consisted of the 8.6 million shares held in escrow and an additional 12.9 million shares received in the sale of Numonyx. In 2011, we sold the remaining Micron shares.

Note 12: Gains (Losses) on Equity Investments, Net

Gains (losses) on equity investments, net included:

(In millions)	2011	2010	2009
Share of equity method investee losses, net	$(204)	$(113)	$(131)
Impairment charges	(132)	(125)	(221)
Gains on sales, net	303	424	80
Other, net	145	162	102
Total gains (losses) on equity investments, net	$ 112	$ 348	$(170)

Environmental

3.38

FMC CORPORATION (DEC)

NOTES TO CONSOLIDATED FINANCIAL STATEMENTS

Note 1: Principal Accounting Policies and Related Financial Information (in part)

Environmental obligations. We provide for environmental-related obligations when they are probable and amounts can be reasonably estimated. Where the available information is sufficient to estimate the amount of liability, that estimate has been used. Where the information is only sufficient to establish a range of probable liability and no point within the range is more likely than any other, the lower end of the range has been used.

Estimated obligations to remediate sites that involve oversight by the United States Environmental Protection Agency ("EPA"), or similar government agencies, are generally accrued no later than when a Record of Decision ("ROD"), or equivalent, is issued, or upon completion of a Remedial Investigation/Feasibility Study ("RI/FS"), or equivalent, that is submitted by us and the appropriate government agency or agencies. Estimates are reviewed quarterly and, if necessary, adjusted as additional information becomes available. The estimates can change substantially as additional information becomes available regarding the nature or extent of site contamination, required remediation methods, and other actions by or against governmental agencies or private parties.

Our environmental liabilities for continuing and discontinued operations are principally for costs associated with the remediation and/or study of sites at which we are alleged to have released hazardous substances into the environment. Such costs principally include, among other items, RI/FS, site remediation, costs of operation and maintenance of the remediation plan, management costs, fees to outside law firms and consultants for work related to the environmental effort, and future monitoring costs. Estimated site liabilities are determined based upon existing remediation laws and technologies, specific site consultants' engineering studies or by extrapolating experience with environmental issues at comparable sites.

Included in our environmental liabilities are costs for the operation, maintenance and monitoring of site remediation plans (OM&M). Such reserves are based on our best estimates for these OM&M plans. Over time we may incur OM&M costs in excess of these reserves. However, we are unable to reasonably estimate an amount in excess of our recorded reserves because we cannot reasonably estimate the period for which such OM&M plans will need to be in place or the future annual cost of such remediation, as conditions at these environmental sites change over time. Such additional OM&M costs could be significant in total but would be incurred over an extended period of years.

Included in the environmental reserve balance, other assets balance and disclosure of reasonably possible loss contingencies are amounts from third party insurance policies which we believe are probable of recovery.

Provisions for environmental costs are reflected in income, net of probable and estimable recoveries from named Potentially Responsible Parties ("PRPs") or other third parties. Such provisions incorporate inflation and are not discounted to their present values.

In calculating and evaluating the adequacy of our environmental reserves, we have taken into account the joint and several liability imposed by Comprehensive Environmental Remediation, Compensation and Liability Act ("CERCLA") and the analogous state laws on all PRPs and have considered the identity and financial condition of the other PRPs at each site to the extent possible. We have also considered the identity and financial condition of other third parties from whom recovery is anticipated, as well as the status of our claims against such parties. Although we are unable to forecast the ultimate contributions of PRPs and other third parties with absolute certainty, the degree of uncertainty with respect to each party is taken into account when determining the environmental reserve on a site-by-site basis. Our liability includes our best estimate of the costs expected to be paid before the consideration of any potential recoveries from third parties. We believe that any recorded recoveries related to PRPs are realizable in all material respects. Recoveries are recorded as either an offset in "Environmental liabilities, continuing and discontinued" or as "Other Assets" in our consolidated balance sheets in accordance with U.S. accounting literature.

Note 7: Restructuring and Other Charges (Income) (in part)

Other Charges (Income), Net (in part)

(In millions)	Year Ended December 31		
	2011	2010	2009
Environmental Charges, Net	$3.1	$14.2	$20.2
Legal Matters	—	1.5	29.9
Other, net	1.3	9.0	1.2
Other Charges (Income), Net	$4.4	$24.7	$51.3

Environmental Charges, Net

Environmental charges represent the net charges associated with environmental remediation at continuing operating sites, see Note 10 for additional details.

Note 9: Discontinued Operations (in part)

Our discontinued operations represent adjustments to retained liabilities primarily related to operations discontinued between 1976 and 2001. The primary liabilities retained include environmental liabilities, other postretirement benefit liabilities, self-insurance and long-term obligations related to legal proceedings.

Our discontinued operations comprised the following:

(In millions)	Year Ended December 31		
	2011	2010	2009
Adjustment for workers' compensation, product liability, and other postretirement benefits related to previously discontinued operations (net of income tax expense of $0.3, $0.4 and $0.2 for 2011, 2010 and 2009, respectively)	$ 0.7	$ 0.8	$ 0.5
Provision for environmental liabilities and legal reserves and expenses related to previously discontinued operations, net of recoveries (net of income tax benefit of $19.9, $24.2 and $11.4 in 2011, 2010 and 2009, respectively)	(32.5)	(39.5)	(18.7)
Income from and adjustment associated with a tax matter related to a previously discontinued operation	$ —	$ 5.1	$ —
Discontinued operations, net of income taxes	$(31.8)	$(33.6)	$(18.2)

Year Ended December 31, 2011

For the year ended December 31, 2011, we recorded a $52.4 million ($32.5 million after-tax) charge to discontinued operations related primarily to environmental issues and legal reserves and expenses. Environmental charges of $25.4 million ($15.8 million after-tax) related primarily to a provision increase for environmental issues at our Front Royal site as well as operating and maintenance activities for a number of environmental sites. See a roll forward of our environmental reserves in Note 10. We also recorded increases to legal reserves and expenses in the amount of $27.0 million ($16.7 million after-tax).

Year Ended December 31, 2010

For the year ended December 31, 2010, we recorded a $63.7 million ($39.5 million after-tax) charge, respectively, to discontinued operations related primarily to environmental issues and legal reserves and expenses. Environmental charges of $38.1 million ($23.6 million after-tax) related primarily to a provision increase for environmental issues at our Middleport site as well as operating and maintenance activities for a number of environmental sites partially offset by recoveries. We also recorded increases to legal reserves and expenses in the amount of $25.6 million ($15.9 million after-tax).

Year Ended December 31, 2009

For the year ended December 31, 2009, we recorded a $30.1 million ($18.7 million after-tax) charge to discontinued operations related primarily to environmental issues and legal reserves and expenses. Environmental charges of $7.1 million ($4.4 million after-tax) relate primarily to a provision increase for environmental issues at our Front Royal and Middleport sites as well as for operating and maintenance activities for a number of environmental sites partially offset by recoveries. We also recorded increases to legal reserves and expenses in the amount of $23.0 million ($14.3 million after-tax).

Note 10: Environmental Obligations (in part)

Environmental liabilities consist of obligations relating to waste handling and the remediation and/or study of sites at which we are alleged to have released or disposed of hazardous substances. These sites include current operations, previously operated sites, and sites associated with discontinued operations. We have provided reserves for potential environmental obligations that we consider probable and for which a reasonable estimate of the obligation can be made. Accordingly, total reserves of $251.2 million and $241.8 million, respectively, before recoveries, existed at December 31, 2011 and 2010. The long-term portion of these reserves is included in "Environmental liabilities, continuing and discontinued" on the consolidated balance sheets, net of recoveries, and amounted to $213.3 million and $209.9 million at December 31, 2011 and 2010, respectively. The short-term portion of our continuing operations obligations is recorded in "Accrued and other liabilities." In addition, we have estimated that reasonably possible environmental loss contingencies, net of expected recoveries may exceed amounts accrued by approximately $110 million at December 31, 2011. This reasonably possible estimate is based upon information available as of the date of the filing and the actual future loses may be higher given the uncertainties regarding the status of laws, regulations, enforcement policies, the impact of potentially responsible parties, technology and information related to individual sites.

To ensure we are held responsible only for our equitable share of site remediation costs, we have initiated, and will continue to initiate, legal proceedings for contributions from other PRPs. We have recorded recoveries, representing probable realization of claims against insurance companies, U.S. government agencies and other third parties, of $82.6 million and $68.6 million at December 31, 2011 and 2010, respectively. The recoveries at December 31, 2011 and 2010, are recorded as either an offset to the "Environmental liabilities, continuing and discontinued" totaling $24.3 million and $16.9 million or as "Other assets" totaling $58.3 million and $51.7 million in the consolidated balance sheets, respectively. Cash recoveries for the years 2011, 2010 and 2009 were $12.4 million, $14.6 million and $13.7 million, respectively.

The table below is a roll forward of our total environmental reserves, continuing and discontinued from December 31, 2008 to December 31, 2011.

(In millions)	Operating and Discontinued Sites Total
Total environmental reserves, net of recoveries at December 31, 2008	$172.7
2009	
Provision	47.5
Spending, net of recoveries	(36.1)
Net Change	11.4
Total environmental reserves, net of recoveries at December 31, 2009	$184.1
2010	
Provision	76.1
Spending, net of recoveries	(35.3)
Net Change	40.8
Total environmental reserves, net of recoveries at December 31, 2010	$224.9
2011	
Provision	45.2
Spending, net of recoveries	(43.2)
Net Change	2.0
Total environmental reserves, net of recoveries at December 31, 2011	$226.9

The table below provides detail of current and long-term environmental reserves, continuing and discontinued.

(In millions)	December 31 2011	December 31 2010
Environmental reserves, current, net of recoveries[1]	$ 13.6	$ 15.0
Environmental reserves, long-term continuing and discontinued, net of recoveries	213.3	209.9
Total environmental reserves, net of recoveries	$226.9	$224.9

[1] "Current" includes only those reserves related to continuing operations. These amounts are included within "Accrued and other liabilities" on the consolidated balance sheets.

Our net environmental provisions relate to costs for the continued cleanup of both operating sites and for certain discontinued manufacturing operations from previous years. The net provisions are comprised as follows:

(In millions)	Year Ended December 31		
	2011	2010	2009
Continuing operations[1]	$ 3.1	$14.2	$20.2
Discontinued operations[2]	25.4	38.1	7.1
Net environmental provision	$28.5	$52.3	$27.3

[1] Recorded as a component of "Restructuring and other charges (income)" on our consolidated statements of income. See Note 7.
[2] Recorded as a component of "Discontinued operations, net" on our consolidated statements of income. See Note 9.

On our consolidated balance sheets, the net environmental provisions are recorded as follows:

(In millions)	Year Ended December 31		
	2011	2010	2009
Environmental reserves[1]	$45.2	$76.1	$47.5
Other assets[2]	(16.7)	(23.8)	(20.2)
Net environmental provision	$28.5	$52.3	$27.3

[1] See above roll forward of our total environmental reserves as presented on our consolidated balance sheets.
[2] Represents certain environmental recoveries. See Note 20 for details of Other assets as presented on our consolidated balance sheets.

Significant Environmental Sites

Front Royal

On October 21, 1999, the Federal District Court for the Western District of Virginia approved a Consent Decree signed by FMC, the EPA (Region III) and the Department of Justice ("DOJ") regarding past response costs and future clean-up work at the discontinued fiber-manufacturing site in Front Royal, Virginia. In January 2010, the EPA issued a Record of Decision (ROD) for Operable Unit 7 (OU-7) primarily addressing waste basins and ground water, which should be the last operable unit to be remediated at the site. The reserve prior to 2011, included a provision for OU-7 and previously approved work for other operable units under the Consent Decree. During 2011 extensive design work occurred, providing the basis for an improved cost estimate for the construction of the groundwater treatment plant. The groundwater treatment plant is an integral component of the remedy required to address the OU-7 ROD. We recorded an increase to the reserve associated with the new treatment plant estimate during the year. As part of a prior settlement, government agencies have reimbursed us for approximately one-third of the clean-up costs due to the government's role at the site, and we expect reimbursement to continue in the future. The amount of the reserve for this site was $36.4 million and $28.5 million at December 31, 2011 and December 31, 2010, respectively.

Pocatello

We have successfully decommissioned our Pocatello plant, completed closure of the RCRA ponds and formally requested that EPA acknowledge completion of work under a June 1999 RCRA Consent Decree. Future remediation costs include completion of one of the CERCLA remedies identified in the Supplemental Feasibility Study (SFS) that addresses ground water contamination and existing waste disposal areas on the Pocatello plant portion of the Eastern Michaud Flats Superfund Site. In April 2010, the EPA presented their recommended alternative from the SFS to the National Remedy Review Board (NRRB). The NRRB has endorsed the selection of this alternative, and the EPA has drafted a proposed plan recommending this remedy.

On September 26, 2011, the EPA issued their Proposed Plan for the site. As expected, the Proposed Plan described the EPA's recommended alternative remedy referred to above. The public comment period on the EPA's Proposed Plan ended in December. The EPA is expected to issue an Interim Amendment to the Record of Decision (ROD) in 2012. Additionally, we continue to conduct work pursuant to CERCLA unilateral administrative orders to address air emissions from beneath the cap of several of the closed RCRA ponds.

The Shoshone-Bannock Tribes ("the Tribes") are objecting to the EPA's Proposed Plan. The Tribes are seeking further investigations and studies to identify a technology to excavate and treat elemental phosphorus in soil. FMC has supported EPA's Proposed Plan on the basis that there is no technology to safely excavate and treat the elemental phosphorus-contaminated soils and further studies will only delay the remediation and development of the site.

The amount of the reserve for this site was $64.8 million and $71.0 million at December 31, 2011 and 2010, respectively.

Middleport

At our facility in Middleport, New York, we have constructed an engineered cover, closed the RCRA regulated surface water impoundments and are collecting and treating both surface water runoff and ground water. A draft corrective measures study (CMS) has been prepared for two off-site areas and is under review by the EPA and New York State Departments of the Environment and Health (collectively referred to as the Agencies). This initial draft CMS for these two areas was submitted in 2010. At the Agencies' request, a second draft of the CMS for these areas was submitted in May 2011.

Next, the Agencies' will issue its preliminary draft Statement of Basis indicating the selected remedial alternatives. There will be a public comment period where FMC will have the opportunity to respond to the selected remedy. Additional costs may result, in the event any remedies other than FMC's preferred remedies are selected. The amount of the reserve for this site is $47.0 million and $46.2 million at December 31, 2011 and 2010, respectively.

SEC 3.38

Sale of Receivables

3.39

ALLIANCE ONE INTERNATIONAL, INC. (MAR)

STATEMENTS OF CONSOLIDATED OPERATIONS AND COMPREHENSIVE INCOME (LOSS) (in part)

(In thousands, except per share data)	Years Ended March 31		
	2011	2010	2009
Sales and other operating revenues	$2,094,062	$2,308,299	$2,258,219
Cost of goods and services sold	1,817,243	1,911,849	1,897,380
Gross profit	276,819	396,450	360,839
Selling, administrative and general expenses	157,920	155,376	156,000
Other income (expense)	37,442	(17,260)	214
Restructuring charges	23,467	—	591
Operating income	132,874	223,814	204,462

NOTES TO CONSOLIDATED FINANCIAL STATEMENTS

(In thousands)

Note 1—Significant Accounting Policies (in part)

Other Income (Expense)

Other Income (Expense) consists primarily of gains on sales of property, plant and equipment and assets held for sale. This caption also includes expenses related to the Company's sale of receivables. See Note 17 "Sale of Receivables" to the "Notes to Consolidated Financial Statements" for further information. During fiscal 2011, the Company recorded a gain of $37,765 on the assignment of approximately 9,000 tobacco suppliers in Southern Brazil and the sale of related assets to the Brazilian affiliate of Philip Morris International, Inc. ("PMI"). The Company expects to continue to supply processed tobacco to PMI and to process tobacco for PMI's Brazilian affiliate under a long-term processing agreement. During fiscal 2010, an estimate of a probable loss in connection with a Foreign Corrupt Practices Act ("FCPA") investigation was recorded. The following table summarizes the significant components of Other Income (Expense).

	Years Ending March 31		
	2011	2010	2009
Malawi other property sales	$ 1,975	$ 1,677	$ —
Turkey storage and other property sales	—	2,567	—
Brazil factory and other property sales to PMI's affiliate	37,765	—	—
Other sales of assets and expenses	97	896	3,762
FCPA loss	—	(19,450)	—
Losses on sale of receivables	(2,395)	(2,950)	(3,548)
	$37,442	$(17,260)	$ 214

Sale of Accounts Receivable

The Company is engaged in a revolving trade accounts receivable securitization arrangement to sell receivables to a third party limited liability company. The Company records the transaction as a sale of receivables, removes such receivables from its financial statements and records a receivable for the beneficial interest in such receivables. The losses on the sale of receivables are recognized in Other Income (Expense). As of March 31, 2011 and 2010, respectively, accounts receivable sold and outstanding were $53,156 and $105,579. See Note 17 "Sale of Receivables" and Note 18 "Fair Value Measurements" to the "Notes to Consolidated Financial Statements" for further information.

Note 17—Sale of Receivables

On April 1, 2010, the Company adopted new accounting guidance on accounting for the transfers of financial assets. This new accounting guidance is intended to improve the information provided in financial statements concerning transfers of financial assets, including the effects of transfers on financial position, financial performance and cash flows, and any continuing involvement of the transferor with the transferred financial assets.

The Company has entered into an accounts receivable securitization program whereby it sells certain of its trade accounts receivable to a third-party bankruptcy-remote special purpose entity ("SPE") which, in turn, sells the receivables to a third-party commercial paper conduit. The SPE was formed for the sole purpose of buying and selling receivables generated by the Company.

The sales price consists of 90% of the face value of the receivable, less contractual dilutions which limit the amount that may be outstanding from any one particular customer and insurance reserves that also have the effect of limiting the risk attributable to any one customer. Upon sale, the Company removes the carrying value of the receivable sold and records the fair value of its beneficial interest in the receivable in accounts receivable. The fair value of the beneficial interest is calculated by applying the commercial paper rate and the servicing rate to the balance of the outstanding receivables in the facility. The Company receives a 0.5% per annum servicing fee on receivables sold and outstanding which is recorded as a reduction of selling, administrative and general expenses. This fee is compensatory and no servicing asset or liability has resulted from the sale. The receivables sold are non-interest bearing. This in conjunction with the short life of the receivables sold and outstanding causes the effects of any prepayments on the value of assets recorded to be inconsequential. Losses on sale of receivables are recorded as a component of Other Income (Expense) in the consolidated statements of operations.

The following table summarizes the Company's accounts receivable securitization information as of March 31:

	2011	2010
Receivables outstanding in facility as of March 31:	$ 53,156	$105,579
Beneficial interest as of March 31	$ 15,797	$ 25,125
Impact on beneficial interest resulting from changes in discount rate:		
10%	$ 25	$ 83
20%	$ 51	$ 165
Criteria to determine beneficial interest as of March 31:		
Weighted average life in days	67	95
Discount rate (inclusive of 0.5% servicing fee)	2.46%	3.00%
Unused balance fee	0.40%	0.25%
Cash proceeds for the twelve months ended March 31:		
Current purchase price	$405,982	$606,772
Deferred purchase price	240,989	232,101
Service fees	504	517
Total	$647,475	$839,390
Loss on sale of receivables	$ 2,395	$ 2,950

It is the Company's intention to maximize the receivables sold under the revolving agreement meaning that amounts collected by the pool would be reinvested in the purchase of additional eligible receivables. The table below indicates the utilization of the revolving agreement:

	Twelve Months Ended March 31	
	2011	2010
Average outstanding balance	$60,203	$76,711
Maximum outstanding balance	99,113	99,712
Minimum outstanding balance	16,738	47,174

Mergers and Acquisitions

3.40

CARPENTER TECHNOLOGY CORPORATION (JUN)

CONSOLIDATED STATEMENTS OF INCOME (in part)

For the Years Ended June 30, 2011, 2010 and 2009

($ in millions, except per share data)	2011	2010	2009
Net sales	$1,675.1	$1,198.6	$1,362.3
Cost of sales	1,426.1	1,053.8	1,155.1
Gross profit	249.0	144.8	207.2
Selling, general and administrative expenses	149.5	133.1	133.8
Acquisition related costs	3.1	—	—
Restructuring charges	—	—	9.4
Operating income	96.4	11.7	64.0

NOTES TO CONSOLIDATED FINANCIAL STATEMENTS

3. Acquisition and Strategic Partnership (in part)

Acquisitions (in part)

Latrobe Specialty Metals, Inc.

On June 20, 2011, the Company entered into an Agreement and Plan of Merger (the "Merger Agreement") to acquire Latrobe Specialty Metals, Inc., a Delaware corporation ("Latrobe"). The closing of the merger is subject to the satisfaction or waiver of certain conditions.

According to the terms of the Merger Agreement, the Company will issue 8.1 million shares of the Company's common stock to Latrobe's stockholders, subject to certain adjustments for working capital and other items. The Company will assume all third party indebtedness incurred by Latrobe, and pay all fees and expenses incurred by Latrobe prior to the Merger in connection with prior proposed securities offerings; provided, however, if the amount of Latrobe's indebtedness assumed by the Company exceeds $160 million, or the amount of Latrobe's prior securities offering related expenses paid by the Company exceeds $4 million, such excess amounts shall reduce the number of shares of Company common stock to be issued to Latrobe's stockholders. In addition, the Company will pay all transaction related expenses of Latrobe; provided, however, that any such amounts in excess of $10 million may reduce the number of shares of Company common stock to be issued to Latrobe's stockholders.

Under the Merger Agreement, a portion of the shares to be issued as merger consideration will be placed into escrow to secure Latrobe's indemnification obligations and to account for pension funding issues of Latrobe. An indemnity escrow equal to $50 million worth of the Company common stock will be created to cover general indemnification claims. Assuming no claims are asserted, half of the indemnity escrow will be released on the first anniversary of the closing and the remaining shares will be released after 24 months. An additional 300,000 shares will be placed into a pension escrow account in connection with Latrobe's Pension Funding Issues. The shares of Company common stock will be released from the pension escrow over a period of 5 years following closing based on the level of a particular fixed income index over such 5-year period.

The Company has agreed that upon consummation of the Merger and until the Company's 2014 annual meeting of stockholders, certain of Latrobe's stockholders will designate two persons who will be appointed to the Company's Board of Directors. Certain of Latrobe's stockholders (including those that have the right to designate directors to the Company's Board of Directors) will, upon consummation of the Merger, agree (i) that during the time that such Latrobe stockholders may appoint designees to the Company's Board of Directors (or shorter in the event such designees resign from the Company's Board of Directors) they will vote the shares of the Company's common stock in favor of the Company's nominees for directors and not contrary to the recommendations of the Company's Board of Directors on other matters, and (ii) for a period of five years following the consummation of the Merger they will not acquire any additional shares of the Company's common stock or, with limited exceptions, sell their shares of the Company's common stock where the result of such sale would be for a third party to own more than 5% of the Company's outstanding common stock. The Company has also agreed to grant limited registration rights in favor of such Latrobe stockholders.

The Merger Agreement may be terminated by Latrobe or the Company in the event the consummation of the Merger has not occurred by September 30, 2011 and the cause for the consummation not occurring is not the terminating party; provided, however, if the Merger has not been consummated solely because the applicable antitrust approvals have not been received, and all other conditions to consummation of the Merger have been satisfied or waived, then the "Termination Date" shall be January 16, 2012. Latrobe also may terminate the Merger Agreement at any time after October 31, 2011 because the applicable antitrust approvals have not been received, although the Company may override such termination. If the override right is exercised and the Merger is not consummated by January 16, 2012, the Company shall be required to pay Latrobe a $5 million fee. In addition, if the Merger Agreement is terminated by Latrobe because applicable antitrust approvals have not, or cannot, be obtained, the Company agreed to reimburse Latrobe for its reasonable out-of-pocket costs related to seeking the applicable antitrust approvals.

In connection with the Merger Agreement, the Company incurred approximately $2.4 million of acquisition related costs in fiscal year 2011.

Amega West Services

On December 31, 2010, the Company acquired all of the members' interests in Amega West Services, LLC ("Amega West"), a Houston-based manufacturer and service provider in the directional drilling industry for a cash purchase price of $41.6 million. In connection with the acquisition, the Company also assumed $12.4 million of Amega West's long-term debt which was paid off in cash concurrently with closing of the purchase. Amega West is a leading manufacturer of high-precision components for measurement while drilling ("MWD") and logging while drilling ("LWD") housings, drill collars, stabilizers and other down-hole tools used for directional drilling. MWD and LWD technology is used to ensure critical data is obtained and transmitted to the surface to monitor progress of the well. The consideration paid has been allocated as follows:

Net working capital, including $4.9 million of accounts payable to Carpenter effectively settled at closing	$ 6.5
Property, plant and equipment	25.9
Customer relationships	5.2
Non-compete agreements	5.4
Trademarks and tradenames	1.9
Goodwill	9.7
Deferred tax liabilities	(0.6)
Long-term debt	(12.4)
Total purchase price	$41.6

Of the goodwill recorded related to the Amega West acquisition, $8.3 million is expected to be deductible for tax purposes.

The purchase agreement includes an earn-out opportunity for certain management equity sellers, designed to drive earnings growth at Amega West. According to the terms of the earn-out, the Company held back approximately $2.8 million of the cash purchase price otherwise payable to the earn-out participants, providing the participants with the opportunity to receive up to two times the holdback amount if certain earnings targets are achieved over a four and a half year period following the acquisition. $2.2 million of the earnout is guaranteed and is therefore considered as part of the total purchase price. The earnout payments in excess of the guaranteed minimum amount, if any, will be treated as compensation related to postcombination services.

The results of operations of Amega West have been included in the Consolidated Statements of Income since the acquisition date and are reported in the Emerging Ventures segment. The acquisition of Amega West is not considered material to the consolidated financial statements and accordingly the Company will not disclose proforma information.

In connection with the Amega West acquisition, the Company incurred approximately $0.7 million of acquisition related costs in fiscal year 2011.

Change in Fair Value of Derivatives

3.41

ANADARKO PETROLEUM CORPORATION (DEC)

CONSOLIDATED STATEMENTS OF INCOME (in part)

	Years Ended December 31		
(Millions except per-share amounts)	2011	2010	2009
Revenues and Other			
Natural-gas sales	$ 3,300	3,420	$2,924
Oil and condensate sales	8,072	5,592	4,022
Natural-gas liquids sales	1,462	997	536
Gathering, processing, and marketing sales	1,048	833	728
Gains (losses) on divestitures and other, net	85	142	133
Reversal of accrual for Deepwater Royalty Relief Act dispute	—	—	657
Total	13,967	10,984	9,000
Costs and Expenses			
Oil and gas operating	993	830	859
Oil and gas transportation and other	891	816	664
Exploration	1,076	974	1,107
Gathering, processing, and marketing	791	615	617
General and administrative	1,060	967	983
Depreciation, depletion, and amortization	3,830	3,714	3,532
Other taxes	1,492	1,068	746
Impairments	1,774	216	115
Deepwater Horizon settlement and related costs	3,930	15	—
Total	15,837	9,215	8,623
Operating Income (Loss)	(1,870)	1,769	377
Other (Income) Expense			
Interest expense	839	855	702
(Gains) losses on commodity derivatives, net	(562)	(893)	408
(Gains) losses on other derivatives, net	1,023	285	(582)
Other (income) expense, net	254	(119)	(43)
Total	1,554	128	485

NOTES TO CONSOLIDATED FINANCIAL STATEMENTS YEARS ENDED DECEMBER 31, 2011, 2010, AND 2009

1. Summary of Significant Accounting Policies (in part)

Derivative Instruments—Anadarko uses derivative instruments to manage its exposure to cash-flow variability from commodity-price and interest-rate risk. All derivatives that do not satisfy the normal purchases and sales exception criteria are carried on the balance sheet at fair value and are included in other current assets, other assets, accrued expenses, or other long-term liabilities, depending on the derivative position and the expected timing of settlement. Where the Company has the contractual right and intends to net settle, derivative assets and liabilities are reported on a net basis.

Realized and unrealized gains and losses on derivative instruments are recognized on a current basis. Net derivative losses attributable to derivatives previously subject to hedge accounting reside in accumulated other comprehensive income and will be reclassified to earnings in future periods as the economic transactions to which the derivatives relate affect earnings. See *Note 10—Derivative Instruments*.

10. Derivative Instruments (in part)

Objective and Strategy—The Company uses derivative instruments to manage its exposure to cash-flow variability from commodity-price and interest-rate risks.

Futures, swaps, and options are used to manage exposure to commodity-price risk inherent in the Company's oil and natural-gas production and natural-gas processing operations (Oil and Natural-Gas Production/Processing Derivative Activities). Futures contracts and commodity-price swap agreements are used to fix the price of expected future oil and natural-gas sales at major industry trading locations, such as Henry Hub for natural gas and Cushing for oil. Basis swaps are used to fix or float the price differential between product prices at one market location versus another. Options are used to establish a floor price, a ceiling price, or a floor and a ceiling price (collar) for expected future oil and natural-gas sales. Derivative instruments are also used to manage commodity-price risk inherent in customer price requirements and to fix margins on the future sale of natural gas and NGLs from the Company's leased storage facilities (Marketing and Trading Derivative Activities).

Interest-rate swaps are used to fix or float interest rates on existing or anticipated indebtedness. The purpose of these instruments is to manage the Company's existing or anticipated exposure to unfavorable interest-rate changes. The fair value of this swap portfolio increases (decreases) when interest rates increase (decrease).

The Company does not apply hedge accounting to any of its derivative instruments. As a result, both realized and unrealized gains and losses associated with derivative instruments are recognized in earnings. Net derivative losses attributable to derivatives previously subject to hedge accounting reside in accumulated other comprehensive income (loss) and are reclassified to earnings as the transactions to which the derivatives relate are recognized in earnings. Accumulated other comprehensive loss balances of $109 million ($70 million after tax) and $125 million ($79 million after tax) at December 31, 2011 and 2010, respectively, relate to interest-rate derivatives that were previously subject to hedge accounting.

Oil and Natural-Gas Production/Processing Derivative Activities. Below is a summary of the Company's derivative instruments related to its Oil and Natural-Gas Production/Processing Activities at December 31, 2011. The natural-gas prices listed below are New York Mercantile Exchange (NYMEX) Henry Hub prices. The crude-oil prices listed below are NYMEX Cushing prices.

	2012	2013
Natural Gas		
Three-Way Collars (thousand MMBtu/d)	—[1]	450
Average price per MMBtu		
Ceiling sold price (call)	$ —	$6.57
Floor purchased price (put)	$ —	$5.00
Floor sold price (put)	$ —	$4.00
Fixed-Price Contracts (thousand MMBtu/d)	1,000	—
Average price per MMBtu	$ 4.69	$ —
Crude Oil		
Three-Way Collars (MBbls/d)	2	—
Average price per barrel		
Ceiling sold price (call)	$92.50	$ —
Floor purchased price (put)	$50.00	$ —
Floor sold price (put)	$35.00	$ —

[1] Includes the effects of offsetting purchased and sold natural-gas three-way collars of 500,000 MMBtu/d.
MMBtu—million British thermal units
MMBtu/d—million British thermal units per day
MBbls/d—thousand barrels per day

A three-way collar is a combination of three options: a sold call, a purchased put, and a sold put. The sold call establishes the maximum price that the Company will receive for the contracted commodity volumes. The purchased put establishes the minimum price that the Company will receive for the contracted volumes unless the market price for the commodity falls below the sold put strike price, at which point the minimum price equals the reference price (e.g., NYMEX) plus the excess of the purchased put strike price over the sold put strike price.

Marketing and Trading Derivative Activities—In addition to the positions in the above tables, the Company also engages in marketing and trading activities, which include physical product sales and related derivative transactions used to manage commodity-price risk. At December 31, 2011 and 2010, the Company had fixed-price physical transactions related to natural gas totaling 22 billion cubic feet (Bcf) and 32 Bcf, respectively, offset by derivative transactions for 21 Bcf and 28 Bcf, respectively, for net positions of 1 Bcf and 4 Bcf, respectively.

Interest-Rate Derivatives—In December 2008 and January 2009, Anadarko entered into interest-rate swap contracts as a fixed-rate payor to mitigate the interest-rate risk associated with anticipated 2011 and 2012 debt issuances. The Company locked in a fixed interest rate in exchange for a floating interest rate indexed to the three-month LIBOR. The swap instruments include a provision that requires both the termination of the swaps and cash settlement in full at the start of the reference period.

Due to rising interest rates in 2009, the fair value of the swap contracts increased. As a result, the Company revised the swap contract terms in the second quarter of 2009 to increase the weighted-average interest rate of the swap portfolio from approximately 3.25% to approximately 4.80%, and realized a $552 million gain. During the third quarter of

2011, in order to better align the swap portfolio with the anticipated timing of future debt refinancing, the Company extended the swap maturity dates from October 2011 to June 2014 for interest-rate swaps with an aggregate notional principal amount of $1.85 billion. In connection with these extensions, the swap interest rates were also adjusted. In addition, interest-rate swap agreements with an aggregate notional principal amount of $150 million were settled for a loss of $57 million in October 2011.

The Company had the following outstanding interest-rate swaps at December 31, 2011.

Millions except percentages	Reference Period		Weighted-Average
Notional Principal Amount	**Start**	**End**	**Interest Rate**
$ 250	October 2012	October 2022	4.91%
$ 750	October 2012	October 2042	4.80%
$ 750	June 2014	June 2024	6.00%
$1,100	June 2014	June 2044	5.57%

*Effect of Derivative Instruments—Statement of Income—*The realized and unrealized gain or loss amounts and classification of derivative instruments for the respective years ended December 31 are as follows:

Millions		(Gain) Loss		
Derivatives	**Classification of (Gain) Loss Recognized**	**Realized**	**Unrealized**	**Total**
2011				
Commodity				
	Gathering, Processing, and Marketing Sales[1]	$ 20	$ (12)	$ 8
	(Gains) Losses on Commodity Derivatives, net	(226)	(336)	(562)
Interest Rate and Other				
	(Gains) Losses on Other Derivatives, net	59	964	1,023
Derivative (Gain) Loss, net		$(147)	$ 616	$ 469
2010				
Commodity				
	Gathering, Processing, and Marketing Sales[1]	$ 3	$ (4)	$ (1)
	(Gains) Losses on Commodity Derivatives, net	(498)	(395)	(893)
Interest Rate and Other				
	(Gains) Losses on Other Derivatives, net	—	285	285
Derivative (Gain) Loss, net		$(495)	$(114)	$ (609)
2009				
Commodity				
	Gathering, Processing, and Marketing Sales[1]	$ (2)	$ 39	$ 37
	(Gains) Losses on Commodity Derivatives, net	(327)	735	408
Interest Rate				
	(Gains) Losses on Other Derivatives, net	(525)	(57)	(582)
Derivative (Gain) Loss, net		$(854)	$ 717	$ (137)

[1] Represents the effect of marketing and trading derivative activities.

Change in Fair Value

3.42

METLIFE, INC. (DEC)

CONSOLIDATED STATEMENTS OF OPERATIONS
(in part)

For the Years Ended December 31, 2011, 2010 and 2009

(In millions, except per share data)

	2011	2010	2009
Revenues			
Premiums	$36,361	$27,071	$26,157
Universal life and investment-type product policy fees	7,806	6,028	5,197
Net investment income	19,606	17,511	14,741
Other revenues	2,532	2,328	2,329
Net investment gains (losses):			
Other-than-temporary impairments on fixed maturity securities	(924)	(682)	(2,432)
Other-than-temporary impairments on fixed maturity securities transferred to other comprehensive income (loss)	(31)	212	939
Other net investment gains (losses)	88	62	(1,408)
Total net investment gains (losses)	(867)	(408)	(2,901)
Net derivative gains (losses)	4,824	(265)	(4,866)
Total revenues	70,262	52,265	40,657

NOTES TO THE CONSOLIDATED FINANCIAL STATEMENTS

1. Business, Basis of Presentation and Summary of Significant Accounting Policies (in part)

Summary of Significant Accounting Policies and Critical Accounting Estimates (in part)

Investments

The accounting policies for the Company's principal investments are as follows:

Fixed Maturity and Equity Securities. The Company's fixed maturity and equity securities are classified as available-for-sale and are reported at their estimated fair value.

Unrealized investment gains and losses on these securities are recorded as a separate component of other comprehensive income (loss), net of policyholder-related amounts and deferred income taxes. All security transactions are recorded on a trade date basis. Investment gains and losses on sales of securities are determined on a specific identification basis.

Interest income on fixed maturity securities is recorded when earned using an effective yield method giving effect to amortization of premiums and accretion of discounts. Dividends on equity securities are recorded when declared. Interest, dividends and prepayment fees are recorded in net investment income.

Included within fixed maturity securities are structured securities including mortgage-backed and asset-backed securities ("ABS"). Amortization of the premium or discount considers the estimated timing and amount of prepayments of the underlying loans. Actual prepayment experience is periodically reviewed and effective yields are recalculated when differences arise between the originally anticipated and the actual prepayments received and currently anticipated.

Prepayment assumptions for single class and multi-class mortgage-backed and ABS are estimated by management using inputs obtained from third-party specialists, including broker-dealers, and based on management's knowledge of the current market. For credit-sensitive mortgage-backed and ABS and certain prepayment-sensitive securities, the effective yield is recalculated on a prospective basis. For all other mortgage-backed and ABS, the effective yield is recalculated on a retrospective basis.

The Company periodically evaluates fixed maturity and equity securities for impairment. The assessment of whether impairments have occurred is based on management's case-by-case evaluation of the underlying reasons for the decline in estimated fair value. The Company's review of its fixed maturity and equity securities for impairments includes an analysis of the total gross unrealized losses by three categories of severity and/or age of the gross unrealized loss, as summarized in Note 3 "—Aging of Gross Unrealized Loss and OTTI Loss for Fixed Maturity and Equity Securities Available-for-Sale."

Management considers a wide range of factors about the security issuer and uses its best judgment in evaluating the cause of the decline in the estimated fair value of the security and in assessing the prospects for near-term recovery. Inherent in management's evaluation of the security are assumptions and estimates about the operations of the issuer and its future earnings potential. Considerations used by the Company in the impairment evaluation process include, but are not limited to: (i) the length of time and the extent to which the estimated fair value has been below cost or amortized cost; (ii) the potential for impairments of securities when the issuer is experiencing significant financial difficulties; (iii) the potential for impairments in an entire industry sector or sub-sector; (iv) the potential for impairments in certain economically depressed geographic locations; (v) the potential for impairments of securities where the issuer, series of issuers or industry has suffered a catastrophic type of loss or has exhausted natural resources; (vi) with respect to fixed maturity securities, whether the Company has the intent to sell or will more likely than not be required to sell a particular security before the decline in estimated fair value below amortized cost recovers; (vii) with respect to structured securities, changes in forecasted cash flows after considering the quality of underlying collateral; expected prepayment speeds; current and forecasted loss severity; consideration of the payment terms of the underlying assets backing a particular security; and the payment priority within the tranche structure of the security; and (viii) other subjective factors, including concentrations and information obtained from regulators and rating agencies.

For fixed maturity securities in an unrealized loss position, an other-than-temporary impairment ("OTTI") is recognized in earnings when it is anticipated that the amortized cost will not be recovered. In such situations, the OTTI recognized in earnings is the entire difference between the fixed maturity security's amortized cost and its estimated fair value only when either: (i) the Company has the intent to sell the fixed maturity security; or (ii) it is more likely than not that the Company will be required to sell the fixed maturity security before recovery of the decline in estimated fair value below amortized cost. If neither of these two conditions exist, the difference between the amortized cost of the fixed maturity security and the present value of projected future cash flows expected to be collected is recognized as an OTTI in earnings ("credit loss"). If the estimated fair value is less than the present value of projected future cash flows expected to be collected, this portion of OTTI related to other-than credit factors ("noncredit loss") is recorded in other comprehensive income (loss). Adjustments are not made for subsequent recoveries in value.

With respect to equity securities, the Company considers in its OTTI analysis its intent and ability to hold a particular equity security for a period of time sufficient to allow for the recovery of its estimated fair value to an amount equal to or greater than cost. If a sale decision is made for an equity security and it is not expected to recover to an amount at least equal to cost prior to the expected time of the sale, the security will be deemed other-than-temporarily impaired in the period that the sale decision was made and an OTTI loss will be recorded in earnings. When an OTTI loss has occurred, the OTTI loss is the entire difference between the equity security's cost and its estimated fair value with a corresponding charge to earnings.

Upon acquisition, the Company classifies perpetual securities that have attributes of both debt and equity as fixed maturity securities if the securities have an interest rate step-up feature which, when combined with other qualitative factors, indicates that the securities have more debt-like characteristics; while those with more equity-like characteristics are classified as equity securities within non-redeemable preferred stock. Many of such securities, commonly referred to as "perpetual hybrid securities," have been issued by non-U.S. financial institutions that are accorded the highest two capital treatment categories by their respective regulatory bodies (i.e. core capital, or "Tier 1 capital" and perpetual deferrable securities, or "Upper Tier 2 capital"). With respect to perpetual hybrid securities, the Company considers in its OTTI analysis whether there has been any deterioration in credit of the issuer and the likelihood of recovery in value of the securities that are in a severe and extended unrealized loss position. The Company also considers whether any perpetual hybrid securities, with an unrealized loss, regardless of credit rating, have deferred any dividend payments. When an OTTI loss has occurred, the OTTI loss is the entire difference between the perpetual hybrid security's cost and its estimated fair value with a corresponding charge to earnings.

The Company's methodology and significant inputs used to determine the amount of the credit loss on fixed maturity securities are as follows:

i. The Company calculates the recovery value by performing a discounted cash flow analysis based on the present value of future cash flows expected to be received. The discount rate is generally the effective interest rate of the fixed maturity security prior to impairment.

ii. When determining the collectability and the period over which value is expected to recover, the Company applies the same considerations utilized in its overall impairment evaluation process which incorporates information regarding the specific security, fundamentals of the industry and geographic area in which the security issuer operates, and overall macroeconomic conditions. Projected future cash flows are estimated using assumptions derived from management's best estimates of likely scenario-based outcomes after giving consideration to a variety of variables that include, but are not limited to: general payment terms of the security; the likelihood that the issuer can service the scheduled interest and principal payments; the quality and amount of any credit enhancements; the security's position within the capital structure of the issuer; possible corporate restructurings or asset sales by the issuer; and changes to the rating of the security or the issuer by rating agencies.

iii. Additional considerations are made when assessing the unique features that apply to certain structured securities such as residential mortgage-backed securities ("RMBS"), commercial mortgage-backed securities ("CMBS") and ABS. These additional factors for structured securities include, but are not limited to: the quality of underlying collateral; expected prepayment speeds; current and forecasted loss severity; consideration of the payment terms of the underlying assets backing a particular security; and the payment priority within the tranche structure of the security.

iv. When determining the amount of the credit loss for U.S. and foreign corporate securities, foreign government securities and state and political subdivision securities, management considers the estimated fair value as the recovery value when available information does not indicate that another value is more appropriate. When information is identified that indicates a recovery value other than estimated fair value, management considers in the determination of recovery value the same considerations utilized in its overall impairment evaluation process as described in (ii) above, as well as private and public sector programs to restructure foreign government securities.

The cost or amortized cost of fixed maturity and equity securities is adjusted for OTTI in the period in which the determination is made. The Company does not change the revised cost basis for subsequent recoveries in value.

In periods subsequent to the recognition of OTTI on a fixed maturity security, the Company accounts for the impaired security as if it had been purchased on the measurement date of the impairment. Accordingly, the discount (or reduced premium) based on the new cost basis is accreted into net investment income over the remaining term of the fixed maturity security in a prospective manner based on the amount and timing of estimated future cash flows.

Trading and Other Securities. Trading and other securities are stated at estimated fair value. Trading and other securities include investments that are actively purchased and sold ("Actively Traded Securities"). These Actively Traded Securities are principally fixed maturity securities. Short sale agreement liabilities related to Actively Traded Securities, included in other liabilities, are also stated at estimated fair value. Trading and other securities also includes securities for which the fair value option ("FVO") has been elected ("FVO Securities"). FVO Securities include certain fixed maturity and equity securities held-for-investment by the general account to support asset and liability matching strategies for certain insurance products. FVO Securities also include contractholder-directed investments supporting unit-linked variable annuity type liabilities which do not qualify for presentation and reporting as separate account summary total assets and liabilities. These investments are primarily mutual funds and, to a lesser extent, fixed maturity and equity securities, short-term investments and cash and cash equivalents. The investment returns on these investments inure to contractholders and are offset by a corresponding change in policyholder account balances ("PABs") through interest credited to policyholder account balances. Changes in estimated fair value of these securities subsequent to purchase are included in net investment income, except for certain fixed maturity securities included in FVO Securities where changes are included in net investment gains (losses). FVO Securities also include securities held by consolidated securitization entities ("CSEs") with changes in estimated fair value subsequent to consolidation included in net investment gains (losses). Interest and dividends related to all trading and other securities are included in net investment income.

Securities Lending. Securities lending transactions, whereby blocks of securities, which are included in fixed maturity securities and short-term investments, are loaned to third parties, are treated as financing arrangements and the associated liability is recorded at the amount of cash received. At the inception of a loan, the Company obtains collateral, usually cash, in an amount generally equal to 102% of the estimated fair value of the securities loaned and maintains it at a level greater than or equal to 100% for the duration of the loan. The Company monitors the estimated fair value of the securities loaned on a daily basis with additional collateral obtained as necessary. Income and expenses associated with securities lending transactions are reported as investment income and investment expense, respectively, within net investment income.

Mortgage Loans—Mortgage Loans Held-For-Investment. For the purposes of determining valuation allowances the Company disaggregates its mortgage loan investments into three portfolio segments: commercial, agricultural, and residential. The accounting and valuation allowance policies that are applicable to all portfolio segments are presented below, followed by the policies applicable to both commercial and agricultural loans, which are very similar, as well as policies applicable to residential loans. Also included in mortgage loans held-for-investment are commercial mortgage loans held by CSEs that were consolidated by the Company on January 1, 2010 upon the adoption of new guidance. The FVO was elected for these commercial mortgage loans, and thus they are stated at estimated fair value with changes in estimated fair value subsequent to consolidation recognized in net investment gains (losses).

Commercial, Agricultural and Residential Mortgage Loans—Mortgage loans held-for-investment are stated at unpaid principal balance, adjusted for any unamortized premium or discount, deferred fees or expenses, and net of valuation allowances. Interest income is accrued on the principal amount of the loan based on the loan's contractual interest rate. Amortization of premiums and discounts is recorded using the effective yield method. Interest income, amortization of premiums and discounts and prepayment fees are reported in net investment income. Interest ceases to accrue when collection of interest is not considered probable and/or when interest or principal payments are past due as follows: commercial—60 days; and agricultural and residential—90 days, unless, in the case of a residential loan, it is both well-secured and in the process of collection. When a loan is placed on non-accrual status, uncollected past due interest is charged-off against net investment income. Generally, the accrual of interest income resumes after all delinquent amounts are paid and management believes all future principal and interest payments will be collected. Cash receipts on non-accruing loans are recorded in accordance with the loan agreement as a reduction of principal and/or interest income. Charge-offs occur upon the realization of a credit loss, typically through foreclosure or after a decision is made to sell a loan, or for residential loans when, after considering the individual consumer's financial status, management believes that uncollectability is other-than-temporary. Gain or loss upon charge-off is recorded, net of previously established valuation allowances, in net investment gains (losses). Cash recoveries on principal amounts previously charged-off are generally recorded as an increase to the valuation allowance, unless the valuation allowance adequately provides for expected credit losses; then the recovery is recorded in net investment gains (losses). Gains and losses from sales of loans and increases or decreases to valuation allowances are recorded in net investment gains (losses).

Mortgage loans are considered to be impaired when it is probable that, based upon current information and events, the Company will be unable to collect all amounts due under the contractual terms of the loan agreement. Specific valuation allowances are established using the same methodology for all three portfolio segments as the excess carrying value of a loan over either (i) the present value of expected future cash flows discounted at the loan's original effective interest rate, (ii) the estimated fair value of the loan's underlying collateral if the loan is in the process of foreclosure or otherwise collateral dependent, or (iii) the loan's observable market price. A common evaluation framework is used for establishing non-specific valuation allowances for all loan portfolio segments; however, a separate non-specific valuation allowance is calculated and maintained for each loan portfolio segment that is based on inputs unique to each loan portfolio segment. Non-specific valuation allowances are established for pools of loans with similar risk characteristics where a property-specific or market-specific risk has not been identified, but for which the Company expects to incur a credit loss. These evaluations are based upon several loan portfolio segment-specific factors, including the Company's experience for loan losses, defaults and loss severity, and loss expectations for loans with similar risk characteristics. These evaluations are revised as conditions change and new information becomes available.

For commercial and agricultural mortgage loans, the Company typically uses 10 years or more of historical experience in establishing non-specific valuation allowances. For commercial mortgage loans, 20 years of historical experience is used which captures multiple economic cycles. For evaluations of commercial mortgage loans, in addition to historical experience, management considers factors that include the impact of a rapid change to the economy, which may not be reflected in the loan portfolio, and recent loss and recovery trend experience as compared to historical loss and recovery experience. For agricultural mortgage loans, ten years of historical experience is used which captures a full economic cycle. For evaluations of agricultural loans, in addition to historical experience, management considers factors that include increased stress in certain sectors, which may be evidenced by higher delinquency rates, or a change in the number of higher risk loans. For commercial and agricultural mortgage loans, on a quarterly basis, management incorporates the impact of these current market events and conditions on historical experience in determining the non-specific valuation allowance established for each portfolio segment level. For evaluations of residential mortgage loans, the key inputs of expected frequency and expected loss reflect current market conditions, with expected frequency adjusted, when appropriate, for differences from market conditions and the Company's experience.

Commercial and Agricultural Mortgage Loans—All commercial loans are reviewed on an ongoing basis which may include an analysis of the property financial statements and rent roll, lease rollover analysis, property inspections, market analysis, estimated valuations of the underlying collateral, loan-to-value ratios, debt service coverage ratios, and tenant creditworthiness. All agricultural loans are monitored on an ongoing basis. The monitoring process focuses on higher risk loans, which include those that are classified as restructured, potentially delinquent, delinquent or in foreclosure, as well as loans with higher loan-to-value ratios and lower debt service coverage ratios. The monitoring process for agricultural loans is generally similar, with a focus on higher risk loans, including reviews on a geographic and property-type basis. Higher risk commercial and agricultural loans are reviewed individually on an ongoing basis for potential credit loss and specific valuation allowances are established using the methodology described above for all loan portfolio segments. Quarterly, the remaining loans are reviewed on a pool basis by aggregating groups of loans that have similar risk characteristics for potential credit loss, and non-specific valuation allowances are established as described above using inputs that are unique to each segment of the loan portfolio.

For commercial loans, the Company's primary credit quality indicator is the debt service coverage ratio, which compares a property's net operating income to amounts needed to service the principal and interest due under the loan. Generally, the lower the debt service coverage ratio, the higher the risk of experiencing a credit loss. The Company also reviews the loan-to-value ratio of its commercial loan portfolio. Loan-to-value ratios compare the unpaid principal balance of the loan to the estimated fair value of the underlying collateral. A loan-to-value ratio greater than 100% indicates that the loan's unpaid principal balance is greater than the collateral value. A loan-to-value ratio of less than 100% indicates an excess of collateral value over the loan's unpaid principal balance. Generally, the higher the loan-to-value ratio, the higher the risk of experiencing a credit loss. The debt service

coverage ratio and loan-to-value ratio, as well as the values utilized in calculating these ratios, are updated annually, on a rolling basis, with a portion of the loan portfolio updated each quarter.

For agricultural loans, the Company's primary credit quality indicator is the loan-to-value ratio. The values utilized in calculating this ratio are developed in connection with the ongoing review of the agricultural loan portfolio and are routinely updated.

Residential Mortgage Loans—The Company's residential loan portfolio is comprised primarily of closed end, amortizing residential loans and home equity lines of credit and it does not hold any optional adjustable rate mortgages, subprime, or low teaser rate loans.

In contrast to the commercial and agricultural loan portfolios, residential loans are smaller-balance homogeneous loans that are collectively evaluated for impairment. Non-specific valuation allowances are established using the evaluation framework described above for pools of loans with similar risk characteristics from inputs that are unique to the residential segment of the loan portfolio. Loan specific valuation allowances are only established on residential loans when they have been restructured and are established using the methodology described above for all loan portfolio segments.

For residential loans, the Company's primary credit quality indicator is whether the loan is performing or non-performing. The Company generally defines non-performing residential loans as those that are 90 or more days past due and/or in non-accrual status. The determination of performing or non-performing status is assessed monthly. Generally, non-performing residential loans have a higher risk of experiencing a credit loss.

Mortgage Loans Modified in a Troubled Debt Restructuring. For a small portion of the portfolio, classified as troubled debt restructurings, concessions are granted related to the borrowers' financial difficulties. Generally, the types of concessions include: reduction of the contractual interest rate, extension of the maturity date at an interest rate lower than current market interest rates and/or a reduction of accrued interest. The amount, timing and extent of the concession granted is considered in determining any impairment or changes in the specific valuation allowance recorded in connection with the troubled debt restructuring. Through the continuous portfolio monitoring process, a specific valuation allowance may have been recorded prior to the quarter when the mortgage loan is modified in a troubled debt restructuring. Accordingly, the carrying value (after specific valuation allowance) before and after modification through a troubled debt restructuring may not change significantly, or may increase if the expected recovery is higher than the pre-modification recovery assessment.

Mortgage Loans—Mortgage Loans Held-For-Sale. This caption includes three categories of mortgage loans:

Residential mortgage loans—held-for-sale. Forward and reverse residential mortgage loans originated with the intent to sell, for which the FVO was elected, are stated at estimated fair value. Subsequent changes in estimated fair value are recognized in other revenues.

Mortgage loans—held-for-sale—lower of amortized cost or estimated fair value. Mortgage loans that were previously designated as held-for-investment, but now are designated as held-for-sale, are stated at the lower of amortized cost or estimated fair value. At the time of transfer to held-for-sale status, such mortgage loans are recorded at the lower of amortized cost or estimated fair value, or for collateral dependent loans, estimated fair value less expected disposition costs, with any loss recognized in net investment gains (losses).

Securitized Reverse Residential Mortgage Loans. Reverse residential mortgage loans originated with the intent to sell which have been sold into Government National Mortgage Association ("GNMA") securitizations, for which the FVO was elected, are stated at estimated fair value. Prior to December 31, 2011, consistent with historical industry practice, these standard form loans were de-recognized from the balance sheet upon the GNMA securitization. However, after an industry led review of the GNMA securitization program, the Company has determined that these securitized reverse residential mortgage loans do not qualify for de-recognition. Therefore, as of December 31, 2011 the Company recorded $7.7 billion of reverse mortgage loans, included within mortgage loans held-for-sale. The FVO was also elected for the $7.6 billion corresponding liability, included within other liabilities. Subsequent changes in estimated fair value of both the asset and liability are recognized in other revenues. The Company's economic exposure is generally limited to its servicing rights. Prior year amounts have not been included in the financial statements as these amounts were not material to such financial statements.

Policy Loans. Policy loans are stated at unpaid principal balances. Interest income on such loans is recorded as earned in net investment income using the contractually agreed upon interest rate. Generally, interest is capitalized on the policy's anniversary date. Valuation allowances are not established for policy loans, as these loans are fully collateralized by the cash surrender value of the underlying insurance policies. Any unpaid principal or interest on the loan is deducted from the cash surrender value or the death benefit prior to settlement of the policy.

Real Estate. Real estate held-for-investment, including related improvements, is stated at cost less accumulated depreciation. Depreciation is provided on a straight-line basis over the estimated useful life of the asset (typically 20 to 55 years). Rental income is recognized on a straight-line basis over the term of the respective leases. The Company classifies a property as held-for-sale if it commits to a plan to sell a property within one year and actively markets the property in its current condition for a price that is reasonable in comparison to its estimated fair value. The Company classifies the results of operations and the gain or loss on sale of a property that either has been disposed of or classified as held-for-sale as discontinued operations, if the ongoing operations of the property will be eliminated from the ongoing operations of the Company and if the Company will not have any significant continuing involvement in the operations of the property after the sale. Real estate held-for-sale is stated at the lower of depreciated cost or estimated fair value less expected disposition costs. Real estate is not depreciated while it is classified as held-for-sale. The Company periodically reviews its properties held-for-investment for impairment and tests properties for recoverability whenever events or changes in circumstances indicate the carrying amount of the asset may not be recoverable and the carrying value of the property exceeds its estimated fair value. Properties whose carrying values are greater than their undiscounted cash flows are written down to their estimated fair value, with the impairment loss included in net investment gains (losses). Impairment losses are based upon the estimated fair value of real estate, which is generally computed using the present value of expected future cash flows discounted at a rate commensurate with the underlying risks. Real estate acquired upon foreclosure is recorded at the lower of estimated fair value or the carrying value of the mortgage loan at the date of foreclosure.

Real Estate Joint Ventures and Other Limited Partnership Interests. The Company uses the equity method of accounting for investments in real estate joint ventures and other limited partnership interests consisting of leveraged buy-out funds, hedge funds and other private equity funds in which it has more than a minor ownership interest or more than a minor influence over the joint venture's or partnership's operations, but does not have a controlling interest and is not the primary beneficiary. The equity method is also used for such investments in which the Company has more than a minor influence or more than a 20% interest. Generally, the Company records its share of earnings using a three-month lag methodology for instances where the timely financial information is not available and the contractual agreements provide for the delivery of the investees' financial information after the end of the Company's reporting period. The Company uses the cost method of accounting for investments in real estate joint ventures and other limited partnership interests in which it has a minor equity investment and virtually no influence over the joint venture's or the partnership's operations. Based on the nature and structure of these investments, they do not meet the characteristics of an equity security. The Company reports the distributions from real estate joint ventures and other limited partnership interests accounted for under the cost method and equity in earnings from real estate joint ventures and other limited partnership interests accounted for under the equity method in net investment income. In addition to the investees performing regular evaluations for the impairment of underlying investments, the Company routinely evaluates its investments in real estate joint ventures and other limited partnerships for impairments. The Company considers its cost method investments for OTTI when the carrying value of real estate joint ventures and other limited partnership interests exceeds the net asset value ("NAV"). The Company takes into consideration the severity and duration of this excess when deciding if the cost method investment is other-than-temporarily impaired. For equity method investees, the Company considers financial and other information provided by the investee, other known information and inherent risks in the underlying investments, as well as future capital commitments, in determining whether an impairment has occurred. When an OTTI is deemed to have occurred, the Company records a realized capital loss within net investment gains (losses) to record the investment at its estimated fair value.

Short-term Investments. Short-term investments include securities and other investments with remaining maturities of one year or less, but greater than three months, at the time of purchase and are stated at estimated fair value or amortized cost, which approximates estimated fair value.

Other Invested Assets. Other invested assets consist principally of freestanding derivatives with positive estimated fair values, leveraged leases, investments in insurance enterprise joint ventures, tax credit partnerships, funding agreements, mortgage servicing rights ("MSRs") and funds withheld.

Freestanding derivatives with positive estimated fair values are described in "—Derivative Financial Instruments" below.

Leveraged leases are recorded net of non-recourse debt. The Company recognizes income on the leveraged leases by applying the leveraged lease's estimated rate of return to the net investment in the lease. The Company regularly reviews residual values and impairs them to expected values.

Joint venture investments represent the Company's investments in entities that engage in insurance underwriting activities and are accounted for under the equity method.

Tax credit partnerships are established for the purpose of investing in low-income housing and other social causes, where the primary return on investment is in the form of income tax credits and are accounted for under the equity method or under the effective yield method. The Company reports the equity in earnings of joint venture investments and tax credit partnerships in net investment income.

Funding agreements represent arrangements where the Company has long-term interest bearing amounts on deposit with third parties and are generally stated at amortized cost.

MSRs are measured at estimated fair value and are either acquired or are generated from the sale of originated residential mortgage loans where the servicing rights are retained by the Company. Changes in estimated fair value of MSRs are reported in other revenues in the period in which the change occurs.

Funds withheld represent a receivable for amounts contractually withheld by ceding companies in accordance with reinsurance agreements. The Company recognizes interest on funds withheld at rates defined by the terms of the agreement which may be contractually specified or directly related to the underlying investments and records it in net investment income.

3. Investments (in part)

Net Investment Gains (Losses)

The components of net investment gains (losses) were as follows:

(In millions)	Years Ended December 31		
	2011	2010	2009
Total gains (losses) on fixed maturity securities:			
Total OTTI losses recognized	$(924)	$(682)	$(2,432)
Less: Noncredit portion of OTTI losses transferred to and recognized in other comprehensive income (loss)	(31)	212	939
Net OTTI losses on fixed maturity securities recognized in earnings[1]	(955)	(470)	(1,493)
Fixed maturity securities—net gains (losses) on sales and disposals	25	215	(165)
Total gains (losses) on fixed maturity securities	(930)	(255)	(1,658)
Other net investment gains (losses):			
Equity securities	(23)	104	(399)
Trading and other securities—FVO general account securities—changes in estimated fair value	(2)	—	—
Mortgage loans	175	22	(442)
Real estate and real estate joint ventures	134	(54)	(164)
Other limited partnership interests	4	(18)	(356)
Other investment portfolio gains (losses)	(7)	(6)	(26)
Subtotal—investment portfolio gains (losses)	(649)	(207)	(3,045)
FVO CSEs—changes in estimated fair value:			
Commercial mortgage loans	(84)	758	—
Securities	—	(78)	—
Long-term debt—related to commercial mortgage loans	97	(722)	—
Long-term debt—related to securities	(8)	48	—
Other gains (losses)[2]	(223)	(207)	144
Subtotal FVO CSEs and other gains (losses)	(218)	(201)	144
Total net investment gains (losses)	$(867)	$(408)	$(2,901)

[1] Investment portfolio gains (losses) for the year ended December 31, 2011 includes intent-to-sell impairments of ($154) million as a result of the pending disposition of certain operations of MetLife Bank and the Caribbean Business. See Note 2.

[2] Other gains (losses) includes a loss of $87 million and $209 million for the years ended December 31, 2011 and 2010, respectively, related to the sale of the Company's investment in MSI MetLife. See Note 2. Other gains (losses) for the year ended December 31, 2011 includes a goodwill impairment loss of $65 million and a loss of $19 million related to the Company's pending sale of the Caribbean Business. See Notes 2 and 7.

See "—Variable Interest Entities" for discussion of CSEs included in the table above.

Gains (losses) from foreign currency transactions included within net investment gains (losses) were $37 million, $230 million and $226 million for the years ended December 31, 2011, 2010 and 2009, respectively.

Proceeds from sales or disposals of fixed maturity and equity securities and the components of fixed maturity and equity securities net investment gains (losses) were as shown in the table below. Investment gains and losses on sales of securities are determined on a specific identification basis.

(In millions)	Years Ended December 31			Years Ended December 31			Years Ended December 31		
	2011	2010	2009	2011	2010	2009	2011	2010	2009
	Fixed Maturity Securities			Equity Securities			Total		
Proceeds	$67,449	$54,514	$38,972	$1,241	$616	$ 940	$68,690	$55,130	$39,912
Gross investment gains	$ 892	$ 831	$ 939	$ 108	$129	$ 134	$ 1,000	$ 960	$ 1,073
Gross investment losses	(867)	(616)	(1,104)	(71)	(11)	(133)	(938)	(627)	(1,237)
Total OTTI losses recognized in earnings:									
Credit-related	(645)	(423)	(1,130)	—	—	—	(645)	(423)	(1,130)
Other[1]	(310)	(47)	(363)	(60)	(14)	(400)	(370)	(61)	(763)
Total OTTI losses recognized in earnings	(955)	(470)	(1,493)	(60)	(14)	(400)	(1,015)	(484)	(1,893)
Net investment gains (losses)	(930)	(255)	$ (1,658)	$ (23)	(104)	$(399)	$ (953)	$ (151)	$ (2,057)

[1] Other OTTI losses recognized in earnings include impairments on equity securities, impairments on perpetual hybrid securities classified within fixed maturity securities where the primary reason for the impairment was the severity and/or the duration of an unrealized loss position and fixed maturity securities where there is an intent to sell or it is more likely than not that the Company will be required to sell the security before recovery of the decline in estimated fair value.

Fixed maturity security OTTI losses recognized in earnings related to the following sectors and industries within the U.S. and foreign corporate securities sector:

(In millions)	Years Ended December 31		
	2011	2010	2009
Sector:			
U.S. and foreign corporate securities—by industry:			
Finance	$ 56	$126	$ 452
Consumer	50	36	211
Communications	41	16	235
Industrial	11	2	30
Utility	10	3	89
Other industries	1	—	26
Total U.S. and foreign corporate securities	169	183	1,043
Foreign government securities	486	—	1
RMBS	214	117	258
ABS	54	84	103
CMBS	32	86	88
Total	$955	$470	$1,493

Equity security OTTI losses recognized in earnings related to the following sectors and industries:

(In millions)	Years Ended December 31		
	2011	2010	2009
Sector:			
Non-redeemable preferred stock	$38	$ 7	$333
Common stock	22	7	67
Total	$60	$14	$400
Industry:			
Financial services industry:			
Perpetual hybrid securities	$38	$ 3	$310
Common and remaining non-redeemable preferred stock	—	—	30
Total financial services industry	38	3	340
Other industries	22	11	60
Total	$60	$14	$400

SEC 3.42

Impairment of Intangibles

3.43

CONSTELLATION BRANDS, INC. (FEB)

CONSOLIDATED STATEMENTS OF OPERATIONS
(in part)

(In millions, except per share data)

	For the Years Ended		
	February 28, 2011	**February 28, 2010**	**February 28, 2009**
Sales	$ 4,096.7	$ 4,213.0	$ 4,723.0
Less—excise taxes	(764.7)	(848.2)	(1,068.4)
Net sales	3,332.0	3,364.8	3,654.6
Cost of product sold	(2,141.9)	(2,220.0)	(2,424.6)
Gross profit	1,190.1	1,144.8	1,230.0
Selling, general and administrative expenses	(640.9)	(682.5)	(832.0)
Impairment of goodwill and intangible assets	(23.6)	(103.2)	(300.4)
Restructuring charges	(23.1)	(47.6)	(68.0)
Operating income	502.5	311.5	29.6

NOTES TO CONSOLIDATED FINANCIAL STATEMENTS

February 28, 2011

1. Summary of Significant Accounting Policies (in part)

Goodwill and Other Intangible Assets (in part)

In accordance with the FASB guidance for intangibles—goodwill and other, the Company reviews its goodwill and indefinite lived intangible assets annually for impairment, or sooner, if events or changes in circumstances indicate that the carrying amount of an asset may not be recoverable. The Company uses January 1 as its annual impairment test measurement date. Indefinite lived intangible assets consist principally of trademarks. Intangible assets determined to have a finite life, primarily customer relationships, are amortized over their estimated useful lives and are subject to review for impairment in accordance with the FASB guidance for property, plant and equipment. Note 8 provides a summary of intangible assets segregated between amortizable and nonamortizable amounts.

In the fourth quarter of fiscal 2011, pursuant to the Company's accounting policy, the Company performed its annual review of indefinite lived intangible assets for impairment. The Company determined that certain trademarks associated primarily with the CWNA segment's Canadian reporting unit were impaired largely due to lower revenue and profitability associated with products incorporating these assets included in long-term financial forecasts developed as part of the strategic planning cycle conducted during the Company's fourth quarter. The Company measured the amount of impairment by calculating the amount by which the carrying value of these assets exceeded their estimated fair values, which were based on projected discounted cash flows (Level 3 fair value measurement—see Note 6). As a result of this review, the Company recorded impairment losses of $16.7 million, which are included in impairment of goodwill

and intangible assets on the Company's Consolidated Statements of Operations. The Company had previously recorded impairment losses of $6.9 million, which are included in impairment of goodwill and intangible assets on the Company's Consolidated Statements of Operations, during its third quarter of fiscal 2011 in connection with its decision to discontinue certain wine brands within its CWNA segment's wine portfolio (Level 3 fair value measurement—see Note 6). In the fourth quarter of fiscal 2010, as a result of its annual review of indefinite lived intangible assets for impairment, the Company determined that certain trademarks associated primarily with the CWAE segment's Australian reporting unit were impaired largely due to lower revenue and profitability associated with products incorporating these assets included in long-term financial forecasts developed as part of the strategic planning cycle conducted during the Company's fourth quarter. The Company measured the amount of impairment by calculating the amount by which the carrying value of these assets exceeded their estimated fair values, which were based on projected discounted cash flows (Level 3 fair value measurement—see Note 6). As a result of this review, the Company recorded impairment losses of $103.2 million, which are included in impairment of goodwill and intangible assets on the Company's Consolidated Statements of Operations. In the fourth quarter of fiscal 2009, as a result of its annual review of indefinite lived intangible assets for impairment, the Company determined that certain trademarks associated primarily with the CWAE segment's U.K. reporting unit were impaired largely due to the aforementioned market declines in the U.K. during the fourth quarter of fiscal 2009, and the resulting lower revenue and profit forecasts associated with products incorporating these assets which reflected the significant fourth quarter deterioration in market conditions in the U.K. The Company measured the amount of impairment by calculating the amount by which the carrying value of these assets exceeded their estimated fair values, which were based on projected discounted cash flows. As a result of this review, the Company recorded impairment losses of $25.9 million, which are included in impairment of goodwill and intangible assets on the Company's Consolidated Statements of Operations. The Company had previously recorded impairment losses of $21.8 million during its second quarter of fiscal 2009 in connection with the Company's Australian Initiative (as defined in Note 21) and the resulting lower revenue and profit forecasts associated with certain brands incorporating these assets impacted by the Australian Initiative.

6. Fair Value of Financial Instruments (in part)

Trademarks:

For the year ended February 28, 2011, in connection with the Company's annual review of indefinite lived intangible assets for impairment, certain trademarks, with a carrying value of $153.9 million, were written down to their fair value of $136.9 million, resulting in an impairment of $16.7 million. In addition, in connection with the Company's third quarter of fiscal 2011 decision to discontinue certain wine brands within its CWNA segment's wine portfolio, certain indefinite-lived trademarks, with a carrying value of $6.9 million, were written down to their estimated fair value resulting in an impairment of $6.9 million. For the year ended February 28, 2010, in connection with the Company's annual review of indefinite lived intangible assets for impairment, certain trademarks, with a carrying value of $266.3 million, were written down to their fair value

of $162.7 million, resulting in an impairment of $103.2 million for the year ended February 28, 2010. These impairments are included in impairment of goodwill and intangible assets on the Company's Consolidated Statements of Operations. For each period, the Company measured the amount of impairment by calculating the amount by which the carrying value of these assets exceeded their estimated fair values. The fair value was determined based on an income approach using the relief from royalty method, which assumes that, in lieu of ownership, a third party would be willing to pay a royalty in order to exploit the related benefits of trademark assets. The cash flow models the Company uses to estimate the fair values of its trademarks involve several assumptions, including (i) projected revenue growth rates; (ii) estimated royalty rates; (iii) calculated after-tax royalty savings expected from ownership of the subject trademarks; and (iv) discount rates used to derive the present value factors used in determining the fair value of the trademarks.

Loss on Extinguishment of Debt

3.44

PHILLIPS-VAN HEUSEN CORPORATION (JAN)

CONSOLIDATED INCOME STATEMENTS (in part)

(In thousands, except per share data)

	2010	2009	2008
Net sales	$4,219,739	$2,070,754	$2,160,716
Royalty revenue	309,642	242,026	236,552
Advertising and other revenue	107,467	85,951	94,667
Total revenue	4,636,848	2,398,731	2,491,935
Cost of goods sold	2,214,897	1,216,128	1,291,267
Gross profit	2,421,951	1,182,603	1,200,668
Selling, general and administrative expenses	2,071,416	938,791	1,028,784
Debt extinguishment costs	6,650	—	—
Other loss	140,490	—	—
Gain on sale of investments	—	—	1,864
Income before interest and taxes	203,395	243,812	173,748

NOTES TO CONSOLIDATED FINANCIAL STATEMENTS

(Currency and share amounts in thousands, except per share data)

6. Debt (in part)

Tender for and Redemption of 2011 Notes and 2013 Notes

The Company commenced tender offers on April 7, 2010 for (i) all of the $150,000 outstanding principal amount of its notes due 2011; and (ii) all of the $150,000 outstanding principal amount of its notes due 2013. The tender offers expired on May 4, 2010. On May 6, 2010, the Company accepted for

purchase all of the notes tendered and made payment to tendering holders and called for redemption all of the balance of its outstanding 7 1/4% senior notes due 2011 and all of the balance of its outstanding 8 1/8% senior notes due 2013. The redemption prices of the notes due 2011 and 2013 were 100.000% and 101.354%, respectively, of the outstanding aggregate principal amount of each applicable note, plus accrued and unpaid interest thereon to the redemption date. On May 6, 2010, the Company made an irrevocable payment, including accrued and unpaid interest, to the trustee for the notes due 2011 and 2013. As a result, such notes were satisfied and effectively discharged as of May 6, 2010.

The Company incurred costs of $6,650 during the second quarter of 2010 on the extinguishment of its 7 1/4% senior notes due 2011 and its 8 1/8% senior notes due 2013.

PENSIONS AND OTHER POSTRETIREMENT BENEFITS

RECOGNITION AND MEASUREMENT

3.45 FASB ASC 715, *Compensation—Retirement Benefits*, requires that an entity recognize the overfunded or underfunded status of a single-employer defined benefit postretirement plan as an asset or a liability in its statement of financial position, recognize changes in that funded status in comprehensive income, and disclose in the notes to the financial statements additional information about net periodic benefit cost. FASB ASC 715 requires an entity to recognize as components of other comprehensive income the gains or losses and prior service costs or credits that arise during a period but are not recognized in the income statement as components of net periodic benefit cost of a period. Those amounts recognized in accumulated other comprehensive income are adjusted as they are subsequently recognized in the income statement as components of net periodic benefit cost. Additionally, FASB ASC 715 requires that an entity measure plan assets and benefit obligations as of the date of its fiscal year-end statement of financial position. An employer whose equity securities are publicly traded is required to initially recognize the funded status of a defined benefit postretirement plan.

DISCLOSURE

3.46 FASB ASC 715 states the disclosure requirements for pensions and other postretirement benefits, including disclosures about the assets, obligations, cash flows, investment strategy, and net periodic benefit cost of defined pension and postretirement plans. FASB ASC 715 also includes disclosures related to multiemployer plans. FASB ASC 715-20 calls for different disclosures about defined benefit plans for public and nonpublic entities.

3.47 The disclosure requirements of FASB ASC 715 include, but are not limited to, the actuarial gains and losses, the assumed health care cost trend rate for other postretirement benefits, the allocation by major category of plan assets, the inputs and valuation techniques used to measure the fair value of plan assets, the effect of fair value measurements using significant unobservable inputs (level 3) on changes in plan assets for the period, and significant concentrations of risk within plan assets.

3.48 In September 2011, FASB issued ASU No. 2011-09, *Compensation—Retirement Benefits—Multiemployer Plans (Subtopic 715-80): Disclosures about an Employer's Participation in a Multiemployer Plan*, to improve transparency about such plans by requiring employers to provide additional disclosures. An entity should include additional details in these disclosures, including plan names and identifying numbers for significant multiemployer plans, the level of employers' participation in the plans, the financial health of the plans, and the nature of the employer commitments to the plans. The amendments in this Update are effective for public and nonpublic entities for fiscal years ending after December 15, 2011, and December 15, 2012, respectively.

PRESENTATION AND DISCLOSURE EXCERPTS

Defined Benefit Plans

3.49

BECTON, DICKINSON AND COMPANY (SEP)

NOTES TO CONSOLIDATED FINANCIAL STATEMENTS

Thousands of dollars, except per share amounts and numbers of shares

Note 8—Benefit Plans (in part)

The Company has defined benefit pension plans covering substantially all of its employees in the United States and certain foreign locations. The Company also provides certain postretirement healthcare and life insurance benefits to qualifying domestic retirees. Postretirement healthcare and life insurance benefit plans in foreign countries are not material. The measurement date used for the Company's employee benefit plans is September 30.

Net pension and other postretirement cost for the years ended September 30 included the following components:

	Pension Plans			Other Postretirement Benefits		
	2011	**2010**	**2009**	**2011**	**2010**	**2009**
Service cost	$ 88,692	$ 72,901	$55,004	$ 5,842	$ 5,007	$ 3,441
Interest cost	93,228	90,432	87,480	13,143	14,190	15,338
Expected return on plan assets	(103,081)	(99,199)	(86,819)	—	—	—
Amortization of prior service (credit) cost	(1,294)	(1,091)	(1,099)	(686)	4	(463)
Amortization of loss (gain)	55,735	41,812	17,235	4,465	3,408	(143)
Amortization of net asset	(34)	(47)	(59)	—	—	—
Curtailment/settlement loss	1,096	—	—	—	—	—
	$134,342	$104,808	$71,742	$22,764	$22,609	$18,173

Net pension cost attributable to foreign plans included in the preceding table was $34,429, $25,820 and $24,971 in 2011, 2010 and 2009, respectively.

The change in benefit obligation, change in fair value of plan assets, funded status and amounts recognized in the Consolidated Balance Sheets for these plans were as follows:

	Pension Plans		Other Postretirement Benefits	
	2011	2010	2011	2010
Change in Benefit Obligation:				
Beginning obligation	$1,911,295	$1,635,334	$ 260,124	$ 249,593
Service cost	88,692	72,901	5,842	5,007
Interest cost	93,228	90,432	13,143	14,190
Plan amendments	(3,683)	60	—	(6,702)
Benefits paid	(108,381)	(101,394)	(25,776)	(25,046)
Actuarial loss	22,146	224,890	8,277	16,233
Other, includes translation	(6,856)	(10,928)	7,848	6,849
Benefit obligation at September 30	$1,996,441	$1,911,295	$ 269,458	$ 260,124
Change in Fair Value of Plan Assets:				
Beginning fair value	$1,413,848	$1,209,135	$ —	$ —
Actual return on plan assets	1,391	109,310	—	—
Employer contribution	53,505	207,775	—	—
Benefits paid	(108,381)	(101,394)	—	—
Other, includes translation	(7,633)	(10,978)	—	—
Plan assets at September 30	$1,352,730	$1,413,848	$ —	$ —
Funded Status at September 30:				
Unfunded benefit obligation	$ (643,711)	$ (497,447)	$(269,458)	$(260,124)
Amounts Recognized in the Consolidated Balance Sheets at September 30:				
Other	$ 3,217	$ 143	$ —	$ —
Salaries, wages and related items	(6,042)	(6,492)	(18,188)	(17,875)
Long-term Employee Benefit Obligations	(640,886)	(491,098)	(251,270)	(242,249)
Net amount recognized	$ (643,711)	$ (497,447)	$(269,458)	$(260,124)
Amounts Recognized in Accumulated Other Comprehensive (Loss) Income Before Income Taxes at September 30:				
Net transition asset	$ 398	$ 513	$ —	$ —
Prior service credit	9,193	6,530	6,013	6,699
Net actuarial loss	(911,146)	(843,284)	(70,653)	(67,009)
Net amount recognized	$ (901,555)	$ (836,241)	$ (64,640)	$ (60,310)

Foreign pension plan assets at fair value included in the preceding table were $419,452 and $402,298 at September 30, 2011 and 2010, respectively. The foreign pension plan projected benefit obligations were $500,969 and $560,640 at September 30, 2011 and 2010, respectively.

Pension plans with accumulated benefit obligations in excess of plan assets and plans with projected benefit obligations in excess of plan assets consist of the following at September 30:

	Accumulated Benefit Obligation Exceeds the Fair Value of Plan Assets		Projected Benefit Obligation Exceeds the Fair Value of Plan Assets	
	2011	2010	2011	2010
Projected benefit obligation	$1,616,534	$1,669,986	$1,862,441	$1,903,939
Accumulated benefit obligation	$1,338,643	$1,410,029		
Fair value of plan assets	$ 989,043	$1,224,095	$1,215,513	$1,406,349

The estimated net actuarial loss and prior service credit for pension benefits that will be amortized from Accumulated other comprehensive (loss) income into net pension costs over the next fiscal year are expected to be $(62,700) and $1,772, respectively. The estimated net actuarial loss and prior service credit for other postretirement benefits that will be amortized from Accumulated other comprehensive (loss) income into net other postretirement costs over the next fiscal year are expected to be $(4,645) and $690, respectively.

The weighted average assumptions used in determining pension plan information were as follows:

	2011	2010	2009
Net Cost			
Discount rate:			
U.S. plans[(A)]	5.20%	5.90%	8.00%
Foreign plans	4.68	5.63	6.03
Expected return on plan assets:			
U.S. plans	8.00	8.00	8.00
Foreign plans	6.31	6.38	6.45
Rate of compensation increase:			
U.S. plans[(A)]	4.50	4.50	4.50
Foreign plans	3.56	3.35	3.56
Benefit Obligation			
Discount rate:			
U.S. plans[(A)]	4.90	5.20	5.90
Foreign plans	5.26	4.68	5.63
Rate of compensation increase:			
U.S. plans[(A)]	4.25	4.50	4.50
Foreign plans	3.61	3.56	3.35

[(A)] Also used to determine other postretirement and postemployment benefit plan information.

At September 30, 2011 the assumed healthcare trend rates were 7.6% pre and post age 65, gradually decreasing to an ultimate rate of 5.0% beginning in 2024. At September 30, 2010 the corresponding assumed healthcare trend rates were 7.8% pre and post age 65, gradually decreasing to an ultimate rate of 4.5% beginning in 2027. A one percentage point increase in assumed healthcare cost trend rates in each year would increase the accumulated postretirement benefit obligation as of September 30, 2011 by $8,566 and the aggregate of the service cost and interest cost components of 2011 annual expense by $828. A one percentage point decrease in the assumed healthcare cost trend rates in each year would decrease the accumulated postretirement benefit obligation as of September 30, 2011 by $7,617 and the aggregate of the 2011 service cost and interest cost by $723.

Expected Rate of Return on Plan Assets

The expected rate of return on plan assets is based upon expectations of long-term average rates of return to be achieved by the underlying investment portfolios. In establishing this assumption, the Company considers many factors, including historical assumptions compared with actual results; benchmark data; expected returns on various plan asset classes, as well as current and expected asset allocations.

Expected Funding

The Company's funding policy for its defined benefit pension plans is to contribute amounts sufficient to meet legal funding requirements, plus any additional amounts that may be appropriate considering the funded status of the plans, tax consequences, the cash flow generated by the Company and other factors. While the Company does not anticipate any significant required contributions to its pension plans in 2012, the Company made a discretionary contribution of $100,000 to its U.S. pension plan in October 2011.

Expected benefit payments are as follows:

	Pension Plans	Other Postretirement Benefits
2012	$128,921	$18,188
2013	96,178	18,708
2014	101,061	19,224
2015	111,483	19,778
2016	116,066	20,199
2017–2021	735,367	102,714

Expected receipts of the subsidy under the Medicare Prescription Drug Improvement and Modernization Act of 2003, which are not reflected in the expected other postretirement benefit payments included in the preceding table, are as follows: 2012, $2,314; 2013, $2,440; 2014, $2,549; 2015, $2,623; 2016, $2,684; 2017–2021, $13,800.

Investments

The Company's primary objective is to achieve returns sufficient to meet future benefit obligations. It seeks to generate above market returns by investing in more volatile asset classes such as equities while at the same time controlling risk with allocations to more stable asset classes like fixed income.

U.S. Plans

The Company's U.S. plans comprise 69% of total benefit plan investments, based on September 30, 2011 market values, and have a target asset mix of 65% equities and 35% fixed income. This mix was established based on an analysis of projected benefit payments and estimates of long-term returns, volatilities and correlations for various asset classes. The mix is reviewed periodically by the named fiduciary of the plans and is intended to provide above-market returns at an acceptable level of risk over time.

The established target mix includes ranges by which the target may deviate in order to accommodate normal market fluctuations. Routine cash flows are used to bring the mix closer to target and a move outside of the acceptable ranges will signal the potential for a formal rebalancing, based on an assessment of current market conditions and transaction costs. Any tactical deviations from the established asset mix require the approval of the named fiduciary.

The U.S. plans may enter into both exchange traded and non-exchange traded derivative transactions in order to manage interest rate exposure, volatility, term structure of interest rates, and sector and currency exposures within the fixed income portfolios. The Company has established minimum credit quality standards for counterparties in such transactions.

The following table provides the fair value measurements of U.S. plan assets, as well as the measurement techniques and inputs utilized to measure fair value of these assets, at September 30, 2011 and 2010.

	Total U.S. Plan Asset Balances at September 30, 2011	Quoted Prices in Active Markets for Identical Assets (Level 1)	Significant Other Observable Inputs (Level 2)	Significant Unobservable Inputs (Level 3)
Fixed Income:				
Mortgage and asset-backed securities[A]	$ 165,042	$ —	$165,042	$ —
Corporate bonds[B]	111,954	—	111,954	—
Government and agency-U.S.[C]	41,885	26,577	15,308	—
Government and agency-Foreign[D]	6,836	—	6,836	—
Other[E]	8,277	—	8,277	—
Equity securities[F]	562,047	435,847	126,200	—
Cash and cash equivalents[G]	37,237	37,237	—	—
Fair value of plan assets	$ 933,278	$499,661	$433,617	$ —

	Total U.S. Plan Asset Balances at September 30, 2010	Quoted Prices in Active Markets for Identical Assets (Level 1)	Significant Other Observable Inputs (Level 2)	Significant Unobservable Inputs (Level 3)
Fixed Income:				
Mortgage and asset-backed securities[A]	$ 160,189	$ —	$160,189	$ —
Corporate bonds[B]	109,331	—	109,331	—
Government and agency-U.S.[C]	41,175	21,416	19,759	—
Government and agency-Foreign[D]	15,960	—	15,960	—
Other[E]	3,337	—	3,337	—
Equity securities[F]	631,877	396,188	235,689	—
Cash and cash equivalents[G]	42,681	42,681	—	—
Fair value of plan assets	$1,004,550	$460,285	$544,265	$ —

[A] Values are based upon a combination of observable prices, independent pricing services and relevant broker quotes.

[B] Values are based upon comparable securities with similar yields and credit ratings.

[C] Values of instruments classified as Level 1 are based on the closing price reported on the major market on which the investments are traded. Values of instruments classified as Level 2 are based upon quoted market prices from observable pricing sources.

[D] Values are based upon quoted market prices from observable pricing sources.

[E] Classification contains various immaterial investments and valuation varies by investment type. Values are primarily based upon quoted market prices from observable pricing sources.

[F] Values of instruments classified as Level 1 are based on the closing price reported on the major market on which the investments are traded. Values of instruments classified as Level 2 are based on the net asset value provided by the fund administrator, which is based on the value of the underlying assets owned by the fund, less its liabilities and then divided by the number of fund units outstanding.

[G] Values are based upon quoted market prices or broker/dealer quotations.

SEC 3.49

The U.S. portion of fixed income assets is invested in mortgage-backed, corporate, government and agency and asset-backed instruments. Mortgage-backed securities consist of residential mortgage pass-through certificates. Corporate bonds are diversified across industry and sector and, while consisting primarily of investment grade instruments, include an allocation to high-yield debt as well. U.S. government investments consist of obligations of the U.S. Treasury and its agencies.

The non-U.S. portion of fixed income investments consists primarily of corporate bonds in developed markets but includes an allocation to emerging markets debt as well. The value of derivative instruments is not material and is included in the "Other" category provided in the table above.

Equity securities included within the plans' assets consist of publicly-traded U.S. and non-U.S. equity securities. In order to achieve appropriate diversification, these portfolios are allocated among multiple asset managers and in-

vested across market sectors, investment styles, capitalization weights and geographic regions.

A portion of the U.S. plans' assets consists of investments in cash and cash equivalents, primarily to accommodate liquidity requirements relating to trade settlement and benefit payment activity.

Foreign Plans

Foreign plan assets comprise 31% of the Company's total benefit plan assets, based on market value at September 30, 2011. Such plans have local independent fiduciary committees, with responsibility for development and oversight of investment policy, including asset allocation decisions. In making such decisions, consideration is given to local regulations, investment practices and funding rules.

The following table provides the fair value measurements of foreign plan assets, as well as the measurement techniques and inputs utilized to measure fair value of these assets, at September 30, 2011 and 2010.

	Total Foreign Plan Asset Balances at September 30, 2011	Quoted Prices in Active Markets for Identical Assets (Level 1)	Significant Other Observable Inputs (Level 2)	Significant Unobservable Inputs (Level 3)
Fixed Income:				
Corporate bonds[A]	$ 34,905	$ —	$34,905	$ —
Government and agency-U.S.[B]	1,065	1,065	—	—
Government and agency-Foreign[C]	77,949	36,687	41,262	—
Other[D]	—	—	—	—
Equity securities[E]	215,309	201,325	13,726	258
Cash and cash equivalents[F]	1,191	1,191	—	—
Real estate[G]	10,688	—	—	10,688
Insurance contracts[H]	78,345	—	—	78,345
Fair value of plan assets	$419,452	$240,268	$89,893	$89,291

	Total Foreign Plan Asset Balances at September 30, 2010	Quoted Prices in Active Markets for Identical Assets (Level 1)	Significant Other Observable Inputs (Level 2)	Significant Unobservable Inputs (Level 3)
Fixed Income:				
Corporate bonds[A]	$ 36,541	$ —	$36,541	$ —
Government and agency-U.S.[B]	—	—	—	—
Government and agency-Foreign[C]	65,561	34,387	31,174	—
Other[D]	8,797	—	8,797	—
Equity securities[E]	220,102	207,577	12,258	267
Cash and cash equivalents[F]	6,478	6,478	—	—
Real estate[G]	9,486	—	—	9,486
Insurance contracts[H]	62,333	—	89	62,244
Fair value of plan assets	$409,298	$248,442	$88,859	$71,997

[A] Values are based upon comparable securities with similar yields and credit ratings.

[B] Values are based on the closing price reported on the major market on which the investments are traded.

[C] Values of instruments classified as Level 1 are based on the closing price reported on the major market on which the investments are traded. Values of instruments classified as Level 2 are based upon quoted market prices from observable pricing sources.

[D] Values are based upon quoted market prices from observable pricing sources.

[E] Values of instruments classified as Level 1 are based on the closing price reported on the major market on which the investments are traded. Values of instruments classified as Level 2 are based on the net asset value provided by the fund administrator, which is based on the value of the underlying assets owned by the fund, less its liabilities and then divided by the number of fund units outstanding.

[F] Values are based upon quoted market prices or broker/dealer quotations.

[G] Values represent the estimated fair value based on the fair value of the underlying investment value or cost, adjusted for any accumulated earnings or losses.

[H] Values approximately represent cash surrender value.

Fixed income investments include corporate, U.S. government and non-U.S. government securities. Equity securities included in the foreign plan assets consist of publicly-traded U.S. and non-U.S. equity securities. Real estate investments consist of investments in funds holding an interest in real

properties. The foreign plans also hold a portion of assets in cash and cash equivalents, in order to accommodate liquidity requirements.

The following table summarizes the changes, for the years ended September 30, 2011 and 2010, in the fair value of foreign pension assets measured using Level 3 inputs:

	Equity Securities	Real Estate	Insurance Contracts	Total Assets
Balance at September 30, 2009	$ 494	$ 8,987	$59,078	$68,559
Actual return on plan assets:				
Relating to assets held at September 30, 2010	—	558	2,075	2,633
Relating to assets sold during the period	(199)	185	—	(14)
Purchases, sales and settlements, net	7	122	—	129
Transfers in (out) from other categories	(3)	—	4,866	4,863
Exchange rate changes	(32)	(366)	(3,775)	(4,173)
Balance at September 30, 2010	$ 267	$ 9,486	$62,244	$71,997
Actual return on plan assets:				
Relating to assets held at September 30, 2011	(4)	46	2,613	2,655
Relating to assets sold during the period	—	—	—	—
Purchases, sales and settlements, net	—	1,363	14,710	16,073
Transfers in (out) from other categories	—	—	92	92
Exchange rate changes	(5)	(207)	(1,314)	(1,526)
Balance at September 30, 2011	$ 258	$10,688	$78,345	$89,291

Defined Contribution Plans

3.50

ALLIANT TECHSYSTEMS INC. (MAR)

NOTES TO THE CONSOLIDATED FINANCIAL STATEMENTS

(Amounts in thousands except share and per share data and unless otherwise indicated)

10. Employee Benefit Plans (in part)

ATK provides defined benefit pension plans and defined contribution plans for the majority of its employees. ATK has tax qualified defined benefit plans, supplemental (nonqualified) defined benefit pension plans, a defined contribution plan, and a supplemental (non-qualified) defined contribution plan. A qualified plan meets the requirements of certain sections of the Internal Revenue Code and, generally, contributions to qualified plans are tax deductible. A qualified plan typically provides benefits to a broad group of employees and may not discriminate in favor of highly compensated employees in coverage, benefits or contributions. In addition, ATK provides medical and life insurance benefits to certain retirees and their eligible dependents through its postretirement plans.

Defined Contribution Plan

ATK also sponsors a defined contribution plan. Participation in this plan is available to substantially all employees. The defined contribution plan is a 401(k) plan to which employees may contribute up to 50% of their pay (highly compen-

sated employees are subject to limitations). Employee contributions are invested, at the employees' direction, among a variety of investment alternatives including an ATK common stock fund. Participants may transfer amounts into and out of the investment alternatives at any time. Effective January 1, 2004, the ATK matching contribution and non-elective contribution to this plan depends on a participant's years of service, pension plan participation, and certain other factors. Participants receive:

- a matching contribution of 100% of the first 3% of the participant's contributed pay plus 50% of the next 2% of the participant's contributed pay, or
- a matching contribution of 50% of the first 6% of the participant's contributed pay,
- an automatic enrollment of a 6% pre-tax contribution rate (of which the participant can either change or opt out) along with a matching contribution of 100% of the first 3% of the participant's contributed pay plus 50% of the next 3% of the participant's contributed pay (subject to one year vesting) and a non-elective contribution based on recognized compensation and age and service (subject to three year vesting), or
- a non-elective contribution based on the recognized compensation, age, and service (subject to three year vesting), or
- no matching contribution.

ATK's contributions to the plan were $36,479 in fiscal 2011, $36,009 in fiscal 2010, and $33,745 in fiscal 2009.

As of March 31, 2011, ATK had more than 15,000 employees. Approximately 10% of these employees were covered by collective bargaining agreements. The majority of represented employees work at three locations. Two of the major collective bargaining agreements have terms that expire in calendar 2011 and will be renegotiated during calendar 2011, and three others expire in calendar 2012.

Supplemental Retirement Plans (SERP)

3.51

GUESS?, INC. (JAN)

NOTES TO CONSOLIDATED FINANCIAL STATEMENTS

(1) Summary of Significant Accounting Policies and Practices (in part)

Supplemental Executive Retirement Plan

In accordance with authoritative accounting guidance for defined benefit pension and other postretirement plans, an asset for a plan's overfunded status or a liability for a plan's underfunded status is recognized in the consolidated balance sheets; plan assets and obligations that determine the plan's funded status are measured as of the end of the Company's fiscal year; and changes in the funded status of defined benefit postretirement plans are recognized in the year in which they occur. Such changes are reported in other comprehensive income and as a separate component of stockholders' equity.

(10) Supplemental Executive Retirement Plan

On August 23, 2005, the Board of Directors of the Company adopted a Supplemental Executive Retirement Plan, which became effective January 1, 2006. The SERP provides select employees who satisfy certain eligibility requirements with certain benefits upon retirement, termination of employment, death, disability or a change in control of the Company, in certain prescribed circumstances. The participants in the SERP are Maurice Marciano, Chairman of the Board, Paul Marciano, Chief Executive Officer and Vice Chairman of the Board, and Carlos Alberini, the Company's former President and Chief Operating Officer. During the year ended January 29, 2011, the Company recorded a $5.8 million charge related to the accelerated amortization of prior service cost resulting from the departure of Mr. Alberini from the Company.

As a non-qualified pension plan, no dedicated funding of the SERP is required; however, the Company has and expects to make periodic payments into insurance policies held in a rabbi trust to fund the expected obligations arising under the non-qualified SERP. The amount of future payments may vary, depending on the future years of service, future annual compensation of the participants and investment performance of the trust. The cash surrender values of the insurance policies are $32.9 million and $22.1 million as of January 29, 2011 and January 30, 2010, respectively, and are included in other assets. As a result of a change in value of the insurance policy investments, the Company recorded gains (losses) of $2.7 million, $3.1 million and $(3.2) million in other income during fiscal 2011, fiscal 2010 and fiscal 2009, respectively.

In accordance with authoritative accounting guidance for defined benefit pension and other postretirement plans, an asset for a plan's overfunded status or a liability for a plan's underfunded status is recognized in the consolidated balance sheet; plan assets and obligations that determine the plan's funded status are measured as of the end of the Company's fiscal year; and changes in the funded status of defined benefit postretirement plans are recognized in the year in which they occur. Such changes are reported in other comprehensive income and as a separate component of stockholders' equity.

The components of net periodic pension cost to comprehensive income for fiscal 2011, fiscal 2010 and fiscal 2009, are (in thousands):

	Year Ended Jan. 29, 2011	Year Ended Jan. 30, 2010	Year Ended Jan. 31, 2009
Service cost	$ 69	$ 213	$ 244
Interest cost	2,177	2,053	2,319
Net amortization of unrecognized prior service cost	1,195	1,743	1,743
Net amortization of actuarial losses	619	—	927
Curtailment expense	5,819	—	—
Net periodic defined benefit pension cost	$9,879	$ 4,009	$ 5,233
Unrecognized prior service cost charged to comprehensive income	$1,195	$ 1,743	$ 1,743
Unrecognized net actuarial loss charged to comprehensive income	619	—	927
Actuarial (losses)/gains	(8,361)	(5,569)	6,826
Curtailment expense	5,819	—	—
Related tax impact	251	1,435	(3,651)
Total periodic costs and other charges to comprehensive income	$ (477)	$(2,391)	$ 5,845

Included in accumulated other comprehensive income, before tax, as of January 29, 2011 and January 30, 2010 were the following amounts that have not yet been recognized in net periodic benefit cost (in thousands):

	Jan. 29, 2011	Jan. 30, 2010
Unrecognized prior service cost	$ 5,545	$12,558
Unrecognized net actuarial loss	15,387	7,645
Net balance sheet impact	$20,932	$20,203

The following chart summarizes the SERP's funded status and the amounts recognized in the Company's consolidated balance sheets (in thousands):

	Jan. 29, 2011	Jan. 30, 2010
Projected benefit obligation	$(47,772)	$(37,165)
Plan assets at fair value[1]	—	—
Net liability (included in other long-term liabilities)	$(47,772)	$(37,165)

[1] The SERP is a non-qualified pension plan and hence the insurance policies are not considered to be plan assets. Accordingly, the table above does not include the insurance policies with market values of $32.9 million and $22.1 million at January 29, 2011 and January 30, 2010, respectively.

The Company assumed a discount rate of 5.5% at January 29, 2011 compared to 6.0% at January 30, 2010, as part of the actuarial valuation performed to calculate the projected benefit obligation disclosed above, based on the timing of cash flows expected to be made in the future to the participants, applied to high quality yield curves. Compensation levels utilized in calculating the projected benefit obligation were derived from expected future compensation as outlined in employment contracts in effect at the time. At January 29, 2011, amounts included in comprehensive income that are expected to be recognized as components of net periodic defined benefit pension cost in fiscal 2012 consist of prior service costs of $1.1 million and actuarial losses of $2.4 million. Benefits projected to be paid in the next five fiscal years amount to $3.6 million with half of such payments to be paid in each of the fourth and fifth years. Aggregate benefits projected to be paid in the following five fiscal years amount to $22.2 million.

Multi-Employer Plans

3.52

ARKANSAS BEST CORPORATION (DEC)

NOTES TO CONSOLIDATED FINANCIAL STATEMENTS

Note I—Employee Benefit Plans (in part)

Multiemployer Plans

Under the provisions of the Taft-Hartley Act, retirement and health care benefits for ABF's contractual employees are provided by a number of multiemployer plans. Due to the inherent nature of multiemployer plans, there are risks associated with participation in these plans that differ from single-employer plans. ABF contributes to multiemployer pension and postretirement benefit plans in accordance with its collective bargaining agreement with the IBT. Other unrelated employers contribute to these multiemployer plans pursuant to their respective collective bargaining agreements. Assets contributed by an employer to a multiemployer plan are not segregated into a separate account and are not restricted to provide benefits only to employees of that contributing employer. If a participating employer to a multiemployer plan no longer contributes to the plan, the unfunded obligations of the plan may be borne by the remaining participating employers. In the event of the termination of a multiemployer pension plan or if ABF withdraws from a multiemployer pension plan, under current law, ABF would have material liabilities for its share of the unfunded vested liabilities of each such plan. Multiemployer plans that enter reorganization status subject contributing employers to an increased contribution requirement, but will generally not require a contribution increase of more than 7% over the level required in the preceding year. ABF has not received notification of any plan termination, and ABF does not currently intend to withdraw from these plans. Therefore, the Company believes the likelihood of events that would require recognition of liabilities for its share of unfunded vested benefits is remote.

ABF currently contributes to 25 multiemployer pension plans, which vary in size and in funded status. The trust funds for these plans are administered by trustees, an equal number of whom generally are appointed by the IBT and certain management carrier organizations or other appointing authorities for employer trustees, as set forth in the fund's trust agreements. ABF contributes to these plans monthly based generally on the time worked by its contractual employees, as specified in the collective bargaining agreement and other related supplemental agreements. ABF recognizes as expense the contractually required contribution for the period and recognizes as a liability any contributions due and unpaid. The Company intends to meet its obligations to the multiemployer plans under its collective bargaining agreement with the IBT.

In 2006, the PPA became law and together with related regulations established new minimum funding requirements for multiemployer pension plans. The PPA mandates that multiemployer pension plans that are below certain funded levels or that have projected funded deficiencies adopt a funding improvement plan or a rehabilitation program to improve the funded levels over a defined period of time. As defined by the PPA, plans in "critical status" (or in the red zone) are generally less than 65% funded, plans in "endangered status" (or in the yellow zone) are less than 80% funded and plans in "neither endangered nor critical status" (or in the green zone) are at least 80% funded. The PPA also accelerates the timing of annual funding notices and requires additional disclosures from multiemployer pension plans if such plans fall below the required funded levels. Based on the most recent annual funding notices the Company has received, most of which are for plan years ended December 31, 2010, approximately 62% of ABF's contributions to multiemployer pension plans, including the Central States, Southeast and Southwest Areas Pension Fund (the "Central States Pension Fund") discussed below, are made to plans that are in "critical status" and approximately 12% of ABF's contributions to multiemployer pension plans are made to plans that are in "endangered status" as defined by the PPA.

In December 2008, the Worker, Retiree, and Employer Recovery Act of 2008 (the "Recovery Act") became law. For plan years beginning October 1, 2008 through September 30, 2009, the Recovery Act allowed multiemployer plans the option to freeze their funded certification based on the funded status of the previous plan year. In addition, the Recovery Act provided multiemployer plans in endangered or critical status in plan years beginning in 2008 or 2009 a three-year extension of the plan's funding improvement or rehabilitation period.

The Preservation of Access to Care for Medicare Beneficiaries and Pension Relief Act of 2010 (the "Pension Relief Act") was signed into law in June 2010. The Pension Relief Act includes provisions that may provide funding relief for multiemployer pension plans that satisfy certain solvency requirements. The Company has not received information from the multiemployer plan administrators regarding the impact, if any, of the Pension Relief Act on the funded status of the multiemployer pension plans to which ABF contributes. Due to their funded positions, certain plans may not be eligible for funding relief provisions of the Pension Relief Act because of the solvency requirements under the law.

ABF's participation in multiemployer pension plans is outlined in the table below. The multiemployer pension funds listed separately in the table represent funds which are individually significant to ABF based on the amount of plan contributions. The severity of a plan's underfunded status was also considered in ABF's analysis of individually significant funds to be separately disclosed. ABF's current collective bargaining agreement with the IBT, which expires March 31, 2013, requires contributions to all of these multiemployer plans.

Significant multiemployer pension funds and key participation information were as follows:

Legal Name of Plan	EIN/Pension Plan Number[a]	Pension Protection Act Zone Status[b]		FIP/RP Status Pending/ Implemented[c]	Contributions[d] ($ thousands)			Surcharge Imposed[e]
		2011	2010		2011	2010	2009	
Central States, Southeast and Southwest Areas Pension Fund	36-6044243	Red	Red	Implemented[1]	$ 70,579	$ 65,091	$ 54,679	No
Western Conference of Teamsters Pension Plan	91-6145047	Green	Green	No[2]	20,807	18,268	15,511	No
Central Pennsylvania Teamsters Defined Benefit Plan	23-6262789	Green	Yellow	Implemented[3]	12,022	10,827	9,892	No
I. B. of T. Union Local No. 710 Pension Fund[4]	36-2377656	Yellow[5]	Green[6]	No	9,265	8,207	7,360	No
All other plans in the aggregate					20,168	18,220	16,474	
Total multiemployer pension contributions paid[7]					$132,841	$120,613	$103,916	

Table Heading Definitions

[a] The "EIN/Pension Plan Number" column provides the Federal Employer Identification Number (EIN) and the three-digit plan number, if applicable.

[b] Unless otherwise noted, the most recent PPA zone status available in 2011 and 2010 is for the plan's year-end status at December 31, 2010 and 2009, respectively. The zone status is based on information that ABF received from the plan and is certified by the plan's actuary.

[c] The "FIP/RP Status Pending/Implemented" column indicates plans for which a financial improvement plan (FIP) or a rehabilitation plan (RP) is either pending or has been implemented.

[d] Contribution amounts reflect payments made in the respective year and differ from amounts expensed during the year, which are disclosed in total within Note I.

[e] Surcharge column indicates if a surcharge was paid by the employer to the plan.

[1] Adopted a rehabilitation plan effective March 25, 2008 and updated rehabilitation plans effective December 31, 2010 (as further discussed in Note I) and December 31, 2011. Utilized amortization extension effective December 31, 2003.

[2] Utilized amortization extension to calculate the zone status beginning with the January 1, 2011 actuarial valuation.

[3] Adopted funding improvement plan effective November 19, 2009.

[4] Pension Protection Act zone status relates to plan years February 1, 2010 - January 31, 2011 and February 1, 2009 - January 31, 2010.

[5] Certified as "endangered" status for the plan year beginning February 1, 2010. The Plan adopted a funding improvement plan effective December 25, 2010. The Plan was subsequently certified on February 1, 2011 as being in "neither endangered nor critical" status. Therefore, it never implemented the Funding Improvement Plan as required for plans certified as "endangered."

[6] Certified as "endangered" for the plan year beginning February 1, 2009. Under Section 204 of the Recovery Act, the Trustees elected to apply the Plan's 2008 funded status, which was "neither endangered nor critical," to the 2009 plan year.

[7] Contribution levels can be impacted by several factors such as changes in business levels and the related time worked by contractual employees, contractual rate increases for pension benefits and the specific funding structure, which differs among funds. The pension contribution rate for contractual employees increased an average of 3.6%, 9.6% and 11.4% effective primarily on August 1, 2011, 2010 and 2009, respectively. The year-over-year increases in multiemployer pension plan contributions presented above were also influenced by growth in ABF's business levels.

ABF was listed in the funding notices of its individually significant multiemployer pension funds as providing more than 5% of the total contributions for the following funds and for the most recent plan years available.

Pension Fund	Plan Years in which ABF's Plan Contributions Exceeded More Than 5 Percent of Total Contributions
Central States, Southeast and Southwest Areas Pension Fund	Plan years ended December 31, 2010 and 2009
Central Pennsylvania Teamsters Defined Benefit Plan	Plan years ended December 31, 2010 and 2009
I. B. of T. Union Local No. 710 Pension Fund	Plan years ended January 31, 2011 and 2010

For 2011, 2010 and 2009, 50% to 55% of ABF's multiemployer pension contributions were made to the Central States Pension Fund. The Central States Pension Fund adopted a rehabilitation plan as a result of its actuarial certification for the plan year beginning January 1, 2008 which placed the Central States Pension Fund in critical status in accordance with the PPA. ABF's current collective bargaining agreement complies with the rehabilitation plan which was adopted by the Central States Pension Fund prior to the April 1, 2008 effective date of the collective bargaining agreement. The Actuarial Certification of Plan Status as of January 1, 2010 certified that the Central States Pension Fund remained in critical status with a funded percentage of 63.4%. In accordance with PPA requirements, the Central States Pension Fund adopted an updated rehabilitation plan effective December 31, 2010, which implements additional measures to improve the plan's funded level, including establishing a minimum retirement age and actuarially adjusting certain pre-age 65 benefits for participants who retire after July 1, 2011. The updated rehabilitation plan also effectively caps the required pension contribution rates at the current levels for the rate class applicable to the National Master Freight Agreement (the "NMFA"); however, any changes to scheduled contribution rate increases under the current labor agreement, which ends on March 31, 2013, would be subject to approval by the bargaining parties. For the August 1, 2011 contractual increase, the supplemental negotiating committee associated with the Central States Pension Fund requested a $0.20 per hour increase for the related health and welfare fund and no increase for the pension fund.

In 2005, the IRS granted an extension of the period of time over which the Central States Pension Fund amortizes unfunded liabilities by ten years subject to the condition that a targeted funding ratio will be maintained by the fund. Due, in part, to the decline in asset values associated with the investment losses in the financial markets during 2008, the funded level of the Central States Pension Fund dropped below the targeted funding ratio set forth as a condition of the ten-year amortization extension beginning with the January 1, 2009 actuarial valuation. However, the amortization extension granted by the IRS in 2005 expressly indicated that modifications of conditions would be considered in the event of unforeseen market fluctuations which cause the plan to fail the funded ratio condition for a certain plan year. Based on information currently available to the Company, the Central States Pension Fund has not received notice of revocation of the ten-year amortization extension granted by the IRS. In the unlikely event that the IRS revokes the extension, revocation would apply retroactively to the 2004 plan year, which would result in a material liability for ABF's share of the resulting funded deficiency, the extent of which is currently unknown to the Company. The Company believes that the occurrence of events that would require recognition of liabilities for ABF's share of a funded deficiency is remote.

Other multiemployer pension plans in which ABF participates, including the plans previously outlined in the table within this note, have adopted or will have to adopt either a funding improvement plan or a rehabilitation program, depending on their current funded status as required by the PPA. The Company believes that the contribution rates under ABF's collective bargaining agreement will comply with any rehabilitation plan that has been or may be adopted by the majority of the multiemployer pension plans in which ABF participates. If the contribution rates in the collective bargaining agreement fail to meet the requirements established by the rehabilitation or funding improvement plan required by the PPA for underfunded plans, the PPA would impose additional contribution requirements on ABF in the form of a surcharge of an additional 5% to 10%. However, under the current collective bargaining agreement, any surcharges that may be required by the PPA are covered by the contractual contribution rate and should not increase ABF's overall contribution obligation.

ABF contributes to 42 multiemployer health and welfare plans which provide healthcare benefits for active employees and retirees covered under ABF's labor agreements. The contribution rate for health and welfare benefits increased by an average of 4.1%, 3.8% and 3.1% primarily on August 1, 2011, 2010 and 2009, respectively, under ABF's current collective bargaining agreement with the IBT. Other than changes in rates and time worked, there have been no significant changes that affect the comparability of the 2011, 2010 and 2009 multiemployer health and welfare contributions.

ABF's aggregate expense related to contributions to the multiemployer health, welfare and pension plans for the years ended December 31 were as follows:

($ thousands)	2011	2010	2009
Health and welfare	$112,043	$103,228	$ 99,282
Pension	131,882	120,154	107,585
Total expense for contributions to multiemployer plans	$243,925	$223,382	$206,867

Under ABF's current collective bargaining agreement, the combined increase in the contribution rate for health, welfare and pension benefit costs effective August 1, 2012 could be up to $1.00 per hour, or an average increase of 6.3%. If the Central States Pension Fund maintains a contribution rate increase consistent with the August 1, 2011 increase previously discussed, the resulting average increase in the contribution rate for time worked for health, welfare and pension benefits effective August 1, 2012 would be approximately 3.7%. The Company cannot determine with any certainty the minimum contributions which will be required under future collective bargaining agreements for its contractual employees that will become effective after March 31, 2013. Furthermore, the Company cannot predict future requirements or the related amounts thereof, if any, to make additional contributions to multiemployer funds to satisfy existing or future statutory or other contractual obligations, including any requirements to remedy plan funding deficiencies.

SEC 3.52

Plan Amendment

3.53

XEROX CORPORATION (DEC)

NOTES TO CONDENSED CONSOLIDATED FINANCIAL STATEMENTS

(In millions, except per-share data and where otherwise noted)

Note 14—Employee Benefit Plans (in part)

We sponsor numerous pension and other post-retirement benefit plans, primarily retiree health, in our domestic and international operations. December 31 is the measurement date for all of our post-retirement benefit plans.

	Pension Benefits		Retiree Health	
	2011	2010	2011	2010
Change in Benefit Obligation:				
Benefit obligation, January 1	$ 9,731	$ 9,194	$ 1,006	$ 1,102
Service cost	186	178	8	8
Interest cost	612	575	47	54
Plan participants' contributions	10	11	33	26
Plan amendments[3]	(2)	(19)	(4)	(86)
Actuarial loss	916	477	26	13
Acquisitions[2]	—	140	—	1
Currency exchange rate changes	(85)	(154)	(3)	6
Curtailments	—	(1)	—	—
Benefits paid/settlements	(870)	(670)	(106)	(118)
Other	7	—	—	—
Benefit Obligation, December 31	$10,505	$ 9,731	$ 1,007	$ 1,006
Change in Plan Assets:				
Fair value of plan assets, January 1	7,940	$ 7,561	$ —	$ —
Actual return on plan assets	694	846	—	—
Employer contribution	556	237	73	92
Plan participants' contributions	10	11	33	26
Acquisitions[2]	—	107	—	—
Currency exchange rate changes	(57)	(144)	—	—
Benefits paid/settlements	(870)	(669)	(106)	(118)
Other	4	(9)	—	—
Fair Value of Plan Assets, December 31	$ 8,277	$ 7,940	$ —	$ —
Net Funded Status at December 31[1]	$ (2,228)	$(1,791)	$(1,007)	$(1,006)
Amounts Recognized in the Consolidated Balance Sheets:				
Other long-term assets	$ 76	$ 92	$ —	$ —
Accrued compensation and benefit costs	(45)	(44)	(82)	(86)
Pension and other benefit liabilities	(2,259)	(1,839)	—	—
Post-retirement medical benefits	—	—	(925)	(920)
Net Amounts Recognized	$ (2,228)	$(1,791)	$(1,007)	$(1,006)

[1] Includes under-funded and non-funded plans.
[2] Primarily ACS's acquired balances.
[3] Refer to the "Plan Amendment" section for additional information.

Plan Amendments

In December 2011, we amended all of our primary U.S. Defined Benefit Pension Plans for salaried employees. Our primary qualified plans had previously been amended to freeze the final average pay formulas within the plans as of December 31, 2012, but a cash balance service credit was expected to continue post December 31, 2012. The 2011 amendments fully freeze any further benefit and service accruals after December 31, 2012 for all of these plans, including the non-qualified plans. As a result of these plan amendments, we recognized a pre-tax curtailment gain of $107 ($66 after-tax). The gain represents the recognition of deferred gains from other prior year amendments ("prior service credits") as a result of the discontinuation of any future benefit or service accrual period. The amendments are not expected to materially impact 2012 pension expense.

In 2011, the Canadian Salary Pension Plan was amended to close the plan to future service accrual effective January 1, 2014. Benefits earned up to January 1, 2014 will not be affected and participants will continue receive the benefit of future salary increases to the extent applicable; therefore, the amendment does not result in a material change to the projected benefit obligation at the re-measurement date, December 31, 2011.

In 2010, we amended our domestic retiree health benefit plan to eliminate the use of the Retiree Drug Subsidy that the Company receives from Medicare as an offset to retiree contributions. This amendment was effective January 1, 2011. The Company instead decided to use this subsidy to reduce its retiree healthcare costs. The amendment resulted in a net decrease of $55 to the retiree medical benefit obligation and a corresponding $34 after tax increase to equity. This amendment reduced 2011 expenses by approximately $13.

In 2010, as a result of a renegotiation of the contract with our largest union, we amended our union pension plan for this population to freeze the final average pay formula of the pension plan effective January 1, 2013 and our union retiree health benefits plan to eliminate a portion of the subsidy currently paid to current and future Medicare-eligible retirees effective January 1, 2011. These amendments are generally consistent with amendments previously made to our salaried employee retirement plans.

POSTEMPLOYMENT BENEFITS

RECOGNITION AND MEASUREMENT

3.54 FASB ASC 712, *Compensation—Nonretirement Postemployment Benefits*, requires that entities providing postemployment benefits to their employees accrue the cost of such benefits. FASB ASC 712 does not require that the amount of other postemployment benefits be disclosed.

PRESENTATION AND DISCLOSURE EXCERPTS

Postemployment Benefits

3.55

ABBOTT LABORATORIES (DEC)

NOTES TO CONSOLIDATED FINANCIAL STATEMENTS

Note 4—Post-Employment Benefits

Retirement plans consist of defined benefit, defined contribution and medical and dental plans. Information for Abbott's major defined benefit plans and post-employment medical and dental benefit plans is as follows: (*dollars in millions*)

	Defined Benefit Plans			Medical and Dental Plans		
	2011	2010	2009	2011	2010	2009
Projected benefit obligations, January 1	$ 8,606	$ 6,852	$ 5,541	$ 1,673	$ 1,705	$ 1,443
Service cost—benefits earned during the year	332	288	221	55	60	45
Interest cost on projected benefit obligations	446	421	368	88	101	94
Losses (gains), primarily changes in discount rates, plan design changes, law changes and differences between actual and estimated health care costs	608	565	747	(104)	(153)	175
Benefits paid	(294)	(289)	(251)	(62)	(74)	(58)
Acquisition of Solvay's pharmaceuticals business	—	1,045	—	—	28	—
Settlement	(776)	—	—	—	—	—
Other, primarily foreign currency translation	41	(276)	226	7	6	6
Projected benefit obligations, December 31	$ 8,963	$ 8,606	$ 6,852	$ 1,657	$ 1,673	$ 1,705
Plans' assets at fair value, January 1	$ 7,451	$ 5,812	$ 3,997	$ 396	$ 341	$ 266
Actual return on plans' assets	29	782	1,096	5	55	62
Company contributions	394	525	862	40	74	71
Benefits paid	(294)	(289)	(251)	(52)	(74)	(58)
Acquisition of Solvay's pharmaceuticals business	—	763	—	—	—	—
Settlement	(776)	—	—	—	—	—
Other, primarily foreign currency translation	157	(142)	108	—	—	—
Plans' assets at fair value, December 31	$ 6,961	$ 7,451	$ 5,812	$ 389	$ 396	$ 341
Projected benefit obligations greater than plans' assets, December 31	$(2,002)	$(1,155)	$(1,040)	$(1,268)	$(1,277)	$(1,364)
Long-term assets	$ 66	$ 27	$ 21	$ —	$ —	$ —
Short-term liabilities	(35)	(34)	(31)	—	—	—
Long-term liabilities	(2,033)	(1,148)	(1,030)	(1,268)	(1,277)	(1,364)
Net liability	$(2,002)	$(1,155)	$(1,040)	$(1,268)	$(1,277)	$(1,364)
Amounts Recognized in Accumulated Other Comprehensive Income (loss):						
Actuarial losses, net	$ 3,822	$ 2,879	$ 2,699	$ 601	$ 713	$ 685
Prior service cost (credits)	25	30	34	(364)	(406)	(184)
Total	$ 3,847	$ 2,909	$ 2,733	$ 237	$ 307	$ 501

The projected benefit obligations for non-U.S. defined benefit plans was $2.3 billion, $3.0 billion and $2.0 billion at December 31, 2011, 2010 and 2009, respectively. The accumulated benefit obligations for all defined benefit plans was $7.7 billion, $7.5 billion and $5.8 billion at December 31, 2011, 2010 and 2009, respectively. For plans where the accumulated benefit obligations exceeded plan assets at December 31, 2011, 2010 and 2009, the aggregate accumulated benefit obligations were $6.7 billion, $2.0 billion and $1.5 billion, respectively; the projected benefit obligations were $7.9 billion, $2.2 billion and $1.8 billion, respectively; and the aggregate plan assets were $5.8 billion, $1.1 billion and $780 million, respectively.

	Defined Benefit Plans			Medical and Dental Plans		
(Dollars in millions)	2011	2010	2009	2011	2010	2009
Service cost—benefits earned during the year	$ 332	$ 288	$ 221	$ 55	$ 60	$ 45
Interest cost on projected benefit obligations	446	421	368	88	101	94
Expected return on plans' assets	(608)	(571)	(506)	(34)	(31)	(24)
Settlement	40	—	—	—	—	—
Amortization of actuarial losses	163	136	52	38	38	30
Amortization of prior service cost (credits)	4	4	4	(42)	(22)	(22)
Total cost	$ 377	$ 278	$ 139	$105	$146	$123

Other comprehensive income (loss) for 2011 includes amortization of actuarial losses and prior service cost of $163 million and $4 million, respectively, and net actuarial losses of $1.1 billion for defined benefit plans and amortization of actuarial losses and prior service credits of $38 million and $42 million, respectively, and net actuarial gains of $66 million for medical and dental plans. Other comprehensive income (loss) for 2010 includes amortization of actuarial losses and prior service cost of $136 million and $4 million, respectively, and net actuarial losses of $305 million for defined benefit plans and amortization of actuarial losses and prior service credits of $38 million and $22 million, respectively, and net actuarial gains of $177 million for medical and dental plans. Other comprehensive income (loss) for 2009 includes amortization of actuarial losses and prior service cost of $52 million and $4 million, respectively, and net actuarial losses of $197 million for defined benefit plans and amortization of actuarial losses and prior service credits of $30 million and $22 million, respectively, and net actuarial losses of $128 million for medical and dental plans. The pretax amount of actuarial losses and prior service cost (credits) included in Accumulated other comprehensive income (loss) at December 31, 2011 that is expected to be recognized in the net periodic benefit cost in 2012 is $253 million and $4 million, respectively, for defined benefit pension plans and $35 million and $(42) million, respectively, for medical and dental plans.

The weighted average assumptions used to determine benefit obligations for defined benefit plans and medical and dental plans are as follows:

	2011	2010	2009
Discount rate	5.0%	5.4%	5.8%
Expected aggregate average long-term change in compensation	5.3%	5.1%	5.2%

The weighted average assumptions used to determine the net cost for defined benefit plans and medical and dental plans are as follows:

	2011	2010	2009
Discount rate	5.4%	5.8%	6.7%
Expected return on plan assets	7.8%	7.8%	8.2%
Expected aggregate average long-term change in compensation	5.1%	4.9%	4.3%

The assumed health care cost trend rates for medical and dental plans at December 31 were as follows:

	2011	2010	2009
Health care cost trend rate assumed for the next year	7%	7%	7%
Rate that the cost trend rate gradually declines to	5%	5%	5%
Year that rate reaches the assumed ultimate rate	2019	2016	2016

The discount rates used to measure liabilities were determined based on high-quality fixed income securities that match the duration of the expected retiree benefits. The health care cost trend rates represent Abbott's expected annual rates of change in the cost of health care benefits and is a forward projection of health care costs as of the measurement date. A one-percentage point increase/(decrease) in the assumed health care cost trend rate would increase/(decrease) the accumulated post-employment benefit obligations as of December 31, 2011, by $231 million/$(188) million, and the total of the service and interest cost components of net post-employment health care cost for the year then ended by approximately $25 million/$(20) million.

The following table summarizes the bases used to measure defined benefit plans' assets at fair value:

(Dollars in millions)	Outstanding Balances	Basis of Fair Value Measurement		
		Quoted Prices in Active Markets	Significant Other Observable Inputs	Significant Unobservable Inputs
December 31, 2011:				
Equities:				
U.S. large cap[a]	$1,470	$1,449	$ 21	$ —
U.S. mid cap[b]	423	152	271	—
International[c]	1,217	485	732	—
Fixed income securities:				
U.S. government securities[d]	857	370	487	—
Corporate debt instruments[e]	527	223	304	—
Non-U.S. government securities[f]	450	228	222	—
Other[g]	45	21	24	—
Absolute return funds[h]	1,709	334	751	624
Commodities[i]	183	8	165	10
Other[j]	80	78	—	2
	$6,961	$3,348	$2,977	$636
December 31, 2010:				
Equities:				
U.S. large cap[a]	$1,523	$1,499	$ 24	$ —
U.S. mid cap[b]	437	162	275	—
International[c]	1,552	758	794	—
Fixed income securities:				
U.S. government securities[d]	793	355	438	—
Corporate debt instruments[e]	524	237	286	1
Non-U.S. government securities[f]	758	172	586	—
Other[g]	40	20	19	1
Absolute return funds[h]	1,426	258	582	586
Commodities[i]	242	5	234	3
Other[j]	156	156	—	—
	$7,451	$3,622	$3,238	$591
December 31, 2009:				
Equities:				
U.S. large cap[a]	$1,267	$1,247	$ 20	$ —
U.S. mid cap[b]	339	105	234	—
International[c]	1,186	455	731	—
Fixed income securities:				
U.S. government securities[d]	753	321	430	2
Corporate debt instruments[e]	478	203	272	3
Non-U.S. government securities[f]	346	163	183	—
Other[g]	46	21	23	2
Absolute return funds[h]	1,296	237	536	523
Other[j]	101	74	27	—
	$5,812	$2,826	$2,456	$530

[a] A mix of index funds that track the S&P 500 (45 percent in 2011 and 2010 and 40 percent in 2009) and separate actively managed equity accounts that are benchmarked to the Russell 1000 (55 percent in 2011 and 2010 and 60 percent in 2009).

[b] A mix of index funds (75 percent) and separate actively managed equity accounts (25 percent) that track or are benchmarked to the S&P 400 midcap index.

[c] Primarily separate actively managed pooled investment accounts that are benchmarked to the MSCI and MSCI emerging market indices.

[d] Index funds not actively managed (45 percent in 2011 and 2010 and 75 percent in 2009) and separate actively managed accounts (55 percent in 2011 and 2010 and 25 percent in 2009).

[e] Index funds not actively managed (40 percent in 2011, 15 percent in 2010 and 75 percent in 2009) and separate actively managed accounts (60 percent in 2011, 85 percent in 2010 and 25 percent in 2009).

[f] Primarily United Kingdom, Japan and Irish government-issued bonds.

[g] Primarily mortgage backed securities.

[h] Primarily funds invested by managers that have a global mandate with the flexibility to allocate capital broadly across a wide range of asset classes and strategies including, but not limited to equities, fixed income, commodities, interest rate futures, currencies and other securities to outperform an agreed upon benchmark with specific return and volatility targets.

[i] Primarily investments in liquid commodity future contracts.

[j] Primarily cash and cash equivalents.

SEC 3.55

Equities that are valued using quoted prices are valued at the published market prices. Equities in a common collective trust or a registered investment company that are valued using significant other observable inputs are valued at the net asset value (NAV) provided by the fund administrator. The NAV is based on the value of the underlying assets owned by the fund minus its liabilities. Fixed income securities that are valued using significant other observable inputs are valued at prices obtained from independent financial service industry-recognized vendors. Absolute return funds and commodities are valued at the NAV provided by the fund administrator.

The following table summarizes the change in the value of assets that are measured using significant unobservable inputs:

(Dollars in millions)	2011	2010	2009
January 1	$591	$530	$303
Transfers (out of) in from other categories	(1)	(37)	3
Actual return on plan assets:			
Assets on hand at year end	(14)	41	99
Assets sold during the year	(1)	(2)	(5)
Purchases, sales and settlements, net	61	59	130
December 31	$636	$591	$530

The investment mix of equity securities, fixed income and other asset allocation strategies is based upon achieving a desired return, balancing higher return, more volatile equity securities, and lower return, less volatile fixed income securities. Investment allocations are made across a range of markets, industry sectors, capitalization sizes, and in the case of fixed income securities, maturities and credit quality. The plans do not directly hold any securities of Abbott. There are no known significant concentrations of risk in the plans' assets. Abbott's medical and dental plans' assets are invested in a similar mix as the pension plan assets.

The plans' expected return on assets, as shown above, is based on management's expectations of long-term average rates of return to be achieved by the underlying investment portfolios. In establishing this assumption, management considers historical and expected returns for the asset classes in which the plans are invested, as well as current economic and capital market conditions.

Abbott funds its domestic pension plans according to IRS funding limitations. International pension plans are funded according to similar regulations. Abbott funded $394 million in 2011, $525 million in 2010 and $862 million in 2009 to defined pension plans. Abbott expects pension funding for its main domestic pension plan of $200 million annually.

Total benefit payments expected to be paid to participants, which includes payments funded from company assets as well as paid from the plans, are as follows: (*dollars in millions*)

	Defined Benefit Plans	Medical and Dental Plans
2012	$ 284	$ 80
2013	297	82
2014	311	87
2015	331	92
2016	351	98
2017 to 2021	2,082	592

The Abbott Stock Retirement Plan is the principal defined contribution plan. Abbott's contributions to this plan were $151 million in 2011, $147 million in 2010 and $137 million in 2009.

Abbott provides certain other post-employment benefits, primarily salary continuation plans, to qualifying domestic employees, and accrues for the related cost over the service lives of the employees.

EMPLOYEE COMPENSATORY PLANS

RECOGNITION AND MEASUREMENT

3.56 FASB ASC 718, *Compensation—Stock Compensation*, establishes accounting and reporting standards for share-based payment transactions with employees, including awards classified as equity, awards classified as liabilities, employee stock ownership plans, and employee stock purchase plans. FASB ASC 718 requires that share-based payment transactions be accounted for using a fair-value-based method. Thus, entities are required to recognize the cost of employee services received in exchange for award of equity instruments based on the grant-date fair value of those awards or the fair value of the liabilities incurred. FASB ASC 718 provides clarification and expanded guidance in several areas, including measuring fair value, classifying an award as equity or a liability, and attributing compensation cost to reporting periods.

PRESENTATION AND DISCLOSURE EXCERPTS

Stock Option Plans

3.57

GENERAL MILLS, INC. (MAY)

NOTES TO CONSOLIDATED FINANCIAL STATEMENTS

Note 11. Stock Plans (in part)

We use broad-based stock plans to help ensure that management's interests are aligned with those of our stockholders. As of May 29, 2011, a total of 16,942,290 shares were available for grant in the form of stock options, restricted shares, restricted stock units, and shares of common stock under the 2009 Stock Compensation Plan (2009 Plan) and the 2006 Compensation Plan for Non-Employee Directors (2006 Director Plan). The 2009 Plan also provides for the issuance of cash-settled share-based units. Stock-based awards now outstanding include some granted under the 1995, 1996, 1998 (senior management), 1998 (employee), 2001, 2003, 2005, and 2007 stock plans and the Executive Incentive Plan (EIP), under which no further awards may be granted. The stock plans provide for full vesting of options, restricted shares, restricted stock units, and cash-settled share-based units upon completion of specified service periods or in certain circumstances, following a change of control.

Stock Options

The estimated fair values of stock options granted and the assumptions used for the Black-Scholes option-pricing model were as follows:

	Fiscal Year		
	2011	2010	2009
Estimated fair values of stock options granted	$4.12	$3.20	$4.70
Assumptions:			
Risk-free interest rate	2.9%	3.7%	4.4%
Expected term	8.5 years	8.5 years	8.5 years
Expected volatility	18.5%	18.9%	16.1%
Dividend yield	3.0%	3.4%	2.7%

The valuation of stock options is a significant accounting estimate that requires us to use judgments and assumptions that are likely to have a material impact on our financial statements. Annually, we make predictive assumptions regarding future stock price volatility, employee exercise behavior, dividend yield, and the forfeiture rate.

We estimate the fair value of each option on the grant date using a Black-Scholes option-pricing model, which requires us to make predictive assumptions regarding future stock price volatility, employee exercise behavior, and dividend yield. We estimate our future stock price volatility using the historical volatility over the expected term of the option, excluding time periods of volatility we believe a marketplace participant would exclude in estimating our stock price volatility. We also have considered, but did not use, implied volatility in our estimate, because trading activity in options on our stock, especially those with tenors of greater than 6 months, is insufficient to provide a reliable measure of expected volatility.

Our expected term represents the period of time that options granted are expected to be outstanding based on historical data to estimate option exercises and employee terminations within the valuation model. Separate groups of employees have similar historical exercise behavior and therefore were aggregated into a single pool for valuation purposes. The weighted-average expected term for all employee groups is presented in the table above. The risk-free interest rate for periods during the expected term of the options is based on the U.S. Treasury zero-coupon yield curve in effect at the time of grant.

Any corporate income tax benefit realized upon exercise or vesting of an award in excess of that previously recognized in earnings (referred to as a windfall tax benefit) is presented in the Consolidated Statements of Cash Flows as a financing cash flow.

Realized windfall tax benefits are credited to additional paid-in capital within the Consolidated Balance Sheets. Realized shortfall tax benefits (amounts which are less than that previously recognized in earnings) are first offset against the cumulative balance of windfall tax benefits, if any, and then charged directly to income tax expense, potentially resulting in volatility in our consolidated effective income tax rate. We calculated a cumulative memo balance of windfall tax benefits from post-1995 fiscal years for the purpose of accounting for future shortfall tax benefits.

Options may be priced at 100 percent or more of the fair market value on the date of grant, and generally vest four years after the date of grant. Options generally expire within 10 years and one month after the date of grant.

Information on stock option activity follows:

	Options Exercisable (Thousands)	Weighted Average Exercise Price Per Share	Options Outstanding (Thousands)	Weighted Average Exercise Price Per Share
Balance as of May 25, 2008	76,389.2	$21.23	106,042.4	$22.68
Granted			6,495.4	31.74
Exercised			(17,548.4)	19.60
Forfeited or expired			(382.4)	27.50
Balance as of May 31, 2009	67,619.2	21.96	94,607.0	23.84
Granted			6,779.4	27.99
Exercised			(20,013.6)	19.87
Forfeited or expired			(268.2)	24.82
Balance as of May 30, 2010	47,726.6	22.89	81,104.6	25.17
Granted			5,234.3	37.38
Exercised			(18,665.4)	22.59
Forfeited or expired			(126.2)	31.26
Balance as of May 29, 2011	39,221.7	$23.78	67,547.3	$26.82

Stock-based compensation expense related to stock option awards was $26.8 million in fiscal 2011, $34.4 million in fiscal 2010, and $40.0 million in fiscal 2009.

Net cash proceeds from the exercise of stock options less shares used for withholding taxes and the intrinsic value of options exercised were as follows:

	Fiscal Year		
(In millions)	2011	2010	2009
Net cash proceeds	$410.4	$388.5	$305.9
Intrinsic value of options exercised	$275.6	$271.8	$226.7

Stock Award Plans

3.58

J. C. PENNEY COMPANY, INC. (JAN)

NOTES TO CONSOLIDATED FINANCIAL STATEMENTS

12) Stock-Based Compensation (in part)

Stock Awards

On March 16, 2010, we made a grant of approximately 964,000 restricted stock unit awards to associates, representing the annual grant under the 2009 Plan. These awards consisted of approximately 574,000 time-based restricted stock units and approximately 390,000 performance-based restricted stock units. The time-based award vests one-third on each of the first three anniversaries of the grant date provided that the associate remains continuously employed with the Company during that time. The performance-based award has a target with a payout matrix ranging from 0% to 200% based on 2010 EPS (defined as per common share income from continuing operations, excluding any unusual and/or extraordinary items as determined by the Human Resources and Compensation Committee (HRCC) of the Board). A payment of 100% of the target award would be achieved at earnings of $1.58 per share and based on the actual 2010 earnings per share adjusted for unusual and extraordinary items determined by the HRCC, the award will payout at 154%, which resulted in an additional 205,000 units granted. In addition to the performance requirement, this award also includes a time-based vesting requirement, which is the same as the requirement for the time-based award. Upon vesting, both the time-based award and the performance-based award will be paid out in shares of jcpenney common stock.

In 2010, we granted approximately 58,000 restricted stock units to non-employee Board members. Restricted stock awards for non-employee directors are expensed when granted since the recipients have the right to receive the shares upon a qualifying termination of service in accordance with the grant. We also granted approximately 150,000 restricted stock units during 2010 consisting of ad-hoc awards to associates and dividend equivalents on outstanding awards.

In addition to individual ad-hoc and Board member stock awards vested during 2010, approximately 111,000 of our March 2008 annual grant of time-based restricted stock unit awards vested.

The following table summarizes our non-vested stock awards as of January 29, 2011 and activity during the year then ended:

(Shares in thousands)	Stock Awards	Weighted-Average Grant Date Fair Value
Non-vested at January 30, 2010	983	$28
Granted	1,377	30
Vested	(288)	43
Forfeited/canceled	(44)	33
Non-vested at January 29, 2011	2,028	27

As of January 29, 2011, we had $28 million of unrecognized compensation expense related to unearned associate stock awards, which will be recognized over the remaining weighted-average vesting period of approximately one year. The aggregate market value of shares vested during 2010, 2009 and 2008 was $8 million, $10 million and $17 million, respectively, compared to an aggregate grant date fair value of $12 million, $24 million and $26 million, respectively.

Savings and Investment Plans

3.59

THE J. M. SMUCKER COMPANY (APR)

NOTES TO CONSOLIDATED FINANCIAL STATEMENTS

(Dollars in thousands, unless otherwise noted, except per share data)

Note I: Savings Plans

ESOP: The Company sponsors an Employee Stock Ownership Plan and Trust ("ESOP") for certain domestic, nonrepresented employees. The Company has entered into loan agreements with the Trustee of the ESOP for purchases by the ESOP of the Company's common shares in amounts not to exceed a total of 1,134,120 unallocated common shares of the Company at any one time. These shares are to be allocated to participants over a period of not less than 20 years.

ESOP loans bear interest at one-half percentage point over prime, are secured by the unallocated shares of the plan, and are payable as a condition of allocating shares to participants. Interest expense incurred on ESOP debt was $127, $115, and $261 in 2011, 2010, and 2009, respectively. A contribution to the plan, representing compensation expense, is made annually in the amount sufficient to fund ESOP debt repayment and was $614 in 2009. Due to the payment by the Company of a $5.00 per share one-time special dividend in 2009, no contribution was necessary in 2011 or 2010 to fund ESOP debt repayment. Dividends on unallocated shares are used to reduce expense and were $262, $281, and $1,461 in 2011, 2010, and 2009, respectively. The principal payments received from the ESOP in 2011, 2010, and 2009 were $735, $761, and $649, respectively.

Dividends on allocated shares are credited to participant accounts and are used to purchase additional common shares for participant accounts. Dividends on allocated and unallocated shares are charged to retained income by the Company.

As permitted by FASB ASC 718, *Compensation— Retirement Benefits,* the Company will continue to recognize future compensation using the cost basis as all shares currently held by the ESOP were acquired prior to 1993. At April 30, 2011, the ESOP held 155,986 unallocated and 856,318 allocated shares. All shares held by the ESOP were considered outstanding in earnings per share calculations for all periods presented.

Defined Contribution Plans: The Company offers employee savings plans for domestic and Canadian employees. The Company's contributions under these plans are based on a specified percentage of employee contributions. Charges to operations for these plans in 2011, 2010, and 2009 were $16,440, $15,625, and $10,900, respectively.

Employee Stock Purchase Plans (ESPP)

3.60

GUESS?, INC. (JAN)

NOTES TO CONSOLIDATED FINANCIAL STATEMENTS

(13) Savings Plan (in part)

In January 2002, the Company established a qualified employee stock purchase plan ("ESPP"), the terms of which allow for qualified employees (as defined) to participate in the purchase of designated shares of the Company's common stock at a price equal to 85% of the lower of the closing price at the beginning or end of each quarterly stock purchase period. See Note 17 for further details.

(17) Share-Based Compensation (in part)

The Company has four share-based compensation plans. The Guess?, Inc. 2004 Equity Incentive Plan (the "Plan") provides that the Board of Directors may grant stock options and other equity awards to officers, key employees and certain consultants and advisors to the Company or any of its subsidiaries. The Plan authorizes grants of options to purchase up to 20,000,000 authorized but unissued shares of common stock. At January 29, 2011 and January 30, 2010, there were 13,723,669 and 13,863,982 shares available for grant under the Plan, respectively. Stock options granted under the Plan have ten-year terms and typically vest and become fully exercisable in increments of one-fourth of the shares granted on each anniversary from the date of grant. The three most recent annual grants have initial vesting periods of ten months, nine months and nine months, respectively, followed by three annual vesting periods. The Guess?, Inc. Employee Stock Purchase Plan ("ESPP") allows for qualified employees to participate in the purchase of designated shares of the Company's common stock at a price equal to 85% of the lower of the closing price at the beginning or end of each quarterly stock purchase period. The Guess?, Inc. 2006 Non-Employee Directors' Stock Grant and Stock Option Plan (the "Director Plan") provides for the grant of certain stock and stock options to non-employee directors. The Director Plan authorizes grants of options to purchase up to 2,000,000 authorized but unissued shares of common stock which consists of 1,000,000 shares that were initially approved for issuance on July 30, 1996 plus an additional

1,000,000 shares that were approved for issuance effective May 9, 2006. At January 29, 2011 and January 30, 2010, there were 951,373 and 973,838 shares available for grant under this plan, respectively. In addition, the Guess?, Inc. 1996 Equity Incentive Plan, under which equity grants have not been permitted since the approval of the Plan in 2004, continues to govern outstanding awards previously made thereunder.

Compensation expense for new stock options and nonvested stock awards is recognized on a straight-line basis over the vesting period. The Company estimates forfeitures in calculating the expense relating to share-based compensation as opposed to recognizing forfeitures as an expense reduction as they occur.

The following table summarizes the share-based compensation expense recognized under all of the Company's stock plans during fiscal 2011, fiscal 2010 and fiscal 2009 (in thousands):

	Year Ended Jan. 29, 2011	Year Ended Jan. 30, 2010	Year Ended Jan. 31, 2009
Stock options	$ 7,755	$ 8,051	$ 5,642
Nonvested stock awards/units	21,199	18,923	16,621
ESPP	358	365	583
Total share-based compensation expense	$29,312	$27,339	$22,846

ESPP

In January 2002, the Company established an ESPP, the terms of which allow for qualified employees (as defined) to participate in the purchase of designated shares of the Company's common stock at a price equal to 85% of the lower of the closing price at the beginning or end of each quarterly stock purchase period. Prior to March 4, 2009, the ESPP was a straight purchase plan with no holding period requirement. Effective March 4, 2009, the ESPP was amended to require participants to hold any shares purchased under the ESPP after April 1, 2009 for a minimum period of six months after purchase. In addition, all Company employees are subject to the terms of the Company's securities trading policy which generally prohibits the purchase or sale of any Company securities during the two weeks before the end of each fiscal quarter through two days after the public announcement by the Company of its earnings for that period. On January 23, 2002, the Company filed with the SEC a Registration Statement on Form S-8 registering 4,000,000 shares of common stock for the ESPP.

During fiscal 2011, fiscal 2010 and fiscal 2009, 42,695, 73,810 and 67,917 shares of the Company's common stock were issued pursuant to the ESPP at an average price of $30.69, $16.92 and $26.03 per share, respectively.

The fair value of stock compensation expense associated with the Company's ESPP was estimated on the date of grant using the Black-Scholes option-pricing valuation model and the following weighted-average assumptions for grants during fiscal 2011, fiscal 2010 and fiscal 2009.

Valuation Assumptions	Year Ended Jan. 29, 2011	Year Ended Jan. 30, 2010	Year Ended Jan. 31, 2009
Risk-free interest rate	0.1%	0.2%	1.7%
Expected stock price volatility	43.4%	62.3%	72.4%
Expected dividend yield	1.6%	2.4%	1.0%
Expected life of ESPP options (in months)	3	3	3

The weighted-average grant-date fair value of ESPP options granted during fiscal 2011, fiscal 2010 and fiscal 2009 was $9.39, $5.19 and $10.60, respectively.

Deferred Compensation Plans

3.61

BROWN SHOE COMPANY, INC. (JAN)

NOTES TO CONSOLIDATED FINANCIAL STATEMENTS

6. Retirement and Other Benefit Plans (in part)

Deferred Compensation Plan

In 2007, the Company established a non-qualified deferred compensation plan (the "Deferred Compensation Plan") for the benefit of certain management employees. The investment funds offered to the participants generally correspond to the funds offered in the Company's 401(k) plan, and the account balance fluctuates with the investment returns on those funds. The Deferred Compensation Plan permits the deferral of up to 50% of base salary and 100% of compensation received under the Company's annual incentive plan. The deferrals are held in a separate trust, which has been established by the Company to administer the Deferred Compensation Plan. The assets of the trust are subject to the claims of the Company's creditors in the event that the Company becomes insolvent. Consequently, the trust qualifies as a grantor trust for income tax purposes (i.e., a "Rabbi Trust"). The liabilities of the Deferred Compensation Plan of $1.4 million in 2010 and $1.0 million in 2009 are presented in employee compensation and benefits in the accompanying consolidated balance sheets. The assets held by the trust of $1.4 million in 2010 and $1.0 million in 2009 are classified as trading securities within prepaid expenses and other current assets in the accompanying consolidated balance sheets, with changes in the deferred compensation charged to selling and administrative expenses in the accompanying consolidated statements of earnings.

Deferred Compensation Plan for Non-Employee Directors

Non-employee directors are eligible to participate in a deferred compensation plan, whereby deferred compensation amounts are valued as if invested in the Company's common stock through the use of phantom stock units ("PSUs"). Under the plan, each participating director's account is credited with the number of PSUs equal to the number of shares of the Company's common stock that the participant could purchase or receive with the amount of the deferred compensation, based upon the fair value (as determined based on the average of the high and low prices) of the Company's common stock on the last trading day of the fiscal quarter when the cash compensation was earned. Dividend equivalents are paid on PSUs at the same rate as dividends on the Company's common stock and are re-invested in additional PSUs at the next fiscal quarter-end. The PSUs are payable in cash based on the number of PSUs credited to the participating director's account, valued on the basis of the fair value at fiscal quarter-end on or following termination of the director's service. The liabilities of the plan of $0.8 million as of January 29, 2011, and $0.7 million as of January 30, 2010, are based on 62,218 and 61,002 outstanding PSUs, respectively, and are presented in other liabilities in the accompanying consolidated balance sheets. Gains and losses resulting from changes in the fair value of the PSUs are charged to selling and administrative expenses in the accompanying consolidated statements of earnings.

Incentive Compensation Plans

3.62

ALLERGAN, INC. (DEC)

NOTES TO CONSOLIDATED FINANCIAL STATEMENTS

Note 10: Employee Stock Plans

The Company has an incentive award plan that provides for the granting of non-qualified stock options, incentive stock options, stock appreciation rights, performance shares, restricted stock and restricted stock units to officers, key employees and non-employee directors.

Stock option grants to officers and key employees under the incentive award plan are generally granted at an exercise price equal to the fair market value at the date of grant, generally expire ten years after their original date of grant and generally become vested and exercisable at a rate of 25% per year beginning twelve months after the date of grant. Restricted share awards to officers and key employees generally become fully vested and free of restrictions four years from the date of grant, except for restricted stock grants pursuant to the Company's executive bonus plan, which generally become fully vested and free of restrictions two years from the date of grant.

Restricted share awards to non-employee directors generally vest and become free of restrictions twelve months after the date of grant.

At December 31, 2011, the aggregate number of shares available for future grant under the incentive award plan for stock options and restricted share awards was approximately 28.0 million shares.

Share-Based Award Activity and Balances

The following table summarizes the Company's stock option activity:

(In thousands, except option exercise price and fair value data)	2011		2010		2009	
	Number of Shares	Weighted Average Exercise Price	Number of Shares	Weighted Average Exercise Price	Number of Shares	Weighted Average Exercise Price
Outstanding, beginning of year	23,856	$51.50	24,897	$47.99	21,238	$48.96
Options granted	5,007	75.95	5,084	59.54	5,790	40.73
Options exercised	(5,496)	48.01	(5,383)	43.12	(1,835)	35.68
Options cancelled	(716)	60.35	(742)	49.70	(296)	52.01
Outstanding, end of year	22,651	57.47	23,856	51.50	24,897	47.99
Exercisable, end of year	12,414	53.05	14,485	51.30	16,628	48.98
Weighted average per share fair value of options granted during the year		$23.30		$18.86		$15.44

The aggregate intrinsic value of stock options exercised in 2011, 2010 and 2009 was $172.5 million, $135.0 million and $35.9 million, respectively.

As of December 31, 2011, the weighted average remaining contractual life of options outstanding and options exercisable are 6.6 years and 5.1 years, respectively, and based on the Company's closing year-end stock price of $87.74 at December 31, 2011, the aggregate intrinsic value of options outstanding and options exercisable are $685.6 million and $430.6 million, respectively. Upon exercise of stock options, the Company generally issues shares from treasury.

The following table summarizes the Company's restricted share activity:

(In thousands, except fair value data)	2011		2010		2009	
	Number of Shares	Weighted Average Grant-Date Fair Value	Number of Shares	Weighted Average Grant-Date Fair Value	Number of Shares	Weighted Average Grant-Date Fair Value
Restricted share awards, beginning of year	886	$51.20	814	$48.99	678	$52.12
Shares granted	277	76.52	352	60.53	455	42.95
Shares vested	(87)	56.12	(212)	58.97	(304)	46.49
Shares cancelled	(41)	54.45	(68)	48.70	(15)	58.96
Restricted share awards, end of year	1,035	57.38	886	51.20	814	48.99

The total fair value of restricted shares that vested was $6.9 million in 2011, $12.8 million in 2010 and $12.7 million in 2009, respectively.

Valuation and Expense Recognition of Share-Based Awards

The Company accounts for the measurement and recognition of compensation expense for all share-based awards made to the Company's employees and directors based on the estimated fair value of the awards.

The following table summarizes share-based compensation expense by award type for the years ended December 31, 2011, 2010 and 2009, respectively:

(In millions)	2011	2010	2009
Employee and director stock options	$ 65.6	$ 56.9	$131.2
Employee and director restricted share awards	15.0	12.5	12.1
Stock contributed to employee benefit plans	5.7	4.5	8.6
Pre-tax share-based compensation expense	86.3	73.9	151.9
Income tax benefit	(28.5)	(23.2)	(50.9)
Net share-based compensation expense	$ 57.8	$ 50.7	$101.0

SEC 3.62

The following table summarizes pre-tax share-based compensation expense by expense category for the years ended December 31, 2011, 2010 and 2009, respectively:

(In millions)	2011	2010	2009
Cost of sales	$ 7.8	$ 7.6	$ 12.1
Selling, general and administrative	56.3	49.7	101.6
Research and development	22.2	16.6	38.2
Pre-tax share-based compensation expense	$86.3	$73.9	$151.9

Share-based compensation expense for 2009 includes $78.6 million of pre-tax compensation expense from stock option modifications related to the 2009 restructuring plan, including incremental pre-tax compensation expense of $ 11.0 million due to the change in fair value from the modifications, consisting of $ 5.0 million of cost of sales, $ 52.6 million in SG&A expenses and $ 21.0 million in R&D expenses.

The Company uses the Black-Scholes option-pricing model to estimate the fair value of share-based awards on the original grant date. The determination of fair value using the Black-Scholes option-pricing model is affected by the Company's stock price as well as assumptions regarding a number of complex and subjective variables, including expected stock price volatility, risk-free interest rate, expected dividends and projected employee stock option exercise behaviors. Stock options granted during 2011, 2010 and 2009 were valued using the Black-Scholes option-pricing model with the following weighted-average assumptions:

	2011	2010	2009
Expected volatility	27.82%	29.10%	39.82%
Risk-free interest rate	2.54%	2.73%	1.64%
Expected dividend yield	0.32%	0.37%	0.40%
Expected option life (in years)	5.85	5.79	5.71

The Company estimates its stock price volatility based on an equal weighting of the Company's historical stock price volatility and the average implied volatility of at-the-money options traded in the open market. The risk-free interest rate assumption is based on observed interest rates for the appropriate term of the Company's stock options. The Company does not target a specific dividend yield for its dividend payments but is required to assume a dividend yield as an input to the Black-Scholes option-pricing model. The dividend yield assumption is based on the Company's history and an expectation of future dividend amounts. The expected option life assumption is estimated based on actual historical exercise activity and assumptions regarding future exercise activity of unexercised, outstanding options.

The Company recognizes shared-based compensation cost over the vesting period using the straight-line single option method. Share-based compensation expense is recognized only for those awards that are ultimately expected to vest. An estimated forfeiture rate has been applied to unvested awards for the purpose of calculating compensation cost. Forfeitures were estimated based on historical experience. These estimates are revised, if necessary, in future periods if actual forfeitures differ from the estimates. Changes in forfeiture estimates impact compensation cost in the period in which the change in estimate occurs.

As of December 31, 2011, total compensation cost related to non-vested stock options and restricted stock not yet recognized was approximately $ 170.0 million, which is expected to be recognized over the next 48 months (31 months on a weighted-average basis). The Company has not capitalized as part of inventory any share-based compensation costs because such costs were negligible as of December 31, 2011, 2010 and 2009.

Employee Stock Ownership Plans (ESOP)

3.63

THE PROCTER & GAMBLE COMPANY (JUN)

NOTES TO CONSOLIDATED FINANCIAL STATEMENTS

Note 8—Postretirement Benefits and Employee Stock Ownership Plan (in part)

Defined Contribution Retirement Plans (in part)

We maintain The Procter & Gamble Profit Sharing Trust (Trust) and Employee Stock Ownership Plan (ESOP) to provide a portion of the funding for the U.S. DC plan and other retiree benefits. Operating details of the ESOP are provided at the end of this Note. The fair value of the ESOP Series A shares allocated to participants reduces our cash contribution required to fund the U.S. DC plan.

Employee Stock Ownership Plan

We maintain the ESOP to provide funding for certain employee benefits discussed in the preceding paragraphs.

The ESOP borrowed $1.0 billion in 1989 and the proceeds were used to purchase Series A ESOP Convertible Class A Preferred Stock to fund a portion of the U.S. DC plan. Principal and interest requirements of the borrowing were paid by the Trust from dividends on the preferred shares and from advances provided by the Company. The original borrowing of $1.0 billion has been repaid in full, and advances from the Company of $144 remain outstanding at June 30, 2011. Each share is convertible at the option of the holder into one share of the Company's common stock. The dividend for the current year was equal to the common stock dividend of $1.97 per share. The liquidation value is $6.82 per share.

In 1991, the ESOP borrowed an additional $1.0 billion. The proceeds were used to purchase Series B ESOP Convertible Class A Preferred Stock to fund a portion of retiree health care benefits. These shares, net of the ESOP's debt, are considered plan assets of the other retiree benefits plan discussed above. Debt service requirements are funded by preferred stock dividends, cash contributions and advances provided by the Company, of which $405 is outstanding at June 30, 2011. Each share is convertible at the option of the holder into one share of the Company's common stock. The dividend for the current year was equal to the common stock dividend of $1.97 per share. The liquidation value is $12.96 per share.

Our ESOP accounting practices are consistent with current ESOP accounting guidance, including the permissible continuation of certain provisions from prior accounting guidance. ESOP debt, which is guaranteed by the Company, is recorded as debt (see Note 4) with an offset to the reserve for ESOP debt retirement, which is presented within shareholders' equity. Advances to the ESOP by the Company are recorded as an increase in the reserve for ESOP debt retirement. Interest incurred on the ESOP debt is recorded as interest expense. Dividends on all preferred shares, net of related tax benefits, are charged to retained earnings.

The series A and B preferred shares of the ESOP are allocated to employees based on debt service requirements, net of advances made by the Company to the Trust. The number of preferred shares outstanding at June 30 was as follows:

Shares in thousands	2011	2010	2009
Allocated	52,281	54,542	56,818
Unallocated	13,006	14,762	16,651
Total Series A	65,287	69,304	73,469
Allocated	20,759	20,752	20,991
Unallocated	40,090	41,347	42,522
Total Series B	60,849	62,099	63,513

For purposes of calculating diluted net earnings per common share, the preferred shares held by the ESOP are considered converted from inception.

Profit Sharing Plans

3.64

TEXAS INSTRUMENTS INCORPORATED (DEC)

NOTES TO FINANCIAL STATEMENTS

6. Profit Sharing Plans

Profit sharing benefits are generally formulaic and determined by one or more subsidiary or company-wide financial metrics. We pay profit sharing benefits primarily under the company-wide TI Employee Profit Sharing Plan. This plan provides for profit sharing to be paid based solely on TI's operating margin for the full calendar year. Under this plan, TI must achieve a minimum threshold of 10 percent operating margin before any profit sharing is paid. At 10 percent operating margin, profit sharing will be 2 percent of eligible payroll. The maximum amount of profit sharing available under the plan is 20 percent of eligible payroll, which is paid only if TI's operating margin is at or above 35 percent for a full calendar year.

We recognized $143 million, $279 million and $102 million of profit sharing expense under the TI Employee Profit Sharing Plan in 2011, 2010 and 2009, respectively.

DEPRECIATION EXPENSE

RECOGNITION AND MEASUREMENT

3.65 FASB ASC 360, *Property, Plant, and Equipment*, defines *depreciation accounting* (the process of allocating the cost of productive facilities over the expected useful lives of the facilities) as a system of accounting that aims to distribute the cost or other basic value of tangible capital assets, less salvage (if any), over the estimated useful life of the unit, which may be a group of assets, in a systematic and rational manner. It is a process of allocation, not valuation.

3.66 FASB ASC 250 requires that a change in depreciation, amortization, or depletion method for long-lived, nonfinancial assets be accounted for as a change in accounting estimate effected by a change in accounting principle. Changes in accounting estimate are accounted for prospectively, not retrospectively as is required for changes in accounting principle.

DISCLOSURE

3.67 FASB ASC 360 stipulates that both the amount of depreciation expense and method(s) of depreciation should be disclosed in the financial statements or notes thereto.

3.68

TABLE 3-3: DEPRECIATION METHODS

Table 3-3 summarizes the methods of depreciation used to allocate the cost of depreciable assets.

	Number of Entities		
	2011	2010	2009
Straight line	490	492	488
Declining balance	9	10	10
Sum of the years' digits	2	2	3
Accelerated method—not specified	9	13	17
Units of production	12	15	16
Group/composite	17	4	10

PRESENTATION AND DISCLOSURE EXCERPTS

Straight-Line and Accelerated Method

3.69

THE HERSHEY COMPANY (DEC)

NOTES TO CONSOLIDATED FINANCIAL STATEMENTS

1. Summary of Significant Accounting Policies (in part)

Property, Plant and Equipment

Property, plant and equipment are stated at cost and depreciated on a straight-line basis over the estimated useful lives of the assets, as follows: 3 to 15 years for machinery and equipment; and 25 to 40 years for buildings and related improvements. Maintenance and repairs are expensed as incurred. We capitalize applicable interest charges incurred during the construction of new facilities and production lines and amortize these costs over the assets' estimated useful lives.

We review long-lived assets for impairment whenever events or changes in circumstances indicate that the carrying amount of such assets may not be recoverable. We measure the recoverability of assets to be held and used by a comparison of the carrying amount of long-lived assets to future undiscounted net cash flows expected to be generated. If these assets are considered to be impaired, we measure impairment as the amount by which the carrying amount of the assets exceeds the fair value of the assets. We report assets held for sale or disposal at the lower of the carrying amount or fair value less cost to sell.

18. Supplemental Balance Sheet Information (in part)

Property, Plant and Equipment

The property, plant and equipment balance included construction in progress of $239.9 million as of December 31, 2011 and $179.8 million as of December 31, 2010. Major classes of property, plant and equipment were as follows:

In thousands of dollars

December 31	2011	2010
Land	$ 92,495	$ 71,060
Buildings	895,859	843,094
Machinery and equipment	2,600,204	2,410,609
Property, plant and equipment, gross	3,588,558	3,324,763
Accumulated depreciation	(2,028,841)	(1,887,061)
Property, plant and equipment, net	$1,559,717	$1,437,702

During 2011, we recorded accelerated depreciation of property, plant and equipment of $33.0 million associated with the Next Century program. As of December 31, 2011, certain real estate with a carrying value or fair value less cost to sell, if lower, of $6.9 million was being held for sale. These assets were associated with the closure of facilities as part of our global supply chain transformation program. During 2011, we recorded an adjustment of $5.8 million to reduce the carrying amount of two properties being held for sale due to a decline in the estimated net realizable value of these properties.

3.70

GENERAL ELECTRIC COMPANY (DEC)

NOTES TO CONSOLIDATED FINANCIAL STATEMENTS

Note 1. Summary of Significant Accounting Policies (in part)

Depreciation and Amortization (in part)

The cost of GE manufacturing plant and equipment is depreciated over its estimated economic life. U.S. assets are depreciated using an accelerated method based on a sum-of-the-years digits formula; non-U.S. assets are generally depreciated on a straight-line basis.

The cost of GECS equipment leased to others on operating leases is depreciated on a straight-line basis to estimated residual value over the lease term or over the estimated economic life of the equipment.

The cost of GECS acquired real estate investments is depreciated on a straight-line basis to the estimated salvage value over the expected useful life or the estimated proceeds upon sale of the investment at the end of the expected holding period if that approach produces a higher measure of depreciation expense.

Note 7. Property, Plant and Equipment (in part)

December 31 (Dollars in millions)	Depreciable Lives— New (in years)	2011	2010
Original cost			
GE			
Land and improvements	8[(a)]	$ 611	$ 573
Buildings, structures and related equipment	8–40	7,823	7,468
Machinery and equipment	4–20	22,071	20,833
Leasehold costs and manufacturing plant under construction	1–10	2,538	1,986
		33,043	30,860
GECS[(b)]			
Land and improvements, buildings, structures and related equipment	1–37[(a)]	3,110	3,510
Equipment leased to others			
Aircraft	19–21	46,240	45,674
Vehicles	1–28	15,278	17,216
Railroad rolling stock	4–50	4,324	4,331
Construction and manufacturing	1–30	2,644	2,586
All other[(c)]	3–30	3,438	5,855
		75,034	79,172
Eliminations		40	—
Total		$108,117	$110,032
Net carrying value			
GE			
Land and improvements		$ 584	$ 550
Buildings, structures and related equipment		3,827	3,617
Machinery and equipment		7,648	6,551
Leasehold costs and manufacturing plant under construction		2,224	1,726
		14,283	12,444
GECS[(b)]			
Land and improvements, buildings, structures and related equipment		1,499	1,665
Equipment leased to others			
Aircraft[(d)]		34,271	34,665
Vehicles		8,772	9,077
Railroad rolling stock		2,853	2,960
Construction and manufacturing		1,670	1,454
All other[(c)]		2,354	3,947
		51,419	53,768
Eliminations		37	—
Total		$ 65,739	$ 66,212

[(a)] Depreciable lives exclude land.

[(b)] Included $1,570 million and $1,571 million of original cost of assets leased to GE with accumulated amortization of $470 million and $531 million at December 31, 2011 and 2010, respectively.

[(c)] Included $2,404 million of original cost and $1,670 million of carrying value at December 31, 2010 related to our CLL marine container leasing business, which was disposed during 2011.

[(d)] The GECAS business of GE Capital recognized impairment losses of $301 million in 2011 and $438 million in 2010 recorded in the caption "Other costs and expenses" in the Statement of Earnings to reflect adjustments to fair value based on an evaluation of average current market values (obtained from third parties) of similar type and age aircraft, which are adjusted for the attributes of the specific aircraft under lease.

Consolidated depreciation and amortization related to property, plant and equipment was $9,185 million, $9,786 million and $10,617 million in 2011, 2010 and 2009, respectively.

SEC 3.70

Units-of-Production Method

3.71

CF INDUSTRIES HOLDINGS, INC. (DEC)

NOTES TO CONSOLIDATED FINANCIAL STATEMENTS

2. Summary of Significant Accounting Policies (in part)

Property, Plant and Equipment

Property, plant and equipment are stated at cost. Depreciation, depletion and amortization are computed using the units-of-production method or the straight-line method. Depreciable lives are as follows:

	Years
Mobile and office equipment	4 to 12
Production facilities and related assets	10 to 25
Distribution facilities	10
Mining assets and phosphogypsum stacks	20
Land improvements	10 to 20
Buildings	10 to 45

We periodically review the depreciable lives assigned to production facilities and related assets, as well as estimated production capacities used to develop units-of-production (UOP) depreciation expense, and we change the estimates to reflect the results of those reviews.

Scheduled inspections, replacements and overhauls of plant machinery and equipment at the Company's continuous process manufacturing facilities are referred to as plant turnarounds. Plant turnarounds are accounted for under the deferral method, as opposed to the direct expense or built-in overhaul methods. Under the deferral method, expenditures related to turnarounds are capitalized into property, plant and equipment when incurred and amortized to production costs on a straight-line basis over the period benefited, which is until the next scheduled turnaround in up to 5 years. If the direct expense method were used, all turnaround costs would be expensed as incurred. Internal employee costs and overhead amounts are not considered turnaround costs and are not capitalized. Turnaround costs are classified as investing activities in the consolidated statements of cash flows. For additional information, see Note 20—Property, Plant and Equipment—Net.

20. Property, Plant and Equipment—Net

Property, plant and equipment—net consist of the following:

(In millions)	December 31 2011	December 31 2010
Land	$ 60.3	$ 60.5
Mineral properties	200.7	200.7
Manufacturing plants and equipment	5,448.0	5,297.2
Distribution facilities and other	272.6	221.3
Construction in progress	201.9	315.1
	6,183.5	6,094.8
Less: Accumulated depreciation, depletion and amortization	2,447.5	2,152.5
	$3,736.0	$3,942.3

Plant turnarounds—Scheduled inspections, replacements and overhauls of plant machinery and equipment at our continuous process manufacturing facilities are referred to as plant turnarounds. The expenditures related to turnarounds are capitalized into property, plant and equipment when incurred and are included in the table above in the line entitled, "Manufacturing plants and equipment." The following is a summary of plant turnaround activity for 2011, 2010 and 2009:

(In millions)	Year Ended December 31 2011	2010	2009
Net capitalized turnaround costs at beginning of the year	$ 66.8	$ 57.4	$ 40.6
Additions	16.2	34.4	41.8
Depreciation	(27.9)	(26.1)	(26.4)
Effect of exchange rate changes	(0.3)	1.1	1.4
Net capitalized turnaround costs at end of the year	$ 54.8	$ 66.8	$ 57.4

Scheduled replacements and overhauls of plant machinery and equipment include the dismantling, repair or replacement and installation of various components including piping, valves, motors, turbines, pumps, compressors, heat exchangers and the replacement of catalyst when a full plant shutdown occurs. Scheduled inspections are also conducted during full plant shutdowns, including required safety inspections which entail the disassembly of various components such as steam boilers, pressure vessels and other equipment requiring safety certifications. Internal employee costs and overhead are not considered turnaround costs and are not capitalized.

INCOME TAXES

RECOGNITION AND MEASUREMENT

3.72 FASB ASC 740, *Income Taxes*, clarifies the accounting for tax positions in an entity's financial statements. FASB ASC 740 prescribes a more-likely-than-not recognition threshold and measurement attribute for the financial statement recognition and measurement of a tax position taken or expected to be taken. Under FASB ASC 740, tax positions will be evaluated for recognition, derecognition, and measurement using consistent criteria. In addition, FASB ASC 740 provides guidance on classification and disclosure. FASB ASC 740 requires, except in certain specified situations, that undistributed earnings of a subsidiary included in consolidated income be accounted for as a temporary difference. Finally, the provisions of FASB ASC 740 provide more information about the uncertainty in income tax assets and liabilities.

DISCLOSURE

3.73 FASB ASC 740 sets forth standards for financial presentation and disclosure of income tax liabilities or assets and expense. These requirements vary for public and nonpublic entities. FASB ASC 740 states that amounts and expiration dates of operating loss and tax credit carryforwards for tax purposes should be disclosed. Any portion of the valuation allowance for deferred tax assets for which subsequently recognized tax benefits will be credited directly to contributed capital should also be disclosed. An entity's temporary difference and carryforward information requires additional disclosure, which differs for public and nonpublic entities.

PRESENTATION AND DISCLOSURE EXCERPTS

Expense Provision

3.74

CAMPBELL SOUP COMPANY (JUL)

CONSOLIDATED STATEMENTS OF EARNINGS
(in part)

(Millions, except per share amounts)	2011	2010	2009
Net sales	$7,719	$7,676	$7,586
Costs and expenses			
Cost of products sold	4,616	4,526	4,558
Marketing and selling expenses	1,007	1,058	1,077
Administrative expenses	612	605	591
Research and development expenses	129	123	114
Other expenses / (income)	13	4	61
Restructuring charges	63	12	—
Total costs and expenses	6,440	6,328	6,401
Earnings before interest and taxes	1,279	1,348	1,185
Interest expense	122	112	110
Interest income	11	6	4
Earnings before taxes	1,168	1,242	1,079
Taxes on earnings	366	398	347
Earnings from continuing operations	802	844	732
Earnings from discontinued operations	—	—	4
Net earnings	802	844	736

NOTES TO CONSOLIDATED FINANCIAL STATEMENTS

(Currency in millions, except per share amounts)

12. Taxes on Earnings (in part)

The provision for income taxes on earnings from continuing operations consists of the following:

	2011	2010	2009
Income taxes:			
Currently payable			
Federal	$ 215	$ 253	$ 145
State	27	46	12
Non-U.S.	78	45	46
	320	344	203
Deferred			
Federal	47	38	142
State	(2)	1	9
Non-U.S.	1	15	(7)
	46	54	144
	$ 366	$ 398	$ 347
Earnings from continuing operations before income taxes:			
United States	$ 944	$1,051	$ 976
Non-U.S.	224	191	103
	$1,168	$1,242	$1,079

The following is a reconciliation of the effective income tax rate on continuing operations with the U.S. federal statutory income tax rate:

	2011	2010	2009
Federal statutory income tax rate	35.0%	35.0%	35.0%
State income taxes (net of federal tax benefit)	1.4	2.5	1.7
Tax effect of international items	(2.1)	(2.5)	(0.8)
Settlement of tax contingencies	(0.5)	(0.7)	(1.0)
Federal manufacturing deduction	(1.8)	(1.3)	(1.0)
Other	(0.7)	(1.0)	(1.7)
Effective income tax rate	31.3%	32.0%	32.2%

During 2011, the company recorded a tax benefit of $8 following the finalization of tax audits.

In the third quarter of 2010, the company recorded deferred tax expense of $10 due to the enactment of U.S. health care legislation in March 2010. The law changed the tax treatment of subsidies to companies that provide prescription drug benefits to retirees. Accordingly, the company recorded the non-cash charge to reduce the value of the deferred tax asset associated with the subsidy.

In 2010, the company recorded a tax benefit of $9 following the finalization of tax audits. The company recorded an additional tax benefit of $2 during the year related to the resolution of other tax contingencies.

In 2009, the company recorded a tax benefit of $11 following the finalization of tax audits.

Credit Provision

3.75

THE GREAT ATLANTIC & PACIFIC TEA COMPANY, INC. (FEB)

(Debtors-in-Possession)

CONSOLIDATED STATEMENTS OF OPERATIONS (in part)

(Dollars in thousands, except per share amounts)

	Fiscal 2010	Fiscal 2009	Fiscal 2008
Sales	$ 8,078,455	$ 8,813,568	$ 9,516,186
Cost of merchandise sold	(5,677,800)	(6,146,808)	(6,613,150)
Gross margin	2,400,655	2,666,760	2,903,036
Store operating, general and administrative expense	(2,737,093)	(2,790,154)	(2,978,099)
Goodwill, trademark and long-lived asset impairment	(114,183)	(477,180)	—
Loss from continuing operations before nonoperating income (loss), interest expense, net, and reorganization items, net	(450,621)	(600,574)	(75,063)
Nonoperating income (loss)	13,777	(9,181)	116,864
Interest expense, net	(218,369)	(192,889)	(157,000)
Reorganization items, net	(21,985)	—	—
Loss from continuing operations before income taxes	(677,198)	(802,644)	(115,199)
Benefit from (provision for) income taxes	3,798	21,994	(2,683)
Loss from continuing operations	(673,400)	(780,650)	(117,882)

NOTES TO CONSOLIDATED FINANCIAL STATEMENTS

Note 17—Income Taxes (in part)

A reconciliation of income taxes from continuing operations at the 35% federal statutory income tax rate for fiscal 2010, fiscal 2009 and fiscal 2008 to income taxes as reported is as follows:

	Fiscal 2010	Fiscal 2009	Fiscal 2008
Income tax benefit from continuing operations computed at federal statutory income tax rate	$ 237,019	$ 280,925	$ 40,318
State and local income taxes, net of federal tax benefit and valuation allowance	(296)	3,975	(2,924)
Permanent difference relating to the sale of canadian assets	—	153,841	—
Permanent differences relating to Pathmark financing and impairments	7,880	(108,168)	40,902
Permanent item relating to Share Lending Agreement	—	—	(9,897)
Valuation allowance	(239,401)	(307,784)	(69,377)
Other	(1,404)	(795)	(1,705)
Income tax benefit (provision), as reported	$ 3,798	$ 21,994	$ (2,683)

The effective tax rate on continuing operations of (0.6%) for fiscal 2010 varied from the statutory rate of 35%, primarily due to state and local income taxes, the increase in our valuation allowance, and the impact of the Pathmark financing and fiscal 2010 impairments. Approximately $3.1 million of the net income tax benefit resulted from the write-off of the deferred tax liability associated with the Pathmark trademark, an indefinite-lived intangible asset, as a result of its impairment during fiscal 2010.

The effective tax rate on continuing operations of (2.7%) for fiscal 2009 varied from the statutory rate of 35%, primarily due to state and local income taxes, the increase in our valuation allowance as our Company could not recognize the benefit from our current losses, the remeasurement of uncertain tax positions, and the impact of the Pathmark financing and fiscal 2009 impairments. Approximately $16.0 million of the net income tax benefit resulted from the write-off of the deferred tax liability associated with the Pathmark trademark, an indefinite-lived intangible asset, as a result of its impairment during fiscal 2009.

The effective tax rate on continuing operations of 2.3% for fiscal 2008 varied from the statutory rate of 35%, primarily due to state and local income taxes, the increase in our valuation allowance and the impact of the Pathmark financing and the adjustment as a result of share lending agreements.

The benefit from (provision for) income taxes from continuing operations consisted of the following:

	Fiscal 2010	Fiscal 2009	Fiscal 2008
Current:			
Federal	$1,183	$ 156,196	$ 2,397
State and local	(455)	6,116	(4,498)
Foreign taxes	12	(36)	(582)
	740	162,276	(2,683)
Deferred:			
Federal	3,058	(140,282)	—
Benefit from (provision for) income taxes	$3,798	$ 21,994	$(2,683)

Operating Loss and Tax Credit Carryforwards

3.76

AUTODESK, INC. (JAN)

NOTES TO CONSOLIDATED FINANCIAL STATEMENTS

Note 5. Income Taxes (in part)

Significant components of Autodesk's deferred tax assets and liabilities are as follows:

	January 31, 2011	January 31, 2010
Nonqualified stock options	$ 69.0	$ 57.5
Research and development tax credit carryforwards	64.0	55.7
Foreign tax credit carryforwards	16.6	26.8
Accrued compensation and benefits	33.7	25.7
Other accruals not currently deductible for tax	18.7	17.8
Purchased technology and capitalized software	22.8	12.7
Fixed assets	15.1	12.0
Tax loss carryforwards	6.3	11.3
Capitalized research and development expenditures	2.5	3.4
Reserves for product returns and bad debts	2.1	2.1
Other	2.6	2.2
Total deferred tax assets	253.4	227.2
Less: valuation allowance	(42.9)	(39.0)
Net deferred tax assets	210.5	188.2
Tax method change on advanced payments	(9.4)	—
Unremitted earnings of foreign subsidiaries	(53.6)	(42.1)
Total deferred tax liability	(63.0)	(42.1)
Net deferred tax assets	$147.5	$146.1

The valuation allowance increased by $3.9 million, $14.3 million and $8.5 million in fiscal 2011, 2010 and 2009, respectively. The fiscal 2011 and fiscal 2010 increase was primarily related to California deferred taxes. During the first quarter of fiscal 2010, the State of California enacted legislation significantly altering California tax law. As a result of the newly enacted legislation, Autodesk expects that in fiscal years 2012 and beyond, income subject to tax in California will be less than under prior tax law and accordingly, deferred tax assets are less likely to be realized. The fiscal 2009 increases were primarily related to Canadian deferred taxes, which Autodesk does not expect to realize.

No provision has been made for federal income taxes on unremitted earnings of certain of Autodesk's foreign subsidiaries (cumulatively $1,030.5 million at January 31, 2011) because Autodesk plans to reinvest such earnings for the foreseeable future. At January 31, 2011, the net unrecognized deferred tax liability for these earnings was approximately $314.5 million.

Realization of the Company's net deferred tax assets of $147.5 million is dependent upon the Company's ability to generate future taxable income in appropriate tax jurisdictions to obtain benefit from the reversal of temporary differences, net operating loss carryforwards and tax credits. The amount of deferred tax assets considered realizable is subject to adjustment in future periods if estimates of future taxable income are reduced.

As of January 31, 2011, Autodesk had $16.9 million of cumulative federal tax loss carryforwards and $351.4 million of cumulative state tax loss carryforwards, which may be available to reduce future income tax liabilities in certain jurisdictions. These federal and state tax loss carryforwards will expire beginning fiscal 2012 through fiscal 2021 and fiscal 2012 through fiscal 2031, respectively.

As of January 31, 2011, Autodesk had $70.4 million of cumulative federal research tax credit carryforwards, $37.6 million of cumulative California state research tax credit carryforwards and $47.9 million of cumulative Canadian federal tax credit carryforwards, which may be available to reduce future income tax liabilities in the respective jurisdictions. The federal credit carryforwards will expire beginning fiscal 2012 through fiscal 2031, the state credit carryforwards may reduce future California income tax liabilities indefinitely, and the Canadian tax credit carryforwards will expire beginning fiscal 2023 through fiscal 2031. Autodesk also has $119.1 million of cumulative foreign tax credit carryforwards, which may be available to reduce future U. S. tax liabilities. The foreign tax credit will expire beginning fiscal 2018 through fiscal 2021.

Utilization of net operating losses and tax credits may be subject to an annual limitation due to ownership change limitations provided in the Internal Revenue Code and similar state provisions. This annual limitation may result in the expiration of net operating losses and credits before utilization.

3.77

CHESAPEAKE ENERGY CORPORATION (DEC)

NOTES TO CONSOLIDATED FINANCIAL STATEMENTS

5. Income Taxes (in part)

Deferred income taxes are provided to reflect temporary differences in the basis of net assets for income tax and finan-

cial reporting purposes. The tax-effected temporary differences and tax loss carryforwards which comprise deferred taxes are as follows:

($ In millions)	Years Ended December 31	
	2011	**2010**
Deferred tax liabilities:		
Natural gas and oil properties	$(2,883)	$(2,074)
Other property and equipment	(634)	(184)
Investments	(56)	—
Volumetric production payments	(1,453)	(1,394)
Contingent convertible debt	(396)	(493)
Deferred tax liabilities	(5,422)	(4,145)
Deferred tax assets:		
Net operating loss carryforwards	1,198	1,386
Derivative instruments	395	115
Asset retirement obligations	123	114
Investments	—	40
Deferred stock compensation	62	84
Accrued liabilities	82	25
Alternative minimum tax credits	257	11
State statutory depletion	121	93
Other	85	32
Deferred tax assets	2,323	1,900
Net deferred tax asset (liability)	(3,099)	(2,245)
Other non-current tax liabilities	(246)	—
Total deferred tax liabilities	$(3,345)[(a)]	$(2,245)
Reflected in accompanying balance sheets as:		
Current deferred income tax asset	$139	$139
Non-current deferred income tax liability	(3,484)	(2,384)
Total	$(3,345)	$(2,245)

[(a)] In addition to the income tax expense of $1.123 billion, activity during 2011 includes an increase to deferred tax liabilities of $26 million related to stock-based compensation, $25 million related to acquisitions and $1 million related to derivative instruments. The activity during 2011 also includes a decrease to deferred tax liabilities of $74 million related to the repurchase of contingent convertible notes and $1 million related to investments. These items were not recorded as part of the provision for income taxes.

As of December 31, 2011 and 2010, we classified $139 million of deferred tax assets as current that were attributable to current temporary differences associated with accrued liabilities, derivative liabilities and other items. As of December 31, 2011 and 2010, non-current deferred tax liabilities on the consolidated balance sheet included net non-current deferred tax liabilities of $3.238 billion and $2.384 billion, respectively. Also, included as of December 31, 2011 was $246 million of non-current liabilities related to uncertain tax positions associated with the federal alternative minimum tax.

Deferred tax assets relating to tax benefits of employee share-based compensation have been reduced related to stock options exercised and restricted stock that vested in periods in which Chesapeake was in a net operating loss position. Some exercises and vestings result in tax deductions in excess of previously recorded benefits based on the stock option or restricted stock value at the time of grant (windfalls). Although these additional tax benefits or windfalls are reflected in net operating loss carryforwards in the tax return, the additional tax benefit associated with the windfalls is not recognized until the deduction reduces taxes payable pursuant to accounting for stock compensation under GAAP. Accordingly, since the tax benefit does not reduce Chesapeake's current taxes payable due to net operating loss carryforwards, these windfall tax benefits are not reflected in Chesapeake's net operating losses in deferred tax assets as of December 31, 2011. Windfalls included in net operating loss carryforwards but not reflected in deferred tax assets as of December 31, 2011 totaled $21.2 million. Any shortfalls resulting from tax deductions that were less than the previously-recorded benefits were recorded as reductions to additional paid-in capital.

At December 31, 2011, Chesapeake had federal income tax net operating loss (NOL) carryforwards of approximately $3.155 billion which excludes the NOL carryforwards related to unrecognized tax benefits and stock compensation windfalls that have not been recognized under GAAP. Additionally, we had $66 million of alternative minimum tax (AMT) NOL carryforwards, net of unrecognized tax benefits, available as a deduction against future AMT income. The NOL carryforwards expire from 2019 through 2031. The value of these carryforwards depends on the ability of Chesapeake to generate taxable income.

The ability of Chesapeake to utilize NOL carryforwards to reduce future federal taxable income and federal income tax is subject to various limitations under the Internal Revenue Code of 1986, as amended. The utilization of such carryforwards may be limited upon the occurrence of certain ownership changes, including the issuance or exercise of rights to acquire stock, the purchase or sale of stock by 5% stockholders, as defined in the Treasury regulations, and the offering of stock by us during any three-year period resulting in an aggregate change of more than 50% in the beneficial ownership of Chesapeake.

In the event of an ownership change (as defined for income tax purposes), Section 382 of the Code imposes an annual limitation on the amount of a corporation's taxable income that can be offset by these carryforwards. The limitation is generally equal to the product of (i) the fair market value of the equity of the Company multiplied by (ii) a percentage approximately equivalent to the yield on long-term tax exempt bonds during the month in which an ownership change occurs. In addition, the limitation is increased if there are recognized built-in gains during any post-change year, but only to the extent of any net unrealized built-in gains (as defined in the Code) inherent in the assets sold. Certain NOLs acquired through various acquisitions are also subject to limitations.

The following table summarizes our net operating losses as of December 31, 2011 and any related limitations:

($ In millions)	Total	Limited	Annual Limitation
Net operating loss	$3,155	$80	$16
AMT net operating loss	$ 66	$66	$15

As of December 31, 2011, we do not believe that an ownership change has occurred. Future equity transactions by Chesapeake or by 5% stockholders (including relatively small transactions and transactions beyond our control)

could cause an ownership change and therefore a limitation on the annual utilization of NOLs.

Accounting guidance for recognizing and measuring uncertain tax positions prescribes a threshold condition that a tax position must meet for any of the benefit of the uncertain tax position to be recognized in the financial statements. Guidance is also provided regarding de-recognition, classification and disclosure of these uncertain tax positions. As of December 31, 2011, the amount of unrecognized tax benefits related to NOL carryforwards associated with uncertain tax positions and AMT associated with uncertain tax positions was $369 million. As of December 31, 2010, the amount of unrecognized tax benefits related to AMT associated with uncertain tax positions was $34 million. If these unrecognized tax benefits are disallowed and we are required to pay additional AMT liabilities, any payments can be utilized as credits against future regular tax liabilities. If these unrecognized tax benefits are disallowed and our NOL carryforwards are reduced, the reduction will be offset by additional tax basis that will generate future deductions. The uncertain tax positions identified would not have a material effect on the effective tax rate. As of December 31, 2011, we had an accrued liability of $12 million for interest related to these uncertain tax positions. Chesapeake recognizes interest related to uncertain tax positions in interest expense. Penalties, if any, related to uncertain tax positions would be recorded in other expenses.

Taxes on Undistributed Earnings

3.78

HANESBRANDS INC. (DEC)

MANAGEMENT'S DISCUSSION AND ANALYSIS OF FINANCIAL CONDITION AND RESULTS OF OPERATIONS

Liquidity and Capital Resources (in part)

Undistributed Earnings from Foreign Subsidiaries

As of December 31, 2011, the cumulative amount of undistributed earnings from our foreign subsidiaries was approximately $1.3 billion, of which less than $1 million of cash and cash equivalents was held by foreign subsidiaries whose undistributed earnings are considered permanently reinvested, and $18 million of cash and cash equivalents was held by foreign subsidiaries whose undistributed earnings are not considered permanently reinvested. Our intention is to reinvest the cash and cash equivalents of those entities whose undistributed earnings we have previously asserted as being permanently reinvested in our international operations. We reassess our reinvestment assertions each reporting period and currently believe that we have sufficient other sources of liquidity to support our assertion that such undistributed earnings held by foreign subsidiaries may be considered to be reinvested permanently.

We repatriated $28 million, $21 million and $23 million in 2011, 2010 and 2009, respectively, from earnings generated in such years. The amount of the current year foreign earnings that we have repatriated in the past has been determined, and the amount that we expect to repatriate during

2012 will be determined, based upon a variety of factors including current year earnings of the foreign subsidiaries, foreign investment needs and the cash flow needs we have in the U.S., such as for the repayment of debt and other domestic obligations. The majority of our repatriation of the earnings of foreign subsidiaries has historically occurred at year-end, although we may always repatriate funds earlier in the year based on the needs of our business. When we repatriate funds to the U.S., we are required to pay taxes on these amounts based on applicable U.S. tax rates, net of any foreign tax that would be allowed to be deducted or taken as a credit against U.S. income tax. We paid $2 million, $2 million and $5 million in additional U.S. federal income taxes in 2011, 2010 and 2009, respectively, as a result of repatriation of foreign earnings generated in such years. We do not currently expect the amount of repatriated foreign earnings or the resulting additional tax expense in 2012 to differ materially from prior fiscal years.

CONSTRUCTION-TYPE AND PRODUCTION-TYPE CONTRACTS

RECOGNITION AND MEASUREMENT

3.79 Accounting and disclosure requirements for construction-type and production-type contracts are discussed in FASB ASC 605-35. In accounting for contracts, the basic accounting policy decision is the choice between the percentage-of-completion method and the completed-contract method. The determination of which is preferable is based on an evaluation of the circumstances.

3.80

TABLE 3-4: METHOD OF ACCOUNTING FOR CONSTRUCTION-TYPE AND PRODUCTION-TYPE CONTRACTS

Table 3-4 shows that usually the percentage of completion method or a modification of this method is used to recognize revenue on long-term contracts.

	Number of Entities		
	2011	2010	2009
Percentage of completion: input based.......	32	43	63
Percentage of completion: output based....	19	32	41
Completed contract.....................................	3	8	20
Other, described..	7	N/C*	N/C*

* N/C = Not compiled. The line item was not included in the table for the year shown.

PRESENTATION AND DISCLOSURE EXCERPTS

Construction and Production Type Contracts

3.81

L-3 COMMUNICATIONS HOLDINGS, INC. (DEC)

CONSOLIDATED STATEMENTS OF OPERATIONS (in part)

(In millions, except per share data)

	Year Ended December 31		
	2011	2010	2009
Net sales:			
Products	$ 7,563	$ 7,596	$ 7,516
Services	7,606	8,084	8,099
Total net sales	15,169	15,680	15,615

NOTES TO CONSOLIDATED FINANCIAL STATEMENTS

2. Summary of Significant Accounting Policies (in part)

Revenue Recognition: Substantially all of the Company's sales are generated from written contractual (revenue) arrangements. The sales price for the Company's revenue arrangements are either fixed price, cost-plus or time-and-material type. Depending on the contractual scope of work, the Company utilizes either contract accounting standards or accounting standards for revenue arrangements with commercial customers to account for these contracts. Approximately 40% of the Company's 2011 sales were accounted for under contract accounting standards, including approximately 30% from fixed-price type contracts and approximately 10% from cost-plus type contracts. For contracts that are accounted for under contract accounting standards, sales and profits are recognized based on: (1) a Percentage-of-Completion (POC) method of accounting (fixed-price contracts), (2) allowable costs incurred plus the estimated profit on those costs (cost-plus contracts), or (3) direct labor hours expended multiplied by the contractual fixed rate per hour plus incurred costs for material (time-and-material contracts).

Sales and profits on fixed-price type contracts that are covered by contract accounting standards are substantially recognized using POC methods of accounting. Sales and profits on fixed-price production contracts under which units are produced and delivered in a continuous or sequential process are recorded as units are delivered based on their contractual selling prices (the "units-of-delivery" method). Sales and profits on each fixed-price production contract under which units are not produced and delivered in a continuous or sequential process, or under which a relatively few number of units are produced, are recorded based on the ratio of actual cumulative costs incurred to the total estimated costs at completion of the contract, multiplied by the total estimated contract revenue, less cumulative sales recognized in prior periods (the "cost-to-cost" method). Under both POC methods of accounting, a single estimated total profit margin is used to recognize profit for each contract over its entire period of performance, which can exceed one year. Losses on contracts are recognized in the period in which they become evident. The impact of revisions of contract estimates, which may result from contract modifications, performance or other reasons, are recognized on a cumulative catch-up basis in the period in which the revisions are made.

Sales and profits on cost-plus type contracts that are covered by contract accounting standards are recognized as allowable costs are incurred on the contract, at an amount equal to the allowable costs plus the estimated profit on those costs. The estimated profit on a cost-plus type contract is fixed or variable based on the contractual fee arrangement. Incentive and award fees are the primary variable fee contractual arrangements. Incentive and award fees on cost-plus type contracts are included as an element of total estimated contract revenues and are recorded to sales when a basis exists for the reasonable prediction of performance in relation to established contractual targets and the Company is able to make reasonably dependable estimates for them.

Sales and profits on time-and-material type contracts are recognized on the basis of direct labor hours expended multiplied by the contractual fixed rate per hour, plus the actual costs of materials and other direct non-labor costs.

Sales on arrangements for (1) fixed-price type contracts that require us to perform services that are not related to the production of tangible assets (Fixed-Price Service Contracts) and (2) certain commercial customers are recognized in accordance with accounting standards for revenue arrangements with commercial customers. Sales for the Company's businesses whose customers are primarily commercial business enterprises are substantially all generated from single element revenue arrangements. Sales are recognized when there is persuasive evidence of an arrangement, delivery has occurred or services have been performed, the selling price to the buyer is fixed or determinable and collectability is reasonably assured. Sales for Fixed-Price Service Contracts that do not contain measurable units of work performed are generally recognized on a straight-line basis over the contractual service period, unless evidence suggests that the revenue is earned, or obligations fulfilled, in a different manner.

Sales for Fixed-Price Service Contracts that contain measurable units of work performed are generally recognized when the units of work are completed. Sales and profit on cost-plus and time-and-material type contracts to perform services are recognized in the same manner as those within the scope of contract accounting standards, except for incentive and award fees. Cost-based incentive fees are recognized when they are realizable in the amount that would be due under the contractual termination provisions as if the contract was terminated. Performance based incentive fees and award fees are recorded as sales when awarded by the customer.

For contracts with multiple deliverables, the Company applies the separation and allocation guidance under the accounting standard for revenue arrangements with multiple deliverables, unless all the deliverables are covered by contract accounting standards, in which case the Company applies the separation and allocation guidance under contract accounting standards. Revenue arrangements with multiple deliverables are evaluated to determine if the deliverables should be separated into more than one unit of accounting. The Company recognizes revenue for each unit of accounting based on the revenue recognition policies discussed above.

Sales and profit in connection with contracts to provide services to the U.S. Government that contain collection risk because the contracts are incrementally funded and subject to the availability of funds appropriated, are deferred until a contract modification is obtained, indicating that adequate funds are available to the contract or task order.

3.82

NORTHROP GRUMMAN CORPORATION (DEC)

CONSOLIDATED STATEMENTS OF OPERATIONS (in part)

$ In millions, except per share amounts	Year Ended December 31		
	2011	2010	2009
Sales and Service Revenues			
Product sales	$15,073	$16,091	$16,004
Service revenues	11,339	12,052	11,646
Total sales and service revenues	26,412	28,143	27,650
Cost of Sales and Service Revenues			
Cost of product sales	11,491	12,558	12,648
Cost of service revenues	9,295	10,291	10,157
General and administrative expenses	2,350	2,467	2,571
Operating income	3,276	2,827	2,274

NOTES TO CONSOLIDATED FINANCIAL STATEMENTS

1. Summary of Significant Accounting Policies (in part)

Revenue Recognition—The majority of the company's business is derived from long-term contracts for production of goods, and services provided to the federal government. In accounting for these contracts, the company extensively utilizes the cost-to-cost and the units-of-delivery measures of the percentage-of-completion method of accounting. Sales under cost-reimbursement contracts and construction-type contracts that provide for delivery at a low volume per year or a small number of units after a lengthy period of time over which a significant amount of costs have been incurred are accounted for using the cost-to-cost method. Under this method, sales, including estimated earned fees or profits, are recorded as costs are incurred. Sales under contracts that provide for delivery at a high volume per year are accounted for using the units-of-delivery method. Under this method, sales are recognized as deliveries are made to the customer generally using unit sales values for delivered units in accordance with the contract terms. The company estimates profit on units-of-delivery contracts as the difference between total estimated revenue and total estimated cost of a contract and recognizes that profit over the life of the contract based on deliveries or as computed on the basis of the estimated final average unit costs plus profit. The company classifies contract revenues as product sales or service revenues depending upon the predominant attributes of the relevant underlying contracts.

Certain contracts contain provisions for price redetermination or for cost and/or performance incentives. Such redetermined amounts or incentives are included in sales when the amounts can reasonably be determined and estimated. Amounts representing contract change orders, claims, requests for equitable adjustment, or limitations in funding are included in sales only when they can be reliably estimated and realization is probable. In the period in which it is determined that a loss will result from the performance of a contract, the entire amount of the estimated ultimate loss is charged against income. Loss provisions are first offset against costs that are included in unbilled accounts receivable or inventoried costs, with any remaining amount reflected in liabilities. Changes in estimates of contract sales, costs, or profits are recognized using the cumulative catch-up method of accounting. This method recognizes in the current period the cumulative effect of the changes on current or prior periods. Hence, the effect of the changes on future periods of contract performance is recognized as if the revised estimate had been used since contract inception.

Changes in contract estimates occur for a variety of reasons including changes in contract scope, unforeseen changes in contract cost estimates due to unanticipated cost growth or risks affecting contract costs and/or the resolution of contract risks at lower costs than anticipated, as well as changes in contract overhead costs over the performance period. The company has an extensive contract management process involving several functional organizations and numerous personnel who are skilled at managing contract activities. Because the company's business involves performing on a broad portfolio of long-term contracts, generally involving complex customized products and services principally for its U.S. Government customers, changes in estimates occur routinely over the contract performance period. Significant changes in estimates on a single contract could have a material effect on the company's consolidated financial position or annual results of operations, and where such changes occur, separate disclosure is made of the nature, underlying conditions and financial impact of the change. Aggregate net changes in contract estimates recognized using the cumulative catch-up method of accounting increased operating income by $738 million ($1.70 per diluted share) in 2011, $675 million ($1.46 per diluted share) in 2010, and $421 million ($0.85 per diluted share) in 2009. No discrete event or adjustments to an individual contract within the aggregate net changes in contract estimates for 2011, 2010 or 2009 was material to the consolidated statement of operations for such annual period.

Revenue under contracts to provide services to non-federal government customers are generally recognized when services are performed. Service contracts include operations and maintenance contracts, and outsourcing-type arrangements, primarily in the Information Systems and Technical Services segments. Revenue under such contracts is generally recognized on a straight-line basis over the period of contract performance, unless evidence suggests that the revenue is earned or the obligations are fulfilled in a different pattern. Costs incurred under these service contracts are expensed as incurred, except that direct and incremental set-up costs are capitalized and amortized over the life of the agreement (see *Outsourcing Contract Costs* below). Operating profit related to such service contracts may fluctuate from period to period, particularly in the earlier phases of the contract. For contracts that include more than one type of product or service, revenue recognition includes the proper identification of separate units of accounting and the allocation of revenue across all elements based on relative fair values.

3.83

GRIFFON CORPORATION (SEP)

CONSOLIDATED STATEMENTS OF OPERATIONS

(in thousands, except per share data)

| | Years Ended September 30 | | |
	2011	2010	2009
Revenue	$1,830,802	$1,293,996	$1,194,050
Cost of goods and services	1,437,341	1,005,692	936,927
Gross profit	393,461	288,304	257,123

NOTES TO CONSOLIDATED FINANCIAL STATEMENTS

(Dollars in thousands, except per share data)

(Unless otherwise indicated, all references to years or year-end refer to Griffon's fiscal period ending September 30)

Note 1—Description of Business and Summary of Significant Accounting Policies (in part)

Revenue Recognition

Revenue is recognized when the following circumstances are satisfied: a) persuasive evidence of an arrangement exists, b) delivery has occurred, title has transferred or services are rendered, c) price is fixed and determinable and d) collectability is reasonably assured. Goods are sold on terms which transfer title and risk of loss at a specified location. Revenue recognition from product sales occurs when all factors are met, including transfer of title and risk of loss, which occurs either upon shipment or upon receipt by customers at the location specified in the terms of sale. Other than standard product warranty provisions, sales arrangements provide for no other significant post-shipment obligations. From time to time and for certain customers rebates and other sales incentives, promotional allowances or discounts are offered, typically related to customer purchase volumes, all of which are fixed or determinable and are classified as a reduction of revenue and recorded at the time of sale. Griffon provides for sales returns allowances based upon historical returns experience.

Telephonics earns a substantial portion of its revenue as either a prime or subcontractor from contract awards with the U.S. Government, as well as non-U.S. governments and other commercial customers. These formal contracts are typically long-term in nature, usually greater than one year. Revenue and profits from these long-term fixed price contracts are recognized under the percentage-of-completion method of accounting. Revenue and profits on fixed-price contracts that contain engineering as well as production requirements are recorded based on the ratio of total actual incurred costs to date to the total estimated costs for each contract (cost-to-cost method).

Using the cost-to-cost method, revenue is recorded at amounts equal to the ratio of actual cumulative costs incurred divided by total estimated costs at completion, multiplied by the total estimated contract revenue, less the cumulative revenue recognized in prior periods. The profit recorded on a contract using this method is equal to the current estimated total profit margin multiplied by the cumulative revenue recognized, less the amount of cumulative profit previously recorded for the contract in prior periods. As this method relies on the substantial use of estimates, these projections may be revised throughout the life of a contract. Components of this formula and ratio that may be estimated include gross profit margin and total costs at completion. The cost performance and estimates to complete on long-term contracts are reviewed, at a minimum, on a quarterly basis, as well as when information becomes available that would necessitate a review of the current estimate. Adjustments to estimates for a contract's estimated costs at completion and estimated profit or loss often are required as experience is gained, and as more information is obtained, even though the scope of work required under the contract may or may not change, or if contract modifications occur. The impact of such adjustments or changes to estimates is made on a cumulative basis in the period when such information has become known. Gross profit is affected by a variety of factors, including the mix of products, systems and services, production efficiencies, price competition and general economic conditions.

Revenue and profits on cost-reimbursable type contracts are recognized as allowable costs are incurred on the contract at an amount equal to the allowable costs plus the estimated profit on those costs. The estimated profit on a cost-reimbursable contract may be fixed or variable based on the contractual fee arrangement. Incentive and award fees on these contracts are recorded as revenue when the criteria under which they are earned are reasonably assured of being met and can be estimated.

For contracts whose anticipated total costs exceed the total expected revenue, an estimated loss is recognized in the period when identifiable. A provision for the entire amount of the estimated loss is recorded on a cumulative basis.

Amounts representing contract change orders or claims are included in revenue only when they can be reliably estimated and their realization is probable, and are determined on a percentage-of-completion basis measured by the cost-to-cost method.

DISCONTINUED OPERATIONS

RECOGNITION AND MEASUREMENT

3.84 FASB ASC 205-20 sets forth the financial accounting and reporting requirements for discontinued operations of a component of an entity. A *component of an entity* comprises operations and cash flows that can be clearly distinguished, operationally and for financial reporting purposes, from the rest of the entity. A component of an entity may be a reportable or an operating segment, a reporting unit, a subsidiary, or an asset group.

3.85 FASB ASC 205-20 uses a single accounting model to account for all long-lived assets to be disposed of (by sale, abandonment, or distribution to owners). This includes asset disposal groups meeting the criteria for presentation as a discontinued operation, as specified in FASB ASC 205-20. A long-lived asset group classified as held for sale should be measured at the lower of its carrying amount or fair value less cost to sell. Additionally, in accordance with FASB ASC 360, a loss shall be recognized for any write-down to fair value less cost to sell. A gain shall be recognized for any subsequent recovery of cost. Lastly, a gain or loss not previously recognized that results from the sale of the asset disposal group should be recognized at the date of sale.

PRESENTATION

3.86 The conditions for determining whether discontinued operations treatment is appropriate and the required income statement presentation are stated in FASB ASC 205-20-45-1, as follows:

> The results of operations of a component of an entity that either has been disposed of or is classified as held for sale . . . [should] be reported in discontinued operations . . . if both of the following conditions are met:
> a. The operations and cash flow of the component have been (or will be) eliminated from the ongoing operations of the entity as a result of the disposal transaction.
> b. The entity will not have any significant continuing involvement in the operations of the component after the disposal transaction.

3.87 In a period in which a component of an entity either has been disposed of or is classified as held for sale, the income statement of a business entity or statement of activities of a not-for-profit entity for current and prior periods should report the results of operations of the component, including any gain or loss recognized from the sale or write-down, in discontinued operations. The results of operations of a component classified as held for sale should be reported in discontinued operations in the period(s) in which they occur. The results of discontinued operations, less applicable income taxes (benefit), should be reported as a separate component of income before extraordinary items (if applicable). For example, the results of discontinued operations may be reported in the income statement of a business entity as follows:

Income from continuing operations before income taxes	$XXXX
Income taxes	XXX
Income from continuing operations	$XXXX
Discontinued operations (Note X):	
Loss from operations of discontinued component X (including loss on disposal of $XXX)	$XXXX
Income tax benefit	XXXX
Loss on discontinued operations	XXXX
Net income	$XXXX

A gain or loss recognized on the disposal should be disclosed either on the face of the income statement or in the notes to the financial statements.

3.88 Illustrations of transactions that should and should not be accounted for as business segment disposals are presented in the implementation guidance and illustrations of FASB ASC 205-20-55.

PRESENTATION AND DISCLOSURE EXCERPTS

Business Component Disposals

3.89

SARA LEE CORPORATION (JUN)

CONSOLIDATED STATEMENTS OF INCOME (in part)

Dollars in millions except per share data	Years Ended	July 2, 2011	July 3, 2010	June 27, 2009
Continuing Operations				
Net sales		$8,681	$8,339	$8,366
Cost of sales		5,868	5,356	5,614
Selling, general and administrative expenses		2,060	2,183	2,072
Net charges for exit activities, asset and business dispositions		105	84	98
Impairment charges		21	28	314
Contingent sale proceeds		—	(133)	(150)
Operating income		627	821	418
Interest expense		117	138	161
Interest income		(32)	(23)	(41)
Debt extinguishment costs		55	—	—
Income from continuing operations before income taxes		487	706	298
Income tax expense		149	124	114
Income from continuing operations		338	582	184
Discontinued Operations				
Income (loss) from discontinued operations net of tax expense (benefit) of $(50), $481 and $109		222	(139)	196
Gain on sale of discontinued operations, net of tax expense of $568, $74 and nil		736	84	—
Net income (loss) from discontinued operations		958	(55)	196
Net income		1,296	527	380
Less: Income from noncontrolling interests, net of tax				
Discontinued operations		9	21	16
Net income attributable to Sara Lee		$1,287	$ 506	$ 364
Amounts attributable to Sara Lee				
Net income from continuing operations		$ 338	$ 582	$ 184
Net income (loss) from discontinued operations		949	(76)	180
Net income attributable to Sara Lee		$1,287	$ 506	$ 364

NOTES TO FINANCIAL STATEMENTS

Note 5—Discontinued Operations (in part)

The businesses that formerly comprised the North American Fresh Bakery and International Household and Body Care segments as well as the North American refrigerated dough operations previously reported as part of the North American Foodservice segment are classified as discontinued operations and are presented in a separate line in the Consolidated Statements of Income for all periods presented. The assets and liabilities of these businesses to be sold meet the accounting criteria to be classified as held for sale and have been aggregated and reported on separate lines of the Condensed Consolidated Balance Sheets for all periods presented.

On November 9, 2010, the corporation signed an agreement to sell its North American fresh bakery business to Grupo Bimbo for $959 million, which includes the assumption of $34 million of debt. Per the agreement, the purchase price is subject to various adjustments, including a reduction by up to $140 million if and to the extent that Grupo Bimbo is required to divest certain assets in connection with obtaining regulatory approval. The regulatory review process is ongoing but may result in a purchase price reduction in excess of $140 million. The agreement will enable Grupo Bimbo to use the Sara Lee brand in the fresh bakery category throughout the world, except Western Europe, Australia and New Zealand, while the corporation retains the brand for all other categories and geographies. The sale also includes a small portion of business that is currently part of the North American Foodservice segment which is not reflected as discontinued operations as it does not meet the definition of a component pursuant to the accounting rules. The transaction, which is subject to customary closing conditions and regulatory clearances, is anticipated to close in the first quarter of 2012.

In the fourth quarter of 2011, steps were taken to market and dispose of the North American refrigerated dough business. This business was classified as held for sale and reported as a discontinued operation. On August 9, 2011, the corporation signed an agreement to sell this business to Ralcorp for $545 million.

As of the end of 2011, the corporation has closed or received binding offers for virtually all of its household and body care businesses—body care, air care, shoe care and insecticides. The corporation has completed the disposition of its global body care and European detergents business, as well as, its Australia/New Zealand bleach business. It has also completed the disposition of a majority of its shoe care and air care businesses. The corporation also entered into an agreement to sell its non-Indian insecticides businesses and received a deposit on the sale. In 2010, the corporation disposed of its Godrej Sara Lee joint venture, an insecticide business in India, which had been part of the household and body care businesses.

Results of Discontinued Operations. The amounts in the tables below reflect the operating results of the businesses reported as discontinued operations. The amounts of any gains or losses related to the disposal of these discontinued operations are excluded.

(In millions)	Net Sales	Pretax Income (Loss)	Income (Loss)
2011			
International Household and Body Care	$1,078	$ 72	$ 36
North American Fresh Bakery	2,037	58	159
North American Refrigerated Dough	307	42	27
Total	$3,422	$172	$ 222
2010			
International Household and Body Care	$2,126	$254	$(199)
North American Fresh Bakery	2,128	32	23
North American Refrigerated Dough	326	56	37
Total	$4,580	$342	$(139)
2009			
International Household and Body Care	$2,000	$245	$ 155
North American Fresh Bakery	2,200	13	10
North American Refrigerated Dough	316	47	31
Total	$4,516	$305	$ 196

With respect to the North American fresh bakery and refrigerated dough businesses, the reported amounts represent a full year of results for each year presented. With respect to the household and body care businesses, the reported results represent less than a full year of results in 2011 and 2010 as certain of these businesses were sold during 2011 and 2010.

In 2011, the North American fresh bakery operations recognized a $122 million tax benefit associated with the excess tax basis related to these assets.

In 2010, the household and body care operations reported $453 million of tax expense which includes the following significant tax amounts: i) a $428 million tax charge related

to the company's third quarter decision to no longer reinvest overseas earnings attributable to overseas cash and the net assets of the household and body care businesses; ii) a $40 million tax benefit related to the reversal of a tax valuation allowance on United Kingdom net operating loss carryforwards as a result of the gain from the household and body care business dispositions; and iii) a $22 million tax benefit related to the anticipated utilization of U.S. capital loss carryforwards available to offset the capital gain resulting from the household and body care business dispositions. Also in 2010, a $10 million pretax curtailment loss was recognized in the results of discontinued operations.

Gain (Loss) on the Sale of Discontinued Operations. The gain (loss) on the sales of discontinued operations recognized in 2011 and 2010 are summarized in the following tables.

(In millions)	Pretax Gain (Loss) on Sale	Tax (Charge)/ Benefit	After Tax Gain (Loss)
2011			
Global Body Care and European Detergents	$ 867	$(376)	$491
Air Care Products	273	(179)	94
Australia/New Zealand Bleach	48	(17)	31
Shoe Care Products	115	4	119
Other Household and Body Care Businesses	1	—	1
Total	$1,304	$(568)	$736
2010			
Godrej Sara Lee joint venture	$ 150	$ (72)	$ 78
Other	8	(2)	6
Total	$ 158	$ (74)	$ 84

The tax expense recognized on the sale of the household and body care businesses in 2011 includes a $190 million charge related to the anticipated repatriation of the cash proceeds received on the disposition of these businesses. In the fourth quarter, a repatriation tax benefit of $79 million was recognized on the gain transactions, which was reflected in the income taxes on the shoe care products gain.

Businesses Sold in 2011

Global Body Care and European Detergents. In December 2010, the corporation completed the disposition of its global body care and European detergents business. Using foreign currency exchange rates on the date of the transaction, the corporation received cash proceeds of $1.6 billion and reported an after tax gain on disposition of $491 million. The corporation entered into a customary transitional services agreement with the purchaser of this business to provide for the orderly separation of the business and the orderly transition of various functions and processes which was completed by the end of 2011.

Air Care Products Business. A majority of the air care products business was sold in July 2010. Using foreign currency exchange rates on the date of the transaction, the corporation has received cash proceeds of $411 million to date, which represents the majority of the proceeds to be received, and reported an after tax gain on disposition of $94 million. When this business was sold, certain operations were retained, primarily in Spain, until production related to non-air care businesses ceases at the facility. Sara Lee will continue to manufacture air care products for the buyer for a period of approximately five months after 2011, at which point the production facility will be sold to the buyer and the final gain on the sale will be recognized. The corporation entered into a customary transition services agreement with the purchaser of this business to provide for the orderly separation of the business and the orderly transition of various functions and processes which completed by the end of the second quarter of 2011.

Australia/New Zealand Bleach. In February 2011, the corporation completed the sale of its Australia/New Zealand bleach business. Using foreign currency exchange rates on the date of the transaction, the corporation received cash proceeds of $53 million and reported an after tax gain on disposition of $31 million.

Shoe Care Business. In May 2011, the corporation completed the sale of the majority of its shoe care businesses. Using foreign currency exchange rates on the date of the transaction, the corporation received cash proceeds of $276 million and reported an after tax gain on disposition of $119 million. The corporation anticipates receiving approximately $70 to $80 million more in future proceeds on delayed sales and working capital adjustments from the buyer in 2012.

Non-Indian Insecticides Business. In December 2010, the corporation entered into an agreement to sell all of its non-Indian insecticides businesses for € 154 million and received a deposit of € 152 million ($203 million—using foreign currency exchange rates on the date of receipt) on the sale of this business. The deposit is recognized as unrestricted cash, with an offsetting liability to the buyer, which is reported in Accrued liabilities—Other in the Consolidated Balance Sheet. However, as a result of competition concerns raised by the European Commission, the parties abandoned the original sale transaction in May 2011. Under the terms of the new sale agreement, the original purchase price remains € 154 million and the corporation will complete the sale of various insecticides businesses outside of the European Union (such as Malaysia, Singapore, Kenya and Russia) to the original buyer. It will transfer the net proceeds from the subsequent divestiture of the European portion of insecticide businesses to the original buyer.

Business Sold in 2010

Godrej Sara Lee Joint Venture. In May 2010, the corporation completed the disposition of its Godrej Sara Lee joint venture business, which was part of the International Household and Body Care segment, and recognized an after tax gain on the disposition. A total of $230 million of cash proceeds was received from the disposition of this business.

Discontinued Operations Cash Flows. The corporation's discontinued operations impacted the cash flows of the corporation as summarized in the table below.

(In millions)	2011	2010	2009
Discontinued operations impact on			
Cash from operating activities	$ 221	$ 498	$ 579
Cash from (used in) investing activities	2,446	119	(105)
Cash used in financing activities	(2,667)	(625)	(468)
Net cash impact of discontinued operations	$ —	$ (8)	$ 6
Cash balance of discontinued operations			
At start of period	—	$ 8	$ 2
At end of period	—	—	8
Increase (decrease) in cash of discontinued operations	$ —	$ (8)	$ 6

The cash used in financing activities primarily represents the net transfers of cash with the corporate office. The net assets of the discontinued operations includes only the cash noted above as most of the cash of those businesses has been retained as a corporate asset.

The following is a summary of the net assets held for sale as of July 2, 2011 and July 3, 2010, which primarily consists of the net assets of the North American fresh bakery and refrigerated dough businesses and the international household and body care businesses.

(In millions)	July 2, 2011	July 3, 2010
Trade accounts receivable	$ 173	$ 200
Inventories	84	240
Other current assets	28	51
Total current assets held for sale	285	491
Property	558	616
Trademarks and other intangibles	263	452
Goodwill	612	1,038
Deferred assets	(91)	—
Other noncurrent assets	49	17
Assets held for sale	$1,676	$2,614
Accounts payable	$ 134	$ 137
Accrued expenses and other current liabilities	157	303
Current maturities of long-term debt	16	20
Total current liabilities held for sale	307	460
Long-term debt	79	92
Other liabilities	194	320
Liabilities held for sale	$ 580	$ 872
Noncontrolling interest	$ 29	$ 28

3.90

CABOT CORPORATION (SEP)

CONSOLIDATED STATEMENTS OF OPERATIONS
(in part)

	Years Ended September 30		
(In millions, except per share amounts)	2011	2010	2009
Net sales and other operating revenues	$3,102	$2,716	$2,108
Cost of sales	2,544	2,206	1,891
Gross profit	558	510	217
Selling and administrative expenses	249	241	205
Research and technical expenses	66	65	66
Income (loss) from operations	243	204	(54)
Interest and dividend income	2	2	3
Interest expense	(39)	(40)	(30)
Other expense	(3)	—	(18)
Income (loss) from continuing operations before income taxes and equity in net earnings of affiliated companies	203	166	(99)
(Provision) benefit for income taxes	(6)	(30)	21
Equity in earnings of affiliated companies, net of tax of $5, $4 and $1	8	7	5
Income (loss) from continuing operations	205	143	(73)
Income (loss) from discontinued operations, net of tax of $29, $16, and ($1)	53	26	(2)
Net income (loss)	258	169	(75)
Net income attributable to noncontrolling interests, net of tax of $4, $3 and $1	22	15	2
Net income (loss) attributable to Cabot Corporation	$ 236	$ 154	$ (77)

NOTES TO CONSOLIDATED FINANCIAL STATEMENTS

Note A. Significant Accounting Policies (in part)

The consolidated financial statements have been prepared in conformity with accounting principles generally accepted in the United States. The significant accounting policies of Cabot Corporation ("Cabot" or "the Company") are described below. Certain changes have been made to operating segment information for prior years to reflect changes made in the fourth quarter of fiscal 2011 related to changes in the Company's reporting segments.

In August 2011, the Company entered into an agreement to sell its Supermetals Business. The applicable assets and liabilities of the business have been classified as held for sale in the Consolidated Balance Sheets as of September 30, 2011 and 2010. Consolidated Statements of Operations for all periods presented have been recast to reflect the presentation of discontinued operations. Unless otherwise indicated, all disclosures and amounts in the Notes to Consolidated Financial Statements relate to the Company's continuing operations.

Note C. Discontinued Operations

Cabot Supermetals Business

In August 2011, the Company entered into a Sale and Purchase Agreement (the "Purchase Agreement") with Global Advanced Metals Pty Ltd., an Australian company ("GAM"), for the sale of substantially all of the assets of the Company's Supermetals Business in exchange for a minimum of $401.5 million comprised of the following: (i) $175 million payable in cash at the closing, subject to certain working capital adjustments at closing, (ii) $175 million of 10.84% interest-bearing two-year promissory notes, which may be pre-paid by GAM at any time prior to maturity for an amount equal to $215 million (consisting of principal, interest and a prepayment premium), secured by liens on the property and assets of the acquired business and guaranteed by the GAM corporate group, (iii) quarterly contingent cash payments to be made in each calendar quarter that the promissory notes are outstanding in an amount equal to 50% of Adjusted EBITDA of the acquired business for the relevant calendar quarter, guaranteed to be at least $11.5 million for the first year following the closing of the transaction, and (iv) the assumption of certain liabilities associated with the Supermetals Business.

The parties expect the transaction to close by the end of calendar year 2011. Completion of the sale is subject to regulatory approval and certain other customary conditions. The Purchase Agreement is not subject to a financing condition.

In connection with the transaction, the parties have entered into a tantalum ore supply agreement under which the Company will sell to GAM all of the tantalum ore mined at the Company's mine in Manitoba, Canada for a period of three years following the closing of the transaction. The Company also entered into a transition services agreement for the Company to provide certain information technology applications and infrastructure and various administrative services to GAM during the transition period of six months from the closing date in exchange for one time and monthly service fees. GAM has the option to terminate such transition services with notice at any time and may elect to extend such services for up to three months. The future continuing cash flows from the disposed business to Cabot resulting from the tantalum ore supply agreement and transition services agreement are not significant and do not constitute a material continuing financial interest in the Supermetals Business.

The Supermetals Business, which had previously been presented as a separate reporting business, meets the criteria for being reported as a discontinued operation and has been segregated from continuing operations. The following table summarizes the results from discontinued operations:

	Years Ended September 30		
(Dollars in millions)	2011	2010	2009
Net sales and other operating revenues	$201	$177	$135
Income (loss) from operations before income taxes	84	42	(3)
(Provision) benefit for income taxes	(31)	(16)	1
Income (loss) from discontinued operations, net of tax	$ 53	$ 26	$ (2)

The following table summarizes the assets held for sale and the liabilities held for sale in the Company's Consolidated Balance Sheets:

	September 30	
(Dollars in millions)	2011	2010
Assets		
Accounts and notes receivable, net of reserve for doubtful accounts	$ 41	$ 36
Inventories	64	66
Prepaid expenses and other current assets	1	1
Total current assets held for sale	$106	$103
Net property, plant and equipment	$ 39	$ 38
Other assets	—	2
Total noncurrent assets held for sale	$ 39	$ 40
Liabilities		
Accounts payable and accrued liabilities	$ 12	$ 16
Total current liabilities held for sale	$ 12	$ 16
Other liabilities	$ 6	$ 6
Total noncurrent liabilities held for sale	$ 6	$ 6

Discontinued Operations—Other

In addition to the divesture of its Supermetals Business, the Company also has classified certain settlements associated with separate businesses divested ten or more years ago as part of Income (loss) from discontinued operations, net of tax in its Consolidated Statements of Operations for the fiscal years ended September 30, 2011 and 2009. These settlements resulted in net charges of less than $1 million in each of these years. No such charges were recorded in fiscal 2010.

Adjustment of Gain or Loss

3.91

QUALCOMM INCORPORATED (SEP)

*NOTES TO CONSOLIDATED FINANCIAL
STATEMENTS*

Note 10. Segment Information

The Company is organized on the basis of products and services. The Company aggregates four of its divisions into the Qualcomm Wireless & Internet segment and three of its divisions into the Qualcomm Strategic Initiatives (QSI) segment. Reportable segments are as follows:

- Qualcomm CDMA Technologies (QCT)—develops and supplies integrated circuits and system software based on CDMA, OFDMA and other technologies for use in voice and data communications, networking, application processing, multimedia and global positioning system products;
- Qualcomm Technology Licensing (QTL)—grants licenses or otherwise provides rights to use portions of the Company's intellectual property portfolio, which includes certain patent rights essential to and/or useful in the manufacture and sale of certain wireless products, including, without limitation, products implementing cdmaOne, CDMA2000, WCDMA, CDMA TDD (including TD-SCDMA), GSM/GPRS/EDGE and/or OFDMA standards, and collects fixed license fees and royalties in partial consideration for such licenses;
- Qualcomm Wireless & Internet (QWI)—comprised of:
  - Qualcomm Internet Services (QIS)—provides content enablement services for the wireless industry and push-to-talk and other products and services for wireless network operators;
  - Qualcomm Government Technologies (QGOV)—provides development, hardware, analytical expertise and services to United States government

agencies involving wireless communications technologies;
  - Qualcomm Enterprise Services (QES)—provides satellite- and terrestrial-based two-way wireless information and position reporting services to transportation and logistics companies and other enterprise companies with fleet vehicles; and
  - Firethorn—builds and manages software applications that enable certain mobile commerce services.
- Qualcomm Strategic Initiatives (QSI)—comprised of the Company's Qualcomm Ventures, Structured Finance & Strategic Investments and FLO TV divisions. QSI makes strategic investments that the Company believes will open new opportunities for its technologies, support the design and introduction of new products or services for voice and data communications or possess unique capabilities or technology. Many of these strategic investments are in early-stage companies. QSI also holds spectrum licenses. The results of QSI's FLO TV business is presented as discontinued operations (Note 11).

The Company evaluates the performance of its segments based on earnings (loss) before income taxes (EBT) from continuing operations. Segment EBT includes the allocation of certain corporate expenses to the segments, including depreciation and amortization expense related to unallocated corporate assets. Certain income and charges are not allocated to segments in the Company's management reports because they are not considered in evaluating the segments' operating performance. Unallocated income and charges include certain investment income (loss); certain share-based compensation; and certain research and development expenses and other selling and marketing expenses that were deemed to be not directly related to the businesses of the segments. Additionally, starting with acquisitions in the third quarter of fiscal 2011, unallocated charges include recognition of the step-up of inventories to fair value and amortization of certain intangible assets. Such charges related to acquisitions that were completed prior to the third quarter of fiscal 2011 are allocated to the respective segments. The table below presents revenues, EBT and total assets for reportable segments (in millions):

	QCT	QTL	QWI	QSI*	Reconciling Items*	Total*
2011						
Revenues	$8,859	$5,422	$656	$ —	$ 20	$14,957
EBT	2,056	4,753	(152)	(132)	(838)	5,687
Total assets	1,569	36	136	2,386	32,295	36,422
2010						
Revenues	$6,695	$3,659	$628	$ —	$ —	$10,982
EBT	1,693	3,020	12	7	(239)	4,493
Total assets	1,085	28	129	2,745	26,585	30,572
2009						
Revenues	$6,135	$3,605	$641	$ —	$ 6	$10,387
EBT	1,441	3,068	20	(54)	(2,072)	2,403
Total assets	892	89	142	1,614	24,708	27,445

* Revenues and EBT for fiscal 2010 and 2009 were adjusted to present discontinued operations (Note 11). Share-based payments that had been included in reconciling items and QSI revenues and EBT have been adjusted to conform for all periods presented.

Segment assets are comprised of accounts receivable and inventories for all reportable segments other than QSI. QSI segment assets include certain marketable securities, notes receivable, spectrum licenses, other investments and all

assets of QSI's consolidated subsidiaries. QSI segment assets related to the discontinued FLO TV business totaled $913 million at September 25, 2011 and $1.3 billion at both September 26, 2010 and September 27, 2009. QSI assets at September 25, 2011, September 26, 2010 and September 27, 2009 also included $20 million, $20 million and $10 million, respectively, related to investments in equity method investees. Reconciling items for total assets included $806 million, $384 million and $389 million at September 25, 2011, September 26, 2010 and September 27, 2009, respectively, of goodwill and other assets related to the Company's QMT division, a nonreportable segment developing display technology for mobile devices and other applications. Total segment assets also differ from total assets on a consolidated basis as a result of unallocated corporate assets primarily comprised of certain cash, cash equivalents, marketable securities, property, plant and equipment, deferred tax assets, goodwill, other intangible assets and assets of nonreportable segments. The net book values of long-lived assets located outside of the United States were $629 million, $221 million and $256 million at September 25, 2011, September 26, 2010 and September 27, 2009, respectively. The net book values of long-lived assets located in the United States were $1.8 billion, $2.2 billion and $2.1 billion at September 25, 2011, September 26, 2010 and September 27, 2009, respectively.

Revenues from each of the Company's divisions aggregated into the QWI reportable segment were as follows (in millions):

	2011	2010	2009
QES	$395	$376	$344
QIS	150	173	229
QGOV	100	74	66
Firethorn	11	7	3
Eliminations	—	(2)	(1)
	$656	$628	$641

Other reconciling items were comprised as follows (in millions):

	2011	2010*	2009*
Revenues			
Elimination of intersegment revenues	$ (3)	$ (10)	$ (15)
Other nonreportable segments	23	10	21
	$ 20	$ —	$ 6
EBT			
Unallocated cost of equipment and services revenues	$(210)	$ (42)	$ (40)
Unallocated research and development expenses	(553)	(401)	(372)
Unallocated selling, general and administrative expenses	(506)	(336)	(293)
Unallocated other operating expenses	—	—	(1,013)
Unallocated investment income (loss), net	756	767	(141)
Other nonreportable segments	(324)	(224)	(206)
Intersegment eliminations	(1)	(3)	(7)
	$(838)	$(239)	$(2,072)

* As adjusted for discontinued operations (Note 11)

Reconciling items for fiscal 2011 included $143 million, $59 million and $6 million of unallocated cost of equipment and services revenue, unallocated selling, general and administrative expenses and unallocated research and development expenses, respectively, related to the step-up of inventories

to fair value and amortization of intangible assets resulting from acquisitions. Other nonreportable segments' losses before taxes during fiscal 2011, 2010 and 2009 were primarily attributable to the Company's QMT division.

Specified items included in segment EBT were as follows (in millions):

	QCT	QTL	QWI	QSI*
2011				
Revenues from external customers	$8,856	$5,422	$656	$—
Intersegment revenues	3	—	—	—
Interest income	1	1	—	20
Interest expense	1	—	—	99
2010				
Revenues from external customers	$6,686	$3,659	$628	$—
Intersegment revenues	9	—	—	—
Interest income	1	2	2	8
Interest expense	1	—	(4)	27
2009				
Revenues from external customers	$6,125	$3,603	$638	$—
Intersegment revenues	10	2	3	—
Interest income	4	12	1	3
Interest expense	—	1	1	—

* As adjusted for discontinued operations (Note 11)

Intersegment revenues are based on prevailing market rates for substantially similar products and services or an approximation thereof, but the purchasing segment may record the cost of revenues at the selling segment's original cost. In that event, the elimination of the selling segment's gross margin is included with other intersegment eliminations in reconciling items. Effectively all equity in earnings (losses) of investees was recorded in QSI in fiscal 2011, 2010 and 2009.

The Company distinguishes revenues from external customers by geographic areas based on the location to which its products, software or services are delivered and, for QTL licensing revenues, the invoiced addresses of its licensees. Sales information by geographic area was as follows (in millions):

	2011	2010*	2009*
China	$ 4,744	$ 3,194	$ 2,378
South Korea	2,887	2,913	3,655
Taiwan	2,550	1,360	831
Japan	1,165	1,018	1,098
United States	897	555	603
Other foreign	2,714	1,942	1,822
	$14,957	$10,982	$10,387

* As adjusted for discontinued operations (Note 11)

Note 11. Discontinued Operations

On December 20, 2010, the Company agreed to sell substantially all of its 700 MHz spectrum for $1.9 billion, subject to the satisfaction of customary closing conditions, including approval by the U.S. Federal Communications Commission (FCC). The agreement terminates on January 13, 2013; however, either party can extend the agreement for another 90 days thereafter if the FCC approval has not been received by then. The agreement followed the Company's previously announced plan to restructure and evaluate strategic options related to the FLO TV business and network. The FLO TV business and network were shut down on March 27, 2011. Since then, the Company has been working to sell the remaining assets and exit contracts. The 700 MHz spectrum with a carrying value of $746 million that the Company has agreed to sell was classified as held for sale, and all other assets were considered disposed of at September 25, 2011. Accordingly, the results of operations of the FLO TV business were presented as discontinued operations at September 25, 2011. Loss from discontinued operations includes share-based payments and excludes certain general corporate expenses allocated to the FLO TV business during the periods presented. The Company's consolidated statements of operations for all prior periods presented have been adjusted to conform.

Summarized results from discontinued operations were as follows (in millions):

	Year Ended		
	September 25, 2011	September 26, 2010	September 27, 2009
Revenues	$ 5	$ 9	$ 29
Loss from discontinued operations	(507)	(459)	(327)
Income tax benefit	194	186	127
Discontinued operations, net of income taxes	$(313)	$(273)	$(200)

The carrying amounts of the major classes of assets and liabilities of discontinued operations in the consolidated balance sheet were as follows (in millions):

	September 25, 2011
Assets	
Current assets	$ 10
Property, plant and equipment, net	156
Assets held for sale	746
Other assets	1
	$913
Liabilities	
Trade accounts payable	$ 2
Payroll and other benefits related liabilities	2
Other current liabilities	75
Other noncurrent liabilities	183
	$262

The Company has a significant number of site leases, and the Company has corresponding capital lease assets, capital lease liabilities and asset retirement obligations (Note 9). The capital lease assets, included in property, plant and equipment, net, were considered disposed of at March 27, 2011 when the Company shut down the FLO TV business.

Restructuring and restructuring-related activities under the Company's plan related to discontinued operations were initiated in the fourth quarter of fiscal 2010 and are expected to be substantially complete by the end of fiscal 2012 as the Company continues to negotiate the exit of certain contracts and removes certain of its equipment from the network sites. During fiscal 2011, the Company recorded $300 million in restructuring-related charges, primarily consisting of asset impairments and accelerated depreciation, and net restructuring charges of $58 million, including $48 million in contract termination costs. Restructuring charges also include certain severance and lease costs. There were no significant restructuring and restructuring-related expenses recognized in fiscal 2010. The Company estimates that it will incur future restructuring and restructuring-related charges of up to $25 million, primarily related to lease exit costs. The Company may also realize certain gains, primarily due to the potential release of liabilities associated with ongoing efforts to exit certain contracts, the amount of which cannot be reasonably estimated at this time. Future cash expenditures are expected to be in the range of $75 million to $115 million.

Changes in the restructuring accrual for fiscal 2011, which is reported as a component of other liabilities, were as follows (in millions):

	Contract Termination Costs	Other Costs	Total
Beginning balance of restructuring accrual	$ —	$—	$—
Initial costs	63	16	79
Adjustments to costs	(2)	(6)	(8)
Cash payments	(22)	(6)	(28)
Ending balance of restructuring accrual	$ 39	$ 4	$43

EXTRAORDINARY ITEMS

RECOGNITION AND MEASUREMENT

3.92 FASB ASC 225-20 defines *extraordinary items* as events and transactions that are distinguished by their unusual nature and the infrequency of their occurrence. Both of the following criteria should be met to classify an event or a transaction as an extraordinary item:

- *Unusual nature.* The underlying event or transaction should possess a high degree of abnormality and be of a type clearly unrelated to or only incidentally related to the ordinary and typical activities of the entity, taking into account the environment in which the entity operates.
- *Infrequency of occurrence.* The underlying event or transaction should be of a type that would not reasonably be expected to recur in the foreseeable future, taking into account the environment in which the entity operates.

PRESENTATION

3.93 FASB ASC 225-20 also addresses the presentation and disclosure of unusual and infrequently occurring items that do not meet the extraordinary criteria. Such items are reported as a separate component of continuing operations either on the face of the income statement or in the notes. FASB ASC 225-20-55 illustrates events and transactions that should and should not be classified as extraordinary items.

3.94

TABLE 3-5: UNUSUAL ITEMS

Table 3-5 shows the nature of items classified as unusual by the survey entities.

	2011	2010
Impairment losses	27	16
Environmental	1	3
Investment losses	2	3
Litigation costs due to takeover attempt	2	1
Discontinued operations	48	N/C*
Other	17	26
No unusual items	408	451

* N/C = Not compiled. The line item was not included in the table for the year shown.

3.95

TABLE 3-6: EXTRAORDINARY ITEMS

Table 3-6 shows the nature of items classified as extraordinary by the survey entities.

	2011	2010	2009
Nature			
Early retirement of debt	—	11	N/C*
Litigation settlement	—	1	N/C*
Discontinued operations	—	N/C*	N/C*
Acquisition of a business	1	N/C*	N/C*
Other	—	12	3
Total Extraordinary Items	**1**	**24**	**3**
Number of Entities			
Presenting extraordinary items	1	24	3
Not presenting extraordinary items	499	476	497
Total Entities	**500**	**500**	**500**

* N/C = Not compiled. The line item was not included in the table for the year shown.

PRESENTATION AND DISCLOSURE EXCERPTS

Extraordinary Items

3.96

HUNTSMAN CORPORATION (DEC)

CONSOLIDATED STATEMENTS OF OPERATIONS AND COMPREHENSIVE (LOSS) INCOME (in part)

(In Millions, Except Per Share Amounts)

	Year Ended December 31		
	2011	2010	2009
Revenues:			
Trade sales, services and fees, net	$11,041	$9,049	$7,569
Related party sales	180	201	96
Total revenues	11,221	9,250	7,665
Cost of goods sold	9,381	7,789	6,587
Gross profit	1,840	1,461	1,078
Operating Expenses:			
Selling, general and administrative	921	861	850
Research and development	166	151	145
Other operating (income) expense	(20)	10	(18)
Restructuring, impairment and plant closing costs	167	29	88
Total expenses	1,234	1,051	1,065
Operating income	606	410	13
Interest expense, net	(249)	(229)	(238)
Loss on accounts receivable securitization program	—	—	(23)
Equity in income of investment in unconsolidated affiliates	8	24	3
Loss on early extinguishment of debt	(7)	(183)	(21)
(Expenses) income associated with the Terminated Merger and related litigation	—	(4)	835
Other income	2	2	—
Income from continuing operations before income taxes	360	20	569
Income tax expense	(109)	(29)	(444)
Income (loss) from continuing operations	251	(9)	125
(Loss) income from discontinued operations, (including gain on disposal of $1 in 2009), net of tax	(1)	42	(19)
Income before extraordinary gain (loss)	250	33	106
Extraordinary gain (loss) on the acquisition of a business, net of tax of nil	4	(1)	6
Net income	254	32	112
Net (income) loss attributable to noncontrolling interests	(7)	(5)	2
Net income attributable to Huntsman Corporation	$ 247	$ 27	$ 114
Net income	$ 254	$ 32	$ 112

NOTES TO CONSOLIDATED FINANCIAL STATEMENTS

3. Business Combinations and Dispositions (in part)

Textile Effects Acquisition

On June 30, 2006, we acquired Ciba's textile effects business and accounted for the Textile Effects Acquisition using the purchase method. As such, we analyzed the fair value of tangible and intangible assets acquired and liabilities assumed and we determined the excess of fair value of net assets over cost. Because the fair value of the acquired assets and liabilities assumed exceeded the purchase price, the valuation of the long-lived assets acquired was reduced to zero. Accordingly, no basis was assigned to property, plant and equipment or any other non-current nonfinancial assets and the remaining excess was recorded as an extraordinary gain, net of taxes (which were not applicable because the gain was

recorded in purchase accounting). During 2011, 2010 and 2009, we recorded an additional extraordinary gain (loss) on the acquisition of $4 million, $(1) million and $6 million, respectively, related to settlement of contingent purchase price consideration, the reversal of accruals for certain restructuring and employee termination costs recorded in connection with the Textile Effects Acquisition and a reimbursement by Ciba of certain costs pursuant to the acquisition agreements.

Unusual Items

3.97

GENCORP INC. (NOV)

CONSOLIDATED STATEMENTS OF OPERATIONS (in part)

(In millions, except per share amounts)	Year Ended		
	2011	2010	2009
Net sales	$918.1	$857.9	$795.4
Operating costs and expenses:			
Cost of sales (exclusive of items shown separately below)	799.3	753.9	674.0
Selling, general and administrative	40.9	26.7	10.2
Depreciation and amortization	24.6	27.9	25.7
Other expense, net	8.9	8.5	2.9
Unusual items			
Executive severance agreements	—	1.4	3.1
Loss on bank amendment	1.3	0.7	0.2
Loss on debt repurchased	0.2	1.2	—
Loss on legal matters and settlements	4.1	2.8	1.3
Gain on legal settlement	—	(2.7)	—
Total operating costs and expenses	879.3	820.4	717.4
Operating income	38.8	37.5	78.0

NOTES TO CONSOLIDATED FINANCIAL STATEMENTS

13. Unusual Items

Charges and gains associated with unusual items are summarized as follows:

(In millions)	Year Ended		
	2011	2010	2009
Aerospace and Defense:			
Loss on legal matters and settlements	$4.1	$2.8	$1.3
Aerospace and defense unusual items	4.1	2.8	1.3
Corporate:			
Executive severance agreements	—	1.4	3.1
Loss on debt repurchased	0.2	1.2	—
Loss on bank amendment	1.3	0.7	0.2
Gain on legal settlement	—	(2.7)	—
Corporate unusual items	1.5	0.6	3.3
Total unusual items	$5.6	$3.4	$4.6

Fiscal 2011 Activity:

The Company recorded a charge of $3.3 million related to a legal settlement and $0.8 million for realized losses and interest associated with the failure to register with the SEC the issuance of certain of its common shares under the defined contribution 401(k) employee benefit plan.

During fiscal 2011, the Company repurchased $22.0 million principal amount of its 2 1 / 4 % Debentures at various prices ranging from 99.0% of par to 99.6% of par resulting in a loss of $0.2 million.

In addition, during fiscal 2011, the Company recorded $1.3 million of losses related to an amendment to the Senior Credit Facility.

Fiscal 2010 Activity:

In fiscal 2010, the Company recorded $1.4 million associated with executive severance. In addition, the Company recorded a charge of $1.9 million related to the estimated unrecoverable costs of legal matters and $0.9 million for realized losses and interest associated with the failure to register with the SEC the issuance of certain of its common shares under the defined contribution 401(k) employee benefit plan. Further, the Company recorded a $2.7 million gain related to a legal settlement.

In addition, during fiscal 2010, the Company recorded $0.7 million of losses related to an amendment to the Senior Credit Facility.

A summary of the Company's losses on the 2 1 / 4 % Debentures repurchased during fiscal 2010 is as follows (in millions):

Principal amount repurchased	$ 77.8
Cash repurchase price	(74.3)
	3.5
Write-off of the associated debt discount	(6.3)
Portion of the 2 1 / 4 % Debentures repurchased attributed to the equity component	2.9
Write-off of the deferred financing costs	(0.4)
Loss on 2 1 / 4 % Debentures repurchased	$ (0.3)

A summary of the Company's losses on the 9 1 / 2 % Notes repurchased during fiscal 2010 is as follows (in millions):

Principal amount repurchased	$ 22.5
Cash repurchase price	(23.0)
Write-off of the deferred financing costs	(0.4)
Loss on 9 1 / 2 % Notes repurchased	$ (0.9)

Fiscal 2009 Activity:

In fiscal 2009, the Company recorded a charge of $1.3 million for realized losses and interest associated with its failure to register with the SEC the issuance of certain of the Company's common shares under its defined contribution 401(k) employee benefit plan. During fiscal 2009, the Company also

incurred a charge of $3.1 million associated with executive severance agreements. Additionally, the Company recorded costs of $0.2 million related to a bank amendment.

3.98

BEAM INC. (DEC)

NOTES TO CONSOLIDATED FINANCIAL STATEMENTS

22. Segment Information

In connection with the Separation Transactions as described in Note 3, *Discontinued Operations*, we re-evaluated our reportable segments as a standalone spirits company. Our three operating segments, which are also our reportable segments, are: North America, EMEA (Europe/Middle East/Africa), and APSA (Asia-Pacific/South America). Our reportable segments are based on internal organization of the business used by management for making operating decisions and assessing performance. Key countries/markets included in North America are: Canada, Mexico, and the U.S. Key countries/markets included in EMEA are: Spain, United Kingdom, Germany, Russia, Turkey, Ireland, Italy, Hungary, Czech Republic, Romania, South Africa, North America Duty Free, and Europe Travel Retail. Key countries/markets included in APSA are: Australia, New Zealand, South East Asia, China, Brazil, India, South Korea and Japan.

Each operating segment derives revenues from the sale of distilled spirits. Segment net sales is net sales excluding items considered by management to be unusual or infrequent in nature ("segment net sales"). The measure of segment profitability regularly reviewed by the chief operating decision maker (segment operating income) is operating income excluding restructuring, restructuring-related expense, and other items considered by management to be unusual or infrequent in nature ("segment income"). Unallocated corporate costs in both periods reflect the estimated, incremental historical Fortune Brands corporate structure as compared to the estimated Beam corporate structure following the Spin-Off.

Financial information for each segment is presented in the tables below. Asset information by segment is not presented as this information is not provided to or reviewed by the Company's chief operating decision maker.

(In millions)	2011	2010	2009
Net sales:			
North America	$1,271.5	$1,161.8	$1,090.9
EMEA	505.9	477.8	489.3
APSA	487.4	455.3	400.1
Segment net sales	$2,264.8	$2,094.9	$1,980.3
One-time impact of Australia distribution agreement	46.3	—	—
Consolidated net sales	$2,311.1	$2,094.9	$1,980.3
Income From Continuing Operations Before Income Taxes:			
North America	$ 360.9	$ 359.8	$ 354.8
EMEA	120.3	98.7	120.2
APSA	91.0	93.8	98.5
Total segment income	$ 572.2	$ 552.3	$ 573.5
Restructuring charges (Note 7)	7.7	15.4	28.8
Other charges (Note 7)	133.0	28.8	97.7
Unallocated corporate costs	36.0	51.9	47.9
Consolidated operating income	$ 395.5	$ 456.2	$ 399.1
Interest expense	117.4	143.7	143.6
Loss on early extinguishment of debt	149.2	—	—
Other (income) expense	(40.4)	(33.2)	7.5
Income from continuing operations before income tax	$ 169.3	$ 345.7	$ 248.0
Depreciation Expense:			
North America	$ 43.9	$ 37.9	$ 33.6
EMEA	24.6	25.3	20.5
APSA	22.4	21.7	17.9
Depreciation expense	$ 90.9	$ 84.9	$ 72.0
Amortization of Intangible Assets:			
North America	$ 7.9	$ 7.2	$ 8.1
EMEA	4.4	4.9	4.9
APSA	4.0	4.2	4.3
Amortization of intangible assets	$ 16.3	$ 16.3	$ 17.3

Refer to Note 7, *Restructuring and Other Charges*, for more information on restructuring charges and other charges.

Net sales and long-lived assets by location are as follows (in millions):

	2011	2010	2009
Net sales[a]:			
United States	$1,163.8	$1,034.6	$ 981.9
Australia	289.7	246.2	243.3
All other countries	857.6	814.1	755.1
Total net sales	$2,311.1	$2,094.9	$1,980.3
Long-lived assets:			
United States	$ 359.8	$ 321.5	
Spain	164.3	173.3	
All other countries	205.6	173.4	
Total long-lived assets	$ 729.7	$ 668.2	

[a] Based on country of destination.

SEC 3.98

23. Quarterly Financial Data (Unaudited)

The Company began reporting its former Golf segment as a discontinued operation beginning in the quarter ended June 30, 2011 and its former Home & Security segment as a discontinued operation beginning in the quarter ended December 31, 2011. Prior period results have been reclassified to conform to the discontinued operations presentation. Selected quarterly financial data for the years ended December 31, 2011 and 2010 are as follows (in millions, except per share data):

	2011			
	First Quarter[b]	Second Quarter[c]	Third Quarter[d]	Fourth Quarter[e]
Net sales[a]	$524.0	$570.4	$579.2	$637.5
Gross profit	294.4	328.7	335.8	364.4
Income (loss) from continuing operations	61.7	62.4	(82.0)	91.2
Income (loss) from discontinued operations	21.5	267.6	495.8	(2.7)
Net income	83.2	330.0	413.8	88.5
Net income attributable to Beam Inc.	81.2	328.6	413.1	88.5
Basic earnings (loss) per Beam Inc. common share				
Continuing operations	$ 0.40	$ 0.40	$ (0.53)	$ 0.59
Discontinued operations	0.13	1.73	3.20	(0.02)
Net income	$ 0.53	$ 2.13	$ 2.67	$ 0.57
Diluted earnings (loss) per Beam Inc. common share				
Continuing operations	$ 0.39	$ 0.40	$(0.53)	$ 0.58
Discontinued operations	0.13	1.69	3.20	(0.02)
Net income	$ 0.52	$ 2.09	$ 2.67	$ 0.56

	2010			
	First Quarter	Second Quarter[f]	Third Quarter[g]	Fourth Quarter[h]
Net sales[a]	$446.7	$503.5	$514.8	$629.9
Gross profit	260.2	304.5	308.8	356.4
Income from continuing operations	42.6	131.3	56.1	79.5
Income from discontinued operations	31.8	98.1	48.6	7.9
Net income	74.4	229.4	104.7	87.5
Net income attributable to Beam Inc.	72.2	227.4	102.6	85.4
Basic earnings per Beam Inc. common share				
Continuing operations	$ 0.28	$ 0.86	$ 0.37	$ 0.52
Discontinued operations	0.20	0.63	0.30	0.04
Net Income	$ 0.48	$ 1.49	$ 0.67	$ 0.56
Diluted earnings per Beam Inc. common share				
Continuing operations	$ 0.28	$ 0.85	$ 0.36	$ 0.51
Discontinued operations	0.19	0.63	0.30	0.04
Net income	$ 0.47	$ 1.48	$ 0.66	$ 0.55

[a] Net sales have been reduced by $148.9 million, $132.5 million, $128.0 million and $151.1 million for the first, second, third, and fourth quarters in 2011, respectively, and by $126.4 million, $128.0 million, $128.3 million and $188.3 million for the first, second, third, and fourth quarters in 2010, respectively, for excise taxes related to continuing operations that were previously within "Cost of goods sold" and are now classified as a reduction of sales as described in Note 1, *Description of Business, Basis of Presentation, and Summary of Significant Accounting Policies—Changes in Basis of Presentation and Accounting.*

[b] Unusual items impacting the quarter ended March 31, 2011 include (on a pre-tax basis): $46.3 million favorable one-time sales impact and $23.6 million favorable one-time operating income impact associated with transition to our new long-term distribution agreement in Australia and $9.2 million related to business separation costs.

[c] Unusual items impacting the quarter ended June 30, 2011 include (on a pre-tax basis): $8.1 million for business separation costs.

[d] Unusual items impacting the quarter ended September 30, 2011 include (on a pre-tax basis): $134.0 million loss on early extinguishment of debt, $68.6 million of business separation costs, $25.0 million of acquisition-related contingent consideration, and $7.6 million gain related to a distribution from our Maxxium investment.

[e] Unusual items impacting the quarter ended December 31, 2011 include (on a pre-tax basis): $31.3 million for impairment of tradenames, $19 million tax benefit related to the resolution of routine foreign tax audits, and $15.2 million loss on early extinguishment of debt.

[f] Unusual items impacting the quarter ended June 30, 2010 include (on a pre-tax basis): $42.4 million tax benefit and $25.6 million tax indemnification income related to the resolution of routine foreign tax audits.

[g] Unusual items impacting the quarter ended September 30, 2010 include (on a pre-tax basis): $14.5 million for restructuring charges and $8.6 million loss on sale of brands and related assets.

[h] Unusual items impacting the quarter ended December 31, 2010 include (on a pre-tax basis): $7.4 million loss on sale of brands and related assets and $5.3 million for income tax credits related to the resolution of a routine foreign tax audit.

EARNINGS PER SHARE

PRESENTATION

3.99 The computation, presentation, and disclosure requirements for earnings per share (EPS) for entities with publicly held common stock or potential common stock are stated in FASB ASC 260, *Earnings Per Share*. The objective of basic EPS is to measure the performance of an entity over the reporting period. The objective of diluted EPS is to measure the performance of an entity over the reporting period while giving effect to all dilutive potential common shares that were outstanding during the period. FASB ASC 260 also discusses the application of EPS guidance to master limited partnerships.

PRESENTATION AND DISCLOSURE EXCERPTS

Earnings Per Share

3.100

CARLISLE COMPANIES INCORPORATED (DEC)

NOTES TO CONSOLIDATED FINANCIAL STATEMENTS

Note 9—Earnings Per Share

On January 1, 2009, the Company adopted the accounting provisions related to determining whether instruments granted in stock-based compensation transactions are participating securities. The Company's unvested restricted shares and restricted stock units contain nonforfeitable rights to dividends and, therefore, are considered participating securities for purposes of computing earnings per share pursuant to the two-class method. The computation below of earnings per share excludes the income attributable to the unvested restricted shares and restricted stock units from the numerator and excludes the dilutive impact of those underlying shares from the denominator. Stock options are included in the calculation of diluted earnings per share utilizing the treasury stock method and performance share awards are included in the calculation of diluted earnings per share using the contingently issuable method. Neither are considered to be participating securities as they do not contain non-forfeitable dividend rights.

The following reflects the Income from continuing operations and share data used in the basic and diluted earnings per share computations using the two-class method:

In millions, except share and per share amounts	2011	2010	2009
Numerator:			
Income from continuing operations	$ 181.9	$ 130.6	$ 155.3
Less: dividends declared—common stock outstanding, unvested restricted shares and restricted share units	(43.5)	(40.6)	(38.6)
Undistributed earnings	138.4	90.0	116.7
Percent allocated to common shareholders[1]	99.0%	98.9%	98.9%
	137.1	89.0	115.4
Add: dividends declared—common stock	43.1	40.2	38.2
Numerator for basic and diluted EPS	$ 180.2	$ 129.2	$ 153.6
Denominator (In thousands):			
Denominator for basic EPS: weighted-average common shares outstanding	61,457	60,901	60,601
Effect of dilutive securities:			
Performance awards	318	92	—
Stock options	720	599	633
Denominator for diluted EPS: adjusted weighted average common shares outstanding and assumed conversion	62,495	61,592	61,234
Per Share Income From Continuing Operations:			
Basic	$ 2.93	$ 2.12	$ 2.53
Diluted	$ 2.88	$ 2.10	$ 2.51
[1]Basic weighted-average common shares outstanding	61,457	60,901	60,601
Basic weighted-average common shares outstanding, unvested restricted shares expected to vest and restricted share units	62,047	61,578	61,269
Percent allocated to common shareholders	99.0%	98.9%	98.9%

To calculate earnings per share for the Income (loss) from discontinued operations and for Net income, the denominator for both basic and diluted earnings per share is the same as used in the above table. The Income (loss) from discontinued operations and the Net income were as follows:

In millions, except share amounts	2011	2010	2009
Income (loss) from discontinued operations attributable to common shareholders for basic and diluted earnings per share	$ (1.6)	$ 14.8	$ (10.6)
Net income attributable to common shareholders for basic and diluted earnings per share	$178.6	$144.0	$ 143.0
Antidilutive stock options excluded from EPS calculation[1]	200.0	715.0	2,454.8

[1] Represents stock options excluded from the calculation of diluted earnings per share as such options had exercise prices in excess of the weighted-average market price of the Company's common stock during these periods. Amounts in thousands.

Section 4: Comprehensive Income

COMPREHENSIVE INCOME IN ANNUAL FILINGS

RECOGNITION AND MEASUREMENT

4.01 Financial Accounting Standards Board (FASB) *Accounting Standards Codification* (ASC) 220, *Comprehensive Income*, requires that items included in other comprehensive income should be classified based on their nature. Other comprehensive income includes the following: foreign currency items, changes in the fair value of certain derivatives, unrealized gains and losses on certain securities, and certain pension or other postretirement benefit items.

PRESENTATION

Author's Note

In June 2011, FASB issued FASB Accounting Standards Update (ASU) No. 2011-05, *Comprehensive Income (Topic 220): Presentation of Comprehensive Income*, which amends FASB ASC by eliminating the option to present the components of OCI as part of the statement of changes in stockholders' equity. Going forward, an entity will present the total of comprehensive income, the components of net income, and the components of OCI either in a single continuous statement of comprehensive income or in two separate but consecutive statements. In either option, an entity should present each component of net income together with total net income, each component of OCI together with a total for OCI, and a total amount for comprehensive income. The amendments to FASB ASC 220, *Comprehensive Income*, in ASU No. 2011-05 do not change which items an entity should present in OCI or when an entity should reclassify an item of OCI to net income. ASU No. 2011-05 is effective for fiscal years, and interim periods within those years, beginning after December 15, 2011. For nonpublic entities, the amendments are effective for fiscal years ending after December 15, 2012, and interim and annual periods thereafter. Early adoption is permitted because the remaining options are already permitted by FASB ASC 220. The amendments do not require any transition disclosures.

ASU No. 2011-05 is the result of a joint project with IASB to improve presentation of comprehensive income.

In December 2011, FASB issued ASU No. 2011-12, *Comprehensive Income (Topic 220): Deferral of the Effective Date for Amendments to the Presentation of Reclassifications of Items Out of Accumulated Other Comprehensive Income in ASU No. 2011-05*. ASU No. 2011-12 defers the changes in ASU No. 2011-05 related only to the presentation of reclassification adjustments. Preparers had argued that these reclassification adjustments would be difficult for preparers and might add unnecessary complexity to the financial statements. FASB issued ASU No. 2011-12 to allow sufficient time for it to redeliberate whether an entity should present the effects of reclassification adjustments on the face of the financial statements for all periods presented. While FASB is considering preparers' concerns, entities should continue to report reclassification adjustments in accordance with the requirements of FASB ASC 220 in effect before issuance of ASU No. 2011-05. The amendments in ASU No. 2011-12 are effective at the same time as the amendments in ASU No. 2011-05.

4.02 FASB ASC 220 requires entities that provide a full set of general-purpose financial statements (that is, financial position, results of operations, and cash flows) report comprehensive income and its components. The FASB ASC glossary defines *comprehensive income* as the change in equity (net assets) of a business entity during a period from transactions and other events and circumstances from nonowner sources. It includes all changes in equity during a period, except those resulting from investments by owners and distributions to owners. *Other comprehensive income* is defined as revenues, expenses, gains, and losses that under generally accepted accounting principles are included in comprehensive income but excluded from net income. If an entity has only net income, it is not required to report comprehensive income. All items that meet the definition of *components of comprehensive income* must be reported in a financial statement for the period in which they are recognized. Further, a total amount for comprehensive income should be displayed in the financial statement when the components of other comprehensive income are reported. No specific required format exists for displaying comprehensive income and its components. However, an entity is encouraged to display the components of other comprehensive income and total comprehensive income below the total for net income in a statement that reports results of operations or in a separate statement of comprehensive income that begins with net income.

4.03 FASB ASC 220 also states that an entity should disclose the amount of income tax expense or benefit allocated to each component of other comprehensive income, including reclassification adjustments, either on the face of the statement in which those components are displayed or in the notes thereto. Also, FASB ASC 810, *Consolidation*, states that if an entity has an outstanding noncontrolling interest (minority interest), the components of other comprehensive income attributable to the parent and noncontrolling interest in a less-than-wholly-owned subsidiary are required to be reported on the face of the financial statement in which comprehensive income is presented, in addition to presenting consolidated comprehensive income.

4.04 FASB ASC 220 also requires that adjustments should be made to avoid double counting in comprehensive income items that are displayed as part of net income for a period that also had been displayed as part of other comprehensive income in that period or earlier periods. For example, gains on investment securities that were realized and included in net income of the current period that also had been included in other comprehensive income as unrealized holding gains in the period in which they arose must be deducted through other comprehensive income of the period in which they are included in net income to avoid including them in comprehensive income twice. These adjustments are called *reclassification adjustments*. An entity may display reclassification adjustments on the face of the financial statement in which comprehensive income is reported, or it may disclose them in the notes to the financial statements (that is, either a gross display on the face of the financial statement or a net display on the face of the financial statement and disclosure of the gross change in the notes to the financial statements).

4.05

TABLE 4-1: COMPREHENSIVE INCOME—REPORTING STATEMENT

Table 4-1 shows the statement in which comprehensive income was presented.

Reporting Format:	2011	2010	2009
Included in statement of changes in stockholders' equity	343	409	405
Separate statement of comprehensive income	133	75	76
Combined statement of income and comprehensive income	15	7	11
	491	491	492
No comprehensive income reported	9	9	8
Total Entities	**500**	**500**	**500**

4.06

TABLE 4-2: OTHER COMPREHENSIVE INCOME—COMPONENTS*

Table 4-2 lists the components of other comprehensive income disclosed by survey entities in the statement used to present comprehensive income for the period reported.

	2011	2010
Foreign currency translation	407	405
Defined benefit postretirement plan adjustments	386	379
Gains and losses on derivatives held as cash flow hedges	286	286
Unrealized gains/losses on securities	218	200
Reclassification adjustments (includes realized gains/losses)	93	83
Outstanding noncontrolling interest	26	17
Share of investee other comprehensive income	7	7
Other	37	31

* Appearing in the statement used to present comprehensive income.

4.07

TABLE 4-3: COMPREHENSIVE INCOME—TAX EFFECT DISCLOSURE

	2011	2010	2009
Tax Effect Disclosure in Any Statement:			
Amount of tax effect allocated to each component	147	175	109
Amount of tax effect allocated to some but not all components	69	84	136
Total amount of tax effect	13	61	9
	229	320	254
Tax Effect Disclosure in Notes:			
Amount of tax effect allocated to each component	76	47	76
Amount of tax effect allocated to some but not all components	11	21	41
Total amount of tax effect	2	6	7
	89	74	124
Tax effect not disclosed in any statement	172	97	114
	490	491	492
No comprehensive income reported	10	9	8
Total Entities	**500**	**500**	**500**

PRESENTATION AND DISCLOSURE EXCERPTS

Combined Statement of Income and Comprehensive Income

4.08

CONVERGYS CORPORATION (DEC)

CONSOLIDATED STATEMENTS OF OPERATIONS AND COMPREHENSIVE INCOME (LOSS)

	Year Ended December 31		
(Amounts in millions except per share amounts)	**2011**	**2010**	**2009**
Revenues	$2,262.0	$2,203.4	$2,421.0
Operating costs and expenses:			
Cost of providing services and products sold[1]	1,420.5	1,340.9	1,461.6
Selling, general and administrative expenses	527.4	575.7	616.4
Research and development costs	49.3	56.2	74.2
Depreciation	86.9	97.3	110.3
Amortization	9.6	10.1	10.9
Restructuring charges	—	36.7	43.3
Asset impairment	—	181.1	3.1
Total costs and expenses	2,093.7	2,298.0	2,319.8
Operating income (loss)	168.3	(94.6)	101.2
Earnings and gain from Cellular Partnerships, net	285.2	47.2	41.0
Other income (expense), net	9.8	8.9	(17.2)
Interest expense	(16.1)	(19.5)	(28.9)
Income (loss) before income taxes	447.2	(58.0)	96.1
Income tax expense	118.9	16.7	11.6
Income (loss) from continuing operations	328.3	(74.7)	84.5
Income (loss) from discontinued operations, net of tax	6.5	21.5	(161.8)
Net income (loss)	$ 334.8	$ (53.2)	$ (77.3)
Other comprehensive income (loss), net of tax:			
Foreign currency translation adjustments	$ (3.9)	$ 11.7	$ 25.4
Change related to pension liability (net of tax benefit (expense) of $6.7, $2.9, and ($2.4))	(7.3)	(3.5)	2.2
Unrealized (loss) gain on hedging activities (net of tax benefit (expense) of $13.0, ($20.0), and ($27.9))	(20.2)	33.5	51.8
Total comprehensive income (loss)	$ 303.4	$ (11.5)	$ 2.1
Basic earnings (loss) per share:			
Continuing operations	$ 2.73	$ (0.61)	$ 0.69
Discontinued operations	0.06	0.18	(1.32)
Net basic earnings (loss) per share	$ 2.79	$ (0.43)	$ (0.63)
Diluted earnings (loss) per share:			
Continuing operations	$ 2.67	$ (0.61)	$ 0.68
Discontinued operations	0.05	0.18	(1.30)
Net diluted earnings (loss) per share	$ 2.72	$ (0.43)	$ (0.62)
Weighted average common shares outstanding:			
Basic	120.2	123.1	122.8
Diluted	122.9	123.1	124.9

[1] Exclusive of depreciation and amortization, with the exception of amortization of deferred charges.

The accompanying notes are an integral part of the Consolidated Financial Statements.

Separate Statement of Comprehensive Income

4.09

ANALOG DEVICES, INC. (OCT)

CONSOLIDATED STATEMENTS OF COMPREHENSIVE INCOME

Years ended October 29, 2011, October 30, 2010 and October 31, 2009

(Thousands)	2011	2010	2009
Income from continuing operations, net of tax	$860,894	$711,225	$247,408
Foreign currency translation adjustment	(647)	6,085	14,840
Net unrealized (losses) gains on securities:			
Net unrealized holding (losses) (net of taxes of $67 in 2011, $6 in 2010 and $347 in 2009) on available-for-sale securities classified as short-term investments	(459)	(50)	(2,456)
Net unrealized holding (losses) gains (net of taxes of $64 in 2011, $175 in 2010 and $197 in 2009) on securities classified as other investments	(118)	325	366
Net unrealized (losses) gains on securities	(577)	275	(2,090)
Derivative instruments designated as cash flow hedges:			
Changes in fair value of derivatives (net of taxes of $539 in 2011, $449 in 2010 and $2,278 in 2009)	3,347	(1,339)	16,215
Realized (gain) loss reclassification (net of taxes of $1,171 in 2011, $458 in 2010 and $1,609 in 2009)	(7,793)	1,863	9,657
Net change in derivative instruments designated as cash flow hedges	(4,446)	524	25,872
Accumulated other comprehensive income (loss)—pension plans:			
Transition asset (obligation) (net of taxes of $1 in 2011, $34 in 2010 and $1 in 2009)	12	(80)	(34)
Net actuarial gain (loss) (net of taxes of $1,770 in 2011, $4,594 in 2010 and $287 in 2009)	13,084	(30,151)	(663)
Net prior service income (net of taxes of $0 in 2011, $0 in 2010 and $1 in 2009)	—	—	5
Net change in accumulated other comprehensive income (loss)—pension plans (net of taxes of $1,771 in 2011, $4,560 in 2010 and $286 in 2009)	13,096	(30,231)	(692)
Other comprehensive income (loss)	7,426	(23,347)	37,930
Comprehensive income from continuing operations	868,320	687,878	285,338
Total income from discontinued operations, net of tax	6,500	859	364
Comprehensive income	$874,820	$688,737	$285,702

See accompanying Notes.

Statement of Comprehensive Income Included With Statement of Changes in Stockholders' Equity

4.10

AIRGAS, INC. (MAR)

CONSOLIDATED STATEMENTS OF STOCKHOLDERS' EQUITY

(In thousands)	Shares of Common Stock	Common Stock	Capital in Excess of Par Value	Retained Earnings	Accumulated Other Comprehensive Income (Loss)	Shares of Treasury Stock	Treasury Stock	Total Stockholders' Equity
					Years Ended March 31, 2011, 2010 and 2009			
Balance—April 1, 2008	84,076	$841	$468,302	$ 983,663	$ (4,713)	(1,788)	$ (34,757)	$1,413,336
Comprehensive income:								
Net earnings				261,088				$ 261,088
Foreign currency translation adjustment					(11,451)			(11,451)
Net change in fair value of interest rate swap agreements (Note 10)					8,325			8,325
Net tax expense of other comprehensive income items					(2,914)			(2,914)
Total comprehensive income								$ 255,048
Shares issued in connection with stock options exercised (Note 13)	1,027	10	16,178					16,188
Dividends paid on common stock ($0.56) (Note 12)				(45,766)				(45,766)
Tax benefit associated with the exercise of stock options			11,846					11,846
Shares issued in connection with the Employee Stock Purchase Plan (Note 13)	439	5	16,502					16,507
Expense related to stock-based compensation (Note 13)			20,202					20,202
Purchase of treasury stock (Note 12)						(2,351)	(115,606)	(115,606)
Balance—March 31, 2009	85,542	$856	$533,030	$1,198,985	$(10,753)	(4,139)	$(150,363)	$1,571,755
Comprehensive income:								
Net earnings				196,300				$ 196,300
Foreign currency translation adjustment					8,629			8,629
Net change in fair value of interest rate swap agreements (Note 10)					8,563			8,563
Net tax expense of other comprehensive income items					(2,997)			(2,997)
Total comprehensive income								$ 210,495
Shares issued in connection with stock options exercised (Note 13)	187	2	(18,561)			1,112	40,422	21,863
Dividends paid on common stock ($0.76) (Note 12)				(62,526)				(62,526)
Tax benefit associated with the exercise of stock options			15,444					15,444
Shares issued in connection with the Employee Stock Purchase Plan (Note 13)	524	5	15,423					15,428
Expense related to stock-based compensation (Note 13)			23,085					23,085
Balance—March 31, 2010	86,253	$863	$568,421	$1,332,759	$ 3,442	(3,027)	$(109,941)	$1,795,544
Comprehensive income:								
Net earnings				249,766				$ 249,766
Foreign currency translation adjustment					2,948			2,948
Net gain on derivative instruments (Note 10)					1,633			1,633
Net tax expense of other comprehensive income items					(443)			(443)
Total comprehensive income								$ 253,904
Shares issued in connection with stock options exercised (Note 13)			(7,964)			812	30,056	$ 22,092
Dividends paid on common stock ($1.01) (Note 12)				(83,797)				(83,797)
Tax benefit associated with the exercise of stock options			8,444					8,444
Shares issued in connection with the Employee Stock Purchase Plan (Note 13)	338	3	14,994					14,997
Expense related to stock-based compensation (Note 13)			23,698					23,698
Purchase of treasury stock (Note 12)						(4,780)	(300,000)	(300,000)
Balance—March 31, 2011	86,591	$866	$607,593	$1,498,728	$ 7,580	(6,995)	$(379,885)	$1,734,882

See accompanying notes to consolidated financial statements.

Tax Effect Disclosure in the Notes

4.11

BROWN SHOE COMPANY, INC. (JAN)

NOTES TO CONSOLIDATED FINANCIAL STATEMENTS

4. Comprehensive Income (Loss)

Comprehensive income (loss) includes changes in equity related to foreign currency translation adjustments, unrealized gains or losses from derivatives used for hedging activities and pension and other postretirement benefits adjustments.

The following table sets forth the reconciliation from net earnings (loss) to comprehensive income (loss) for the periods ended January 29, 2011, January 30, 2010 and January 31, 2009:

($ thousands)	2010	2009	2008
Net earnings (loss)	$37,060	$10,443	$(134,813)
Other comprehensive income (loss) ("OCI"), net of tax:			
Foreign currency translation adjustment	2,150	3,437	(10,372)
Pension and other postretirement benefits adjustments, net of tax of $2,197, $2,485 and $7,150 in 2010, 2009 and 2008, respectively	3,433	3,509	(11,233)
Unrealized gains (losses) on derivative financial instruments, net of tax of $63, $481 and $200 in 2010, 2009 and 2008, respectively	171	(1,146)	409
Net loss (gain) from derivatives reclassified into earnings, net of tax of $124, $82 and $11 in 2010, 2009 and 2008, respectively	233	161	(11)
	5,987	5,961	(21,207)
Comprehensive income (loss)	$43,047	$16,404	$(156,020)
Less: Comprehensive (loss) income attributable to noncontrolling interests	(150)	946	(1,403)
Comprehensive income (loss) attributable to Brown Shoe Company, Inc.	$43,197	$15,458	$(154,617)

The following table sets forth the balance in accumulated other comprehensive income (loss) for the Company at January 29, 2011, January 30, 2010 and January 31, 2009:

($ thousands)	2010	2009	2008
Foreign currency translation gains	$6,281	$ 4,154	$ 720
Unrealized (losses) gains on derivative financial instruments, net of tax	(313)	(717)	268
Pension and other postretirement benefits, net of tax	173	(3,260)	(6,769)
Accumulated other comprehensive income (loss)	$6,141	$ 177	$(5,781)

See additional information related to derivative financial instruments in Note 1, Note 13 and Note 14 to the consolidated financial statements and additional information related to pension and other postretirement benefits in Note 6 to the consolidated financial statements.

Tax Effect Disclosure on the Face of the Financial Statements

4.12

COLLECTIVE BRANDS, INC. (JAN)

CONSOLIDATED STATEMENTS OF SHAREOWNERS'
EQUITY AND COMPREHENSIVE INCOME (LOSS)
(in part)

| | Collective Brands, Inc. Shareowners' | | | | | | | |
| | Outstanding Common Stock | | Additional Paid-In Capital | Retained Earnings | Accumulated Other Comprehensive Income (Loss) | Non-Controlling Interests | Total Equity | Comprehensive Income (Loss) |
(Dollars in millions, shares in thousands)	Shares	Dollars						
Balance at February 2, 2008	63,753	$0.7	$ —	$708.1	$(5.9)	$17.2	$720.1	
Net (loss) earnings	—	—	—	(68.7)	—	8.7	(60.0)	$(60.0)
Translation adjustments	—	—	—	—	(18.9)	(0.7)	(19.6)	(19.6)
Net change in fair value of derivative, net of taxes of $0.8 (Note 5)	—	—	—	—	1.2	—	1.2	1.2
Changes in unrecognized amounts of pension benefits, net of taxes of $7.1 (Note 7)	—	—	—	—	(12.0)	—	(12.0)	(12.0)
Issuances of common stock under stock plans	433	—	1.2	—	—	—	1.2	
Purchases of common stock	(153)	—	(1.9)	—	—	—	(1.9)	
Amortization of unearned nonvested shares	—	—	11.1	—	—	—	11.1	
Stock option expense	—	—	9.5	—	—	—	9.5	
Restricted stock cancellation	(308)	—	(2.1)	—	—	—	(2.1)	
Contributions from noncontrolling interests	—	—	—	—	—	4.6	4.6	
Distributions to noncontrolling interests	—	—	—	—	—	(6.1)	(6.1)	
Comprehensive loss								(90.4)
Comprehensive income attributable to noncontrolling interests								(8.0)
Comprehensive loss attributable to Collective Brands, Inc.								(98.4)
Balance at January 31, 2009	63,725	0.7	17.8	639.4	(35.6)	23.7	646.0	
Net earnings	—	—	—	82.7	—	5.6	88.3	88.3
Translation adjustments	—	—	—	—	8.0	0.1	8.1	8.1
Net change in fair value of derivatives, net of taxes of $2.2 (Note 5)	—	—	—	—	3.9	—	3.9	3.9
Changes in unrecognized amounts of pension benefits, net of taxes of $0.3 (Note 7)	—	—	—	—	1.4	—	1.4	1.4
Issuances of common stock under stock plans	882	—	8.2	—	—	—	8.2	
Purchases of common stock	(389)	—	(7.6)	—	—	—	(7.6)	
Amortization of unearned nonvested shares	—	—	5.4	—	—	—	5.4	
Stock option expense	—	—	10.9	—	—	—	10.9	
Restricted stock cancellation	(62)	—	—	—	—	—	—	
Contributions from noncontrolling interests	—	—	—	—	—	5.5	5.5	
Distributions to noncontrolling interests	—	—	—	—	—	(6.2)	(6.2)	
Comprehensive income								101.7
Comprehensive income attributable to noncontrolling interests								(5.7)
Comprehensive income attributable to Collective Brands, Inc.								$96.0
Balance at January 30, 2010	64,156	$0.7	$34.7	$722.1	$(22.3)	$28.7	$763.9	

(continued)

(Dollars in millions, shares in thousands)	Collective Brands, Inc. Shareowners'							
	Outstanding Common Stock		Additional Paid-In Capital	Retained Earnings	Accumulated Other Comprehensive Income (Loss)	Non-Controlling Interests	Total Equity	Comprehensive Income (Loss)
	Shares	Dollars						
Balance at January 30, 2010	64,156	$0.7	$34.7	$722.1	$(22.3)	$28.7	$763.9	
Net earnings	—	—	—	112.8	—	9.8	122.6	$122.6
Translation adjustments	—	—	—	—	6.2	0.7	6.9	6.9
Net change in fair value of derivatives, net of taxes of $2.7 (Note 5)	—	—	—	—	5.0	—	5.0	5.0
Changes in unrecognized amounts of pension benefits, net of taxes of $0.7 (Note 7)	—	—	—	—	1.0	—	1.0	1.0
Issuances of common stock under stock plans	1,183	—	10.7	—	—	—	10.7	
Purchases of common stock	(3,834)	(0.1)	(63.8)	—	—	—	(63.9)	
Amortization of unearned nonvested shares	—	—	7.9	—	—	—	7.9	
Stock option expense	—	—	8.0	—	—	—	8.0	
Restricted stock cancellation	(39)	—	—	—	—	—	—	
Contributions from noncontrolling interests	—	—	—	—	—	3.1	3.1	
Distributions to noncontrolling interests	—	—	—	—	—	(10.8)	(10.8)	
Comprehensive income								135.5
Comprehensive income attributable to noncontrolling interests								(10.5)
Comprehensive income attributable to Collective Brands, Inc.								$125.0
Balance at January 29, 2011	61,466	$0.6	$(2.5)	$834.9	$(10.1)	$31.5	$854.4	

Foreign Currency Translation

4.13

CONSTELLATION BRANDS, INC. (FEB)

CONSOLIDATED STATEMENTS OF CHANGES IN STOCKHOLDERS' EQUITY

(In millions, except share data)

	Common Stock		Additional Paid-In Capital	Retained Earnings	Accumulated Other Comprehensive Income (Loss)	Treasury Stock	Total
	Class A	Class B					
Balance, February 29, 2008	$2.2	$0.3	$1,344.0	$1,306.0	$736.0	$(622.6)	$2,765.9
Comprehensive loss:							
Net loss for Fiscal 2009	—	—	—	(301.4)	—	—	(301.4)
Other comprehensive (loss) income, net of income tax effect:							
Foreign currency translation adjustments	—	—	—	—	(683.5)	—	(683.5)
Unrealized loss on cash flow hedges:							
Net derivative losses	—	—	—	—	(16.4)	—	(16.4)
Reclassification adjustments	—	—	—	—	0.8	—	0.8
Net loss recognized in other comprehensive income							(15.6)
Pension/postretirement:							
Net actuarial gains	—	—	—	—	44.3	—	44.3
Reclassification adjustments	—	—	—	—	12.0	—	12.0
Net gain recognized in other comprehensive income							56.3
Other comprehensive loss, net of income tax effect							(642.8)
Comprehensive loss							(944.2)

(continued)

	Common Stock		Additional Paid-In Capital	Retained Earnings	Accumulated Other Comprehensive Income (Loss)	Treasury Stock	Total
	Class A	Class B					
Adjustments to apply change in measurement date provision of compensation—retirement benefits, net of income tax effect	$ —	$ —	$ —	$ (1.1)	$ 1.0	$ —	$ (0.1)
Conversion of 33,660 Class B Convertible Common shares to Class A Common shares	—	—	—	—	—	—	—
Exercise of 2,254,660 Class A stock options	—	—	27.1	—	—	—	27.1
Employee stock purchases of 376,297 treasury shares	—	—	3.6	—	—	2.0	5.6
Grant of 460,036 Class A Common shares—restricted stock awards	—	—	(2.4)	—	—	2.4	—
Stock-based employee compensation	—	—	47.5	—	—	—	47.5
Tax benefit on stock-based employee compensation awards	—	—	6.5	—	—	—	6.5
Balance, February 28, 2009	$2.2	$0.3	$1,426.3	$1,003.5	$ 94.2	$(618.2)	$1,908.3
Comprehensive income:							
Net income for Fiscal 2010	—	—	—	99.3	—	—	99.3
Other comprehensive income (loss), net of income tax effect:							
Foreign currency translation adjustments	—	—	—	—	497.5	—	497.5
Unrealized gain on cash flow hedges:							
Net derivative gains	—	—	—	—	60.2	—	60.2
Reclassification adjustments	—	—	—	—	(11.6)	—	(11.6)
Net gain recognized in other comprehensive income							48.6
Pension/postretirement:							
Net actuarial losses	—	—	—	—	(57.7)	—	(57.7)
Reclassification adjustments	—	—	—	—	4.6	—	4.6
Net loss recognized in other comprehensive income							(53.1)
Other comprehensive income, net of income tax effect							493.0
Comprehensive income							592.3
Conversion of 14,657 Class B Convertible Common shares to Class A Common shares	—	—	—	—	—	—	—
Exercise of 1,453,431 Class A stock options	0.1	—	12.2	—	—	—	12.3
Employee stock purchases of 388,294 treasury shares	—	—	2.5	—	—	2.0	4.5
Grant of 1,365,460 Class A Common shares—restricted stock awards	—	—	(7.3)	—	—	7.3	—
Vesting of 27,145 restricted stock units (17,645 treasury shares and 9,500 Class A Common shares), net of 11,110 shares withheld to satisfy tax withholding requirements	—	—	(0.2)	—	—	0.1	(0.1)
Cancellation of 136,497 restricted Class A Common shares	—	—	0.7	—	—	(0.7)	—
Stock-based employee compensation	—	—	56.8	—	—	—	56.8
Tax benefit on stock-based employee compensation awards	—	—	2.2	—	—	—	2.2
Balance, February 28, 2010	$2.3	$0.3	$1,493.2	$1,102.8	$587.2	$(609.5)	$2,576.3

(continued)

	Common Stock		Additional Paid-In Capital	Retained Earnings	Accumulated Other Comprehensive Income (Loss)	Treasury Stock	Total
	Class A	Class B					
Comprehensive income:							
Net income for Fiscal 2011	$ —	$ —	$ —	$ 559.5	$ —	$ —	$ 559.5
Other comprehensive income (loss), net of income tax effect:							
Foreign currency translation adjustments:							
Net gains					178.2		178.2
Reclassification adjustments					(657.1)		(657.1)
Net loss recognized in other comprehensive income							(478.9)
Unrealized loss on cash flow hedges:							
Net derivative gains	—	—	—	—	9.1	—	9.1
Reclassification adjustments	—	—	—	—	(24.5)	—	(24.5)
Net loss recognized in other comprehensive income							(15.4)
Pension/postretirement:							
Net actuarial gains	—	—	—	—	9.3	—	9.3
Reclassification adjustments	—	—	—	—	86.6	—	86.6
Net gain recognized in other comprehensive income							95.9
Other comprehensive loss, net of income tax effect							(398.4)
Comprehensive income							161.1
Repurchase of 17,240,101 Class A Common shares	—	—	—	—	—	(300.3)	(300.3)
Conversion of 116,879 Class B Convertible Common shares to Class A Common shares	—	—	—	—	—	—	—
Exercise of 5,100,677 Class A stock options	—	—	62.3	—	—	—	62.3
Employee stock purchases of 305,207 treasury shares	—	—	2.6	—	—	1.7	4.3
Grant of 739,388 Class A Common shares—restricted stock awards	—	—	(3.9)	—	—	3.9	—
Vesting of 53,780 restricted stock units (43,085 treasury shares and 10,695 Class A Common shares), net of 23,628 shares withheld to satisfy tax withholding requirements	—	—	(0.6)	—	—	0.2	(0.4)
Cancellation of 37,864 restricted Class A Common shares	—	—	0.2	—	—	(0.2)	—
Stock-based employee compensation	—	—	47.0	—	—	—	47.0
Tax benefit on stock-based employee compensation awards	—	—	1.6	—	—	—	1.6
Balance, February 28, 2011	$2.3	$0.3	$1,602.4	$1,662.3	$188.8	$(904.2)	$2,551.9

The accompanying notes are an integral part of these statements.

NOTES TO CONSOLIDATED FINANCIAL STATEMENTS

February 28, 2011

1. Summary of Significant Accounting Policies: (in part)

Foreign Currency Translation

The "functional currency" of the Company's subsidiaries outside the U.S. is the respective local currency. The translation from the applicable foreign currencies to U.S. dollars is performed for balance sheet accounts using exchange rates in effect at the balance sheet date and for revenue and expense accounts using a weighted average exchange rate for the period. The resulting translation adjustments are recorded as a component of Accumulated Other Comprehensive Income (Loss) ("AOCI"). As a result of the January 2011 CWAE Divestiture, the Company reclassified $657.1 million, net of income tax effect, from AOCI to selling, general and administrative expenses on the Company's Consolidated Statements of Operations (see Note 7, Note 19). Gains or losses resulting from foreign currency denominated transactions are also included in selling, general and administrative expenses on the Company's Consolidated Statements of Operations. The Company engages in foreign currency denominated transactions with customers and suppliers, as well as between subsidiaries with different functional currencies. Aggregate foreign currency transaction net losses were $2.3 million, $4.6 million and $26.3 million for the years ended February 28, 2011, February 28, 2010, and February 28, 2009, respectively.

19. Accumulated Other Comprehensive (Loss) Income:

Other comprehensive (loss) income, net of income tax effect, includes the following components:

(In millions)	Before Tax Amount	Tax (Expense) or Benefit	Net of Tax Amount
Other comprehensive (loss) income, February 28, 2009:			
Foreign currency translation adjustments	$(676.6)	$ (6.9)	$(683.5)
Unrealized loss on cash flow hedges:			
Net derivative losses	(2.8)	(13.6)	(16.4)
Reclassification adjustments	2.4	(1.6)	0.8
Net loss recognized in other comprehensive income	(0.4)	(15.2)	(15.6)
Pension/postretirement:			
Net gains	64.8	(20.5)	44.3
Reclassification adjustments	16.5	(4.5)	12.0
Net gain recognized in other comprehensive income	81.3	(25.0)	56.3
Other comprehensive loss, February 28, 2009	$(595.7)	$(47.1)	$(642.8)
Other comprehensive income (loss), February 28, 2010:			
Foreign currency translation adjustments	$ 500.6	$ (3.1)	$ 497.5
Unrealized gain on cash flow hedges:			
Net derivative gains	91.3	(31.1)	60.2
Reclassification adjustments	(19.1)	7.5	(11.6)
Net gain recognized in other comprehensive income	72.2	(23.6)	48.6
Pension/postretirement:			
Net losses	(79.3)	21.6	(57.7)
Reclassification adjustments	6.2	(1.6)	4.6
Net loss recognized in other comprehensive income	(73.1)	20.0	(53.1)
Other comprehensive income, February 28, 2010	$ 499.7	$ (6.7)	$ 493.0
Other comprehensive (loss) income, February 28, 2011:			
Foreign currency translation adjustments:			
Net gains	$ 201.5	$(23.3)	$ 178.2
Reclassification adjustments	(678.8)	21.7	(657.1)
Net loss recognized in other comprehensive income	(477.3)	(1.6)	(478.9)
Unrealized loss on cash flow hedges:			
Net derivative gains	11.4	(2.3)	9.1
Reclassification adjustments	(49.4)	24.9	(24.5)
Net loss recognized in other comprehensive income	(38.0)	22.6	(15.4)
Pension/postretirement:			
Net gains	12.9	(3.6)	9.3
Reclassification adjustments	121.0	(34.4)	86.6
Net gain recognized in other comprehensive income	133.9	(38.0)	95.9
Other comprehensive loss, February 28, 2011	$(381.4)	$(17.0)	$(398.4)

Accumulated other comprehensive income (loss), net of income tax effect, includes the following components:

(In millions)	Foreign Currency Translation Adjustments	Net Unrealized Gains (Losses) on Derivatives	Pension Postretirement Adjustments	Accumulated Other Comprehensive Income (Loss)
Balance, February 28, 2010	$ 672.9	$ 19.6	$(105.3)	$ 587.2
Current period change	(478.9)	(15.4)	95.9	(398.4)
Balance, February 28, 2011	$ 194.0	$ 4.2	$ (9.4)	$ 188.8

Pension and Postretirement Adjustments

4.14

AK STEEL HOLDING CORPORATION (DEC)

CONSOLIDATED STATEMENTS OF COMPREHENSIVE INCOME (LOSS)

Years Ended December 31, 2011, 2010 and 2009

(Dollars in millions)

	2011	2010	2009
Other comprehensive income (loss), before tax:			
Foreign currency translation gain (loss)	$ (0.7)	$ (0.8)	$ 1.0
Cash flow hedges:			
Gains (losses) arising in period	(21.0)	(23.2)	(19.3)
Reclassification of losses (gains) to net income (loss)	4.0	29.1	62.2
Unrealized holding gains (losses) on securities:			
Unrealized holding gains (losses) arising in period	(0.5)	1.7	3.7
Reclassification of losses (gains) to net income (loss)	—	0.3	—
Pension and OPEB plans:			
Prior service cost arising in period	(20.6)	1.1	0.3
Reclassification of prior service cost (credits) included in net income (loss)	(58.5)	(76.0)	(75.9)
Gains (losses) arising in period	(319.4)	(64.8)	23.0
Reclassification of losses (gains) included in net income (loss)	272.0	13.1	14.6
Other comprehensive income (loss), before tax	(144.7)	(119.5)	9.6
Income tax provision (benefit)	(54.8)	(44.2)	1.3
Other comprehensive income (loss)	(89.9)	(75.3)	8.3
Net income (loss) attributable to AK Steel Holding Corporation	(155.6)	(128.9)	(74.6)
Comprehensive income (loss) attributable to AK Steel Holding Corporation	$(245.5)	$(204.2)	$(66.3)

See notes to consolidated financial statements.

NOTES TO CONSOLIDATED FINANCIAL STATEMENTS

(Dollars in millions, except per share amounts or as otherwise specifically noted)

Note 1—Summary of Significant Accounting Policies (in part)

Pension and Other Postretirement Benefits: The Company recognizes in income, as of the Company's measurement date, any unrecognized actuarial net gains or losses that exceed 10% of the larger of the projected benefit obligations or the plan assets, defined as the "corridor." Prior to January 31, 2009, amounts inside this corridor were amortized over the average remaining service life of active plan participants. Effective January 31, 2009, the date of the "lock and freeze" of a defined benefit pension plan covering all salaried employees, the Company began to amortize actuarial gains and losses over the plan participants' life expectancy. Actuarial net gains and losses occur when actual experience differs from the assumptions used to value the plans.

Note 6—Pension and Other Postretirement Benefits (in part)

Summary

The Company provides noncontributory pension and various healthcare and life insurance benefits to a significant portion of its employees and retirees. Benefits are provided through defined benefit and defined contribution plans administered by the Company, as well as multiemployer plans for certain union members. The pension plan is not fully funded and, based on current assumptions, the Company plans to contribute approximately $170.0 to the master pension trust during 2012. Of this total, $28.7 was made in the first quarter of 2012, leaving approximately $141.3 to be made during the remainder of 2012. The Company made $170.0 in contributions during 2011. The Company expects to make approximately $79.8 in other postretirement benefit payments in 2012, as well as VEBA payments of $31.7 pursuant to the Butler Retiree Settlement.

Plan Obligations

The schedules below include amounts calculated based on benefit obligation and asset valuation measurement dates of December 31, 2011 and 2010.

	Pension Benefits		Other Benefits	
	2011	2010	2011	2010
Change in benefit obligations:				
Benefit obligations at beginning of year	$ 3,529.2	$ 3,494.8	$ 795.4	$ 876.6
Service cost	3.2	3.4	4.2	4.1
Interest cost	180.8	191.5	37.9	43.1
Plan participants' contributions	—	—	29.4	29.5
Actuarial loss (gain)	141.4	156.2	18.1	27.9
Amendments	—	7.5	20.7	(8.6)
Contributions to Middletown and Butler retirees VEBAs	—	—	(87.6)	(65.0)
Benefits paid	(314.9)	(326.9)	(111.1)	(123.1)
Medicare subsidy reimbursement received	—	—	6.2	8.1
Special/contractual termination benefits	—	3.1	—	1.2
Incremental benefits paid related to preliminary injunction	—	—	—	1.6
Foreign currency exchange rate changes	(0.2)	(0.4)	—	—
Benefit obligations at end of year	$ 3,539.5	$ 3,529.2	$ 713.2	$ 795.4
Change in plan assets:				
Fair value of plan assets at beginning of year	$ 2,472.9	$ 2,370.1	$ —	$ 1.0
Actual gain on plan assets	47.6	314.9	—	—
Employer contributions	172.3	114.8	75.5	84.5
Plan participants' contributions	—	—	29.4	29.5
Benefits paid	(314.9)	(326.9)	(111.1)	(123.1)
Medicare subsidy reimbursement received	—	—	6.2	8.1
Fair value of plan assets at end of year	$ 2,377.9	$ 2,472.9	$ —	$ —
Funded status	$(1,161.6)	$(1,056.3)	$(713.2)	$(795.4)
Amounts recognized in the consolidated balance sheets:				
Current liabilities	$ (23.6)	$ (5.3)	$(106.4)	$(140.4)
Noncurrent liabilities	(1,138.0)	(1,051.0)	(606.8)	(655.0)
Net amount recognized	$(1,161.6)	$(1,056.3)	$(713.2)	$(795.4)
Amounts recognized in accumulated other comprehensive income, before tax:				
Actuarial loss (gain)	$ 351.1	$ 336.8	$ 1.0	$ (32.1)
Prior service cost (credit)	16.7	20.6	(385.9)	(468.9)
Net amount recognized	$ 367.8	$ 357.4	$(384.9)	$(501.0)

The accumulated benefit obligation for all defined benefit pension plans was $3,526.3 and $3,514.1 at December 31, 2011 and 2010. All of the Company's pension plans have an accumulated benefit obligation in excess of plan assets.

Assumptions used to value benefit obligations and determine net periodic benefit cost are as follows:

	Pension Benefits			Other Benefits		
	2011	2010	2009	2011	2010	2009
Assumptions used to determine benefit obligations at December 31:						
Discount rate	4.74%	5.36%	5.75%	4.72%	5.26%	5.50%
Rate of compensation increase	4.00%	4.00%	4.00%	4.00%	4.00%	4.00%
Subsequent year healthcare cost trend rate				7.50%	8.00%	8.00%
Ultimate healthcare cost trend rate				4.50%	4.50%	4.50%
Year ultimate healthcare cost trend rate begins				2018	2018	2014
Assumptions used to determine net periodic benefit cost for the year ended December 31:						
Discount rate	5.36%	5.75%	6.25%	5.18%	5.50%	6.25%
Expected return on plan assets	8.50%	8.50%	8.50%			
Rate of compensation increase	4.00%	4.00%	4.00%	4.00%	4.00%	4.00%

Periodic Benefit Costs

The components of net periodic benefit costs for the years 2011, 2010 and 2009 are as follows:

	Pension Benefits			Other Benefits		
	2011	2010	2009	2011	2010	2009
Components of net periodic benefit cost:						
Service cost	$ 3.2	$ 3.4	$ 3.7	$ 4.2	$ 4.1	$ 4.0
Interest cost	180.8	191.5	207.7	37.9	43.1	55.2
Expected return on plan assets	(207.5)	(195.7)	(180.8)	—	—	—
Amortization of prior service cost (credit)	4.0	2.9	3.0	(76.6)	(78.9)	(78.9)
Reversal of prior amortization related to Butler Retiree Settlement	—	—	—	14.2	—	—
Recognized net actuarial loss (gain):						
Annual amortization	18.8	17.3	17.9	(1.0)	(4.2)	(3.4)
Pension corridor charge	268.1	—	—	—	—	—
Settlement gain	—	—	—	(14.0)	—	—
Special termination benefits	—	3.1	—	—	1.2	—
Incremental benefits paid related to preliminary injunction[a]	—	—	—	—	1.6	—
Net periodic benefit cost (credit)	$ 267.4	$ 22.5	$ 51.5	$(35.3)	$(33.1)	$(23.1)

[a] The amount is a result of a preliminary injunction issued on January 29, 2010, in a case filed by three former hourly workers retired from the Company's Butler Works. The preliminary injunction barred the Company from effecting any further benefit reductions or new healthcare charges for Butler Works retirees. A further discussion of the case can be found below.

In July 2009, the Company reached a final settlement (the "Middletown Retiree Settlement") of a class action filed on behalf of certain retirees from the Company's Middletown Works relating to the Company's other postretirement benefit ("OPEB") obligations to such retirees. Under terms of the Middletown Retiree Settlement, the Company has transferred to a Voluntary Employees Beneficiary Association ("VEBA") trust all OPEB obligations owed to the covered retirees under the Company's applicable health and welfare plans and will have no further liability for any claims incurred by those retirees after the effective date of the Middletown Retiree Settlement relating to their OPEB obligations. For accounting purposes, a settlement of the Company's OPEB obligations related to the Middletown Retiree Settlement was deemed to have occurred in the first quarter of 2011 when the Company made the final payment of $65.0 to the VEBA trust created under the terms of that settlement. In 2011, the Company recognized the settlement accounting and recorded a non-cash gain of $14.0 in the Consolidated Statements of Operations. The amount recognized was prorated based on the portion of the total liability as of March 2008 that was settled pursuant to the Middletown Retiree Settlement.

In January 2011, the Company reached a final settlement agreement (the "Butler Retiree Settlement") of a class action filed on behalf of certain retirees from the Company's Butler Works relating to the Company's OPEB obligations to such retirees. On June 18, 2009, three former hourly members of the Butler Armco Independent Union filed a purported class action against AK Steel alleging that AK Steel did not have a right to make changes to their healthcare benefits. The named plaintiffs sought, among other things, injunctive relief for themselves and the other members of a proposed class, including an order retroactively rescinding certain changes to retiree healthcare benefits negotiated by AK Steel with its union. Pursuant to the Butler Retiree Settlement, AK Steel agreed to continue to provide company-paid health and life insurance to Class Members through December 31, 2014,

and to make combined lump sum payments totaling $91.0 to a VEBA trust and to plaintiffs' counsel. AK Steel agreed to make three cash contributions to the VEBA trust as follows: $22.6 on August 1, 2011, which has been paid; $31.7 on July 31, 2012; and $27.6 on July 31, 2013. The balance of the lump sum payments were paid to plaintiffs' attorneys on August 1, 2011, to cover plaintiffs' obligations with respect to attorneys' fees. Effective January 1, 2015, AK Steel will transfer to the VEBA trust all OPEB obligations owed to the Class Members under the Company's applicable health and welfare plans and will have no further liability for any claims incurred by the Class Members after December 31, 2014, relating to their OPEB obligations. The VEBA trust will be utilized to fund all such future OPEB obligations to the Class Members. Trustees of the VEBA trust will determine the scope of the benefits to be provided to the Class Members. The effect of the settlement on the Company's total OPEB liability (prior to any funding of a VEBA trust created under the terms of the settlement) was an increase in that liability of approximately $29.6 in 2011. With respect to this increase, a one-time, pre-tax charge of $14.2 was recorded in 2011 to reverse previous amortization of the prior plan amendment. The remaining portion was recognized in other comprehensive income and will be amortized into earnings over approximately five years. For accounting purposes, a settlement of the Company's OPEB obligations will be deemed to have occurred when the Company makes the final benefit payments in 2014.

The estimated net loss and prior service cost for the defined benefit pension plans that will be amortized from accumulated other comprehensive income into net periodic benefit cost over the next fiscal year are $24.5 and $3.8, respectively. The estimated net loss and prior service credit for the other postretirement benefit plans that will be amortized from accumulated other comprehensive income into net periodic benefit cost over the next fiscal year are $0.1 and $(77.4), respectively.

As a result of the enactment of the Patient Protection and Affordable Care Act and the Health Care and Education Reconciliation Act of 2010 (collectively, the "Health Care Acts"), the Company recorded a non-cash charge of $25.3 in 2010. The charge was due to a reduction in the value of the Company's deferred tax asset as a result of a change to the tax treatment associated with Medicare Part D reimbursements. The Company expects to continue to receive Medicare Part D reimbursements despite passage of the Health Care Acts.

Note 12—Comprehensive Income (Loss)

Accumulated other comprehensive income, net of tax, is as follows:

	2011	2010
Foreign currency translation	$ 2.8	$ 3.5
Cash flow hedges	(10.9)	(0.4)
Unrealized holding gain (loss) on securities	(0.6)	(0.3)
Pension and OPEB plans	11.4	89.8
Accumulated other comprehensive income	$ 2.7	$ 92.6

The tax effects allocated to each component of other comprehensive income (loss) are as follows:

	2011	2010	2009
Cash flow hedges:			
Gains (losses) arising in period	$ (8.0)	$ (7.0)	$ (6.9)
Reclassification of loss (gain) to net income (loss)	1.5	12.0	22.1
Unrealized holding gain (loss) on securities:			
Unrealized holding gain (loss) arising in period	(0.2)	0.6	1.4
Reclassification of loss (gain) to net income (loss)	—	0.1	—
Pension and OPEB plans:			
Prior service cost arising in period	(7.5)	(0.5)	0.1
Reclassification of prior service cost (credits) included in net income (loss)	(22.3)	(29.5)	(29.7)
Gains (losses) arising in period	(122.2)	(25.8)	8.8
Reclassification of losses (gains) included in net income (loss)	103.9	5.9	5.5
Income tax (benefit) allocated to other comprehensive income	$ (54.8)	$(44.2)	$ 1.3

4.15

DEERE & COMPANY (OCT)

STATEMENT OF CHANGES IN CONSOLIDATED STOCK-HOLDERS' EQUITY

For the Years Ended October 31, 2009, 2010 and 2011

(In millions of dollars)

		Deere & Company Stockholders					
	Total Stockholders' Equity	Comprehensive Income (Loss)	Common Stock	Treasury Stock	Retained Earnings	Accumulated Other Comprehensive Income (Loss)	Non-controlling Interests
Balance October 31, 2008	$6,537.2		$2,934.0	$(5,594.6)	$10,580.6	$(1,387.3)	$ 4.5
Net income (loss)	872.9	$ 873.5			873.5		(.6)
Other comprehensive income (loss)							
Retirement benefits adjustment	(2,536.6)	(2,536.6)				(2,536.6)	
Cumulative translation adjustment	327.4	326.8				326.8	.6
Unrealized loss on derivatives	(4.0)	(4.0)				(4.0)	
Unrealized gain on investments	7.8	7.8				7.8	
Total comprehensive income	(1,332.5)	$(1,332.5)					

(continued)

	Total Stockholders' Equity	Deere & Company Stockholders					Non-controlling Interests
		Comprehensive Income (Loss)	Common Stock	Treasury Stock	Retained Earnings	Accumulated Other Comprehensive Income (Loss)	
Repurchases of common stock	$ (3.2)			$ (3.2)			
Treasury shares reissued	33.1			33.1			
Dividends declared	(473.6)				(473.6)		
Stock options and other	61.8		62.2				(.4)
Balance October 31, 2009	4,822.8		2,996.2	(5,564.7)	10,980.5	(3,593.3)	4.1
Net income	1,874.3	$ 1,865.0			1,865.0		9.3
Other comprehensive income (loss)							
Retirement benefits adjustment	158.0	158.0				158.0	
Cumulative translation adjustment	35.7	35.8				35.8	(.1)
Unrealized gain on derivatives	14.9	14.9				14.9	
Unrealized gain on investments	5.0	5.0				5.0	
Total comprehensive income	2,087.9	$ 2,078.7					9.2
Repurchases of common stock	(358.8)			(358.8)			
Treasury shares reissued	134.0			134.0			
Dividends declared	(492.7)				(492.3)		(.4)
Stock options and other	110.2		110.1		(.1)		.2
Balance October 31, 2010	6,303.4		3,106.3	(5,789.5)	12,353.1	(3,379.6)	13.1
Net income	2,807.8	$ 2,799.9			2,799.9		7.9
Other comprehensive income (loss)							
Retirement benefits adjustment	(338.4)	(338.4)				(338.4)	
Cumulative translation adjustment	17.8	17.8				17.8	
Unrealized gain on derivatives	20.9	20.9				20.9	
Unrealized gain on investments	1.3	1.3				1.3	
Total comprehensive income	2,509.4	$ 2,501.5					7.9
Repurchases of common stock	(1,667.0)			(1,667.0)			
Treasury shares reissued	163.7			163.7			
Dividends declared	(638.0)				(633.5)		(4.5)
Stock options and other	143.4		145.4		(.1)		(1.9)
Balance October 31, 2011	$ 6,814.9		$3,251.7	$(7,292.8)	$14,519.4	$(3,678.0)	$14.6

The notes to consolidated financial statements are an integral part of this statement.

NOTES TO CONSOLIDATED FINANCIAL STATEMENTS

7. Pension and Other Postretirement Benefits (in part)

The company has several defined benefit pension plans covering its U.S. employees and employees in certain foreign countries. The company has several postretirement health care and life insurance plans for retired employees in the U.S. and Canada. The company uses an October 31 measurement date for these plans.

The components of net periodic pension cost and the assumptions related to the cost consisted of the following in millions of dollars and in percents:

	2011	2010	2009
Pensions			
Service cost	$ 197	$ 176	$ 124
Interest cost	492	510	563
Expected return on plan assets	(793)	(761)	(739)
Amortization of actuarial losses	148	113	1
Amortization of prior service cost	46	42	25
Early-retirement benefits			4
Settlements/curtailments	1	24	27
Net cost	$ 91	$ 104	$ 5
Weighted-Average Assumptions			
Discount rates	5.0%	5.5%	8.1%
Rate of compensation increase	3.9%	3.9%	3.9%
Expected long-term rates of return	8.1%	8.3%	8.3%

The components of net periodic postretirement benefits cost and the assumptions related to the cost consisted of the following in millions of dollars and in percents:

	2011	2010	2009
Health Care and Life Insurance			
Service cost	$ 44	$ 44	$ 28
Interest cost	326	337	344
Expected return on plan assets	(113)	(122)	(118)
Amortization of actuarial losses	271	311	65
Amortization of prior service credit	(16)	(16)	(12)
Early-retirement benefits			1
Settlements/curtailments			(1)
Net cost	$ 512	$ 554	$ 307
Weighted-Average Assumptions			
Discount rates	5.2%	5.6%	8.2%
Expected long-term rates of return	7.7%	7.8%	7.8%

The above benefit plan costs in net income and other changes in plan assets and benefit obligations in other comprehensive income in millions of dollars were as follows:

	Pensions			Health Care and Life Insurance		
	2011	2010	2009	2011	2010	2009
Net costs	$ 91	$ 104	$ 5	$ 512	$ 554	$ 307
Retirement benefits adjustments included in other comprehensive (income) loss:						
Net actuarial losses (gains)	848	227	2,087	132	(28)	2,024
Prior service cost (credit)	9	14	147			(60)
Amortization of actuarial losses	(148)	(113)	(1)	(271)	(311)	(65)
Amortization of prior service (cost) credit	(46)	(42)	(25)	16	16	12
Settlements/curtailments	(1)	(24)	(27)			1
Total (gain) loss recognized in other comprehensive (income) loss	662	62	2,181	(123)	(323)	1,912
Total recognized in comprehensive (income) loss	$ 753	$ 166	$2,186	$ 389	$ 231	$2,219

In 2011, the company decided to participate in a prescription drug plan to provide group benefits under Medicare Part D as an alternative to collecting the retiree drug subsidy. This change, which will take effect in 2013, is expected to result in future cost savings to the company greater than the Medicare retiree drug subsidies over time. The change is included in the health care postretirement benefit obligation in 2011. The participants' level of benefits will not be affected.

The benefit plan obligations, funded status and the assumptions related to the obligations at October 31 in millions of dollars follow:

	Pensions		Health Care and Life Insurance	
	2011	2010	2011	2010
Change in Benefit Obligations				
Beginning of year balance	$(10,197)	$ (9,708)	$(6,467)	$(6,318)
Service cost	(197)	(176)	(44)	(44)
Interest cost	(492)	(510)	(326)	(337)
Actuarial losses	(656)	(517)	(113)	(69)
Amendments	(9)	(14)		
Benefits paid	648	681	340	325
Health care subsidy receipts			(14)	(15)
Settlements/curtailments			1	17
Foreign exchange and other	(23)	30	(28)	(9)
End of year balance	(10,925)	(10,197)	(6,652)	(6,467)
Change in Plan Assets (Fair Value)				
Beginning of year balance	$ 9,504	$ 8,401	$ 1,637	$ 1,666
Actual return on plan assets	600	1,054	95	219
Employer contribution	79	763	43	73
Benefits paid	(648)	(681)	(340)	(325)
Settlements	(1)	(17)		
Foreign exchange and other	18	(16)	24	4
End of year balance	9,552	9,504	1,459	1,637
Funded status	$ (1,373)	$ (693)	$(5,193)	$(4,830)
Weighted-Average Assumptions				
Discount rates	4.4%	5.0%	4.4%	5.2%
Rate of compensation increase	3.9%	3.9%		

The amounts recognized at October 31 in millions of dollars consist of the following:

	Pensions		Health Care and Life Insurance	
	2011	2010	2011	2010
Amounts Recognized in Balance Sheet				
Noncurrent asset	$ 30	$ 147		
Current liability	(60)	(55)	$ (23)	$ (27)
Noncurrent liability	(1,343)	(785)	(5,170)	(4,803)
Total	$(1,373)	$(693)	$(5,193)	$(4,830)
Amounts Recognized in Accumulated Other Comprehensive Income—Pretax				
Net actuarial losses	$4,473	$3,774	$2,067	$2,206
Prior service cost (credit)	147	184	(64)	(80)
Total	$4,620	$3,958	$2,003	$2,126

The total accumulated benefit obligations for all pension plans at October 31, 2011 and 2010 was $10,363 million and $9,734 million, respectively.

The accumulated benefit obligations and fair value of plan assets for pension plans with accumulated benefit obligations in excess of plan assets were $10,168 million and $9,321 million, respectively, at October 31, 2011 and $1,039 million and $583 million, respectively, at October 31, 2010.

The projected benefit obligations and fair value of plan assets for pension plans with projected benefit obligations in excess of plan assets were $10,784 million and $9,381 million, respectively, at October 31, 2011 and $6,407 million and $5,567 million, respectively, at October 31, 2010.

The amounts in accumulated other comprehensive income that are expected to be amortized as net expense (income) during fiscal 2012 in millions of dollars follow:

	Pensions	Health Care and Life Insurance
Net actuarial losses	$201	$239
Prior service cost (credit)	42	(15)
Total	$243	$224

The company expects to contribute approximately $439 million to its pension plans and approximately $27 million to its health care and life insurance plans in 2012, which include direct benefit payments on unfunded plans.

The benefits expected to be paid from the benefit plans, which reflect expected future years of service, and the Medicare subsidy expected to be received are as follows in millions of dollars:

	Pensions	Health Care and Life Insurance	Health Care Subsidy Receipts*
2012	$ 680	$ 360	$17
2013	677	375	3
2014	684	391	
2015	680	406	
2016	684	418	
2017 to 2021	3,723	2,244	

* Medicare Part D subsidy.

The annual rates of increase in the per capita cost of covered health care benefits (the health care cost trend rates) used to determine accumulated postretirement benefit obligations were based on the trends for medical and prescription drug claims for pre- and post-65 age groups due to the effects of Medicare. At October 31, 2011, the weighted-average composite trend rates for these obligations were assumed to be a 7.3 percent increase from 2011 to 2012, gradually decreasing to 5.0 percent from 2017 to 2018 and all future years. The obligations at October 31, 2010 and the cost in 2011 assumed a 7.7 percent increase from 2010 to 2011, gradually decreasing to 5.0 percent from 2016 to 2017 and all future years. An increase of one percentage point in the assumed health care cost trend rate would increase the accumulated postretirement benefit obligations by $900 million and the aggregate of service and interest cost component of net periodic postretirement benefits cost for the year by $55 million. A decrease of one percentage point would decrease the obligations by $695 million and the cost by $43 million.

The discount rate assumptions used to determine the postretirement obligations at October 31, 2011 and 2010 were based on hypothetical AA yield curves represented by a series of annualized individual discount rates. These discount rates represent the rates at which the company's benefit obligations could effectively be settled at the October 31 measurement dates.

SEC 4.15

25. Other Comprehensive Income Items

Other comprehensive income items are transactions recorded in stockholders' equity during the year, excluding net income and transactions with stockholders. Following are the items included in other comprehensive income (loss) for Deere & Company and the related tax effects in millions of dollars:

	Before Tax Amount	Tax (Expense) Credit	After Tax Amount
2009			
Retirement benefits adjustment:			
Net actuarial losses and prior service cost	$(4,198)	$1,587	$(2,611)
Reclassification of actuarial losses and prior service cost to net income	105	(31)	74
Net unrealized loss	(4,093)	1,556	(2,537)
Cumulative translation adjustment	326	1	327
Unrealized loss on derivatives:			
Hedging loss	(90)	31	(59)
Reclassification of realized loss to net income	84	(29)	55
Net unrealized loss	(6)	2	(4)
Unrealized gain on investments:			
Holding loss	(793)	278	(515)
Reclassification of realized loss to net income	805	(282)	523
Net unrealized gain	12	(4)	8
Total other comprehensive income (loss)	$(3,761)	$1,555	$(2,206)
2010			
Retirement benefits adjustment:			
Net actuarial losses and prior service cost	$ (213)	$ 77	$ (136)
Reclassification of actuarial losses and prior service cost to net income	474	(180)	294
Net unrealized gain	261	(103)	158
Cumulative translation adjustment	49	(13)	36
Unrealized loss on derivatives:			
Hedging loss	(56)	19	(37)
Reclassification of realized loss to net income	79	(27)	52
Net unrealized gain	23	(8)	15
Unrealized holding gain and net unrealized gain on investments	8	(3)	5
Total other comprehensive income (loss)	$ 341	$ (127)	$ 214
Retirement benefits adjustment:			
Net actuarial losses and prior service cost	$ (989)	$ 368	$ (621)
Reclassification of actuarial losses and prior service cost to net income	450	(167)	283
Net unrealized loss	(539)	201	(338)
Cumulative translation adjustment	14	4	18
Unrealized gain on derivatives:			
Hedging gain	31	(11)	20
Reclassification of realized loss to net income	1		1
Net unrealized gain	32	(11)	21
Unrealized holding gain and net unrealized gain on investments	2	(1)	1
Total other comprehensive income (loss)	$ (491)	$ 193	$ (298)

Net Change in Unrealized Gains and Losses on Available-for-Sale Securities

4.16

ST. JUDE MEDICAL, INC. (DEC)

CONSOLIDATED STATEMENTS OF SHAREHOLDERS' EQUITY

(In thousands, except share amounts)

	Common Stock		Additional Paid-In Capital	Retained Earnings	Accumulated Other Comprehensive Income (Loss)	Total Share-holders' Equity
	Number of Shares	Amount				
Balance at January 3, 2009	345,332,272	$34,533	$ 219,041	$2,977,630	$ 4,702	$ 3,235,906
Comprehensive income:						
Net earnings				777,226		777,226
Other comprehensive income:						
Unrealized gain on available-for-sale securities, net of taxes of $3,369					5,865	5,865
Reclassification of realized loss on derivative financial instruments to net earnings, net of taxes of $247					411	411
Foreign currency translation adjustment, net of taxes of $(173)					83,056	83,056
Other comprehensive income						89,332
Comprehensive income						866,558
Repurchases of common stock	(27,154,078)	(2,715)	(433,632)	(563,653)		(1,000,000)
Stock-based compensation			59,795			59,795
Common stock issued under stock plans and other, net	6,359,387	636	125,620			126,256
Tax benefit from stock plans			35,036			35,036
Balance at January 2, 2010	324,537,581	$32,454	$ 5,860	$3,191,203	$ 94,034	$ 3,323,551
Comprehensive income:						
Net earnings				907,436		907,436
Other comprehensive income (loss):						
Unrealized gain on available-for-sale securities, net of taxes of $1,893					6,187	6,187
Reclassification of realized gain on available-for-sale securities, net of taxes of $1,848					(3,081)	(3,081)
Foreign currency translation adjustment, net of taxes of $314					(13,136)	(13,136)
Other comprehensive loss						(10,030)
Comprehensive income						897,406
Repurchases of common stock	(15,388,500)	(1,539)	(623,712)			(625,251)
Stock-based compensation			69,586			69,586
Common stock issued under stock plans and other, net	6,293,732	629	151,144			151,773
Common stock issued in connection with acquisition	13,575,353	1,358	532,289			533,647
Tax benefit from stock plans			20,959			20,959
Balance at January 1, 2011	329,018,166	$32,902	$ 156,126	$4,098,639	$ 84,004	$ 4,371,671
Comprehensive income:						
Net earnings				825,793		825,793
Cash dividends declared on common stock, $0.84 per share				(271,868)		(271,868)
Other comprehensive income (loss):						
Unrealized gain on available-for-sale securities, net of taxes of $1,894					2,780	2,780
Foreign currency translation adjustment, net of taxes of $(475)					(71,064)	(71,064)
Other comprehensive loss						(68,284)
Comprehensive income						485,641
Repurchases of common stock	(18,314,774)	(1,831)	(504,271)	(268,642)		(774,744)
Stock-based compensation			76,313			76,313
Common stock issued under stock plans and other, net	8,912,573	890	301,587			302,477
Tax benefit from stock plans			13,258			13,258
Balance at December 31, 2011	319,615,965	$31,961	$ 43,013	$4,383,922	$ 15,720	$ 4,474,616

See notes to the consolidated financial statements

NOTES TO THE CONSOLIDATED FINANCIAL STATEMENTS

Note 1—Summary of Significant Accounting Policies (in part)

Marketable Securities: Marketable securities consist of publicly-traded equity securities that are classified as available-for-sale securities and investments in mutual funds that are classified as trading securities. On the balance sheet, available-for-sale securities and trading securities are classified as other current assets and other assets, respectively.

The following table summarizes the components of the balance of the Company's available-for-sale securities at December 31, 2011 and January 1, 2011 (in thousands):

	December 31, 2011	January 1, 2011
Adjusted cost	$ 9,236	$ 9,116
Gross unrealized gains	29,649	24,988
Gross unrealized losses	(228)	(359)
Fair value	$38,657	$33,745

Available-for-sale securities are recorded at fair value based upon quoted market prices (see Note 12). Unrealized gains and losses, net of related incomes taxes, are recorded in accumulated other comprehensive income in shareholders' equity. Upon the sale of an available-for-sale security, the unrealized gain (loss) is reclassified out of accumulated other comprehensive income and reflected as a realized gain (loss) in net earnings. Realized gains (losses) are computed using the specific identification method and recognized as other income (expense). During 2010, the Company sold an available-for-sale security, recognizing a realized after-tax gain of $3.1 million. The total pre-tax gain of $4.9 million was recognized as other income (see Note 9). There were no realized gains (losses) from the sale of available-for-sale securities recorded during fiscal years 2011 or 2009. Additionally, when the fair value of an available-for-sale security falls below its original cost and the Company determines that the corresponding unrealized loss is other-than-temporary, the Company recognizes an impairment loss to net earnings in the period the determination is made.

The Company's investments in mutual funds are recorded at fair market value based upon quoted market prices (see Note 12) and are held in a rabbi trust, which is not available for general corporate purposes and is subject to creditor claims in the event of insolvency. These investments are specifically designated as available to the Company solely for the purpose of paying benefits under the Company's deferred compensation plan (see Note 11).

Gains and Losses on Derivatives Held as Cash Flow Hedges

4.17

CHESAPEAKE ENERGY CORPORATION (DEC)

CONSOLIDATED STATEMENTS OF COMPREHENSIVE INCOME

	Years Ended December 31		
($ In millions)	2011	2010	2009
Net income (loss)	$1,757	$1,774	$(5,805)
Other comprehensive income (loss), net of income tax:			
Change in fair value of derivative instruments, net of income taxes of $137 million, $129 million and $413 million	224	212	677
Reclassification of (gain) loss on settled derivative instruments, net of income taxes of ($139) million, ($298) million and ($540) million	(225)	(491)	(885)
Ineffective portion of derivatives qualifying for cash flow hedge accounting, net of income taxes of $3 million, $9 million and ($14) million	4	14	(23)
Unrealized (gain) loss on available-for-sale securities, net of income taxes of ($1) million, ($3) million and $14 million	(1)	(5)	23
Reclassification of loss on investments, net of income taxes of $0, $0 and $26 million	—	—	43
Other comprehensive income (loss)	2	(270)	(165)
Comprehensive income (loss)	1,759	1,504	(5,970)
Net income attributable to noncontrolling interests	(15)	—	(25)
Comprehensive income (loss) available to Chesapeake	$1,744	$1,504	$(5,995)

The accompanying notes are an integral part of these consolidated financial statements.

NOTES TO CONSOLIDATED FINANCIAL STATEMENTS

1. Basis of Presentation and Summary of Significant Accounting Policies (in part)

Derivatives

Chesapeake uses commodity price and financial risk management instruments to mitigate a portion of our exposure to price fluctuations in natural gas and oil prices and changes in interest rates and foreign exchange rates. Results of commodity derivative transactions are reflected in natural gas and oil sales, and results of interest rate and foreign exchange rate derivative transactions are reflected in interest expense.

We have established the fair value of our derivative instruments utilizing established index prices, volatility curves and discount factors. These estimates are compared to our counterparty values for reasonableness. Derivative transactions are subject to the risk that counterparties will be unable to meet their obligations. Such non-performance risk is considered in the valuation of our derivative instruments, but to date has not had a material impact on the values of our derivatives. The values we report in our financial statements are as of a point in time and subsequently change as these estimates are revised to reflect actual results, changes in market conditions and other factors.

Accounting guidance for derivative instruments and hedging activities establishes accounting and reporting standards requiring that derivative instruments (including certain derivative instruments embedded in other contracts) be recorded at fair value and included in the consolidated balance sheet as assets or liabilities. The accounting for changes in the fair value of a derivative instrument depends on the intended use of the derivative and the resulting designation, which is established at the inception of a derivative. For derivative instruments designated as natural gas and oil cash flow hedges, changes in fair value, to the extent the hedge is effective, are recognized in other comprehensive income until the hedged item is recognized in earnings as natural gas and oil sales. Any change in the fair value resulting from ineffectiveness is recognized immediately in natural gas and oil sales. For interest rate derivative instruments designated as fair value hedges, changes in fair value are recorded on the consolidated balance sheets as assets

(liabilities), and the debt's carrying value amount is adjusted by the change in the fair value of the debt subsequent to the initiation of the derivative. Differences between the changes in the fair values of the hedged item and the derivative instrument, if any, represent gains or losses on ineffectiveness and are reflected currently in interest expense. Hedge effectiveness is measured at least quarterly based on the relative changes in fair value between the derivative contract and the hedged item over time. Changes in fair value of contracts that do not qualify as hedges or are not designated as hedges are recognized currently in earnings. Cash settlements of our derivative arrangements are generally classified as operating cash flows unless the derivative is deemed to contain, for accounting purposes, a significant financing element at contract inception, in which case these cash settlements are classified as financing cash flows in the accompanying consolidated statement of cash flows.

9. Derivatives and Hedging Activities (in part)

Cash Flow Hedges

A reconciliation of the components of accumulated other comprehensive income (loss) in the consolidated statements of stockholders' equity related to our cash flow hedges is presented below.

	Years Ended December 31					
	2011		2010		2009	
($ In millions)	Before Tax	After Tax	Before Tax	After Tax	Before Tax	After Tax
Balance, beginning of period	$(291)	$(181)	$ 134	$ 84	$ 505	$ 315
Net change in fair value	368	228	364	226	1,054	654
Gains reclassified to income	(364)	(225)	(789)	(491)	(1,425)	(885)
Balance, end of period	$(287)	$(178)	$(291)	$(181)	$ 134	$ 84

The following table presents the pre-tax gain (loss) recognized in, and reclassified from, accumulated other comprehensive income (AOCI) related to instruments designated as cash flow derivatives:

($ In millions)		Years Ended December 31		
Cash Flow Derivatives	Location of Gain (Loss)	2011	2010	2009
Gain (Loss) Recognized in AOCI (Effective Portion)				
Commodity contracts	AOCI	$392	$386	$ 958
Foreign currency contracts	AOCI	(24)	(22)	96
		$368	$364	$1,054
Gain (Loss) Reclassified from AOCI (Effective Portion)				
Commodity contracts	Natural gas and oil sales	$402	$789	$1,425
Foreign currency contracts	Interest expense	(18)	—	—
Foreign currency contracts	Loss on purchase of debt	(20)	—	—
		$364	$789	$1,425
Gain (Loss) Recognized in income				
Commodity contracts				
Ineffective portion	Natural gas and oil sales	$ (7)	$ (23)	$ 36
Amount initially excluded from effectiveness testing	Natural gas and oil sales	22	4	157
		$ 15	$ (19)	$ 193

4.18

HASBRO, INC. (DEC)

NOTES TO CONSOLIDATED FINANCIAL STATEMENTS

(Thousands of dollars and shares except per share data)

(1) Summary of Significant Accounting Policies (in part)

Risk Management Contracts

Hasbro uses foreign currency forward contracts to mitigate the impact of currency rate fluctuations on firmly committed and projected future foreign currency transactions. These over-the-counter contracts, which hedge future purchases of inventory and other cross-border currency requirements not denominated in the functional currency of the business unit, are primarily denominated in United States and Hong Kong dollars, and Euros and are entered into with a number of counterparties, all of which are major financial institutions. The Company believes that a default by a counterparty would not have a material adverse effect on the financial condition of the Company. Hasbro does not enter into derivative financial instruments for speculative purposes.

At the inception of the contracts, Hasbro designates its derivatives as either cash flow or fair value hedges. The Company formally documents all relationships between hedging instruments and hedged items as well as its risk management objectives and strategies for undertaking various hedge transactions. All hedges designated as cash flow hedges are linked to forecasted transactions and the Company assesses, both at the inception of the hedge and on an on-going basis, the effectiveness of the derivatives used in hedging transactions in offsetting changes in the cash flows of the forecasted transaction. The ineffective portion of a hedging derivative, if any, is immediately recognized in the consolidated statements of operations.

The Company records all derivatives, such as foreign currency exchange contracts, on the balance sheet at fair value. Changes in the derivative fair values that are designated as cash flow hedges and are effective are deferred and recorded as a component of Accumulated Other Comprehensive (Loss) Earnings ("AOCE") until the hedged transactions occur and are then recognized in the consolidated statements of operations. The Company's foreign currency contracts hedging anticipated cash flows are designated as cash flow hedges. When it is determined that a derivative is not highly effective as a hedge, the Company discontinues hedge accounting prospectively. Any gain or loss deferred through that date remains in AOCE until the forecasted transaction occurs, at which time it is reclassified to the consolidated statements of operations. To the extent the transaction is no longer deemed probable of occurring, hedge accounting treatment is discontinued and amounts deferred would be reclassified to the consolidated statements of operations. In the event hedge accounting requirements are not met, gains and losses on such instruments are included currently in the consolidated statements of operations. The Company uses derivatives to economically hedge intercompany loans denominated in foreign currencies. The Company does not use hedge accounting for these contracts as changes in the fair value of these contracts are substantially offset by changes in the fair value of the intercompany loans.

(2) Other Comprehensive Loss

The Company's other comprehensive loss for the years 2011, 2010 and 2009 consist of the following:

	2011	2010	2009
Foreign currency translation adjustments	$(21,844)	(32,457)	23,782
Changes in value of available-for-sale securities, net of tax	—	—	504
Gain (loss) on cash flow hedging activities, net of tax	(8,689)	10,444	(24,446)
Changes in unrecognized pension and postretirement amounts, net of tax	(20,237)	(1,812)	8,356
Reclassifications to earnings, net of tax:			
Net (gains) losses on cash flow hedging activities	3,338	(15,422)	(18,657)
Loss on available-for-sale securities	—	—	147
Amortization of unrecognized pension and postretirement amounts	3,340	(11,235)	6,689
Other comprehensive loss	$(44,092)	(50,482)	(3,625)

In 2011, 2010 and 2009, net losses on cash flow hedging activities reclassified to earnings, net of tax, included losses of $100, $109 and $679, respectively, as a result of hedge ineffectiveness.

The related tax benefit of other comprehensive earnings items was $8,581, $5,327 and $1,322 for the years 2011, 2010 and 2009, respectively. Income tax expense (benefit) related to reclassification adjustments from other comprehensive earnings of $(1,571), $8,767 and $(331) in 2011, 2010 and 2009, respectively, were included in these amounts.

At December 25, 2011, the Company had remaining deferred gains on hedging instruments, net of tax, of $10,081 in AOCE. These instruments hedge inventory purchased during the fourth quarter of 2011 or forecasted to be purchased during 2012 and 2013 and intercompany expenses and royalty payments expected to be paid or received during 2012 and 2013. These amounts will be reclassified into the consolidated statement of operations upon the sale of the related inventory or receipt or payment of the related royalties or expenses. Of the amount included in AOCE at December 25,

2011, the Company expects approximately $8,307 to be reclassified to the consolidated statement of operations within the next 12 months. However, the amount ultimately realized in earnings is dependent on the fair value of the hedging instruments on the settlement dates.

Components of AOCE at December 25, 2011 and December 26, 2010 are as follows:

	2011	2010
Foreign currency translation adjustments	$ 40,798	62,642
Gain on cash flow hedging activities, net of tax	10,081	15,432
Unrecognized pension and postretirement amounts, net of tax	(86,822)	(69,925)
Total AOCE	$(35,943)	8,149

(16) Derivative Financial Instruments (in part)

Cash Flow Hedges

Hasbro uses foreign currency forward contracts to reduce the impact of currency rate fluctuations on firmly committed and projected future foreign currency transactions. All of the Company's designated foreign currency forward contracts are considered to be cash flow hedges. These instruments hedge a portion of the Company's currency requirements associated with anticipated inventory purchases and other cross-border transactions in 2012 and 2013.

At December 25, 2011 and December 26, 2010, the notional amounts and fair values of assets (liabilities) for the Company's foreign currency forward contracts designated as cash flow hedging instruments were as follows:

	2011		2010	
	Notional Amount	Fair Value	Notional Amount	Fair Value
Hedged Transaction				
Inventory purchases	$379,688	7,974	593,953	11,074
Intercompany royalty transactions	117,192	2,126	179,308	5,344
Other	29,517	(360)	17,047	533
Total	$526,397	9,740	790,308	16,951

The Company has a master agreement with each of its counterparties that allows for the netting of outstanding forward contracts. The fair values of the Company's foreign currency forward contracts designated as cash flow hedges are recorded in the consolidated balance sheet at December 25, 2011 and December 26, 2010 as follows:

	2011	2010
Prepaid Expenses and Other Current Assets		
Unrealized gains	$11,965	24,710
Unrealized losses	(4,187)	(9,229)
Net unrealized gain	7,778	15,481
Other Assets		
Unrealized gains	2,113	4,403
Unrealized losses	(92)	(2,933)
Net unrealized gain	2,021	1,470
Total asset derivatives	$ 9,799	16,951
Accrued Liabilities		
Unrealized gains	$ 12	—
Unrealized losses	(50)	—
Net unrealized loss	(38)	—
Other liabilities		
Unrealized gains	—	—
Unrealized losses	(21)	—
Net unrealized loss	(21)	—
Total liability derivatives	$ (59)	—

During the years ended December 25, 2011, December 26, 2010 and December 27, 2009, the Company reclassified net (losses) gains from AOCE to net earnings of $(2,936), $17,780 and $21,240, respectively. Of the amount reclassified in 2011, 2010 and 2009, $(6,158), $13,249 and $17,173 were reclassified to cost of sales and $2,895, $4,663 and $4,785 were reclassified to royalty expense, respectively. In addition, $436 was reclassified to net revenues in 2011. Net losses of $(109), $(132) and $(718) were reclassified to earnings as a result of hedge ineffectiveness in 2011, 2010 and 2009, respectively. Other (income) expense for the year ended December 25, 2011 includes a loss of approximately $3,700 related to certain derivatives which no longer qualified for hedge accounting.

Reclassification Adjustments

4.19

BOYD GAMING CORPORATION (DEC)

CONSOLIDATED STATEMENTS OF CHANGES IN STOCKHOLDERS' EQUITY

For the years ended December 31, 2011, 2010 and 2009

		Boyd Gaming Corporation Stockholders' Equity						
(In thousands, except share data)	Other Com-prehensive Income (Loss)	Common Stock Shares	Amount	Additional Paid-In Capital	Retained Earnings	Accumulated Other Com-prehensive Loss, Net	Non-Controlling Interests	Total Stock-Holders' Equity
Balances, January 1, 2009		87,814,061	$878	$616,304	$546,358	$(20,018)	$ —	$1,143,522
Net income	$ 4,241	—	—	—	4,241	—	—	4,241
Derivative instruments fair value adjustment, net of taxes of $979	1,892	—	—	—	—	1,892	—	1,892
Comprehensive income	$ 6,133							
Stock options exercised		29,797	—	160	—	—	—	160
Settlement of restricted stock units		11,281	—	—	—	—	—	—
Tax effect of share-based compensation arrangements		—	—	(1,384)	—	—	—	(1,384)
Share-based compensation costs		—	—	15,888	—	—	—	15,888
Dividends paid on common stock		(1,724,685)	(17)	(7,933)	—	—	—	(7,950)
Balances, December 31, 2009		86,130,454	861	623,035	550,599	(18,126)	—	1,156,369
Net income	$12,250	—	—	—	10,310	—	1,940	12,250
Derivative instruments fair value adjustment, net of taxes of $5,824	6,416	—	—	—	—	10,532	(4,116)	6,416
Comprehensive income	18,666							
Comprehensive loss attributable to noncontrolling interests	2,176	—	—	—	—	—	—	—
Comprehensive income attributable to Boyd Gaming Corporation	$20,842							
Stock options exercised		114,524	1	669	—	—	—	670
Share-based compensation costs		—	—	11,324	—	—	—	11,324
Noncontrolling interest attributable to Borgata		—	—	—	—	—	219,256	219,256
Noncontrolling interest attributable to LVE		—	—	—	—	—	(44,916)	(44,916)
Balances, December 31, 2010		86,244,978	862	635,028	560,909	(7,594)	172,164	1,361,369
Net income	$ (7,999)	—	—	—	(3,854)	—	(4,145)	(7,999)
Derivative instruments fair value adjustment, net of taxes of $4,230	11,562	—	—	—	—	7,594	3,968	11,562
Comprehensive income	3,563							
Comprehensive income attributable to noncontrolling interests	177	—	—	—	—	—	—	—
Comprehensive income attributable to Boyd Gaming Corporation	$ 3,740							
Stock options exercised		72,757	1	396	—	—	—	397
Award of restricted stock units		254,363	—	(383)	—	—	—	(383)
Tax effect of share-based compensation arrangements		—	—	(863)	—	—	—	(863)
Share-based compensation costs		—	—	9,996	—	—	—	9,996
Balances, December 31, 2011		86,572,098	$863	$644,174	$557,055	$ —	$171,987	$1,374,079

The accompanying notes are an integral part of these consolidated financial statements.

NOTES TO CONSOLIDATED FINANCIAL STATEMENTS

As of December 31, 2011 and 2010 and for the years ended December 31, 2011, 2010 and 2009

Note 1. Summary of Significant Accounting Policies (in part)

Derivative Instruments

The Company applies hedge accounting to certain derivative instruments, which is conditional upon satisfying specific documentation and performance criteria. In particular, the underlying hedged item must expose the Company to risks associated with market fluctuations and the instrument used as the hedging derivative must generate offsetting effects in prescribed magnitudes. If these criteria are not met, a change in the market value of the financial instrument and all associated settlements would be recognized as gains or losses in the period of change.

Under cash flow hedge accounting, effective derivative results are initially recorded in other comprehensive income ("OCI") and later reclassified to earnings, coinciding with the income recognition relating to the variable interest payments being hedged (i.e., when the interest expense on the variable-rate liability is recorded in earnings). Any hedge ineffectiveness (which represents the amount by which hedge results exceed the variability in the cash flows of the forecasted transaction due to the risk being hedged) is recorded in current period earnings.

During the years ended December 31, 2011, 2010 and 2009, the Company had certain derivative instruments that were not designated to qualify for hedge accounting. The periodic change in the mark-to-market of these derivative instruments is recorded in current period earnings.

Derivatives are included in the consolidated balance sheets as assets or liabilities at fair value. Certain interest rate swap contract liabilities included in our consolidation of LVE are recorded in other liabilities on the consolidated balance sheets at December 31, 2011 and 2010.

Accumulated Other Comprehensive Income (Loss)

Comprehensive income includes net income and all other non-stockholder changes in equity, or other comprehensive income. Components of the Company's comprehensive income are reported in the accompanying consolidated statements of stockholders' equity. The cumulative balance of other comprehensive income consists solely of fair value adjustments related to hedged derivative instruments.

Note 12. Derivative Instruments (in part)

Hedge Accounting

These derivative instruments have been accounted for as cash flow hedges through September 30, 2010. Accounting for cash flow hedging requires determining a division of hedge results deemed effective and deemed ineffective. However, most of the Company's hedges were designed in such a way so as to perfectly offset specifically-defined interest payments, such that no ineffectiveness has occurred, nor would any ineffectiveness occur, as long as the forecasted cash flows of the designated hedged items and the associated swap contracts remain unchanged.

However, on October 1, 2010, in anticipation of the refinancing of our bank credit facility, we de-designated all of our interest rate swap agreements as cash flow hedges. Concurrent with the de-designation of the hedging relationship, hedge accounting was suspended and the amount remaining in accumulated other comprehensive loss associated with this cash flow hedging relationship was frozen. This amount is being amortized into interest expense over the respective remaining term of the associated debt. Prospectively, all changes in the fair value of these interest rate swaps will be recognized immediately in earnings.

Fair Value

Fair value approximates the amount the Company would pay if these contracts were settled at the respective valuation dates. Fair value is estimated based upon current, and predictions of future, interest rate levels along a yield curve, the remaining duration of the instruments and other market conditions, and therefore, is subject to significant estimation and a high degree of variability and fluctuation between periods. The fair value is adjusted, to reflect the impact of credit ratings of the counterparties or the Company, as applicable. These adjustments resulted in a reduction in the fair values as compared to their settlement values.

Credit risk relating to derivative counterparties is mitigated by using multiple, highly rated counterparties, and the credit quality of each is monitored on an ongoing basis.

The fair values of our derivative instruments at December 31, 2010 included approximately $0.2 million of credit valuation adjustments to reflect the impact of the credit ratings of both the Company and our counterparties, based primarily upon the market value of the credit default swaps of the respective parties. These credit valuation adjustments resulted in a reduction in the fair values of our derivative instruments as compared to their settlement values.

Classification of Changes in Fair Value

The effect of derivative instruments on the consolidated statements of operations for the years ended December 31, 2011, 2010 and 2009 was as follows:

Derivatives in a Cash Flow Hedging Relationship—Interest Rate Swap Contracts	Gain (Loss) Recognized in OCI on Derivative (Effective Portion)	Location of Gain (Loss) Reclassified From AOCI Into Income (Ineffective Portion)	Gain (Loss) Reclassified From AOCI Into Income (Ineffective Portion)
	(In thousands)		(In thousands)
December 31, 2011	$ —	Interest expense	$(11,824)
December 31, 2010	16,356	Interest expense	(4,580)
December 31, 2009	2,871	Interest expense	2,081

4.20

PEABODY ENERGY CORPORATION (DEC)

CONSOLIDATED STATEMENTS OF COMPREHENSIVE INCOME

	Year Ended December 31		
(Dollars in millions)	2011	2010	2009
Net income	$ 946.3	$ 802.2	$ 463.0
Other comprehensive income, net of income taxes:			
Net unrealized losses on available-for-sale securities (net of $3.9 tax benefit for 2011)			
Unrealized holding losses on available-for-sale securities	(5.8)	—	—
Less: Reclassification for realized gains included in net income	(0.9)	—	—
Unrealized losses on available-for-sale securities	(6.7)	—	—
Unrealized gains on cash flow hedges (net of $6.2 tax benefit for 2011 and $129.5 and $220.9 tax provision for 2010 and 2009, respectively)			
Increase in fair value of cash flow hedges	291.9	229.9	235.2
Less: Reclassification for realized (gains) losses included in net income	(251.0)	(102.4)	84.6
Unrealized gains on cash flow hedges	40.9	127.5	319.8
Postretirement plans and workers' compensation obligations (net of $63.4, $2.1 and $71.8 tax benefit for 2011, 2010, and 2009, respectively)			
Net actuarial loss for the period	(149.2)	(46.2)	(128.4)
Amortization of actuarial loss and prior service cost	40.5	34.3	13.6
Postretirement plan and worker's compensation obligations	(108.7)	(11.9)	(114.8)
Other comprehensive (loss) income	(74.5)	115.6	205.0
Comprehensive income	871.8	917.8	668.0
Less: Comprehensive (loss) income attributable to noncontrolling interests	(11.4)	28.2	14.8
Comprehensive income attributable to common stockholders	$ 883.2	$ 889.6	$ 653.2

NOTES TO CONSOLIDATED FINANCIAL STATEMENTS

(1) Summary of Significant Accounting Policies Discussion (in part)

Derivatives (in part)

Gains or losses on derivative financial instruments designated as cash flow hedges are recorded as a separate component of stockholders' equity until the hedged transaction occurs (or until hedge ineffectiveness is determined), at which time gains or losses are reclassified to earnings in conjunction with the recognition of the underlying hedged item. To the extent that the periodic changes in the fair value of the derivatives exceed the changes in the hedged item, the ineffective portion of the periodic non-cash changes are recorded in earnings in the period of the change. If the hedge ceases to qualify for hedge accounting, the Company prospectively recognizes the mark-to-market movements in earnings in the period of the change. The potential for hedge ineffectiveness is present in the design of the Company's cash flow hedge relationships and is discussed in detail in Notes 6 and 7.

(6) Derivatives and Fair Value Measurements (in part)

Risk Management—Non Coal Trading Activities (in part)

The Company is exposed to various types of risk in the normal course of business, including price risk on commodities utilized in the Company's operations, interest rate risk on long-term debt, and foreign currency exchange rate risk for non-U.S. dollar expenditures. In most cases, commodity price risk (excluding coal trading activities) related to the sale of coal is mitigated through the use of long-term, fixed-price contracts rather than through the use of financial instruments. For the price risk exposure on other commodities, as well as for the interest rate risk and foreign currency exchange rate risk, the Company utilizes financial derivative instruments to manage the risks related to these fluctuations. All of these risks are actively monitored in an effort to ensure compliance with the risk management policies of the Company.

Hedge Ineffectiveness (in part). The Company assesses, both at inception and at least quarterly thereafter, whether the derivatives used in hedging activities are highly effective at offsetting the changes in the anticipated cash flows of the hedged item. The effective portion of the change in the fair value is recorded in "Accumulated other comprehensive loss" until the hedged transaction impacts reported earnings, at which time any gain or loss is also reclassified to earnings. To the extent that the periodic changes in the fair value of the derivatives exceed the changes in the hedged item, the ineffective portion of the periodic non-cash changes are recorded in earnings in the period of the change. If the hedge ceases to qualify for hedge accounting, the Company prospectively recognizes the mark-to-market movements in earnings in the period of the change.

A measure of ineffectiveness is inherent in hedging future diesel fuel purchases with derivative positions based on crude oil and refined petroleum products as a result of location and product differences.

The Company's derivative positions for the hedging of future explosives purchases are based on natural gas, which is the primary price component of explosives. However, a small measure of ineffectiveness exists as the contractual purchase price includes manufacturing fees that are subject to periodic adjustments. In addition, other fees, such as transportation surcharges, can result in ineffectiveness, but have historically changed infrequently and comprise a small portion of the total explosives cost.

The Company's derivative positions for the hedging of forecasted foreign currency expenditures contain a small measure of ineffectiveness due to timing differences between the hedge settlement and the purchase transaction, which could differ by less than a day and up to a maximum of 30 days.

The tables below show the classification and amounts of pre-tax gains and losses related to the Company's non-trading hedges during the years ended December 31, 2011, 2010 and 2009:

Year Ended December 31, 2011

Financial Instrument	Income Statement Classification Gains (Losses)—Realized	Gain (Loss) Recognized in Income on Non-Designated Derivatives[1]	Gain (Loss) Recognized in Other Comprehensive Income on Derivative (Effective Portion)	Gain (Loss) Reclassified From Other Comprehensive Income Into Income (Effective Portion)	Gain (Loss) Reclassified From Other Comprehensive Income Into Income (Ineffective Portion)
		(Dollars in millions)			
Commodity swaps and options	Operating costs and expenses	$ —	$ 30.7	$ 42.7	$4.8
Foreign currency cash flow hedge contracts:					
—Operating costs	Operating costs and expenses	—	193.4	342.2	—
—Capital expenditures	Depreciation, depletion and amortization	—	(0.5)	—	—
Foreign currency economic hedge contracts	Acquisition costs related to Macarthur Coal Limited	$(32.8)	$ —	$ —	$ —
Total		$(32.8)	$223.6	$384.9	$4.8

[1] Relates to foreign currency contracts associated with the acquisition of Macarthur shares under the takeover process.

Year Ended December 31, 2010

Financial Instrument	Income Statement Classification Gains (Losses)—Realized	Gain (Loss) Recognized in Income on Non-Designated Derivatives[2]	Gain (Loss) Recognized in Other Comprehensive Income on Derivative (Effective Portion)	Gain (Loss) Reclassified From Other Comprehensive Income Into Income (Effective Portion)	Gain (Loss) Reclassified From Other Comprehensive Income Into Income (Ineffective Portion)
		(Dollars in millions)			
Interest rate swaps cash flow hedge contracts	Interest expense	$(8.5)	$ 0.8	$ (0.5)	$ —
Commodity swaps and options	Operating costs and expenses	—	29.9	(36.2)	(1.1)
Foreign currency cash flow hedge contracts	Operating costs and expenses	—	622.2	188.2	—
Total		$(8.5)	$652.9	$151.5	$(1.1)

[2] Amounts relate to swaps that were de-designated and terminated in conjunction with the refinancing of the Company's previous credit facility.

	Income Statement Classification Gains (Losses)—Realized	Year Ended December 31, 2009			
		Gain (Loss) Recognized in Income on Non-Designated Derivatives[3]	Gain (Loss) Recognized in Other Comprehensive Income on Derivative (Effective Portion)	Gain (Loss) Reclassified From Other Comprehensive Income Into Income (Effective Portion)	Gain (Loss) Reclassified From Other Comprehensive Income Into Income (Ineffective Portion)
Financial Instrument					
		(Dollars in millions)			
Interest rate swaps cash flow hedge contracts	Interest expense	$ —	$ 0.2	$ (5.5)	$ —
Commodity swaps and options:					
—Cash flow hedges	Operating costs and expenses	—	65.5	(98.3)	0.7
—Economic hedges	Operating costs and expenses	(2.7)	—	—	—
Foreign currency cash flow hedge contracts	Operating costs and expenses	—	458.0	(30.8)	—
Total		$(2.7)	$523.7	$(134.6)	$0.7

[3] Amounts relate to diesel fuel and explosives hedge derivatives that were de-designated in 2009.

Based on the net fair value of the Company's non-coal trading positions held in "Accumulated other comprehensive loss" at December 31, 2011, unrealized gains to be reclassified from comprehensive income to earnings over the next 12 months associated with the Company's foreign currency and diesel fuel hedge programs are expected to be approximately $266 million and $43 million, respectively. The unrealized losses to be realized under the explosives hedge program are expected to be approximately $6 million. As these unrealized gains are associated with derivative instruments that represent hedges of forecasted transactions, the amounts reclassified to earnings will partially offset the realized transactions, while the unrealized losses will add incremental expense to the consolidated statements of income.

(7) Coal Trading (in part)

Risk Management (in part)

The Company engages in direct and brokered trading of coal, ocean freight and fuel-related commodities in over-the-counter markets (coal trading), some of which is subsequently exchange-cleared and some of which is bilaterally-settled. Except those for which the Company has elected to apply a normal purchases and normal sales exception, all derivative coal trading contracts are accounted for on a fair value basis.

The Company's policy is to include instruments associated with coal trading transactions as a part of its trading book. Trading revenues are recorded in "Other revenues" in the consolidated statements of income and include realized and unrealized gains and losses on derivative instruments, including coal deliveries related to contracts accounted for under the normal purchases and normal sales exception. Therefore, the Company has elected the trading exemption to reflect the disclosures for its coal trading activities.

Hedge Ineffectiveness. The Company assesses, both at inception and at least quarterly thereafter, whether the derivatives used in hedging activities are highly effective at offsetting the changes in the anticipated cash flows of the hedged item. The effective portion of the change in the fair value is recorded in "Accumulated other comprehensive loss" until the hedged transaction impacts reported earnings, at which time gains and losses are also reclassified to earnings. To the extent that the periodic changes in the fair value of the derivatives exceed the changes in the hedged item, the ineffective portion of the periodic non-cash changes are recorded in earnings in the period of the change. If the hedge ceases to qualify for hedge accounting, the Company prospectively recognizes the mark-to-market movements in earnings in the period of the change.

In some instances, the Company has designated an existing coal trading derivative as a hedge and, thus, the derivative has a non-zero fair value at hedge inception. The "off-market" nature of these derivatives, which is best described as an embedded financing element within the derivative, is a source of ineffectiveness. In other instances, the Company uses a coal trading derivative that settles at a different time, has different quality specifications, or has a different location basis than the occurrence of the cash flow being hedged. These collectively yield ineffectiveness to the extent that the derivative hedge contract does not exactly offset changes in the fair value or expected cash flows of the hedged item.

Forecasted Transactions No Longer Probable. During 2011, the Company reclassified losses of $10.0 million out of "Accumulated other comprehensive loss" to earnings as the underlying forecasted transactions were deemed no longer probable of occurring.

(18) Accumulated Other Comprehensive Income (Loss)

The following table sets forth the after-tax components of comprehensive income (loss):

(Dollars in millions)	Foreign Currency Translation Adjustment	Net Actuarial Loss Associated With Postretirement Plans and Workers' Compensation Obligations	Prior Service Cost Associated With Postretirement Plans	Cash Flow Hedges	Available-For-Sale Securities	Total Accumulated Other Comprehensive Loss
December 31, 2008	$3.1	$(220.4)	$(18.7)	$(152.5)	$ —	$(388.5)
Net change in fair value	—	—	—	235.2	—	235.2
Reclassification from other comprehensive income to earnings	—	11.8	1.8	84.6	—	98.2
Current period change	—	(134.9)	6.5	—	—	(128.4)
December 31, 2009	3.1	(343.5)	(10.4)	167.3	—	(183.5)
Net change in fair value	—	—	—	229.9	—	229.9
Reclassification from other comprehensive income to earnings	—	31.8	2.5	(102.4)	—	(68.1)
Current period change	—	(41.3)	(4.9)	—	—	(46.2)
December 31, 2010	3.1	(353.0)	(12.8)	294.8	—	(67.9)
Net change in fair value	—	—	—	291.9	(5.8)	286.1
Reclassification from other comprehensive income to earnings	—	38.2	2.3	(251.0)	(0.9)	(211.4)
Current period change	—	(150.1)	0.9	—	—	(149.2)
December 31, 2011	$3.1	$(464.9)	$ (9.6)	$ 335.7	$(6.7)	$(142.4)

Comprehensive income (loss) differs from net income by the amount of unrealized gain or loss resulting from valuation changes of the Company's cash flow hedges (see Note 6 and Note 7 for information related to the Company's cash flow hedges), changes in the fair value of available-for-sale securities (see Note 5 for information related to the Company's investments in available-for-sale securities) and the change in actuarial loss and prior service cost during the periods. The values of the Company's cash flow hedging instruments are primarily affected by changes in diesel fuel and coal prices, and the U.S. dollar/Australian dollar exchange rate.

Section 5: Stockholders' Equity

FORMAT OF STOCKHOLDERS' EQUITY IN ANNUAL FILINGS

PRESENTATION

5.01 *Equity* (sometimes referred to as net assets) is the residual interest in the assets of an entity that remains after deducting its liabilities. As discussed in Financial Accounting Standards Board (FASB) *Accounting Standards Codification* (ASC) 505, *Equity*, if both financial position and results of operations are presented, disclosure of changes in (*a*) the separate accounts comprising stockholders' equity (in addition to retained earnings) and (*b*) the number of shares of equity securities during at least the most recent annual fiscal period and any subsequent interim period presented is required in order to make the financial statements sufficiently informative. Disclosure of such changes may take the form of separate statements or may be made in the basic financial statements or notes thereto. Most public entities present a statement of stockholders' equity to conform with Rule 3-04 of Securities and Exchange Commission (SEC) Regulation S-X. As shown in Table 5-1, which summarizes the presentation formats used by the survey entities to present changes in retained earnings, changes in retained earnings are most frequently presented in a Statement of Stockholders' Equity.

5.02 FASB ASC 505 explains that additional paid-in capital, however created, should not be used to relieve income of the current or future years of charges that would otherwise be made to the income statement. In accounting for a stock dividend, a corporation should transfer from retained earnings to the category of capital stock and additional paid-in capital an amount equal to the fair value of the additional shares issued.

5.03 Rule 5-02 of Regulation S-X requires separate captions for additional paid-in capital, other additional capital, and retained earnings. If appropriate, additional paid-in capital and other additional capital may be combined with the stock caption to which it applies.

DISCLOSURE

5.04 FASB ASC 505, *Equity*, states that an entity should explain the pertinent rights and privileges of the various securities outstanding. Examples are dividend and liquidation preferences; contractual rights of security holders to receive dividends or returns from the security issuer's profits, cash flows, or returns on investments; participation rights; call prices and dates; conversion or exercise prices or rates and pertinent dates; sinking-fund requirements; unusual voting rights; and significant terms of contracts to issue additional shares.

5.05 FASB ASC 505 also requires disclosure of changes in the separate accounts comprising shareholders' equity (in addition to retained earnings) and of the changes in the number of shares of equity securities during at least the most recent annual fiscal period. Disclosure of such changes may take the form of separate statements or may be made in the basic financial statements or notes thereto.

5.06

TABLE 5-1: FORMAT OF CHANGES IN STOCKHOLDERS' EQUITY

	2011	2010	2009
Statement of stockholders' equity	486	489	490
Separate statement of retained earnings	4	5	2
Combined statement of income and retained earnings	1	1	2
Schedule in notes	9	5	6
Total Entities	**500**	**500**	**500**

5.07

TABLE 5-2: PRESENTATION OF CHANGES IN ADDITIONAL PAID-IN CAPITAL

Table 5-2 summarizes the presentation formats used by the survey entities to present changes in additional paid-in capital.

	2011	2010	2009
Statement of stockholders' equity	456	455	446
Schedule in notes	7	8	8
Statement of additional paid-in capital only	—	1	N/C*
Balance unchanged during the year	2	—	1
	465	464	455
Additional paid-in capital account not presented	35	36	45
Total Entities	**500**	**500**	**500**

* N/C = Not compiled. The line item was not included in the table for the year shown.

PRESENTATION AND DISCLOSURE EXCERPTS

Stock Option Awards and Employee Stock Purchase Plan (ESPP)

5.08

ATMEL CORPORATION (DEC)

CONSOLIDATED STATEMENTS OF STOCKHOLDERS' EQUITY AND COMPREHENSIVE INCOME (LOSS)

(In thousands)	Common Stock Shares	Par Value	Additional Paid-In Capital	Accumulated Other Comprehensive Income	Retained Earnings (Accumulated Deficit)	Total
Balances, December 31, 2008	448,872	$449	$1,238,796	$113,999	$(551,160)	$ 802,084
Comprehensive loss:						
Net loss	—	—	—	—	(109,498)	(109,498)
Actuarial gain related to defined benefit pension plans	—	—	—	413	—	413
Unrealized gains on investments, net of tax	—	—	—	327	—	327
Foreign currency translation adjustments	—	—	—	25,731	—	25,731
Total comprehensive loss						(83,027)
Stock-based compensation expense	—	—	37,730	—	—	37,730
Exercise of stock options	1,206	1	3,262	—	—	3,263
Issuance of common stock under employee stock purchase plan	2,139	2	6,481	—	—	6,483
Common stock issued in lieu of 2008 bonus awards	632	1	1,944	—	—	1,945
Vested restricted stock units	3,014	3	—	—	—	3
Shares withheld for employee taxes related to vested restricted stock units	(1,277)	(1)	(4,073)	—	—	(4,074)
Balances, December 31, 2009	454,586	$455	$1,284,140	$140,470	$(660,658)	$ 764,407
Comprehensive income:						
Net income	—	—	—	—	423,075	423,075
Actuarial loss related to defined benefit pension plans	—	—	—	(788)	—	(788)
Unrealized losses on investments, net of tax	—	—	—	(2,102)	—	(2,102)
Recognition of cumulative foreign CTA adjustments (See Note 10)	—	—	—	(99,779)	—	(99,779)
Foreign currency translation adjustments	—	—	—	(21,472)	—	(21,472)
Total comprehensive income						298,934
Stock-based compensation expense	—	—	58,487	—	—	58,487
Tax benefit on stock-based compensation expense	—	—	1,664	—	—	1,664
Exercise of stock options	5,344	5	22,493	—	—	22,498
Issuance of common stock under employee stock purchase plan	2,028	2	7,411	—	—	7,413
Vested restricted stock units	4,816	5	—	—	—	5
Shares withheld for employee taxes related to vested restricted stock units	(1,418)	(1)	(11,138)	—	—	(11,139)
Common stock issued to former employees of Quantum (See Note 3)	3,152	3	—	—	—	3
Repurchase of common stock	(11,720)	(12)	(89,204)	—	—	(89,216)
Balances, December 31, 2010	456,788	$457	$1,273,853	$ 16,329	$(237,583)	$1,053,056
Comprehensive income:						
Net income	—	—	—	—	314,990	314,990
Actuarial loss related to defined benefit pension plans	—	—	—	(197)	—	(197)
Unrealized gains on investments, net of tax	—	—	—	179	—	179
Foreign currency translation adjustments	—	—	—	(6,863)	—	(6,863)
Total comprehensive income	—	—	—	—	—	308,109
Stock-based compensation expense	—	—	69,102	—	—	69,102
Tax benefit on stock-based compensation expense	—	—	939	—	—	939
Exercise of stock options	4,285	4	19,336	—	—	19,340
Issuance of common stock under employee stock purchase plan	1,514	2	9,404	—	—	9,406
Vested restricted stock units	6,345	6	—	—	—	6
Vested performance-based restricted stock units	8,485	8	—	—	—	8
Shares withheld for employee taxes related to vested restricted stock units	(6,252)	(6)	(73,280)	—	—	(73,286)
Repurchase of common stock	(28,776)	(29)	(304,207)	—	—	(304,236)
Balances, December 31, 2011	442,389	$442	$ 995,147	$ 9,448	$ 77,407	$1,082,444

The accompanying notes are an integral part of these Consolidated Financial Statements.

SEC 5.08

NOTES TO CONSOLIDATED FINANCIAL STATEMENTS

Note 9 Stockholders' Equity (in part)

Stock Option Awards (in part)

Range of Exercise Price	Options Outstanding				Options Exercisable			
	Number Outstanding	Weighted-Average Remaining Contractual Term (Years)	Weighted-Average Exercise Price	Aggregate Intrinsic Value	Number Exercisable	Weighted-Average Remaining Contractual Term (Years)	Weighted-Average Exercise Price	Aggregate Intrinsic Value
(In thousands, except per share prices and life data)								
$1.68–3.24	981	3.95	$2.73	$ 5,270	905	3.76	$2.69	$ 4,901
3.26–3.29	512	3.62	3.28	2,465	505	3.58	3.28	2,432
3.32–3.32	1,090	6.21	3.32	5,210	1,005	6.19	3.32	4,803
3.41–4.20	926	6.66	4.13	3,676	592	6.58	4.12	2,358
4.23–4.40	820	4.95	4.25	3,157	332	5.12	4.27	1,224
4.43–4.43	1,000	7.71	4.43	3,670	413	7.71	4.43	1,516
4.56–4.89	1,528	5.19	4.82	5,013	1,443	5.01	4.82	4,729
4.92–5.75	826	4.79	5.39	2,234	826	5.01	5.39	2,111
5.96–8.89	520	4.97	6.38	870	396	4.57	6.42	638
10.01–10.01	14	8.88	10.01	—	3	8.88	10.01	—
	8,217	5.48	$4.26	$31,565	6,420	5.21	$4.22	$24,712

The number of options exercisable under Atmel's stock option plans at December 31, 2011, 2010 and 2009 were 6.4 million, 8.5 million and 11.1 million, respectively. For the years ended December 31, 2011, 2010 and 2009, the number of stock options that were forfeited, but were not available for future stock option grants due to the expiration of these shares under the 1986 Stock Plan was not material.

For the years ended December 31, 2011, 2010 and 2009, the number of stock options that were exercised were 4.3 million, 5.3 million and 1.2 million, respectively, which had a total intrinsic value at the date of exercise of $42.0 million, $24.8 million and $1.5 million, respectively, and had an aggregate exercise price of $19.3 million, $22.5 million and $3.3 million, respectively.

Employee Stock Purchase Plan

Under the 1991 Employee Stock Purchase Plan ("1991 ESPP"), qualified employees are entitled to purchase shares of Atmel's common stock at the lower of 85% of the fair market value of the common stock at the date of commencement of the six-month offering period or at 85% of the fair market value on the last day of the offering period. Purchases are limited to 10% of an employee's eligible compensation. There were 0.8 million, 2.0 million and 2.1 million shares purchased under the 1991 ESPP for the years ended December 31, 2011, 2010 and 2009, at an average price per share of $4.85, $3.65 and $3.03, respectively. The remaining 1.9 million shares available under the 1991 ESPP expired in the three months ended March 31, 2011. In 2010, the Company's stockholders approved a new 2010 Employee Stock Purchase Plan ("2010 ESPP") and authorized an additional 25.0 million shares for issuance under the 2010 ESPP. There

were 0.7 million shares purchased under the 2010 ESPP for the year ended December 31, 2011 at an average price per share of $8.56. Of the 25.0 million shares authorized for issuance under the 2010 ESPP, 24.3 million shares were available for issuance at December 31, 2011. The 1991 ESPP and the 2010 ESPP are collectively referred to as the "Company's ESPPs."

The fair value of each purchase under the Company's ESPPs is estimated on the date of the beginning of the offering period using the Black-Scholes option pricing model. The following assumptions were utilized to determine the fair value of the Company's ESPPs shares:

	Years Ended		
	December 31, 2011	December 31, 2010	December 31, 2009
Risk-free interest rate	0.12%	0.18%	0.35%
Expected life (years)	0.50	0.50	0.50
Expected volatility	46%	45%	73%
Expected dividend yield	—	—	—

The weighted-average fair value of the rights to purchase shares under the Company's ESPPs for offering periods started for the years ended December 31, 2011, 2010 and 2009 was $2.70, $0.89 and $0.86, respectively. Cash proceeds for the issuance of shares under the Company's ESPPs were $9.4 million, $7.4 million and $6.5 million for the years ended December 31, 2011, 2010 and 2009, respectively.

Common Stock Issued to Employees

5.09

JUNIPER NETWORKS, INC. (DEC)

CONSOLIDATED STATEMENTS OF CHANGES IN EQUITY

(In thousands)

	Shares	Amount	Additional Paid-In Capital	Accumulated Other Comprehensive Income (Loss)	Accumulated Deficit	Non-controlling Interest	Total Equity
			Juniper Networks				
Balance at December 31, 2008	526,752	$5	$ 8,811,497	$ (4,245)	$(2,905,852)	$ —	$5,901,405
Consolidated net income (loss)	—	—	—	—	116,999	(1,771)	115,228
Change in unrealized loss on investments, net	—	—	—	(2,757)	—	—	(2,757)
Change in foreign currency translation adjustments, net	—	—	—	5,569	—	—	5,569
Consolidated comprehensive income	—	—	—	—	—	—	118,040
Purchase of subsidiary shares by noncontrolling interest	—	—	—	—	—	4,400	4,400
Issuance of shares in connection with Employee Stock Purchase Plan	3,221	—	39,164	—	—	—	39,164
Issuance of shares in connection with vesting of restricted share units	1,432	—	—	—	—	—	—
Exercise of stock options by employees, net of repurchases	8,651	—	126,284	—	—	—	126,284
Repurchase and retirement of common stock	(20,715)	—	(6,216)	—	(447,672)	—	(453,888)
Share-based compensation expense	—	—	139,659	—	—	—	139,659
Adjustment related to tax benefit from employee stock option plans	—	—	(50,299)	—	—	—	(50,299)
Balance at December 31, 2009	519,341	5	9,060,089	(1,433)	(3,236,525)	2,629	5,824,765
Consolidated net income	—	—	—	—	618,402	971	619,373
Change in unrealized loss on investments, net	—	—	—	(317)	—	—	(317)
Change in foreign currency translation adjustments, net	—	—	—	499	—	—	499
Consolidated comprehensive income	—	—	—	—	—	—	619,555
Return of capital to noncontrolling interest	—	—	—	—	—	(3,000)	(3,000)
Issuance of shares in connection with Employee Stock Purchase Plan	1,974	—	41,829	—	—	—	41,829
Issuance of shares in connection with vesting of restricted share units	2,224	—	—	—	—	—	—
Exercise of stock options by employees, net of repurchases	21,568	—	409,395	—	—	—	409,395
Shares assumed in connection with business acquisitions	—	—	2,355	—	—	—	2,355
Repurchase and retirement of common stock	(19,654)	—	(75,242)	—	(488,284)	—	(563,526)
Repurchases related to net issuances	(75)	—	(17)	—	(1,930)	—	(1,947)
Share-based compensation expense	—	—	177,825	—	—	—	177,825
Adjustment related to tax benefit from employee stock option plans	—	—	101,549	—	—	—	101,549
Balance at December 31, 2010	525,378	5	9,717,783	(1,251)	(3,108,337)	600	6,608,800
Consolidated net income (loss)	—	—	—	—	425,136	(124)	425,012
Change in unrealized loss on investments, net	—	—	—	(9,980)	—	—	(9,980)
Change in foreign currency translation adjustments, net	—	—	—	(6,359)	—	—	(6,359)
Consolidated comprehensive income	—	—	—	—	—	—	408,673
Issuance of shares in connection with Employee Stock Purchase Plan	2,400	—	51,687	—	—	—	51,687
Issuance of shares in connection with vesting of restricted share units	2,431	—	—	—	—	—	—
Exercise of stock options by employees, net of repurchases	13,904	—	293,856	—	—	—	293,856
Repurchase and retirement of common stock	(17,500)	—	(256,372)	—	(284,866)	—	(541,238)
Repurchases related to net issuances	(204)	—	(3,017)	—	(4,335)	—	(7,352)
Share-based compensation expense	—	—	217,761	—	—	—	217,761
Adjustment related to tax benefit from employee stock option plans	—	—	57,471	—	—	—	57,471
Balance at December 31, 2011	526,409	$5	$10,079,169	$(17,590)	$(2,972,402)	$ 476	$7,089,658

See accompanying Notes to Consolidated Financial Statements.

NOTES TO CONSOLIDATED FINANCIAL STATEMENTS

Note 12. Employee Benefit Plans (in part)

Share-Based Compensation Plans

The Company's share-based compensation plans include the 2006 Equity Incentive Plan (the "2006 Plan"), the 2000 Nonstatutory Stock Option Plan (the "2000 Plan"), the Amended and Restated 1996 Stock Plan (the "1996 Plan"), various equity incentive plans assumed through acquisitions, the 2008 Employee Stock Purchase Plan (the "2008 Purchase Plan"), and the 1999 Employee Stock Purchase Plan ("1999 Purchase Plan"). Under these plans, the Company has granted (or in the case of acquired plans, assumed) stock options, RSUs, and PSAs.

As of December 31, 2011, a total of approximately 105.2 million shares of common stock were reserved for future issuance upon exercise of stock options and for the future grant of share-based compensation awards under the Company's equity incentive plans and the 2008 Purchase Plan.

The 2006 Plan, adopted and approved by the Company's stockholders in May 2006, had an initial authorized share reserve of 64.5 million shares of common stock plus the addition of any shares subject to options under the 2000 Plan and the 1996 Plan that were outstanding as of May 18, 2006, and that subsequently expire unexercised, up to a maximum of an additional 75.0 million shares. In the second quarters of 2011 and 2010, the Company's stockholders' approved amendments to the 2006 Plan that increased the number of shares reserved for issuance thereby increasing the authorized share reserve by 30.0 million shares in May 2011 and 2010. As of December 31, 2011, the 2006 Plan had 58.2 million shares subject to currently outstanding equity awards and 41.1 million shares available for future issuance. Options granted under the 2006 Plan have a maximum term of seven years from the grant date, and generally vest and become exercisable over a four-year period. Subject to the terms of change of control severance agreements, and except for a limited number of shares allowed under the 2006 Plan, RSUs or PSAs that vest solely based on continuing employment or provision of services will vest in full no earlier than three years from the grant date, or in the event vesting is based on factors other than continued future provision of services, such awards will vest in full no earlier than one year from the grant date.

In connection with past acquisitions, the Company assumed stock option and RSU awards under the stock plans of the acquired companies. The Company exchanged those awards for Juniper Networks' stock options and RSUs. As of December 31, 2011, stock options and RSUs covering approximately 1.4 million shares of common stock were outstanding under awards assumed through the Company's past acquisitions.

The Company adopted the 2008 Purchase Plan, in May 2008, which replaced the 1999 Purchase Plan. The Board reserves an aggregate of 12.0 million shares of the Company's common stock for issuance under this plan. The 2008 Purchase Plan is generally similar to the 1999 Purchase Plan, except that under the 2008 Purchase Plan, any increases to the number of shares reserved for issuance must be approved by the Company's stockholders. The 2008 Purchase Plan permits eligible employees to acquire shares of the Company's common stock at a 15% discount to the offering price (as determined in the 2008 Purchase Plan) through periodic payroll deductions of up to 10% of base compensation, subject to individual purchase limits of 6,000 shares in any twelve-month period or $25,000 worth of stock, determined at the fair market value of the shares at the time the stock purchase option is granted, in one calendar year.

In December 2005, the Board amended the Juniper Networks 1999 Employee Stock Purchase Plan that was approved by the Board in April 1999. Under the 1999 Purchase Plan, the Board authorized a maximum number of 12.0 million shares, plus an annual increase to be added on the first day of the Company's fiscal year beginning in 2000 equal to the lesser of (1) 3.0 million shares or (2) 1% of the outstanding shares on such date or (3) a lesser amount determined by the Board. The 1999 Purchase Plan permits eligible employees to acquire shares of the Company's common stock through periodic payroll deductions of up to 10% of base compensation.

Stock Option Activities (in part)

Since 2006, the Company has granted stock option awards that have a maximum contractual life of seven years from the date of grant. Prior to 2006, stock option awards generally had a ten-year contractual life from the date of grant. The following table summarizes the Company's stock option activity and related information as of and for the three years ended December 31, 2011 (in millions, except for per share amounts and years):

	Outstanding Options			
	Number of Shares	Weighted Average Exercise Price per Share	Weighted Average Remaining Contractual Term (In Years)	Aggregate Intrinsic Value
Balance at December 31, 2008	73.6	$21.24		
Options granted	9.9	17.86		
Options canceled	(2.3)	21.57		
Options exercised	(8.6)	14.59		
Options expired	(5.2)	34.91		
Balance at December 31, 2009	67.4	20.84	4.6	$451.2
Options granted	6.2	29.15		
Options assumed[1]	0.5	31.65		
Options canceled	(2.3)	22.03		
Options exercised	(21.6)	18.99		
Options expired	(0.8)	61.48		
Balance at December 31, 2010	49.4	21.90	4.1	$744.5
Options granted	5.6	37.17		
Options canceled	(1.9)	26.76		
Options exercised	(13.9)	21.13		
Options expired	(0.6)	34.32		
Balance at December 31, 2011	38.6	$23.98	3.7	$ 75.3
As of December 31, 2011:				
Vested or expected-to-vest options	36.9	$23.66	3.7	$ 74.2
Exercisable options	26.1	$21.51	3.0	$ 61.7

[1] Stock options assumed in connection with the acquisition of Ankeena and Altor.

Aggregate intrinsic value represents the difference between the Company's closing stock price on the last trading day of the period, which was $20.41 per share as of December 31, 2011 and the exercise price multiplied by the number of related options. The pre-tax intrinsic value of options exercised, representing the difference between the fair market value of the Company's common stock on the date of the exercise and the exercise price of each option, was $249.8 million, $260.3 million, and $83.6 million for 2011, 2010, and 2009, respectively. Total fair value of options vested during 2011, 2010, and 2009 was $80.7 million, $83.2 million, and $88.9 million, respectively.

Employee Stock Purchase Plan

The Company's 2008 Purchase Plan is implemented in a series of offering periods, each six months in duration, or a shorter period as determined by the Board. Employees purchased approximately 2.4 million, 2.0 million, and 3.2 million shares of common stock through the 2008 Purchase Plan and 1999 Purchase Plan at an average exercise price of $21.53, $21.20, and $12.16 per share during fiscal years 2011, 2010, and 2009, respectively.

As of December 31, 2011, approximately 6.0 million shares had been issued and 6.0 million shares remained available for future issuance under the 2008 Purchase Plan.

Share-Based Compensation Expense

The weighted-average assumptions used and the resulting estimates of fair value for employee stock options and the employee stock purchase plan during the three years ended December 31, 2011 were:

	Years Ended December 31		
	2011	2010	2009
Employee Stock Options:			
Volatility factor	43%	38%	50%
Risk-free interest rate	1.5%	2.0%	1.6%
Expected life (years)	4.1	4.3	4.2
Dividend yield	—	—	—
Weighted-average fair value per share	$13.17	$9.77	$7.41
Employee Stock Purchase Plan:			
Volatility factor	41%	35%	54%
Risk-free interest rate	0.2%	0.2%	0.4%
Expected life (years)	0.5	0.5	0.5
Dividend yield	—	—	—
Weighted-average fair value per share	$ 7.48	$6.55	$5.54

The Company's share-based compensation expense associated with stock options, employee stock purchases, RSUs, and PSAs is recorded in the following cost and expense categories for the three years ended December 31, 2011 (in millions):

	Years Ended December 31		
	2011	2010	2009
Cost of revenues—Product	$ 4.6	$ 4.4	$ 3.9
Cost of revenues—Service	15.7	13.5	10.5
Research and development	97.7	78.5	59.3
Sales and marketing	70.9	54.9	43.1
General and administrative	33.3	30.7	22.9
Total	$222.2	$182.0	$139.7

The following table summarizes share-based compensation expense by award type (in millions):

	Years Ended December 31		
	2011	2010	2009
Options	$ 76.2	$ 81.5	$ 81.2
Assumed options	—	0.8	—
RSUs and PSAs	123.1	81.8	44.1
Assumed RSUs	—	0.6	—
Employee stock purchase plan	18.5	13.1	14.4
Other acquisition-related compensation	4.4	4.2	—
Total	$222.2	$182.0	$139.7

As of December 31, 2011, approximately $94.8 million of unrecognized compensation cost, adjusted for estimated forfeitures, related to unvested stock options will be recognized over a weighted-average period of approximately 2.3 years while approximately $247.4 million of unrecognized compensation cost, adjusted for estimated forfeitures, related to unvested RSUs and PSAs will be recognized over a weighted-average period of approximately 2.1 years.

Common Stock Issued in a Public Offering

5.10

SUNOCO, INC. (DEC)

CONSOLIDATED STATEMENTS OF COMPREHENSIVE INCOME (LOSS) AND EQUITY

(Dollars in millions, shares in thousands)

		Sunoco, Inc. Shareholders' Equity							
	Compre-hensive Income (Loss)*	Common Stock		Capital in Excess of Par Value	Retained Earnings	Accumulated Other Compre-hensive Loss	Common Stock Held in Treasury		Non-Controlling Interests
		Shares	Par Value				Shares	Cost	
At December 31, 2008		281,141	$281	$1,667	$6,010	$(477)	164,263	$4,639	$438
Net income (loss)	$(200)	—	—	—	(329)	—	—	—	129
Other comprehensive loss:									
Reclassifications of settlement and curtailment losses and prior service cost and actuarial loss amortization to earnings (net of related tax expense of $65)	95	—	—	—	—	95	—	—	—
Retirement benefit plans funded status adjustment (net of related tax expense of $33) (Note 9)	48	—	—	—	—	48	—	—	—
Net hedging losses (net of related tax benefit of $7)	(9)	—	—	—	—	(9)	—	—	—
Reclassifications of net hedging losses to earnings (net of related tax expense of $10)	13	—	—	—	—	13	—	—	—
Net decrease in unrealized loss on available-for-sale securities (net of related tax expense of $1)	1	—	—	—	—	1	—	—	—
Cash dividends and distributions	—	—	—	—	(140)	—	—	—	(94)
Issued under stock-based incentive plans	—	65	—	—	—	—	—	—	—
Net increase in equity related to unissued shares under stock-based incentive plans	—	—	—	9	—	—	—	—	—
Net proceeds from Sunoco Logistics Partners L.P. public equity offering (Note 16)	—	—	—	22	—	—	—	—	88
Other	—	—	—	5	—	—	(2)	—	1
Total	$ (52)								

(continued)

	Compre-hensive Income (Loss)*	Common Stock Shares	Common Stock Par Value	Capital in Excess of Par Value	Retained Earnings	Accumulated Other Compre-hensive Loss	Common Stock Held in Treasury Shares	Common Stock Held in Treasury Cost	Non-controlling Interests
At December 31, 2009		281,206	$281	$1,703	$5,541	$(329)	164,261	$4,639	$562
Net income	$ 428	—	—	—	234	—	—	—	194
Other comprehensive loss:									
Reclassifications of settlement and curtailment losses and prior service cost and actuarial loss amortization to earnings (net of related tax expense of $34)	51	—	—	—	—	51	—	—	—
Retirement benefit plans funded status adjustment (net of related tax expense of $5) (Note 9)	29	—	—	—	—	29	—	—	—
Net hedging losses (net of related tax benefit of $3)	(3)	—	—	—	—	(3)	—	—	—
Reclassifications of net hedging losses to earnings (net of related tax expense of $1)	1	—	—	—	—	1	—	—	—
Net increase in unrealized gain on available-for-sale securities (net of related tax expense of $—)	2	—	—	—	—	2	—	—	—
Cash dividends and distributions	—	—	—	—	(73)	—	—	—	(123)
Issued under stock-based incentive plans	—	57	—	—	—	—	—	—	—
Net increase in equity related to unissued shares under stock-based incentive plans	—	—	—	12	—	—	—	—	—
Contribution to pension plans	—	—	—	(161)	—	—	(3,593)	(251)	—
Distribution in connection with modification of incentive distribution rights (Note 16)	—	—	—	75	—	—	—	—	(121)
Net proceeds from Sunoco Logistics Partners L.P. public equity offering (Note 16)	—	—	—	76	—	—	—	—	162
Noncontrolling interest attributable to the consolidation of pipeline acqusitions (Note 16)	—	—	—	—	—	—	—	—	80
Other	—	2	—	(6)	—	—	2	(1)	(1)
Total	$ 508								
At December 31, 2010		281,265	$281	$1,699	$5,702	$(249)	160,670	$4,387	$753
Net income (loss)	$(1,509)	—	—	—	(1,684)	—	—	—	175
Other comprehensive loss:									
Reclassifications of settlement and curtailment losses and prior service cost and actuarial loss amortization to earnings (net of related tax expense of $30)	43	—	—	—	—	43	—	—	—
Retirement benefit plans funded status adjustment (net of related tax benefit of $37) (Note 9)	(55)	—	—	—	—	(55)	—	—	—
Net hedging gains (net of related tax expense of $1)	1	—	—	—	—	1	—	—	—
Reclassifications of net hedging losses to earnings (net of related tax expense of $1)	2	—	—	—	—	2	—	—	—
Cash dividends and distributions	—	—	—	—	(71)	—	—	—	(122)
Purchases for treasury	—	—	—	—	—	—	14,412	500	—
Issued under stock-based incentive plans	—	308	—	5	—	—	—	—	—
Net increase in equity related to unissued shares under stock-based incentive plans	—	—	—	15	—	—	—	—	—
Noncontrolling interest attributable to the consolidation of pipeline acquisition (Note 16)	—	—	—	—	—	—	—	—	20
SunCoke Energy, Inc. initial public offering (Note 16)	—	—	—	80	—	—	—	—	112
Issuance of Sunoco Logistics Partners L.P. deferred distribution units (Note 16)	—	—	—	7	—	—	—	—	(12)
Purchase of Indiana Harbor noncontrolling interest (Note 16)	—	—	—	(6)	—	—	—	—	(24)
Other	—	351	1	11	—	—	30	2	5
Total	$(1,518)								
At December 31, 2011		281,924	$282	$1,811	$3,947	$(258)	175,112	$4,889	$907

* Comprehensive income (loss) attributable to Sunoco shareholders amounted to $(1,693), $314 and $(181) million for the years ended December 31, 2011, 2010 and 2009, respectively.

(See Accompanying Notes)

SEC 5.10

NOTES TO CONSOLIDATED FINANCIAL STATEMENTS

16. Noncontrolling Interests (in part)

Cokemaking Operations

On July 12, 2011, Sunoco borrowed $300 million from an affiliate of one of SunCoke Energy's IPO underwriters. On July 26, 2011, an IPO of 13.34 million shares of SunCoke Energy common stock was completed at an offering price of $16 per share. Sunoco's $300 million borrowing was satisfied at the closing of the SunCoke IPO through an exchange of the 13.34 million shares of SunCoke Energy stock valued at $213 million and a cash payment of $87 million. Sunoco also incurred underwriters' commissions and other expenses totaling $21 million in connection with the offering. At December 31, 2011, Sunoco maintained a controlling financial interest in SunCoke Energy through its ownership of 81 percent of the outstanding shares of SunCoke Energy common stock. In connection with the SunCoke IPO, Sunoco recorded a $112 million increase in noncontrolling interests and an $80 million increase in capital in excess of par value. On January 17, 2012, the Company completed the separation of SunCoke Energy from Sunoco by distributing its remaining shares of SunCoke Energy common stock to Sunoco shareholders by means of a spin-off. The distribution was in the form of a pro rata stock dividend which entitled Sunoco shareholders of record on January 5, 2012 to receive 0.53 of a share of SunCoke Energy common stock for each share of Sunoco common stock held. The results of operations of the Coke business will be classified as discontinued operations in the consolidated statements of operations effective with the distribution date. This transaction will be accounted for as a reduction to equity at carrying value in accordance with current accounting guidance. SunCoke Energy generally assumed all liabilities associated with Sunoco's cokemaking and coal businesses prior to the date of the spin-off. SunCoke Energy is also responsible for all tax liabilities related to Sunoco's cokemaking and coal businesses prior to the spin-off. However, SunCoke Energy is not entitled to any refunds which may occur that are applicable to such periods.

In September 2011, SunCoke Energy purchased a portion of the noncontrolling interest in its Indiana Harbor cokemaking operations for $34 million. The transaction was accounted for as an equity transaction and resulted in a $24 million decrease in noncontrolling interests and a $6 million decrease in capital in excess of par value, net of income taxes. The noncontrolling interest in the Indiana Harbor cokemaking operations declined from 34 percent to 15 percent as a result of this transaction.

Common Stock Issued for an Acquisition

5.11

PHILLIPS-VAN HEUSEN CORPORATION (JAN)

CONSOLIDATED STATEMENTS OF CHANGES IN STOCKHOLDERS' EQUITY

(In thousands, except share and per share data)

	Preferred Stock	Common Stock Shares	Common Stock $1 Par Value	Additional Paid In Capital- Common Stock	Retained Earnings	Accumulated Other Comprehensive Income (Loss)	Treasury Stock	Stockholders' Equity
February 3, 2008		56,505,842	$56,506	$558,960	$558,538	$(17,384)	$(200,337)	$956,283
Net income					91,771			91,771
Change related to retirement and benefit plans costs, net of tax (benefit) of $(32,342)						(53,368)		(53,368)
Foreign currency translation adjustments, net of tax (benefit) of $(1,378)						(2,268)		(2,268)
Total comprehensive income								36,135
Adoption of the measurement date provisions of retirement benefits guidance, net of tax (benefit) of $(224)					(366)			(366)
Settlement of awards under stock plans		202,866	203	2,616				2,819
Tax benefits from awards under stock plans				1,184				1,184
Stock-based compensation expense				10,527				10,527
Cash dividends					(7,760)			(7,760)
Acquisition of 634 treasury shares							(27)	(27)

(continued)

	Preferred Stock	Common Stock Shares	$1 Par Value	Additional Paid In Capital-Common Stock	Retained Earnings	Accumulated Other Comprehensive Income (Loss)	Treasury Stock	Stockholders' Equity
February 1, 2009		56,708,708	$56,709	$ 573,287	$642,183	$(73,020)	$(200,364)	$ 998,795
Net income					161,910			161,910
Change related to retirement and benefit plans costs, net of tax (benefit) of $(5,281)						(8,690)		(8,690)
Foreign currency translation adjustments, net of tax expense of $767						1,262		1,262
Total comprehensive income								154,482
Settlement of awards under stock plans		430,522	430	7,648				8,078
Tax benefits from awards under stock plans				953				953
Stock-based compensation expense				14,456				14,456
Cash dividends					(7,811)			(7,811)
Acquisition of 14,327 treasury shares							(400)	(400)
January 31, 2010		57,139,230	57,139	596,344	796,282	(80,448)	(200,764)	1,168,553
Net income					53,805			53,805
Change related to retirement and benefit plans costs, net of tax (benefit) of $(481)						(772)		(772)
Foreign currency translation adjustments, net of tax (benefit) of $(915)						148,353		148,353
Liquidation of foreign operation, net of tax expense of $318						523		523
Unrealized losses on derivative financial instruments, net of tax (benefit) of $(256)						(11,899)		(11,899)
Total comprehensive income								190,010
Common stock offering, including the sale of 5,250,000 treasury shares		500,000	500	162,573			201,456	364,529
Issuance of restricted stock		350,861	351	(351)				—
Issuance of common stock in connection with the acquisition of Tommy Hilfiger		7,872,980	7,873	467,734				475,607
Issuance of 8,000 preferred shares	$188,595							188,595
Exercise of warrant, net of withholding of 140,207 treasury shares		320,000	320	8,640			(8,960)	—
Settlement of awards under stock plans		1,051,496	1,052	22,887				23,939
Tax benefits from awards under stock plans				10,539				10,539
Stock-based compensation expense				33,281				33,281
Cash dividends					(10,015)			(10,015)
Acquisition of 41,868 treasury shares							(2,481)	(2,481)
January 30, 2011	$188,595	67,234,567	$67,235	$1,301,647	$840,072	$ 55,757	$ (10,749)	$2,442,557

See notes to consolidated financial statements.

SEC 5.11

NOTES TO CONSOLIDATED FINANCIAL STATEMENTS

(Currency and share amounts in thousands, except per share data)

2. Acquisitions (in part)

Acquisition of Tommy Hilfiger (in part)

The Company acquired on May 6, 2010 all of the outstanding equity interests of Tommy Hilfiger. The results of Tommy Hilfiger's operations have been included in the Company's consolidated financial statements since that date. Tommy Hilfiger designs, sources and markets men's, women's and children's sportswear and activewear, jeanswear and other products worldwide and licenses its brands worldwide over a broad range of products.

The Company believes Tommy Hilfiger's established international platform in Europe will be a strategic complement to the Company's strong North American presence and provides the Company with the resources and expertise needed to grow its heritage brands and businesses internationally.

Fair Value of the Acquisition Consideration

The acquisition date fair value of the consideration paid, based on applicable exchange rates in effect on the closing date, totaled $2,961,383, which consisted of the following:

Cash	$2,485,776
Common stock (7,873 shares, par value $1.00 per share)	475,607
Total fair value of the acquisition consideration	$2,961,383

The fair value of the 7,873 common shares issued was equal to the aggregate value of the shares at the closing market price of the Company's common stock on May 5, 2010 (the day prior to the closing). The value is not the same as the value of the shares as determined pursuant to the acquisition agreement, due to the fluctuation in the market price of the Company's common stock between the date of the acquisition agreement and the date of the acquisition closing.

The Company funded the cash portion and related costs of the Tommy Hilfiger acquisition with cash on hand and the net proceeds of the following activities: (i) the sale on April 28, 2010 of 5,750 shares of the Company's common stock; (ii) the issuances of an aggregate of 8 shares of Series A convertible preferred stock, which are convertible into 4,189 shares of the Company's common stock, for an aggregate gross purchase price of $200,000; (iii) the issuance of $600,000 of 7 3/8% senior notes due 2020; and (iv) the borrowing of approximately $1,900,000 of term loans under new credit facilities.

Please see the notes entitled "Goodwill and Other Intangible Assets," "Debt" and "Stockholders' Equity" for a further discussion of these aspects of the acquisition.

The Company incurred certain pre-tax costs directly associated with the acquisition, totaling approximately $72,000, which are included within selling, general and administrative expenses in its financial statements. The Company also recorded a loss of $140,490 during the year ended January 30, 2011 associated with hedges against the Euro to United States dollar exchange rate relating to the purchase price. The Company incurred costs totaling $29,251 associated with the issuance of the common and preferred shares related to the acquisition, which were deducted from the recognized proceeds of issuance within stockholders' equity. The Company incurred costs totaling $71,533 associated with the issuance of debt related to the acquisition, which will be amortized over the term of the related debt agreement.

Tommy Hilfiger had total revenue of $1,945,230 and net income, after short-lived non-cash valuation amortization charges and transaction and integration costs, of $72,488 for the period from the date of acquisition through January 30, 2011. These amounts are included in the Company's results of operations for the year then ended.

Common Stock Issued Upon Conversion of Convertible Debt

5.12

AMKOR TECHNOLOGY, INC. (DEC)

CONSOLIDATED STATEMENTS OF STOCKHOLDERS' EQUITY AND COMPREHENSIVE INCOME

(In thousands)	Common Stock		Additional Paid-In Capital	Accumulated Deficit	Accumulated Other Comprehensive Income	Treasury Stock		Total Amkor Stockholders' Equity	Non-controlling Interest in Subsidiaries	Total Equity
	Shares	Par Value				Shares	Cost			
Balance at December 31, 2008	183,035	$183	$1,496,976	$(1,278,221)	$18,201	—	$ —	$237,139	$6,024	$243,163
Net income	—	—	—	155,980	—	—	—	155,980	303	156,283
Adjustments to unrealized components of defined benefit pension plan, net of tax	—	—	—	—	(12,632)	—	—	(12,632)	—	(12,632)
Cumulative translation adjustment	—	—	—	—	(548)	—	—	(548)	165	(383)

(continued)

(In thousands)	Common Stock Shares	Par Value	Additional Paid-In Capital	Accumulated Deficit	Accumulated Other Comprehensive Income	Treasury Stock Shares	Cost	Total Amkor Stockholders' Equity	Non-controlling Interest in Subsidiaries	Total Equity
Comprehensive income								$142,800	$ 468	$143,268
Issuance of stock through share-based compensation plans	136	—	693	—	—	—	—	693	—	693
Share-based compensation expense	—	—	2,577	—	—	—	—	2,577	—	2,577
Balance at December 31, 2009	183,171	$183	$1,500,246	$(1,122,241)	$ 5,021	—	$ —	$383,209	$6,492	$389,701
Net income	—	—	—	231,971	—	—	—	231,971	176	232,147
Adjustments to unrealized components of defined benefit pension plan, net of tax	—	—	—	—	2,270	—	—	2,270	—	2,270
Cumulative translation adjustment	—	—	—	—	8,166	—	—	8,166	—	8,166
Comprehensive income								242,407	176	242,583
Treasury stock acquired through surrender of shares for tax withholding	—	—	—	—	—	(47)	(284)	(284)	—	(284)
Issuance of stock through share-based compensation plans	296	—	1,166	—	—	—	—	1,166	—	1,166
Share-based compensation expense	—	—	3,515	—	—	—	—	3,515	—	3,515
Balance at December 31, 2010	183,467	$183	$1,504,927	$ (890,270)	$15,457	(47)	$ (284)	$630,013	$6,668	$636,681
Net income	—	—	—	91,808	—	—	—	91,808	1,287	93,095
Adjustments to unrealized components of defined benefit pension plan, net of tax	—	—	—	—	(5,800)	—	—	(5,800)	—	(5,800)
Cumulative translation adjustment	—	—	—	—	1,192	—	—	1,192	—	1,192
Comprehensive income								87,200	1,287	88,487
Conversion of debt to common stock	13,351	13	100,484	—	—	—	—	100,497	—	100,497
Repurchase of common stock	—	—	—	—	—	(28,573)	(129,500)	(129,500)	—	(129,500)
Treasury stock acquired through surrender of shares for tax withholding	—	—	—	—	—	(111)	(776)	(776)	—	(776)
Issuance of stock through share-based compensation plans	541	1	821	—	—	—	—	822	—	822
Share-based compensation expense	—	—	5,010	—	—	—	—	5,010	—	5,010
Balance at December 31, 2011	197,359	$197	$1,611,242	$ (798,462)	$10,849	(28,731)	$(130,560)	$693,266	$7,955	$701,221

The accompanying notes are an integral part of these statements.

NOTES TO CONSOLIDATED FINANCIAL STATEMENTS

12. Debt (in part)

Debt of Amkor Technology, Inc. (in part)

Senior Subordinated and Subordinated Notes (in part)

In November 2005, we issued $100.0 million of our 6.25% Convertible Subordinated Notes due December 2013 (the "December 2013 Notes") in a private placement to Mr. James J. Kim, our Executive Chairman of the Board of Directors, and certain Kim family members. The December 2013 Notes were convertible at any time prior to the maturity date into our common stock at a price of approximately $7.49 per share (the market price of our common stock on the date of issuance of the December 2013 Notes was $6.20 per share). The December 2013 Notes were subordinate to the prior payment in full of all of our senior and senior subordinated debt. The proceeds from the sale of the December 2013 Notes were used to purchase a portion of existing debt. In January 2011, holders of all $100.0 million of the outstanding December 2013 Notes converted their notes into an aggregate of 13,351,131 shares of our common stock. There was no gain or loss recorded as a result of the conversion. Forfeited accrued interest of $0.9 million and unamortized deferred debt costs of $0.4 million were included in the net carrying amount of the debt recorded to our capital accounts upon conversion in 2011.

Warrants

5.13

XILINX, INC. (MAR)

*CONSOLIDATED STATEMENTS OF STOCKHOLDERS'
EQUITY*

(In thousands, except per share amounts)	Common Stock Outstanding Shares	Amount	Additional Paid-In Capital	Retained Earnings	Accumulated Other Comprehensive Income (Loss)	Total Shareholders' Equity
Balance as of March 29, 2008	280,519	$2,805	$1,160,278	$800,310	$ 5,804	$1,969,197
Components of comprehensive income:						
Net income	—	—	—	361,719	—	361,719
Change in net unrealized loss on available-for-sale securities, net of tax benefit of $9,272	—	—	—	—	(14,888)	(14,888)
Change in net unrealized loss on hedging transactions, net of taxes	—	—	—	—	(2,039)	(2,039)
Cumulative translation adjustment	—	—	—	—	(7,735)	(7,735)
Total comprehensive income						337,057
Issuance of common shares under employee stock plans	5,811	58	96,338	—	—	96,396
Repurchase and retirement of common stock	(10,823)	(108)	(156,635)	(118,257)	—	(275,000)
Early extinguishment of convertible debentures	—	—	(72,593)	—	—	(72,593)
Stock-based compensation expense	—	—	54,509	—	—	54,509
Stock-based compensation capitalized in inventory	—	—	(396)	—	—	(396)
Adjustment to accounting for uncertain tax position adoption entry	—	—	—	(10,120)	—	(10,120)
Cash dividends declared ($0.56 per common share)	—	—	—	(154,534)	—	(154,534)
Tax benefit from exercise of stock options	—	—	4,244	—	—	4,244
Balance as of March 28, 2009	275,507	2,755	1,085,745	879,118	(18,858)	1,948,760
Components of comprehensive income:						
Net income	—	—	—	357,484	—	357,484
Change in net unrealized loss on available-for-sale securities, net of tax benefit of $9,115	—	—	—	—	14,756	14,756
Change in net unrealized loss on hedging transactions, net of taxes	—	—	—	—	(541)	(541)
Cumulative translation adjustment	—	—	—	—	3,422	3,422
Total comprehensive income						375,121
Issuance of common shares under employee stock plans	4,183	42	60,046	—	—	60,088
Repurchase and retirement of common stock	(6,203)	(62)	(95,526)	(54,409)	—	(149,997)
Stock-based compensation expense	—	—	56,481	—	—	56,481
Stock-based compensation capitalized in inventory	—	—	17	—	—	17
Cash dividends declared ($0.60 per common share)	—	—	—	(165,648)	—	(165,648)
Reduction of tax benefit from exercise of stock options	—	—	(4,352)	—	—	(4,352)
Balance as of April 3, 2010	273,487	2,735	1,102,411	1,016,545	(1,221)	2,120,470
Components of comprehensive income:						
Net income	—	—	—	641,875	—	641,875
Change in net unrealized loss on available-for-sale securities, net of tax benefit of $2,176	—	—	—	—	3,537	3,537
Change in net unrealized loss on hedging transactions, net of taxes	—	—	—	—	6,776	6,776
Cumulative translation adjustment	—	—	—	—	1,425	1,425
Total comprehensive income						653,613

(continued)

(In thousands, except per share amounts)	Common Stock Outstanding		Additional Paid-In Capital	Retained Earnings	Accumulated Other Comprehensive Income (Loss)	Total Shareholders' Equity
	Shares	Amount				
Issuance of common shares under employee stock plans	8,870	$ 89	$ 170,264	$ —	$ —	$ 170,353
Repurchase and retirement of common stock	(17,755)	(178)	(217,461)	(251,304)	—	(468,943)
Stock-based compensation expense	—	—	60,258	—	—	60,258
Stock-based compensation capitalized in inventory	—	—	394	—	—	394
Equity component of 2.625% Debentures, net	—	—	108,094	—	—	108,094
Purchase of call options	—	—	(112,319)	—	—	(112,319)
Issuance of warrants	—	—	46,908	—	—	46,908
Cash dividends declared ($0.64 per common share)	—	—	—	(169,072)	—	(169,072)
Tax benefit from exercise of stock options	—	—	4,861	—	—	4,861
Balance as of April 2, 2011	264,602	$2,646	$1,163,410	$1,238,044	$10,517	$2,414,617

See notes to consolidated financial statements.

NOTES TO CONSOLIDATED FINANCIAL STATEMENTS

Note 14. Convertible Debentures and Revolving Credit Facility (in part)

2.625% Senior Convertible Debentures (in part)

To hedge against potential dilution upon conversion of the 2.625% Debentures, the Company also purchased call options on its common stock from the hedge counterparties. The call options give the Company the right to purchase up to 19.8 million shares of its common stock at $30.29 per share. The Company paid an aggregate of $112.3 million to purchase these call options. The call options will terminate upon the earlier of the maturity of the 2.625% Debentures or the last day any of the 2.625% Debentures remain outstanding. To reduce the hedging cost, under separate transactions the Company sold warrants to the hedge counterparties, which give the hedge counterparties the right to purchase up to 19.8 million shares of the Company's common stock

at $42.91 per share. These warrants expire on a gradual basis over a specified period starting on September 13, 2017. The Company received an aggregate of $46.9 million from the sale of these warrants. In accordance to the authoritative guidance issued by the FASB on determining whether an instrument (or embedded feature) is indexed to an entity's own stock, the Company concluded that the call options and warrants were indexed to the Company's stock. Therefore, the call options and warrants were classified as equity instruments and will not be marked to market prospectively. The net amount of $65.4 million paid to the hedge counterparties, less the applicable tax benefit related to the call options of $41.7 million, was recorded as a reduction to additional paid-in capital. The settlement terms of the call options and warrants provide for net share settlement.

Tax Benefits of Stock-Based Compensation

5.14

SONOCO PRODUCTS COMPANY (DEC)

CONSOLIDATED STATEMENTS OF CHANGES IN TOTAL EQUITY

(Dollars and shares in thousands)	Total Equity	Common Shares		Capital in Excess of Stated Value	Accumulated Other Comprehensive Loss	Retained Earnings	Non-controlling Interests
		Outstanding	Amount				
January 1, 2009	$1,174,518	99,732	$7,175	$404,939	$(454,679)	$1,205,540	$11,543
Net income	155,145					151,482	3,663
Other comprehensive income/(loss):							
Translation gain	80,780				79,535		1,245
Defined benefit plan adjustment[1]	56,149				56,149		
Derivative financial instruments[1]	8,526				8,526		
Other comprehensive income	145,455				144,210		1,245
Dividends	(108,979)					(108,979)	
Dividends paid to noncontrolling interests	(2,202)						(2,202)
Issuance of stock awards	9,316	468		9,316			
Shares repurchased	(1,239)	(51)		(1,239)			
Stock-based compensation	8,616			8,616			

(continued)

SEC 5.14

(Dollars and shares in thousands)	Total Equity	Common Shares		Capital in Excess of Stated Value	Accumulated Other Comprehensive Loss	Retained Earnings	Non-controlling Interests
		Outstanding	Amount				
December 31, 2009	$1,380,630	100,149	$7,175	$421,632	$(310,469)	$1,248,043	$14,249
Net income	201,474					201,053	421
Other comprehensive income/(loss):							
Translation gain	8,119				6,887		1,232
Defined benefit plan adjustment[1]	13,621				13,621		
Derivative financial instruments[1]	(2,906)				(2,906)		
Other comprehensive income	18,834				17,602		1,232
Dividends	(112,941)					(112,941)	
Issuance of stock awards	28,550	1,099		28,550			
Shares repurchased	(24,658)	(738)		(24,658)			
Stock-based compensation	15,804			15,804			
December 31, 2010	$1,507,693	100,510	$7,175	$441,328	$(292,867)	$1,336,155	$15,902
Net income	218,044					217,517	527
Other comprehensive income/(loss):							
Translation gain	(39,051)				(38,962)		(89)
Defined benefit plan adjustment[1]	(127,798)				(127,798)		
Derivative financial instruments[1]	(672)				(672)		
Other comprehensive loss	(167,521)				(167,432)		(89)
Dividends	(116,237)					(116,237)	
Issuance of stock awards	26,487	1,100		26,487			
Shares repurchased	(49,442)	(1,399)		(49,442)			
Stock-based compensation	12,102			12,102			
Purchase of noncontrolling interest	(5,718)			(2,991)			(2,727)
December 31, 2011	$1,425,408	100,211	$7,175	$427,484	$(460,299)	$1,437,435	$13,613

[1] Net of tax.

The Notes beginning on page F-6 are an integral part of these financial statements.

NOTES TO THE CONSOLIDATED FINANCIAL STATEMENTS

(Dollars in thousands except per share data)

11. Share-Based Compensation Plans (in part)

The Company provides share-based compensation to certain of its employees and non-employee directors in the form of stock options, stock appreciation rights, restricted stock units and other share-based awards. Awards issued prior to 2009 were issued pursuant to the 1991 Key Employee Stock Plan (the "1991 Plan") or the 1996 Non-Employee Directors Stock Plan (the "1996 Plan"). Awards issued after 2008 were issued pursuant to the Sonoco Products Company 2008 Long-Term Incentive Plan (the "2008 Plan"), which became effective upon approval by the shareholders on April 16, 2008. The maximum number of shares of common stock that may be issued under the 2008 Plan was set at 8,500,000 shares, subject to certain adjustments, which includes all awards that were granted, forfeited or expired during 2008 under all previous plans. At December 31, 2011, a total of 3,154,693 shares remain available for future grant under the 2008 Plan. After the effective date of the 2008 Plan, no awards may be granted under any previous plan. The Company issues new shares for stock option and stock appre-

ciation right exercises and stock unit conversions. Although the Company from time to time has repurchased shares to replace its authorized shares issued under its stock compensation plans, there is no specific schedule or policy to do so. The Company's stock-based awards to non-employee directors have not been material.

Accounting For Share-Based Compensation

For stock appreciation rights granted to retiree-eligible employees, the service completion date is assumed to be the grant date; therefore, expense associated with share-based compensation to these employees is recognized at that time.

Total compensation cost for share-based payment arrangements was $12,102, $15,804 and $8,616, for 2011, 2010 and 2009, respectively. The related tax benefit recognized in net income was $4,421, $5,936 and $3,254, for the same years, respectively. Share-based compensation expense is included in "Selling, general and administrative expenses" in the Consolidated Statements of Income.

An "excess" tax benefit is created when the tax deduction for an exercised stock option, exercised stock appreciation right or converted stock unit exceeds the compensation cost that has been recognized in income. The excess tax benefit is not recognized on the income statement, but rather on the balance sheet as "Capital in excess of stated value." The additional net excess tax benefit realized was $4,018, $4,209 and $1,030 for 2011, 2010 and 2009, respectively.

Equity-Based Compensation Expenses

5.15

LAM RESEARCH CORPORATION (JUN)

CONSOLIDATED STATEMENTS OF STOCKHOLDERS' EQUITY

(In thousands)

	Common Stock Shares	Common Stock	Additional Paid-In Capital	Treasury Stock	Accumulated Other Comprehensive Income (Loss)	Retained Earnings	Total
Balance at June 29, 2008	125,187	125	1,332,159	(1,490,701)	10,620	1,926,394	1,778,597
Sale of common stock	1,806	2	12,012	—	—	—	12,014
Purchase of treasury stock	(1,367)	(1)	—	(30,945)	—	—	(30,946)
Income tax benefit on equity-based compensation plans	—	—	(14,294)	—	—	—	(14,294)
Reissuance of treasury stock	906	1	(6,157)	25,953	—	—	19,797
Equity-based compensation expense	—	—	53,511	—	—	—	53,511
Components of comprehensive loss:							
Net loss	—	—	—	—	—	(302,148)	(302,148)
Foreign currency translation adjustment	—	—	—	—	(58,587)	—	(58,587)
Unrealized loss on fair value of derivative financial instruments, net	—	—	—	—	(6,633)	—	(6,633)
Unrealized gain on financial instruments, net	—	—	—	—	1,192	—	1,192
Less: Reclassification adjustment for losses included in earnings	—	—	—	—	501	—	501
Change in retiree medical benefit	—	—	—	—	85	—	85
Total comprehensive loss	—	—	—	—	—	—	(365,590)
Balance at June 28, 2009	126,532	$127	$1,377,231	$(1,495,693)	$(52,822)	$1,624,246	$1,453,089
Sale of common stock	1,619	1	13,386	—	—	—	13,387
Purchase of treasury stock	(2,982)	(3)	—	(106,531)	—	—	(106,534)
Income tax benefit on equity-based compensation plans	—	—	10,635	—	—	—	10,635
Reissuance of treasury stock	777	1	1,224	20,807	—	(4,579)	17,453
Equity-based compensation expense	—	—	50,463	—	—	—	50,463
Components of comprehensive income:							
Net income	—	—	—	—	—	346,669	346,669
Foreign currency translation adjustment	—	—	—	—	(13,868)	—	(13,868)
Unrealized loss on fair value of derivative financial instruments, net	—	—	—	—	(414)	—	(414)
Unrealized gain on financial instruments, net	—	—	—	—	2,062	—	2,062
Less: Reclassification adjustment for gains included in earnings	—	—	—	—	(645)	—	(645)
Change in retiree medical benefit	—	—	—	—	(4,162)	—	(4,162)
Total comprehensive income	—	—	—	—	—	—	329,642
Balance at June 27, 2010	125,946	$126	$1,452,939	$(1,581,417)	$(69,849)	$1,966,336	$1,768,135

(continued)

	Common Stock Shares	Common Stock	Additional Paid-In Capital	Treasury Stock	Accumulated Other Comprehensive Income (Loss)	Retained Earnings	Total
Sale of common stock	1,744	$ 2	$ 12,404	$ —	$ —	$ —	$ 12,406
Purchase of treasury stock	(4,790)	(5)	(149,589)	(197,840)	—	—	(347,434)
Income tax benefit on equity-based compensation plans	—	—	28,775	—	—	—	28,775
Reissuance of treasury stock	679	1	3,549	17,666	—	2	21,218
Equity-based compensation expense	—	—	53,012	—	—	—	53,012
Issuance of convertible notes	—	—	110,655	—	—	—	110,655
Sale of warrants			133,830				133,830
Purhcase of convertible note hedge			(114,110)				(114,110)
Components of comprehensive income:							
Net income	—	—	—	—	—	723,748	723,748
Foreign currency translation adjustment	—	—	—	—	80,695	—	80,695
Unrealized gain on fair value of derivative financial instruments, net	—	—	—	—	6,994	—	6,994
Unrealized gain on financial instruments, net	—	—	—	—	621	—	621
Less: Reclassification adjustment for gains included in earnings	—	—	—	—	(7,514)	—	(7,514)
Change in retiree medical benefit	—	—	—	—	(1,186)	—	(1,186)
Total comprehensive income							803,358
Balance at June 26, 2011	123,579	$124	$1,531,465	$(1,761,591)	$ 9,761	$2,690,086	$2,469,845

See Notes to Consolidated Financial Statements.

NOTES TO CONSOLIDATED FINANCIAL STATEMENTS

June 26, 2011

Note 2: Summary of Significant Accounting Policies (in part)

Equity-based Compensation—Employee Stock Purchase Plan ("ESPP") and Employee Stock Plans: The Company recognizes the fair value of equity-based awards as employee compensation expense. The fair value of the Company's restricted stock units was calculated based upon the fair market value of Company stock at the date of grant. The fair value of the Company's stock options and ESPP awards was estimated using a Black-Scholes option valuation model. This model requires the input of highly subjective assumptions, including expected stock price volatility and the estimated life of each award. The fair value of equity-based awards is amortized over the vesting period of the award and the Company has elected to use the straight-line method of amortization.

The Company makes quarterly assessments of the adequacy of its tax credit pool related to equity-based compensation to determine if there are any deficiencies that require recognition in its consolidated statements of operations. The Company will only recognize a benefit from stock-based compensation in paid-in-capital if an incremental tax benefit is realized after all other tax attributes currently available to us

have been utilized. In addition, the Company has elected to account for the indirect benefits of stock-based compensation on the research tax credit through the income statement rather than through paid-in-capital. The Company has also elected to net deferred tax assets and the associated valuation allowance related to net operating loss and tax credit carryforwards for the accumulated stock award tax benefits. The Company tracks these stock award attributes separately and recognizes these attributes through paid-in-capital.

Note 11: Equity-Based Compensation Plans

The Company has adopted stock plans that provide for the grant to employees of equity-based awards, including stock options and restricted stock units ("RSUs"), of Lam Research Common Stock. In addition, these plans permit the grant of nonstatutory equity-based awards to consultants and outside directors. An option is a right to purchase the Company's stock at a set price. An RSU award is an agreement to issue shares of the Company's stock at the time of vesting. Pursuant to the plans, the equity-based award price is determined by the Board of Directors or its designee, the plan administrator, but in no event will the exercise price for any option be less than the fair market value of the Company's Common Stock on the date of grant. Equity-based awards granted under the plans vest over a period determined by the Board of Directors or the plan administrator, typically over a period of two years or less. The Company also has an ESPP that allows employees to purchase shares of its Common

Stock through payroll deduction at a discounted price. A summary of stock plan transactions is as follows:

| | Available for Grant | Options Outstanding | | Restricted Stock Units Outstanding | |
		Number of Shares	Weighted-Average Exercise Price	Number of Shares	Weighted-Average FMV at Grant
June 29, 2008	15,839,806	2,606,694	$21.60	1,696,224	$46.51
Granted	(2,592,679)	476,094	$20.21	2,116,585	$27.29
Exercised		(731,934)	$16.42		
Canceled	981,297	(760,538)	$24.97	(220,759)	$43.98
Expired	(3,516,323)				
Vested restricted stock				(1,071,987)	$47.26
June 28, 2009	10,712,101	1,590,316	$22.10	2,520,063	$30.32
Granted	(1,383,941)	—	$ —	1,383,941	$34.71
Exercised		(642,861)	$20.91		
Canceled	259,579	(62,030)	$41.36	(197,549)	$33.23
Vested restricted stock				(965,693)	$35.29
June 27, 2010	9,587,739	885,425	$21.61	2,740,762	$30.50
Granted	(922,210)	—	$ —	922,210	$50.11
Exercised		(572,182)	$21.68		
Canceled	157,495	(3,310)	$20.35	(154,185)	$32.20
Expired	(68,869)				
Vested restricted stock				(1,177,447)	$27.03
June 26, 2011	8,754,155	309,933	$21.50	2,331,340	$39.90

Outstanding and exercisable options presented by price range at June 26, 2011 are as follows:

| Range of Exercise Prices | Options Outstanding | | | Options Exercisable | |
	Number of Options Outstanding	Weighted-Average Remaining Life (Years)	Weighted-Average Exercise Price	Number of Options Exercisable	Weighted-Average Exercise Price
$16.14–$19.25	10,315	0.18	$16.52	10,315	$16.52
$20.21–$22.79	220,258	2.63	$20.23	220,258	$20.23
$23.61–$24.69	51,200	0.18	$24.00	51,200	$24.00
$25.98–$26.19	3,060	0.23	$26.02	3,060	$26.02
$27.79–$29.06	25,100	3.45	$29.05	25,100	$29.05
$16.14–$29.06	309,933	2.26	$21.50	309,933	$21.50

The 2007 Stock Incentive Plan provides for the grant of non-qualified equity-based awards to eligible employees, consultants and advisors, and non-employee directors of the Company and its subsidiaries. Additional shares are reserved for issuance pursuant to awards previously granted under the Company's 1997 Stock Incentive Plan and its 1999 Stock Option Plan. As of June 26, 2011 there were a total of 2,641,273 shares subject to options and restricted stock units issued and outstanding under the Company's Stock Plans. As of June 26, 2011, there were a total of 8,754,155 shares available for future issuance under the 2007 Stock Incentive Plan.

The ESPP allows employees to designate a portion of their base compensation to be deducted and used to purchase the Company's Common Stock at a purchase price per share of the lower of 85% of the fair market value of the Company's Common Stock on the first or last day of the applicable purchase period. Typically, each offering period lasts 12 months and comprises three interim purchase dates. Key provisions of the ESPP include (i) an annual increase in the number of shares available for issuance under the plan by a specific amount on a one-for-one basis with shares of Common Stock that the Company repurchases for such purpose and (ii) authorization of the Plan Administrator (the Compensation Committee of the Board) to set a limit on the number of shares a plan participant can purchase on any single plan exercise date. The automatic annual increase provides that the number of shares in the plan reserve available for issuance shall be increased on the first business day of each calendar year commencing with 2004, on a one-for-one basis with each share of Common Stock that the Company repurchases, and designates for this purpose, by a number of shares equal to the lesser of (i) 2,000,000, (ii) one and one-half percent (1.5%) of the number of shares of all classes of Common Stock of the Company outstanding on the first business day of such calendar year, or (iii) a lesser number determined by the Plan Administrator. During fiscal years 2011, 2010, and 2009, the number of shares of Lam Research Common Stock reserved for issuance under the 1999 ESPP increased by 1.9 million each year.

During fiscal year 2011, a total of 679,406 shares of the Company's Common Stock were sold to employees under the 1999 ESPP. At June 26, 2011, 9,672,531 shares were available for purchase under the 1999 ESPP.

The estimated fair value of the Company's stock-based awards, less expected forfeitures, is amortized over the awards' vesting period on a straight-line basis. The Company recognized or realized the following equity-based compensation expenses and benefits during the fiscal years noted:

	Year Ended		
(In millions)	June 26, 2011	June 27, 2010	June 28, 2009
Equity-based compensation expense	$53.0	$50.5	$53.0
Income tax benefit recognized in the Consolidated Statement of Operations related to equity-based compensation	$ 8.6	$ 8.3	$ 9.1
Tax benefit realized from the exercise and vesting of options and RSUs	$16.3	$11.1	$ 8.1

Stock Options and Restricted Stock Units

Stock Options

The Company did not grant any stock options during fiscal years 2011 or 2010. The fair value of the Company's stock options granted during fiscal year 2009 was estimated using a Black-Scholes option valuation model. This model requires the input of highly subjective assumptions, including

expected stock price volatility and the estimated life of each award. The Company assumed no expected dividends and the following assumptions were used to value these stock options:

Expected term	4.0 years
Expected volatility	46.9%
Risk-free interest rate	2.07%

The year-end intrinsic value relating to stock options for fiscal years 2011, 2010, and 2009 is presented below:

	Year Ended		
(Millions)	June 26, 2011	June 27, 2010	June 28, 2009
Intrinsic value—options outstanding	$ 6.73	$16.50	$6.70
Intrinsic value—options exercisable	$ 6.73	$ 6.96	$4.50
Intrinsic value—options exercised	$16.70	$ 9.98	$7.20

As of June 26, 2011, all stock options outstanding are fully vested and all related compensation expense has been recognized. Cash received from stock option exercises was $12.4 million, $13.4 million, and $12.0 million during fiscal years 2011, 2010, and 2009, respectively.

Restricted Stock Units

The fair value of the Company's restricted stock units was calculated based upon the fair market value of the Company's stock at the date of grant. As of June 26, 2011, there was $58.7 million of total unrecognized compensation cost related to unvested restricted stock units granted; that cost is expected to be recognized over a weighted average remaining vesting period of 1.3 years.

ESPP

ESPP rights were valued using the Black-Scholes model. During fiscal years 2011, 2010, and 2009 ESPP was valued assuming no expected dividends and the following weighted-average assumptions:

	Year Ended		
	June 26, 2011	June 27, 2010	June 28, 2009
Expected life (years)	0.68	0.78	0.68
Expected stock price volatility	42.25%	59.07%	74.00%
Risk-free interest rate	0.61%	0.61%	0.41%

As of June 26, 2011, there was $1.2 million of total unrecognized compensation cost related to the ESPP that is expected to be recognized over a remaining vesting period of 2 months.

Share Repurchase Program

5.16

HEWLETT-PACKARD COMPANY (OCT)

CONSOLIDATED STATEMENTS OF STOCKHOLDERS' EQUITY

(In millions, except number of shares in thousands)	Common Stock Number of Shares	Par Value	Additional Paid-In Capital	Retained Earnings	Accumulated Other Comprehensive (Loss) Income	Total HP Stock- holders' Equity	Non- controlling Interests	Total
Balance October 31, 2008	2,415,303	$24	$14,012	$24,971	$ (65)	$38,942	$237	$39,179
Net earnings				7,660		7,660	78	7,738
Net unrealized gain on available-for-sale securities					16	16		16
Net unrealized loss on cash flow hedges					(971)	(971)		(971)
Net unrealized components of defined benefit pension plans					(2,531)	(2,531)		(2,531)
Net cumulative translation adjustment					304	304		304
Comprehensive income						4,478	78	4,556
Issuance of common stock in connection with employee stock plans and other	69,157	1	1,783			1,784		1,784
Repurchases of common stock	(119,651)	(1)	(2,789)	(1,922)		(4,712)		(4,712)
Net excess tax benefits from employee stock plans			163			163		163
Cash dividends declared				(766)		(766)		(766)
Stock-based compensation expense			635			635		635
Cumulative effect of change in accounting principle				(7)		(7)		(7)
Changes in ownership of non-controlling interests							(68)	(68)
Balance October 31, 2009	2,364,809	$24	$13,804	$29,936	$(3,247)	$40,517	$247	$40,764
Net earnings				8,761		8,761	109	8,870
Net unrealized gain on available-for-sale securities					16	16		16
Net unrealized loss on cash flow hedges					(32)	(32)		(32)
Net unrealized components of defined benefit pension plans					(602)	(602)		(602)
Net cumulative translation adjustment					28	28	4	32
Comprehensive income						8,171	113	8,284
Issuance of common stock in connection with employee stock plans and other	80,335	1	2,606			2,607		2,607
Repurchases of common stock	(241,246)	(3)	(5,809)	(5,259)		(11,071)		(11,071)
Net excess tax benefits from employee stock plans			300			300		300
Cash dividends declared				(743)		(743)	(28)	(771)
Stock-based compensation expense			668			668		668
Balance October 31, 2010	2,203,898	$22	$11,569	$32,695	$(3,837)	$40,449	$332	$40,781
Net earnings				7,074		7,074	74	7,148
Net unrealized gain on available-for-sale securities					17	17		17
Net unrealized gain on cash flow hedges					160	160		160
Net unrealized components of defined benefit pension plans					116	116		116
Net cumulative translation adjustment					46	46	(17)	29
Comprehensive income						7,413	57	7,470
Issuance of common stock in connection with employee stock plans and other	45,461	1	751			752		752
Repurchases of common stock	(258,853)	(3)	(6,296)	(3,669)		(9,968)		(9,968)
Net excess tax benefits from employee stock plans			128			128		128
Cash dividends declared				(834)		(834)	(10)	(844)
Stock-based compensation expense			685			685		685
Balance October 31, 2011	1,990,506	$20	$ 6,837	$35,266	$(3,498)	$38,625	$379	$39,004

The accompanying notes are an integral part of these Consolidated Financial Statements.

NOTES TO CONSOLIDATED FINANCIAL STATEMENTS

Note 15: Stockholders' Equity (in part)

Share Repurchase Program

HP's share repurchase program authorizes both open market and private repurchase transactions. In fiscal 2011, HP executed share repurchases of 259 million shares. Repurchases of 262 million shares were settled for $10.1 billion, which included 4 million shares repurchased in transactions that were executed in fiscal 2010 but settled in fiscal 2011. HP had no shares repurchased in the fourth quarter of fiscal 2011 that will be settled in the next fiscal year. In fiscal 2010, HP executed share repurchases of 241 million shares. Repurchases of 240 million shares were settled for $11.0 billion, which included 3 million shares repurchased in transactions that were executed in fiscal 2009 but settled in fiscal 2010. In fiscal 2009, HP completed share repurchases of approximately 120 million shares. Repurchases of approximately 132 million shares were settled for $5.1 billion, which included approximately 14 million shares repurchased in transactions that were executed in fiscal 2008 but settled in fiscal 2009. The foregoing shares repurchased and settled in fiscal 2011, fiscal 2010 and fiscal 2009 were all open market repurchase transactions.

In fiscal 2011, HP's Board of Directors authorized an additional $10 billion for future share repurchases. In fiscal 2010, HP's Board of Directors authorized an additional $18.0 billion for future share repurchases. In fiscal 2009, there was no additional authorization for future share repurchases by HP's Board of Directors. As of October 31, 2011, HP had remaining authorization of approximately $10.8 billion for future share repurchases.

Dividends

5.17

MARRIOTT INTERNATIONAL, INC. (DEC)

CONSOLIDATED STATEMENTS OF SHAREHOLDERS' EQUITY

Fiscal Years 2011, 2010, and 2009

(In millions)

Common Shares Outstanding		Total	Equity Attributable to Marriott Shareholders					Equity Attributable to Noncontrolling Interests
			Class A Common Stock	Additional Paid-In Capital	Retained Earnings	Treasury Stock, at Cost	Accumulated Other Comprehensive Income (Loss)	
353.4	Balance at year-end 2008	$1,391	$5	$3,590	$3,565	$(5,765)	$(15)	$11
—	Net loss	(353)	—	—	(346)	—	—	(7)
—	Other comprehensive income	28	—	—	—	—	28	—
—	Dividends	(33)	—	—	(125)	92	—	—
4.8	Employee stock plan issuance	113	—	(5)	9	109	—	—
—	Other	(4)	—	—	—	—	—	(4)
—	Purchase of treasury stock	—	—	—	—	—	—	—
358.2	Balance at year-end 2009	1,142	5	3,585	3,103	(5,564)	13	—
	Impact of adoption of ASU 2009-16 and ASU							
—	2009-17[1]	(146)	—	—	(146)	—	—	—
358.2	Opening balance 2010	996	5	3,585	2,957	(5,564)	13	—
—	Net income	458	—	—	458	—	—	—
—	Other comprehensive loss	(15)	—	—	—	—	(15)	—
—	Dividends	(76)	—	—	(76)	—	—	—
10.2	Employee stock plan issuance	279	—	59	(53)	273	—	—
(1.5)	Purchase of treasury stock	(57)	—	—	—	(57)	—	—
366.9	Balance at year-end 2010	1,585	5	3,644	3,286	(5,348)	(2)	—
—	Net income	198	—	—	198	—	—	—
—	Other comprehensive loss	(24)	—	—	—	—	(24)	—
—	Dividends	(135)	—	—	(135)	—	—	—
9.5	Employee stock plan issuance	182	—	9	(137)	310	—	—
(43.4)	Purchase of Treasury stock	(1,425)	—	—	—	(1,425)	—	—
	Spin-off of Marriott Vacations Worldwide Corporation	(1,162)	—	(1,140)	—	—	(22)	—
333.0	Balance at year-end 2011	$ (781)	$5	$2,513	$3,212	$(6,463)	$(48)	$ —

[1] The abbreviation ASU means Accounting Standards Update.

See Notes to Consolidated Financial Statements.

NOTES TO CONSOLIDATED FINANCIAL STATEMENTS

1. Summary of Significant Accounting Policies (in part)

Basis of Presentation (in part)

On November 21, 2011 ("the spin-off date"), the Company completed a spin-off of its timeshare operations and timeshare development business through a special tax-free dividend to our shareholders of all of the issued and outstanding common stock of our wholly owned subsidiary Marriott Vacations Worldwide Corporation ("MVW"). On the spin-off date, Marriott shareholders of record as of the close of business on November 10, 2011 received one share of MVW common stock for every ten shares of Marriott common stock. As of the spin-off date, Marriott does not beneficially own any shares of MVW common stock and does not consolidate MVW's financial results for periods after the spin-off date as part of its financial reporting. However, because of Marriott's significant continuing involvement in MVW future operations (by virtue of license and other agreements between Marriott and MVW), our former Timeshare segment's historical financial results prior to the spin-off date will continue to be included in Marriott's historical financial results as a component of continuing operations. See Footnote No. 17, "Spin-off," for additional information on the spin-off.

17. Spin-Off

On November 21, 2011, we completed a spin-off of our timeshare operations and timeshare development business through a special tax-free dividend to our shareholders of all of the issued and outstanding common stock of our wholly owned subsidiary MVW. In connection with the spin-off, we entered into several agreements with MVW, and, in some cases, certain of its subsidiaries, that govern our post-spin-off relationship with MVW, including a Separation and Distribution Agreement, two License Agreements for the use of Marriott and Ritz-Carlton marks and intellectual property, an Employee Benefits and Other Employment Matters Allocation Agreement, a Tax Sharing and indemnification Agreement, a Marriott Rewards Affiliation Agreement, and a Non-Competition Agreement. Under license agreements with us, MVW is both the exclusive developer and operator of timeshare, fractional, and related products under the Marriott brand and the exclusive developer of fractional and related products under The Ritz-Carlton brand.

MVW filed a Form 10 registration statement with the SEC which, as amended, describes the spin-off and was declared effective on October 27, 2011. As a result of the spin-off, MVW is an independent company whose common shares are listed on the New York Stock Exchange under the symbol "VAC." On the spin-off date, Marriott shareholders of record as of the close of business on November 10, 2011 received one share of MVW common stock for every ten shares of Marriott common stock. Fractional shares of MVW common stock to which Marriott shareholders of record would have otherwise been entitled were aggregated and sold in the open market, and shareholders received cash payments in lieu of those fractional shares. The distribution of shares of MVW common stock did not result in the recognition, for U.S. federal income tax purposes, of income, gain or loss by us or our shareholders, except, in the case of our shareholders, for cash received in lieu of fractional shares.

As of the spin-off date, Marriott does not beneficially own any shares of MVW common stock and does not consolidate MVW's financial results for periods after the spin-off date as part of its financial reporting. However, because of Marriott's significant continuing involvement in MVW future operations (by virtue of the license and other agreements between Marriott and MVW), our former Timeshare segment's historical financial results for periods prior to the spin-off date continue to be included in Marriott's historical financial results as a component of continuing operations.

Under the license agreements we receive license fees consisting of a fixed annual fee of $50 million plus two percent of the gross sales price paid to MVW for initial developer sales of interests in vacation ownership units and residential real estate units and one percent of the gross sales price paid to MVW for resales of interests in vacation ownership units and residential real estate units, in each case that are identified with or use the Marriott or Ritz-Carlton marks.

The license fee also includes a periodic inflation adjustment.

Our shareholders' equity decreased by $1,162 million as a result of the spin-off of MVW. We show the components of the decrease, which was primarily noncash and principally comprised of the net book value of the net assets that we contributed to MVW in connection with the spin-off, in the following table:

($ in millions)	2011
Cash and equivalents	$ 52
Accounts and notes receivable	247
Inventory	982
Other current assets	293
Property and equipment and other	284
Loans to timeshare owners	987
Other current liabilities	(533)
Current portion of long-term debt	(122)
Long-term debt	(773)
Other long-term liabilities	(255)
Spin-off of MVW	$1,162

For 2011, we recognized $34 million of transaction-related expenses associated with the spin-off. While MVW did not complete its typical notes securitization in 2011 prior to the spin-off, we received net proceeds of approximately $122 million prior to the spin-off under a $300 million secured warehouse credit facility that MVW put in place during the third quarter of 2011 to provide short-term financing for receivables originated in connection with the sale of timeshare interests. Also, on October 26, 2011, MVW US Holdings, Inc., a wholly owned subsidiary of MVW, issued $40 million of its cumulative redeemable Series A preferred stock ("Preferred Stock") to Marriott as part of Marriott's internal reorganization completed in preparation for the spin-off. On October 28, 2011, Marriott sold all of the Preferred Stock to third-party investors, resulting in $38 million in net proceeds to Marriott, and when combined with the cash under the MVW warehouse facility, Marriott received a total of approximately $160 million in a cash distribution prior to the completion of the spin-off. This had no impact to Marriott's earnings.

Conversion of Common Shares

5.18

SPRINT NEXTEL CORPORATION (DEC)

CONSOLIDATED STATEMENTS OF SHAREHOLDERS' EQUITY

(In millions)

	Common Shares		Paid-In Capital	Treasury Shares		Accumulated Deficit	Accumulated Other Comprehensive Loss	Total
	Shares[1]	Amount		Shares	Amount			
Balance, December 31, 2008	2,951	$5,902	$47,332	94	$(1,939)	$(30,856)	$(524)	$19,915
Net loss						(2,436)		(2,436)
Other comprehensive income, net of tax							172	172
Issuance of common shares, net				(20)	491	(487)		4
Share-based compensation expense			78					78
Conversion of series 2 to series 1 common shares	(40)	(80)	(785)	(40)	865			
Equity consideration related to Virgin Mobile acquisition	96	193	186					379
Other, net			(18)		1			(17)
Balance, December 31, 2009	3,007	$6,015	$46,793	34	$ (582)	$(33,779)	$(352)	$18,095
Net loss						(3,465)		(3,465)
Other comprehensive loss, net of tax							(150)	(150)
Issuance of common shares, net	1	1	(1)	(14)	355	(347)		8
Share-based compensation expense			59					59
Other, net			(10)			9		(1)
Balance, December 31, 2010	3,008	$6,016	$46,841	20	$ (227)	$(37,582)	$(502)	$14,546
Net loss						(2,890)		(2,890)
Other comprehensive loss, net of tax							(290)	(290)
Issuance of common shares, net	7	14	—	(1)	21	(17)		18
Share-based compensation expense			43					43
Conversion of series 2 to series 1 common shares	(19)	(38)	(168)	(19)	206			—
Balance, December 31, 2011	2,996	$5,992	$46,716	—	$ —	$(40,489)	$(792)	$11,427

[1] See note 14 for information regarding common shares.

See Notes to the Consolidated Financial Statements.

NOTES TO THE CONSOLIDATED FINANCIAL STATEMENTS

Note 14. Shareholders' Equity and Per Share Data (in part)

Our articles of incorporation authorize 6,620,000,000 shares of capital stock as follows:

- 6,000,000,000 shares of Series 1 voting common stock, par value $2.00 per share;
- 500,000,000 shares of Series 2 voting common stock, par value $2.00 per share;
- 100,000,000 shares of non-voting common stock, par value $0.01 per share; and
- 20,000,000 shares of preferred stock, no par value per share.

Classes of Common Stock

Series 1 Common Stock

The holders of our Series 1 common stock are entitled to one vote per share on all matters submitted for action by the shareholders. There were about 3.0 billion shares of Series 1 common stock outstanding as of December 31, 2011.

Series 2 Common Stock

The holders of our Series 2 common stock are entitled to 10% of one vote per share, but otherwise have rights that are substantially identical to those of the Series 1 common stock. In 2009, certain holders of our Series 2 common stock exercised their rights to convert 39.8 million Series 2 shares to 39.8 million Series 1 shares, resulting in an $80 million and $785 million reduction to common shares and paid-in capital, respectively, and a corresponding $865 million reduction in treasury shares. In 2011, the remaining 35 million Series 2 shares were converted to 35 million Series 1 shares, resulting in a $38 million and $168 million reduction in common shares and paid-in capital, respectively, and a corresponding $206 million reduction in treasury shares. As a result, there were no shares of Series 2 common stock outstanding as of December 31, 2011.

Redemption of Convertible Preferred Stock

5.19

METLIFE, INC. (DEC)

CONSOLIDATED STATEMENTS OF EQUITY (in part)

For the Year Ended December 31, 2011

(In millions)

	Pre-ferred Stock	Convertible Preferred Stock	Common Stock	Additional Paid-In Capital	Retained Earnings	Treasury Stock at Cost	Net Unrealized Investment Gains (Losses)	Other-Than-Temporary Impair-ments	Foreign Currency Translation Adjustments	Defined Benefit Plans Adjust-ment	Total MetLife, Inc.'s Stock-holders' Equity	Non-controlling Interests[1]	Total Equity
							Accumulated Other Comprehensive Income (Loss)						
Balance at December 31, 2010	$1	$—	$ 10	$26,423	$21,363	$(172)	$3,356	$(366)	$(541)	$(1,449)	$48,625	$371	$48,996
Redemption of convertible preferred stock		—		(2,805)							(2,805)		(2,805)
Preferred stock redemption premium					(146)						(146)		(146)
Common stock issuance—newly issued shares			1	2,949							2,950		2,950
Stock-based compensation				215							215		215
Dividends on preferred stock					(122)						(122)		(122)
Dividends on common stock					(787)						(787)		(787)
Change in equity of noncontrolling interests												38	38
Comprehensive income (loss):													
Net income (loss)					6,981						6,981	3	6,984
Other comprehensive income (loss):													
Unrealized gains (losses) on derivative instruments, net of income tax							1,022				1,022		1,022
Unrealized investment gains (losses), net of related offsets and income tax							4,542	(75)			4,467	(5)	4,462
Foreign currency translation adjustments, net of income tax									(109)		(109)	(33)	(142)
Defined benefit plans adjustment, net of income tax										(494)	(494)		(494)
Other comprehensive income (loss)											4,886	(38)	4,848
Comprehensive income (loss)											11,867	(35)	11,832
Balance at December 31, 2011	$1	$—	$ 11	$26,782	$27,289	$(172)	$8,920	$(441)	$(650)	$(1,943)	$59,797	$374	$60,171

[1] Net income (loss) attributable to noncontrolling interests excludes gains (losses) of redeemable noncontrolling interests in partially owned consolidated subsidiaries of ($13) million.

See accompanying notes to the consolidated financial statements.

NOTES TO THE CONSOLIDATED FINANCIAL STATEMENTS

2. Acquisitions and Dispositions (in part)

2010 Acquisition of ALICO (in part)

Description of Transaction

On the Acquisition Date, MetLife, Inc. acquired all of the issued and outstanding capital stock of American Life from AM Holdings, a subsidiary of AIG, and DelAm from AIG for a total purchase price of $16.4 billion, which consisted of (i) cash of $7.2 billion (includes settlement of intercompany balances and certain other adjustments), and (ii) securities of MetLife, Inc. valued at $9.2 billion.

The $7.2 billion cash portion of the purchase price was funded through the issuance of common stock as described in Note 18, fixed and floating rate senior debt as described in Note 11 as well as cash on hand. The securities issued to AM Holdings included (a) 78,239,712 shares of MetLife, Inc.'s common stock; (b) 6,857,000 shares of Series B Contingent Convertible Junior Participating Non-Cumulative Perpetual Preferred Stock (the "convertible preferred stock") of MetLife, Inc.; and (c) 40 million common equity units of MetLife, Inc. (the "Equity Units") with an aggregate stated amount at issuance of $3.0 billion, initially consisting of (i) three purchase contracts (the "Series C Purchase Contracts," the "Series D Purchase Contracts" and the "Series E Purchase Contracts" and, together, the "Purchase Contracts"), obligating the holder to purchase, on specified future settlement dates, a variable number of shares of MetLife, Inc.'s common stock for a fixed price; and (ii) an interest in each of three series of debt securities (the "Series C Debt Securities," the "Series D Debt Securities" and the "Series E Debt Securities," and, together, the "Debt Securities") issued by MetLife, Inc. Distributions on the Equity Units will be made quarterly, through contract payments on the Purchase Contracts and interest payments on the Debt Securities, initially at an aggregate annual rate of 5.00% (an average annual rate of 3.02% on the Purchase Contracts and an average annual rate of 1.98% on the Debt Securities) as described in Note 14.

On March 8, 2011, AM Holdings sold, in public offering transactions, all the shares of common stock and Equity Units it received as consideration from MetLife in connection with the Acquisition. The Company did not receive any of the proceeds from the sale of either the shares of common stock or the Equity Units owned by AM Holdings. On March 8, 2011, MetLife, Inc. issued 68,570,000 shares of common stock for gross proceeds of $3.0 billion, which were used to repurchase and cancel 6,857,000 shares of convertible preferred stock received as consideration by AM Holdings from MetLife in connection with the Acquisition. See Note 18.

ALICO is an international life insurance company, providing consumers and businesses with products and services for life insurance, accident and health insurance, retirement and wealth management solutions. The Acquisition significantly broadened the Company's diversification by product, distribution and geography, meaningfully accelerated MetLife's global growth strategy, and provides the opportunity to build an international franchise leveraging the key strengths of ALICO.

Fair Value and Allocation of Purchase Price

The computation of total purchase consideration and the amounts recognized for each major class of assets acquired and liabilities assumed, based upon their respective fair values at the Acquisition Date, and the resulting goodwill, are presented below:

(In millions)	November 1, 2010
Cash	$ 6,800
MetLife, Inc.'s common stock (78,239,712 shares)[1]	3,200
MetLife, Inc.'s convertible preferred stock[1],[2]	2,805
MetLife, Inc.'s Equity Units ($3.0 billion aggregate stated amount)[3]	3,189
Total cash paid and securities issued to AM Holdings	$15,994
Contractual purchase price adjustments[4]	396
Total purchase price	$16,390
Effective settlement of pre-existing relationships[5]	(186)
Contingent consideration[6]	88
Total purchase consideration for ALICO	$16,292

[1] Fair value is based on the opening price of MetLife, Inc.'s common stock of $40.90 on the New York Stock Exchange ("NYSE") on November 1, 2010.

[2] On March 8, 2011, MetLife, Inc. repurchased and canceled all of the convertible preferred stock.

[3] The Equity Units include the Debt Securities and the Purchase Contracts that will settle in MetLife, Inc.'s common stock on specified future dates. See Note 14.

[4] Relates to the cash settlement of intercompany balances prior to the Acquisition for amounts in excess of certain agreed-upon thresholds and certain other adjustments.

[5] Effective settlement of debt securities issued by MetLife, Inc. that were owned by ALICO on the Acquisition Date and which reduced the total purchase consideration. Such debt securities were sold to a third party in the second quarter of 2011.

[6] Estimated fair value of potential payments related to the adequacy of reserves for guarantees on the fair value of a fund of assets backing certain United Kingdom ("U.K.") unit-linked contracts.

At the Acquisition Date, management expected the aggregate amount of MetLife, Inc.'s common stock to be issued to AM Holdings to be between 214.6 million to 231.5 million shares, consisting of 78.2 million shares issued at closing, 68.6 million shares to be issued upon conversion of the convertible preferred stock and between 67.8 million and 84.7 million shares of common stock, in total, issuable upon settlement of the Purchase Contracts forming part of the Equity Units. On March 8, 2011, MetLife, Inc. issued 68.6 million shares of common stock and used the gross proceeds to repurchase and cancel the convertible preferred stock. On the same date, AM Holdings sold, in a public offering, all the Equity Units it received as consideration from MetLife in connection with the Acquisition. See Notes 14 and 18.

COMMON STOCK

DISCLOSURE

5.20 Rule 5-02 of Regulation S-X requires stating on the face of the balance sheet the number of shares issued or outstanding, as appropriate, and the dollar amount. The number of shares authorized should be disclosed on the balance sheet or in the notes. As shown in Table 5-3, consistent with prior years, the majority of the survey entities show common stock at par value.

5.21

TABLE 5-3: COMMON STOCK

Table 5-3 summarizes the reporting bases of common stock.

	2011	2010	2009
Par Value Stock			
Par value...	453	424	467
Amount in excess of par.............................	5	12	11
Assigned per share amount..........................	3	13	—
No Par Value Stock			
Assigned per share amount.........................	3	5	5
No assigned per share amount.....................	32	43	47
Other...	5	5	N/C*
Issues Outstanding...................................	501	502	530

* N/C = Not compiled. Line item was not included in the table for the year shown.

PREFERRED STOCK

PRESENTATION

5.22 FASB ASC 505-10-50 requires that if preferred stock or other senior stock has a preference in involuntary liquidation, the entity should disclose the liquidation preference of the stock (the relationship between the preference in liquidation and the par or stated value of the shares). That disclosure should be made in the "Equity" section of the balance sheet in the aggregate, either parenthetically or in short.

5.23 FASB ASC 480 requires that an issuer classify certain financial instruments with characteristics of both liabilities and equity as liabilities. Some issuances of stock, such as mandatorily redeemable preferred stock, impose unconditional obligations requiring the issuer to transfer assets or issue its equity shares. FASB ASC 480 requires an issuer to classify such financial instruments as liabilities.

DISCLOSURE

5.24 FASB ASC 505-10-50 requires disclosure of both of the following either on the face of the balance sheet or in the notes thereto:
- The aggregate or per-share amounts at which preferred stock may be called or is subject to redemption through sinking-fund operations or otherwise
- The aggregate and per-share amounts of arrearages in cumulative preferred dividends

Rule 5-02 of SEC Regulation S-X also calls for disclosure of the number of shares authorized and the number of shares issued or outstanding, as appropriate.

5.25

TABLE 5-4: PREFERRED STOCK

Table 5-4 summarizes the reporting bases of preferred stock.

	Number of Entities		
	2011	2010	2009
Par value preferred stock shown at:			
Par value...	17	14	12
Liquidation or redemption value....................	5	5	7
No assigned per share amount.....................	—	—	3
Assigned per share amount.........................	3	1	—
Other...	—	2	—
No par value preferred stock shown at:			
No assigned per share amount.....................	4	5	7
Liquidation or redemption value....................	4	3	6
Assigned per share amount.........................	2	4	3
Number of Entities			
Preferred stock outstanding.............................	35	28	36
No preferred stock outstanding........................	465	472	464
Total Entities..	500	500	500

PRESENTATION AND DISCLOSURE EXCERPTS

Preferred Stock

5.26

RITE AID CORPORATION (FEB)

CONSOLIDATED STATEMENTS OF STOCKHOLDERS' (DEFICIT)/EQUITY

For the Years Ended February 26, 2011, February 27, 2010 and February 28, 2009

(In thousands)

	Preferred Stock-Series G		Preferred Stock-Series H		Preferred Stock-Series I		Common Stock		Additional Paid-In Capital	Accumulated Deficit	Accumulated Other Comprehensive Income (Loss)	Total
	Shares	Amount	Shares	Amount	Shares	Amount	Shares	Amount				
Balance March 1, 2008	1,393	$139,253	1,352	$135,202	4,820	$116,415	830,209	$830,209	$4,047,499	$(3,537,276)	$(20,117)	$1,711,185
Net loss										(2,915,420)		(2,915,420)
Other comprehensive income:												
Changes in Defined Benefit Plans											(21,662)	(21,662)
Comprehensive loss												(2,937,082)
Exchange of restricted shares for taxes								(1,741)	(1,741)	(1,113)			(2,854)
Issuance of restricted stock								2,646	2,646	(2,646)			—
Cancellation of restricted stock								(967)	(967)	967			—
Amortization of restricted stock balance										17,913			17,913
Stock-based compensation expense										13,535			13,535
Stock options exercised								516	516	601			1,117
Dividends on preferred stock	100	10,006	83	8,296					(18,302)			
Conversion of Series G and I preferred stock	(1,493)	(149,258)			(4,820)	(116,415)	55,450	55,450	210,223			—
Cash dividends paid on preferred shares										(3,466)			(3,466)
Balance February 28, 2009	—	$ 1	1,435	$143,498	—	$ —	886,113	$886,113	$4,265,211	$(6,452,696)	$(41,779)	$(1,199,652)
Net loss										(506,676)		(506,676)
Other comprehensive income:												
Changes in Defined Benefit Plans											10,459	10,459
Comprehensive loss												(496,217)
Exchange of restricted shares for taxes								(1,198)	(1,198)	(343)			(1,541)
Issuance of restricted stock								3,289	3,289	(3,289)			—
Cancellation of restricted stock								(642)	(642)	642			—
Amortization of restricted stock balance										11,772			11,772
Stock-based compensation expense										12,022			12,022
Stock options exercised								74	74	(8)			66
Dividends on preferred stock			88	8,806					(8,807)			(1)
Balance February 27, 2010	—	$ 1	1,523	$152,304	—	$ —	887,636	$887,636	$4,277,200	$(6,959,372)	$(31,320)	$(1,673,551)
Net loss										(555,424)		(555,424)
Other comprehensive income:												
Changes in Defined Benefit Plans											1,178	1,178
Comprehensive loss												(554,246)
Exchange of restricted shares for taxes								(1,103)	(1,103)	(29)			(1,132)
Issuance of restricted stock								3,905	3,905	(3,905)			—
Cancellation of restricted stock								(385)	(385)	385			—
Amortization of restricted stock balance										6,053			6,053
Stock-based compensation expense										11,283			11,283
Stock options exercised								244	244	(18)			226
Dividends on preferred stock			93	9,346					(9,346)			—
Balance February 26, 2011	—	$ 1	1,616	$161,650	—	$ —	890,297	$890,297	$4,281,623	$(7,514,796)	$(30,142)	$(2,211,367)

The accompanying notes are an integral part of these consolidated financial statements.

NOTES TO CONSOLIDATED FINANCIAL STATEMENTS

For the Years Ended February 26, 2011, February 27, 2010 and February 28, 2009

(In thousands, except per share amounts)

13. Capital Stock

As of February 26, 2011, the authorized capital stock of the Company consists of 1,500,000 shares of common stock and 20,000 shares of preferred stock, each having a par value of $1.00 per share. Preferred stock is issued in series, subject to terms established by the Board of Directors.

In fiscal 2006, the Company issued 4,820 shares of Series I Mandatory Convertible Preferred Stock ("Series I preferred stock") at an offering price of $25 per share. Dividends on the Series I preferred stock were $1.38 per share per year, and were due and payable on a quarterly basis in either cash or common stock or a combination of both at the Company's election. In the first quarter of fiscal 2009 the Company entered into agreements with several of the holders of the Series I preferred stock to convert 2,404 shares into Rite Aid common stock earlier than the mandatory conversion date, November 17, 2008, at a rate of 5.6561 which resulted in the issuance of 14,648 shares of Rite Aid common stock. On the mandatory conversion date, the remaining outstanding 2,416 shares of Series I preferred stock automatically converted at a rate of 5.6561 which resulted in the issuance of 13,665 shares of Rite Aid common stock.

The Company also has outstanding Series G and Series H preferred stock. The Series G preferred stock has a liquidation preference of $100 per share and pays quarterly dividends at 7% of liquidation preference. In the fourth quarter of 2009, at the election of the holder, substantially all of the Series G preferred stock was converted into 27,137 common shares, at a conversion rate of $5.50 per share. The remaining Series G preferred stock can be redeemed at the Company's election after January 2009. The Company has not elected to redeem the remaining Series G preferred stock as of February 26, 2011.

The Series H preferred stock pays dividends of 6% of liquidation preference and can be redeemed at the Company's election after January 2010. All dividends can be paid in either cash or in additional shares of preferred stock, at the election of the Company. Any redemptions are at 105% of the liquidation preference of $100 per share, plus accrued and unpaid dividends. The Series H shares are convertible into common stock of the Company, at the holder's option, at a conversion rate of $5.50 per share. The Company has not elected to redeem the Series H preferred stock as of February 26, 2011.

DIVIDENDS

PRESENTATION

5.27 For public entities with respect to any dividends, Rule 3-04 of Regulation S-X requires the amount per share and in the aggregate for each class of shares to be stated. This may be stated on the financial statements or within the note disclosures. Further, Rule 4-08 of Regulation S-X requires disclosure of any restrictions that limit the payment of dividends.

5.28 An entity may distribute certain stock purchase rights that enable the holders of such rights to purchase additional equity in an entity if an outside party acquires or tenders for a substantial minority interest in the subject entity. These are commonly referred to as "poison pill arrangements."

5.29

TABLE 5-5: DIVIDENDS

Table 5-5 shows the nature of distributions made by the survey entities to their shareholders.

	Number of Entities		
	2011	2010	2009
Cash Dividends Paid to Common Stock Shareholders			
Per share amount disclosed in financial statements	235	178	176
Per share amount disclosed in footnote disclosures	108	158	152
Total	**343**	**336**	**328**
Cash Dividends Paid to Preferred Stock Shareholders			
Per share amount disclosed in financial statements	15	6	7
Per share amount disclosed in footnote disclosures	18	22	15
Total	**33**	**28**	**22**
Stock Dividends	2	5	—
Dividends in Kind	1	2	3
Stock Purchase Rights Plan Adopted/Extended	6	11	12

PRESENTATION AND DISCLOSURE EXCERPTS

Cash Dividends

5.30

H.J. HEINZ COMPANY (APR)

CONSOLIDATED STATEMENTS OF EQUITY

(Amounts in thousands, expect per share amounts)	April 27, 2011 Shares	Dollars	April 28, 2010 Shares	Dollars	April 29, 2009 Shares	Dollars
Preferred stock						
Balance at beginning of year	7	$ 70	7	$ 70	7	$ 72
Conversion of preferred into common stock	—	(1)	—	—	—	(2)
Balance at end of year	7	69	7	70	7	70
Authorized shares—April 27, 2011	7					
Common stock						
Balance at beginning of year	431,096	107,774	431,096	107,774	431,096	107,774
Balance at end of year	431,096	107,774	431,096	107,774	431,096	107,774
Authorized shares—April 27, 2011	600,000					
Additional capital						
Balance at beginning of year		657,596		737,917		617,811
Conversion of preferred into common stock		(39)		(29)		(95)
Stock options exercised, net of shares tendered for payment		(26,482)[4]		(21,717)[4]		98,736[4]
Stock option expense		9,447		7,897		9,405
Restricted stock unit activity		(8,119)		(9,698)		(538)
Tax settlement[1]		—		—		8,537
Purchase of subsidiary shares from noncontrolling interests[2]		(2,411)		(54,209)		—
Other, net[3]		(625)		(2,565)		4,061
Balance at end of year		629,367		657,596		737,917
Retained earnings						
Balance at beginning of year		6,856,033		6,525,719		6,129,008
Net income attributable to H.J. Heinz Company		989,510		864,892		923,072
Cash dividends:						
Preferred (per share $1.70 per share in 2011, 2010 and 2009)		(12)		(9)		(12)
Common (per share $1.80, $1.68, and $1.66 in 2011, 2010 and 2009, respectively)		(579,606)		(533,543)		(525,281)
Other[5]		(1,247)		(1,026)		(1,068)
Balance at end of year		7,264,678		6,856,033		6,525,719
Treasury stock						
Balance at beginning of year	(113,404)	(4,750,547)	(116,237)	(4,881,842)	(119,628)	(4,905,755)
Shares reacquired	(1,425)	(70,003)	—	—	(3,650)	(181,431)
Conversion of preferred into common stock	1	40	1	29	3	97
Stock options exercised, net of shares tendered for payment	4,495	203,196	2,038	94,315	6,179	178,559
Restricted stock unit activity	296	13,756	470	21,864	485	15,026
Other, net[3]	218	10,196	324	15,087	374	11,662
Balance at end of year	(109,819)	$(4,593,362)	(113,404)	$(4,750,547)	(116,237)	$(4,881,842)

[1] See Note No. 6 for further details.
[2] See Note No. 4 for further details.
[3] Includes activity of the Global Stock Purchase Plan.
[4] Includes income tax benefit resulting from exercised stock options.
[5] Includes adoption of the measurement date provisions of accounting guidance for defined benefit pension and other postretirement plans and unpaid dividend equivalents on restricted stock units.
[6] Comprised of unrealized translation adjustment of $337,075, pension and post-retirement benefits net prior service cost of $(7,232) and net losses of $(619,708), and deferred net gains on derivative financial instruments of $(9,699).

See Notes to Consolidated Financial Statements.

CONSOLIDATED STATEMENTS OF EQUITY

(Amounts in thousands, expect per share amounts)	April 27, 2011		April 28, 2010		April 29, 2009	
	Shares	Dollars	Shares	Dollars	Shares	Dollars
Other comprehensive (loss)/income						
Balance at beginning of year		$ (979,581)		$(1,269,700)		$ (61,090)
Net pension and post-retirement benefit gains/(losses)		77,355		78,871		(301,347)
Reclassification of net pension and post-retirement benefit losses to net income		53,353		38,903		24,744
Unrealized translation adjustments		563,060		193,600		(944,439)
Net change in fair value of cash flow hedges		9,790		(32,488)		33,204
Net hedging (gains)/losses reclassified into earnings		(21,365)		13,431		(20,772)
Purchase of subsidiary shares from noncontrolling interests[2]		(2,176)		(2,198)		—
Balance at end of year		(299,564)[6]		(979,581)		(1,269,700)
Total H.J. Heinz company shareholders' equity		3,108,962		1,891,345		1,219,938
Noncontrolling interest						
Balance at beginning of year		57,151		59,167		65,727
Net income attributable to the noncontrolling interest		16,438		17,451		14,889
Other comprehensive income, net of tax:						
Net pension and post-retirement benefit losses		(57)		(1,266)		(464)
Unrealized translation adjustments		4,816		8,411		(8,110)
Net change in fair value of cash flow hedges		(395)		(788)		131
Net hedging losses/(gains) reclassified into earnings		571		254		(56)
Purchase of subsidiary shares from noncontrolling interests[2]		(1,750)		(5,467)		—
Dividends paid to noncontrolling interest		(3,270)		(20,611)		(12,950)
Balance at end of year		73,504		57,151		59,167
Total equity		$3,182,466		$ 1,948,496		$1,279,105
Comprehensive income						
Net income		$1,005,948		$ 882,343		$937,961
Other comprehensive income, net of tax:						
Net pension and post-retirement benefit gains/(losses)		77,298		77,605		(301,811)
Reclassification of net pension and post-retirement benefit losses to net income		53,353		38,903		24,744
Unrealized translation adjustments		567,876		202,011		(952,549)
Net change in fair value of cash flow hedges		9,395		(33,276)		33,335
Net hedging (gains)/losses reclassified into earnings		(20,794)		13,685		(20,828)
Total comprehensive income/(loss)		1,693,076		1,181,271		(279,148)
Comprehensive income attributable to the noncontrolling interest		(21,373)		(24,062)		(6,390)
Comprehensive income/(loss) attributable to H.J. Heinz company		$1,671,703		$ 1,157,209		$ (285,538)

[1] See Note No. 6 for further details.
[2] See Note No. 4 for further details.
[3] Includes activity of the Global Stock Purchase Plan.
[4] Includes income tax benefit resulting from exercised stock options.
[5] Includes adoption of the measurement date provisions of accounting guidance for defined benefit pension and other postretirement plans and unpaid dividend equivalents on restricted stock units.
[6] Comprised of unrealized translation adjustment of $337,075, pension and post-retirement benefits net prior service cost of $(7,232) and net losses of $(619,708), and deferred net gains on derivative financial instruments of $(9,699).

See Notes to Consolidated Financial Statements.

SEC 5.30

SELECTED FINANCIAL DATA

The following table presents selected consolidated financial data for the Company and its subsidiaries for each of the five fiscal years 2007 through 2011. All amounts are in thousands except per share data.

	Fiscal Year Ended				
	April 27, 2011 (52 Weeks)	April 28, 2010 (52 Weeks)	April 29, 2009 (52 Weeks)	April 30, 2008 (52 Weeks)	May 2, 2007 (52 Weeks)
Sales[1]	$10,706,588	$10,494,983	$10,011,331	$9,885,556	$8,800,071
Interest expense[1]	275,398	295,711	339,635	364,808	333,037
Income from continuing operations[1]	1,005,948	931,940	944,400	858,176	794,398
Income from continuing operations per share attributable to H.J. Heinz Company common shareholders—diluted[1]	3.06	2.87	2.91	2.62	2.34
Income from continuing operations per share attributable to H.J. Heinz Company common shareholders—basic[1]	3.09	2.89	2.95	2.65	2.37
Short-term debt and current portion of long-term debt	1,534,932	59,020	65,638	452,708	468,243
Long-term debt, exclusive of current portion[2]	3,078,128	4,559,152	5,076,186	4,730,946	4,413,641
Total assets	12,230,645	10,075,711	9,664,184	10,565,043	10,033,026
Cash dividends per common share	1.80	1.68	1.66	1.52	1.40

[1] Amounts exclude the operating results related to the Company's private label frozen desserts business in the U.K. as well as the Kabobs and Appetizers And, Inc. businesses in the U.S., which were divested in Fiscal 2010 and have been presented as discontinued operations.

[2] Long-term debt, exclusive of current portion, includes $150.5 million, $207.1 million, $251.5 million, $198.3 million, and $71.0 million of hedge accounting adjustments associated with interest rate swaps at April 27, 2011, April 28, 2010, April 29, 2009, April 30, 2008, and May 2, 2007, respectively. H.J. Heinz Finance Company's ("HFC") mandatorily redeemable preferred shares of $350 million in Fiscals 2011-2009 and $325 million in Fiscals 2008 and 2007 are classified as long-term debt.

MANAGEMENT'S DISCUSSION AND ANALYSIS OF FINANCIAL CONDITION AND RESULTS OF OPERATIONS

Fiscal Year 2010 Operating Results By Business Segment (in part)

Liquidity and Financial Position (in part)

- Dividend payments totaled $580 million this year, compared to $534 million for the same period last year, reflecting a 7.1% increase in the annualized dividend per common share to $1.80.

On May 26, 2011, the Company announced that its Board of Directors approved a 6.7% increase in the quarterly dividend on common stock from 45 cents to 48 cents, an annual indicative rate of $1.92 per share for Fiscal 2012, effective with the July 2011 dividend payment. Fiscal 2012 dividend payments are expected to be approximately $620 million.

Non-Cash Dividends

5.31

EASTMAN CHEMICAL COMPANY (DEC)

*NOTES TO THE AUDITED CONSOLIDATED
FINANCIAL STATEMENTS*

17. Stockholders' Equity (in part)

A reconciliation of the changes in stockholders' equity for 2009, 2010, and 2011 is provided below:

(Dollars in millions)	Common Stock at Par Value[1] $	Paid-in Capital $	Retained Earnings[1] $	Accumulated Other Comprehensive Income (Loss) $	Treasury Stock at Cost $	Total Stockholders' Equity $
Balance at December 31, 2008	2	638	2,562	(335)	(1,314)	1,553
Net Earnings	—	—	136	—	—	136
Cash Dividends Declared[2]	—	—	(128)	—	—	(128)
Other Comprehensive Loss	—	—	—	(50)	—	(50)
Share-based Compensation Costs[3]	—	19	—	—	—	19
Stock Option Exercises	—	7	—	—	—	7
Other[4]	—	(3)	—	—	—	(3)
Stock Repurchases	—	—	—	—	(21)	(21)
Balance at December 31, 2009	2	661	2,570	(385)	(1,335)	1,513
Net Earnings	—	—	438	—	—	438
Cash Dividends Declared[2]	—	—	(129)	—	—	(129)
Other Comprehensive Loss	—	—	—	(47)	—	(47)
Share-based Compensation Costs[3]	—	24	—	—	—	24
Stock Option Exercises	—	102	—	—	—	102
Other[4]	—	6	—	—	—	6
Stock Repurchases	—	—	—	—	(280)	(280)
Balance at December 31, 2010	2	793	2,879	(432)	(1,615)	1,627
Net Earnings	—	—	696	—	—	696
Cash Dividends Declared[2]	—	—	(139)	—	—	(139)
Other Comprehensive Loss	—	—	—	(106)	—	(106)
Share-based Compensation Costs[3]	—	39	—	—	—	39
Stock Option Exercises	—	59	—	—	—	59
Other[4]	—	9	—	—	1	10
Stock Repurchases	—	—	—	—	(316)	(316)
Balance at December 31, 2011	2	900	3,436	(538)	(1,930)	1,870

[1] Common Stock at Par Value and Retained Earnings have been adjusted for the two-for-one stock split on October 3, 2011.
[2] Includes cash dividends paid and dividends declared, but unpaid.
[3] Includes the fair value of equity share-based awards recognized for share-based compensation.
[4] Includes tax benefits/charges relating to the difference between the amounts deductible for federal income taxes over the amounts charged to income for book value purposes have been adjusted to paid-in capital and other items.

On August 5, 2011, the Company's Board of Directors declared a two-for-one split of the Company's common stock. The stock split was in the form of a 100 percent stock dividend and was distributed on October 3, 2011 to stockholders of record as of September 15, 2011. Stockholders were issued one additional share for each share owned. Treasury shares were treated as shares outstanding in the stock split. All shares and per share amounts in this Annual Report on Form 10-K have been adjusted for all periods presented for the stock split.

STOCK SPLITS

RECOGNITION AND MEASUREMENT

5.32 The FASB ASC glossary defines a *stock split* as an issuance by a corporation of its own common shares to its common shareholders without consideration and under conditions indicating that such action is prompted mainly by a desire to increase the number of outstanding shares for the purpose of effecting a reduction in their unit market price and, thereby, of obtaining wider distribution and improved marketability of the shares. It is also sometimes called a stock split-up.

5.33 FASB ASC 505-20 addresses the accounting for stock splits, as well as stock dividends, and provides guidance on determining whether a stock dividend or stock split should be accounted for according to its form or whether it should be accounted for differently.

PRESENTATION AND DISCLOSURE EXCERPTS

Stock Split

5.34

HORMEL FOODS CORPORATION (OCT)

CONSOLIDATED STATEMENTS OF CHANGES IN SHAREHOLDERS' INVESTMENT

	Hormel Foods Corporation Shareholders								
(In thousands, except per share amounts)	Common Stock		Treasury Stock		Additional Paid-In Capital	Retained Earnings	Accumulated Other Comprehensive Income (Loss)	Non-controlling Interest	Total Share holders' Investment
	Shares*	Amount	Shares*	Amount					
Balance at October 26, 2008	269,041	$7,883	0	$ 0	$ 0	$2,112,873	$(114,016)	$6,535	$2,013,275
Comprehensive income									
Net earnings						342,813		3,165	345,978
Foreign currency translation							(862)	12	(850)
Deferred hedging, net of reclassification adjustment							27,763		27,763
Pension and other benefits							(117,954)		(117,954)
Comprehensive income								3,177	254,937
ASC 715 measurement date adjustment (net of $912 tax effect)						(11,793)	1,459		(10,334)
Purchases of common stock			(2,305)	(38,147)					(38,147)
Stock-based compensation expense					12,054				12,054
Exercise of stock options/nonvested shares	452	13	(1)	(15)	2,553				2,551
Shares retired	(2,306)	(68)	2,306	38,162	(14,607)	(23,487)			0
Distribution to noncontrolling interest								(7,999)	(7,999)
Declared cash dividends—$.38 per share*						(102,016)			(102,016)
Balance at October 25, 2009	267,187	$7,828	0	$0	$0	$2,318,390	$(203,610)	$1,713	$2,124,321
Comprehensive income									
Net earnings						395,587		4,189	399,776
Foreign currency translation							5,468	80	5,548
Deferred hedging, net of reclassification adjustment							33,372		33,372
Pension and other benefits							(11,140)		(11,140)
Comprehensive income								4,269	427,556
Purchases of common stock			(3,407)	(69,574)					(69,574)
Stock-based compensation expense					14,402				14,402
Exercise of stock options/nonvested shares	2,198	65	(15)	(308)	22,007				21,764
Shares retired	(3,422)	(100)	3,422	69,882	(36,409)	(33,373)			0
Declared cash dividends—$.42 per share*						(111,830)			(111,830)
Balance at October 31, 2010	265,963	$7,793	0	$ 0	$ 0	$2,568,774	$(175,910)	$5,982	$2,406,639

(continued)

Hormel Foods Corporation Shareholders

(In thousands, except per share amounts)	Common Stock Shares*	Common Stock Amount	Treasury Stock Shares*	Treasury Stock Amount	Additional Paid-In Capital	Retained Earnings	Accumulated Other Comprehensive Income (Loss)	Non-controlling Interest	Total Shareholders' Investment
Comprehensive income									
Net earnings						$474,195		$5,001	$479,196
Foreign currency translation							843	251	1,094
Deferred hedging, net of reclassification adjustment							(3,476)		(3,476)
Pension and other benefits							3,060		3,060
Comprehensive income								5,252	479,874
Purchases of common stock			(5,497)	(152,930)					(152,930)
Stock-based compensation expense					17,229				17,229
Exercise of stock options/nonvested shares	3,503	102	(6)	(163)	53,100				53,039
Shares retired	(5,503)	(161)	5,503	153,093	(70,329)	(82,603)			0
Distribution to noncontrolling interest								(8,000)	(8,000)
Declared cash dividends—$.51 per share						(136,035)			(136,035)
Balance at October 30, 2011	263,963	$7,734	0	$0	$0	$2,824,331	$(175,483)	$3,234	$2,659,816

* Shares and per share figures have been restated, as appropriate, to reflect the two-for-one stock split effected February 1, 2011.

See Notes to Consolidated Financial Statements.

NOTES TO CONSOLIDATED FINANCIAL STATEMENTS

October 30, 2011

Note A—Summary of Significant Accounting Policies (in part)

Stock Split: On November 22, 2010, the Company's Board of Directors authorized a two-for-one split of the Company's common stock, which was subsequently approved by shareholders at the Company's Annual Meeting on January 31, 2011, and effected on February 1, 2011. The Company's common stock was reclassified by reducing the par value from $.0586 per share to $.0293 per share and the number of authorized shares was increased from 400,000,000 to 800,000,000 shares, in order to effect a two-for-one stock split. The number of authorized shares of nonvoting common stock and preferred stock was also increased to 400,000,000 shares and 160,000,000 shares, respectively, with no change in the par value of those shares.

Unless otherwise noted, all prior year share amounts and per share calculations throughout this Annual Report have been restated to reflect the impact of this split, and to provide data on a basis comparable to fiscal 2011. Such restatements include calculations regarding the Company's weighted-average shares, earnings per share, and dividends per share, as well as disclosures regarding the Company's stock-based compensation plans and share repurchase activity.

Reverse Stock Split

5.35

UNIFI, INC. (JUN)

CONSOLIDATED STATEMENTS OF CHANGES IN SHAREHOLDERS' EQUITY

Fiscal Years ended June 26, 2011, June 27, 2010, and June 28, 2009

(Amounts in thousands)

	Shares Outstanding[1]	Common Stock[1]	Capital in Excess of Par Value[1]	Retained Earnings	Accumulated Other Comprehensive Income	Total Shareholders' Equity
Balance June 29, 2008	20,229	$2,023	$29,177	$254,494	$19,975	$305,669
Options exercised	456	46	3,785	—	—	3,831
Share-based compensation	—	—	1,425	—	—	1,425
Other comprehensive (loss)	—	—	—	—	(16,960)	(16,960)
Net loss	—	—	—	(48,996)	—	(48,996)

(continued)

	Shares Outstanding[1]	Common Stock[1]	Capital in Excess of Par Value[1]	Retained Earnings	Accumulated Other Comprehensive Income	Total Share-holders' Equity
Balance June 28, 2009	20,685	$2,069	$34,387	$205,498	$3,015	$244,969
Purchase of stock	(628)	(63)	(4,932)	—	—	(4,995)
Share-based compensation	—	—	2,124	—	—	2,124
Other comprehensive income	—	—	—	—	7,113	7,113
Net income	—	—	—	10,685	—	10,685
Balance June 27, 2010	20,057	$2,006	$31,579	$216,183	$10,128	$259,896
Purchase of stock	—	—	(1)	—	—	(1)
Options exercised	19	2	144	—	—	146
Share-based compensation	—	—	875	—	—	875
Stock option tax benefit	—	—	2	—	—	2
Conversion of restricted stock units	4	—	—	—	—	—
Other comprehensive income	—	—	—	—	13,648	13,648
Net income	—	—	—	25,089	—	25,089
Balance June 26, 2011	20,080	$2,008	$32,599	$241,272	$23,776	$299,655

[1] All share amounts and computations using such amounts have been retroactively adjusted to reflect the November 3, 2010 1-for-3 reverse stock split.

See accompanying notes to Consolidated Financial Statements.

NOTES TO CONSOLIDATED FINANCIAL STATEMENTS

Fiscal Years ended June 26, 2011, June 27, 2010 and June 28, 2009

(Amounts in thousands, except per share amounts)

15. Shareholders' Equity (in part)

On October 27, 2010, the shareholders of the Company approved a reverse stock split of the Company's common stock (the "reverse stock split") at a ratio of 1-for-3. The reverse stock split became effective November 3, 2010. The Company had 20,060 shares of common stock issued and outstanding immediately following the completion of the reverse stock split. The Company is authorized in its Restated Certificate of Incorporation to issue up to a total of 500,000 shares of common stock at a $0.10 par value per share which was unchanged by the amendment. All share and per share amounts have been retroactively adjusted to reflect the reverse stock split.

CHANGES TO RETAINED EARNINGS

RECOGNITION AND MEASUREMENT

5.36 The retained earnings account is affected by direct charges and credits. The most frequent direct charges to retained earnings are net loss for the year, losses on treasury stock transactions, and cash or stock dividends. The most common direct credit to retained earnings is net income for the year.

PRESENTATION

5.37 In addition to direct charges and credits, the retained earnings account is also affected by opening balance adjustments. Reasons for which the opening balance of retained earnings is properly restated include certain changes in accounting principles, changes in the reporting entity, and corrections of an error in previously issued financial statements.

5.38 FASB ASC 250, *Accounting Changes and Error Corrections*, requires, unless impracticable or otherwise specified by applicable authoritative guidance, retrospective application to prior periods' financial statements of a change in accounting principle. *Retrospective application* is the application of a different accounting principle to prior accounting periods as if that principle had always been used. More specifically, retrospective application involves the following:

- The cumulative effect of the change on periods prior to those presented should be reflected in the carrying amount of assets and liabilities as of the beginning of the first period presented.
- An offsetting adjustment, if any, shall be made to the opening balance of retained earnings or other appropriate component of equity or net assets in the statement of financial position for that period.
- Financial statements for each individual prior period presented should be adjusted to reflect the period-specific effects of applying the new accounting principle.

5.39 FASB ASC 250 also requires any accounting error in the financial statements of a prior period discovered after the financial statements are issued or available to be issued to be reported as an error correction by restating the prior period financial statements. Restatement involves similar requirements as those specified for retrospective application of a change in accounting principle.

5.40 SEC Staff Accounting Bulletin (SAB) No. 108 provides guidance on the consideration of the effects of prior year misstatements in quantifying current year misstatements for the purpose of assessing materiality. SAB No. 108 requires that registrant entities determine the quantitative effect of a financial statement misstatement by using both an income statement ("rollover") and a balance sheet ("iron curtain") approach and evaluate whether, under either approach, the error is material after considering all relevant quantitative and qualitative factors.

5.41

TABLE 5-6: CREDITS AND CHARGES TO ADDITIONAL PAID-IN CAPITAL*

Table 5-6 summarizes credits and charges to additional paid-in capital.

	Number of Entities		
	2011	2010	2009
Credits			
Common stock issued			
Employee benefits	339	272	303
Public offerings	26	20	38
Business combinations	17	24	20
Debt conversions/extinguishments	8	12	14
Preferred stock conversions	5	5	8
Compensation recognized	237	344	310
Stock compensation tax benefits	174	138	137
Warrants issued or exercised	14	30	6
Treasury stock purchased or retired	16	13	N/C^
Market value adjustment for employee benefit trust	—	2	N/C^
Other—described	77	86	70
Charges			
Treasury stock issued for less than cost	57	58	86
Purchase or retirement of capital stock	130	112	84
Stock compensation tax benefits	29	22	66
Restricted stock	64	52	64
Other employee benefits	41	31	52
Conversion of preferred stock	5	6	4
Stock issue expense	16	25	N/C^
Business combination consummated in current year	9	9	N/C^
Stock splits	1	2	N/C^
Dividends	18	15	N/C^
Other—described	101	100	59

* Appearing in the statement of stockholders' equity or notes to the financial statements, or both.
^ N/C = Not compiled. The line item was not included in the table for the year shown.

PRESENTATION AND DISCLOSURE EXCERPTS

Change in Accounting Principle

5.42

LOCKHEED MARTIN CORPORATION (DEC)

CONSOLIDATED STATEMENTS OF STOCKHOLDERS' EQUITY

(In millions, except per share data)	Common Stock	Additional Paid-In Capital	Retained Earnings	Accumulated Other Comprehensive Loss	Total Stockholders' Equity	Comprehensive Income (Loss)
Balance at December 31, 2008	$393	$—	$11,621	$ (9,149)	$2,865	
Cumulative effect of a change in accounting principle (see Note 1)	—	—	(112)	—	(112)	
Balance at December 31, 2008, as adjusted	393	—	11,509	(9,149)	2,753	

(continued)

SEC 5.38

(In millions, except per share data)	Common Stock	Additional Paid-In Capital	Retained Earnings	Accumulated Other Comprehensive Loss	Total Stockholders' Equity	Comprehensive Income (Loss)
Net earnings	$ —	$ —	$ 2,973	$ —	$2,973	$2,973
Repurchases of common stock	(25)	(440)	(1,386)	—	(1,851)	—
Common stock dividends declared ($2.34 per share)	—	—	(908)	—	(908)	—
Stock-based awards and ESOP activity	5	440	—	—	445	—
Other comprehensive income (loss):						
Postretirement benefit plans:						
Unrecognized amounts in 2009, net of tax of $121 million	—	—	—	214	214	214
Recognition of previously deferred amounts, net of tax of $158 million	—	—	—	281	281	281
Other, net	—	—	—	59	59	59
Balance at December 31, 2009	373	—	12,188	(8,595)	3,966	$3,527
Net earnings	—	—	2,878	—	2,878	$2,878
Repurchases of common stock	(33)	(514)	(1,936)	—	(2,483)	—
Common stock dividends declared ($2.64 per share)	—	—	(969)	—	(969)	—
Stock-based awards and ESOP activity	6	514	—	—	520	—
Other comprehensive income (loss):						
Postretirement benefit plans:						
Unrecognized amounts in 2010, net of tax benefit of $531 million	—	—	—	(983)	(983)	(983)
Recognition of previously deferred amounts, net of tax of $304 million	—	—	—	553	553	553
Other, net	—	—	—	15	15	15
Balance at December 31, 2010	346	—	12,161	(9,010)	3,497	$2,463
Net earnings	—	—	2,655	—	2,655	$2,655
Repurchases of common stock	(32)	(589)	(1,781)	—	(2,402)	—
Common stock dividends declared ($3.25 per share)	—	—	(1,098)	—	(1,098)	—
Stock-based awards and ESOP activity	7	589	—	—	596	—
Other comprehensive income (loss):						
Postretirement benefit plans:						
Unrecognized amounts in 2011, net of tax benefit of $1.6 billion	—	—	—	(2,858)	(2,858)	(2,858)
Recognition of previously deferred amounts, net of tax of $364 million	—	—	—	666	666	666
Other, net	—	—	—	(55)	(55)	(55)
Balance at December 31, 2011	$321	$ —	$11,937	$(11,257)	$1,001	$ 408

See accompanying Notes to Consolidated Financial Statements.

NOTES TO CONSOLIDATED FINANCIAL STATEMENTS

Note 1—Significant Accounting Policies (in part)

Sales and earnings (in part)

We record net sales and estimated profits for approximately 95% of our contracts using the percentage-of-completion (POC) method (as described below) for cost-reimbursable and fixed-price contracts for design, development, and production (DD&P) activities, and services contracts with the U.S. Government. Sales are recorded on all time-and-materials contracts as the work is performed based on agreed-upon hourly rates and allowable costs. We account for our services contracts with non-U.S. Government customers using the services method of accounting (as described below). We classify net sales as products or services on our Statements of Earnings based on the attributes of the underlying contracts.

POC Method of Accounting—The POC method for DD&P contracts depends on the nature of the products provided under the contract. For example, for contracts that require us to perform a significant level of development effort in comparison to the total value of the contract and/or to deliver minimal quantities, sales are recorded using the cost-to-cost method to measure progress toward completion. Under the cost-to-cost method of accounting, we recognize sales and an estimated profit as costs are incurred based on the proportion that the incurred costs bear to total estimated costs. For contracts that require us to provide a substantial number of similar items without a significant level of development, we record sales and an estimated profit on a POC basis using units-of-delivery as the basis to measure progress toward completing the contract. For contracts to provide services to the U.S. Government, sales are generally recorded using the cost-to-cost method.

Award fees and incentives, as well as penalties related to contract performance, are considered in estimating sales and profit rates on contracts accounted for under the POC method. Estimates of award fees are based on past experience and anticipated performance. We record incentives or penalties when there is sufficient information to assess anticipated contract performance. Incentive provisions that increase or decrease earnings based solely on a single significant event are not recognized until the event occurs.

Accounting for contracts under the POC method requires judgment relative to assessing risks, estimating contract revenues and costs (including estimating award and incentive fees and penalties related to performance), and making assumptions for schedule and technical issues. Due to the scope and nature of the work required to be performed on many of our contracts, the estimation of total revenue and cost at completion is complicated and subject to many variables and, accordingly, is subject to change. When adjustments in estimated contract revenues or estimated costs at completion are required, any changes from prior estimates are recognized in the current period for the inception-to-date effect of such changes. When estimates of total costs to be incurred on a contract exceed total estimates of revenue to be earned, a provision for the entire loss on the contract is recorded in the period in which the loss is determined.

At the outset of each contract, we estimate the initial profit booking rate. The initial profit booking rate of each contract is based on the initial estimated costs at completion considering risks surrounding the ability to achieve the technical requirements (for example, a newly-developed product versus a mature product), schedule (for example, the number and type of milestone events), and costs by contract requirements. Profit booking rates may increase during the performance of the contract if we successfully retire risks surrounding the technical, schedule, and costs aspects of the contract, or may decrease if we are not successful in retiring risks and, as a result, our estimated costs at completion increase.

Our net profit booking rate adjustments resulting from changes in estimates increased operating profit, net of state taxes, by approximately $1.6 billion in 2011, $1.4 billion in 2010, and $1.6 billion in 2009. These adjustments increased net earnings by approximately $1.0 billion ($3.00 per share) in 2011, $890 million ($2.40 per share) in 2010, and $1.0 billion ($2.60 per share) in 2009.

Change in Accounting Principle and Adoption of New Accounting Standard (in part)

On January 1, 2011, we changed the way we account for our services contracts with the U.S. Government. We now recognize sales on those contracts using the POC method (as described above). All prior period amounts have been adjusted to reflect the new method of accounting. The effect of this change in accounting was not material to our consolidated results of operations or financial position for any period, including 2011, and did not impact cash flows. At December 31, 2010, the cumulative effect of adopting the new method was a reduction in retained earnings of $211 million, which reflects the inception-to-date timing differences between the two methods. We believe the POC method is preferable to the service accounting method we previously used, as consistent sales recognition for all contracts with the U.S. Government better reflects the underlying economics of those contracts and aligns our financial reporting with other companies in our industry.

Correction of an Error or Misstatement

5.43

LA-Z-BOY INCORPORATED (APR)

CONSOLIDATED STATEMENT OF CHANGES IN EQUITY

(Amounts in thousands)	Common Shares	Capital in Excess of Par Value	Retained Earnings	Accumulated Other Comprehensive Income (Loss)	Non-Controlling Interests	Total
At April 26, 2008 (previously reported)	$51,428	$209,388	$188,203	$ (943)	$3,298	$451,374
Cumulative effect of accounting corrections			(2,411)	(6)		(2,417)
At April 26, 2008 (as revised)	$51,428	$209,388	$185,792	$ (949)	$3,298	$448,957
Comprehensive loss						
Net income (loss)			(122,665)		252	
Unrealized loss on marketable securities arising during the period (net of tax)				(4,332)		
Reclassification adjustment for loss on marketable securities included in net loss				5,180		
Translation adjustment				(370)	(408)	
Change in fair value of cash flow hedge				(723)		
Net actuarial loss				(21,974)		
Total comprehensive loss						(145,040)
Stock issued for stock and employee benefit plans, net of cancellations	50	(7,262)	7,077			(135)
Stock option, restricted stock and performance based stock expense		3,819				3,819
Dividends declared			(5,177)			(5,177)
Change in noncontrolling interest upon consolidation of VIE and other changes in noncontrolling interests					995	995

(continued)

(Amounts in thousands)	Common Shares	Capital in Excess of Par Value	Retained Earnings	Accumulated Other Comprehensive Income (Loss)	Non-Controlling Interests	Total
At April 25, 2009	$51,478	$205,945	$ 65,027	$(23,168)	$4,137	$303,419
Comprehensive income						
Net income (loss)			32,701		(1,342)	
Unrealized gain on marketable securities arising during the period				2,685		
Reclassification adjustment for gain on marketable securities included in net income				(97)		
Translation adjustment				(190)	404	
Change in fair value of cash flow hedge				146		
Net pension amortization and net actuarial loss				340		
Total comprehensive income						34,647
Stock issued for stock and employee benefit plans, net of cancellations	292	(9,294)	8,738			(264)
Stock option, restricted stock and performance based stock expense		5,222				5,222
Change in noncontrolling interest					90	90
At April 24, 2010	51,770	201,873	106,466	(20,284)	3,289	343,114
Comprehensive income						
Net income (loss)			24,047		(6,674)	
Unrealized gain on marketable securities arising during the period				1,085		
Reclassification adjustment for gain on marketable securities included in net income				(495)		
Translation adjustment				(298)	353	
Change in fair value of cash flow hedge				548		
Net pension amortization and net actuarial loss				640		
Total comprehensive income						19,206
Stock issued for stock and employee benefit plans, net of cancellations	139	(4,001)	3,757			(105)
Stock option and restricted stock expense		3,717				3,717
Acquisition of VIE and other			(8,573)		8,633	60
Cumulative effect of change in accounting for noncontrolling interests			925		(2,777)	(1,852)
At April 30, 2011	$51,909	$201,589	$126,622	$(18,804)	$2,824	$364,140

The accompanying Notes to Consolidated Financial Statements are an integral part of these statements.

NOTES TO CONSOLIDATED FINANCIAL STATEMENTS

Note 1: Accounting Policies (in part)

Principles of Consolidation

Our consolidated financial statements include the accounts of La-Z-Boy Incorporated and its majority-owned subsidiaries. All inter-company transactions have been eliminated. Additionally, our consolidated financial statements include the accounts of certain entities in which we hold a controlling interest based on exposure to economic risks and potential rewards (variable interests) for which we are the primary beneficiary.

In June 2009, the Financial Accounting Standards Board amended its guidance on accounting for VIEs. The new accounting guidance resulted in a change in our accounting policy effective April 25, 2010. Among other things, the new guidance requires more qualitative than quantitative analyses to determine the primary beneficiary of a VIE and requires continuous assessments of whether an enterprise is the primary beneficiary of a VIE. Under the new guidance, a VIE must be consolidated if the enterprise has both (a) the power to direct the activities of the VIE that most significantly impact the entity's economic performance, and (b) the obligation to absorb losses or the right to receive benefits from the VIE that could potentially be significant to the VIE. We adopted this new accounting guidance and it was effective for us on April 25, 2010, the first day of our current fiscal year. This guidance is being applied prospectively.

We consolidate entities that are VIEs when we are deemed to be the primary beneficiary of the VIE. We will continuously evaluate our VIEs' primary beneficiaries as facts and circumstances change to determine if such changes warrant a change in our status as primary beneficiary.

On April 25, 2010, we deconsolidated our Toronto, Ontario VIE as a result of the above mentioned change in accounting policy. This entity is an independent La-Z-Boy Furniture Galleries® dealer operating eight stores and had previously been consolidated due to certain lease guarantees and other financial support we have provided. Although these financial arrangements result in our holding a majority of the variable interests in this VIE, they do not empower us to direct the activities of the VIE that most significantly impact the VIE's economic performance. Consequently, subsequent to this change in accounting policy, we deconsolidated this VIE.

Sales and operating income, net of eliminations, for our Toronto, Ontario VIE for fiscal 2010 were $20.4 million and $3.4 million, respectively. The most significant impacts on our Consolidated Balance Sheet were a decrease to current assets of $6.9 million, a decrease to long-term assets of $5.0 million, and a decrease to noncontrolling interest of $2.8 million. We recognized a non-cash gain of $0.9 million at April 25, 2010. This gain was categorized as a cumulative effect to retained earnings during fiscal 2011. There was no impact on earnings per share as a result of the deconsolidation.

During fiscal 2011, we corrected our historical financial statements for errors primarily related to inventory, intercompany accounts payable and lease expense related to our VIEs. These corrections did not impact our net income attributable to La-Z-Boy Incorporated on a per share basis for fiscal 2011 or fiscal 2010. These corrections resulted in a $0.5 million increase to our net loss attributable to La-Z-Boy Incorporated for fiscal 2009. Certain of these corrections related to periods prior to fiscal 2009 and as such have been reflected in the accompanying financial statements as an adjustment to our opening retained earnings account.

Also during fiscal 2011, we corrected our historical financial statements for lease expense for stores that we are subleasing to an independent dealer which were not recorded on a straight-line basis. This revision resulted in a $0.1 million decrease in our net income attributable to La-Z-Boy Incorporated for fiscal 2010 and $0.1 million increase in our net loss attributable to La-Z-Boy Incorporated for fiscal 2009.

As a result of above mentioned corrections, during the second quarter of fiscal 2011, we also revised our historical financial statements to correct a previously disclosed out-of-period reduction to cost of goods sold, with a corresponding adjustment to accumulated other comprehensive loss. This revision resulted in a $0.6 million decrease in our net income attributable to La-Z-Boy Incorporated for fiscal 2010 and a $0.6 million decrease in our net loss attributable to La-Z-Boy Incorporated for fiscal 2009.

Additionally, during fiscal 2011 it was determined that our tax rate for fiscal 2010 did not reflect a deduction due to write-offs of certain inventory when completing our tax provision for fiscal 2010, and that our tax rate and corresponding tax expense were therefore overstated. This correction resulted in a $0.9 million increase to our net income attributable to La-Z-Boy Incorporated for fiscal 2010.

We determined that the cumulative impact of recording the corrections mentioned above in fiscal 2011 would be material to our fiscal 2011 full year results. However, we determined that the corrections were not material, either individually or in the aggregate, to any of our prior fiscal years or interim periods. Consequently, we revised our historical financial statements for the related prior periods. Because our analysis concluded that these corrections were immaterial to any prior period, we have not amended any of our previous filings with the Securities and Exchange Commission.

The following tables set forth the significant impacts of the corrections to our Consolidated Statement of Operations for fiscal 2010 and fiscal 2009, and our Consolidated Balance Sheet as of April 24, 2010:

| | Year Ended 4/24/2010 | | |
	4/24/2010 (As Previously Reported)	Adjustments	4/24/2010 (As Adjusted)
(Amounts in thousands, except per share data)			
Net income attributable to La-Z-Boy Incorporated	$32,538	$163	$32,701
Diluted net income attributable to La-Z-Boy Incorporated per share	$ 0.62	$ —	$ 0.62

| | Year Ended 4/25/2009 | | |
	4/25/2009 (As Previously Reported)	Adjustments	4/25/2009 (As Adjusted)
(Amounts in thousands, except per share data)			
Net loss attributable to La-Z-Boy Incorporated	$(122,672)	$ 7	$(122,665)
Diluted net loss attributable to La-Z-Boy Incorporated per share	$ (2.39)	$ —	$ (2.39)

| | As of 04/24/10 | | |
	04/24/10 (As Previously Reported)	Adjustments	04/24/10 (As Adjusted)
(Amounts in thousands)			
Inventories, net	$134,187	$(1,707)	$132,480
Other current assets	$ 18,159	$ 703	$ 18,862
Other long-term liabilities	$ 68,381	$ 2,064	$ 70,445
Retained earnings	$108,707	$(2,241)	$106,466
Accumulated other comprehensive loss	$ (20,251)	$ (33)	$ (20,284)
Noncontrolling interests	$ 4,141	$ (852)	$ 3,289

SEC 5.43

5.44

THE DUN & BRADSTREET CORPORATION (DEC)

*CONSOLIDATED STATEMENT OF SHAREHOLDERS'
EQUITY (DEFICIT)*

(Dollar amounts in millions, except per share data)	Common Stock ($0.01 Par Value)	Capital Surplus	Retained Earnings	Treasury Stock	Cumulative Translation Adjustment	Defined Benefit Plans	Derivative Financial Instrument	Total D&B Sharehold-ers' Equity (Deficit)	Non-Controlling Interest	Total Equity (Deficit)
For the Years Ended December 31, 2011, 2010 and 2009										
Balance, January 1, 2009	$0.8	$206.1	$1,582.8	$(1,924.4)	$(204.3)	$(514.2)	$(3.5)	$(856.7)	$ 6.1	$(850.6)
Net Income	0.0	0.0	319.4	0.0	0.0	0.0	0.0	319.4	2.6	322.0
Adjustment to Opening Retained Earnings, net of tax $14.0 (Note 1)	0.0	0.0	(23.2)	0.0	0.0	0.0	0.0	(23.2)	0.0	(23.2)
Purchase of shares	0.0	0.0	0.0	0.0	0.0	0.0	0.0	0.0	3.2	3.2
Payment to noncontrolling interest	0.0	0.0	0.0	0.0	0.0	0.0	0.0	0.0	(0.5)	(0.5)
Equity-Based Plans	0.0	(3.1)	0.0	52.3	0.0	0.0	0.0	49.2	0.0	49.2
Treasury Shares Acquired	0.0	0.0	0.0	(225.6)	0.0	0.0	0.0	(225.6)	0.0	(225.6)
Pension Adjustments, net of tax of $2.3	0.0	0.0	0.0	0.0	0.0	(10.4)	0.0	(10.4)	0.0	(10.4)
Dividend Declared	0.0	0.0	(71.5)	0.0	0.0	0.0	0.0	(71.5)	0.0	(71.5)
Adjustments to Legacy Tax Matters	0.0	6.5	0.0	0.0	0.0	0.0	0.0	6.5	0.0	6.5
Change in Cumulative Translation Adjustment	0.0	0.0	0.0	0.0	42.9	0.0	0.0	42.9	0.3	43.2
Derivative Financial Instruments, no tax impact	0.0	0.0	0.0	0.0	0.0	0.0	0.5	0.5	0.0	0.5
Balance, December 31, 2009	$0.8	$209.5	$1,807.5	$(2,097.7)	$(161.4)	$(524.6)	$(3.0)	$(768.9)	$11.7	$(757.2)
Net Income	0.0	0.0	252.1	0.0	0.0	0.0	0.0	252.1	(1.2)	250.9
Purchase of shares	0.0	(0.3)	0.0	0.0	0.0	0.0	0.0	(0.3)	(0.2)	(0.5)
Payment to noncontrolling interest	0.0	0.0	0.0	0.0	0.0	0.0	0.0	0.0	(1.9)	(1.9)
Equity-Based Plans	0.0	11.6	0.0	18.4	0.0	0.0	0.0	30.0	0.0	30.0
Treasury Shares Acquired	0.0	0.0	0.0	(134.8)	0.0	0.0	0.0	(134.8)	0.0	(134.8)
Pension Adjustments, net of tax of $16.5	0.0	0.0	0.0	0.0	0.0	8.6	0.0	8.6	0.0	8.6
Dividend Declared	0.0	0.0	(70.1)	0.0	0.0	0.0	0.0	(70.1)	0.0	(70.1)
Adjustments to Legacy Tax Matters	0.0	6.5	0.0	0.0	0.0	0.0	0.0	6.5	0.0	6.5
Change in Cumulative Translation Adjustment	0.0	0.0	0.0	0.0	(0.7)	0.0	0.0	(0.7)	0.4	(0.3)
Balance, December 31, 2010	$0.8	$227.3	$1,989.5	$(2,214.1)	$(162.1)	$(516.0)	$(3.0)	$(677.6)	$8.8	$(668.8)

(continued)

(Dollar amounts in millions, except per share data)	Common Stock ($0.01 Par Value)	Capital Surplus	Retained Earnings	Treasury Stock	Cumulative Translation Adjustment	Defined Benefit Plans	Derivative Financial Instrument	Total D&B Sharehold- ers' Equity (Deficit)	Non- Controlling Interest	Total Equity (Deficit)
					For the Years Ended December 31, 2011, 2010 and 2009					
Net Income	$0.0	$ 0.0	$ 260.3	$ 0.0	$ 0.0	$ 0.0	$0.0	$ 260.3	$(0.1)	$ 260.2
Sale of Noncontrolling Interest	0.0	0.0	0.0	0.0	0.0	0.0	0.0	0.0	1.7	1.7
Noncontrolling Interest Reclassed to Liability Held for Sale	0.0	0.0	0.0	0.0	0.0	0.0	0.0	0.0	(4.7)	(4.7)
Equity-Based Plans	0.0	5.2	0.0	43.2	0.0	0.0	0.0	48.4	0.0	48.4
Treasury Shares Acquired	0.0	0.0	0.0	(185.4)	0.0	0.0	0.0	(185.4)	0.0	(185.4)
Pension Adjustments, net of tax of $80.4	0.0	0.0	0.0	0.0	0.0	(122.4)	0.0	(122.4)	0.0	(122.4)
Dividends Declared	0.0	0.0	(70.5)	0.0	0.0	0.0	0.0	(70.5)	(0.7)	(71.2)
Adjustments to Legacy Tax Matters	0.0	6.5	0.0	0.0	0.0	0.0	0.0	6.5	0.0	6.5
Derivative Financial instruments, no tax impact	0.0	0.0	0.0	0.0	0.0	0.0	3.0	3.0	0.0	3.0
Change in Cumulative Translation Adjustment	0.0	0.0	0.0	0.0	(6.2)	0.0	0.0	(6.2)	(1.3)	(7.5)
Balance, December 31, 2011	$0.8	$239.0	$2,179.3	$(2,356.3)	$(168.3)	$(638.4)	$0.0	$(743.9)	$ 3.7	$(740.2)

The accompanying notes are an integral part of the consolidated financial statements.

NOTES TO CONSOLIDATED FINANCIAL STATEMENTS

(Tabular dollar amounts in millions, except per share data)

Note 1. Description of Business and Summary of Significant Accounting Policies (in part)

Basis of Presentation (in part)

For the year ended December 31, 2011, we revised our financial statements to reflect the impact for certain ratable contracts which were previously accounted for using a convention in which a full month's revenue was recorded irrespective of the contract's actual effective date. As a result, the December 31, 2011 revenue and net income include an out of period adjustment of approximately $2.1 million and $1.3 million, respectively, relating to the year ended December 2010 and approximately $2.6 million and $1.6 million, respectively, relating to the year ended December 2009.

Additionally, to adjust for the impact prior to 2009, management recorded the following non-cash adjustments: a $23.2 million reduction to opening retained earnings, $14.0 million increase to deferred taxes and $37.2 increase to the December 31, 2010 deferred revenue balance. In accordance with accounting guidance found in Accounting Standards Codification ("ASC") 250-110 (SEC Staff Accounting Bulletin No. 99, Materiality), we assessed the materiality of the adjustments and concluded that the errors were not material to any of our previously issued financial statements.

Other Changes in Retained Earnings: Share Repurchase Programs

5.45

COMPUTER SCIENCES CORPORATION (MAR)

CONSOLIDATED STATEMENTS OF CHANGES IN EQUITY

(Amounts in millions, except shares in thousands)	Common Stock Shares	Common Stock Amount	Additional Paid-In Capital	Earnings Retained for Use in Business	Accumulated Other Comprehensive Income (Loss)	Common Stock in Treasury	Total CSC Equity	Non-Controlling Interest	Total Equity
Balance at March 28, 2008	159,219	$159	$1,771	$3,802	$101	$(371)	$5,462	$159	$5,621
Comprehensive income:									
Net income				1,115			1,115	8	1,123
Currency translation adjustment					(638)		(638)		(638)
Unfunded pension obligation					(467)		(467)		(467)
Comprehensive income							10	8	18
Stock based compensation expense			54				54		54
Acquisition of treasury stock						(4)	(4)		(4)
Stock option exercises and other common stock transactions	470	1	11				12		12
Change in pension valuation date per ASC 715				(24)			(24)		(24)
Non controlling interest distributions								(59)	(59)
Balance at April 3, 2009	159,689	160	1,836	4,893	(1,004)	(375)	5,510	108	5,618
Comprehensive income:									
Net income				817			817	17	834
Currency translation adjustment					242		242		242
Unfunded pension obligation					(290)		(290)		(290)
Comprehensive Income							769	17	786
Stock based compensation expense			64				64		64
Acquisition of treasury stock						(4)	(4)		(4)
Stock option exercises and other common stock transactions	2,545	2	106				108		108
Non controlling interest distributions and Other				(1)			(1)	(63)	(64)
Balance at April 2, 2010	162,234	162	2,006	5,709	(1,052)	(379)	6,446	62	6,508
Comprehensive income:									
Net income				740			740	19	759
Currency translation adjustment					261		261		261
Unfunded pension obligation					101		101		101
Comprehensive income							1,102	19	1,121
Stock based compensation expense			56				56		56
Acquisition of treasury stock						(6)	(6)		(6)
Repurchase of common stock	(1,353)	(1)	(19)	(45)			(65)		(65)
Stock option exercises and other common stock transactions	1,992	2	77				79		79
Cash dividends declared				(108)			(108)		(108)
Non controlling interest distributions								(25)	(25)
Balance at April 1, 2011	162,873	$163	$2,120	$6,296	$(690)	$(385)	$7,504	$ 56	$7,560

(See notes to consolidated financial statements)

NOTES TO CONSOLIDATED FINANCIAL STATEMENTS

Note 13—Stockholders' Equity (in part)

Stock Repurchase Program

In December 2010, the Company's board of directors approved a share repurchase program authorizing up to $1 billion in share repurchases of the Company's outstanding common stock. CSC expects to implement the program through purchases made in open market transactions in compliance with Securities and Exchange Commission rules, market conditions, and applicable state and federal legal requirements. The timing, volume, and nature of share repurchases will be at the discretion of management, and may be suspended or discontinued at any time. No end date has been established for the repurchase program.

In the fourth quarter, 1,353,000 shares were purchased through open market purchases for an aggregate consideration of $65 million at a weighted average price of $48.01 per share. The shares repurchased were retired immediately and included in the category of authorized but unissued shares. The excess of purchase price over par value of the shares repurchased was allocated between additional paid-in capital and retained earnings.

Other Changes in Retained Earnings: Stock Split

5.46

FLOWERS FOODS, INC. (DEC)

CONSOLIDATED STATEMENTS OF CHANGES IN STOCKHOLDERS' EQUITY

(Amounts in thousands, except share data)	Common Stock		Capital in Excess of Par Value	Retained Earnings	Accumulated Other Comprehensive Income (Loss)	Treasury Stock		Non-controlling Interest	Total
	Number of Shares Issued	Par Value				Number of Shares	Cost		
Balances at January 3, 2009	101,659,924	$199	$525,201	$369,397	$(102,279)	(8,913,142)	$(157,799)	$9,335	$644,054
Net income				130,297				3,415	133,712
Derivative instruments, net of tax					28,940				28,940
Pension and postretirement plans, net of tax					8,667				8,667
Comprehensive income									
Comprehensive income attributable to noncontrolling interest									
Comprehensive income attributable to Flowers Foods, Inc.									
Stock repurchases						(1,793,534)	(40,531)		(40,531)
Exercise of stock options			(1,552)			232,024	4,166		2,614
Issuance of performance-contingent restricted stock awards			(4,416)			248,680	4,416		—
Issuance of deferred stock awards			(352)			19,450	352		—
Amortization of share-based compensation awards			11,792						11,792
Income tax benefits related to share-based payments			1,522						1,522
Conversion of deferred compensation (Note 11)			95						95
Issuance of deferred compensation			(146)			6,135	146		—
Distributions from noncontrolling interest to owners								(669)	(669)
Dividends paid—$0.450 per common share				(62,170)					(62,170)

(continued)

(Amounts in thousands, except share data)	Common Stock Number of Shares Issued	Par Value	Capital in Excess of Par Value	Retained Earnings	Accumulated Other Comprehensive Income (Loss)	Treasury Stock Number of Shares	Cost	Non-controlling Interest	Total
Balances at January 2, 2010	101,659,924	$199	$532,144	$437,524	$(64,672)	(10,200,387)	$(189,250)	$12,081	$728,026
Deconsolidation of Variable Interest Entity (Note 12)								(12,081)	(12,081)
Net income				137,047					137,047
Derivative instruments, net of tax					35,769				35,769
Pension and postretirement plans, net of tax					(4,806)				(4,806)
Comprehensive income									
Stock repurchases						(1,548,771)	(39,184)		(39,184)
Exercise of stock options			(1,202)			486,887	9,086		7,884
Issuance of performance-contingent restricted stock awards			(4,102)			220,640	4,102		—
Issuance of deferred stock awards			(631)			33,920	631		—
Amortization of share-based compensation awards			12,995						12,995
Income tax benefits related to share-based payments			1,022						1,022
Performance-contingent restricted stock awards forfeitures and cancellations			83			(4,425)	(83)		—
Issuance of deferred compensation			(15)			642	15		—
Dividends paid—$0.517 per common share				(70,882)					(70,882)
Balances at January 1, 2011	101,659,924	$199	$540,294	$503,689	$(33,709)	(11,011,494)	$(214,683)	$—	$795,790
Net income				123,428					123,428
Derivative instruments, net of tax					(38,813)				(38,813)
Pension and postretirement plans, net of tax					(39,525)				(39,525)
Comprehensive income									
Adjustment for 3 for 2 stock split (Note 14)	50,828,084		(39)			(5,375,912)			(39)
Stock repurchases						(1,155,103)	(26,598)		(26,598)
Exercise of stock options			(2,512)			803,090	15,445		12,933
Issuance of performance-contingent restricted stock awards			(4,213)			216,050	4,213		—
Issuance of deferred stock awards			(1,160)			56,505	1,119		(41)
Amortization of share-based compensation awards			12,982						12,982
Income tax benefits related to share-based payments			2,932						2,932
Performance-contingent restricted stock awards forfeitures and cancellations			961			(51,630)	(961)		—
Issuance of deferred compensation			(219)			11,672	219		—
Contingent acquisition consideration			(5,000)						(5,000)
Dividends paid—$0.583 per common share				(79,081)					(79,081)
Balances at December 31, 2011	152,488,008	$199	$544,065	$547,997	$(112,047)	(16,506,822)	$(221,246)	$—	$758,968

See Accompanying Notes to Consolidated Financial Statements.

NOTES TO CONSOLIDATED FINANCIAL STATEMENTS

Note 14. Stockholders' Equity (in part)

Stock Split

On May 25, 2011, the board of directors declared a 3-for-2 stock split of the company's common stock. The record date for the split was June 10, 2011, and new shares were issued on June 24, 2011. All share and per share information has been restated for all prior periods presented giving retroactive effect to the stock split. The company revised certain historical amounts when it recorded the 3-for-2 stock split. The amounts were immaterial and reclassified within stockholders' equity between par value and capital in excess of par.

SPINOFFS

RECOGNITION AND MEASUREMENT

5.47 The distributions of nonmonetary assets that constitute a business to owners of an entity are commonly referred to as spinoffs. A *business* is defined as an integrated set of activities and assets that is capable of being conducted and managed for the purpose of providing a return in the form of dividends, lower costs, or other economic benefits directly to investors or other owners, members, or participants. Spinoffs are discussed in FASB ASC 505-60.

5.48 The accounting for the distribution of nonmonetary assets to owners of an entity in a spinoff should be based on the recorded amount (after reduction, if appropriate, for an indicated impairment of value). An entity's distribution of the shares of a wholly owned or consolidated subsidiary to its shareholders should be recorded based on the carrying value of the subsidiary. Regardless of whether the spun-off operations will be sold immediately after the spinoff, the transaction should not be accounted for as a sale of the accounting spinnee followed by a distribution of the proceeds. In order to determine the required accounting and reporting in a spinoff transaction, an entity needs to determine which party is the accounting spinnor and which is the accounting spinnee. The accounting spinnee should be reported as a discontinued operation by the accounting spinnor if the spinnee is a component of an entity and meets the conditions for such reporting.

PRESENTATION AND DISCLOSURE EXCERPTS

Spinoffs

5.49

ITT CORPORATION (DEC)

CONSOLIDATED STATEMENTS OF CHANGES IN SHAREHOLDERS' EQUITY

(In millions) Years Ended December 31	Shares			Dollars		
	2011	2010	2009	2011	2010	2009
Common Stock						
Common stock, beginning balance	91.5	90.8	90.3	$ 92	$ 91	$ 90
Activity from stock incentive plans	1.6	0.7	0.5	1	1	1
Common stock, ending balance	93.1	91.5	90.8	$ 93	$ 92	$ 91
Retained Earnings						
Retained earnings, beginning balance				$ 5,441	$ 4,762	$ 4,242
Net (loss) income				(130)	804	629
Cash dividends declared on common stock				(147)	(184)	(154)
Activity from stock incentive plans				97	59	45
Distribution of Exelis and Xylem				(4,409)	—	—
Retained earnings, ending balance				$ 852	$ 5,441	$ 4,762
Accumulated Other Comprehensive Loss						
Postretirement benefit plans, beginning balance				$(1,359)	$(1,388)	$(1,529)
Net change in postretirement benefit plans				(508)	29	141
Distribution of Exelis and Xylem				1,714	—	—
Postretirement benefit plans, ending balance				$ (153)	$(1,359)	$(1,388)
Cumulative translation adjustments, beginning balance				$ 276	$ 350	$ 224
Net foreign currency translation adjustment				(40)	(74)	126
Distribution of Exelis and Xylem				(333)	—	—

(continued)

(In millions)	Shares			Dollars		
Years Ended December 31	2011	2010	2009	2011	2010	2009
Cumulative translation adjustments, ending balance				$ (97)	$ 276	$ 350
Unrealized gain on investment securities, beginning balance				$ 11	$ 12	$ 1
Net change in unrealized gains on investment securities				(12)	(1)	11
Unrealized gain on investment securities, ending balance				$ (1)	$ 11	$ 12
Total accumulated other comprehensive loss				$ (251)	$(1,072)	$(1,026)
Total Shareholders' Equity						
Total shareholders' equity, beginning balance				$4,461	$ 3,827	$ 3,028
Net change in common stock				1	1	—
Net change in retained earnings				(4,589)	679	520
Net change in accumulated other comprehensive income				821	(46)	279
Total shareholders' equity, ending balance				$ 694	$ 4,461	$ 3,827

The accompanying Notes to Consolidated Financial Statements are an integral part of the above statements of changes in shareholders' equity.

NOTES TO CONSOLIDATED FINANCIAL STATEMENTS

(Dollars and share amounts in millions, unless otherwise stated)

Note 1—Description of Business, Basis of Presentation and Summary of Significant Accounting Policies (in part)

Basis of Presentation

On October 31, 2011, ITT Corporation made a pro rata distribution to its shareholders consisting of all the shares of common stock of Xylem Inc. (Xylem, previously referred to as the water-related businesses), which held ITT's interests in the water businesses, and all the shares of common stock of Exelis Inc. (Exelis, previously referred to as ITT's Defense & Information Solutions segment), which held ITT's interests in the defense businesses (the Distribution). These financial statements have been reclassified to present the financial position, results of operations and cash flows of Exelis and Xylem as discontinued operations in all periods presented. For further information on the discontinued operations of Exelis and Xylem, see Note 4, "Discontinued Operations." In addition, in conjunction with the Distribution, we implemented changes to our management structure and changed our segment reporting structure.

On October 31, 2011, we completed a one-for-two reverse stock split (1:2 Reverse Stock Split) of ITT's issued and outstanding common stock, as approved by our Board of Directors. The par value of our common stock remained $1 per share following the 1:2 Reverse Stock Split. All common stock shares authorized, issued and outstanding, as well as share prices and earnings per share give effect to the 1:2 Reverse Stock Split in all periods presented.

In addition to the reclassification effects from the Distribution, certain other prior year amounts have been reclassified to conform to the current year presentation as described within these Notes to the Consolidated Financial Statements.

Note 3—Company Transformation

As mentioned in Note 1, on October 31, 2011, the Company completed the legal and structural separation of Exelis and Xylem from the Company into two independent, publicly traded companies via a tax-free Distribution to shareholders. The Distribution was made pursuant to a Distribution Agreement, dated October 25, 2011, among ITT, Exelis and Xylem (the Distribution Agreement). With the completion of these separations, the Company disposed of its water-related businesses and Defense segment in their entirety and ceased to consolidate their financial position and results of operations in its consolidated financial statements. Accordingly, the Company has presented the financial position and results of operations of its former water-related businesses and Defense segment as discontinued operations in the consolidated financial statements for all periods presented. See Note 4, "Discontinued Operations," for additional information. The water-related businesses include the Water & Wastewater division, including its analytical instrumentation component, and the Residential & Commercial Water division previously reported within the Fluid Technology segment, as well as the Flow Control division that was previously reported within the Motion & Flow segment. The Industrial Process division, which was previously reported within the Fluid Technology segment, was not included in the Distribution and is now reported as a segment of ITT.

During 2011, we recognized pre-tax expenses of $636 in connection with activities taken to complete the Distribution and to create the revised organizational structure (referred to herein as Transformation costs). We have presented $396 of the pre-tax transformation costs within income from continuing operations and $240 within income from discontinued operations. Amounts presented within discontinued operations are costs directly related to the Distribution and provide no future benefit to the Company. The components of transformation costs incurred during 2011 are presented below.

	Continuing Operations	Discontinued Operations	Total
Loss on extinguishment of debt (see Note 16)	$297	$ —	$297
Advisory fees	—	139	139
Non-cash asset impairment[a]	57	8	65
IT costs	—	46	46
Employee retention and other compensation costs[b]	37	20	57
Lease termination and other real estate costs	4	10	14
Other costs	1	17	18
Transformation costs before income tax expense	396	240	636
Tax-related separation costs	4	7	11
Tax benefit	(143)	(74)	(217)
Total transformation costs, net of tax benefit	$257	$173	$430

[a] Includes a $55 million non-cash impairment charge related to a decision to discontinue development of an information technology consolidation initiative.

[b] Includes $17 of compensation costs recognized within continuing operations in connection with the retirement of Steven R. Loranger, our former Chairman, President and Chief Executive Officer in October 2011.

The table included below provides a rollforward of the accrual for Transformation costs for the year ended 2011.

Transformation accrual—January 1	$ 2
Charges for actions during the period:	
Continuing operations	396
Discontinued operations	240
Cash payments	(559)
Asset impairment and other non-cash charges, net	(45)
Transformation accrual—December 31	$ 34

Note 4—Discontinued Operations (in part)

On October 31, 2011, the Company completed the Distribution of Exelis and Xylem (see Note 1). ITT was designated as the accounting and legal spinnor with respect to the Distribution. In connection with the Distribution, ITT received a net cash transfer (the Contribution) of $683 and $988 from Exelis and Xylem, respectively. No gain or loss was recognized in connection with the Distribution. While we are a party to a Distribution Agreement and several other agreements, including a Tax Matters Agreement, Benefits and Compensation Matters Agreement and Master Transition Services Agreement, we have determined we do not have significant continuing involvement in the operations of Xylem or Exelis, nor do we expect significant continuing cash flows from Exelis or Xylem. As a result, the operating results of Exelis and Xylem through the date of the Distribution have been classified in the consolidated financial statements as discontinued operations for all periods presented.

The table below provides the major components of assets and liabilities at December 31, 2010 that were included in the Distribution and includes those assets and liabilities that were distributed to Exelis and Xylem which were not part of their historical operations.

	Exelis	Xylem	Total
Cash and cash equivalents	$ 18	$ 808	$ 826
Receivables, net	958	690	1,648
Inventories, net	239	389	628
Other current assets	188	167	355
Total current assets	1,403	2,054	3,457
Plant, Property and Equipment, net	462	465	927
Goodwill	2,156	1,617	3,773
Other intangible assets	258	416	674
Other non-current assets	243	248	491
Total assets	4,522	4,800	9,322
Accounts payable	326	321	647
Accrued liabilities and other current liabilities	884	361	1,245
Total current liabilities	1,210	682	1,892
Postretirement benefits	1,223	257	1,480
Other non-current liabilities	113	324	437
Total liabilities	$2,546	$1,263	$3,809

In order to effect the Distribution and govern ITT's relationship with Exelis and Xylem after the Distribution, ITT entered into a distribution agreement and several other agreements, including a tax matters agreement, employee benefits and compensation agreement and master transition services agreement. Information on the agreements utilized to effectuate the Distribution are provided below.

Distribution Agreement

The Distribution Agreement between ITT and Exelis and Xylem contains the key provisions relating to the separation of the businesses of Exelis and Xylem from ITT and the distribution of the shares of Exelis and Xylem common stock to our shareholders. The Distribution Agreement provides the framework for the allocation, transfer and assumption of assets and liabilities among ITT, Exelis and Xylem as well as the settlement or extinguishment of certain liabilities and other obligations between and among ITT, Exelis and Xylem. Under the Distribution Agreement, we agreed to indemnify Exelis and Xylem and their respective subsidiaries and affiliates, subject to limited exceptions with respect to certain employee claims, against claims and liabilities related to the past operation of ITT's business (other than the liabilities of the divested businesses) and Exelis and Xylem agreed to indemnify us against claims and liabilities related to their respective businesses. The Distribution Agreement establishes that certain liabilities, e.g., the bond litigation, referenced in Note 20, "Commitments and Contingencies," will be shared 21% to ITT, 40% to Exelis, and 39% to Xylem.

In connection with the Distribution, ITT retained certain material contingent legacy liabilities involving asbestos and environmental matters. See Note 20, "Commitments and Contingencies," for information regarding asbestos and environmental related contingencies.

Tax Matters Agreement

On October 25, 2011, we entered into a Tax Matters Agreement with Exelis and Xylem that governs the respective rights, responsibilities and obligations of the companies after the Distribution with respect to tax liabilities and benefits, tax attributes, tax contests and other tax sharing regarding U.S. Federal, state, local and foreign income taxes, other tax matters and related tax returns. Exelis and Xylem have liability with ITT to the U.S. Internal Revenue Service (IRS) for the consolidated U.S. Federal income taxes of the ITT consolidated group relating to the taxable periods in which Exelis and Xylem were part of that group. However, the Tax Matters Agreement specifies the portion, if any, of this tax liability for which ITT, Exelis and Xylem will bear responsibility, and ITT, Exelis and Xylem agreed to indemnify each other against any amounts for which they are not responsible. The Tax Matters Agreement also provides special rules for allocating tax liabilities in the event that the Distribution is determined to not be tax-free. The Tax Matters Agreement provides for certain covenants that may restrict our ability to pursue strategic or other transactions that otherwise could maximize the value of our business and may discourage or delay a change of control that may be considered favorable. Though valid as between the parties, the Tax Matters Agreement will not be binding on the IRS.

Pursuant to the Tax Matters Agreement, as the shared income tax liabilities are settled, ITT will make payments up to certain specified thresholds, with payments in excess of those specified thresholds shared among ITT, Exelis, and Xylem. If payments to the taxing authorities are less than certain specified thresholds, ITT will make payments up to the remaining specified thresholds to Exelis and Xylem. Settlement is expected to occur as the audit process by applicable taxing authorities is completed for the impacted years and cash payments are made. Given the nature of the shared tax liabilities, the maximum amount of potential future payments is not determinable. Any such cash payments, when they occur, will reduce the liability for uncertain tax positions as such payments represent an equivalent reduction of risk. At December 31, 2011, ITT's accrual for uncertain tax positions includes amounts related to certain shared tax liabilities; however, no receivables from Exelis or Xylem have been recorded as our estimate of their portion of the shared tax liabilities is not more than the amounts currently accrued for the uncertain tax position. If our estimate of exposures to the shared tax liabilities increases above the specified threshold, a receivable would be recorded. At December 31, 2011, there is a tax indemnification liability recorded of $4 due to Xylem.

Adjustments in the future for the impact of filing final income tax returns in certain jurisdictions where those returns include a combination of ITT, Exelis and Xylem legal entities and for certain amended income tax returns for the periods prior to the Distribution may be recorded to either shareholders' equity or the statement of income depending on the specific item giving rise to the adjustment.

Benefits and Compensation Matters Agreement

On October 25, 2011, we entered into a Benefits and Compensation Matters Agreement with Exelis and Xylem that governs the respective rights, responsibilities and obligations of Exelis, Xylem and ITT after the Distribution with respect to transferred employees, defined benefit pension plans, defined contribution pension plans, nonqualified pension plans, employee health and welfare benefit plans, incentive plans, corporate-owned life insurance, stock equity awards, foreign benefit plans, director plans and collective bargaining agreements. The Benefits and Compensation Matters Agreement provides for the allocation and treatment of assets and liabilities arising out of incentive plans, pension plans and employee welfare benefit programs in which Exelis and Xylem employees participated prior to the Distribution. Generally, Exelis and Xylem assumed or retained sponsorship of, and liabilities relating to, employee compensation and benefit programs relating to Exelis and Xylem current employees.

The Benefits and Compensation Matters Agreement also provided that outstanding ITT equity awards would be equitably adjusted in connection with the Distribution. All outstanding ITT equity awards held by employees of Exelis as of the Distribution Date were substituted for Exelis equity awards and all outstanding ITT equity awards held by employees of Xylem as of the Distribution Date were substituted for Xylem equity awards. As described in Note 18, "Long-Term Incentive Employee Compensation," the substitution preserved the economic value of the cancelled ITT equity awards for employees of Exelis and Xylem as of the Distribution Date. Subject to the applicable transition period with respect to certain benefit plans or programs, after the Distribution, employees of Exelis and Xylem no longer participate in ITT's plans or programs, and Exelis and Xylem have established or maintained plans or programs for their employees.

Master Transition Services Agreement

On October 25, 2011, we entered into a Master Transition Services Agreement with Exelis and Xylem, under which each of Exelis and Xylem or their respective affiliates provide us with certain services (including information technology, financial, procurement and human resource services, benefits support services and other specified services), and we or certain of our affiliates provide each of Exelis and Xylem certain services (including information technology, human resources services and other specified services). These services will initially be provided at cost with scheduled, escalating increases to up to cost plus 10% and generally extend for a period of 3 to 24 months and are intended to help ensure an orderly transition for each of Exelis, Xylem and ITT following the Distribution.

During November and December of 2011, we billed Exelis and Xylem approximately $22, primarily relating to active employee health benefits which continued to be administered by ITT. On January 1, 2012, the administration of the employee health benefit plans was transferred to Exelis and Xylem. Total billings by Exelis and Xylem to ITT, following the Distribution, amount to less than $1. As of December 31, 2011, we have an aggregate receivable and payable, associated with transactions related to the Master Transition Services Agreement, of less than $1 each.

TREASURY STOCK

PRESENTATION

5.50 Repurchased common stock is often referred to as treasury stock or treasury shares. FASB ASC 505-30 discusses the balance sheet presentation of treasury stock and states that if a corporation's stock is acquired for purposes other than retirement (formal or constructive), or if ultimate disposition has not yet been decided, the cost of acquired stock may be shown separately as a deduction from the total of capital stock, additional paid-in capital, and retained earnings or may be accorded the accounting treatment appropriate for retired stock.

5.51 A repurchase of shares at a price significantly in excess of the current market price creates a presumption that the repurchase price includes amounts attributable to items other than the shares repurchased. A repurchase of shares at a price significantly in excess of the current market price may require an entity to allocate amounts to other elements of the transaction. As shown in Table 5-7, the prevalent balance sheet presentation of treasury stock is to show the cost of treasury stock as a reduction of stockholders' equity.

5.52

TABLE 5-7: TREASURY STOCK—BALANCE SHEET PRESENTATION

	2011	2010	2009
Common Stock			
Cost of treasury stock shown as stockholders' equity deduction	316	292	316
Cost of treasury stock deducted from total capital	14	18	N/C*
Cost of treasury stock deducted from stock of the same class	6	12	5
Par or stated value of treasury stock deducted from issued stock of the same class	4	—	19
Other	1	1	—
Total Presentations	**341**	**323**	**340**
Preferred Stock			
Par value of treasury stock deducted from stock of the same class	—	1	N/C*
Other	1	—	—
Total Presentations	**1**	**1**	**—**
	Number of Entities		
Disclosing treasury stock	341	323	340
Not disclosing treasury stock	159	177	160
Total Entities	**500**	**500**	**500**

* N/C = Not compiled. Line item was not included in the table for the year shown.

PRESENTATION AND DISCLOSURE EXCERPTS

Treasury Stock

5.53

AIR PRODUCTS AND CHEMICALS, INC. (SEP)

CONSOLIDATED BALANCE SHEETS (in part)

30 September

(Millions of dollars, except for share data)	2011	2010
Air products shareholders' equity		
Common stock (par value $1 per share; issued 2011 and 2010—249,455,584 shares)	249.4	249.4
Capital in excess of par value	805.6	802.2
Retained earnings	8,599.5	7,852.2
Accumulated other comprehensive loss	(1,253.4)	(1,159.4)
Treasury stock, at cost (2011—39,270,328 shares; 2010—35,652,719 shares)	(2,605.3)	(2,197.5)
Total Air Products Shareholders' Equity	5,795.8	5,546.9
Noncontrolling Interests	142.9	150.7
Total equity	5,938.7	5,697.6

NOTES TO THE CONSOLIDATED FINANCIAL STATEMENTS

(Millions of dollars, except for share data)

17. Capital Stock

Authorized capital stock consists of 25 million preferred shares with a par value of $1 per share, none of which was outstanding at 30 September 2011, and 300 million shares of common stock with a par value of $1 per share.

In 2007, the Board of Directors authorized the repurchase of up to $1,000 of our outstanding common stock. We repurchase shares pursuant to Rules 10b5-1 and 10b-18 under the Securities Exchange Act of 1934, as amended, through repurchase agreements established with several brokers. During fiscal year 2011, we purchased 7.4 million of our outstanding shares at a cost of $649.2, which completed our 2007 $1,000 share repurchase program.

On 15 September 2011, the Board of Directors authorized a new $1,000 share repurchase program. At 30 September 2011, $1,000 in share repurchase authorization remains.

The following table reflects the changes in common shares:

Year Ended 30 September	2011	2010	2009
Number of Common Shares Outstanding			
Balance, beginning of year	213,802,865	211,260,264	209,334,627
Purchase of treasury shares	(7,433,612)	—	—
Issuance of treasury shares for stock option and award plans	3,816,003	2,542,601	1,925,637
Balance, end of year	210,185,256	213,802,865	211,260,264

OTHER COMPONENTS OF STOCKHOLDERS' EQUITY

PRESENTATION

5.54 For public entities, Rule 3-04 of Regulation S-X requires that an analysis of the changes in each caption of stockholders' equity and noncontrolling interests presented in the balance sheets should be given in a note or separate statement. This analysis should be presented in the form of a reconciliation of the beginning balance to the ending balance for each period for which an income statement is required to be filed, with all significant reconciling items described by appropriate captions and contributions from, and distributions to, owners shown separately.

5.55 Many of the survey entities present accounts other than capital stock, additional paid-in capital, retained earnings, accumulated other comprehensive income, and treasury stock in the "Stockholders' Equity" section of the balance sheet. Other stockholders' equity accounts appearing on the balance sheets of the survey entities include, but are not limited to, guarantees of employee stock ownership plan debt, unearned or deferred compensation related to employee stock award plans, and amounts owed to an entity by employees for loans to buy company stock, in each instance pursuant to relevant FASB ASC requirements. Other items, such as foreign currency translation adjustments, unrealized gains and losses on certain investments in debt and equity securities, and defined benefit postretirement plan adjustments, are considered components of other comprehensive income. FASB ASC 220, *Comprehensive Income*, permits the presentation of components of other comprehensive income and total comprehensive income in a statement of changes in stockholders' equity.

Author's Note

In June 2011, FASB issued FASB Accounting Standards Update (ASU) No. 2011-05, *Comprehensive Income (Topic 220): Presentation of Comprehensive Income*, which amends FASB ASC by eliminating the option to present the components of OCI as part of the statement of changes in stockholders' equity. Going forward, an entity will present the total of comprehensive income, the components of net income, and the components of OCI either in a single continuous statement of comprehensive income or in two separate but consecutive statements. In either option, an entity should present each component of net income together with total net income, each component of OCI together with a total for OCI, and a total amount for comprehensive income. The amendments to FASB ASC 220, *Comprehensive Income*, in ASU No. 2011-05 do not change which items an entity should present in OCI or when an entity should reclassify an item of OCI to net income. ASU No. 2011-05 is effective for fiscal years, and interim periods within those years, beginning after December 15, 2011. For nonpublic entities, the amendments are effective for fiscal years ending after December 15, 2012, and interim and annual periods thereafter. Early adoption is permitted because the remaining options are already permitted by FASB ASC 220. The amendments do not require any transition disclosures.

ASU No. 2011-05 is the result of a joint project with IASB to improve presentation of comprehensive income.

In December 2011, FASB issued ASU No. 2011-12, *Comprehensive Income (Topic 220): Deferral of the Effective Date for Amendments to the Presentation of Reclassifications of Items Out of Accumulated Other Comprehensive Income in ASU No. 2011-05.* ASU No. 2011-12 defers the changes in ASU No. 2011-05 related only to the presentation of reclassification adjustments. Preparers had argued that these reclassification adjustments would be difficult for preparers and might add unnecessary complexity to the financial statements. FASB issued ASU No. 2011-12 to allow sufficient time for it to redeliberate whether an entity should present the effects of reclassification adjustments on the face of the financial statements for all periods presented. While FASB is considering preparers' concerns, entities should continue to report reclassification adjustments in accordance with the requirements of FASB ASC 220 in effect before issuance of ASU No. 2011-05. The amendments in ASU No. 2011-12 are effective at the same time as the amendments in ASU No. 2011-05.

DISCLOSURE

5.56 In addition, FASB ASC 220 allows disclosure of accumulated balances, by component, included in accumulated other comprehensive income in a statement of changes in stockholders' equity.

5.57 FASB ASC 810, *Consolidation*, establishes accounting and reporting standards for the noncontrolling interest in a subsidiary. It clarifies that a *noncontrolling interest in a subsidiary* is an ownership interest in the consolidated entity that should be reported as equity in the consolidated financial statements but separate from the parent's equity, and clearly identified and labeled. In addition, FASB ASC 810 requires expanded disclosures in the consolidated financial statements that clearly identify and distinguish between the interests of the parent's owners and the interests of the noncontrolling owners of a subsidiary. Those expanded disclosures include a reconciliation of the beginning and ending balances of the equity attributable to the parent and noncontrolling owners and a schedule showing the effects of changes in a parent's ownership interest in a subsidiary on the equity attributable to the parent.

5.58

TABLE 5-8: OTHER STOCKHOLDERS' EQUITY ACCOUNTS

Table 5-8 shows the number of survey company balance sheets presenting other stockholders' equity accounts.

	Number of Entities		
	2011	**2010**	**2009**
Noncontrolling interests	261	240	156
Warrants	12	2	30
Unearned compensation	10	12	17
Employee benefit trusts	12	10	11
Guarantees of employee stock ownership plan debt	8	12	10
Receivables from the sale of stock	2	2	3
Other, described	16	20	N/C*

* N/C = Not compiled. Line item was not included in the table for the year shown.

PRESENTATION AND DISCLOSURE EXCERPTS

Unearned Compensation

5.59

THE SHERWIN-WILLIAMS COMPANY (DEC)

CONSOLIDATED BALANCE SHEETS (in part)

(Thousands of dollars)

	December 31		
	2011	**2010**	**2009**
Shareholders' Equity:			
Common stock—$1.00 par value: 103,854,234, 107,020,728 and 109,436,869 shares outstanding at December 31, 2011, 2010 and 2009, respectively	107,454	231,346	228,647
Preferred stock—convertible, no par value: 160,273, 216,753 and 216,753 shares outstanding at December 31, 2011, 2010 and 2009, respectively	160,273	216,753	216,753
Unearned ESOP compensation	(160,273)	(216,753)	(216,753)
Other capital	1,297,625	1,222,909	1,068,963
Retained earnings	756,372	4,824,489	4,518,428
Treasury stock, at cost	(276,654)	(4,390,983)	(4,007,633)
Cumulative other comprehensive loss	(367,878)	(278,321)	(317,455)
Total shareholders' equity	1,516,919	1,609,440	1,490,950

STATEMENTS OF CONSOLIDATED SHAREHOLDERS' EQUITY AND COMPREHENSIVE INCOME

(Thousands of dollars except per common share data)

	Common Stock	Preferred Stock	Unearned ESOP Compen- sation	Other Capital	Retained Earnings	Treasury Stock	Cumulative Other Compre- hensive Loss	Total
Balance at January 1, 2009	$227,147	$216,753	$(216,753)	$1,016,362	$4,245,141	$(3,472,384)	$(410,618)	$1,605,648
Comprehensive income:								
Net income					435,848			435,848
Foreign currency translation							75,622	75,622
Net actuarial gains (losses) and prior service costs recognized for employee benefit plans, net of taxes of ($10,285)							17,168	17,168
Unrealized net gains on securities and derivative instruments used in cash flow hedges, net of taxes of ($144)							373	373
Comprehensive income								529,011
Treasury stock purchased						(530,363)		(530,363)
Income tax effect of ESOP				(13,411)				(13,411)
Stock options exercised	1,071			35,525		(4,886)		31,710
Income tax effect of stock options exercised				7,645				7,645
Restricted stock and stock option grants (net activity)	429			22,842				23,271
Cash dividends–$1.42 per common share					(162,561)			(162,561)
Balance at December 31, 2009	228,647	216,753	(216,753)	1,068,963	4,518,428	(4,007,633)	(317,455)	1,490,950
Comprehensive income:								
Net income					462,485			462,485
Foreign currency translation							25,131	25,131
Net actuarial gains (losses) and prior service costs recognized for employee benefit plans, net of taxes of ($8,948)							13,527	13,527
Unrealized net gains on securities, net of taxes of ($183)							476	476
Comprehensive income								501,619
Treasury stock purchased						(375,677)		(375,677)
Income tax effect of ESOP				(7,515)				(7,515)
Stock options exercised	2,351			99,857		(7,673)		94,535
Income tax effect of stock options exercised				19,676				19,676
Restricted stock and stock option grants (net activity)	348			41,928				42,276
Cash dividends–$1.44 per common share					(156,424)			(156,424)
Balance at December 31, 2010	231,346	216,753	(216,753)	1,222,909	4,824,489	(4,390,983)	(278,321)	1,609,440
Comprehensive income:								
Net income					441,860			441,860
Foreign currency translation							(65,632)	(65,632)
Net actuarial gains (losses) and prior service costs recognized for employee benefit plans, net of taxes of $17,321							(23,370)	(23,370)
Unrealized net losses on securities, net of taxes of $214							(555)	(555)
Comprehensive income								352,303
Treasury stock purchased						(367,372)		(367,372)
Treasury stock retired	(125,426)				(4,356,465)	4,481,891		
Redemption of preferred stock		(56,480)	56,480					
Income tax effect of ESOP*				(54,420)				(54,420)
Stock options exercised	1,234			68,302		(190)		69,346
Income tax effect of stock options exercised				12,958				12,958
Restricted stock and stock option grants (net activity)	300			47,876				48,176
Cash dividends–$1.46 per common share					(153,512)			(153,512)
Balance at December 31, 2011	$107,454	$160,273	$(160,273)	$1,297,625	$756,372	$ (276,654)	$(367,878)	$1,516,919

* Includes $51,209 reduction in Other capital related to IRS Settlement. See Note 15 for more information on the IRS Settlement.

See notes to consolidated financial statements.

NOTES TO CONSOLIDATED FINANCIAL STATEMENTS

(Thousands of dollars unless otherwise indicated)

Note 1—Significant Accounting Policies (in part)

Employee Stock Purchase and Savings Plan and preferred stock. The Company accounts for the Employee Stock Purchase and Savings Plan (ESOP) in accordance with the Employee Stock Ownership Plans Subtopic of the Compensation—Stock Ownership Topic of the ASC. The Company recognized compensation expense for amounts contributed to the ESOP and the ESOP used dividends on unallocated preferred shares to service debt. Unallocated preferred shares held by the ESOP were not considered outstanding in calculating earnings per share of the Company. See Note 12.

Note 12—Stock Purchase Plan And Preferred Stock

As of December 31, 2011, 26,694 employees contributed to the Company's ESOP, a voluntary defined contribution plan available to all eligible salaried employees. Participants are allowed to contribute, on a pretax or after-tax basis, up to the lesser of twenty percent of their annual compensation or the maximum dollar amount allowed under the Internal Revenue Code. Prior to July 1, 2009, the Company matched one hundred percent of all contributions up to six percent of eligible employee contributions. Effective July 1, 2009, the ESOP was amended to change the Company match to one-hundred percent on the first three percent of eligible employee contributions and fifty percent on the next two percent of eligible contributions. Effective July 1, 2011, the ESOP was amended to reinstate the Company match up to six percent of eligible employee contributions. Such participant contributions may be invested in a variety of mutual funds or a Company common stock fund and may be exchanged between investments as directed by the participant. Participants are permitted to diversify both future and prior Company matching contributions previously allocated to the Company common stock fund into a variety of mutual funds.

The Company made contributions to the ESOP on behalf of participating employees, representing amounts authorized by employees to be withheld from their earnings, of $79,266, $70,601 and $70,025 in 2011, 2010 and 2009, respectively. The Company's matching contributions to the ESOP charged to operations were $48,816, $37,894 and $44,587 for 2011, 2010 and 2009, respectively.

At December 31, 2011, there were 16,508,933 shares of the Company's common stock being held by the ESOP, representing 15.9 percent of the total number of voting shares outstanding. Shares of Company common stock credited to each member's account under the ESOP are voted by the trustee under instructions from each individual plan member. Shares for which no instructions are received are voted by the trustee in the same proportion as those for which instructions are received.

On August 1, 2006, the Company issued 500,000 shares of convertible serial preferred stock, no par value (Series 2 Preferred stock) with cumulative quarterly dividends of $11.25 per share, for $500,000 to the ESOP. The ESOP financed the acquisition of the Series 2 Preferred stock by borrowing $500,000 from the Company at the rate of 5.5 percent per annum. This borrowing is payable over ten years in equal quarterly installments. Each share of Series 2 Preferred stock is entitled to one vote upon all matters presented to the Company's shareholders and generally votes with the common stock together as one class. The Series 2 Preferred stock is held by the ESOP in an unallocated account. As the value of compensation expense related to contributions to the ESOP is earned, the Company has the option of funding the ESOP by redeeming a portion of the preferred stock or with cash. Contributions are credited to the members' accounts at the time of funding. The Series 2 Preferred stock is redeemable for cash or convertible into common stock or any combination thereof at the option of the ESOP based on the relative fair value of the Series 2 Preferred and common stock at the time of conversion. At December 31, 2011, 2010 and 2009, there were no allocated or committed-to-be released shares of Series 2 Preferred stock outstanding. In 2011, the Company redeemed 56,480 shares of the Series 2 Preferred stock for cash. In 2010 and 2009, the Company elected to fund the ESOP with cash. The fair value of the Series 2 Preferred stock is based on a conversion/redemption formula outlined in the preferred stock terms and was $328,495, $411,655, and $315,659 at December 31, 2011, 2010, and 2009 respectively.

Note 15—Income Taxes (in part)

The IRS was auditing transactions related to the Company's Leveraged ESOP transactions that were implemented on August 1, 2006 and August 27, 2003. See Note 12. At various times, principal and interest on the debt related to the transactions was forgiven as a mechanism for funding Company contributions of elective deferrals and matching contributions to the ESOP. The Company claimed income tax deductions for the forgiven principal on the debt along with interest and dividends. The benefit related to tax deductions for forgiven principal and interest was reflected in equity and did not flow through the provision for income taxes.

In October 2011, the Company reached a settlement of the IRS' audit of the Company's ESOP. The Company has fully resolved all IRS issues for the 2003 through 2009 tax years relating to the matters challenging the ESOP related federal income tax deductions claimed by the Company and proposing substantial excise taxes and penalties. The settlement (including interest), which resolved all ESOP related tax issues, resulted in an after-tax charge related to federal and state income taxes totaling approximately $74,982, or $.70 per diluted common share, and an additional reduction in Shareholders' equity of approximately $51,209 in the Company's fourth quarter. The Department of Labor's investigation of the Leveraged ESOP Transactions remains open. The Company paid $60,000 of the settlement to the IRS during 2011 and expects to make a final payment of approximately $73,105 during 2012.

Deferred Compensation

5.60

GRIFFON CORPORATION (SEP)

CONSOLIDATED STATEMENTS OF SHAREHOLDERS' EQUITY AND COMPREHENSIVE INCOME (LOSS)

(In thousands)	Common Stock Shares	Common Stock Par Value	Capital in Excess of Par Value	Retained Earnings	Treasury Shares Shares	Treasury Shares Cost	Accumulated Other Comprehensive Income (Loss)	Deferred ESOP & Other Compensation	Total	Comprehensive Income (Loss)
Balance at 9/30/2008	71,567	$17,892	$433,744	$403,284	12,440	$(213,310)	$25,469	$(1,749)	$665,330	
Net income	—	—	—	18,708	—	—	—	—	18,708	$18,708
Common stock issued for options exercised/shares vested	33	7	(7)	—	—	—	—	—	—	
Tax benefit/credit from the exercise/forfeiture of stock options	—	—	217	—	—	—	—	—	217	
Amortization of deferred compensation	—	—	—	—	—	—	—	818	818	
Common stock acquired	—	—	—	—	26	(250)	—	—	(250)	
Restricted stock awards granted, net	1,209	302	(1,034)	—	—	—	—	—	(732)	
ESOP purchase of common stock	—	—	—	—	—	—	—	(4,370)	(4,370)	
ESOP allocation of common stock	—	—	(22)	—	—	—	—	—	(22)	
Stock-based compensation	—	—	4,092	—	—	—	—	53	4,145	
Issuance of common stock pursuant to rights offering, net of financing costs	854	214	1,711	—	—	—	—	—	1,925	
Issuance of convertible debt, net	—	—	(263)	—	—	—	—	—	(263)	
Translation of foreign financial statements	—	—	—	—	—	—	11,836	—	11,836	11,836
Pension OCI, net of tax	—	—	—	—	—	—	(9,135)	—	(9,135)	(9,135)
Balance at 9/30/2009	73,663	18,415	438,438	421,992	12,466	(213,560)	28,170	(5,248)	688,207	$21,409
Net income	—	—	—	9,592	—	—	—	—	9,592	9,592
Common stock issued for options exercised/shares vested	48	13	329	—	—	—	—	—	342	
Tax benefit/credit from the exercise/forfeiture of stock options	—	—	325	—	—	—	—	—	325	
Amortization of deferred compensation	—	—	—	—	—	—	—	744	744	
Restricted stock awards granted, net	630	157	(627)	—	—	—	—	—	(470)	
Issuance of convertible debt, net	—	—	13,694	—	—	—	—	—	13,694	
ESOP allocation of common stock	—	—	266	—	—	—	—	—	266	
Stock-based compensation	—	—	5,765	—	—	—	—	13	5,778	
Issuance of common stock pursuant to acquisition	239	60	2,765	—	—	—	—	—	2,825	
Translation of foreign financial statements	—	—	—	—	—	—	(9,677)	—	(9,677)	(9,677)
Pension OCI, net of tax	—	—	—	—	—	—	(911)	—	(911)	(911)
Balance at 9/30/2010	74,580	18,645	460,955	431,584	12,466	(213,560)	17,582	(4,491)	710,715	$(996)
Net income (loss)	—	—	—	(7,431)	—	—	—	—	(7,431)	$(7,431)
Common stock issued for options exercised/shares vested	339	85	2,425	—	—	—	—	—	2,510	
Tax benefit/credit from the exercise/forfeiture of stock options	—	—	7	—	—	—	—	—	7	
Amortization of deferred compensation	—	—	—	—	—	—	—	668	668	
Common stock acquired	—	—	—	—	1,968	(18,139)	—	—	(18,139)	
Restricted stock awards granted, net	1,265	316	(588)	—	—	—	—	—	(272)	
ESOP purchase of common stock	—	—	—	—	—	—	—	(19,973)	(19,973)	
ESOP allocation of common stock	—	—	173	—	—	—	—	—	173	
Stock-based compensation	—	—	8,956	—	—	—	—	—	8,956	
Translation of foreign financial statements	—	—	—	—	—	—	(11,232)	—	(11,232)	(11,232)
Pension OCI, net of tax	—	—	—	—	—	—	(14,074)	—	(14,074)	(14,074)
Balance at 9/30/2011	76,184	$19,046	$471,928	$424,153	14,434	$(231,699)	$(7,724)	$(23,796)	$651,908	$(32,737)

The accompanying notes to consolidated financial statements are an integral part of these statements.

NOTES TO CONSOLIDATED FINANCIAL STATEMENTS

(Dollars in thousands, except per share data)
(Unless otherwise indicated, all references to years or year-end refer to Griffon's fiscal period ending September 30)

Note 10—Notes Payable, Capitalized Leases and Long-Term Debt (in part)

(d) Griffon's Employee Stock Ownership Plan ("ESOP") entered into a loan agreement in August 2010 to borrow $20,000 over a one-year period, to be used to purchase Griffon common stock in the open market. The loan bears interest at a) LIBOR plus 2.5% or b) the lender's prime rate, at Griffon's option. In November 2011, Griffon converted the outstanding loan to a five-year term; principal is payable in quarterly installments of $250, beginning December 2011, with the remainder due at maturity (November 2016). The loan is secured by shares purchased with the proceeds of the loan, and repayment is guaranteed by Griffon. At September 30, 2011, 1,874,737 shares have been purchased and the outstanding balance was $19,973.

In addition, the ESOP has a loan agreement, guaranteed by Griffon, which requires quarterly principal payments of $156 and interest through the expiration date of September 2012 at which time the $3,900 balance of the loan, and any outstanding interest, will be payable. The primary purpose of this loan was to purchase 547,605 shares of Griffon's common stock in October 2008. The loan is secured by shares purchased with the proceeds of the loan, and repayment is guaranteed by Griffon. The loan bears interest at rates based upon the prime rate or LIBOR. At September 30, 2011, $4,375 was outstanding.

Note 11—Employee Benefit Plans (in part)

Griffon has an ESOP that covers substantially all domestic employees. All employees of Griffon, who are not members of a collective bargaining unit, automatically become eligible to participate in the plan on the October 1st following completion of one year of service. Griffon's securities are allocated to participants' individual accounts based on the proportion of each participant's aggregate compensation (not to exceed $245 for the plan year ended September 30, 2011), bears to the total of all participants' compensation. Shares of the ESOP which have been allocated to employee accounts are charged to expense based on the fair value of the shares transferred and are treated as outstanding in earnings per share. Compensation expense under the ESOP was $841 in 2011, $1,011 in 2010 and $796 in 2009. The cost of the shares held by the ESOP and not yet allocated to employees is reported as a reduction of Shareholders' Equity. The fair value of the unallocated ESOP shares as of September 30, 2011 and 2010 based on the closing stock price of Griffon's stock was $19,761 and $7,640, respectively.

The ESOP shares were as follows:

	At September 30	
	2011	**2010**
Allocated shares	2,158,009	2,213,122
Unallocated shares	2,415,754	626,725
	4,573,763	2,839,847

Stock Compensation

5.61

DONALDSON COMPANY, INC. (JUL)

CONSOLIDATED STATEMENTS OF CHANGES IN SHAREHOLDERS' EQUITY

(Thousands of dollars, except per share amounts)	Common Stock	Additional Paid-In Capital	Retained Earnings	Stock Compensation Plans	Accumulated Other Comprehensive Income (Loss)	Treasury Stock	Total
Balance July 31, 2008	$443,216	$ —	$522,476	$27,065	$112,883	$(365,605)	$740,035
Comprehensive income							
Net earnings			131,907				131,907
Foreign currency translation					(63,385)		(63,385)
Pension liability adjustment, net of deferred taxes					(58,593)		(58,593)
Net loss on cash flow hedging derivatives					(582)		(582)
Comprehensive income							9,347
Treasury stock acquired						(32,773)	(32,773)
Stock options exercised		(2,998)	(6,151)			12,104	2,955
Deferred stock and other activity		(529)	(88)	(4,344)		3,710	(1,251)
Performance awards		(266)	(60)	(2,827)		1,932	(1,221)
Stock option expense			4,143				4,143
Tax reduction—employee plans		3,793					3,793
Adjustment to adopt retirement benefit compensation guidance, net of tax			(887)				(887)
Dividends ($0.460 per share)			(35,523)				(35,523)
Balance July 31, 2009	443,216	—	615,817	19,894	(9,677)	(380,632)	688,618

(continued)

(Thousands of dollars, except per share amounts)	Common Stock	Additional Paid-In Capital	Retained Earnings	Stock Compen-sation Plans	Accumulated Other Comprehensive Income (Loss)	Treasury Stock	Total
Comprehensive income							
Net earnings			$166,163				$166,163
Foreign currency translation					(15,961)		(15,961)
Pension liability adjustment, net of deferred taxes					(14,780)		(14,780)
Net loss on cash flow hedging derivatives					(68)		(68)
Comprehensive income							135,354
Treasury stock acquired						(66,696)	(66,696)
Stock options exercised		(5,608)	(7,678)	2,676		22,951	12,341
Deferred stock and other activity		(704)	(30)	(244)		1,707	729
Performance awards		7	(7)				—
Stock option expense			6,891				6,891
Tax reduction—employee plans		6,305					6,305
Dividends ($0.480 per share)			(36,909)				(36,909)
Balance July 31, 2010	443,216	—	744,247	22,326	(40,486)	(422,670)	746,633
Comprehensive income							
Net earnings			225,291				225,291
Foreign currency translation					72,505		72,505
Pension liability adjustment, net of deferred taxes					7,166		7,166
Net gain on cash flow hedging derivatives					842		842
Comprehensive income							305,804
Treasury stock acquired						(108,929)	(108,929)
Stock options exercised		(10,792)	(7,854)	1,862		30,604	13,820
Deferred stock and other activity		(1,418)	174	548		2,185	1,489
Performance awards		(7)	7				—
Stock option expense			6,462				6,462
Tax reduction—employee plans		12,217					12,217
Dividends ($0.560 per share)			(42,785)				(42,785)
Balance July 31, 2011	$443,216	$ —	$925,542	$24,736	$ 40,027	$(498,810)	$934,711

The accompanying notes are an integral part of these Consolidated Financial Statements.

NOTES TO CONSOLIDATED FINANCIAL STATEMENTS

Note H—Shareholders' Equity (in part)

Stock Compensation Plans The Stock Compensation Plans in the Consolidated Statements of Changes in Shareholders' Equity consist of the balance of amounts payable to eligible participants for stock compensation that was deferred to a Rabbi Trust pursuant to the provisions of the 2010 Master Stock Incentive Plan, as well as performance awards payable in common stock discussed further in Note I.

Note I—Stock Option Plans

Employee Incentive Plans In November 2010 shareholders approved the 2010 Master Stock Incentive Plan (the "Plan") that replaced the 2001 Plan that was scheduled to expire on December 31, 2010 and provided for similar awards. The Plan extends through September 2020 and allows for the granting of nonqualified stock options, incentive stock options, restricted stock, restricted stock units, stock appreciation rights ("SAR"), dividend equivalents, and other stock-based awards. Options under the Plan are granted to key employees at market price at the date of grant. Options are exercisable for up to 10 years from the date of grant. The

Plan also allows for the granting of performance awards to a limited number of key executives. As administered by the Human Resources Committee of the Company's Board of Directors, these performance awards are payable in common stock and are based on a formula which measures performance of the Company over a three-year period. Performance award expense under these plans totaled $1.8 million in Fiscal 2011 and $0.5 million in Fiscal 2010. The Company recorded a net reversal of performance award expense in Fiscal 2009 of $3.1 million due to the reversal of $3.6 million of Long-Term Compensation Plan expense recognized in prior periods based upon actual and forecasted results.

Stock options issued from Fiscal 2001 to Fiscal 2011 become exercisable for non-executives in equal increments over three years. Stock options issued in Fiscal 2011 become exercisable for executives in equal increments over three years. Stock options issued from Fiscal 2001 to Fiscal 2010 became exercisable for most executives immediately upon the date of grant. Certain other stock options issued to executives during Fiscal 2004, 2006, and 2007 became exercisable in equal increments over three years. For Fiscal 2011, the Company recorded pretax compensation expense associated with stock options of $6.5 million and recorded $2.4 million of related tax benefit. For Fiscal 2010 and 2009, the Company recorded pretax compensation expense associated with stock options of $6.9 million and $4.1 million, respectively, and $2.5 million and $1.5 million, respectively, of related tax benefit.

Stock-based employee compensation cost is recognized using the fair-value based method. The Company determined the fair value of these awards using the Black-Scholes option pricing model, with the following weighted average assumptions:

	2011	2010	2009
Risk-free interest rate	<0.12–3.1%	<0.01–3.9%	1.4–4.0%
Expected volatility	25.5–34.7%	24.4–32.3%	21.6–25.5%
Expected dividend yield	1.0%	1.0%	1.0%
Expected life			
Director original grants without reloads	8 years	8 years	8 years
Non-officer original grants	8 years	7–8 years	7 years
Officer original grants with reloads	—	4 years	4 years
Reload grants	<8 years	<8 years	<5 years
Officer original grants without reloads	8 years	8 years	7 years

Reload grants are grants made to officers or directors who exercised a reloadable option during the fiscal year and made payment of the purchase price using shares of previously owned Company stock. The reload grant is for the number of shares equal to the shares used in payment of the purchase price and/or withheld for minimum tax withholding. Beginning in Fiscal 2011 options no longer have a reload provision for officers and directors.

Black-Scholes is a widely accepted stock option pricing model; however, the ultimate value of stock options granted will be determined by the actual lives of options granted and the actual future price levels of the Company's common stock. The weighted average fair value for options granted during Fiscal 2011, 2010, and 2009 is $17.26, $13.23, and $8.56 per share, respectively, using the Black-Scholes pricing model.

The following table summarizes stock option activity:

	Options Outstanding	Weighted Average Exercise Price
Outstanding at July 31, 2008	5,181,778	$25.62
Granted	366,588	34.23
Exercised	(505,363)	17.64
Canceled	(44,878)	39.04
Outstanding at July 31, 2009	4,998,125	26.94
Granted	643,974	42.41
Exercised	(848,990)	20.84
Canceled	(21,297)	41.94
Outstanding at July 31, 2010	4,771,812	30.04
Granted	551,601	57.22
Exercised	(1,121,751)	23.10
Canceled	(7,665)	47.20
Outstanding at July 31, 2011	4,193,997	35.44

The total intrinsic value of options exercised during Fiscal 2011, 2010, and 2009 was $34.2 million, $19.5 million, and $9.1 million, respectively.

Shares reserved at July 31, 2011 for outstanding options and future grants were 8,307,431. Shares reserved consist of shares available for grant plus all outstanding options. Upon shareholder approval of the 2010 Master Stock Incentive Plan, 4,600,000 shares were added to shares reserved. Remaining shares available for grant under the 2001 plan were removed from the shares reserved calculation.

The following table summarizes information concerning outstanding and exercisable options as of July 31, 2011:

Range of Exercise Prices	Number Outstanding	Weighted Average Remaining Contractual Life (Years)	Weighted Average Exercise Price	Number Exercisable	Weighted Average Exercise Price
$12 to $22	658,066	1.19	$17.89	658,066	$17.89
$22 to $32	1,102,423	2.94	30.12	1,086,511	30.09
$32 to $42	1,121,686	5.67	34.95	1,101,164	34.96
$42 and above	1,311,822	8.23	49.15	655,381	44.34
	4,193,997	5.05	35.44	3,501,122	32.00

At July 31, 2011, the aggregate intrinsic value of shares outstanding and exercisable was $85.0 million and $81.9 million, respectively.

SEC 5.61

The following table summarizes the status of options which contain vesting provisions:

	Options	Weighted Average Grant Date Fair Value
Non-vested at July 31, 2010	407,453	$12.89
Granted	482,250	18.45
Vested	(189,913)	12.27
Canceled	(6,915)	15.42
Non-vested at July 31, 2011	692,875	16.90

The total fair value of shares vested during Fiscal 2011, 2010, and 2009 was $10.5 million, $8.0 million, and $7.9 million, respectively.

As of July 31, 2011, there was $6.1 million of total unrecognized compensation cost related to non-vested stock options granted under the Plan. This unvested cost is expected to be recognized during Fiscal 2012, Fiscal 2013, and Fiscal 2014.

Warrants

5.62

LEAR CORPORATION (DEC)

CONSOLIDATED BALANCE SHEETS (in part)

(In millions, except share data)

	Successor	
December 31	2011	2010
Equity:		
Preferred stock, 100,000,000 shares authorized (including 10,896,250 shares of Series A convertible preferred stock authorized); no shares outstanding	—	—
Common stock, $0.01 par value, 300,000,000 shares authorized; 107,486,539 and 105,498,880 shares issued as of December 31, 2011 and 2010, respectively[1]	1.1	1.1
Additional paid-in capital, including warrants to purchase common stock[1]	2,150.6	2,116.0
Common stock held in treasury, 6,799,597 and 322,130 shares as of December 31, 2011 and 2010, respectively, at cost[1]	(305.6)	(13.4)
Retained earnings	922.3	434.5
Accumulated other comprehensive loss	(332.0)	(78.0)
Lear Corporation stockholders' equity	2,436.4	2,460.2
Noncontrolling interests	124.7	108.6
Equity	2,561.1	2,568.8

[1] Share data as of December 31, 2010, has been retroactively adjusted to reflect the two-for-one stock split described in Note 11, "Capital Stock and Equity," to these consolidated financial statements.

NOTES TO CONSOLIDATED FINANCIAL STATEMENTS

(11) Capital Stock and Equity (in part)

Warrants

On November 9, 2009, in connection with the Plan, the Company issued 8,157,249 Warrants. As of December 31, 2011 and 2010, there were 396,102 and 942,333 Warrants outstanding, respectively, exercisable into 792,204 and 1,884,666 shares of common stock (after giving effect to the two-for-one stock split described above). In accordance with GAAP, the Company accounts for the Warrants as equity instruments. The Company estimated the initial fair value of the Warrants issued to be $305.9 million using a Monte Carlo simulation pricing model with the following assumptions (after giving effect to the two-for-one stock split described above): exercise price of $0.005; implied stock price of $19.36; expected volatility of 60.0%; expected dividend rate of 0.0%; risk free interest rate of 2.3%; expiration date of five years and aggregate reorganization value of Successor Common Stock and Warrants of $1,636.2 million. The following is a description of the Warrants:

- *Exercise*—Each Warrant entitles its holder to purchase two shares of common stock at an exercise price of $0.005 per share of common stock (adjusted for the two-for-one stock split described above) (the "Exercise Price"), subject to adjustment. All Warrants are exercisable until November 9, 2014 (warrant expiration date).
- *No Rights as Stockholders*—Prior to the exercise of the Warrants, no holder of Warrants (solely in its capacity as a holder of Warrants) is entitled to any rights as a stockholder of the Company, including, without limitation, the right to vote, receive notice of any meeting of stockholders or receive dividends, allotments or other distributions.
- *Adjustments*—The number of shares of common stock for which a Warrant is exercisable, the Exercise Price and the Trigger Price (as defined in the warrant agreement) will be subject to adjustment from time to time upon the occurrence of certain events, including an increase in the number of outstanding shares of common stock by means of a dividend consisting of shares of common stock, a subdivision of the Company's outstanding shares of common stock into a larger number of shares of common stock or a combination of the Company's outstanding shares of common stock into a smaller number of shares of common stock. In addition, upon the occurrence of certain events constituting a reorganization, recapitalization, reclassification, consolidation, merger or similar event, each holder of a Warrant will have the right to receive, upon exercise of a Warrant (if then exercisable), an amount of securities, cash or other property receivable by a holder of the number of shares of common stock for which a Warrant is exercisable immediately prior to such event.

Noncontrolling Interest

5.63

GREIF, INC. (OCT)

CONSOLIDATED STATEMENTS OF CHANGES IN SHAREHOLDERS' EQUITY

(Amounts in thousands, except per share amounts)

	Capital Stock		Treasury Stock		Retained Earnings	Non-Controlling Interests	Accumulated Other Comprehensive Income (Loss)	Share-holders' Equity
	Shares	Amount	Shares	Amount				
As of October 31, 2008 (as previously reported)	46,644	$86,446	30,198	$(112,931)	$1,183,925	$3,729	$(72,820)	$1,088,349
Correction of an error							$(19,547)	$ (19,547)
As of October 31, 2008 (as restated)(1)	46,644	$86,446	30,198	$(112,931)	$1,183,925	$3,729	$(92,367)	$1,068,802
Net income					110,646	3,186		113,832
Other comprehensive income (loss):								
—foreign currency translation							32,868	32,868
—interest rate and other derivatives, net of income tax expense of $1,707							4,226	4,226
—minimum pension liability adjustment, net of income tax benefit of $28,580							(51,092)	(51,092)
Comprehensive income								99,834
Change in pension measurement date, net of income tax benefit of $590							(1,428)	(1,428)
Acquisitions of noncontrolling interests and other						82		82
Dividends paid					(87,957)			(87,957)
Treasury shares acquired	(100)		100	(3,145)				(3,145)
Stock options exercised	133	1,749	(133)	266				2,015
Tax benefit of stock options		575						575
Long-term incentive shares issued	260	7,734	(260)	533				8,267
As of October 31, 2009 (as restated)(1)	46,937	$96,504	29,905	$(115,277)	$1,206,614	$6,997	$(107,793)	$1,087,045
Net income					209,985	5,472		215,457
Other comprehensive income (loss):								
—foreign currency translation							26,760	26,760
—interest rate and other derivatives, net of income tax expense of $149							370	370
—minimum pension liability adjustment, net of income tax benefit of $1,279							3,020	3,020
Comprehensive income								245,607
Acquisitions and noncontrolling interests and other						88,919		88,919
Dividends paid					(93,122)			(93,122)
Treasury shares acquired	(50)		50	(2,696)				(2,696)
Stock options exercised	133	1,729	(133)	273				2,002
Tax benefit of stock options		17						17
Long-term incentive shares issued	149	7,807	(149)	306				8,113

(continued)

	Capital Stock		Treasury Stock		Retained Earnings	Non-Controlling Interests	Accumulated Other Comprehensive Income (Loss)	Share-holders' Equity
	Shares	Amount	Shares	Amount				
As of October 31, 2010 (as restated)[1]	47,169	$106,057	29,673	$(117,394)	$1,323,477	$101,388	$(77,643)	$1,335,885
Net income					176,040	1,134		177,174
Other comprehensive income (loss):								
—foreign currency translation						14,572	(46,742)	(32,170)
—interest rate and other derivatives, net of income tax benefit of $562							1,384	1,384
—minimum pension liability adjustment, net of income tax expense of $9,652							(25,150)	(25,150)
Comprehensive income								121,238
Acquisitions and noncontrolling interests						39,728		39,728
Dividends paid					(97,817)			(97,817)
Treasury shares acquired	(300)		300	(15,062)				(15,062)
Stock options exercised	168	2,196	(168)	344				2,540
Restricted stock directors	11	697	(11)	22				719
Restricted stock executives	5	308	(5)	10				318
Tax benefit of stock options and other		2,192						2,192
Long-term incentive shares issued	40	2,349	(40)	83				2,432
As of October 31, 2011	47,093	$113,799	29,749	$(131,997)	$1,401,700	$156,822	$(148,151)	$1,392,173

[1] The consolidated balance sheet as of October 31, 2010 and the consolidated statements of changes in shareholders' equity as of October 31, 2009 and 2010 have been restated to correct prior period errors. The corrections did not impact total assets, consolidated net income, or cash flows of the Company. Refer to Note 19 for additional discussion.

Refer to the accompanying Notes to Consolidated Financial Statements.

NOTES TO CONSOLIDATED FINANCIAL STATEMENTS

Note 1—Basis of Presentation and Summary of Significant Accounting Policies (in part)

Equity Earnings (Losses) of Unconsolidated Affiliates, Net of Tax and Noncontrolling Interests Including Variable Interest Entities (in part)

The Company accounts for equity earnings (losses) of unconsolidated affiliates, net of tax and noncontrolling interests under ASC 810, "Consolidation." ASC 810 establishes accounting and reporting standards for the noncontrolling interest in a subsidiary and for the deconsolidation of a subsidiary. ASC 810 also changes the way the consolidated financial statements are presented, establishes a single method of accounting for changes in a parent's ownership interest in a subsidiary that do not result in deconsolidation, requires that a parent recognize a gain or loss in net income when a subsidiary is deconsolidated and expands disclosures in the consolidated financial statements that clearly identify and distinguish between the parent's ownership interest and the interest of the noncontrolling owners of a subsidiary. Refer to Note 16 for additional information regarding the Company's unconsolidated affiliates and noncontrolling interests.

On September 29, 2010, Greif, Inc. and its indirect subsidiary Greif International Holding Supra C.V. ("Greif Supra"), a Netherlands limited partnership, completed a Joint Venture Agreement with Dabbagh Group Holding Company Limited ("Dabbagh"), a Saudi Arabia corporation and Na-

tional Scientific Company Limited ("NSC"), a Saudi Arabia limited liability company and a subsidiary of Dabbagh, referred to herein as the Flexible Packaging JV. The joint venture owns the operations in the Flexible Products & Services segment, with the exception of the North American multi-wall bag business. Greif Supra and NSC have equal economic interests in the joint venture, notwithstanding the actual ownership interests in the various legal entities. All investments, loans and capital injections are shared 50 percent by Greif and the Dabbagh entities. Greif has deemed this joint venture to be a VIE based on the criteria outlined in ASC 810. Greif exercises management control over this joint venture and is the primary beneficiary due to supply agreements and broader packaging industry customer risks and rewards. Therefore, Greif has fully consolidated the operations of this joint venture as of the formation date of September 29, 2010 and has reported Dabbagh's share in the profits and losses in this joint venture as from this date on the Company's income statement under net income attributable to noncontrolling interests.

Note 16—Equity Earnings (Losses) of Unconsolidated Affiliates, Net of Tax and Net Income Attributable to Noncontrolling Interests (in part)

Net Income Attributable to Noncontrolling Interests

Net income attributable to noncontrolling interests represent the portion of earnings or losses from the operations of the Company's consolidated subsidiaries attributable to unrelated third party equity owners that were deducted from net income to arrive at net income attributable to the Company. One of the companies acquired in 2011 is a joint venture. The

Company does not own 100 percent of this acquired company, and it is not a VIE. The Company does, however, exert control over this acquired company, and accordingly, the operations of this acquired company are consolidated with the Company's operations. Noncontrolling interests from this acquisition were recorded for $25.9 million for the year ended October 31, 2011. Net income attributable to noncontrolling interests for the years ended October 31, 2011, 2010 and 2009 was $1.1 million, $5.5 million and $3.2 million, respectively.

Section 6: Statement of Cash Flows

GENERAL

PRESENTATION

6.01   Financial Accounting Standards Board (FASB) *Accounting Standards Codification* (ASC) 230, *Statement of Cash Flows*, requires entities to present a statement of cash flows that classifies cash receipts and payments by operating, investing, and financing activities. The information provided in a statement of cash flows, if used with related disclosures and information in the other financial statements, should help investors, creditors, and others do the following:
- Assess the entity's ability to generate positive future net cash flows
- Assess the entity's ability to meet its obligations, its ability to pay dividends, and its needs for external financing
- Assess the reasons for differences between net income and associated cash receipts and payments
- Assess the effects on an entity's financial position of both its cash and noncash investing and financing transactions during the period

6.02   Paragraphs 4–6 of FASB ASC 230-10-45 provide that the statement of cash flows explains the change in cash and cash equivalents during a period. *Cash equivalents* are defined by the FASB ASC glossary to be short-term, highly liquid investments that have both of the following characteristics:
- Readily convertible to known amounts of cash
- So near their maturity that they present an insignificant risk of changes in value because of changes in interest rates

Generally, only investments with original maturities of three months or less qualify under that definition. *Original maturity* means original maturity to the entity holding the investment.

6.03   FASB ASC 230-10-45 states that the amount of cash and cash equivalents at the beginning and end of the period reported on a statement of cash flows should agree with the amount of cash and cash equivalents reported on a statement of financial position. Because not all investments that qualify are required to be treated as cash equivalents, an entity should establish a policy concerning which short-term, highly liquid investments that satisfy the definition of *cash equivalents* are treated as such.

6.04   Paragraphs 7–9 of FASB ASC 230-10-45 explain that generally, cash receipts and payments should be reported separately and not netted. For certain items, the turnover is quick, the amounts are large, and the maturities are short. For certain other items, such as demand deposits of a bank and customer accounts payable of a broker-dealer, the entity is substantively holding or disbursing cash on behalf of its customers. Only the net changes during the period in assets and liabilities with those characteristics need be reported because knowledge of the gross cash receipts and payments related to them may not be necessary to understand the entity's operating, investing, and financing activities. Specifically, provided that the original maturity of the asset or liability is three months or less, cash receipts and payments pertaining to investments (other than cash equivalents), loans receivable, and debt qualify for net reporting based on this rationale.

6.05   FASB ASC 830-230-45-1 specifies that the effect of exchange rate changes on cash balances held in foreign currencies be reported as a separate part of the reconciliation of the change in cash and cash equivalents during the period in the statement of cash flows. Further, a statement of cash flows of an entity with foreign exchange transactions or foreign operations should report the reporting currency equivalent of foreign currency cash flows using the exchange rates in effect at the time of the cash flows. An appropriately weighted average exchange rate for the period may be used for translation if the result is substantially the same as if the rates at the dates of the cash flows were used.

DISCLOSURE

6.06   FASB ASC 230-10-50-1 explains that an entity should disclose its policy regarding cash equivalent classification, and any change to that policy is a change in accounting principle that should be affected by restating financial statements for earlier years presented for comparative purposes. If the indirect method is used, amounts of interest (net of capitalized amounts) and income tax payments during the period are required to be disclosed.

6.07   Paragraphs 3–6 of FASB ASC 230-10-50 require the disclosure of information about noncash investing and financing activities. Examples of noncash investing and financing transactions include converting debt to equity; acquiring assets by assuming directly-related liabilities, such as purchasing a building by incurring a mortgage to the seller: obtaining an asset by entering into a capital lease; obtaining a building or investment asset by receiving a gift; and exchanging noncash assets or liabilities for other noncash assets or liabilities. If only a few noncash transactions exist, it may be convenient to include them on the same page as the statement of cash flows. Otherwise, the transactions may be reported elsewhere in the financial statements and clearly referenced to the statement of cash flow.

6.08

TABLE 6-1: PRESENTATION OF INTEREST AND INCOME TAX PAYMENTS

Table 6-1 shows where in the financial statements interest and income tax payments are disclosed.

	2011	2010	2009
Interest Payments			
Notes to financial statements............................	207	219	244
Bottom of statement of cash flows..................	257	243	235
Within statement of cash flows........................	7	9	6
Amount not disclosed......................................	29	29	15
Total Entities...	**500**	**500**	**500**
Income Tax Payments			
Notes to financial statements............................	207	223	252
Bottom of statement of cash flows..................	262	249	241
Within statement of cash flows........................	7	11	7
Amount not disclosed......................................	24	17	—
Total Entities...	**500**	**500**	**500**

PRESENTATION AND DISCLOSURE EXCERPTS

Cash and Cash Equivalents

6.09

THE SHAW GROUP INC. (AUG)

CONSOLIDATED BALANCE SHEETS (in part)

	At August 31	
(In thousands, except share amounts)	2011	2010
Assets		
Current assets:		
Cash and cash equivalents ($78.6 million and $82.3 million related to variable interest entities (VIEs))	$ 674,080	$ 912,736
Restricted and escrowed cash and cash equivalents ($0.0 million and $4.5 million related to VIEs)	38,721	33,926
Short-term investments ($7.8 million and $10.1 million related to VIEs)	226,936	551,960
Restricted short-term investments	277,316	321,056
Accounts receivable, including retainage, net ($7.5 million and $28.3 million related to VIEs)	772,242	833,574
Inventories	245,044	228,891
Costs and estimated earnings in excess of billings on uncompleted contracts, including claims	552,502	637,651
Deferred income taxes	367,045	319,712
Investment in Westinghouse	999,035	967,916
Prepaid expenses and other current assets	138,260	64,468
Total current assets	4,291,181	4,871,890

NOTES TO CONSOLIDATED FINANCIAL STATEMENTS

Note 2—Cash, Cash Equivalents and Short-Term Investments

Our major types of investments are as follows:

Money market mutual funds—We invest in money market funds that seek to maintain a stable net asset value of $1 per share, while limiting overall exposure to credit, market and liquidity risks.

Certificates of deposit—Certificates of deposit are short-term interest-bearing debt instruments issued by various financial institutions with which we have an established banking relationship.

Foreign government and foreign government guaranteed securities—We invest in foreign government and foreign government guaranteed securities that are publicly traded and valued.

Corporate bonds—We evaluate our corporate debt securities based on a variety of factors including, but not limited to, the credit rating of the issuer. Our corporate debt securities are publicly traded debt rated at least A/A2 or better by S&P and/or Moody's, respectively, with maturities up to two years at the time of purchase. Losses in this category are due primarily to market liquidity.

At August 31, 2011, the components of our cash, cash equivalents, and short-term investments were as follows (in thousands):

| | Cost Basis | Unrealized Gain | Unrealized (Loss) | Recorded Basis | Balance Sheet Classifications | |
					Cash and Cash Equivalents	Short-Term Investments
Cash	$653,979	$—	$ —	$653,979	$653,979	$ —
Money market mutual funds	17,350	—	—	17,350	17,350	—
Certificates of deposit	211,910	—	—	211,910	2,751	209,159
Available-for-sale securities:						
Corporate bonds	17,853	40	(116)	17,777	—	17,777
Total	$901,092	$40	$(116)	$901,016	$674,080	$226,936

At August 31, 2010, the components of our cash, cash equivalents, and short-term investments were as follows (in thousands):

| | Cost Basis | Unrealized Gain | Unrealized (Loss) | Recorded Basis | Balance Sheet Classifications | |
					Cash and Cash Equivalents	Short-Term Investments
Cash	$ 401,277	$ —	$ —	$ 401,277	$401,277	$ —
Money market mutual funds	509,781	—	—	509,781	509,781	—
Certificates of deposit	325,668	—	—	325,668	1,678	323,990
Available-for-sale securities:						
Bond mutual funds	75,236	738	—	75,974	—	75,974
Foreign government and foreign government guaranteed securities	42,570	217	—	42,787	—	42,787
Corporate bonds	109,270	320	(381)	109,209	—	109,209
Total	$1,463,802	$1,275	$(381)	$1,464,696	$912,736	$551,960

Gross realized gains and losses from sales of available-for-sale securities are determined using the specific identification method and are included in other income (expense), net. During the fiscal year ending August 31, 2011, the proceeds and realized gains and losses were as follows (in thousands):

Proceeds	$389,837
Realized gains	$ 1,171
Realized losses	$ 3,925

There were no transfers of securities between available for sale and trading classifications during the fiscal year ending August 31, 2011.

We evaluate whether unrealized losses on investments in securities are other-than-temporary, and if we believe the unrealized losses are other-than-temporary, we record an impairment charge. There were no material other-than-temporary impairment losses recognized during the fiscal ending August 31, 2011.

Gross unrealized losses on investment securities and the fair value of those securities that have been in a continuous loss position for which we have not recognized an impairment charge at August 31, 2011, were as follows (in thousands):

| | Less Than 12 Months | |
	Fair Value	Unrealized Loss
Available-for-sale:		
Corporate bonds	1,889	(39)
	$1,889	$(39)

At August 31, 2011, maturities of debt securities classified as available-for-sale were as follows (in thousands):

	Cost Basis	Estimated Fair Value
Due in one year or less	$15,770	$15,715
Due in one to two years	2,083	2,062
	$17,853	$17,777

Note 3—Restricted and Escrowed Cash and Cash Equivalents and Restricted Short-Term Investments

At August 31, 2011, the components of our restricted and escrowed cash and cash equivalents and restricted short-term investments were as follows (in thousands):

	Recorded Basis	Holding Period (Loss)	Balance Sheet Classification	
			Restricted and Escrowed Cash and Cash Equivalents	Restricted Short-Term Investments
Cash	$ 16,358	$ —	$16,358	$ —
Money market mutual funds	22,363	—	22,363	—
Certificates of deposit	252,627	—	—	252,627
Trading securities:				
Stock and bond mutual funds	6,473	272	—	6,473
U.S. government and agency securities	1,806	(82)	—	1,806
Corporate bonds	16,410	(390)	—	16,410
Total	$316,037	$(200)	$38,721	$277,316

At August 31, 2010, the components of our restricted and escrowed cash and cash equivalents and restricted short-term investments were as follows (in thousands):

	Recorded Basis	Holding Period (Loss)	Balance Sheet Classification	
			Restricted and Escrowed Cash and Cash Equivalents	Restricted Short-Term Investments
Cash	$ 7,769	$ —	$ 7,769	$ —
Money market mutual funds	26,157	—	26,157	—
Certificates of deposit	296,874	—	—	296,874
Trading securities:				
Stock and bond mutual funds	6,156	101	—	6,156
U.S. government and agency securities	4,350	(127)	—	4,350
Corporate bonds	13,676	(304)	—	13,676
Total	$354,982	$(330)	$33,926	$321,056

Our restricted and escrowed cash and cash equivalents and restricted short-term investments were restricted for the following (in thousands):

	August 31, 2011	August 31, 2010
Contractually required by projects	$ 14,696	$ 6,232
Voluntarily used to secure letters of credit	252,628	296,873
Secure contingent obligations in lieu of letters of credit	20,626	23,353
Assets held in trust and other	28,087	28,524
	$316,037	$354,982

We voluntarily cash collateralize certain letters of credit if the bank fees avoided on those letters of credit exceed the return on other investment opportunities. We are able to access cash we have pledged to secure various letters of credit by replacing them with letters of credit issued under our Credit Facility. See Note 10—Debt and Revolving Lines of Credit for additional information.

Foreign Currency Cash Flows

6.10

HARMAN INTERNATIONAL INDUSTRIES, INCORPORATED (JUN)

CONSOLIDATED STATEMENTS OF CASH FLOWS (in part)

	Year Ended June 30		
(In thousands)	2011	2010	2009
Net cash provided by operating activities	331,750	240,439	74,451
Net cash (used in) provided by investing activities	(434,500)	66,701	(67,012)
Net cash (used in) provided by financing activities	(8,378)	(222,260)	375,986
Effect of exchange rate changes on cash	69,450	(25,669)	(20,175)
Net (decrease) increase in cash and cash equivalents	(41,678)	59,211	363,250
Cash and cash equivalents at beginning of period	645,570	586,359	223,109
Cash and cash equivalents at end of period	$603,892	$645,570	$586,359

NOTES TO THE CONSOLIDATED FINANCIAL STATEMENTS

(Dollars in thousands, except per-share data and unless otherwise indicated)

Note 1—Summary of Significant Accounting Policies (in part)

Foreign Currency Translation: The financial statements of subsidiaries located outside of the United States generally are measured using the local currency as the functional currency. Assets, including goodwill, and liabilities of these subsidiaries are translated at the rates of exchange at the balance sheet date. The resulting translation adjustments are included in accumulated other comprehensive income ("AOCI") in our Consolidated Balance Sheets. Income, expense and cash flow items are translated at average monthly exchange rates. Gains and losses from foreign currency transactions of these subsidiaries are included in net income attributable to Harman International Industries, Incorporated in our Consolidated Statements of Operations.

Derivative Financial Instruments: We are exposed to market risks from changes in foreign currency exchange rates and interest rates which could affect our operating results, financial condition and cash flows. We manage our exposure to these risks through our regular operating and financial activities and when appropriate, through the use of derivative financial instruments. These derivatives are utilized to hedge economic exposures, as well as to reduce earnings and cash flow volatility resulting from shifts in market rates. We enter into limited types of derivative contracts, including foreign currency spot and forward and option contracts and an interest rate swap, to manage foreign currency and interest rate exposures. Our primary foreign currency exposure is the Euro. The fair market value of all our derivative contracts change with fluctuations in interest rates and currency rates, and are designed so that changes in their values are offset by changes in the values of the underlying exposures. Derivative financial instruments are held solely as risk management tools and not for trading or speculative purposes. We do not utilize derivatives that contain leverage features. On the date that we enter into a derivative that qualifies for hedge accounting, the derivative is designated as a hedge of the identified exposure. We document all relationships between hedging instruments and hedged items for which we apply hedge accounting treatment and assess the effectiveness of our hedges at inception and on an ongoing basis.

We record all derivative instruments as either assets or liabilities at fair value in our Consolidated Balance Sheets. Certain of these derivative contracts have been designated as cash flow hedges, whereby gains and losses are reported within AOCI in our Consolidated Balance Sheets, until the underlying transaction occurs, at which point they are reported in earnings as gains or losses in our Consolidated Statements of Operations. Certain of our derivatives, for which hedge accounting is not applied, are effective as economic hedges. These derivative contracts are required to be recognized each period at fair value, with gains and losses reported in earnings in our Consolidated Statements of Operations and therefore do result in some level of earnings volatility. The level of volatility will vary with the type and amount of derivative hedges outstanding, as well as fluctuations in the currency and interest rate markets during the period. The related cash flow impacts of all our derivative activities are reflected as cash flows from operating activities in our Consolidated Statements of Cash Flows. Refer to Note 10—*Derivatives* for more information.

Foreign Currency Management: The fair value of foreign currency related derivatives is included in our Consolidated Balance Sheets in other current assets and accrued liabilities. The earnings impact of cash flow hedges relating to forecasted purchases of inventory in foreign currency is reported in cost of sales to match the underlying transaction being hedged. Unrealized gains and losses on these instruments are deferred in AOCI in our Consolidated Balance Sheets until the underlying transaction is recognized in earnings. The earnings impact of cash flow hedges relating to the variability in cash flows associated with foreign currency denominated assets and liabilities is reported in cost of sales, SG&A or other expense in our Consolidated Statements of Operations, depending on the nature of the assets or liabilities being hedged. The amounts deferred in AOCI in our Consolidated Balance Sheets associated with these instruments relate to spot-to-spot foreign currency differentials from the date of designation until the hedged transaction takes place.

Note 10—Derivatives

We are exposed to market risk from changes in foreign currency exchange rates and interest rates, which could affect our operating results, financial condition and cash flows. We manage our exposure to these risks through our regular operating and financial activities and, when appropriate, through the use of derivative financial instruments. These derivative instruments are utilized to hedge economic exposures, as well as to reduce earnings and cash flow volatility resulting from shifts in market rates. We enter into limited types of derivative contracts, including foreign currency spot, forward and option contracts and an interest rate swap, to manage foreign currency and interest rate exposures. Our primary foreign currency exposure is the Euro. The fair market values of all our derivative contracts change with fluctuations in interest rates and currency rates and are designed so that any changes in their values are offset by changes in the values of the underlying exposures. Derivative financial instruments are held solely as risk management tools and not for trading or speculative purposes.

We record all derivative instruments as either assets or liabilities at fair value in our Consolidated Balance Sheets. Certain of these derivative contracts have been designated as cash flow hedges, whereby gains and losses are reported within AOCI in our Consolidated Balance Sheets, until the underlying transaction occurs, at which point they are reported in earnings as gains and losses in our Consolidated Statements of Operations. Certain of our derivatives, for which hedge accounting is not applied, are effective as economic hedges. These derivative contracts are required to be recognized each period at fair value, with gains and losses reported in earnings in our Consolidated Statements of Operations and therefore do result in some level of earnings volatility. The level of volatility will vary with the type and amount of derivative hedges outstanding, as well as fluctuations in the currency and interest rate markets during the period. The related cash flow impacts of all our derivative activities are reflected as cash flows from operating activities.

Derivatives, by their nature, involve varying degrees of market and credit risk. The market risk associated with these instruments resulting from currency exchange and interest rate movements is expected to offset the market risk of the underlying transactions, assets and liabilities being hedged. We do not believe there is significant risk of loss in the event of non-performance by the counterparties associated with these instruments, because these transactions are executed with a diversified group of major financial institutions. Furthermore, our policy is to contract only with counterparties having a minimum investment grade or better credit rating. Credit risk is managed through the continuous monitoring of exposure to such counterparties.

Foreign Exchange Risk Management

We use foreign exchange contracts to hedge the price risk associated with foreign denominated forecasted purchases of materials used in our manufacturing process and to manage currency risk associated with operating costs in certain operating units, including foreign currency denominated intercompany loans and other foreign currency denominated assets. These contracts generally mature in one year or less. A portion of these contracts are designated as cash flow hedges.

At June 30, 2011 and 2010, we had outstanding foreign exchange contracts, including forward and option contracts, which are summarized below:

	June 30, 2011		June 30, 2010	
	Gross Notional Value	Fair Value Asset/ (Liability)[1]	Gross Notional Value	Fair Value Asset/ (Liability)[1]
Currency Hedged (Buy/Sell):				
U.S. Dollar/Euro	$612,400	$(33,760)	$511,600	$25,852
Swiss Franc/U.S. Dollar	41,647	516	13,922	922
British Pound/U.S. Dollar	20,700	(152)	0	0
British Pound/Swiss Franc	15,408	(574)	0	0
Euro/British Pound	11,604	163	7,343	(32)
U.S. Dollar/Brazilian Real	10,400	(1,249)	0	0
U.S. Dollar/British Pound	8,500	(76)	2,250	(52)
Chinese Yuan/U.S. Dollar	6,188	84	0	0
Euro/U.S. Dollar	8,200	146	1,378	(123)
U.S. Dollar/Japanese Yen	900	(22)	900	(55)
Japanese Yen/Euro	0	0	6,786	137
Swiss Franc/Euro	0	0	9,282	772
Swedish Krona/Euro	0	0	5,389	7
Danish Krone/Euro	0	0	1,150	10
Total	$735,947	$(34,924)	$560,000	$27,438

[1] Represents the net receivable/(payable) included in our Consolidated Balance Sheets.

Cash Flow Hedges

We designate a portion of our foreign exchange contracts as cash flow hedges of foreign currency denominated purchases. As of June 30, 2011 and June 30, 2010, we had $528.4 million and $511.6 million of forward and option contracts maturing through June 2012 and June 2011, respectively. These contracts are recorded at fair value in the accompanying Consolidated Balance Sheets. The changes in fair value for these contracts on a spot to spot basis are reported in AOCI and are reclassified to either Cost of sales or SG&A, depending on the nature of the underlying asset or liability that is being hedged, in our Consolidated Statements of Operations, in the period or periods during which the underlying transaction occurs. If it becomes apparent that an underlying forecasted transaction will not occur, the amount recorded in AOCI related to the hedge is reclassified to Miscellaneous, net, in our Consolidated Statements of Operations, in the then-current period. Amounts relating to such reclassifications were immaterial for the years ended June 30, 2011, 2010 and 2009.

Changes in the fair value of the derivatives are highly effective in offsetting changes in the cash flows of the hedged items because the amounts and the maturities of the derivatives approximate those of the forecasted exposures. Any ineffective portion of the derivative is recognized in the current period in our Consolidated Statements of Operations, in the same line item in which the foreign currency gain or loss on the underlying hedged transaction was recorded. We recognized less than $0.1 million of ineffectiveness in our Consolidated Statements of Operations for each of the fiscal years ended June 30, 2011, 2010 and 2009 and all components of each derivative's gain or loss, with the exception of forward points (see below), were included in the assessment of hedge ineffectiveness. At June 30, 2011 and 2010, the fair value of these contracts was a net liability of $25.2 million and a net asset of $21.5 million, respectively. The amount associated with these hedges that is expected to be reclassified from AOCI to earnings within the next 12 months is a loss of $29.4 million.

We elected to exclude forward points from the effectiveness assessment. At the end of the reporting period we calculate the excluded amount, which is the fair value relating to the change in forward points that is recorded in current earnings as Miscellaneous, net in our Consolidated Statements of Operations. For the years ended June 30, 2011, 2010 and 2009, we recognized $1.2 million, $0.1 million and $2.4 million, respectively, in net gains related to the change in forward points.

Economic Hedges

When hedge accounting is not applied to derivative contracts, or after former cash flow hedges have been de-designated as balance sheet hedges, we recognize the gain or loss on the associated contracts directly in current period earnings in either Miscellaneous, net or Cost of sales according to the underlying exposure in our Consolidated Statements of Operations as unrealized exchange gains and losses. As of June 30, 2011 and 2010, we had $207.5 million and $47.5 million, respectively, of forward contracts maturing through June 2012 and November 2010, respectively, in various currencies to hedge foreign currency denominated intercompany loans and other foreign currency denominated assets. At June 30, 2011 and 2010, the fair value of these contracts was a liability of $9.7 million and $1.6 million, respectively. Adjustments to the carrying value of the foreign currency forward contracts offset the gains and losses on the underlying loans and other foreign denominated assets in Miscellaneous, net.

Interest Rate Risk Management

We have one interest rate swap contract with a notional amount of $24.5 million and $21.7 million at June 30, 2011 and 2010, respectively, in order to manage our interest rate exposure and effectively convert interest on an operating lease from a variable rate to a fixed rate. The objective of the swap is to offset changes in rent expenses caused by interest rate fluctuations. The interest rate swap contract is designated as a cash flow hedge. At the end of each reporting period, the discounted fair value of the swap contract is calculated and recorded in AOCI and reclassified to rent expense, within SG&A in our Consolidated Statements of Operations, in the then current period. If the hedge is determined to be ineffective, the ineffective portion will be reclassified from AOCI and recorded as rent expense, within SG&A. We recognized less than $0.1 million of ineffectiveness in our Consolidated Statements of Operations in each of the fiscal years ended June 30, 2011, 2010 and 2009. All components of the derivative loss were included in the assessment of the hedges effectiveness. The amount associated with the swap contract that is expected to be recorded as rent expense in the next 12 months is a loss of $0.8 million.

Fair Value of Derivatives

The following tables provide a summary of the fair value amounts of our derivative instruments as of June 30, 2011 and 2010:

	Balance Sheet Location	Fair Value June 30, 2011	Fair Value June 30, 2010
Derivatives Designated as Cash Flow Hedges, Gross:			
Other assets:			
Foreign exchange contracts	Other current assets	$ 95	$24,969
Other liabilities:			
Foreign exchange contracts	Accrued liabilities	25,335	3,429
Interest rate swap	Accrued liabilities	625	709
Interest rate swap	Other non-current liabilities	554	1,129
Total liabilities		26,514	5,267
Net (liability) asset for derivatives designated as hedging instruments		(26,419)	19,702
Derivatives Designated as Economic Hedges, Gross:			
Other assets:			
Foreign exchange contracts	Other current assets	1,032	6,223
Other liabilities:			
Foreign exchange contracts	Accrued liabilities	10,716	325
Net (liability) asset for economic hedges:		(9,684)	5,898
Total net derivative (liability) asset		$(36,103)	$25,600

Derivative Activity:

The following tables show derivative activity for derivatives designated as cash flow hedges for the years ended June 30, 2011, 2010 and 2009:

Derivative	Location of Derivative Gain/(Loss) Recognized in Income	Gain/(Loss) Reclassified From AOCI Into Income (Effective Portion) 2011	2010	2009	Gain/(Loss) Recognized in Income on Derivatives (Ineffective Portion) 2011	2010	2009	Gain/(Loss) from Amounts Excluded From Effectiveness Testing 2011	2010	2009
Foreign exchange contracts	Cost of sales	$(34,063)	$(2,028)	$4,890	$ 0	$ 0	$ 0	$ 15	$ 19	$ 0
Foreign exchange contracts	SG&A	0	2,203	347	21	14	0	(330)	(231)	(71)
Foreign exchange contracts	Other expense	0	0	0	0	0	0	0	0	(1,160)
Interest rate swap	Rent expense	(758)	(827)	(51)	(9)	(8)	(6)	0	0	0
Total cash flow hedges		$(34,821)	$ (652)	$5,186	$12	$ 6	$(6)	$(315)	$(212)	$(1,231)

(Years Ended June 30)

| | Gain/(Loss) Recognized in OCI (Effective Portion) | | |
| | Years Ended June 30 | | |
Derivative	2011	2010	2009
Foreign exchange contracts	$(82,165)	$27,967	$(5,355)
Interest rate swap	(105)	(983)	(2,666)
Total cash flow hedges	$(82,270)	$26,984	$(8,021)

The following table summarizes gains and losses from our derivative instruments that are not designated as hedging instruments for the years ended June 30, 2011, 2010 and 2009:

| | Location of Derivative | Years Ended June 30 | | |
Derivative	Gain/(Loss)	2011	2010	2009
Foreign exchange contracts	Other expense	$(1,938)	$3,357	$ 0
Foreign exchange contracts	Cost of sales	$ (260)	$ 311	$(287)

Interest and Income Tax Payments

6.11

3M COMPANY (DEC)

CONSOLIDATED STATEMENT OF CASH FLOWS

Years ended December 31

(Millions)	2011	2010	2009
Cash Flows From Operating Activities			
Net income including noncontrolling interest	$ 4,357	$ 4,163	$ 3,244
Adjustments to reconcile net income including noncontrolling interest to net cash provided by operating activities			
Depreciation and amortization	1,236	1,120	1,157
Company pension and postretirement contributions	(582)	(618)	(792)
Company pension and postretirement expense	555	322	223
Stock-based compensation expense	253	274	217
Deferred income taxes	177	(170)	701
Excess tax benefits from stock-based compensation	(53)	(53)	(14)
Changes in assets and liabilities			
Accounts receivable	(205)	(189)	55
Inventories	(196)	(404)	453
Accounts payable	(83)	146	109
Accrued income taxes (current and long-term)	(45)	255	(147)
Product and other insurance receivables and claims	9	49	64
Other—net	(139)	279	(329)
Net cash provided by operating activities	5,284	5,174	4,941
Cash Flows From Investing Activities			
Purchases of property, plant and equipment (PP&E)	(1,379)	(1,091)	(903)
Proceeds from sale of PP&E and other assets	55	25	74
Acquisitions, net of cash acquired	(649)	(1,830)	(69)
Purchases of marketable securities and investments	(4,162)	(3,287)	(2,240)
Proceeds from sale of marketable securities and investments	1,679	1,995	718
Proceeds from maturities of marketable securities	1,738	1,565	683
Other investing	—	(3)	5
Net cash used in investing activities	(2,718)	(2,626)	(1,732)

(continued)

(Millions)	2011	2010	2009
Cash Flows From Financing Activities			
Change in short-term debt—net	$ 11	$ (24)	$ (536)
Repayment of debt (maturities greater than 90 days)	(1,429)	(556)	(519)
Proceeds from debt (maturities greater than 90 days)	1,111	108	41
Purchases of treasury stock	(2,701)	(854)	(17)
Proceeds from issuances of treasury stock pursuant to stock option and benefit plans	902	666	431
Dividends paid to shareholders	(1,555)	(1,500)	(1,431)
Excess tax benefits from stock-based compensation	53	53	14
Other—net	(67)	(77)	3
Net cash used in financing activities	(3,675)	(2,184)	(2,014)
Effect of exchange rate changes on cash and cash equivalents	(49)	(27)	(4)
Net increase/(decrease) in cash and cash equivalents	(1,158)	337	1,191
Cash and cash equivalents at beginning of year	3,377	3,040	1,849
Cash and cash equivalents at end of year	$ 2,219	$ 3,377	$ 3,040

The accompanying Notes to Consolidated Financial Statements are an integral part of this statement.

NOTES TO CONSOLIDATED FINANCIAL STATEMENTS

Note 7. Supplemental Cash Flow Information

(Millions)	2011	2010	2009
Cash income tax payments, net of refunds	$1,542	$1,509	$834
Cash interest payments	219	178	233
Capitalized interest	19	17	27

Cash interest payments include interest paid on debt and capital lease balances, including net interest payments/ receipts related to accreted debt discounts/premiums, as well as net interest payments/receipts associated with interest rate swap contracts.

Individual amounts in the Consolidated Statement of Cash Flows exclude the impacts of acquisitions, divestitures and exchange rate impacts, which are presented separately. "Other—net" in the Consolidated Statement of Cash Flows within operating activities in 2011, 2010 and 2009 includes changes in liabilities related to 3M's restructuring actions (Note 4).

Transactions related to investing and financing activities with significant non-cash components are as follows:
- During 2010, Sumitomo 3M purchased a portion of its shares held by its noncontrolling interest, Sumitomo Electric Industries, Ltd. (SEI), by paying cash of 5.8 billion Japanese Yen and entering into a note payable to SEI of 17.4 billion Japanese Yen. The cash paid as a result of the purchase of Sumitomo 3M shares from SEI was classified as other financing activity in the consolidated statement of cash flows. The remainder of the purchase financed by the note payable to SEI was considered non-cash financing activity in the first quarter of 2010. This is described in Note 6 in the section entitled "Purchase and Sale of Subsidiary Shares and Transfers of Ownership Interests Involving Non-Wholly Owned Subsidiaries."
- Also in 2010, as discussed in Note 2, the Company recorded a financed liability of 1.7 billion Japanese Yen related to the A-One acquisition.
- During 2009, 3M recorded a capital lease asset and obligation of approximately $50 million related to an IT investment with an amortization period of seven years and contributed $600 million to its U.S. defined benefit pension plan in shares of the Company's common stock.

Noncash Activities

6.12

SEALED AIR CORPORATION (DEC)

CONSOLIDATED STATEMENTS OF CASH FLOWS

(In millions)	Year Ended December 31		
	2011	2010	2009
Cash flows from operating activities:			
Net earnings available to common stockholders	$ 149.1	$ 255.9	$ 244.3
Adjustments to reconcile net earnings to net cash provided by operating activities:			
Depreciation and amortization	189.5	154.7	154.5
Share-based incentive compensation	25.0	30.6	38.8
Costs related to the acquisition of Diversey	64.8	—	—
Amortization of senior debt related items and other	4.9	1.7	1.0
Loss on debt redemption	—	38.5	3.4
Provisions for bad debt	8.6	6.4	6.8

(continued)

	Year Ended December 31		
(In millions)	2011	2010	2009
Provisions for inventory obsolescence	9.2	2.1	6.6
Deferred taxes, net	(55.6)	(3.3)	(16.6)
Excess tax benefit from share-based incentive compensation	(2.6)	—	—
Net loss on sales of small product lines	—	—	0.2
Net gain on disposals of property and equipment and other	(6.3)	(0.8)	(3.0)
(Net gains on sale) other-than-temporary impairment of available-for-sale securities	—	(5.9)	4.0
Changes in operating assets and liabilities, net of effects of businesses acquired:			
Changes in restricted cash	(6.3)	—	—
Receivables, net	(116.0)	(33.9)	115.2
Accounts receivable securitization program	—	—	(80.0)
Inventories	(9.0)	(19.4)	109.7
Other assets, net	47.1	16.3	9.6
Accounts payable	(14.4)	19.0	(68.4)
Other liabilities	104.1	21.2	25.9
Net cash provided by operating activities	392.1	483.1	552.0
Cash flows from investing activities:			
Capital expenditures for property and equipment	(124.5)	(87.6)	(80.3)
Acquisition of Diversey, net of cash and cash equivalents acquired	(1,983.1)	—	—
Investment in Diversey preferred stock	(262.9)	—	—
Other businesses acquired in purchase transactions, net of cash and cash equivalents acquired and equity investment in 2011 and 2010	(12.0)	(24.1)	—
Proceeds from sale of available-for-sale securities	—	12.6	—
Proceeds from sales of property and equipment	10.4	4.2	7.2
Other investing activities	1.7	(2.0)	2.8
Net cash used in investing activities	(2,370.4)	(96.9)	(70.3)
Cash flows from financing activities:			
Changes in restricted cash	262.9	—	—
Payments of long-term debt	(1,753.6)	(276.1)	(585.3)
Proceeds from long-term debt	3,706.4	—	766.6
Dividends paid on common stock	(87.4)	(79.7)	(75.7)
Acquisition of common stock for tax withholding obligations under our 2005 contingent stock plan	(12.2)	—	—
Net payments of short-term borrowings	(43.9)	(4.4)	(8.3)
Payments of debt issuance costs	(51.2)	—	(7.0)
Repurchases of common stock	—	(9.8)	—
Excess tax benefit from share-based incentive compensation	2.6	—	—
Other financing activities	—	(3.0)	—
Net cash provided by (used in) financing activities	2,023.6	(373.0)	90.3
Effect of foreign currency exchange rate changes on cash and cash equivalents	1.9	(32.1)	(6.4)
Cash and cash equivalents:			
Balance, beginning of period	$ 675.6	$ 694.5	$ 128.9
Net change during the period	47.2	(18.9)	565.6
Balance, end of period	$ 722.8	$ 675.6	$ 694.5
Supplemental Cash Flow Information:			
Interest payments, net of amounts capitalized	$ 135.3	$ 128.7	$ 100.9
Income tax payments	$ 129.8	$ 86.6	$ 114.3
Non-cash items:			
Non-cash items associated with the acquisition of Diversey:			
31.7 million shares of Sealed Air common stock issued in connection with the Diversey acquisition	$ 512.9	$ —	$ —
Fair value of Diversey preferred stock investment	$ 262.9	$ —	$ —
Fair-value-based measure of the portion of the SARs attributed to pre-acquisition service	$ 50.8	$ —	$ —
Other non-cash items:			
Transfers of shares of our common stock from Treasury as part of our 2009 and 2008 profit-sharing plan contributions	$ —	$ 7.2	$ 5.9
Net unrealized (losses) gains on available-for-sale securities	$ —	$ (7.0)	$ 7.0

See accompanying notes to consolidated financial statements.

NOTES TO CONSOLIDATED FINANCIAL STATEMENTS

Note 3 Acquisition of Diversey Holdings, Inc. (in part)

Description of Transaction

On October 3, 2011, we completed the acquisition of 100% of the outstanding stock of Diversey. We acquired Diversey to position us to capture growth opportunities by developing end-to-end service-based solutions for the food processing and food service industries, to leverage combined research and development investments to develop broader growth initiatives in the food processing and food service industries and to improve access to under-developed markets and increase access to developing regions.

Under the terms of the acquisition agreement, we paid in aggregate $2.1 billion in cash consideration and an aggregate of approximately 31.7 million shares of Sealed Air common stock to the shareholders of Diversey. We financed the payment of the cash consideration and related fees and expenses through (a) borrowings under our new Credit Facility, (b) proceeds from our issuance of the Notes and (c) cash on hand. In connection with the acquisition, we also used our new borrowings and cash on hand to retire $1.6 billion of existing indebtedness of Diversey. The new Credit Facility and Notes are described further in Note 11, "Debt and Credit Facilities."

Consideration Transferred

The following table summarizes the consideration transferred at the acquisition date.

Cash	$2,098.7
31.7 million shares of Sealed Air common stock (at October 3, 2011 average price of $16.18 per share)	512.9
Fair value of Diversey preferred stock investment[1]	262.9
Fair-value-based measure of the portion of the SARs attributed to pre-acquisition service[2]	50.8
Total consideration	$2,925.3

[1] On October 3, 2011, prior to the closing of the acquisition, we used cash on hand in the amount of $262.9 million to purchase preferred stock of Diversey (the "Preferred Stock Issuance") and this amount has been included in the consideration transferred. Diversey elected to exercise its covenant defeasance option with respect to its 10.50% senior notes due 2020 (the "DHI Notes"), and Diversey, Inc., a subsidiary of Diversey, elected to exercise its covenant defeasance option with respect to its 8.25% senior notes due 2019 (the "DI Notes"). In addition, Diversey elected to redeem 35% of the aggregate accreted value of the DHI Notes using a portion of the proceeds of the Preferred Stock Issuance, and Diversey, Inc. elected to redeem 35% of the aggregate principal amount of the DI Notes using a portion of the proceeds of the Preferred Stock Issuance that had been contributed to the equity capital of Diversey, Inc. Each such redemption occurred on November 2, 2011 (the "Equity Claw Redemption Date").

On the Equity Claw Redemption Date, 35% of the DHI Notes were redeemed at a price of 110.50% of their accreted value, plus accrued and unpaid interest to the Equity Claw Redemption Date. Additionally, 35% of the DI Notes were redeemed at a price of 108.25% of their principal amount, plus accrued and unpaid interest to the Equity Claw Redemption Date. Following the completion of these redemptions Diversey and Diversey, Inc. notified The Depository Trust Company and Wilmington Trust (the "Trustee") that they would be redeeming the remaining 65% of the DHI Notes and the DI Notes pursuant to the make-whole redemption provisions of the indentures governing the DHI Notes and the DI Notes. Each such redemption occurred on December 2, 2011.

[2] In connection with the acquisition, Sealed Air exchanged Diversey's cash-settled stock appreciation rights and stock options that were unvested as of May 31, 2011 and unexercised at October 3, 2011 into cash-settled stock appreciation rights based on Sealed Air common stock ("SARs"). The number of SARs was determined based on the ratio of the per share merger consideration value of $24.50 and the fair value of Sealed Air's common stock on September 30, 2011 of $16.70, or an exchange fraction of 1.46722. This resulted in granting 13.0 million SARs.

CASH FLOWS FROM OPERATING ACTIVITIES

PRESENTATION

6.13 FASB ASC 230-10-45 defines those transactions and events that constitute operating cash receipts and payments. Cash inflows from operating activities include the following:

- Cash receipts from sales of goods or services, including receipts from the collection or sale of accounts and both short- and long-term notes receivable from customers arising from those sales. Goods include certain loans and other debt and equity instruments of other entities that are acquired specifically for resale.

- Cash receipts from returns on loans, other debt instruments of other entities, and equity securities—interest and dividends.
- All other cash receipts that do not stem from transactions defined as investing or financing activities, such as amounts received to settle lawsuits; proceeds of insurance settlements, except for those that are directly related to investing or financing activities, such as destruction of a building; and refunds from suppliers.

Cash outflows from operating activities include the following:
- Cash payments to acquire materials for manufacture or goods for resale, including principal payments on accounts and both short- and long-term notes payable to suppliers for those materials or goods. Goods include certain loans and other debt and equity instruments of other entities that are acquired specifically for resale.

- Cash payments to other suppliers and employees for other goods or services.
- Cash payments to governments for taxes, duties, fines, and other fees or penalties and the cash that would have been paid for income taxes if increases in the value of equity instruments issued under share-based payment arrangements that are not included in the cost of goods or services recognizable for financial reporting purposes also had not been deductible in determining taxable income.
- Cash payments to lenders and other creditors for interest.
- Cash payment made to settle an asset retirement obligation.
- All other cash payments that do not stem from transactions defined as investing or financing activities, such as payments to settle lawsuits, cash contributions to charities, and cash refunds to customers.

6.14 FASB ASC 230-10-45 recommends that the direct method be used to report net cash flow from operating activities, which includes reporting major classes or gross cash receipts and payments and their arithmetic sum. Entities that choose not to provide information about major classes of operating cash receipts and payments by the direct method should determine and report the same amount for net cash flow from operating activities indirectly by adjusting net income of a business entity to reconcile it to net cash flow from operating activities (the indirect or reconciliation method). Regardless of whether the direct or indirect method is used, a reconciliation of net income to net cash flow from operating activities is required to be presented.

6.15 FASB ASC 230-10-45-28 also notes that when reconciling net income to net cash flow from operating activities, a business entity should adjust net income to remove past operating cash receipts and payments and accruals of expected future operating cash receipts and payments, including changes during the period in inventory and receivables and payables pertaining to operating activities. Additionally, all items that are included in net income, such as depreciation and amortization expense, that do not affect net cash provided from, or used for, operating activities should be adjusted for.

6.16

TABLE 6-2: METHOD OF REPORTING CASH FLOWS FROM OPERATING ACTIVITIES

Table 6-2 shows the methods used to report cash flows from operating activities.

	2011	2010	2009
Indirect method	495	492	495
Direct method	5	8	5
Total Entities	**500**	**500**	**500**

6.17

TABLE 6-3: CASH FLOWS FROM OPERATING ACTIVITIES—INCOME STATEMENT RECONCILING ITEMS

Table 6-3 lists the major types of income statement items used by the survey entities to reconcile net income to net cash flow from operating activities.

	2011	2010	2009
Depreciation and/or amortization	496	497	498
Deferred taxes	440	420	438
Employee related costs	406	366	422
Write-down of assets	123	191	189
Gain or loss on sale of property	200	213	173
Tax benefit from share-based compensation plans	167	159	153
Equity in investee's earnings	131	110	137
Gain or loss on sale of assets other than property	130	94	128
Provision for doubtful accounts	117	118	128
Intangible asset impairment	127	89	114
Intangible asset amortization	132	133	111
Gain or loss from discontinued operations	50	102	111
Restructuring	89	93	101
Gain or loss on debt extinguishments	85	88	N/C*
Cash surrender value	7	9	N/C*
Cumulative effect of accounting change	—	1	N/C*
Minority interest/noncontrolling interest	14	19	N/C*
Debt discount/premium/issue cost amortization	63	69	N/C*
Accretion of discount/premium on marketable securities/investments	10	17	N/C*
Unrealized gain/loss on marketable securities/derivatives	40	29	N/C*
Foreign currency translation/transaction	44	50	N/C*
Purchased research and/or development cost	4	10	N/C*
Litigation	14	18	N/C*
Other, described	182	200	N/C*

* N/C = Not compiled. The line item was not included in the table for the year shown.

6.18

TABLE 6-4: CASH FLOWS FROM OPERATING ACTIVITIES—BALANCE SHEET RECONCILING ITEMS

Table 6-4 lists the major types of balance sheet items used by the survey entities to reconcile net income to net cash flow from operating activities.

	2011	2010	2009
Accounts receivable	430	407	460
Inventories	408	369	423
Accounts receivable combined with inventories and/or other items	37	64	27
Accounts payable	267	236	275
Accounts payable combined with other items	192	231	207
Income taxes payable	106	218	205
Employee-related liabilities	94	99	112
Current assets and current liabilities are netted	14	16	N/C*
Marketable securities or restricted cash	8	8	N/C*
Deferred income taxes	72	28	N/C*
Other assets, described	165	135	N/C*
Other liabilities, described	252	192	N/C*

* N/C = Not compiled. The line item was not included in the table for the year shown.

PRESENTATION AND DISCLOSURE EXCERPTS

Direct Method

6.19

EMC CORPORATION (DEC)

CONSOLIDATED STATEMENTS OF CASH FLOWS

(In thousands)

	For the Year Ended December 31		
	2011	**2010**	**2009**
Cash Flows From Operating Activities:			
Cash received from customers	$ 21,144,690	$ 17,585,447	$ 14,647,691
Cash paid to suppliers and employees	(15,218,678)	(12,830,684)	(11,032,859)
Dividends and interest received	135,971	102,912	109,525
Interest paid	(70,071)	(76,711)	(73,430)
Income taxes paid	(323,097)	(232,121)	(316,542)
Net cash provided by operating activities	5,668,815	4,548,843	3,334,385
Cash Flows From Investing Activities:			
Additions to property, plant and equipment	(801,375)	(745,412)	(411,579)
Capitalized software development costs	(442,341)	(362,956)	(304,520)
Purchases of short- and long-term available-for-sale securities	(7,180,169)	(6,329,894)	(5,494,540)
Sales of short- and long-term available-for-sale securities	5,121,454	3,625,260	5,256,412
Maturities of short- and long-term available-for-sale securities	1,130,321	437,297	704,653
Business acquisitions, net of cash acquired	(536,624)	(3,194,611)	(2,664,141)
(Increase) decrease in strategic and other related investments	(300,476)	123,867	(163,757)
Purchase of leasehold interest	(151,083)	—	—
VCE company funding	(383,211)	(29,600)	(19,200)
Other, net	—	—	1,184
Net cash used in investing activities	(3,543,504)	(6,476,049)	(3,095,488)
Cash Flows From Financing Activities:			
Issuance of EMC's common stock from the exercise of stock options	673,389	780,732	366,361
Issuance of VMware's common stock from the exercise of stock options	337,618	431,306	227,666
EMC repurchase of EMC's common stock	(1,999,968)	(999,924)	—
EMC purchase of VMware's common stock	(399,984)	(399,224)	—
VMware repurchase of VMware's common stock	(526,203)	(338,527)	—
Repayments of proceeds from securities lending	—	—	(412,321)
Excess tax benefits from stock-based compensation	361,632	281,872	46,082
Payment of long-term and short-term obligations	(27,089)	(4,128)	(20,835)
Proceeds from long-term and short-term obligations	3,096	4,066	4,969
Interest rate contracts settlement	(140,993)	—	—
Net cash (used in) provided by financing activities	(1,718,502)	(243,827)	211,922
Effect of exchange rate changes on cash and cash equivalents	5,089	(12,328)	7,995
Net increase (decrease) in cash and cash equivalents	411,898	(2,183,361)	458,814
Cash and cash equivalents at beginning of year	4,119,138	6,302,499	5,843,685
Cash and cash equivalents at end of year	$ 4,531,036	$ 4,119,138	$6,302,499

(continued)

	For the Year Ended December 31		
	2011	2010	2009
Reconciliation of net income to net cash provided by operating activities:			
Net income	$ 2,608,885	$ 1,969,686	$1,121,801
Adjustments to reconcile net income to net cash provided by operating activities:			
Depreciation and amortization	1,421,598	1,167,550	1,073,135
Non-cash interest expense on convertible debt	102,907	105,649	108,347
Non-cash restructuring and other special charges	(1,484)	6,861	25,050
Stock-based compensation expense	822,576	667,728	600,537
Provision for doubtful accounts	20,255	18,965	14,351
Deferred income taxes, net	(19,423)	(49,787)	27,198
Excess tax benefits from stock-based compensation	(361,632)	(281,872)	(46,082)
Gain on Data Domain and SpringSource common stock	—	—	(25,822)
Other, net	4,573	(21,250)	(13,906)
Changes in assets and liabilities, net of acquisitions:			
Accounts and notes receivable	(391,672)	(405,758)	241,069
Inventories	(393,156)	(114,111)	(158,482)
Other assets	(61,830)	(54,469)	3,600
Accounts payable	34,871	154,496	140,376
Accrued expenses	158,467	4,162	(80,642)
Income taxes payable	336,711	455,964	(91,142)
Deferred revenue	1,508,520	957,114	366,361
Other liabilities	(121,351)	(32,085)	28,636
Net cash provided by operating activities	$ 5,668,815	$ 4,548,843	$3,334,385
Non-cash investing and financing activity:			
Issuance of common stock and stock options exchanged in business acquisitions	$ 3,224	$ 28,668	$ 83,780

The accompanying notes are an integral part of the consolidated financial statements.

Indirect/Reconciliation Method

6.20

AVON PRODUCTS, INC. (DEC)

CONSOLIDATED STATEMENTS OF CASH FLOWS

(In millions)

Years Ended December 31	2011	2010	2009
Cash Flows From Operating Activities			
Net income	$ 517.8	$ 609.3	$ 628.2
Discontinued operations, net of tax	8.6	(14.1)	(9.0)
Income from continuing operations	$ 526.4	$ 595.2	$ 619.2
Adjustments to reconcile net income to net cash provided by operating activities:			
Depreciation	174.0	145.2	127.8
Amortization	65.6	49.6	47.5
Provision for doubtful accounts	247.2	215.7	221.2
Provision for obsolescence	128.1	131.1	120.0
Share-based compensation	36.6	57.6	54.9
Foreign exchange losses (gains)	12.8	(9.4)	(1.5)
Deferred income taxes	(196.6)	(103.1)	(166.3)
Impairment of goodwill and intangible asset	263.0	—	—
Charge for Venezuelan monetary assets and liabilities	—	46.1	—
Other	39.9	26.6	57.6

(continued)

Years Ended December 31	2011	2010	2009
Changes in assets and liabilities:			
Accounts receivable	(241.5)	(280.3)	(259.5)
Inventories	(210.3)	(189.8)	(127.8)
Prepaid expenses and other	24.6	(4.9)	(90.4)
Accounts payable and accrued liabilities	(55.7)	76.7	145.0
Income and other taxes	(50.7)	(63.2)	16.1
Noncurrent assets and liabilities	(107.6)	(4.1)	(9.1)
Net cash provided by operating activities of continuing operations	655.8	689.0	754.7
Cash Flows From Investing Activities			
Capital expenditures	(276.7)	(331.2)	(296.3)
Disposal of assets	17.1	11.9	11.2
Acquisitions and other investing activities	(13.0)	(785.8)	5.8
Proceeds from sale of investments	33.7	11.3	61.9
Purchases of investments	(28.8)	(1.9)	(.9)
Net cash used by investing activities of continuing operations	(267.7)	(1,095.7)	(218.3)
Cash Flows From Financing Activities*			
Cash dividends	(403.4)	(384.1)	(364.7)
Debt, net (maturities of three months or less)	635.7	(3.6)	(507.6)
Proceeds from debt	88.9	661.5	957.8
Repayment of debt	(614.6)	(53.2)	(450.5)
Proceeds from exercise of stock options	16.8	23.9	13.1
Excess tax benefit realized from share-based compensation	(.2)	4.3	(.7)
Repurchase of common stock	(7.7)	(14.1)	(8.6)
Net cash (used) provided by financing activities of continuing operations	(284.5)	234.7	(361.2)
Cash Flows From Discontinued Operations			
Net cash provided by operating activities of discontinued operations	—	13.0	27.3
Net cash (used) provided by investing activities of discontinued operations	(1.2)	61.3	(.6)
Net cash used by financing activities of discontinued operations	—	(.3)	(.6)
Net cash (used) provided by discontinued operations	(1.2)	74.0	26.1
Effect of exchange rate changes on cash and equivalents	(37.2)	(33.7)	5.6
Net change in cash and equivalents	65.2	(131.7)	206.9
Cash and equivalents at beginning of year[1]	$1,179.9	$1,311.6	$1,104.7
Cash and equivalents at end of year[2]	$1,245.1	$1,179.9	$1,311.6
Cash paid for:			
Interest, net of amounts capitalized	$ 137.4	$ 133.4	$ 127.5
Income taxes, net of refunds received	$ 423.8	$ 387.3	$ 377.9

* —Non-cash financing activities included the change in fair market value of interest-rate swap agreements of $53.2 in 2011, $66.8 in 2010, and $(55.7) in 2009 (see Note 5, Debt and Other Financing).

[1] —Includes cash and cash equivalents of discontinued operations of $13.5 and $3.2 at the beginning of the year in 2010 and 2009 respectively.

[2] —Includes cash and cash equivalents of discontinued operations of $13.5 at the end of the year in 2009.

The accompanying notes are an integral part of these statements.

Adjustments to Reconcile Net Income: Depreciation and Amortization

6.21

BROWN SHOE COMPANY, INC.

CONSOLIDATED STATEMENTS OF CASH FLOWS
(in part)

($ thousands)	2010	2009	2008
Operating Activities			
Net earnings (loss)	$ 37,060	$ 10,443	$(134,813)
Adjustments to reconcile net earnings (loss) to net cash (used for) provided by operating activities:			
Depreciation	33,149	36,459	39,937
Amortization of capitalized software	10,506	7,867	7,812
Amortization of intangibles	6,667	6,774	7,124
Amortization of debt issuance costs	2,195	2,195	1,637
Share-based compensation expense	6,144	4,673	2,601
Tax deficiency (benefit) related to share-based plans	87	58	(498)
Loss on disposal of facilities and equipment	1,089	1,180	1,065
Impairment charges for facilities and equipment	2,762	3,928	2,657
Impairment of goodwill and intangible assets	—	—	149,150
Deferred rent	(4,191)	(2,845)	249
Deferred income taxes	27,229	15,414	(51,248)
Provision for doubtful accounts	516	727	548
Foreign currency transaction (gains) losses	(18)	(106)	131
Undistributed loss of nonconsolidated affiliate	—	—	216
Changes in operating assets and liabilities:			
Receivables	(30,088)	(714)	35,644
Inventories	(66,568)	11,166	(29,196)
Prepaid expenses and other current and noncurrent assets	(9,440)	(1,601)	(373)
Trade accounts payable	(10,754)	24,987	(27,213)
Accrued expenses and other liabilities	2,668	285	22,406
Income taxes	(5,993)	2,742	(336)
Other, net	(5,332)	(5,554)	6,836
Net cash (used for) provided by operating activities	(2,312)	118,078	34,336

Adjustments to Reconcile Net Income: Gain/Loss on Discontinued Operations/ Sale of Business

6.22

BOSTON SCIENTIFIC CORPORATION (DEC)

CONSOLIDATED STATEMENTS OF CASH FLOWS
(in part)

	Year Ended December 31		
(In millions)	2011	2010	2009
Operating Activities			
Net income (loss)	$ 441	$(1,065)	$(1,025)
Adjustments to reconcile net income (loss) to cash provided by operating activities			
Gain on sale of businesses	(778)		
Depreciation and amortization	717	816	834
Deferred income taxes	46	(110)	(64)
Stock-based compensation expense	128	150	144
Goodwill impairment charges	697	1,817	
Intangible asset impairment charges	21	65	12
Net (gains) losses on investments and notes receivable	(27)	12	(9)
Purchased research and development			21
Contingent consideration expense	7	2	
Other, net	(7)	11	(3)
Increase (decrease) in cash flows from operating assets and liabilities:			
Trade accounts receivable	42	52	1
Inventories	(54)	(5)	(92)
Other assets	(60)	132	276
Accounts payable and accrued expenses	(271)	(1,148)	462
Other liabilities	106	(404)	278
Cash provided by operating activities	1,008	325	835

Adjustments to Reconcile Net Income: Restructuring Expense

6.23

ALLIANCE ONE INTERNATIONAL, INC. (MAR)

STATEMENTS OF CONSOLIDATED CASH FLOWS (in part)

(In thousands)	Years Ended March 31		
	2011	2010	2009
Operating Activities			
Net Income (Loss)	$(72,148)	$79,946	$133,237
Adjustments to reconcile net income to net cash provided by operating activities of continuing operations:			
Net income from discontinued operations, net of tax	—	—	(407)
Depreciation and amortization	28,216	29,113	29,277
Debt amortization/interest	12,959	13,104	4,979
Debt retirement cost	4,584	40,353	954
Restructuring charges (recovery)	10,323	—	(87)
(Gain) loss on foreign currency transactions	(8,387)	(12,288)	21
Gain on disposition of fixed assets	(4,355)	(5,981)	(3,706)
Gain on other sales of assets	(37,765)	—	—
Bad debt expense	3,002	81	—
Stock based compensation	4,609	448	5,632
Changes in operating assets and liabilities, net:			
Trade and other receivables	(100,711)	(28,974)	(38,575)
Inventories and advances to suppliers	60,123	(61,324)	10,383
Prepaid expenses	321	(3,352)	(693)
Deferred items	99,646	(14,947)	(76,019)
Recoverable income taxes	(535)	(6,711)	(3,069)
Payables and accrued expenses	(95,239)	30,828	(250)
Advances from customers	(84,832)	57,844	(47,511)
Current derivative asset	(16)	(1,699)	(10,839)
Current derivative liability	—	641	25,670
Income taxes	(1,416)	(7,773)	7,012
Other operating assets and liabilities	(1,620)	1,142	(575)
Other, net	224	868	(2,366)
Net cash provided (used) by operating activities of continuing operations	(183,017)	111,319	33,068
Net cash provided by operating activities of discontinued operations	—	—	562
Net cash provided (used) by operating activities	(183,017)	111,319	33,630

Adjustments to Reconcile Net Income: Cash Surrender Value

6.24

STEELCASE INC. (FEB)

CONSOLIDATED STATEMENTS OF CASH FLOWS (in part)

(In millions)

	Year Ended		
	February 25, 2011	February 26, 2010	February 27, 2009
Operating Activities			
Net income (loss)	$ 20.4	$(13.6)	$(11.7)
Adjustments to reconcile net income to net cash (used in) provided by operating activities:			
Depreciation and amortization	64.4	74.2	87.3
Goodwill and intangible assets impairment charges	—	—	65.2
Changes in cash surrender value of COLI	(13.5)	(38.0)	39.0
(Gain) loss on disposal of fixed assets	(5.7)	3.4	10.7
Gain from IDEO ownership transition	(13.2)	—	—
Deferred income taxes	11.3	(18.2)	(4.8)
Pension and post-retirement benefit cost	4.0	5.9	5.7
Restructuring charges (payments), net	16.7	(5.8)	11.0
Excess tax expense (benefit) from vesting of stock awards	(0.4)	1.0	(0.4)
Other	1.3	1.0	(1.8)
Changes in operating assets and liabilities, net of acquisitions, divestures, and deconsolidations:			
Accounts receivable	(65.2)	44.7	70.2
Inventories	(28.5)	33.9	3.6
Other assets	10.9	2.5	(8.1)
Accounts payable	34.2	(16.7)	(50.0)
Employee compensation	41.7	(62.0)	(52.5)
Employee benefit obligations	(23.0)	(3.7)	(22.7)
Accrued expenses and other liabilities	17.3	(19.5)	(36.5)
Net cash provided by (used in) operating activities	72.7	(10.9)	104.2

Adjustments to Reconcile Net Income: Deferred Taxes

6.25

L-3 COMMUNICATIONS HOLDINGS, INC. (DEC)

CONSOLIDATED STATEMENTS OF CASH FLOWS (in part)

(In millions)

| | Year Ended December 31 | | |
	2011	2010	2009
Operating Activities:			
Net income	$ 968	$ 966	$ 911
Depreciation of property, plant and equipment	173	164	158
Amortization of intangibles and other assets	74	67	60
Deferred income tax provision	107	111	74
Stock-based employee compensation expense	64	82	74
Contributions to employee savings plans in L-3 Holdings' common stock	137	143	139
Amortization of pension and postretirement benefit plans net loss and prior service cost	48	41	52
Amortization of bond discounts (included in interest expense)	4	24	23
Amortization of deferred debt issue costs (included in interest expense)	9	12	11
Non-cash portion of debt retirement charge	11	5	—
Goodwill impairment charge	43	—	—
Equity in losses (earnings) of unconsolidated subsidiaries	12	(8)	(4)
Other non-cash items	2	(2)	1
Subtotal	1,652	1,605	1,499
Changes in operating assets and liabilities, excluding acquired and divested amounts:			
Billed receivables	56	(109)	107
Contracts in process	(89)	(136)	(79)
Inventories	(14)	2	14
Accounts payable, trade	(30)	(2)	(118)
Accrued employment costs	(40)	22	(59)
Accrued expenses	48	47	(39)
Advance payments and billings in excess of costs incurred	(15)	63	(15)
Income taxes	(1)	78	27
Excess income tax benefits related to share-based payment arrangements	(2)	(7)	(4)
Other current liabilities	17	23	9
Pension and postretirement benefits	(83)	(78)	43
All other operating activities	(15)	(47)	22
Subtotal	(168)	(144)	(92)
Net cash from operating activities	1,484	1,461	1,407

Adjustments to Reconcile Net Income: Settlement of Receivables and Related Charges

6.26

JABIL CIRCUIT, INC. (AUG)

CONSOLIDATED STATEMENTS OF CASH FLOWS (in part)

(In thousands)

| | Fiscal Year Ended August 31 | | |
	2011	2010	2009
Cash Flows From Operating Activities:			
Net income (loss)	$ 382,958	$ 170,766	$(1,166,031)
Adjustments to reconcile net income (loss) to net cash provided by operating activities:			
Depreciation and amortization	319,179	283,284	291,997
Recognition of stock-based compensation expense	76,230	104,609	44,026
Loss on disposal of subsidiaries	23,944	18,671	—
Settlement of receivables and related charges	12,673	—	—
Other, net	9,910	9,488	18,902
Loss on early extinguishment of debt	—	—	10,522
Deferred income taxes	2,266	2,331	102,375
Restructuring and impairment charges	628	8,217	51,894
Goodwill impairment charges	—	—	1,022,821
Change in operating assets and liabilities, exclusive of net assets acquired:			
Trade accounts receivable	48,232	(247,133)	169,741
Inventories	(158,545)	(969,348)	283,816
Prepaid expenses and other current assets	(212,265)	(143,639)	40,950
Other assets	3,205	448	(7,604)
Accounts payable and accrued expenses	305,814	1,172,770	(292,671)
Income taxes payable	13,780	16,946	(13,429)
Net cash provided by operating activities	828,009	427,410	557,309

Adjustments to Reconcile Net Income: Impairment/Write-Down of Assets

6.27

FOOT LOCKER, INC. (JAN)

CONSOLIDATED STATEMENTS OF CASH FLOWS
(in part)

(In millions)	2010	2009	2008
From Operating Activities			
Net income (loss)	$169	$ 48	$(80)
Adjustments to reconcile net income (loss) to net cash provided by operating activities of continuing operations:			
Discontinued operations, net of tax	—	(1)	1
Non-cash impairment and other charges	10	36	259
Depreciation and amortization	106	112	130
Share-based compensation expense	13	12	9
Deferred tax provision (benefit)	84	2	(44)
Qualified pension plan contributions	(32)	(100)	(6)
Change in assets and liabilities:			
Merchandise inventories	(19)	111	128
Accounts payable	7	23	(39)
Other accruals	35	(30)	(4)
Income taxes	(9)	9	(7)
Payment on the settlement of the net investment hedge	(24)	—	—
Proceeds from the termination of interest rate swaps	—	19	—
Other, net	(14)	105	36
Net cash provided by operating activities of continuing operations	326	346	383

CASH FLOWS FROM INVESTING ACTIVITIES

PRESENTATION

6.28 FASB ASC 230 defines those transactions and events that constitute investing cash receipts and payments. Investing activities include making and collecting loans and acquiring and disposing of debt or equity instruments and property, plant, and equipment (PPE) and other productive assets. Investing activities exclude acquiring and disposing of certain loans or other debt or equity instruments that are acquired specifically for resale. Cash flows from purchases, sales, and maturities of available-for-sale securities should be classified as cash flows from investing activities and reported gross in the statement of cash flows. The following are considered cash receipts and payments from investing activities:

- Receipts from collections or sales of loans made by the entity and of other entities' debt instruments, other than cash equivalents and certain debt instruments that are acquired specifically for resale, that were purchased by the entity.
- Receipts from sales of equity instruments of other entities, other than certain equity instruments carried in a trading account, and from returns of investment in those instruments.
- Receipts from sales of PPE and other productive assets.
- Receipts from sales of loans that were not specifically acquired for resale. If loans were acquired as investments, cash receipts from sales of those loans shall be classified as investing cash inflows, regardless of a change in the purpose for holding those loans.
- Disbursements for loans made by the entity and payments to acquire debt instruments of other entities, other than cash equivalents and certain debt instruments that are acquired specifically for resale.
- Payments to acquire equity instruments of other entities, other than certain equity instruments carried in a trading account.
- Payments at the time of purchase or soon before or after purchase to acquire PPE and other productive assets, including interest capitalized as part of the cost of those assets. Generally, only advance payments, the down payment, or other amounts paid at the time of purchase or soon before or after the purchase of PPE and other productive assets are investing cash outflows. However, incurring directly-related debt to the seller is a financing transaction; thus, subsequent payments of principal on that debt are financing cash outflows.

PRESENTATION AND DISCLOSURE EXCERPTS

Acquisitions

6.29

JOY GLOBAL INC. (OCT)

CONSOLIDATED STATEMENT OF CASH FLOWS
(in part)

(In thousands)

	Fiscal Years Ended		
	October 28, 2011	October 29, 2010	October 30, 2009
Investing Activities:			
Acquisition of businesses, net of cash acquired	(1,048,908)	—	(11,184)
Property, plant and equipment acquired	(110,523)	(73,474)	(94,128)
Proceeds from sale of property, plant and equipment	6,160	418	1,779
Proceeds from sale of LeTourneau Technologies Drilling Systems, Inc.	375,000	—	—
Investment in International Mining Machinery shares	(376,724)	—	—
Deposits of cash into escrow	(866,000)	—	—
Other, net	(882)	(1,859)	(481)
Net cash used by investing activities—continuing operations	(2,021,877)	(74,915)	(104,014)
Net cash used by investing activities—discontinued operations	—	—	—
Net cash used by investing activities	(2,021,877)	(74,915)	(104,014)

NOTES TO CONSOLIDATED FINANCIAL STATEMENTS

October 28, 2011

3. Acquisitions

Acquisition of LeTourneau Technologies, Inc.

We completed the acquisition of LeTourneau Technologies, Inc. ("LeTourneau") on June 22, 2011. LeTourneau historically operated in three businesses, mining equipment, steel products and drilling products. Subsequent to the acquisition, we entered into a definitive agreement to sell the drilling products business of LeTourneau and that transaction closed on October 24, 2011. The results of operations for LeTourneau have been included in the accompanying consolidated financial statements from the acquisition date forward, with results of the drilling products business being included as results of discontinued operations while the mining equipment and steel products business results are included in continuing operations as part of the surface mining equipment segment.

We purchased all of the outstanding shares of LeTourneau. The purchase price for the acquisition was as follows:

(In thousands)	
Cash consideration	$1,100,000
Working capital purchase price adjustments	(46,323)
	$1,053,677

The purchase price has been finalized, yet the allocation of the purchase price is subject to change for certain potential adjustments related to working capital. The preliminary allocation of the purchase price to the assets acquired and liabilities assumed is based upon the estimated fair values at the date of acquisition. The fair values of the assets and liabilities included in the table below are preliminary and subject to change principally as we are currently in the process of finalizing the disposition of certain assets and liabilities related to the drilling products business.

The excess of the purchase price over the net tangible and identifiable intangible assets is reflected as goodwill. The amount allocated to intangible assets and goodwill for tax purposes is expected to be tax deductible as a result of our election under Section 338(h)(10) of the Internal Revenue Code. The following table summarizes the preliminary fair value of the assets acquired and the liabilities assumed as of the acquisition date:

(In thousands)

Assets Acquired:	
Cash and cash equivalents	$ 4,769
Accounts receivable	52,910
Inventories	200,050
Other current assets	187
Current assets of discontinued operations	331,412
Property, plant and equipment	106,394
Other intangible assets and goodwill	519,628
Other non-current assets	2,776
Non-current assets of discontinued operations	233,096
Total assets acquired	1,451,222
Liabilities Assumed:	
Accounts payable	(37,217)
Employee compensation and benefits	(10,576)
Advance payments and progress billings	(97,228)
Other accrued liabilities	(63,016)
Current liabilities of discontinued operations	(189,508)
Total liabilities assumed	(397,545)
	$1,053,677

The fair value for acquired assets was primarily determined based upon discounted expected cash flows. Of the $519.6 million of intangible assets and goodwill related to continuing operations, $181.2 million has been assigned to intangible assets that are being amortized and $37.2 million has been assigned to trademarks which are not being amortized. The determination of the useful life was based upon historical experience, economic factors, and future cash flows of the assets acquired. The intangible assets have been assigned to the following categories and are being amortized over a weighted-average useful life of 18 years:

(In thousands)

Customer relationships	$ 76,500
Patents	69,900
Unpatented technology	31,600
Backlog	3,200
	$181,200

The results of LeTourneau have been included in the consolidated financial statements since the date of acquisition. From the date of acquisition until our fiscal year end, the mining equipment and steel products businesses of LeTourneau had combined net sales of $144.9 million and operating income of $23.2 million. We incurred $10.4 million of acquisition costs related to LeTourneau.

The following unaudited pro forma financial information for the years ended October 28, 2011 and October 29, 2010 reflect the results of continuing operations as if the acquisition had been completed on October 30, 2010 and October 31, 2009, respectively. Pro forma adjustments have been made for changes in depreciation and amortization expenses related to the valuation of the acquired fixed and intangible assets at fair value, the elimination of non-recurring items, the addition of incremental costs related to debt used to finance the acquisition, and the tax benefits related to the increased costs.

	Year Ended	
(In thousands, except per share data)	October 28, 2011	October 29, 2010
Net sales	$4,620,059	$3,785,543
Income from continuing operations	$ 913,474	$ 480,116
Basic earnings per share from continuing operations	$ 6.12	$ 4.65
Diluted earnings per share from continuing operations	$ 6.02	$ 4.58

The unaudited pro forma financial information is presented for information purposes only. It is not necessarily indicative of what our financial position or results of operations actually would have been had we completed the acquisition at the dates indicated, nor does it purport to project the future financial position or operating results of the combined company.

Investments

6.30

ANALOG DEVICES, INC. (OCT)

CONSOLIDATED STATEMENTS OF CASH FLOWS (in part)

Years ended October 29, 2011, October 30, 2010 and October 31, 2009

(Thousands)	2011	2010	2009
Investing Activities			
Cash flows from investing:			
Purchases of short-term available-for-sale investments	(4,289,304)	(3,478,025)	(2,812,094)
Maturities of short-term available-for-sale investments	3,436,284	2,801,727	2,274,254
Sales of short-term available-for-sale investments	282,861	234,718	74,880
Additions to property, plant and equipment, net	(122,996)	(111,557)	(56,095)
Net proceeds (expenditures) related to sale of businesses	10,000	63,036	(1,653)
Payments for acquisitions	(13,988)	—	(8,360)
(Increase) decrease in other assets	(6,595)	4,276	(5,661)
Net cash used for investing activities	(703,738)	(485,825)	(534,729)

NOTES TO CONSOLIDATED FINANCIAL STATEMENTS

Years ended October 29, 2011, October 30, 2010 and October 31, 2009

(All tabular amounts in thousands except per share amounts)

2. Summary of Significant Accounting Policies (in part)

b. Cash, Cash Equivalents and Short-Term Investments

Cash and cash equivalents are highly liquid investments with insignificant interest rate risk and maturities of three months or less at the time of acquisition. Cash, cash equivalents and short-term investments consist primarily of institutional money market funds and corporate obligations such as commercial paper and bonds. They also include bank time deposits.

The Company classifies its investments in readily marketable debt and equity securities as "held-to-maturity," "available-for-sale" or "trading" at the time of purchase. There were no transfers between investment classifications in any of the fiscal years presented. Held-to-maturity securities, which are carried at amortized cost, include only those securities the Company has the positive intent and ability to hold to maturity. Securities such as bank time deposits, which by their nature are typically held to maturity, are classified as such. The Company's other readily marketable cash equivalents and short-term investments are classified as available-for-sale. Available-for-sale securities are carried at fair value with unrealized gains and losses, net of related tax, reported in accumulated other comprehensive (loss) income.

The Company's deferred compensation plan investments are classified as trading. See Note 7 for additional information on the Company's deferred compensation plan investments. There were no cash equivalents or short-term investments classified as trading at October 29, 2011 or October 30, 2010.

The Company periodically evaluates its investments for impairment. There were no other-than-temporary impairments of short-term investments in any of the fiscal years presented.

Realized gains or losses recognized in nonoperating income from the sales of available-for-sale securities were not material during any of the fiscal years presented.

Unrealized gains and losses on available-for-sale securities classified as short-term investments at October 29, 2011 and October 30, 2010 were as follows:

	2011	2010
Unrealized gains on securities classified as short-term investments	$ 22	$ 165
Unrealized losses on securities classified as short-term investments	(600)	(217)
Net unrealized losses on securities classified as short-term investments	$(578)	$ (52)

Unrealized gains and losses in fiscal years 2011 and 2010 relate to corporate obligations.

The components of the Company's cash and cash equivalents and short-term investments as of October 29, 2011 and October 30, 2010 were as follows:

	2011	2010
Cash and Cash Equivalents:		
Cash	$ 17,857	$ 37,460
Available-for-sale	1,374,069	1,020,993
Held-to-maturity	13,174	11,547
Total cash and cash equivalents	$1,405,100	$1,070,000
Short-Term Investments:		
Available-for-sale	$2,186,782	$1,587,768
Held-to-maturity (less than one year to maturity)	580	30,000
Total short-term investments	$2,187,362	$1,617,768

See Note 2j for additional information on the Company's cash equivalents and short-term investments.

j. Fair Value (in part)

The table below sets forth by level the Company's financial assets and liabilities, excluding accrued interest components, that were accounted for at fair value on a recurring basis as of October 29, 2011 and October 30, 2010. The table excludes cash on hand and assets and liabilities that are measured at historical cost or any basis other than fair value.

	October 29, 2011				October 30, 2010		
	Fair Value Measurement at Reporting Date Using				Fair Value Measurement at Reporting Date Using		
	Quoted Prices in Active Markets for Identical Assets (Level 1)	Significant Other Observable Inputs (Level 2)	Significant Other Unobservable Inputs (Level 3)	Total	Quoted Prices in Active Markets for Identical Assets (Level 1)	Significant Other Observable Inputs (Level 2)	Total
Assets							
Cash equivalents:							
Available-for-sale:							
Institutional money market funds	$1,278,121	$ —	$ —	$1,278,121	$921,034	$ —	$ 921,034
Corporate obligations[1]	—	95,948	—	95,948	—	99,959	99,959

(continued)

| | October 29, 2011 | | | | October 30, 2010 | | |
| | Fair Value Measurement at Reporting Date Using | | | | Fair Value Measurement at Reporting Date Using | | |
	Quoted Prices in Active Markets for Identical Assets (Level 1)	Significant Other Observable Inputs (Level 2)	Significant Other Unobservable Inputs (Level 3)	Total	Quoted Prices in Active Markets for Identical Assets (Level 1)	Significant Other Observable Inputs (Level 2)	Total
Short—term investments:							
Available-for-sale:							
Securities with one year or less to maturity:							
Corporate obligations[1]	$ —	$2,169,078	$ —	$2,169,078	$ —	$1,520,220	$1,520,220
Floating rate notes, issued at par	—	—	—	—	—	50,000	50,000
Floating rate notes[1]	—	17,704	—	17,704	—	—	—
Securities with greater than one year to maturity:							
Floating rate notes[1]	—	—	—	—	—	17,548	17,548
Other assets:							
Forward foreign currency exchange contracts[2]	—	2,472	—	2,472	—	7,256	7,256
Deferred compensation investments	26,410	—	—	26,410	8,690	—	8,690
Other investments	1,135	—	—	1,135	1,317	—	1,317
Interest rate swap agreements	—	22,187	—	22,187	—	26,801	26,801
Total assets measured at fair value	$1,305,666	$2,307,389	$ —	$3,613,055	$931,041	$1,721,784	$2,652,825
Liabilities							
Long-term debt							
$375 million aggregate principal 5.0% debt[3]	$ —	$ 396,337	$ —	396,337	$ —	$ 400,635	$ 400,635
Contingent consideration	—	—	13,973	13,973	—	—	—
Total liabilities measured at fair value	$ —	$ 396,337	$13,973	$ 410,310	$ —	$ 400,635	$ 400,635

[1] The amortized cost of the Company's investments classified as available-for-sale as of October 29, 2011 and October 30, 2010 was $2,284.9 million and $1,639.1 million, respectively.

[2] The Company has a master netting arrangement by counterparty with respect to derivative contracts. As of October 29, 2011 and October 30, 2010, contracts in a liability position of $0.8 million in each year, were netted against contracts in an asset position in the consolidated balance sheets.

[3] Equal to the accreted notional value of the debt plus the fair value of the interest rate component of the long-term debt. The fair value of the long-term debt as of October 29, 2011 and October 30, 2010 was $413.4 million and $416.3 million, respectively.

The following methods and assumptions were used by the Company in estimating its fair value disclosures for financial instruments:

Cash equivalents and short-term investments—These investments are adjusted to fair value based on quoted market prices or are determined using a yield curve model based on current market rates.

Deferred compensation plan investments and other investments—The fair value of these mutual fund, money market fund and equity investments are based on quoted market prices.

Long-term debt — The fair value of long-term debt is based on quotes received from third-party banks.

Interest rate swap agreements—The fair value of interest rate swap agreements is based on quotes received from third-party banks. These values represent the estimated amount the Company would receive or pay to terminate the agreements taking into consideration current interest rates as well as the creditworthiness of the counterparty.

Forward foreign currency exchange contracts—The estimated fair value of forward foreign currency exchange contracts, which includes derivatives that are accounted for as cash flow hedges and those that are not designated as cash flow hedges, is based on the estimated amount the Company would receive if it sold these agreements at the reporting date taking into consideration current interest rates as well as the creditworthiness of the counterparty for assets and the Company's creditworthiness for liabilities.

Business Combinations

6.31

CARDINAL HEALTH, INC. (JUN)

CONSOLIDATED STATEMENTS OF CASH FLOWS
(in part)

(In millions)	Fiscal Year Ended June 30		
	2011	**2010**	**2009**
Cash Flows From Investing Activities:			
Proceeds from divestitures and sale of property and equipment	3.0	158.6	136.2
Acquisition of subsidiaries, net of cash acquired	(2,299.5)	(32.0)	(128.6)
Purchase of held-to-maturity investment securities	(155.6)	0.0	0.0
Additions to property and equipment	(291.3)	(260.3)	(421.2)
Proceeds from sale of CareFusion common stock	705.9	270.7	0.0
Proceeds from maturities of held-to-maturity securities	9.5	0.0	0.0
Net cash provided by/(used in) investing activities—continuing operations	(2,028.0)	137.0	(413.6)
Net cash used in investing activities—discontinued operations	0.0	(9.9)	(129.3)
Net cash provided by/(used in) investing activities	(2,028.0)	127.1	(542.9)

NOTES TO CONSOLIDATED FINANCIAL STATEMENTS

1. Basis of Presentation and Summary of Significant Accounting Policies (in part)

Business Combinations. The purchase price of an acquired business is allocated to the assets acquired and liabilities assumed based on their estimated fair values as of the date of acquisition, including identifiable intangible assets. When an acquisition involves contingent consideration, we recognize a liability equal to the fair value of the contingent consideration obligation at the date of acquisition. The excess of the purchase price over the estimated fair value of the net tangible and identifiable intangible assets acquired is recorded as goodwill. We base the fair values of identifiable intangible assets on detailed valuations that require management to make significant judgments, estimates and assumptions. Critical estimates and assumptions include: expected future cash flows for trade names, customer relationships and other identifiable intangible assets; discount rates that reflect the risk factors associated with future cash flows; and estimates of useful lives. See Note 2 for additional information regarding our acquisitions, including the contingent consideration related to the P4 Healthcare acquisition.

2. Acquisitions

Fiscal 2011

During fiscal 2011, we completed several acquisitions, the most significant of which are described in more detail below. The results of the acquisitions described below are included within our Pharmaceutical segment. We also completed other acquisitions during this period that were not significant, individually or in the aggregate. The valuation of identifiable intangible assets utilizes significant unobservable inputs and thus represents a Level 3 fair value measurement. The fair value measurements of assets acquired and liabilities assumed as of the acquisition dates were completed during fiscal 2011. The consolidated financial statements include

the results of operations from these business combinations from the date of acquisition. For fiscal 2011, these three acquisitions increased revenues by $2.9 billion and operating earnings by $61.3 million, compared to fiscal 2010.

Kinray. On December 21, 2010, we completed the acquisition of privately held Kinray, Inc. ("Kinray") for $1.3 billion in an all-cash transaction. Kinray is a wholesale pharmaceutical distribution company which serves retail independent pharmacies primarily in the New York metropolitan area.

Yong Yu. On November 29, 2010, we completed the acquisition of what is now our Yong Yu subsidiary for $457.7 million, including the assumption of $57.4 million in debt. Yong Yu is a health care distribution business headquartered in Shanghai, China.

P4 Healthcare. On July 15, 2010, we completed the acquisition of privately held Healthcare Solutions Holding, LLC ("P4 Healthcare") for $506.1 million in cash and certain contingent consideration. P4 Healthcare serves key participants across the chain of specialty care, including physicians, pharmaceutical companies and payors by providing essential tools, services and data to help improve the quality of patient outcomes and increase efficiency in the delivery of health care services.

In accordance with the agreement, the former owners of P4 Healthcare have the right to receive certain contingent payments based on targeted earnings before interest, taxes, depreciation, and amortization ("EBITDA"). The contingent consideration was to be earned over four measurement periods, which spanned three years, and each measurement period had specific targets and payout amounts. The contingent consideration payout was limited to $150.0 million. Subsequent to June 30, 2011, we amended the agreement with the former owners to extend the fourth measurement period (beginning January 1, 2013) from six months to eighteen months and reduce the maximum contingent consideration payout to $100.0 million.

We determined the estimated fair value of the contingent consideration obligation based on a probability-weighted income approach derived from EBITDA estimates and probability assessments with respect to the likelihood of achieving the various EBITDA targets. The fair value measurement is based on significant inputs not observable in the market and thus represents a Level 3 fair value measurement. At each reporting date, we revalue the contingent consideration obligation to estimated fair value and record changes in fair value as income or expense in our consolidated statement of earnings as acquisition-related costs. Changes in the fair value of the contingent consideration obligation may result from changes in the terms of the contingent payments, changes in discount periods and rates, changes in the timing and amount of EBITDA estimates, and changes in probability assumptions with respect to the timing and likelihood of achieving the EBITDA targets. Actual progress toward achieving the

EBITDA targets for the remaining measurement periods may be different than our expectations of performance in future measurement periods. Failure to meet current expectations of progress could increase the probability of not achieving the targets within the measurement periods and result in a material reduction in the fair value of the contingent consideration obligation. The fair value of the contingent consideration obligation was $75.4 million as of June 30, 2011, compared to the initial valuation of $92.0 million. The $16.6 million decrease in the contingent consideration liability reflects a cash payment of $10.2 million for the first measurement period and changes in our estimate of performance in future measurement periods.

The following table summarizes the fair values of the assets acquired and liabilities assumed as of the acquisition date for the three acquisitions described above:

(In millions)	Kinray	Yong Yu	P4 Healthcare
Identifiable intangible assets			
Trade names[1]	$ 16.8	$ 4.3	$ 16.0
Customer relationships[2]	116.0	51.7	163.0
Non-compete agreements[3]	0.0	0.0	9.7
Other[4]	0.0	0.0	37.0
Total identifiable intangible assets acquired	132.8	56.0	225.7
Cash and equivalents	0.0	3.9	0.0
Trade receivables, net	297.3	243.8	9.2
Inventories	180.8	133.1	0.1
Property and equipment, net	3.5	3.7	2.3
Other assets	18.8	52.0	2.8
Accounts payable	(268.5)	(218.8)	(1.2)
Other accrued liabilities	(12.4)	(55.8)	(8.3)
Short-term borrowings	0.0	(56.1)	0.0
Long-term obligations	0.0	(1.3)	0.0
Contingent consideration obligation	0.0	0.0	(92.0)
Total identifiable net assets acquired	352.3	160.5	138.6
Goodwill	983.7	239.8	367.5
Total net assets acquired	$1,336.0	$ 400.3	$506.1

[1] The weighted average lives of the trade names relating to the Kinray and Yong Yu acquisitions range from two to three years. P4 Healthcare trade names have indefinite lives.
[2] The weighted average lives of customer relationships range from 4 to 15 years.
[3] The weighted average life of non-compete agreements is five years.
[4] The weighted average lives of other identified intangible assets range from 2 to 10 years.

Fiscal 2010

During fiscal 2010, we completed an acquisition that individually was not significant. The aggregate purchase price of this acquisition, which was paid in cash, was $32.0 million, including the assumption of $1.9 million of liabilities. The consolidated financial statements include the results of operations from this business combination from the date of the acquisition.

Fiscal 2009

During fiscal 2009, we completed an acquisition that individually was not significant. The aggregate purchase price of this acquisition, which was paid in cash, was $128.6 million. Assumed liabilities of this acquired business were $102.1 million. The consolidated financial statements include the

results of operations from this business combination from the date of acquisition.

Acquisition-Related Costs

We classify costs incurred in connection with acquisitions as acquisition-related costs. These costs consist primarily of transaction costs, integration costs and changes in the fair value of contingent payments. Transaction costs are incurred during the initial evaluation of a potential targeted acquisition and primarily relate to costs to analyze, negotiate and consummate the transaction as well as financial and legal due diligence activities. Integration costs relate to activities needed to combine the operations of an acquired enterprise into our operations. As described above, we record changes in the fair value of contingent payments relating to acquisitions as income or expense in our acquisition-related costs.

Sale of Discontinued Operations

6.32

A. O. SMITH CORPORATION (DEC)

CONSOLIDATED STATEMENT OF CASH FLOWS
(in part)

Years ended December 31 (dollars in millions)

	2011	2010	2009
Investing Activities			
Acquisition of businesses	(421.1)	(11.8)	(71.4)
Proceeds from sale of investments	—	4.6	8.9
Proceeds on sale of assets	—	3.0	2.0
Net cash distributed with spinoff of discontinued SICO businesses	—	—	(7.1)
Capital expenditures	(53.5)	(53.5)	(42.7)
Cash used in investing activities—continuing operations	(474.6)	(57.7)	(110.3)
Cash provided by (used in) investing activities—discontinued operations	600.2	(8.8)	(6.7)
Cash Provided by (Used in) Investing Activities	125.6	(66.5)	(117.0)

NOTES TO CONSOLIDATED FINANCIAL STATEMENTS

1. Organization and Significant Accounting Policies (in part)

Organization (in part)

On August 22, 2011, the company sold its Electrical Products (EPC) business to Regal Beloit Corporation (RBC) for approximately $760 million in cash and approximately 2.83 million shares of RBC common stock. Due to the sale, EPC has been reported separately as a discontinued operation.

2. Discontinued Operations

On August 22, 2011, the company completed the sale of EPC to RBC for $759.9 million in cash and approximately 2.83 million of RBC shares. Included in the $759.9 million of cash is a final working capital adjustment of $7.4 million which is recorded as a receivable from RBC. The value of the RBC shares on the date of the closing of the sale was $140.6 million. See Note 13 for further discussion regarding the company's investment in RBC stock. The company has paid $126.5 million in income taxes and $21.4 million in commissions and other sale related payments as of December 31, 2011 and estimates it will pay $34.2 million in income taxes in 2012.

Included in the gain on sale of EPC was an additional income tax accrual of $56.5 million due to the company's assertion that certain foreign earnings derived from the sale of EPC were not considered permanently reinvested by the company. The accrual is included in long term deferred income taxes in continuing operations. Also included in the gain on sale is a $10.9 million gain related to cumulative translation adjustments associated with EPC's foreign subsidiaries.

The results of EPC including all prior years have been reported separately as discontinued operations.

The components of the net assets of EPC discontinued operations were:

(Dollars in millions)	December 31, 2010
Current Assets	
Trade receivables	$110.8
Inventory	135.9
Deferred taxes	2.2
Derivative contracts asset	17.4
Other current assets	6.0
Total current assets	272.3
Net property, plant and equipment	148.1
Goodwill	248.4
Other intangibles	2.8
Total assets	$671.6
Current Liabilities	
Trade payables	$ 89.5
Accrued payroll and benefits	15.2
Accrued liabilities	11.1
Product warranties	4.3
Income taxes	2.5
Total current liabilities	122.6
Deferred taxes	77.2
Other liabilities	1.3
Total liabilities	201.1
Total net assets	$470.5

Current liabilities-net of $31.5 million and long-term liabilities-net of $8.7 million of the EPC discontinued operations at December 31, 2011 consist primarily of certain retained product liabilities, employee obligations such as workers' compensation and disability and income tax liabilities associated with EPC.

The condensed statement of earnings of the EPC discontinued operations is:

(Dollars in millions)

Years Ended December 31	2011	2010	2009
Net sales	$531.8	$701.8	$616.5
Cost of products sold	415.6	544.0	510.5
Gross profit	116.2	157.8	106.0
Selling, general and administrative expenses	61.5	84.2	74.8
Restructuring and other	—	0.1	(1.6)
Interest expense	2.2	3.6	4.7
Other (income) expense—net	(6.0)	(0.7)	0.3
	58.5	70.6	27.8
Provision (benefit) for income taxes	15.5	16.2	(1.3)
Net earnings	$ 43.0	$ 54.4	$ 29.1

Consolidated interest expense not directly attributable to other operations was allocated to discontinued operations based on the ratio of EPC net assets to be sold to the sum of consolidated net assets plus consolidated debt not directly attributable to other operations.

The cash flow provided by EPC discontinued operations is as follows:

(Dollars in millions)

Years Ended December 31	2011	2010	2009
Operating Activities			
Earnings	$ 43.0	$ 54.4	$ 29.1
Adjustments to reconcile earnings to net cash provided by discontinued operating activities:			
Depreciation and amortization	16.5	26.1	29.2
Gain on sale of assets	(4.8)	(0.2)	(2.0)
Net changes in operating assets and liabilities			
Current assets and liabilities	(56.2)	(23.3)	74.5
Noncurrent assets and liabilities	0.9	4.5	9.9
Other	(1.7)	—	(0.7)
Cash (used in) provided by discontinued operating activities	(2.3)	61.5	140.0
Investing Activities			
Capital expenditures	(10.5)	(14.3)	(14.3)
Proceeds on sale of assets	6.1	5.5	7.6
Proceeds from sale of operations	752.5	—	—
Payments associated with sale	(147.9)	—	—
Cash provided by (used in) discontinued investing activities	600.2	(8.8)	(6.7)
Cash flow provided by discontinued operations	$ 597.9	$ 52.7	$133.3

In the second quarter of 2011, the company sold a facility in China and recognized a gain of $4.8 million.

Capitalized Software

6.33

LOCKHEED MARTIN CORPORATION (DEC)

CONSOLIDATED STATEMENTS OF CASH FLOWS
(in part)

	Year Ended December 31		
(In millions)	2011	2010	2009
Investing Activities			
Expenditures for property, plant and equipment	(814)	(820)	(852)
Expenditures for capitalized internal-use software	(173)	(254)	(314)
Net cash provided by (used for) short-term investment transactions	510	(171)	(279)
Net proceeds from sale of EIG	—	798	—
Acquisitions of businesses/investments in affiliates	(649)	(148)	(435)
Other, net	313	22	48
Net cash used for investing activities	(813)	(573)	(1,832)

NOTES TO CONSOLIDATED FINANCIAL STATEMENTS

Note 1—Significant Accounting Policies (in part)

Capitalized software—We capitalize certain costs associated with the development or purchase of internal-use software. The amounts capitalized are included in other assets on our Balance Sheets and are amortized on a straight-line basis over the estimated useful life of the resulting software, which ranges from two to six years. As of December 31, 2011 and 2010, capitalized software totaled $864 million and $899 million, net of accumulated amortization of $1.3 billion and $1.1 billion. Amortization expense related to capitalized software was $211 million in 2011, $211 million in 2010, and $160 million in 2009. In 2011, we revised the classification of cash payments associated with the development or purchase of internal-use software from operating cash flows to investing cash flows. Cash flows for all years above have been adjusted for this change. Cash payments for internal-use software were $173 million in 2011, $254 million in 2010, and $314 million in 2009.

Restricted Cash

6.34

MICRON TECHNOLOGY, INC. (AUG)

CONSOLIDATED STATEMENTS OF CASH FLOWS
(in part)

(In millions)

For the Year Ended	September 1, 2011	September 2, 2010	September 3, 2009
Cash Flows From Investing Activities			
Expenditures for property, plant and equipment	(2,550)	(616)	(488)
Acquisition of noncontrolling interests in TECH	(159)	—	—
Additions to equity method investments	(31)	(165)	(408)
Decrease (increase) in restricted cash	330	(240)	(56)
Proceeds from sales of property, plant and equipment	127	94	26
Return of equity method investment	48	—	41
Proceeds from sale of interest in Hynix JV	—	423	—
Cash acquired from acquisition of Numonyx	—	95	—
Proceeds from maturities of available-for-sale securities	—	—	130
Other	34	(39)	81
Net cash used for investing activities	(2,201)	(448)	(674)

*MANAGEMENT'S DISCUSSION AND ANALYSIS
OF FINANCIAL CONDITION AND RESULTS
OF OPERATIONS*

Liquidity and Capital Resources (in part)

Investing Activities

Net cash used for investing activities was $2,201 million for 2011, which consisted primarily of cash expenditures of $2,550 million for property, plant and equipment and $159 million for the acquisition of noncontrolling interests in TECH, partially offset by $330 million released from restricted cash. We believe that to develop new product and process technologies, support future growth, achieve operating efficiencies and maintain product quality, we must continue to invest in manufacturing technologies, facilities and capital equipment and research and development. We estimate that capital spending for 2012 will be approximately $2 billion, the majority of which is expected to be incurred in the first half of 2012. The actual amounts for 2012 will vary depending on market conditions. As of September 1, 2011, we had commitments of approximately $600 million for the acquisition of property, plant and equipment, substantially all of which is expected to be paid within one year.

Amounts released to us from restricted cash in 2011 included the following:
- $250 million of restricted cash collateral released to us in connection with the termination of our guarantee of a loan for a former joint venture as a result of the underlying loan being repaid, and
- $ 60 million of previously restricted cash that was released to us as a result of our prepayment of the TECH credit facility in 2011.

Insurance Proceeds

6.35

SMITHFIELD FOODS, INC. (APR)

*CONSOLIDATED STATEMENTS OF CASH FLOWS
(in part)*

(In millions)

	Fiscal Years		
	2011	2010	2009
Cash Flows From Investing Activities:			
Capital expenditures	(176.8)	(174.7)	(179.3)
Dispositions, including Butterball, LLC	261.5	23.3	587.0
Insurance proceeds	120.6	9.9	—
Net disposals (additions) of breeding stock	26.2	(8.0)	4.8
Proceeds from sale of property, plant and equipment	22.8	11.7	21.4
Dividends received	—	5.3	56.5
Investments in partnerships	—	(1.3)	(31.7)
Business acquisitions, net of cash acquired	—	—	(17.4)
Net cash flows from investing activities	254.3	(133.8)	441.3

NOTES TO CONSOLIDATED FINANCIAL STATEMENTS

Note 17: Regulation and Contingencies (in part)

Fire Insurance Settlement

In July 2009 (fiscal 2010), a fire occurred at the primary manufacturing facility of our subsidiary, Patrick Cudahy, Inc. (Patrick Cudahy), in Cudahy, Wisconsin. The fire damaged a portion of the facility's production space and required the temporary cessation of operations, but did not consume the entire facility. Shortly after the fire, we resumed production activities in undamaged portions of the plant, including the distribution center, and took steps to address the supply needs for Patrick Cudahy products by shifting production to other Company and third-party facilities.

We maintain comprehensive general liability and property insurance, including business interruption insurance. In December 2010 (fiscal 2011), we reached an agreement with our insurance carriers to settle the claim for a total of $208.0 million, of which $70.0 million had been advanced to us in fiscal 2010. We allocated these proceeds to first recover the book value of the property lost, out-of-pocket expenses incurred and business interruption losses that resulted from the fire. The remaining proceeds were recognized as an involuntary conversion gain of $120.6 million in the Corporate segment in the third quarter of fiscal 2011. The involuntary conversion gain was classified in a separate line item on the consolidated statement of income.

Based on an evaluation of business interruption losses incurred, we recognized $15.8 million and $31.8 million in fiscal 2011 and fiscal 2010, respectively, of the insurance proceeds in cost of sales in our Pork segment to offset business interruption losses incurred.

Of the $208.0 million in insurance proceeds received to settle the claim, $120.6 million and $9.9 million has been classified in net cash flows from investing activities in the consolidated statements of cash flows for fiscal 2011 and fiscal 2010, respectively, which represents the portion of proceeds related to destruction of the facility. The remainder of the proceeds was recorded in net cash flows from operating activities in the consolidated statements of cash flows and was attributed to business interruption recoveries and reimbursable costs covered under our insurance policy.

In-Process Research & Development (IPRD)

6.36

ELI LILLY AND COMPANY (DEC)

CONSOLIDATED STATEMENTS OF CASH FLOWS
(in part)

	Year Ended December 31		
(Dollars in millions)	**2011**	**2010**	**2009**
Cash Flows From Investing Activities			
Purchases of property and equipment	(672.0)	(694.3)	(765.0)
Disposals of property and equipment	25.3	24.6	17.7
Net change in short-term investments	(250.9)	(686.5)	399.1
Proceeds from sales and maturities of noncurrent investments	2,138.5	584.7	1,107.8
Purchases of noncurrent investments	(4,459.4)	(1,067.2)	(432.3)
Purchase of product rights	(632.9)	(442.4)	—
Purchases of in-process research and development	(388.0)	(50.0)	(90.0)
Cash paid for acquisitions, net of cash acquired	(307.8)	(609.4)	—
Loan to collaboration partner	(165.0)	—	—
Other investing activities, net	(112.2)	(219.3)	(94.5)
Net cash (used for) provided by investing activities	(4,824.4)	(3,159.8)	142.8

NOTES TO CONSOLIDATED FINANCIAL STATEMENTS

(Dollars in millions, except per-share data)

Note 1: Summary of Significant Accounting Policies (in part)

Goodwill and Other Intangibles (in part):

The cost of in-process research and development (IPR&D) projects acquired directly in a transaction other than a business combination is capitalized if the projects have an alternative future use; otherwise, they are expensed. The fair values of IPR&D projects acquired in business combinations are capitalized as other intangible assets. There are several methods that can be used to determine the estimated fair value of the IPR&D acquired in a business combination. We utilized the "income method," which applies a probability weighting that considers the risk of development and commercialization, to the estimated future net cash flows that are derived from projected sales revenues and estimated costs. These projections are based on factors such as relevant market size, patent protection, historical pricing of similar products, and expected industry trends. The estimated future net cash flows are then discounted to the present value using an appropriate discount rate. This analysis is performed for each project independently. These assets are treated as indefinite-lived intangible assets until completion or abandonment of the projects, at which time the assets will be amortized over the remaining useful life or written off, as appropriate. We also capitalize milestone payments incurred at or after the product has obtained regulatory approval for marketing and amortize those amounts over the remaining estimated useful life of the underlying asset.

Note 3: Acquisitions (in part)

During 2011 and 2010, we completed the acquisitions of the animal health business of Janssen Pharmaceutica NV (Janssen), Avid Radiopharmaceuticals, Inc. (Avid), Alnara Pharmaceuticals, Inc. (Alnara), and a group of animal health product lines. These acquisitions were accounted for as business combinations under the acquisition method of accounting. The assets acquired and liabilities assumed were recorded at their respective fair values as of the acquisition date in our consolidated financial statements. The determination of estimated fair value required management to make significant estimates and assumptions. The excess of the purchase price over the fair value of the acquired net assets, where applicable, has been recorded as goodwill. The results of operations of these acquisitions are included in our consolidated financial statements from the date of acquisition. None of these acquisitions were material to our consolidated financial statements.

Most of these acquisitions included IPR&D, which represented compounds, new indications, or line extensions under development that had not yet achieved regulatory approval for marketing. As discussed in Note 1, the fair values of IPR&D assets acquired as part of the acquisition of a business are capitalized as intangible assets. Accordingly, we capitalized IPR&D assets acquired in business combinations totaling $30.9 million and $598.0 million for the years ended December 31, 2011 and 2010, respectively. Once the Avid and Alnara products are launched, the amortization of the respective acquired IPR&D assets will not be deductible for tax purposes. The ongoing expenses with respect to each of these assets in development are not material to our total research and development expense currently and are not expected to be material to our total research and development expense on an annual basis in the future.

Some of these acquisitions included contingent consideration, which is recorded at fair value in other liabilities as of the acquisition date. The fair value of the contingent consideration was determined by utilizing a probability weighted estimated cash flow stream discounted for the expected timing of each payment. Subsequent to the acquisition date, on a quarterly basis we remeasure the contingent consideration at current fair value with changes recorded in other—net, expense in the statement of operations.

In addition to the acquisitions of businesses, we also acquired several assets in development which are discussed below in Product Acquisitions and in Note 4. The acquired IPR&D related to these products of $388.0 million, $50.0 million, and $90.0 million for the years ended December 31, 2011, 2010, and 2009, respectively, was written off by a charge to income immediately upon acquisition because the products had no alternative future use.

Note 4: Collaborations (in part)

Diabetes Collaboration

In January 2011, we and Boehringer entered into a global agreement to jointly develop and commercialize a portfolio of diabetes compounds. Included are Boehringer 's two oral diabetes agents, linagliptin and empagliflozin (BI 10773). Subsequently in 2011, linagliptin was approved and launched in the U.S. (tradename Tradjenta), Japan (tradename Trazenta), Europe (tradename Trajenta), and other countries. Empagliflozin is currently in Phase III clinical testing. Also included in the agreement is our new insulin glargine product and our novel basal insulin analog, both of which began Phase III clinical testing in the second half of 2011; and an option granted to Boehringer to co-develop and co-commercialize our anti-TGF-beta monoclonal antibody, which is currently in Phase II clinical testing. Under the terms of the agreement, we made an initial one-time payment to Boehringer of $388.0 million and recorded an acquired IPR&D charge, which was included as expense in the first quarter of 2011 and is deductible for tax purposes.

In connection with the approval of linagliptin in the U.S., Japan, and Europe, in 2011 we paid $478.7 million in success-based regulatory milestones, all of which were capitalized as intangible assets and are being amortized to cost of sales. We may pay up to approximately €300 million in additional success-based regulatory milestones for empagliflozin. We will be eligible to receive up to a total of $650.0 million in success-based regulatory milestones on our two insulin products. Should Boehringer elect to opt in to the Phase III development and potential commercialization of the anti-TGF-beta monoclonal antibody, we would be eligible for up to $525.0 million in opt-in and success-based regulatory milestone payments. The companies share ongoing development costs equally. The companies also share in the commercialization costs and gross margin for any product resulting from the collaboration that receives regulatory approval. We record our portion of the gross margin as collaboration and other revenue, and we record our portion of the commercialization costs as marketing, selling, and administrative expense. Each company will also be entitled to potential performance payments on sales of the molecules they contribute to the collaboration. Revenue related to this collaboration has not been significant to date.

CASH FLOWS FROM FINANCING ACTIVITIES

PRESENTATION

6.37 FASB ASC 230-10-45 defines those transactions and events that constitute financing cash receipts and payments. The following are considered cash receipts and payments from financing activities:

- Proceeds from issuing equity instruments.
- Proceeds from issuing bonds, mortgages, and notes and from other short- or long-term borrowing.
- Receipts from contributions and investment income that, by donor stipulation, are restricted for the purposes of acquiring, constructing, or improving PPE or other long-lived assets or establishing or increasing a permanent or term endowment.
- Proceeds received from derivative instruments that include financing elements at inception, regardless of whether the proceeds were received at inception or over the term of the derivative instrument, other than a financing element inherently included in an at-the-market derivative instrument with no prepayments.
- Cash that is recognizable for financial reporting purposes because it is retained as a result of the tax deductibility of increases in the value of equity instruments issued under share-based payment arrangements that are not included in the cost of goods or services. For this purpose, excess tax benefits should be determined on an individual award (or portion thereof) basis.
- Payments of dividends or other distributions to owners, including outlays to reacquire the entity's equity instruments.
- Repayments of borrowed amounts.
- Other principal payments to creditors who have extended long-term credit.
- Distributions to counterparties of derivative instruments that include financing elements at inception, other than a financing element inherently included in an at-the-market derivative instrument with no prepayments. The distributions may be either at inception or over the term of the derivative instrument.
- Payments for debt issue costs.

PRESENTATION AND DISCLOSURE EXCERPTS

Debt Proceeds/Repayments

6.38

ROCK-TENN COMPANY (SEP)

CONSOLIDATED STATEMENTS OF CASH FLOWS
(in part)

	Year Ended September 30		
(In millions)	2011	2010	2009
Financing Activities:			
Proceeds from issuance of notes	—	—	100.0
Additions to revolving credit facilities	802.6	189.7	230.8
Repayments of revolving credit facilities	(564.5)	(197.7)	(244.6)
Additions to debt	2,877.4	154.3	119.6
Repayments of debt	(1,966.3)	(366.3)	(552.1)
Debt issuance costs	(43.8)	(0.2)	(4.4)
Cash paid for debt extinguishment costs	(37.9)	—	(5.2)
Restricted cash and investments	—	—	19.2
Issuances of common stock, net of related minimum tax withholdings	25.2	(0.6)	(0.1)
Purchases of common stock	—	(3.6)	—
Excess tax benefits from share-based compensation	—	4.3	5.5
Capital contributed to consolidated subsidiary from noncontrolling interest	—	1.4	1.7
Advances from (repayments to) unconsolidated entity	1.7	1.7	(7.0)
Cash dividends paid to shareholders	(37.6)	(23.4)	(15.3)
Cash distributions paid to noncontrolling interests	(5.2)	(6.9)	(4.8)
Net cash provided by (used for) financing activities	1,051.6	(247.3)	(356.7)

NOTES TO CONSOLIDATED FINANCIAL STATEMENTS

Note 9. Debt

The following were individual components of debt (in millions):

	September 30, 2011	September 30, 2010
8.20% secured notes due August 2011[a]	$ —	$155.8
5.625% secured notes due March 2013[b]	80.9	81.1
9.25% unsecured notes due March 2016[c]	299.2	299.1
Term loan facilities[d]	2,223.1	470.1
Revolving credit and swing facilities[d]	238.0	11.3
Receivables-backed financing facility[e]	559.0	75.0
Industrial development revenue bonds, bearing interest at variable rates (2.54% at September 30, 2011 and 2.06% at September 30, 2010)[f]	17.4	17.4
Other debt	28.2	19.1
Total debt	3,445.8	1,128.9
Less current portion of debt	143.3	231.6
Long-term debt due after one year	$3,302.5	$897.3

A portion of the debt classified as long-term, which includes the term loans, receivables-backed, revolving and swing facilities, may be paid down earlier than scheduled at our discretion without penalty. During fiscal 2011, 2010, and 2009, amortization of debt issuance costs charged to interest expense was $7.7 million, $6.1 million, and $6.9 million, respectively.

(a) We repaid the remaining balance of our $250.0 million aggregate principal amount of our 8.20% notes due on August 15, 2011 at maturity.

(b) In March 2003, we sold $100.0 million in aggregate principal amount of our 5.625% notes due March 2013 ("March 2013 Notes"). Interest on the March 2013 Notes is payable in arrears each September and March. The March 2013 Notes are redeemable prior to maturity, subject to certain rules and restrictions, and are not subject to any sinking fund requirements. The March 2013 Notes are senior, secured obligations and rank equally with all other secured debt as they share generally, on a pro-rata basis, in the same collateral that was granted to the banks as part of the Credit Facility. The indenture related to the March 2013 Notes restricts us and our subsidiaries from incurring certain liens and entering into certain sale and leaseback transactions, subject to a number of exceptions. We are amortizing debt issuance costs of approximately $0.8 million over the term of the March 2013 Notes. In the first quarter of fiscal 2010, we repurchased $19.5 million of our March 2013 Notes at an average price of approximately 98% of par and recorded an aggregate gain on extinguishment of debt of approximately $0.5 million. The amount in the table above is net of hedge adjustments resulting from terminated interest rate swaps and unamortized discount. Giving effect to the amortization of the original issue discount, the terminated fair value hedge adjustments and the debt issuance costs, the effective interest rate on the March 2013 Notes is approximately 5.37%.

(c) On March 5, 2008, we issued $200.0 million aggregate principal amount of 9.25% senior notes due March 2016 ("March 2016 Notes"). Interest on our March 2016 Notes is payable in arrears each March and September. The March 2016 Notes are redeemable prior to maturity, subject to certain rules and restrictions, and are not subject to any sinking fund requirements. The indenture related to the March 2016 Notes contains incurrence based financial and restrictive covenants applicable to the notes, including limitations on: restricted payments, dividend and other payments affecting restricted subsidiaries (as defined therein), incurrence of debt, asset sales, transactions with affiliates, liens, sale and leaseback transactions and the creation of unrestricted subsidiaries. The March 2016 Notes were originally issued at a discount of $1.4 million and incurred debt issuance costs of $4.7 million. On May 29, 2009, we issued an additional $100.0 million aggregate principal amount of March 2016 Notes (the "Additional Notes") and as a result incurred debt issuance costs of approximately $2.7 million related to the Additional Notes; these debt issuance costs, together with the original issue debt discount and debt issuance costs, are being amortized through the maturity date of the March 2016 Notes. Giving effect to the amortization of the original issue discount and the debt issuance costs, the effective interest rate of the March 2016 Notes and the Additional Notes is approximately 9.63%.

(d) On May 27, 2011, we entered into a Credit Agreement (the "Credit Facility") with an original maximum principal amount of $3.7 billion. The Credit Facility includes a $1.475 billion, 5-year revolving credit facility, a $1.475 billion, 5-year term loan A facility, and a $750 million, 7-year term loan B facility. The Credit Facility is pre-payable at any time. The borrowings under the Credit Facility were primarily used to finance the Smurfit-Stone Acquisition in part, to repay certain outstanding indebtedness of Smurfit-Stone, to refinance certain of our existing credit facilities, to pay for fees and expenses incurred in connection with the acquisition, and for other corporate purposes. We may borrow amounts under the revolving credit facility to provide for working capital and general corporate requirements, including acquisitions permitted pursuant to the Credit Facility. Up to $250.0 million under the revolving credit facility may be used for the issuance of letters of credit. In addition, up to $300.0 million of the revolving credit facility may be used to fund borrowings in Canadian dollars. At September 30, 2011, the amount committed under the Credit Facility for loans to a Canadian subsidiary was $300.0 million. At September 30, 2011, available borrowings under the revolving credit portion of the Credit Facility, reduced by outstanding letters of credit not drawn upon of approximately $91.1 million, were approximately $1,145.9 million.

At our option, borrowings under the Credit Facility bear interest at either a base rate or at the London Interbank Offered Rate ("LIBOR"), plus, in each case, an applicable margin. In addition, advances in Canadian dollars may be made by way of purchases of bankers' acceptances. We are required to pay fees in respect of outstanding letters of credit at a rate equal to the applicable margin for LIBOR-based borrowings based upon a Credit Agreement Leverage Ratio. The following table summarizes the applicable margins and percentages related to the revolving credit facility and term loan A of the Credit Facility:

	Range	September 30, 2011
Applicable margin/percentage for determining:		
LIBOR-based loans and banker's acceptance advances interest rate[1]	1.50%–2.25%	2.0%
Base rate-based borrowings[1]	0.50%–1.25%	1.0%
Facility commitment[2]	0.25%–0.35%	0.35%

[1] The rates vary based on our Leverage Ratio, as defined in the Credit Agreement.

[2] Applied to the aggregate borrowing availability based on the Leverage Ratio, as defined below.

The variable interest rate, including the applicable margin, on our term loan A facility, before the effect of interest rate swaps, was 2.23% at September 30, 2011. Interest rates on our revolving credit facility for borrowings both in the U.S. and Canada ranged from 3.25% to 4.00% at September 30, 2011.

Borrowings under the term loan B facility have applicable margins of 2.75% for LIBOR-based loans (with LIBOR to be no lower than 0.75%) and 1.75% for base rate-based loans. The interest rate for borrowings under the term loan B facility was 3.50% at September 30, 2011.

All obligations under the Credit Facility are fully and unconditionally guaranteed by our existing and future wholly-owned U.S. subsidiaries, including those acquired in the Smurfit-Stone Acquisition, other than certain present and future unrestricted subsidiaries and certain other limited exceptions as well as a pledge of subsidiary stock of certain wholly-owned subsidiaries. In addition, the obligations of Rock-Tenn Company of Canada are guaranteed by Rock-Tenn Company and all such wholly-owned U.S. subsidiaries, as well as by wholly-owned Canadian subsidiaries of Rock-Tenn, including those acquired in the Smurfit-Stone Acquisition, other than certain present and future unrestricted subsidiaries and certain other limited exceptions.

The Credit Facility contains certain prepayment requirements and customary affirmative and negative covenants. The negative covenants include covenants that, subject to certain exceptions, contain: limitations on liens and further negative pledges; limitations on sale-leaseback transactions; limitations on debt and prepayments, redemptions or repurchases of certain debt and equity; limitations on mergers and asset sales; limitations on sales, transfers and other dispositions of assets; limitations on loans and certain other investments; limitations on restrictions affecting subsidiaries; (i) limitations on transactions with affiliates; (ii) limitations on changes to accounting policies or (iii) fiscal periods; limitations on speculative hedge transactions; and restrictions on modification or waiver of material documents in a manner materially adverse to the lenders.

In addition, the term loan A and the revolving credit facility include financial covenants requiring that we maintain a maximum total leverage ratio and minimum interest coverage ratio. The terms of the Credit Facility require us to maintain a leverage ratio (which is the ratio of our total funded debt less certain amounts of unrestricted cash, to Credit Agreement EBITDA, as defined, for the preceding four fiscal quarters ("Leverage Ratio")) of not greater than 3.75 to 1.00 for fiscal quarters ending from June 30, 2011 through June 30, 2012, and not greater than 3.50 to 1.00 for fiscal quarters ending thereafter. In addition, we must maintain an interest coverage ratio (which is the ratio of Credit Agreement EBITDA for the preceding four fiscal quarters to cash interest expense for such period) of not less than 3.50 to 1.00 for any fiscal quarters ending on or after September 30, 2011. Credit Agreement EBITDA is calculated in accordance with the definition contained in our Credit Agreement. Credit Agreement EBITDA is generally defined as consolidated net income of RockTenn for any fiscal period plus the following to the extent such amounts are deducted in determining such consolidated net income: (i) consolidated interest expense, (ii) consolidated tax expenses, (iii) depreciation and amortization expenses, (iv) financing expenses and write-offs, including remaining portions of original issue discount on prepayment of indebtedness, prepayment premiums and commitment fees, (v) inventory expenses associated with the write up of Smurfit-Stone inventory acquired in the merger and other permitted acquisitions, (vi) all other non-cash charges, (vii) all legal, accounting and professional advisory expenses incurred in respect of the Smurfit-Stone Acquisition and other permitted acquisitions and related financing transactions, (vii) certain expenses and costs incurred in connection with the Smurfit-Stone Acquisition and associated synergies, restructuring charges, and certain other charges and expenses, subject to certain limitations specified in the Credit Facility, (viii) certain other charges and expenses unrelated to the Smurfit-Stone Acquisition subject to certain specified limitations in the Credit Facility, and (ix) for certain periods, run-rate synergies expected to be achieved due to the Smurfit-Stone Acquisition not already included in EBITDA and adjustments to include Smurfit-Stone EBITDA as outlined in the Credit Agreement related to periods prior to the acquisition ("Credit Agreement EBITDA"). We test and report our compliance with these covenants each quarter. We are in compliance with all of our covenants.

The credit facilities also contain certain customary events of default, including relating to non-payment, breach of representations, warranties or covenants, default on other material debt, bankruptcy and insolvency events, invalidity or impairment of loan documentation, collateral or subordination provisions, change of control and customary ERISA defaults. The term "ERISA" means the Employee Retirement

Income Security Act of 1974, as amended, and the rules and regulations thereunder.

On May 27, 2011, at the effective time of the Smurfit-Stone Acquisition, in connection with our entry into the Credit Facility, we terminated our existing credit agreement, dated as of March 5, 2008, as amended (the "Terminated Credit Facility"), following the payment in full of all outstanding indebtedness under the Terminated Credit Facility. There were no material early termination penalties incurred as a result of the termination of the Terminated Credit Facility. We recorded a loss on extinguishment of debt of $39.5 million primarily for fees paid to certain creditors and third parties and to write-off certain unamortized deferred financing costs related to the Terminated Credit Facility and capitalized approximately $43.3 million of debt issuance costs in other assets related to the new credit agreements, including amounts related to our receivables-backed financing facility.

(e) On May 27, 2011, we increased our receivables-backed financing facility (the "Receivables Facility") to $625.0 million from $135.0 million. The Receivables Facility has been amended to include the trade receivables of additional Rock-Tenn subsidiaries. In addition, the maturity date of the Receivables Facility has been extended until the third anniversary of the Smurfit-Stone Acquisition. The borrowings are classified as long-term at September 30, 2011 and September 30, 2010. The borrowing rate, which consists of a blend of the market rate for asset-backed commercial paper and the one month LIBOR rate plus a utilization fee, was 1.36% and 2.08% as of September 30, 2011 and September 30, 2010, respectively. The commitment fee for this facility was 0.30% and 1.00% as of September 30, 2011 and September 30, 2010, respectively. Borrowing availability under this facility is based on the eligible underlying accounts receivable and certain covenants. The agreement governing the Receivables Facility contains restrictions, including, among others, on the creation of certain liens on the underlying collateral. We test and report our compliance with these covenants monthly. We are in compliance with all of our covenants. At September 30, 2011 and September 30, 2010, maximum available borrowings, excluding amounts outstanding, under this facility were approximately $559.9 million and $135.0 million, respectively. The carrying amount of accounts receivable collateralizing the maximum available borrowings at September 30, 2011 was approximately $881.1 million. We have continuing involvement with the underlying receivables as we provide credit and collections services pursuant to the securitization agreement.

(f) The industrial development revenue bonds ("IDBs") are issued by various municipalities in which we maintain facilities. Each series of bonds is secured by a direct pay letter of credit, or collateralized by a mortgage interest and collateral interest in specific property or a combination thereof. As of September 30, 2011, the outstanding amount of direct pay letters of credit supporting all IDBs was $17.7 million. The letters of credit are renewable at our request so long as no default or event of default has occurred under the Credit Facility. On October 3, 2011 we repaid all of these outstanding IDBs.

SEC 6.38

Capital Stock Proceeds/Payments

6.39

THE PNC FINANCIAL SERVICES GROUP, INC.
(DEC)

CONSOLIDATED STATEMENT OF CASH FLOWS
(in part)

(In millions)	Year Ended December 31		
	2011	**2010**	**2009**
Financing Activities			
Net change in			
Noninterest-bearing deposits	$ 8,909	$ 5,872	$ 7,169
Interest-bearing deposits	(4,863)	(8,844)	(9,849)
Federal funds purchased and repurchase agreements	(1,151)	152	(1,173)
Federal Home Loan borrowings	1,000	(280)	280
Other borrowed funds	(562)	380	(1,726)
Sales/issuances			
Federal Home Loan borrowings	1,000		2,092
Bank notes and senior debt	1,244	3,230	2,461
Other borrowed funds	10,025	4,820	234
Preferred stock	988		
Supervisory Capital Assessment Program—common stock			624
Common and treasury stock	72	3,486	247
Repayments/maturities			
Federal Home Loan borrowings	(1,076)	(4,373)	(9,671)
Bank notes and senior debt	(2,612)	(2,808)	(3,887)
Subordinated debt	(1,942)	(257)	(1,000)
Other borrowed funds	(8,977)	(4,677)	(211)
Preferred stock—TARP		(7,579)	
Redemption of noncontrolling interest and other preferred stock		(100)	
Acquisition of treasury stock	(73)	(204)	(188)
Preferred stock cash dividends paid	(56)	(146)	(388)
Common stock cash dividends paid	(604)	(204)	(430)
Net cash provided (used) by financing activities	1,322	(11,532)	(15,416)

*NOTES TO CONSOLIDATED FINANCIAL
STATEMENTS*

Note 18 Equity (in part)

Preferred Stock

Information related to preferred stock is as follows:

Preferred Stock—Issued and Outstanding

December 31 Shares in thousands	Liquidation Value per Share	Preferred Shares	
		2011	**2010**
Authorized			
$1 par value		16,588	16,588
Issued and outstanding			
Series B	$ 40	1	1
Series K	10,000	50	50
Series L	100,000	2	2
Series O	100,000	10	
Total issued and outstanding		63	53

Our Series B preferred stock is cumulative and is not redeemable at our option. Annual dividends on Series B preferred stock total $1.80 per share. Holders of Series B preferred stock are entitled to 8 votes per share, which is equal to the number of full shares of common stock into which the Series B Preferred Stock is convertible.

Our Series K preferred stock was issued in May 2008 in connection with our issuance of $500 million of Depositary Shares, each representing a fractional interest in a share of the Fixed-to-Floating Non-Cumulative Perpetual Preferred Stock, Series K. Dividends are payable if and when declared each May 21 and November 21 until May 21, 2013. After that date, dividends will be payable each 21 st of August, November, February and May. Dividends will be paid at a rate of 8.25% prior to May 21, 2013 and at a rate of three-month LIBOR plus 422 basis points beginning May 21, 2013. The Series K preferred stock is redeemable at our option on or after May 21, 2013.

Our 9.875% Fixed-to-Floating Rate Non-Cumulative Preferred Stock, Series L was issued in connection with the National City transaction in exchange for National City's Fixed-to-Floating Rate Non-Cumulative Preferred Stock, Series F. Dividends on the Series L preferred stock are payable if and when declared each 1 st of February, May, August and November. Dividends will be paid at a rate of 9.875% prior to February 1, 2013 and at a rate of three-month LIBOR plus 633 basis points beginning February 1, 2013. The Series L is redeemable at PNC's option, subject to Federal Reserve approval, if then applicable, on or after February 1, 2013 at a redemption price per share equal to the liquidation preference plus any declared but unpaid dividends.

Our Series O preferred stock was issued on July 27, 2011, when we issued one million depositary shares, each representing a 1/100 th interest in a share of our Fixed-to-Floating Rate Non-Cumulative Perpetual Preferred Stock, Series O for gross proceeds before commissions and expenses of $1 billion. Dividends are payable when, as, and if declared by our board of directors or an authorized committee of our board, semi-annually on February 1 and August 1 of each year until August 1, 2021 at a rate of 6.75%. After that date, dividends will be payable on February 1, May 1, August 1 and November 1 of each year beginning on November 1, 2021 at a rate of three-month LIBOR plus 3.678% per annum. The Series O preferred stock is redeemable at our option on or after August 1, 2021 and at our option within 90 days of a regulatory capital treatment event as defined in the designations.

We have authorized but unissued Series H, I, J and M preferred stock. As described in Note 13 Capital Securities of Subsidiary Trusts and Perpetual Trust Securities, under the terms of two of the hybrid capital vehicles we issued that currently qualify as capital for regulatory purposes (the Trust II Securities and the Trust III Securities), these Trust Securities are automatically exchangeable into shares of PNC preferred stock (Series I and Series J, respectively) in each case under certain conditions relating to the capitalization or the financial condition of PNC Bank, N.A. and upon the direction of the Office of the Comptroller of the Currency. The Series preferred stock of PNC REIT Corp. is also automatically exchangeable under similar conditions into shares of PNC Series H preferred stock.

As a part of the National City transaction, we established the PNC Non-Cumulative Perpetual Preferred Stock, Series M, which mirrors in all material respects the former National City Non-Cumulative Perpetual Preferred Stock, Series E. PNC has designated 5,751 preferred shares, liquidation value $100,000 per share, for this series. No shares have yet been issued; however, National City issued stock purchase contracts for 5,001 shares of its Series E Preferred Stock (now replaced by the PNC Series M as part of the National City transaction) to the National City Preferred Capital Trust I in connection with the issuance by that Trust of $500 million of 12.000% Fixed-to-Floating Rate Normal Automatic Preferred Enhanced Capital Securities (the Normal APEX Securities) in January 2008 by the Trust. It is expected that the Trust will purchase 5,001 of the Series M preferred shares pursuant to these stock purchase contracts on December 10, 2012 or on an earlier date and possibly as late as December 10, 2013. The Trust has pledged the $500,100,000 principal amount of National City 8.729% Junior Subordinated Notes due 2043 held by the Trust and their proceeds to secure this purchase obligation.

If Series M shares are issued prior to December 10, 2012, any dividends on such shares will be calculated at a rate per annum equal to 12.000% until December 10, 2012, and thereafter, at a rate per annum that will be reset quarterly and will equal three-month LIBOR for the related dividend period plus 8.610%. Dividends will be payable if and when declared by the Board at the dividend rate so indicated applied to the liquidation preference per share of the Series M Preferred Stock. The Series M is redeemable at PNC's option, subject to Federal Reserve approval, if then applicable, on or after December 10, 2012 at a redemption price per share equal to the liquidation preference plus any declared but unpaid dividends.

The replacement capital covenants with respect to the Normal APEX Securities, our Series M shares and our 6,000,000 of Depositary Shares (each representing 1/4000th of an interest in a share of our 9.875% Fixed-to-Floating Rate Non-Cumulative Preferred Stock, Series L) were terminated on November 5, 2010 as a result of a successful consent solicitation.

After receiving all required approvals, on February 10, 2010, we redeemed all 75,792 shares of our Fixed Rate Cumulative Perpetual Preferred Stock, Series N that had been issued on December 31, 2008 to the US Treasury under the US Treasury's Troubled Asset Relief Program (TARP) Capital Purchase Program.

In connection with the redemption of the Series N Preferred Stock, we accelerated the accretion of the remaining issuance discount on the Series N Preferred Stock, recorded a corresponding reduction in retained earnings of $250 million during the first quarter of 2010 and paid dividends of $89 million to the US Treasury. This resulted in a noncash reduction in net income attributable to common shareholders and related basic and diluted earnings per share.

During 2010, PNC called its Series A, C and D cumulative convertible preferred stock for redemption in accordance with the terms of that stock. Effective September 10, 2010, PNC redeemed 1,777 outstanding shares of Series A at a redemption price of $40.00 per share. Effective October 1, 2010, PNC redeemed 18,118 outstanding shares of Series C and 26,010 shares of Series D at a redemption price of $20.00 per share.

Stock-Based Compensation

6.40

ELECTRONIC ARTS INC. (MAR)

CONSOLIDATED STATEMENTS OF CASH FLOWS
(in part)

	Year Ended March 31		
(In millions)	2011	2010	2009
Financing Activities			
Proceeds from issuance of common stock	34	39	89
Excess tax benefit from stock-based compensation	1	14	2
Repurchase and retirement of common stock	(58)	—	—
Net cash provided by (used in) financing activities	(23)	53	91

NOTES TO CONSOLIDATED FINANCIAL STATEMENTS

(13) Stock-Based Compensation and Employee Benefit Plans (in part)

Stock-Based Compensation Expense

Employee stock-based compensation expense recognized during the fiscal years ended March 31, 2011, 2010 and 2009 was calculated based on awards ultimately expected to vest and has been reduced for estimated forfeitures. In subsequent periods, if actual forfeitures differ from those estimates, an adjustment to stock-based compensation expense will be recognized at that time.

The following table summarizes stock-based compensation expense resulting from stock options, restricted stock, restricted stock units and the ESPP included in our Consolidated Statements of Operations (in millions):

	Year Ended March 31		
	2011	2010	2009
Cost of goods sold	$ 2	$ 2	$ 2
Marketing and sales	21	16	20
General and administrative	40	33	47
Research and development	111	110	134
Restructuring and other charges	2	26	—
Stock-based compensation expense	$176	$187	$203

During the fiscal years ended March 31, 2011, 2010 and 2009, we did not recognize any provision for or benefit from income taxes related to our stock-based compensation expense.

As of March 31, 2011, our total unrecognized compensation cost related to stock options was $36 million and is expected to be recognized over a weighted-average service period of 1.5 years. As of March 31, 2011, our total unrecognized compensation cost related to restricted stock, restricted stock units and notes payable in shares of common stock (collectively referred to as "restricted stock rights") was $255 million and is expected to be recognized over a weighted-average service period of 1.9 years. Of the $255

million of unrecognized compensation cost noted above, $24 million relates to performance-based restricted stock units for which we ceased recognizing stock-based compensation expense during fiscal year 2010 because we determined that the performance attainment was neither probable nor improbable of achievement.

For the fiscal year ended March 31, 2011, we recognized $2 million of tax costs from the exercise of stock options, net of $3 million of deferred tax write-offs; of this amount $1 million of excess tax benefit related to stock-based compensation was reported in the financing activities on our Consolidated Statements of Cash Flows. For the fiscal year ended March 31, 2010, we recognized $14 million of tax benefits from the exercise of stock options for which we did not have any deferred tax asset write-offs; all of which represented excess tax benefits related to stock-based compensation and was reported in financing activities. For the fiscal year ended March 31, 2009, we recognized $2 million of tax benefits from the exercise of stock options for which we did not have any deferred tax asset write-offs; all of which represented excess tax benefits related to stock-based compensation and was reported in financing activities.

Dividends

6.41

AMPHENOL CORPORATION (DEC)

CONSOLIDATED STATEMENTS OF CASH FLOW
(in part)

(Dollars in thousands)

	Year Ended December 31		
	2011	2010	2009
Cash Flow From Financing Activities:			
Long-term borrowings under credit facilities (Note 2)	873,200	793,406	609,648
Repayments of long-term debt	(301,900)	(748,017)	(1,241,582)
Borrowings under senior notes	—	—	598,878
Settlement of interest rate swap agreements	—	—	(4,575)
Payment of fees and expenses related to debt financing	(2,125)	(6,975)	(4,650)
Purchase and retirement of treasury stock	(672,191)	—	—
Proceeds from exercise of stock options	26,086	46,616	25,481
Excess tax benefits from stock-based payment arrangements	5,995	14,692	16,085
Payment of contingent acquisition-related obligations	(40,000)	—	—
Distributions to and purchases of noncontrolling interests	(29,931)	(24,588)	(23,328)
Dividend payments	(10,282)	(10,413)	(10,279)
Cash flow (used in) provided by financing activities	(151,148)	64,721	(34,322)

NOTES TO CONSOLIDATED FINANCIAL STATEMENTS

(Dollars in thousands, except per share data)

Note 7—Equity (in part)

Dividends:

After declaration by the Board of Directors, the Company paid a quarterly dividend on its common stock of $.015 per share in 2010 and 2011. The Company paid its fourth quarterly dividend in the amount of $2,447 or $.015 per share on January 3, 2012 to shareholders of record as of December 14, 2011. Cumulative dividends declared during 2011 and 2010 were $10,097 and $10,449, respectively. Total dividends paid in 2011 were $10,282, including those declared in 2010 and paid in 2011, and total dividends paid in 2010

were $10,413, including those declared in 2009 and paid in 2010. On January 26, 2012, the Company's Board of Directors approved the first quarter 2012 dividend on its common stock in the amount of $.105 per share. This represents an increase in the quarterly dividend rate from $.015 to $.105 per share effective with the first quarter 2012 dividend, which will be paid in April 2012.

Debt Issuance Costs

6.42

AMKOR TECHNOLOGY, INC. (DEC)

CONSOLIDATED STATEMENTS OF CASH FLOWS
(in part)

	For the Year Ended December 31		
(In thousands)	2011	2010	2009
Cash Flows From Financing Activities:			
Borrowings under revolving credit facilities	6,567	3,261	41,410
Payments under revolving credit facilities	(6,567)	(34,253)	(10,171)
Borrowings under short-term credit facilities	20,000	15,000	15,000
Payments under short-term credit facilities	(15,000)	(15,000)	—
Proceeds from issuance of long-term debt	387,512	611,007	100,000
Proceeds from issuance of long-term debt, related party	75,000	—	150,000
Payments of long-term debt, net of redemption premiums and discounts	(392,191)	(663,433)	(338,104)
Payments for debt issuance costs	(5,875)	(7,487)	(8,479)
Payments for repurchase of common stock	(128,368)	—	—
Proceeds from issuance of stock through share-based compensation plans	821	1,048	693
Payments of tax withholding for restricted shares	(776)	—	—
Net cash used in financing activities	(58,877)	(89,857)	(49,651)

MANAGEMENT'S DISCUSSION AND ANALYSIS OF FINANCIAL CONDITION AND RESULTS OF OPERATIONS

Cash Flows (in part)

Financing activities: Our net cash used in financing activities in 2011 decreased by $31.0 million from 2010. Cash used in financing activities during 2011 consisted principally of $392.2 million of repayments, made up of $264.3 million of principal, and $7.8 million in tender premiums, on the 9.25% Senior Notes due 2016, $42.6 million for our 2.50% Convertible Senior Subordinated Notes due May 2011, $62.9 million of our Korean term loans and $14.6 million of other foreign amortizing debt. We incurred $5.9 million in debt issuance costs in 2011 associated with the issuance of our 6.625% Senior Notes due in 2021. Cash provided by financing activities during 2011 included the issuance of $400.0 million of our 2021 Notes and proceeds of $62.5 million in Korean term loans. Additionally, we used cash to repurchase $128.4 million of common stock under our stock repurchase program.

Cash used in financing activities during 2010 consisted principally of the repurchase of an aggregate $537.5 million principal amount of our senior notes and $99.9 million in repayments of our Korean term loans. Financing cash flows in 2010 also included $6.7 million of debt retirement costs for transactions classified as financing activities. We also

incurred $7.5 million in debt issuance costs in 2010, primarily associated with the issuance of our 7.375% Senior Notes due 2018. Cash provided by financing activities during 2010 included the issuance of $345.0 million of our 7.375% Senior Notes due 2018 and proceeds from a $180.0 million Korean term loan and a Taiwanese term loan of approximately $47.0 million.

NOTES TO CONSOLIDATED FINANCIAL STATEMENTS

12. Debt (in part)

Debt of Amkor Technology, Inc. (in part)

Senior Notes (in part)

In May 2010, we issued $345.0 million of our 7.375% Senior Notes due 2018 (the "2018 Notes"). The 2018 Notes were issued at par and are senior unsecured obligations. Interest is payable semi-annually on May 1 and November 1 of each year, commencing on November 1, 2010. We incurred $7.1 million of debt issuance costs associated with the 2018 Notes in the year ended December 31, 2010.

In May 2011, we issued $400.0 million of the 2021 Notes. The 2021 Notes were issued at par and are senior unsecured obligations. Interest is payable semi-annually on June 1 and December 1 of each year at a rate of 6.625%, commencing on December 1, 2011. Mr. James J. Kim, our Executive Chairman of the Board of Directors and our largest stockholder, and an affiliate of Mr. James J. Kim (collectively, the "Kim Purchasers") purchased $75.0 million aggregate principal amount of the 2021 Notes in the offering. In addition, we entered into a letter agreement with the Kim Purchasers pursuant to which we agreed to register the resale of their 2021 Notes with the U.S. Securities and Exchange Commission upon request of the Kim Purchasers at any time after May 20, 2012. We incurred $5.9 million of debt issuance costs associated with the 2021 Notes in the year ended December 31, 2011.

Financial Instrument Settlements—Credit Facility

6.43

GREIF, INC. (OCT)

CONSOLIDATED STATEMENTS OF CASH FLOWS
(in part)

(Dollars in thousands)

For the Years Ended October 31	2011	2010	2009
Cash Flows From Financing Activities:			
Proceeds from issuance of long-term debt	3,859,401	3,731,683	3,170,212
Payments on long-term debt	(3,465,834)	(3,637,945)	(2,983,534)
Proceeds from (payments of) short-term borrowings, net	74,308	3,878	(25,749)
Proceeds from (payments of) trade accounts receivable credit facility, net	(5,000)	135,000	(120,000)
Dividends paid	(97,817)	(93,122)	(87,957)
Acquisitions of treasury stock and other	(15,062)	(2,696)	(3,145)
Exercise of stock options	2,540	2,002	2,015
Debt issuance costs paid	(4,394)	(10,902)	(13,588)
Settlement of derivatives, net	—	17,985	(3,574)
Net cash provided by (used in) financing activities	348,142	145,883	(65,320)

NOTES TO CONSOLIDATED FINANCIAL STATEMENTS

Note 9—Long-Term Debt (in part)

Long-term debt is summarized as follows (Dollars in thousands):

	October 31, 2011	October 31, 2010
Credit Agreement	$ 355,447	$273,700
Senior Notes due 2017	302,853	303,396
Senior Notes due 2019	242,932	242,306
Senior Notes due 2021	280,206	—
Trade accounts receivable credit facility	130,000	135,000
Other long-term debt	46,200	11,187
	1,357,638	965,589
Less current portion	(12,500)	(12,523)
Long-term debt	$1,345,138	$953,066

United States Trade Accounts Receivable Credit Facility

On December 8, 2008, the Company entered into a trade accounts receivable credit facility with a financial institution. This facility was amended on September 19, 2011, which decreased the amount available to the borrowers from $135.0 million to $130.0 million and extended the termination date of the commitment to September 19, 2014. The credit facility is secured by certain of the Company's trade accounts receivable in the United States and bears interest at a variable rate based on the applicable base rate or other agreed-upon rate plus a margin amount (1.01% as of October 31, 2011). In addition, the Company can terminate the credit facility at any time upon five days prior written notice. A significant portion of the initial proceeds from this credit facility was used to pay the obligations under the previous trade accounts receivable credit facility, which was terminated. The remaining proceeds were and will be used to pay certain fees, costs and expenses incurred in connection with the credit facility and for working capital and general corporate purposes. As of October 31, 2011, there was $130.0 million outstanding under the credit facility. The agreement for this receivables financing facility contains financial covenants that require the Company to maintain the same leverage ratio and fixed charge coverage ratio as set forth in the Credit Agreement. As of October 31, 2011, the Company was in compliance with these covenants.

Greif Receivables Funding LLC ("GRF"), an indirect subsidiary of the Company, has participated in the purchase and transfer of receivables in connection with these credit facilities and is included in the Company's consolidated financial statements. However, because GRF is a separate

and distinct legal entity from the Company and its other subsidiaries, the assets of GRF are not available to satisfy the liabilities and obligations of the Company and its other subsidiaries, and the liabilities of GRF are not the liabilities or obligations of the Company and its other subsidiaries. This entity purchases and services the Company's trade accounts receivable that are subject to this credit facility.

Issuance of Noncontrolling Interest

6.44

EL PASO CORPORATION (DEC)

CONSOLIDATED STATEMENTS OF CASH FLOWS
(in part)

(In millions)

	Year Ended December 31		
	2011	2010	2009
Cash Flows From Financing Activities			
Net proceeds from issuance of debt and other financing obligations	5,942	3,360	1,618
Payments to retire long-term debt and other financing obligations	(5,692)	(3,127)	(1,668)
Net proceeds from issuance of noncontrolling interests (Note 14)	948	1,340	212
Net proceeds from the issuance of preferred stock of subsidiary	30	120	145
Dividends paid	(38)	(65)	(177)
Distributions to noncontrolling interest holders	(200)	(96)	(48)
Distributions to holders of preferred stock of subsidiary	(15)	(21)	—
Proceeds from stock option exercises	68	8	1
Other	1	1	(6)
Net cash provided by financing activities	1,044	1,520	77

NOTES TO CONSOLIDATED FINANCIAL STATEMENTS

14. Equity and Noncontrolling Interests (in part)

Noncontrolling Interests. We are the general partner of EPB, a master limited partnership (MLP). As of December 31, 2011, we own a 44 percent interest in EPB (a 2 percent general partner interest and a 42 percent limited partner interest). During the years ended December 31, 2011, 2010, and 2009 EPB issued noncontrolling interests, net of issuance costs, of $0.9 billion, $1.3 billion and $0.2 billion in conjunction with our contribution to EPB of additional ownership interests in CIG, SNG, Southern LNG Company, L.L.C. (SLNG), which owns the Elba Island LNG receiving terminal, and El Paso Elba Express Company, L.L.C. (Elba Express), which owns the Elba Express Pipeline. As of December 31, 2011, our MLP owns 100 percent of each of these entities, except for CIG, of which it owns 86 percent. The issuance of the EPB common units were reflected in our consolidated statements of equity at December 31, 2011 as an increase of $610 million to noncontrolling interests and an increase of $213 million, net of deferred tax liability, to El Paso Corporation's additional paid in capital. Our net income attributable to El Paso Corporation, together with the increase in El Paso Corporation's additional paid-in capital for the year ended December 31, 2011 totaled $354 million.

In accordance with its partnership agreement, EPB is obligated to make quarterly distributions of available cash to its unitholders. We receive our share of these cash distributions through our limited partner ownership interest, general partner interest, and incentive distribution rights (IDR's) we hold as the general partner. Prior to February 15, 2011, we held subordinated units in EPB. Upon payment of the quarterly cash distribution for the fourth quarter of 2010, the financial tests required for the conversion of subordinated units into common units were satisfied. As a result, our subordinated units were converted on February 15, 2011 into common units on a one-for-one basis effective January 3, 2011.

To the extent that the consideration for the sales of assets to EPB is not in the form of additional equity in EPB, our interest in our assets becomes diluted over time. However our economic interest will benefit from the receipt of incentive distributions in accordance with the partnership agreement.

Our IDRs pay an increasing percentage interest in quarterly distributions of cash based on the level of distribution to all unitholders. As the holder of these rights we can elect to relinquish the right to receive incentive distribution payments and reset, at higher levels, the minimum quarterly distribution amount and cash target distribution levels upon which the incentive distribution payments would be set. We are currently entitled to receive the maximum level of incentive distributions.

For additional information regarding our master limited partnership, see Note 11.

Net Income Attributable to Noncontrolling Interests. The components of net income attributable to noncontrolling interests on our statements of income for the year ended December 31, are as follows:

(In millions)	2011	2010	2009
EPB	$221	$118	$60
Preferred Stock of Cheyenne Plains (Note 18)	15	21	5
Preferred Stock of Ruby (Note 18)	50	27	—
Net income attributable to noncontrolling interests	$286	$166	$65

Section 7: Independent Auditors' Report

Author's Note

In this section, readers will find guidance for both nonissuers, the audits of which are performed under generally accepted auditing standards (GAAS) issued by the Auditing Standards Board (ASB), and issuers, the audits of which are performed under standards issued by the Public Company Accounting Oversight Board (PCAOB). Under each topic within this section, guidance for both nonissuers and issuers is presented separately, unless noted otherwise. All illustrative reporting excerpts are from the survey entities included in this edition (all of which are public companies) and are, thus, based on PCAOB standards. Illustrative reporting examples based on GAAS can be found in the AICPA's *Audit and Accounting Manual* and *The Auditor's Report: Comprehensive Guidance and Examples*.

In an effort to make GAAS easier to read, understand, and apply, the ASB launched the Clarity Project in 2011. As a result of this project, all existing AU sections under the AICPA's *Professional Standards* have been redrafted and will be effective for audits of financial statements for periods ending on or after December 15, 2012. The issuance of the clarified standards reflects the ASB's established clarity drafting conventions that include, among other improvements, more clearly stated objectives of the auditor and the requirements with which the auditor has to comply when conducting an audit in accordance with GAAS. As the ASB redrafted the standards for clarity, it also converged the standards with International Standards on Auditing issued by the International Auditing and Assurance Standards Board.

Given the effective date of the clarified auditing standards, the following guidance for nonissuers is based on the extant standards (that is, those that are superseded by the clarified standards).

PRESENTATION IN ANNUAL REPORT

PRESENTATION

7.01 This section reviews the format and content of independent auditors' reports appearing in the annual reports of the 500 survey entities. AU section 508, *Reports on Audited Financial Statements* (AICPA, *Professional Standards*), applies to auditors' reports issued in connection with audits of historical financial statements that are intended to present the financial position, results of operations, and cash flows in conformity with generally accepted accounting principles (GAAP). As stated above, AICPA Professional Standards apply to audits of nonissuers. PCAOB Auditing Standards apply to audits of issuers.

7.02 Section 103(a) of the Sarbanes-Oxley Act of 2002 authorized the Public Company Accounting Oversight Board (PCAOB) to establish auditing and related professional practice standards to be used by public accounting firms registered with the PCAOB. PCAOB Rule 3100, *Compliance With Auditing and Related Professional Practice Standards* (AICPA, *PCAOB Standards and Related Rules*, Select Rules of the Board), requires auditors to comply with all applicable auditing and related professional practice standards of the PCAOB. On an initial, transitional basis, the PCAOB adopted, as interim standards, the generally accepted auditing standards described in AU section 150, *Generally Accepted Auditing Standards* (AICPA, *Professional Standards*), in existence on April 16, 2003, to the extent not superseded or amended by the PCAOB.

TITLE AND ADDRESSEE

PRESENTATION

Author's Note

There are no differences in the following guidance related to audit requirements on title and addressee for issuers and nonissuers.

7.03 Paragraph .08(a) of AU section 508 states that the title of an auditor's report should include the word *independent*.

7.04 Paragraph .09 of AU section 508 states the following:

The report may be addressed to the company whose financial statements are being audited or to its board of directors or stockholders. A report on the financial statements of an unincorporated entity should be addressed as circumstances dictate, for example, to the partners, to the general partner, or to the proprietor. Occasionally, an auditor is retained to audit the financial statements of a company that is not a client; in such a case, the report is customarily addressed to the client and not to the directors or stockholders of the company whose financial statements are being audited.

AUDITORS' REPORTS

PRESENTATION

Nonissuers

7.05 Paragraph .08 of AU section 508 presents examples of auditors' standard reports for single-year financial statements and comparative two-year financial statements. The examples presented in paragraph .08 of AU section 508 follows:

INDEPENDENT AUDITORS' REPORT (single year)

We have audited the accompanying balance sheet of X Company as of December 31, 20XX, and the related statements of income, retained earnings, and cash flows for the year then ended. These financial statements are the responsibility of the Company's management. Our responsibility is to express an opinion on these financial statements based on our audit.

We conducted our audit in accordance with auditing standards generally accepted in the United States of America. Those standards require that we plan and perform the audit to obtain reasonable assurance about whether the financial statements are free of material misstatement. An audit includes examining, on a test basis, evidence supporting the amounts and disclosures in the financial statements. An audit also includes assessing the accounting principles used and significant estimates made by management, as well as evaluating the overall financial statement presentation. We believe that our audit provides a reasonable basis for our opinion.

In our opinion, the financial statements referred to above, present fairly, in all material respects, the financial position of X Company as of [at] December 31, 20XX, and the results of its operations and its cash flows for the year then ended in conformity with accounting principles generally accepted in the United States of America.

[*Signature*]
[*Date*]

INDEPENDENT AUDITORS' REPORT (comparative)

We have audited the accompanying balance sheets of X Company as of December 31, 20X2 and 20X1, and the related statements of income, retained earnings, and cash flows for the years then ended. These financial statements are the responsibility of the Company's management. Our responsibility is to express an opinion on these financial statements based on our audits.

We conducted our audits in accordance with auditing standards generally accepted in the United States of America. Those standards require that we plan and perform the audit to obtain reasonable assurance about whether the financial statements are free of material misstatement. An audit includes examining, on a test basis, evidence supporting the amounts and disclosures in the financial statements. An audit also includes assessing the accounting principles used and significant estimates made by management, as well as evaluating the overall financial statement presentation. We believe that our audits provide a reasonable basis for our opinion.

In our opinion, the financial statements referred to above, present fairly, in all material respects, the financial position of X Company as of [at] December 31, 20X2 and 20X1, and the results of its operations and its cash flows for the years then ended in conformity with accounting principles generally accepted in the United States of America.

[*Signature*]
[*Date*]

When performing an integrated audit of financial statements and internal control over financial reporting, if the auditor issues separate reports on the company's financial statements and on internal control over financial reporting, the following paragraph should be added to the auditor's report on the company's financial statements:

We also have audited, in accordance with the standards of the Public Company Accounting Oversight Board (United States), the effectiveness of X Company's internal control over financial reporting as of December 31, 20x3, based on [identify control criteria] and our report dated [date of report, which should be the same as the date of the report on the financial statements] expressed [include nature of opinions].

7.06 Most of the survey entities present a balance sheet for two years and the other basic financial statements for three years. Footnote 8 to paragraph .08 of AU section 508 explains that if statements of income, retained earnings, and cash flows are presented on a comparative basis for one or more periods, but the balance sheet(s) as of the end of one or more of the prior period(s) is not presented, the phrase "for the years then ended" should be changed to indicate that the auditor's opinion applies to each period for which statements of income, retained earnings, and cash flows are presented, such as "for each of the three years in the period ended [date of latest balance sheet]."

7.07 Financial Accounting Standards Board (FASB) *Accounting Standards Codification* (ASC) 220, *Comprehensive Income*, permits entities to report components of comprehensive income in either a separate financial statement or a combined statement of income and comprehensive income. Alternatively, FASB ASC 220 allows components of comprehensive income to be reported in a statement of stockholders' equity. Although an entity may include the term *comprehensive income* in the title of the statement in which it is presented, FASB ASC 220 does not require the use of the term in an entity's financial statements. FASB ASC 220 acknowledges the use of equivalent terms.

Author's Note

In June 2011, FASB issued FASB Accounting Standards Update (ASU) No. 2011-05, *Comprehensive Income (Topic 220): Presentation of Comprehensive Income*, which amends FASB ASC by eliminating the option to present the components of OCI as part of the statement of changes in stockholders' equity. Going forward, an entity will present the total of comprehensive income, the components of net income, and the components of OCI either in a single continuous statement of comprehensive income or in two separate but consecutive statements. In either option, an entity should present each component of net income together with total net income, each component of OCI together with a total for OCI, and a total amount for comprehensive income. The amendments to FASB ASC 220, *Comprehensive Income*, in ASU No. 2011-05 do not change which items an entity should present in OCI or when an entity should reclassify an item of OCI to net income. ASU No. 2011-05 is effective for fiscal years, and interim periods within those years, beginning after December 15, 2011. For nonpublic entities, the amendments are effective for fiscal years ending after December 15, 2012, and interim and annual periods thereafter. Early adoption is permitted because the remaining options are already permitted by FASB ASC 220. The amendments do not require any transition disclosures.

ASU No. 2011-05 is the result of a joint project with IASB to improve presentation of comprehensive income.

In December 2011, FASB issued ASU No. 2011-12, *Comprehensive Income (Topic 220): Deferral of the Effective Date for Amendments to the Presentation of Reclassifications of Items Out of Accumulated Other Comprehensive Income in ASU No. 2011-05.* ASU No. 2011-12 defers the changes in ASU No. 2011-05 related only to the presentation of reclassification adjustments. Preparers had argued that these reclassification adjustments would be difficult for preparers and might add unnecessary complexity to the financial statements. FASB issued ASU No. 2011-12 to allow sufficient time for it to redeliberate whether an entity should present the effects of reclassification adjustments on the face of the financial statements for all periods presented. While FASB is considering preparers' concerns, entities should continue to report reclassification adjustments in accordance with the requirements of FASB ASC 220 in effect before issuance of ASU No. 2011-05. The amendments in ASU No. 2011-12 are effective at the same time as the amendments in ASU No. 2011-05.

7.08 FASB ASC 505-10-50-2 allows for changes in the separate accounts comprising stockholders' equity to be presented either on the face of the basic financial statements or in the form of a separate statement, such as a statement of changes in stockholders' equity.

Issuers

7.09 For audits of public entities (that is, *issuers*, as defined by the Sarbanes-Oxley Act of 2002, and other entities, when prescribed by the rules of the Securities and Exchange Commission [SEC]), PCAOB Auditing Standard No. 1, *References in Auditors' Reports to the Standards of the Public Company Accounting Oversight Board* (AICPA, *PCAOB Standards and Related Rules*, Auditing Standards), directs auditors to state that the engagement was conducted in accordance with "the standards of the Public Company Accounting Oversight Board (United States)" whenever the auditor has performed the engagement in accordance with the PCAOB's standards. An example of a standard independent registered auditor's report presented in the appendix, "Illustrative Reports," of Auditing Standard No. 1 follows:

REPORT OF INDEPENDENT REGISTERED PUBLIC ACCOUNTING FIRM

We have audited the accompanying balance sheets of X Company as of December 31, 20X3 and 20X2, and the related statements of operations, stockholders' equity, and cash flows for each of the three years in the period ended December 31, 20X3. These financial statements are the responsibility of the Company's management. Our responsibility is to express an opinion on these financial statements based on our audits.

We conducted our audits in accordance with the standards of the Public Company Accounting Oversight Board (United States). Those standards require that we plan and perform the audit to obtain reasonable assurance about whether the financial statements are free of material misstatement. An audit includes examining, on a test basis, evidence supporting the amounts and disclosures in the financial statements. An audit also includes assessing the accounting principles used and significant estimates made by management, as well as evaluating the overall financial statement presentation. We believe that our audits provide a reasonable basis for our opinion.

In our opinion, the financial statements referred to above present fairly, in all material respects, the financial position of the company as of [at] December 31, 20X3 and 20X2, and the results of its operations and its cash flows for each of the three years in the period ended December 31, 20X3, in conformity with U.S. generally accepted accounting principles.

[*Signature*]
[*City and State or Country*]
[*Date*]

7.10 For audit requirements on reporting on internal controls over financial reporting, refer to paragraph 7.50.

7.11

TABLE 7-1: INFORMATION RELATED TO AUDITOR'S AND MANAGEMENT'S REPORTS*

	Number of Entities	
	2011	2010
Auditor's Opinion		
Unqualified opinion, clean..............................	480	469
Unqualified opinion with emphasis of a matter paragraph..	20	31
Total...	500	500
Management's Report on Internal Control Over Financial Reporting		
Presented in regular audit report....................	105	47
Presented as separate report.........................	394	453
Not presented..	1	—
Total...	500	500
Auditor's Report on Internal Control Over Financial Reporting		
Presented in regular audit report....................	271	226
Presented as separate report.........................	226	272
Not presented..	3	2
Total...	500	500
Additional Matters With Regard to Auditor's Reports		
One paragraph presentation of audit report...	80	94
Reference to report of other auditors..............	5	2
Opinion expressed on supplemental information..	87	63
Report of management on financial statement...	130	35
Report on internal control over financial reporting indicated ineffective controls........	1	2
Dual dating of report.......................................	1	N/C*

* N/C = Not compiled. Line item was not included in the table for the year shown.

7.12

TABLE 7-2: INTERNAL CONTROL FRAMEWORK*

Table 7-2 shows whether the entities use an internal control framework established by COSO or not.

	2011
Framework established by COSO in internal control—integrated framework.....................................	498
Other..	2
Total..	500

* Note: This item was not tracked in previous editions, so no prior year data are available.

PRESENTATION AND DISCLOSURE EXCERPTS

PricewaterhouseCoopers LLP Auditors' Report

Author's Note

Although most audit reports use the exact format and order of paragraphs, PricewaterhouseCoopers uses a variation of the standard auditor's report that rearranges the standard elements into one paragraph for use in their unqualified opinions only.

7.13

BROWN-FORMAN CORPORATION (APR)

REPORT OF INDEPENDENT REGISTERED PUBLIC ACCOUNTING FIRM

To the Board of Directors and Stockholders of Brown-Forman Corporation

In our opinion, the accompanying consolidated balance sheets and the related consolidated statements of operations, comprehensive income, cash flows, and stockholders' equity present fairly, in all material respects, the financial position of Brown-Forman Corporation and its subsidiaries (the "Company") at April 30, 2011 and April 30, 2010, and the results of their operations and their cash flows for each of the three years in the period ended April 30, 2011 in conformity with accounting principles generally accepted in the United States of America. Also in our opinion, the Company maintained, in all material respects, effective internal control over financial reporting as of April 30, 2011, based on criteria established in *Internal Control—Integrated Framework* issued by the Committee of Sponsoring Organizations of the Treadway Commission (COSO). The Company's management is responsible for these financial statements, for maintaining effective internal control over financial reporting and for its assessment of the effectiveness of internal control over financial reporting, included in Management's Report on Internal Control over Financial Reporting appearing on page 68 of this Annual Report to Stockholders. Our responsibility is to express opinions on these financial statements and on the Company's internal control over financial reporting based on our integrated audits. We conducted our audits in accordance with the standards of the Public Company Accounting Oversight Board (United States). Those standards require that we plan and perform the audits to obtain reasonable assurance about whether the financial statements are free of material misstatement and whether effective internal control over financial reporting was maintained in all material respects. Our audits of the financial statements included examining, on a test basis, evidence supporting the amounts and disclosures in the financial statements, assessing the accounting principles used and significant estimates made by management, and evaluating the overall financial statement presentation. Our audit of internal control over financial reporting included obtaining an understanding of internal control over financial reporting, assessing the risk that a material weakness exists, and testing and evaluating the design and operating effectiveness of internal control based on the assessed risk. Our audits also included performing such other procedures as we considered necessary in the circumstances. We believe that our audits provide a reasonable basis for our opinions.

A company's internal control over financial reporting is a process designed to provide reasonable assurance regarding the reliability of financial reporting and the preparation of financial statements for external purposes in accordance with generally accepted accounting principles. A company's internal control over financial reporting includes those policies and procedures that (i) pertain to the maintenance of records that, in reasonable detail, accurately and fairly reflect the transactions and dispositions of the assets of the company; (ii) provide reasonable assurance that transactions are recorded as necessary to permit preparation of financial statements in accordance with generally accepted accounting principles, and that receipts and expenditures of the company are being made only in accordance with authorizations of management and directors of the company; and (iii) provide reasonable assurance regarding prevention or timely detection of unauthorized acquisition, use, or disposition of the company's assets that could have a material effect on the financial statements.

Because of its inherent limitations, internal control over financial reporting may not prevent or detect misstatements. Also, projections of any evaluation of effectiveness to future periods are subject to the risk that controls may become inadequate because of changes in conditions, or that the degree of compliance with the policies or procedures may deteriorate.

Statement of Operations and Comprehensive Income

7.14

UNIFI, INC. (JUN)

REPORT OF INDEPENDENT REGISTERED PUBLIC ACCOUNTING FIRM

The Board of Directors and Stockholders of Unifi, Inc.

We have audited the accompanying consolidated balance sheet of Unifi, Inc. and subsidiaries as of June 26, 2011, and the related consolidated statements of operations, comprehensive income (loss), changes in shareholders' equity, and cash flows for year ended June 26, 2011. These consolidated financial statements are the responsibility of the Company's management. Our responsibility is to express an opinion on these consolidated financial statements based on our audit.

We conducted our audit in accordance with the standards of the Public Company Accounting Oversight Board (United States). Those standards require that we plan and perform the audit to obtain reasonable assurance about whether the financial statements are free of material misstatement. An audit includes examining, on a test basis, evidence supporting the amounts and disclosures in the financial statements. An audit also includes assessing the accounting principles used and significant estimates made by management, as well as

evaluating the overall financial statement presentation. We believe that our audit provides a reasonable basis for our opinion.

In our opinion, the consolidated financial statements referred to above present fairly, in all material respects, the financial position of Unifi, Inc. and subsidiaries as of June 26, 2011, and the results of their operations and their cash flows for year ended June 26, 2011, in conformity with U.S. generally accepted accounting principles.

We also have audited, in accordance with the standards of the Public Company Accounting Oversight Board (United States), Unifi, Inc. and subsidiaries' internal control over financial reporting as of June 26, 2011, based on criteria established in *Internal Control—Integrated Framework* issued by the Committee of Sponsoring Organizations of the Treadway Commission (COSO), and our report dated September 9, 2011 expressed an unqualified opinion on the effectiveness of the Company's internal control over financial reporting.

Statement of Changes in Shareholders' Equity

7.15

SYSCO CORPORATION (JUN)

REPORT OF INDEPENDENT REGISTERED PUBLIC ACCOUNTING FIRM ON CONSOLIDATED FINANCIAL STATEMENTS

To the Board of Directors and Shareholders of Sysco Corporation

We have audited the accompanying consolidated balance sheets of Sysco Corporation (a Delaware Corporation) and subsidiaries (the "Company") as of July 2, 2011 and July 3, 2010, and the related consolidated results of operations, shareholders' equity, and cash flows for each of the three years in the period ended July 2, 2011. These financial statements are the responsibility of the Company's management. Our responsibility is to express an opinion on these financial statements based on our audits.

We conducted our audits in accordance with the standards of the Public Company Accounting Oversight Board (United States). Those standards require that we plan and perform the audit to obtain reasonable assurance about whether the financial statements are free of material misstatement. An audit includes examining, on a test basis, evidence supporting the amounts and disclosures in the financial statements. An audit also includes assessing the accounting principles used and significant estimates made by management, as well as evaluating the overall financial statement presentation. We believe that our audits provide a reasonable basis for our opinion.

In our opinion, the financial statements referred to above present fairly, in all material respects, the consolidated financial position of the Company at July 2, 2011 and July 3, 2010, and the consolidated results of their operations and their cash flows for each of the three years in the period ended July 2, 2011, in conformity with U.S. generally accepted accounting principles.

We also have audited, in accordance with the standards of the Public Company Accounting Oversight Board (United States), Sysco Corporation and its subsidiaries' internal control over financial reporting as of July 2, 2011, based on criteria established in *Internal Control—Integrated Framework* issued by the Committee of Sponsoring Organizations of the Treadway Commission and our report dated August 30, 2011 expressed an unqualified opinion thereon.

REFERENCE TO THE REPORT OF OTHER AUDITORS

PRESENTATION

Nonissuers

7.16 AU section 543, *Part of Audit Performed by Other Independent Auditors* (AICPA, *Professional Standards*), establishes requirements and provides guidance for the independent auditor in deciding (*a*) whether he or she may serve as principal auditor and use the work and reports of other independent auditors who have audited the financial statements of one or more subsidiaries, divisions, branches, components, or investments included in the financial statements presented and (*b*) the form and content of the principal auditor's report in these circumstances. When considering whether to refer to the report of other auditors, it is important to first determine whether the auditor may serve as principal auditor. He or she may have performed all but a relatively minor portion of the work, or significant parts of the audit may have been performed by other auditors. In the latter case, the auditor must decide whether his or her own participation is sufficient to enable him or her to serve as the principal auditor and to report as such on the financial statements, in accordance with AU section 543. In deciding this question, the auditor should consider, among other things, the materiality of the portion of the financial statements he or she has audited in comparison with the portion audited by other auditors, the extent of his or her knowledge of the overall financial statements, and the importance of the components he or she audited in relation to the enterprise as a whole.

7.17 When the opinion of a principal auditor is based, in part, on the report of another auditor, paragraph .07 of AU section 543 states that his report should indicate clearly, in both the introductory, scope and opinion paragraphs, the division of responsibility as between that portion of the financial statements covered by his own audit and that covered by the audit of the other auditor. The report should disclose the magnitude of the portion of the financial statements audited by the other auditor. This may be done by stating the dollar amounts or percentages of one or more of the following: total assets, total revenues, or other appropriate criteria, whichever most clearly reveals the portion of the financial statements audited by the other auditor. The other auditor may be named but only with his express permission and provided his report is presented together with that of the principal auditor.

7.18 When the principal auditor decides not to make reference to the audit of the other auditor, he or she should consider whether to perform one or more of the following procedures:

- Visit the other auditor and discuss the audit procedures followed and results thereof.
- Review the audit programs of the other auditor. In some cases, it may be appropriate to issue instructions to the other auditor about the scope of his or her audit work.
- Review the working papers of the other auditor, including the understanding of internal control and the assessment of control risk.

7.19 Paragraphs .12–.13 of AU section 508 reaffirm the requirements of AU section 543. Paragraph .13 of AU section 508 and paragraph .09 of AU section 543 present examples of auditors' reports referring to the report of other auditors.

Issuers

7.20 Although the information in paragraphs 7.15–.18 apply to issuers, as well, paragraphs C8–C11 of PCAOB Auditing Standard No. 5, *An Audit of Internal Control Over Financial Reporting That Is Integrated with An Audit of Financial Statements* (AICPA, *PCAOB Standards and Related Rules*, Auditing Standards), provide guidance based, in part, on the report of another auditor in an audit of internal control over financial reporting. Paragraphs C8–C11 of Auditing Standard No. 5 state the following:

- If the auditor decides it is appropriate to serve as the principal auditor of the financial statements, then that auditor also should be the principal auditor of the company's internal control over financial reporting. When serving as the principal auditor of internal control over financial reporting, the auditor should decide whether to make reference in the report on internal control over financial reporting to the audit of internal control over financial reporting performed by the other auditor. In these circumstances, the auditor's decision is based on factors analogous to those of the auditor who uses the work and reports of other independent auditors when reporting on a company's financial statements, as described in paragraphs 7.15–.16.
- The decision about whether to make reference to another auditor in the report on the audit of internal control over financial reporting might differ from the corresponding decision as it relates to the audit of the financial statements. For example, the audit report on the financial statements may make reference to the audit of a significant equity investment performed by another independent auditor, but the report on internal control over financial reporting might not make a similar reference because management's assessment of internal control over financial reporting ordinarily would not extend to controls at the equity method investee.
- When the auditor decides to make reference to the report of the other auditor as a basis, in part, for his or her opinion on the company's internal control over financial reporting, the auditor should refer to the report of the other auditor when describing the scope of the audit and expressing the opinion.

7.21 In addition to the suggested procedures in paragraph 7.17, when the principal auditor decides not to make reference to the audit of the other auditor, he or she must obtain and review and retain the following information from the other auditor, as prescribed in PCAOB AU section 508, *Reports on Audited*

Financial Statements (AICPA, *PCAOB Standards and Related Rules,* Interim Standards):

- An engagement completion document consistent with paragraphs 12–13 of PCAOB Auditing Standard No. 3, *Audit Documentation* (AICPA, *PCAOB Standards and Related Rules,* Auditing Standards). This engagement completion document should include all cross-referenced supporting audit documentation.
- A list of significant risks, the auditor's responses, and the results of the auditor's related procedures.
- Sufficient information relating to significant findings or issues that are inconsistent with or contradict the auditor's final conclusions, as described in paragraph 8 of Auditing Standard No. 3.
- Any findings affecting the consolidating or combining of accounts in the consolidated financial statements.
- Sufficient information to enable the office issuing the auditor's report to agree or reconcile the financial statement amounts audited by the other firm to the information underlying the consolidated financial statements.
- A schedule of accumulated misstatements, including a description of the nature and cause of each accumulated misstatement, and an evaluation of uncorrected misstatements, including the quantitative and qualitative factors the auditor considered to be relevant to the evaluation.
- All significant deficiencies and material weaknesses in internal control over financial reporting, including a clear distinction between those two categories.
- Letters of representations from management.
- All matters to be communicated to the audit committee.

7.22 The auditor's report for five survey entities made reference to the report of other auditors. The reference to other auditors in both of these reports is related to investments in unconsolidated affiliates.

PRESENTATION AND DISCLOSURE EXCERPTS

Reference to Other Auditors

7.23

BASSETT FURNITURE INDUSTRIES, INCORPORATED (NOV)

REPORT OF INDEPENDENT REGISTERED PUBLIC ACCOUNTING FIRM

The Board of Directors and Shareholders of Bassett Furniture Industries, Incorporated

We have audited the accompanying consolidated balance sheets of Bassett Furniture Industries, Incorporated and subsidiaries as of November 26, 2011 and November 27, 2010, and the related consolidated statements of operations, shareholders' equity, and cash flows for each of the three years in the period ended November 26, 2011. Our audits also included the financial statement schedule listed in the Index at Item 15(a). These financial statements and schedule are the responsibility of the Company's management. Our responsibility is to express an opinion on these financial statements and schedule based on our audits. The financial

statements of International Home Furnishings Center, Inc. (a corporation in which the Company had a 47% interest until it was sold on May 2, 2011) for each of the two years in the period ended November 27, 2010 have been audited by other auditors whose report has been furnished to us, and our opinion on the consolidated financial statements, insofar as it relates to the amounts included for International Home Furnishings Center, Inc., is based solely on the report of the other auditors. In the consolidated financial statements, the Company's investment in International Home Furnishings Center, Inc. is stated at $(7,356,000) at November 27, 2010, and the Company's equity in the net income of International Home Furnishings Center, Inc. is stated at $4,535,000 and $4,705,000 for each of the two years in the period ended November 27, 2010.

We conducted our audits in accordance with the standards of the Public Company Accounting Oversight Board (United States). Those standards require that we plan and perform the audit to obtain reasonable assurance about whether the financial statements are free of material misstatement. An audit includes examining, on a test basis, evidence supporting the amounts and disclosures in the financial statements. An audit also includes assessing the accounting principles used and significant estimates made by management, as well as evaluating the overall financial statement presentation. We believe that our audits and the report of other auditors provide a reasonable basis for our opinion.

In our opinion, based on our audits and the report of other auditors, the financial statements referred to above present fairly, in all material respects, the consolidated financial position of Bassett Furniture Industries, Incorporated and subsidiaries at November 26, 2011 and November 27, 2010, and the consolidated results of their operations and their cash flows for each of the three years in the period ended November 26, 2011, in conformity with U.S. generally accepted accounting principles. Also, in our opinion, the related financial statement schedule, when considered in relation to the basic financial statements taken as a whole, presents fairly in all material respects the information set forth therein.

We also have audited, in accordance with the standards of the Public Company Accounting Oversight Board (United States), Bassett Furniture Industries, Incorporated's internal control over financial reporting as of November 26, 2011, based on criteria established in Internal Control-Integrated Framework issued by the Committee of Sponsoring Organizations of the Treadway Commission and our report dated February 3, 2012 expressed an unqualified opinion thereon.

UNCERTAINTIES

PRESENTATION

Author's Note

There are no differences in the following guidance for issuers and nonissuers when referring to the report of other auditors.

7.24 Paragraph .30 of AU section 508 does not require an explanatory paragraph for *uncertainties*, as defined in paragraph .29 of AU section 508. This does not apply to uncertainties related to going concern situations, for which AU section 341, *The Auditor's Consideration of an Entity's Ability to Continue as a Going Concern* (AICPA, *Professional Standards*), provides guidance.

7.25

TABLE 7-3: REFERENCES TO UNCERTAINTIES IN AUDITORS' REPORTS

Table 7-3 summarizes the nature of uncertainties for which an explanatory paragraph was included in an auditors' report.

	2011	2010	2009
Going concern	4	—	8
Consistency	1	N/C*	N/C*
Change in accounting method/policy	25	N/C*	N/C*
Fresh start accounting/reorganization	3	N/C*	N/C*
Other	10	19	—
Total Uncertainties	**43**	**19**	**8**

* N/C = Not compiled. Line item was not included in the table for the year shown.

PRESENTATION AND DISCLOSURE EXCERPTS

Going Concern

7.26

LEE ENTERPRISES, INCORPORATED (SEP)

REPORT OF INDEPENDENT REGISTERED PUBLIC ACCOUNTING FIRM

The Board of Directors and Stockholders
of Lee Enterprises, Incorporated

We have audited the accompanying consolidated balance sheets of Lee Enterprises, Incorporated and subsidiaries (the Company) as of September 25, 2011 and September 26, 2010, and the related consolidated statements of operations and comprehensive income (loss), stockholders' equity (deficit), and cash flows for each of the 52-week periods ended September 25, 2011, September 26, 2010, and September 27, 2009. These consolidated financial statements are the responsibility of the Company's management. Our responsibility is to express an opinion on these consolidated financial statements based on our audits. We did not audit the consolidated financial statements of Madison Newspapers, Inc., and subsidiary (MNI), a 50 percent owned investee company, as of September 25, 2011 and September 26, 2010, and for the 52-week periods then ended. The Company's investment in MNI at September 25, 2011 and September 26, 2010, was $23,451,000, and $23,798,000, respectively, and its equity in earnings of MNI was $3,053,000 and $3,566,000 for the 52-week periods then ended, respectively. The consolidated financial statements of MNI for these periods were audited by other auditors whose report has been furnished to us, and our opinion, insofar as it relates to the amounts included for MNI as of and for the 52-week periods ended September 25, 2011 and September 26, 2010, is based solely on the report of the other auditors.

We conducted our audits in accordance with the standards of the Public Company Accounting Oversight Board (United States). Those standards require that we plan and perform the audit to obtain reasonable assurance about whether the financial statements are free of material misstatement. An audit includes examining, on a test basis, evidence supporting the amounts and disclosures in the financial statements. An audit also includes assessing the accounting principles used and significant estimates made by management, as well as evaluating the overall financial statement presentation. We believe that our audits and the report of the other auditors provide a reasonable basis for our opinion.

In our opinion, based on our audits and the report of the other auditors, the consolidated financial statements referred to above present fairly, in all material respects, the financial position of Lee Enterprises, Incorporated and subsidiaries as of September 25, 2011 and September 26, 2010, and the results of their operations and their cash flows for each of the 52-week periods ended September 25, 2011, September 26, 2010, and September 27, 2009, in conformity with U.S. generally accepted accounting principles.

The accompanying consolidated financial statements have been prepared assuming that the Company will continue as a going concern. As discussed in Notes 1 and 4 to the consolidated financial statements, the Company has short-term obligations that cannot be satisfied by available funds, which raises substantial doubt about its ability to continue as a going concern. Management's plans in regard to this matter are also described in Note 4. The consolidated financial statements do not include any adjustments that might result from the outcome of this uncertainty.

We also have audited, in accordance with the standards of the Public Company Accounting Oversight Board (United States), Lee Enterprises, Incorporated and subsidiaries internal control over financial reporting as of September 25, 2011, based on criteria established in *Internal Control—Integrated Framework* issued by the Committee of Sponsoring Organizations of the Treadway Commission (COSO), and our report dated December 9, 2011, expressed an unqualified opinion on the effectiveness of the Company's internal control over financial reporting.

NOTES TO CONSOLIDATED FINANCIAL STATEMENTS

1 Significant Accounting Policies (in part)

Basis of Presentation

The Consolidated Financial Statements include our accounts and those of our subsidiaries, all of which are wholly-owned, except for our 50% interest in TNI Partners ("TNI"), 50% interest in Madison Newspapers, Inc. ("MNI") and 82.5% interest in INN Partners, L.C. ("INN").

We have prepared the Consolidated Financial Statements on the basis that the Company will continue as a going concern. As discussed more fully in Note 4, since our refinancing process was not completed at the time of the filing of our Annual Report on Form 10-K, there is significant uncertainty about our ability to operate as a going concern. Accordingly, the opinion of our independent registered accounting firm on our Consolidated Financial Statements contains explanatory going concern language. Our ability to operate as a going concern is dependent on our ability to obtain approval by the U. S. Bankruptcy Court of the refinancing plan approved by creditors and to generate cash flows and maintain liquidity sufficient to service our debt.

4 Debt (in part)

Debt is summarized as follows:

(Thousands of dollars)	September 25, 2011	Balance September 26, 2010	Interest Rate September 25, 2011
Credit Agreement:			
A Term Loan	569,335	635,665	4.25
Revolving credit facility	286,425	285,425	4.25
Pulitzer Notes:			
Principal amount	138,500	160,500	10.05
Unaccreted fair value adjustment	290	837	
	994,550	1,082,427	
Less current maturities	994,550	81,500	
	—	1,000,927	

At September 25, 2011, our weighted average cost of debt is 5.1 %.

Status of Debt Refinancing and Liquidity

At September 25, 2011, we had $286,425,000 outstanding under the revolving credit facility, and after consideration of the 2009 Amendments and letters of credit, have approximately $75,677,000 available for future use. Including cash and restricted cash, our liquidity at September 25, 2011 totals $104,204,000. This liquidity amount excludes any future cash flows. Since February 2009, we have satisfied all interest payments and substantially all principal payments due under our debt facilities with our cash flows.

In April 2011, we announced a plan to offer to qualified institutional buyers, subject to market conditions, $680,000,000 of first priority lien senior secured notes due in 2017, $375,000,000 of second priority lien senior secured notes due in 2018 (the "Notes Offering") and up to 8,928,175 shares of Common Stock. The proceeds from the offerings, net of offering costs, would have been used to refinance the Credit Agreement and Pulitzer Notes. As a result of market conditions, we terminated the offering process in May 2011 and charged $5,120,000 of related debt financing costs to expense in 2011.

In September 2011, we announced a plan to amend our current Credit Agreement and extend the April 2012 maturity in a structure of first and second lien debt. The first lien debt will consist of a term loan of $689,510,000, along with a $40,000,000 revolving credit facility that is not expected to be drawn at closing. The second lien debt will be a $175,000,000 term loan.

The first lien term loan will bear interest at LIBOR plus 6.25%, with a LIBOR floor of 1.25%. Principal payments for the first lien term loan will be required quarterly beginning in June 2012 and total $10,000,000 annually in the twelve month period ending March 2013, increasing to $12,000,000 in the following twelve months and to $13,500,000 annually thereafter. A quarterly cash flow sweep will also be used to reduce first lien debt. Covenants include a minimum interest

coverage ratio, maximum total leverage ratio and capital expenditure limitation. The maturity is in December 2015.

Interest on the revolving credit facility, when used, will be at LIBOR plus 5.5%, with a LIBOR floor of 1.25%. The revolving credit facility will also support issuance of letters of credit. The maturity is in December 2015.

The second lien term loan will bear interest at 15.0% and mature in April 2017. It requires no amortization and has no affirmative financial covenants. Lenders under the second lien term loan will share in the issuance of approximately 6,744,000 shares of our Common Stock, an amount equal to 13% of outstanding shares on a pro forma basis as of the closing date.

As a condition to the refinancing of the Credit Agreement, we were expected to refinance the remaining $138,000,000 of our current Pulitzer Notes debt with a separate $175,000,000 loan to be arranged in the leveraged loan or high yield markets. Subsequent credit market conditions did not allow for that debt to be refinanced on acceptable terms, and as a result, we chose to amend the Pulitzer Notes and extend the maturity with the existing Noteholders.

Under the agreement with the Noteholders, which was announced in December 2011, the amended Pulitzer Notes will carry an interest rate of 10.55%, increasing 0.75% in January 2013 and January of each year thereafter. Annual mandatory principal payments will total $6,400,000 per year. A quarterly cash flow sweep will also be used to reduce the balance of the Pulitzer Notes. Covenants include a minimum EBITDA ratio and capital expenditure limitation. After consideration of unscheduled principal payments totaling $15,145,000 (of which $10,145,000 were made in December 2011), offset by $3,500,000 of non-cash fees to be paid to the Noteholders in the form of additional Pulitzer Notes debt, the amended Pulitzer Notes will have a balance of $126,355,000 at the closing of the transaction. The maturity is in December 2015.

Substantially all of our assets will secure the debt, as is the case today. Our weighted average cost of debt will increase from 5.1% at September 25, 2011 to approximately 9.2% under the refinanced agreements. Mandatory annual principal payments will total $11,400,000 in 2012. Cash payments to the Lenders, Noteholders and legal and professional fees are expected to total approximately $40,000,000, of which $6,273,000 was paid in 2011, $721,000 was charged to expense in 2011 and the remainder of which will be paid and charged to expense in 2012 upon consummation of the transactions. In addition, previously capitalized financing costs of $4,514,000 at September 25, 2011 will be charged to expense in 2012 prior to, or upon consummation of, the transactions. The terms of the amended agreements require that substantially all future cash flows be directed toward repayment of the Credit Agreement or Pulitzer Notes and that cash flows of Pulitzer are largely segregated from those of the Credit Parties.

The Credit Agreement and Pulitzer Notes require 100% Lender or Noteholder approval, respectively, for key changes, including extension of maturities. Because credit market conditions dictated the need to extend the Pulitzer Notes with current Noteholders, we were not able to increase the Pulitzer Notes facility to $175,000,000 as discussed above. Consequently, we were unable to redeem the interests of the last 6% of non-consenting Lenders under the Credit Agreement for cash.

As a result, we will make use of a voluntary, prepackaged filing under Chapter 11 of the U.S. Bankruptcy Code on or about December 12, 2011 to effect the amendments to the Credit Agreement and Pulitzer Notes discussed above. This process is not expected to have an adverse effect on our governance or operations. Immediately upon filing, we will request authority to pay all suppliers and other vendors without delay, which request is commonly approved in similar situations. All our digital and print products will be published as usual and no employees will be impacted. Our 50% owned equity interests in Tucson, AZ and Madison, WI are not included in the filing. Lender and Noteholder balloting related to the Chapter 11 process is expected to be completed on or before December 12, 2011.

We expect to complete the restructuring process quickly and without disruption to our business, likely in 60 days or less from the date of filing. We have received commitments for a $40,000,000 debtor-in-possession financing facility that will provide additional liquidity during the restructuring process and will, subject to the satisfaction of certain conditions, be converted into the revolving credit facility under the amended Credit Agreement upon our emergence from Chapter 11 proceedings.

Support agreements have been executed by 94% of Lenders under the Credit Agreement and 100% of Noteholders of the Pulitzer Notes and are in effect as of September 8, 2011 and December 2, 2011, respectively. Such support agreements require the Lenders and Noteholders to support the amendments to the Credit Agreement and Pulitzer Notes, respectively, contemplated in the prepackaged filing. An amendment to the Credit Agreement to allow unscheduled principal payments on the Pulitzer Notes and to facilitate other aspects of the refinancing process was declared effective on December 2, 2011.

We do not expect the refinancing process to affect the trading of our Common Stock on the New York Stock Exchange ("NYSE"). We are currently operating under an approved plan, which is subject to periodic reassessment by the NYSE, to address non-compliance issues, including the need to increase the average closing price of our Common Stock to $1 per share.

Since our refinancing process was not completed at the time of the filing of our Annual Report on Form 10-K, there is significant uncertainty about our ability to operate as a going concern. Accordingly, the opinion of our independent registered accounting firm on our Consolidated Financial Statements contains explanatory going concern language. Our ability to operate as a going concern is dependent on our ability to obtain approval by the U. S. Bankruptcy Court of the refinancing plan approved by creditors and to generate cash flows and maintain liquidity sufficient to service our debt.

There are numerous potential consequences under the Credit Agreement, and Guaranty Agreement and Note Agreement related to the Pulitzer Notes, if an event of default, as defined, occurs and is not remedied. Many of those consequences are beyond our control, and the control of Pulitzer and PD LLC, respectively. The occurrence of one or more events of default would give rise to the right of the Lenders or the Noteholders, or both of them, to exercise their remedies under the Credit Agreement and the Note and Guaranty Agreements, respectively, including, without limitation, the right to accelerate all outstanding debt and take actions authorized in such circumstances under applicable collateral security documents.

In 2010, we filed a Form S-3 shelf registration statement ("Shelf") with the SEC, which has been declared effective. The Shelf gives us the flexibility to issue and publicly distribute various types of securities, including preferred stock, common stock, secured or unsecured debt securities, purchase contracts and units consisting of any combination of such securities, from time to time, in one or more offerings, up to an aggregate amount of $750,000,000. In July 2011, the SEC announced changes to the issuer eligibility rules which will require us to have a public float of at least $75,000,000 in order to use the Shelf. If the market price of our Common Stock increases sufficiently, the Shelf may enable us to sell securities quickly and efficiently when market conditions are favorable or financing needs arise. Net proceeds from the sale of any securities must be used generally to reduce debt subject to conditions of existing debt agreements.

Fresh-Start Accounting

7.27

VISTEON CORPORATION (DEC)

REPORT OF INDEPENDENT REGISTERED PUBLIC ACCOUNTING FIRM

To the Board of Directors and Shareholders
of Visteon Corporation

In our opinion, the accompanying consolidated balance sheets as of December 31, 2011 and 2010 and the related consolidated statements of operations, shareholders' equity (deficit) and cash flows for the year ended December 31, 2011 and the three months ended December 31, 2010 present fairly, in all material respects, the financial position of Visteon Corporation and its subsidiaries (Successor Company) at December 31, 2011 and 2010, and the results of their operations and their cash flows for the year ended December 31, 2011 and the three months ended December 31, 2010 in conformity with accounting principles generally accepted in the United States of America. In addition, in our opinion, the financial statement schedule listed in the index appearing under Item 15 (a) (2) for the year ended December 31, 2011 and the three months ended December 31, 2010 presents fairly, in all material respects, the information set forth therein when read in conjunction with the related consolidated financial statements. Also in our opinion, the Company maintained, in all material respects, effective internal control over financial reporting as of December 31, 2011, based on criteria established in *Internal Control—Integrated Framework* issued by the Committee of Sponsoring Organizations of the Treadway Commission (COSO). The Company's management is responsible for these financial statements and financial statement schedule, for maintaining effective internal control over financial reporting and for its assessment of the effectiveness of internal control over financial reporting, included in the accompanying Management's Report on Internal Control over Financial Reporting. Our responsibility is to express opinions on these financial statements, on the financial statement schedule, and on the Company's internal control over financial reporting based on our integrated audits. We conducted our audits in accordance with the standards of the Public Company Accounting Oversight Board (United States). Those standards require that we plan and perform the audits to obtain reasonable assurance about whether the financial statements are free of material misstatement and whether effective internal control over financial reporting was maintained in all material respects. Our audits of the financial statements included examining, on a test basis, evidence supporting the amounts and disclosures in the financial statements, assessing the accounting principles used and significant estimates made by management, and evaluating the overall financial statement presentation. Our audit of internal control over financial reporting included obtaining an understanding of internal control over financial reporting, assessing the risk that a material weakness exists, and testing and evaluating the design and operating effectiveness of internal control based on the assessed risk. Our audits also included performing such other procedures as we considered necessary in the circumstances. We believe that our audits provide a reasonable basis for our opinions.

As discussed in Note 1 to the consolidated financial statements, Visteon Corporation and certain of its U.S. subsidiaries (the "Debtors") voluntarily filed a petition on May 28, 2009 with the United States Bankruptcy Court for the District of Delaware for reorganization under Chapter 11 of the Bankruptcy Code. The Company's Fifth Amended Joint Plan of Reorganization (the "Plan") was confirmed on August 31, 2010. Confirmation of the Plan resulted in the discharge of certain claims against the Debtors that arose before May 28, 2009 and substantially alters rights and interests of equity security holders as provided for in the Plan. The Plan was substantially consummated on October 1, 2010 and the Company emerged from bankruptcy. In connection with its emergence from bankruptcy, the Company adopted fresh start accounting on October 1, 2010.

A company's internal control over financial reporting is a process designed to provide reasonable assurance regarding the reliability of financial reporting and the preparation of financial statements for external purposes in accordance with generally accepted accounting principles. A company's internal control over financial reporting includes those policies and procedures that (i) pertain to the maintenance of records that, in reasonable detail, accurately and fairly reflect the transactions and dispositions of the assets of the company; (ii) provide reasonable assurance that transactions are recorded as necessary to permit preparation of financial statements in accordance with generally accepted accounting principles, and that receipts and expenditures of the company are being made only in accordance with authorizations of management and directors of the company; and (iii) provide reasonable assurance regarding prevention or timely detection of unauthorized acquisition, use, or disposition of the company's assets that could have a material effect on the financial statements.

Because of its inherent limitations, internal control over financial reporting may not prevent or detect misstatements. Also, projections of any evaluation of effectiveness to future periods are subject to the risk that controls may become inadequate because of changes in conditions, or that the degree of compliance with the policies or procedures may deteriorate.

NOTES TO CONSOLIDATED FINANCIAL STATEMENTS

Note 1. Basis of Presentation (in part)

The Company adopted fresh-start accounting upon emergence from the Chapter 11 Proceedings and became a new entity for financial reporting purposes as of the Effective Date. Therefore, the consolidated financial statements for the reporting entity subsequent to the Effective Date (the "Successor") are not comparable to the consolidated financial statements for the reporting entity prior to the Effective Date (the "Predecessor"). Additional details regarding the adoption of fresh-start accounting are included herein under Note 4, "Fresh-Start Accounting."

Reorganization Under Chapter 11 of the U.S. Bankruptcy Code

On May 28, 2009, Visteon and certain of its U.S. subsidiaries (the "Debtors") filed voluntary petitions for reorganization relief under chapter 11 of the United States Bankruptcy Code (the "Bankruptcy Code") in the United States Bankruptcy Court for the District of Delaware (the "Court") in response to sudden and severe declines in global automotive production during the latter part of 2008 and early 2009 and the resulting adverse impact on the Company's cash flows and liquidity. On August 31, 2010 (the "Confirmation Date"), the Court entered an order (the "Confirmation Order") confirming the Debtors' joint plan of reorganization (as amended and supplemented, the "Plan"). On October 1, 2010 (the "Effective Date"), all conditions precedent to the effectiveness of the Plan and related documents were satisfied or waived and the Company emerged from bankruptcy. Additional details regarding the status of the Company's Chapter 11 Proceedings are included herein under Note 3, "Voluntary Reorganization under Chapter 11 of the United States Bankruptcy Code."

Visteon UK Limited Administration

On March 31, 2009, in accordance with the provisions of the United Kingdom Insolvency Act of 1986 and pursuant to a resolution of the board of directors of Visteon UK Limited, a company organized under the laws of England and Wales (the "UK Debtor") and an indirect, wholly-owned subsidiary of the Company, representatives from KPMG (the

"Administrators") were appointed as administrators in respect of the UK Debtor (the "UK Administration"). The UK Administration was initiated in response to continuing operating losses of the UK Debtor and mounting labor costs and their related demand on the Company's cash flows. The effect of the UK Debtor's entry into administration was to place the management, affairs, business and property of the UK Debtor under the direct control of the Administrators.

As of March 31, 2009, total assets of $64 million, total liabilities of $132 million and related amounts deferred as accumulated other comprehensive income of $84 million, were deconsolidated from the Company's balance sheet resulting in a deconsolidation gain of $152 million. The Company also recorded $57 million for contingent liabilities related to the UK Administration, including $45 million of costs associated with former employees of the UK Debtor, for which the Company was reimbursed from the escrow account on a 100% basis.

Additional amounts related to these items or other contingent liabilities for potential claims under the UK Administration, which may result from (i) negotiations; (ii) actions of the Administrators; (iii) resolution of contractual arrangements, including unexpired leases; (iv) assertions by the UK Pensions Regulator; and, (v) material adverse developments; or other events, may be recorded in future periods. No assurance can be provided that the Company will not be subject to future litigation and/or liabilities related to the UK Administration, including assertions by the UK Pensions Regulator. Additional liabilities, if any, will be recorded when they become probable and estimable and could materially affect the Company's results of operations and financial condition in future periods.

Transactions with Ford Motor Company

On September 29, 2010, the Company entered into a Global Settlement and Release Agreement (the "Release Agreement") with Ford and Automotive Components Holdings, LLC ("ACH") conditioned on the effectiveness of the Company's Plan. The Release Agreement provides, among other things, for: (i) the termination of the Company's future obligations to reimburse Ford for certain pension and retiree benefit costs; (ii) the resolution of and release of claims and causes of actions against the Company and certain claims, liabilities, or actions against the Company's non-debtor affiliates; (iii) withdrawal of all proofs of claim, with a face value of approximately $163 million, including a claim for pension and retiree benefit liabilities described above, filed against the Company by Ford and/or ACH and an agreement to not assert any further claims against the estates, other than with respect to preserved claims; (iv) the rejection of all purchase orders under which the Company is not producing component parts and other agreements which would not provide a benefit to the reorganized Company and waiver of any claims against the Company arising out of such rejected agreements; (v) the reimbursement by Ford of up to $29 million to the Company for costs associated with restructuring initiatives in various parts of the world; and (vi) a commitment by Ford and its affiliates to source the Company new and replacement business totaling approximately $600 million in annual sales for vehicle programs launching through 2013.

In exchange for these benefits, the Company assumed all outstanding purchase orders and related agreements under which the Company is currently producing parts for Ford and/or ACH and agreed to continue to produce and deliver

component parts to Ford and ACH in accordance with the terms of such purchase orders to ensure Ford continuity of supply. The Company also agreed to release Ford and ACH from any claims, liabilities, or actions that the Company may potentially assert against Ford and/or ACH.

On July 26, 2010, the Company, Visteon Global Technologies, Inc., ACH and Ford entered into an agreement (the "ACH Termination Agreement") to terminate each of (i) the Master Services Agreement, dated September 30, 2005 (as amended); (ii) the Visteon Salaried Employee Lease Agreement, dated October 1, 2005 (as amended); and, (iii) the Visteon Hourly Employee Lease Agreement, dated October 1, 2005 (as amended). On August 17, 2010, the Court approved the ACH Termination Agreement, pursuant to which Ford released Visteon from certain OPEB obligations related to employees previously leased to ACH resulting in a $9 million gain during the third quarter of 2010.

Note 3. Voluntary Reorganization Under Chapter 11 of the United States Bankruptcy Code (in part)

The Chapter 11 Proceedings were initiated in response to sudden and severe declines in global automotive production during the latter part of 2008 and early 2009 and the adverse impact on the Company's cash flows and liquidity. The reorganization cases are being jointly administered as Case No. 09-11786 under the caption "In re Visteon Corporation, et al". On August 31, 2010, the Court entered the Confirmation Order confirming the Debtors' Plan and on the Effective Date all conditions precedent to the effectiveness of the Plan and related documents were satisfied or waived and the Company emerged from bankruptcy.

Plan of Reorganization (in part)

A plan of reorganization determines the rights and satisfaction of claims of various creditors and security holders, but the ultimate settlement of certain claims will be subject to the uncertain outcome of litigation, negotiations and Court decisions up to and for a period of time after a plan of reorganization is confirmed. The following is a summary of the substantive provisions of the Plan and related transactions and is not intended to be a complete description of, or a substitute for a full and complete reading of, the Plan.

- Cancellation of any shares of Visteon common stock and any options, warrants or rights to purchase shares of Visteon common stock or other equity securities outstanding prior to the Effective Date;
- Issuance of approximately 45,000,000 shares of Successor common stock to certain investors in a private offering (the "Rights Offering") exempt from registration under the Securities Act for proceeds of approximately $1.25 billion;
- Execution of an exit financing facility including $500 million in funded, secured debt and a $200 million asset-based, secured revolver that was undrawn at the Effective Date; and,
- Application of proceeds from such borrowings and sales of equity along with cash on hand to make settlement distributions contemplated under the Plan, including;
  - cash settlement of the pre-petition seven-year secured term loan claims of approximately $1.5 billion, along with interest of approximately $160 million;

— cash settlement of the U.S. asset-backed lending facility ("ABL") and related letters of credit of approximately $128 million;

— establishment of a professional fee escrow account of $68 million; and

— cash settlement of other claims and fees of approximately $119 million;

- Issuance of approximately 2,500,000 shares of Successor common stock to holders of pre-petition notes, including 7% Senior Notes due 2014, 8.25% Senior Notes due 2010, and 12.25% Senior Notes due 2016; holders of the 12.25% senior notes also received warrants to purchase up to 2,355,000 shares of reorganized Visteon common stock at an exercise price of $9.66 per share;

- Issuance of approximately 1,000,000 shares of Successor common stock and warrants to purchase up to 1,552,774 shares of Successor common stock at an exercise price of $58.80 per share for Predecessor common stock interests;

- Issuance of approximately 1,700,000 shares of restricted stock to management under a post-emergence share-based incentive compensation program; and,

- Reinstatement of certain pre-petition obligations including certain OPEB liabilities and administrative, general and other unsecured claims.

Financial Statement Classification

Financial reporting applicable to a company in chapter 11 of the Bankruptcy Code generally does not change the manner in which financial statements are prepared. However, financial statements for periods including and subsequent to a chapter 11 bankruptcy filing must distinguish between transactions and events that are directly associated with the reorganization proceedings and the ongoing operations of the business. Accordingly, revenues, expenses, realized gains and losses and provisions for losses that can be directly associated with the reorganization of the business have been reported separately as Reorganization items, net in the Company's statement of operations.

Note 4. Fresh-Start Accounting

The application of fresh-start accounting results in the allocation of reorganization value to the fair value of assets and is permitted only when the reorganization value of assets immediately prior to confirmation of a plan of reorganization is less than the total of all post-petition liabilities and allowed claims and the holders of voting shares immediately prior to the confirmation of the plan of reorganization receive less than 50% of the voting shares of the emerging entity. The Company adopted fresh-start accounting as of the Effective Date, which represents the date that all material conditions precedent to the Plan were resolved, because holders of existing voting shares immediately before filing and confirmation of the plan received less than 50% of the voting shares of the emerging entity and because its reorganization value

is less than post-petition liabilities and allowed claims, as shown below:

(Dollars in millions)	October 1, 2010
Post-petition liabilities	$ 2,763
Liabilities subject to compromise	3,121
Total post-petition liabilities and allowed claims	5,884
Reorganization value of assets	(5,141)
Excess post-petition liabilities and allowed claims	$ 743

Reorganization Value

The Company's reorganization value includes an estimated enterprise value of approximately $2.4 billion, which represents management's best estimate of fair value within the range of enterprise values contemplated by the Court of $2.3 billion to $2.5 billion. The range of enterprise values considered by the Court was determined using certain financial analysis methodologies including the comparable companies analysis, the precedent transactions analysis and the discounted cash flow analysis. The application of these methodologies requires certain key judgments and assumptions, including financial projections, the amount of cash available to fund operations and current market conditions.

The comparable companies analysis estimates the value of a company based on a comparison of such company's financial statistics with the financial statistics of publicly-traded companies with similar characteristics. Criteria for selecting comparable companies for this analysis included, among other relevant characteristics, similar lines of business, geographic presence, business risks, growth prospects, maturity of businesses, market presence, size and scale of operations. The comparable companies analysis established benchmarks for valuation by deriving financial multiples and ratios for the comparable companies, standardized using common metrics of (i) EBITDAP (Earnings Before Interest, Taxes, Depreciation, Amortization and Pension expense) and (ii) EBITDAP minus capital expenditures. EBITDAP based metrics were utilized to ensure that the analysis allowed for valuation comparability between companies which sponsor pensions and those that do not. The calculated range of multiples for the comparable companies was used to estimate a range which was applied to the Company's projected EBITDAP and projected EBITDAP minus capital expenditures to determine a range of enterprise values. The multiples ranged from 4.6 to 7.8 depending on the comparable company for EBITDAP and from 6.1 to 14.6 for EBITDAP minus capital expenditures. Because the multiples derived excluded pension expense, the analysis further deducted an estimated amount of pension underfunding totaling $455 million from the resulting enterprise value.

The precedent transactions analysis is based on the enterprise values of companies involved in public or private merger and acquisition transactions that have operating and financial characteristics similar to Visteon. Under this methodology, the enterprise value of such companies is determined by an analysis of the consideration paid and the debt assumed in the merger, acquisition or restructuring transaction. As in a comparable companies valuation analysis, the precedent transactions analysis establishes benchmarks for valuation by deriving financial multiples and ratios, standardized using common variables such as revenue or EBITDA (Earnings Before Interest, Taxes, Depreciation and Amortization). In performing the precedent transactions analysis an EBITDAP metric was not able to be used due to the unavailability of pension expense information for the transactions analyzed. Therefore, the precedent transactions analysis relied on derived EBITDA multiples, which were then applied to the Company's operating statistics to determine enterprise value. Different than the comparable companies analysis in that the EBITDA metric is already burdened by pension costs, the precedent transactions analysis did not need to separately deduct pension underfunding in order to calculate enterprise value. The calculated multiples used to estimate a range of enterprise values for the Company, ranged from 4.0 to 7.1 depending on the transaction.

The discounted cash flow analysis estimates the value of a business by calculating the present value of expected future cash flows to be generated by such business. This analysis discounts the expected cash flows by an estimated discount rate. This approach has three components: (i) calculating the present value of the projected unlevered after-tax free cash flows for a determined period of time, (ii) adding the present value of the terminal value of the cash flows and (iii) subtracting the present value of projected pension payments in excess of the terminal year pension expense through 2017, due to the underfunded status of such pension plans. These calculations were performed on unlevered after-tax free cash flows, using an estimated tax rate of 35%, for the period beginning July 1, 2010 through December 31, 2013 (the "Projection Period"), discounted to the assumed effective date of June 30, 2010.

The discounted cash flow analysis was based on financial projections as included in the Fourth Amended Disclosure Statement (the "Financial Projections") and included assumptions for the weighted average cost of capital (the "Discount Rate"), which was used to calculate the present value of future cash flows and a perpetuity growth rate for the future cash flows, which was used to determine the enterprise value represented by the time period beyond the Projection Period. The Discount Rate was calculated using the capital asset pricing model resulting in Discount Rates ranging from 14% to 16%, which reflects a number of Company and market-specific factors. The perpetuity growth rate was calculated using the perpetuity growth rate method resulting in a perpetuity growth rate for free cash flow of 0% to 2%. Projected pension payments were discounted on a similar basis as the overall discounted cash flow Discount Rate range.

The estimated enterprise value was based upon an equally weighted average of the values resulting from the comparable companies, precedent transactions and discounted cash flow analyses, as discussed above, and was further adjusted for the estimated value of non-consolidated joint ventures and the estimated amounts of available cash (i.e. cash in excess of estimated minimum operating requirements). The value of non-consolidated joint ventures was calculated using a discounted cash flow analysis of the dividends projected to be received from these operations and also includes

a terminal value based on the perpetuity growth method, where the dividend is assumed to continue into perpetuity at an assumed growth rate. This discounted cash flow analysis utilized a discount rate based on the cost of equity range of 13% to 21% and a perpetuity growth rate after 2013 of 2% to 4%. Application of this valuation methodology resulted in an estimated value of non-consolidated joint ventures of $195 million, which was incremental to the estimated enterprise value. Projected global cash balances were utilized to determine the estimated amount of available cash of $242 million, which was incremental to the estimated enterprise value. Amounts of cash expected to be used for settlements under the terms of the Plan and the estimated minimum level of cash required for ongoing operations were deducted from total projected cash to arrive at an amount of remaining or available cash. The estimated enterprise value, after adjusting for the estimated fair values of non-debt liabilities, is intended to approximate the reorganization value, or the amount a willing buyer would pay for the assets of the company immediately after restructuring.

A reconciliation of the reorganization value is provided in the table below.

Components of Reorganization Value	October 1, 2010
	(Dollars in millions)
Enterprise value	$2,390
Non-debt liabilities	2,751
Reorganization value	$5,141

The value of a business is subject to uncertainties and contingencies that are difficult to predict and will fluctuate with changes in factors affecting the prospects of such a business. As a result, the estimates set forth herein are not necessarily indicative of actual outcomes, which may be significantly more or less favorable than those set forth herein. These estimates assume that the Company will continue as the owner and operator of these businesses and related assets and that such businesses and assets will be operated in accordance with the business plan, which is the basis for Financial Projections. The Financial Projections are based on projected market conditions and other estimates and assumptions including, but not limited to, general business, economic, competitive, regulatory, market and financial conditions, all of which are difficult to predict and generally beyond the Company's control. Depending on the actual results of such factors, operations or changes in financial markets, these valuation estimates may differ significantly from that disclosed herein.

The Company's reorganization value was first allocated to its tangible assets and identifiable intangible assets and the excess of reorganization value over the fair value of tangible and identifiable intangible assets was recorded as goodwill. Liabilities existing as of the Effective Date, other than deferred taxes, were recorded at the present value of amounts expected to be paid using appropriate risk adjusted interest rates. Deferred taxes were determined in conformity with applicable income tax accounting standards. Accumulated depreciation, accumulated amortization, retained deficit, common stock and accumulated other comprehensive loss attributable to the predecessor entity were eliminated.

Adjustments recorded to the predecessor entity to give effect to the Plan and to record assets and liabilities at fair value pursuant to the adoption of fresh-start accounting are summarized below (dollars in millions):

	Predecessor 10/1/2010	Reorganization Adjustments[a]	Fair Value Adjustments[b]	Successor 10/1/2010
Assets				
Cash and equivalents	$ 918	$ (52)[c]	$ —	$ 866
Restricted cash	195	(105)[d]	—	90
Accounts receivable, net	1,086	(4)[e]	—	1,082
Inventories, net	395	—	4[q]	399
Other current assets	283	(11)[f]	(14)[r], [aa]	258
Total current assets	2,877	(172)	(10)	2,695
Property and equipment, net	1,812	—	(240)[s]	1,572
Equity in net assets of non-consolidated affiliates	378	5[g]	13[t]	396
Intangible assets, net	6	—	361[u]	367
Goodwill	—	—	38[v]	38
Other non-current assets	74	13[h]	(14)[w], [aa]	73
Total assets	$ 5,147	$ (154)	$ 148	$5,141
Liabilities and Stockholders' (Deficit) Equity				
Short-term debt, including current portion of long-term debt	$ 128	$ 5[k]	$ —	$ 133
Accounts payable	1,043	—	—	1,043
Accrued employee liabilities	196	19[i]	3[x]	218
Other current liabilities	326	95[j]	(58)[y]	363
Total current liabilities	1,693	119	(55)	1,757
Long-term debt	12	473[k]	—	485
Employee benefits	632	154[l]	(63)[x]	723
Deferred income taxes	175	(5)[m]	27[aa]	197
Other non-current liabilities	251	(5)[n]	(39)[y], [aa]	207
Liabilities subject to compromise	3,121	(3,121)[o]	—	—
Common stock—Successor	—	1[p]	—	1
Stock warrants—Successor	—	41[p]	—	41
Common stock—Predecessor	131	(131)[p]	—	—
Stock warrants—Predecessor	127	(127)[p]	—	—
Additional paid-in capital	3,407	(2,175)[p]	(169)[p]	1,063
Accumulated deficit	(4,684)	4,619[p]	65[p]	—
Accumulated other comprehensive loss	(74)	—	74[p]	—
Treasury stock	(3)	3[p]	—	—
Total Visteon shareholders' (deficit) equity	(1,096)	2,231	(30)	1,105
Non-controlling interests	359	—	308[z]	667
Total shareholders' (deficit) equity	(737)	2,231	278	1,772
Total liabilities and shareholders' (deficit) equity	$ 5,147	$ (154)	$ 148	$5,141

[a] Records adjustments necessary to give effect to the Plan, including the receipt of cash proceeds associated with the Rights Offering and Exit Facility, settlement of liabilities subject to compromise, elimination of Predecessor equity and other transactions as contemplated under the Plan. These adjustments resulted in a pre-tax gain on the settlement of liabilities subject to compromise of $956 million in the nine-month Predecessor period ended October 1, 2010 (see explanatory note o., as follows). The Company recorded a $5 million income tax benefit attributable to cancellation of inter-company indebtedness with foreign affiliates pursuant to the Plan.

[b] Records adjustments necessary to reflect assets and liabilities at fair value and to eliminate Accumulated deficit and Accumulated other comprehensive income/(loss). These adjustments resulted in a pre-tax gain of $106 million in the nine-month Predecessor period ended October 1, 2010. Adjustments to record assets and liabilities at fair value on the Effective Date are as follows (dollars in millions):

Inventory	$ 4
Property and equipment	(240)
Equity in net assets of non-consolidated affiliates	13
Intangible assets	361
Goodwill	38
Other assets	(14)
Employee benefits	60
Other liabilities	97
Non-controlling interests	(308)
Elimination of Predecessor accumulated other comprehensive loss and other equity	95
Pre-tax gain on fair value adjustments	$ 106
Net tax expense related to fresh-start adjustments	(41)
Net income on fresh-start adjustments	$ 65

(continued)

(c) This adjustment reflects the net use of cash on the Effective Date and in accordance with the Plan (dollars in millions):

Rights offering proceeds	$1,250
Exit financing proceeds, net	482
Net release of restricted cash	105
Total sources	1,837
Seven year secured term loan and interest	1,660
ABL and letters of credit	128
Rights offering fees	49
Payment of administrative and professional claims	23
Debt issue fees	10
Claim settlements and other	19
Total uses	1,889
Net decrease in cash	$ (52)

(d) The decrease in restricted cash reflects the release of $173 million of cash that was restricted under various orders of the Bankruptcy Court, partially offset by the establishment of a professional fee escrow account of $68 million.
(e) This adjustment reflects the settlement of a receivable in connection with the Release Agreement.
(f) This adjustment relates to the Rights Offering commitment premium deposit paid in July 2010.
(g) This adjustment records additional equity in net income of non-consolidated affiliates related to the nine-month Predecessor period ended October 1, 2010.
(h) This adjustment records $13 million of estimated debt issuance costs capitalized in connection with the exit financing facility.
(i) This adjustment reflects the reinstatement of OPEB and non-qualified pension obligations expected to be paid within 12 months.
(j) This adjustment reflects the establishment of a liability for the payment of $122 million of allowed general unsecured and other claims in accordance with the Plan partially offset by $23 million of accrued reorganization items that were paid on the Effective Date and $4 million for amounts settled in connection with the Release Agreement.
(k) This adjustment reflects the new $500 million secured term loan, net of $10 million original issuance discount and $12 million of fees paid to the lenders.
(l) This adjustment represents the reinstatement of $154 million of other postretirement employee benefit ("OPEB") and non-qualified pension obligations from Liabilities subject to compromise in accordance with the terms of the Plan.
(m) This adjustment reflects the deferred tax impact of certain intercompany liabilities subject to compromise that were cancelled in accordance with the Plan.
(n) This adjustment eliminates incentive compensation accruals for terminated Predecessor compensation plans.
(o) This adjustment reflects the settlement of liabilities subject to compromise ("LSC") in accordance with the Plan, as shown below (dollars in millions):

	LSC September 30, 2010	Settlement per Fifth Amended Plan	Gain on Settlement of LSC
Debt	$2,490	$1,717	$773
Employee liabilities	324	218	106
Interest payable	183	160	23
Other claims	124	70	54
	$3,121	$2,165	$956
Income tax benefit			5
After-tax gain on settlement of LSC			$961

(p) The cancellation of Predecessor Visteon common stock in accordance with the Plan and elimination of corresponding shareholders' deficit balances, are shown below (dollars in millions):

	Predecessor Shareholders' Deficit September 30, 2010	Reorganization Adjustments	Fresh-Start Adjustments	Successor Shareholders' Equity October 1, 2010
Common stock				
Predecessor	$ 131	$ (131)	$ —	$ —
Successor	—	1	—	1
Stock warrants				
Predecessor	127	(127)	—	—
Successor	—	41	—	41
Additional paid-in capital				
Predecessor	3,407	(3,407)	—	—
Successor	—	1,232	(169)	1,063
Accumulated deficit	(4,684)	4,619	65	—
Accumulated other comprehensive loss	(74)	—	74	—
Treasury stock	(3)	3	—	—
Visteon Shareholders' (deficit) equity	$(1,096)	$ 2,231	$ (30)	$1,105

This adjustment also reflects the issuance of Successor common stock.

   A reconciliation of the reorganization value of assets to the Successor's common stock is shown below (dollars in millions, except per share amounts):

(continued)

Reorganization value of assets	$	5,141
Less: fair value of debt		(618)
Less: fair value of non-controlling interests		(667)
Less: fair value of liabilities (excluding debt)		(2,751)
Successor common stock and warrants	$	1,105
Less: fair value of warrants		(41)
Successor common stock	$	1,064
Shares outstanding at October 1, 2010		48,642,520
Per share value	$	21.87

The per-share value of $21.87 was utilized to determine the value of shares issued for settlement of allowed claims.

(q) Inventory was recorded at fair value and was estimated to exceed book value by approximately $26 million. Raw materials were valued at current replacement cost. Work-in-process was valued at estimated finished goods selling price less estimated disposal costs, completion costs and a reasonable profit allowance for selling effort. Finished goods were valued at estimated selling price less estimated disposal costs and a reasonable profit allowance for selling effort. Additionally, fresh-start accounting adjustments for supply and spare parts inventory items of $22 million were a partial offset.

(r) The adjustment to other current assets includes a $7 million prepaid insurance balance and $2 million of other deferred fee amounts with no future benefit to the Successor. Additionally, this adjustment includes a $5 million decrease in deferred tax assets associated with fair value adjustments (see explanatory note aa for additional details related to deferred tax adjustments).

(s) The Company estimates that the book value of property and equipment exceeds the fair value by $240 million after giving consideration to the highest and best use of the assets. Fair value estimates were based on a combination of the cost or market approach, as appropriate. Fair value under the market approach was based on recent sale transactions for similar assets, while fair value under the cost approach was based on the amount required to construct or purchase an asset of equal utility, considering physical deterioration, functional obsolescence and economic obsolescence.

(t) Investments in non-consolidated affiliates were recorded at fair value primarily based on an income approach utilizing the dividend discount model. Significant assumptions included estimated future dividends for each applicable non-consolidated affiliate and discount rates.

(u) Identifiable intangible assets are primarily comprised of developed technology, customer-related intangibles and trade names. Fair value estimates of intangible assets were based on income approaches utilizing projected financial information consistent with the Fourth Amended Disclosure Statement, as described below:

- Developed technology and trade name intangible assets were valued using the relief from royalty method, which estimates the value of an intangible asset to be equal to the present value of future royalties that would be paid for the right to use the asset if it were not owned. Significant assumptions included estimated future revenues for each technology category and trade name, royalty rates, tax rates and discount rates.
- Customer related intangible assets were valued using the multi-period excess earnings method, which estimates the value of an intangible asset to be equal to the present value of future earnings attributable to the asset group after recognition of required returns to other contributory assets. Significant assumptions included estimated future revenues for existing customers, retention rates based on historical experience, tax rates, discount rates, and contributory asset charges including employee intangibles.

(v) Reorganization value in excess of the fair value allocated to identifiable tangible and intangible assets was recorded as goodwill. In adjusting the balance sheet accounts to fair value, the Company estimated excess reorganization value of approximately $38 million, which has been reflected as goodwill and was determined as follows (dollars in millions):

Enterprise value	$2,390
Add: Estimated fair value of non-debt liabilities	2,751
Reorganization value	5,141
Less: Estimated fair value of assets	5,103
Reorganization value in excess of fair value of assets	$ 38

(w) Adjustments to other non-current assets included a decrease of $10 million related to deferred tax assets associated with fair value adjustments and a decrease of $4 million related to discounting of amounts due in future periods (see explanatory note aa for additional details related to deferred tax adjustments).

(x) The adjustments to accrued employee liabilities and employee benefits are related to the remeasurement of pension and OPEB obligations at the Effective Date, based on certain assumptions including discount rates.

(y) The adjustments to other current and other non-current liabilities include decreases of $51 million and $31 million, respectively, to eliminate deferred revenue, which was initially recorded in connection with payments received from customers under various support and accommodation agreements. The decrease in other current liabilities also includes $5 million for discounting of future obligations, while the decrease in non-current liabilities also includes $8 million for non-income tax liabilities and $5 million for tax liabilities, partially offset by $6 million related to leasehold intangibles (see explanatory note aa for additional details related to deferred tax adjustments).

(z) Non-controlling interests are recorded at fair value based on publicly available market values, where possible, and based on other customary valuation methodologies where publicly available market values are not possible, including comparable company and discounted cash flow models. The Company estimates that the fair value of non-controlling interests exceeds book value by $308 million.

(aa) Deferred tax impacts associated with fresh-start adjustments result from changes in the book values of tangible and intangible assets while the tax basis in such assets remains unchanged. The Company anticipates that a full valuation allowance will be maintained in the U.S.; accordingly this adjustment relates to the portion of fresh-start adjustments applicable to certain non-U.S. jurisdictions where the Company is subject to and pays income taxes. Additionally, the amount of non-U.S. accumulated earnings considered permanently reinvested was modified in connection with the adoption of fresh-start accounting, resulting in a decrease in deferred tax liabilities associated with foreign withholding taxes of approximately $30 million. Deferred tax adjustments include the following (dollars in millions):

Balance Sheet Account Classification:	
Other current assets	$ 2
Other non-current assets	10
Deferred income taxes	27
Net increase in deferred tax liabilities	39
Other balance sheet adjustments	2
Net tax expense related to fresh-start adjustments	$41

LACK OF CONSISTENCY

PRESENTATION

Nonissuers

7.28 As required by paragraphs.16–.18 of AU section 508, if there has been a change in accounting principles or the method of their application that has a material effect on the comparability of the company's financial statements, the auditor should refer to the change in an explanatory paragraph of the report. Such paragraph should follow the opinion paragraph and identify the nature of the change and refer the reader to the note in the financial statements that discusses the change in detail.

7.29 The explanatory paragraph in the auditor's report is required in reports on financial statements of subsequent years, as long as the year of the change is presented and reported on. However, if the accounting change is accounted for by retroactive restatement of the financial statements affected, the additional paragraph is required only in the year of the change.

Issuers

7.30 Although the information in paragraphs 7.22–.23 apply to issuers, as well, PCAOB Auditing Standard No. 6, *Evaluating Consistency of Financial Statements* (AICPA, *PCAOB Standards and Related Rules*, Auditing Standards), further states that the auditor should evaluate a change in accounting principle to determine whether the
- newly adopted accounting principle is a generally accepted accounting principle (GAAP).
- method of accounting for the effect of the change is in conformity with GAAP.
- disclosures related to the accounting change are adequate.
- company has justified that the alternative accounting principle is preferable.

7.31 Auditing Standard No. 6 further states that if the auditor concludes that the criteria in paragraph 7.24 for a change in accounting principle are not met, the auditor should consider the matter to be a departure from GAAP and, if the effect of the change in accounting principle is material, should issue a qualified or an adverse opinion.

7.32 In addition to a change in accounting principle, a lack of consistency can also be the result of a correction of a material misstatement in previously issued financial statements. Paragraphs .18A–.18C of PCAOB AU section 508 state that the correction of a material misstatement in previously issued financial statements should be recognized in the auditor's report on the audited financial statements through the addition of an explanatory paragraph following the opinion paragraph.

7.33 The explanatory paragraph should include a
- statement that the previously issued financial statements have been restated for the correction of a misstatement in the respective period.
- reference to the company's disclosure of the correction of the misstatement.

7.34 This type of explanatory paragraph in the auditor's report should be included in reports on financial statements when the related financial statements are restated to correct the prior

material misstatement. The paragraph need not be repeated in subsequent years.

7.35

TABLE 7-4: REFERENCES TO LACK OF CONSISTENCY IN AUDITORS' REPORTS

Table 7-4 summarizes the accounting changes for which auditors expressed unqualified opinions but included explanatory language (following the opinion paragraph) in their reports.

	2011	2010	2009
Income tax uncertainties	1	8	185
Employee benefits	5	10	107
Consolidations/noncontrolling interests	2	19	66
Business combinations	10	31	38
Fair value measurements	1	2	24
Convertible instruments	1	14	21
Stock-based compensation	—	—	11
Earnings per share	—	5	9
Accounting errors/misstatements	5	3	8
Inventories	2	4	3
Impairment of long-lived assets	1	3	2
Variable interest entities	7	16	2
Derivative financial instruments	—	1	2
Revenue recognition	5	5	2
Transfer/servicing of financial assets	3	6	1
Multiple element revenue transactions	1	N/C*	N/C*
Other—described	8	33	19
Total Entities	**48**	**112**	**290**

* N/C = Not compiled. Line item was not included in the table for the year shown.

PRESENTATION AND DISCLOSURE EXCERPTS

Correction of Errors and Restatement

7.36

GREIF, INC. (OCT)

REPORT OF INDEPENDENT REGISTERED PUBLIC ACCOUNTING FIRM

The Board of Directors and Shareholders of Greif, Inc.

We have audited the accompanying consolidated balance sheets of Greif, Inc. and subsidiaries as of October 31, 2011 and 2010, and the related consolidated statements of income, shareholders' equity, and cash flows for each of the three years in the period ended October 31, 2011. Our audits also included the financial statement schedule listed in the Index at Item 15(a)(2). These consolidated financial statements are the responsibility of the Company's management. Our responsibility is to express an opinion on these financial statements based on our audits.

We conducted our audits in accordance with the standards of the Public Company Accounting Oversight Board

(United States). Those standards require that we plan and perform the audit to obtain reasonable assurance about whether the financial statements are free of material misstatement. An audit includes examining, on a test basis, evidence supporting the amounts and disclosures in the financial statements. An audit also includes assessing the accounting principles used and significant estimates made by management, as well as evaluating the overall financial statement presentation. We believe that our audits provide a reasonable basis for our opinion.

In our opinion, the financial statements referred to above present fairly, in all material respects, the consolidated financial position of Greif, Inc. and subsidiaries at October 31, 2011 and 2010, and the consolidated results of their operations and their cash flows for each of the three years in the period ended October 31, 2011, in conformity with U.S. generally accepted accounting principles. Also, in our opinion, the related financial statement schedule, when considered in relation to the basic consolidated financial statements taken as a whole, presents fairly in all material respects the information set forth therein.

As discussed in Note 19 to the consolidated financial statements, the Company has restated the October 31, 2010 and 2009 consolidated financial statements.

We also have audited, in accordance with the standards of the Public Company Accounting Oversight Board (United States), Greif Inc.'s internal control over financial reporting as of October 31, 2011, based on criteria established in Internal Control-Integrated Framework issued by the Committee of Sponsoring Organizations of the Treadway Commission and our report dated December 16, 2011 expressed an unqualified opinion thereon.

NOTES TO CONSOLIDATED FINANCIAL STATEMENTS

Note 19—Correction of Errors and Restatement

In the fourth quarter of 2011, the Company corrected a prior period error related to the incorrect balance sheet elimination of certain intercompany balances occurring in 2003. The effect of the error impacted both foreign currency translation within other comprehensive income (loss), which had been overstated by $19.6 million, and accounts payable, which had been understated by $19.6 million. The Company has corrected the error for all periods presented by restating the consolidated statements of changes in shareholders' equity and the consolidated balance sheets. The correction of the error did not impact total assets, consolidated net income, or cash flows.

During the third quarter of 2011, the Company recorded an out-of-period correction of an error in both noncontrolling interest, which had been understated by $24.7 million, and foreign currency translation within other comprehensive income (loss), which had been overstated by $24.7 million, as of October 31, 2010. Since the Company restated its consolidated financial statements for the intercompany error noted above, the consolidated balance sheet as of October 31, 2010 and the consolidated statements of changes in shareholders' equity have also been restated to reflect this correction as of October 31, 2010. The correction of the error did not impact total assets, consolidated net income, or cash flows.

The following are the previously stated and corrected balances on the consolidated balance sheets as of October 31, 2009 and 2010:

| | October 31, 2009 | | |
Consolidated Balance Sheet	As Previously Reported	Correction	As Restated
Current liabilities			
Accounts payable	335,816	19,547	355,363
Current liabilities	562,097	19,547	581,644
Shareholders' equity			
Accumulated other comprehensive income (loss):			
Foreign currency translation	(6,825)	(19,547)	(26,372)
Other comprehensive loss	(88,246)	(19,547)	(107,793)
Noncontrolling interests	6,997	—	6,997
Total shareholders' equity	1,106,592	(19,547)	1,087,045
Total liabilities and shareholders' equity	2,823,929	—	2,823,929

| | October 31, 2010 | | |
Consolidated Balance Sheet	As Previously Reported	Correction	As Restated
Current liabilities			
Accounts payable	448,310	19,547	467,857
Current liabilities	761,811	19,547	781,358
Shareholders' equity			
Accumulated other comprehensive income (loss):			
Foreign currency translation	44,612	(44,224)	388
Other comprehensive loss	(33,419)	(44,224)	(77,643)
Noncontrolling interests	76,711	24,677	101,388
Total shareholders' equity	1,355,432	(19,547)	1,335,885
Total liabilities and shareholders' equity	3,498,445	—	3,498,445

Pension and Other Postretirement Benefit Obligations

7.37

ASHLAND INC. (SEP)

REPORT OF INDEPENDENT REGISTERED PUBLIC ACCOUNTING FIRM

To The Board of Directors and Stockholders of Ashland Inc. and consolidated subsidiaries

In our opinion, the consolidated financial statements listed in the accompanying index present fairly, in all material respects, the financial position of Ashland Inc. and its subsidiaries at September 30, 2011 and September 30, 2010, and the results of their operations and their cash flows for each of the three years in the period ended September 30, 2011 in conformity with accounting principles generally accepted in the United States of America. In addition, in our opinion, the financial statement schedule listed in the accompanying index presents fairly, in all material respects, the information set forth therein when read in conjunction with the related consolidated financial statements. Also in our opinion, the Company maintained, in all material respects, effective internal control over financial reporting as of September 30, 2011, based on criteria established in *Internal Control—Integrated Framework* issued by the Committee of Sponsoring Organizations of the Treadway Commission (COSO). The Company's management is responsible for these financial statements and financial statement schedule, for maintaining effective internal control over financial reporting and for its assessment of the effectiveness of internal control over financial reporting, included in the accompanying Management's Report on Internal Control over Financial Reporting. Our responsibility is to express opinions on these financial statements, on the financial statement schedule, and on the Company's internal control over financial reporting based on our integrated audits. We conducted our audits in accordance with the standards of the Public Company Accounting Oversight Board (United States). Those standards require that we plan and perform the audits to obtain reasonable assurance about whether the financial statements are free of material misstatement and whether effective internal control over financial reporting was maintained in all material respects. Our audits of the financial statements included examining, on a test basis, evidence supporting the amounts and disclosures in the financial statements, assessing the accounting principles used and significant estimates made by management, and evaluating the overall financial statement presentation. Our audit of internal control over financial reporting included obtaining an understanding of internal control over financial reporting, assessing the risk that a material weakness exists, and testing and evaluating the design and operating effectiveness of internal control based on the assessed risk. Our audits also included performing such other procedures as we considered necessary in the circumstances. We believe that our audits provide a reasonable basis for our opinions.

As described in Note A to the consolidated financial statements, Ashland changed the manner in which it accounts for pension and other postretirement benefit obligations and inventory costing in 2011.

A company's internal control over financial reporting is a process designed to provide reasonable assurance regarding the reliability of financial reporting and the preparation of financial statements for external purposes in accordance with generally accepted accounting principles. A company's internal control over financial reporting includes those policies and procedures that (i) pertain to the maintenance of records that, in reasonable detail, accurately and fairly reflect the transactions and dispositions of the assets of the company; (ii) provide reasonable assurance that transactions are recorded as necessary to permit preparation of financial statements in accordance with generally accepted accounting principles, and that receipts and expenditures of the company are being made only in accordance with authorizations of management and directors of the company; and (iii) provide reasonable assurance regarding prevention or timely detection of unauthorized acquisition, use, or disposition of the company's assets that could have a material effect on the financial statements.

Because of its inherent limitations, internal control over financial reporting may not prevent or detect misstatements. Also, projections of any evaluation of effectiveness to future periods are subject to the risk that controls may become inadequate because of changes in conditions, or that the degree of compliance with the policies or procedures may deteriorate.

As described in Management's Report on Internal Control over Financial Reporting, management has excluded International Specialty Products Inc., which was acquired in August 2011, from its assessment of internal control over financial reporting as of September 30, 2011. We have also excluded International Specialty Products Inc. from our audit of internal control over financial reporting. International Specialty Products Inc. is a wholly-owned subsidiary of Ashland Inc. whose total assets and total sales represent 35% and 3%, respectively, of the related consolidated financial statement amounts of Ashland Inc. as of and for the year ended September 30, 2011.

NOTES TO CONSOLIDATED FINANCIAL STATEMENTS

Note A—Significant Accounting Policies (in part)

Change in Accounting Policy Regarding Pension and Other Postretirement Benefits

During 2011, Ashland elected to change its method of recognizing actuarial gains and losses for its defined benefit pension plans and other postretirement benefit plans. Previously, Ashland recognized the actuarial gains and losses as a component of Stockholders' Equity within the Consolidated Balance Sheet on an annual basis and amortized the gains and losses into operating results over the average future service period of active employees within the related plans. Ashland has elected to immediately recognize the change in the fair value of plan assets and net actuarial gains and losses annually in the fourth quarter of each fiscal year and whenever a plan is determined to qualify for a remeasurement during a fiscal year. The remaining components of pension and other postretirement benefits expense will be recorded on a quarterly basis. While Ashland's historical policy of recognizing pension and other postretirement benefit expense is considered acceptable under U.S. GAAP, Ashland believes that the new policy is preferable as it eliminates the delay in recognizing gains and losses within operating results. This change will also improve transparency within Ashland's operating results by immediately recognizing the effects of economic and interest rate trends on plan investments and assumptions in the year these gains and losses are actually incurred. This change in accounting policy has been applied retrospectively, adjusting all prior periods presented.

In connection with this change in accounting policy for pension and other postretirement benefits, Ashland also elected to change its method of accounting for certain costs included in inventory. Ashland has elected to exclude the amount of its pension and other postretirement benefit costs applicable to inactive participants from inventoriable costs and charge them directly to cost of sales. While Ashland's historical policy of including all pension and other postretirement benefit costs as a component of inventoriable costs was acceptable, Ashland believes that the new policy is preferable, as inventoriable costs will only include costs that are directly attributable to current employees. Applying this change retrospectively, in connection with the change in accounting for pension and other postretirement benefit costs, did not have a significant impact on previously reported inventory, cost of sales or segment reported results in any of the prior period financial statements.

The impact of these accounting policy changes on Ashland's consolidated financial statements are summarized below:

Statements of Consolidated Income

	Year Ended September 30, 2011		
(In millions except per share data)	Previous Method	Effect of Change	As Reported
Sales	$6,502	$ —	$6,502
Costs and expenses			
Cost of sales	4,813	77	4,890
Selling, general and administrative expense	1,267	175	1,442
Research and development expense	89	—	89
	6,169	252	6,421
Equity and other income	49	—	49
Operating income	382	(252)	130
Net interest and other financing expense	(121)	—	(121)
Net gain on acquisitions and divestitures	(5)	—	(5)
Other income	(1)	—	(1)
Income from continuing operations before income taxes	255	(252)	3
Income tax expense (benefit)	43	(96)	(53)
Income from continuing operations	212	(156)	56
Income from discontinued operations	309	49	358
Net income	$ 521	$ (107)	$ 414
Earnings per share from continuing operations			
Basic	$ 2.70	$(1.98)	$ 0.72
Diluted	$ 2.65	$(1.95)	$ 0.70
Earnings per share from net income			
Basic	$ 6.65	$(1.37)	$ 5.28
Diluted	$ 6.51	$(1.34)	$ 5.17

(In millions except per share data)	Year Ended September 30, 2010		
	As Reported	Effect of Change	As Amended
Sales	$5,741	$ —	$5,741
Costs and expenses			
Cost of sales	4,058	66	4,124
Selling, general and administrative expense	1,168	162	1,330
Research and development expense	86	—	86
	5,312	228	5,540
Equity and other income	48	—	48
Operating income	477	(228)	249
Net interest and other financing expense	(197)	—	(197)
Net gain on acquisitions and divestitures	21	—	21
Other income	2	—	2
Income from continuing operations before income taxes	303	(228)	75
Income tax expense (benefit)	62	(75)	(13)
Income from continuing operations	241	(153)	88
Income from discontinued operations	91	(38)	53
Net income	$ 332	$ (191)	$ 141
Earnings per share from continuing operations			
Basic	$ 3.10	$(1.96)	$ 1.14
Diluted	$ 3.04	$(1.93)	$ 1.11
Earnings per share from net income			
Basic	$ 4.26	$(2.44)	$ 1.82
Diluted	$ 4.18	$(2.40)	$ 1.78

(In millions except per share data)	Year Ended September 30, 2009		
	As Reported	Effect of Change	As Amended
Sales	$5,220	$ —	$5,220
Costs and expenses			
Cost of sales	3,732	118	3,850
Selling, general and administrative expense	1,115	284	1,399
Research and development expense	96	—	96
	4,943	402	5,345
Equity and other income	34	—	34
Operating income (loss)	311	(402)	(91)
Net interest and other financing expense	(205)	—	(205)
Net gain on acquisitions and divestitures	59	—	59
Other income	(86)	—	(86)
Income (loss) from continuing operations before income taxes	79	(402)	(323)
Income tax expense (benefit)	52	(135)	(83)
Income (loss) from continuing operations	27	(267)	(240)
Income (loss) from discontinued operations	44	(65)	(21)
Net income (loss)	$ 71	$ (332)	$ (261)
Earnings per share from continuing operations			
Basic	$ 0.38	$(3.69)	$(3.31)
Diluted	$ 0.37	$(3.68)	$(3.31)
Earnings per share from net income (loss)			
Basic	$ 0.98	$(4.58)	$(3.60)
Diluted	$ 0.96	$(4.56)	$(3.60)

SEC 7.37

Consolidated Balance Sheet

(In millions)	At September 30, 2011		
	Previous Method	Effect of Change	As Reported
Retained earnings	$3,952	$(752)	$3,200
Accumulated other comprehensive loss	(445)	752	307

(In millions)	At September 30, 2010		
	As Reported	Effect of Change	As Amended
Deferred income taxes (noncurrent asset)	$ 336	$ (1)	$ 335
Employee benefit obligations	1,372	(5)	1,367
Retained earnings	3,482	(645)	2,837
Accumulated other comprehensive loss	(345)	649	304

Statement of Consolidated Cash Flows

(In millions)	Year Ended September 30, 2011		
	Previous Method	Effect of Change	As Reported
Cash Flows Provided by Operating Activities From Continuing Operations			
Net income	$ 521	$(107)	$ 414
(Income) loss from discontinued operations (net of income taxes)	(309)	(49)	(358)
Deferred income tax (benefit)	39	(96)	(57)
Actuarial loss on pension and postretirement plans	—	318	318
Change in operating assets and liabilities	(370)	(66)	(436)

(In millions)	Year Ended September 30, 2010		
	As Reported	Effect of Change	As Amended
Cash Flows Provided by Operating Activities From Continuing Operations			
Net income	$332	$(191)	$ 141
(Income) loss from discontinued operations (net of income taxes)	(91)	38	(53)
Deferred income tax (benefit)	9	(76)	(67)
Actuarial loss on pension and postretirement plans	—	268	268
Change in operating assets and liabilities	(72)	(39)	(111)

(In millions)	Year Ended September 30, 2009		
	As Reported	Effect of Change	As Amended
Cash Flows Provided by Operating Activities From Continuing Operations			
Net income (loss)	$ 71	$(332)	$(261)
(Income) loss from discontinued operations (net of income taxes)	(44)	65	21
Deferred income tax (benefit)	12	(135)	(123)
Actuarial loss on pension and postretirement plans	—	409	409
Change in operating assets and liabilities	243	(7)	236

Statements of Consolidated Stockholders' Equity

(In millions)	Year Ended September 30, 2011		
	Previous Method	Effect of Change	As Reported
Retained Earnings			
Net income	$ 521	$(107)	$ 414
Balance at September 30, 2011	3,952	(752)	3,200
Accumulated Other Comprehensive Loss			
Pension and postretirement obligation adjustment	(690)	752	62
Balance at September 30, 2011	(445)	752	307
Total Comprehensive Income (Loss)			
Net income	521	(107)	414
Pension and postretirement obligation adjustment, net of tax	(70)	103	33
Balance at September 30, 2011	421	(4)	417

(In millions)	Year Ended September 30, 2010		
	As Reported	Effect of Change	As Amended
Retained Earnings			
Net income	$ 332	$(191)	$ 141
Balance at September 30, 2010	3,482	(645)	2,837
Accumulated Other Comprehensive Loss			
Pension and postretirement obligation adjustment	(620)	649	29
Balance at September 30, 2010	(345)	649	304
Total Comprehensive Income (Loss)			
Net income	332	(191)	141
Pension and postretirement obligation adjustment, net of tax	(158)	178	20
Balance at September 30, 2010	110	(13)	97

(In millions)	Year Ended September 30, 2009		
	As Reported	Effect of Change	As Amended
Retained Earnings			
Balance at September 30, 2008	$3,138	$(122)	$3,016
Net income	71	(332)	(261)
Balance at September 30, 2009	3,185	(454)	2,731
Accumulated Other Comprehensive Loss			
Balance at September 30, 2008	30	118	148
Pension and postretirement obligation adjustment, net of tax	(462)	471	9
Balance at September 30, 2009	(123)	471	348
Total Comprehensive Income (Loss)			
Net income	71	(332)	(261)
Pension and postretirement obligation adjustment, net of tax	(355)	353	(2)
Balance at September 30, 2009	(82)	21	(61)

Variable Interest Entities

7.38

DELL INC. (JAN)

REPORT OF INDEPENDENT REGISTERED PUBLIC ACCOUNTING FIRM

To the Board of Directors and Shareholders of Dell Inc.

In our opinion, the consolidated financial statements listed in the accompanying index present fairly, in all material respects, the financial position of Dell Inc. and its subsidiaries (the "Company") at January 28, 2011 and January 29, 2010, and the results of their operations and their cash flows for each of the three years in the period ended January 28, 2011 in conformity with accounting principles generally accepted in the United States of America. Also, in our opinion, the Company maintained, in all material respects, effective internal control over financial reporting as of January 28, 2011, based on criteria established in *Internal Control—Integrated Framework* issued by the Committee of Sponsoring Organizations of the Treadway Commission (COSO). The Company's management is responsible for these financial statements, for maintaining effective internal control over financial reporting and for its assessment of the effectiveness of internal control over financial reporting, included in Management's Report on Internal Control Over Financial Reporting appearing under Item 9A. Our responsibility is to express opinions on these financial statements, and on the Company's internal control over financial reporting based on our integrated audits. We conducted our audits in accordance with the standards of the Public Company Accounting Oversight Board (United States). Those standards require that we plan and perform the audits to obtain reasonable assurance about whether the financial statements are free of material misstatement and whether effective internal control over financial reporting was maintained in all material respects. Our audits of the financial statements included examining, on a test basis, evidence supporting the amounts and disclosures in the financial statements, assessing the accounting principles used and significant estimates made by management, and evaluating the overall financial statement presentation. Our audit of internal control over financial reporting included obtaining an understanding of internal control over financial reporting, assessing the risk that a material weakness exists, and testing and evaluating the design and operating effectiveness of internal control based on the assessed risk. Our audits also included performing such other procedures as we considered necessary in the circumstances. We believe that our audits provide a reasonable basis for our opinions.

As described in Note 1, in Fiscal 2011, the Company changed the manner in which it accounts for variable interest entities and transfers of financial assets and extinguishments of liabilities; and, in Fiscal 2010, the Company changed the manner in which it accounts for business combinations.

A company's internal control over financial reporting is a process designed to provide reasonable assurance regarding the reliability of financial reporting and the preparation of financial statements for external purposes in accordance with generally accepted accounting principles. A company's internal control over financial reporting includes those policies and procedures that (i) pertain to the maintenance of records that, in reasonable detail, accurately and fairly reflect the transactions and dispositions of the assets of the company; (ii) provide reasonable assurance that transactions are recorded as necessary to permit preparation of financial statements in accordance with generally accepted accounting principles, and that receipts and expenditures of the company are being made only in accordance with authorizations of management and directors of the company; and (iii) provide reasonable assurance regarding prevention or timely detection of unauthorized acquisition, use, or disposition of the company's assets that could have a material effect on the financial statements.

Because of its inherent limitations, internal control over financial reporting may not prevent or detect misstatements. Also, projections of any evaluation of effectiveness to future periods are subject to the risk that controls may become inadequate because of changes in conditions, or that the degree of compliance with the policies or procedures may deteriorate.

NOTES TO CONSOLIDATED FINANCIAL STATEMENTS

Note 1—Description of Business and Summary of Significant Accounting Policies (in part)

Asset Securitization—Dell enters into securitization transactions to transfer certain financing receivables for fixed-term leases and loans to special purpose entities. During Fiscal 2011, Dell adopted the new accounting guidance that removes the concept of a qualifying special purpose entity and removes the exception from applying variable interest entity accounting. The adoption of the new guidance requires an entity to perform an ongoing analysis to determine whether the entity's variable interest or interests give it a controlling financial interest in a variable interest entity. The adoption of the new guidance resulted in Dell's consolidation of its two qualifying special purpose entities with asset securitizations now being accounted for as secured borrowings. See Note 4 of Notes to Consolidated Financial Statements for additional information on the impact of the consolidation.

Prior to Fiscal 2011, these receivables were removed from the Consolidated Statement of Financial Position at the time they were sold. Receivables were considered sold when the receivables were transferred beyond the reach of Dell's creditors, the transferee had the right to pledge or exchange the assets, and Dell had surrendered control over the rights and obligations of the receivables. Gains and losses from the sale of fixed-term leases and loans were recognized in the period the sale occurred, based upon the relative fair value of the assets sold and the remaining retained interest. Retained interest was recognized at fair value with any changes in fair value recorded in earnings. In estimating the value of retained interest, Dell made a variety of financial assumptions, including pool credit losses, payment rates, and discount rates. These assumptions were supported by both Dell's historical experience and anticipated trends relative to the particular receivable pool.

Recently Issued and Adopted Accounting Pronouncements (in part)

Variable Interest Entities and Transfers of Financial Assets and Extinguishments of Liabilities—In June 2009, the FASB issued a new pronouncement on transfers of financial assets and extinguishments of liabilities which removes the concept of a qualifying special purpose entity and removes the exception from applying variable interest entity accounting to qualifying special purpose entities. See "Asset Securitization" above for more information.

Note 4—Financial Services (in part)

Dell Financial Services L.L.C.

Dell offers or arranges various financing options and services for its business and consumer customers in the U.S. through Dell Financial Services L.L.C. ("DFS"), a wholly-owned subsidiary of Dell. DFS's key activities include the origination, collection, and servicing of customer receivables related to the purchase of Dell products and services. New financing originations, which represent the amounts of financing provided to customers for equipment and related software and services through DFS, were approximately $3.7 billion, for both fiscal years ended January 28, 2011, and January 29, 2010, and $4.5 billion during the fiscal year ended January 30, 2009.

Dell transfers certain customer financing receivables to special purpose entities ("SPEs"). The SPEs are bankruptcy remote legal entities with separate assets and liabilities. The purpose of the SPEs is to facilitate the funding of customer receivables in the capital markets. These SPEs have entered into financing arrangements with multi-seller conduits that, in turn, issue asset-backed debt securities in the capital markets. Dell's risk of loss related to securitized receivables is limited to the amount of Dell's right to receive collections for assets securitized exceeding the amount required to pay interest, principal, and other fees and expenses related to the asset-backed securities. Dell provides credit enhancement to the securitization in the form of over-collateralization. Prior to Fiscal 2011, the SPE that funds revolving loans was consolidated, and the two SPEs that fund fixed-term leases and loans were not consolidated. In accordance with the new accounting guidance on variable interest entities ("VIEs"), and transfers of financial assets and extinguishment of financial liabilities, Dell determined that these two SPEs would be consolidated as of the beginning of Fiscal 2011. The primary factors in this determination were the obligation to absorb losses due to the interest Dell retains in the assets transferred to the SPEs in the form of over-collateralization, and the power to direct activities through the servicing role performed by Dell. Dell recorded the assets and liabilities at their carrying amount as of the beginning of Fiscal 2011, with a $1 million cumulative effect adjustment decrease to the opening balance of retained earnings in Fiscal 2011.

Dell's securitization programs contain standard structural features related to the performance of the securitized receivables. These structural features include defined credit losses, delinquencies, average credit scores, and excess collections above or below specified levels. In the event one or more of these criteria are not met and Dell is unable to restructure the program, no further funding of receivables will be permitted and the timing of Dell's expected cash flows from over-collateralization will be delayed. At January 28, 2011, these criteria were met.

Trade Receivables Securitization

7.39

AIRGAS, INC. (MAR)

REPORT OF INDEPENDENT REGISTERED PUBLIC ACCOUNTING FIRM

The Board of Directors and Stockholders of Airgas, Inc.

We have audited the consolidated financial statements of Airgas, Inc. and subsidiaries as listed in the accompanying index. In connection with our audits of the consolidated financial statements, we also have audited the financial statement

schedule as listed in the accompanying index. We also have audited Airgas, Inc.'s internal control over financial reporting as of March 31, 2011, based on criteria established in *Internal Control—Integrated Framework* issued by the Committee of Sponsoring Organizations of the Treadway Commission (COSO). Airgas, Inc.'s management is responsible for these consolidated financial statements and financial statement schedule, for maintaining effective internal control over financial reporting, and for its assessment of the effectiveness of internal control over financial reporting, included in the accompanying Management's Report on Internal Control Over Financial Reporting. Our responsibility is to express an opinion on these consolidated financial statements and financial statement schedule and an opinion on the Company's internal control over financial reporting based on our audits.

We conducted our audits in accordance with the standards of the Public Company Accounting Oversight Board (United States). Those standards require that we plan and perform the audits to obtain reasonable assurance about whether the financial statements are free of material misstatement and whether effective internal control over financial reporting was maintained in all material respects. Our audits of the consolidated financial statements included examining, on a test basis, evidence supporting the amounts and disclosures in the financial statements, assessing the accounting principles used and significant estimates made by management, and evaluating the overall financial statement presentation. Our audit of internal control over financial reporting included obtaining an understanding of internal control over financial reporting, assessing the risk that a material weakness exists, and testing and evaluating the design and operating effectiveness of internal control based on the assessed risk. Our audits also included performing such other procedures as we considered necessary in the circumstances. We believe that our audits provide a reasonable basis for our opinions.

A company's internal control over financial reporting is a process designed to provide reasonable assurance regarding the reliability of financial reporting and the preparation of financial statements for external purposes in accordance with generally accepted accounting principles. A company's internal control over financial reporting includes those policies and procedures that (1) pertain to the maintenance of records that, in reasonable detail, accurately and fairly reflect the transactions and dispositions of the assets of the company; (2) provide reasonable assurance that transactions are recorded as necessary to permit preparation of financial statements in accordance with generally accepted accounting principles, and that receipts and expenditures of the company are being made only in accordance with authorizations of management and directors of the company; and (3) provide reasonable assurance regarding prevention or timely detection of unauthorized acquisition, use, or disposition of the company's assets that could have a material effect on the financial statements.

Because of its inherent limitations, internal control over financial reporting may not prevent or detect misstatements. Also, projections of any evaluation of effectiveness to future periods are subject to the risk that controls may become inadequate because of changes in conditions, or that the degree of compliance with the policies or procedures may deteriorate.

In our opinion, the consolidated financial statements referred to above present fairly, in all material respects, the financial position of Airgas, Inc. and subsidiaries as of March 31, 2011 and 2010, and the results of their operations and their cash flows for each of the years in the three-year period ended March 31, 2011, in conformity with U.S. generally accepted accounting principles. Also in our opinion, the related financial statement schedule, when considered in relation to the basic consolidated financial statements taken as a whole, presents fairly, in all material respects, the information set forth therein. Also in our opinion, Airgas, Inc. maintained, in all material respects, effective internal control over financial reporting as of March 31, 2011, based on criteria established in *Internal Control—Integrated Framework* issued by the Committee of Sponsoring Organizations of the Treadway Commission.

As discussed in Note 2 to the consolidated financial statements, the Company changed its method of accounting for its trade receivable securitization agreement due to the adoption of Accounting Standards Update No. 2009-16, *Transfers and Servicing (Topic 860): Accounting for Transfers of Financial Assets*, as of April 1, 2010.

NOTES TO CONSOLIDATED FINANCIAL STATEMENTS

(2) Accounting and Disclosure Changes (in part)

(a) Recently Adopted Accounting Pronouncements

On April 1, 2010, the Company adopted Accounting Standards Update ("ASU") No. 2009-16, *Transfers and Servicing (Topic 860): Accounting for Transfers of Financial Assets* ("ASU 2009-16"), which affected the accounting treatment of its trade receivables securitization program. The Company currently participates in a trade receivables securitization agreement (the "Securitization Agreement") with three commercial banks to which it sells qualifying trade receivables on a revolving basis. The amount of receivables securitized under the Securitization Agreement was $295 million at both March 31, 2011 and 2010. Under the new guidance, proceeds received under the Securitization Agreement are treated as secured borrowings, whereas previously they were treated as proceeds from the sale of trade receivables. The impact of the new accounting treatment resulted in the recognition of both the trade receivables securitized under the program and the borrowings they collateralize on the Consolidated Balance Sheet, which led to a $295 million increase in trade receivables and long-term debt. Additionally, net new borrowings under the Securitization Agreement are classified as financing activities on the Company's Consolidated Statement of Cash Flows. Prior to April 1, 2010, they were treated as proceeds from the sale of trade receivables and reflected net of collections on the Consolidated Statement of Cash Flows as operating activities. With respect to the Company's Consolidated Statement of Earnings, the amounts previously recorded within the line item "Discount on securitization of trade receivables," which represented the difference between the proceeds from the sale and the carrying value of the receivables under the Securitization Agreement, are now reflected within "Interest expense, net" as borrowing costs, consistent with the new accounting treatment. There was no impact to the Company's consolidated net earnings as a result of the change in accounting principle. Additionally, the Company's debt covenants were not impacted by the balance sheet recognition of the borrowings

as a result of the new accounting guidance, as borrowings under the Securitization Agreement were already factored into the debt covenant calculations.

Prior to the adoption of ASU 2009-16, the funding transactions under the Securitization Agreement were accounted for as sales of trade receivables. The Company retained a subordinated interest in the trade receivables sold, which was recorded at the trade receivables' previous carrying value. Subordinated retained interests of approximately $142 million, net of an allowance for doubtful accounts of $23 million, were included in trade receivables on the accompanying Consolidated Balance Sheet at March 31, 2010. Under the previous accounting treatment, management calculated the fair value of the retained interest based on management's best estimate of the undiscounted expected future cash collections on the trade receivables, with changes in the fair value recognized as bad debt expense.

On April 1, 2010, the Company adopted ASU No. 2009-17, *Consolidations (Topic 810): Improvements to Financial Reporting by Enterprises Involved with Variable Interest Entities* ("ASU 2009-17"). ASU 2009-17 established new standards that changed the consolidation model for variable interest entities ("VIEs"), including (1) changes in considerations as to whether an entity is a VIE, (2) a qualitative rather than quantitative assessment to identify the primary beneficiary of a VIE, (3) an ongoing rather than event-driven assessment of the VIE's primary beneficiary, and (4) the elimination of the qualified special purpose entity scope exception. The new guidance did not result in the deconsolidation of the Company's existing VIE, which is the bankruptcy-remote special purpose entity used to collateralize trade receivables under the Securitization Agreement.

Comprehensive Income

7.40

VULCAN MATERIALS COMPANY (DEC)

REPORT OF INDEPENDENT REGISTERED PUBLIC ACCOUNTING FIRM

The Board of Directors and Shareholders of Vulcan Materials Company

We have audited the accompanying consolidated balance sheets of Vulcan Materials Company and its subsidiary companies (the "Company") as of December 31, 2011 and December 31, 2010, and the related consolidated statements of comprehensive income, equity, and cash flows for each of the years in the three-year period ended December 31, 2011. These financial statements are the responsibility of the Company's management. Our responsibility is to express an opinion on the financial statements based on our audits.

We conducted our audits in accordance with the standards of the Public Company Accounting Oversight Board (United States). Those standards require that we plan and perform the audit to obtain reasonable assurance about whether the financial statements are free of material misstatement. An audit includes examining, on a test basis, evidence supporting the amounts and disclosures in the financial statements. An audit also includes assessing the accounting principles used and significant estimates made by management, as well as evaluating the overall financial statement presentation. We believe that our audits provide a reasonable basis for our opinion.

In our opinion, such consolidated financial statements present fairly, in all material respects, the financial position of Vulcan Materials Company and its subsidiary companies as of December 31, 2011 and 2010, and the results of their operations and their cash flows for each of the years in the three-year period ended December 31, 2011 in conformity with accounting principles generally accepted in the United States of America.

As discussed in Note 1 to the consolidated financial statements, the Company has changed its presentation of earnings (loss) and comprehensive income (loss) to be included in a single, continuous statement of comprehensive income (loss) due to the adoption of *Accounting Standards Update 2011-05, Presentation of Comprehensive Income.*

We have also audited, in accordance with the standards of the Public Company Accounting Oversight Board (United States), the Company's internal control over financial reporting as of December 31, 2011, based on criteria established in *Internal Control—Integrated Framework,* issued by the Committee of Sponsoring Organizations of the Treadway Commission, and our report dated February 29, 2012 expressed an unqualified opinion on the Company's internal control over financial reporting.

NOTES TO CONSOLIDATED FINANCIAL STATEMENTS

Note 1: Summary of Significant Accounting Policies (in part)

New Accounting Standards (in part)

Accounting Standards Recently Adopted (in part)

2011—PRESENTATION OF OTHER COMPREHENSIVE INCOME As of the annual period ended December 31, 2011, we adopted ASU No. 2011-05, "Presentation of Comprehensive Income." This standard eliminates the option to present components of other comprehensive income (OCI) as part of the statement of equity. The amendments in this standard require that all nonowner changes in equity be presented either in a single continuous statement of comprehensive income or in two separate but consecutive statements. In December 2011, the Financial Accounting Standards Board (FASB) issued ASU No. 2011-12, "Deferral of the Effective Date for Amendments to the Presentation of Reclassifications of Items Out of Accumulated Other Comprehensive Income in ASU No. 2011-05." ASU No. 2011-12 indefinitely defers the requirement in ASU No. 2011-05 to present reclassification adjustments out of accumulated other comprehensive income by component in the Consolidated Statement of Comprehensive Income. Our accompanying Consolidated Statements of Comprehensive Income conform to the presentation requirements of these standards.

Multiple Deliverable Revenue Arrangements

7.41

UNITED CONTINENTAL HOLDINGS, INC. (DEC)

REPORT OF INDEPENDENT REGISTERED PUBLIC ACCOUNTING FIRM

The Board of Directors and Stockholders of United Continental Holdings, Inc.

We have audited the accompanying consolidated balance sheets of United Continental Holdings, Inc. (the "Company") as of December 31, 2011 and December 31, 2010, and the related statements of consolidated operations, comprehensive income (loss), cash flows, and stockholders' equity (deficit) for each of the two years in the period ended December 31, 2011. Our audits also included the financial statement schedule listed in the Index at Item 15(a) for the years ended December 31, 2011 and 2010. These financial statements and the financial statement schedule are the responsibility of the Company's management. Our responsibility is to express an opinion on these financial statements and financial statement schedule based on our audits.

We conducted our audits in accordance with the standards of the Public Company Accounting Oversight Board (United States). Those standards require that we plan and perform the audit to obtain reasonable assurance about whether the financial statements are free of material misstatement. An audit includes examining, on a test basis, evidence supporting the amounts and disclosures in the financial statements. An audit also includes assessing the accounting principles used and significant estimates made by management, as well as evaluating the overall financial statement presentation. We believe that our audits provide a reasonable basis for our opinion.

In our opinion, the consolidated financial statements referred to above present fairly, in all material respects, the consolidated financial position of the Company at December 31, 2011 and December 31, 2010, and the consolidated results of its operations and its cash flows for each of the two years in the period ended December 31, 2011, in conformity with U.S. generally accepted accounting principles. Also, in our opinion, such financial statement schedule, when considered in relation to the basic consolidated financial statements taken as a whole, presents fairly, in all material respects, the information set forth therein.

As discussed in Note 2 to the consolidated financial statements, the Company elected to change its method of accounting for frequent flyer award breakage in 2010.

As discussed in Note 2 to the consolidated financial statements, the Company has changed its method of accounting for multiple deliverable revenue recognition as a result of the adoption of the amendments to the FASB Accounting Standards Codification resulting from Accounting Standards Update No. 2009-13, Multiple Deliverable Revenue Arrangements, effective January 1, 2011.

We also have audited, in accordance with the standards of the Public Company Accounting Oversight Board (United States), the Company's internal control over financial reporting as of December 31, 2011, based on criteria established in *Internal Control—Integrated Framework* issued by the Committee of Sponsoring Organizations of the Treadway

Commission and our report dated February 22, 2012, expressed an unqualified opinion thereon.

COMBINED NOTES TO CONSOLIDATED FINANCIAL STATEMENTS

Note 2—Significant Accounting Policies (in part)

The following policies are applicable to UAL, United and Continental, except as noted below under *Continental Predecessor Accounting Policies,* for accounting policies followed by Continental Predecessor that are materially different than the Company's accounting policies.

(c) *Frequent Flyer Accounting*—United and Continental have frequent flyer programs that are designed to increase customer loyalty. Program participants earn mileage credits ("miles") by flying on United, Continental and certain other participating airlines. Program participants can also earn miles through purchases from other non-airline partners that participate in the Company's loyalty programs. We sell miles to these partners, which include credit card issuers, retail merchants, hotels, car rental companies, and our participating airline partners. Miles can be redeemed for free, discounted or upgraded air travel and non-travel awards. The Company records its obligation for future award redemptions using a deferred revenue model.

Miles Earned in Conjunction with Flights

In the case of the sale of air services, the Company recognizes a portion of the ticket sales as revenue when the air transportation occurs and defers a portion of the ticket sale representing the value of the related miles. The adoption of Accounting Standards Update 2009-13, Multiple-Deliverable Revenue Arrangements—a consensus of the FASB Emerging Issues Task Force ("ASU 2009-13") resulted in the revision of this accounting, effective January 1, 2011.

Under the Company's prior accounting policy, the Company estimated the weighted average equivalent ticket value by assigning a fair value to the miles that were issued in connection with the sale of air transportation. The equivalent ticket value is a weighted average ticket value of each outstanding mile, based upon projected redemption patterns for available award choices when such miles are consumed. The fair value of the miles was deferred and the residual amount of ticket proceeds was recognized as passenger revenue at the time the air transportation was provided.

The Company began applying the new guidance in 2011 and determines the estimated selling price of the air transportation and miles as if each element is sold on a separate basis. The total consideration from each ticket sale is then allocated to each of these elements individually on a pro rata basis. The estimated selling price of miles is computed using an estimated weighted average equivalent ticket value that is adjusted by a sales discount that considers a number of factors, including ultimate fulfillment expectations associated with miles sold in flight transactions to various customer groups.

Generally, as compared to the historical accounting policy, the new accounting policy decreases the value of miles that the Company records as deferred revenue and increases the passenger revenue recorded at the time air transportation is provided. The application of the new accounting method to passenger ticket transactions resulted in the following estimated increases to revenue (in millions, except per share amounts):

	Year Ended December 31, 2011		
	UAL	**United**	**Continental**
Operating revenue	$340	$215	$125
Per basic share	1.03	NM	NM
Per diluted share	0.89	NM	NM

Co-branded Credit Card Partner Mileage Sales

United and Continental also each have significant contracts to sell frequent flyer miles to their co-branded credit card partner, Chase Bank USA, N.A. ("Chase"). On June 9, 2011, these contracts were modified and the Company entered into The Consolidated Amended and Restated Co-Branded Card Marketing Services Agreement dated June 9, 2011, (the "Co-Brand Agreement") with Chase.

The Company historically had two primary revenue elements, marketing and air transportation, in the case of miles sold to non-airline third parties. The Company applied the material modification provisions of ASU 2009-13 to the Co-Brand Agreement in June 2011 when the contract was amended. After the adoption of ASU 2009-13, the Company identified five revenue elements in the Co-Brand Agreement: the air transportation element represented by the value of the mile (generally resulting from its redemption for future air transportation); use of the United brand and access to frequent flyer member lists; advertising; baggage services; and airport lounge usage (together, excluding "the air transportation element", the "marketing-related deliverables").

The fair value of the elements is determined using management's estimated selling price of each element. The objective of using the estimated selling price based methodology is to determine the price at which we would transact a sale if the product or service were sold on a stand-alone basis. Accordingly, we determine our best estimate of selling price by considering multiple inputs and methods including, but not limited to, discounted cash flows, brand value, volume discounts, published selling prices, number of miles awarded and number of miles redeemed. The Company estimated the selling prices and volumes over the term of the Co-Brand Agreement in order to determine the allocation of proceeds to each of the multiple elements to be delivered.

The estimated selling price of miles is calculated generally consistent with the methodology as described in *Miles Earned in Conjunction with Flights*, above.

Under accounting prior to the adoption of ASU 2009-13, the Company used an equivalent ticket value to determine the fair value of miles. The new guidance changed the allocation of arrangement consideration to the number of units of accounting; however, the pattern and timing of revenue recognition for those units did not change. The Company records passenger revenue related to the air transportation element when the transportation is delivered. The other elements are generally recognized as other operating revenue when earned. Pending new or materially modified contracts after January 1, 2011, certain other non-airline partners who participate in the loyalty programs and to which we sell miles remain subject to our historical residual accounting method.

Generally, as compared to the historical accounting policy, the new accounting policy decreases the value of the air transportation deliverable related to the Co-Brand Agreement that the Company records as deferred revenue (and ultimately, passenger revenue when redeemed awards are flown) and increases the value primarily of the marketing-related deliverables recorded in other revenue at the time these marketing-related deliverables are provided. The annual impact of this accounting change on operating revenue will decrease over time. Our ability to project the annual decline for each year is significantly impacted by credit card sales volumes, frequent flyer redemption patterns and other factors. Excluding the effects disclosed in the "Special Revenue Item" section below, the impact of adoption of ASU 2009-13 resulted in the following estimated increases to revenue (in millions, except per share amounts):

	Year Ended December 31, 2011		
	UAL	United	Continental
Operating revenue	$260	$180	$80
Per basic share	0.79	NM	NM
Per diluted share	0.68	NM	NM

Given the impact from the adoption of ASU 2009-13 on total revenue, there was a total impact on the Company's profit sharing of approximately $90 million.

Special Revenue Item

The transition provisions of ASU 2009-13 require that the Company's existing deferred revenue balance be adjusted retroactively to reflect the value of any undelivered element remaining at the date of contract modification as if we had been applying ASU 2009-13 since the initiation of the Co-Brand Agreement. We applied this transition provision by revaluing the undelivered air transportation element using its new estimated selling price as determined in connection with the contract modification. This estimated selling price was lower than the rate at which the undelivered element had been deferred under the previous contracts and, as a result, we recorded the following one-time non-cash adjustment to decrease frequent flyer deferred revenue and increase special revenue (in millions, except per share amounts):

	Year Ended December 31, 2011		
	UAL	United	Continental
Special revenue item	$ 107	$ 88	$ 19
Per basic share	0.33	NM	NM
Per diluted share	0.28	NM	NM

Expiration of Miles

United accounts for miles sold and awarded that will never be redeemed by program members, which we referred to as "breakage," using the redemption method. UAL reviews its breakage estimates annually based upon the latest available information regarding redemption and expiration patterns. During the first quarter of 2010, United obtained additional historical data, previously unavailable, which enabled it to refine its estimate of the amount of breakage in its population of miles, increasing the estimate of miles in the population expected to expire. Both the change in estimate and methodology have been applied prospectively effective January 1, 2010. UAL and United estimate these changes increased passenger revenue by approximately $250 million, or $1.21 per UAL basic share ($0.99 per UAL diluted share), in the year ended December 31, 2010.

The Company's estimate of the expected expiration of miles requires significant management judgment. Current and future changes to expiration assumptions or to the expiration policy, or to program rules and program redemption opportunities, may result in material changes to the deferred revenue balance as well as recognized revenues from the programs.

Other Information

The following table summarizes information related to the Company's frequent flyer deferred revenue (in millions, except rates):

	UAL	United	Continental
Frequent flyer deferred revenue at December 31, 2011	$5,658	$3,502	$2,156
% of miles earned expected to expire or go unredeemed	24%	24%	25%
Impact of 1% change in outstanding miles or estimated selling price on deferred revenue	$ 74	$ 33	$ 41

In 2011, the Company announced that MileagePlus will be the loyalty program for the Company beginning in 2012. Moving to a single loyalty program will be a significant milestone in the integration of the two airlines. Continental's loyalty program will formally end in the first quarter of 2012 at which point United will automatically enroll OnePass members in MileagePlus and deposit into those MileagePlus accounts award miles equal to their OnePass award miles balance. The Company currently does not expect a material impact in redemptions when moving to a single loyalty program.

Also, effective January 1, 2012, United updated its estimated selling price for miles to the contractual rate at which we sell miles to our Star Alliance partners participating in reciprocal frequent flyer programs, as the estimated selling price for miles. Management believes this change is a change in estimate, and as such, the change will be applied prospectively effective January 1, 2012.

The following table provides additional information related to amounts recorded related to UAL's frequent flyer programs (in millions):

Year Ended December 31	Cash Proceeds From Miles Sold	Other Revenue Recognized Upon Award of Miles to Third-Party Customers[b]	Increase in Frequent Flyer Deferred Revenue for Miles Awarded[c]	Net Increase in Advanced Purchase of Miles[d]
2011 United	$1,823	$376	$1,249	$198
2011 Continental Successor	1,348	190	1,158	—
2011 UAL[a]	$3,171	$566	$2,407	$198
2010 United	$1,863	$300	$1,477	$ 86
2010 Continental Successor	293	31	262	—
2010 UAL[a]	$2,156	$331	$1,739	$ 86
2009 UAL/United	$1,703	$256	$1,377	$ 70

[a] Continental's results are included in UAL's results from October 1, 2010 to December 31, 2011.

[b] This amount represents other revenue recognized during the period from the sale of miles to third parties, representing the marketing services component of the sale.

[c] This amount represents the increase to frequent flyer deferred revenue during the period.

[d] This amount represents the net increase in the advance purchase of miles obligation due to cash payments for the sale of miles in excess of miles awarded to customers.

EMPHASIS OF A MATTER

PRESENTATION

Author's Note

There are no differences in the following guidance for issuers and nonissuers when referring to an emphasis of a matter.

7.42 Paragraph .19 of AU section 508 states the following:

In any report on financial statements, the auditor may emphasize a matter regarding the financial statements. Such explanatory information should be presented in a separate paragraph of the auditors' report. Phrases such as "with the foregoing [following] explanation" should not be used in the opinion paragraph if an emphasis paragraph is included in the auditors' report. Emphasis paragraphs are never required; they may be added solely at the auditors' discretion. Examples of matters the auditor may wish to emphasize are—

- That the entity is a component of a larger business enterprise.
- That the entity has had significant transactions with related parties.
- Unusually important subsequent events.
- Accounting matters, other than those involving a change or changes in accounting principles, affecting the comparability of the financial statements with those of the preceding period.

The auditors' reports for 20 survey entities included explanatory information emphasizing a matter regarding the financial statements.

PRESENTATION AND DISCLOSURE EXCERPTS

Emphasis of a Matter

7.43

ILLINOIS TOOL WORKS INC. (DEC)

REPORT OF INDEPENDENT REGISTERED PUBLIC ACCOUNTING FIRM

To the Board of Directors and Stockholders of Illinois Tool Works Inc.

We have audited the accompanying statement of financial position of Illinois Tool Works Inc. and Subsidiaries (the "Company") as of December 31, 2011 and 2010, and the related statements of income, income reinvested in the business, comprehensive income, and cash flows for each of the three years in the period ended December 31, 2011. We also have audited the Company's internal control over financial reporting as of December 31, 2011, based on criteria established in *Internal Control—Integrated Framework* issued by the Committee of Sponsoring Organizations of the Treadway Commission. The Company's management is responsible for these financial statements, for maintaining effective internal control over financial reporting, and for its assessment of the effectiveness of internal control over financial reporting, included in the accompanying management report on internal control over financial reporting. Our responsibility is to express an opinion on these financial statements and an opinion on the Company's internal control over financial reporting based on our audits.

We conducted our audits in accordance with the standards of the Public Company Accounting Oversight Board (United States). Those standards require that we plan and perform the audit to obtain reasonable assurance about whether the financial statements are free of material misstatement and whether effective internal control over financial reporting was maintained in all material respects. Our audits of the financial statements included examining, on a test basis, evidence supporting the amounts and disclosures in the financial statements, assessing the accounting principles used and significant estimates made by management, and evaluating the overall financial statement presentation. Our audit of internal control over financial reporting included obtaining an understanding of internal control over financial reporting, assessing the risk that a material weakness exists, and testing and evaluating the design and operating effectiveness of internal control based on the assessed risk. Our audits also included performing such other procedures as we considered necessary in the circumstances. We believe that our audits provide a reasonable basis for our opinions.

A company's internal control over financial reporting is a process designed by, or under the supervision of, the company's principal executive and principal financial officers, or persons performing similar functions, and effected by the company's board of directors, management, and other personnel to provide reasonable assurance regarding the reliability of financial reporting and the preparation of financial statements for external purposes in accordance with generally accepted accounting principles. A company's internal control over financial reporting includes those policies and procedures that (1) pertain to the maintenance of records that, in reasonable detail, accurately and fairly reflect the transactions and dispositions of the assets of the company; (2) provide reasonable assurance that transactions are recorded as necessary to permit preparation of financial statements in accordance with generally accepted accounting principles, and that receipts and expenditures of the company are being made only in accordance with authorizations of management and directors of the company; and (3) provide reasonable assurance regarding prevention or timely detection of unauthorized acquisition, use, or disposition of the company's assets that could have a material effect on the financial statements.

Because of the inherent limitations of internal control over financial reporting, including the possibility of collusion or improper management override of controls, material misstatements due to error or fraud may not be prevented or detected on a timely basis. Also, projections of any evaluation of the effectiveness of the internal control over financial reporting to future periods are subject to the risk that the controls may become inadequate because of changes in conditions, or that the degree of compliance with the policies or procedures may deteriorate.

In our opinion, the consolidated financial statements referred to above present fairly, in all material respects, the financial position of Illinois Tool Works Inc. and Subsidiaries as of December 31, 2011 and 2010, and the results of their operations and their cash flows for each of the three years in the period ended December 31, 2011, in conformity with accounting principles generally accepted in the United States of America. Also, in our opinion, the Company maintained, in all material respects, effective internal control over financial reporting as of December 31, 2011, based on the criteria established in *Internal Control—Integrated Framework* issued by the Committee of Sponsoring Organizations of the Treadway Commission.

As discussed in the International Reporting Lag note within the Notes to Financial Statements, on January 1, 2011, the Company elected to change its method of accounting to eliminate a one-month lag for reporting its international operations outside of North America, which was retrospectively adjusted in the Company's 2010 and 2009 consolidated financial statements.

NOTES TO FINANCIAL STATEMENTS

International Reporting Lag—Prior to 2011, the Company's international operations outside of North America had a fiscal reporting period that began on December 1 and ended on November 30. Effective January 1, 2011, the Company eliminated the one month lag for the reporting of its international operations outside of North America. As a result, the Company is now *reporting both North American and international results on a calendar year basis*. The Company determined that the elimination of the one month reporting lag was preferable because the same period-end reporting date improves overall financial reporting as the impact of current events, economic conditions and global trends are consistently reflected in the financial statements of the North American and international business units.

The Company has applied this change in accounting principle retrospectively to all prior financial statement periods presented. The impact of the elimination of the one month reporting lag for international operations outside of North America for the years ended December 31, 2010 and 2009 was as follows:

Increase (Decrease)		
(In thousands except per share amounts)	**2010**	**2009**
Operating revenues	$(21,796)	$91,574
Income from continuing operations	(24,877)	26,023
Income from continuing operations per diluted share	(0.04)	0.05
Net income	(24,241)	25,688
Net income per diluted share	(0.04)	0.05

The cumulative effect of adopting this change in accounting principle was recorded as an after-tax increase of $7,274,000 to income reinvested in the business as of January 1, 2009.

DEPARTURES FROM UNQUALIFIED OPINIONS

PRESENTATION

Author's Note

There are no differences in the following guidance for issuers and nonissuers when referring to departures from unqualified opinions.

7.44 AU section 508 does not require auditors to express qualified opinions about the effects of uncertainties or lack of consistency. Under AU section 508, departures from unqualified opinions include opinions qualified because of a scope limitation or departure from GAAP, including inadequate disclosures; adverse opinions; and disclaimers of opinion. Paragraphs .20–.63 of AU section 508 discuss these departures. None of the auditors' reports issued in connection with the financial statements of the survey entities contained a *departure*, as defined by AU section 508.

REPORTS ON COMPARATIVE FINANCIAL STATEMENTS

PRESENTATION

Author's Note

There are no differences in the following guidance for issuers and nonissuers when referring to the reports on comparative financial statements.

7.45 Paragraphs .65–.74 of AU section 508 discuss reports on comparative financial statements. None of the auditors' reports for the survey entities expressed an opinion on prior-year financial statements that differed from the opinion originally expressed and none of the auditor reports indicated that a change in auditors had occurred in the current year.

OPINION EXPRESSED ON SUPPLEMENTARY FINANCIAL INFORMATION

PRESENTATION

Author's Note

Because the report on supplementary financial information is applicable only for issuers, the following guidance is not intended for nonissuers.

7.46 Annual reports to security holders may be combined with the required information of SEC Form 10-K and are suitable for filing with the SEC if certain conditions are satisfied. Accordingly, many survey entities prepare an integrated annual report or simply provide to stockholders a copy of Form 10-K in lieu of the annual report. Form 10-K requires inclusion of certain supplementary financial information, including schedules (Article 12 of Regulation S-X), that must be audited. The report on the audit of schedules may be a separate report or combined with the report on the audit of the basic financial statements.

PRESENTATION AND DISCLOSURE EXCERPTS

Supplementary Financial Information

7.47

GENERAL DYNAMICS CORPORATION (DEC)

REPORT OF INDEPENDENT REGISTERED PUBLIC ACCOUNTING FIRM

The Board of Directors and Shareholders of General Dynamics Corporation

We have audited the accompanying Consolidated Balance Sheets of General Dynamics Corporation and subsidiaries as of December 31, 2010 and 2011, and the related Consolidated Statements of Earnings, Shareholders' Equity, and Cash Flows for each of the years in the three-year period ended December 31, 2011. In connection with our audits of the consolidated financial statements, we also have audited financial statement Schedule II. These consolidated financial statements and financial statement schedule are the responsibility of the company's management. Our responsibility is to express an opinion on these consolidated financial statements and financial statement schedule based on our audits.

We conducted our audits in accordance with the standards of the Public Company Accounting Oversight Board (United States). Those standards require that we plan and perform the audit to obtain reasonable assurance about whether the financial statements are free of material misstatement. An audit includes examining, on a test basis, evidence supporting the amounts and disclosures in the financial statements. An audit also includes assessing the accounting principles used and significant estimates made by management, as well as evaluating the overall financial statement presentation. We believe that our audits provide a reasonable basis for our opinion.

In our opinion, the consolidated financial statements referred to above present fairly, in all material respects, the financial position of General Dynamics Corporation and subsidiaries as of December 31, 2010 and 2011, and the results of their operations and their cash flows for each of the years in the three-year period ended December 31, 2011, in conformity with U.S. generally accepted accounting principles. Also, in our opinion, the related financial statement schedule, when considered in relation to the basic consolidated financial statements taken as a whole, presents fairly, in all material respects, the information set forth therein.

We also have audited, in accordance with the standards of the Public Company Accounting Oversight Board (United States), General Dynamics Corporation's internal control over financial reporting as of December 31, 2011, based on the criteria established in Internal Control—Integrated Framework issued by the Committee of Sponsoring Organizations of the Treadway Commission (COSO), and our report dated February 17, 2012, expressed an unqualified opinion on the effectiveness of the company's internal control over financial reporting.

SCHEDULE II—VALUATION AND QUALIFYING ACCOUNTS

(Dollars in millions)	2009	2010	2011
Balance on January 1	$ 98	$108	$122
Charged to costs and expenses	10	18	48
Deductions from reserves	(2)	1	(14)
Other adjustments*	2	(5)	(4)
Balance on December 31	$108	$122	$152

* Includes amounts assumed in business combinations and foreign currency translation adjustments.

Allowance and valuation accounts consist of accounts receivable allowance for doubtful accounts and valuation allowance on deferred tax assets. These amounts are deducted from the assets to which they apply.

DATING OF REPORT

PRESENTATION

Nonissuers

7.48 AU section 530, *Dating of the Independent Auditor's Report* (AICPA, *Professional Standards*), discusses dating of the independent auditor's report. Paragraphs .01 and .05 of AU section 530 state the following:

> **.01** The auditor's report should not be dated earlier than the date on which the auditor has obtained sufficient appropriate audit evidence to support the opinion. Paragraph .05 describes the procedure to be followed when a subsequent event occurring after the date of the auditor's report is disclosed in the financial statements.

> **.05** The independent auditor has two methods available for dating the report when a subsequent event disclosed in the financial statements occurs after the original date of the auditor's report but before the issuance of the related financial statements. The auditor may use "dual dating," for example, "February 16, 20_____, except for Note_____, as to which the date is March 1, 20_____," or may date the report as of the later date. In the former instance, the responsibility for events occurring subsequent to the original report date is limited to the specific event referred to in the note (or otherwise disclosed). In the latter instance, the independent auditor's responsibility for subsequent events extends to the date of the report and, accordingly, the procedures outlined in section 560.12 generally should be extended to that date.

> Footnote 1 of paragraph .01 of AU section 530 explains that among other things, sufficient appropriate audit evidence includes evidence that the audit documentation has been reviewed and that the entity's financial statements, including disclosures, have been prepared and that management has asserted that they have taken responsibility for them.

Issuers

7.49 Amendments were made to the preceding paragraphs in order to conform terminology to the PCAOB's risk assessment standards (Auditing Standard No. 8, *Audit Risk* [AICPA, *PCAOB Standards and Related Rules*, Auditing Standards] through Auditing Standard No. 15, *Audit Evidence* [AICPA, *PCAOB Standards and Related Rules*, Auditing Standards]) and update references to auditing standards that are being superseded or amended. The risk assessment standards are effective for audits of fiscal years beginning on or after December 15, 2010. Paragraphs .01 and .05 of PCAOB AU section 530, *Dating of the Independent Auditor's Report* (AICPA, *PCAOB Standards and Related Rules*, Interim Standards), state the following:

> **.01** The auditor should date the audit report no earlier than the date on which the auditor has obtained sufficient appropriate evidence to support the auditor's opinion. Paragraph .05 describes the procedure to be followed when a subsequent event occurring after the report date is disclosed in the financial statements.

Note: When performing an integrated audit of financial statements and internal control over financial reporting, the auditor's reports on the company's financial statements and on internal control over financial reporting should be dated the same date.

Note: If the auditor concludes that a scope limitation will prevent the auditor from obtaining the reasonable assurance necessary to express an opinion on the financial statements, then the auditor's report date is the date that the auditor has obtained sufficient appropriate evidence to support the representations in the auditor's report.

> **.05** The independent auditor has two methods for dating the report when a subsequent event disclosed in the financial statements occurs after the auditor has obtained sufficient appropriate evidence on which to base his or her opinion, but before the issuance of the related financial statements. The auditor may use "dual dating," for example, "February 16, 20_____, except for Note_____, as to which the date is March 1, 20_____," or may date the report as of the later date. In the former instance, the responsibility for events occurring subsequent to the original report date is limited to the specific event referred to in the note (or otherwise disclosed). In the latter instance, the independent auditor's responsibility for subsequent events extends to the later report date and, accordingly, the procedures outlined in section 560.12 generally should be extended to that date.

PRESENTATION AND DISCLOSURE EXCERPTS

Dating of Report

7.50

JABIL CIRCUIT, INC. (AUG)

REPORT OF INDEPENDENT REGISTERED PUBLIC ACCOUNTING FIRM

The Board of Directors and Stockholders of Jabil Circuit, Inc.

We have audited the accompanying consolidated balance sheet of Jabil Circuit, Inc. and subsidiaries as of August 31, 2010, and the related consolidated statements of operations, comprehensive income (loss), stockholders' equity, and cash flows for each of the years in the two-year period ended August 31, 2010. In connection with our audit of the consolidated financial statements, we also have audited financial statement schedule II for each of the years in the two-year period ended August 31, 2010. These consolidated financial statements and financial statement schedule are the responsibility of the Company's management. Our responsibility is to express an opinion on these consolidated financial statements and financial statement schedule based on our audits.

We conducted our audits in accordance with the standards of the Public Company Accounting Oversight Board (United States). Those standards require that we plan and perform the audit to obtain reasonable assurance about whether the financial statements are free of material misstatement. An audit includes examining, on a test basis, evidence supporting the amounts and disclosures in the financial statements. An audit also includes assessing the accounting principles used and significant estimates made by management, as well as evaluating the overall financial statement presentation. We believe that our audits provide a reasonable basis for our opinion.

In our opinion, the consolidated financial statements referred to above present fairly, in all material respects, the financial position of Jabil Circuit and subsidiaries as of August 31, 2010, and the results of their operations and their cash flows for each of the years in the two-year period ended August 31, 2010, in conformity with U.S. generally accepted accounting principles. Also in our opinion, the related financial statement schedule for each of the years in the two-year period ended August 31, 2010, when considered in relation to the basic consolidated financial statements taken as a whole, presents fairly, in all material respects, the information set forth therein.

/s/ KPMG LLP

October 21, 2010, except with respect to Note 6 and Note 11b, as to which the date is as of October 27, 2011

Tampa, Florida

Certified Public Accountants

AUDITORS' REPORTS ON INTERNAL CONTROL OVER FINANCIAL REPORTING

PRESENTATION

Author's Note

Because the report on internal control over financial reporting is required only for issuers, the following guidance is not applicable for nonissuers.

7.51 Section 404(a) of the Sarbanes-Oxley Act of 2002 requires that management of a public entity assess the effectiveness of the entity's internal control over financial reporting as of the end of the entity's most recent fiscal year and include in the entity's annual report management's conclusions about the effectiveness of the entity's internal control structure and procedures. Management is required to state a direct conclusion about whether the entity's internal control over financial reporting is effective. Management's report on internal control over financial reporting is required to include the following:

- A statement of management's responsibility for establishing and maintaining adequate internal control over financial reporting for the entity
- A statement identifying the framework used by management to conduct the required assessment of the effectiveness of the entity's internal control over financial reporting
- An assessment of the effectiveness of the entity's inter-

nal control over financial reporting as of the end of the entity's most recent fiscal year, including an explicit statement about whether that internal control over financial reporting is effective
- A statement that the registered public accounting firm that audited the financial statements included in the annual report has issued an attestation report on management's assessment of the entity's internal control over financial reporting

7.52 Under Section 404(b) of the Sarbanes-Oxley Act of 2002, the auditor who audits the public entity's financial statements included in the annual report is required to audit the entity's internal control over financial reporting. In addition, the auditor is required to audit and report on management's assessment of the effectiveness of internal control over financial reporting. Under PCAOB Auditing Standard No. 5, *An Audit of Internal Control Over Financial Reporting That is Integrated with an Audit of Financial Statements* (AICPA, *PCAOB Standards and Related Rules,* Auditing Standards), the auditor's objective in an audit of internal control over financial reporting is to express an opinion on the effectiveness of the entity's internal control over financial reporting. The audit of internal control over financial reporting should be integrated with the audit of the financial statements. Accordingly, independent auditors engaged to audit the financial statements of such entities also are required to audit and report on the entity's internal control over financial reporting as of the end of such fiscal year. Further, if the auditor determines that elements of management's annual report on internal control over financial reporting are incomplete or improperly presented, the auditor should modify the report to include an explanatory paragraph describing the reasons for this determination and identify and fairly describe any material weakness. Paragraph 86 of Auditing Standard No. 5 allows the auditor to issue a combined report (that is, one report containing both an opinion on the financial statements and an opinion on internal control over financial reporting) or separate reports on the entity's financial statements and internal control over financial reporting.

7.53 In September 2010, the SEC approved a final rule related to the Dodd-Frank Wall Street Reform and Consumer Protection Act (Dodd-Frank Act). The Dodd-Frank Act provides that Section 404(b) of the Sarbanes-Oxley Act of 2002 shall not apply with respect to any audit report prepared for an issuer that is neither an accelerated filer nor a large accelerated filer. Prior to the Dodd-Frank Act, a nonaccelerated filer would have been required, under existing SEC rules, to include an attestation report of its registered public accounting firm on internal control over financial reporting in the filer's annual report filed with the SEC for fiscal years ending on or after June 15, 2010. During 2011, 499 of the entities surveyed presented a management's report on internal control over financial reporting, and 497 presented an auditor's report on internal control over financial reporting; 271 of those entities had the auditor's report on internal control over financial reporting combined with the auditor's report on financial statements. The auditor's report on internal control over financial reporting for one of the entities surveyed indicated internal control was not effective.

PRESENTATION AND DISCLOSURE EXCERPTS

Separate Report on Internal Control

7.54

PILGRIM'S PRIDE CORPORATION (DEC)

REPORT OF INDEPENDENT REGISTERED PUBLIC ACCOUNTING FIRM ON INTERNAL CONTROL OVER FINANCIAL REPORTING

The Board of Directors and Stockholders of Pilgrim's Pride Corporation

We have audited Pilgrim's Pride Corporation's internal control over financial reporting as of December 25, 2011, based on criteria established in *Internal Control—Integrated Framework* issued by the Committee of Sponsoring Organizations of the Treadway Commission (the COSO criteria). Pilgrim's Pride Corporation's management is responsible for maintaining effective internal control over financial reporting, and for its assessment of the effectiveness of internal control over financial reporting included in the accompanying *Management's Report on Internal Control Over Financial Reporting*. Our responsibility is to express an opinion on the company's internal control over financial reporting based on our audit.

We conducted our audit in accordance with the standards of the Public Company Accounting Oversight Board (United States). Those standards require that we plan and perform the audit to obtain reasonable assurance about whether effective internal control over financial reporting was maintained in all material respects. Our audit included obtaining an understanding of internal control over financial reporting, assessing the risk that a material weakness exists, testing and evaluating the design and operating effectiveness of internal control based on the assessed risk, and performing such other procedures as we considered necessary in the circumstances. We believe that our audit provides a reasonable basis for our opinion.

A company's internal control over financial reporting is a process designed to provide reasonable assurance regarding the reliability of financial reporting and the preparation of financial statements for external purposes in accordance with generally accepted accounting principles. A company's internal control over financial reporting includes those policies and procedures that (1) pertain to the maintenance of records that, in reasonable detail, accurately and fairly reflect the transactions and dispositions of the assets of the company; (2) provide reasonable assurance that transactions are recorded as necessary to permit preparation of financial statements in accordance with generally accepted accounting principles, and that receipts and expenditures of the company are being made only in accordance with authorizations of management and directors of the company; and (3) provide reasonable assurance regarding prevention or timely detection of unauthorized acquisition, use, or disposition of the company's assets that could have a material effect on the financial statements.

Because of its inherent limitations, internal control over financial reporting may not prevent or detect misstatements. Also, projections of any evaluation of effectiveness to future periods are subject to the risk that controls may become inadequate because of changes in conditions, or that the degree of compliance with the policies or procedures may deteriorate.

In our opinion, Pilgrim's Pride Corporation maintained, in all material respects, effective internal control over financial reporting as of December 25, 2011, based on the COSO criteria.

We also have audited, in accordance with the standards of the Public Company Accounting Oversight Board (United States), the consolidated balance sheets of Pilgrim's Pride Corporation as of December 25, 2011 and December 26, 2010, and the related consolidated statements of operations, comprehensive income, stockholders' equity, and cash flows for the years ended December 25, 2011 and December 26, 2010, the three months ended December 27, 2009, and the year ended September 26, 2009 of Pilgrim's Pride Corporation and our report dated February 17, 2012 expressed an unqualified opinion thereon.

Combined Report on Financial Statements and Internal Control

7.55

ANNTAYLOR STORES CORPORATION (JAN)

REPORT OF INDEPENDENT REGISTERED PUBLIC ACCOUNTING FIRM

To the Board of Directors and Stockholders of AnnTaylor Stores Corporation

New York, NY

We have audited the accompanying consolidated balance sheets of AnnTaylor Stores Corporation and its subsidiaries (the "Company") as of January 29, 2011 and January 30, 2010, and the related consolidated statements of operations, stockholders' equity, and cash flows for each of the three fiscal years in the period ended January 29, 2011. We also have audited the Company's internal control over financial reporting as of January 29, 2011, based on criteria established in *Internal Control—Integrated Framework* issued by the Committee of Sponsoring Organizations of the Treadway Commission. The Company's management is responsible for these financial statements, for maintaining effective internal control over financial reporting, and for its assessment of the effectiveness of internal control over financial reporting, included in the accompanying Management's Report on Internal Control over Financial Reporting. Our responsibility is to express an opinion on these financial statements and an opinion on the Company's internal control over financial reporting based on our audits.

We conducted our audits in accordance with the standards of the Public Company Accounting Oversight Board (United States). Those standards require that we plan and perform the audit to obtain reasonable assurance about whether the financial statements are free of material misstatement and whether effective internal control over financial reporting was maintained in all material respects. Our audits of the financial statements included examining, on a test basis, evidence supporting the amounts and disclosures in the financial statements, assessing the accounting principles used and significant estimates made by management, and evaluating the overall financial statement presentation. Our audit of internal control over financial reporting included obtaining an understanding of internal control over financial reporting, assessing the risk that a material weakness exists, and testing and evaluating the design and operating effectiveness of internal control based on the assessed risk. Our audits also included performing such other procedures as we considered necessary in the circumstances. We believe that our audits provide a reasonable basis for our opinions.

A company's internal control over financial reporting is a process designed by, or under the supervision of, the company's principal executive and principal financial officers, or persons performing similar functions, and effected by the company's board of directors, management, and other personnel to provide reasonable assurance regarding the reliability of financial reporting and the preparation of financial statements for external purposes in accordance with generally accepted accounting principles. A company's internal control over financial reporting includes those policies and procedures that (1) pertain to the maintenance of records that, in reasonable detail, accurately and fairly reflect the transactions and dispositions of the assets of the company; (2) provide reasonable assurance that transactions are recorded as necessary to permit preparation of financial statements in accordance with generally accepted accounting principles, and that receipts and expenditures of the company are being made only in accordance with authorizations of management and directors of the company; and (3) provide reasonable assurance regarding prevention or timely detection of unauthorized acquisition, use, or disposition of the company's assets that could have a material effect on the financial statements.

Because of the inherent limitations of internal control over financial reporting, including the possibility of collusion or improper management override of controls, material misstatements due to error or fraud may not be prevented or detected on a timely basis. Also, projections of any evaluation of the effectiveness of the internal control over financial reporting to future periods are subject to the risk that the controls may become inadequate because of changes in conditions, or that the degree of compliance with the policies or procedures may deteriorate.

In our opinion, the consolidated financial statements referred to above present fairly, in all material respects, the financial position of AnnTaylor Stores Corporation and its subsidiaries as of January 29, 2011 and January 30, 2010, and the results of its operations and its cash flows for each of the three years in the period ended January 29, 2011, in conformity with accounting principles generally accepted in the United States of America. Also, in our opinion, the Company maintained, in all material respects, effective internal control over financial reporting as of January 29, 2011, based on the criteria established in *Internal Control—Integrated Framework* issued by the Committee of Sponsoring Organizations of the Treadway Commission.

Audit Report with Specific Items Excluded

7.56

POLO RALPH LAUREN CORPORATION (MAR)

REPORT OF INDEPENDENT REGISTERED PUBLIC ACCOUNTING FIRM

To the Board of Directors and Stockholders of Polo Ralph Lauren Corporation

We have audited Polo Ralph Lauren Corporation and subsidiaries' (the "Company's") internal control over financial reporting as of April 2, 2011, based on criteria established in Internal Control—Integrated Framework issued by the Committee of Sponsoring Organizations of the Treadway Commission (the "COSO criteria"). The Company's management is responsible for maintaining effective internal control over financial reporting, and for its assessment of the effectiveness of internal control over financial reporting, included in the accompanying Management's Report of Internal Control Over Financial Reporting. Our responsibility is to express an opinion on the Company's internal control over financial reporting based on our audit.

We conducted our audit in accordance with the standards of the Public Company Accounting Oversight Board (United States). Those standards require that we plan and perform the audit to obtain reasonable assurance about whether effective internal control over financial reporting was maintained in all material respects. Our audit included obtaining an understanding of internal control over financial reporting, assessing the risk that a material weakness exists, testing and evaluating the design and operating effectiveness of internal control based on the assessed risk, and performing such other procedures as we considered necessary in the circumstances. We believe that our audit provides a reasonable basis for our opinion.

A company's internal control over financial reporting is a process designed to provide reasonable assurance regarding the reliability of financial reporting and the preparation of financial statements for external purposes in accordance with generally accepted accounting principles. A company's internal control over financial reporting includes those policies and procedures that (1) pertain to the maintenance of records that, in reasonable detail, accurately and fairly reflect the transactions and dispositions of the assets of the company; (2) provide reasonable assurance that transactions are recorded as necessary to permit preparation of financial statements in accordance with generally accepted accounting principles, and that receipts and expenditures of the company are being made only in accordance with authorizations of management and directors of the company; and (3) provide reasonable assurance regarding prevention or timely detection of unauthorized acquisition, use, or disposition of the company's assets that could have a material effect on the financial statements.

Because of its inherent limitations, internal control over financial reporting may not prevent or detect misstatements. Also, projections of any evaluation of effectiveness to future periods are subject to the risk that controls may become inadequate because of changes in conditions, or that the degree of compliance with the policies or procedures may deteriorate.

As indicated in the accompanying Management's Report of Internal Control Over Financial Reporting, management's assessment of and conclusion on the effectiveness of Internal control over financial reporting did not include the internal controls of the South Korea Licensed Operations Acquisition, which is included in the 2011 consolidated financial statements of Polo Ralph Lauren Corporation and subsidiaries and constituted 2% of total assets as of April 2, 2011 and less than 1% of revenues and net income for the year then ended. Our audit of internal control over financial reporting of Polo Ralph Lauren Corporation and subsidiaries also did not include an evaluation of the internal control over financial reporting of the South Korea Licensed Operations Acquisition.

In our opinion, the Company maintained, in all material respects, effective internal control over financial reporting as of April 2, 2011, based on the COSO criteria.

We also have audited, in accordance with the standards of the Public Company Accounting Oversight Board (United States), the consolidated balance sheets of the Company as of April 2, 2011 and April 3, 2010, and the related consolidated statements of operations, equity, and cash flows for each of the three years in the period ended April 2, 2011 and our report dated May 26, 2011 expressed an unqualified opinion thereon.

Ineffective Internal Controls

7.57

KOHL'S CORPORATION (JAN)

REPORT OF INDEPENDENT REGISTERED PUBLIC ACCOUNTING FIRM

The Board of Directors and Shareholders of Kohl's Corporation

We have audited Kohl's Corporation's internal control over financial reporting as of January 29, 2011, based on criteria established in Internal Control—Integrated Framework issued by the Committee of Sponsoring Organizations of the Treadway Commission (the COSO criteria). Kohl's Corporation's management is responsible for maintaining effective internal control over financial reporting, and for its assessment of the effectiveness of internal control over financial reporting included in the accompanying Management's Annual Report on Internal Control over Financial Reporting. Our responsibility is to express an opinion on the company's internal control over financial reporting based on our audit.

We conducted our audit in accordance with the standards of the Public Company Accounting Oversight Board (United States). Those standards require that we plan and perform the audit to obtain reasonable assurance about whether effective internal control over financial reporting was maintained in all material respects. Our audit included obtaining an understanding of internal control over financial reporting, assessing the risk that a material weakness exists, testing and evaluating the design and operating effectiveness of internal control based on the assessed risk, and performing such other procedures as we considered necessary in the

circumstances. We believe that our audit provides a reasonable basis for our opinion.

A company's internal control over financial reporting is a process designed to provide reasonable assurance regarding the reliability of financial reporting and the preparation of financial statements for external purposes in accordance with generally accepted accounting principles. A company's internal control over financial reporting includes those policies and procedures that (1) pertain to the maintenance of records that, in reasonable detail, accurately and fairly reflect the transactions and dispositions of the assets of the company; (2) provide reasonable assurance that transactions are recorded as necessary to permit preparation of financial statements in accordance with generally accepted accounting principles, and that receipts and expenditures of the company are being made only in accordance with authorizations of management and directors of the company; and (3) provide reasonable assurance regarding prevention or timely detection of unauthorized acquisition, use or disposition of the company's assets that could have a material effect on the financial statements.

Because of its inherent limitations, internal control over financial reporting may not prevent or detect misstatements. Also, projections of any evaluation of effectiveness to future periods are subject to the risk that controls may become inadequate because of changes in conditions, or that the degree of compliance with the policies or procedures may deteriorate.

In our report dated March 18, 2011, we expressed an unqualified opinion on internal control over financial reporting. As described in the following paragraph, a material weakness was subsequently identified as a result of the restatement of the previously issued financial statements. Accordingly, management has revised its assessment about the effectiveness of the Company's internal control over financial reporting and our present opinion on the effectiveness of the Company's internal control over financial reporting as of January 29, 2011, as expressed herein, is different from that expressed in our previous opinion.

A material weakness is a deficiency, or combination of deficiencies, in internal control over financial reporting, such that there is a reasonable possibility that a material misstatement of the company's annual or interim financial statements will not be prevented or detected on a timely basis. The following material weakness has been identified and included in management's assessment. Management has identified a material weakness in controls related to the company's accounting for leases. We also have audited, in accordance with the standards of the Public Company Accounting Oversight Board (United States), the consolidated balance sheets of the Company as of January 29, 2011 and January 30, 2010, and the related consolidated statements of income, changes in shareholders' equity, and cash flows for each of the three years in the period ended January 29, 2011. This material weakness was considered in determining the nature, timing and extent of audit tests applied in our audit of the consolidated financial statements as of and for the year ended January 29, 2011 and this report does not affect our report dated March 18, 2011, except for Note 2, as to which the date is September 13, 2011, which expressed an unqualified opinion on those financial statements.

In our opinion, because of the effect of the material weakness described above on the achievement of the objectives of the control criteria, Kohl's Corporation has not maintained effective internal control over financial reporting as of January 29, 2011, based on the COSO criteria.

/s/ ERNST & YOUNG LLP

Milwaukee, Wisconsin

March 18, 2011, except for the effects of the material weakness as to which the date is

September 13, 2011

GENERAL MANAGEMENT AND SPECIAL-PURPOSE COMMITTEE REPORTS

PRESENTATION

7.58 A total of 130 survey entities presented a report of management on financial statements. These reports may include the following:
- Description of management's responsibility for preparing the financial statements
- Identification of independent auditors
- Statement about management's representations to the independent auditors
- Statement about financial records and related data made available to the independent auditors
- Description of special-purpose committees of the board of directors
- General description of the entity's system of internal control
- Description of the entity's code of conduct

Occasionally, survey entities presented a report of a special-purpose committee, such as the audit committee or compensation committee.

PRESENTATION AND DISCLOSURE EXCERPTS

Report of Management on Financial Statements

7.59

EMERSON ELECTRIC CO. (SEP)

REPORT OF MANAGEMENT

The Company's management is responsible for the integrity and accuracy of the financial statements. Management believes that the financial statements for the three years ended September 30, 2011 have been prepared in conformity with U.S. generally accepted accounting principles appropriate in the circumstances. In preparing the financial statements, management makes informed judgments and estimates where necessary to reflect the expected effects of events and transactions that have not been completed. The

Company's disclosure controls and procedures ensure that material information required to be disclosed is recorded, processed, summarized and communicated to management and reported within the required time periods.

In meeting its responsibility for the reliability of the financial statements, management relies on a system of internal accounting control. This system is designed to provide reasonable assurance that assets are safeguarded and transactions are executed in accordance with management's authorization and recorded properly to permit the preparation of financial statements in accordance with U.S. generally accepted accounting principles. The design of this system recognizes that errors or irregularities may occur and that estimates and judgments are required to assess the relative cost and expected benefits of the controls. Management believes that the Company's internal accounting controls provide reasonable assurance that errors or irregularities that could be material to the financial statements are prevented or would be detected within a timely period.

The Audit Committee of the Board of Directors, which is composed solely of independent directors, is responsible for overseeing the Company's financial reporting process. The Audit Committee meets with management and the Company's internal auditors periodically to review the work of each and to monitor the discharge by each of its responsibilities. The Audit Committee also meets periodically with the independent auditors, who have free access to the Audit Committee and the Board of Directors, to discuss the quality and acceptability of the Company's financial reporting, internal controls, as well as non-audit-related services.

The independent auditors are engaged to express an opinion on the Company's consolidated financial statements and on the Company's internal control over financial reporting. Their opinions are based on procedures that they believe to be sufficient to provide reasonable assurance that the financial statements contain no material errors and that the Company's internal controls are effective.

Report of the Audit Committee

7.60

PFIZER INC. (DEC)

AUDIT COMMITTEE REPORT

The Audit Committee reviews the Company's financial reporting process on behalf of the Board of Directors. Management has the primary responsibility for the financial statements and the reporting process, including the system of internal controls.

In this context, the Committee has met and held discussions with management and the independent registered public accounting firm regarding the fair and complete presentation of the Company's results and the assessment of the Company's internal control over financial reporting. The Committee has discussed significant accounting policies applied by the Company in its financial statements, as well as alternative treatments. Management has represented to the Committee that the Company's consolidated financial statements were prepared in accordance with accounting principles generally accepted in the United States of America, and the Committee has reviewed and discussed the consolidated financial statements with management and the independent registered public accounting firm. The Committee has discussed with the independent registered public accounting firm matters required to be discussed by Statement on Auditing Standards No. 114.

In addition, the Committee has reviewed and discussed with the independent registered public accounting firm the auditor's independence from the Company and its management. As part of that review, the Committee has received the written disclosures and the letter required by applicable requirements of the Public Company Accounting Oversight Board regarding the independent accountant's communications with the Audit Committee concerning independence, and the Committee has discussed the independent registered public accounting firm's independence from the Company.

The Committee also has considered whether the independent registered public accounting firm's provision of non-audit services to the Company is compatible with the auditor's independence. The Committee has concluded that the independent registered public accounting firm is independent from the Company and its management.

As part of its responsibilities for oversight of the Company's Enterprise Risk Management process, the Committee has reviewed and discussed Company policies with respect to risk assessment and risk management, including discussions of individual risk areas, as well as an annual summary of the overall process.

The Committee has discussed with the Company's Internal Audit Department and independent registered public accounting firm the overall scope of and plans for their respective audits. The Committee meets with the Chief Internal Auditor, Chief Compliance Officer and representatives of the independent registered public accounting firm, in regular and executive sessions to discuss the results of their examinations, the evaluations of the Company's internal controls, and the overall quality of the Company's financial reporting and compliance programs.

In reliance on the reviews and discussions referred to above, the Committee has recommended to the Board of Directors, and the Board has approved, that the audited financial statements be included in the Company's Annual Report on Form 10-K for the year ended December 31, 2011, for filing with the SEC. The Committee has selected, and the Board of Directors has ratified, the selection of the Company's independent registered public accounting firm for 2012.

Appendix of 500 Entities

List of 500 Survey Entities and Where in the Text Excerpts From Their Annual Reports Can Be Found

The following table lists the 500 entities surveyed in alphabetical order, as well as where in the text their annual reports are excerpted.

Company Name	Month of Fiscal Year End	Accounting Technique Illustration
3M Company	December	6.11
A. O. Smith Corporation	December	6.32
A. Schulman, Inc.	August	
Abbott Laboratories	December	3.55
ABM Industries Incorporated	October	
Acuity Brands, Inc.	August	
Adobe Systems Incorporated	November	
Advanced Micro Devices, Inc.	December	
AGCO Corporation	December	2.86
Air Products and Chemicals, Inc.	September	1.49, 5.53
Airgas, Inc.	March	1.29, 4.10, 7.38
AK Steel Holding Corporation	December	4.14
Alcoa Inc.	December	1.109, 2.180
Allegheny Technologies Incorporated	December	
Allergan, Inc.	December	3.62
Alliance One International, Inc.	March	2.110, 3.39, 6.23
Alliant Techsystems Inc.	March	3.50
Altria Group, Inc.	December	1.107, 3.25
Amazon.com, Inc.	December	
American Greetings Corporation	February	
American International Group, Inc.	December	1.33, 1.37, 1.106
AMETEK, Inc.	December	
Amgen Inc.	December	
Amkor Technology, Inc.	December	5.12, 6.42
Ampco-Pittsburgh Corporation	December	
Amphenol Corporation	December	6.41
Anadarko Petroleum Corporation	December	3.41
Analog Devices, Inc.	October	4.09, 6.30
AnnTaylor Stores Corporation	January	7.55
Apache Corporation	December	2.178
Apple Inc.	September	1.39, 1.113
Applied Industrial Technologies, Inc.	June	
Applied Materials, Inc.	October	1.48
Archer Daniels Midland Company	June	1.72, 2.149, 2.188
Arden Group, Inc.	December	
Arkansas Best Corporation	December	3.52
Armstrong World Industries, Inc.	December	1.34, 2.127
Arrow Electronics, Inc.	December	
Ashland Inc.	September	7.36
AT&T Inc.	December	2.91
Atmel Corporation	December	5.08
Autodesk, Inc.	January	3.76
Automatic Data Processing, Inc.	June	1.36, 2.75
AutoNation, Inc.	December	1.66, 2.63
AutoZone, Inc.	August	
Avery Dennison Corporation	December	
Avis Budget Group, Inc.	December	
Avnet, Inc.	June	
Avon Products, Inc.	December	6.20

Company Name	Month of Fiscal Year End	Accounting Technique Illustration
Badger Meter, Inc.	December	
Baker Hughes Incorporated	December	
Ball Corporation	December	
Barnes & Noble, Inc.	April	
Bassett Furniture Industries, Incorporated	November	2.30, 2.76, 2.103, 7.23
Baxter International Inc.	December	
BE Aerospace, Inc.	December	
Beam Inc.	December	3.03, 3.98
Becton, Dickinson and Company	September	3.49
Belden Inc.	December	
Bemis Company, Inc.	December	
Berkshire Hathaway Inc.	December	3.16
Best Buy Co., Inc.	February	
BMC Software, Inc.	March	
Boeing Company, The	December	2.106
Bon-Ton Stores, Inc., The	January	1.25, 1.145
Boston Scientific Corporation	December	2.85, 6.22
Boyd Gaming Corporation	December	2.152, 3.13, 4.19
Breeze-Eastern Corporation	March	
Briggs & Stratton Corporation	June	
Brinker International, Inc.	June	
Brink's Company, The	December	
Bristol-Myers Squibb Company	December	
Brown Shoe Company, Inc.	January	3.61, 4.11, 6.21
Brown-Forman Corporation	April	1.28, 7.13
Brunswick Corporation	December	1.38, 2.185
C. R. Bard, Inc.	December	
CA, Inc.	March	2.133
Cablevision Systems Corporation	December	1.157, 2.64
Cabot Corporation	September	1.31, 3.90
CACI International Inc	June	2.88
Cameron International Corporation	December	
Campbell Soup Company	July	3.32, 3.74
Cardinal Health, Inc.	June	1.40, 6.31
Career Education Corporation	December	2.96, 2.161
Carlisle Companies Incorporated	December	3.100
Carpenter Technology Corporation	June	3.40
Caterpillar Inc.	December	
CBS Corporation	December	
CenturyLink, Inc.	December	1.92
Cenveo, Inc.	December	1.148
CF Industries Holdings, Inc.	December	3.71
Chesapeake Energy Corporation	December	2.27, 3.77, 4.17
Chevron Corporation	December	
Children's Place Retail Stores, Inc., The	January	
Chiquita Brands International, Inc.	December	
Church & Dwight Co., Inc.	December	
Cintas Corporation	May	
Cisco Systems, Inc.	July	2.22, 2.28, 3.07
Citigroup Inc.	December	2.23, 3.08
Cliffs Natural Resources Inc.	December	
Clorox Company, The	June	2.10
Coach, Inc.	June	1.61
Coca-Cola Company, The	December	
Coca-Cola Enterprises Inc.	December	
Coherent, Inc.	September	
Colgate-Palmolive Company	December	
Collective Brands, Inc.	January	4.12
Comcast Corporation	December	
Commercial Metals Company	August	1.147, 3.31
Computer Sciences Corporation	March	1.75, 2.104, 5.45

Company Name	Month of Fiscal Year End	Accounting Technique Illustration
ConAgra Foods, Inc.	May	1.84, 3.17
ConocoPhillips	December	1.68
Constellation Brands, Inc.	February	2.69, 3.43, 4.13
Convergys Corporation	December	4.08
Con-way Inc.	December	
Cooper Tire & Rubber Company	December	
Corn Products International, Inc.	December	
Corning Incorporated	December	
Costco Wholesale Corporation	August	
Covance Inc.	December	
Cracker Barrel Old Country Store, Inc.	July	
Crane Co.	December	1.114, 2.179
Crown Holdings, Inc.	December	
CSP Inc.	September	
Cummins Inc.	December	2.176
CVS Caremark Corporation	December	
Cytec Industries Inc.	December	
D.R. Horton, Inc.	September	
Dana Holding Corporation	December	
Danaher Corporation	December	
Darden Restaurants, Inc.	May	1.133
Dean Foods Company	December	
Deere & Company	October	2.111, 4.15
Dell Inc.	January	7.37
Delta Air Lines, Inc.	December	
Devon Energy Corporation	December	
Dillard's, Inc.	January	
DIRECTV	December	3.09
Discovery Communications, Inc.	December	2.56
Domino's Pizza, Inc.	December	3.24
Donaldson Company, Inc.	July	5.61
Dover Corporation	December	
Dow Chemical Company, The	December	1.110, 2.29
Dun & Bradstreet Corporation, The	December	2.90, 5.44
E. I. du Pont de Nemours and Company	December	
E. W. Scripps Company, The	December	
Eastman Chemical Company	December	5.31
Eastman Kodak Company	December	2.128
Eaton Corporation	December	
eBay Inc.	December	
Ecolab Inc.	December	
El Paso Corporation	December	1.96, 6.44
Electronic Arts Inc.	March	1.101, 2.138, 6.40
Eli Lilly and Company	December	6.36
EMC Corporation	December	6.19
EMCOR Group, Inc.	December	1.67, 2.54
Emerson Electric Co.	September	2.187, 7.59
Energizer Holdings, Inc.	September	1.98, 1.161
Equifax Inc.	December	
Estee Lauder Companies Inc., The	June	2.189
Exide Technologies	March	
Express Scripts, Inc.	December	
Exxon Mobil Corporation	December	
Family Dollar Stores, Inc.	August	
Federal-Mogul Corporation	December	
FedEx Corporation	May	
Fidelity National Information Services, Inc.	December	1.99, 3.35
First Solar, Inc.	December	1.69, 1.149
Fiserv, Inc.	December	
Flowers Foods, Inc.	December	5.46
Fluor Corporation	December	

Company Name	Month of Fiscal Year End	Accounting Technique Illustration
FMC Corporation	December	3.38
Foot Locker, Inc.	January	6.27
Ford Motor Company	December	3.15
Fred's, Inc.	January	2.46, 2.162
Freeport-McMoRan Copper & Gold Inc.	December	3.30
Frontier Communications Corporation	December	
Furniture Brands International, Inc.	December	
GameStop Corp.	January	2.154, 3.34
Gannett Co., Inc.	December	
Gap, Inc., The	January	
Gardner Denver, Inc.	December	
GenCorp Inc.	November	3.97
General Cable Corporation	December	2.47
General Dynamics Corporation	December	3.22, 7.47
General Electric Company	December	1.70, 1.140, 3.26, 3.70
General Mills, Inc.	May	3.57
Genuine Parts Company	December	3.29
Georgia Gulf Corporation	December	
Goldman Sachs Group, Inc., The	December	
Goodrich Corporation	December	2.45
Goodyear Tire & Rubber Company, The	December	
Google Inc.	December	
Great Atlantic & Pacific Tea Company, Inc., The	February	2.155, 3.28, 3.75
Greif, Inc.	October	2.36, 3.12, 5.63, 6.43, 7.36
Griffon Corporation	September	2.160, 2.175, 3.83, 5.60
Guess?, Inc.	January	3.51, 3.60
H.J. Heinz Company	April	2.97, 5.30
Halliburton Company	December	
Hanesbrands Inc.	December	3.78
Harley-Davidson, Inc.	December	
Harman International Industries, Incorporated	June	2.151, 6.10
Harris Corporation	June	1.89
Harsco Corporation	December	
Hasbro, Inc.	December	4.18
Health Net, Inc.	December	
Herman Miller, Inc.	May	
Hershey Company, The	December	3.69
Hess Corporation	December	3.23
Hewlett-Packard Company	October	1.47, 2.136, 5.16
Hill-Rom Holdings, Inc.	September	3.36
HNI Corporation	December	
Home Depot, Inc., The	January	
Honeywell International Inc.	December	
Hormel Foods Corporation	October	3.11, 5.34
Hovnanian Enterprises, Inc.	October	1.144, 3.18
Hubbell Incorporated	December	
Humana Inc.	December	
Huntsman Corporation	December	1.60, 3.96
IAC/InterActiveCorp	December	2.123
IDT Corporation	July	1.41
Illinois Tool Works Inc.	December	7.43
Ingram Micro Inc.	December	1.108
Insperity, Inc.	December	2.99, 2.119
Intel Corporation	December	1.23, 2.89, 3.37
International Business Machines Corporation	December	
International Flavors & Fragrances Inc.	December	2.101, 2.131
International Paper Company	December	
Interpublic Group of Companies, Inc., The	December	
Intuit Inc.	July	
Iron Mountain Incorporated	December	
ITT Corporation	December	5.49

Company Name	Month of Fiscal Year End	Accounting Technique Illustration
J. C. Penney Company, Inc.	January	3.58
J. M. Smucker Company, The	April	2.55, 3.59
Jabil Circuit, Inc.	August	1.64, 6.26, 7.50
Jack in the Box Inc.	September	2.163
Jacobs Engineering Group Inc.	September	
Jarden Corporation	December	2.37
JDS Uniphase Corporation	June	1.63, 1.102
Johnson & Johnson	December	1.112
Johnson Controls, Inc.	September	1.85
Jones Group Inc., The	December	
Joy Global Inc.	October	6.29
JPMorgan Chase & Co.	December	1.146, 2.07, 2.24
Juniper Networks, Inc.	December	5.09
KB Home	November	3.27
Kellogg Company	December	2.124
Kelly Services, Inc.	December	
Kimball International, Inc.	June	
Kimberly-Clark Corporation	December	
KLA-Tencor Corporation	June	1.115
Kohl's Corporation	January	1.74, 2.72, 3.21, 7.57
Kraft Foods Inc.	December	1.71
Kroger Co., The	January	2.137
L.S. Starrett Company, The	June	2.100
L-3 Communications Holdings, Inc.	December	3.81, 6.25
Lam Research Corporation	June	2.98, 5.15
Las Vegas Sands Corp.	December	
La-Z-Boy Incorporated	April	5.43
Lear Corporation	December	1.94, 5.62
Lee Enterprises, Incorporated	September	7.26
Leggett & Platt, Incorporated	December	
Lennar Corporation	November	
Lennox International Inc.	December	
Lexmark International, Inc.	December	
Liberty Media Corporation	December	
Liz Claiborne, Inc.	December	2.87
Lockheed Martin Corporation	December	5.42, 6.33
Louisiana-Pacific Corporation	December	
Lowe's Companies, Inc.	January	
LSI Corporation	December	
Macy's, Inc.	January	
Manitowoc Company, Inc., The	December	1.76
Manpower Inc.	December	
Marriott International, Inc.	December	1.153, 5.17
Martin Marietta Materials, Inc.	December	
Masco Corporation	December	
MasterCard Incorporated	December	
Mattel, Inc.	December	
McClatchy Company, The	December	
McCormick & Company, Incorporated	November	
McDonald's Corporation	December	
McGraw-Hill Companies, Inc., The	December	
McKesson Corporation	March	1.91, 1.132
MeadWestvaco Corporation	December	
Medtronic, Inc.	April	2.92, 2.140
Merck & Co., Inc.	December	2.102
Meredith Corporation	June	
Meritage Homes Corporation	December	
Meritor, Inc.	September	2.118
MetLife, Inc.	December	3.42, 5.19
Mettler-Toledo International Inc.	December	
Micron Technology, Inc.	August	2.70, 6.34

Company Name	Month of Fiscal Year End	Accounting Technique Illustration
Microsoft Corporation	June	
Mohawk Industries, Inc.	December	
Molex Incorporated	June	2.141
Molson Coors Brewing Company	December	
Monsanto Company	August	1.30, 1.65
Morgan Stanley	December	
Mosaic Company, The	May	1.27, 1.154, 2.144
Motorola Solutions, Inc.	December	
Mueller Industries, Inc.	December	
Murphy Oil Corporation	December	
NACCO Industries, Inc.	December	1.156
Nash-Finch Company	December	
National Oilwell Varco, Inc.	December	
National Semiconductor Corporation	May	
NCR Corporation	December	
NetApp, Inc.	April	1.150
Netflix, Inc.	December	
New York Times Company, The	December	
Newell Rubbermaid Inc.	December	
NewMarket Corporation	December	3.14
Newmont Mining Corporation	December	
News Corporation	June	1.155
NIKE, Inc.	May	
Noble Energy, Inc.	December	
Nordstrom, Inc.	January	
Northrop Grumman Corporation	December	3.82
Nucor Corporation	December	
NVR, Inc.	December	
Occidental Petroleum Corporation	December	
Office Depot, Inc.	December	
Olin Corporation	December	
Omnicom Group Inc.	December	
Oracle Corporation	May	
Owens-Illinois, Inc.	December	2.139
PACCAR Inc	December	
Pall Corporation	July	2.184
Parker-Hannifin Corporation	June	
Paychex, Inc.	May	
Peabody Energy Corporation	December	4.20
Pentair, Inc.	December	
PepsiCo, Inc.	December	
PerkinElmer, Inc.	December	1.59
Pfizer Inc.	December	7.60
Phillips-Van Heusen Corporation	January	3.10, 3.44, 5.11
Pilgrim's Pride Corporation	December	7.54
Pitney Bowes Inc.	December	
Plum Creek Timber Company, Inc.	December	1.131
PNC Financial Services Group, Inc., The	December	1.135, 6.39
Polaris Industries Inc.	December	
Polo Ralph Lauren Corporation	March	2.173, 7.56
PolyOne Corporation	December	
Potlatch Corporation	December	
PPG Industries, Inc.	December	
Praxair, Inc.	December	
Precision Castparts Corp.	March	2.53
priceline.com Incorporated	December	
Procter & Gamble Company, The	June	3.63
Prudential Financial, Inc.	December	
PulteGroup, Inc.	December	1.111
QUALCOMM Incorporated	September	2.52, 3.91
Quanex Building Products Corporation	October	2.172

Company Name	Month of Fiscal Year End	Accounting Technique Illustration
Quantum Corporation	March	
Quiksilver, Inc.	October	
R.R. Donnelley & Sons Company	December	
RadioShack Corporation	December	
Raytheon Company	December	
Regal Beloit Corporation	December	2.142
Regal Entertainment Group	December	1.151
Republic Services, Inc.	December	2.174
Reynolds American Inc.	December	
Rite Aid Corporation	February	2.150, 5.26
Robbins & Myers, Inc.	August	1.90
Robert Half International Inc.	December	
Rock-Tenn Company	September	2.120, 2.186, 6.38
Rockwell Automation, Inc.	September	2.143
Rockwell Collins, Inc.	September	2.50
RPM International Inc.	May	
Ruddick Corporation	September	
Ryder System, Inc.	December	
Ryland Group, Inc., The	December	
Safeway Inc.	December	
SanDisk Corporation	December	
Sanmina-SCI Corporation	September	
Sara Lee Corporation	June	3.89
Schnitzer Steel Industries, Inc.	August	2.177
Scholastic Corporation	May	
Scotts Miracle-Gro Company, The	September	1.100
Seaboard Corporation	December	
Sealed Air Corporation	December	6.12
Sealy Corporation	November	1.73
Sears Holdings Corporation	January	
Service Corporation International	December	2.181
Shaw Group Inc., The	August	6.09
Sherwin-Williams Company, The	December	5.59
Silgan Holdings Inc.	December	
Smithfield Foods, Inc.	April	1.32, 6.35
Snap-on Incorporated	December	
Snyder's-Lance, Inc.	December	
Sonic Automotive, Inc.	December	
Sonoco Products Company	December	5.14
Southwest Airlines Co.	December	
Span-America Medical Systems, Inc.	September	
Sparton Corporation	June	
Spectrum Brands Holdings, Inc.	September	1.158, 2.105
Sprint Nextel Corporation	December	3.33, 5.18
SPX Corporation	December	
St. Jude Medical, Inc.	December	2.71, 4.16
Standard Pacific Corp.	December	
Standard Register Company, The	December	1.62
Standex International Corporation	June	
Stanley Black & Decker, Inc.	December	
Staples, Inc.	January	
Starbucks Corporation	September	
Starwood Hotels & Resorts Worldwide, Inc.	December	
Steel Dynamics, Inc.	December	1.95
Steelcase Inc.	February	6.24
Stryker Corporation	December	
Sunoco, Inc.	December	5.10
SuperMedia Inc.	December	2.84
SUPERVALU INC.	February	
Symantec Corporation	March	
SYNNEX Corporation	November	

Company Name	Month of Fiscal Year End	Accounting Technique Illustration
Sysco Corporation	June	7.15
Target Corporation	January	
Tech Data Corporation	January	
Teleflex Incorporated	December	
Tellabs, Inc.	December	
Tenet Healthcare Corporation	December	
Tenneco Inc.	December	2.35
Terex Corporation	December	
Tesoro Corporation	December	
Texas Industries, Inc.	May	
Texas Instruments Incorporated	December	3.64
Textron Inc.	December	
Thermo Fisher Scientific Inc.	December	
Thomas & Betts Corporation	December	
Thor Industries, Inc.	July	
Tiffany & Co.	January	1.35
Time Warner Inc.	December	
Timken Company, The	December	
TJX Companies, Inc., The	January	
Toll Brothers, Inc.	October	
Toro Company, The	October	
Trinity Industries, Inc.	December	
TRW Automotive Holdings Corp.	December	
Tupperware Brands Corporation	December	
Tutor Perini Corporation	December	2.135
Twin Disc, Incorporated	June	
Tyson Foods, Inc.	September	
Unifi, Inc.	June	1.97, 5.35, 7.14
Union Pacific Corporation	December	
Unisys Corporation	December	1.24
United Continental Holdings, Inc.	December	7.41
United Parcel Service, Inc.	December	
United States Steel Corporation	December	
United Stationers Inc.	December	
United Technologies Corporation	December	
UnitedHealth Group Incorporated	December	
Universal Corporation	March	1.26, 1.116, 2.51
Universal Forest Products, Inc.	December	
Universal Health Services, Inc.	December	
URS Corporation	December	
USG Corporation	December	
V.F. Corporation	December	
Valassis Communications, Inc.	December	
Valero Energy Corporation	December	
Varian Medical Systems, Inc.	September	2.132
VeriSign, Inc.	December	
Verizon Communications Inc.	December	
Viacom Inc.	September	
Viad Corp	December	
Visa Inc.	September	
Vishay Intertechnology, Inc.	December	
Visteon Corporation	December	7.27
Vulcan Materials Company	December	7.40
W. R. Grace & Co.	December	
W.W. Grainger, Inc.	December	
Walgreen Co.	August	
Wal-Mart Stores, Inc.	January	
Walt Disney Company, The	September	
Walter Energy, Inc.	December	
Warnaco Group, Inc., The	December	
Washington Post Company, The	December	

Company Name	Month of Fiscal Year End	Accounting Technique Illustration
Waste Management, Inc.	December	
Wausau Paper Corp.	December	
Weis Markets, Inc.	December	
WellPoint, Inc.	December	
Wendy's Company, The	December	
Werner Enterprises, Inc.	December	
Western Digital Corporation	June	
Western Refining, Inc.	December	
Western Union Company, The	December	
Weyerhaeuser Company	December	
Whirlpool Corporation	December	
Whole Foods Market, Inc.	September	
Williams-Sonoma, Inc.	January	2.57
Winn-Dixie Stores, Inc.	June	
Winnebago Industries, Inc.	August	2.134
Wolverine World Wide, Inc.	December	
Worthington Industries, Inc.	May	2.171
Wyndham Worldwide Corporation	December	
Wynn Resorts, Limited	December	
Xerox Corporation	December	3.53
Xilinx, Inc.	March	1.42, 5.13
Yahoo! Inc.	December	
YUM! Brands, Inc.	December	
Zimmer Holdings, Inc.	December	

No.	Title	Paragraph

FASB ACCOUNTING STANDARDS CODIFICATION™ (ASC)

No.	Title	Paragraph
Notice to Constituents (NTC)		1.11
105-10	*Generally Accepted Accounting Principles—Overall*	1.07–1.09
205-10	*Presentation of Financial Statements—Overall*	1.15, 1.16, 1.20, 2.05
205-20	*Presentation of Financial Statements—Discontinued Operations*	3.84–3.86, 3.88
210	*Balance Sheet*	2.73, 2.93, 2.112, 2.121, 2.164
210-10	*Balance Sheet—Overall*	2.03, 2.60
210-20	*Balance Sheet—Offsetting*	1.17, 2.04
220	*Comprehensive Income*	2.182, 3.02, 4.01–4.04, 5.55, 5.56, 7.08
225	*Income Statement*	3.93
225-20	*Income Statement—Extraordinary and Unusual Items*	3.92, 3.93
230	*Statement of Cash Flows*	6.01, 6.28
230-10	*Statement of Cash Flows—Overall*	6.02–6.04, 6.06, 6.07, 6.13–6.15, 6.37
235	*Notes to Financial Statements*	1.19
235-10	*Notes to Financial Statements—Overall*	1.19
250	*Accounting Changes and Error Corrections*	1.16, 1.50, 3.01, 3.66, 5.38, 5.39
250-10	*Accounting Changes and Error Corrections—Overall*	1.20, 1.51–1.57
255	*Changing Prices*	1.159
260	*Earnings Per Share*	3.99
275	*Risks and Uncertainties*	1.21

No.	Title	Paragraph
280	Segment Reporting	1.43
280-10	Segment Reporting—Overall	1.43–1.45
310	Receivables	2.25, 2.26
310-10	Receivables—Overall	2.26
320	Investments—Debt and Equity Securities	2.11, 2.13
320-10	Investments—Debt and Equity Securities—Overall	2.12, 2.14, 2.15
323	Investments—Equity Method and Joint Ventures	2.65
323-10	Investments—Equity Method and Joint Ventures—Overall	2.66, 2.67
330	Inventory	2.38, 2.41
330-10	Inventory—Overall	2.39
350	Intangibles—Goodwill and Other	2.77–2.79, 2.81
350-20	Intangibles—Goodwill and Other—Goodwill	1.45, 2.59, 2.78, 2.80
360	Property, Plant, and Equipment	2.62, 3.65, 3.67, 3.85
360-10	Property, Plant, and Equipment—Overall	2.62
360-20	Property, Plant, and Equipment—Real Estate Sales	2.58
440	Commitments	1.93, 2.146
450-20	Contingencies—Loss Contingencies	1.103
450-30	Contingencies—Gain Contingencies	1.104
470	Debt	2.107, 2.125, 2.126, 2.145, 2.146
470-10	Debt—Overall	2.145
480	Distinguishing Liabilities from Equity	2.165, 5.23
505	Equity	5.01, 5.02, 5.04, 5.05
505-10	Equity—Overall	5.22, 5.24, 7.08
505-20	Equity—Stock Dividends and Stock Splits	5.33
505-30	Equity—Treasury Stock	5.50
505-60	Equity—Spinoffs and Reverse Spinoffs	5.47
605-10	Revenue Recognition—Overall	3.04
605-25	Revenue Recognition—Multiple-Element Arrangements	3.05
605-35	Revenue Recognition—Construction-Type and Production-Type Contracts	3.79
712	Compensation—Nonretirement Postemployment Benefits	3.54
715	Compensation—Retirement Benefits	2.115, 2.116, 3.45–3.47
715-20	Compensation—Retirement Benefits—Defined Benefit Plans—General	3.46

No.	Title	Paragraph
718	Compensation—Stock Compensation	3.56
740	Income Taxes	3.72, 3.73
740-10	Income Taxes—Overall	2.121, 2.122
805	Business Combinations	1.86
805-10	Business Combinations—Overall	1.87
805-20	Business Combinations—Identifiable Assets and Liabilities, and Any Noncontrolling Interest	2.60
805-30	Business Combinations—Goodwill or Gain from Bargain Purchase, Including Consideration Transferred	1.86
810	Consolidation	1.78, 1.79, 2.02, 4.03, 5.57
810-10	Consolidation—Overall	1.77, 1.78, 1.80—1.83, 2.58
815	Derivatives and Hedging	1.11, 1.117, 1.119, 1.120, 1.122, 1.124
815-10	Derivatives and Hedging—Overall	1.17, 2.04
815-15	Derivatives and Hedging—Embedded Derivatives	1.117
815-20	Derivatives and Hedging—Hedging—General	1.121, 1.124
820	Fair Value Measurements and Disclosures	1.136, 2.17, 2.74
820-10	Fair Value Measurements and Disclosures—Overall	1.137—1.139, 2.18, 2.19
825	Financial Instruments	1.118, 1.125, 2.16, 2.20, 2.26, 2.74, 2.109, 2.114, 2.126, 2.147
825-10	Financial Instruments—Overall	2.16, 2.74
830-230	Foreign Currency Matters—Statement of Cash Flows	6.05
835-20	Interest—Capitalization of Interest	2.58
840	Leases	2.156
840-20	Leases—Operating Leases	2.158, 2.159
840-30	Leases—Capital Leases	2.157, 2.159
845-10	Nonmonetary Transactions—Overall	1.81
850	Related Party Disclosures	1.152
860	Transfers and Servicing	2.31, 2.32, 2.34
860-50	Transfers and Servicing—Servicing Assets and Liabilities	2.34
946	Financial Services—Investment Companies	1.138
985-20	Software—Costs of Software to Be Sold, Leased, or Marketed	2.59, 2.61

No.	Title	Paragraph
FASB ACCOUNTING STANDARDS UPDATE (ASU)		
No. 2009-16	*Transfers and Servicing (Topic 860): Accounting for Transfers of Financial Assets*	2.33
No. 2011-03	*Transfers and Servicing (Topic 860): Reconsideration of Effective Control for Repurchase Agreements*	2.33
No. 2011-04	*Fair Value Measurement (Topic 820): Amendments to Achieve Common Fair Value Measurement and Disclosure Requirements in GAAP and IFRSs*	1.136, 2.19
No. 2011-05	*Comprehensive Income (Topic 220): Presentation of Comprehensive Income*	2.182, 3.02, 4.01, 5.55, 7.07
No. 2011-08	*Intangibles-Goodwill and Other (Topic 350): Testing Goodwill for Impairment*	2.78
No. 2011-09	*Compensation-Retirement Benefits-Multiemployer Plans (Subtopic 715-80): Disclosures about an Employer's Participation in a Multiemployer Plan*	2.117, 3.48
No. 2011-10	*Property, Plant, and Equipment (Topic 360): Derecognition of in Substance Real Estate-a Scope Clarification*	2.58
No. 2011-11	*Balance Sheet (Topic 210): Disclosures about Offsetting Assets and Liabilities*	1.17, 2.04
No. 2011-12	*Comprehensive Income (Topic 220): Deferral of the Effective Date for Amendments to the Presentation of Reclassifications of Items Out of Accumulated Other Comprehensive Income in ASU No. 2011-05*	2.182, 3.02, 4.01, 5.55, 7.07
FASB CONCEPTS STATEMENTS		
No. 5	*Recognition and Measurement in Financial Statements of Business Enterprises*	3.04
No. 6	*Elements of Financial Statements—a replacement of FASB Concepts Statement No. 3 (incorporating an amendment of FASB Concepts Statement No. 2)*	3.19, 7.30, 7.31
FASB STATEMENTS		
No. 168	*The FASB Accounting Standards Codification™ and the Hierarchy of Generally Accepted Accounting Principles—a replacement of FASB Statement No. 162*	1.10
CODIFICATION OF AICPA STATEMENTS ON AUDITING STANDARDS		
AU Section 150	*Generally Accepted Auditing Standards*	7.02
AU Section 341	*The Auditor's Consideration of an Entity's Ability to Continue as a Going Concern*	7.24
AU Section 431	*Adequacy of Disclosure in Financial Statements*	1.18
AU Section 508	*Reports on Audited Financial Statements*	7.01, 7.03–7.06, 7.19, 7.21, 7.24, 7.28, 7.32, 7.42, 7.44, 7.45
AU Section 530	*Dating of the Independent Auditor's Report*	7.48, 7.49

No.	Title	Paragraph
AU Section 543	*Part of Audit Performed by Other Independent Auditors*	7.16, 7.17, 7.19
AU Section 560	*Subsequent Events*	7.49

SARBANES-OXLEY ACT OF 2002

No.	Title	Paragraph
Section 103(a)	*Auditing, Quality Control, Ethics Standards*	7.02
Section 404(a)	*Management Assessment of Internal Control—Rules Required*	7.51
Section 404(b)	*Management Assessment of Internal Control—Internal Control Evaluation*	7.52, 7.53

PCAOB AUDITING STANDARDS

No.	Title	Paragraph
No. 1	*References in Auditors' Reports to the Standards of the Public Company Accounting Oversight Board*	7.09
No. 3	*Audit Documentation*	7.21
No. 5	*An Audit of Internal Control Over Financial Reporting That is Integrated with an Audit of Financial Statements*	7.20, 7.52
No. 6	*Evaluating Consistency of Financial Statements*	7.30, 7.31
No. 8	*Audit Risk*	7.49
No. 15	*Audit Evidence*	7.49

PCAOB RULES

No.	Title	Paragraph
Rule 3100	*Compliance With Auditing and Related Professional Practice Standards*	7.02

SEC GUIDANCE

No.	Title	Paragraph
SEC Regulation S-K	*Standard Instructions for Filing Forms Under the Securities Act of 1933, Securities Exchange Act of 1934 and Energy Policy and Conservation Act of 1975*	1.14, 1.18, 2.01
SEC Regulation S-X	*Accounting Rules—Form and Content of Financial Statements*	1.16, 1.18, 2.01, 2.94, 2.146, 2.153, 2.166
Item 303		1.160
Article 8		2.01
SEC Rule 3-01(a)		2.02
SEC Rule 3-04		5.01, 5.27, 5.54
SEC Rule 3A-02		2.02
SEC Rule 4-08		5.27
SEC Rule 5-02		1.104, 2.62, 2.80, 2.94, 2.108, 2.113, 2.129, 2.165, 2.166, 2.167, 5.03, 5.20, 5.24

No.	Title	Paragraph
SEC Rule 5-02.1		2.09
SEC Rule 5-02.6		2.40–2.42
SEC Rule 5-02.8		2.48
SEC Rule 14a-3		1.14, 1.16
Staff Accounting Bulletin No. 108		5.40
Topic 5(BB)	*Inventory Valuation Allowances*	2.39

———————————

Subject Index

A

Accelerated depreciation method, 3.69–3.70

Accounting changes and error corrections
auditing report lack of consistency, 7.36
business combinations, 1.60
changes in accounting estimates, 1.72–1.73
changes in accounting principle, 1.59–1.63
comprehensive income, 1.68
consolidation, 1.71
disclosure, 1.57–1.58
errors, correction of, 1.74–1.76
goodwill, 1.69
interest and penalties related to uncertain tax
positions, 1.61
inventory, 1.62
lack of consistency in independent auditors' report,
7.36
multi-employer pension plans, 1.66
noncontrolling interests, 1.61
pensions and other postretirement benefits,
1.59
presentation, 1.50–1.56
presentation and disclosure excerpts, 1.59–1.76
prior period adjustments, 1.56, 1.57
restatement, 7.36
retained earnings, 5.39, 5.40, 5.43–5.44
revenue recognition, 1.63–1.64
share-based compensation, 1.59
transfers of financial assets and variable interest
entities, 1.64
troubled debt restructuring, 1.70

Accounting corrections. *See* Accounting changes and
error corrections

Accounting estimates
changes in, 1.72–1.73
changes in, distinguishing from changes in
accounting principles, 1.55
depreciation expense, 3.66
disclosure, 1.57
prospective application, 1.54

significant accounting policies and estimates, 1.39
use of, 1.37–1.39

Accounting policies
critical accounting policies, 1.32
disclosure, 1.19, 1.22, 1.33
significant accounting policies and estimates, 1.39

Accounting principles
business combinations, 1.60
changes in, and retained earnings, 5.42
changes in, distinguishing from change in
accounting estimates, 1.55
changes in, generally, 1.59–1.63
changes in, when permitted, 1.52
disclosure, 1.57
evaluating changes in, independent auditors'
report, 7.30–7.35
exceptions, 1.53
financial assets, transfers, 1.64
inventory, 1.62
nonauthoritative accounting guidance sources, 1.08
noncontrolling interests, 1.61
pensions and other postretirement benefits, 1.59
retained earnings, 5.38, 5.42
retrospective application, 1.54, 5.48
revenue recognition, 1.63–1.64
share-based compensation, 1.59
variable interest entities, transfers, 1.64

Accounting standards, new, 1.30

Accounting Standards Board (ASB), clarified auditing
standards, 7.01

Accounts receivable. *See* Current receivables;
Receivables; Receivables sold or
collateralized

Accretion on asset retirement obligations, 3.30

Accumulated depreciation, 2.62

Accumulated other comprehensive income. *See also*
Comprehensive income; Other comprehensive
income
balance sheet, 2.182–2.189

in equity section of balance sheet, 2.184–2.185
in notes to consolidated financial statements, 2.188–2.189
pension plans, recognition and measurement, 3.45
presentation, 2.182–2.183
presentation and disclosure excerpts, 2.184–2.189
in statement of changes in equity, 2.186–2.187, 5.56

Acquisitions. *See also* Business combinations
acquisition-related items, other current liabilities, 2.140
business combinations, 1.86, 1.87
cash flows from investing activities, 6.29
common stock issued for an, 5.11
expenses and losses, 3.40
merger agreements, 1.158
subsequent events, 1.150

Actuarial gains and losses, pension plan disclosures, 3.47

Additional paid-in capital
caption for, 5.03
changes in, 5.07
changes to retained earnings, 5.41
credits and charges to, 5.02, 5.07

Addressee of auditors' report, 7.04

Adjustment of gain or loss, discontinued operations, 3.91

Advances
other current assets, 2.51
other current liabilities, 2.132

Advertising
expenses, 3.24
royalty, licensing and marketing obligations, 1.101

Allowances for doubtful accounts, 2.26

Amendments to pension plans, 3.53

Amortization
adjustments to reconcile net income, 6.21
depreciation expense, 3.66
intangible assets, 2.77
of software, 3.35

Annual filings, comprehensive income in, 4.01–4.20

Annual reports
auditors' report, presentation in, 7.01–7.02
required contents, 1.14–1.16
stockholders' equity, 5.01–5.19

Areas of discontinued operations, 2.96

ASB. *See* Accounting Standards Board

ASC. See *FASB Accounting Standards Codification* (ASC)

Asset group, discontinued operations, 3.84

Asset retirement obligations
accretion on, 3.30
other current liabilities, 2.144
other noncurrent liabilities, 2.178

Assets
accretion on asset retirement obligations, 3.30
current assets, 2.93
current assets of discontinued operations, 2.53
deferred tax assets, 3.73
derecognition by parent companies, 1.81
fair value measurement, 1.137, 1.139
financial assets, transfer, 1.64
gain on disposals, 3.12
held for disposal, 2.62
held for sale, 2.52
impairment of assets, 6.27
income taxes, disclosure, 3.73
intangible. *See* Intangible assets
noncurrent assets, 2.115
as offset to liabilities, 1.17
other current. *See* Other current assets
other noncurrent. *See* Other noncurrent assets
pension plan disclosures, 3.46, 3.47
servicing assets, fair value, 2.32, 2.34
write-down of. *See* Write-down of assets

Assets held for sale. *See* Held for sale

Audit committee's report, 7.60

Auditors' report. *See* Independent auditors' report

Available-for-sale securities, 2.12, 2.14, 2.22, 4.16, 6.28

Average cost inventory, 2.41, 2.42, 2.47

B

Balance sheet
accumulated other comprehensive income, 2.182–2.189
annual report requirements, 1.14
cash and cash equivalents, 2.08–2.10
changes to retained earnings, 5.40
classified balance sheets, 2.03
credit agreements, 2.153–2.155
current amount of long-term debt, 2.125–2.128
current receivables, 2.25–2.30
employee-related liabilities, 2.115–2.121
format and classification, 2.06
general considerations, 2.01–2.07
income tax liability, 2.121–2.124
intangible assets, 2.77–2.92
inventory, 2.38–2.47
long-term debt, 2.145–2.152
long-term leases, 2.156–2.163
marketable securities, 2.11–2.24
other current assets, 2.48–2.57
other current liabilities, 2.129–2.144
other noncurrent assets, 2.93–2.106
other noncurrent liabilities, 2.164–2.181
presentation, 2.01–2.03, 2.129
presentation and disclosure excerpts, 2.07
receivables sold or collateralized, 2.31–2.37
short-term debt, 2.107–2.111
trade accounts payable, 2.112–2.114

Banks, borrowings from, 2.129

Bargain purchase gain, 3.13

Billings in excess of costs, 2.135

Business, defined, 5.47

Business combinations. *See also* Acquisitions
cash flows from investing activities, 6.31
changes in accounting principle, 1.60
disclosure, 1.87–1.88
merger agreements, 1.158
presentation and disclosure excerpts, 1.89–1.92
recognition and measurement, 1.86
tangible verses intangible assets acquired, 2.60

Business components disposals, 3.89–3.90

Business segment disposals, 3.88

C

Callable debt
balance sheet presentation, 2.125
short-term debt, 2.107

Capital leases, 2.156, 2.157, 2.159

Capital resources, 1.29

Capital stock, proceeds or payments, 6.39

Capitalized interest in property, plant, and equipment, 2.58

Capitalized software, 2.59, 2.61, 2.79, 6.33

Carryforwards and carrybacks
net operating loss carryforward, 1.115
operating loss carryforward, 1.115, 3.76–3.77
tax credits, 3.73, 3.76–3.77
tax credits and other tax carryforwards, 1.114–1.115
value-added tax (VAT) credits, 1.116

Cash and cash equivalents
balance sheet, 2.08–2.10
cash equivalents defined, 2.08, 6.02
disclosure, 2.09, 6.06–6.08
presentation, 2.08, 6.01–6.05
presentation and disclosure excerpts, 2.10, 6.09
restricted cash, 2.09

Cash dividends, 5.30

Cash flows from financing activities
capital stock proceeds or payments, 6.39
debt issuance costs, 6.42
debt proceeds or repayments, 6.38
dividends, 6.41
financial instrument settlements, credit facility, 6.44
issuance of noncontrolling interest, 6.44
presentation, 6.37
presentation and disclosure excerpts, 6.38–6.44
statement of cash flows, 6.37–6.44
stock-based compensation, 6.40

Cash flows from investing activities

acquisitions, 6.30
business combinations, 6.31
capitalized software, 6.33
hedging instruments, 1.121
in-process research and development (IPRD), 6.36
insurance proceeds, 6.35
investments, 6.30
pension plan disclosures, 3.46
presentation, 6.28
presentation and disclosure excerpts, 6.29–6.36
restricted cash, 6.34
sale of discontinued operations, 6.32
statement of cash flows, 6.29–6.36

Cash flows from operating activities
adjustments to reconcile net income, 6.21–6.27
amortization, 6.21
balance sheet reconciling items, 6.18
cash inflows, 6.13
cash outflows, 6.13
cash surrender value, 6.24
deferred taxes, 6.25
depreciation, 6.21
direct method to report, 6.14, 6.16, 6.19
discontinued operations gain or loss, 6.22
impairment of assets, 6.27
income statement reconciling items, 6.17
indirect/reconciliation method to report, 6.14, 6.15, 6.16, 6.20
presentation, 6.13–6.18
presentation and disclosure excerpts, 6.19–6.27
provision for losses on accounts receivable, 6.26
reconciling items, 6.18
reporting methods, 6.14–6.16
restructuring expense, 6.23
sale of business gain or loss, 6.22
settlement of receivables and related charges, 6.26
statement of cash flows, 6.13–6.27
write-down of assets, 6.27

Cash flows statement. *See* Statement of cash flows

Cash surrender value
adjustments to reconcile net income, 6.24
of life insurance, 2.93, 2.101

Changes
in accounting estimates. *See* Accounting estimates, changes in
in accounting principles. *See* Accounting principles
in additional paid-in capital, 5.07
in fair value, 3.41, 3.42
to retained earnings, 5.36–5.46
in stockholders' equity, 5.06, 5.36–5.46

Clarity Project, Accounting Standards Board (ASB), 7.01

Classified balance sheets, 2.03

Collateralized long-term debt, 2.150–2.151

Combined report on financial statements and internal controls, 7.55

Commercial paper, 2.109, 2.129

Commitments
balance sheet presentation, 2.167
disclosure, 1.93, 2.146

leasing commitments, 1.99
presentation and disclosure excerpts, 1.94–1.102
purchase agreements, 1.102
restrictive covenants, 1.94–1.98
royalty, licensing and marketing obligations, 1.101
sales and marketing agreements, 1.100

Commodity contracts, 1.129

Common stock
balance sheet presentation, 5.21
conversion of shares, stockholders' equity, 5.18
disclosure, 5.20–5.21
issued for an acquisition, 5.11
issued in a public offering, 5.10
issued to employees, 5.09
issued upon conversion of convertible debt, 5.12
repurchased. See Treasury stock
stockholders' equity, 5.20–5.21

Comparative financial statements, 2.01, 7.45

Components
of an entity, 3.84
of comprehensive income, 4.02
of other comprehensive income, 4.06
of stockholders' equity, 5.54–5.63

Comprehensive income
accounting changes and error corrections, 1.68
accumulated. See Accumulated other
comprehensive income
in annual filings, 4.01–4.20
combined statement of income and comprehensive
income, 4.08
components of, 4.02
defined, 4.02
disclosure, 4.06–4.07
foreign currency translation, 4.13
gains and losses on derivatives held as cash flow
hedges, 4.17–4.18
lack of consistency in independent auditors' report,
7.40
net change in unrealized gains and losses on
available-for-sale securities, 4.16
other. See Other comprehensive income
pension and postretirement adjustments, 4.14–4.15
pension plans, 3.45
presentation, 4.01–4.07
presentation and disclosure excerpts, 4.08–4.20
presentation in auditors' report, 7.08
reclassification adjustments, 4.04, 4.19–4.20
recognition and measurement, 4.01
reporting requirements, 3.02
reporting statement presentation, 4.05
separate statement of, 4.09
statement of, inclusion with statement of changes
in stockholders' equity, 4.10
tax effect disclosure in the notes, 4.03, 4.11
tax effect disclosure on the face of the financial
statements, 4.12
tax effect disclosures, 4.07, 4.11, 4.12

Computer software. See Software

Consistency. See Lack of consistency

Consolidated financial statements. See also
Consolidation

disclosures, 1.82–1.83, 5.57
presumption of meaning, 2.02
purpose, 1.77
when required, 1.78, 2.02

Consolidated tax returns, 1.152

Consolidation
accounting changes and error corrections, 1.71
disclosure, 1.82–1.83
financial statements. See Consolidated financial
statements
presentation, 1.80–1.81
presentation and disclosure excerpts, 1.84–1.85
recognition and measurement, 1.77–1.79

Construction-type and production-type contracts
accounting methods, 3.80
income statement, 3.79–3.83
presentation and disclosure excerpts, 3.81–3.83
production-type commodity contracts, 1.129,
3.79–3.83
recognition and measurement, 3.79–3.80

Content rights, 2.56

Contingencies
defined, 1.103
disclosures, 1.103, 1.104
environmental matters, 1.109–1.110
gain. See Gain contingencies
investigations and regulatory action, 1.112
legal matters, 1.106–1.107
loss. See Loss contingencies
net operating loss carryforward, 1.115
operating loss carryforward, 1.115, 3.76–.3.77
presentation and disclosure excerpts, 1.106–1.117
recognition and measurement, 1.103–1.04
self-insurance, 1.111
tax contingencies, 1.107–1.108
tax credits and other tax carryforwards,
1.114–1.115
value-added tax (VAT) credits, 1.116
warranties, 1.113

Contingent liabilities, 2.167

Contracts. See also Construction-type and
production-type contracts
customer contracts and relationships, 2.88
interest rate contracts, 1.137
other current assets, 2.106

Controlling financial interests, 1.78

Convertible debt
common stock, issuance upon conversion, 5.12
conversion of common shares, 5.18
convertible long-term debt, 2.152

Corporate officers or directors, related party
transactions, 1.155

Correction of errors. See Accounting changes and
error corrections

Cost method, 2.38, 2.71

Costs in excess of billings, 2.54

Covenants
debt included with, 2.107, 2.125

long-term debt, 2.152
  restrictive covenants, 1.94–1.98

Credit agreements
  balance sheet, 2.153–2.155
  disclosure, 2.108, 2.153
  line of credit, 1.141–1.142
  presentation and disclosure excerpts, 2.154–2.155
  revolving credit agreements, 2.107, 2.125

Credit derivatives, 1.124

Credit facility, financial instrument settlements, 6.44

Credit provision, income tax, 3.75

Credit-risk-related features, derivatives, 1.124, 1.125

Credits
  additional paid-in capital, 5.02
  deferred credits, 2.166, 2.169, 2.170, 2.181
  tax credits. See Tax credits and other tax carryforwards

Current amount of long-term debt
  balance sheet, 2.125–2.128
  disclosure, 2.126
  presentation, 2.125
  presentation and disclosure excerpts, 2.127–2.128

Current assets
  on balance sheet, 2.03, 2.93
  of discontinued operations, 2.53

Current liabilities
  on balance sheet, 2.03, 2.112
  employee-related liabilities, 2.115
  long-term debt, 2.145

Current receivables
  balance sheet, 2.25–2.30
  disclosure, 2.26
  finance receivables, 2.28
  insurance claims, 2.29
  presentation, 2.25
  presentation and disclosure excerpts, 2.27–2.30
  receivables from related parties, 2.27
  sale of assets—escrow receivable, 2.29

Customer contracts and relationships, 2.88

D

Dating of auditors' report, 7.48–7.50
  issuers, 7.49
  nonissuers, 7.48

Debt
  callable debt, 2.107, 2.125
  cash flows from financing activities, 6.42
  collateralized long-term debt, 2.152
  convertible. See Convertible debt
  debt reduction obligations, 1.93
  extinguishment, gains or losses, 3.18, 3.44
  increasing-rate debt, 2.107, 2.125
  issuance costs, 2.105, 6.42
  long-term. See Long-term debt
  proceeds or repayments, 6.38

short-term. See Short-term debt
  troubled debt restructuring, 1.70

Deferred compensation
  employee compensatory plans, 3.61
  other components of stockholders' equity, 5.60
  other noncurrent assets, 2.98

Deferred credits, 2.166, 2.169, 2.170, 2.181

Deferred income, 2.166

Deferred net revenue, 2.138

Deferred tax assets, 3.73

Deferred tax credits, 2.166

Deferred taxes
  cash flows from operating activities, 6.25
  income taxes, 2.133, 2.166, 2.171
  long-term deferred income tax asset, 2.100
  other current assets, 2.50

Defined benefit pension plans, 3.46, 3.49

Defined contribution pension plans, 3.50

Departures from unqualified opinions, 7.44

Depletion, depreciation expense, 3.66

Deposits, 2.99

Depreciable assets. See Property, plant, and equipment

Depreciation
  accelerated methods, 3.69–3.70, 6.21
  income statement, 3.68–3.70
  straight-line methods, 3.69–3.70
  units-of-production methods, 3.70

Depreciation accounting, defined, 3.65

Depreciation expense
  disclosure, 3.67–3.68
  income statement, 3.65–3.71
  presentation and disclosure excerpts, 3.69–3.71
  property, plant, and equipment, 2.62
  recognition and measurement, 3.65–3.66

Derivative financial instruments (derivatives)
  changes in fair value, 3.41
  classified as other current assets, 2.55
  classified as other current liabilities, 2.142
  classified as other noncurrent assets, 2.102
  classified as other noncurrent liabilities, 2.180
  credit derivatives, 1.124
  credit-risk-related features, 1.124, 1.125
  disclosure, 1.119–1.130
  forward contracts, 1.134
  interest rate hedging instruments, 1.133
  other current liabilities, 2.142
  plain English references, 1.11
  presentation and disclosure excerpts, 1.131–1.140
  recognition and measurement, 1.117
  revenues and gains, 3.15

Description of business, 1.36

Direct method to report cash flows from operating activities, 6.14, 6.16, 6.19

Discontinued operations
  adjustments of gain or loss, 3.91
  adjustments to reconcile net income, 6.22
  business components disposals, 3.89–3.90
  income statement, 3.84–3.91
  other noncurrent assets, 2.96
  other noncurrent liabilities, 2.175
  presentation, 3.86–3.88
  presentation and disclosure excerpts, 3.89–3.91
  recognition and measurement, 3.84–3.85
  subsequent events, 1.147–1.148
  write-down of assets, 3.85, 3.87

Dividends
  cash dividends, 5.30
  cash flows from financing activities, 6.41
  cumulative preferred stock dividends in arrears, 1.93
  non-cash dividends, 5.31
  other current liabilities, 2.131
  presentation, 5.27–5.29
  presentation and disclosure excerpts, 5.30–5.31
  restrictions, 1.93
  revenues and gains, 3.09
  stock dividends, 5.02, 5.33
  stockholders' equity, 5.17, 5.27–5.31

Doubtful accounts, allowances for, 2.26

E

Earned revenues and gains, 3.04

Earnings, income taxes on undistributed, 3.78

Earnings per share (EPS), income statement, 3.99–3.100

Emerging Issues Task Force, 1.09

Emphasis of a matter in auditors' report, 7.42–7.43

Employee compensatory plans
  common stock issued to employees, 5.09
  deferred compensation plans, 3.61
  employee stock ownership plans (ESOP), 3.63
  employee stock purchase plans (ESPP), 3.60, 5.08
  incentive compensation plans, 3.62
  income statement, 3.56–3.64
  multi-employer pension plans (MEPP), 1.66, 3.46, 3.48, 3.52
  postemployment benefits, 3.54–3.55
  presentation and disclosure excerpts, 3.57–3.64
  profit sharing plans, 3.64
  recognition and measurement, 3.56
  savings and investment plans, 3.59
  stock award plans, 3.58
  stock option awards, 5.08
  stock option plans, 3.57

Employee stock ownership plans (ESOP), 3.63

Employee stock purchase plans (ESPP), 3.60, 5.08

Employee-related liabilities
  balance sheet, 2.115–2.121
  disclosure, 2.116–2.117
  other noncurrent liabilities related to, 2.168

  presentation, 2.115
  presentation and disclosure excerpts, 2.118–2.120

Entities selected for survey, 1.01–1.06

Environmental matters
  contingencies, 1.109–1.110
  expenses and losses, 3.38
  other current liabilities, 2.139
  other noncurrent liabilities, 2.177

EPS. See Earnings per share (EPS)

Equity. See also Stock; Stockholders' equity
  defined, 5.01
  disclosure, 5.04–5.08
  in earnings of affiliates, 3.11
  losses of investees, 3.37
  presentation, 5.01–5.03
  presentation and disclosure excerpts, 5.08–5.19
  rights and privileges, 5.04
  statement of changes in shareholders' equity, 1.15, 2.186–2.187, 7.15
  statement of comprehensive income included with statement if changes in shareholder's equity, 4.10

Equity method
  disclosure, 2.67–2.79
  joint ventures, 2.65–2.72
  presentation, 2.66
  presentation and disclosure excerpts, 2.69–2.72
  recognition and measurement, 2.65

Equity section of balance sheet, 2.184–2.185

Equity transactions, 1.80

Equity-based compensation expenses, 5.15

Errors. See Accounting changes and error corrections

ESOP. See Employee stock ownership plans

ESPP. See Employee stock purchase plans

Estimated earnings in excess of billings, 2.54

Events. See Subsequent events

Exchange agreements, 1.158

Expenses and losses. See also Losses
  accretion on asset retirement obligation, 3.30
  advertising, 1.101, 3.24
  changes in fair value, 3.41, 3.42
  changes in fair value of derivatives, 3.41
  defined, 3.19
  disclosure, 3.20
  environmental, 3.38
  equity in losses of investees, 3.37
  equity-based compensation expenses, 5.15
  exploration, 3.23
  foreign currency, 3.34
  impairment of intangibles, 3.43
  income statement, 3.19–3.53
  income tax provisions, 3.74
  income taxes, 3.73
  intangible asset amortization, 3.33
  interest, 3.28, 3.29
  interest and penalties related to unrecognized tax benefits, 3.29
  litigation, 3.36

loss on extinguishment of debt, 3.44
mergers and acquisitions, 3.40
presentation, 3.19–3.20
presentation and disclosure excerpts, 3.21–3.44
provision for losses, 3.26
research and development, 2.92, 6.36
restructuring, 3.32, 6.23
sale of receivables, 3.39
selling, general, and administrative, 3.21–3.22
software amortization, 3.35
taxes other than income taxes, 3.25
warranties, 3.27
write-down of assets, 3.31

Exploration expenses and losses, 3.23

Extraordinary items
classification of, 3.95
defined, 3.92
income statement, 3.92–3.98
presentation, 3.93–3.95
presentation and disclosure excerpts, 3.96–3.98
recognition and measurement, 3.92
unusual items, 3.92, 3.94, 3.97–3.98

F

Fair value
changes in, 3.41, 3.42
commercial paper, 2.109
current amount of long-term debt, 2.126
debt and equity securities investments, 2.16
defined, 1.136, 2.17
derivatives, 1.122, 1.123, 3.41
disclosure, 1.139
discontinued operations, 3.85
employee compensatory plans, 3.56
expenses and losses, 3.41, 3.42
hedging instruments, 1.121, 1.123
held for sale asset group, 3.85
investment in joint ventures, accounting for, 2.72
loans payable, 2.109
long-term debt, 2.147
marketable securities, 2.16–2.20
of marketable securities, 2.18
noncurrent receivables, 2.74
pension plan disclosures, 3.47
presentation and disclosure excerpts, 1.140
receivables sold or collateralized, 2.32
recognition and measurement, 1.118, 1.136–1.138
revenues and gains, 3.05
servicing assets and liabilities, 2.32, 2.34
short-term notes payable, 2.109
trade accounts payable, 2.114
trade receivables, 2.26

Fair value option, 1.118, 1.125, 2.19

FASB Accounting Standards Codification (ASC),
referencing in financial statements, 1.13,
1.25–1.26

FIFO. *See* First-in, first-out (FIFO) inventory

Filing classifications of survey entities, 1.05

Finance receivables, 2.28

Financial condition. *See* Management's discussion
and analysis (MD&A) of financial condition and
results of operations

Financial data
five year, 1.27
quarterly, 1.26

Financial guarantees, 1.126, 1.141–1.142

Financial institutions, borrowings from, 2.129

Financial instrument settlements, credit facility, 6.44

Financial instruments
commodity contracts, 1.129
derivatives. *See* Derivative financial instruments
(derivatives)
disclosure, 1.119–1.35
financial guarantees and indemnifications, 1.126,
1.141–1.142
foreign currency contracts, 1.128
hedging. *See* Hedging instruments
hybrid financial instruments, 1.117
interest rate contracts, 1.127
line of credit, 1.132–1.133
other financial instruments, 1.130
presentation and disclosure excerpts, 1.131–1.140
recognition and measurement, 1.117–1.118
standby letters of credit, 1.135

Financial statements
accounting policies, disclosure, 1.19, 1.22, 1.33
Accounting Standards Codification (ASC)
referencing in, 1.13, 1.25–1.26
annual report contents, 1.14–1.16
balance sheet. *See* Balance sheet
cash flows. *See* Statement of cash flow
combined report on financial statements and
internal controls, 7.55
comparability, 1.16
consolidated. *See* Consolidated financial
statements
critical accounting policies, 1.32
description of business, 1.36
disclosure, 1.18–1.22
estimates, use of, 1.37–1.39
financial performance. *See* Statement of financial
performance
financial position. *See* Statement of financial
position
forward-looking information, 1.28
general considerations, 1.23–1.46
income. *See* Income statement
liquidity and capital resources, 1.29
management's discussion and analysis. *See*
Management's discussion and analysis (MD&A)
of financial condition and results of operations
market risk information, 1.31
nature of operations, 1.34–1.35
new accounting standards, 1.30
plain English references, 1.11, 1.13, 1.23–1.24
presentation, 1.14–1.17
presentation and disclosure excerpts, 1.23–1.46
presentation in auditors' report, 7.06
quarterly financial data, 1.26–1.26

recognition and measurement, 1.07–1.13
selected information for five years, 1.27
significant accounting policies and estimates, 1.39
single-period financial statements *versus* comparative financial statements, 2.01
statement of changes in shareholders' equity, 1.15, 2.186–2.187, 7.15
statement of stockholders' equity, 5.01, 7.08
tax effect disclosure on the face of, 4.12
tax effects disclosures, 4.03
vulnerability due to certain concentrations, 1.40–1.42

First-in, first-out (FIFO) inventory, 2.41, 2.42, 2.45

Fixed assets. *See* Property, plant, and equipment

Foreign currency
contracts, 1.128
expenses and losses, 3.34
hedges, 1.121
on statement of cash flows, 6.05, 6.10
translation, comprehensive income, 4.13

Forward contracts, 1.134

Forward-looking information, 1.28

Fresh-start accounting, 7.27

G

Gain contingencies, 1.103, 1.104

Gains. *See also* Revenues and gains
actuarial gains, pension plan disclosures, 3.47
adjustments of, discontinued operations, 3.91
adjustments to reconcile net income, 6.22
on asset disposals, 3.12
debt extinguishment, 3.18
derivatives, 1.123, 1.124
derivatives held as cash flow hedges, 4.17–4.18
disclosure, 3.06
discontinued operations, 3.85, 3.87, 6.22
sale of business, 6.22
unrealized, net change on available-for-sale securities, 4.16
unrealized, on marketable securities, 2.12

General management committee reports, 7.58–7.60

Going concern, 7.26

Goodwill. *See also* Intangible assets
accounting changes and error corrections, 1.69
business combinations, 1.86
disclosure, 2.81
intangible assets, 2.84–2.85
presentation, 2.80
recognition and measurement, 2.77

H

Hedging instruments
disclosure, 1.119, 1.121, 1.123, 1.124

interest rate hedging instruments, 1.133
plain English references, 1.11
recognition and measurement, 1.117

Held for disposal, 2.62

Held for sale
discontinued operations, 3.85, 3.86, 3.87
long-term assets, 3.85
other current assets, 2.52

Held-to-maturity securities, 2.12

Hybrid financial instruments, 1.117

I

IFRS. *See* International Financial Reporting Standards

Impairment
of assets, 6.27
of intangibles, 3.43
of investments, 2.13

Incentive employee compensation plans, 3.62

Incentives, returns, and rebates, 2.143

Income. *See* Comprehensive income

Income statement
annual report requirements, 1.14, 1.15
cash flows from operating activities, reconciling items, 6.17
changes to retained earnings, 5.40
combined statement of income and comprehensive income, 4.08
construction-type and production-type contracts, 3.79–3.83
depreciation expense, 3.65–3.71
discontinued operations, 3.84–3.91
earnings per share, 3.99–3.100
employee compensatory plans, 3.56–3.64
expenses and losses, 3.19–3.53
extraordinary items, 3.92–3.98
format, 3.01–3.03
incomes taxes, 3.72–3.78
pensions and other postretirement benefits, 3.45–3.53
postemployment benefits, 3.54–3.55
presentation, 3.01–3.03
presentation and disclosure excerpts, 3.03
presentation in auditors' report, 7.06
reclassifications, 3.03
revenues and gains, 3.04–3.18

Income tax liability
balance sheet, 2.121–2.124
disclosure, 2.122, 4.03
presentation, 2.121
presentation and disclosure excerpts, 2.123–2.124

Income taxes
credit provision, 3.75
disclosure, 3.73
expense provision, 3.74
income statement, 3.72–3.78

operating loss and tax credit carryforwards, 3.76–3.77
payment of, 6.10
presentation and disclosure excerpts, 3.74–3.78
presentation on statement of cash flows, 6.08, 6.11
recognition and measurement, 3.72
on undistributed earnings, 3.78

Increasing-rate debt, 2.107, 2.125

Indebtedness. *See* Debt

Indemnifications, 1.126, 1.141–1.142

"Independent," in title of auditors' report, 7.03

Independent auditors' report
audit committee's report, 7.60
dating of report, 7.48–7.50
departures from unqualified opinions, 7.44
emphasis of a matter, 7.42–7.43
evaluating changes in accounting principle, 7.30–7.35
fresh-start accounting, 7.27
general management and special-purpose committee reports, 7.58–7.60
generally, 7.01
going concern, 7.26
information related to, 7.11
internal control framework, 7.12
internal control over financial reporting, 7.51–7.57
for issuers, 7.09–7.12
lack of consistency, 7.28–7.41
management's report on financial statements, 7.59
management's reports on financial statements, 7.11
for nonissuers, 7.05–7.08
opinions expressed on supplementary financial information, 7.46–7.47
presentation, 7.03–7.04, 7.05–7.12
presentation and disclosure excerpts, 7.13, 7.13–7.15
presentation in annual report, 7.01–7.02
PricewaterhouseCoopers LLP auditors' report, 7.12
reference to the report of other auditors, 7.16–7.23
reports on comparative financial statements, 7.45
sample language, 7.05
statement of changes in shareholders' equity, 7.15
statement of operations and comprehensive income, 7.13
title and addressee, 7.03–7.04
uncertainties, 7.24–7.27

Indirect/reconciliation method reporting cash flows from operating activities, 6.14, 6.15, 6.16, 6.20

Industry classifications of survey entities, 1.04

Inflationary accounting, 1.61, 1.159–1.60

Infrequency of occurrence, extraordinary items, 3.92

In-process research and development (IPRD), 2.92, 6.36

Insurance
cash surrender value of life insurance, 2.93, 2.101
claims, 2.29
life insurance cash surrender value, 2.93, 2.101
other noncurrent liabilities, 2.174

proceeds from, 6.35
recoveries from, 3.17

Intangible assets
amortization, 3.33
amortization period, 2.83
balance sheet, 2.77–2.92
customer contracts and relationships, 2.88
disclosure, 2.81–2.83
goodwill as, 2.84–2.85
impairment, 3.43
in-process research and development (IPRD), 2.92
licenses, 2.91
merchandising rights, 2.87
presentation, 2.80
presentation and disclosure excerpts, 2.84–2.92
recognition and measurement, 2.77–2.79
software, 2.59, 2.90
technology, 2.89
trademarks, 2.86
tradenames and other intangibles, 2.86

Interest
changes in accounting principles, 1.61
expenses and losses, 3.28, 3.29, 6.08, 6.11
and penalties related to unrecognized tax benefits, 3.29
presentation and disclosure excerpts, 6.10
revenues and gains, 3.08

Interest rate contracts, 1.127

Interest rate hedging instruments, 1.133

Internal controls
audit report with specific items excluded, 7.56
auditor's report framework, 7.12
combined report on financial statements and internal controls, 7.55
ineffective internal controls, 7.57
over financial reporting, 7.51–7.57
presentation, 7.51–7.53
presentation and disclosure excerpts, 7.54–7.57
separate report on internal control, 7.54

International Financial Reporting Standards (IFRS), 1.08

Inventory
average cost inventory, 2.41, 2.42, 2.47
balance sheet, 2.38–2.47
changes in accounting principle, 1.62
cost determination
disclosure, 2.41–2.44
first-in first-out (FIFO), 2.45
last-in first-out (LIFO), 2.41, 2.42, 2.46
presentation, 2.40
presentation and disclosure excerpts, 2.45–2.47
recognition and measurement, 2.38–2.39

Investigations, contingencies, 1.112

Investments
cash flows from investing activities, 6.30
equity in earnings of affiliates, 3.11
equity in losses of investees, 3.37
fair value estimates, 1.138
gains, 3.16
impairment, 2.13

joint ventures, accounting method. *See* Joint
    ventures
noncurrent investments, 2.68
other noncurrent assets, 2.93
pension plan strategies disclosure, 3.46
transaction between reporting entity and investee,
    1.153

Involuntary liquidation, 5.22

IPRD. *See* In-process research and development

J

Joint ventures
    cost method, 2.71
    disclosure, 2.67–2.68
    equity method, 2.65–2.72
    fair value, 2.72
    noncurrent investments—carrying bases, 2.68
    presentation, 2.66
    presentation and disclosure excerpts, 2.69–2.72
    recognition and measurement, 2.65

L

Lack of consistency in independent auditors' report
    comprehensive income, 7.40
    correction of errors and restatement, 7.36
    issuers, 7.30–7.35
    multiple deliverable revenue arrangements, 7.41
    nonissuers, 7.28–7.29
    pension and other postretirement benefit
        obligations, 7.37
    presentation, 7.28–7.35
    presentation and disclosure excerpts, 7.35
    trade receivables securitization, 7.39
    variable interest entities, 7.38

Land, 2.93. *See also* Property, plant, and equipment

Last-in, first-out (LIFO) inventory, 2.41, 2.42, 2.44,
    2.46

Lawsuits. *See* Litigation

Leases
    lessee leases, 2.160–2.162
    lessor leases, 2.163
    long-term. *See* Long-term leases
    operating leases, 2.156, 2.158, 2.159

Leasing commitments, 1.99

Legal matters, contingencies, 1.106–1.107

Lessee leases, 2.160–2.162

Lessor leases, 2.163

Letters of credit, 1.93, 1.135

Liabilities
    contingent liabilities, 2.167
    current liabilities, 2.03, 2.112, 2.115, 2.145

employee compensatory plans, 3.56
fair value measurement, 1.138, 1.139
income taxes, disclosure, 3.73
noncurrent liabilities, 2.115
offsetting with assets, 1.17
other current. *See* Other current liabilities
other noncurrent. *See* Other noncurrent liabilities
pension plan disclosures, 3.46
preferred stock classified as, 5.23
servicing liabilities, fair value, 2.32, 2.34

Licenses and licensing, 1.101, 2.91

Life insurance cash surrender value, 2.93, 2.101

LIFO. *See* Last-in, first-out (LIFO) inventory

Line of credit, 1.141–1.142

Liquidity, 1.29

Litigation
    expenses and losses, 3.36
    other current liabilities, 2.141
    other noncurrent liabilities, 2.179
    revenues and gains, 3.14
    subsequent events, 1.146

Loans. *See also* Credit agreements; Debt
    due-on-demand arrangements, 2.107, 2.125
    loans payable, 2.109

Long-term assets held for sale. *See* Held for sale

Long-term debt
    balance sheet, 2.145–2.152
    collateralized, 2.150–2.151
    convertible, 2.152
    covenants, 2.152
    current amount, 2.125–2.128
    disclosure, 2.146–2.148
    presentation, 2.145
    presentation and disclosure excerpts, 2.149–2.152
    unsecured, 2.149

Long-term deferred income tax asset, 2.100

Long-term leases
    balance sheet, 2.156–2.163
    commitments, 1.93
    disclosure, 2.159
    lessee leases, 2.160–2.162
    lessor leases, 2.163
    presentation, 2.157–2.158
    presentation and disclosure excerpts, 2.160–2.163
    recognition and measurement, 2.156

Long-term prepayments, 2.93

Long-term receivables, 2.75

Loss contingencies, 1.103, 1.104

Losses. *See also* Expenses and losses
    actuarial gains, pension plan disclosures, 3.47
    adjustments of, discontinued operations, 3.91
    adjustments to reconcile net income, 6.22
    debt extinguishment, 3.44
    defined, 3.19
    derivatives, 1.123, 1.124
    derivatives held as cash flow hedges, 4.17–4.18
    discontinued operations, 3.85, 3.87, 6.22

impairment of investments, 2.13
provision for, 3.26
sale of business, 6.22
unrealized, net change on available-for-sale securities, 4.16
unrealized, on marketable securities, 2.12

M

Management's discussion and analysis (MD&A) of financial condition and results of operations, 1.14

Management's reports on financial statements
in auditors' report, 7.59
information related to, 7.11

Mandatorily redeemable preferred stock, 2.165, 5.23

Market risk information, 1.31

Marketable securities. *See also* Trading securities
available-for-sale securities, 2.12, 2.14, 2.22, 4.16, 6.28
balance sheet, 2.11–2.24
classification of, 2.12
disclosure, 2.15–2.19
fair value inputs for debt and equity securities, 2.21
held-to-maturity securities, 2.12
presentation, 2.14
presentation and disclosure excerpts, 2.22–2.24
recognition and measurement, 2.11–2.13

Marketing
royalty, licensing and marketing obligations, 1.101
sales and marketing agreements, 1.100

Master limited partnerships, 3.99

Materiality, 1.152

MD&A. *See* Management's discussion and analysis (MD&A) of financial condition and results of operations

MEPP. *See* Multi-employer pension plans

Merchandising rights, 2.87

Merger agreements, 1.158. *See also* Acquisitions; Business combinations

Minority interest. *See* Noncontrolling interest

Misstatements, correction of, 5.40, 5.43–5.44

Multi-employer pension plans (MEPP), 1.66, 3.46, 3.48, 3.52

Multiple deliverable revenue arrangements, 7.40

Multiple element arrangements, transactions, 3.05

Multistep income statement form, 3.01

N

Natural business year, 1.12

Natural resources, 2.93

Nature of operations, 1.34–1.35

Net assets. *See* Equity; Stockholders' equity

Net income, cash flow reconciliation adjustments
cash surrender value, 6.24
deferred taxes, 6.25
depreciation and amortization, 6.21
discontinued operations or sale of business, gain or loss, 6.22
impairment of assets, 6.27
provision for losses on accounts receivable, 6.26
restructuring expense, 6.23
settlement of receivables and related charges, 6.26
write-down of assets, 6.27

Net income reporting requirements, 3.01

Net operating loss carryforward, 1.115

Noncash activities, 6.07, 6.12

Non-cash dividends, 5.31

Noncontrolling interest
business combinations, 1.86
changes in accounting principle, 1.61
components of other comprehensive income, 4.03
consolidated financial statements, 1.79
defined, 1.79
disclosures, 1.83
issuance of, 6.44
other components of stockholders' equity, 5.63
parent company ownership interest changes, 1.80
stockholders' equity, 5.57
in a subsidiary, 5.57

Noncurrent assets, employee-related, 2.115

Noncurrent investments, carrying bases, 2.68

Noncurrent liabilities, employee-related, 2.115

Noncurrent receivables
long-term receivable, 2.75
notes receivable, 2.76
presentation, 2.73–2.74
presentation and disclosure excerpts, 2.75–2.76

Nonpublic entities, fair value disclosures, 2.16, 2.19

Nonrecognized subsequent events, 1.141

Notes receivable, 2.76

Notes to financial statements
accumulated other comprehensive income, 2.188–2.189
annual report requirements, 1.15
common stock, 5.20
dividends, 5.27
pension plan disclosures, 2.116
pension plans, recognition and measurement, 3.45
restricted cash, 2.09
tax effects disclosures, 4.03, 4.11

O

Obligations. *See* Liabilities

Operating leases, 2.156, 2.158, 2.159

Operating loss, disclosure of, 3.73

Operating loss carryforward, 1.115, 3.76–3.77

Operating segments of public entities, 1.43–1.44

Operations, discontinued. *See* Discontinued operations

Opinions, 7.46–7.47. *See also* Independent auditors' report

Original maturity, 6.03

Other additional capital, 5.03

Other changes in retained earnings, 5.45

Other components of stockholders' equity
  deferred compensation, 5.60
  disclosure, 5.56–5.58
  noncontrolling interest, 5.63
  presentation, 5.54–5.55
  presentation and disclosure excerpts, 5.59–5.63
  stock compensation, 5.61
  unearned compensation, 5.59
  warrants, 5.13, 5.62

Other comprehensive income
  accumulated. *See* Accumulated other comprehensive income
  components disclosed, 4.06
  comprehensive. *See* Comprehensive income
  defined, 4.02
  items included in, 4.01, 5.55

Other current assets
  advances, 2.51
  assets held for sale, 2.52
  balance sheet, 2.48–2.57
  content rights, 2.56
  contracts, 2.106
  costs and estimated earnings in excess of billings, 2.54
  current assets of discontinued operations, 2.53
  debt issuance costs, 2.105
  deferred taxes, 2.50
  deposits, 2.99
  derivatives, 2.55
  held for sale, 2.52
  long-term deferred income tax asset, 2.100
  prepaid expenses, 2.57
  presentation, 2.48–2.49
  presentation and disclosure excerpts, 2.50–2.57
  retail real estate, 2.103
  software, 2.104

Other current liabilities
  acquisition-related items, 2.140
  advances, 2.132
  asset retirement obligation, 2.144
  balance sheet, 2.129–2.144
  billings in excess of costs and estimated earnings, 2.135
  deferred income taxes, 2.133
  deferred net revenue, 2.138
  derivatives, 2.142
  dividends, 2.131
  environment, 2.139
  litigation, 2.141
  presentation, 2.129–2.130
  presentation and disclosure excerpts, 2.131–2.144
  restructuring, 2.136
  returns, rebates and incentives, 2.143
  self-insurance reserves, 2.137
  warranties, 2.134

Other income, disclosure of, 3.06

Other noncurrent assets
  areas of discontinued operations, 2.96
  balance sheet, 2.93–2.106
  cash surrender value of life insurance, 2.93, 2.101
  deferred compensation arrangements, 2.98
  derivatives, 2.102
  disclosure, 2.94–2.95
  pension asset, 2.97
  presentation and disclosure excerpts, 2.96–2.106
  recognition and measurement, 2.93

Other noncurrent liabilities
  asset retirement obligations, 2.178
  balance sheet, 2.164–2.181
  deferred credits, 2.181
  deferred income taxes, 2.171
  derivatives, 2.180
  discontinued operations, 2.175
  environmental, 2.177
  insurance, 2.174
  litigation, 2.179
  presentation, 2.164–2.170
  presentation and disclosure excerpts, 2.171–2.181
  related to employees, 2.168, 2.170
  tax uncertainties, 2.173
  taxes payable, 2.172
  warranties, 2.176

Other postretirement benefit obligations, 7.37

Other-than-temporary impairments, 2.13

P

Parent companies
  changes in ownership interest, 1.80
  deconsolidation of subsidiaries, 1.81
  derecognition of asset group, 1.81
  disclosures, 1.83

Penalties
  changes in accounting principles, 1.61
  related to unrecognized tax benefits, 3.29

Pending Content, fair value of marketable securities, 2.18–2.19

Pensions and other postretirement benefits. *See also* Employee-related liabilities
  adjustments, comprehensive income, 4.14–4.15
  changes in accounting principle, 1.59
  commitments, 1.93
  defined benefit plans, 3.46, 3.49
  defined contribution plans, 3.50
  disclosure, 3.46–3.48

income statement, 3.45–3.53
lack of consistency in independent auditors' report, 7.37
multi-employer pension plans, 1.66, 3.46, 3.48, 3.52
other noncurrent assets, 2.97
plan amendment, 3.53
presentation and disclosure excerpts, 3.49–3.53
recognition and measurement, 3.45
supplemental retirement plans (SERP), 3.51

Performance share grants, subsequent events, 1.151

Plain English references, 1.11, 1.13, 1.23–1.24

Poison pill arrangements, 5.28

Postemployment benefits, 3.54–3.55

PPE. See Property, plant, and equipment

Preferred stock
disclosure, 5.24–5.25
mandatorily redeemable preferred stock, 2.165, 5.23
presentation, 5.22–5.23
presentation and disclosure excerpts, 5.26
redemption of convertible, 5.19
stockholders' equity, 5.22–5.26

Prepaid expenses, 2.57

Prepayments, long-term, 2.93

PricewaterhouseCoopers LLP auditors' report, 7.12

Prior period adjustments, 1.56, 1.57

Production-type contracts. See Construction-type and production-type contracts

Professional association pronouncements, 1.08

Profit sharing plans, 3.64

Property, plant, and equipment (PPE)
acquisitions, cash flows from investing activities, 6.28
defined, 2.58
disclosure, 2.62
plant acquisition, 1.93
presentation, 2.60–2.61
presentation and disclosure excerpts, 2.63–2.64
recognition and measurement, 2.58–2.59

Property held for sale. See Held for sale

Public entities
auditors' report (sample language), 7.07, 7.51–7.57
business combinations, 1.87
segment reporting, 1.43

Public offering, common stock issued in a, 5.10

Purchase and sale agreements, 1.102

Purchases, disclosure of commitment, 1.93

R

R&D. See Research and development (R&D)

Real estate, retail, 2.103

Realized/realizable revenues and gains, 3.04

Rebates, incentives, and returns, 2.143

Receivables
adjustments to reconcile net income, 6.26
current. See Current receivables
noncurrent. See Noncurrent receivables
from related parties, 2.25–2.30
sold or collateralized. See Receivables sold or collateralized
trade receivables, 2.26, 2.74, 7.39

Receivables sold or collateralized
balance sheet, 2.31–2.37
disclosure, 2.34
expenses and losses, 3.39
presentation and disclosure excerpts, 2.35–2.37
recognition and measurement, 2.31–2.33

Reclassification
adjustments, comprehensive income, 4.04, 4.19–4.20
balance sheet presentation, 2.05, 2.07, 2.10
disclosure, 1.20
income statement presentation, 3.03

Recognized subsequent events, 1.141

Reconciliation
cash flows from operating activities, 6.17, 6.18
consolidated financial statements, 1.83
segment reporting, 1.45
stockholders' equity, 5.54

Redeemable preferred stock, 2.165, 5.23

Redemption of convertible preferred stock, 5.19

Reference to report of other auditors
issuers, 7.20–7.22
nonissuers, 7.16–7.19
presentation, 7.16–7.22
presentation and disclosure excerpts, 7.23

References in Plain English, 1.11, 1.13, 1.23–1.24

Regulatory agencies, 1.08, 1.112

Related party transactions
agreements, 1.157
disclosure, 1.152
major stockholder transactions, 1.154
merger agreement and exchange agreement, 1.158
other current liabilities, 2.129
presentation and disclosure excerpts, 1.153–1.158
related party receivables, 2.27
transaction between reporting entity and investee, 1.153
transaction between reporting entity and officer/director, 1.155
transaction between reporting entity and variable interest entity, 1.156

Remeasurement (new basis) events, 1.117

Repayments, 6.38

Reporting entities, 1.57, 1.155, 1.156

Reporting methods, 6.14–6.16

Repurchased common stock. *See* Treasury stock

Research and development (R&D), 2.92, 6.36

Restatements, 7.36

Restricted cash
    cash flows from investing activities, 6.34
    disclosure, 2.09
    other noncurrent assets, 2.93

Restricted stock and performance share grants, 1.151

Restrictive covenants, 1.94–1.98

Restructuring
    expenses and losses, 3.32, 6.23
    other current liabilities, 2.136
    subsequent events, 1.149
    troubled debt restructuring, 1.70

Results of operations. *See* Management's discussion
    and analysis (MD&A) of financial condition and
    results of operations

Retail real estate, 2.103

Retained earnings, caption for, 5.03

Retained earnings, changes to
    additional paid-in capital, 5.41
    changes in accounting principle, 5.38, 5.42
    correction of an error or misstatement, 5.39, 5.40,
        5.43–5.44
    opening balance adjustments, 5.37
    other changes in retained earnings, 5.45–5.46
    presentation, 5.37–5.41
    presentation and disclosure excerpts, 5.42–5.46
    recognition and measurement, 5.36
    share repurchase programs, 5.45
    stock split, 5.46
    stockholders' equity, 5.36–5.46

Retirement benefits. *See* Pensions and other
    postretirement benefits

Returns, rebates and incentives, 2.143

Revenue of survey entities, 1.04, 1.06

Revenue recognition, 1.63–1.64

Revenues and gains. *See also* Gains
    bargain purchase gain, 3.13
    debt extinguishment, 3.18
    derivatives, 3.15
    disclosure, 3.06
    dividends, 3.09
    equity in earnings of affiliates, 3.11
    gain on asset disposals, 3.12
    gains on extinguishment of debt, 3.18
    income statement, 3.04–3.18
    insurance recoveries, 3.17
    interest, 3.08
    investment gains, 3.16
    litigation, 3.14
    presentation and disclosure excerpts, 3.07–3.18
    recognition and measurement, 3.04–.06
    revenues, 3.07
    royalty revenue, 3.10

Reverse stock split, 5.35

Revolving credit agreements, 2.107, 2.125

Risks and uncertainties. *See also* Tax uncertainties
    in auditors' report, 7.24–7.27
    derivatives, 1.121, 1.124, 1.125
    disclosure, 1.21
    hedging instruments, 1.121
    income taxes, recognition and measurement, 3.72
    market risk information, 1.31
    pension plan disclosures, 3.47
    risk assessment standards, 7.49

Royalty obligations, 1.101

Royalty revenue, 3.10

S

Sale agreements, 1.102

Sales
    of assets, escrow receivable, 2.29
    of business, 6.22
    of discontinued operations, 6.32
    of equity instruments, 6.28
    future revenue, 2.107, 2.125
    of loans, 6.28
    of receivables. *See* Receivables sold or
        collateralized

Sales and marketing agreements, 1.100

Savings and investment plans, 3.59

SEC. *See* Securities and Exchange Commission

Securities and Exchange Commission (SEC), 1.09

Security for loans, 1.93

Segment reporting
    presentation, 1.43–1.46
    presentation and disclosure excerpts, 1.47–1.49
    segment information, 1.46, 1.47–1.49

Segmentation of transactions, 3.05

Self-insurance, 1.111

Self-insurance reserves, 2.137

Selling, general, and administrative expenses,
    3.21–3.22

Separate accounts, changes in, 5.05

Separate report on internal control, 7.54

SERP. *See* Supplemental retirement plans

Servicing assets and liabilities, 2.32, 2.34

Share repurchase programs, 5.16, 5.45

Share-based compensation, 1.59

Shareholders' equity, statement of changes in, 1.15,
    2.186–2.187, 7.15

Shares. *See* Stock

Short-term debt
    balance sheet, 2.107–2.111
    disclosure, 2.108–2.109
    obligations expected to be refinanced on a
      long-term basis, 2.125
    presentation, 2.107
    presentation and disclosure excerpts, 2.110–2.111

Short-term notes payable, 2.109

Single-step income statement form, 3.01

Software
    amortization, as expense, 3.35
    capitalized costs, 2.59, 2.61, 2.79, 6.33
    intangible assets, 2.59, 2.90
    other current assets, 2.104

Special-purpose committee reports, 7.58–7.60

Spinoffs
    defined, 5.47
    presentation and disclosure excerpts, 5.49
    recognition and measurement, 5.47–5.48
    stockholders' equity, 5.47–5.49

Staff Accounting Bulletins (SEC), 1.09

Standby letters of credit, 1.135

Statement of cash flows
    annual report requirements, 1.14
    cash and cash equivalents, 6.09
    cash flows from financing activities, 6.37–6.44
    cash flows from investing activities, 6.29–6.36
    cash flows from operating activities, 6.13–6.27
    disclosure, 6.06–6.08
    foreign currency cash flows, 6.05, 6.10
    interest and income tax payments, 6.08, 6.11
    noncash activities, 6.12
    presentation, 6.01–6.05
    presentation and disclosure excerpts, 6.09–6.12
    presentation in auditors' report, 7.06

Statement of changes in shareholders' equity, 1.15,
    2.186–2.187, 7.15. See also Statement of
    stockholders' equity

Statement of comprehensive income, 4.09, 4.10

Statement of financial performance, 1.122

Statement of financial position
    annual report requirements, 1.15
    derivatives, 1.117, 1.122
    pension plans, recognition and measurement, 3.45

Statement of operations and comprehensive income,
    7.13

Statement of retained earnings, 7.06

Statement of stockholders' equity, 5.01, 7.08. See
    also Statement of changes in shareholders'
    equity

Stock
    capital stock, proceeds or payments, 6.39
    common. See Common stock
    employee compensatory plans, 3.57, 3.58
    employee stock ownership plan (ESOP), 3.63
    employee stock purchase plan (ESPP), 3.60, 5.08
    preferred. See Preferred stock

    restricted, and performance share grants
      subsequent event, 1.151
    splits. See Stock splits
    stock-based compensation, 5.14, 6.40
    treasury stock. See Treasury stock

Stock award plans, 3.58

Stock compensation, 5.61

Stock dividends, 5.02, 5.33

Stock option awards, 5.08

Stock option plans, 3.57

Stock splits
    changes to retained earnings, 5.46
    defined, 5.32
    presentation and disclosure excerpts, 5.34
    recognition and measurement, 5.32–5.33
    reverse, 5.35
    stockholders' equity, 5.32–5.34

Stock-based compensation, 5.14, 6.40

Stockholders' equity
    changes to retained earnings, 5.36–5.46
    common stock, 5.20–5.21
    components, 5.54–5.63
    conversion of common shares, 5.18
    disclosure, 5.04–5.08
    dividends, 5.17, 5.27–5.31
    equity-based compensation expenses, 5.15
    format if changes in, 5.06
    format in annual filings, 5.01–5.19
    other stockholders' equity accounts, 5.58
    preferred stock, 5.22–5.26
    presentation, 5.01–5.03
    presentation and disclosure excerpts, 5.08–5.19
    redemption of convertible preferred stock,
      5.19
    share repurchase program, 5.16, 5.45
    spinoffs, 5.47–5.49
    statement of, 5.01, 7.08
    stock splits, 5.32–5.34
    tax benefits of stock-based compensation, 5.14
    Treasury stock, 5.50–5.53
    warrants, 5.13, 5.62

Stockholders in related party transactions, 1.154

Straight-line depreciation methods, 3.69–3.70

Subsequent events
    acquisitions, 1.150
    defined, 1.141
    disclosure, 1.142–1.143
    discontinued operations, 1.147–1.148
    litigation, 1.146
    nonrecognized subsequent events, 1.141, 1.142
    presentation and disclosure excerpts, 1.144–1.151
    recognition and measurement, 1.141
    restricted stock and performance share grants,
      1.151
    restructuring, 1.149
    term loan and credit facilities, 1.145

Subsidiaries, consolidation, 1.81

Supplemental retirement plans (SERP), 3.51

Supplementary financial information, 7.46–7.47

Survey entities, 1.01–1.06

T

Tax contingencies, 1.107–1.108

Tax credits and other tax carryforwards
    contingencies, 1.114–1.115
    deferred credits, 2.166
    income taxes, 3.73, 3.76–3.77
    tax credit carryforward, 1.114–1.115
    value-added tax (VAT) credits, 1.116

Tax effects, disclosure, 4.07, 4.11, 4.12

Tax returns, 1.152

Tax uncertainties, 2.173

Taxes
    benefits of stock-based compensation, 5.14
    deferred. *See* Deferred taxes
    interest and penalties related to uncertain tax
        positions, 1.61
    other than income taxes, 3.25

Taxes payable, 2.172

Technical Practice Aids (AICPA), 1.08

Technology
    computer software. *See* Software
    intangible assets, 2.89

Term loan and credit facilities, 1.145

Title of auditors' report, 7.03

Trade accounts, 2.113, 2.114

Trade accounts payable
    disclosure, 2.114
    presentation, 2.113
    recognition and measurement, 2.112

Trade creditors, 2.129

Trade receivables, securitization, 7.39

Trade receivables and payables, 2.26, 2.74, 7.39

Trademarks, 2.86

Trading securities. *See also* Marketable securities
    available-for-sale securities, 2.12, 2.14, 2.22, 4.16,
        6.28
    gains and losses, 2.12, 2.13
    held-to-maturity securities, 2.12

Transfer of financial assets, 1.64

Treasury stock
    balance sheet presentation, 5.52
    presentation, 5.50–5.52
    presentation and disclosure excerpts, 5.53
    stockholders' equity, 5.50–5.53

Troubled debt restructuring, 1.70

U

Uncertainties. *See also* Risks and uncertainties
    fresh-start accounting, 7.26
    going concern, 7.26
    in independent auditors' report, 7.24–7.27
    presentation, 7.24
    presentation and disclosure excerpts, 7.26–7.27

Uncertainty tax positions, interest and penalties
    related to, 1.61

Undistributed earnings, income taxes on, 3.78

Unearned compensation, 5.59

Units-of-production depreciation methods, 3.70

Unsecured long-term debt, 2.149

Unusual items, 3.92, 3.94, 3.97–3.98. *See also*
    Extraordinary items

V

Value-added tax (VAT) credits, 1.116

Variable interest entities (VIEs)
    changes in accounting principle, 1.64
    consolidated financial statements, 1.78
    related party transactions, 1.156

VAT. *See* Value-added tax (VAT) credits

VIEs. *See* Variable interest entities (VIEs)

Voting interests, 1.78, 1.87

Vulnerability due to certain concentrations, 1.40–1.42

W

Warranties
    contingencies, 1.113
    expenses and losses, 3.27
    other current liabilities, 2.134
    other noncurrent liabilities, 2.176

Warrants, 5.13, 5.62

Websites, 2.79

Working capital, 1.93

Write-down of assets
    adjustments to reconcile net income, 6.27
    discontinued operations, 3.85, 3.87
    expenses and losses, 3.31

Powerful Online Research Tools

The AICPA Online Professional Library offers the most current access to comprehensive accounting and auditing literature, as well business and practice management information, combined with the power and speed of the Web. Through your online subscription, you'll get:

- Cross-references within and between titles — smart links give you quick access to related information and relevant materials
- First available updates — no other research tool offers access to new AICPA standards and conforming changes more quickly, guaranteeing that you are always current with all of the authoritative guidance!
- Robust search engine — helps you narrow down your research to find your results quickly
- And much more…

Choose from two comprehensive libraries or select only the titles you need!

With the *Essential A&A Research Collection*, you gain access to the following:
- AICPA Professional Standards
- AICPA Technical Practice Aids
- PCAOB Standards & Related Rules
- All current AICPA Audit and Accounting Guides
- All current Audit Risk Alerts
One-year individual online subscription
Item # ORS-XX

OR

***Premium A&A Research Collection* and get everything from the *Essential A&A Research Collection* plus:**
- AICPA Audit & Accounting Manual
- All current Checklists & Illustrative Financial Statements
- eXacct: Financial Reporting Tools & Techniques
- IFRS Accounting Trends & Techniques
One-year individual online subscription
Item # WAL-BY

You can also add the FASB *Accounting Standards Codification*™ and the GASB Library to either collection.

Take advantage of a 30-day free trial!
See for yourself how these powerful online libraries can improve your productivity and simplify your accounting research.

Visit **cpa2biz.com/library** for details or to subscribe.

Additional Publications

Audit Risk Alerts/Financial Reporting Alerts
Find out about current economic, regulatory and professional developments before you perform your audit engagement. AICPA industry-specific Audit Risk Alerts will make your audit planning process more efficient by giving you concise, relevant information that shows you how current developments may impact your clients and your audits. For financial statement preparers, AICPA also offers a series of Financial Reporting Alerts. For a complete list of Audit Risk Alerts available from the AICPA, please visit **cpa2biz.com/ara**.

Checklists and Illustrative Financial Statements
Updated to reflect recent accounting and auditing standards, these industry-specific practice aids are invaluable tools to both financial statement preparers and auditors. For a complete list of Checklists available from the AICPA, please visit **cpa2biz.com/checklists**.